CAMBRIDGE CLASSICAL TEXTS AND
COMMENTARIES

EDITORS

J. DIGGLE   E. W. HANDLEY   H. D. JOCELYN
M. D. REEVE   D. N. SEDLEY   R. J. TARRANT

29

EURIPIDES: PHOENISSAE

EURIPIDES

PHOENISSAE

EDITED WITH INTRODUCTION
AND COMMENTARY

BY

DONALD J. MASTRONARDE

Professor of Classics, University of California, Berkeley

CAMBRIDGE
UNIVERSITY PRESS

Published by the Press Syndicate of the University of Cambridge
The Pitt Building, Trumpington Street, Cambridge CB2 1RP
40 West 20th Street, New York, NY 10011–4211, USA
10 Stamford Road, Oakleigh, Melbourne 3166, Australia

First published 1994

Printed in Great Britain at the University Press, Cambridge

Cambridge University Press acknowledges with gratitude the kind
permission of B. G. Teubner Verlagsgesellschaft, Stuttgart and
Leipzig, to print in this volume a very slightly adapted version of
D. J. Mastronarde's text as it appears in his Teubner edition,
Euripides. Phoenissae (Leipzig, 1988).

A catalogue record for this book is available from the British Library

Library of Congress cataloguing in publication data
Euripides.
[Phoenician women] Phoenissae / Euripides; edited with introduction
and commentary by Donald J. Mastronarde.
p.   cm. – (Cambridge classical texts and commentaries; v. 29)
Includes bibliographical references (p.) and indexes.
ISBN 0 521 41071 1 (hardback)
1. Seven against Thebes (Greek mythology) – Drama.
I. Mastronarde, Donald J. II. Title. III. Series.
PA3973.P6   1993   882.01–dc20
93–3247   CIP

ISBN 0 521 41071 1 hardback

CONTENTS

PREFACE

It is over fifteen years since I first decided that I would attempt to write a detailed commentary on *Phoenissae*. In the intervening years there have been detours for study of the textual tradition and then for the Teubner edition, and delays occasioned by other projects, family life, and administrative duties. Now that the project has come to an end, I feel relief mixed with exhaustion, and I am also humbled by the sense that I cannot avoid leaving some questions unanswered, or even unasked, and some insights of fellow scholars unnoticed.

Portions of this work were first drafted as long ago as 1979, a major chunk was completed in 1986, and the commentary itself reached virtual completion at the end of 1991. Many months of 1992 were devoted to a final process of pruning, updating, and adding cross-references as well as to compiling or revising sections of the Introduction. I have in general taken account of bibliography through 1991, although I have been able to make use of, or at least add references to, some later material.

From the beginning it was my goal to produce a commentary on a scale that would allow consideration of a full spectrum of issues, from literary and dramaturgic to stylistic and textual. The literary interpretation of a work like *Phoenissae* is not neatly separable from or posterior to the problem of establishing its text, which for this play includes the difficult attempt to determine the extent of interpolation that the play has suffered. I argue for a relatively conservative position in the interpolation controversy, but hope that I have informed the reader adequately of the main approaches and arguments so that he or she may form a personal judgment or carry on the debate from a secure foundation. Accepting the desirability of not letting an already large book grow even more unwieldy, I have knowingly tolerated some unevenness of treatment: on some points I give a fuller view of the history of approaches to a problem or quote parallels at length, while on others the comment may be much more condensed and the parallels left for the reader to pursue in other books. Brevity will not, I hope, be taken as a sign of dogmatism or of disrespect for works or views which I have not had room to cite.

I would like to express here my gratitude to the editors of the series for their encouragement and patience. James Diggle, in particular, has been tireless in supplying me with corrections, supplements, and advice of all kinds: only a fraction of these points are actually signalled by the appearance of the initials JD in the commentary. I am all the more grateful for our cordial correspondence because I know that his *Phoenissae* in volume III of the OCT will differ in many points from mine. I am again indebted to Michael Haslam for sharing with me yet another papyrus scrap of this play. At various points over the years I have had Berkeley graduate students perform some grimly tedious tasks for me (checking collations, compiling conjectures, proof-reading), and I here thank Costas Yialoucas, Nancy Marlowe, James Astorga, and Kate Gilhuly for this help. Earlier phases of my work were supported by fellowships from the American Council of Learned Societies and the John Simon Guggenheim Foundation. From the University of California, Berkeley, I have received assistance with computers and minor expenses, sabbatical leaves, and a Regents Humanities Fellowship, as well as a fine library collection and a wonderful place to work.

Finally, I dedicate this book to my wife Joan: οὐ μὲν γὰρ τοῦ γε κρεῖσσον καὶ ἄρειον . . .

Berkeley, California   D. J. M.
December 1992

INTRODUCTION

I THE PLAY

Like several other plays of Euripides, especially those of his later years, *Phoenissae* shows marked tendencies toward an 'open' form of composition and away from the 'closed' form. The latter is more typical of 'classical' forms of drama and, under the influence of Aristotle and of modern ideologies of order and coherence, has generally been preferred by influential critics.[1] The closed form tends toward concentration and self-containment, creating an impression of totality and unity through a simply organized structure with a single rhythm of rise and fall and through restriction to the deliberate actions of a few figures. The open form tends in the opposite direction, diminishing concentration and hierarchy in various ways. Event (what happens because of outside forces) becomes as prominent as, or more prominent than, action (what occurs because of the deliberate choice of a figure); the number of figures involved in the action is increased and their separate influence on the course of events reduced; the rhythm of complication and resolution is varied and multiplied; the interconnection of the acts or scenes is to be understood by an inductive movement that notes juxtapositions and implicit parallels and contrasts rather than by a deductive movement that recognizes a causal connection in terms of 'necessity or probability'. The open structure is not to be viewed as a failed effort at closed structure, but rather as a divergent choice that consciously plays against the world-view of closure and simple order.

Phoenissae is a complex but well-organized dramatic

---

[1] For a clear brief presentation of 'open' vs. 'closed' forms in drama, see M. Pfister, *The Theory and Analysis of Drama* (Cambridge 1988) (transl. of *Das Drama* (Frankfurt 1977)) 239–45.

structure.[1] It does not concentrate solely on the strife and death of the sons of Oedipus, as the play's severest critics expected or demanded that it should.[2] Rather, it engages a whole ensemble of figures from the families of Oedipus and Creon in exploring themes of selfishness and blindness, familial disaster, familial loyalty, political duties and loyalties, divine–human interaction, and the lability of human wisdom. This is not the place for a detailed reading of the play, and it would be uneconomical to repeat here all the observations that are made about structure and function in the commentary, especially in the remarks that introduce each scene or ode (there, too, are addressed many of the complaints found in much traditional criticism of the play). This section is therefore confined to a sketch of my understanding of the play.[3]

The action is shaped most of all by two elements, the search for salvation and the interplay of loyalties to self, to kin, and to country in the various figures in their various situations.[4] From the beginning, the danger to the family from Laius'

---

[1] See in particular Strohm on the interconnection of the episodes (against the claim that the episodes are self-standing) and Ludwig on symmetrical structure.

[2] Cf. Morus and esp. Hermann's *praefatio*, which has been very influential. On their view, *Phoen.* should have been a simple variation on *Septem*: after the first 637 lines, Eur. should have reported the duel and death of the brothers.

[3] For fuller discussion, see my Toronto dissertation, *Studies in Euripides' Phoinissai* (1974), esp. 267–96 ('The Problem of Unity'); cf. also Mueller-Goldingen, 1–5, 267–71; Foley, 112–32; Arthur; Saïd.

[4] Recognition of the importance of the themes of family and fatherland is a key element of Hartung's defence of the play against Hermann's strictures (*Euripides Restitutus* II.442–4). Cf. P. Voigt, *NJPP* 153 (1896) 817–43, who argues somewhat one-sidedly that all figures in the play except Menoeceus are shown failing the city for various selfish reasons. In an interpretation distorted by Nazi ideology, Riemschneider makes the city the 'hero' of the play and judges all the figures as defenders or enemies of the state. The best discussion of this complex of themes is that of E. Rawson, 'Family and Fatherland in Euripides' *Phoenissae*', *GRBS* 11 (1970) 109–27.

disobedience and from Oedipus' curse threatens not only the brothers but also the city. Jocasta's prologue naturally concentrates on the family's salvation, but her action is not in conflict with the best interests of the city. After an imagistic evocation of the danger to the city in the teichoskopia, the first episode develops the dilemma of Polynices' position (the misery of exile is both partly based on his love of fatherland and a cause of his attack on his fatherland) and the intransigence of both brothers. Despite Jocasta's noble effort at validating a world-view of order and equality sponsored by the gods, the interests of both city and family are shown to be secondary to the personal desires of the brothers, and the only new result of the meeting is that the brothers are eager to face each other in battle. Yet the attack of the Seven and the fratricidal duel are strikingly postponed. The next movement of the play, in the second and third episodes, brings about a split between the fate of the royal family and that of the city. Eteocles' strategy-session with Creon works in contrast to the famous central scene of Aeschylus' *Septem*: it is Creon who is aware of the latest military intelligence and Creon who suggests the strategy of defence at the seven gates, while Eteocles' σοφία is exposed as shallow; and the final instructions of Eteocles ensure that he himself will not know of Tiresias' advice and that his hatred will carry on beyond his death. In the Menoeceus-episode the salvation of the city is successfully separated from that of the royal family. By incorporating the legend of Cadmus into the background of this play, Euripides has contrived to establish a communal guilt that threatens to reinforce the Labdacid guilt. But this communal guilt can be separately appeased by the generous patriotism of the idealistic youth, which contrasts strongly with the selfishness of the brothers, with the inability of Creon to maintain his professed patriotism when confronted with danger to his own kin, and with the polluting rescue brought to the city by Oedipus long ago. The separation between city and royal family is then realized in the separate narratives of battle and duel in the fourth and fifth episodes: the main battle is won with the brothers unexpectedly still alive, but a challenge to a duel (displaced from its 'proper' position before the full-scale battle) leads finally to the expected conclusion. This sequence also allows Jocasta to make a second futile attempt at saving her sons, parallel to the first. After the death of the brothers and the suicide of Jocasta there follows a lyric lament, and Oedipus, whose presence in the house has been evoked throughout the play, is brought forth. In the final scene (if its main lines of action are accepted as Euripidean) various themes are rounded off. The exile of Oedipus is the last in a series and a renewal of his earlier state. The argument over the treatment of Polynices' corpse answers to the earlier portrayal of both Antigone and Polynices, and it highlights the familial loyalty of Antigone in contrast to the very narrow sympathies of Creon, who denies an appeal in the name of his own sister. The betrothal to Haemon, introduced in the second episode and then exploited in the third to deflect the demand for sacrifice onto Menoeceus, serves here as the linking device between Antigone's abandoned purpose of burying her brother and the new purpose of attending her blind father in exile.[1] The play ends, as often in Euripides, with the grief-stricken survivors clinging to each other, having only their human solidarity as a compensation for their suffering.

The interlocking sequences of the plot are drawn together by shared scenic and verbal motifs and repeated general motifs.[2] Systems of repeated imagery do not constitute the

---

[1] In his treatment of Antigone, therefore, Eur. features both a movement from sheltered innocence to engagement in brutal action (cf. Ion, Iphigenia in *IA*) and a reinterpretation of her traditional heroism (cf. Heracles). For the motif of Antigone as sheltered or secluded maiden, see 88–201n., 88–102n., 196–201n., 1067–283n. *ad fin.*, 1265n., 1582–709n., 1691n.

[2] See, e.g., Strohm, Ludwig, and Saïd, 513–18; also Podlecki, though his treatment seems to me somewhat mechanical and too inclusive.

unity of a literary work, but they serve to underscore the
analogies between disparate events and to lead an audience
toward a recognition of latent connections of similarity and
contrast. Among the scenic gestures may be mentioned old
man and young girl joining hands (teichoskopia, exit-lyric),
a daughter leading a blind father (Tiresias-scene and exodos),
a speaker checking the departure of a reluctant informer
(Creon and Tiresias, Jocasta and the first messenger), and
supplication (Creon to Tiresias, Antigone to Creon). The
most striking verbal parallels include the chorus' comment
on Jocasta's love of her child (355–6 φιλότεκνον) and Creon's
remark about his own (965 φιλότεκνος); Eteocles' ἐρρέτω
πρόπας δόμος in 624 and Creon's χαιρέτω πόλις in 919;
Eteocles' οὐκ ἂν τύχοις in 615 (rejecting Polynices' desire to
see his father) and Creon's οὐ γὰρ ἂν τύχοις τάδε in 1666
(rejecting Antigone's supplication on behalf of Polynices);
Jocasta's πότερα τυραννεῖν ἢ πόλιν σῶισαι θέλεις in 560 (to
Eteocles) and Tiresias' ἢ γὰρ παῖδα σῶισον ἢ πόλιν in 952
(to Creon), Creon's οὐδ' ἂν τὸν αὑτοῦ παῖδά τις δοίη κτανεῖν
in 966 (trying to save Menoeceus) and οὐ φονεύσεις παῖδ' ἐμόν
in 1682 (protecting Haemon).

Probably the most pervasive repeated motif in the play is
that of kinship, made all the more striking by the ironic
juxtaposition of the horrors of infanticide, patricide, incest,
and father's curse with extreme devotion. The audience
observes the loyalty of Jocasta to her sons and son/husband,
the devotion of Antigone to Polynices and her father, Polynices' references to his family (both the present Jocasta and
the absent father and sisters), the brother/sister tie between
Creon and Jocasta and the special foster-mother tie between
Menoeceus and Jocasta, and the kinship of Tyrians and
Thebans through Io.[1] Related to this motif are those of

---

[1] Examples are too numerous to list in full; see esp. 11n., 156n., 202–6on.,
288–90n., 291–2n., 433–4n., 436n., 615–16n., 691n., 769n., 784–833n.,
987–8n., 1284–1307n., 1323n., 1427–79n.

marriage, birth, and fertility,[1] shading off into the motif of disastrous marriage, incest, and monstrous births (Spartoi, Sphinx, Oedipus and his children). Fratricide, like incest, is a drastic perversion of kinship-ties, and the mutual slaughter of the Spartoi is presented as a prototype of the fratricidal duel. Exile and arrival are repeatedly evoked, and the important arrivals are ambivalent (Cadmus as founder/sinner, Oedipus as saviour/polluter, Polynices as much-loved son/attacker) or openly baneful (Sphinx). The repeated motif suggests a long-standing pattern of doom in which apparent successes mask guilt and disaster and in which the human agents, though conquerors of savage beasts, are ultimately like the beasts.[2] Similarly ironic motifs are the wisdom that is shallow, ineffectual, or disastrous[3] and the victory that is tarnished or ignoble instead of 'fair'.[4]

The ambivalence in these actions is closely related to the double-faced relationship of the gods as benefactors and persecutors to the figures of Theban myth and the Labdacid clan. Apollo sends the founder Cadmus and saviour Oedipus and his oracle induces the Argive marriage of Polynices. Ares provides the stock of the Spartoi who people Thebes, and Earth provides the fertile plains and waters that sustain its prosperity, but the dragon and the Spartoi oppose the foundation of a human city and leave a trace of divine wrath as a stain upon the city. Epaphus, son of Io (herself once recipient of special divine persecution and favour), is summoned

---

[1] E.g., 1–87n., 301–54n., 638–89n., 649–56n., 666–9n., 673n., 757–65n., 784–833n., 801–2n., 814–17n., 820–1n., 1019–66n., 1043n., 1352–3n., 1436–7n., 1570–6n., 1582–1709n., 1672n., 1732n.

[2] For the arrival-motif see 201–60n., 295n., 638–83n., 638n., 1019–66n., 1019n.

[3] Note the uses of σοφία, σοφός and other words of intellect in 453, 460, 472, 495, 498, 499, 530, 735–6, 746, 1259, 1408, 1728–31; conversely, words of folly in 395, 569, 570, 584, 763, 1612; also, the 'wisdom' of the gods, disappointing in 86, superior to the blindness of mortals acting in conformity to fate (414, 871).

[4] See 1019–66n., 1048n.

with Demeter and Kore to help, but the Sphinx too is a visitation from the gods. Dionysus, product of a strange birth himself and sponsor of a magical fertility, represents a memory of the frenzy of joyful worship that is now expelled by a frenzy of war and grief. Some have interpreted the divine elements, which are found especially in the choral odes, as a mythological alternative that is played off against, but does not mesh with or reduce the validity of, the psychologically credible human choices and actions that produce the disaster.[1] But the pattern of fated doom is in fact present in the episodes of the play as well (especially in Tiresias' speeches, but also in minor hints elsewhere, concluding in the reference to an oracle in 1703–7), and from the tragic audience's perspective such patterning may serve to undercut the apparent freedom of the human figures and to suggest that they are often blind to the ways they are fulfilling a destiny, or to offer a surplus of possible causations that is not meant to be resolved.[2]

Another important feature of *Phoenissae*, again one shared by many of the contemporary plays of Euripides, is its self-consciousness about its relation to the literary and dramatic tradition.[3] In small ways, the drama imitates, evokes, or produces variations on the teichoskopia in the *Iliad* and the self-sacrifice in *Erectheus*. Both *Antigone* and *OT* are evoked in the confrontation of Creon and Tiresias, and the burial-argument and reinterpretation of Antigone's heroism depend on allusion to Sophocles' masterpiece. The reconciliation attempt of Jocasta probably owes something to Stesichorus' poem on the quarrel of the brothers. The most important model, however, for intertextual allusion is Aeschylus' *Septem*.

---

[1] For the best exposition of the view of mythological and realistic elements as distinct, see Conacher, Chapter 13, and cf. Parry, *Lyric Poems* 173.

[2] For the particular problem of the effectiveness or irrelevance of the sacrifice of Menoeceus, see 1067–283n., 1198n., 1308–479n., and esp. 1427–79n.

[3] These are brought out especially in the discussions of Foley and Saïd.

9

We have already noted how Creon and Menoeceus are used to alter fundamentally Eteocles' responsibility for the defence and salvation of Thebes. The exotic foreign chorus makes possible a more distanced reaction to events, on the one hand not deflecting attention from the specific individuals seen on stage to the Theban citizenry as a collective and on the other reinforcing the long-term view of Theban history that provides depth and complexity to the disaster of this day. *Septem* allowed the audience to see and hear Eteocles alone, but *Phoenissae* puts Polynices on stage and explicitly argues the justice of the dispute. Related to this innovation is the evocation of contemporary political concerns by the use of language of political ambition and strife and Jocasta's countervailing appeal to principles of ἰσονομία.

Phoenissae, then, offers a complex, but not incoherent, presentation of the downfall of the Theban dynasty, giving full weight to the complication of the event, in human terms and in divine terms, in familial terms and in public terms, with both the apparent immediacy of a wholly new situation and the inevitability of a pattern perceived through generations. There is no single narrowly defined event or single person as focus, as 'classical' critics have so often desired. Rather, the several figures are made weaker as agents by their number, the briefness of their appearances, and the separation of their actions. They often act in partial ignorance or in vain: Eteocles seems not to know of Menoeceus' sacrifice, Creon mourns his son in ignorance of the duel, Jocasta fails in her first attempt at reconciliation and arrives too late for the second, the duel does not produce a winner and even fails to end the conflict between the two armies, Creon's actions in the exodos are not entirely his own, Antigone and Polynices are not reunited until the moment of his death, his appeal for burial in Theban soil goes for nought, various prayers to the gods for help are unanswered. Like other late plays of Euripides, *Phoenissae* is thus more engaged in presenting and exploring a generalized tragic world-view than in studying in depth one or two figures of extraordinary personality or isolated suffering.

II THE PROBLEM OF DATE AND COMPANION PLAYS

Were no other evidence available, one would speculate that *Phoenissae* belongs to the last decade of Euripides' life because of many features of dramatic construction and technique, such as the use of trochaic tetrameters, the large number of speaking roles, the overall length of the piece, the presence of two messenger-scenes and the length of the rheseis in them, the 'dithyrambic' style of the choral lyrics, the extensive use of polymetric astrophic actor's songs. The most reliable criterion of dating for Euripidean tragedies, the number and nature of the resolutions in his iambic trimeters, also clearly establishes *Phoen.* as a late work.[1] The resolution rate is closest to that of *Helen*, and likewise in the number of resolution-types not attested in the 'severe' and 'semi-severe' styles our play is closest in behaviour to *Helen* and *IT* and somewhat less free than *Or.*, *Ba.*, and *IA*.[2]

Of the two pieces of external evidence that bear on the question of date, the didascalic hypothesis of 'Aristophanes' (Teubner arg. 7) is too corrupt to be useful, while the scholion on *Frogs* 53, without contradicting the evidence based on resolutions, provides a *terminus post quem* but no reliable narrowing of the range of possible dates. The latter, commenting

---

[1] For the most recent and convincing discussion of dating by resolution-rate, see Cropp and Fick. In my own study of the resolutions in *Phoen.* (in which I have received the generous help of Martin Cropp), I count 1163 trimeters (excluding various corrupt lines and those deleted in my text) and 405 resolutions, for a rate of 34.83% (of trimeters; compare the rate cited by Cropp and Fick, 6.96% of eligible feet = 34.80% of trimeters).

[2] Cropp and Fick, 60–1.

on Dionysus' mention of recently reading *Andromeda*, reads διὰ τί δὲ μὴ ἄλλο τι τῶν πρὸ ὀλίγου διδαχθέντων καὶ καλῶν, Ὑψιπύλης, Φοινισσῶν, Ἀντιόπης; ἡ δὲ Ἀνδρομέδα ὀγδόωι ἔτει προ⟨ει⟩σῆλθεν [*TrGF* DID C 15(c)] and shows that *Phoen.* is later than 412, the year of *Andromeda* and *Helen*. The words πρὸ ὀλίγου make 409 and later years seem more probable than 411 or 410, but it may be unsafe to place so much weight on the precision of scholiastic language. As for the hypothesis, the Nausicrates cited there as archon is not found in the archon list for this period,[1] and various restorations eliminate the name (ἐπὶ Γλαυκίππου Snell)[2] or make Nausicrates choregus (Bergk) or the father of Diocles, archon in 408 (Luppe).[3]

References to contemporary events have sometimes been used to support a particular date of production. The maidens' route in the parodos has been taken to allude to Athenian interest in Carthage as an ally against Sicily (202–60n. at end), the discussion of the ills of exile has been referred to Alcibiades (388–407n.), and an allusion to a victory at Cyzicus has been proposed (854–5n.). As is usual for tragedy, however, the political relevance of the play is on a very general level, and the detection of specific allegories is to be rejected.[4] The political strife of the period leading up to

---

[1] It is probable that in the didascalic lists 411/10 was recorded as ἐπὶ Θεοπόμπου, the archon of the final ten months of the year who replaced Mnasilochus, elected under the 400: cf. G. F. Hill, R. Meiggs, A. Andrewes, *Sources for Greek History between the Persian and Peloponnesian Wars* (Oxford 1951) 400. From Diodorus Sic. 13.43 and Σ*Or.* 371 it is clear that Theopompus was the name recorded in the chronological lists used by ancient historians and scholars.

[2] Snell was following up the implications of Wilam.'s theory that the play was performed in 409 (see p. 13, n. 3 below).

[3] 'Zur Datierung der *Phoinissai* des Euripides', *RhMus* 130 (1987) 29–34. The fatal flaw in Luppe's proposal is the question how the archon's father's name could have been known. Archon lists would not have contained such information, as the case of the two Calliases (cited by Luppe, 31) shows.

[4] See also Mueller-Goldingen, 11–13.

the oligarchic revolution of 411 provides a poignant contemporary background for the rivalry of the brothers,[1] and the play's political language reflects contemporary concerns (e.g., 464n., 532n.), but to establish this fact does not permit us to say even that 411 is 'too early' for the play to have been conceived.

There have been two major theories about the companion plays of *Phoen.* Kirchhoff restored the hypothesis as saying that *Oenomaus, Chrysippus,* and *Phoen.* belonged to the same tetralogy, the satyr-play of which (name lost) was not preserved (⟨οὐ⟩ σώιζεται). The same loosely connected trilogy is accepted by, e.g., Wilamowitz, Robert, Zielinski ('de Euripidis Thebaide'), and most recently Snell, who provides in *TrGF* a restoration *exempli gratia.* The metrical argument often cited against this grouping is not valid, but there are other reasons to doubt that *Phoen.* could have followed *Chrysippus* (see section V below). The other theory holds that the scholiast on *Frogs* 53 cited three tragedies that he found listed under a single year and that *Antiope,*[2] *Hypsipyle,* and *Phoen.* formed a loosely connected trilogy.[3] Such a trilogy would belong to 411 or 410 or 409, on the common (but not unassailable) assumptions that *Orestes* is a tragedy from a different trilogy performed in 408 and that no Euripidean plays were produced in Athens between spring 408 and the death of Euripides less than two years later. But C. W. Müller has recently revived the idea that *Orestes* was the 'prosatyric' fourth play in a tetralogy with *Antiope, Hyps.,* and *Phoen.*

---

[1] See esp. de Romilly, 'Les Phéniciennes'.

[2] Note, however, that Cropp and Fick, 75–6, have suggested that the scholion should be emended to refer to *Antigone* instead of *Antiope.*

[3] Cf. T. B. L. Webster, 'Three Plays by Euripides', in L. Wallach, ed., *The Classical Tradition. Literary and Historical Studies in Honor of Harry Caplan* (Ithaca 1966) 83–97; R. L. Hunter, *ZPE* 41 (1981) 21 n. 18; R. Kannicht, addendum to DID C 16, p. 344 in *TrGF* I² (1986). Note that Wilam. (apud H. Schaal, *de Euripidis Antiopa* (Jena 1914) 51) once speculated that the ancient scholar picked one title from each year in a list and that *Hyps.* belonged to 410, *Phoen.* to 409, *Antiope* to 408.

produced in 408.[1] I find it hard to believe that a play as long as *Or.* was presented as 'prosatyric' after tragedies of the great length of *Hyps.* and *Phoen.*, and I do not accept the principle by which Müller rules out a production in 409,[2] so I am inclined to discount this hypothesis.

Thus *Phoen.* was most likely performed in one of the years 411–409, although a later production is not impossible. Of these years, 409 best suits the phrase πρὸ ὀλίγου, but the criterion of resolution suggests a date closer to *Helen* in 412 than to *Orestes* in 408. Given the state of our evidence, I see no reason to place confidence in assignment to any particular year or to any particular grouping of plays (but I doubt the collocation of *Chrysippus* and *Phoen.*).

III FEATURES OF THE ORIGINAL PRODUCTION

The original production made use of the normal convention of the skene-background as a palace façade with one usable

---

[1] *Zur Datierung des sophokleischen Ödipus* [Akad. d. Wiss. Mainz, Abh. der Geistes- und sozialwissenschaftlichen Kl., 1984:5] 66–9. Curiously, the same grouping was proposed long ago by Hartung, who used Σ*Frogs* 53 to group *Antiope* and *Hypsipyle* with *Phoen.* and, unaware that he was dealing with Thoman scholia (*not* scholia in Rf, as Mueller-Goldingen, 9, states), understood the phrase ἐν τῶι τρίτωι δράματι in Σ^Thom. *Or.* 1472 and 1492 as placing *Phoen.* as third play in the same production with Orestes. Cf. *Euripides' Werke* ed. J. A. Hartung, 4. Bändchen: Orestes (Leipzig 1849) v–vii, repeated in his edn of *Phoen.*, p. xi.

[2] Müller makes the valid general observation that the major tragedians seem to have produced, on the average, one tetralogy every two years. But it is an unjustified step to assume that this observation applies exactly to any specific short period of time. It is quite obvious that artists are capable of intense spurts of production and of fallow periods, and we have no way to predict when these may have occurred in Eur.'s life. And even if a poet has a production in hand for the upcoming Dionysia, he may well be working simultaneously on a new tetralogy for a future competition (Mueller-Goldingen, 10, assuming that new work does not

door. This is the Labdacid palace, into which go and out of which appear Jocasta (1, 87, 301, 637, 1072), Antigone (1270), Oedipus (1539), and Eteocles (637, 690). In the teichoskopia two actors appear on the bare stage-roof, arriving and departing by a trap-door or a ladder from behind (88ff. staging n.). Other entrances and exits are from the side, perhaps with a distinction between a side that leads to the city-walls and a gate to the outside (Polynices (261, 637), Eteocles (443, 783), Creon (695), Menoeceus (1012), messengers (1067, 1283, 1332), Jocasta (1283), Antigone (1283, 1480, 1736), Oedipus (1736)) and a side that leads to other places within the city, such as Creon's house, Tiresias' house, and the lodging of the Phoenician maidens (chorus (202), Tiresias with daughter (834, 959), Menoeceus (834), Creon (990, 1308), second messenger (1479)).[1]

There were probably at least two simple prop-altars near, but not in front of, the door (274n.), and possibly prop-statues of gods were placed behind the altars (632n.), including perhaps an image of Apollo in his function as Agyieus (631n.). The remaining props include swords and armour, Tiresias' prophetic lots, the staffs used by Tiresias and Oedipus, and dummy corpses (on litters) of Eteocles, Polynices, and Jocasta (if these were not represented by silent extras).

Masks and costumes are readily inferable from the text. Jocasta is an old woman in mourning (dark robes, shorn hair). The Servant is an old man in slave's garb. Antigone is

---

begin until after the Dionysia, suggests that a poet could not easily have composed a full tetralogy in the time between one Dionysia and the selection for the next festival at the beginning of the new archon-year).

[1] Cf. the *actio* in Teubner edn, except that there I had Tir. come and go by the side leading to the walls. The play ends with the chorus still in the orchestra and probably with the soldiers and bodies still on stage ('cancelled ending'); the bodies, still present at 1702, might be carried in and off at 1710, but I doubt this (1744n.). It is not clear whether Creon departs at 1682 (by which exit?) or lingers in the background to the end (1682n.).

a young maiden with saffron robe and head-dress in her first two appearances, but in the exodos she returns without head-dress and with the upper part of her robe let down, and perhaps with a different mask expressive of grief. The chorus of maidens apparently has exotic robes (278–9n.). Eteocles and Polynices are bearded young men wearing swords, Menoeceus a beardless youth. Creon is an old man, and Tiresias and Oedipus are blind old men. The messengers are both soldiers.

The roles can be divided in several different ways. If the scholiasts are to be believed (88–102n.), the same actor played Jocasta and Antigone in the opening scenes. One might accordingly speculate that a protagonist who was a skilled singer took Jocasta's role, Antigone's role in teicho-skopia and exodos (but not in 1270–83), and (e.g.) Tiresias' part, while the deuteragonist played the Servant, Polynices, Creon, and the first messenger, and the tritagonist Eteocles, Menoeceus, Antigone in 1270–83, the second messenger, and Oedipus. But the scholiasts may be wrong, in which case one could consider divisions in which Antigone is played entirely by the deuteragonist or tritagonist: e.g., protagonist as Jocasta, Tiresias, second messenger, Oedipus; deuterago-nist as Servant, Polynices, Creon, first messenger; tritagonist as Antigone, Eteocles, Menoeceus.[1] Silent extras are needed to play attendants of Eteocles in the first and second episodes, the daughter of Tiresias in the third, and as soldiers carrying the corpses in the exodos; it is uncertain whether Creon is attended at 1308.

---

[1] This is the assignment proposed by B. Arnold, *De Euripidis re scenica pars* II (Nordhausen 1879) 18–20 (also listing earlier proposals). For other possibilities see, e.g., A. Pickard-Cambridge, *The Dramatic Festivals of Athens*, 2nd edn rev. J. Gould and D. M. Lewis (Oxford 1968) 147; Craik, 46 (though she wrongly states that there is reason to assign Et. and Tir. to the same actor).

IV THEBAID MYTH AND
PHOENISSAE

Most previous attempts[1] to deal with the poorly documented background of Thebaid myth from which the tragedians drew (and against which they may have innovated) have been bedevilled by the desire to reconstruct specific literary artefacts of the archaic period and to trace a historical development in variations in the legend. Even if such reconstructions inspired more confidence than they do, they would give a misleading impression of the 'sources' of Thebaid myth. For we must recognize that the literary distillations which survived in written form represented only a part of a larger oral tradition, a tradition that varied according to time, locale, and artistic temperament of the bards. Nor is our knowledge of the literary artefacts known to later generations of Greeks at all satisfactory. Proclus informs us that in the *Cypria* Nestor told Menelaus ἐν παρεκβάσει ... τὰ περὶ Οἰδίπουν, but we know nothing more of this. We have the scantiest possible fragments of the epic *Oedipodeia*, while those of the *Thebaid* are so few and uninformative that it can be debated whether they represent one or two poems.[2] As for the controversial

---

[1] Several important treatments of this topic are included in the bibliography: see esp. March, Robert, Bethe, Burkert, Edmunds. For further bibliography on Thebaid myth, see A. Bernabé's Teubner *Poetae Epici Graeci* I (Leipzig 1988) xxiii–xxiv; March, 171–2. Relevant fragments are in Bernabé, 17–32, and M. Davies, *Epicorum Graecorum Fragmenta* (Göttingen 1988) 21–7. As far as Eur.'s treatment is concerned, on most details I am in agreement with the useful presentation of Stephanopoulos, 99–126; see also Mueller-Goldingen, 14–36.

[2] I think it quite likely that more than one *Thebaid* was recited in archaic Greece, but I am doubtful that two separate *Thebaid* poems were known in detail to Hellenistic scholars. Wehrli, *MusHelv* 14 (1957) 113 n. 27, argues that an older *Thebaid* and a younger *Cyclic Thebaid* are to be distinguished because a poem beginning Ἄργος ἄειδε θεὰ πολυδίψιον

Peisander-scholion, its reliability as a reflection of an archaic source or sources is very doubtful (see the next section). Moreover, the loss of almost all of archaic and fifth-century choral lyric, which may have been a major force in diffusion and adaptation of mythic variants, hampers every attempt to identify the specific sources of tragic myth. The Lille Thebaid fragment, which I assume to be by Stesichorus, presents features no one would have guessed to be present in a sixth-century version and leaves open new questions about how the poet treated other details. Equally, our scant knowledge of local cults and of the stories attached to them (whether by long-standing tradition or by recent poetic aetiology) must create caution if not despair.[1]

In this section, rather than enter into exposition and debate of all the issues raised by the evidence for Thebaid myth surviving from archaic and classical times, I wish to highlight the more important choices that Eur. seems to have made in presenting various details in *Phoen.* For the sake of brevity, I state my considered opinion and leave most of the controversy to the footnotes.

First, Euripides follows well-established if not unanimous traditions in regard to several key features of the story.

(1) As in Pindar (*O.* 2.38–40) and tragedy in general, the

ἔνθεν ἄνακτες could not, he thinks, contain a comprehensive treatment of Oedipus' fate and because two forms of citation exist (*Thebaid* in Pausanias, Apollodorus, and the *Certamen*; *Cyclic Thebaid* in Athenaeus and scholiasts on Pindar and Sophocles). But 'cyclic' may be used not because the poem itself was a comprehensive, chronologically ordered treatment of Theban legend, but because the poem together with other archaic epics formed a comprehensive cycle of heroic myth. Huxley, 41–6, supporting the view that a single *Thebaid* is reflected by our fragments, suggests that 'cyclic' is used to distinguish the work from Antimachus' poem; cf. Burkert, 29–30.

[1] My main reaction to March's chapter about Oedipus is that it envisages a too harmonious archaic tradition and too easily concentrates the major innovations in the story in Aeschylus' Theban tetralogy.

oracle to Laius comes from Delphic Apollo.[1] It is conditional
or imperative in form, as in Aesch. (*Septem* 745–9) and Eur.'s
own *Oedipus* (fr. 539a Snell: Φοίβου ποτ᾽ οὐκ ἐῶντος ἔσπειρεν
τέκνον), not starkly unconditional as in Soph. (*OT* 713–14,
853–4; *OC* 969–70) and perhaps Pindar. There is no clear
hint in *Phoen.* as to why Laius was destined to die at his son's
hand, and in stories of this type (fathers or grandfathers
exposing babies because of a prediction of the baby's future
actions) no reason need be given. In some versions Laius'
disobedience may itself have been viewed as a misdeed. The
only other misdeed recorded in extant sources is the kidnapping and rape of Chrysippus, which led the boy to commit
suicide in shame. The evidence for this story and for the plot
of Eur.'s *Chrysippus* is examined in the next section. Pelops'
curse upon Laius probably occurred in *Chrysippus*, but I do
not think it probable that *Chrysippus* belonged to the same
production as *Phoen.*; and if it did not, Eur. certainly was
under no compulsion to assume the events of that play as
background to *Phoen.*

(2) Neither in earlier sources nor in *Phoen.* can we trace
any explicit sponsor of the Sphinx as persecutor of the
Thebans.[2] The lack of explicit reason for her arrival con-
forms to the tragic preference for multiple and inscrutable
causation. In myth some monsters appear as punishment for
misdeeds, others are simply present in a locale as a chaotic,
destructive force which must be conquered by a god or hero
so that human civilization can be founded or maintained. In
OT an audience may infer that the Sphinx, like the plague

---

[1] As for earlier versions, Robert, 69f., argues that Tiresias predated Apollo
as the oracle-giver in the Oedipus-legend; Nilsson, *GGA* 184 (1922) 41,
regards Tiresias as a figure added under influence of the Delphic version.

[2] Later sources mention Hera (Apollodorus 3.5.8; Dio Chrys. *Or.* 11.8;
Peisander: see next section), Dionysus (ΣHes. *Th.* 326; Σ1031, restored
by Unger to refer to Eur. *Antigone* (fr. 178)), or Ares (Thomas Mag.,
Teubner arg. 12).

and the timely death of Polybus, is sent by Apollo or the gods to assist or coerce the course of Oedipus' fate. *Phoen.* 1031–2 (φόνιος ἐκ θεῶν ὅς τάδ' ἦν ὁ πράξας) is vague, and 810–11 (τὰν ὁ κατὰ χθονὸς Ἀΐδας Καδμείοις ἐπιπέμπει) need mean no more than that the Sphinx was destructive, a bringer of death (cf. *Hec.* 1077, Bond on *Her.* 562). *Phoen.* also follows standard tragic myth in viewing Oedipus as a riddle-solver.[1] In the earlier tradition, the slaying of the monster may have been a feat of strength and valour, the intellectual element of the riddle being a later addition.[2] Yet it is unnecessary and unsafe to assume a subtle (or careless) reference to physical slaying in the phrase σῶμα φονεύσας at *Phoen.* 1507 (see *ad loc.*), and the illustrations on vases which have been thought to document the version without the riddle are both later in date than illustrations of the riddle and open to other interpretations.[3]

(3) Oedipus' incest with his mother is a universal assump-

---

[1] On the place of the Sphinx within the legend of Oedipus, see Edmunds, *Sphinx*, 12–15, who argues on the basis of the traditional patricide/ mother-incest legends that the Sphinx's presence in the story may be an additional (overdetermining) element in the Greek tradition. We know of no Greek version in which it was absent.

[2] Cf. Corinna (*PMG* 672, from Σ26): Oedipus killed both the Sphinx and the Teumessian fox, the latter certainly a feat of physical skill.

[3] Moret, 1–2, 79–91. Moret, 80 n. 2, reports that several experts have agreed that one of the most frequently cited vase-paintings of the combat (on Boston lekythos inv. 97.374) is in fact a forgery. Scenes of the Thebans confronting the (riddling) Sphinx date from as early as 540– 530, and Moret cites two vases (*c.* 520–510 and 470) with words that appear to reflect hexameter riddles, though the words καὶ τρι[πουν] on the later vase cannot be assumed to be from the hexameter riddle we have (= Teubner arg. 5). See A. Lesky, *Gesammelte Schriften* (Bern 1966) 318ff. (who argues on the basis of vocabulary that it does not go back to an archaic epic, as Robert, 56f., 168, supposed); H. Lloyd-Jones, *Dionysiaca* 60–1. Both consider a fifth-century tragedy to be a likely source for our version (not Eur. *Oed.*, which has a different hexameter riddle, fr. 83.ii.22–5 Austin). It is not impossible that oral tradition carried several versions independent of literary context, verses that would be taught to children and recited in the symposium.

tion of the Greek tradition so far as we know it.[1] It is not clear whether offspring of the incestuous union, assumed in all the tragic versions, is an equally old feature.[2] March has recently argued that the epic tradition was consistent in attributing Oedipus' children to a second, non-incestuous union and that the incestuous offspring first appeared in Aeschylus' Theban tetralogy. It was, however, in the interest of families who claimed descent from Polynices' son Thersandros to give Polynices a non-incestuous mother, and it may have been in the interest of Homeric decorum to adopt a similar view or at least be silent about the offspring of incest. On the other hand, it was in the interest of tragedy and perhaps of other pre-tragic narratives to concentrate the horrors within a single family for stronger effects. Epikaste and Iokaste are rightly taken to be variant names of the same figure. She is identified as daughter of Menoeceus and sister of Creon only in Soph. and Eur., but this genealogy is probably older (cf. Σ942 = Aesch. fr. dub. 488; Creon appears in the epic *Oedipodeia* and in *Septem* 474). Euryganeia (or Eurygane), the daughter of Hyperphas (Paus. 9.5.11) or Periphas (Σ53 = Pherecydes *FGrHist* 3 F 95), is a separate figure,[3] a second wife who (explicitly in the *Oedipodeia*, according to Pausanias' source; implicitly in *Od.* 11.271–4 (ἀφὰρ δ' ἀνάπυστα)) bore the four well-known children of Oedipus after Jocasta's death.[4] We cannot say how the early

---

[1] For speculation on whether the incest is a secondary element and on possible significances of the motif, see F. Wehrli, *MusHelv* 14 (1957) 108–17; Nilsson, *GGA* 184 (1922) 38–9; Robert, 1.44–7; Edmunds, *HSCP* 85 (1981) 221–38.

[2] The parallel legends cited by Edmunds would imply that they are.

[3] Robert's view that Euryganeia/Eurygane is a further variant of the incestuous wife and mother has rightly had few followers.

[4] This is the one detail in the Peisander-scholion certainly identifiable with the *Oedipodeia*, though the use of φασὶ δέ makes it uncertain whether Peisander himself supplied or used this tradition. Euryganeia was depicted by Onasias in a mid-fifth-century painting of the Argive expedition against Thebes (Paus. 9.4.2, 9.5.11). When Pherecydes adds a third

oral tradition, the epic *Thebaid*, or Stesichorus[1] treated this detail. Where children are mentioned, the four well-known names are all but universally recognized.[2]

(4) All the tragedians feature the blind Oedipus, and this feature was, I believe, already attested in the *Thebaid*.[3] Oedipus is not blind in the version alluded to in *Il.* 23.679, if δεδουπότος is 'fell in battle',[4] and the same may have been true of other sources which refer to the funeral of Oedipus at Thebes (Hes. fr. 192, perhaps fr. 193.4) or to battle during Oedipus' reign.[5] Whether Oedipus was blind in the *Oedipo-*

---

wife Astymedousa, he is probably forcing a conflation of variant traditions. Astymedousa may have been referred to in Hes. fr. 193 M–W (see M. L. West, *The Hesiodic Catalogue of Women* (Oxford 1985) 110f.). She is given as a second wife after Jocasta in Σ^A *Il.* 4.376. Deubner (1942) unconvincingly assigns all three wives to the epic *Oedipodeia*.

[1] If ἐπ' ἄλγεσι in 201 means 'in addition to ⟨previous⟩ pains' rather than 'with attendant pains', then such previous pains could, but need not, include the discovery of incest. March has argued that the woman in the Lille poem is definitely Eurygane. Aélion, *Quelques grands mythes* 40–1, simply assumes that the mother in Stesichorus is Jocasta/Epicasta.

[2] Only Pherecydes mentions Phrastor and Laonytus (as children of incest, the others being children of Euryganeia): they seem to come from the epic tradition of the wars between Thebes and the Minyans, since they died at the hands of the Minyans.

[3] So, e.g., Burkert, 30. This has been denied by March, 126, who alleges that φράσθη in fr. 2.5 does not hint at blindness but means simply 'recognized'; but she ignores the parody, *TrGF* adesp. 458 (quoted in the same sch. on *OC* 1375 that contains *Thebaid* fr. 2), which implies the reading of φράσθη as 'noticed ⟨because unable to see⟩'.

[4] Burkert, 33, quotes Leumann's explanation of how δεδουπότος might simply mean 'having died'.

[5] Hes. *Op.* 163 μαρναμένους μήλων ἕνεκ' Οἰδιπόδαο: from the context (destruction of the race of heroes in war at Thebes and at Troy), I believe we should assume a reference to the war of the Seven 'for the sake of the flocks [=wealth, estate] of ⟨dead⟩ Oedipus' (so West; Burkert, 32–3; March, 134). But a number of scholars insist that this is a reference to Boeotian wars involving or prompted by heroic cattle-raiding during Oedipus' lifetime (e.g. Robert, 1.113; more recently, Robert J. Buck, *A History of Boiotia* (Alberta 1979), 62; S. Symeonoglou, *The Topography of Thebes from the Bronze Age to Modern Times* (Princeton 1985), 64, 67).

deia or in Stesichorus is unknown, though many infer from the fact of a second marriage and continued rule that Oedipus cannot have been blind in the former. Oedipus continues to be king in Homer and the *Oedipodeia* and probably in Hesiod; he loses power in the *Thebaid*[1] and in tragedy.[2]

(5) The tragedians all use Oedipus' curse upon his sons, which goes back at least to the *Thebaid*, the two substantial fragments of which contain two curses that overlap in their effect (eternal strife over their inheritance, and death at each other's hands). In these lines we find an Oedipus blind and dependent on his sons, although we cannot say whether he was in any sense imprisoned by them. The dishonour done to him may not in context have been so trivial as it seemed to the Sophocles scholiast (Didymus?), if there was some sacral meaning in the heirlooms presented to Oedipus and in the portion of meat offered to him.[3] But the tragedians too seem to prefer to offer their own explanations of the curse rather than repeat the details of the *Thebaid*. In *Phoen.* Euripides has perhaps imitated most closely the situation of the *Thebaid*, making detention by his sons the dishonour that drives the distraught father to curse them. The timing and motivation of the curse in *Septem* are uncertain because of textual corruption, but recent studies have made a case for the view that the curse followed immediately on Oedipus' discovery of the truth.[4] In *OC* 431ff. there is a suggestion of

---

[1] March seems to assume that Oed. continued to rule in the epic *Thebaid*, on the a priori assumption that it agreed with the *Oedipodeia*. The actions that prompt the curses suggest, however, that Oed. is dependent on his sons. The incidents in which Oedipus is angered by his sons perhaps reflect some sacral power (either residual or acquired through his extraordinary experiences): cf. Edmunds, *HSCP* 85 (1981) 229 n. 31; a sacral significance in the items which prompt Oedipus' curse is also detected by E. Simon, *Das Satyrspiel Sphinx des Aischylos* (Sitzungsberichte Heidelberg 1981:5), p. 10 n. 13.

[2] See, however, 63n.   [3] Cf. note 1 above.

[4] Cf. West's reconstruction of *Se.* 782–4 (with patricide and incest as the two evils causing the mental disturbance in which the curse is uttered:

detention of Oedipus by his sons (cf. perhaps the end of *OT*), but the curse in *OC* seems to emerge from the circumstances of the play itself (421ff., 788–9, 1370–6: πρόσθ᾽ in 1375 probably refers to 421ff.). As for earlier sources, the references in Homer and Hesiod are too vague to be connected certainly with the curse or even with a quarrel between the sons, although ἄλγεα πάσχων in *Od.* 11.275 seems to me to imply something more than warfare with neighbours.[1] Wherever a son named Polynices appeared, however, one may assume the existence of a quarrel if not also of a curse (e.g., *Oedipodeia*). In Stesichorus there is clearly a quarrel (206, 233) and Tiresias has given prophecies which involve the city as well as the brothers and which relate the quarrel to fated troubles of the family (217, 228, 230–1). Since the property and kingship can be divided, it is best to assume that Oedipus is dead, but there is no sign in the extant lines of any action on his part that has brought about the quarrel and the need to consult Tiresias.

(6) The exile of Oedipus at the end of *Phoen.* is a slight adaptation of a pre-existing motif. Exile was absent, certainly or probably, from the early Theban tradition and from

---

Studies in Aeschylus (Stuttgart 1990) 116–18); or the view of Hutchinson, comm. pp. xxiv–xxv, and March, 143 (the two evils are that Oedipus at the time of discovery both blinded himself and cursed his sons because of their incestuous origin – 785–6 ἀθλίας ... ἐπίκοτος τροφᾶς). In *Se.* 778–9 I prefer to punctuate after γάμων, not before μέλεος, as Hutchinson does. ΣSoph. *OC* 1375 (Didymus?), on the other hand, refers τροφᾶς to the meat-portion provided by the sons in the *Thebaid* fragment which is there quoted; so too Wilamowitz and others. This requires a chronological separation of self-blinding and curse. In this scenario, the sons may begin quarrelling after the fall of Oed. but before he curses them. If the curse is simultaneous with the self-blinding, there is no room for forceful detention of Oedipus (at least as a crucial event); but one might guess that the brothers have already been quarrelling and that the pre-existing quarrel suggests to Oed. the specific content of the curse.

[1] March, 122, considers suffering caused by 'haunting knowledge' of his sins or by objectionable actions of his sons or by local warfare.

the epic tradition based on it (and from Stesichorus and Aeschylus' Theban plays?); but the existence of cults in other locations will have given rise to (or arisen from) tales of wandering, and it is not justifiable to regard all of these as particularly late inventions.[1] Sophocles alludes to the tradition of Oedipus as exile throughout *OT* (even though the end of the play leaves Oedipus' final condition undecided or at least postponed),[2] and it is a natural, if insecure, inference from *P.* 4.263 that Pindar knew of Oedipus in exile.[3]

In some features of the story Eur. has been mildly innovative:

(1) Familiar as we are with *Od.* 11.277–9, *Septem*, and Soph.'s Theban plays, it strikes us as remarkable to see Jocasta still alive at the opening of *Phoen.*, and her role in the agon seems a typically Euripidean invention. Yet we do not know what was her fate in the *Thebaid*, and in Stesichorus the name of the mother does not survive.[4] If Eur. is the first to make Jocasta live on after the discovery of the incest, one effect, as March notes, is to reinforce the notion that her action was not really culpable, since it was done in ignorance (cf. 53–4). As for a mother's mediation between her sons, this

---

[1] For a highly speculative but intriguing argument for the antiquity of the connection of Oedipus with Colonus see Kirsten. See also 1707n.

[2] See March, 148–54, for a revival of the theory that *OT* did end in Oed.'s departure for exile and that the return into the house is the result of interpolation.

[3] March, 145–7, suggests that Aeschylus created the connection of Oedipus with Attica and that Pindar's allusion to exile is a reference to Aeschylus' idea (such borrowing strikes me as unlikely for Pindar in itself and as intolerably obscure for Pindar's aristocratic, non-Attic audience). There is no way to assign a date to the details in Androtion (*FGrHist* 324 F 62) that differ from those of *OC*, but I see no reason to think (with Deubner (1942) and March) they may be taken from Aeschylus (Jacoby points out how confused the author of the ἱστορία is and how uncertain it is what part of it is from Androtion).

[4] See March, 127–31, for argument that Stesichorus presented Euryganeia, the second, non-incestuous wife.

is shared with Stesichorus,[1] although in *Phoen.* it is located not at the time when the deal was struck but after the deal has collapsed and on the eve of battle. And in surviving to witness the battle between her sons, the Jocasta of *Phoen.* is simply doing what Euryganeia did in Onasias' painting (as already perhaps in *Oedipodeia*).

(2) The timing of the reconciliation-attempt in *Phoen.* requires that Polynices enter the hostile city under truce, apparently an innovation; but the incident may be modelled on the embassy of Tydeus to Thebes (*Il.* 4.365ff., 5.801ff.) and that of Menelaus and Odysseus to Troy (*Il.* 3.205ff., 11.139–41; Bacchyl. 15). In both of those violence was threatened or an ambush actually attempted, just as Polynices fears in our play.

(3) In Eur.'s treatment of the quarrel between the brothers the compact providing for annual alternation of rule over Thebes seems to be an innovation. The brothers' strife could easily have been motivated without a curse[2] and without a compact intended to forestall predicted trouble: Sophocles and Pherecydes (Σ71 = *FGrHist* 3 F 96), for instance, have Polynices driven out by force. In the background to *Septem* as well the brothers were possibly quarrelling about the division of wealth and kingdom before Oedipus' curse, for he invokes an 'equal division' that entails the death of both. The fact that Polynices' shield in *Septem* represents Dike leading the exile home suggests to me that there either no compact existed or Eteocles violated it: that is, we can exclude the notion

---

[1] Mueller-Goldingen, 34–5, argues that Eur. shows specific awareness of Stesichorus' poem in three details: the maxim in 86–7 is taken to reflect lines 204–8 in Stesichorus; Tir.'s admonitions to the sons in the past (878–9) match his role in the Stesichorus; and Jocasta's determination to die with her sons (1283) is comparable to the mother's wish to die before witnessing their fatal strife (lines 211–17). Since the first item is a maxim and the third involves two distinct topoi, the claim is far from established.

[2] Or have begun before the curse: see above p. 23, n. 4.

that Polynices agreed to take possessions in lieu of kingship and then came to desire the kingship as well. The compact providing for permanent division of kingship on the one hand and possessions on the other was probably found in the *Thebaid* tradition, where Polynices' gift to Eriphyle may imply acceptance of possessions in lieu of kingship. Such a compact is explicitly attested in Stesichorus and Hellanicus (Σ71 = *FGrHist* 4 F 98): the mother proposes it in the former, Eteocles in the latter. Likewise, in Eur.'s own *Su.* Polynices is in voluntary exile and has been wronged by his brother in regard to χρήματα (150–3, 930–1): this implies a compact in which Eteocles still had some obligation to his brother after his departure (e.g., regular payment for his sustenance in exile), but cannot easily be taken to imply alternation of kingship and exile.[1]

(4) Related to the innovation about the compact between the brothers is the extremity of Eur.'s portrayal of Eteocles and the degree of sympathy accorded to Polynices. The injustice of Eteocles, so accentuated in *Phoen.*, is better viewed as an extension of earlier portrayals (*Septem?*,[2] Pherecydes, *Su.*) rather than a wholesale revaluation.[3] Conversely, the

---

[1] Stephanopoulos, 113–14, argues that the passages in *Su.* already imply the alternation of rule and exile and that, since there is no reason for Eur. to have innovated on this point in *Su.*, the notion must have come from an earlier source. But *Su.* 152–3 (ἀλλ' οἱ μένοντες τοὺς ἀπόντας ἠδίκουν. – οὔ πού σφ' ἀδελφὸς χρημάτων νοσφίζεται;) are hard to reconcile with the notion that Polynices has been deprived of his turn at the kingship.

[2] Like Aélion, *Euripide* 1.211–18, I do not subscribe to interpretations of *Septem* that view Eteocles as simply the good man who defends his country and dies because of the quarrelsomeness of his unjust brother.

[3] In *Phoen.* Polynices is explicitly the younger brother, whereas the relative age of the brothers in the earlier sources is unknown. The fact that both make a claim on the kingship perhaps suggests that the brothers were originally twins (cf. Romulus and Remus; Robert, 1.143, speculates that Et. and Pol. may have been patterned on the quarrelling Argive twins Proetus and Acrisius). In *OC* 1294 Soph. makes Polynices the elder, but that may be his innovation to suit his realistically political version of the quarrel rather than a reassertion of tradition against *Phoen.*

lengths to which Eur. goes to win sympathy for Polynices are not matched in any other source that we know of.[1]

(5) Whereas the fact of Oedipus' exile appears not to have been new, the extension of his life and the timing of his exile seem to be innovations. It is known or may, I think, be assumed that in all previous versions Oedipus died before his sons.[2] In *Phoen.* he is kept alive and present to regret his curse, to underscore the innocence of his polluting actions, to worry about the outcome of the battle, to hear the terrible news, and to have the final suffering of exile imposed on him by Creon. Oedipus' suffering follows the pattern of Polynices' rather than vice versa as in *OC*. His exile is postponed to a point where it serves as the final, capping instance of exile in the history of the dynasty, and where it opens up the possibility for a different treatment of Antigone.

Finally, in the actual selection and ordering of events presented in the play, there are a number of strikingly new features:

(1) Several factors suggest that Menoeceus is a creation of Euripides for this play.[3] First, his name is a simple duplication of his grandfather's name, a convenient device for grafting new figures on to a traditional stemma (cf. Lycus in *Her.* 31). Second, he is younger than Haemon, whereas Haemon seems to be the younger son in *Ant.* (and perhaps already in the *Oedipodeia*, to judge from κάλλιστόν τε καὶ ἱμεροέστατον), and Men. has lost his mother in infancy (a detail designed to create a special link to Jocasta for thematic points special to this play). Third, Euripides anachronistically alludes early in the Menoeceus-scene to the self-sacrifice legend connected to

---

[1] See 257–60n., 261–442n., 438–42n., 511n., 690–783n. Cf. Mueller-Goldingen, 36 and *passim*.

[2] In *OC* the hero's death and even his curse upon his sons have been postponed to the very moment of the Argive expedition, perhaps under the influence of Euripides' recent treatment of the theme.

[3] See in particular Schmitt, 88–92; Stephanopoulos, 115–22; O'Connor-Visser, 82–7.

the war between Erectheus and Eumolpus: this is perhaps a sly admission of the source from which he borrowed the motif. Fourth, the need for the sacrifice arises only in a play involving the complex of distant and recent causation which we find in *Phoen*. Menoeceus has sometimes been regarded as the same legendary figure as Megareus, most recently and with fullest argument by F. Vian,[1] but the argument is not successful. Vian underestimates the importance of the scene and its degree of connection to the rest of the play and overestimates the oddity of certain details (the continued wrath of Ares, its coupling with a sacrifice to Earth, the impossibility of choosing Haemon), and thus he prefers to detect an effort to adapt pre-existing material. If Apollodorus 3.6.7 diverges from Euripides to such a degree that a separate source seems likely, this does not prove that the other source is pre-Euripidean. Nor is an interpretation of *Ant*. 992–6 and 1303 which assumes that Tiresias had required the sacrifice of Megareus inevitable or even probable: in the former place, Creon's acknowledgment of gratitude does not sound like an allusion to the death of his own son, and in the latter, if κλεινὸν λάχος is restored (rather than κενὸν λέχος, preferred with reason by Lloyd-Jones and Wilson), it would more likely allude to Megareus' selection as a champion at one of the gates of Thebes (as in *Septem* 473ff.).

(2) The separation of the duel between the brothers from the famous assault of the Seven is surely a Euripidean innovation, designed to diminish Eteocles' status as general and as controller of Thebes' destiny and to make even sharper the distinction between the salvation of the city and the salvation of the royal family. This choice is one of the ways in which Euripides most obviously seeks an effect of contrast between his treatment of the story and that in *Septem*.

(3) Our ignorance of the origins of stories involving

---

[1] Vian, 208–14; Vian's view is followed by Aélion, *Euripide* 1201–3, *Quelques grands mythes* 101–3.

Antigone is total. All we can say is that in *Ant.* she buries her brother and dies in Thebes (and there is no hint that she has been abroad at an earlier time). In the interpolated closing scene of *Septem* (whatever its date) the same story seems to be assumed; and in Euripides' own *Antigone* there seems to have been no room for exile. Her decision to accompany her father is impossible without the extension of Oedipus' life to this very late date (see above), and this decision seems to be part of a reinterpretation of her heroism in which burial of her brother has been effectively blocked (an innovation if Antigone's main role in earlier myth was to bury her brother). Thus Antigone's exile is presumably a Euripidean innovation, followed by Sophocles in *OC*.[1] But we must admit that in any detailed treatment of Oedipus as both blind and wandering in exile it would be necessary to explain who guides him on his way.[2]

(4) In considering innovations, we must also take account of Euripides' decision to emphasize the distant past, the arrival of Cadmus and the story of the Spartoi, details which provide prototypes for other arrivals, feats of conquest, and incest and fratricide, as well as a causal chain that additionally threatens the city and necessitates Menoeceus' sacrifice. Through these shifts and innovations Euripides has created a complex interaction of a large number of closely related individuals, none of whom has truly decisive power to affect the events of this critical day in Theban history.

---

[1] March, 147, in reconstructing Aeschylus' *Oed.* as a play involving the hero's exile, contemplates having a daughter attend him in exile and bring back news of his death.

[2] Solitary wandering is, to be sure, envisioned in *OT*, where Oedipus seems to want to be escorted out of Theban territory and abandoned to wander helplessly or to perish on Cithaeron (1410f., 1436, 1451f., 1518; cf. *Phoen.* 1687 πεσὼν ὅπου μοι μοῖρα κείσομαι πέδωι), but this desire is conditioned by his immediate despair.

V THE PEISANDER-SCHOLION
AND CHRYSIPPUS

This section has two purposes: first, to review some of the evidence for the story of the rape of Chrysippus by Laius, and second, to consider whether the story in general or Eur.'s lost play *Chrysippus* in particular is relevant to the understanding of *Phoen.*

Using the Peisander-scholion (Teubner arg. 11 = Σ1760), Bethe reconstructed an *Oedipodeia* in which the rape of Chrysippus played an important role, but the method and implications of his argument were strongly and justifiably attacked by Robert. It is still necessary, however, to consider the narrative offered by this scholion and to ask whether it might be based on a single literary source or, if not, whether it might nevertheless carry clues to pre-Euripidean versions of Thebaid myth.

The *Suda* identifies two authors named Peisander: an archaic (sixth-century?) epic poet from Camirus in Rhodes who wrote a *Heracleia* (Theocr. *Epigr.* 22 Gow), to whom were ascribed some further poems known to be spurious; and a much later (early third century A.D.) epic poet from Laranda in Lycaonia who wrote a sixty-book universal genealogy entitled Ἡρωϊκαὶ θεογαμίαι (the article ends with the phrase καὶ ἄλλα καταλογάδην, which may refer to yet another Peisander). Macrobius 5.2.4–5 records a poet of a universal Greek mythography supposedly used as a source by Virgil, and it is unclear whether he is referring to one of the spurious works alluded to in the *Suda* or to a prose mythography about which his source misled him or whether some further confusion is involved.[1] Peisander of Laranda is not likely to have been used as a source in the Euripides-scholia (here and

---

[1] Cf. Jacoby's introduction to his comm. on *FGrHist* 16, with the Nachträge, pp. 544–7.

Σ834) or the scholia to Ap. Rhod. (seven times, *FGrHist* 16 F 2–8). Nor would we expect the scholiastic sources to refer to spurious poems under the name of the earlier Peisander without some further qualification.[1] Therefore, the mythographic notes in the scholia have reasonably been assigned to an otherwise unknown writer, probably of Hellenistic date.[2] There is no reason to expect such a writer to follow a single source; rather, as Jacoby and de Kock argued, we expect a learned conflation of earlier motifs. Moreover, within the scholiastic tradition, the original kernel of Peisander's narrative will not only have been expanded with explanatory additions but also reworded and perhaps truncated in other places. Hence, although a large proportion of what falls between ἱστορεῖ Πείσανδρος and ταῦτά φησι Πείσανδρος may be his, we can never be sure exactly how much.

Just as Bethe used the scholion to reconstruct the *Oedipodeia*, so Deubner wished to reconstruct the *Chrysippus* of Eur. from the first half of the scholion (through ἀπελθὼν τοίνυν ἐφονεύθη … ἐπειδὴ ἔτυψε τῆι μάστιγι τὸν Οἰδίποδα). His reconstruction fails because of a basic misreading of the chronological sequence implied by the Greek.[3] The suicide of

---

[1] For the scholiasts' usual method of referring to epic works whose authorship was disputed, see Schwartz's index to the Euripides scholia, II. 391.

[2] So Jacoby, *FGrHist* 16; also Keydell, *RE* 19:1 (1937) 144–7 s.v. Peisandros [13]; Huxley, *Greek Epic Poetry* 101. For the view that the Peisander of the scholion is the archaic poet, see Lamer, 474–81, Thalmann, 15. If we were faced solely with Σ1760, there might be some economy in supposing that the source was an archaic epic, rightly or wrongly ascribed to Peisander (though the manner of reference would still be abnormal). But the number and variety of fragments assembled by Jacoby make this less attractive.

[3] The first sentence (κατὰ χόλον τῆς Ἥρας … οὐκ ἐτιμωρήσαντο) is a summary of several events which are preliminary to the main narrative (kidnapping, rape, Theban inaction, Hera's wrath, arrival of Sphinx). Appended to this is a description of the Sphinx and her action which has long been recognized as parenthetic (ἦν δὲ ἡ Σφὶγξ … καὶ οἱ ἄλλοι μνηστῆρες). The next two brief sentences are also explanations appended to the first sentence and not a resumption of the narrative, as

Chrysippus, in shame over the rape, must have occurred at the first possible opportunity after the rape: for the story-type cf. Phaedra's false accusation in *Hipp.* and Lucretia in Livy 1.58 – the victim of violent sexual assault demonstrates an exalted sense of honour by refusing to live on once her/his body has been violated. Thus the Theban inaction punished by Hera (first sentence) is later in time than the suicide (sixth sentence, within digression). In Deubner's reconstruction, on the other hand, Chrysippus dallies for a time at Thebes and commits suicide only after the Sphinx's arrival makes it known that his relationship with Laius is despised by the gods and harmful to the Thebans. This sequence fails to satisfy either the words of the scholion or the logic of the story-type. De Kock, who views the story as Peisander's own unified narrative and not as an outline of Eur.'s *Chrysippus*, still makes the same error about the timing of Chrysippus' suicide.[1]

As de Kock argues, the plot (or at least the 'Dicaearchan' hypothesis) of Eur. *Chrysippus* is much more likely to be reflected in the fragmentary summary (Teubner arg. 8) transmitted in VRf and in the similar details of Hyp. III (Smith) to *Septem* (lines 11–16: these lines or their source were used by Thomas, Teubner arg. 12): this summary implies a scene in Pisa, a failed attempt by Laius to persuade Chrysippus, the secret departure of Laius for Thebes with the kidnapped boy, Pelops' uncertainty about the fate of his son resolved by a report of his son's suicide, and a curse against Laius (made presumably in the final scene of the play during a *threnos* for the boy). Laius was represented in the play as the first mortal

---

Deubner (1942) believed. They tell us that Laius was the first mortal pederast and that Chrysippus committed suicide in shame. Only with μὲν οὖν in the next sentence (τότε μὲν οὖν ὁ Τειρεσίας κτλ.) do we return to the situation and time-sequence established by the first sentence: the particles mark the intervening sentences as parenthetic or digressive.

[1] In Webster's reconstruction (*The Tragedies of Euripides* (London 1967) 111–13), I find the suggested confrontation of Laius and Pelops *after* the death of Chrysippus highly improbable.

to practise pederasty (Aelian, *NA* 6.15; Hyp. III to *Septem*, whence Thomas in arg. 12). Two details in the VRf-version, however, give cause for doubt: the emphasis on the passage of time (ἐπὶ πολὺ θρηνοῦντος, ὕστερον ἔμαθε) and the anonymity of the curse (τῶι αὐτὸν ἀνελόντι) do not seem appropriate to a tragedy. Hyp. *Se.* III, on the other hand, has ὅπερ ὁ Πέλοψ μαθὼν τὸν Λάιον κατηράσατο ἐξ οἰκείας φονευθῆναι γονῆς. If the play ended with Pelops' curse, it is hard to see how Hera was involved, unless she appeared as *dea ex machina* (cf. the end of *Andr.*) and because of her own anger at Laius assured Pelops that his curse would be effective. Neither the crime of kidnapping nor the content of the curse, however, requires the intervention of Hera as god of marriage. Rather Pelops' curse and Hera's wrath are probably alternatives as responses to the rape, each used to motivate further trouble for Laius in different versions. If so, Hera probably had no role in Eur.'s *Chrysippus*.

The appearance of Hera in *Phoen.* 24 (see *ad loc.*) was one of the chief points that prompted Bethe to believe that Peisander was following an early epic source. Even when most of Bethe's case is exploded, the suspicion must remain that Hera is named for a reason that was elaborated somewhere in the tradition earlier than *Phoen.* Two other features of Peisander's narrative are possibly old. (1) The site of the patricide seems to be on Cithaeron,[1] whereas the Phocian crossroad was canonical in versions which emphasized the Delphic connection.[2] (2) Hera's use of the Sphinx may be

---

[1] Robert, 160f., unconvincingly argues that the scholion means that looking toward Parnassus from a high spot on Cithaeron Oedipus pointed out in the far distance the site of the murder.

[2] It is reasonable to argue that the Delphic connection is an intrusion upon an older myth. Apollo is also connected to the story of Pelops and Laius by the undatable hexameter oracle (Teubner arg. 4): its longer version, instead of ending ὡς γὰρ ἔνευσα, has ἔνευσε / Ζεὺς Κρονίδης Πέλοπος στυγεραῖς ἀραῖσι πιθήσας, / οὗ φίλον ἥρπασας υἱόν. Fontenrose, *The Delphic Oracle* 362–3 (no. L17), notes that it is reasonable to assume that the scholiasts understood this to be a Delphic oracle, though it is

related to the fact that she made use of the Nemean lion, which is the sibling of the Sphinx in Hesiod, *Th.* 326–8.

The most serious difficulty in regard to the story of Chrysippus is the question whether and how early in the Greek tradition pederasty could have been shown as *per se* objectionable. Euripides is cited by Aelian as the authority for Laius as the first human pederast: this suggests that Aelian knew of no earlier *important* literary source, but does not prove that Eur. originated the claim. On a priori grounds one would not expect disapproval of pederasty *per se* in archaic Greek myth (cf. Pindar's attitude in *O.* 1 and archaic love-poems to boys by Solon, Anacreon, and others). Nor, if Laius was married at the time of his passion for Chrysippus, would a homosexual liaison constitute, in Greek eyes, in and of itself a violation of the sanctity of marriage. An offence could have been committed in word rather than deed if Laius made a statement derogating sexual union with woman in marriage in comparison with pederasty: such a statement could enrage Hera and call forth punishment. In *Chrysippus* (as recon-structed above), however, the act of abduction and the use of force in themselves would render Laius' actions criminal: Zeus Xenios would be an appropriate sponsor of vengeance (and Zeus is in fact mentioned in the oracle, Teubner arg. 4). The shame which Chrysippus felt perhaps implies disap-proval of homosexuality in general, but it may simply be a re-flex of the double standard by which the passive partner could be subject to disapproval while the active partner was not. A wider disapproval is, however, explicit in the words of Peisan-der (ἀσεβήσαντα, παράνομον). In phrasing if not in plot-device this detail seems not to be older than the time of Eur.

Several scholars[1] have argued that the rape of Chrysippus

---

not explicitly so identified (P alone has ἀπολλῶνος χρησμός; F has ὁ παρὰ τοῦ διὸς χρησμός, which fits the oracle in its shorter version of three lines with ἔνευσα, as in *Anth. Pal.* 14.67).

[1] E.g., Lamer, 474–81; H. Lloyd-Jones, *Justice of Zeus*, 120f.; Thalmann, 15–17 (with further references p. 155 n. 46).

was used by Aeschylus[1] in his Theban trilogy as the original transgression on account of which the fateful oracular command was addressed to Laius. This motif is nowhere explicit in *Septem*, and it need not be implicit in the reference to Laius' παρβασία. Indeed, the emphasis of τρὶς εἰπόντος in *Septem* 746 suggests to me (1) that the transgression was disobedience, not an offence against Chrysippus and Pelops; (2) that no reason was given for the oracular command, for if one were, there would be no need to inquire a second and third time. But nothing can be proved either way *ex silentio*. I merely record that I am sceptical of the claim. I agree with Hutchinson (*Septem* comm., xxiii) that the most probable content of A.'s *Laius* is the events leading to his death at Oedipus' hands and that, like the oracle, the incident with Chrysippus (if mentioned at all) lay in the prehistory of the play. It is also worth noting that Thucydides (1.9.2) casually assumed and Hellanicus (*FGrHist* 4 F 157 = Σ^A *Il.* 2.105) narrated the version in which Chrysippus was killed by his half-brothers Atreus and Thyestes.[2]

Finally, we must address the issue of whether, even if we can guess the plot of *Chrysippus*, its story had any importance for *Phoen*. Many scholars have believed in a loosely connected trilogy consisting of *Oenomaus*, *Chrysippus*, and *Phoen.*,[3] with the theme of curse carried through all three plays. Two

---

[1] H. Lloyd-Jones, 121–4, revives the view of Perrotta that the rape of Chrysippus and a consequent curse upon Laius are assumed in certain passages of Soph. *OT*. I cannot share this view; cf. Stinton in *Greek Tragedy and its Legacy* 72–4.

[2] Pelops' curse on the murderer(s) occurs in Hellanicus' version; the curse is presumably an old motif; it may have been transferred from the familial version to the Laius version or vice versa. Hyginus 85 combines the traditions: Laius kidnaps Chrysippus and Pelops recovers him by warfare, but the boy is then killed by his half-brothers at the urging of Hippodameia. This combination is not likely to be old, but even if it is, it leaves no room for a curse upon Laius.

[3] See section II above.

considerations may be cited to justify scepticism about such a trilogy.

(1) Most important is the lack of reference in *Phoen.* to the strain of causation connected with Pelops' curse on Laius. The play is replete with glimpses of the past, provided by Jocasta, Tiresias, Antigone, Oedipus, and the chorus, all serving to illuminate present events. Yet amidst all this the only possible allusion to the Chrysippus-story comes very late and is very brief: 1611 ἀρὰς παραλαβὼν Λαΐου καὶ παισὶ δούς. The passage is regarded by some as spurious, but I am inclined to grant its authenticity. Whether Euripidean or not, the passage is open to more than one interpretation (see *ad loc.*). I prefer an explication that does without Pelops' curse on Laius; but it cannot be denied that if *Chrysippus* was performed just before *Phoen.*, an audience could have understood an allusion to Pelops' curse. It would be circular reasoning, however, to regard 1611 as evidence that *Chrysippus* was part of the same trilogy.

In arguing for the trilogy *Oenomaus*, *Chrysippus*, and *Phoen.*, Zielinski, 198, cited the parallel of *Tro.* to justify the scant allusion to the action of *Chrysippus* in *Phoen.* But in *Tro.* there is no competing nexus of causation that rivals the role of Paris in bringing disaster upon Troy. The Judgment is implicit at many points (*Tro.* 23–4, 122ff., 211, 368, 398) and explicitly developed in 919–31, with a clear allusion to the exposure of the baby which had been revealed as unsuccessful in *Alexandros*. Deubner unconvincingly ascribes the lack of allusion in *Phoen.* to Jocasta's embarrassment and the chorus' foreign origin. To me it seems that the internal evidence of *Phoen.* speaks fairly strongly against production with *Chrysippus*.

(2) The scrap of the 'Aristophanic' didascalic hypothesis (Teubner arg. 7) is woefully corrupt, but a didascalic reference to a trilogy would normally be in the form of a listing of the three titles in the dative after the poet's name. So we would expect to find δεύτερος Εὐριπίδης Οἰνομάωι, Χρυσίππωι, Φοινίσσαις. Instead the titles survive in the

nominative in a subsequent sentence. One may strongly suspect that the names occurred in a further remark (cf. the Aristophanic hyp. to *Alc.* and *Hipp.*) which bore no implication for the question of the trilogy.

A third point sometimes cited against the hypothesis of a relationship between *Chrysippus* and *Phoen.* is the lack of resolutions in the few extant fragments of *Chrysippus* and *Oenomaus*. The trimeter fragments are all gnomic, and we have passages of 8, 5, and 4 lines in length for *Oenomaus* as well as very few shorter pieces. In a sophisticated study of resolution rates in fragmentary plays, Cropp and Fick have justifiably drawn no conclusions for any play represented by so few fragments.[1] They point out that one could pick out a number of resolution-free passages of 8, 5, and 4 lines (such as survive for *Oenomaus*) from *Phoen.* One might try to reinstate the intuitive impression of earlier critics by considering the probability of picking *at random* from *Phoen.* a group of resolutionless passages comprising 8, 5, 4, 3, 2, 1 and 1 lines respectively (as exist for *Oenomaus*).[2] But since the surviving fragments have not been selected at random, such a calculation is not in fact probative.[3]

---

[1] Cropp and Fick, 16; (for *Chrysippus* and *Oenomaus* in particular) 77–8, 86.

[2] I quote the following from a personal communication of Martin Cropp (who correctly maintains the need to distinguish between probabilities for a random sampling and the actual case under consideration): 'It can be shown that the probability of this [sc. picking from *Phoen.* such a set of resolutionless passages] is of the order of 1 in 4,800, whereas the probability of picking a similar set from *Medea* is of the order of 1 in 6, or some 800 times greater. For the *Chrysippus* fragments the analogous probabilities are 1 in 20 and 1 in 2 – that is, the probability of picking four resolutionless couplets at random from *Medea* is around ten times the probability of picking them from *Phoenissae*. (It follows that the probability of randomly picking the *Oenomaus* fragments *plus* the *Chrysippus* fragments from a trilogy with the resolution-rate of *Medea* is some 8,000 times greater than the probability of picking them from a trilogy with the resolution-rate of *Phoenissae*!)'

[3] I quote again from Cropp: 'It must be stressed that the fragments which we have are not only few but also very far from being randomly selected.

VI THE PROBLEM OF INTERPOLATION

As a matter of principle, each separate instance of suspected interpolation deserves to be judged on its own, and general beliefs about the history of transmission, the habits of interpolators,[1] or the degree to which a particular play's text has been subject to alteration should play only a secondary role. Thus, detailed arguments about interpolation are reserved for the commentary. Nevertheless, some general issues may be reviewed here.

One area of great uncertainty is the early transmission of the tragic texts, from the time of production to the collecting activities of the newly founded Alexandrian library.[2] In D. L. Page's well-known discussion in *Actors' Interpolations*, a key assumption is that the book tradition of tragedies essentially depended on the theatre tradition:[3] on this view, plays survived mainly because actors kept them alive in production, booksellers made their texts by taking dictation from actors, and readers who wanted a text simply wanted it

---

They are exclusively gnomic; we cannot be sure that they do not come from limited segments of their respective plays; and they consist exclusively of complete sentences. The value of analysing the fragments statistically as if they were a representative sample is therefore quite uncertain, although it can still be said that the total absence of resolutions from the fragments of *Oenomaus* and *Chrysippus* would be to some undefinable extent surprising if these plays were contemporary with *Phoenissae*.'

[1] E.g., the alleged family of ὅθεν-interpolations (27n.); the tendency of elliptical ἀλλ' ὅμως at the end of a trimeter to induce interpolation of a following line (1069–71n.); the elaboration of vocatives (1–2n., 291–2n.).

[2] On this subject see esp. Wilamowitz, *Her.* comm. vol. 1 [= *Einleitung in die griechische Tragödie*] chap. 3; Barrett's *Hipp.*, pp. 45–8; M. Griffith, *The Authenticity of the Prometheus Bound* (Cambridge 1977) 226–34.

[3] A similar assumption is found at least as early as A. Boeckh (1808) 10–12.

because of interest aroused in seeing the play performed and wanted the text of the most recently performed version of a play. I think it more likely that there were, at least from the later part of Euripides' career onward, parallel traditions of booksellers' texts and actors' texts. The large number of plays surviving to be collected in Alexandria can hardly be explained without an independent tradition of readers' texts, for the actors' tradition would have been confined to the plays that were in the active repertory. The booksellers' tradition will not, in addition, have been so closely tied to theatre practice, if it is correct to assume that the readers of books of tragedy were a relatively restricted group of literary enthusiasts (cf., albeit in caricature, Dionysus in *Frogs*), scholars, and teachers, whose desire for the books did not in fact depend on contemporary reperformances. For many plays, indeed, the source of the booksellers' tradition must have been a copy obtained from the playwright's family. Finally, it is not certain that even for the popular, reperformed plays, book-producers would have used actors for dictation to their scribes. If a view of this sort is correct, it does not mean that actors' changes could not get into the tradition, only that the tradition was not completely at the mercy of the contemporary theatre and that histrionic changes did not necessarily have easy access and did not necessarily replace any sounder tradition.[1]

We may imagine, then, that the text of *Phoen.*, like that of

---

[1] This view also implies that those following the dictates of the decree of Lycurgus (Plut. *Mor.* 841F) had the possibility of obtaining texts from other sources than the actors themselves and that they should be assumed to have used actors' texts only as a last resort, after the booksellers' tradition, large personal libraries, and the playwrights' descendants had been checked. The decree also implies, in my view, that there were previously no archival copies in the possession of the city (*contra* H. Erbse, in H. Hunger *et al.*, *Geschichte der Textüberlieferung der antiken und mittelalterlichen Literatur* I (Zurich 1961) 218, who supposes that poets who were assigned a chorus were required to deposit a copy of their plays with the city; similarly, J. Davison, *Phoenix* 16 (1962) 226).

other plays, was subject to contamination from the theatre tradition before the time when Alexandrian scholars worked on it. It cannot be excluded, however, that such contamination may occasionally have occurred later; and, more important, it must be recognized that histrionic interpolation is not the only kind that has affected our texts of tragedy. While any larger interpolation will inevitably be classified as histrionic, many smaller ones should not be. Expansions that make ellipses clearer for a reader or student or introduce proper names most likely come from the collation of copies designed for and used by readers, teachers, and pupils. Gnomologic expansion, though perhaps sometimes due to the taste of later actors or audiences, will at other times have been due to accidental incorporation of marginal parallels recorded in readers' copies.[1] Some additions are so late or were so narrowly represented in the later ancient tradition that we have scholia implying a text in which the addition was not yet found.

The first serious student of interpolation in Greek tragedy was L. C. Valckenaer in his massive 1755 commentary on *Phoen.*: his suspicions were directed at various single lines of this play and a few couplets or triplets (1116–18, 1262–3, 1369–71, 1758–9), but did not bear on the overall structure of the play. In 1771 S. F. N. Morus became the first to suggest an extensive interpolation (1104–40). In a monograph of 1808 A. Boeckh dealt with many issues related to authors' revisions and actors' interpolations; of *Phoen.* in particular, he declared 1759–66 spurious but defended the exodos as a whole with the unsatisfactory explanation that everything after Jocasta's death is not part of the action proper, but was included by Euripides to arouse audience interest in a future production of his *Antigone*. J. A. Hartung was the first to

---

[1] For an interesting suggestion of non-accidental rhetorical expansion, see R. J. Tarrant, 'The Reader as Author: Collaborative Interpolation in Latin Poetry', in *Editing Gk. and Lat. Texts* 121–62.

propose a more significant disturbance in the exit-lyric, but
it was only in the second half of the nineteenth century that
attempts were made to respond to the long-standing critical
dissatisfaction with the structure of the play by attributing
major portions to post-Euripidean revision. Paley and H.
Leidloff were the first to do this: Paley deleted or suspected
753–5 and 763–5, 1221–58, 1268ff., 1595–626, 1635–8;
Leidloff suspected the entire third episode and exodos and
the entrance of Creon at 1308ff. Numerous studies followed,
concentrated mainly on the exodos and the burial-motif. The
introductions of the commentaries of Wecklein (1894) and
Powell (1911) provide fair examples of the thinking of contemporary critics who were inclined to believe in large-scale
interpolations in the play.

In the twentieth century the play itself has more or less
dropped out of the curriculum, partly from changing fashions
and from the radical changes in schools that have diminished
the presence of Greek, and partly from a general impression
that we cannot be sure how Euripidean the play is. *Phoenissae*
is thus now mainly the object of high-level professional study.
A new level of sophistication in interpolation research was
reached with the work of W. H. Friedrich and particularly
Eduard Fraenkel. The latter in particular has prompted
extensive responses on the one hand[1] and defences and ex-
tensions on the other,[2] and in recent years there has been a
revival of interest in the problems of the play. The main areas
of disagreement continue to be the exodos and testament of
Eteocles (748–83), but Fraenkel's work also revived in a serious way questions about Tiresias' role and Creon's appearance at 1308. Of less far-reaching import is the controversy over the catalogue of the Seven in 1104–40; and less
problematic (because, in my view, so much less justified) are

---

[1] E.g., Diller, Erbse, my own Toronto dissertation (1974), Mueller-
Goldingen.
[2] E.g., Reeve, Dihle, Willink.

the doubts directed at the teichoskopia. These problems all receive detailed treatment in the notes on particular sections or passages of the play.

There are several kinds of evidence or argument that come to bear on disputes about interpolation, and almost every kind is subject to limitations. External evidence of various sorts is provided by papyri, scholia, mss, and quotations in other authors. No surviving ancient comment on *Phoen.* explicitly records a claim of inauthenticity.[1] But some verses are missing in papyri or mss or said to have been unevenly attested in copies known to ancient commentators. Such absence justifiably arouses suspicion, but each case still needs to be evaluated on its merits, and I do not believe that deletion is invariably justified: for absence in papyri, see 291–2n.; for ἐν ἐνίοις οὐ φέρεται or the like, see 375n.; for absence in some mss, see 1346n. Absence of a line from a quotation in an ancient author is a much less secure index of suspicion, since we must always take into account the vagaries of the gnomologic tradition and the rhetorical purposes of the citing author: see 547–8n., 1376n. Inferences about spuriousness from comments in the scholia are also subject to doubt. It is easy to establish that the commentator on 1226 did not have 1225 in his text, but scholia are written (or survive) in such a truncated and 'short-sighted' style (narrowly addressing particular words, often without much awareness of the wider context) that this is a rarity. Hartung often misused scholia to support his suspicions, and I believe that Murray did so in deleting 562 (see n.). Another uncertainty with scholiastic evidence pertains to a notation of περισσότης, which may or may not have been a justification for athetesis suggested by an ancient scholar, which in turn may or may not have been a consequence of some other evidence now lost to us: 428n., 794n.

---

[1] Unless μέρος οὐκ ἔστι δράματος in Arg. 3 is so interpreted: see 88–201n. Authenticity.

Among internal indices which are commonly cited in discussing possible interpolations are problems of coherence or consistency and obscurities or oddities of syntax and vocabulary. Problems of coherence are usually identified within a fairly narrow range of context (the single speech or short passage). One species of this kind of problem involves offences against the 'grammar' of dramatic conventions. Observation of the use of particles, of identifiable speech-formulae, and of other conventions can make a useful contribution to the elucidation of tragic texts, but it remains problematic in some cases whether compliance with a 'rule' is to be enforced by deletion or 'violation' of the rule is to be interpreted as aimed at a particular effect.[1] Occasionally, problems of consistency are seen only when a much broader range of text is considered. For instance, it may be argued that a character who has said A in a given scene should not be saying B a few hundred lines later.[2] Coherence and consistency of assumptions are certainly necessary criteria for the critic (they are powerfully used in impugning the ending of *Septem*, and I deploy such considerations at several points in the commentary). But there is ample room for uncertainty. First, different scholars will not always agree that one position is logically inconsistent with another.[3] Second, and more important in the case of Euripides, the assumption that dramatic characters are to be expected to be fully consistent in their values,

---

[1] Cf. 376–8n., 753n., 1012n., 1265–9n., 1584n., 1615n., 1708n.

[2] For instance, the common argument that the Antigone who speaks impressively of the unwritten laws in *Ant.* 450ff. should not be quibbling about husbands and children vs. brothers in a speech 450 lines later; similarly, the claim that a Creon who speaks *Phoen.* 1320–1 should not later speak so harshly to Ant. in the burial-argument of the exodos.

[3] For instance, is it inconsistent for Hippolytus to speak of someone teaching women to be σώφρων (*Hipp.* 667) after the remarks in his dedication to Artemis (79–81)? Is Polynices' concern with wealth and poverty in 438–42 (see n.) inconsistent with his status as son-in-law of Adrastus?

beliefs, and arguments is far from secure. Certain inconsistencies may be tolerated in the interest of attaining given immediate effects, while others may be flaunted openly as a realistic or ironic representation of typical human partiality or lack of self-awareness.

Symmetry and repetition of various kinds have often been cited in interpolation-arguments. I regard it as misguided either to seek exact equality of length in paired speeches by deleting surplus lines or to recommend a deletion by noting that it produces equal speeches. Some believe that Polynices' and Eteocles' speeches in the agon should have precisely the same number of lines (and even that Jocasta's speech should be exactly twice as long). Yet what matters in the aesthetic reception of these dramatic speeches is the perception that they are roughly equal (and that Jocasta's is roughly twice as long); there is no advantage to the poet or audience in making the number of lines actually identical. Similarly, irregularities in stichomythia deserve attention, but it is not always the case that a deletion to create perfect regularity is justified.[1] Repeated words, phrases, and lines have also been sources of suspicion for many critics, but nowadays it is widely accepted that there are many kinds of repetition, some casual and inoffensive to the Greeks (if not to some moderns), some meaningful, some due to corruption or interpolation. Each case must be carefully weighed on its own.[2]

Obscurities and oddities of language are the staple of the textual critic, and no one can reasonably edit a text on the assumption that every oddity is possible and original. Final decisions can be based on diligent collection of comparative data, but there will often be an irreducible element of individual judgment and an unavoidable evaluation of probabilities.

---

[1] Cf. 710–11n., 912n., 1323n.
[2] See, e.g., 22n., 143n. (with refs. therein), 439–40n., 478n., 630n., 697n., 710–11n.

Although there are logical rules of grammar, actual language is sometimes not strictly logical, and a great deal of the communicative power of language lies in delivery and in context (which includes ideas that are not spoken). In poetry, even in Euripides, despite his reputation for simplicity and clarity, there is as well a deliberate deviation from the ordinary, an enhancement or strain of language that marks the special nature of the poetic artefact. Thus, if the meaning of a word is otherwise unattested or a construction rare, we cannot be certain that this is due to corruption or a clumsy interpolator. Throughout the commentary, I have tried to pay special attention to rare and unusual meanings and to demonstrate how context helps to determine meaning,[1] in order to demonstrate that oddities of various kinds are not uncommon in Euripidean poetry, occurring in unsuspected passages as well as in passages that have been subjected to meticulous scrutiny by those testing the hypothesis of interpolation. The noting of *hapax legomena* has long been an interest and tool of scholars debating authorship and authenticity, and I have tried to establish claims of hapax status as firmly as is practical.[2] Yet I hope I have established that the way J. U. Powell, for instance, used *hapax legomena* in examining the authenticity of the teichoskopia is seriously flawed. Even the more cautious guidelines suggested by Reeve for assessing

---

[1] See, for instance, 946n.

[2] Since 1986 I have made use of copyrighted text data in electronic form under licence to my campus from the Thesaurus Linguae Graecae (University of California, Irvine); I have searched this data with UNIX-based programs developed at the Department of the Classics of Harvard University. The set of data available to me was approximately the same as that on the TLG CD-ROM version C. It must be emphasized here that this set represents a very large proportion of surviving Greek literature, but is incomplete, being as yet deficient especially in scholia and lexicographic materials. Furthermore, because of the complexities of Greek inflection and the texts themselves, the search programs currently available have various limitations, and thus some claims of rarity may be subject to correction.

when a word occurring once in an author may be suspect seem to me too inclined toward ready suspicion.[1]

Metrical anomalies would appear to be more reliable for establishing spuriousness, since the form of tragic trimeters is relatively rigid and has been well studied. Yet metrical faults can arise through corruption as well as through incompetent interpolation, and so a metrical argument cannot be decisive by itself, although it may be strong in conjunction with other considerations (547–8n., 1233–5n., 1637–8n.). Nor does the incidence of resolution make any reliable contribution to the problem of separating interpolations from genuine Euripides. I have conducted an experimental study of resolution-rates within separate episodes and parts of episodes and within the lines of separate characters. None of the variation appears to be great enough to support any conclusions, especially in the absence of comparative analyses of nearly contemporary plays of Euripides. It may be noted, however, that the iambic exodos as a whole is in line with the rest of the play in its resolution-rate, so that if the whole is post-Euripidean it is written in a style that imitates the habits of late Euripides.[2]

---

[1] Reeve (1972) 260: 'In trimeters suspicion falls on words of the following classes: (1) words common at the time but otherwise absent from poetry; (2) words otherwise found only in epic or lyric; (3) words common elsewhere in the poet in a different sense; (4) words common in later Greek but otherwise absent from the language of the time; (5) words not found elsewhere in the poet but common in the other tragedians.' Apart from the problem of the uncertainty caused by the loss of the majority of Euripides' works and the vast body of fifth-century Attic drama and other Attic poetry, one may object that Eur. was the tragedian most likely to use a word avoided by the other tragedians as too colloquial or too prosaic, that a poet (like other speakers of a language) is under no compulsion to use the same word at all times in precisely the same sense, and the like. For the insecurity of reason (5), cf. the comment of O. Taplin, *HSCP* 76 (1972) 72 n. 48, on the unique occurrence of σιωπάω in Aesch. fr. 132b.8. See also 51–2n.

[2] The rate in the exodos is 41.80%, compared to 34.83% (for the whole play, including the exodos) or 32.08% (for the portion preceding the exodos). Compare the rates for the prologue (40.96%), for the scene 355–445 (46.07%), and for the agon 446–587 (50%). Another curiosity

47

I have emphasized here the limitations inherent in the kinds of evidence or arguments adduced in supporting deletion of a passage as interpolated, not in order to claim that such arguments are useless, but merely to indicate that they may be less reliable than some of their proponents have believed. In some discussions, the proponent of deletion is said to be sceptical (i.e., of the reliability of the tradition), but I think there is also a proper place for scepticism of our ability to arrive at a confident decision, given the nature of the evidence. In discussing possible interpolations, I have tried to indicate which arguments I believe are factually erroneous or so subjective as to be of little help, and I have tried to show which are singly weak or inadequate. I would also maintain that in some cases a critic who is inclined to delete will seek for and find objections by operating with a fineness of scrutiny that might well unearth similar oddities almost everywhere in a text, if it were consistently applied. Thus the number of objections alleged against a passage may be somewhat misleading. Nevertheless, as has been well pointed out,[1] separately inadequate arguments can combine to form a substantial case in favour of deletion. Individual judgments will still differ in the weighting of various factors and the assessment of their cumulative force. That I am relatively conservative in these matters will be obvious to the reader. Yet I hope that I have presented the information necessary for others to make their own judgments, and that

---

is that in the first rhesis of the first messenger there is a concentration of resolutions in the suspect passage 1104–40 (64.71%) because of proper names and, by contrast, a relative dearth of resolutions in the rest of the speech (16.67%). If 1104–40 are spurious, the overall rate for the play changes very little, but the rate for this scene (22.73%) is strikingly lower than for any comparable section of the play, the reduced rhesis has a rate far below that of any other lengthy rhesis in the play, and the first messenger's lines as a group exhibit a lower rate (22.73%) than the body of lines spoken by any other character with a substantial role.

[1] Reeve (1972) 256.

the need for brevity has not made my views seem more dogmatic than they are.

VII THE TEXT

Extensive information about the textual tradition of the *Phoenissae* has been presented in *Text. Trad.* and in the *praefatio* of the Teubner edition. For significant comments, corrections, and supplementary material, the reader should consult in particular the review of *Text. Trad.* by K. Matthiessen in *Byzantinische Zeitschrift* 79 (1986) 344–6, the review of the Teubner edition by Diggle (1990a), and Diggle's *Text. Trad. Or.* The purpose of this section is not to repeat detailed arguments,[1] but to explain the simplified apparatus of this edition.

Normally the third play in the sequence of select plays of Euripides (cf. MBV, gV) and hence the third in the

---

[1] One additional manuscript of *Phoen.* came to my attention in 1988 through the kindness of D. Harlfinger: codex Bodmer 64, containing arg. Phoen., Phoen., and (to fill the verso of the last folio) the iambic hypothesis to *OT* and *Anth. gr.* 9.387, 9.388, 5.78 (the folios are unnumbered). This was formerly part of Phillipps ms 3086, recorded but not examined by Turyn (*The Byzantine Manuscript Tradition of the Tragedies of Euripides* [Illinois Studies in Language and Literature, 43 (Urbana, Illinois 1957)] 387–8). I have examined the ms in microfilm: it is basically a witness of the χ-class, although it has no scholia. On the basis of the particular selection of prefatory material and the inclusion of the *OT* hypothesis, Bodmer 64 may be related somehow to Vat. Pal. gr. 42, which also has these items; but I have not been able to make any closer examination of the latter, and there are too many late mss of the χ-class that I have never examined. For further details on Phillipps 3086 see Mark L. Sosower, 'A Greek Codex of Sir Thomas Phillipps once in the Clermont Library', *Syllecta Classica* 2 (1990) 95–102; he suggests that the ms was produced in Venice, and speculates that the Euripides portion might have been copied from one of the mss known to have been in Cardinal Bessarion's collection. (I can determine that it is not a copy of Marc. gr. 468 (F), or of Marc. gr. 469 (Yv), but I have no information about Marc. gr. 470.)

'Byzantine triad', *Phoen.* is preserved in about 115 mss dating from the tenth or eleventh century to 1600. Although various degrees of affiliation can be established among small groups of mss, the tradition is characterized by so much horizontal contamination that it is not possible to draw a useful stemma. Mss may be placed in three broad classes. The most important class includes the *veteres*, mostly earlier than 1260, the approximate date of the second Byzantine (Palaeologan) renaissance: HMBOVC, constantly cited in the apparatus of this edition. Second in importance is the class of *recentiores*, mss generally later than 1260: in this edition, nineteen of these mss are taken into account, but for simplicity most citations actually take the form of the group symbol **r** (two or more of the group), and subgroups identified in *Text. Trad.* and used in the Teubner apparatus do not appear here.[1]

The third class consists of those mss associated because of their scholia with Manuel Moschopulus, Thomas Magister, and Demetrius Triclinius. The ' Moschopulean' form of text, referred to here as χ,[2] is reconstructed from the common ancestor of XXaXb, the earliest of which is considerably later than the possible date of Moschopulus' activity as a writer of scholia. Moschopulus' scholia were written earlier than Thomas', and Triclinius' use of readings from χ may suggest that χ was in existence at least as early as 1305. But there can be no assurance that χ is an accurate descendant of the form of text on which Moschopulus wrote his commentary (and made conjectures, if he in fact did so).[3] The χ-text should be viewed as one which contains inherited material not sur-

---

[1] In response to the criticisms of Matthiessen and Diggle I now include AMt with the other *recentiores* and mark no special connection of A with χ, although it is still my impression that A reflects a scholarly milieu which may also have given rise to some of the features of the ancestor of XXaXb (cf. *Text. Trad.* 113–14).

[2] ξ in the apparatus of *Hecuba* in the OCT of Diggle and in *Text. Trad. Or.*

[3] See Diggle, *Text. Trad. Or.* chaps. 8–9, esp. pp. 65–6, 80; also *Text. Trad.* 89–90, 92, 94, 99–100, 119–20.

viving elsewhere as well as peculiar careless errors, corrections of Palaeologan date (or of earlier date but first visible to us in χ), and a fairly consistent style of 'learned' orthography. Even if the term 'Moschopulean' must be abandoned or always used with the attenuation marked by inverted commas, χ is still, to some degree, a product of Palaeologan research and scholarship, presumably connected with the circle of Planudes. The mss with Thoman scholia are a more diverse group and much less important.[1] Their evidence is usually conveyed by the group symbol ζ or **z** (for two or more of the group). The readings of T, the manuscript which reflects the work of Triclinius, are cited mainly for the lyric passages; for the iambic portions of the play, its evidence is adduced only when it carries an emendation or shares a reading with only a few other witnesses.

The text of this edition is virtually the same as that of the Teubner edition. Typographical errors or misplaced accents have been corrected as follows: 142 σημεῖ᾽, 194 ἐπεὶ, 522 ζεύγνυσθε, 673 ξυνῆψε, 1100 Τευμησσὸν, 1141 τόξοισι, 1184 ῎Ολυμπον, 1342 εἰσηκούσατ᾽, 1615 δῆθ᾽, 1681 ξυνθανοῦμαί, 1724 γέροντά μ᾽. I have changed my mind on the following points: 86 βροτῶν, 174 capitalize Γῆς, 301 κλυοῦσ᾽ (West), 437 σὲ κἀμὲ (Π²²), 453 ἀνύτουσιν (Porson), 683 καὶ (Major), 821 ὀδοντοφυὰ (L. Dindorf), 827 comma and 839 colon, 916 πέφηνε (Camper), 970 (990, 1708) εἶα (breathing), 1038 ἄλλον ἐποτότυζε (Π⁷), 1064 ὁρμάσασ᾽ (Willink), 1212 κλυεῖν (West), 1317 μετὰ, 1404 ἐνθένδε, 1530 ὀτοτοτοῖ (Kirchhoff). I of course have doubts or second thoughts about other details of the Teubner text, but I think it is more useful to keep this text as close as possible to my Teubner and to reserve doubts for the commentary.

---

[1] West (1990) 312 suggests that Zm is an apograph rather than *gemellus* of Zv (just as, for the adjacent Aeschylean pages in each, Fc (= Zm) is an apograph of Fb (= Zv)). This is hard to square with the evidence at line 1284 (/——— αἲ αἲ Zm (horizontal stroke reflecting a space left by erasure in the exemplar), / αἲ αἲ Zv), cited in *GRBS* 26 (1985) 102.

For the apparatus criticus of this edition, I have omitted most singular readings that are clearly wrong and most orthographic details. I tacitly print οἰκτίρω, -πίτνω, ηὗρε, κᾱς, νυν, δύο, γιγν-, ἱππῆς, ἀριστῆς, ἄρη, πολυνείκη, μειξ-, κληι- for οἰκτείρω, -πιτνῶ / -πίπτω, εὗρε, κεῖς, νῦν, δύω, γιν-, ἱππεῖς, ἀριστεῖς, ἄρην, πολυνείκην, μιξ-, κληϊ- / κλει-, and do not record variations such as ὦ / ὤ, ἐτεοκλῆς / ἐτεοκλέης, ἄρ(α) / ἅρ(α), -αισι / -ησι, presence or absence of nu-movable in -σι(ν) or -ε(ν) (or -εν vs. elision of -ε). Testimonia are not always cited when they merely confirm a reading of the mss adopted in the text, and multiple testimonia are often cited with ' test.' (implying reference to the Teubner or *Text. Trad.* for details) rather than in full. Likewise, the evidence of the papyri is cited here with some reduction in inessential detail; moreover, when a minority variant or emendation is recorded 'negatively' in the apparatus, the agreement of a papyrus with an adopted majority reading of the mss will not be evident. Thus no inference about papyrus readings should be made from the silence of this apparatus.

TEXT

SIGLA

PAPYRI

Π^1	M. P. E. R. 5 (1892) 74–7
Π^2	P. Oxy. 2.224 and P. Ryl. 3.547
Π^3	P. Lit. Lond. 75
Π^4	P. Oxy. 9.1177 and P. Oxy. 53.3714
Π^5	P. Strasb. WG 307
Π^6	P. Wurzb. 1
Π^7	PSI 11.1193
Π^8	M. P. E. R. n. s. 3 (1939) 21
Π^9	P. Berol. inv. 11868
Π^{10}	P. Merton 2.54
Π^{11}	P. Ant. 2.74
Π^{12}	P. Berol. 17018 and 21218
Π^{13}	P. Berol. 21169
Π^{14}	BASP 12 (1975) 71–4
Π^{15}	P. Oxy. 44.3153
Π^{16}	P. Oxy. 47.3321
Π^{17}	P. Oxy. 47.3322
Π^{18}	P. Berol. 21207
Π^{19}	P. Oxy. 53.3712
Π^{20}	P. Oxy. 53.3713
Π^{21}	P. Oxy. 53.3715
Π^{22}	P. Oxy. 60.4012[1]
Π^{aa}	P. Herc. 1609 I 127
Π^{a}	P. Vat. gr. 11
Π^{b}	M. P. E. R. n. s. 1 (1932) 23
Π^{c}	P. Cairo inv. 65445
Π^{d}	O. Edfu 3.326

---

[1] I know of this through the kindness of M. W. Haslam. This scrap of a parchment codex of the fifth century has remnants of 430–7 (with 436 apparently omitted) and 461–7.

Π^e PSI 13.1303
Π^f YCS 15 (1957) 183
Π^g P. Oxy. 27.2455
Π^h P. Oxy. 31.2544
Π^i P. Oxy. 33.2661
Π^j P. Oxy. 42.3004
Π^k PSI ined.[1]

MANUSCRIPTS

veteres

H	Jerusalem, Patriarchike Bibliotheke, 36	10–11th cent.
M	Venice, Biblioteca Nazionale Marciana, gr. 471	11th cent.
B	Paris, Bibliothèque Nationale, gr. 2713	10–11th cent.
O	Florence, Biblioteca Medicea-Laurenziana, plut. 31.10	*c.* 1175
V	Vatican, Biblioteca Apostolica Vaticana, gr. 909	*c.* 1250–80
C	Turin, Biblioteca Nazionale, B.IV.13	1300–50

recentiores

A	Paris, Bibliothèque Nationale, gr. 2712	*c.* 1300
Aa	Milan, Biblioteca Ambrosiana, C 44 sup.	14th cent.
Ab	Milan, Biblioteca Ambrosiana, F 74 sup.	*c.* 1300

---

[1] Diggle (1990a) has brought to my attention the attestation of *Phoen.* 499–500 and 515–17 in a gnomology of the second or third century A.D.; preliminary publication of this Florentine papyrus (eventually to appear in PSI) is made by Bartoletti, 8, 13–14. There are no variants of consequence, but see 499n.

Cr	Cremona, Biblioteca	
	Governativa, 130	14th cent.
F	Venice, Biblioteca Nazionale	
	Marciana, gr. 468	late 13th cent.
G	Milan, Biblioteca Ambrosiana,	
	L 39 sup.	*c.* 1320
L	Florence, Biblioteca Medicea-	
	Laurenziana, plut. 32.2	1300–20
Mn	Munich, Bayerische	
	Staatsbibliothek, gr. 560	14th cent.
Mt	Madrid, Biblioteca Nacional,	
	4677	14th cent.
P	Florence, Biblioteca Medicea-	
	Laurenziana, conv. soppr. 172	1320–25
Pr	Reims, Bibliothèque de la ville,	
	1306	late 13th cent.
R	Vatican, Biblioteca Apostolica	
	Vaticana, gr. 1135	mid/late 13th cent.
Rf	Florence, Biblioteca Medicea-	
	Laurenziana, plut. 32.33	*c.* 1300
Rv	Vatican, Biblioteca Apostolica	
	Vaticana, gr. 1331	14th cent.
Rw	Vienna, Österreichische	
	Nationalbibliothek, phil. gr.	
	119	*c.* 1300
S	Salamanca, Biblioteca	
	Universitaria, 31	1326
Sa	Vatican, Biblioteca Apostolica	
	Vaticana, gr. 1345	late 13th cent.
Vr	Vatican, Biblioteca Apostolica	
	Vaticana, Pal. gr. 343	*c.* 1500
W	Athos, Mone Iberon, 209	*c.* 1300

'*Moschopulean*' *manuscripts*

| X | Oxford, Bodleian Library, Auct. | |
| | F.3.25 | 1330–40 |

Xa	Oxford, Bodleian Library,	
	Barocci 120	1320–30
Xb	Florence, Biblioteca Medicea-	
	Laurenziana, conv. soppr. 71	14th cent.

'Thomano-Triclinian' manuscripts

Z	Cambridge, University Library,	
	Nn.3.14	14th cent.
Zb	Vatican, Biblioteca Apostolica	
	Vaticana, gr. 51	1320–30
Zc	Copenhagen, Det Kongelige	
	Bibliotek, Gamle Kongelig	
	Samling 3549	early 14th cent.
Zm	Milan, Biblioteca Ambrosiana, I	
	47 sup.	14th cent.
Zu	Uppsala, Universitetsbibliotek,	
	gr. 15	1300–50
T	Rome, Biblioteca Angelica, gr.	
	14	1300–25

Composite symbols

Ω = all mss listed above

Ω̣ = all mss except the one or two cited for a different reading

ω = HMBOVC

ω̣ = ω except the one cited for a different reading

ω+ = ω plus several codd. of the other groups below (ρχζ)
likewise, (e.g.) MB+ = MB plus several codd. of the other
groups below

ρ = all *recentiores* listed above

r = two or more of *recentiores* just listed

χ = agreement of XXaXb

x = two of XXaXb

ζ = all, or almost all, of Thomano-Triclinian witnesses listed
above, or all except T

z = two or more of Thomano-Triclinian codd.

* after test. or specific author cited for testimonium indicates some mss of the test. author(s)

Modifications of symbols

A^1	first hand in manuscript A
A^2, A^3	second, third hand in A
A^c	corrector in A
A^r	rubricator in A
A^s	above the line in A
A^g	supralinear gloss in A
$A^{\gamma\rho}$	variant or correction in A introduced by γρ(άφεται/άφε) (καὶ)
A^{marg}	in the margin in A
A^{ac}	A before correction
A^{pc}	A after correction
A^{uv}	A *ut videtur*
Σ	scholion, scholiast on *Phoen.*
$Σ^A$	scholion as found in manuscript A
$^{le}Σ$	lemma of Σ
$^iΣ$	reading implied by interpretation of Σ
$^pΣ$	word or form used in paraphrase of Σ
$^gΣ$	gloss used in Σ
$^{\gamma\rho}Σ$	γράφεται variant in Σ

ΤΑ ΤΟΥ ΔΡΑΜΑΤΟΣ ΠΡΟΣΩΠΑ

ΙΟΚΑΣΤΗ
ΘΕΡΑΠΩΝ
ΑΝΤΙΓΟΝΗ
ΧΟΡΟΣ ΕΚ ΦΟΙΝΙΣΣΩΝ
ΠΟΛΥΝΕΙΚΗΣ
ΕΤΕΟΚΛΗΣ
ΚΡΕΩΝ
ΤΕΙΡΕΣΙΑΣ
ΜΕΝΟΙΚΕΥΣ
ΑΓΓΕΛΟΣ
ΕΤΕΡΟΣ ΑΓΓΕΛΟΣ
ΟΙΔΙΠΟΥΣ

indicem personarum fere sic praebent **r**XαζT, confuso ordine ω**r** (om. **x**L)
θεράπων (vide ad 88): παιδαγωγός Ω

ΦΟΙΝΙΣΣΑΙ

ΙΟΚΑΣΤΗ

{῝Ω τὴν ἐν ἄστροις οὐρανοῦ τέμνων ὁδὸν
καὶ χρυσοκολλήτοισιν ἐμβεβὼς δίφροις,}
῞Ηλιε, θοαῖς ἵπποισιν εἱλίσσων φλόγα,
ὡς δυστυχῆ Θήβαισι τῆι τόθ᾽ ἡμέραι
ἀκτῖν᾽ ἐφῆκας, Κάδμος ἡνίκ᾽ ἦλθε γῆν   5
τήνδ᾽, ἐκλιπὼν Φοίνισσαν ἐναλίαν χθόνα·
ὃς παῖδα γήμας Κύπριδος Ἁρμονίαν ποτὲ
Πολύδωρον ἐξέφυσε, τοῦ δὲ Λάβδακον
φῦναι λέγουσιν, ἐκ δὲ τοῦδε Λάιον.
ἐγὼ δὲ παῖς μὲν κλήιζομαι Μενοικέως,   10
{Κρέων τ᾽ ἀδελφὸς μητρὸς ἐκ μιᾶς ἔφυ,}
καλοῦσι δ᾽ Ἰοκάστην με· τοῦτο γὰρ πατὴρ
ἔθετο. γαμεῖ δὲ Λάιός μ᾽· ἐπεὶ δ᾽ ἄπαις
ἦν χρόνια λέκτρα τἄμ᾽ ἔχων ἐν δώμασιν,
ἐλθὼν ἐρωτᾶι Φοῖβον ἐξαιτεῖ θ᾽ ἅμα   15
παίδων ἐς οἴκους ἀρσένων κοινωνίαν.
ὁ δ᾽ εἶπεν· ῏Ω Θήβαισιν εὐίπποις ἄναξ,
μὴ σπεῖρε τέκνων ἄλοκα δαιμόνων βίαι·
εἰ γὰρ τεκνώσεις παῖδ᾽, ἀποκτενεῖ σ᾽ ὁ φύς,
καὶ πᾶς σὸς οἶκος βήσεται δι᾽ αἵματος.   20
ὁ δ᾽ ἡδονῆι ⟨᾿ν⟩δοὺς εἴς τε βακχείαν πεσὼν
ἔσπειρεν ἡμῖν παῖδα· καὶ σπείρας βρέφος,

1–2 om. Π¹⁶Π¹⁷, del. Haslam; v. 3 ut initium fabulae citat Πᵍ, cf. Πᵈ, sch. Hephaest. 267, 297 Consbr.   4 Θήβησι L   5 ἀφῆκας V   8 τοῦδε OVrz   11 del. Paley; partem versus habere videtur Π¹⁶, totum habet Π¹⁷   μητρὸς ἐκ μιᾶς fere ω+: ἐκ μιᾶς γαστρὸς r   16 παίδων Π¹⁶ω+: τέκνων rz   κοιρανίαν r   18 τέκνων fere Ω, test.: παίδων Π¹⁶, test.   αὔλακα V, test.*   βίαι Π¹⁶Ω, test.: ἄτερ Max. Tyr. 1.19, 368*   19 ἦν γὰρ Max. Tyr.   φυτεύσεις/-ηις test.*   20 αἱμάτων Orig. Cels. 2.20*   21 ᾿νδοὺς Markland: δοὺς Π¹⁶Ω, test.   βακχείαν F¹ (coni. von Arnim): βακχεῖον ΩFᶜ, test.: βακχιον Π¹⁶   22 παῖδα Π¹⁶ω+: τέκνον r   βρέφος fere Π¹⁶Ω: φρενὸς anon., γόνον Wecklein, τάλας Hartung (cf. 25)

61

ΦΟΙΝΙΣΣΑΙ

γνοὺς τἀμπλάκημα τοῦ θεοῦ τε τὴν φάτιν,
λειμῶν᾽ ἐς Ἥρας καὶ Κιθαιρῶνος λέπας
δίδωσι βουκόλοισιν ἐκθεῖναι βρέφος,   25
σφυρῶν σιδηρᾶ κέντρα διαπείρας μέσων·
ὅθεν νιν Ἑλλὰς ὠνόμαζεν Οἰδίπουν.
Πολύβου δέ νιν λαβόντες ἱπποβουκόλοι
φέρουσ᾽ ἐς οἴκους εἴς τε δεσποίνης χέρας
ἔθηκαν. ἡ δὲ τὸν ἐμὸν ὠδίνων πόνον   30
μαστοῖς ὑφεῖτο καὶ πόσιν πείθει τεκεῖν.
ἤδη δὲ πυρσαῖς γένυσιν ἐξανδρούμενος
παῖς οὑμὸς ἢ γνοὺς ἤ τινος μαθὼν πάρα
ἔστειχε τοὺς φύσαντας ἐκμαθεῖν θέλων
πρὸς δῶμα Φοίβου, Λάιός θ᾽ οὑμὸς πόσις   35
τὸν ἐκτεθέντα παῖδα μαστεύων μαθεῖν
εἰ μηκέτ᾽ εἴη. καὶ ξυνάπτετον πόδα
εἰς ταὐτὸν ἄμφω Φωκίδος σχιστῆς ὁδοῦ.
καί νιν κελεύει Λαΐου τροχηλάτης·
Ὦ ξένε, τυράννοις ἐκποδὼν μεθίστασο.   40
ὁ δ᾽ εἷρπ᾽ ἄναυδος, μέγα φρονῶν. πῶλοι δέ νιν
χηλαῖς τένοντας ἐξεφοίνισσον ποδῶν.
ὅθεν – τί τἄκτος τῶν κακῶν με δεῖ λέγειν; –
παῖς πατέρα καίνει καὶ λαβὼν ὀχήματα
Πολύβωι τροφεῖ δίδωσιν. ὡς δ᾽ ἐπεζάρει   45
Σφὶγξ ἁρπαγαῖσι πόλιν ἐμός τ᾽ οὐκ ἦν πόσις,
Κρέων ἀδελφὸς τἀμὰ κηρύσσει λέχη,
ὅστις σοφῆς αἴνιγμα παρθένου μάθοι,
τούτωι ξυνάψειν λέκτρα. τυγχάνει δέ πως

25 βρέφος Π¹⁶Ω: πατὴρ Camper   26–27 del. Paley (27 Valck.)
26 διασπείρας OCF¹   μέσων Π¹⁶z: μέσον fere ω+, Σ805: μέσα Cr:
(σφυροῖν…) μέσοιν Blaydes   27 ᾠνόμαξεν Π¹⁶: ὠνόμασεν rz   30 τὸν
ἐμὸν Π¹⁶χLz: τὸν ἐμῶν Or, Σᴮⱽ1606: τῶν ἐμῶν ω+, Σᴹ1606   πόνων
M¹(corr. M²)Saᵃᶜ, Σˢ1606   31 πόσει Sa   τρέφειν Nagel   34
τεκόντας Posidonius (apud Strab. 16.38)   36 μαθεῖν ω+(xʸᵖ): ἰδεῖν
Bʸᵖrχ: ἰδὼν Vʸᵖ: ι[..]ν vel ι[…]ν Π¹⁶   40 ξένε Π¹⁶ωr: ξένιε MᵃᶜO: ξεῖνε
rχζ   42 ποδοῖν r   43 τάχθος r   45 ἐπεζάρει χΖ: ἐπεβάρει MᵍO
47 κρέων Π¹⁷Orχz: κρέων δ᾽ Π¹⁷ˢωr: κρέων τ᾽ rz   48 μάθη(ι) rz
49 -άψει Vr: -άπτειν z

μούσας ἐμὸς παῖς Οἰδίπους Σφιγγὸς μαθών,   50
{ὅθεν τύραννος τῆσδε γῆς καθίσταται}
καὶ σκῆπτρ' ἔπαθλα τῆσδε λαμβάνει χθονός.
γαμεῖ δὲ τὴν τεκοῦσαν οὐκ εἰδὼς τάλας,
οὐδ' ἡ τεκοῦσα παιδὶ συγκοιμωμένη.
τίκτω δὲ παῖδας παιδὶ δύο μὲν ἄρσενας,   55
Ἐτεοκλέα κλεινήν τε Πολυνείκους βίαν,
κόρας τε δισσάς· τὴν μὲν Ἰσμήνην πατὴρ
ὠνόμασε, τὴν δὲ πρόσθεν Ἀντιγόνην ἐγώ.
μαθὼν δὲ τἀμὰ λέκτρα μητρώιων γάμων
ὁ πάντ' ἀνατλὰς Οἰδίπους παθήματα   60
εἰς ὄμμαθ' αὑτοῦ δεινὸν ἐμβάλλει φόνον,
χρυσηλάτοις πόρπαισιν αἱμάξας κόρας.
ἐπεὶ δὲ τέκνων γένυς ἐμῶν σκιάζεται,
κλήιθροις ἔκρυψαν πατέρ', ἵν' ἀμνήμων τύχη
γένοιτο πολλῶν δεομένη σοφισμάτων·   65
ζῶν δ' ἔστ' ἐν οἴκοις. πρὸς δὲ τῆς τύχης νοσῶν
ἀρὰς ἀρᾶται παισὶν ἀνοσιωτάτας,
θηκτῶι σιδήρωι δῶμα διαλαχεῖν τόδε.
τὼ δ' εἰς φόβον πεσόντε μὴ τελεσφόρους
εὐχὰς θεοὶ κραίνωσιν οἰκούντων ὁμοῦ   70
ξυμβάντ' ἔταξαν τὸν νεώτερον πάρος
φεύγειν ἑκόντα τήνδε Πολυνείκη χθόνα,
Ἐτεοκλέα δὲ σκῆπτρ' ἔχειν μένοντα γῆς,
ἐνιαυτὸν ἀλλάσσοντ'. ἐπεὶ δ' ἐπὶ ζυγοῖς
καθέζετ' ἀρχῆς, οὐ μεθίσταται θρόνων,   75
φυγάδα δ' ἀπωθεῖ τῆσδε Πολυνείκη χθονός.

---

50 μούσας Π¹⁷V²ᵞᴾΣᵞᴾ: αἴνιγμ' Ω   51–2 del. Leutsch, 51 Valck, 52
Bergk (52 om. Π¹⁷, hab. Π¹⁶Π¹⁹)   52 var. lect. καὶ σκῆπτρα χώρας ἆθλα
⟨τῆσδε λαμβάνει⟩ cognovit Σ   55 ἄρσενας VG: ἄρρενας Π¹⁹Ω
57 ἰσμήνην M: ἰσμ- Ω: εισμ- Π¹⁹   59 μητρῶιον γάμον VPz
60 del. Valck. (hab. Π¹⁶Π¹⁷Π¹⁹)   62 del. Fraenkel (hab. Π¹⁶Π¹⁹)
χρυσηλάταις MO   70 εὐχὰς ω +: ἀρὰς r: ὀργὰς V   οἰκούντοιν (dat.)
Elmsley   73 σκῆπτρον V   74 ζυγῶ L   75 ἄρχων z   76
φυγάδα δ' M¹ᴾᶜB²V +: φυγάδα B¹: φυγάδ' rxz: φυγὰς δ' fort. Mᵃᶜ: φυγᾶι δ'
OCr

ὁ δ᾽ Ἄργος ἐλθών, κῆδος Ἀδράστου λαβών,
πολλὴν ἀθροίσας ἀσπίδ᾽ Ἀργείων ἄγει.
ἐπ᾽ αὐτὰ δ᾽ ἐλθὼν ἑπτάπυλα τείχη τάδε
πατρῶι᾽ ἀπαιτεῖ σκῆπτρα καὶ μέρη χθονός.   80
ἐγὼ δ᾽ ἔριν λύουσ᾽ ὑπόσπονδον μολεῖν
ἔπεισα παιδὶ παῖδα πρὶν ψαῦσαι δορός.
ἥξειν δ᾽ ὁ πεμφθεὶς φησιν αὐτὸν ἄγγελος.
    ἀλλ᾽, ὦ φαεννᾶς οὐρανοῦ ναίων πτυχάς
Ζεῦ, σῶισον ἡμᾶς, δὸς δὲ σύμβασιν τέκνοις·   85
χρὴ δ᾽, εἰ σοφὸς πέφυκας, οὐκ ἐᾶν βροτῶν
τὸν αὐτὸν αἰεὶ δυστυχῆ καθεστάναι.   87

ΘΕΡΑΠΩΝ

ὦ κλεινὸν οἴκοις Ἀντιγόνη θάλος πατρί,   88
ἐπεί σε μήτηρ παρθενῶνας ἐκλιπεῖν
μεθῆκε μελάθρων ἐς διῆρες ἔσχατον   90
στράτευμ᾽ ἰδεῖν Ἀργεῖον ἱκεσίαισι σαῖς,
ἐπίσχες, ὡς ἂν προὐξερευνήσω στίβον,
μή τις πολιτῶν ἐν τρίβωι φαντάζεται,
κἀμοὶ μὲν ἔλθηι φαῦλος ὡς δούλωι ψόγος,
σοὶ δ᾽ ὡς ἀνάσσηι. πάντα δ᾽ ἐξειδὼς φράσω   95
ἅ τ᾽ εἶδον εἰσήκουσά τ᾽ Ἀργείων πάρα,
σπονδὰς ὅτ᾽ ἦλθον σῶι κασιγνήτωι φέρων
ἐνθένδ᾽ ἐκεῖσε δεῦρό τ᾽ αὖ κείνων πάρα.
    ἀλλ᾽ οὔτις ἀστῶν τοῖσδε χρίμπτεται δόμοις·
κέδρου παλαιὰν κλίμακ᾽ ἐκπέρα ποδί,   100
σκόπει δὲ πεδία καὶ παρ᾽ Ἰσμηνοῦ ῥοὰς
Δίρκης τε νᾶμα πολεμίων στράτευμ᾽ ὅσον.   102

---

77 κῆδος τ᾽ **rζ**   79 ἐπ᾽ ω+: ἐς/εἰς **rχz**   84 φαεινὰς **rχz** πτυχὰς
Pr^uv: πτύχας ω+: πύλας χ   85 σύμβασιν VS^ac: ξύμ- Ω   86 βροτῶν
Ab^ac, sch. Dion. Thr. (*Gramm. Gr.* 1:3.289, 20–1)* (coni. Markland,
Valck.): βροτὸν Ω   88–201 Euripidi abiudicant Verrall, Dihle   88^n
θεράπων scripsi (post Robert): παιδαγωγός Ω   90 μελάθρων δ᾽ **r**   92
τρίβον V   94 ἔλθοι **rZ**   97 = 143 (vide ad 141–4)   98 κείνων V,
cf. ^PΣ: κείνου Ω   99 τοῖσδ᾽ ἐγχρί- fere V**rz**   101 ἰσμηνοῦ M:
ἰσμ- Ω

ΑΝΤΙΓΟΝΗ

οῦ ὄρεγέ νυν ὄρεγε γεραιὰν νέαι   103
    χεῖρ' ἀπὸ κλιμάκων
    ποδὸς ἴχνος ἐπαντέλλων.   105
Θε. ἰδοὺ ξύναψον, παρθέν'· εἰς καιρὸν δ' ἔβης·
    κινούμενον γὰρ τυγχάνει Πελασγικὸν
    στράτευμα, χωρίζουσι δ' ἀλλήλων λόχους.
Αν. ἰὼ πότνια παῖ
    Λατοῦς Ἑκάτα, κατάχαλκον ἅπαν   110
    πεδίον ἀστράπτει.
Θε. οὐ γάρ τι φαύλως ἦλθε Πολυνείκης χθόνα,
    πολλοῖς μὲν ἵπποις, μυρίοις δ' ὅπλοις βρέμων.
Αν. ἆρα πύλαι κλῄθροις χαλκόδετά τ' ἔμβολα
    λαϊνέοισ⟨ιν⟩ Ἀμφίονος ὀργάνοις   115
    τείχεος ἥρμοσται;
Θε. θάρσει· τά γ' ἔνδον ἀσφαλῶς ἔχει πόλις.
    ἀλλ' εἰσόρα †τὸν πρῶτον, εἰ βούλῃ μαθεῖν†.
Αν. τίς οὗτος ὁ λευκόλοφας,
    πρόπαρ ὃς ἁγεῖται στρατοῦ,   120
    πάγχαλκον ἀσπίδ' ἀμφὶ βραχίονι
    κουφίζων;   121-2
Θε. λοχαγός, ὦ δέσποινα.   Αν. τίς πόθεν γεγώς;
    αὔδησον, ὦ γεραιέ, τίς ὀνομάζεται;

---

105 ποδὸς del. Bothe   ἐπαντέλλων **Brz**, Hsch. ε 4198: ἐπανατ-
ω+   108 χωρίζουσι δ' Ω: χωριζουσιν Π³   λόχοις V: λοχος
Π³   109 ἰὼ Ω: ω Π³ᵘ\ᵛ   109-10 πότνια παῖ Λατοῦς Π³Ω: παῖ Λ.
πότνια L   110-11 κατάχαλκον ... ἀστράπτει Ω: παταχαλκον ...
αστραπται Π³: κατέσχον ... ἀστραπαῖς Eust. 471, 42   111 πεδίον Ω:
οπλοις πεδιον Π³, cf. Heliod. 9.14.1   112 γάρ τοι Vr   φαῦλος
CMtᵃᶜ**z**   113 δ' om. Π³   114 ἆρ' αἱ **r**   χαλκόδετά τ' ἔμβολα
Ω(δ' **r**): χαλ]κοτ...εμβ[ολ]α Π³: χαλκόδέτ' ἔμβολα (sic) O: χαλκόδετ'
ἔμβολά τε Seidler   115 λαϊνέοισιν Bothe, Burges, sch. Thom. Soph. *Ai.*
596: λαϊνέοις Ω: λαινοις Π³   118 τὸν Ω: τὸ A. Schoene (τὸ πεδίον anon.):
versum del. Diggle   120 ἁγεῖται fere ω+: ἄγει **r**   121-2 πάγχαλκον
δ' CL²   βραχίονι ω+: -ίονα **Crχz**, Σᴹᶜ111   123-4 del.
Dindorf   124 αὔδησον Matthiae: αὔδασον Ω

Θε. οὗτος Μυκηναῖος μὲν αὐδᾶται γένος,   125
      Λερναῖα δ᾽ οἰκεῖ νάμαθ᾽, Ἱππομέδων ἄναξ.

Αν. ἒ ἔ, ὡς γαῦρος, ὡς φοβερὸς εἰσιδεῖν,
      γίγαντι γηγενέται προσόμοιος
      ἀστερωπὸς ⟨ὡς⟩ ἐν γραφαῖσιν, οὐχὶ πρόσ-
      φορος ἀμερίωι γένναι.   130

Θε. τὸν δ᾽ ἐξαμείβοντ᾽ οὐχ ὁρᾶις Δίρκης ὕδωρ
      λοχαγόν; Αν. ἄλλος ἄλλος ὅδε τευχέων τρόπος.
      τίς δ᾽ ἐστὶν οὗτος; Θε. παῖς μὲν Οἰνέως ἔφυ,
      Τυδεύς, Ἄρη δ᾽ Αἰτωλὸν ἐν στέρνοις ἔχει.

Αν. οὗτος ὁ τᾶς Πολυνείκεος, ὦ γέρον,   135
      αὐτοκασιγνήται νύμφας
      ὁμόγαμος κυρεῖ;
      ὡς ἀλλόχρως ὅπλοισι, μειξοβάρβαρος.

Θε. σακεσφόροι γὰρ πάντες Αἰτωλοί, τέκνον,
      λόγχαις τ᾽ ἀκοντιστῆρες εὐστοχώτατοι.   140

{Αν. σὺ δ᾽, ὦ γέρον, πῶς αἰσθάνηι σαφῶς τάδε;

Θε. σημεῖ᾽ ἰδὼν τότ᾽ ἀσπίδων ἐγνώρισα,
      σπονδὰς ὅτ᾽ ἦλθον σῶι κασιγνήτωι φέρων·
      ἃ προσδεδορκὼς οἶδα τοὺς ὡπλισμένους.}

Αν. τίς δ᾽ οὗτος ἀμφὶ μνῆμα τὸ Ζήθου περᾶι,   145
      καταβόστρυχος, ὄμμασι γοργὸς
      εἰσιδεῖν νεανίας,
      λοχαγός, ὡς ὄχλος νιν ὑστέρωι ποδὶ
      πάνοπλος ἀμφέπει;

---

125 μὲν om. M¹(corr. M²)OCSa   127 ἒ ἔ vel ἒ ἔ ω+: αῖ αῖ **r**
128 γίγαντι γηγενέται fere Ω: γεγονοτα γηγενεθλαν Π³: γίγαντι del.
Nauck   129 ἀστερωπὸς **r**X: ἀστρωπὸς Dindorf   ὡς addidi (post
Nauck)   130 ἀμερίων Mt^{pc}χT, cf. ᴾΣ^{VG} et Et. gen. s.v. ἡμέριοι
132 λοχαγόν **Brz**: λοχαγος Π³: λοχ. om. ωρχz   133 δ᾽ om. Π³Zb,
del. Burges   ουτος εστι transp. Π³   134 ἄρη(ν) δ᾽ αἰτωλὸν fere Ω:
αρης δ αιτολος Π³   136 αὐτοκασιγνήται Reiske: -γνητα Π³: -γνήτας fere
Ω   138 ως δ Π³   141–4 del. Stahl (post Bergk), 143 (=97) Burges,
143–4 Busche, Pearson   145 τὸ ω+: τοῦ V¹(in ras.)**r**: om. **r**
146 γοργός τ᾽ **rχz**   147 ἐσιδεῖν χ   148 Ant. continuant R¹LT et
(incertum an consulto) C: totum v. servo trib. M¹(qui etiam 149 Ant.
trib.)**Or**: λοχαγός servo, ὡς κτλ. Ant. trib. M²BVR²+   λοχαγός om.
T

Θε. ὅδ' ἐστὶ Παρθενοπαῖος, Ἀταλάντης γόνος.   150
Αν. ἀλλά νιν ἁ κατ' ὄρη μετὰ ματέρος
      Ἄρτεμις ἱεμένα τόξοις δαμάσασ' ὀλέσειεν,
      ὃς ἐπ' ἐμὰν πόλιν ἔβα πέρσων.
Θε. εἴη τάδ', ὦ παῖ. σὺν δίκηι δ' ἥκουσι γῆν·
      ὃ καὶ δέδοικα μὴ σκοπῶσ' ὀρθῶς θεοί.   155
Αν. ποῦ δ' ὃς ἐμοὶ μιᾶς ἐγένετ' ἐκ ματρὸς
      πολυπόνωι μοίραι;
      ὦ φίλτατ', εἰπέ, ποῦ 'στι Πολυνείκης, γέρον;
Θε. ἐκεῖνος ἑπτὰ παρθένων τάφου πέλας
      Νιόβης Ἀδράστωι πλησίον παραστατεῖ.   160
      ὁρᾶις; Αν. ὁρῶ δῆτ' οὐ σαφῶς, ὁρῶ δέ πως
      μορφῆς τύπωμα στέρνα τ' ἐξηικασμένα.
      ἀνεμώκεος εἴθε δρόμον νεφέλας
      ποσὶν ἐξανύσαιμι δι' αἰθέρος
      πρὸς ἐμὸν ὁμογενέτορα – περὶ δ' ὠλένας   165
      δέραι φιλτάται βάλοιμι χρόνωι –
      φυγάδα μέλεον. ὡς
      ὅπλοισι χρυσέοισιν ἐκπρεπής, γέρον,
      ἑώιοις ὅμοια φλεγέθων βολαῖς ἀελίου.
Θε. ἥξει δόμους τούσδ', ὥστε σ' ἐμπλῆσαι χαρᾶς,   170
      ἔνσπονδος. Αν. οὗτος δ', ὦ γεραιέ, τίς κυρεῖ,
      ὃς ἅρμα λευκὸν ἡνιοστροφεῖ βεβώς;
Θε. ὁ μάντις Ἀμφιάραος, ὦ δέσποιν', ὅδε·
      σφάγια δ' ἅμ' αὐτῶι, Γῆς φιλαίματοι ῥοαί.
Αν. ὦ λιπαροζώνου θύγατερ Ἀελίου   175
      Σελαναία, χρυσεόκυκλον φέγγος,

153 ἐπ' om. V   ἔβαν V: ἐπέβα r   156 ποῦ ποῦ δ' Vrᵖᶜz: ποῖ
ποῖ δ' A   ματρὸς Hermann: ματέρος fere Ω   158 'στι vel ἐστι fere
Ω(V²ʸᵖ): μοι V¹   161 ὁρᾶις om. r   162 μορφᾶς fere Lζ   163
δρόμω C: δρόμου r   165–6 ὠλέναις δέρην φιλτάταις V²ˢ   166
βάλ(λ)οιμι Ω: βάλοιμ' ἐν Hermann: βάλοιμεν Diggle   167 var. lect. ὡς
ἴδω cognovit Σ   168 εὐπρεπής rχz   ἀελίου del. Wecklein   170
ὥστε σ' ω+: ὥστ' Or   ἐκπλῆσαι rz   171 τίς κυρεῖ T: τίς πόθεν Π⁴χ:
πόθεν κυρεῖ z: τίς πόθεν κυρεῖ ωρz   174 φιλαίματοι Π⁴ω+: φιλαιμάτου
rζ, ʸᵖΣ: φιλαιμάτοιο ʸᵖΣ   χοαί Musgrave   176 χρυσόκυκλον VRχ
(χρ]υσεονκυκλοιν Π⁴)

ὡς ἀτρεμαῖα κέντρα καὶ σώφρονα
πώλοις μεταφέρων ἰθύνει.
ποῦ δ᾽ ὃς τὰ δεινὰ τῇδ᾽ ἐφυβρίζει πόλει,
Καπανεύς; Θε. ἐκεῖνος προσβάσεις τεκμαίρεται   180
πύργων ἄνω τε καὶ κάτω τείχη μετρῶν.

Αν. ἰώ,
Νέμεσι καὶ Διὸς βαρύβρομοι βρονταὶ
κεραύνιόν τε φῶς αἰθαλόεν, σύ τοι
μεγαληγορίαν ὑπεράνορα κοιμίζεις·
ὅδ᾽ ἐστίν, αἰχμαλωτίδας   185
ὃς δορὶ Θηβαίας Μυκηνῇσιν
⟨   ⟩
Λερναίαι τε δώσειν τριαίναι,
Ποσειδανίοις Ἀμυμωνίοις
ὕδασι δουλείαν περιβαλών.
μήποτε μήποτε τάνδ᾽, ὦ πότνια,   190
χρυσεοβόστρυχον ὦ Διὸς ἔρνος,
Ἄρτεμι, δουλοσύναν τλαίην.

Θε. ὦ τέκνον, εἴσβα δῶμα καὶ κατὰ στέγας
ἐν παρθενῶσι μίμνε σοῖς, ἐπεὶ πόθου
εἰς τέρψιν ἦλθες ὧν ἔχρῃζες εἰσιδεῖν.   195
ὄχλος γάρ, ὡς ταραγμὸς εἰσῆλθεν πόλιν,
χωρεῖ γυναικῶν πρὸς δόμους τυραννικούς.
φιλόψογον δὲ χρῆμα θηλειῶν ἔφυ,

178 ἰθύνει ⟨δρόμον⟩ post Paley Wilam.   180 ἐκεῖνος Valck. (et Π⁴ᵘᵛ):
ἐκεῖνος ἑπτὰ Ω   τεκμαίρεται Π⁴Ω: σκοπεῖ Τ (= χᵍζᵍ)   182bis νέμεσι
MB²VC, fere test.: νέμεσις Β¹Ο +, Suda ε 1062*   καὶ διὸς Ω: καὶ τὸ διὸς
Suda ε 1062: om. (τε post βαρύβρ. add.) test. alia   183 κεραυνοῦ Bothe,
Hermann (-ῶν Nauck)   φῶς Π⁴ω +: πῦρ rχΤ   184 μεγαληγορίαν
Valck. et Toup e Σ: μεγαλανορίαν Ω (μεγαλάνορα ὑπερηνορίαν Eust. 462,
4)   κοιμίζοις Β³V²ˢrz: κομίζεις χΖ   186–9 lacunam alicubi latere vid.
Hermann, Matthiae   186 Μυκηνῇσιν Kirchhoff: μυκήνησι ΜΟ:
μυκήναισι(ν) Ω   187 δωσε[Π⁴: δώσει Canter: δώσων (deleto ὃς)
King   188 ποσειδανίοις VP: -δων(ε)ίοις ω+: -δωνίοισι(ν) rΖ   τ᾽
post ποσειδ. add. rΖc   ἀμυμων(ε)ίοις ω+: -ονίοις Π¹⁴VRf: -ωνίοισι(ν)
vel -ονίοισι(ν) rz   190 μήποτε semel r   191 -βόστρυχον Brz:
-βόστρυχε ω+   197 χώρει VCr, cf. Σ   198 δὲ ΜΟ, Stob. 4.22g. 198:
τι gV: γὰρ Ω

σμικράς τ' ἀφορμὰς ἢν λάβωσι τῶν λόγων,
πλείους ἐπεισφέρουσιν· ἡδονὴ δέ τις   200
γυναιξὶ μηδὲν ὑγιὲς ἀλλήλας λέγειν.   201

ΧΟΡΟΣ

Τύριον οἶδμα λιποῦσ' ἔβαν   στρ. α 202
   ἀκροθίνια Λοξίαι
   Φοινίσσας ἀπὸ νάσου,
   Φοίβωι δούλα μελάθρων   205
   ἵν' ὑπὸ δειράσι νιφοβόλοις
   Παρνασσοῦ κατενάσθη,
   Ἰόνιον κατὰ πόντον ἐλάται πλεύσασα, περιρρύτων
   ὑπὲρ ἀκαρπίστων πεδίων   210
   Σικελίας Ζεφύρου πνοαῖς
   ἱππεύσαντος ἐν οὐρανῶι
   κάλλιστον κελάδημα.   213

πόλεος ἐκπροκριθεῖσ' ἐμᾶς   ἀντ. α 214
   καλλιστεύματα Λοξίαι   215
   Καδμείων ἔμολον γᾶν,
   κλεινῶν Ἀγηνοριδᾶν
   ὁμογενεῖς ἐπὶ Λαΐου
   πεμφθεῖσ' ἐνθάδε πύργους.
   ἴσα δ' ἀγάλμασι χρυσοτεύ-   220
   κτοις Φοίβωι λάτρις ἐγενόμαν·
   ἔτι δὲ Κασταλίας ὕδωρ
   περιμένει με κόμας ἐμᾶς

---

199 τ' MχT: δ' BVC+, Stob.: om. ORf   λόγων Ω, gV, Stob.*:
ψόγων Stob.*   201 ἀλλήλας BVCr, Stob.: -αις MB¹ˢO+, gV, test.
alia   205 φοίβου rχ   μελάθρω A   206 -βόλοις ω+, Hsch. ν 597:
-βόλοιο r: -βόλου Rw   207 κατενάσθη Ad (coni. Thirlby): -σθην
Ω   209 περιρρύτων Ω(etiam Mᵘᵛ): -ρύτων [sic] V   213 var. lect.
ἐξ οὐρανοῦ testari vid. Σ   214 πόλεος Musgrave: -εως Ω   216
καδμείων BCr: καδμείων δ' MOV+   217 ἀγηνοριδῶν B²rχz   218
συγγενεῖς MʸᵖCʸᵖ   220 χρυσο- Vr: χρυσεο- ω+   221 γενόμαν
Rfχ: γενοίμαν V²F   223 περιμένει MOr: ἐπιμ- BVC+

δεῦσαι παρθένιον χλιδὰν
Φοιβείαισι λατρείαις.   225

ὦ λάμπουσα πέτρα πυρὸς   ἐπωιδ. 226
δικόρυφον σέλας ὑπὲρ ἄκρων
βακχείων Διονύσου,
οἶνα θ᾽ ἃ καθαμέριον
στάζεις, τὸν πολύκαρπον οἰ-   230
νάνθας ἱεῖσα βότρυν,
ζάθεά τ᾽ ἄντρα δράκοντος οὔ-
ρειαί τε σκοπιαὶ θεῶν
νιφόβολόν τ᾽ ὄρος ἱερόν, εἱ-
λίσσων ἀθανάτας θεοῦ   235
χορὸς γενοίμαν ἄφοβος,
παρὰ μεσόμφαλα γύαλα Φοί-
βου Δίρκαν προλιποῦσα.   238

νῦν δέ μοι πρὸ τειχέων   στρ. β 239
θούριος μολὼν Ἄρης   240
  αἷμα δάϊον φλέγει
  τᾷδ᾽ – ὃ μὴ τύχοι – πόλει·
κοινὰ γὰρ φίλων ἄχη,
  κοινὰ δ᾽, εἴ τι πείσεται
ἑπτάπυργος ἅδε γᾶ,   245
  Φοινίσσαι χῶραι. φεῦ φεῦ.
κοινὸν αἷμα, κοινὰ τέκεα
τᾶς κερασφόρου πέφυκεν Ἰοῦς·
ὧν μέτεστί μοι πόνων.   249

ἀμφὶ δὲ πτόλιν νέφος   ἀντ. β 250
ἀσπίδων πυκνὸν φλέγει

---

226 ὦ Π⁴ᵘᵛζᵍ: ἰὼ Ω   228 βακχείων V²rζ: βακχειῶν ω+, Σ: βακχεῖον
Rwᵃᶜ (coni. Kirchhoff, una cum 227 δικορύφων)   230 στάζεις τὸν Ω:
περκάζεις Nauck   235 ἀθανάτου rζ   ἀθανάτας θεοῦ multis suspectum   237 παρ μεσ- MO   239 δὲ ω+: γὰρ r (e Σ)   242 τύχηι
MOr: τύχοι (-ηι) ποτὲ rz   244 πείσεται rT: πείσεθ᾽ fere ω+   245
γαῖα fere z   246 φοίνισσα χώρα r, ʸᵖΣ   247 τέκνα rζ   250 πτόλιν
Π²⁰MBR (coni. Heath): πόλιν OVC+

σχῆμα φοινίου μάχας,
ἂν Ἄρης τάχ᾽ εἴσεται,
παισὶν Οἰδίπου φέρων
πημονὰν Ἐρινύων.   255
Ἄργος ὦ Πελασγικόν,
    δειμαίνω τὰν σὰν ἀλκὰν
καὶ τὸ θεόθεν· οὐ γὰρ ἄδικον
εἰς ἀγῶνα τόνδ᾽ ἔνοπλος ὁρμᾶι {παῖς}
ὃς μετέρχεται δόμους.   260

ΠΟΛΥΝΕΙΚΗΣ
    τὰ μὲν πυλωρῶν κλῆιθρά μ᾽ εἰσεδέξατο   261
δι᾽ εὐπετείας τειχέων ἔσω μολεῖν·
ὃ καὶ δέδοικα μή με δικτύων ἔσω
λαβόντες οὐκ ἐκφρῶσ᾽ ἀναίμακτον χρόα.
ὧν οὔνεκ᾽ ὄμμα πανταχῆι διοιστέον   265
κἀκεῖσε καὶ τὸ δεῦρο, μὴ δόλος τις ἦι.
ὡπλισμένος δὲ χεῖρα τῶιδε φασγάνωι
τὰ πίστ᾽ ἐμαυτῶι τοῦ θράσους παρέξομαι.
    ὠή, τίς οὗτος; ἢ κτύπον φοβούμεθα;
ἅπαντα γὰρ τολμῶσι δεινὰ φαίνεται,   270
ὅταν δι᾽ ἐχθρᾶς πούς ἀμείβηται χθονός.
πέποιθα μέντοι μητρί, κοὐ πέποιθ᾽ ἅμα,
ἥτις μ᾽ ἔπεισε δεῦρ᾽ ὑπόσπονδον μολεῖν.
    ἀλλ᾽ ἐγγὺς ἀλκή – βώμιοι γὰρ ἐσχάραι
πέλας πάρεισι –, κοὐκ ἔρημα δώματα·   275
φέρ᾽ ἐς σκοτεινὰς περιβολὰς μεθῶ ξίφος
καὶ τάσδ᾽ ἔρωμαι τίνες ἐφεστᾶσιν δόμοις.
    ξέναι γυναῖκες, εἴπατ᾽, ἐκ ποίας πάτρας
Ἑλληνικοῖσι δώμασιν πελάζετε;

---

252 σῆμα **r** (coni. Heimsoeth)   φονίου MO**rχ**   μάχας Blaydes: μάχης
Ω   253 οἴσεται **rχz**   257 τᾶν· σᾶν M^γρ   259 ἔνοπλον B^γρVC**r**:
ἐν ὅπλοις **z**   παῖς del. Tricl.   263 μή με Ω(M^γρ): μήτε MO   264
οὐκ ἐκφρῶσ᾽ Bergk, Dindorf: οὐκ ἐκφρῶσιν ^γρΣ^BV (= Philoxenus): οὐ μεθῶσ᾽
MOT: οὐ μεθῶσιν BVC+   265 πανταχοῦ B²**rχ**   269 ἢ OVC+: ἤ
MB**rz**, Σ   277 ἔρωμ᾽ αἵτινες B²**r**: ἔρωμαι τὰς V²**r**   ἐφεστώσας vel
-τάσας V²**rz**: ἐφεστίους Sa   δόμους **rχ**

ΦΟΙΝΙΣΣΑΙ

Χο. Φοίνισσα μὲν γῆ πατρὶς ἡ θρέψασά με,   280
Ἀγήνορος δὲ παῖδες ἐκ παίδων δορὸς
Φοίβωι μ' ἔπεμψαν ἐνθάδ' ἀκροθίνιον.
μέλλων δὲ πέμπειν μ' Οἰδίπου κλεινὸς γόνος
μαντεῖα σεμνὰ Λοξίου τ' ἐπ' ἐσχάρας,
ἐν τῶιδ' ἐπεστράτευσαν Ἀργεῖοι πόλιν.   285
σὺ δ' ἀντάμειψαί μ', ὅστις ὢν ἐλήλυθας
ἑπτάστομον πύργωμα Θηβαίας χθονός.
Πο. πατὴρ μὲν ἡμῖν Οἰδίπους ὁ Λαΐου,
ἔτικτε δ' Ἰοκάστη με, παῖς Μενοικέως·
καλεῖ δὲ Πολυνείκη με Θηβαῖος λεώς.   290
Χο. ὦ συγγένεια τῶν Ἀγήνορος τέκνων,
ἐμῶν τυράννων, ὧν ἀπεστάλην ὕπο·
– γονυπετεῖς ἕδρας προσπίτνω σ', ἄναξ,
τὸν οἴκοθεν νόμον σέβουσα·
ἔβας ὦ χρόνωι γᾶν πατρώιαν.   295
ἰὼ ἰώ· πότνια, μόλε πρόδομος,
ἀμπέτασον πύλας.
κλύεις, ὦ τεκοῦσα τόνδε μᾶτερ;
τί μέλλεις ὑπώροφα μέλαθρα περᾶν
θιγεῖν τ' ὠλέναις⟨ι⟩ τέκνου;   300
Ιο. Φοίνισσαν βοὰν   301
κλυοῦσ', ὦ νεάνιδες, γηραιῶι
ποδὶ τρομερὰν ἕλκω {ποδὸς} βάσιν·

---

284 ἐσχάραις **r**, *lex. Vind.* ε 141   285 ἀργείων Μ¹(corr. Μ²ˢ): ἀργεῖαν
Ο   πόλει **r**, Eust. 236, 36–7   292–1 om. Π¹³, spurios iud.
Haslam   291 ξυγ- **rz**   292 ὑπεστάλην **Cr**   293 paragraphum
addidi   293 -πίτνω Dindorf (Elmsley ad *Hcld.* 77): -πιτνῶ fere Ω:
-πιπτω Π¹³   294 fere σεβίζουσα **r**   295 ἔβας semel (Π¹³ᵘᵛ)ΜʸᵖBrz:
bis ωΒʸᵖ+   ὦ Hermann: ὦ fere ω+(Π¹³ᵘᵛ): ὦ πολυνείκη **rz**
296 ἰὼ ἰὼ bis ω**r**: semel **Brχζ** (plura verba quam codd. habuit
Π¹³)   πρόδομος Μ²BOVr**ζ**: πρόδρομος Π¹³Μ¹Crχ   297–8 aliqua
verba quae in codd. extant non hab. Π¹³ (297 omisisse Π¹³ coni. et spurium
iud. Haslam)   297 ἀμπ- V (coni. Hermann, Seidler): ἀναπ- Ω,
test.   300 ὠλέναισι Hermann: -ναις Ω   301–2 φοίν. βοὰν κλ. ὦ
νεανίδες fere MOCr: φοίν. ὦ νεαν. βοὰν ἔσω δόμων κλύουσα τῶνδε fere
BVC+   κλυοῦσ' West: κλύουσ(α) Ω   302–3 γηραιῶι ποδὶ τρ. ἕ.
ποδὸς fere ω+: γηραιῶι τρ. ἕ. ποδὶ Rwᵃᶜχ: γήραι τῶ παιδὶ τρ. ἕ. ποδὸς
Ο: γήραι τρ. ἕ. ποδὸς **r**   ποδὸς del. Kirchhoff

72

ἰὼ τέκνον, χρόνωι σὸν ὄμ-
μα μυρίαις τ' ἐν ἁμέραις   305
προσεῖδον· ἀμφίβαλλε μα-
στὸν ὠλέναισι ματέρος,
παρηίδων τ' ὄρεγμα βο-   308
στρύχων τε κυανόχρωτα χαί-   308bis
τας πλόκαμον, σκιάζων δέραν ἁμάν.
ἰὼ ἰώ, μόλις φανεὶς   310
ἄελπτα κἀδόκητα ματρὸς ὠλέναις.
τί φῶ σε; πῶς ἁπάνται
καὶ χερσὶ καὶ λόγοισι
πολυέλικτον ἁδονὰν
ἐκεῖσε καὶ τὸ δεῦρο   315
περιχορεύουσα τέρψιν παλαιᾶν λάβω χαρμονᾶν;
ἰὼ τέκος,
ἔρημον πατρῷον ἔλιπες δόμον
φυγὰς ἀποσταλεὶς ὁμαίμου λώβαι,
ἦ ποθεινὸς φίλοις,   320
ἦ ποθεινὸς Θήβαις.
ὅθεν ἐμάν τε λευκόχροα κείρομαι
δακρυόεσσ' ἀνεῖσα πένθει κόμαν,
ἄπεπλος φαρέων λευκῶν, τέκνον,
δυσόρφναια δ' ἀμφὶ τρύχη τάδε   325
σκότι' ἀμείβομαι.
ὁ δ' ἐν δόμοισι πρέσβυς ὀμματοστερὴς
ἀπήνας ὁμοπτέρου τᾶς ἀπο-
ζυγείσας δόμων

---

304 ἰὼ MBO + : ὦ VCrχz   305 τ' MO + : om. BVCrχz   307 ματρὸς
fere rz   308bis τε om. Sa, del. Hartung   309 χαίταις Π⁸ (coni.
Brodaeus)   ἀμάν Wecklein: ἀμάν MO: ἐμάν Π⁸Ω   310 ἰὼ bis ω + :
semel rχz   μόγις rz   312 σε del. Hartung   ἁπάνται Wecklein:
ἅπαντα Ω   313 λόγοισι ω + : fere κόμαισι rχT (ex Hec. 837)   316–17
παλαιᾶν ... χαρμονᾶν M²B³V²rχT: -ᾶν ... -ᾶν fere ωrζ   317 ἰὼ τέκος
ἐμὸν τέκος r   322 post κείρομαι add. χαίταν Σ371   323 δακρυόεσσ'
ἀνεῖσα πένθει post Valck. Hermann et Dindorf e Σ: δακρυόεσσαν ἰεῖσα
πενθήρη fere Ω, Σ alter (etiam -εσσαν εἰς σ' ἀπένθη et -εσσαν εἰς σὰ πένθη
Σ)   324 ⟨ὦ⟩ τέκνον Dindorf   325 τ' Pᵃᶜ, Wakefield   ἀμφὶ τρύχη
BV + , Σ: ἀμφιτρύχη fere MOCr, test.: ἀμφιτρίχη Gχ

πόθον ἀμφιδάκρυτον ἀεὶ κατέχων   330
ἀνῇξε μὲν ξίφους ἐπ' αὐ-
τόχειρά τε σφαγὰν ὑπὲρ
τέραμνά τ' ἀγχόνας, στενάζων ἀρὰς τέκνοις·
σὺν ἀλαλαῖσι δ' αἰὲν αἱαγμάτων   335
σκότια κρύπτεται.
σὲ δ', ὦ τέκνον, καὶ γάμοισι δὴ κλύω
ζυγέντα παιδοποιὸν ἀδονὰν
ξένοισιν ἐν δόμοις ἔχειν
ξένον τε κῆδος ἀμφέπειν,   340
ἄλαστα ματρὶ τᾶιδε Λα-
ΐου τε τοῦ πάλαι γένει,
γάμων ἐπακτὸν ἄταν.
ἐγὼ δ' οὔτε σοι πυρὸς ἀνῆψα φῶς
νόμιμον ἐν γάμοις   345
ὡς πρέπει ματέρι μακαρίαι·
ἀνυμέναια δ' Ἰσμηνὸς ἐκηδεύθη
λουτροφόρου χλιδᾶς, ἀνὰ δὲ Θηβαίαν
πόλιν ἐσιγάθη σᾶς ἔσοδοι νύμφας.

---

330 ἀεὶ **rz**: αἰεὶ ω+   331 ξίφος Or   335 ἀλαλαῖσι ωrx: ἀλαλαγαῖσι fere B³Vrζ   αἰὲν hoc loco MO+: post σκοτ. **rz**: post αἱαγμάτων T: om. BVC**r**   336 σκότια PZu: σκοτία(ι) Ω   337 καὶ del. Hermann (hab. Π¹³Π⁸ᵘᵛ)   γάμοισι δὴ Ω: γαμοις ηδη Π¹³:]...γδη Π⁸   340 ξένων **r**   δε Π¹³   341 ματρὶ Π¹³**z**: μητρὶ fere ω+   τᾶιδε T (coni. post Valck. Heath): τάδε Ω, Σ   341–2 Λαΐου τε τοῦ πάλαι γένει Hermann: Λαΐωι τε τῶι παλαιγενεῖ fere Π⁸Π¹³Ω   343 γάμων Π¹³V+: γάμον ω ἐπακτὸν MBO: ἐπακτὰν Sa, fort. B²: ἐπακτὰν fere VC+   344 οὔτε Π¹³ ω+, test.: ουδε Π⁶: οὔτι **rx**: οὔτε post σοι transp. Plut. *Mor*. 606ϝ   πυρὸς ἀνῆψα φῶς Π¹³Ω, test.: πῦρ ἀνῆψα Plut.   345 γόνιμον Plut.   ἐν γάμοις Π¹³Ω, test.: om. sch. Ap. Rhod. 4.808–9   346 ὡς πρέπει del. Nauck (totum versum om. Plut.)   ματέρι Seidler: ματρὶ vel μητρὶ Π¹³Ω, sch. Ap. Rhod.   347 ἀνυμέναιος Cr   Ἰσμ- scripsi (cf. 57, 101): ἰσμ-Ω, Plut.   ἰσμ. ἐκηδ. Π¹³Ω, Plut.: εκηδευθη ισμηνος Π⁶   348 θηβαίων **r**   349 ἐσιγάθη fere Ω, Hsch. ε 6214: ἐσιγάθησαν Bᵞᵖ, ᵞᵖΣ: ἐσίγαθεν Willink   ἔσοδοι Π¹³ (Kirchhoff): εἴσοδοι ωι: εἴσοδος B+: ἔσοδος Hermann, Seidler

ὄλοιτο, τάδ᾽ εἴτε σίδαρος   350
εἴτ᾽ ἔρις εἴτε πατὴρ ὁ σὸς αἴτιος,
εἴτε τὸ δαιμόνιον κατεκώμασε
δώμασιν Οἰδιπόδα·
πρὸς ἐμὲ γὰρ κακῶν ἔμολε τῶνδ᾽ ἄχη.   354

Χο. δεινὸν γυναιξὶν αἱ δι᾽ ὠδίνων γοναί,   355
    καὶ φιλότεκνόν πως πᾶν γυναικεῖον γένος.

Πο. μῆτερ, φρονῶν εὖ κοὔ φρονῶν ἀφικόμην
    ἐχθροὺς ἐς ἄνδρας· ἀλλ᾽ ἀναγκαίως ἔχει
    πατρίδος ἐρᾶν ἅπαντας· ὃς δ᾽ ἄλλως λέγει,
    λόγοισι χαίρει, τὸν δὲ νοῦν ἐκεῖσ᾽ ἔχει.   360
    οὕτω δ᾽ ἐτάρβησ᾽ εἰς φόβον τ᾽ ἀφικόμην
    μή τις δόλος με πρὸς κασιγνήτου κτάνηι,
    ὥστε ξιφήρη χεῖρ᾽ ἔχων δι᾽ ἄστεως
    κυκλῶν πρόσωπον ἦλθον. ἐν δέ μ᾽ ὠφελεῖ,
    σπονδαί τε καὶ σὴ πίστις, ἥ μ᾽ εἰσήγαγεν   365
    τείχη πατρῷα. πολύδακρυς δ᾽ ἀφικόμην
    χρόνιος ἰδὼν μέλαθρα καὶ βωμοὺς θεῶν
    γυμνάσιά θ᾽ οἷσιν ἐνετράφην Δίρκης θ᾽ ὕδωρ·
    ὧν οὐ δικαίως ἀπελαθεὶς ξένην πόλιν
    ναίω, †δι᾽ ὅσσων ὄμμ᾽† ἔχων δακρυρροοῦν.   370
    ἀλλ᾽ – ἐκ γὰρ ἄλγους ἄλγος αὖ – σὲ δέρκομαι
    κάρα ξυρῆκες καὶ πέπλους μελαγχίμους
    ἔχουσαν· οἴμοι τῶν ἐμῶν ἐγὼ κακῶν·
    ὡς δεινὸν ἔχθρα, μῆτερ, οἰκείων φίλων·
    {καὶ δυσλύτους ἔχουσα τὰς διαλλαγάς}   375

350–1 εἴτε σίδαρος εἴτ᾽ ἔρις Π¹³ω+: εἴτ᾽ ἔρις εἴτε σίδαρος **rz**
353 δόμοισιν **r**   οἰδιπόδαο **rχ**   359 δ᾽ ἐρᾶν V   361 δ᾽ ἐτάρβησ᾽
Rw (coni. Hermann): δὲ τάρβος T: δὲ τάρβους Ω: δ᾽ ἐτάρβουν Porson
363 ἄστεως Favorinus *de exilio* 7 (Π^α) (Dindorf): ἄστεος Ω   366 τ᾽
r   368 θ᾽¹ Π¹³Ω: δ᾽ Plut. *Mor.* 526F   οἷς **r**   ἐτράφην LT
([ο]ι[...]ετ[ρα]φ[η]ν Π¹³, i.e. aut οις aut ετραφην habebat)   370 ναι]ων
Π¹³   ὄμμ᾽ Π¹³Ω, Eust. 432, 12: αἶμ᾽ L   ἔχω Eust.   372 del.
Kirchhoff, coll. *Alc.* 427   375 del. post Valck. Usener (Σ: ἔν τισιν οὐ
φέρεται)   ἔχουσι Π¹³Zc

τί γὰρ πατήρ μοι πρέσβυς ἐν δόμοισι δρᾶι,
σκότον δεδορκώς; τί δὲ κασίγνηται δύο;
ἦ που στένουσι τλήμονες φυγὰς ἐμάς;

Ιο. κακῶς θεῶν τις Οἰδίπου φθείρει γένος·
ούτω γὰρ ἤρξατ', ἄνομα μὲν τεκεῖν ἐμέ,   380
κακῶς δὲ γῆμαι πατέρα σὸν φῦναί τε σέ.
ἀτὰρ τί ταῦτα; δεῖ φέρειν τὰ τῶν θεῶν.
ὅπως δ' ἔρωμαι, μή τι σὴν δάκω φρένα,
δέδοιχ', ἃ χρήιζω· διὰ πόθου δ' ἐλήλυθα.

Πο. ἀλλ' ἐξερώτα, μηδὲν ἐνδεὲς λίπηις·   385
ἃ γὰρ σὺ βούληι, ταῦτ' ἐμοί, μῆτερ, φίλα.

Ιο. καὶ δή σ' ἐρωτῶ πρῶτον ὧν χρήιζω τυχεῖν·
τί τὸ στέρεσθαι πατρίδος; ἦ κακὸν μέγα;

Πο. μέγιστον· ἔργωι δ' ἐστὶ μεῖζον ἢ λόγωι.

Ιο. τίς ὁ τρόπος αὐτοῦ; τί φυγάσιν τὸ δυσχερές;   390

Πο. ἓν μὲν μέγιστον· οὐκ ἔχει παρρησίαν.

Ιο. δούλου τόδ' εἶπας, μὴ λέγειν ἅ τις φρονεῖ.

Πο. τὰς τῶν κρατούντων ἀμαθίας φέρειν χρεών.

Ιο. καὶ τοῦτο λυπρόν, συνασοφεῖν τοῖς μὴ σοφοῖς.

Πο. ἀλλ' εἰς τὸ κέρδος παρὰ φύσιν δουλευτέον.   395

Ιο. αἱ δ' ἐλπίδες βόσκουσι φυγάδας, ὡς λόγος.

Πο. καλοῖς βλέπουσαί γ' ὄμμασιν, μέλλουσι δέ.

Ιο. οὐδ' ὁ χρόνος αὐτὰς διεσάφησ' οὔσας κενάς;

Πο. ἔχουσιν Ἀφροδίτην τιν' ἡδεῖαν κακῶν.

Ιο. πόθεν δ' ἐβόσκου, πρὶν γάμοις εὑρεῖν βίον;   400

376–8 del. Usener   376 δώμασι VC**r**   378 ἦ ΜΜηχ   τλήμονος
Tˢ: τλήμονας Brunck   380 οὗτος M¹ᵖᶜOᵃᶜ   381 φῦσαί **r**Zu (coni.
Hermann)   382 τί τάδε; δεῖ γὰρ φέρειν τὰ τοῦ θεοῦ **r** (τάδε etiam
z)   384 διὰ πόνου B   386 ταῦτ' Bothe: ταῦτ' fere **r**: ταῦτ' ω+,
gV   387 om. Π¹³, spurium iud. Haslam   τυχεῖν ω+: μαθεῖν
r   388 ἦ BVC+: ἦ MO**rz**, gV   389 μεῖζον fere Ω, gV, test.: μαλλο[ν
Π¹³   390 δυσχερές ω+, Stob. 3.39.17: δυστυχές MᵞᵖCᵞᵖ**rχz**, Plut. Mor.
605ᶠ   393 τήν … ἀμαθίαν Plut. Mor. 605ᶠ   κρατούντων Ω, gV, test.:
πολιτῶν ᵞᵖΣ   395 ἀλλ' εἰς Ω, gV: ὅπου Plut. Demetr. 14, Lucian Apol.
3   397 βλέπουσαί γ' Hermann (cf. ᴾΣ): βλέπουσί γ' Ω, Σ alter, Plut.
Mor. 606ᴅ: βλέπουσιν P, gV   399 ἡδεῖαν Ω: εὐδίαν Jackson   κακῶν
ω+: θεόν **r**: νόσον Musgrave

ΦΟΙΝΙΣΣΑΙ

Πο. ποτὲ μὲν ἐπ' ἦμαρ εἶχον, εἶτ' οὐκ εἶχον ἄν.

Ιο. φίλοι δὲ πατρὸς καὶ ξένοι σ' οὐκ ὠφέλουν;

Πο. εὖ πρᾶσσε· τὰ φίλων δ' οὐδέν, ἤν τις δυστυχῆι.

Ιο. οὐδ' ηὐγένειά σ' ἦρεν εἰς ὕψος μέγαν;

Πο. κακὸν τὸ μὴ ἔχειν· τὸ γένος οὐκ ἔβοσκέ με.   405

Ιο. ἡ πατρίς, ὡς ἔοικε, φίλτατον βροτοῖς.

Πο. οὐδ' ὀνομάσαι δύναι' ἂν ὡς ἔστιν φίλον.

Ιο. πῶς δ' ἦλθες Ἄργος; τίν' ἐπίνοιαν ἔσχεθες;

Πο. ἔχρησ' Ἀδράστωι Λοξίας χρησμόν τινα.

Ιο. ποῖον; τί τοῦτ' ἔλεξας; οὐκ ἔχω μαθεῖν.   410

Πο. κάπρωι λέοντί θ' ἁρμόσαι παίδων γάμους.

Ιο. καὶ σοὶ τί θηρῶν ὀνόματος μετῆν, τέκνον;

Πο. οὐκ οἶδ'· ὁ δαίμων μ' ἐκάλεσεν πρὸς τὴν τύχην.

Ιο. σοφὸς γὰρ ὁ θεός· τίνι τρόπωι δ' ἔσχες λέχος;

Πο. νὺξ ἦν, Ἀδράστου δ' ἦλθον εἰς παραστάδας.   415

Ιο. κοίτας ματεύων, ἧι φυγὰς πλανώμενος;

Πο. ἦν ταῦτα· κᾆτά γ' ἦλθεν ἄλλος αὖ φυγάς.

Ιο. τίς οὗτος; ὡς ἄρ' ἄθλιος κἀκεῖνος ἦν.

Πο. Τυδεύς, ὃν Οἰνέως φασὶν ἐκφῦναι πατρός.

Ιο. τί θηρσὶν ὑμᾶς δῆτ' Ἄδραστος ἤικασεν;   420

Πο. στρωμνῆς ἐς ἀλκὴν οὕνεκ' ἤλθομεν πέρι.

Ιο. ἐνταῦθα Ταλαοῦ παῖς συνῆκε θέσφατα;

Πο. κἄδωκέ γ' ἡμῖν δύο δυοῖν νεάνιδας.

Ιο. ἆρ' εὐτυχεῖς οὖν τοῖς γάμοις ἢ δυστυχεῖς;

Πο. οὐ μεμπτὸς ἡμῖν ὁ γάμος εἰς τόδ' ἡμέρας.   425

Ιο. πῶς δ' ἐξέπεισας δεῦρό σοι σπέσθαι στρατόν;

Πο. δισσοῖς Ἄδραστος ὤμοσεν γαμβροῖς τόδε,

---

403 δ' om. Πᵃ a.c., Ab (del. Valck.)   τι δυστυχῆις Planud. *Rhet. Gr.* 5.422, 11 Walz, anon. *Rhet. Gr.* 7:2.813 Walz (coni. Elmsley)   404 μέγαν Wecklein: μέγα Ω, test.   407 δύναι' ἂν Markland (cf. Mᵍ δύναιτό τις): fere δύναιμ' ἂν Ω, test.   φίλον ω+, gV, test.: μέγα **r**   408 δ' om. Br   ἔσχεθες MBV+: ἔσχες OC**rz**: ἔ(σ)χων **r**   412 θηρὸς Rwx   413–14 ante 409 transp. Jacobs   416 ματεύων B²**rx**: μαστ- ω+   ἧι Vrᵞᵖ, ed. Ald.: ἢ Ω, Σ   417 γ' ω+: δ' Πᵍ**rxz**   420 θηρσὶν Cr (coni. Valck.): θηρσὶ δ' ω+   423 κἄδωκέ γ' Schaefer: κἄδωκεν Ω   426 σοι ἔπεσθαι VLZc: ἔπεσθαι σοι **z**   427 τάδε **rxζ**

77

ΦΟΙΝΙΣΣΑΙ

{Τυδεῖ τε κἀμοί· σύγγαμος γάρ ἐστ᾽ ἐμός·}
ἄμφω κατάξειν εἰς πάτραν, πρόσθεν δ᾽ ἐμέ.
πολλοὶ δὲ Δαναῶν καὶ Μυκηναίων ἄκροι   430
πάρεισι, λυπρὰν χάριν ἀναγκαίαν δέ μοι
διδόντες· ἐπὶ γὰρ τὴν ἐμὴν στρατεύομαι
πόλιν. θεοὺς δ᾽ ἐπώμοσ᾽ ὡς ἀκουσίως
τοῖς φιλτάτοις ἑκοῦσιν ἠράμην δόρυ.
ἀλλ᾽ εἰς σὲ τείνει τῶνδε διάλυσις κακῶν,   435
μῆτερ, διαλλάξασαν ὁμογενεῖς φίλους
παῦσαι πόνων σὲ κἀμὲ καὶ πᾶσαν πόλιν.
πάλαι μὲν οὖν ὑμνηθέν, ἀλλ᾽ ὅμως ἐρῶ·
τὰ χρήματ᾽ ἀνθρώποισι τιμιώτατα,
δύναμίν τε πλείστην τῶν ἐν ἀνθρώποις ἔχει.   440
ἀγὼ μεθήκω δεῦρο μυρίαν ἄγων
λόγχην· πένης γὰρ οὐδὲν εὐγενὴς ἀνήρ.
Χο. καὶ μὴν Ἐτεοκλῆς εἰς διαλλαγὰς ὅδε
χωρεῖ· σὸν ἔργον, μῆτερ Ἰοκάστη, λέγειν
τοιούσδε μύθους οἷς διαλλάξεις τέκνα.   445

ΕΤΕΟΚΛΗΣ
μῆτερ, πάρειμι· τὴν χάριν δέ σοι διδοὺς
ἦλθον. τί χρὴ δρᾶν; ἀρχέτω δέ τις λόγου·
ὡς ἀμφὶ τείχη ⟨
                                    ⟩ καὶ ξυνωρίδας λόχων
τάσσων ἐπέσχον †πόλιν† ὅπως κλύοιμί σου
κοινὰς βραβείας, αἷς ὑπόσπονδον μολεῖν   450
τόνδ᾽ εἰσεδέξω τειχέων πείσασά με.
Ιο. ἐπίσχες· οὔτοι τὸ ταχὺ τὴν δίκην ἔχει,

428 del. Jortin (περισσὸν iud. Σ)   σύγγαμβρος Vᵃᶜrχᵍζᵍ   ἐμοὶ
r   431 δέ μοι Wecklein: δ᾽ ἐμοὶ Ω   434 ἑκοῦσιν ʸᵖΣᴮ: τοκεῦσιν ΩⱽᴿΣᴹ:
τεκοῦσιν Π²²Vr (cf. falsam lect. in Σⱽᶜ)   436 omisisse vid. Π²², del.
Nauck, Haslam (παῦσον 437 Wecklein)   437 σ]εκἀμε[Π²², coni.
Elmsley: με καὶ σὲ Ω   438–42 del. Hartung (olim) et Leidloff   439
ἀνθρώποισιν εὑρίσκειν φίλους Plut. Mor. 497ʙ (una cum 440 ἔχειν)
444 χωρεῖ ω+: ἥκει MʸᵖCʸᵖrz   445 συναλλάξεις Mn   446 δέ σοι
BV+: δὲ σοὶ MOCr, Σ   448 lacunam stat. Paley   λόχων Ω(V²):
λοχῶν V¹Z   449 πόλιν om. Lz: πάλιν Hartung: μόλις Badham
452 οὔτι rχ

78

βραδεῖς δὲ μῦθοι πλεῖστον ἀνύτουσιν σοφόν.
σχάσον δὲ δεινὸν ὄμμα καὶ θυμοῦ πνοάς·
οὐ γὰρ τὸ λαιμότμητον εἰσορᾶις κάρα   455
Γοργόνος· ἀδελφὸν εἰσορᾶις ἥκοντα σόν.
σύ τ' αὖ πρόσωπον πρὸς κασίγνητον στρέφε,
Πολύνεικες· εἰς γὰρ ταὐτὸν ὄμμασιν βλέπων
λέξεις τ' ἄμεινον τοῦδέ τ' ἐνδέξηι λόγους.
παραινέσαι δὲ σφῶιν τι βούλομαι σοφόν·   460
ὅταν φίλος τις ἀνδρὶ θυμωθεὶς φίλωι
εἰς ἓν συνελθὼν ὄμματ' ὄμμασιν διδῶι,
ἐφ' οἷσιν ἥκει, ταῦτα χρὴ μόνον σκοπεῖν,
κακῶν δὲ τῶν πρὶν μηδενὸς μνείαν ἔχειν.
λόγος μὲν οὖν σὸς πρόσθε, Πολύνεικες τέκνον·   465
σὺ γὰρ στράτευμα Δαναϊδῶν ἥκεις ἄγων,
ἄδικα πεπονθώς, ὡς σὺ φήις· κριτὴς δέ τις
θεῶν γένοιτο καὶ διαλλακτὴς κακῶν.
Πο. ἁπλοῦς ὁ μῦθος τῆς ἀληθείας ἔφυ,
κοὺ ποικίλων δεῖ τἄνδιχ' ἑρμηνευμάτων·   470
ἔχει γὰρ αὐτὰ καιρόν· ὁ δ' ἄδικος λόγος
νοσῶν ἐν αὑτῶι φαρμάκων δεῖται σοφῶν.
ἐγὼ δὲ πατρὸς δωμάτων προὐσκεψάμην
τοὐμόν τε καὶ τοῦδ', ἐκφυγεῖν χρήιζων ἀρὰς
ἃς Οἰδίπους ἐφθέγξατ' εἰς ἡμᾶς ποτε·   475
ἐξῆλθον ἔξω τῆσδ' ἑκὼν αὐτὸς χθονός,
δοὺς τῶιδ' ἀνάσσειν πατρίδος ἐνιαυτοῦ κύκλον,
ὥστ' αὐτὸς ἄρχειν αὖθις ἀνὰ μέρος λαβὼν
καὶ μὴ δι' ἔχθρας τῶιδε καὶ φθόνου μολὼν
κακόν τι δρᾶσαι καὶ παθεῖν, ἃ γίγνεται.   480

---

453 ἀνύτουσιν Hermann (ἀνύτ- Porson): ἀνύουσι(ν) Ω, gV, test.   456
ἀδελφὸν Br: ἀδελφὸν δ' ω+   457 τρέπε ΜᵧᵖΒᵧᵖ   459 τ'¹ om.
rχ ἐκδέξηι rz λόγοις V   464 μηδενὸς ω+, gV: μηδαμῶς
rζ   470 δεῖ τἄνδιχ' fere rχz, test.: ambigue δεῖτ'ἄνδιχ' fere ωrz, gV:
δεῖτ' ἄνδιχ' (δεῖται ἄνδιχά) ᵧᵖΣ, fere Ioh. Philop. CAG 13:1.37, 15   472
αὑτῶι Β²rχ, test.: αὐτῶι ω+   473–80 alii alios versus del.   473
πατρὸς δωμάτων multis suspectum   474 χρήιζων ⟨τ'⟩ Musgrave, ⟨δ'⟩
Matthiae   476 κἀξῆλθον Barnes   479 φθόνου ΜᵧᵖCˢGᵧᵖ: φόνου fere
Ω

ὁ δ' αἰνέσας ταῦθ' ὁρκίους τε δοὺς θεοὺς
ἔδρασεν οὐδὲν ὧν ὑπέσχετ', ἀλλ' ἔχει
τυραννίδ' αὐτὸς καὶ δόμων ἐμὸν μέρος.
καὶ νῦν ἕτοιμός εἰμι τἀμαυτοῦ λαβὼν
στρατὸν μὲν ἔξω τῆσδ' ἀποστεῖλαι χθονός,   485
οἰκεῖν δὲ τὸν ἐμὸν οἶκον ἀνὰ μέρος λαβὼν
καὶ τῶιδ' ἀφεῖναι τὸν ἴσον αὖθις ⟨εἰς⟩ χρόνον,
καὶ μήτε πορθεῖν πατρίδα μήτε προσφέρειν
πύργοισι πηκτῶν κλιμάκων προσαμβάσεις,
ἃ μὴ κυρήσας τῆς δίκης πειράσομαι   490
δρᾶν. μάρτυρας δὲ τῶνδε δαίμονας καλῶ,
ὡς πάντα πράσσων σὺν δίκηι δίκης ἄτερ
ἀποστεροῦμαι πατρίδος ἀνοσιώτατα.
ταῦτ' αὔθ' ἕκαστα, μῆτερ, οὐχὶ περιπλοκὰς
λόγων ἀθροίσας εἶπον, ἀλλὰ καὶ σοφοῖς   495
καὶ τοῖσι φαύλοις ἔνδιχ', ὡς ἐμοὶ δοκεῖ.
Χο. ἐμοὶ μέν, εἰ καὶ μὴ καθ' Ἑλλήνων χθόνα
τεθράμμεθ', ἀλλ' οὖν ξυνετά μοι δοκεῖς λέγειν.
Ετ. εἰ πᾶσι ταὐτὸ καλὸν ἔφυ σοφόν θ' ἅμα,
οὐκ ἦν ἂν ἀμφίλεκτος ἀνθρώποις ἔρις·   500
νῦν δ' οὔθ' ὅμοιον οὐδὲν οὔτ' ἴσον βροτοῖς
πλὴν ὀνομάσαι· τὸ δ' ἔργον οὐκ ἔστιν τόδε.
ἐγὼ γὰρ οὐδέν, μῆτερ, ἀποκρύψας ἐρῶ·
ἄστρων ἂν ἔλθοιμ' αἰθέρος πρὸς ἀντολὰς
καὶ γῆς ἔνερθε, δυνατὸς ὢν δρᾶσαι τάδε,   505
τὴν θεῶν μεγίστην ὥστ' ἔχειν Τυραννίδα.
τοῦτ' οὖν τὸ χρηστόν, μῆτερ, οὐχὶ βούλομαι
ἄλλωι παρεῖναι μᾶλλον ἢ σώιζειν ἐμοί·

---

481 ταῦθ' ω+: τάδ' **rz**   483 ἐμὸν Za (Grotius): ἐμῶν Ω   487 εἰς
Jackson: αὖ ZbT: om. Ω   488 μήτε² **rz**: μηκέτι MOR: μήτε τι
BVC+   492 ὡς M²OB+: καὶ M¹VC   494 ταῦτ' αὔθ' ἕκαστα fere
ω+: καιταυθ'εκ[Π¹²: ταῦθ' ἕκ. **r**: ταῦτ' οὖν (θ') ἕκ. V, gV   498 δοκεῖ
r   502 ὀνομάσαι Ω: ὀνόμασιν Markland, Porson   503 σ' ἐρῶ Rw
(ᴾΣ)   504 αἰθέρος Stob. 4.6.3: ἡλίου Ω, Σ, Plut. *Mor.* 481A   ἀντολὰς
BLTᵖᶜ, Stob., Plut.*: ἀνατ- ω+, Plut.*   506 τὴν Π¹²ω+, test.: τῶν **rz**:
τὴν τῶν Vr, Plut.*

ἀνανδρία γάρ, τὸ πλέον ὅστις ἀπολέσας
τοὔλασσον ἔλαβε. πρὸς δὲ τοῖσδ' αἰσχύνομαι   510
ἐλθόντα σὺν ὅπλοις τόνδε καὶ πορθοῦντα γῆν
τυχεῖν ἃ χρῄζει· ταῖς γὰρ ἂν Θήβαις τόδε
γένοιτ' ὄνειδος εἰ Μυκηναίου δορὸς
φόβωι παρείην σκῆπτρα τἀμὰ τῶιδ' ἔχειν.
χρῆν δ' αὐτὸν οὐχ ὅπλοισι τὰς διαλλαγάς,   515
μῆτερ, ποιεῖσθαι· πᾶν γὰρ ἐξαιρεῖ λόγος
ὃ καὶ σίδηρος πολεμίων δράσειεν ἄν.
ἀλλ', εἰ μὲν ἄλλως τήνδε γῆν οἰκεῖν θέλει,
ἔξεστ'· ἐκεῖνο δ' οὐχ ἑκὼν μεθήσομαι –
ἄρχειν παρόν μοι, τῶιδε δουλεύσω ποτέ;   520
πρὸς ταῦτ' ἴτω μὲν πῦρ, ἴτω δὲ φάσγανα,
ζεύγνυσθε δ' ἵππους, πεδία πίμπλαθ' ἁρμάτων,
ὡς οὐ παρήσω τῶιδ' ἐμὴν τυραννίδα.
εἴπερ γὰρ ἀδικεῖν χρή, τυραννίδος πέρι
κάλλιστον ἀδικεῖν, τἄλλα δ' εὐσεβεῖν χρεών.   525
Χο. οὐκ εὖ λέγειν χρὴ μὴ 'πὶ τοῖς ἔργοις καλοῖς·
      οὐ γὰρ καλὸν τοῦτ', ἀλλὰ τῆι δίκηι πικρόν.
Ιο.   ὦ τέκνον, οὐχ ἅπαντα τῶι γήραι κακά,
      Ἐτεόκλεες, πρόσεστιν· ἀλλ' ἡμπειρία
      ἔχει τι λέξαι τῶν νέων σοφώτερον.   530
      τί τῆς κακίστης δαιμόνων ἐφίεσαι
      Φιλοτιμίας, παῖ; μὴ σύ γ'· ἄδικος ἡ θεός·
      πολλοὺς δ' ἐς οἴκους καὶ πόλεις εὐδαίμονας
      εἰσῆλθε κἀξῆλθ' ἐπ' ὀλέθρωι τῶν χρωμένων·

---

509 ἀνανδρίαι V   515 χρὴ Orion *anth.* 1.8   516 ἐξαιρεῖ B¹Vr, test.,
ⁱΣ: ἐξαίρει MB³OC+, Themist. *or.* 2.37b*, 16.207d   519 ἐκεῖνου [sic] O
(ἐκείνου coni. Valck.)   520 del. Kirchhoff   δουλεύσω ω+, Σ:
δουλεῦσαι **r**χ   521 μὲν ω+: μοι **r**: γε Philo *Joseph.* 78*   φάσγανον
rz, Philo   522 ζεύγνυσθ' ἵππους MOA   πί(μ)πλάσθ' fere **r**ζ
523 μεθήσω **rz**   527 τοῦτ' ω+, gV: τόδ' **r**, Stob. 3.13.13   πικρόν Ω,
gV: βαρύ Stob. χᵍ   528 γήραι Ω, gV, test.: βίωι *proleg. Voss. (Gramm.
Gr.* 1:3.7, 1–3)   529 ἐμπειρία R, test.*: ἐμπειρίαι ᵞᵖΣ   530 δεῖξαι
Stob. 4.50a.1, Sext. Emp. *adv. math.* 1.62*   532 φιλοτιμίας Ω, Πᵃ Πᶜ,
Plut. *Sulla* 4: πλεονεξίας Dio Chrys. 17.9   534 κἀξῆλθ' om. Πᵃ, Dio
Chrys.: καὶ εισηλθε Πᶜ   κτωμένων O (corr. O¹ˢ)

ἐφ' ἧι σὺ μαίνηι. κεῖνο κάλλιον, τέκνον,　　　　　535
'Ισότητα τιμᾶν, ἢ φίλους ἀεὶ φίλοις
πόλεις τε πόλεσι συμμάχους τε συμμάχοις
συνδεῖ· τὸ γὰρ ἴσον νόμιμον ἀνθρώποις ἔφυ,
τῶι πλέονι δ' αἰεὶ πολέμιον καθίσταται
τοὐλασσον ἐχθρᾶς θ' ἡμέρας κατάρχεται.　　　　540
καὶ γὰρ μέτρ' ἀνθρώποισι καὶ μέρη σταθμῶν
'Ισότης ἔταξε κἀριθμὸν διώρισεν,
νυκτός τ' ἀφεγγὲς βλέφαρον ἡλίου τε φῶς
ἴσον βαδίζει τὸν ἐνιαύσιον κύκλον,
κοὐδέτερον αὐτῶν φθόνον ἔχει νικώμενον.　　　　545
εἶθ' ἥλιος μὲν νύξ τε δουλεύει βροτοῖς,
σὺ δ' οὐκ ἀνέξηι δωμάτων ἔχων ἴσον
καὶ †τῶιδ' ἀπονεῖμαι†; κᾆτα ποῦ 'στιν ἡ δίκη;
τί τὴν τυραννίδ', ἀδικίαν εὐδαίμονα,
τιμᾶις ὑπέρφευ καὶ μέγ' ἥγησαι τόδε;　　　　　550
περιβλέπεσθαι τίμιον; κενὸν μὲν οὖν.
ἢ πολλὰ μοχθεῖν πόλλ' ἔχων ἐν δώμασιν
βούληι; τί δ' ἐστὶ τὸ πλέον; ὄνομ' ἔχει μόνον·
ἐπεὶ τά γ' ἀρκοῦνθ' ἱκανὰ τοῖς γε σώφροσιν.
οὔτοι τὰ χρήματ' ἴδια κέκτηνται βροτοί,　　　　555
τὰ τῶν θεῶν δ' ἔχοντες ἐπιμελούμεθα·

---

535 κεῖνο κάλλιον, τέκνον Ω (κάλλιστον χ): τοῦτο κάλλιστον βροτοῖς Dio
Chrys.　　536 ἢ fere Ω: καὶ Πᵃ, Dio Chrys.　　ἀεὶ Ω, test.: εἶναι Plut.
Mor. 481Α*, Dio Chrys.　　φίλοις fere Ω, test.: φίλους Πᵃ　　537 συμ-...
συμ- **rζ**, test.: ξυμ-... ξυμ- ω +　　-μάχους...-μάχοις Ω, Plut *Mor.* 481Α,
test. alia: -μάχοις...-μάχος Dio Chrys.*, Plut. *Mor.* 643F　　538 συνδεῖν
Dio Chrys.　　μόνιμον Plut. *Mor.* 481Α* (cf. 484Β)　　540 θ' om. **r**: δ'
Brz, gV　　544 βαδίζειν **r**　　545 αὐτοῖν **rz**, fort. recte ἔχειν
r　　546 εἶθ' Ω, test.: ὡς Isid. Pelus. *PG* 78.1113　　βροτοῖς Ω, test.:
μέτροις Weil　　547 ἔχειν Rfχˢ, ʸᵖΣ, Oenom. apud Euseb. *praep. evang.*
6.7.30; Theodoret. *therap.* 4.40　　548 del. Schoene, Paley, fort. recte
(hab. Π¹²)　　ἀπονεῖμαι ωrζ, Doxopatr. *Anec. Oxon.* 4.163, 4–6: ἀπονέμειν
rχ, ʸᵖΣ: ἀπονέμων Α, ʸᵖΣ (coni. Markland): (τῶιδε) νεῖμαι Salmasius:
ἀπονεμεῖς Porson　　553 ἔχειν Mᵃᶜ**r**　　554 τοῖς γε ω +: τοῖς **r**, Stob.
4.32a.4*: τοῖσι χ**z**　　555–8 susp. Valck., del. Nauck (555–7 Wecklein)
555 κτήματ' **rz**　　556 δ' om. LVr, Plut. *Mor.* 116Α*

ὅταν δὲ χρήιζωσ', αὖτ' ἀφαιροῦνται πάλιν.
{ὁ δ' ὄλβος οὐ βέβαιος, ἀλλ' ἐφήμερος.}
ἄγ', ἤν σ' ἔρωμαι δύο λόγω προθεῖσ' ἅμα,
πότερα τυραννεῖν ἢ πόλιν σῶισαι θέλεις,   560
ἐρεῖς τυραννεῖν; ἢν δὲ νικήσηι σ' ὅδε
Ἀργεῖά τ' ἔγχη δόρυ τὸ Καδμείων ἕληι,
ὄψηι δαμασθὲν ἄστυ Θηβαῖον τόδε,
ὄψηι δὲ πολλὰς αἰχμαλωτίδας κόρας
βίαι πρὸς ἀνδρῶν πολεμίων πορθουμένας.   565
δαπανηρὸς ἄρ' ὁ πλοῦτος ὃν ζητεῖς ἔχειν
γενήσεται Θήβαισι, φιλότιμος δὲ σύ.
    σοὶ μὲν τάδ' αὐδῶ, σοὶ δέ, Πολύνεικες, λέγω·
ἀμαθεῖς Ἄδραστος χάριτας εἰς σ' ἀνήψατο,
ἀσύνετα δ' ἦλθες καὶ σὺ πορθήσων πόλιν.   570
φέρ', ἢν ἕληις γῆν τήνδ' – ὃ μὴ τύχοι ποτέ –,
πρὸς θεῶν, τροπαῖα πῶς ἀναστήσεις Διί;
πῶς δ' αὖ κατάρξηι θυμάτων, ἑλὼν πάτραν,
καὶ σκῦλα γράψεις πῶς ἐπ' Ἰνάχου ῥοαῖς;
Θήβας πυρώσας τάσδε Πολυνείκης θεοῖς   575
ἀσπίδας ἔθηκε; μήποτ', ὦ τέκνον, κλέος
τοιόνδε σοι γένοιθ' ὑφ' Ἑλλήνων λαβεῖν.
ἢν δ' αὖ κρατηθῆις καὶ τὰ τοῦδ' ὑπερδράμηι,
πῶς Ἄργος ἥξεις μυρίους λιπὼν νεκρούς;
ἐρεῖ δὲ δή τις· Ὦ κακὰ μνηστεύματα   580

---

558 del. Valck. (hab. Π¹⁵)   559 λόγωι OVMt: λόγους **r**   προθεῖσ'
ω+: προσθεῖσ' V**rxz**   560 σώσειν MO   562 del. Harberton,
Murray   ἔγχει MO   563 θηβαῖον MB²OC+: θηβαίων B¹V**rχ**:
καδμεῖον vel -είων **r**   565 λεληισμένας M^{γρ}B^{γρ}C^{γρ}: ὠθουμένας G
566 δαπανηρὸς Π¹⁵Mn^s, ^{γρ}Σ^B (vol. M^{γρ}C^{γρ}): ὀδυνηρὸς Ω   567 del.
Valck. (566–7 Dindorf) (hab. Π¹²Π¹⁵)   569 χάριτας ἄδραστος transp.
r   ἀμείψατο **r**: ἠμείψατο χ   570 πόλιν Ω: πάτραν Oenom. apud
Euseb. *praep. ev.* 6.7.29   571 φερε· αν ελης δ[Π¹⁵   τύχηι M^{γρ}C**r**
572 διί Rw^s, Σ^{Mn}S, coni. Kirchhoff: om. S: δή MVC: δορός BOV²^{γρ}+
573 δ' αὖ fere Ω: δαι Π¹⁵   κατάρξεις **rχz**   πάτραν ω+: πόλιν
r   575 πυρώσας Π¹⁵BO+: πυρσώσας MVC**rζ**   577 γένοιθ' **rz**:
γένοιτ' ἄν ω+   578 ὑπερδρ- **r** (cf. ᴾΣ), coni. Canter: ὑπεκδρ- ω+
580 δή om. MO

Ἄδραστε προσθείς, διὰ μιᾶς νύμφης γάμον
ἀπωλόμεσθα. δύο κακὼ σπεύδεις, τέκνον,
κείνων στέρεσθαι τῶνδέ τ' ἐν μέσωι πεσεῖν.
   μέθετον τὸ λίαν, μέθετον· ἀμαθία δυοῖν,
εἰς ταῦθ' ὅταν μόλητον, ἔχθιστον κακόν.   585
Χο. ὦ θεοί, γένοισθε τῶνδ' ἀπότροποι κακῶν
καὶ ξύμβασίν τιν' Οἰδίπου τέκνοις δότε.
Ετ. μῆτερ, οὐ λόγων ἔθ' ἀγών, ἀλλ' ἀναλοῦται χρόνος
οὖν μέσωι μάτην, περαίνει δ' οὐδὲν ἡ προθυμία·
οὐ γὰρ ἂν ξυμβαῖμεν ἄλλως ἢ 'πὶ τοῖς εἰρημένοις,   590
ὥστ' ἐμὲ σκήπτρων κρατοῦντα τῆσδ' ἄνακτ' εἶναι
   χθονός·
τῶν μακρῶν δ' ἀπαλλαγεῖσα νουθετημάτων μ' ἔα.
καὶ σὺ τῶνδ' ἔξω κομίζου τειχέων, ἢ κατθανῆι.
Πο. πρὸς τίνος; τίς ὧδ' ἄτρωτος ὅστις εἰς ἡμᾶς ξίφος
φόνιον ἐμβαλὼν τὸν αὐτὸν οὐκ ἀποίσεται μόρον;   595
Ετ. ἐγγύς, οὐ πρόσω βέβηκεν· εἰς χέρας λεύσσεις ἐμάς;
Πο. εἰσορῶ· δειλὸν δ' ὁ πλοῦτος καὶ φιλόψυχον κακόν.
Ετ. κᾆτα σὺν πολλοῖσιν ἦλθες πρὸς τὸν οὐδὲν ἐς μάχην;
Πο. ἀσφαλὴς γάρ ἐστ' ἀμείνων ἢ θρασὺς στρατηλάτης.
Ετ. κομπὸς εἶ σπονδαῖς πεποιθώς, αἵ σε σώιζουσιν
   θανεῖν.   600
Πο. καὶ σέ· δεύτερον δ' ἀπαιτῶ σκῆπτρα καὶ μέρη χθονός.
Ετ. οὐκ ἀπαιτούμεσθ'· ἐγὼ γὰρ τὸν ἐμὸν οἰκήσω δόμον.
Πο. τοῦ μέρους ἔχων τὰ πλείω;   Ετ. φήμ'·
   ἀπαλλάσσου δὲ γῆς.

582 κακὰ V¹(corr. V²)**r**   584 ἀμαθίαι M²BV²ˢ**rχ**, ᴾΣ   585 ταῦθ'
Brunck: ταῦθ' fere BV²**rχ**, Σ: ταῦθ' ω+   αἴσχιστον **rz**   588 ἔθ' ἀγών
post Canter Musgrave: ἐστ' ἀγών Ω   ἀναλοῦται Valck.: ἀνάλωται
Ω   590 ξυμβῶμεν **r**   591 ὥστ' ἐμὲ MO: ὥστε με Ω   593 ἧι VRf:
ἢ S   594 τίς VC+: τίς δ' MBO**rζ**   596 οὐ B³ᵞᴾV²**rχ**, ¹ᶜΣᶜ: οὖ ω+
(utrumque Σ)   βέβηκεν Π¹²Rˢ (coni. Heath, Brunck): βέβηκ' Mt:
βέβηκας Ω, Σ   χέρας King: χεῖρας Π¹²Ω   597 δειλὸν M²B¹ˢV+, test.:
δεινὸν ω**r**, gV, test.   600 κομπὸς MB²OV²C+: κόμπος B¹Mn: κόμπος
V¹**rxz**, Et. magn. 527, 48: κομψὸς ᵞᴾΣⱽ   601 καὶ σέ M (punctum add.
Wilam.): καὶ σὲ **r**: καί σε ω+   δ' Wilam.: γ' Ω: om. C   603 τὰ πλείω
post Maehler scripsi (ταπλ[Π¹²): τὸ πλεῖον ω+: τὸ πλεῖστον **r**

ΦΟΙΝΙΣΣΑΙ

Πο. ὦ θεῶν βωμοὶ πατρῴων, Ετ. οὓς σὺ πορθήσων πάρει.

Πο. κλύετέ μου, Ετ. τίς δ᾽ ἂν κλύοι σου πατρίδ᾽ ἐπεστρατευμένου; 605

Πο. καὶ θεῶν τῶν λευκοπώλων δώματ᾽, Ετ. οἳ στυγοῦσί σε.

Πο. ἐξελαυνόμεσθα πατρίδος, Ετ. καὶ γὰρ ἦλθες ἐξελῶν.

Πο. ἀδικίαι γ᾽, ὦ θεοί. Ετ. Μυκήναις, μὴ ᾽νθάδ᾽ ἀνακάλει θεούς.

Πο. ἀνόσιος πέφυκας Ετ. ἀλλ᾽ οὐ πατρίδος, ὡς σύ, πολέμιος.

Πο. ὅς μ᾽ ἄμοιρον ἐξελαύνεις. Ετ. καὶ κατακτενῶ γε πρός. 610

Πο. ὦ πάτερ, κλύεις ἃ πάσχω; Ετ. καὶ γὰρ οἷα δρᾷς κλύει.

Πο. καὶ σύ, μῆτερ; Ετ. ἀθέμιτόν σοι μητρὸς ὀνομάζειν κάρα.

Πο. ὦ πόλις. Ετ. μολὼν ἐς Ἄργος ἀνακάλει Λέρνης ὕδωρ.

Πο. εἶμι, μὴ πόνει· σὲ δ᾽ αἰνῶ, μῆτερ. Ετ. ἔξιθι χθονός.

Πο. ἔξιμεν· πατέρα δέ μοι δὸς εἰσιδεῖν. Ετ. οὐκ ἂν τύχοις. 615

Πο. ἀλλὰ παρθένους ἀδελφάς. Ετ. οὐδὲ τάσδ᾽ ὄψηι ποτέ.

Πο. ὦ κασίγνηται. Ετ. τί ταύτας ἀνακαλεῖς ἔχθιστος ὤν;

Πο. μῆτερ, ἀλλά μοι σὺ χαῖρε. Ιο. χαρτὰ γοῦν πάσχω, τέκνον.

Πο. οὐκέτ᾽ εἰμὶ παῖς σός. Ιο. εἰς πόλλ᾽ ἀθλία πέφυκ᾽ ἐγώ.

---

604 πατρῴων T: πατρῶιοι Ω   607 ἐξελῶν **Br**χ, Σ: ἐξελὼν ω+
608 γ᾽ ὦ MtχT: γε σῆι ὦ fere ω+   610 κατακτανῶ B+: κτανῶ
rχ   σε **rz**   612 ἀθέμιτόν Bothe: οὐ θεμιτόν Ω, Σ619: οὐ θέμις
Grotius   615 ἔξιμεν Musgrave: ἔξειμι Ω   τύχης M^{ac}**r**   618 μῆτερ
post χαῖρε hab. V(corr. V^{r})   μοι σὺ ω+: σύ μοι **r**: συ με Π^{12}
619 πόλλ᾽ **r**χT: πολλά γ᾽ ω+

85

Πο. ὅδε γὰρ εἰς ἡμᾶς ὑβρίζει.   Ετ. καὶ γὰρ
ἀνθυβρίζομαι.   620
Πο. ποῦ ποτε στήσηι πρὸ πύργων;   Ετ. ὡς τί μ᾽
ἱστορεῖς τόδε;
Πο. ἀντιτάξομαι κτενῶν σε.   Ετ. κἀμὲ τοῦδ᾽ ἔρως ἔχει.
Ιο. ὦ τάλαιν᾽ ἐγώ· τί δράσετ᾽, ὦ τέκν᾽;   Πο. αὐτὸ
σημανεῖ.
Ιο. πατρὸς οὐ φεύξεσθ᾽ Ἐρινῦς;   Ετ. ἐρρέτω
πρόπας δόμος.
Πο. ὡς τάχ᾽ οὐκέθ᾽ αἱματηρὸν τοὐμὸν ἀργήσει ξίφος.   625
τὴν δὲ θρέψασάν με γαῖαν καὶ θεοὺς μαρτύρομαι
ὡς ἄτιμος οἰκτρὰ πάσχων ἐξελαύνομαι χθονός,
δοῦλος ὥς, ἀλλ᾽ οὐχὶ ταὐτοῦ πατρὸς Οἰδίπου γεγώς·
κἂν τί σοι, πόλις, γένηται, μὴ 'μέ, τόνδε δ᾽ αἰτιῶ·
οὐχ ἑκὼν γὰρ ἦλθον, ἄκων δ᾽ †ἐξελαύνομαι
χθονός.†   630
καὶ σύ, Φοῖβ᾽ ἄναξ Ἀγυιεῦ, καὶ μέλαθρα, χαίρετε,
ἥλικές θ᾽ οὑμοί, θεῶν τε δεξίμηλ᾽ ἀγάλματα·
οὐ γὰρ οἶδ᾽ εἴ μοι προσειπεῖν αὖθις ἔσθ᾽ ὑμᾶς ποτε·
ἐλπίδες δ᾽ οὔπω καθεύδουσ᾽, αἷς πέποιθα σὺν θεοῖς
τόνδ᾽ ἀποκτείνας κρατήσειν τῆσδε Θηβαίας
χθονός.   635
Ετ. ἔξιθ᾽ ἐκ χώρας· ἀληθῶς δ᾽ ὄνομα Πολυνείκη πατὴρ
ἔθετό σοι θείαι προνοίαι νεικέων ἐπώνυμον.   637

Χο.   Κάδμος ἔμολε τάνδε γᾶν   στρ. 638
Τύριος, ὧι τετρασκελὴς

---

621 τάδε **r**   622 κτενῶν vel -ών fere ω+ : κτανῶν vel -ών **rζ**
623b Pol. trib. MOV+ : Et. trib. BC**rx**   624b Et. trib. C, fort. Xᵃᶜ: Pol.
trib. Ω: notam om. Mᵃᶜ, et Et. et Pol. notas praef. M¹ᵖᶜ   625 Pol. trib.
M¹ᵖᶜC: Et. trib. (et 626 Pol. trib.) BᵃᶜV²**r**: nullam notam hab. (Pol.
continuant) MᵃᶜBᵖᶜOV¹+   626 γαῖαν Ω: πάτραν fere MʸᵖBʸᵖCʸᵖ
628 γεγώς Π⁴B¹ˢV¹+ : μολών ω(V²ʸᵖ)Rw   629 μὴ 'μέ Porson: μή με fere
Ω   τόνδε δ᾽ **Br**T: τῶνδε δ᾽ Saχ: τῶνδ᾽ **rz**: τόνδ᾽ ω**rz**
630 ἐξελαύνομαι χθονός (]αι χθονος Π⁴) e 627 repetitum vidit
Schoene   633 αὖθις om. **Orz**   ἔσθ᾽ ὑμᾶς Ω (]ς υμας ποτ[Π⁴, i.e. ἔσθ᾽
om.?): ἔξεσται Paley   635 θηβαίων χ   636 ἔξιθ᾽ ἐκ **rχz**: ἔξιθι
ω+   639 τετρασκελής Ω: -λὲς Bergk

μόσχος ἀδάματον πέσημα   640
δίκε τελεσφόρον διδοῦσα
χρησμόν, οὗ κατοικίσαι
πεδία νιν τὸ θέσφατον
πυροφόρα δόμων ἔχρη,
καλλιπόταμος ὕδατος ἵνα τε   645
νοτὶς ἐπέρχεται †γύας†
Δίρκας χλοηφόρους
καὶ βαθυσπόρους γύας·
Βρόμιον ἔνθα τέκετο μά-
τηρ Διὸς γάμοισιν,   650
κισσὸς ὃν περιστεφὴς
ἑλικτὸς εὐθὺς ἔτι βρέφος
χλοηφόροισιν ἔρνεσιν
κατασκίοισιν ὀλβίσας ἐνώτισεν,.
Βάκχιον χόρευμα παρθέ-   655
νοισι Θηβαΐσι   655bis
καὶ γυναιξὶν εὐίοις.   656

ἔνθα φόνιος ἦν δράκων   ἀντ. 657
Ἄρεος ὠμόφρων φύλαξ
νάματ᾽ ἔνυδρα καὶ ῥέεθρα
χλοερὰ δεργμάτων κόραισι   660
πολυπλάνοις ἐπισκοπῶν·

---

640 ἀδάματον Elmsley: ἀδάμαστον Π⁶Ω: ἀδάματος post King
Bergk   642 κατοικίσαι ʸᵖΣᴹᴮᶜ: κατώικισε(ν) ω+: κατώικησεν
rz   643 νιν post Morum Dindorf: μὲν Ω, Σ   644 δόμων
suspectum   ἔχρη Bergk, Hermann: ἔχρησε(ν) Ω   646 γύας Valck.:
γυίας ω: om. S: γαίας fere B²**r**ζ: γᾶς fere MᵐᵃʳᵍCˢ**r**χ: ῥυτᾶς
Hermann   647 fort. χλοηφόρου L¹ (coni. Grotius)   648 βαθυσπόρου
r   γύας Barnes: γυίας ω+: om. T: χώρας OCˢ: γέας Sa   649 τέκετο
bis Or: τέκε Vr: τέτοκε L   650 lacunam post μάτηρ stat. Musgrave,
alii   γάμοις **r**   652 ἕλικος Bergk, Hermann   εὐθὺς hoc loco
Π²ω+: post βρέφος hab. **r**: post ἔτι Z   653 χλοηφόροις **r**   ἔρνεσι
φύλοιο C: ἔρνεσι φύλλοις L²   654 καικατασκ[Π²   655 Βάκχιον
Valck.: βακχεῖον Π²Ω   θηβαΐσι post Hermann Conradt: θηβαῖσι
fere Ω (θηβαίαις Rw, coni. Hermann)   656 εὐίαις **z**   657 φοίνιος
M¹ᵖᶜ**r**   658 ἄρεος V+: αρε]ος υιος Π⁶: ἄρεως MBCF: ἄρες
O   ὁμόφρων V¹(corr. V²)**r**   659 εὔυδρα Mtχ

ὃν ἐπὶ χέρνιβας μολών
  Κάδμος ὄλεσε μαρμάρωι
  κρᾶτα φόνιον ὀλεσίθηρος
  ὠλένας δικὼν βολαῖς,   665
δίας ⟨δ'⟩ ἀμάτορος
  Παλλάδος ⟨δίκεν⟩ φραδαῖς   667
  εἰς βαθυσπόρους γύας   669
  γαπετεῖς {δικὼν} ὀδόντας.   668
ἔνθεν ἐξανῆκε Γᾶ   670
  πάνοπλον ὄψιν ὑπὲρ ἄκρων
  ὅρων χθονός· σιδαρόφρων
  δέ νιν φόνος πάλιν ξυνῆψε Γᾶι φίλαι.
αἵματος δ' ἔδευσε Γαῖαν,   674
  ἅ νιν εὐαλίοισι   674bis
  δεῖξεν αἰθέρος πνοαῖς.   675

καὶ σέ, τὸν προμάτορος   ἐπωιδ. 676
  Ἰοῦς ποτ' ἔκγονον
  Ἔπαφον, ὦ Διὸς γένεθλον, ἐκάλεσ' ἐκάλεσα   678–9
  βαρβάρωι βοᾶι,   679bis
  ἰώ,   680
  βαρβάροις λιταῖς·   680bis
  βᾶθι βᾶθι τάνδε γᾶν·
  σοί νιν ἔκγονοι κτίσαν
  καὶ διώνυμοι θεαί,

---

663 ὄλεσε S (coni. Bergk, Hermann): ὤλεσε(ν) Ω   665 ὠλένας (vel -ης)
rζ, ⁱΣ^M: -ῶν B¹ˢ**r**ˢ**x**ˢ, ⁱΣ^BV: -αις ω+   666 ⟨δ'⟩ Brunck: ⟨τ'⟩
Rauchenstein   667 ⟨δίκεν⟩ post Wilam. addidi   φραδαῖς T: -αῖσι(ν)
Ω, Σι062, Hsch. φ 822   669 transposui (post Conradt): del. (una cum
648) Wilam.   γύας Valck.: γυίας ω+: γαίας **r**   668 δικὼν seclus.
Conradt, Wilam.: δίκ' Heath: ἔδικεν Rauchenstein   670 ἔνθεν δ' fere
MC**r**   673 πάλιν om. PRw   ξυνῆκε Mtχ   γᾶι φίλαι T: φίλα(ι)
γᾶ(ι) fere Ω (φίλα ξυνῆψε γᾶ transp. PRw)   674 δ' om. **r**: τ'
P   674bis εὐαλίοισι Hermann: εὐηλίοισι fere ω+: εὐηλίησι **r**: εὐείλοισι
Musgrave   679 ἐκάλεσ' del. Bothe   680bis βαρβάροισι **r**: -ραις
Mn^γρ   λιταῖς ω+: βοαῖς M^γρC^γρ: βοαῖς λιταῖς **r**   682 σῶι ...
ἐκγόνωι ^γρΣ   683 καὶ Major, Hartung: ἅι vel ἅ ω+, Σ: ὥ **r**: αἵ Σ

Περσέφασσα καὶ φίλα
Δαμάτηρ θεά,   685
πάντων ἄνασσα,   686
πάντων δὲ Γᾶ τροφός,   686bis
κτήσαντο· πέμπε πυρφόρους θεάς,
ἄμυνε τᾶιδε γαίαι.
πάντα δ᾽ εὐπετῆ θεοῖς.   689

Ετ. χώρει σὺ καὶ κόμιζε τὸν Μενοικέως   690
Κρέοντ᾽, ἀδελφὸν μητρὸς Ἰοκάστης ἐμῆς,
λέγων τάδ᾽, ὡς οἰκεῖα καὶ κοινὰ χθονὸς
θέλω πρὸς αὐτὸν συμβαλεῖν βουλεύματα
πρὶν εἰς μάχην τε καὶ δορὸς τάξιν μολεῖν.
καίτοι ποδῶν σῶν μόχθον ἐκλύει παρών·   695
ὁρῶ γὰρ αὐτὸν πρὸς δόμους στείχοντ᾽ ἐμούς.

ΚΡΕΩΝ
ἦ πόλλ᾽ †ἐπῆλθόν† εἰσιδεῖν χρῄζων σ᾽, ἄναξ
Ἐτεόκλεες, πέριξ δὲ Καδμείων πύλας
φυλακάς τ᾽ ἐπῆλθον σὸν δέμας θηρώμενος.
Ετ. καὶ μὴν ἐγώ σ᾽ ἔχρηιζον εἰσιδεῖν, Κρέον·   700
πολλῶι γὰρ ηὗρον ἐνδεεῖς διαλλαγὰς
ὡς εἰς λόγους συνῆψα Πολυνείκει μολών.
Κρ. ἤκουσα μεῖζον αὐτὸν εἰς Θήβας φρονεῖν,
κήδει τ᾽ Ἀδράστου καὶ στρατῶι πεποιθότα.
ἀλλ᾽ εἰς θεοὺς χρὴ ταῦτ᾽ ἀναρτήσαντ᾽ ἔχειν·   705
ἃ δ᾽ ἐμποδὼν μάλιστα, ταῦθ᾽ ἥκω φράσων.
Ετ. τὰ ποῖα ταῦτα; τὸν λόγον γὰρ ἀγνοῶ.
Κρ. ἥκει τις αἰχμάλωτος Ἀργείων πάρα.

---

686 πάντων[1] ω + : ἀπάντων **r**   687 κτήσαντο Porson: ἐκτήσαντο **rχz**:
ἐκτίσαντο ω +   πυρφ. πέμπε transp. O   πυροφόρους ΜΜ^{γρ}VC^{γρ}**rχ**
688 ἄμυνε Hermann (cf. ^{γρ}Σ ἀμύνεται δὲ γᾶ): ἀμῦναι fere Ω   γαίαι
Mrz: γᾶι ω +   689 εὐπ(ε)ιθῆ **r**   θεοῖσι(ν) **MOrz**   693 θέλω
Π^{12}Ω: ἔχω(ν) lex. Vind. ξ 2   695 σὸν P   697 ἐπῆλθον Π^{12}Ω: ἐμόχθουν
Valck.   699 φυλακάς **Mrχz**   701 πολλῶν **r** (coni. Burges)
703 εἰς Wecklein: ἦ Ω, Σ   704 πεποιθέναι **r**   708 τις Ald.: τίς fere
Ω

Ετ. λέγει δὲ δὴ τί τῶν ἐκεῖ νεώτερον;

Κρ. μέλλειν πέριξ †πύργοισι† Καδμείων πόλιν   710
    ὅπλοις ἑλίξειν αὐτίκ᾽ Ἀργείων στρατόν.

Ετ. ἐξοιστέον τἄρ᾽ ὅπλα Καδμείων πόλει.

Κρ. ποῖ; μῶν νεάζων οὐχ ὁρᾶις ἃ χρή σ᾽ ὁρᾶν;

Ετ. ἐκτὸς τάφρων τῶνδ᾽, ὡς μαχουμένους τάχα.

Κρ. σμικρὸν τὸ πλῆθος τῆσδε γῆς, οἱ δ᾽ ἄφθονοι.   715

Ετ. ἐγᾦδα κείνους τοῖς λόγοις ὄντας θρασεῖς.

Κρ. ἔχει τιν᾽ ὄγκον τἄργος Ἑλλήνων πάρα.

Ετ. θάρσει· τάχ᾽ αὐτῶν πεδίον ἐμπλήσω φόνου.

Κρ. θέλοιμ᾽ ἄν· ἀλλὰ τοῦθ᾽ ὁρῶ πολλοῦ πόνου.

Ετ. ὡς οὐ καθέξω τειχέων εἴσω στρατόν.   720

Κρ. καὶ μὴν τὸ νικᾶν ἐστι πᾶν εὐβουλία.

Ετ. βούληι τράπωμαι δῆθ᾽ ὁδοὺς ἄλλας τινάς;

Κρ. πάσας γε, πρὶν κίνδυνον εἰς ἅπαξ μολεῖν.

Ετ. εἰ νυκτὸς αὐτοῖς προσβάλοιμεν ἐκ λόχου;

Κρ. εἴπερ σφαλείς γε δεῦρο σωθήσηι πάλιν.   725

Ετ. ἴσον φέρει νύξ, τοῖς δὲ τολμῶσιν πλέον.

Κρ. ἐνδυστυχῆσαι δεινὸν εὐφρόνης κνέφας.

Ετ. ἀλλ᾽ ἀμφὶ δεῖπνον οὖσι προσβάλω δόρυ;

Κρ. ἔκπληξις ἂν γένοιτο· νικῆσαι δὲ δεῖ.

Ετ. βαθύς γέ τοι Διρκαῖος ἀναχωρεῖν πόρος.   730

Κρ. ἅπαν κάκιον τοῦ φυλάσσεσθαι καλῶς.

Ετ. τί δ᾽, εἰ καθιππεύσαιμεν Ἀργείων στρατόν;

Κρ. κἀκεῖ πέφαρκται λαὸς ἅρμασιν πέριξ.

Ετ. τί δῆτα δράσω; πολεμίοισι δῶ πόλιν;

Κρ. μὴ δῆτα· βουλεύου δ᾽, ἐπείπερ εἶ σοφός.   735

---

709 δὴ τί **rχ**ζ: δή τι ω**r**   710–11 alii alia delent vel emendant (710 del.
Burges, Dindorf; 711 del. Kirchhoff)   710 πύργοισι Ω: πυκνοῖσι
Reiske   711 ἀργεῖον CRfˢ   713 πῆ **Lz**   χρῆν Fᵃᶜ
714 μαχουμένοις Or (coni. Porson)   717 τἄργος MC+: ἄργος BOV**rχ**,
ˡᶜΣ   721 εὐβουλίαι BCX, ᴾΣ: εὐβουλίας F. G. Schoene, fort. Σ   724 εἰ
ω+: ἢ **r**ζ   προσβάλοιμ᾽ ἂν V²ˢGχ   725 σφαλῆις MV²**rz**
728 προσβάλλω Π¹²Br**ζ**   730 δέ **r**   732 ἀργεῖον **Or**   733
πέφαρκται Dindorf: πέφρακται Ω   734 -ίοισι δῶ BVC+, ˡᶜΣᶜ: -ίοις
δώσω MO**rχz**, ˡᶜΣᴹ, ᴾΣᴹ

Ετ. τίς οὖν πρόνοια γίγνεται σοφωτέρα;
Κρ. ἕπτ᾽ ἄνδρας αὐτοῖς φασιν, ὡς ἤκουσ᾽ ἐγώ,
Ετ. τί προστετάχθαι δρᾶν; τὸ γὰρ σθένος βραχύ.
Κρ. †λόχων ἀνάσσειν† ἑπτὰ προσκεῖσθαι πύλαις.
Ετ. τί δῆτα δρῶμεν; ἀπορίαν γὰρ οὐ μενῶ.   740
Κρ. ἕπτ᾽ ἄνδρας αὐτοῖς καὶ σὺ πρὸς πύλαις ἑλοῦ.
Ετ. λόχων ἀνάσσειν ἢ μονοστόλου δορός;
Κρ. λόχων, προκρίνας οἵπερ ἀλκιμώτατοι.
Ετ. ξυνῆκ᾽· ἀμύνειν τειχέων προσαμβάσεις.
Κρ. καὶ ξυστρατήγους ⟨γ᾽⟩· εἷς δ᾽ ἀνὴρ οὐ πάνθ᾽
    ὁρᾶι.   745
Ετ. θάρσει προκρίνας ἢ φρενῶν εὐβουλίαι;
Κρ. ἀμφότερον· ἀπολειφθὲν γὰρ οὐδὲν θάτερον.
Ετ. ἔσται τάδ᾽· ἐλθὼν ἑπτάπυργον ἐς στόμα
    τάξω λοχαγοὺς πρὸς πύλαισιν, ὡς λέγεις,
    ἴσους ἴσοισι πολεμίοισιν ἀντιθείς.   750
    ὄνομα δ᾽ ἑκάστου διατριβὴ πολλὴ λέγειν,
    ἐχθρῶν ὑπ᾽ αὐτοῖς τείχεσιν καθημένων.
    ἀλλ᾽ εἶμ᾽, ὅπως ἂν μὴ καταργῶμεν χέρα.
    καί μοι γένοιτ᾽ ἀδελφὸν ἀντήρη λαβεῖν
    καὶ ξυσταθέντα διὰ μάχης ἑλεῖν δορί.   755
    {κτανεῖν θ᾽ ὃς ἦλθε πατρίδα πορθήσων ἐμήν}
    γάμους δ᾽ ἀδελφῆς Ἀντιγόνης παιδός τε σοῦ

---

737 αὐτοῖς om. LZm, post φασιν transp. Rw   738 προστέτακται
V³**rz**   739 λόχων ἄνακτας Matthiae: λοχαγετοῦντας Wecklein
χἄπτὰ Meineke   πρ]οσκειν[ται Π¹²   741 αὐτὸς Grotius: εὐθὺς
Zakas   πύλας V**r**   742 μονοστόλους O   744 προσαμβάσεις **r**ζ, 'Σ:
προσεμβ- O: πρὸς ἀμβάσεις fere ω+, 'Σ alter   745 γ᾽ add.
Lenting   δ᾽ del. Polle   746 θράσει Μ^{γρ}C^{γρ}**r**   747 ἀμφότερα **r**:
-τερ᾽· ἐν (Burges) cum θατέρου (Reiske) Wecklein   748 ἐλθὼν om. (et
μολὼν in fine versus add.) Or**χ**   ἑπτάπ- MBC+: δ᾽ ἑπτάπ- V**rz** :
ἑπτάπ- δ᾽ O**r**   ἑπτάπυλον **r**   στόμα Jackson: πόλιν Ω   750
ἀντιτιθεὶς MOG   751–3 del. Trendelenburg   751 διατριβὴν πολλὴν
ἔχει Μ¹(fere corr. Μ²): διατριβὴ πολλὴ ἔχει fere **r**   753–6 del. Paley,
post 773 transp. Walter   755 ἑλεῖν δορί MV+: ἐλθεῖν δορί Μ^{γρ}BOC**r**ζ:
ἐλθεῖν δορός G: ἔχειν δόρυ Β^{γρ}   756 (= 1376) del. Valck.   ἐμοί B:
φίλην Β^{γρ}   757 τ᾽ MO**r**

Αἵμονος, ἐάν τι τῆς τύχης ἐγὼ σφαλῶ,
σοὶ χρὴ μέλεσθαι· τὴν δόσιν δ᾽ ἐχέγγυον
τὴν πρόσθε ποιῶ νῦν ἐπ᾽ ἐξόδοις ἐμαῖς.   760
μητρὸς δ᾽ ἀδελφὸς εἶ· τί δεῖ μακρηγορεῖν;
τρέφ᾽ ἀξίως νιν σοῦ τε τήν τ᾽ ἐμὴν χάριν.
πατὴρ δ᾽ ἐς αὑτὸν ἀμαθίαν ὀφλισκάνει,
ὄψιν τυφλώσας· οὐκ ἄγαν σφ᾽ ἐπήινεσα·
ἡμᾶς δ᾽ ἀραῖσιν, ἢν τύχηι, κατακτενεῖ.   765
ἓν δ᾽ ἐστὶν ἡμῖν ἀργόν, εἴ τι θέσφατον
οἰωνόμαντις Τειρεσίας ἔχει φράσαι,
τοῦδ᾽ ἐκπυθέσθαι ταῦτ᾽· ἐγὼ δὲ παῖδα σὸν
Μενοικέα, σοῦ πατρὸς αὐτεπώνυμον,
λαβόντα πέμψω δεῦρο Τειρεσίαν, Κρέον·   770
σοὶ μὲν γὰρ ἡδὺς ἐς λόγους ἀφίξεται,
ἐγὼ δὲ τέχνην μαντικὴν ἐμεμψάμην
ἤδη πρὸς αὐτόν, ὥστε μοι μομφὰς ἔχειν.
πόλει δὲ καὶ σοὶ ταῦτ᾽ ἐπισκήπτω, Κρέον·
ἤνπερ κρατήσηι τἀμά, Πολυνείκους νέκυν   775
μήποτε ταφῆναι τῆιδε Θηβαίαι χθονί,
θνήισκειν δὲ τὸν θάψαντα, κἂν φίλων τις ἦι.
{σοὶ μὲν τάδ᾽ εἶπον· προσπόλοις δ᾽ ἐμοῖς λέγω·}
ἐκφέρετε τεύχη πάνοπλά τ᾽ ἀμφιβλήματα,
ὡς εἰς ἀγῶνα τὸν προκείμενον δορὸς   780
ὁρμώμεθ᾽ ἤδη ξὺν δίκηι νικηφόρωι.
τῆι δ᾽ Εὐλαβείαι, χρησιμωτάτηι θεῶν,
προσευχόμεσθα τήνδε διασῶισαι πόλιν.   783

759 δ᾽ om. **r**: τ᾽ MB**r**   760 ποιῶν MO**r**   761 τ᾽ **r**   εἶ ω +: εἶ σύ
rχ   763–5 del. Helmbold, Fraenkel, 764 Friedrich   762 τήν τ᾽ B +:
τήνδ᾽ ω**r**   763 ἁμαρτίαν MC^γρ   ὀφλισκάνει Ω: optativum reddit
Σ   765 τ᾽ O**r**   -κτενεῖ BVC**r**: -κτανεῖ MO +   766 ἡμῖν ἀργὸν
ἐστὶν M**r**: ἡμῖν ἐστὶν ἀργόν **z**   769 ἀντεπώνυμον M²**r**   774–7 del.
Walter (hab. Π¹⁰)   777 τε C   φιλοις Π¹⁰   778 om. Π¹⁰, del.
Kirchhoff   τάδ᾽ αὐδῶ M**r**   781 om. Π¹⁰, del. Haslam   ὁρμώμεν
r   782–3 Creonti trib. Pohlenz   782 θεων Π¹⁰   783 προσευχ-
Π¹⁰MAa: προσευξ- Ω   -όμε(σ)θα ω +: -ώμε(σ)θα **r**Xa**z**   διασῶσαι
Π¹⁰BVC +: -σώζειν MO**r**

Χο. ὦ πολύμοχθος Ἄρης, τί ποθ' αἵματι   στρ. 784
     καὶ θανάτωι κατέχηι Βρομίου παράμουσος
     ἑορταῖς;   785
     οὐκ ἐπὶ καλλιχόροις στεφάνοισι νεάνιδος ὥρας
     βόστρυχον ἀμπετάσας λωτοῦ κατὰ πνεύματα μέλπηι
     μοῦσαν ἐν ἇι χάριτες χοροποιοί,
     ἀλλὰ σὺν ὁπλοφόροις στρατὸν Ἀργείων ἐπιπνεύσας
     αἵματι Θήβας   790
     κῶμον ἀναυλότατον προχορεύεις.   790bis
     οὐδ' ὑπὸ θυρσομανεῖ νεβρίδων μέτα δίναι,
     †ἅρμασι καὶ† ψαλίοις τετραβάμοσι μώνυχα πῶλον
     Ἱσμηνοῦ τ' ἐπὶ χεύμασι βαίνων
        ἱππείαισι θοάζεις, Ἀργείοις ἐπιπνεύσας
        Σπαρτῶν γένναν,   795
     ἀσπιδοφέρμονα †θίασον ἔνοπλον†,
        ἀντίπαλον κατὰ λάινα τείχεα   797
        χαλκῶι κοσμήσας.   797bis
     ἢ δεινά τις Ἔρις θεός, ἃ τάδε
     μήσατο πήματα γᾶς βασιλεῦσιν,
     Λαβδακίδαις πολυμόχθοις.   800

     ὦ ζαθέων πετάλων πολυθηρότα-   ἀντ. 801
        τον νάπος, Ἀρτέμιδος χιονοτρόφον ὄμμα
           Κιθαιρών,

---

785 βρομίαις R   786 καλλιφοροις Π¹⁰   ὥρας Π¹⁰, e Σ restit. King: ὥραις Ω, Σ alter   787 λοτοῦ OV²ˢr, Eust. 344, 35f. (aliter Eust. 905, 19)   μέλπηι fere Ω(Mʸᴾ)(με[Π¹⁰): πέμπηι MSa   788 ἇι fere Ω: αις Π¹⁰   χοροποιοί MᵖᶜOr, ⁱΣ: χαροποιοί MᵃᶜBC+: μελοποιοί MʸᴾBʸᴾVCʸᴾ   790 θήβαις V²ˢ, ᴾΣ alter   791 δίναι Hermann: δινεύεις Ω: δινεῖς Geel   792 ἅρμασι καὶ ω+: ἅρμασι δὲ καὶ BˢV²ˢR: ἀλλ' ἅρμασι καὶ rζ (Mˢ λείπει τὸ ἀλλά): e.g. ἀλλὰ κροτῶν conicio   ψαλ(λ)ίοις fere BˢV²ˢrχζ: ψαλ(λ)ίων ωr, Σ   -βάμοσι fere ω+, Σ: -βάμονος R: -βάμων r, ᴾΣ: -βάμονα Hartung   μώνυχα πῶλον OV²r: μώνυχα πῶλων MBVˢCr: μωνύχων πώλων B²ˢVrχζ   793 τ' om. r: δ' Cr   794 ἱππείαισι MO+: ἱππείαις BVCrζ   ἀργείοις M (cf. ⁱΣ): -ους Ω(M²), ⁱΣᵛ795   ἀργ. ἐπιπνεύσας del. Seidler, Hermann   795 γένναν MOr, ⁱΣ: γέννα(ι) BVC+, Σ alter   796 ἔνοπλον Π¹⁰Ω: εὔοπλον T: ἐνόπλιον post Schoene Murray   797bis del. Tricl. (hab. Π¹⁰)   799 πήματα . . . βασιλεῦσιν del. Nauck   800 om. Π¹⁰, del. Nauck, Wecklein

μήποτε τὸν θανάτωι προτεθέντα, λόχευμ᾽ Ἰοκάστας,
ὤφελες Οἰδιπόδαν θρέψαι, βρέφος ἔκβολον οἴκων,
χρυσοδέτοις περόναις ἐπίσαμον,   805
μηδὲ τὸ παρθένιον πτερόν, οὔρειον τέρας, ἐλθεῖν
πένθεα γαίας   807
Σφιγγὸς ἀμουσοτάταισι σὺν ὠιδαῖς,   807bis
ἃ ποτε Καδμογενῆ τετραβάμοσι χαλαῖς
τείχεσι χριμπτομένα φέρεν αἰθέρος εἰς ἄβατον φῶς
γένναν, τὰν ὁ κατὰ χθονὸς Ἅιδας   810
    Καδμείοις ἐπιπέμπει· δυσδαίμων δ᾽ ἔρις ἄλλα
    θάλλει παίδων
Οἰδιπόδα κατὰ δώματα καὶ πόλιν.

    οὐ γὰρ ὃ μὴ καλὸν οὔποτ᾽ ἔφυ καλόν,
    οὐδ᾽ οἱ μὴ νόμιμοι   815
†παῖδες ματρὶ λόχευμα, μίασμα πατρός·
    ἡ δὲ συναίμονος εἰς λέχος ἦλθεν†   817
⟨   ⟩   817bis

ἔτεκες, ὦ Γαῖ᾽, ἔτεκές ποτε,   ἐπωιδ. 818
    βάρβαρον ὡς ἀκοὰν ἐδάην ἐδάην ποτ᾽ ἐν οἴκοις,
τὰν ἀπὸ θηροτρόφου φοινικολόφοιο δράκοντος   820
γένναν ὀδοντοφυᾶ, Θήβαις κάλλιστον ὄνειδος·
    Ἁρμονίας δέ ποτ᾽ εἰς ὑμεναίους
ἤλυθον οὐρανίδαι, φόρμιγγί τε τείχεα Θήβας
τᾶς Ἀμφιονίας τε λύρας ὕπο πύργος ἀνέσταν

---

803 μήποτε bis MCᵖᶜr   804 οἰδιπόδαν θρέψαι fere BOCr: οἰδίποδ᾽
ἀνθρέψαι V: οἰδίποδα θρέψαι fere M+   805 χρυσοδέταις r   806
οὔρειον fere Ω: ουδεί/[ον Π¹⁰   808 lacunam stat. Reiske, alii (accepto
791–2 δινεύεις, ἀλλ᾽); iam -βάμοσιν ἐν χηλαῖσιν T   χαλαῖς Hermann:
χηλαῖς r: χαλ- vel χηλαῖσι ω+   810 τὰν T: θ᾽ ἂν Sa: ἂν Ω   ἅιδας
(post Tricl.) Grotius: ἁίδης G: ἁίδης fere Ω   811 δ᾽ om. r   813
οἰδίποδος r   816–17 locus desperatus, etiam lacunosus, nisi 800
deleatur   816 μίασμα τε T   817 ἡ δὲ (vel ἦδε vel ἢ δὲ) ω+: ἢ δὴ Gχ:
ἦτε Hermann: οἱ δὲ fort. Σ alter, Zcˢ   συναίμονος MBVCr, Σ: σύναιμος
O: σύναιμον fere HMʸᵖ+   ἦλθεν Ω, Σ: ἦλθον Zc, Σ alter   818 Γαῖ᾽
Murray: γαῖ· H: γᾶι M: γᾶ Ω   820 θηρότροφον V²ˢ, Σ alter   821
= φυᾶ L. Dindorf: —φυῆ Ω   823 ἦλθον Hrχ   824 πύργοι r
ἀνέσταν MᵃᶜVCr, Σᵛ: ἀνέστα HMᵖᶜBO+, Σᴮ, ᴳΣ

διδύμων ποταμῶν πόρον ἀμφὶ μέσον, 825
Δίρκα χλοεροτρόφον ἅι πεδίον
πρόπαρ Ἰσμηνοῦ καταδεύει,
Ἰώ θ', ἅ κερόεσσα προμάτωρ,
Καδμείων βασιλῆας ἐγείνατο·
μυριάδας δ' ἀγαθῶν ἑτέροις ἑτέ- 830
ρας μεταμειβομένα
πόλις ἅδ' ἐπ' ἄκροις ἕστακ' Ἀρηΐοις στεφάνοισιν. 833

ΤΕΙΡΕΣΙΑΣ
ἡγοῦ πάροιθε, θύγατερ· ὡς τυφλῶι ποδὶ 834
ὀφθαλμὸς εἶ σύ, ναυβάταισιν ἄστρον ὥς· 835
δεῦρ' εἰς τὸ λευρὸν πέδον ἴχνος τιθεῖσ' ἐμόν,
πρόβαινε, μὴ σφαλῶμεν· ἀσθενὴς πατήρ·
κλήρους τέ μοι φύλασσε παρθένωι χερί,
οὓς ἔλαβον οἰωνίσματ' ὀρνίθων μαθὼν
θάκοισιν ἐν ἱεροῖσιν, οὗ μαντεύομαι. 840
τέκνον Μενοικεῦ, παῖ Κρέοντος, εἰπέ μοι
πόση τις ἡπίλοιπος ἄστεως ὁδὸς
πρὸς πατέρα τὸν σόν· ὡς ἐμὸν κάμνει γόνυ,
πυκνὴν δὲ βαίνων ἤλυσιν μόλις περῶ.
Κρ. θάρσει· πέλας γάρ, Τειρεσία, φίλοισι σοῖς 845
εἰσώρμισαι σὸν πόδα· λαβοῦ δ' αὐτοῦ, τέκνον·

---

826 Δίρκα Burges: δίρκας fere Ω   ἅι πεδίον Burges: ἅ πεδίον M¹ᵖᶜB²rχ:
πεδίον **r**: ἀμπεδίον HMᵃᶜM²B¹OCL²: ἀμπεδίον ἅ Vζ   827 πρόπαν
rz   καταρδεύει **r**   828 δ' Wecklein, Blaydes   830 δ' om. **r**: τ'
Wecklein   830–1 ἑτέροις ἑτέρας ῳrζ: ἑτέρας ἑτέροις fere **Mr**: ἑτέρας
ἑτέραις GχT   832 ἕστακεν T: ἔστ' BOL   832–3 ἀρηίοισι Z: Ἄρεως
Hermann: Ἄρεος Porson   στεφάνοις VZT   834 προπάροιθε OV**r**
835 ναύταισιν **Mrz**: ναυτίλοισιν **z**T   836 λευκὸν CP   πέδον
Barnes: πεδίον Ω   838 τε μοι **Mr**: τ' ἐμοὶ ω+   842 πόση Ω: πρόσω
LT   ἄστεως B³r**χ**: ἄστεος ω+: ἄστεος γ' **z**   843 ὥστ' HO   844
περῶ μόλις transp. O   846 εἰσώρμισαι ego et West (ἐσορμίσαι Nauck):
ἔσθ' ὁρμίσαι Κνίçala: ἐξώρμισαι **rζ**: ἐξόρμισαι B²V¹rχ, Σ: ἐξορμίσαι fere
ῳ(V²)**r**   δ' om. H

ὡς πᾶσ᾽ ἀπήνη πούς τε πρεσβύτου φιλεῖ
χειρὸς θυραίας ἀναμένειν κουφίσματα.

Τε. εἶέν, πάρεσμεν· τί με καλεῖς σπουδῇι, Κρέον;

Κρ. οὔπω λελήσμεθ᾽· ἀλλὰ σύλλεξαι σθένος   850
καὶ πνεῦμ᾽ ἄθροισον, αἶπος ἐκβαλὼν ὁδοῦ.

Τε. κόπωι παρεῖμαι γοῦν Ἐρεχθειδῶν ἄπο
δεῦρ᾽ ἐκκομισθεὶς τῆς πάροιθεν ἡμέρας·
κἀκεῖ γὰρ ἦν τις πόλεμος Εὐμόλπου δορός,
οὗ καλλινίκους Κεκροπίδας ἔθηκ᾽ ἐγώ·   855
καὶ τόνδε χρυσοῦν στέφανον, ὡς ὁρᾷς, ἔχω
λαβὼν ἀπαρχὰς πολεμίων σκυλευμάτων.

Κρ. οἰωνὸν ἐθέμην καλλίνικα σὰ στέφη·
ἐν γὰρ κλύδωνι κείμεθ᾽, ὥσπερ οἶσθα σύ,
δορὸς Δαναϊδῶν, καὶ μέγας Θήβαις ἀγών.   860
βασιλεὺς μὲν οὖν βέβηκε κοσμηθεὶς ὅπλοις
ἤδη πρὸς ἀλκὴν Ἐτεοκλῆς Μυκηνίδα·
ἐμοὶ δ᾽ ἐπέσταλκ᾽ ἐκμαθεῖν σέθεν πάρα
τί δρῶντες ἂν μάλιστα σώισαιμεν πόλιν.

Τε. Ἐτεοκλέους μὲν οὔνεκ᾽ ἂν κλήισας στόμα   865
χρησμοὺς ἐπέσχον· σοὶ δ᾽, ἐπεὶ χρήιζεις μαθεῖν,
λέξω. νοσεῖ γὰρ ἥδε γῆ πάλαι, Κρέον,
ἐξ οὗ ᾽τεκνώθη Λάιος βίαι θεῶν
πόσιν τ᾽ ἔφυσε μητρὶ μέλεον Οἰδίπουν·
αἵ θ᾽ αἱματωποὶ δεργμάτων διαφθοραὶ   870
θεῶν σόφισμα κἀπίδειξις Ἑλλάδι.
ἃ συγκαλύψαι παῖδες Οἰδίπου χρόνωι
χρήιζοντες, ὡς δὴ θεοὺς ὑπεκδραμούμενοι,

---

847 πᾶσ᾽ ἀπήνη multis suspectum   849 σπουδῇι om. **r**: ἐν σπουδῇι
H   850 σύλλεξον P   851 αἶπος HV**r**, Hsch. α 2054: ἄπος fere
MBOV²ˢC**r**, Eust. 381, 19: κᾶπος fere **r**χζ   852 παρεῖμαι Μ⁽ʸᵖ⁾Β⁽ʸᵖ⁾**r**χ,
Hsch. π 772: πάρειμι fere ω+   γοῦν ω+: γῆς fere **r**ζ: γόνατ᾽ post
Porson Matthiae   853 ἐκκομ- Ω: εἰσκομ- Herwerden   857 ἀπαρχὴν
O   864 μάλιστα om. O: κάλ(λ)ιστα VC**r**   866 σὺ δ᾽ BVC**rz**
867 κρέον πάλαι transp. **r**   869–80 del Fraenkel (868–80 Reeve)
869 τ᾽ om. **x**: δ᾽ **r**ζ   870 αἵ δ᾽ P (αἵ δ᾽ Paley): ἔνθ᾽ V¹(corr. V²ˢ)
871 κἀπόδειξις MB**r**   ἑλλάδος HOr**χ**   873 ὑπερδραμ- **r** (coni.
Zakas)

ἥμαρτον ἀμαθῶς· οὔτε γὰρ γέρα πατρὶ
οὔτ' ἔξοδον διδόντες, ἄνδρα δυστυχῆ   875
ἐξηγρίωσαν· ἐκ δ' ἔπνευσ' αὐτοῖς ἀρὰς
δεινάς, νοσῶν τε καὶ πρὸς ἠτιμασμένος.
ἀγὼ τί οὐ δρῶν, ποῖα δ' οὐ λέγων ἔπη
εἰς ἔχθος ἦλθον παισὶ τοῖσιν Οἰδίπου;
ἐγγὺς δὲ θάνατος αὐτόχειρ αὐτοῖς, Κρέον·   880
πολλοὶ δὲ νεκροὶ περὶ νεκροῖς πεπτωκότες
Ἀργεῖα καὶ Καδμεῖα μείξαντες βέλη
πικροὺς γόους δώσουσι Θηβαίαι χθονί,
σύ τ' ὦ τάλαινα συγκατασκάπτηι πόλις,
εἰ μὴ λόγοισι τοῖς ἐμοῖς τις πείσεται.   885
ἐκεῖνο μὲν γὰρ πρῶτον ἦν, τῶν Οἰδίπου
μηδένα πολίτην μηδ' ἄνακτ' εἶναι χθονός,
ὡς δαιμονῶντας κἀνατρέψοντας πόλιν.
ἐπεὶ δὲ κρεῖσσον τὸ κακόν ἐστι τἀγαθοῦ,
μί' ἐστὶν ἄλλη μηχανὴ σωτηρίας.   890
ἀλλ' – οὐ γὰρ εἰπεῖν οὔτ' ἐμοὶ τόδ' ἀσφαλὲς
πικρόν τε τοῖσι τὴν τύχην κεκτημένοις
πόλει παρασχεῖν φάρμακον σωτηρίας –
ἄπειμι. χαίρεθ'· εἷς γὰρ ὢν πολλῶν μέτα
τὸ μέλλον, εἰ χρή, πείσομαι· τί γὰρ πάθω;   895
Κρ. ἐπίσχες αὐτοῦ, πρέσβυ.   Τε.   μὴ 'πιλαμβάνου.
Κρ. μεῖνον, τί φεύγεις;   Τε.   ἡ τύχη σ', ἀλλ' οὐκ ἐγώ.
Κρ. φράσον πολίταις καὶ πόλει σωτηρίαν.
Τε. βούληι σὺ μέντοι κοὐχὶ βουλήσηι τάχα.
Κρ. καὶ πῶς πατρώιαν γαῖαν οὐ σῶισαι θέλω;   900

874 γέρα VCrζ: γέρας HMBO+   877 γε z   878 κἀγὼ King   τί
οὐ H^marg rχ^s: τί μὴ V^2γρRw, ^γρΣ: τί ω+   ποῖα H^margP, ^γρΣ, ^lcΣ^M.: ὁποῖα
Ω   879 εἰς ὄχλον H^γρB^γρ, ^γρΣ   881 παρὰ rχ^sζ   νεκροὺς
HOrχ^s   882 μέλη Markland, Earle   884 δ' Vrz   πόλις rχζ: πόλι
M^1pcBOVr: πόλει HM^acCSa   885 λόγοις Mr   886–90 del.
Fraenkel   888 κάνατρ- BC+: κάναστρ- HMOV+   -ψοντας M+:
-ψαντας ω(H incertum)r   891 οὐδ' r   892 δὲ rζ (coni. anon.)
896 αὐτοῦ H   μή τι λαμ- H^ac   897 φεύγεις μ' z   σ' MBO+: δ'
HVCRw: γ' CrZc   899 τάχα Π^12ω+: τάδε V^1sr

ΦΟΙΝΙΣΣΑΙ

Τε. θέλεις ἀκοῦσαι δῆτα καὶ σπουδὴν ἔχεις;
Κρ. εἰς γὰρ τί μᾶλλον δεῖ προθυμίαν ἔχειν;
Τε. κλύοις ἂν ἤδη τῶν ἐμῶν θεσπισμάτων· –
πρῶτον δ' ἐκεῖνο βούλομαι σαφῶς μαθεῖν,
ποῦ 'στιν Μενοικεύς, ὅς με δεῦρ' ἐπήγαγεν;   905
Κρ. ὅδ' οὐ μακρὰν ἄπεστι, πλησίον δὲ σοῦ.
Τε. ἀπελθέτω νυν θεσφάτων ἐμῶν ἑκάς.
Κρ. ἐμὸς πεφυκὼς παῖς ἃ δεῖ σιγήσεται.
Τε. βούληι παρόντος δῆτά σοι τούτου φράσω;
Κρ. κλύων γὰρ ἂν τέρποιτο τῆς σωτηρίας.   910
Τε. ἄκουε δή νυν θεσφάτων ἐμῶν ὁδόν·
{ἃ δρῶντες ἂν μάλιστα σώισαιμεν πόλιν}
σφάξαι Μενοικέα τόνδε δεῖ σ' ὑπὲρ πάτρας,
σὸν παῖδ', ἐπειδὴ τὴν τύχην αὐτὸς καλεῖς.
Κρ. τί φήις; τίν' εἶπας τόνδε μῦθον, ὦ γέρον;   915
Τε. ἅπερ πέφηνε, ταῦτα· κἀνάγκη σε δρᾶν.
Κρ. ὦ πολλὰ λέξας ἐν βραχεῖ χρόνωι κακά.
Τε. σοί γ', ἀλλὰ πατρίδι μεγάλα καὶ σωτήρια.
Κρ. οὐκ ἔκλυον, οὐκ ἤκουσα· χαιρέτω πόλις.
Τε. ἀνὴρ ὅδ' οὐκέθ' αὐτός· ἐκνεύει πάλιν.   920
Κρ. χαίρων ἴθ'· οὐ γὰρ σῶν με δεῖ μαντευμάτων.
Τε. ἀπόλωλεν ἡ ἀλήθει', ἐπεὶ σὺ δυστυχεῖς;
Κρ. ὦ πρός σε γονάτων καὶ γερασμίου τριχός,
Τε. τί προσπίτνεις με; δυσφύλακτ' †αἰτῇ† κακά.

---

902 γάρ τι OV¹(corr. V²)CP   μ' ἄλλο V¹(corr. V²)rχ, fort. Σ alter
903–4 del. Zipperer   904 μαθεῖν σαφῶς transp. Or   905 ἀπήγαγεν
OV¹(corr. V²ˢ)Crz   906 δέ που BᵃᶜOV¹(corr. V²ˢ)   907 νυν (vel νῦν)
ω(V²ˢ) + : δὴ V¹r   909 σοι τούτου MV²ˢ + : σοι τοῦτο OV¹Cr: τοῦτό
σοι B   911 ὁδούς P   912 (≈864) del. Kirchhoff (om. Sa)   μάλ.
σώσαιμεν πόλιν r: μάλ. σώσαιμεν πόλιν καδμείων M: μάλ. σώσαιτε πόλιν
R: σώσαιτε καδμείων πόλιν ω +   915 sic Ω: τί φής; ἐμὸν παῖδ' ἕνεκα γῆς
σφάξαι θέλεις; Mnʸᵖ, ʸᵖΣ   916 πέφηνε Camper: πέφυκε Ω   post
ταῦτα dist. Hermann   σὲ Murray   917 λόγωι Nauck   920 ἀνὴρ
Hermann (ὁ ἀνὴρ Pᵃᶜ): ἀνὴρ Ω, test.   δ' ὅδ' MOCr   οὐκέθ' αὐτός
Valck.: οὐκέτ' αὐτός Ω, test.   921 θεσπισμάτων rz   923 τριχὸς
γερασμίου transp. O   924 αἰτεῖς r: αἴνει anon. Cantabrig.

98

Κρ. σίγα· πόλει δὲ τούσδε μὴ λέξῃς λόγους.   925
Τε. ἀδικεῖν κελεύεις μ'· οὐ σιωπήσαιμεν ἄν.
Κρ. τί δή με δράσεις; παῖδά μου κατακτενεῖς;
Τε. ἄλλοις μελήσει ταῦτ', ἐμοὶ δ' εἰρήσεται.
Κρ. ἐκ τοῦ δ' ἐμοὶ τόδ' ἦλθε καὶ τέκνωι κακόν;
Τε. ὀρθῶς μ' ἐρωτᾶις κἀς ἀγῶν' ἔρχῃ λόγων·   930
    δεῖ τόνδε θαλάμαις, οὗ δράκων ὁ γηγενὴς
    ἐγένετο Δίρκης ναμάτων ἐπίσκοπος,
    σφαγέντα φόνιον αἷμα γῆι δοῦναι χοάς,
    Κάδμου παλαιῶν Ἄρεος ἐκ μηνιμάτων,
    ὃς γηγενεῖ δράκοντι τιμωρεῖ φόνον.   935
    καὶ ταῦτα δρῶντες σύμμαχον κτήσεσθ' Ἄρη·
    χθὼν δ' ἀντὶ καρποῦ καρπὸν ἀντί θ' αἵματος
    αἷμ' ἢν λάβηι βρότειον, ἕξετ' εὐμενῆ
    Γῆν, ἥ ποθ' ἡμῖν χρυσοπήληκα στάχυν
    Σπαρτῶν ἀνῆκεν· ἐκ γένους δὲ δεῖ θανεῖν   940
    τοῦδ', ὃς δράκοντος γένυος ἐκπέφυκε παῖς.
    σὺ δ' ἐνθάδ' ἡμῖν λοιπὸς εἶ Σπαρτῶν γένους
    ἀκέραιος, ἔκ τε μητρὸς ἀρσένων τ' ἄπο,
    οἱ σοί τε παῖδες· Αἵμονος μὲν οὖν γάμοι
    σφαγὰς ἀπείργουσ'. οὐ γάρ ἐστιν ἥιθεος·   945
    κεἰ μὴ γὰρ εὐνῆς ἥψατ', ἀλλ' ἔχει λέχος.
    οὗτος δὲ πῶλος τῆιδ' ἀνειμένος πόλει
    θανὼν πατρώιαν γαῖαν ἐκσώισειεν ἄν.
    πικρὸν δ' Ἀδράστωι νόστον Ἀργείοισί τε
    θήσει, μέλαιναν κῆρ' ἐπ' ὄμμασιν βαλών,   950
    κλεινάς τε Θήβας. τοῖνδ' ἑλοῦ δυοῖν πότμοιν
    τὸν ἕτερον· ἢ γὰρ παῖδα σῶισον ἢ πόλιν.

---

925 πόλει δὲ ω + : πόλει **r**: πολίταις **r**   926 μ' om. **r**   927 δή με ω + :
δῆτα **z** (coni. Wecklein)   κατακτανεῖς **rζ**   929 δέ μοι **r**
931 θαλάμοις **rζ**   933 φοίνιον Ο**rχ**   933–4 sic dist. Ω, Σ: post Κάδμου
dist. Π¹², Reiske   934 Κάδμωι Valck.   ἄρεως ΜΟ**Cr**   936
κτήσασθ' V**Cr**: κτησόμεθ' Rf   937 δ' Ω: τ' Pr   939 ὑμῖν Ο**rχ**
940 ἐγγόνους Ο   945 ἐστ' ΟΡ**z**   ἥιθεος Tricl., Barnes: ἤϊθεος fere Ω,
Eust. 500, 34   946 del. Valck. (om. Μt^{ac})

τὰ μὲν παρ' ἡμῶν πάντ' ἔχεις· ἡγοῦ, τέκνον,
πρὸς οἶκον. ὅστις δ' ἐμπύρωι χρῆται τέχνηι,
μάταιος· ἢν μὲν ἐχθρὰ σημήνας τύχηι,   955
πικρὸς καθέστηχ' οἷς ἂν οἰωνοσκοπῆι·
ψευδῆ δ' ὑπ' οἴκτου τοῖσι χρωμένοις λέγων
ἀδικεῖ τὰ τῶν θεῶν. Φοῖβον ἀνθρώποις μόνον
χρῆν θεσπιωιδεῖν, ὃς δέδοικεν οὐδένα.

Χο. Κρέον, τί σιγᾶις γῆρυν ἄφθογγον σχάσας;   960
κἀμοὶ γὰρ οὐδὲν ἧσσον ἔκπληξις πάρα.

Κρ. τί δ' ἄν τις εἴποι; δῆλον οἵ γ' ἐμοὶ λόγοι·
ἐγὼ γὰρ οὔποτ' εἰς τόδ' εἶμι συμφορᾶς
ὥστε σφαγέντα παῖδα προσθεῖναι πόλει.
πᾶσιν γὰρ ἀνθρώποισι φιλότεκνος βίος,   965
οὐδ' ἂν τὸν αὑτοῦ παῖδά τις δοίη κτανεῖν.
μή μ' εὐλογείτω τἀμά τις κτείνων τέκνα.
αὐτὸς δ' – ἐν ὡραίωι γὰρ ἕσταμεν βίου –
θνήισκειν ἕτοιμος πατρίδος ἐκλυτήριον.
ἀλλ' εἶα, τέκνον, πρὶν μαθεῖν πᾶσαν πόλιν,   970
ἀκόλαστ' ἐάσας μάντεων θεσπίσματα,
φεῦγ' ὡς τάχιστα τῆσδ' ἀπαλλαχθεὶς χθονός·
λέξει γὰρ ἀρχαῖς καὶ στρατηλάταις τάδε,
πύλας ἐφ' ἑπτὰ καὶ λοχαγέτας μολών·
κἂν μὲν φθάσωμεν, ἔστι σοι σωτηρία·   975
ἢν δ' ὑστερήσηις, οἰχόμεσθα, κατθανῆι.

ΜΕΝΟΙΚΕΥΣ
ποῖ δῆτα φεύγω; τίνα πόλιν; τίνα ξένων;
Κρ. ὅπου χθονὸς τῆσδ' ἐκποδὼν μάλιστ' ἔσηι.

---

953 ἡμῖν PRw   πάντ' ω+: ταῦτ' z, fort. L¹   954 δ' del.
Fraenkel   956 πικρὸς ω+: ἐχθρὸς Lζ(etiam MᵍVᵍrᵍ)   957 θ'
O   959 χρὴ Saz, Plut. *Mor.* 407D   961 γὰρ Ω: μὲν O   ἧσσον
Brunck: ἧττον Ω   964 παῖδα ω+: τόνδε r   προθεῖναι MᵖᶜBᵖᶜr
966 αὑτοῦ x: αὐτοῦ fere ω+   τις om. Rf: post δοίη transp. rζ
968 γὰρ om. r: μὲν P   ἕσταμεν vel ἔσταμεν ωrz: ἵσταμαι M¹ᵖᶜBʸᵖrχz:
ἵσταμεν r: ἔσταμαι r   βίου Reiske: βίωι Ω   970 εἶα Radt: εἷα vel εἶα
Ω (item 990, 1708)   971 μάντεως rχζ   972 ἀπαλλαγεὶς fere
B¹ᵘᵛrz   974 susp. Valck., del. Wecklein (cf. Σ: περιττός)   975 ἔσται
O   977 ποῦ r: πῆ Lζ   ξένον Vrζ

Με. οὔκουν σὲ φράζειν εἰκός, ἐκπονεῖν δ' ἐμέ;
Κρ. Δελφοὺς περάσας – Με. ποῖ με χρή, πάτερ,
μολεῖν; 980
Κρ. Αἰτωλίδ' εἰς γῆν. Με. ἐκ δὲ τῆσδε ποῖ περῶ;
Κρ. Θεσπρωτὸν οὖδας. Με. σεμνὰ Δωδώνης βάθρα;
Κρ. ἔγνως. Με. τί δὴ τόδ' ἔρυμά μοι γενήσεται;
Κρ. πόμπιμος ὁ δαίμων. Με. χρημάτων δὲ τίς πόρος;
Κρ. ἐγὼ πορεύσω χρυσόν. Με. εὖ λέγεις, πάτερ. 985
Κρ. χώρει νυν. Με. ὡς σὴν πρὸς κασιγνήτην μολών,
ἧς πρῶτα μαστὸν εἵλκυσ', Ἰοκάστην λέγω,
μητρὸς στερηθεὶς ὀρφανός τ' ἀποζυγείς,
προσηγορήσας εἶμι καὶ σώισω βίον.
Κρ. ἀλλ' εἶα, χώρει· μὴ τὸ σὸν κωλυέτω. 990

Με. γυναῖκες, ὡς εὖ πατρὸς ἐξεῖλον φόβον,
κλέψας λόγοισιν, ὥσθ' ἃ βούλομαι τυχεῖν·
ὅς μ' ἐκκομίζει, πόλιν ἀποστερῶν τύχης,
καὶ δειλίαι δίδωσι. καὶ συγγνωστὰ μὲν
γέροντι, τοὐμὸν δ' οὐχὶ συγγνώμην ἔχει, 995
προδότην γενέσθαι πατρίδος ἥ μ' ἐγείνατο.
ὡς οὖν ἂν εἰδῆτ', εἶμι καὶ σώισω πόλιν
ψυχήν τε δώσω τῆσδ' ὑπερθανεῖν χθονός.
αἰσχρὸν γάρ· οἱ μὲν θεσφάτων ἐλεύθεροι
κοὐκ εἰς ἀνάγκην δαιμόνων ἀφιγμένοι 1000
στάντες παρ' ἀσπίδ' οὐκ ὀκνήσουσιν θανεῖν,
πύργων πάροιθε μαχόμενοι πάτρας ὕπερ,
ἐγὼ δέ πατέρα καὶ κασίγνητον προδοὺς
πόλιν τ' ἐμαυτοῦ δειλὸς ὡς ἔξω χθονὸς

---

979 οὔκουν Wecklein: οὐκοῦν (sine interrog.) Ω   980 περάσας MB¹Cz:
περάσας φεῦγε B²OV+   πῆ r   με om. AP   πάτερ om. LχT, del.
V²   981 ποῦ Rw: πῆ r   982 θεσπρωτὸν MBV²ˢCrz: θεσπρωτῶν
BˢOV¹+   983 δὴ τόδ' Musgrave: δῆτ' Ω   ἔρυγμά V: ἔρυμά T
(Wilam.): (δῆτα) ῥῦμά Valck.   985 παρέξω r   986–91 personarum
vices sic fere Ω: Men. continuat Musgrave, pers. notis 986, 990, 991
deletis   989 προσηγορήσας Hartung: -ρήσων Ω, Σ   σώσω GXbT:
σώσων ω+, Σ: σῶσον rx   991 ἐξῆλθον V   993 πόλεως r   997–8
del. Herwerden (retentis 1013–18)   998 δὲ r   999 εἰ μὲν rz

ἄπειμ', ὅπου δ' ἂν ζῶ κακὸς φανήσομαι;   1005
μὰ τὸν μετ' ἄστρων Ζῆν' Ἄρη τε φοίνιον,
ὃς τοὺς ὑπερτείλαντας ἐκ γαίας ποτὲ
Σπαρτοὺς ἄνακτας τῆσδε γῆς ἱδρύσατο·
ἀλλ' εἶμι καὶ στὰς ἐξ ἐπάλξεων ἄκρων
σφάξας ἐμαυτὸν σηκὸν εἰς μελαμβαθῆ   1010
δράκοντος, ἔνθ' ὁ μάντις ἐξηγήσατο,
ἐλευθερώσω γαῖαν· εἴρηται λόγος.
{στείχω δέ, θανάτου δῶρον οὐκ αἰσχρὸν πόλει
δώσων, νόσου δὲ τήνδ' ἀπαλλάξω χθόνα.
εἰ γὰρ λαβὼν ἕκαστος ὅ τι δύναιτό τις   1015
χρηστὸν διέλθοι τοῦτο κἀς κοινὸν φέροι
πατρίδι, κακῶν ἂν αἱ πόλεις ἐλασσόνων
πειρώμεναι τὸ λοιπὸν εὐτυχοῖεν ἄν.}   1018

Χο.   ἔβας ἔβας,   στρ. 1019
        ὦ πτεροῦσσα, γᾶς λόχευ-   1019bis
        μα νερτέρου τ' Ἐχίδνας,   1020
    Καδμείων ἁρπαγά,
        πολύφθορος πολύστονος
    μειξοπάρθενος,   1023
        δάιον τέρας,   1023bis
        φοιτάσι πτεροῖς
        χαλαῖσί τ' ὠμοσίτοις·   1025
    Διρκαίων ἃ ποτ' ἐκ
        τόπων νέους πεδαίρουσ'
        ἄλυρον ἀμφὶ μοῦσαν
    ὀλομέναν τ' Ἐρινὺν

1005 signum interrog. add. Matthiae   1006 μὰ ω + : οὐ μὰ V^marg**rz**: οὐ
z   1010 μελεμβ- **rζ**   -βαθῆ BVC**r**: -βαφῆ MO +   1013–18 del.
Scheurleer (1017–18 exstant in Π²)   1013 θανάτωι Gχ   1014 δώσω
CR**v**^pc   ἀπαλλάξων R**f** (coni. Scaliger): -ξαι **r**   1016 φέρει O**rz**,
Stob. 4.1.1   1019bis πτερρῦσσα Π²BA (Barnes): πτερόεσσα **r**χ^g:
πτερῦσα Π⁶ω +   1020 τ' Π²Ω: δ' Π⁶Sa   1021 ἁρπαγά Π²C**r** (coni.
Tyrwhitt): ἁρπαγᾶ(ι) fere Ω, Σ   1022 πολύστονος πολύφθορος transp.
r: πολύστ. πολύμοχθος **r**χ   1023 -πάρθενος Π²Π⁶Ω: -πάρθενον Aa¹
(coni. Valck.)   1024 φοιτάσι **r**χ**z**: φοιτᾶσι ω +, Σ: φοιτασιν Π²   1029
οὐλομέναν MG   τ' del. Hartung (hab. Π²)

ἔφερες ἔφερες ἄχεα πατρίδι   1030
   φόνια· φόνιος ἐκ θεῶν
   ὃς τάδ᾿ ἦν ὁ πράξας.
ἰάλεμοι δὲ ματέρων,
   ἰάλεμοι δὲ παρθένων
   ἐστέναζον οἴκοις·   1035
ἰηϊήιον βοάν,
   ἰηϊήιον μέλος,
ἄλλος ἄλλον ἐποτότυζε   1038
   διαδοχαῖς ἀνὰ πτόλιν.   1038bis
βροντᾷ δὲ στεναγμὸς
   ἀχᾷ τ᾿ ἦν ὅμοιος   1040
   ὁπότε πόλεος ἀφανίσειεν
   ἁ πτεροῦσσα παρθένος τιν᾿ ἀνδρῶν.   1042

χρόνωι δ᾿ ἔβα   ἀντ. 1043
   Πυθίαις ἀποστολαῖ-   1043bis
   σιν Οἰδίπους ὁ τλάμων
Θηβαίαν τάνδε γᾶν   1045
   τότ᾿ ἀσμένοις, πάλιν δ᾿ ἄχη·
ματρὶ γὰρ γάμους   1047
   δυσγάμους τάλας   1047bis
   καλλίνικος ὢν
   αἰνιγμάτων συνάπτει,
μιαίνει δὲ πτόλιν·   1050
   δι᾿ αἱμάτων δ᾿ ἀμείβει
   μυσαρὸν εἰς ἀγῶνα

1035 εστεναξαν Π²Π⁷   ἐν οἴκοις **r**ζ   1036–7 ιηιηιον utroquo loco Π²ᵖᶜ, priore loco Π⁷ (ιηιη altero loco): ιηιηιηιον Π²ᵃᶜ: ἰήιον fere Ω, Eust. 500, 41–3   βοάν βοάν ... μέλος μέλος Τ   1038 ἄλλον fere Π²Π⁷Ω: ἄλλοτ᾿ Diggle: ἀλλ᾿ Battier (retento ἐπωτότυζε)   εποτο[Π⁷ (ἐποτότυζε coni. Brunck): ἐπωτότυζε fere **Br**χ: επωτοτυξε Π²: ἐπετότυζε fere ω(B¹ˢ) +   1038bis πόλιν **rz**   1039 δὲ om. **Mr**: δὲ καὶ **O**   1040 ἀχᾷ Musgrave et fort. Π⁷: αχαί Π²: ἰαχάω+: ἰαχᾷ **MV²r**   1041 πόλεος Π² (Musgrave): πόλιος **Rw**: πόλεως Π⁷Ω   1042 πτεροῦσσα Π²Π⁷M¹ˢB¹ˢ (Barnes): πτερουῖσα Ω   1044 τλάμων Π⁷Ω: τάλας Mᵧᵖ   1046 ποτ᾿ **G**: τοτε μεν Π⁶   ἄσμενος **rx**   1047 ματρὶ Π⁷**Or**: μητρὶ fere ω+   γὰρ Π⁷ω+: δὲ **z**: τε V²   1047bis τάλας Τ, fort. **Pr**: ὁ τάλας Ω   1050 πτόλιν Τ: πόλιν Ω

ΦΟΙΝΙΣΣΑΙ

καταβαλών ἀραῖσι
τέκεα μέλεος. ἀγάμεθ' ἀγάμεθ'
ὃς ἐπὶ θάνατον οἴχεται   1055
γᾶς ὑπὲρ πατρώιας,
Κρέοντι μὲν λιπὼν γόους,
τὰ δ' ἑπτάπυργα κλῆιθρα γᾶς
καλλίνικα θήσων.
γενοίμεθ' ὧδε ματέρες,   1060
γενοίμεθ' εὔτεκνοι, φίλα
Παλλάς, ἃ δράκοντος αἷμα   1062
λιθόβολον κατηργάσω,   1062bis
Καδμείαν μέριμναν
ὁρμάσασ' ἐπ' ἔργον,
ὅθεν ἐπέσυτο τάνδε γαῖαν   1065
ἁρπαγαῖσι δαιμόνων τις ἄτα.   1066

ΑΓΓΕΛΟΣ Α'
    ὠή, τίς ἐν πύλαισι δωμάτων κυρεῖ;   1067
    ἀνοίγετ', ἐκπορεύετ' Ἰοκάστην δόμων.
    ὠὴ μάλ' αὖθις· διὰ μακροῦ μέν, ἀλλ' ὅμως
    ἔξελθ', ἄκουσον, Οἰδίπου κλεινὴ δάμαρ,   1070
    λήξασ' ὀδυρμῶν πενθίμων τε δακρύων.
Ιο. ὦ φίλτατ', οὔ που ξυμφορὰν ἥκεις φέρων
    Ἐτεοκλέους θανόντος, οὗ παρ' ἀσπίδα
    βέβηκας αἰεὶ πολεμίων εἴργων βέλη;

1054 τέκνα **z** (M^g)   1058 ἑπτάπυλα Lζ: ἑπτὰ **r**   1061 φίλα fere
M^{γρ}BV²ˢC^{γρ}+: φίλαι ωr   1062–62bis αἷμα λιθ. Ω: λιθ. εἷμα sch.^A
Il. 3.354   1062bis κατηργάσω Wackernagel, *Kl. Schr.* 1.583: κατειργ-
Ω, test.   -είργασαι Gx   1063 καδμείων B¹(vel Bᵃᶜ)**r**
1064 ὁρμάσασ' Willink (ad *Or.* 1288): ὁρμήσασ' Ω   1065 ἐπέσυτο M**tz**:
ἐπέσσυτο fere ω+   γαῖαν Battier: γᾶν Ω   1069–73 incertum an Σ^{BV}
ἐν τοῖς πολλοῖς ἀντιγράφοις οὐ φέρεται ὁ στίχος οὗτος ad unum horum
versuum pertinet (ad 1075 rettulit Valck.); 1070 del. Bruhn, 1070–1
Reeve   1070 κυδρὴ M^{γρ}**r**   1072 οὔ που Kirchhoff: ἢ που fere Ω
(οπου Fᵃᶜ)   ξυμφορὰς **r**   1073 οὔπερ O   1074 εἴργων δόρυ
B¹(corr. B²ˢ)

{τί μοί ποθ' ἥκεις καινὸν ἀγγελῶν ἔπος; }   1075
τέθνηκεν ἢ ζῇ παῖς ἐμός; σήμαινέ μοι.
Αγ.ᵅ   ζῇι, μὴ τρέσῃις τόδ', ὥς σ' ἀπαλλάξω φόβου.
Ιο.   τί δ'; ἑπτάπυργοι πῶς ἔχουσι περιβολαί;
Αγ.ᵅ   ἑστᾶσ' ἄθραυστοι, κοὐκ ἀνήρπασται πόλις.
Ιο.   ἦλθον δὲ πρὸς κίνδυνον Ἀργείου δορός;   1080
Αγ.ᵅ   ἀκμήν γ' ἐπ' αὐτήν· ἀλλ' ὁ Καδμείων Ἄρης
κρείσσων κατέστη τοῦ Μυκηναίου δορός.
Ιο.   ἓν εἰπὲ πρὸς θεῶν, εἴ τι Πολυνείκους πέρι
οἶσθ'· ὡς μέλει μοι καὶ τόδ', εἰ λεύσσει φάος.
Αγ.ᵅ   ζῇ σοι ξυνωρὶς εἰς τόδ' ἡμέρας τέκνων.   1085
Ιο.   εὐδαιμονοίης. πῶς γὰρ Ἀργείων δόρυ
πυλῶν ἀπεστήσασθε πυργηρούμενοι;
λέξον, γέροντα τυφλὸν ὡς κατὰ στέγας
ἐλθοῦσα τέρψω, τῆσδε γῆς σεσωμένης.
Αγ.ᵅ   ἐπεὶ Κρέοντος παῖς ὁ γῆς ὑπερθανὼν   1090
πύργων ἐπ' ἄκρων στὰς μελάνδετον ξίφος
λαιμῶν διῆκε τῆιδε γῆι σωτήριον,
λόχους ἔνειμεν ἑπτὰ καὶ λοχαγέτας
πύλας ἐφ' ἑπτά, φύλακας Ἀργείου δορός,
σὸς παῖς, ἐφέδρους ⟨θ'⟩ ἱππότας μὲν
ἱππόταις   1095
ἔταξ', ὁπλίτας δ' ἀσπιδηφόροις ἔπι,
ὡς τῶι νοσοῦντι τειχέων εἴη δορὸς
ἀλκὴ δι' ὀλίγου. περγάμων δ' ἀπ' ὀρθίων
λεύκασπιν εἰσορῶμεν Ἀργείων στρατὸν

1075 del. Hartung   ἀγγέλλων BOrz   1077 τοῦδ' Rf (coni.
Markland, Porson)   ὥς σ' B³rχζ: ὡς ωr   1078 ἐπτάπυλοι
V²ˢr   1080 ἦλθεν FᶜP   1081 γ' om. rz: δ' r   ἐπ' Ω: ἐς B   1082
κατέστη fere Ω:]π[ε]στη Π⁹   1084 μέλλει Vr   μοι om. Rw: μου
V   τοῦδ' B³Vrζ   1086 αργειον Π⁹ (coni. Fix)   1089 σεσωμενης
Π⁹ (Wecklein): σεσωσμ- Ω   1090 ὑπερβαλὼν z   1092 λαιμὸν B³ˢOr:
λαιμωι Π⁹   τῆσδε γῆς Orχˢ   1095 σὸς παῖς om. V¹, ἐφέδρους om.
O, totum versum om. r   θ' add. Valck., Reiske: δ' add. Grotius
1096 ἔταξ' Ω: τάξας Hermann (θ' non addito 1095)   δ' om. r
ἀσπιδηφόρους fere MᵃᶜBOCr   1098 sic dist. B³rχζ: post ἀλκή dist.
MBV²Cr: nullum punctum hab. OV¹Rw   ὀλίγων P   δ' om. C,
Σ1095: τ' rχ

Τευμησσὸν ἐκλιπόντα, καὶ τάφρου πέλας   1100
†δρόμωι ξυνῆψαν† ἄστυ Καδμείας χθονός.
παιὰν δὲ καὶ σάλπιγγες ἐκελάδουν ὁμοῦ
ἐκεῖθεν ἔκ τε τειχέων ἡμῶν πάρα.
καὶ πρῶτα μὲν προσῆγε Νηίσταις πύλαις
λόχον πυκναῖσιν ἀσπίσιν πεφρικότα   1105
ὁ τῆς κυναγοῦ Παρθενοπαῖος ἔκγονος,
ἐπίσημ' ἔχων οἰκεῖον ἐν μέσωι σάκει,
ἑκηβόλοις τόξοισιν Ἀταλάντην κάπρον
χειρουμένην Αἰτωλόν. εἰς δὲ Προιτίδας
πύλας ἐχώρει σφάγι' ἔχων ἐφ' ἅρματι   1110
ὁ μάντις Ἀμφιάραος, οὐ σημεῖ' ἔχων
ὑβρισμέν' ἀλλὰ σωφρόνως ἄσημ' ὅπλα.
Ὠγύγια δ' εἰς πυλώμαθ' Ἱππομέδων ἄναξ
ἔστειχ' ἔχων σημεῖον ἐν μέσωι σάκει
στικτοῖς Πανόπτην ὄμμασιν δεδορκότα,   1115
τὰ μὲν σὺν ἄστρων ἐπιτολαῖσιν ὄμματα
βλέποντα, τὰ δὲ κρύπτοντα δυνόντων μέτα,
ὡς ὕστερον θανόντος εἰσορᾶν παρῆν.
Ὁμολωίσιν δὲ τάξιν εἶχε πρὸς πύλαις
Τυδεύς, λέοντος δέρος ἔχων ἐπ' ἀσπίδος   1120
χαίτηι πεφρικός· δεξιᾶι δὲ λαμπάδα
Τιτὰν Προμηθεὺς ἔφερεν ὡς πρήσων πόλιν.
ὁ σὸς δὲ Κρηναίαισι Πολυνείκης πύλαις

1100–3 spurios iud. Dihle (1101 del. Kirchhoff, 1100–1 susp. Wecklein; omnes hab. Π¹) 1100 τευμ- Π¹ωr: τελμ- M²+ -μησσὸν Π¹MBCRwz: -μησὸν OV+ ἐκλείποντα VCrz 1101 -ῆψαν Π¹RˢRw, cf. ᵍΣ: -ῆψεν Ω καδμείας Π¹ˢΩ: -ειων Π¹ 1104–40 susp. Morus, del. post Walter et Wecklein Powell 1104 νηίσταις Π¹C (coni. Unger): νηίταις Ω: νηϊ*ταῖς Hsch. ν 458 1110 ἅρμασι(ν) V²ˢrχ 1113 δ' Ω: θ' B 1114 ἔστειχ' BOC+: ἔστηχ' MVrz: ἔστηκ' fere r 1116–18 del. Bergk (1118 iam Valck.) 1116 ὄμματα Ω: ὄμματ' ἦν Valck.: ὄμμασιν (cum τοῖς μὲν) Paley 1117 βλέποντα Π¹²ᵘᵛΩ: κλήιοντα post Seidler Blaydes: οἴγοντα Geel κρύπτοντα Ω: κύπτοντα Markland: μύοντα Geel: (δ') ἀγρυπνοῦντα Kirchhoff 1120 δέρας rz: δέμας Lenting ἀσπίδος Orχz: ἀσπίδι ωrz: αὐχένι (cum 1121 ἐν σάκει δὲ λαμπ.) Pearson 1122 ὡς Mn, Σ alter, Musgrave

Ἄρη προσῆγε· Ποτνιάδες δ' ἐπ' ἀσπίδι
ἐπίσημα πῶλοι δρομάδες ἐσκίρτων φόβωι,   1125
εὖ πως στρόφιγξιν ἔνδοθεν κυκλούμεναι
πόρπαχ' ὑπ' αὐτόν, ὥστε μαίνεσθαι δοκεῖν.
ὁ δ' οὐκ ἔλασσον Ἄρεος εἰς μάχην φρονῶν
Καπανεὺς προσῆγε λόχον ἐπ' Ἠλέκτραις πύλαις·
σιδηρονώτοις δ' ἀσπίδος τύποις ἐπῆν   1130
γίγας ἐπ' ὤμοις γηγενὴς ὅλην πόλιν
φέρων μοχλοῖσιν ἐξανασπάσας βάθρων,
ὑπόνοιαν ἡμῖν οἷα πείσεται πόλις.
ταῖς δ' ἑβδόμαις Ἄδραστος ἐν πύλαισιν ἦν,
ἑκατὸν ἐχίδναις ἀσπίδ' ἐκπληρῶν γραφῆι,   1135
{ὕδρας ἔχων λαιοῖσιν ἐν βραχίοσιν}
Ἀργεῖον αὔχημ'· ἐκ δὲ τειχέων μέσων
δράκοντες ἔφερον τέκνα Καδμείων γνάθοις.
παρῆν δ' ἑκάστου τῶνδέ μοι θεάματα
ξύνθημα παρφέροντι ποιμέσιν λόχων.   1140
καὶ πρῶτα μὲν τόξοισι καὶ μεσαγκύλοις
ἐμαρνάμεσθα σφενδόναις θ' ἑκηβόλοις
πέτρων τ' ἀραγμοῖς· ὡς δ' ἐνικῶμεν μάχηι,
ἔκλαγξε Τυδεὺς καὶ σὸς ἐξαίφνης γόνος·
Ὦ τέκνα Δαναῶν, πρὶν κατεξάνθαι βολαῖς,   1145
τί μέλλετ' ἄρδην πάντες ἐμπίπτειν πύλαις,
γυμνῆτες ἱππῆς ἁρμάτων τ' ἐπιστάται;
ἠχῆς δ' ὅπως ἤκουσαν, οὔτις ἀργὸς ἦν·
πολλοὶ δ' ἔπιπτον κρᾶτας αἱματούμενοι,

1126 στρόφιγξί γ' **r**   1127 αὐτὴν O   1128 ἄρεως **Cr**   1130
σιδηρονωτου (coni. Valck.)... κυκλοις Π¹   δ' om. CF: post τύποις
transp. G   1132 ἐξαναρπάσας P   βάθρων fere Π¹MʸᴾCʸᴾ**r**: βίαι ω+,
fort. Π¹ᵃᶜ   1133 del. Valck.   υπονοιαϋμιν Π¹   1134 δ' om.
MA   1135 ἑκατὸν δ' O**r**   γραφὴν cod. Harlei. 6300, coni. Valck.
(dist. post ἐκπληρῶν)   1136 del. post Wecklein Murray (hab. Π¹, cf.
Virg. *Aen.* 7.657–8)   υδραν Π¹: ὕδρας **z**   1137 ἀργείων V**rz**
1140 παρφέρ- BV¹**rz**: παραφέρ- MOV²ˢC**rχ**: προφέρ- **z**: προσφέρ-
T   1143 πέτρων Wecklein: πετρῶν Ω, Σ   1144 χὠ σὸς fere
M**z**   1147 τ' om. VG (del. Valck.)

ἡμῶν τ' ἐς οὖδας εἶδες ἂν πρὸ τειχέων   1150
πυκνοὺς κυβιστητῆρας ἐκπεπνευκότας·
ξηρὰν δ' ἔδευον γαῖαν αἵματος ῥοαῖς.
ὁ δ' Ἀρκάς, οὐκ Ἀργεῖος, Ἀταλάντης γόνος
τυφὼς πύλαισιν ὥς τις ἐμπεσὼν βοᾶι
πῦρ καὶ δικέλλας, ὡς κατασκάψων πόλιν·   1155
ἀλλ' ἔσχε μαργῶντ' αὐτὸν ἐναλίου θεοῦ
Περικλύμενος παῖς λᾶαν ἐμβαλὼν κάραι
ἁμαξοπληθῆ, γεῖσ' ἐπάλξεων ἄπο·
ξανθὸν δὲ κρᾶτα διεπάλυνε καὶ ῥαφὰς
ἔρρηξεν ὀστέων, ἄρτι δ' οἰνωπὸν γένυν   1160
καθηιμάτωσεν· οὐδ' ἀποίσεται βίον
τῆι καλλιτόξωι μητρὶ Μαινάλου κόρηι.
ἐπεὶ δὲ τάσδ' εἰσεῖδεν εὐτυχεῖς πύλας,
ἄλλας ἐπήιει παῖς σός, εἱπόμην δ' ἐγώ.
ὁρῶ δὲ Τυδέα καὶ παρασπιστὰς πυκνοὺς   1165
Αἰτωλίσιν λόγχαισιν εἰς ἄκρον στόμα
πύργων ἀκοντίζοντας, ὥστ' ἐπάλξεων
λιπεῖν ἐρίπνας φυγάδας· ἀλλά νιν πάλιν
κυναγὸς ὡσεὶ παῖς σὸς ἐξαθροίζεται,
πύργοις δ' ἐπέστησ' αὖθις. εἰς δ' ἄλλας πύλας   1170
ἠπειγόμεσθα, τοῦτο παύσαντες νοσοῦν.
Καπανεὺς δὲ πῶς εἴποιμ' ἂν ὡς ἐμαίνετο;
μακραύχενος γὰρ κλίμακος προσαμβάσεις
ἔχων ἐχώρει, καὶ τοσόνδ' ἐκόμπασεν,
μηδ' ἂν τὸ σεμνὸν πῦρ νιν εἰργαθεῖν Διὸς   1175
τὸ μὴ οὐ κατ' ἄκρων περγάμων ἑλεῖν πόλιν.
καὶ ταῦθ' ἅμ' ἠγόρευε καὶ πετρούμενος

1150 δ' **r**   εἶδες MOV+: ἤιδες BV²ˢC   1151 ἐκπεπτωκότας
Madvig   1152 τ' W   1155 δίκελλαν Ο**rχ**   κατασκάψω **rχ**
1158 om. M¹, in marg. add. M²   1162 κόρηι Ω: χθόνα ʸᵖΣ   1164 παῖς
σός MBO+, Σᴹ1095: σὸς παῖς VC**r**, Σᴮⱽᶜ1095   1166 αἰτωλοῖσι(ν)
V**r**   1170 δ'¹ Ω: τ' F¹ᵖᶜ (coni. Lenting)   1171 παύσοντες **z**   1173
πρὸς ἀμβάσεις Β**r**   1175 εἰργαθεῖν Elmsley: εἰργάθειν fere Ω   1176 μὴ
οὐ ω+, Tzetzes in Lyc. *Alex.* 436: μὴ **rζ**   1177 πτερούμενος
MV²ˢ

ΦΟΙΝΙΣΣΑΙ

ἀνεῖρῳ' ὑπ' αὐτὴν ἀσπίδ' εἱλίξας δέμας,
κλίμακος ἀμείβων ξέστ' ἐνηλάτων βάθρα.
ἤδη δ' ὑπερβαίνοντα γεῖσα τειχέων   1180
βάλλει κεραυνῶι Ζεύς νιν· ἐκτύπησε δὲ
χθών, ὥστε δεῖσαι πάντας· ἐκ δὲ κλιμάκων
ἐσφενδονᾶτο χωρὶς †ἀλλήλων† μέλη,
{κόμαι μὲν εἰς Ὄλυμπον, αἷμα δ' εἰς χθόνα}
χεῖρες δὲ καὶ κῶλ' ὡς κύκλωμ' Ἰξίονος   1185
εἱλίσσετ'· εἰς γῆν δ' ἔμπυρος πίπτει νεκρός.
ὡς δ' εἶδ' Ἄδραστος Ζῆνα πολέμιον στρατῶι,
ἔξω τάφρου καθεῖσεν Ἀργείων στρατόν.
οἱ δ' αὖ παρ' ἡμῶν δεξιὸν Διὸς τέρας
ἰδόντες ἐξήλαυνον ἁρμάτων ὄχοι   1190
ἱππῆς ὁπλῖται, κὰς μέσ' Ἀργείων ὅπλα
συνῆψαν ἔγχη· πάντα δ' ἦν ὁμοῦ κακά·
ἔθνηισκον ἐξέπιπτον ἀντύγων ἄπο,
τροχοί τ' ἐπήδων ἄξονές τ' ἐπ' ἄξοσιν,
νεκροὶ δὲ νεκροῖς ἐξεσωρεύονθ' ὁμοῦ.   1195
πύργων μὲν οὖν γῆς ἔσχομεν κατασκαφὰς
εἰς τὴν παροῦσαν ἡμέραν· εἰ δ' εὐτυχὴς
ἔσται τὸ λοιπὸν ἥδε γῆ, θεοῖς μέλει·
καὶ νῦν γὰρ αὐτὴν δαιμόνων ἔσωισέ τις.
Χο. καλὸν τὸ νικᾶν· εἰ δ' ἀμείνον' οἱ θεοὶ   1200
γνώμην ἔχουσιν, εὐτυχὴς εἴην ἐγώ.
Ιο. καλῶς τὰ τῶν θεῶν καὶ τὰ τῆς τύχης ἔχει·
παῖδές τε γάρ μοι ζῶσι κἀκπέφευγε γῆ.
Κρέων δ' ἔοικε τῶν ἐμῶν νυμφευμάτων

1183–5 del. Nauck   1183 ἀλλήλων Ω: e.g. ἐκβάλλων, ἐκτείνων?
1184 del. Geel   αἱματοσταγεῖς Harry   1186 εἱλίσσετ' Z (coni.
Heath): ἐλ- fere Ω   1188 ἀργεῖον O   1189 τέρας διός transp.
V   1190 ὄχοι Musgrave: ὄχους fere Ω   1193 ἔθνηισκον Ω: ἔθρωισκον
Earle   1194 τ'¹ Ω: δ' SaZ (coni. Blaydes)   τ'² om. A: δ' **r**
1195 δὲ Ω: τε Fritzsche (cum 1194 ἄξονες δ') 1199 hab. M, add. in
marg. L²: om. Ω; susp. vel del. multi   1200–1 obscuri, fort.
corrupti   1201 ἔχοιεν M^{γρ}OV**r**   ἔχουσ', εἴην ἂν εὐτυχὴς ἐγώ
Conradt   1202 ἔχοι M   1203 κἀκπέφευγε V**rz**: κἀπέφευγε M**rz**: καὶ
πέφευγε BO**rχ**

τῶν τ᾽ Οἰδίπου δύστηνος ἀπολαῦσαι κακῶν,　　1205
παιδὸς στερηθείς, τῆι πόλει μὲν εὐτυχῶς,
ἰδίαι δὲ λυπρῶς. ἀλλ᾽ ἄνελθέ μοι πάλιν,
τί τἀπὶ τούτοις παῖδ᾽ ἐμὼ δρασείετον.

Αγ.ᵃ　ἔα τὰ λοιπά· δεῦρ᾽ ἀεὶ γὰρ εὐτυχεῖς.
Ιο.　τοῦτ᾽ εἰς ὕποπτον εἶπας· οὐκ ἐατέον.　　1210
Αγ.ᵃ　μεῖζον τί χρήιζεις παῖδας ἢ σεσωμένους;
Ιο.　καὶ τἀπίλοιπά γ᾽ εἰ καλῶς πράσσω κλυεῖν.
Αγ.ᵃ　μέθες μ᾽· ἔρημος παῖς ὑπασπιστοῦ σέθεν.
Ιο.　κακόν τι κεύθεις καὶ στέγεις ὑπὸ σκότωι.
Αγ.ᵃ　κοὐκ ἄν γε λέξαιμ᾽ ἐπ᾽ ἀγαθοῖσι σοῖς κακά.　　1215
Ιο.　ἢν μή γε φεύγων ἐκφύγηις πρὸς αἰθέρα.
Αγ.ᵃ　αἰαῖ· τί μ᾽ οὐκ εἴασας ἐξ εὐαγγέλου
φήμης ἀπελθεῖν, ἀλλὰ μηνῦσαι κακά;
τὼ παῖδε τὼ σὼ μέλλετον, τολμήματα
αἴσχιστα, χωρὶς μονομαχεῖν παντὸς
στρατοῦ,　　1220
λέξαντες Ἀργείοισι Καδμείοισί τε
εἰς κοινὸν οἷον μήποτ᾽ ὤφελον λόγον.
Ἐτεοκλέης δ᾽ ὑπῆρξ᾽ ἀπ᾽ ὀρθίου σταθεὶς
πύργου, κελεύσας σῖγα κηρῦξαι στρατῶι·
{ἔλεξε δ᾽· ῏Ω γῆς Ἑλλάδος στρατηλάται}　　1225
Δαναῶν ἀριστῆς, οἵπερ ἤλθετ᾽ ἐνθάδε,
Κάδμου τε λαός, μήτε Πολυνείκους χάριν
ψυχὰς ἀπεμπολᾶτε μήθ᾽ ἡμῶν ὕπερ.
ἐγὼ γὰρ αὐτὸς τόνδε κίνδυνον μεθεὶς

1209 τὸ λοιπόν Σ*Or.* 1663　　1211 μεῖζόν τι Vr　　σεσωμένους Aa
(Wecklein): σεσωσμ- Ω　　1212 κλυεῖν West: κλύειν Ω　　1214 κακόν τί
R　　1215 κοὐκ ω+: οὐκ **rχz**, gV　　γε ω(B²ˢ)+, gV: τε B¹: τι Aa: σε
Z　　σοι Reiske　　1216 εἰ μή **r**　　με **Br**ζ　　1218 σημῆναι fere
rz　　1221–58 del. Paley, Powell (1221–63 del. Page)　　1223 δ᾽ ὑπῆρξ᾽
ω+: ὑπῆρξ᾽ Vr (et δ᾽ del. Fraenkel): προὔπῆρξ᾽ Vr　　ἀπ᾽ ω+, Hsch.
α 6577: ἐπ᾽ B²Gχ　　1224 fere σιγᾶν ... στρατόν Rw**z**　　1225 del. post
Geel Hartung (Σ οὗτος δὲ οὐ φέρεται ἐν τοῖς πολλοῖς ἀντιγράφοις· cf. Σ
alterum)　　1226 δαναῶν τ᾽ Lχ**z**　　1227 μήτε ω+: μήποτε **rz**　　1228
ὑμῶν M**r**　　1229 αὐτὸν Rw

μόνος συνάψω συγγόνωι τὠμῶι μάχην·   1230
κἂν μὲν κτάνω τόνδ', οἶκον οἰκήσω μόνος,
ἡσσώμενος δὲ τῶιδε παραδώσω πόλιν.
ὑμεῖς δ' ἀγῶν' ἀφέντες, Ἀργεῖοι, χθόνα
νίσεσθε, βίοτον μὴ λιπόντες ἐνθάδε,
Σπαρτῶν τε λαὸς ἅλις ὅσος κεῖται νεκρός.   1235
τοσαῦτ' ἔλεξε· σὸς δὲ Πολυνείκης γόνος
ἐκ τάξεων ὤρουσε κἀπήινει λόγους.
πάντες δ' ἐπερρόθησαν Ἀργεῖοι τάδε
Κάδμου τε λαὸς ὡς δίκαι' ἡγούμενοι.
ἐπὶ τοῖσδε δ' ἐσπείσαντο, κἀν μεταιχμίοις   1240
ὅρκους συνῆψαν ἐμμενεῖν στρατηλάται.
ἤδη δ' ἔκρυπτον σῶμα παγχάλκοις ὅπλοις
δισσοὶ γέροντος Οἰδίπου νεανίαι·
φίλοι δ' ἐκόσμουν, τῆσδε μὲν πρόμον χθονὸς
Σπαρτῶν ἀριστῆς, τὸν δὲ Δαναϊδῶν ἄκροι.   1245
ἔσταν δὲ λαμπρὼ χρῶμά τ' οὐκ ἠλλαξάτην
μαργῶντ' ἐπ' ἀλλήλοισιν ἱέναι δόρυ.
παρεξιόντες δ' ἄλλος ἄλλοθεν φίλων
λόγοις ἐθάρσυνόν τε κἀξηύδων τάδε·
Πολύνεικες, ἐν σοὶ Ζηνὸς ὀρθῶσαι βρέτας   1250
τροπαῖον Ἄργει τ' εὐκλεᾶ δοῦναι λόγον·
Ἐτεοκλέα δ' αὖ· Νῦν πόλεως ὑπερμαχεῖς,

1230 μόνωι Rwˢ (coni. Valck.)   τὠμῶι Ω: μόνωι Pierson
1232 πόλιν Ο+: μόνος MB¹ᵘᵛ Cr: μόνος πόλιν V¹: μόνωι B²ᵘᵛV²ˢrz: δόμον
V²ʸᴾL¹   1233–5 del. Fraenkel (tantum 1235 Valck.)   1233 ἡμεῖς
VSaz   ἀργεῖοι ωr: ἀργείων rz: ἀργείαν Ο+   1235 τε om. Cr: δὲ
r   ὅσος rχΤ: ὃς ω+, ˡᶜΣ   νεκρός ω+: θανών rχζ   1236 ἔλεξ' ὁ
r   1237 τάξεως r   ὄρουσε ΜΟr   λόγους Ω: τάδε Ο   1238–9
del. Fraenkel   1240 τοῖσδε δ' MBGz: τοῖσι δ' OVr: τοῖσδ' rχz   κἀν
B+: om. Rw: καὶ ωr, ˡᶜΣ   1241 ἐμμενεῖν Markland, Elmsley: ἐμμένειν
fere Ω, ᵖΣ   στρατηλάται V²ˢrz, Σ: -λάτας ω+: -λάταις V¹W, ʸᴾΣ
1242–58 del. Fraenkel   1243 δισσοὶ ω+: οἱ τοῦ Οr (cf. Bʸᴾ οἵ
τοι)   1244–5 del. Mueller–Goldingen   1244 χθονὸς πρόμον transp.
Ο: πρόμαχον χθ. r (Mᵍrᵍ)   1248 ἄλλοι r   1249 λόγοις ἐθάρσυνόν
τε fere MBrz: λόγοισι θαρσύνοντε fere V²Gx: λόγοισι θαρσύνοντες
BʸᴾOV¹+   κἀξηύδων ω+: ἐξηύδων Orz: προσηύδων rχ: κἄλεγον
Bʸᴾ(rᵍ)   1251 δ' rz

νῦν καλλίνικος γενόμενος σκήπτρων κρατεῖς.
τάδ' ἠγόρευον παρακαλοῦντες εἰς μάχην.
μάντεις δὲ μῆλ' ἔσφαζον, ἐμπύρου τ' ἀκμῆς   1255
ῥήξεις {τ'} ἐνώμων, ὑγρότητ' ἐναντίαν,
ἄκραν τε λαμπάδ', ἢ δυοῖν ὅρους ἔχει,
νίκης τε σῆμα καὶ τὸ τῶν ἡσσωμένων.
ἀλλ' εἴ τιν' ἀλκὴν ἢ σοφοὺς ἔχεις λόγους
ἢ φίλτρ' ἐπωιδῶν, στεῖχ', ἐρήτυσον τέκνα   1260
δεινῆς ἁμίλλης· ὡς ὁ κίνδυνος μέγας
καὶ τᾶθλα δεινά· δάκρυά σοι γενήσεται
δισσοῖν στερείσηι τῆιδ' ἐν ἡμέραι τέκνοιν.
Ιο. ὦ τέκνον ἔξελθ' Ἀντιγόνη δόμων πάρος·
οὐκ ἐν χορείαις οὐδὲ παρθενεύμασιν   1265
νῦν σοι προχωρεῖ δαιμόνων κατάστασις,
ἀλλ' ἄνδρ' ἀρίστω καὶ κασιγνήτω σέθεν
εἰς θάνατον ἐκνεύοντε κωλῦσαί σε δεῖ
ξὺν μητρὶ τῆι σῆι μὴ πρὸς ἀλλήλοιν θανεῖν.
Αν. τίν', ὦ τεκοῦσα μῆτερ, ἔκπληξιν νέαν   1270
φίλοις ἀυτεῖς τῶνδε δωμάτων πάρος;
Ιο. ὦ θύγατερ, ἔρρει σῶν κασιγνήτων βίος.
Αν. πῶς εἶπας; Ιο. αἰχμὴν ἐς μίαν καθέστατον.
Αν. οἲ ἐγώ, τί λέξεις, μῆτερ; Ιο. οὐ φίλ', ἀλλ' ἕπου.
Αν. ποῖ, παρθενῶνας ἐκλιποῦσ'; Ιο. ἀνὰ στρατόν.   1275
Αν. αἰδούμεθ' ὄχλον. Ιο. οὐκ ἐν αἰσχύνηι τὰ σά.
Αν. δράσω δὲ δὴ τί; Ιο. συγγόνων λύσεις ἔριν.
Αν. τί δρῶσα, μῆτερ; Ιο. προσπίτνουσ' ἐμοῦ μέτα.
  – ἡγοῦ σὺ πρὸς μεταίχμι'· οὐ μελλητέον. –

1253 σκῆπτρον r   1255 τε Orχz   ἐμπύρου τ' ἀκμῆς post Burges
Geel: ἐμπύρους τ' ἀκμὰς fere Ω (δ' r)   1256 τ' del. Burges,
Geel   ἐναντίων χ   1258 τὸ ὠ+: τὰ Orχ   1262–3 del. Valck.
(1263 Kirchhoff)   1263 στερείσηι Reiske: στερήσηι Ω, Σ   1264
πάρος δόμων transp. L   1265–9 del. Fraenkel   1265 οὐδὲ rχT: οὐδ'
ἐν ω+   1266 δαίμονος Markland, Hermann, alii alia   1268 σε om.
M: δὲ r   1269 del. Wecklein   ἀλλήλων B²ˢr: -οις r   1275 πῆ
L   1276 τὰ σά Ω: τάδε χʸʳ   1277 δή τι BOr   1279 Ioc.
continuant Jackson, Kassel: 1279 Ant., 1280 Ioc. trib. Ω

ἔπειγ᾽ ἔπειγε, θύγατερ· ὡς ἦν μὲν φθάσω   1280
παῖδας πρὸ λόγχης, οὑμὸς ἐν φάει βίος·   1281
θανοῦσι δ᾽ αὐτοῖς συνθανοῦσα κείσομαι.   1283

Χο. αἰαῖ αἰαῖ, τρομερὰν φρίκαι   στρ. 1284
     τρομερὰν φρέν᾽ ἔχω· διὰ σάρκα δ᾽
     ἐμὰν   1285-6
     ἔλεος ἔλεος ἔμολε ματέρος δειλαίας.
     δίδυμα τέκεα πότερος ἄρα πότερον αἱμάξει –
     ἰώ μοι πόνων,
     ἰὼ Ζεῦ, ἰὼ γᾶ –   1290
     ὁμογενῆ δέραν, ὁμογενῆ ψυχὰν
     δι᾽ ἀσπίδων, δι᾽ αἱμάτων;
     τάλαιν᾽ ἐγὼ τάλαινα,
     πότερον ἄρα νέκυν ὀλόμενον ἰαχήσω;   1294-5

     φεῦ δᾶ φεῦ δᾶ, δίδυμοι θῆρες,   ἀντ. 1296
     φόνιαι ψυχαὶ δορὶ παλλόμεναι   1297-8
     πέσεα πέσεα δάι᾽ αὐτίχ᾽ αἱμάξετον.
     τάλανες, ὅ τι ποτὲ μονομάχον ἐπὶ φρέν᾽
     ἠλθέτην,   1300
     βοᾶι βαρβάρωι
     ἰαχὰν στενακτὰν
     μελομέναν νεκροῖς δάκρυσι θρηνήσω.
     σχεδὸν τύχα, πέλας φόνος·

1280 μὲν ω+: γε **r**   1281/1283 sic **Orz**T: post 1281 versum 976 ἦν δ᾽
ὑστερήσηις, οἰχόμεσθα, κατθανῆι (= 1282) inserunt ω+ (cf. Σᴮ ἐν πολλοῖς
οὐ φέρεται)   1284 αἰαῖ αἰαῖ Dindorf: αῖ vel αῖ quater M**B**r (et O, addito
ἔ ἔ): octies V: ter **r**: bis **rχz**: ἔ ἔ fere **rz**   φρῖκα fere B, Σ alter: φρίκαν
r   1285-6 sic **r**T: post ἔχω add. αῖ (vel αῖ vel ἔ) quater ω+, decies V,
bis **rχz**   1287 ματέρος T: ματρὸς fere Ω   1288 δίδυμα τέκνα **r**:
διδύμων τέκνων **r** (falso e Σ)   1290 ἰὼ² Ω: ὤ (cum ἀχὰν 1302)
Wecklein   1292 αἱμάτων multis suspectum   1294-5 πότερον ἄρα
πότερον O   ἀχήσω post Elmsley Dindorf   1298 παλλομένωι Diggle
1299 δάϊδ᾽ fere **Mr**   1300 τάλανες B³**rχz**: τάλαινες ωr   ὅ τι ω+:
τί **rχz**   μονομάχων OG   ἐπὶ om. Cr: εἰς O   ἠλυθέτην Rf: ἐπηλθ-
O**W**z: ἐπηλυθ- **r**   1302 ἰαχὰν στενακτὰν fere O**r**χz: στενακτὰν ἰαχὰν **r**:
ἰαχὰν ωr   μελομένα testari vid. Σ alter   νεκρῶν O**r**χz   1304 φόνος
Scaliger: φόνου Ω

κρινεῖ ξίφος τὸ μέλλον. 1305
ἄποτμος ἄποτμος ὁ φόνος ἕνεκ᾽ Ἐρινύων. 1306-7

— ἀλλὰ γὰρ Κρέοντα λεύσσω τόνδε δεῦρο συννεφῆ 1308
πρὸς δόμους στείχοντα, παύσω τοὺς παρεστῶτας
γόους.

Κρ. οἴμοι, τί δράσω; πότερ᾽ ἐμαυτὸν ἢ πόλιν 1310
στένω δακρύσας, ἣν πέριξ ἔχει νέφος
τοιοῦτον ὥστε δι᾽ Ἀχέροντος ἰέναι;
ἐμός τε γὰρ παῖς γῆς ὄλωλ᾽ ὑπερθανών,
τοὔνομα λαβὼν γενναῖον, ἀνιαρὸν δ᾽ ἐμοί·
ὃν ἄρτι κρημνῶν ἐκ δρακοντείων ἑλὼν 1315
αὐτοσφαγῆ δύστηνος ἐκόμισ᾽ ἐν χεροῖν,
βοᾶι δὲ δῶμα πᾶν· ἐγὼ δ᾽ ἥκω μετὰ
γέρων ἀδελφὴν γραῖαν Ἰοκάστην, ὅπως
λούσηι προθῆταί τ᾽ οὐκέτ᾽ ὄντα παῖδ᾽ ἐμόν.
τοῖς γὰρ θανοῦσι χρὴ τὸν οὐ τεθνηκότα 1320
τιμὰς διδόντα χθόνιον εὐσεβεῖν θεόν.

Χο. βέβηκ᾽ ἀδελφὴ σὴ δόμων ἔξω, Κρέον,
κόρη τε μητρὸς Ἀντιγόνη κοινῶι ποδί.

Κρ. ποῖ; κἀπὶ ποίαν συμφοράν; σήμαινέ μοι.

Χο. ἤκουσε τέκνα μονομάχωι μέλλειν δορὶ 1325
εἰς ἀσπίδ᾽ ἥξειν βασιλικῶν δόμων ὕπερ.

Κρ. πῶς φήις; νέκυν τοι παιδὸς ἀγαπάζων ἐμοῦ
οὐκ εἰς τόδ᾽ ἦλθον ὥστε καὶ τάδ᾽ εἰδέναι.

1305 κρινεῖ MB³V²+, ᴾΣ: κρίνει B¹OV¹r   ξίφος Hermann: φάος Ω,
Σ   1306-7 ἄποτμος¹ Ω: πότμος Dindorf   ἕνεκεν Vr   1308ff.
spurios iud. Leidloff, 1308-34 et 1338-49 del. Fraenkel   1308 δεῦρο
τόνδε transp. r: δεῦρο om. r   1309 γόους ω+: λόγους Vr   1312 del.
Kirchhoff   τοσοῦτον rζ   ἰέναι rχ, ¹Σ: ἰέναι ω+   1313 γὰρ παῖς
γῆς fere Ω (γῆς om. Or): παῖς γῆς τῆσδ᾽ post Heimsoeth Pearson   1316
δύστηνον Or   1317 μετὰ rZc: μέτα ω+: μετα- rz   1317-18 μετὰ
(μέτα) / γέρων ω+: μεταστέλλων fere rz: μεταστέλλων γέρων r   1318
γραῖαν om. Or: γηραιᾶν r   1319 λούσηι ω+: λουτρὰ R: κλαύσηι
Mʸᵖr   1320 τεθνεῶσιν vel τεθνηκόσιν Stob. 4.57.9   χρὴ Ω: ἆρ᾽ ἦν
Stob.   1322 δόμων ἔξω κρέον O+: κρέων ἔξω δόμων G (coni. Brunck):
κρέον ἔξω δόμων ωr   1324 πῆ L   1325 ἤκουσα r   1327 τοι fere
Ω: τε OG   1328 τάδ᾽ ω+: τόδ᾽ rz

Χο.   ἀλλ' οἴχεται μὲν σὴ κασιγνήτη πάλαι·
      δοκῶ δ' ἀγῶνα τὸν περὶ ψυχῆς, Κρέον,   1330
      ἤδη πεπρᾶχθαι παισὶ τοῖσιν Οἰδίπου.

Κρ.   οἴμοι, τὸ μὲν σημεῖον εἰσορῶ τόδε,
      σκυθρωπὸν ὄμμα καὶ πρόσωπον ἀγγέλου
      στείχοντος, ὃς πᾶν ἀγγελεῖ τὸ δρώμενον.

ΑΓΓΕΛΟΣ Β΄
      ὦ τάλας ἐγώ, τίν' εἴπω μῦθον ἢ τίνας γόους;   1335
Κρ.   οἰχόμεσθ'· οὐκ εὐπροσώποις φροιμίοις ἄρχηι
          λόγου.
Αγ.ᵝ   ὦ τάλας, δισσῶς αὐτῶ· μεγάλα γὰρ φέρω κακά.
Κρ.   πρὸς πεπραγμένοισιν ἄλλοις πήμασιν. λέγεις δὲ τί;
Αγ.ᵝ   οὐκέτ' εἰσὶ σῆς ἀδελφῆς παῖδες ἐν φάει, Κρέον.
Χο.   αἰαῖ·   1340
      μεγάλα μοι θροεῖς πάθεα καὶ πόλει.
Κρ.   ὦ δώματ' εἰσηκούσατ' Οἰδίπου τάδε,
      παίδων ὁμοίαις συμφοραῖς ὀλωλότων;
Χο.   ὥστ' ἐκδακρῦσαί γ', εἰ φρονοῦντ' ἐτύγχανεν.
Κρ.   οἴμοι ξυμφορᾶς βαρυποτμωτάτας.   1345
      {οἴμοι κακῶν δύστηνος· ὦ τάλας ἐγώ.}
Αγ.ᵝ   εἰ καὶ τὰ πρὸς τούτοισί γ' εἰδείης κακά.
Κρ.   καὶ πῶς γένοιτ' ἂν τῶνδε δυσποτμώτερα;

1333 πρόσοψιν Xa   1334 πᾶν ω+   (cf. *Chr. Pat.* 147): ἡμῖν **r**
1335 μῦθον ω+: λόγον **r**(V²ᵍ**r**ᵍχʸ)   τίνας γόους B**r**: τίνας λόγους ω+:
τίνα λόγον **r**   1336 εὐπρόσωπος **r**   ἄρχηι **r**: ἀρχὴ ω(B²)+:
utrumque B¹   λόγων W   1338 totum v. Creonti trib. fere Ω: πρὸς
... πήμασιν nuntio trib. Wᵃᶜ, Hermann   ἄλλο vel ἄλλα **r**   δέ τι
O   1340 choro trib. ω+: Creonti **r**   αἰαῖ Dindorf: αἶ αἶ vel αἶ αἶ ω+:
ἒ ἒ fere Mˢ**rz**   1341 μοι ω+: γάρ μοι **r**   πένθεα LZc   1342 Creonti
trib. ω+: nuntio V**r**: choro anon. et Hermann (cf. Mtᵃᶜ): nullam notam
hab. **rz**   1343 del. vel post 1341 transp. Valck.   1344 ὥστ' ἐκδα- fere
O**rx**: ὥστε δα- MBV+: ὥστ' ἂν δα- Hartung   ἐτύγχανεν ω**rz**: -νον
B³V+   1345 ξυμφορᾶς MV¹(corr. V²)Zc   βαρυποτμωτάτας M**rx**:
-οτάτας fere ω+   1346 om. MᵃᶜBᵃᶜV¹**r**, del. post Burges Murray: hab.
O+, add. MᵐᵃʳᵍBᵐᵃʳᵍV²   ὤμοι Or**z**   ὦ fere BOV¹+: ὁ MV²**r**
1347 nuntio trib. Ω: choro O¹ᶜ   τούτοισιν εἰδείης O**rz**   1348
δυσποτμότερα M²V**rz**

ΦΟΙΝΙΣΣΑΙ

Αγ.β τέθνηκ' ἀδελφὴ σὴ δυοῖν παίδοιν μέτα.

Χο.   ἀνάγετ' ἄγετε κωκυτὸν ἐπὶ   1350
      κρᾶτά τε λευκοπήχεις κτύπους χεροῖν.

Κρ.   ὦ τλῆμον, οἷον τέρμον', Ἰοκάστη, βίου
      γάμων τε τῶν σῶν Σφιγγὸς αἰνιγμοὺς ἔτλης.
      πῶς καὶ πέπρακται διπτύχων παίδων φόνος
      ἀρᾶς τ' ἀγώνισμ' Οἰδίπου; σήμαινέ μοι.   1355

Αγ.β τὰ μὲν πρὸ πύργων εὐτυχήματα χθονὸς
      οἶσθ'· οὐ μακρὰν γὰρ τειχέων περιπτυχαί.
      {ὥστ' οὐχ ἅπαντά σ' εἰδέναι τὰ δρώμενα}
      ἐπεὶ δὲ χαλκέοις σῶμ' ἐκοσμήσανθ' ὅπλοις
      οἱ τοῦ γέροντος Οἰδίπου νεανίαι,   1360
      ἔστησαν ἐλθόντ' εἰς μέσον μεταίχμιον
      {δισσὼ στρατηγὼ καὶ διπλὼ στρατηλάτα}
      ὡς εἰς ἀγῶνα μονομάχου τ' ἀλκὴν δορός.
      βλέψας δ' ἐπ' Ἄργος ἧκε Πολυνείκης ἀράς·
      Ὦ πότνι' Ἥρα – σὸς γάρ εἰμ', ἐπεὶ γάμοις   1365
      ἔζευξ' Ἀδράστου παῖδα καὶ ναίω χθόνα –
      δός μοι κτανεῖν ἀδελφόν, ἀντήρη δ' ἐμὴν
      καθαιματῶσαι δεξιὰν νικηφόρον· –
      αἴσχιστον αἰτῶν στέφανον, ὁμογενῆ κτανεῖν.

1350 ἀνάγετ' ἄγετε post Hermann scripsi: ἀνάγετ' ἀνάγετε fere Ω
1351 κρᾶτα fere Mᵧᵖ+: κάρα fere MBVr: κατάρα OCr   τε om.
GXaZ   χεροῖν del. Bothe, Burges, post 1350 κωκυτὸν transp.
Hermann   1352–3 susp. Fraenkel   1352 Creontis notam om. r
τέρμον' ωCrᵃᶜZm¹: τέρμ' vel τέρμα B²+: τέρμ' ἄρ' G   1353 αἰνιγ. ωr:
τ' αἰνιγ. Crχζ: αἰνιγ. τ' ORT: αἰνιγμῶν z: αἰνιγμάτων Aa: αἰνιγμοῖς
Geel, αἰνιγμοῦ τ' Valck.   1354 καὶ πῶς transp. rT   1357 nonnullos
post οὐ distinxisse testatur Σ   1358 del. Wecklein   ὡς τὸ οὐχ 'Σᴹ, ut
vid.: ὡς μὴ οὐχ Donaldson: τὸ μὴ οὐχ Shilleto   ἅπαντας Mr: ἅπαντ(α)
rXa   1359 ἐκόσμησαν θ' MMtx: ἐκόσμησαν Or   1360 del. post
Valck. Kirchhoff (cf. 1243)   1362 del. Valck.   στρατηγὼ fere Ω:
ξυναίμω Valck.: γ' ἀδελφὼ post King Heath   διπλὼ Ω: fere δισσὼ
CrL   1363 μονομάχου τ' ᵧᵖΣᴿᶠ, coni. Pierson, Valck. (cf. ¹Σ et V²ᵧᵖ
et Arist. fr. 570 K–A): μονομάχου τ' Rv²χ: μονομαχοῦντ' fere ω+:
μονομαχεῖν M   1364 δ' om. Diod. Sic. 10.9.8   ἐπ' M: ἐς vel εἰς Ω,
Diod., ˡᶜΣᴹⱽ   1367 γ' Sa: τ' Blaydes   1369–71 del. Valck. (1369
Porson, 1370–1 Kirchhoff)   1369 αἰτῶν z (coni. Canter): αἰτῶ ω+

116

πολλοῖς δ' ἐπήιει δάκρυα τῆς τύχης ὅση,　　　　1370
κἄβλεψαν ἀλλήλοισι διαδόντες κόρας.
Ἐτεοκλέης δὲ Παλλάδος χρυσάσπιδος
βλέψας πρὸς οἶκον ηὔξατ'· ῍Ω Διὸς κόρη,
δὸς ἔγχος ἡμῖν καλλίνικον †ἐκ χερὸς†
εἰς στέρν' ἀδελφοῦ τῆσδ' ἀπ' ὠλένης βαλεῖν.　　　1375
{κτανεῖν θ' ὃς ἦλθε πατρίδα πορθήσων ἐμήν}
ἐπεὶ δ' ἀνήφθη πυρσὸς ὡς Τυρσηνικῆς
σάλπιγγος ἠχὴ σῆμα φοινίου μάχης,
ἧιξαν δράμημα δεινὸν ἀλλήλοις ἔπι·
κάπροι δ' ὅπως θήγοντες ἀγρίαν γένυν　　　　1380
ξυνῆψαν, ἀφρῶι διάβροχοι γενειάδας·
ἧισσον δὲ λόγχαις· ἀλλ' ὑφίζανον κύκλοις
ὅπως σίδηρος ἐξολισθάνοι μάτην.
εἰ δ' ὄμμ' ὑπερσχὸν ἴτυος ἅτερος μάθοι,
λόγχην ἐνώμα, στόματι προφθῆναι θέλων.　　　1385
ἀλλ' εὖ προσῆγον ἀσπίδων κεγχρώμασιν
ὀφθαλμόν, ἀργὸν ὥστε γίγνεσθαι δόρυ.
πλείων δὲ τοῖς ὁρῶσιν ἐστάλασσ' ἱδρὼς
ἢ τοῖσι δρῶσι διὰ φίλων ὀρρωδίαν.
Ἐτεοκλέης δὲ ποδὶ μεταψαίρων πέτρον　　　　1390
ἴχνους ὑπόδρομον κῶλον ἐκτὸς ἀσπίδος
τίθησι· Πολυνείκης δ' ἀπήντησεν δορί,

1370 τῆς εὐχῆς Hermann　　ὅσηι M: ὅσα z: ὅσοι r　　1371 διδόντες
BVrz: (-οισιν) ἐνδόντες T　　1373 ηὔχετο fere r　　1374 ἐκ χερὸς fere Ω:
εὐστόχως Wecklein　　1376 del. Valck. (non legisse vid. Diod.) (cf.
756)　　κτεῖναί M^{γρ}r: καταθανεῖν O　　θ' om. M: δ' r　　1377 ἀνήφθη
Diggle: ἀφείθη Ω, Σ, test.　　ὡς Musgrave: ὡς (et dist. ante ὡς) Ω,
Σ, test.　　1378 ἠχῆι MO　　φοινίου Brx, test.: φονίου ω+　　1379
δράμημα Cobet: δρόμημα Ω　　ἀλλήλους z　　1380 post hunc v. λοξὸν
βλέποντες (τ') ἐμπύροισιν ὄμμασιν inser. post Valck. Burges et Hermann,
coll. Greg. Naz. de vita sua 1806　　1383 ἐξολισθάνοι r (Porson): -θαίνοι
ω+: -θαίνη fere Vr　　1384 ὑπερσχὼν r, ^{ρ}Σ^{B}: -σχόντ' r: -σχὼν τ'
Pr　　ἴτυος post ἅτερος transp. r, post μάθοι R^{γρ}　　μάθηι B²P　　1385
sic dist. Geel, ^{i}Σ: post στόματι dist. ^{i}Σ alter　　κεγχρώμασι(ν) Ω, Hsch. κ
1972: κερχνώμασι Hsch. κ 2371　　1388-9 del. Wecklein (1389 Nauck)
1388 πλεῖον r: πλέον W　　ἐστάλαζ' rZ (coni. Bothe): ἐστάλαξ' rz
1391 ἴχνος B¹(corr.B²)r, ^{ic}Σ^{B}, fort. ^{i}Σ　　1392 πολυνείκους S

πληγὴν σιδήρωι παραδοθεῖσαν εἰσιδών,
κνήμην τε διεπέρασεν Ἀργεῖον δόρυ·
στρατὸς δ' ἀνηλάλαξε Δαναϊδῶν ἅπας.　　　　1395
κἀν τῶιδε μόχθωι γυμνὸν ὦμον εἰσιδών
ὁ πρόσθε τρωθεὶς †στέρνα Πολυνείκους βίαι†
διῆκε λόγχην κἀπέδωκεν ἡδονὰς
Κάδμου πολίταις, ἀπὸ δ' ἔθραυσ' ἄκρον δόρυ.
εἰς δ' ἄπορον ἥκων δορὸς ἐπὶ σκέλος πάλιν　　1400
χωρεῖ, λαβὼν δ' ἀφῆκε μάρμαρον πέτρον
μέσον τ' ἄκοντ' ἔθραυσεν· ἐξ ἴσου δ' Ἄρης
ἦν, κάμακος ἀμφοῖν χεῖρ' ἀπεστερημένοιν.
ἐνθένδε κώπας ἁρπάσαντε φασγάνων
εἰς ταὐτὸν ἧκον, συμβαλόντε δ' ἀσπίδας　　　1405
πολὺν ταραγμὸν ἀμφιβάντ' εἶχον μάχης.
καί πως νοήσας Ἐτεοκλῆς τὸ Θεσσαλὸν
ἐσήγαγεν σόφισμ' ὁμιλίαι χθονός.
ἐξαλλαγεὶς γὰρ τοῦ παρεστῶτος πόνου
λαιὸν μὲν εἰς τοὖπισθεν ἀμφέρει πόδα,　　　1410
πρόσω τὰ κοῖλα γαστρὸς εὐλαβούμενος,
προβὰς δὲ κῶλον δεξιὸν δι' ὀμφαλοῦ
καθῆκεν ἔγχος σφονδύλοις τ' ἐνήρμοσεν.
ὁμοῦ δὲ κάμψας πλευρὰ καὶ νηδὺν τάλας
σὺν αἱματηραῖς σταγόσι Πολυνείκης πίτνει.　　1415
ὁ δ', ὡς κρατῶν δὴ καὶ νενικηκὼς μάχηι,

1393 ἐσιδών Vr　　1394 κνήμην Orχ: κνήμης ωrζ　　δὲ r
διεσπάρασσεν fere BʸᵖOW　　1395 ἀνηλάλαζε r　　δαναῶν V　　1396
κἀν Ω: καὶ WL²　　ἐσιδών Vr　　1397 στέρνα Πολ. ἔπι Paley, alii
alia βίαι om. M　　1398 κἀντέδωκεν Herwerden　　1399 ἀπὸ Ω: ὑπο
GZb¹ᵖᶜ　　1400 εἰς ω+: ὡς r　　1402 τ' W (coni. Valck.): δ' Ω
1403-μένοιν rχT: -μένων Orχᵍ, cf. Σ: -μένοις ω+, Σᴮ　　1404 ἐνθένδε rχ:
ἔνθεν δὲ ω+　　ἁρπάσαντε Orχ: -σαντες ω+　　1405 συμβαλόντες
BVr　　1406 τ' ἀραγμὸν r　　1407 θεσσ- ω+, test.: θεττ- Pz,
test.　　-λὸν Ω, test.: -λῶν test.　　1408 ὁμιλίαι Ω, Hsch. ο 729, Σⱽ Or.
1082: -ίας Σᴹᴮᶜ Or. 1082　　1409 ἀπαλλαγεὶς Or　　1410 ἀμφέρει Vrχ:
ἀναφέρει ω+, lex. Vind. α 62: μεταφέρει ζT　　1411 πρόσω τὰ Ω: τὰ
πρόσω explic. Σ　　1412 προσβὰς BV　　1413 σπονδύλοις rζ　　δ'
P　　1414 πλευρὰ ωr: πλευρὰν fere M+　　1415 αἱματηρᾶ σταγόνι fere
r　　1416 μάχην Wz

ξίφος δικὼν εἰς γαῖαν ἐσκύλευέ νιν
τὸν νοῦν πρὸς αὑτὸν οὐκ ἔχων, ἐκεῖσε δέ.
ὃ καί νιν ἔσφηλ'· ἔτι γὰρ ἐμπνέων βραχύ,
σώιζων σίδηρον ἐν λυγρῶι πεσήματι,   1420
μόλις μέν, ἐξέτεινε δ' εἰς ἧπαρ ξίφος
Ἐτεοκλέους ὁ πρόσθε Πολυνείκης πεσών.
γαῖαν δ' ὀδὰξ ἑλόντες ἀλλήλων πέλας
πίπτουσιν ἄμφω κοὐ διώρισαν κράτος.

Χο.   φεῦ φεῦ, κακῶν σῶν, Οἰδίπου, σ' ὅσον στένω·   1425
τὰς σὰς δ' ἀρὰς ἔοικεν ἐκπλῆσαι θεός.

Αγ.ᵝ   ἄκουε δή νυν καὶ τὰ πρὸς τούτοις κακά·
ἐπεὶ τέκνω πεσόντ' ἐλειπέτην βίον,
ἐν τῶιδε μήτηρ ἡ τάλαινα προσπίτνει,
{σὺν παρθένωι τε καὶ προθυμίαι ποδός}   1430
τετρωμένους δ' ἰδοῦσα καιρίους σφαγὰς
ὤιμωξεν· Ὦ τέκν', ὑστέρα βοηδρόμος
πάρειμι. προσπίτνουσα δ' ἐν μέρει τέκνα
ἔκλαι', ἐθρήνει, τὸν πολὺν μαστῶν πόνον
στένουσ', ἀδελφή θ' ἡ παρασπίζουσ' ὁμοῦ·   1435
Ὦ γηροβοσκὼ μητρός. – Ὦ γάμους ἐμοὺς
προδόντ' ἀδελφὼ φιλτάτω. στέρνων δ' ἄπο
φύσημ' ἀνεὶς δύσθνητον Ἐτεοκλῆς ἄναξ
ἤκουσε μητρός, κἀπιθεὶς ὑγρὰν χέρα
φωνὴν μὲν οὐκ ἀφῆκεν, ὀμμάτων δ' ἄπο   1440
προσεῖπε δακρύοις, ὥστε σημῆναι φίλα.

1418 αὐτὸν r**χ**z, Σ: αὐτὸν **ω**rz, Σ, Thom. Mag. 140, 16 Ritschl
1423 ἑλόντες Ω: λαβόντες RʸᵖZ   ἀλλήλοιν O**r**   1425 Creonti trib.
Rv, cf. Σ τινὲς Κρέων   οἰδίπους **r**z, fort. B¹ᵖᶜ   σ' ὅσον B² (post
Elmsley Hermann): ὅσον MʸᵖV²ʸᵖ**r**z et (post οἰδίπους) **r**z, fort. B¹ᵖᶜ: σὸς
ὢν MBᵃᶜV**r**: γ' ὅσον χZ: om. O   1426 ἐκπλήσ(σ)ειν O**r**   1428 ἐπεὶ
ω+: ὡς γὰρ MʸᵖBʸᵖO**r**   τέκνω πεσόντ(ε) ω+: πεσόντε τέκν' O:
πεσόντε παῖδ(ε) fere Mʸᵖ**r**   ἐλιπέτην M**r**ζ: λιπέτην MʸᵖBʸᵖSa
1429 προσπίπτοι M   1430 del. Markland, Valck.   τε om.
O**r**   1431 τετρωμένω **z**   καιρίας σφαγὰς **r**ζ: καιρίοις (vel -ίαις)
σφαγαῖς **r**   1432 ὤμοξεν MV¹(corr. V²)**r**   1435 δ' V**r**   1436 sic
dist. Geel, Diggle   1437 τ' A   1438 δύσθνητον M (cf. ᵍΣ):
δύστλητον Ω: δυσθνῄισκον Hermann   1439 λυγρὰν M²O**r**z
1440 δ' om. M

ὁ δ' ἦν ἔτ' ἔμπνους, πρὸς κασιγνήτην δ' ἰδὼν
γραῖάν τε μητέρ' εἶπε Πολυνείκης τάδε·
Ἀπωλόμεσθα, μῆτερ· οἰκτίρω δὲ σὲ
καὶ τήνδ' ἀδελφὴν καὶ κασίγνητον νεκρόν·   1445
φίλος γὰρ ἐχθρὸς ἐγένετ', ἀλλ' ὅμως φίλος.
θάψον δέ μ', ὦ τεκοῦσα, καὶ σύ, σύγγονε,
ἐν γῆι πατρώιαι, καὶ πόλιν θυμουμένην
παρηγορεῖτον, ὡς τοσόνδε γοῦν τύχω
χθονὸς πατρώιας, κεἰ δόμους ἀπώλεσα.   1450
ξυνάρμοσον δὲ βλέφαρά μου τῆι σῆι χερί,
μῆτερ – τίθησι δ' αὐτὸς ὀμμάτων ἔπι –
καὶ χαίρετ'· ἤδη γάρ με περιβάλλει σκότος.
ἄμφω δ' ἅμ' ἐξέπνευσαν ἄθλιον βίον.
μήτηρ δ', ὅπως ἐσεῖδε τήνδε συμφοράν,   1455
ὑπερπαθήσασ', ἥρπασ' ἐκ νεκρῶν ξίφος
κἄπραξε δεινά· διὰ μέσου γὰρ αὐχένος
ὠθεῖ σίδηρον, ἐν δὲ τοῖσι φιλτάτοις
θανοῦσα κεῖται περιβαλοῦσ' ἀμφοῖν χέρας.
ἀνῆιξε δ' ὀρθὸς λαὸς εἰς ἔριν λόγων,   1460
ἡμεῖς μὲν ὡς νικῶντα δεσπότην ἐμόν,
οἱ δ' ὡς ἐκεῖνον. ἦν δ' ἔρις στρατηλάταις,
οἱ μὲν πατάξαι πρόσθε Πολυνείκη δορί,
οἱ δ' ὡς θανόντων οὐδαμοῦ νίκη πέλοι.
κἄν τῶιδ' ὑπεξῆλθ' Ἀντιγόνη στρατοῦ δίχα.   1465
οἱ δ' εἰς ὅπλ' ἦισσον· εὖ δέ πως προμηθίαι
καθῆστο Κάδμου λαὸς ἀσπίδων ἔπι·

1442 δ'² om. Sa   1444 δὲ σὲ Valck.: δέ σε Ω   1447 σύ om. BSaZb:
τὸ (σύγγονον) Teles* (Stob. 3.60.8)   1448 πόλει θυμουμένη V¹(corr.
V²)**r**   1449 τοσοῦδε Teles*   γοῦν ω+, Teles: δὴ Bʸᵖ**r**, ʸᵖΣᴹ
1450 κἄν O   post hunc v. Teletem legisse καὶ γῆς φίλης ὄχθοισι
κρυφθῆναι τάφωι credunt quidam (vide comm.)   1451 μοι **r**: μου ante
βλέφ. transp. gBgE, Teles   1455 εἰσεῖδε **r**ζ: ἐπεῖδε B   1456 ἥρπασ' ἐκ
νεκρῶν ξίφος OV+(νεκροῦ **r**): ἥρπασεν νεκρῶν ξ. M: ἐκ ν. ξ. ἥρπασε Lz:
ἐκ ν. λάβε ξ. B: ἐκ ν. εἷλε ξ. **r**·   1458 ἐν δὲ τοῖσι Ω: σὺν τέκνοις δὲ
Bʸᵖ   1459 ἀμφοῖν χέρας fere Ω: ἀμφὼ τέκνα Bʸᵖ   1460 ὀρθῶς
Vᵃᶜ(corr. V¹)**r**   1464 πέλει BV**r**ζ   1465 del. Valck. (lacuna statuta)

κἄφθημεν οὔπω τεύχεσιν πεφαργμένον
Ἀργεῖον εἰσπεσόντες ἐξαίφνης στρατόν.
κοὐδεὶς ὑπέστη, πεδία δ᾽ ἐξεπίμπλασαν   1470
φεύγοντες, ἔρρει δ᾽ αἷμα μυρίων νεκρῶν
λόγχαις πιτνόντων. ὡς δ᾽ ἐνικῶμεν μάχῃ,
οἱ μὲν Διὸς τροπαῖον ἵστασαν βρέτας,
οἱ δ᾽ ἀσπίδας συλῶντες Ἀργείων νεκρῶν
σκυλεύματ᾽ εἴσω τειχέων ἐπέμπομεν.   1475
ἄλλοι δὲ τοὺς θανόντας Ἀντιγόνης μέτα
νεκροὺς φέρουσιν ἐνθάδ᾽ οἰκτίσαι φίλοις.
πόλει δ᾽ ἀγῶνες οἱ μὲν εὐτυχέστατοι
τῇδ᾽ ἐξέβησαν, οἱ δὲ δυστυχέστατοι.

Χο.   οὐκ εἰς ἀκοὰς ἔτι δυστυχία   1480
     δώματος ἥκει· πάρα γὰρ λεύσσειν
     πτώματα νεκρῶν τρισσῶν ἤδη
     τάδε πρὸς μελάθροις κοινῷ θανάτωι
     σκοτίαν αἰῶνα λαχόντων.

Αν.   οὐ προκαλυπτομένα βοτρυχώδεος ἁβρὰ
     παρῇδος   1485–6
     οὐδ᾽ ὑπὸ παρθενίας τὸν ὑπὸ βλεφά-
     ροις φοίνικ᾽, ἐρύθημα προσώπου,
     αἰδομένα φέρομαι βάκχα νεκύ-
     ων, κράδεμνα δικοῦσα κόμας ἀπ᾽ ἐ-   1490
     μᾶς, στολίδος κροκόεσσαν ἀνεῖσα τρυφάν,

1468 πεφαργμ- Dindorf: πεφραγμ- Ω   1471 μυρίον **rx**   1472 μάχην
Mt^{ac}Zu   1473 ἔστησαν fere RfXa   1474 νεκρῶν ω+: στρατῶν **r**:
στρατοῦ Cr   1477 φίλοις ω**r**: φίλους O+   1481 δωμάτων
Orz   1482 πτώματα ω+, Phryn. *ecl.* 352 Fischer: σώματα V²ʸᵖ**r**:
σωμάτων πτώματα R   1485–766 retractatos vel spurios iud. Dihle
(vide ad 1582)   1485–6 προσκαλ- **r**   βοτρυχ- **z**: βοστρυχ- ω+, Σ,
test.: βοτρυώδεος Porson   ἁβρᾶι OCr   παρῇδος Hartung: παρῆιδος
Ω, test.   1489 ἀδομένα **r**: αἰδουμένα **rx**   νεκρῶν M   1490 κόμας
ω+: κάρας **r**   1491 στολίδος ... τρυφάν Porson: στολίδα ... τρυφᾶς
fere Ω

ἀγεμόνευμα νεκροῖσι πολύστονον. αἰαῖ,
   ἰώ μοι.   1492–3
ὦ Πολύνεικες, ἔφυς ἄρ' ἐπώνυμος· ὤμοι, Θῆβαι·
σὰ δ' ἔρις – οὐκ ἔρις, ἀλλὰ φόνωι φόνος –   1495
  Οἰδιπόδα δόμον ὤλεσε κρανθεῖσ'
αἵματι δεινῶι,   1497
αἵματι λυγρῶι.   1497bis
τίνα προσωιδὸν
  ἢ τίνα μουσοπόλον στοναχὰν ἐπὶ
δάκρυσι δάκρυσιν, ὦ δόμος, ὦ δόμος,   1500
ἀγκαλέσωμαι,
τρισσὰ φέρουσα τάδ' αἵματα σύγγονα,
μάτερα καὶ τέκνα, χάρματ' Ἐρινύος;
ἃ δόμον Οἰδιπόδα πρόπαν ὤλεσε,
  τᾶς ἀγρίας ὅτε   1505
δυσξυνέτου ξυνετὸν μέλος ἔγνω
Σφιγγὸς ἀοιδοῦ σῶμα φονεύσας.
ἰώ μοι μοι, {πάτερ,}
  τίς Ἑλλὰς ἢ βάρβαρος ἢ
τῶν προπάροιθ' εὐγενετᾶν   1510

1492 αἰαῖ Dindorf: αῖ αῖ vel αῖ αῖ ω+: αῖ quater Pχz   1493–4
ἰώ μοι ὦ ωρζ: ἰώ μοι ἰὼ Or: ἰὼ χ   1494 ὤμοι Orz: ὤμοιμοι fere ω+:
ὦ **r**   Θήβαις Hermann (Θῆβαι SAa)   1496 οἰδιπόδαο Prχ
κρανθεῖσ' fere OV²**r**, Σ: κρανθεὶς MB+, Σ: κρανθείς/σ' V¹: κραθεὶς
rχ   1497 del. Dindorf   1497bis om. **r**   1498 del. Paley   τίνα
ω+: τίνα δὲ Orχz: τίνα δὴ **r**   πρὸς ὠιδὸν B, Σ alter   1499
μουσοπόλων Valck., -πόλου Burges   ἐπὶ Ω: ἔπι possis   1500 ὦ ...
ὦ fere Ω (ὦ² om. **r**): ω vel ιω ... ιω Π⁵   1501 ἀγκαλ- metricus cod.
Parm. 154 (post Paley Herwerden): ἀνακαλ-Π⁵Ω   -καλέσωμαι Π⁵BV²ˢ**r**:
-καλέσομαι ω+   1502 inter -καλέσωμαι et σύγγονα aliquid om.
Π⁵   τάδ' αἵματα Wᵖᶜ (coni. Markland, Musgrave): τάδ' αἵμακτὰ **r**:
τάδε σώματα ω+: σώματα **r**: γε σώματα T: πεσήματα Kirchhoff
1503 χάρμα τ' Σ   1503–4 ἐρινννύων αἶ L¹(corr. L²)   1504 δώμαθ' Cr:
δῶμ' Jackson   οἰδιπόδαο Gχ: οἰδίποδος Br   πρόπαντ' Zc²: πρόπαρ
rZ   ὤλεσαν PᵃᶜL   1506 δυσξύνετον Rf, cf. ᴾΣ   ξυνετὸς Gχ
ἔγνως Mtχ   1507 σῶμα φονεύσας del. Nauck (hab. Π⁵ᵘᵛ)   1508 μοι
μοι ωrz: μοι O+   πάτερ ω+: μᾶτερ fere **r**ζ: del. Hermann, non hab.
Π⁵   1509 ἕλλην MnʸᵖZb (Ἕλλαν coni. Murray)   ἢ¹ Π⁵Ω: τίς A
1510 προπάροιθ(εν) Π⁵ω+: πάροιθ(εν) **rz**

ἕτερος ἔτλα κακῶν τοσῶνδ'
αἵματος ἀμερίου
τοιάδ' ἄχεα φανερά;
τάλαιν', ὡς ἐλελίζω·
τίς ἄρ' ὄρνις δρυὸς ἢ   1515
ἐλάτας ἀκροκόμοις ἐν πετάλοις {ἑζομένα}
†μονομάτερος ὀδυρμοῖς†
ἐμοῖς ἄχεσι συνωιδός;
αἴλινον αἰάγμασιν ἃ
τούσδε προκλαίω μονάδ' αἰ-   1520
ῶνα διάξουσα τὸν αἰεὶ χρόνον ἐν
λειβομένοισιν δάκρυσιν.
{ἰαχήσω}
τίν' ἐπὶ πρῶτον ἀπὸ χαί-
τας σπαραγμοῖς ἀπαρχὰς βάλω;   1525
ματρὸς ἐμᾶς ἢ διδύμοισι γάλακ-
τος παρὰ μαστοῖς

1511–12 sic fere Π⁵Ω (sed inter ετλα et]ντοσωνδε spatium ca. 16 litt. hab.
Π⁵): ἕτερος αἵματος ἀμ. transp. Wecklein, alii alia   1511 ἔτλαν V¹(corr.
V²)   τοσῶνδ' fere Π⁵ω(B²)+: τόσων δι' fere B¹r: τοσῶνδε δι'
r   1512 ἀμερίου fere Ω: ενθαμεριου Π⁵: ἀμετέρου Kirchhoff   1513
φανερα φανερα Π⁵   1514 ἐλελίζω rχT: -ζει fere ωr, Σ, Eust. 125, 28: -ζηι
fere Π⁵ᵘᵛr: -ξει r: -ξηι ζ   1515 τίς τ' ἄρ' Bχ   δρυὸς Π⁵r: ἢ δρυὸς
ω+   1516 εμπεταλοις Π⁵, cf. ᴾΣ: κλάδοις M, fort. Fᵃᶜ: ἀμφὶ κλάδοις Ω
(ἀμφὶ ... ὀδυρμοῖς bis hab. A)   ἑζομένα om. Π⁵B, etiam A priore
loco   1517 μονομάτερος fere ω+: -τορος z: μουνα / [Π⁵: μονομάτορσιν
Wilam.   ὀδυρμοῖς Ω: (μουνα / [c. 14–15 litt.)]ρημα Π⁵: del.
Seidler   1518 συνωιδο[Π⁵   1520 τουσδε Π⁵: τοῖσδε Ω, Σ
προκλαίω Π⁵MVr: προσκλαίω BO+   μονάδ' B²Vrζ: μόνα δ'
ωrχ   1521 δι]αζωουσα Π⁵ (διαζῶσα coni. Paley)   1522 λειβομένοις
T   δακρυοις Π⁵: -ύοισιν rχ   1523 ἰαχήσω del. Burges, Dindorf, non
hab. Π⁵   1524 τίν' ἐπὶ Ω: ετινα Π⁵   ἀπὸ Π⁵ω+: ἐπὶ Or
1524–5 ἀπὸ χαίτας σπαρ. ἀπ. Ω: [c. 14]γμοναποχαιτας Π⁵
1525 σπαραγμοῖς rZ: -οῖσιν fere ω+:]γμον Π⁵   βάλω fere Π⁵ω+
(βαλῶ Orz): βάλλω rT   1526 ματέρος Orz   ἐμᾶς om. Pr   ἢ
King: ἐν fere Π⁵ω+: om. vel del. r   διδύμοις Π⁵r   γάλακτος Π⁵Ω:
τάλαινας Nauck: ἀγαλάκτοις Headlam   1527 μαστοῖς T: μασ[τ]οισ[Π⁵:
-οῖσιν Ω: παγαῖς post Reiske Schenkl

ἢ πρὸς ἀδελφῶν
οὐλόμεν' αἰκίσματα νεκρῶν;

ὀτοτοτοῖ· λεῖπε σοὺς   1530
δόμους, ἀλαὸν ὄμμα φέρων,
πάτερ γεραιέ, δεῖξον,
Οἰδιπόδα, σὸν αἰῶνα μέλεον, ὃς ἔτι
δώμασιν ἀέριον σκότον ὄμμασι
σοῖσι βαλὼν ἕλκεις μακρόπνουν ζοάν.   1535
κλύεις, ὦ κατ' αὐλὰν   1536
ἀλαίνων γεραιὸν   1536bis
πόδ' ἢ δεμνίοις
δύστανος ἰαύων;   1538

ΟΙΔΙΠΟΥΣ
τί μ', ὦ παρθένε, βακτρεύμασι τυφλοῦ   1539
ποδὸς ἐξάγαγες εἰς φῶς   1540
λεχήρη σκοτίων ἐκ θαλάμων οἰκ-
τροτάτοισιν δακρύοισιν,
πολιὸν αἰθέρος ἀφανὲς εἴδωλον ἢ
νέκυν ἔνερθεν ἢ
πτανὸν ὄνειρον;   1545
Αν. δυστυχὲς ἀγγελίας ἔπος οἴσῃ,
πάτερ· οὐκέτι σοι τέκνα λεύσσει

1529]λομενααπεισματα Π⁵   νεκρῶν ωr: δισσῶν Π⁵Μγρrχζ
1530 ὀτοτοτοῖ Kirchhoff: ὀτοττοτοί M: variis modis scr. Π⁵Ω   λεῖπε
ω+: λίπε Π⁵rχz   1533 οἰδιπόδα σὸν fere Ω (οἰδίπου r): οιδιποδασον
Π⁵   μέλεον ὃς fere Ω (μέλεος Wᵃᶜ, ὃς om. R): μελεαμελεοσον Π⁵   ετι
Π⁵: ἐπὶ Ω: ἐνὶ Scholefield   1535 μακρόπουν Π⁵rχ   ζοάν Π⁵V: ζωάν Ω
1537 πόδ' ἢ Schoene: πόδα Ω   1537–8 δεμνίοις δύστανος L (coni.
Valck.): δεμνίοις δύστανον ωrZc: δύστανον δεμνίοις rχz:
δυστηνοισιδεμνιοις Π⁵ (δυστάνοις coni. Paley)   1539 τί δ' χ
1541–2 οἰκτροτάτοις rzT   1542 δακρύοις ZT: δάκρυσι Vr
1543 αἰθέρος ἀφανὲς Ω (αἰθέριον cod. Harl. 6300): αἰθεροφαὲς Diggle: ἀφανὲς
del. Hartung   1545 ποτανὸν Seidler   ὄνειρον Ω: nescioquid
confusum vel deletum Π⁵   1546 εἴσῃι Battier

ΦΟΙΝΙΣΣΑΙ

φάος οὐδ' ἄλοχος, παραβάκτροις
ἃ πόδα σὸν τυφλόπουν θεραπεύμασιν αἰὲν ἐμόχθει,
⟨ὦ⟩ πάτερ, ὤμοι.   1550

Οι.   ὤμοι ἐμῶν παθέων· πάρα γὰρ στενάχειν
         τάδ', αὐτεῖν.   1551–2
         τρισσαὶ ψυχαί· ποίαι μοίραι
         πῶς ἔλιπον φάος; ὦ τέκνον, αὔδα.

Αν.   οὐκ ἐπ' ὀνείδεσιν οὐδ' ἐπιχάρμασιν,   1555
         ἀλλ' ὀδύναισι λέγω· σὸς ἀλάστωρ
         ξίφεσιν βρίθων
         καὶ πυρὶ καὶ σχετλίαισι μάχαις ἐπὶ παῖδας ἔβα σούς,
         ὦ πάτερ, ὤμοι.

Οι.   αἰαῖ· Αν. τί τόδε καταστένεις;   1560
Οι.   τέκνα. Αν. δι' ὀδύνας ἔβας·
         εἰ δὲ τέθριππά γ' ἔθ' ἅρματα λεύσσων
         ἀελίου τάδε σώματα νεκρῶν
         ὄμματος αὐγαῖς σαῖς ἐπενώμας;

Οι.   τῶν μὲν ἐμῶν τεκέων φανερὸν κακόν·   1565
         ἃ δὲ τάλαιν' ἄλοχος τίνι μοι, τέκνον, ὤλετο μοίραι;

1548–9 παραβ. ἃ **Brz**: ᾇ παραβ. **r**: ᾇ παραβ. ἃ ῳ+: παραβ. Π⁵
παραβάκτροις **Or**: παρὰ βάκτροις ῳ+   τυφλόπουν fere ω+: τυφλὸν
Bʸᵖ**rχz** 1550 ὦ add. Hermann, Seidler   1551–2 Oed. notam hic
(Π⁵)ω+: ante 1550 ὤμοι **rz**   ὤμοι fere **M**ʸᵖ**O**+: ... ọι Π⁵: ὤμοιμοι fere
ῳ**rz**   ἐμῶν fere Π⁵Ω: τῶν ἐμῶν V: ἐγὼ **M**ʸᵖ**W**   στενάζειν **Xaz**:
στοναχαῖς Geel   τάδ' Ω: καὶ τάδ' **T**: πάρ' Portus   αὐταῖς **Sa**: αὐτῆι
Wecklein: αὐτει Jackson (dist. ante τάδ')   1553 μιᾶι μοίραι **B**ʸᵖ**V**²ˢ
1554 πῶς ἔλιπον φάος ὦ fere Ω: φως ελιπον ταδε μοι Π⁵   1555
ἐπιχάρμασιν **MVrXa**: ἐπὶ χάρμ. **BO**+   1556 σὸς Π⁵**T**: ὁ σὸς Ω
1557 ξίφεσιν **M**: -εσι Π⁵Ω   1558 σχετλίαισι fere ω+: φονίαισι fere
Bʸᵖ**rz**   1559 ὤμοι **T** et fere Π⁵: ὤμοι ἐγὼ **M**ʸᵖ**W**: ἰώμοι(μοι) vel sim.
Ω   1560 Oed. notam hic Seidler (Π⁵): post 1559 πάτερ Ω   αἰαῖ
Dindorf: αἲ vel αἶ bis ω+: quater **r**: ε Π⁵: om. **r**   τοδε Π⁵: τάδε
Ω   1561 δι' ὀδ. Ω: δ]ιαιọ...[Π⁵   ἄρα ἔβας **Sa**: ἂν ἔβας **T**: ἔβας ἂν **r**
(coni. Hartung), cf. Σ   1562 δὲ Wilam.: τὰ Ω   γ' Ω: δ' **Rf** (coni.
Jackson): τ' **Sa**   ἔθ' Hermann, Seidler: ἐς fere Ω   1563 ἀελίου Ω:
αελιου φαος Π⁵   τάδε σώματα νεκρῶν om. Π⁵ (aut transp., aliis verbis
omissis)   1565 μὲν om. **rxZb**   τέκνων **Rfr**ᵍ**χ**ʸ   1566 μοι om. **r**,
del. Markland

Αν. δάκρυα γοερὰ φανερὰ πᾶσι τιθεμένα,
τέκεσι μαστὸν ἔφερεν ἔφερεν
ἱκέτις ἱκέτιν ὀρομένα.

ηὗρε δ' ἐν Ἠλέκτραισι πύλαις τέκνα   1570
λωτοτρόφον κατὰ λείμακα λόγχαις
κοινὸν ἐνυάλιον
μάτηρ, ὥστε λέοντας ἐναύλους,
μαρναμένους ἐπὶ τραύμασιν, αἵματος
ἤδη ψυχρὰν λοιβὰν φόνιον,   1575
ἂν ἔλαχ' Ἅιδας, ὤπασε δ' Ἄρης·
χαλκόκροτον δὲ λαβοῦσα νεκρῶν πάρα φάσγανον
εἴσω
σαρκὸς ἔβαψεν, ἄχει δὲ τέκνων ἔπεσ' ἀμφὶ τέκνοισι.
πάντα δ' ἐν ἄματι τῷδε συνάγαγεν,
ὦ πάτερ, ἁμετέροισιν ἄχη μελάθροις θεὸς   1580
ὃς τάδ' ἐκτελευτᾷ.   1581

Χο. πολλῶν κακῶν κατῆρξεν Οἰδίπου δόμοις   1582
τόδ' ἦμαρ· εἴη δ' εὐτυχέστερος βίος.

Κρ. οἴκτων μὲν ἤδη λήγεθ', ὡς ὥρα τάφου

1567 δάκ. φαν. γο. transp. **r**Z, φαν. δάκ. γο. Zb παισὶ
O**r**T τεθειμένα **r** 1569 ἱκέτιν M**r**ζ:]σιν Π⁵: ἱκέταν V**r**: ἱκέτην BO**r**
χ ὀρομένα fere Π⁵M, ʸᵖΣ, cf. ᵍΣ: ὀρω- fere B¹ᵘᵛV²ˢ**r**: αἱρο- fere
MˢMʸᵖBʸᵖB³OV+, ⁱΣ 1570 ἐπ' Ἠλ. Herwerden 1574 ἐπὶ Ω: ἐν
Aa τραύμασιν Ω, Σ: τραύμασι τ' Ο (θ' Paley, δ' Musgrave) 1575
ψυχρὰν Ω, Σ: τύχην ˡᶜΣˢ, Σⱽˢ 1575 φονιον Π⁵: φονίαν V+: φοινίαν
ω(V²)**r**Zm 1576 Ἅ(ι)δας **r**, Porson: ἄίδας fere ω+: αρης Π⁵
1578 ἔβαψεν BʸᵖVʸᵖ+: ἔβαλεν M: ἔπεμψε(ν) Π⁵ω**rz** ἄχει Π⁵BO**r**: ἄχη
fere MV**r**: ἄγχι fere B²V²ʸᵖ+ τέκνοις Τ: τε]κνα Π⁵: νεκροῖς Markland
(νεκροῖσιν Eldik) 1579 αἵματι **r**Zbʸᵖ, fort. B¹ συνάγαγεν **rz**Τ:
-ήγαγεν Π⁵ω+ 1580 αμετεροισιν αχη μελαθροις Π⁵: ἁμετέροισι
δόμοισιν ἄχη fere Ω θεὸς om. Π⁵ 1581 ὅς γε τάδε Τ τάδ'
ἐκτελευτᾷ Page, Haslam: τάδε τελευτᾷ Ω: τάδ' ἐπιτελευτᾷ WSa:
ταδε[1–2]ελευ[ται Π⁵ 1582–766 omnino vel maxima ex parte Eur.
abiud. Leidloff, Wecklein, alii; alii alios versus secludunt 1582–3 del.
Geel 1582 κακῶν om. GᵃᶜSᵃᶜ: post οἰδ. transp. O**r**, post -ῆρξε
r ὑπῆρξ- **r**χΤ οἰδιπόδου M δόμος V¹(corr. V²)L: τέκνοις **r**:
ἢ τέκνοις ἢ γένει BʸᵖVˢ: δόμωι Schenkl 1583 εὐτυχέστερος βίος Ω: αὖθις
εὐτυχέστερος Hartung: εὐτυχὴς ἐμοὶ βίος Geel: εὐτυχέστερον τέλος
Gebauer 1584–614 spurios vel retractatos iud. Pearson 1584 ὧσθ'
fere **r**

μνήμην τίθεσθαι· τῶνδε δ', Οἰδίπου, λόγων   1585
ἄκουσον· ἀρχὰς τῆσδε γῆς ἔδωκέ μοι
'Ετεοκλέης παῖς σός, γάμων φερνὰς διδοὺς
Αἵμονι κόρης τε λέκτρον 'Αντιγόνης σέθεν.
οὔκουν σ' ἐάσω τήνδε γῆν οἰκεῖν ἔτι·
σαφῶς γὰρ εἶπε Τειρεσίας οὐ μή ποτε   1590
σοῦ τήνδε γῆν οἰκοῦντος εὖ πράξειν πόλιν.
ἀλλ' ἐκκομίζου· καὶ τάδ' οὐχ ὕβρει λέγω
οὐδ' ἐχθρὸς ὢν σός, διὰ δὲ τοὺς ἀλάστορας
τοὺς σοὺς δεδοικὼς μή τι γῆ πάθηι κακόν.

Οι. ὦ μοῖρ', ἀπ' ἀρχῆς ὥς μ' ἔφυσας ἄθλιον·   1595
{καὶ τλήμον', εἴ τις ἄλλος ἀνθρώπων ἔφυ}
ὃν καὶ πρὶν εἰς φῶς μητρὸς ἐκ γονῆς μολεῖν,
ἄγονον 'Απόλλων Λαΐωι μ' ἐθέσπισεν
φονέα γενέσθαι πατρός· ὦ τάλας ἐγώ.
ἐπεὶ δ' ἐγενόμην, αὖθις ὁ σπείρας πατὴρ   1600
κτείνει με νομίσας πολέμιον πεφυκέναι·
χρῆν γὰρ θανεῖν νιν ἐξ ἐμοῦ· πέμπει δέ με
μαστὸν ποθοῦντα θηρσὶν ἄθλιον βοράν·
οὗ σωιζόμεσθα – Ταρτάρου γὰρ ὤφελεν
ἐλθεῖν Κιθαιρὼν εἰς ἄβυσσα χάσματα,   1605
ὅς μ' οὐ διώλεσ', ἀλλὰ δουλεῦσαί †τε μοι
δαίμων ἔδωκε Πόλυβον ἀμφὶ δεσπότην.†

1585 τῶνδ' οἰδ. λόγων Vr: τόνδε δ' οἰδ. λόγον L   1586b ἀρχὰς – 1590a
γὰρ del. Fraenkel   1586 δέδωκέ Sa   1587 σὸς παῖς transp.
r   1592 τόδ' G   1593 σοί Orx   1595-626 del. Paley, 1595-614
Kitto, Fraenkel   1596 del. Valck., L. Dindorf   τλήμων ... ἔφυν
O   1597 ὃν καὶ Ω: οὐ καὶ Porson   μητρὸς om. rζ (addito in nonnullis
ποτε vel ἔτι post μολεῖν)   1598 μ' Ω: γ' Burges: del. Kirchhoff
('τεθεσπίκει)   1599 πατρὸς ὅς μ' ἐγείνατο ΥΡΣΒ1597: μητρί τ' ἀναβῆναι
λέχος Βυρ   1600 αὐτίχ' Geel, εὐθὺς Seyffert, αὐτὸς Nauck
1601 πεφυκέναι ΜυρVυρO+: δυσδαίμονα ωrz   1602 νιν om.
MBr   1603 ἀθλίαν Aa²χT   1604-7 del. Hartung (1606-7
Apitz)   1604 ταρτάρω B   δ' ἄρ' Heimsoeth   1606-7 locus
desperatus   1606 ὥς μ' M   οὐκ ὤλεσ' r   lacunam post ἀλλὰ stat.
Murray   δουλεῦσαί τε μοι fere ω+: δουλ. τε με Or: δουλεύσοντά
με post Valck. Porson, alii alia   1607 δαίμων ἔδωκε πόλυβον fere ω+
(δέδωκε A, ἔθηκε Lenting, ἔσωιζε Wecklein): δαίμων πόλυβον ἔδωκεν AaZb:
πόλ. ἐξέδωκεν χ: πρὸς πόλ. ἐξέδωκεν T

κτανὼν δ᾽ ἐμαυτοῦ πατέρ᾽ ὁ δυσδαίμων ἐγὼ
εἰς μητρὸς ἦλθον τῆς ταλαιπώρου λέχος,
παῖδάς τ᾽ ἀδελφοὺς ἔτεκον, οὓς ἀπώλεσα,   1610
ἀρὰς παραλαβὼν Λαΐου καὶ παισὶ δούς.
οὐ γὰρ τοσοῦτον ἀσύνετος πέφυκ᾽ ἐγὼ
ὥστ᾽ εἰς ἔμ᾽ ὄμματ᾽ εἴς τ᾽ ἐμῶν παίδων βίον
ἄνευ θεῶν του ταῦτ᾽ ἐμηχανησάμην.
εἶέν· τί δράσω δῆθ᾽ ὁ δυσδαίμων ἐγώ;   1615
τίς ἡγεμών μοι ποδὸς ὁμαρτήσει τυφλοῦ;
ἥδ᾽ ἡ θανοῦσα; ζῶσά γ᾽ ἂν σάφ᾽ οἶδ᾽ ὅτι.
ἀλλ᾽ εὔτεκνος ξυνωρίς; ἀλλ᾽ οὐκ ἔστι μοι.
ἀλλ᾽ ἔτι νεάζων αὐτὸς εὕροιμ᾽ ἂν βίον;
πόθεν; τί μ᾽ ἄρδην ὧδ᾽ ἀποκτείνεις, Κρέον;   1620
ἀποκτενεῖς γάρ, εἴ με γῆς ἔξω βαλεῖς.
οὐ μὴν ἐλίξας γ᾽ ἀμφὶ σὸν χεῖρας γόνυ
κακὸς φανοῦμαι· τὸ γὰρ ἐμόν ποτ᾽ εὐγενὲς
οὐκ ἂν προδοίην, οὐδέ περ πράσσων κακῶς.

Κρ. σοί τ᾽ εὖ λέλεκται γόνατα μὴ χρώιζειν ἐμά,   1625
ἐγὼ δὲ ναίειν σ᾽ οὐκ ἐάσαιμ᾽ ἂν χθόνα.
νεκρῶν δὲ τῶνδε τὸν μὲν εἰς δόμους χρεὼν
ἤδη κομίζειν, τόνδε δ᾽, ὃς πέρσων πόλιν
πατρίδα σὺν ἄλλοις ἦλθε, Πολυνείκους νέκυν
ἐκβάλετ᾽ ἄθαπτον τῆσδ᾽ ὅρων ἔξω χθονός.   1630
κηρύξεται δὲ πᾶσι Καδμείοις τάδε·
ὃς ἂν νεκρὸν τόνδ᾽ ἢ καταστέφων ἁλῶι

1608 δ᾽ om. G: θ᾽ B: τ᾽ **r** (coni. Elmsley)   1610 δ᾽ **r**   1611 del.
Dindorf   1612–14 del. Schenkl   1613 ἔμ᾽ Ω: τάδ᾽ Reeve (qui 1595–
614 delere maluit)   ἐμὸν M   του ταῦτ᾽ Ω: τοσαῦτ᾽ O   1617 γ᾽
ἂν ω(B^γρ) +: γὰρ B**rχ**   1618 ἔστ᾽ ἔτι Kirchhoff   1619 αὐτὸς om. V
1620 ἀποκτείνεις **rχ**ζ: -κτενεῖς ω**r**   1621 del. Kirchhoff   1622 οὐ μὴν
Ω: οὔκουν g V   γ᾽ om. H**r**, gV: ante ἐλίξας transp. OV   1624 οὐδέπω
r   1625–45 spurios vel retractatos iud. Pearson; 1627–34 del. Balsamo,
Friedrich, Fraenkel, 1631–8 Walter   1625 γ᾽ Mt (coni. Valck.)
χρήζειν **rz**   1626 τε Zc (coni. Markland, Valck.)   σ᾽ om.
rz   1628 ἤδη om. Rv: δμῶας M^γρV²γρ**r**   1628–9 δ᾽ ὃς … ἦλθε del.
Porson (scripto τὸν δὲ)   1629 σὺν ὅπλοις King   πολυνείκη(ν)
V¹(corr. V²γρ)**r**   1631 κηρύξεται MB¹ᵖᶜV²ˢ**rχ**: -ετε HV¹**r**: -ατε Orζ
(cum δὲ δὴ **z**): fort. -άτω B^ac

128

ἢ γῆι καλύπτων, θάνατον ἀνταλλάξεται.
{ἐὰν δ' ἄκλαυτον, ἄταφον, οἰωνοῖς βοράν}
σὺ δ' ἐκλιποῦσα τριπτύχους θρήνους νεκρῶν   1635
κόμιζε σαυτήν, Ἀντιγόνη, δόμων ἔσω.
{καὶ παρθενεύου τὴν ἐπιοῦσαν ἡμέραν
μένουσ', ἐν ἧι σε λέκτρον Αἵμονος μένει.}

Αν.   ὦ πάτερ, ἐν οἵοις κείμεθ' ἄθλιοι κακοῖς·
ὡς σὲ στενάζω τῶν τεθνηκότων πλέον·   1640
οὐ γὰρ τὸ μέν σοι βαρὺ κακῶν, τὸ δ' οὐ βαρύ,
ἀλλ' εἰς ἅπαντα δυστυχὴς ἔφυς, πάτερ.
ἀτὰρ σ' ἐρωτῶ τὸν νεωστὶ κοίρανον·
τί τόνδ' ὑβρίζεις πατέρ' ἀποστέλλων χθονός;
τί θεσμοποιεῖς ἐπὶ ταλαιπώρωι νεκρῶι;   1645

Κρ.   Ἐτεοκλέους βουλεύματ', οὐχ ἡμῶν τάδε.

Αν.   ἄφρονά γε, καὶ σὺ μῶρος ὃς ἐπίθου τάδε.

Κρ.   πῶς; τἀντεταλμέν' οὐ δίκαιον ἐκπονεῖν;

Αν.   οὔκ, ἢν πονηρά γ' ἦι κακῶς τ' εἰρημένα.

Κρ.   τί δ'; οὐ δικαίως ὅδε κυσὶν δοθήσεται;   1650

Αν.   οὐκ ἔννομον γὰρ τὴν δίκην πράσσεσθέ νιν.

Κρ.   εἴπερ γε πόλεως ἐχθρὸς ἦν οὐκ ἐχθρὸς ὤν.

Αν.   οὔκουν ἔδωκε †τῆι τύχηι τὸν δαίμονα†;

Κρ.   καὶ τῶι τάφωι νυν τὴν δίκην παρασχέτω.

1634 del. Valck. (cf. Soph. *Ant.* 29–30)   ἄκλαυτον B¹OL: -αυστον
HMB³V +   ἄθαπτον r   1635–6 del. post Paley Stadtmueller
1635 τριπτύχους νεκρῶν γόους r: τριπτύχων νεκρῶν γόους MᵞᴾBᵞᴾr:
τριπτύχους τύπους νεκρῶν A   1636 ἔσω ω +: σέθεν r   1637–8 del.
Dindorf (tantum 1637 Paley, 1638 Marchant)   1637 ἐπιοῦσαν B +:
εἰσιοῦσαν ωr: ἰοῦσαν r: ἔτ' οὔσαν Marchant   1638 μένει MV¹rζ: μενεῖ
OV²rχ, fort. H: μένεῖ Br   1639–82 del. Fraenkel, 1639–72 Balsamo,
Friedrich   1639 ἄθλιοι Barnes: ἀθλίοις Ω   1641 κακὸν Bᵃᶜ(corr.
B¹)Or   1643 αὐτὰρ fere Mr   κοίρανον fere ω +: τύραννον
HV²Sa   1644 del. Valck.   1646–82 retractatos iud. Pearson
1647 γε ω +: τε Saχ   ἐπίθου V¹r: ἐπείθου ω(V²) +   1648 ἐκπονεῖν
ω +: ἐκτελεῖν Orχz   1649 γ' ω +: τ' r   ἦι ω +: ἦ Or   τ' om. OAa
1650 ὅδε Ω: ὅ γε B   1651 δίκην ω +: κρίσιν r   1652 εἴπερ Ω: εἰ
μή Σᵘᵛ   γε om. Hr   1653–4 del. Harberton   1653 οὔκουν V¹A:
οὔκοῦν fere HMOV² +: utrumque B   ἔδωκε Ω: ἔτισε Hartung   1654
τὴν τύχην W

Αν. τί πλημμελήσας, τὸ μέρος εἰ μετῆλθε γῆς;   1655
Κρ. ἄταφος ὅδ᾽ ἀνήρ, ὡς μάθηις, γενήσεται.
Αν. ἐγώ σφε θάψω, κἂν ἀπεννέπηι πόλις.
Κρ. σαυτὴν ἄρ᾽ ἐγγὺς τῶιδε συνθάψεις νεκρῶι.
Αν. ἀλλ᾽ εὐκλεές τοι δύο φίλω κεῖσθαι πέλας.
Κρ. λάζυσθε τήνδε κἀς δόμους κομίζετε.   1660
Αν. οὐ δῆτ᾽, ἐπεὶ τοῦδ᾽ οὐ μεθήσομαι νεκροῦ.
Κρ. ἔκριν᾽ ὁ δαίμων, παρθέν᾽, οὐχ ἃ σοὶ δοκεῖ.
Αν. κἀκεῖνο κέκριται, μὴ ἐφυβρίζεσθαι νεκρούς.
Κρ. ὡς οὔτις ἀμφὶ τῶιδ᾽ ὑγρὰν θήσει κόνιν.
Αν. ναὶ πρός σε τῆσδε μητρὸς Ἰοκάστης, Κρέον.   1665
Κρ. μάταια μοχθεῖς· οὐ γὰρ ἂν τύχοις τάδε.
Αν. σὺ δ᾽ ἀλλὰ νεκρῶι λουτρὰ περιβαλεῖν μ᾽ ἔα.
Κρ. ἓν τοῦτ᾽ ἂν εἴη τῶν ἀπορρήτων πόλει.
Αν. ἀλλ᾽ ἀμφὶ τραύματ᾽ ἄγρια τελαμῶνας βαλεῖν.
Κρ. οὐκ ἔσθ᾽ ὅπως σὺ τόνδε τιμήσεις νέκυν.   1670
Αν. ὦ φίλτατ᾽, ἀλλὰ στόμα γε σὸν προσπτύξομαι.
Κρ. οὐ μὴ εἰς γάμους σοὺς συμφορὰν κτήσηι γόοις;
Αν. ἦ γὰρ γαμοῦμαι ζῶσα παιδὶ σῶι ποτε;
Κρ. πολλή σ᾽ ἀνάγκη· ποῖ γὰρ ἐκφεύξηι λέχος;
Αν. νὺξ ἄρ᾽ ἐκείνη Δαναΐδων μ᾽ ἕξει μίαν.   1675
Κρ. εἶδες τὸ τόλμημ᾽ οἷον ἐξωνείδισεν;
Αν. ἴστω σίδηρος ὅρκιόν τε μοι ξίφος.
Κρ. τί δ᾽ ἐκπροθυμῆι τῶνδ᾽ ἀπηλλάχθαι γάμων;
Αν. συμφεύξομαι τῶιδ᾽ ἀθλιωτάτωι πατρί.

1656 ἀνήρ Porson: ἀνήρ Ω   1658 ἄρ᾽ ω+: ἂν **r**   συνάψεις
rZ   1659 τοι ω+: τι **rz**   1661 ἐπειδὴ δ᾽ οὐ O   1662 παρθένε post
σοὶ transp. Or   ἃ Ω: ὡς L   1663 κέκρικε **r**   1664 τῶιδ᾽ ω+: τῶ
H: σῶμ᾽ **z**   1666 τύχηις HO**rζ**   1667 λουτρὰ νεκρῶι transp.
V**r**   1669 τελαμῶνα χ   1670 τιμήσηις BO**r**   νεκρόν **r**   1671 γε
om. V   1672 οὐ μὴ Kirchhoff: οὐκ Ω, Σ   γόου **r**: γόους **r**
1673 ἦ MV[1](corr. V[2]): οὐ Rf   1674 σ᾽ MBV**r**: γ᾽ O[ac]+: τ᾽ O[1c]W[ac]:
(cum πολλῆς) σ᾽ vel γ᾽ H   πῆ Z: ποῦ Rf   1675–8 del.
Harberton   1675 γ᾽ ἄρ᾽ Sa   δαναΐδων HMB[2]Or: δαναιδῶν B[1]V +
μ᾽ om. **r**   ἕξει μίαν fere Ω (μία HMV[1]F): ἔσται μία H[s]Vr[γρ]   1676
εἴδετε W[ac]   1677 σίδηρος Ω, Eust. 92, 12: ζεὺς Eust. 809, 15   δέ μοι
Eust. (utroque loco)

Κρ. γενναιότης σοι, μωρία δ' ἔνεστί τις.   1680
Αν. καὶ ξυνθανοῦμαί γ', ὡς μάθηις περαιτέρω.
Κρ. ἴθ'· οὐ φονεύσεις παῖδ' ἐμόν· λεῖπε χθόνα.

Οι. ὦ θύγατερ, αἰνῶ μέν σε τῆς προθυμίας.
Αν. ἀλλ' εἰ γαμοίμην, σὺ δὲ μόνος φεύγοις, πάτερ;
Οι. μέν' εὐτυχοῦσα· τἄμ' ἐγὼ στέρξω κακά.   1685
Αν. καὶ τίς σε τυφλὸν ὄντα θεραπεύσει, πάτερ;
Οι. πεσὼν ὅπου μοι μοῖρα κείσομαι πέδωι.
Αν. ὁ δ' Οἰδίπους ποῦ καὶ τὰ κλείν' αἰνίγματα;
Οι. ὄλωλ'· ἓν ἦμάρ μ' ὤλβισ', ἓν δ' ἀπώλεσεν.
Αν. οὔκουν μετασχεῖν κἀμὲ δεῖ τῶν σῶν κακῶν;   1690
Οι. αἰσχρὰ φυγὴ θυγατρὶ σὺν τυφλῶι πατρί.
Αν. οὔ, σωφρονούσηι γ', ἀλλὰ γενναία, πάτερ.
Οι. προσάγαγέ νυν με, μητρὸς ὡς ψαύσω σέθεν.
Αν. ἰδού, παρειᾶς φιλτάτης ψαῦσον χερί.
Οι. ὦ μῆτερ, ὦ ξυνάορ' ἀθλιωτάτη.   1695
Αν. οἰκτρὰ πρόκειται, πάντ' ἔχουσ' ὁμοῦ κακά.
Οι. Ἐτεοκλέους δὲ πτῶμα Πολυνείκους τε ποῦ;
Αν. τώδ' ἐκτάδην σοι κεῖσθον ἀλλήλοιν πέλας.
Οι. πρόσθες τυφλὴν χεῖρ' ἐπὶ πρόσωπα δυστυχῆ.
Αν. ἰδού, θανόντων σῶν τέκνων ἅπτου χερί.   1700
Οι. ὦ φίλα πεσήματ' ἄθλι' ἀθλίου πατρός.
Αν. ὦ φίλτατον δῆτ' ὄμμα Πολυνείκους ἐμοί.

1682 λεῖπε OV (coni. Valck.): λίπε Ω   1684 εἰ ω+: ἢ HᴾᶜB²: ἢ
RfᴾᶜZm δὲ om. P φεύγοις MW, ⁱΣ, fort. H: φεύγεις fere BOV+,
ᴾΣ 1685–6 om., in marg. scr. V 1685 τἄμ' ἐγὼ ω+:
τἀμὰ δὲ **r**: τἀμὰ δ' ἐγὼ **z** 1687 πεσὼν Ω: θανὼν HᵞᴾMnˢᵘᵛ ὅπα
M μοι om. O πέδωι ω+: θανὼν OV²ˢ**r**χᵞᴾ 1688–9 del.
Müller, Robert 1689 μ' om. HV**r** ἓν δ' Ω: ἠδ' ᵞᴾΣ 1690 οὔκουν
Porson: οὐκοῦν fere Ω κἀμὲ δεῖ **r**χΤ: δεῖ κἀμὲ ω+ κακῶν ω+:
πόνων H**r** 1691 πατρὶ τυφλῶι transp. V**r** 1692 γενναίαι M**r**
1693 πρόσαγε HO**r** ψαύσω Ω: θάψω Rᵞᴾ 1694 παρειᾶς F. W.
Schmidt: γεραιᾶς Ω: γεραιᾶ Rfᵘᵛ (γεραιᾶι coni. Valck.) φιλτάτηι
χ 1695 ξυνάορ' HMB²V²+: ξυνάορ fere B¹OV¹**r**ζ 1697 δὲ ω+:
τε H**r** τε Ω: δὲ HRf 1698 ἀλλήλων H**r**χˢ 1699 χερ' H**r**:
χειρῶν O 1701 ἄθλι' ἀθλίου πατρός ω+: ἀθλίου πατρὸς τέκνα
rζ 1702 ὄμμα Purgold, Hartung: ὄνομα Ω

ΦΟΙΝΙΣΣΑΙ

Οι. νῦν χρησμός, ὦ παῖ, Λοξίου περαίνεται.
Αν. ὁ ποῖος; ἀλλ᾽ ἦ πρὸς κακοῖς ἐρεῖς κακά;
Οι. ἐν ταῖς Ἀθήναις κατθανεῖν μ᾽ ἀλώμενον.   1705
Αν. ποῦ; τίς σε πύργος Ἀτθίδος προσδέξεται;
Οι. ἱερὸς Κολωνός, δώμαθ᾽ ἱππίου θεοῦ.
    ἀλλ᾽ εἶα, τυφλῶι τῶιδ᾽ ὑπηρέτει πατρί,
    ἐπεὶ προθυμῆι τῆσδε κοινοῦσθαι φυγῆς.   1709

Αν. ἴθ᾽ εἰς φυγὰν τάλαιναν· ὄρεγε χέρα φίλαν,   1710–11
    πάτερ γεραιέ, πομπίμαν
    ἔχων ἔμ᾽ ὥστε ναυσιπομπὸν αὖραν.

Οι. ἰδού,   1714
    πορεύομαι, τέκνον· σύ μοι   1714bis
    ποδαγὸς ἀθλία γενοῦ.   1715

Αν. γενόμεθα γενόμεθ᾽, ἄθλιοί
    γε δῆτα Θηβαιᾶν μάλιστα παρθένων.

Οι. πόθι γεραιὸν ἴχνος τίθημι;
    βάκτρα πόθι φέρω, τέκνον;

Αν. τᾶιδε τᾶιδε βᾶθί μοι,   1720
    τᾶιδε τᾶιδε πόδα τίθει,
    ὥστ᾽ ὄνειρον ἰσχύν {ἔχων}.

1703–7 del. Leidloff, Walter   1704 ἦ BV²+: ἦ ωΑ   1705 μ᾽ om.
L   ἀλώμενον MOr   1707 δῶμα θ᾽ fere rζ, cf. Σ   ἱππίου rχz:
ἱππείου ωrz, Σ   1708 πατρί Ω: ποδί L   1709 φυγῆς ω+: χθονός
r   1710–66 del. Balsamo; 1710–27, 1732–46, 1758–66 Wecklein; alii
alios versus secludunt; vide ad 1737–66   1710 τάλαιν(α) r   χέρα Τ
(et post φίλαν transp. W): χεῖρα Π⁵Ω   1712 ὦ πάτερ r   γηραιέ
r   1713 ἔχε r   μ᾽ Or   1713–15 nescioquid omisisse vid.
Π⁵   1714 ἰδού ⟨ἰδού⟩ Hermann: fort. spurium iud. Haslam   1714bis
πορεύσομαι W   μοι om. LT: μου Mr   1715 ποδαγωγὸς fere
rχ   ἀθλίωι GχˢZm: ἀθλίου r   1716 γενόμεθα γενόμεθ᾽ fere Π⁵MB+:
γενόμεσθα γενόμεσθ᾽ fere OVrχz, cf. Σ   ἄθλιοί Porson: ἄθλιαί
Ω   1717 γε om. Τ   δῆτα om. r   θηβαίων fere B²OVr
παρθένων Or: παρθ. δή ω+   1718 πουθυ[..]...τιθημιιχνος Π⁵
γηραιὸν r   1719 ποθιφερω (vel ποσιφερω?) Π⁵: πρόσφερ᾽ ὦ fere
Ω   1720 et 1721 τᾶι τᾶιδε Ο   1721 τίθει Π⁵MVr (et LT, ante πόδα
transp.): τίθει πάτερ ΒΟ+   1722 ἀντόνειρον Wecklein   ισχυν Π⁵
(coni. Hermann): ἰσχὺν ἔχων fere Ω

132

Οι.　ἰὼ ἰώ, δυστυχεστάτας φυγὰς
　　　ἀλαίνειν τὸν γέροντά μ' ἐκ πάτρας.
　　　ἰὼ ἰώ, δεινὰ δείν' ἐγὼ τλάς.　　　　　　　1725

Αν.　τί τλάς; τί τλάς; οὐχ ὁρᾶι Δίκα κακούς,
　　　οὐδ' ἀμείβεται βροτῶν ἀσυνεσίας.

Οι.　ὅδ' εἰμὶ μοῦσαν ὃς ἐπὶ καλ-
　　　λίνικον οὐράνιον ἔβαν
　　　⟨μειξο⟩παρθένου κόρας　　　　　　　　　　1730
　　　αἴνιγμ' ἀσύνετον εὑρών.

Αν.　Σφιγγὸς ἀναφέρεις ὄνειδος;
　　　ἄπαγε τὰ πάρος εὐτυχήματ' αὐδῶν·
　　　τάδε σ' ἐπέμενε μέλεα πάθεα
　　　φυγάδα πατρίδος ἄπο γενόμενον,　　　　　1735
　　　ὦ πάτερ, θανεῖν που.
　　　{ποθεινὰ δάκρυα παρὰ φίλαισι παρθένοις
　　　λιποῦσ' ἄπειμι πατρίδος ἀποπρὸ γαίας
　　　ἀπαρθένευτ' ἀλωμένα.

Οι.　φεῦ τὸ χρήσιμον φρενῶν.　　　　　　　　　1740

Αν.　εἰς πατρός γε συμφορὰς
　　　εὐκλεᾶ με θήσει·
　　　τάλαιν' ἐγὼ ⟨σῶν⟩ συγγόνου θ' ὑβρισμάτων

1723 ἰὼ ἰὼ δεινᾶς δυστ. Or　　φυγὰς Rζ (coni. Hermann): φυγᾶς
ω+　　1724 ἀλαίνειν Musgrave: ἐλαύνων Ω　　1725 δεινὰ δείν' fere
(Π⁵ᵘᵛ)rz: δειν(ὰ) ω+ (post ἐγὼ transp. r)　　τλάς Π⁵ω+: ὁ τλάς V²ˢRfχ:
τάλας OWᵃᶜ　　1726 τι τλας semel Π⁵　　1727 om. P　　βροτῶν Ω:
ἀνδρῶν OW (cum ἀμείβετ' W)　　1728 ὃς ἐπὶ om. vel ante μοῦσαν transp.
Π⁵　　1729 οὐράνιον Orχ: οὐράνιόν τ' ω+: τ' οὐράνιόν τ' r: οὐρανόν
τ' Sa: ουρανον[Π⁵: οὐράνιος Burges　　1730–2 nescioquot verba om.
Π⁵　　1730 ⟨μειξο⟩ add. Wilam.: παρθένου omisisse Π⁵ et spurium esse
coni. Haslam　　1731 αἴνιγμα συνετὸν r　　1732 omisisse Π⁵ et spurium
esse coni. Haslam　　1733 α.δω Π⁵: ἀοιδῶν Vrʸᵖ, ʸᵖΣᴹⁿ　　1734 τάδε
σ' fere BV²+: τὰ δὲ σ' ω　　ἀπέμενε Sa　　1737–66 del. Kampfhenkel
(monente Kirchhoff), Wilam.; nihil post 1736 scripsisse vid. Π⁵; inde a 1740
omnia spuria iud. olim Hartung, a 1743 Pohlenz, a 1744 Robert, a 1747
Hartung　　1739 ἀπαρθένευτος G　　1740 Oed., 1741 Ant. trib. Ω: Ant.
continuat Z, cf. BᵐᵃʳᵍVᵐᵃʳᵍ τινὲς καὶ τοῦτο τῆς ἀντιγόνης　　φεῦ φεῦ
LT　　1741 συμφορᾶς MOr　　1743 ἐγὼ ⟨σῶν⟩ Matthiae (⟨σοῦ⟩
Musgrave), cf. ᵖΣ: ἐγὼ Ω: ἔγωγε T: ἐμῶν post Brunck Nauck

ΦΟΙΝΙΣΣΑΙ

ὃς ἐκ δόμων νέκυς ἄθαπτος οἴχεται
μέλεος, ὅν, εἴ με καὶ θανεῖν, πάτερ, χρεών,　　1745
σκότια γᾶι καλύψω.
Οι.　πρὸς ἥλικας φάνηθι σάς.　　1747
Αν.　κόρον ἔχουσ’ ἐμῶν κακῶν.　　1750
Οι.　σὺ δ’ ἀμφὶ βωμίους λιτὰς –　　1749
Αν.　ἅλις ὀδυρμάτων ἐμῶν.　　1748
Οι.　ἴθ’ ἀλλὰ Βρόμιος ἵνα τε ση-　　1751
κὸς ἄβατος ὄρεσι μαινάδων.
Αν.　Καδμείαν ὧι
νεβρίδα στολιδωσαμένα ποτ’ ἐγώ
Σεμέλας θίασον　　1755
ἱερὸν ὄρεσιν ἀνεχόρευσα
χάριν ἀχάριτον εἰς θεοὺς διδοῦσα;　　1757
Οι.　ὦ πάτρας κλεινῆς πολῖται, λεύσσετ’, Οἰδίπους ὅδε, 1758
ὃς τὰ κλείν’ αἰνίγματ’ ἔγνω καὶ μέγιστος ἦν ἀνήρ,
ὃς μόνος Σφιγγὸς κατέσχον τῆς μιαιφόνου κράτη,　　1760
νῦν ἄτιμος αὐτὸς οἰκτρὸς ἐξελαύνομαι χθονός.
ἀλλὰ γὰρ τί ταῦτα θρηνῶ καὶ μάτην ὀδύρομαι;
τὰς γὰρ ἐκ θεῶν ἀνάγκας θνητὸν ὄντα δεῖ φέρειν.　　1763

1744 νέκυς post ἄθαπτος transp. **r**Zb: post οἴχεται LZT　　1745 με om.
O　με κατθανεῖν **r**ζ　χρεώ MV²ʸᵖ　1746 σκότια Fᶜᵘᵛ, coni.
Hermann: σκοτία(ι) Ω　1750 et 1748 inter se transposui (1749 et 1747
inter se transp. post Burges Murray)　1750 om. R, in marg. post 1747
scr. R²　κόρους **r**　1749 ἀμφιβωμίους Elmsley (ἀμφιβωμίοις λιταῖς
Wecklein, quo accepto 1749 ante 1747 transp. Diggle)　1748 om., in
marg. scr. O　ἅλις ω+, Eust. 554, 34: ἅλις ἔχουσα **r**　ὀδυρμῶν
Eust.　ἐμῶν ω+, Eust.: ἐμοὶ χ, ᴾΣ　1751 Βρομίου Musgrave　ἵνα
γε χ　1752 μαινάδος B¹(corr. B²)**r**　1753 καδμείων **r**, fort. Bᵃᶜ　ὧι
M²B¹ᵖᶜV+: ὠὴ M¹**r**ζ: ἰωὴ O　1754 στολισαμέν- V²**r**ζ, ᴾΣ　1756
οὔρεσιν O**r**　1757 ἀχάριτον Hermann, Elmsley: ἀχάριστον Ω: ἄχαριν
T　δοῦσα ZbT　1758-63 del. Boeckh (1758-9 Valck., 1759 Porson)
1758 κλεινῆς **r**χ: κλεινοὶ ω+　ὅδε Ω: τάδε RʸᵖVrʸᵖ　1759 om.,
inter lin. scr. W　ἔγνω ω+, sch. Soph. OT 1525: ἔγνων V**r**, coni.
Musgrave　1760 κατέσχε P　1761 νῦν δ’ O**rz**　αὐτὸς om. O
οἰκτρὸς om. Pr　αὐτὸς οἰκτρῶς post Hermann Nauck　1762
ἀλλὰ γὰρ **r**χ: ἀλλὰ B²ˢ: ἀτὰρ ω+: om. gV

134

Χο.   ὦ μέγα σεμνὴ Νίκη, τὸν ἐμὸν   1764
      βίοτον κατέχοις
      καὶ μὴ λήγοις στεφανοῦσα.}   1766

1764–6 susp. Valck, del. Boeckh (cf. *IT* 1497–9, *Or.* 1691–3, *Hipp.* ad fin.
[V²A])   1764 σεμνὴ νίκη ω+, Eust. 476, 32 et Lucian. *Pisc.* 39*: σεμνὰ
νίκα Lucian.*   1766 λήγοις Ω(B²), test.: λόγοις B¹Sᵘᵛ

135

COMMENTARY

1–87: PROLOGUE-MONOLOGUE

An actor wearing the mask of an old woman (with hair shorn in the style of mourning) and dark robes emerges from the door of the skene (here representing a palace) and delivers a monologue more or less directly to the audience, closing however with a prayer that shows the character fully involved in the world of the play's action. The monologue is framed by invocations directed to the heavens, both of which feature the central theme of the speech, δυστυχία (3–4n.). Some critics (most notably L. Méridier, *Le prologue dans la tragédie d'Euripide* (Bordeaux 1911), *passim*) have found the speech cold and full of irrelevant touches; but it sets forth in a dignified, unself-pitying tone the background of the events of this day, all the more necessary because of the variety of the earlier mythic tradition and because of innovations in details or in their combination (see Introd. IV). Nor is the monologue detachable and dispensable for Euripides' purpose: apart from the information conveyed, the scene lays the groundwork for the portrayal of Jocasta's involvement and moral seriousness; without it the audience would be poorly prepared for her role in the agon (528–85) or for her final futile intervention and suicide (1259–83, 1427–59).

The order of the narrative is chronological, but the story is also structured by a group of parallels and repetitions. Just as the choral odes bring to light several parallelisms of incident and motif in the mythic history of Thebes, so the prologue intimates, at a number of levels, that there is a pattern or repetitiousness in the sufferings of the Labdacids. In each of the three generations a marriage is crucial (12ff., 53ff., 77ff.); the coming-of-age of the sons in the two later generations is described in similar terms (32, 63) and brings fateful action both times; crucial realizations occur at four points (23, 33, 50, 59); there are two attempts to circumvent the force of prophecy or curse (23ff., 69ff.), two refusals to give way (40, 75), two woundings with piercing instruments (26, 62), three references to naming (12, 27, 58). Some of these features are individually slight, but taken together and reinforced by later repetitions (see e.g. on 673 for the motif of 'joining' conveyed by συνάπτω), they seem to reflect a deliberate artistic purpose: the human characters are presented as enacting, blindly and with apparent freedom and responsibility, a coherent scheme of inescapable destruction (see also Introd. I, 33n., 49n., 86–7n., 413n.).

[1–2] The spuriousness of these lines is strongly indicated by external evidence, as was well shown by Haslam (1975) 149ff. (a) The ἀρχή of the play is given as line 3 in a collection of epitomes of Euripidean plays: cf. arg. 1 (a) (revised decipherment in Haslam). Even if these summaries do not go back to Dicaearchus,[1] the technique of ἀρχή-reference was present in Callimachus' πίνακες and presumably even earlier in the first Alexandrian attempts to collect and classify Attic tragedies. It is a permissible assumption that Callimachus and Aristophanes of Byzantium had reason to consider line 3 the ἀρχή of *Phoen*. (b) Two ancient copies (Π¹⁶ and Π¹⁷) now present the text beginning at line 3. (c) Line 3 is very strongly attested in the indirect tradition, and it was used in ways (e.g. by metricians) which suggest that it was the first line of the play.[2] Attestations of lines 1–2 are few and uncertain.[3] (d) The scholiast reports 'an ancient opinion' that Sophocles criticized Eur. for *not* prefixing lines 1–2 to the play. The cumulative force of these considerations has not been shaken by M. van der Valk, *GRBS* 23 (1982) 235–40 or Erbse, *Studien zum Prolog der euripideischen Tragödie* (Berlin 1984) 224–7.

Internally, there is nothing suspicious or unEuripidean about the content or language of 1–2 (see below), but when added to 3 they produce an odd heaping of participles in which the third phrase is somewhat otiose, and they create an aesthetic imbalance between the ornateness of the invocation and the matter-of-fact tone of the following genealogical narra-

---

[1] Haslam argued that they do; *contra*, J. Rusten, *GRBS* 23 (1982) 357–67, with whom I agree, despite W. Luppe in *Aristoteles Werk und Wirkung Paul Moreaux gewidmet* 1 (Berlin 1985) 610–12 (Luppe argues that identification of each epitomized play by ἀρχή would have been necessary only before a complete edition of Euripides was prepared; but the complete edition will have been available to very few readers, and the readers who were apt to use the epitomes were unlikely to have access to a complete edition, and so the identification would still have been useful to ensure that a reader intrigued by a summary could locate the genuine Euripidean play). See also R. Kassel, 'Hypothesis', in W. J. Aerts *et al.*, eds., *ΣΧΟΛΙΑ. Studia ad criticam interpretationemque ... D. Holwerda oblata* (Groningen 1985) 53–9; Luppe, *Anagennesis* 4 (1986) 37–8.

[2] An additional attestation has been adduced by C. Habicht, *GRBS* 31 (1990) 177–82 (an inscription from Pergamum, second cent. A.D.).

[3] The ornate language in *Eccl.* 1–2 mimics hymnal invocation in general or Eur.'s hymnal invocation in particular, but cannot be identified as a specific allusion to *Phoen.* 1–2. Discussions of fragment 1 of Accius' *Phoenissae*, a loose translation of Eur.'s opening, are inconclusive: Haslam believes Accius had only 3ff. before him, but Latinists have argued that Accius has modified 1ff. for various reasons: cf. Haslam, 133 n. 32; G. Paduano, *ASNP* ser. 3, 3 (1973) 827–35; J. Dangel, *Euphrosyne* 16 (1988) 71–86. Mueller-Goldingen, 39 n. 1, argues that Accius knew of a controversy about lines 1–2 and alluded to it by translating principally 3ff., but including a detail from 1–2.

tive. The latter is a subjective impression: some have instead seen a deliberate contrast between solemn, dazzling opening and dry narrative of woes. The ring-structure formed by invocation to Helios and final prayer to Zeus is present with or without 1–2.

The lines cannot be dated with any precision. The scholion commenting on them, as presently phrased, is probably of Imperial date (cf. Haslam (1975) 162 n. 48 on ὅτι μή and the optative ἐπιτιμήσειεν). The Hellenistic theory that ἄστρα means 'constellations' is of uncertain relevance (1n.). Eparchides (fourth or third cent. acc. to Jacoby; date unknown acc. to Page, *Further Gk. Epigr.* (Cambridge 1981), 129) quotes an epitaph ascribed to Eur. (Athen. 61A–B = *FGrHist* 437 F 2 = Page, *Epigr. Gr.* 478–81 or *Further Gk. Epigr.* p. 156): the first line is ὦ τὸν ἀγήραντον πόλον αἰθέρος ῞Ηλιε τέμνων, and if it were a little closer in form, one might speculate that the poem was foisted on Eur. because 1–2 were already in a text of *Phoen.* If the 'ancient opinion' of the Σ was not an invention of an earlier critic faced with explaining two versions of the text (see 264n. for scholiastic invention), it may reflect a comedy modelled on *Frogs*, an imaginative biography or literary-critical dialogue, or a spurious letter written as a rhetorical exercise (one of the extant pseudo-Euripidean letters is addressed to Sophocles).

1 ἄστροις If the intended meaning is 'you who cut your ⟨annual⟩ path amidst the ⟨zodiacal⟩ constellations' (as Haslam insists), then the lines cannot be earlier than the Hellenistic age, for learned Alexandrians used ἄστρον to mean 'constellation' (Call. fr. 110, 64; Aratus, *Phaen.* 414, 436, etc.; cf. Nonnus' usage, Peek, *Lex. Dion. Nonnos* s.v.), and ancient grammarians proclaimed a distinction between ἀστήρ = 'star' and ἄστρον = 'constellation' (Σ*Il.* 5.5; the lexica cited by Schwartz in his apparatus on Σ*Phoen.* 1 and by van der Valk on Eust. 446, 43ff. on *Il.* 4.75). But this distinction has no basis in etymology (cf. *LfgrE* s.v.) or in classical usage, and a few scholars knew the doctrine was wrong (the scholiast Achilles on Aratus, p. 51, 11ff. Maass; Galen 17:1, p. 16 Kühn). Furthermore, not even in learned Hellenistic use does ἄστρα mean specifically *zodiacal* constellations (Σ1 misuses *Phaen.* 543, where 'zodiacal' is supplied by the context). The Alexandrians may have arrived at their peculiar usage by incorrect interpretation of a lost passage (or even of the present passage, not yet a part of *Phoen.*?) or borrowed it from the technical language of astronomers and astrologers (J. Egli, *Heteroklisie im Griechischen mit besonderer Berücksichtigung der Fälle von Gelenkheteroklisie* (Zurich 1954), 37–9). The intended meaning must, however, be 'you who cut your ⟨daily⟩ path amidst the stars'. The Greeks knew that the stars were in heaven even by day, obscured by the sun (Hesiod, *Op.* 417–19; Heraclitus 22 B99 D–K, on which see D. R. Dicks, *Early Greek Astronomy to Aristotle* (Ithaca 1970), 49; Thuc. 2.28); and, *pace* Haslam, passages such as *Hel.* 1095–6 (πρὸς οὐρανὸν ... ἵν' οἰκεῖς ἀστέρων ποικίλματα), *Or.* 1684–5, *Trach.* 1106, *Phoen.* 1006 do imply that both the gods and the stars are located in the heavens by day as well as by night.

οὐρανοῦ may be taken with ἄστροις, as *Septem* 401 (cf. epic formula οὐρανὸς ἀστερόεις; *Prom.* 1049–50 τῶν οὐρανίων ἄστρων διόδους, Critias *TrGF* 43 F 19.33 ἀστρωπὸν οὐρανοῦ δέμας), but is less otiose with ὁδόν, 'heavenly path', cf. 842 below ἄστεως ὁδός, *Prom.* 394 οἶμον αἰθέρος, and probably *Or.* 1003–4 κέλευθον οὐρανοῦ.

τέμνων ὁδόν a poetic metaphor derived, it seems, from epic τέμνειν πέλαγος / κύματα *Od.* 3.174–5, 13.88 (itself a metaphor from ploughing), via ἠέρα τέμνον *Hom.h.Dem.* 383 (cf. Richardson *ad loc.*). ὁδόν is abstract acc. of result, as is κέλευθον in *Andromeda* fr. 124.3. Contrast prosaic τέμνειν ὁδόν = 'build a road' with concrete acc. of object effected.[1]

2 χρυσοκολλήτοισιν 'inlaid with gold'; this epithet is chiefly responsible for the elevated tone of 1–2. Eur. could have used such a formation: χρυσόκολλος Soph. fr. 378, Eur. fr. 587, -κόλλητος *Rhes.* 305, Antiphanes fr. 105.2 and 234.2 K–A. On the Greek poets' fondness for compounds which are *apparent* derivatives of denominative verbs cf. Wilam. on *Her.* 290; Diggle on *Phaethon* 263; Hopkinson on Call. *Hymn* 6.124. Tragic idiom affects elevated epithets in χρυσ(ε)ο- + verbal root in -τος, and in late Eur. the second element is often recherché (*Or.* 840 χρυσεοπήνητος, *IA* 219 χρυσοδαίδαλτος, both lyric).

3–4 *Phoen.* begins with an invocation of Helios as an appropriate witness and sounding-board. An invocation is a convenient and traditional rhetorical device for initiating a prologue-speaker's rhesis or other monologue (e.g. *Prom.* 88ff., *Alc.* 1, *Andr.* 1, *El.* 1), but an address such as this may also reflect a true tendency of the Greeks to share their deepest feelings with the elements (*Med.* 56–8; Barrett on *Hipp.* 601). It is also traditional for a human prologue-speaker to begin with the motif of πόνοι / δυστυχία to set the mood for the whole play (*Ag.*, *Trach.*, *Or.*), and with the contrast 'formerly fortunate, now wretched' *Andr.*, *El.*, Eur. *Antigone* fr. 157, 158; *Cycl.* has a burlesque version featuring both invocation and πόνοι-motif). Here the theme is given emphatic position in 4 and recurs in the admonition with which Jocasta ends her speech. This opening is also like that of *Med.* in another way: *Med.* has an explicit syllogism involving an ἀρχὴ κακῶν, here there is an implicit contrary-to-fact condition – 'had you not

---

[1] The idiom of Hdt. 7.124 and 9.89.4 is different: Schwyzer II.112 is correct against LSJ and J. E. Powell, *A Lexicon to Herodotus* (Cambridge 1938).

shed your rays on that first day of Theban misfortune, none of this would have followed'.

3 Ἥλιε initial dactyl in a proper name, with word-end after the dactyl, is not uncommon in Eur. (cf. 456 Γοργόνος, 758, 1588 Αἵμονος / -ι), and for Ἥλιος so placed see Fraenkel, *Ag.* comm. II.8 n.2, Diggle on *Phaethon* 3. See also on 39-40.

θοαῖς ἵπποισιν same instrumental dat. phrase in *IT* 2; in poetry, teams of swift horses are commonly feminine, 'a question not of sex but of gender' – Barrett on *Hipp.* 231.

εἰλίσσων here of revolution (cf. *Her.* 927, *Hel.* 1362, *Or.* 1379) rather than rotation (*Her.* 868, *Phoen.* 1186), 'carrying on a circular path', as *Prom.* 1091-2 ὦ πάντων αἰθὴρ κοινὸν φάος [sc. ἡλίου] εἰλίσσων, *IA* 1571 (Artemis-Selene) τὸ λαμπρὸν εἰλίσσουσ᾽ ἐν οὐρανῶι φάος. The sound-echo in Ἥλιε . . . εἰλίσσων perhaps verges on etymological play.

4 Θήβαισι L here offers Θήβηισι; on dat. pl. -ηισι/-ηισι in Eur. see Barrett on *Hipp.* 101; other instances listed in *Text. Trad.* 177 (add 91 Cr ἱκεσιήισι), including in lyric 674, 1066, 1570.

5 Κάδμος Although genealogical detail is a mannerism of the Euripidean prologue, there are some cases in which we can see a tailoring of the genealogy to the specific needs of the play. In *IT*, where Iphigenia begins with Pelops and his violent marriage, she later recalls her own 'marriage' in similar terms (214-17), and Pelops' spear plays a clinching role in the recognition scene (822-6). In *Or.*, however, her sister begins with Tantalus, whose crime bears some relation to the 'sick' use of speech and argument in that play and whose punishment is evoked in Electra's aria (982ff.). In *Phoen.* the choral odes and the very identity of the chorus throw emphasis on the continuity of past and present misfortunes, and Cadmus' 'first day' provides the most ancient prototype of Theban misfortune in general and of fratricidal battle in particular (638-89n.). Hence his position at the head of the prologue's genealogy.

6 ἐναλίαν Hdt. 2.49.3 indicates that Cadmus was known to fifth-century Greeks not only as Phoenician, but as specifically Tyrian; hence, although ἐνάλιος at times means no more than 'sea-fringed' (*IA* 165, cf. *Hel.* 1130), the audience would here understand 'his sea-girt land'.

7 Harmonia, daughter of Aphrodite and Ares (Hes. *Th.* 937) and attendant of her mother along with the Horae and Charites (*Hom.h.Ap.* 195) or Pothos and Peitho (Aesch. *Su.* 1041), is a figure without well-known mythology or attributes, except in relation to Cadmus (marriage: 822-3n.; exile: *Ba.* 1332). As a personification of civic concord and unity she goes well with Cadmus the city-founder (cf. Vian, 141-3).

8-9 The genealogy is the same as that in Hdt. 5.59 and *OT* 267 (implicit also in Hes. *Th.* 978); but in *Ba.*, in a different field of Theban

143

legend, Cadmus has no male issue. For pronominal τοῦ with φῦναι in a prologue genealogy cf. *IT* 4, *Or.* 11 (with γίγνεται fr. 14.2).

10–12 παῖς μὲν ... καλοῦσι δ' μὲν ... δέ ... as if ἔφυν μὲν ... ὄνομα δέ μοι ... (so rightly Wecklein; cf. the pattern of naming-triplets, 288–90n).

10 κλήιζομαι Active κλήιζειν = 'celebrate, glorify' can have the weaker sense 'say with pride' (*Med.* 836, *Her.* 340); passive = 'be renowned as' can be equivalent to the copula spoken with a sense of pride (*IT* 917, *Hyps.* 1.iv.26) or be weakened even to a colourless copula (*Or.* 1402, perhaps *Ion* 234). The tone of the context suggests that κλήιζομαι should not be given too strong a sense here.

Μενοικέως this name was probably present in early epic, but is first extant in *Her.* 8 (though ascribed to Aesch. in fr. dub. 488). In *Her.* M. is father of Creon and grandfather of Megara (Creon is father of Megara already in *Od.* 11.269, cf. *Scutum* 83). Unlike later mythographers, the poets seem to have kept separate the compartments of Theban myth (Heracles-legend and Labdacid-legend) in which the pair Menoeceus–Creon was found.[1] The upper reaches of the stemma lead to the Spartoi in both traditions (*Her.* 7–9 is vague; Σ942 gives the stemma Echion–Pentheus–Oclasus–Menoeceus). See Robert, *Oidipus* 1.168, 11.65–6; Vian, 183ff.

[11] With some reluctance I bracket this line as spurious, influenced more by the addition of the not-altogether-clear evidence of Π¹⁶ to the traditional arguments than by force of those arguments *per se* (these were first framed by Geel, though he emended and Paley was the first to delete). Although Π¹⁷ must have had a full line here, Π¹⁶ is incomplete: Haslam reported the papyrus as vacant after κρεωνδ'αδελφοc (the words would then appear to be a gloss on its way to becoming an interpolated verse [428n.]; δ' would either be an addition to the original gloss or be present because the whole phrase was borrowed from 47), but a re-examination shows traces of ink (9 letters?) before the vacant area (Bremer and Worp, 258). This gives some support to the view of defenders of the line that Π¹⁶ may present us with an isolated testimony of physical damage in its *Vorlage*. The internal arguments are: (a) the line is detachable; (b) the connection with τ' is loose and informal (instead of παῖς μὲν ... ἀδελφή τε ... there is a mild anacoluthon: cf. Pearson); (c) Creon is identified as brother in 47, which is therefore assumed to be the first mention of him; (d) from μητρὸς ἐκ μιᾶς some infer that the line might deny Menoeceus' paternity; (e) textual variation in the second half of the line has been deemed suspicious.

---

[1] A possible exception arises if P.Oxy. 44.3317 is really from Eur. *Antigone*: see Luppe, *ZPE* 42 (1981) 27–30 for an argument that the fragment is from *Antiope*; *contra*, Scodel, *ZPE* 46 (1982) 37–42.

(a), (b), and (e) are weak grounds. Repetition of relationship (c) occurs elsewhere in prologues: *Phoen.* 12, 35; *Andr.* 4, 6; *Hec.* 3, 30–1; *El.* 9, 13; *Ion* 28, 36–7. As in *Ion* the brotherly relationship is mentioned a second time to explain why Hermes performed the favour for Apollo, so in *Phoen.* 47 the repetition could explain why Creon has the authority to do what he does. 'Of the same mother' (d) implies nothing about the father (either in general or in this context where Menoeceus has been named as a father and the mother has not been named): it merely emphasizes the closeness of the kinship-tie (cf. *Il.* 19.293, ὁμομήτριος in Xen. *Anab.* 3.1.17; 156n.). Critics who wish to defend line 11 may point to the importance of the kinship-motif in the play (see Introd. I), may argue that δ' in Π¹⁶ is more easily explained if Π¹⁶ descends from a version with a full line in which physical damage obscured the end of the line (and caused variation in the tradition?), and may object to the jingle κλῄζομαι / καλοῦσι which occurs when 11 is removed.

μιᾶς = τῆς αὐτῆς (156n.). If 11 is spurious, the phrase μητρὸς ἐκ μιᾶς was probably borrowed from 156; if the line is retained, the echo contributes to emphasizing the kinship-motif.

12–13 τοῦτο . . . ἔθετο if this clause is meant to underline divergence from traditions in which Oedipus' mother was Epikaste and his (second) wife Euryganeia (so Σ), it is odd that Eur. bothered with the detail. It may be present rather for the sake of parallelism with 57–8 (1–87n.). For the phrase, cf. *Od.* 18.5 (Irus/Arnaeus) τὸ γὰρ θέτο πότνια μήτηρ (also *Hom.h.Dem.* 122).

13 γαμεῖ the so-called 'registering' use of the present indicative, as often in tragedy to describe relationships of kinship, marriage-tie, inhabitation, and the like. Cf. Wackernagel, *Syntax* I.162–5; Schwyzer II.272; Rijksbaron (1991) 1–4.

14 χρόνια predicative and equivalent to an adverb (here 'for a long time'), as usual (Kannicht on *Hel.* 345).

λέκτρα 'having my marriage-bed in the house' is a bland way of saying 'sleeping with me as husband with wife'; cf. *Ion* 304 χρόνι' ἔχοντ' εὐνήματα and the more direct *Ion* 64 χρόνια . . . σπείρας λέχη. λέκτρα is used in many tragic periphrases for marriage and intercourse and sometimes comes to mean 'intercourse' (*Ba.* 958) or '(female) sexual partner' (*Andr.* 928, *Hel.* 572, fr. 520.2).

16 παίδων . . . κοινωνίαν 'shared possession of male children for the house', not 'union producing male children' (Craik); 'for the house' because males inherit and carry on the family. The sharing is between Laius and Jocasta, not between Laius and the offspring. The best parallel is Plato *Symp.* 209c πολὺ μείζω κοινωνίαν τῆς τῶν παίδων πρὸς ἀλλήλους οἱ τοιοῦτοι ἴσχουσι καὶ φιλίαν βεβαιοτέραν, ἅτε καλλιόνων καὶ ἀθανατωτέρων παίδων κεκοινωνηκότες (cf. *Laws* 722D, where παίδων κοινωνίαν καὶ γένεσιν is a hysteron-proteron). Children are a bond or pledge between man and wife: cf. Orestes as κύριος πιστωμάτων *Ag.* 878; Aesch. fr. 99.6 παίδων δ' ἐζύγην ξυνάονι; Lys. 1.6 ἡγούμενος ταύτην [birth of a common child] οἰκειότητα μεγίστην εἶναι; Dion. Hal. *Ant.Rom.* 4.79.2 (of Tarquinius' murdered wife) γυναῖκα σώφρονα καὶ τέκνων κοινωνὸν γεγονυῖαν; for the pledge gone wrong, cf. Jason and Medea. Laius' request implies that he wants a legitimate heir and that he is a loyal husband concerned for Jocasta's childlessness as well as his own (contrast *Ion* 817–20).

παίδων forms of παῖς and τέκνον intrude upon one another against the metre in 22 (FSa), *Med.* 1311 (BD), 1313 (D). Here and in 18 metre does not decide, and in 18 the variation is ancient. Cf. 1428n.

17 Θήβαισιν perhaps a true dative indicating possession (Schwyzer II.153; cf. on 88 πατρί), but the construction overlaps with locative dat. used with verbs of ruling, leading, etc. (Schwyzer II.169).

18 μὴ σπεῖρε the tense conveys 'do not be continually trying to sow'.

τέκνων ἄλοκα 'the furrow from which children are born'. Overtranslating or bowdlerizing, LSJ gives 'wife' for ἄλοξ here and *OT* 1211; but the ploughing metaphor applied to procreation is used in the marriage-formula παίδων ἐπ' ἀρότωι and is otherwise common (Tucker on *Septem* 753 (his 739); J. Taillardat, *Les Images d'Aristophane: études de langue et de style* (Paris 1962) 119, 171–2), and metaphor is typical of oracular utterance.

20 βήσεται δι' αἵματος either vividly 'will make its way through blood' (cf. *Hcld.* 625 'excellence makes its way through toils') or more mildly 'will be involved in bloodshed, will experience a bloody fate' on the analogy of διὰ φιλίας (ἔχθρας, etc.) ἰέναι (ἐλθεῖν, μολεῖν, χωρεῖν; for βαίνειν cf. 1561 δι' ὀδύνας ἔβας), an idiom well discussed by Barrett on *Hipp.* 542–4. Some translate 'will perish through bloodshed', but the sense 'go off, disappear, perish' is normally confined to the perfect stem βέβηκα, and other tenses approach this sense only because of an accompanying participle (*Il.* 1.391, 2.302) or epithet (*OT* 832 βαίην ἄφαντος).[1]

21 ἡδονῆι ⟨'ν⟩δούς so Markland (along with ⟨'κ⟩δούς); cf. the paraphrase of this line in sch. Arist. *Acharn.* 243a (p. 43, 1–4 Wilson) Λάϊος ἐνδούς (v.l. ἐκδούς) ἑαυτὸν μέθηι. The intransitive/absolute use of normally transitive verbs is more common with compounds than with simplicia (K–G 1.90–6, Schwyzer II.219–20); cf. in particular Plato *Phdr.* 250E (of procreation) ἡδονῆι παραδούς, Thuc. 3.37.2 οἴκτωι ἐνδῶτε, and *Tro.* 692 ἐνδόντες τύχηι (where, however, αὐτούς is present in 693 as obj. of the main

---

[1] Exceptions seem to be confined to epic: *Il.* 2.339 and 8.229 of oaths and promises going unfulfilled; the obscure passage *Il.* 17.392.

verb). Many keep simplex δούς, and Wilam. on *Her.* 200 cites it as *Musterbeispiel* for διδόναι = *preisgeben* used without expressed object, while K–G 1.92 falsely notes for this use 'häufiger dicht[erisch]'. But if δούς is true, it is bold and unique in classical Greek. Thuc. 4.108.4 is not another example (cf. Classen: οὗ μὲν ἐπιθυμοῦσιν is object), nor is Plut. *Mor.* 547A ('it is to be permitted to these men', not 'one should give oneself over to these men'); Josephus *AJ* 17.332 is plausibly restored as διδοὺς δέ τι τῆι ἐλπίδι (τι A¹, τῆι A² rell., τι τῆι Niese) on the basis of the parallel passage *BJ* 2.106. δούς is present in Π¹⁶ and was imitated by Philostratus *Vit. Soph.* 1.12 (496) ἡδοναῖς ἐδεδώκει; cf. Plut. *Publ.* 13.4 δόντα τῆι ῥύμηι of a charioteer giving in to horses out of control (ἐνδόντα coni. anonymus). Prodelision of ἐν except after μή, ἤ, ἦ, ἦ is rare, but not unexampled: Eur. *Su.* 69 is a secure case, though in a number of other passages 'ν or 'ν- has been conjectured unnecessarily or much less securely. Cf. M. Platnauer, *CQ* 10 (1960) 140–4; Diggle, *Studies* 33; Fraenkel and Denniston–Page on *Ag.* 431.

βακχείαν conjectured by von Arnim (45), the truth barely survives in Fᵃᶜ. The meaning 'revelry under the influence of wine' can be obtained only from the *nomen actionis* βακχεία (*Choe.* 698, *Ba.* 232), not from βακχεῖον. The latter is either substantivalized adj. with τέλος or ἱερόν understood (so Arist. *Frogs* 357; cf. Plut. *Ant.* 90.3, Aristides *Smyrn.* 230, 17 Jebb (2, 24 Keil = 1.373 Dind.), and see Dodds on *Ba.* 126 for the alternate form βάκχια) or a noun in -εῖον corresponding to *nomen agentis* in -εύς and verb in -εύω (cf. A. Debrunner, *Griechische Wortbildungslehre* (Heidelberg 1917) ¶290; Chantraine, *Formation des noms* ¶48; Schwyzer 1.470). As a noun, it has three legitimate meanings: (1) place related to Bacchic activity, as Hesych. βακχεῖον· τελεστήριον; perhaps *Phoen.* 228 (see *ad loc.*) and Arist. *Lys.* 1 (but ἱερόν or τέλος could be understood, as in line 2); (2) instrument related to Bacchic activity, e.g. Hesych. βακχεῖον· ... νάρθηξ; (3) a group devoted to Bacchic activity, a thiasos, e.g. Diod. 4.3.3 βακχεῖά τε γυναικῶν ἀθροίζεσθαι and two inscriptions cited in LSJ s.v. 2a (F. Poland, *Geschichte der griechischen Vereinswesens* (Leipzig 1909) 68, adds an Attic example, Dittenberger, *Syll.*² 737 (2nd cent. A.D.)); Et. magn. 453, 57 s.v. θίασ{μ}ος (cf. Kannicht on *Hel.* 173–6 for repersonified abstracts in -εῖον or -ήριον).

22 σπείρας βρέφος βρέφος has been suspected for several reasons, and some emendations also seek to eliminate σπείρας, but the objections are less than conclusive. (1) βρέφος was defined by Aristophanes of Byzantium (an authority περὶ ὀνομασίας ἡλικιῶν: frr. 37–219 Slater) as τὸ ἄρτι γεγονός (fr. 37), and 'beget a new-born babe' would be odd (hence Wecklein's σπείρας γόνον). But Eur. sometimes uses the word as a (pathetic?) substitute for παῖς (*Andr.* 722 and *Tro.* 1165 of Astyanax, who can talk, sing, walk, etc.; *Tro.* 557 of children who can cling to their mother's robes). (2) σπείρας βρέφος after ἔσπειρεν ... παῖδα is not an intolerable repetition (cf. *Ion* 16 τεκοῦσ' ἐν οἴκοις παῖδ' ἀπήνεγκεν βρέφος), but may be a deliberate effect of narrative linkage in which the main action of a sentence is resumed in a participial phrase leading off the next sentence, here with *variatio* of the object-noun. This technique is typical of simple (Ionic or Ionicizing) narrative styles (Homer and prose), but sometimes occurs in tragedy (e.g., *Her.* 33, *Hec.* 25–6, 369; *OT* 1404, *OC* 982–3; cf. *Prom.* 468–9, *Choe.* 760ff., *Septem* 177–8): see W. A. A. van Otterlo, *Untersuchungen über Begriff, Anwendung, und Entstehung der gr. Ringkomposition* [Med. Ned. Akad. Wet., Letterkunde, n.R. 7:3 (Amsterdam 1944)] 21–31, esp. 21 n.2 and 23. Thus σπείρας is certainly sound, though Diggle (1990a) finds βρέφος vacuous and notes that the use of repeated participle alone is idiomatic (for repeated object, *OC* 982–3, with emotional force). (3) Appearance of the same word at the end of 22 and 25 is not necessarily suspicious: von Arnim, 35–7, lists eighteen passages from only four plays in which the same word appears at line-end with only one or two verses intervening; see also Di Benedetto on *Or.* 1128–9 (same word ending consecutive verses); Jackson, *Marg. Scaen.* 220–2 (indifference to repetition in various positions); Diggle on *Phaethon* 56. But it is unusual that the shared obj. of participle and main verb is expressed twice. There is one parallel, *Trach.* 1193–7 χρὴ τοὐμὸν ἐξάραντά σε / σῶμ' ... σῶμα τοὐμὸν ἐμβαλεῖν, on which Kamerbeek notes 'the repetition ... is very natural in this strict and emphatic instruction'.[1] If the repetition is sound here, it may be due to the intervention of the participial phrase with different object in 23, and βρέφος in 25 may also be pathetic. If emendation is deemed necessary, I prefer to emend in 25 (e.g. Camper's πατήρ). Emendations here, such as σπείρας, φρενός, create a punctuation-break after the 10th element of the trimeter, which is very rare in Eur.: Denniston (1936); in *Phoen.* only 1233 and 1318 (and perhaps 697).

23 γνούς ... τὴν φάτιν either a slight zeugma 'recognizing his error and understanding (the full import, the applicability of) the god's saying' or hendiadys of the two nouns 'recognizing his error through application of the god's warning'. φάτις is often an oracle or other weighty saying, as *OT* 151 Διὸς ἁδυεπὲς φάτι.

24 λειμών' ... λέπας by hendiadys 'to the sacred meadow of Hera on the rocky mountain Cithaeron'. By synecdoche λέπας can refer to an entire rugged mountain rather than a bare crag of rock (Dodds on *Ba.* 677–8; Stevens on *Andr.* 295). Mountain-peaks or whole mountains are often sacred to one or more gods, and for sacred meadows cf. *Hyps.* i.iv.20

---

[1] Wunder removed the repetition by deleting *Trach.* 1195–8.

(Zeus), *IA* 1463 (Artemis; cf. *Hipp.* 73ff.), and the similar, often metaphorical, use of κῆπος, and in general A. Motte, *Prairies et jardins de la Grèce antique: de la religion à la philosophie* [Mémoires de l'Acad. roy. des sciences ... Classes des lettres, 2ᵉ série, 61:5 (Brussels 1973)] 1ᵉ partie. Hera Cithaeronia was prayed to before the battle of Plataea (Plut. *Arist.* 11.3), and a primitive image at Thespiae is mentioned by Clemens Alex. *protr.* 40P = cap. IV, 46.3 (35, 19 Stählin): cf. Schachter, *Cults of Boiotia* 1.242–4. But the site of her meadow is unknown, and Paus. 9.2.4 tells us that no one knew where on Cithaeron Oedipus was exposed. Motte, 111–12, makes the attractive suggestion that the meadow of Hera was a site of the hierogamy of Zeus and Hera (their union has various locations in Greek myth; Cithaeron is involved in a story of their reconciliation after a quarrel: different versions in Paus. 9.3.1–8, Plut. apud Euseb. *praep. ev.* 3.1.6). Bethe, 8–10 (rejected by Robert, *Oidipus* 1.165), speculated that mention of Hera here is a remnant of a version in which Hera Gamostolos punishes Laius for his pederasty (see Introd. V). Exposure in a meadow on a mountain is, however, a standard motif of heroic myth (Motte, 194–7, cites Paris, Asclepius, Ion; Iamos, not on a mountain).

25 βρέφος 22n.

26 Paley was the first to delete this verse; Fraenkel gives the fullest statement of objections. The grounds for suspicion are inadequate. (a) διαπείρω is hapax in tragedy and perhaps in classical Greek (but cf. *Il.* 16.405 διὰ δ' αὐτοῦ πεῖρεν ὀδόντων), although πείρω and ἀναπείρω are found in early poetry, the latter also in *Rhes.* 514 (ἐμπείρας codd., corr. edd., cf. Hsch. α 3775 ἀμπείρας· διχάσας) and Arist. *Acharn.* 796, 1007. (b) The syntax of διαπείρω here 'is without precedent in Attic Greek' (Paley); but the construction is obvious and has adequate analogies. (c) μέσων with δια- is semi-redundant; but tragic style often affects fullness of expression. (d) There is a factual contradiction between σιδηρᾶ κέντρα and χρυσοδέτοις περόναις 805 (which refers to piercing of feet, not blinding of eyes: see *ad loc.*). Fraenkel considers this most significant; but since it is known that the tragedians allowed inconsistencies of minor detail, esp. in regard to matters in the past or off-stage, he postulates a special rule for prologues whereby the poet 'jede Mitteilung einer Tatsache genau bedenken [wird] und wird späterhin nichts bringen, das mit einer ausdrücklichen Angabe des Prologs im Widerspruch steht'. Against this *petitio principii* at least two Euripidean examples can be cited: at *Hel.* 5 Proteus' palace is on an island, later this fact is forgotten (*Hel.* 460, 1039–42; Kannicht follows Dingelstad in deleting 5, Dale on *Hel.* 460 does not); at *Ion* 16 Creusa is said to have borne her child ἐν οἴκοις (also 344, 898–9), but in 948–9, for pathetic effect, the birth is located κατ' ἄντρον (the couplet was deleted by A. Wiskemann, *de nonnullis locis Ionis fabulae*

Eur. (Marburg 1872), 33–4, but editors have rightly not followed him).[1]
It is the scholarly reader (or scholiast) who notices and worries about such
details; in performance such inconsistencies are of no importance. If Eur.
wrote both 26 and 805, each epithet was intended to have its own effect
in context: iron is cold and sinister (350n.) and goes well with the brutality
of διαπείρας and κέντρα (normally connected with animals and used for
pricking, not piercing); in late Eur. lyric, with its 'pretty' style and paradoxical combination of violence and imagery of luxuriant beauty, the more
ornate epithet is suitable at 805.

σφυρῶν ... κέντρα διαπείρας the usual construction of πείρω and
its compounds is with acc. of the person (or part of body) and instrumental
dat. (thus with διαπείρω Plut. *Art.* 14.2, cf. Luc. 59.38, but not Paus.
10.5.3, a paraphrase of our line); but *Il.* 16.405 διὰ δ' αὐτοῦ πεῖρεν ὀδόντων
could be interpreted as 'Patroclus [subj. of the preceding and following
verbs] drove (the spear) [understood from ἔγχεϊ 404] through his teeth',
an exact' parallel for the construction here,[2] and διαπείρω with acc. of
implement (ὀβέλους, βελόνην) and prepositional phrase is found in late
medical writers and Iamblichus (TLG). Even without Homeric precedent
and later parallels, διαπείρας is being used in an obvious way as a colourful
substitute for διίημι (cf. 1091–2 ξίφος λαιμῶν διῆκε), and in general verbs
of striking and transfixing have two possible constructions: *Il.* 13.518 ὁ δ'
Ἀσκάλαφον βάλε δουρί vs. 5.346 χαλκὸν ἐνὶ στήθεσσι βαλών; *IT* 1430
σκόλοψι πήξομεν δέμας vs. *Od.* 11.129 γαίῃ πήξας εὐῆρες ἐρετμόν (cf.

---

[1] Less certain is the case of *IT* 41, 72, 623–6, 725–6, 1154–5: the second
passage implies that the human sacrifices take place outside the temple,
the others imply or are consistent with the notion that the sacrifice is
carried out inside (as the cremation of the victim certainly is); Monk
deleted 41 (which occurs in a difficult passage in which some interpolation is likely), but the inconsistency may perhaps be felt even without 41
and would serve dramatic goals (horror of Orestes and Pylades at 72;
convenience of movements inside and outside to the recognition and
intrigue). Other kinds of inconsistencies and misdirections are also found
in prologues: the oracle in *Phil.*; an oath demanded in Soph. *El.* 47 is not
later given (673ff.); Aphrodite's δείξω δὲ Θησεῖ πρᾶγμα (Barrett on
Hipp. 42); Apollo's plan for recognition of Ion by Creusa, *Ion* 71–3.

[2] For our purpose here it does not matter that the epic poet may have
intended 'Patroclus pierced [absolute] (with the spear)' or 'and (the
spear) pierced [intransitive] through his teeth'. The normal pattern in
description of fatal wounding is 'A struck B in part X of his body with
weapon Y; Y (subj.) did certain damage; B (subj. or obj.) collapsed
dying'. But *Il.* 16.401–10 is not a simple example of the pattern in any
case.

Schwyzer ii.155–6, 160); likewise, in later Greek, both ἐμπείρω and περιπείρω (cf. LSJ).

σφυρῶν   although Eur. uses σφυρόν in lyric (*Alc.* 586, *IA* 225) by synecdoche for 'foot' (cf. Pindar *I.* 7.13), he uses it in its literal sense in *Ba.* 936, and I see no reason to think the use here is anything but literal (*pace* Dawe on *OT* 718). The puncture is located between ankle-joint and Achilles tendon, as in *Il.* 22.396–7: 42n.

μέσων σφυρῶν ... μέσων is the normal way to say 'middle of the ankles'; μέσων is in Π¹⁶ (coni. Reiske) and was probably discovered as a variant by Triclinius. Since Kirchhoff, most editors favour μέσον, assuming μέσων to be a Byzantine correction (but not Jebb on *OT* 718). But if μέσον is a substantive, the double acc. with δια-compound is difficult (1092n., 1394n., 1398n.), and σφυρῶν μέσον is abnormal idiom: the anarthrous substantive with dependent gen. occurs only in Homeric locative μέσσωι and after prepositions (ἐς, ἐν). If it is instead an adverb 'in the middle' there are a few parallels: *Or.* 983 and *Rhes.* 530 [μέσα for metre] (both lyric, both equivalent to ἐν μέσωι + gen.); *Il.* 12.167 σφῆκες μέσον αἰόλοι (*Od.* 14.300 [a ship ἔθεεν] μέσσον ὑπὲρ Κρήτης: understand πέλαγος?). But why, in trimeters, would Eur. (or anyone else) prefer this to idiomatic μέσων?

27   If 26 is deleted, then 27 must go with it. But the case against 26 is not cogent, and 27 alone has been deleted by many since Valckenaer's rambling indictment. It is true that etymological interpolations are present in *Hel.* 9b–10a and *Tro.* 13–14 (the former, I think, surely non-histrionic, the latter possibly so), and that some critics believe in a family of ὅθεν-interpolations (von Leutsch (1870) 447: 'Lieblingswort des Fälschern'; Page, *Actors' Interp.* 26); but the specific faults alleged here are nugatory. (a) The etymology is not explained, as it is in Sen. *Oed.* 812–13. But Seneca writes Latin; the explanation is self-evident in Greek.[1] (b) Eust. 650, 39–51 on *Il.* 6.403 contrasts unfavourably the etymologizing of Hesiod with the subtle technique of *Phoen.* 805 (taken by Eust. as alluding to Oedipus' name). *Pace* Valckenaer, this implies nothing about the authenticity of *Phoen.* 27. (c) ὅθεν in general and causal ὅθεν in particular are alleged to be rare in Eur. (Valck.; Fraenkel, 12 n.1). The fact is that ὅθεν and ὅθενπερ occur more than thirty-five times in Eur., and there seem to me to be ten or eleven instances in which the antecedent of ὅθεν is the whole previous sentence and the meaning is 'as a result of which' or 'from which source' or 'for which reason', sometimes shading into a temporal sense 'after which' (not recognized by LSJ, K–G, Schwyzer): *Su.* 894, *IT* 35 (temporal?),

---

[1] Varro *de ling. lat.* 7.82 has a perceptive remark on the need to clarify an etymology translated from the Greek.

1366, *Ion* 24, *Phoen.* 43, 322 (causal/temporal?), perhaps 1065, *Or.* 816 (temporal?), 995, 1001, *IA* 587. For ὅθεν introducing an etymology in a context never suspected of interpolation, cf. Aesch. fr. 313 χλιδῶν τε πλόκαμος ὥστε παρθένοις ἁβραῖς· ὅθεν καλεῖν Κουρῆτα λαὸν ἥινεσαν. (d) For νιν in consecutive verses, cf. *Hec.* 265–6, *Hel.* 537–8, *Andr.* 1031–2 (lyric), and twice in three verses *Andr.* 294–6, *Ba.* 286–8, etc. (e) The name was given by Merope, and ὀνομάζω is oddly used, according to Valckenaer. But ὀνομάζω with collective noun as subject means 'call by the name of', 'know by the name of' (*Hcld.* 87, *IT* 1452, *IA* 281), not 'assign the name' (as in 58 below, *Ion* 661, etc.), and Ἑλλάς = Ἕλληνες is attested at *Hcld.* 219, *Andr.* 304, 681 (note ὄντες in 682 agreeing κατὰ σύνεσιν), *Her.* 222, etc. (on the metonymy see K–G 1.12; Breitenbach 177–8). (f) Valckenaer's question why the Corinthians are not the subject of ὠνόμαζεν rather than Hellas may imply some disquiet about the imperfect tense, which at first glance seems more suitable if Oedipus is dead or if the line is an annotation; but see below. For anyone still inclined to delete, the line must have entered the text earlier than Diodorus' use of the prologue (4.64.1).

27 Ἑλλάς Oedipus was famous throughout the Greek world (*OT* 8); cf. ἐπίδειξις Ἑλλάδι (871 n.).

ὠνόμαζεν either the imperfect has the force 'knew him by the name Oedipus (when he was famous as conqueror of Sphinx and king of Thebes)' (Diggle), or this is an extension of the special imperfect of naming ('assign the name') used where we might expect an aorist. For the latter cf. Fraenkel on *Ag.* 681, Lloyd-Jones, *CR* 15 (1965) 242 n.1 on Soph. *Inach.* fr. 269c.18 (σ' ἐθρόει); *Naupactia* fr. 1; Pindar, *P.* 2.44; Eur. *Su.* 1218, *Cycl.* 692, *IA* 416, fr. 2. *Hcld.* 87 has a similar imperfect: 'By what name did the people of Mycenae call you (when you were living there)?' or simply 'By what name did they call you?' For another unusual imperfect, cf. ἔτικτε 289n.

28 ἱπποβουκόλοι perhaps a Eur. coinage, since several ancient sources who explain the word cite Eur. (Pollux alone cites Soph., perhaps in error: fr. 1149a). Since Hesych. glosses the acc. pl., this will not have been the only appearance of the word. It is a mark of royal wealth to have herds of horses (cf. *El.* 623), and I follow the usual view that ἱπποβουκόλοι are horse-herders (the -βου- being frozen or generic); Craik believes they are cowherds on horseback, Greek 'cowboys'.[1]

---

[1] The literary and epigraphic evidence for ancient 'cowboys' is post-classical in date and refers only to rodeo-style stunts (jumping from horse-back to tackle a bull by the horns: ταυροκαθάψια); the earliest artistic evidence for the stunt is on Thessalian coins of the last third of the fifth century (C. M. Kraay, *Greek Coins* (London 1966) pl. 148, no. 466). See P.

Πολύβου a figure known in myth mainly for the marriages of his daughters and for his role in the Oedipus-legend: *RE* 21 (1952) 1584–92. Both his city and the name of his wife are variously reported, and Eur. here avoids identifying either by name.

30 τὸν ἐμὸν ὠδίνων πόνον ἐμόν for ἐμῶν by a frequent form of enallage involving a possessive adj.: cf. K–G 1.263; V. Bers, *Enallage and Greek Style* [Mnem. Supp. 29 (Leiden 1974)], 23. Perhaps ὠδίνων πόνον is viewed as a single concept, 'labour-pain-product' = 'child' (but Bers, 5, criticizes such explanations). See also the commentators cited by Diggle on *Phaethon*, p. 177. It is unclear whether ἐμόν in the mss is Moschopulus' emendation or a reading discovered by collation and properly adopted in his circle: *Text. Trad.* 90. πόνος is sometimes used as abstract for concrete to mean the thing produced through hard work: μελισσᾶν ... τρητὸς πόνος (honeycomb) Pindar, *P.* 6.54; τεκτόνων πόνον Aesch. fr. 357, *Or.* 1570, *Pers.* 751–2 πλούτου πόνος οὑμός (in *Ag.* 54 πόνον ὀρταλίχων ὀλέσαντες is best taken as abstract). Eur. here extends the usage to a child, with the precedent ὠδίς = 'child' *Ag.* 1468, cf. *Her.* 1039–40 ἄπτερον ... ὠδῖνα τέκνων, etc. The whole phrase carries a muted emotion, for it implies that another woman knew the pleasant toil of nursing the baby which Jocasta should have had (cf. *Ion* 961–3). In tragedy, esp. Eur., it is customary to evoke the emotional bond between mother and child by referring to the pain of childbirth and the act of nursing: e.g. *Ag.* 1418, *Choe.* 896–8, Eur. *Su.* 920, *Ion* 319, *Phoen.* 355, 1434, 1527, 1568.

31 ὑφεῖτο use of the middle for a human mother's nursing is an adaptation of Homeric active ὑφίημι = 'put young (animals) to the mother's teat' (*Od.* 9.245, 309, whence Theocr. 4.4) and is not attested elsewhere.[1]

πόσιν πείθει τεκεῖν 'persuaded her husband that she had given birth ⟨to my child⟩': for indirect discourse inf. after active πείθω = 'convince that' cf. Hdt. 3.155.4, 4.154.2, Xen. *Mem.* 1.2.49, *Rhes.* 838. As in many such stories, the adopting mother has herself just given birth,[2] either to a child who dies (Hdt. 1.112) or to a female which she is willing to exchange for a male, and the substitution may be made without the husband's

---

Vigneron, *Le Cheval dans l'antiquité gréco-romaine* 1 (Nancy 1968) 216–18. There is no evidence for the practical use of horses in routine herding of cattle, but if this existed, it was presumably in the open plains of Thessaly and not in southern Greece.

[1] I doubt that ὑποβάλλομαι used of supposititious children is based on this image, as LSJ suggest.

[2] Craik thinks instead of lactation without previous parturition, needlessly, I think, and implausibly (this phenomenon will have been just as rare or impossible in the ancient world as it is in the modern world).

knowledge: cf. Stith Thompson, *Motif-Index of Folk Literature* rev. edn
(Bloomington, Ind. 1955–8) K1920ff. ('substituted children'), esp. 1923.5;
also L100ff. ('unpromising hero') for nurturing a maimed child. Wonder-
ing how the woman could pass off the injured baby as her own without
the husband's knowledge, Nagel proposed τρέφειν, needlessly removing
the folklore-motif. Eur. is free to give as little detail as he wishes about such
a matter, and if the audience troubles itself (as it normally does not do) to
fill in other details of the story, it must do so in some way which respects
the details provided. For other cases of scholarly worry about the details
Eur. did not give, cf. 51–2n. and 62n.

32 πυρσαῖς γένυσιν the first growth of a Greek youth's beard is
typically referred to as πυρσός (Gow on Theocr. 6.3); cf. 63n.

ἐξανδρούμενος as a factitative verb (ἀπ-) /(ἐξ-) ἀνδρόω is more common in aorist or perfect (Schwyzer 1.727 ¶3; Ernst Fraenkel, *Griechische
Denominativa in ihrer geschichtlichen Entwicklung und Verbreitung* (Göttingen
1906) 108). If the present here has the expected progressive or inceptive
meaning, the sense is 'when my son was already beginning to be marked
by the yellowish-red cheeks of early manhood' (cf. Hdt. 1.123.1 'as Cyrus
was coming to manhood'?). But the part. may be 'timeless', equivalent to
ἐξηνδρωμένος, as apparently in Arist. *Knights* 1241 τέχνην δὲ τίνα ποτ' εἶχες
ἐξανδρούμενος (cf. Soph. *El.* 1344 τελουμένων εἴποιμ' ἄν, 'after the deed is
done'; Stevens on *Andr.* 998).

33 The polar contrast τινος μαθών πάρα lends retrospective precision
to γνούς so that it conveys ἀφ' ἑαυτοῦ γνούς. Vagueness about the motivation puts the emphasis on the result itself, which contributes to the impression that the human agents are willy-nilly fulfilling a divine scheme (cf. 49
and 413n.).

34 φύσαντας οἱ τεκόντες is far more common in Eur. than οἱ φύσαντες;
hence Posidonius' (or Strabo's) τεκόντας is a trivialization.

36 μαστεύων μαθεῖν the parallelism (with *variatio*) with ἐκμαθεῖν θέλων
34 is deliberate. Like Pindar, Eur. uses for metrical convenience either
μαστεύω (*Hec.* 754, *Hel.* 597, and in anapaests *Telephus* 147 fr. 1, 8 and 11
Austin) or ματεύω (Soph. has the latter only; for Aesch. cf. West's Teubner
praefatio xlviii). ματ- is often corrupted to μαστ-: 416 below, *Ag.* 1094, etc.
The origin of the error ἰδεῖν/ἰδών is unclear.

37 εἰ μηκέτ' μή appears in indirect questions with εἰ here, *Eum.* 468,
612 (both εἰ ... εἴτε μή) and in Arist. (prose uses both μή and οὐ).

ξυνάπτετον πόδα here only 'X and Y meet', elsewhere συνάπτειν τινι
πόδα is 'X meets Y'; the same flexibility of usage is found in συνάπτειν
μάχην (*Alc.* 502 vs. *Hcld.* 831) and συνάπτειν λέκτρα (*Phoen.* 49 vs. *Her.*
1316–17). Eur. is fond of the verb in any case, but repetitions within this
play seem significant (673n.).

38 ταὐτὸν ἄμφω juxtaposition of semi-redundant words to give rhetorical weight to a contrast (esp. a quantitative one) is a favourite device of Greek style (Fraenkel on *Ag.* 1455, Kannicht on *Hel.* 731–2; Fehling, 281).

Φωκίδος probably adj. with ὁδοῦ rather than partitive gen. noun (sc. γῆς) in locative use (as Schwyzer II.114). The 'Split Way' (or 'Triple Crossroads', *OT* 730) of Phocis connects Daulis (NE), Delphi (W), and Lebadeia, Thebes, etc. (SE): see Paus. 10.5.3–4 with Fraser's comm. (v.231–2 and map X in vol. VI); Robert, *Oidipus* I.82–92. The partitive gen. ὁδοῦ indicates that the name applies to the neighbourhood of the crossroad (cf. *OT* 800–1 τριπλῆς ὅτ' ἦ κελεύθου . . . πέλας). Cf. 42n.

40 Ὦ ξένε although this address is polite enough, the brevity of the command and the dignified allusive plural τυράννοις (K–G I.18; not quite 'the royal entourage', as Craik translates) suggests an imperious tone which, coming from a driver, might offend a young prince. The line-initial dactylic-shaped word or word-group is very rare in Aesch., Soph., and early Eur., but not uncommon in late Eur. (cf. Cropp and Fick, 32–5, shapes 2.1aD and 2.2aD); in *Phoen.*, in addition to the four instances with proper name (3n.), cf. 576, 776, 887, 984, 1179, 1314, 1619, 1639, 1701.[1]

μεθίστασο present rather than aorist imperative solely for metrical reasons, as in *Alc.* 1122; on aspectual distinctions in the imperative cf. 1530n.

41–2 νιν . . . τένοντας object of the whole and of the part: see Wilam. and Bond on *Her.* 162.

τένοντας . . . ποδῶν since the horses wound the back of Oedipus' ankles (for τένοντες = 'Achilles' tendon' cf. *Il.* 22.396, *Med.* 1166, *Ba.* 938, *Cycl.* 400; the gloss of M τὰ ἐπάνω τῶν ποδῶν is incorrect), it is clear that Laius, travelling more swiftly in a chariot, overtakes Oedipus, who is going in the same direction. Eur. does not (and need not) tell us by what route Oedipus has reached this point. In *OT* 794ff. Oedipus has already received his oracle and, leaving Delphi, meets Laius head-on. The difference of Eur.'s version heightens the participants' ignorance, making Oedipus' action more plausible psychologically and the fateful meeting itself more pathetic. The specific wound mentioned here is, I think, intended to recall the earlier wounding of Oedipus by Laius.

---

[1] Some of these lines are suspected by various critics; it is interesting that the same metrical characteristics occur both in the unsuspected and suspected portions of the play. If Fraenkel's deletions were accepted, the remaining text of *Phoen.* would be rather stricter than its contemporaries in this phenomenon.

ἐξεφοίνισσον   a rare compound, also found in *IT* 259 (which I would retain, emending 258) and later in [Aristot.], *Physiognom.* 812a37.

43 τί . . . δεῖ λέγειν;   a rhetorical gesture which emphasizes the unpleasantness of the story in the eyes of the speaker (cf. *Or.* 14, 16).

τἀκτὸς τῶν κακῶν   some take κακῶν as object of ἐκτός ('that which lies outside the sad issue' – Pearson; cf. Craik's 'matters irrelevant to the disaster'), but for that sense I would expect the singular τοῦ κακοῦ. Others assume, rightly I think, a partitive gen.: τἀκτὸς κακά would include the brawl and the killing of Laius' attendant(s); Jocasta views the whole episode as one of κακά but will mention only the essential point of patricide. For such use of ἐκτός cf. Theocr. 10.9 τῶν ἔκτοθεν (Gow: 'matters unconnected with his work' (i.e. with the specific function of the ἐργάτης)) and ἐκτός = 'foreign, external' (LSJ s.v. ΙΙ).

44–5   presentation of the spoils to Polybus is also in Antimachus, *Lyde* fr. 70 Wyss (from Σ44) and Peisander (Teubner, arg. 11); τροφεῖ implies that the gift is payment of τροφεῖα (θρεπτήρια in Antimachus). The detail may derive from an epic source, but it is also typical of Eur. to attend selectively to small details to project a sense of realism (Oedipus could not arrive in Thebes with Laius' chariot).

45 ἐπεζάρει   apparently 'attack, vex', for we cannot be sure exactly what this word meant to Eur. *Rhes.* 441 (ἐπεζάρει restored with certainty for ἐπεζάτει) makes it probable that the verb itself has a violent sense (here reinforced by modal ἁρπαγαῖσι). The word must have been extant in at least a third passage, since Hesych. glosses the form ἐπεζάρηκεν.[1] The ancient theory that the word is Arcadian (Eust. 381, 19ff. and 909, 28ff., Hesych. s.v.)[2] is not supported by analogy: ζέρεθρον = βάραθρον and ζέλλειν = βάλλειν would support ἐπιζερέω not ἐπιζαρέω (M. Lejeune, *Traité de phonétique grecque* (Paris 1947) ¶38; Hoffmann, *Gr. Dialekte* I.102). The etymology provided in Σ (ζάρος ὄρνεόν ἐστι ἁρπακτικόν) is probably a scholiastic fabrication.[3]

46 ἁρπαγαῖσι   cf. 1021, 1066.

47   The reason for the intrusion of δ' (already Π¹⁷ˢ) is unclear (a mere slip ΔΑΔ for ΑΔ?), but the text without δ'/τ' is likely to be correct. Apodotic

---

[1] Herwerden conjectured ἐπιζαρεῖ in *IT* 987.

[2] For a rare dialect-word used in trimeters, JD points to *El.* 625 ἔροτιν (alleged to be Aeolic or Cyprian).

[3] Chantraine and Frisk leave the word unexplained; J. Pokorny, *Indogermanisches etymologisches Wörterbuch* I (Bern 1959) 501, follows Hoffmann's suggestion of a root related to ζῆλος, ζῶρος, etc. (*erregt sein, bestrafen, rächen*).

δέ and repeated δέ after an ἐπεί-clause are very rare in tragedy (Denniston, *GP²* 179, 183; Dawe, *Studies* I.258–9), and the few examples are not closely parallel: δέ at the start of a new stanza after a long temporal clause (*Ag.* 205 (*Septem* 750 variant)); δέ with a resumptive demonstrative (ὥσπερ ... ὡσαύτως δέ Soph. *El.* 27, *Trach.* 116, as in prosaic examples).

κηρύσσει two constructions are combined: (1) 'proclaim publicly' with object λέχη, the prize (as in invitations to a sale or contest, e.g. *Aj.* 1240); (2) 'announce', here with indirect statement object[1] ὅστις ... τούτωι ξυνάψειν λέκτρα (cf. *Hel.* 1491ff. καρύξατ' ἀγγελίαν ... ὅτι) rather than the more usual inf. of command.

48 σοφῆς ... παρθένου both cleverness and unmarried status are standard allusive clues in reference to the Sphinx (806, 1023, 1042, 1506, 1730–1; *OT* 1199). Eternal virginity is probably a token of her dreadful appearance and powers (as for the Erinyes, *Eum.* 69–70, *Aj.* 835).

αἴνιγμα ... μάθοι cf. 50 μούσας ... μαθών, 1506 μέλος ἔγνω, 1731 αἴνιγμ' ... εὑρών, *OT* 393–4 αἴνιγμ' ... διειπεῖν; to understand, recognize, discover, or tell fully a riddle is to solve it because αἴνιγμα includes both the riddling statement and its hidden meaning; only a person who has the correct interpretation really knows the riddle.

49 πῶς another event essential to the fulfilment of the family's fated ruin is presented in language which seems to deny full recognition by the human character of the destined pattern (cf. 33n.). τυγχάνει itself need not imply chance or randomness (Gomme–Sandbach on Men. *Mis.* 230), though such periphrasis frequently has the effect of denying to the subject a full intentionality or full awareness of the ramifications of the action conveyed by the participle (e.g. *Andr.* 76 πατὴρ ἔτ' ἐν Δελφοῖσι τυγχάνει μένων: Neoptolemus is unaware that his remaining absent is so harmful to his son).

50 μούσας in the mss the prosaic αἴνιγμ' has ousted the truth. The riddle was in verse (hexameter in the known versions: Introd. IV), and the poets often allude to the Sphinx as singer: 807 ὠιδαῖς, 1028 μοῦσαν, 1506–7 μέλος ... ἀοιδοῦ; *OT* 36 σκληρᾶς ἀοιδοῦ, 130 ποικιλωιδὸς, 391 ῥαψωιδὸς ... κύων, 1200 χρησμωιδόν.

51–2 Fraenkel deletes both lines (as already von Leutsch (1870) 447, *PhilAnz* 8 (1877) 478–9). Line 53 could easily follow 50, but the argument that the kingship is not explicitly mentioned in 47–9 proves nothing against mention of kingship between 50 and 53: the audience will easily infer not

---

[1] The ὅστις-clause can be taken ἀπὸ κοινοῦ with κηρύσσει, as in *El.* 33 χρυσὸν εἴφ' ὃς ἂν κτάνηι.

a contradiction of the previous information, but a natural supplement to it.[1]

Eur. presumably wrote either 51 or 52, not both: the tautology is too great. Diodorus read line 52 when he used the prologue of *Phoen.* as his main source in 4.64–5, for he uses ἔπαθλον; and the lexicographic research[2] which lies behind the note of Σ παρ' οὐδενὶ κεῖται τὸ ἔπαθλα ἢ μόνωι τῶι Εὐριπίδηι probably reflects Hellenistic scholarship of an even earlier date.[3] On the other hand, Π17 (of *c.* 100 A.D.) has line 51 but not 52. Since *ex hypothesi* one line was written to substitute for the other, the existence of a witness like Π17 does not determine which line is spurious (it cannot be claimed that every ancient text will either have had the genuine line only or have carried the dittography, as a scholarly text would do). We are left, then, to weigh the intrinsic merits or defects of each line. Many (e.g. the editor of Π17 and Haslam (1976) 52) believe it decisive that ἔπαθλον is otherwise attested only from the time of Diodorus onward;[4] but

---

[1] Mueller-Goldingen, 45 n. 12, rejects Fraenkel's fallacious argument, but still deletes because he thinks the solution of the riddle and the marriage should not be separated by any intervening detail. He regards 51 as a verse interpolated for added clarity and 52 as a competing addition made by someone who knew 51 to be suspect.

[2] Aristophanes of Byzantium and Didymus are both known to have studied tragic vocabulary (Pfeiffer, *Hist. Cl. Schol.* 197, 278), but an observation of this kind could also have appeared in a *hypomnema* or some individual *zetema*. Aristophanes seems to have referred to prose writers as well as poets in his lexical studies, but of course any such statement about usage would have been based on *surviving* literature or on *surviving* works by the canonical authors.

[3] Same doctrine in sch. Dem. 4.5 (#33 Dilts) ἔπαθλα δὲ οὐχ εὕρηται, εἰ μὴ ἅπαξ παρ' Εὐριπίδηι; for ἔπαθλον as Koine vocable, Pollux 3.143 καὶ τὰ μὲν ὀνομαζόμενα ὑπὸ τῶν πολλῶν ἔπαθλα ἆθλα καλοῖτ' ἂν κοινῶς ἐπ' ἀμφοῖν [both athletic and musical competitions] καὶ νικητήρια καὶ ἐπίχειρα καὶ γέρα.

[4] The word was not used in 1262 (see *ad loc.*). As far as surviving texts go, TLG confirms the scholiast's παρ' οὐδενί (of those before Diodorus; if the word is due to an interpolator, it may still be an attestation two or three centuries earlier than Diod.). We cannot be sure how much literature the ancient lexicographer examined. οὐδείς can mean 'no other ⟨known and studied⟩ author' (Σ*Tro.* 448; Arist. Byz. hyp. Or. παρ' οὐδενὶ κεῖται ἡ μυθοποιία (no other poet? or equivalent to παρ' οὐδετέρωι, as in hyp. Eum., Alc., Med., 'in neither of the other two tragedians'?)); for omission of ἄλλος cf. K–G II.304 Anm. 4; the fuller παρ' οὐδενὶ ἑτέρωι occurs in the life of Soph., ¶1 (cf. οὐδενὶ ἄλλωι sch.

Eur. is the first to attest many words and meanings which reappear in later poetry or later prose (within the prologue cf. 26 διαπείρω, 42 ἐκφοινίσσω, 63 σκιάζω), and of serious poets he is the most likely to have adopted a colloquial or vulgar word which was avoided by other poets and even by classical prose authors. Since ἔπαθλα is possibly, but not decisively, suspect, other factors need to be weighed. (1) 51 contains ὅθεν, alleged by Valckenaer to be a favourite of interpolators and to be rare in this causal sense. The latter claim is false (27n.), the former inconclusive. (2) We know that ἔπαθλα bothered some so much that they rewrote 52 to remove it.[1] Thus if 52 is genuine, there was a reason for the creation of 51 as a substitute for it. If 51 is genuine, there is no comparable reason for substituting 52. (3) 51 is flat, 52 more lively, using the metaphor of a prize in a contest, also present in 1048, 1728–9 (and cf. 47n. κήρυσσει, 1262n.). The choice is hard, but I am inclined to accept 52.

53 οὐκ εἰδὼς τάλας the phrase bears a separate emphasis, so that it is easy for the omitted verb (ᾔδει) of the next clause to be supplied from the participle (cf. *IT* 963: ἔλαβεν understood from λαβών 962).

54 συγκοιμωμένη only occurrence in extant Eur. (so too in this speech 26 διαπείρας, 28 ἱπποβουκόλοι, 60 ἀνατλάς, 64 ἀμνήμων in a passive sense; cf. 23 ἀμπλάκημα, 45 ἐπεζάρει, which occur in *Rhes.*).

56 κλεινήν τε Πολυνείκους βίαν this epicism is not found elsewhere in Eur. (Aesch. and Soph. use it) and probably lends special dignity to the phrase. Pol.'s epithet is the one implied by etymology to be appropriate to his brother (who here receives no epithet); this unequal treatment, like many other details of the first 442 lines, may be designed to counteract any

---

Call. Hymn. 2.38, p. 50 Pfeiffer). For the qualification ἢ μόνωι τῶι Εὐριπίδηι or (sch. Dem.) εἰ μὴ ἅπαξ παρ᾽ Εὐρ., cf. Moeris 191.23 Bekker (≈ Phrynichus 83 Fischer) ἀκμὴν οὐδεὶς τῶν Ἀττικῶν ⟨ἀντὶ τοῦ⟩ ἔτι, ἢ μόνος Ξενοφῶν ἐν τῆι Ἀναβάσει (4.3.26) (a disputed doctrine: Aesch. fr. 339a, Hyperides fr. 116, Menander fr. 715a); sch. *Od.* 24.1 Κυλλήνιος δὲ οὐδαμοῦ εἴρηται, εἰ μὴ ἅπαξ; sch. *Il.* 10.298b οὐ γέγονε νεκρῶν ἀναίρεσις εἰ μὴ ἅπαξ.

[1] For this cf. sch. *Il.* 3.54a ὅτι τινὲς μὴ εὑρίσκοντες κατὰ τὴν ποίησιν τὸν Ἀλέξανδρον κιθαρίζοντα μετέγραψαν κίδαρις. In the Homeric scholia, mention that a word or phenomenon is hapax is not invariably (or even in a majority of cases) associated with a suggestion of athetesis (see the index to Erbse's edition of sch. *Il.*); but two cases where athetesis is supported by reference to a hapax are sch. *Il.* 7.475a and 24.304a. In our case, it is possible that interest in ἔπαθλον as hapax arose in the context of a dispute about authenticity which was based on other grounds (e.g. textual variation), but this is not the only possibility.

unfavourable preconceptions an audience might have about the exiled brother.

57 τε corresponding to μέν 55 (Denniston, *GP²* 374ff.).

57–8 τὴν μὲν ... πατὴρ ὠνόμασε, τὴν δὲ ... ἐγώ the shared naming is a striking detail, perhaps implying harmony and almost equality of husband and wife, a notion reinforced by the balanced structure of 55–8 as a whole. Eur. seems to delight in the paradox of matter-of-fact familial loyalty, love, and harmony juxtaposed with patricide, incest (here the ominous παῖδας παιδί: cf. on 82), and fratricide. Naming was normally the prerogative of the father (cf. 12–13 above).[1] Ten days after the birth the father, presiding at the δεκάτη (LSJ s.v. 3) in the presence of relatives and guests, acknowledged legitimacy and assigned the name. Names often descended patrilineally, but sometimes the mother or the maternal family had influence: cf. Autolycus' naming of Odysseus (*Od.* 19.399ff.); Athenian Cypselus and Cleisthenes; Arist. *Clouds* 60–7 shows the humorous possibilities; also Dem. 43.74–8. See W. K. Lacey, *The Family in Classical Greece* (Ithaca 1968) 111–12, 172, 287 n. 83, 311 n. 128. Van Looy, 351, suggests that τὴν πρόσθεν Ἀντιγόνην is meant to convey an etymology; but although ἀντί is related to Latin *ante*, there is no evidence in the Greek tradition of the temporal meaning 'before' for ἀντί.

59 μαθὼν ... τἀμὰ λέκτρα μητρώιων γάμων 'learning that my marriage-bed was one of incest'; ὄντα is understood (Pearson on *Hcld.* 332; Diggle, *Studies* 12), with defining predicate gen.

60 Valckenaer complained that πάντα is inaccurate and noted that he would not miss the verse if it were absent, and a few editors subsequently bracketed it. But an explicit subject is needed here, and πάντα is used for rhetorical effect (cf. *Hel.* 53 ἡ δὲ πάντα τλᾶσ' ἐγώ; *Her.* 1250 ὁ πολλὰ δὴ τλὰς Ἡρακλῆς). ἀνατλάς, frequent in *Od.* and used once in each of the tragedians, is an epic reminiscence suitable to the enduring Oedipus of this play. If the tense of the participle is relative to the verb ἐμβάλλει, the sense is 'Oedipus, he who had already suffered all miseries, ⟨went even further and⟩'; but sometimes an attributive participle's tense is relative to

---

[1] The wishes of the mother were no doubt usually taken into account. *Od.* 8.552–4 mentions both parents (554 ἀλλ' ἐπὶ πᾶσι [sc. ὄνομα] τίθενται, ἐπεί κε τέκωσι, τοκῆες). When the mother gives the name elsewhere, special circumstances are usually involved: *Od.* 18.5 (Arnaeus/Irus named by his mother, presumably because he was a bastard whose father was not known; same formula in *Hom.h.Dem.* 122, where no such implication is present); Eur. fr. 2 (Theseus named by his mother in the absence of the father); Pindar *O.* 6.56–7 (Iamus; divine father absent).

the speaker or writer (Goodwin, *MT* ¶152), in which case the sense is 'Oedipus, the man who has ⟨in his life⟩ suffered all miseries'.

61 ἐμβάλλει φόνον the combination of this vivid verb with the abstract noun is quite unusual (concrete object such as ξίφος, χέρα is common; emotion instilled as object in ἐμβ. φόβον); such a combination could stand by itself in e.g. Senecan Latin, but in Euripidean Greek I think it virtually requires the amplification given in 62 (see below).

62 for a theatre-audience or normal reader, the question scarcely arises as to where Oedipus obtained golden fibulae to destroy his eyes (they are of course a convenient tool for such mutilation, as *Hec.* 1117 indicates). But the scholarly reader[1] is tempted to press too hard upon details which are ἔξω τοῦ δράματος: hence Zielinski's claim (*Tragodoumenon libri tres* (Cracow 1925) 32) that the fibulae reflect the version of *OT* in which Jocasta had committed suicide and that Eur. has here carelessly combined inconsistent sources,[2] and Fraenkel's claim that the verse is interpolated because Eur. cannot have been responsible for the 'inconsistency' of referring to the brooches taken from the corpse in *OT* when Joc. is very much alive. If one insists on recuperating from details in the text a fuller narrative of the past (flirting thereby with the documentary fallacy), it seems perverse to reconstruct an illogical or inconsistent story rather than to infer a self-consistent one (31n. and 51–2n.). Once interpolation is established to Fraenkel's satisfaction, he often suggests how the interpolator cobbled together his line from snatches of genuine verses. Such a suggestion should not be counted as an argument in favour of recognizing the interpolation; Fraenkel himself does not do so, though some critics have in some cases. Hence, I do not regularly comment on such suggestions. In general, the language and style of tragedy is 'formulaic' enough that similar expressions may genuinely occur without specific imitation or allusion. In this case, αἱμάξας κόρας is also found in *Hec.* 1117, but the coincidence in expression of the same idea in two plays written over a decade apart is not at all surprising (both words are favourites of Eur.). *OT* 1268–9 mentions χρυσηλάτους περόνας, but χρυσήλατος is a standard epithet of royal possessions, used in trimeters not only where there is some special point (*Andr.* 166, *Ion* 25) but also where no special point is apparent (*Hipp.* 862 and here).

63 γένυς . . . σκιάζεται as in 32 above, the first growth of beard marks

---

[1] So already the scholiasts devote inappropriate attention to minor details: e.g. Σ27, 31, 44, 71; cf. Elsperger, 17, 23–4.

[2] Similarly, Mueller-Goldingen, 47, who regards this detail, like Oed.'s incomplete trip to Delphi, as a passing allusion to the version in *OT* that Eur. does not care to integrate fully into his narrative.

the youth's readiness for manly pursuits: cf. *Od.* 18.269, the coming-of-age of Telemachus; Pindar *O.* 1.68 λάχναι νιν μέλαν γένειον ἔρεφον, coming-of-age of Pelops. σκιάζειν seems not to be used elsewhere in this sense until *Anth. gr.* 12.26.5 (Flaccus, first cent. B.C. or early first cent. A.D.); 309 below and *IT* 1151 are different. The audience is left to assume that between Oedipus' blinding and this point Creon was κύριος of family and city.[1]

64 κλήιθροις 'by means of closing-devices', 'by means of closed doors' (*Andr.* 951, *Hel.* 288, Arist. *Lys.* 264), here equivalent to 'behind closed doors'; cf. 114n.

ἀμνήμων passive 'forgotten' here only. Adjs. formed from verbal root and suffix -μων tend to be active in meaning; but alpha-privative derivatives of these can have active or passive meaning according to context (cf. ἀπήμων, ἀπράγμων; on flexibility of Greek compound adjs. in general see Barrett on *Hipp.* 677–9). The motive of the sons is shame, as Diod. 4.65.1 makes explicit; cf. in a humorous vein the family's shame in Call. *Hymn* 6.

65 πολλῶν δεομένη σοφισμάτων 'requiring many clever shifts to be forgotten'; 'to be forgotten' is understood from the context (for the full idiom cf. Heliod. 4.6.26 πολλῆς μὲν βουλῆς ὥστε πρεπόντως ἀνυσθῆναι, πολλῆς δὲ διασκευῆς ὥστε ἀσφαλῶς πραχθῆναι δεόμενον). The participle is perhaps concessive. With πολλῶν in emphatic position, the phrase probably marks the futility of the sons' attempt (cf. Tiresias' similar judgment of futility ὡς δὴ θεοὺς ὑπεκδραμούμενοι 873) rather than a desire to exculpate them, as Wecklein thought. σοφίσματα are cunning, often underhanded contrivances (1408, *IT* 1031, *Ba.* 30, 489); the noun occurs twelve times in Eur., only once in Soph. (of Odysseus, *Phil.* 14) and Aesch. (*Palamedes* fr. 181a), plus five instances in *Prom.*

66 ζῶν this detail is probably a surprise to the audience (see Introd. IV).

πρὸς δὲ τῆς τύχης νοσῶν either (a) 'mentally distraught because of this treatment' (with rare causal πρός as in *Ant.* 51, 170, *OT* 1236, Eur. fr. 682.2; τύχη = specifically 'what had just happened to him', rather than generally 'from ill-fortune', as Craik) or (b) 'although his affliction was the fault of fortune (he blamed his sons)' (with τύχη personified and common πρός of agency). In the latter reading Jocasta exculpates her sons, in the former Oedipus (if anyone). I prefer (a).[2] The weak position of παισίν in

---

[1] Mueller-Goldingen, 36, believes that Eur. here leaves open the possibility that Oed. continued to rule after his blinding until his sons imprisoned him; this would be a modification of the older sources in which, not blinded, Oed. ruled in Thebes after the death of Epicasta/Jocasta.

[2] This agrees with Tiresias' view in 874ff., but some doubt the authenticity of those lines and in any case an audience has not heard them yet when it hears 66–7.

67 hardly supports the antithesis that (b) requires, and 'mentally distraught' is more likely in this context than a colourless 'afflicted' (cf. 67 ἀνοσιωτάτας and 327–36).

67 ἀρὰς ἀρᾶται *figura etymologica* for emphasis; classified lists of examples in Eur. in J. E. Nussbaumer, *Die Figuren des Gleichklangs bei Euripides* (Sarnen 1938) 88–93.

68 both σιδήρωι and (δια)λαχεῖν are traditional in quotation or paraphrase of the curse (*Septem* 730, 788–9, 816–17). Cf. 350n.

70 κραίνωσιν on the meaning see Fraenkel on *Ag.* 369; D. Bain, *Actors and Audience* (Oxford 1977) 14 n. 1.

οἰκούντων ὁμοῦ gen. absolute with substantive understood from the context (K–G II.81, Schwyzer II.400–1; Headlam on Herodas 2.85; Diggle, *PCPS* 208 (1982) 57, 61), developed from passages like *Il.* 5.665–7, 15.190–1 (where it may be debated whether the original composer viewed the gen. as absolute). Other instances of masc. participles so used in tragedy: *Septem* 247 κυκλουμένων, *Ant.* 909 κατθανόντος, *OT* 506 μεμφομένων (neuter part.: *Septem* 274, Soph. *El.* 1344, *Andr.* 998, (*IA* 1022 corrupt)). As in *Ant.* 909 (and many prose exx.) the omitted noun is here definite; here it is also the same as the subject of the main clause (cf. in prose exx. the omission of pronoun referring to the subject of the previous sentence). Elmsley proposed dative οἰκούντοιν, comparing *Septem* 801–2 Οἰδίπου γένει κραίνων παλαιὰς Λαΐου δυσβουλίας; this could also be taken here as gen. (JD). If the gen. is correct, it gives the phrase more independence as the essential condition 'if they dwelt together'; if the plural is correct, it avoids additional emphasis on duality.[1]

71 νεώτερον on the relative age of the brothers see Introd. IV.

72 Πολυνείκη since no passage in Attic drama requires -ην for -η in a consonant-declension noun and since tragic style is conservative and Eur.'s own speech-habits were formed in the first half of the century, it may be assumed that Eur. always used -η, although -ην may have been making inroads in late fifth-century Attic (inscr. evidence first in the fourth century: Meisterhans³ 136 n.1192). Cf. Collard on *Su.* 928–9. Cf. 134n. for ἄρη.

74 ἐνιαυτὸν ἀλλάσσοντ' punctuation (before or after ἐνιαυτὸν) and construction (dual nom. or sing. acc. part.) have been variously interpreted, but the best rendering is 'with the two continuously exchanging a year ⟨of each condition: exile or rule⟩'. The sentence thus begins with dual ξυμβάντ', describes the separate assignments (71b–72 and 73), and returns

---

[1] Of eleven participles in -ντοιν extant in tragedy (TLG) 8 are accompanied by δυοῖν (δισσοῖν) and one by νῷν: exceptions *Or.* 1066, *OT* 1473.

to the dual ἀλλάσσοντ'. It is clear enough in context that Eteocles is the subject of 74b–75, despite the intervening dual participle. If ἀλλάσσοντα is understood ('Eteocles ... giving ⟨to Pol.⟩ in exchange ⟨for exile⟩ a year ⟨of sovereignty⟩'), the present part. is inappropriate (one would expect ἀλλάξοντ').

74–5 ἐπὶ ζυγοῖς ... ἀρχῆς the metaphor of ruler as helmsman is as old as *Il.* 4.166 ὑψίζυγος (Σ); cf. Fraenkel on *Ag.* 1617f.

75–6 The pact breaks down when Pol. returns at the end of the first year and is driven into involuntary exile; the latter is the exile referred to in 319 and 388–442. The ancient scholar (Σ71) who detected inconsistency in Eur.'s story and explained it by saying that Eur. followed Pherecydes in one scene and Hellanicus in another was careless and illogical (cf. Elsperger, 23–4).

77–8 accumulation of participles, as already in 32–4 and 69–74, but more noticeable because in such a short space; see Bond on *Her.* 700 and cf. *Hel.* 597–9.

77 κῆδος cf. 409ff.

78 ἀσπίδ' used for στρατόν, a metonymy borrowed from military language (Hdt., Xen.; cf. ἵππος = 'cavalry'). Eur. also uses λόγχη (442 below) and αἰχμή (*Held.* 276) in this way.

79 ἐπ' αὐτὰ ... τείχη τάδε the point of αὐτά is that after the marriage Pol. made no attempt to negotiate by emissaries or by mere threats that he would mount an invasion.

ἑπτάπυλα the seven gates are traditional in the story of the Seven and the Epigoni, and both ἑπτάπυλος and ἑπτάπυργος are standard epithets which serve as clues in antonomasia, as here. For the gates, see Appendix on Topography.

80 μέρη 'portions' of (inherited?) land or property, which for Pol. are inseparable from the kingship whose dignity their wealth supports (same pairing in 483, 601, and cf. 439–42n.). Without being a legal technical term, μέρος is used in legal contexts of the proportionate division of an inheritance (Dem. 48.6, cf. 41.11). The same connotation is seen in this play (esp. 603 τοῦ μέρους ἔχων τὰ πλείω) and elsewhere (*Ant.* 146–7 ἔχετον κοινοῦ θανάτου μέρος ἄμφω; Soph. *El.* 1135 τύμβου πατρώιου κοινὸν εἰληχὼς μέρος); but there is no need to enforce a legalistic consistency by emending to μέρος here and in 601 (Wecklein).

81 λύουσ' conative meaning of the present stem.

82 ἔπεισα Pol. refers to this persuasion as a source of uneasy confidence (272, 365); it later (451) appears that the persuasion was applied to Eteocles as well.

παιδὶ παῖδα the echo of 55 παῖδας παιδί may suggest the similarity or repetitiousness of the family's woes; incest and fraternal strife are expressed in like terms (συνάπτει, 673n.).

πρὶν ψαῦσαι δορός 'begin battle', like *Ba.* 304 πρὶν λόγχης θιγεῖν, both expressions unique to Eur. (Thuc. 5.61.2 ἅπτεσθαι χρῆναι τοῦ πολέμου is different.)

83 ἥξειν Pol.'s appearance on stage, probably a major innovation (see Introd. IV), is prepared for both here and in 170. The present line also prepares for the appearance of the old Servant which follows 87. This play has more than the usual amount of preparation for expected entrances: Pol. is also referred to in 258-60, just before his entrance; notice is given of the expected arrival of Tiresias and Menoeceus (768-70) and of Antigone with the corpses (1476-7); the chorus' suspicion that the duel is already over (1330-1) functions similarly as preparation for the arrival of the messenger at 1335; and there is an unusual announcement of the approach of the chorus (196-201n.). In a play with a large number of characters and frequent comings and goings, these details underline the logical concatenation of the complex action.

84-7 invocation of a god in his remote, eternally bright setting marks a heightening of pathos, and reference to that setting intensifies the natural human doubt that the god will deign to intervene and contrasts effectively with the dark immediacy of the human suffering. This is the first of three futile prayers for divine help in settling the dispute amicably (467-8, 586-7).

84 φαεννάς tragedy adopts φαεννός from lyric *Kunstsprache* rather than epic φαεινός (v.l. here, *Andr.* 1086, and fr. 119); only *Prom.* 537 has Attic φανός.

πτυχάς whether Eur. intended a form of πτύξ or of πτυχή was already unknowable to the Alexandrians, unless they had instances in which metre decided and which provided adequate grounds for extrapolation (Σ knew of no way to make an informed choice). But the exclusive use of dat. πτυχαῖς and the transmitted line-ending πτυχὰς ἔχων in Soph. fr. 144 suggest that Elmsley was right to argue that tragedy favoured πτυχαί in the plural (on the sing. see Collard on *Su.* 979; in disputing Elmsley's rule, Kannicht on *Hel.* 605-6 ascribes too much weight to the accents added in the mss tradition in the ninth century). οὐρανοῦ πτυχαί is a type of expression which appealed to (late) Eur.: cf. *Phaethon* 174, αἰθέρος πτ. *Hel.* 44, 605, *Or.* 1636. The connotation in these passages is of remoteness and invisibility or concealment: the sky is apparently viewed as having recesses or folds not obvious from an earthly perspective (or, as Kannicht on *Hel.* 44 suggests, the blue depths between and behind clouds gave this impression). Cf. perhaps Pindar *O.* 13.88 (Bellerophon on Pegasus) αἰθέρος ψυχρῶν ἀπὸ κόλπων ἐρήμου. Different images are conveyed by οὐρανοῦ / ἡλίου / αἰθέρος ἀναπτυχαί = 'open (unfolded) expanses' (Soph. fr. 956, *Hipp.* 601, *Ion* 1445) and ἡλίου περιπτυχαί = perhaps 'realms enfolded by the sun', 'open air' (*Ion* 1516). On the error πύλας see *Text. Trad.* 94; it probably results from graphic confusion, but psychological error is also possible ('gates of heaven': *Il.* 5.749, Luc. 21.33; from patristic Greek, Lampe cites *Testamentum Levi* 5.1, Gregent. *disp.* 4 (86.776D Migne)).[1]

86–7 It is typical of Euripidean characters in certain situations to adopt an admonitory tone toward the gods in the hope that the gods will behave with the wisdom and reasonableness which can be expected from the best sort of human being. This futile projection of human ideals upon intractable amoral powers is an essential element of Jocasta's personal tragedy, as it is for many of Eur.'s most pathetic figures.[2] For the condition εἰ σοφὸς πέφυκας addressed to a god, cf. *Her.* 655–6, *Hel.* 851 (also *IA* 1034 as emended by Diggle, *PCPS* 200 (1974) 33; JD also cites *Her.* 347, *IT* 570, *IA* 394a for divine wisdom or unwisdom). Here it is more a token of Jocasta's moral seriousness than an indictment of the gods' moral levity, for no further reference is made to Zeus' σοφία and the humans are otherwise shown to be ironically unaware of the fated pattern they fulfill. Contrast the more famous examples of 'nouthetetic' prayer or complaint: the servant's request in *Hipp.* 117–20 is implicitly denied in advance by the self-characterization of Aphrodite in the prologue; Orestes' protest in *El.* 971–2 is confirmed by that of the Dioscuri in 1245–6, 1296–7, 1302; Amphitryon's accusation of neglect in *Her.* 339–47 is ultimately proven by the cruel reversal which results from Zeus' disastrously incomplete rendering of aid.[3] Jocasta's admonition would be somewhat sharper in tone if Valckenaer's χρῆν were accepted (proposed on the basis of ὤφειλε in Athen. *leg. de Christ.* 5.1 (Eur. fr. 900, quoted 87n.).

86 δ' equivalent to γάρ (Denniston, *GP*² 169).

σοφός implying, as often in Eur., a correct moral stance (opposite of σκαιός, ἀμαθής). On the intellectualism of some Greek moral language cf. Dodds, 16–17; (on specific words) K. J. Dover, *Greek Popular Morality in the Time of Plato and Aristotle* (Berkeley and Los Angeles 1974) 116–24.

οὐκ ἐᾶν the negative goes with χρή but is postponed to give a different emphasis: 'you ought not (as you seem to be doing) to permit . . .'; Pearson well compares *Hipp.* 507, *Andr.* 214.

βροτῶν (accepted by Craik and Diggle 1990a) is more stylish than βροτόν and is prob. correct: cf. *Rhes.* 106–7 ἀλλ' οὐ γὰρ αὐτὸς πάντ' ἐπίστασθαι βροτῶν / πέφυκεν, Soph. *El.* 917 οὐχ αὑτὸς αἰεὶ δαιμόνων

---

[1] I do not accept West's αἰθέρος πύλαις in *Or.* 1631: 'Actors on High', 287 n. 15.

[2] Cf. 'Optimistic Rationalist'.

[3] Cf. *Hcld.* 718–19, *Her.* 1341–6, *IT* 389–91, *Hel.* 1097–106, 1441–50, *Ion* 436–51; see Dale, *Maia* 15 (1963) 312–13.

παραστατεῖ, *Choe.* 119 ἐλθεῖν τιν' αὐτοῖς δαίμον' ἢ βροτῶν τινα, *Andr.* 100 χρὴ δ' οὔποτ' εἰπεῖν οὐδέν' ὄλβιον βροτῶν.

87 τὸν αὐτόν even if βροτῶν τὸν αὐτόν is completely general, Jocasta must have in mind application to a specific individual (herself or Oedipus) rather than the whole Labdacid race. A reference to Oedipus, though it could be a token of her loyalty to her miserable son, is far-fetched after seventeen lines devoted to the brothers. By generalizing instead of referring to herself directly, Jocasta appears less 'selfish' in her complaint. For the sentiment cf. *Hel.* 1448 ὀφείλω δ' οὐκ ἀεὶ πράσσειν κακῶς, fr. 900 ὤφειλε δῆθεν, εἴπερ ἔστ' ἐν οὐρανῶι / Ζεύς, μὴ τὸν αὐτὸν δυστυχῆ καθίστασθαι, and the more common converse *Hcld.* 610–11 [φημι] οὐδὲ τὸν αὐτὸν ἀεὶ ⟨'μ⟩βεβάναι δόμον εὐτυχίαι; Hdt. 1.207.2 κύκλος τῶν ἀνθρωπηίων ἐστὶ πρηγμάτων, περιφερόμενος δὲ οὐκ ἐᾶι αἰεὶ τοὺς αὐτοὺς εὐτυχέειν. See also Introd. IV p. 26, n. 1 (on Stes. 204–8).

88–201: TEICHOSKOPIA

Several aspects of the structure and function of this scene are treated in more detail in the following sections (on authenticity and on metre); here it will suffice to make a few brief points and to consider the literary ancestry of the scene.

The scene is carefully framed by the speeches of the old Servant. These underline by repetition Antigone's eager interest and the Servant's concern for her sheltered virginal life; they also link the scene backwards and forwards by identifying the Servant as the man named at the end of Jocasta's speech and by announcing the approach of the chorus. Within this frame, the astrophic iambic/lyric amoibaion is much more informally structured: the initiative in pointing or questioning passes from the Servant to Antigone; the Seven are treated at various lengths and with a varying mixture of emotions. Apart from characterizing the initial state of Antigone (from which she will be forced to grow by later events) and adumbrating the justice of Polynices' cause, the scene advances the exposition by evoking the wider vista[1] of the beleaguered Theban landscape, the strength and fearsomeness (and partly ferocity) of the attacking army and its leaders, and the fear of the potential captives within the city. It also provides the variety of texture which is common to all tragedy but especially affected

---

[1] There are ten verbs of seeing in the scene, and the environs of Thebes are brought before the audience's mental eye by reference to the major mythologically defined topographic features of the place (Dirce, Hismenus, tomb of Amphion and Zethus, tomb of Niobids).

by late Euripides: after the sober iambic narrative of Jocasta comes a scene featuring excited actor's song and dazzling imagery.

Two literary precedents would probably have been present to the viewing audience as well as in the mind of the poet. Antigone's worried reaction to the sight of the encircling Argive army recalls the parodos of *Septem* with its portrayal of the near-panic of the young women at the sounds of the approaching Argives.[1] By transferring this expository function from chorus to Antigone, Euripides has freed his chorus for the singing of odes with a generally more detached, objective, and 'historical' perspective on the events of this day. But whereas in *Septem* sound is almost exclusively the medium of the chorus' awareness of the attack (the dust raised in the sky, 81–2, is the only visual evidence), Euripides here borrows from the teichoskopia of *Iliad* 3 the device of observing the enemy army from a high place and of creating a conversation between knowledgeable and unknowledgeable interlocutors. In *Phoen.* the roles are reversed between male and female, and of course this dialogue lacks the emotional and ironic resonances of Helen's self-reproach and the Trojans' ambivalent attitude toward her role as cause of the war. Helen's uncertainty about her brothers, whom she does not see among the Greeks, may, however, have suggested to Euripides the use of such a scene to establish Antigone's tie to Polynices and perhaps even the detail of her inability to see him clearly (see on 161).

AUTHENTICITY OF THE SCENE

The comment of an anonymous[2] ancient critic (arg. 3) ἥ τε ἀπὸ τῶν τειχέων Ἀντιγόνη θεωροῦσα μέρος οὐκ ἔστι δράματος should not be taken

---

[1] Cf. Foley, 117, who notes that the Servant's concern for the proprieties of Ant.'s position may be an echo of Eteocles' emphasis in *Septem* on the proper place of women.

[2] This comment is transmitted separately from the remnant of the didascalic hypothesis of *Phoen.* ascribed to Aristophanes of Byzantium and is, I think, considerably later in date than Aristophanes. It is sometimes said that among the elements of the Aristophanic didascalic hypothesis of each play there might appear 'critical comments' on the play: see Wilam. *Her.* 1.147; T. Achelis, *Phil* 73 (1914) 132–5; Zuntz, *Political Plays* 130–1 (with further refs. 130 n. 3); A. W. A. M. Budé, *De Hypotheseis der griekse Tragedies en Komedies. Een Onderzoek naar de Hypotheseis van Dicaearchus* (Nijmegen 1977) 33–9. Since the Aristophanic material has undergone changes in a long tradition, there is in fact no assurance that any of the 'critical judgments', whether short ones like τὸ δὲ δρᾶμα τῶν

to impugn the authenticity of this scene. It is uncertain whether Scaliger assumed the meaning 'is not ⟨a genuine⟩ part of the play' or 'is not ⟨an integral⟩ part of the action' when he placed ἐπεὶ καὶ παραπληρωματικόν after δράματος; but in an age dominated by Aristotelian criticism of tragedy, the latter is much more likely. Valckenaer and Hermann added τοῦ before δράματος (presumably independently of ms S), but neither understood the phrase as an allegation of spuriousness. Valckenaer, who translates *nam nec pars est fabulae quae spectat de moenibus Antigone neque quidquam est causae cur etc.*, was the chief originator of interpolation-research yet never adduced this judgment or doubted this scene. Hermann, following (as on other points) Morus' critical judgment of the play, assumed the meaning 'is not a⟨n artistically justified⟩ part of the play'. Among moderns Dihle, 60, is alone in inferring from the phrase athetesis of the passage by ancient critics. An accusation of spuriousness would, however, be expected to feature different language (e.g. νόθος, νοθεύειν, οὐκ Εὐριπίδου εἶναι),[1] and the run of the sentence (ἥ τε ... μέρος οὐκ ἔστι δράματος, καὶ ... οὐδενὸς ἕνεκα παραγίνεται, ὅ τε ... προσέρραπται διὰ κενῆς) ensures that the author meant to criticize the artistic quality of what he believed Euripides to have written. The criticism may have been that the scene is inorganic to the plot (cf. Valckenaer above, Morus (1771, 8–11),Wecklein (1894), and Tuilier, *Studi Classici in onore di Quintino Cataudella* (Catania 1972) 1.353, 'ne fait pas partie de l'action'), but this will require τοῦ δράματος (as in Arist. *Poet.* 1453b32 ἔξω τοῦ δράματος, 1460a31 ἐν τῶι δράματι) and μέρος

πρώτων (*Hipp.*) or τὸ δὲ δρᾶμα ἐγκώμιον Ἀθηνῶν (*Su.*) or longer ones like τὸ δὲ δρᾶμά ἐστι σατυρικώτερον κτλ. (*Alc.*) go back to Aristophanes. All the longer ones strike me as reflecting the rhetorical and pedagogical interests of the schools and of later commentators who worked with a corpus of many fewer plays than the full collection. Aristophanes' didascalic hypotheseis were, I believe, designed for scholarly readers, not the general public, and confined themselves to bare facts laconically expressed. A. Nauck, *Aristophanis Byzantii Grammatici Alexandrini Fragmenta* (Halle 1848) 252–63, prints only items labelled in the mss as by Aristophanes and considers the fragments much altered or falsely ascribed. With even greater distrust of the tradition, W. J. Slater, *Aristophanis Byzantii Fragmenta* [Sammlung gr. u. lat. Grammatiker, 6] (Berlin 1986), omits the dramatic material entirely.

[1] The only similar phrase containing μέρος which I have been able to find is in sch.[T] *Il.* 10 *ad init.*: φασὶ τὴν ῥαψωιδίαν ὑφ' Ὁμήρου ἰδίαι τετάχθαι καὶ μὴ εἶναι μέρος τῆς Ἰλιάδος, ὑπὸ δὲ Πεισιστράτου τετάχθαι εἰς τὴν ποίησιν. Here again not being a μέρος entails lack of artistic unity, not different authorship.

will be the equivalent of οἰκεῖον μέρος, as it is in the scholion cited in note 1 of p. 169.[1]

The fantasies of Verrall, who first attacked the scene, need not be discussed. Powell assembled what he thought were linguistic objections to the scene, but ultimately concluded that the scene was genuine. His discussion contains four basic kinds of argument: (1) *hapax legomena*; (2) awkward or harsh constructions; (3) repetition of line, phrase, word, or motif elsewhere in the play; (4) textual uncertainty. Powell's discussion of the first serves only to demonstrate the futility of the careless application of this criterion: if we pay attention to the context and style of the passage and the type of word found as hapax, there is no reason to view these words as non-Euripidean, and some of them, if the passage had been discovered on papyrus with no indication of author or title, could have been cited to suggest Euripidean authorship (see on προὐξερευνάω 92, λευκολόφας 119, ἀκοντιστήρ 140, καταβόστρυχος 146, ὁμογενέτωρ 165, χρυσεόκυκλος 176, χρυσεοβόστρυχος 191; ἡνιοστροφέω 172 and λιπαρόζωνος 175 are not hapax after all; see also on ἐπαντέλλων 105, πρόσφορος 129–30, προσβάσεις 180). Judgments of awkwardness and boldness (2) are highly subjective and no safe guide to authorship in late Eur. lyrics: see e.g. on 88, 94–5, 162, 177–8. Of the repetitions (3), that of 143 = 97 gives evidence of interpolation within the scene but has no relevance to the question of the scene's authenticity; others point to consistency of characterization and the deliberate underlining of important motifs (89 ∼ 1279; 196 ∼ 1276); see also 155n. Nor can intractable corruptions (4) that have naturally crept into an astrophic text be fairly counted against Euripidean authorship: there are just as many bold, difficult, and corrupt features in Jocasta's aria, which (so far) no one has ever doubted.

Dihle, 60–72, has now argued that the scene contains features that point to a post-classical origin and passages that can only be understood as modifications of information contained in 1104–40, a passage most critics (including Dihle) now consider post-Euripidean. He considers it a virtuoso piece composed for performance by itself (yet it is more reasonable to believe that virtuoso entertainers extracted genuine scenes of 'classic' works and performed them with music and dance).

---

[1] Before I was aware of this parallel, I believed that the text without τοῦ might be correct and that the critic might have had in mind the epic forebear of this scene and meant to say that the scene was 'not a section/scene of a drama', but proper rather to an epic composition (this involves a sense of μέρος that is well established: cf. *Poet.* 12 and the Hellenistic use of μέρος for 'act').

Before considering objections, it will be useful to note some general features which point to authenticity:

1. It would be extraordinary to have only the monologue of Jocasta preceding the entrance of the chorus. In tragedy the *prologos* (as defined in *Poet.* 12) normally contains at least two scenes (or, in the *Oresteia*, a scene spoken by one actor but articulated into two sections by some action/event): exceptions are Soph. *Ant.* and *Phil.* (which both feature lively dialogue-scenes), Eur. *Su.* (where the chorus is already on stage during the monologue of Aethra), *Her.* (where in a scene of supplication there are in fact two 'scenes' without an entrance: the monologue, and the debate between Megara and Amphitryon), and *Ba.* (Dionysus summons the chorus at the end of his monologue). (*IA* does not provide reliable evidence.) The rule holds equally for the fragmentary plays of Eur. of which enough is known to allow approximate reconstruction. It may also be noted that in eight of twelve cases in Eur. (nine of thirteen including *Phoen.*) the second or third prologue-scene contains actors' lyrics or anapaests (cf. *Prom.*, Soph. *El.*; among the fragmentary plays *Hyps.* has a monody before the parodos).

2. The amoibaion featuring a male voice speaking in trimeters and a female voice singing (esp. in dochmiac and related metres) is a typically Euripidean form (see below on Metre).

3. The ingenuity of the scene, both in its use of this metrical form and in its performing functions that could have been more routinely performed by a messenger or *kataskopos* (as in *Septem*) or by a chorus, is quite Euripidean: compare Ion's monody, the Phrygian's aria, the departure of the suppliant Helen and the chorus into the scene-building at *Hel.* 385, the experimentation with the trochaic tetrameter in several late plays (esp. *IA* 317ff., *Ba.* 604ff.).

4. Sympathetic readers of the play have understood that the scene is not, as other critics have alleged, unrelated to the rest of the play but serves important dramatic functions. (a) After Joc.'s scrupulously objective description of the quarrel, this scene begins the careful development of the theme of Pol.'s just claim and does so in the mouth of an unbiased observer (154–5: cf. 257–60, 319, 497–8, 526–7; from Pol. himself 369, 469–72, 490–3, 495–6, 608a). (b) The spontaneous affection of Ant. (with the Servant's acceptance of it as natural: 170) prepares us to view Pol. as quite different from the monster painted by the Aeschylean Eteocles or the Sophoclean Creon. (c) This affection is also a preparation for Ant.'s accompanying Joc. to the scene of the duel, for her reception of Pol.'s final request and her subsequent attempt to satisfy it, and for her role as chief mourner. (Ismene, on the other hand, is forgotten after line 616.) (d) The theme of maidenly modesty so emphatically developed by the Servant provides the starting-point from which Ant. grows into a role in which such

modesty must be abandoned (cf. 1266–76, 1485–91), a growth which is paralleled in that of Ion (from his monody to his ineffectual argument against his 'father' (585–647) to his involvement in barely averted violent action in the final scene) and of the Iphigenia of *IA*.

Where we can detect several Euripidean characteristics and such strong reasons for Euripides himself to have written the scene, and where on the other hand we have no plausible reason for an interpolator to have wanted to add the scene (whence Dihle's desperate hypothesis that the scene was never meant to be part of the play), linguistic and dramatic oddities would have to be both numerous and severe to justify suspicion.

Dihle's strongest arguments, if accepted as sound at all, would be those which allege post-classical content or usage or imitation of the passage 1104–40, which many critics view as post-Euripidean (I here grant the hypothesis for the sake of the present argument). (1) The syncretism of Artemis and Hecate implied in 110 is, according to Dihle, otherwise unambiguously attested only much later than Eur. Our source material for Greek cult and religion, even in Athens, is so fragmentary and unsatisfactory that it is very unwise to attack the earliest extant testimony for a detail on the ground that that detail is not otherwise attested until much later. In any case, it requires special pleading to deny the relevance of the combination Artemis Hecate found in Aeschylus and in inscriptions older than *Phoen.* (110n.). (2) The same general principle applies to Dihle's doubt of the genealogy of Selene as daughter of Helios: there is no real justification for denying the notion to Aeschylus, but even if we do, the loss of so much archaic poetry makes it unsafe to deny the notion to Eur. on the ground that *Phoen.* provides the only early extant testimony (175n.). (3) The notion that the Aetolians are '*half*-barbarous' (138) does not, as Dihle suggests, call into doubt their Hellenic descent and so suit only the polemics of Hellenistic Greece; it merely characterizes their culture and military habits in a way quite well known to the Athenians of Eur.'s time (134n.). (4) I explain *ad locc.* how I think 129 can be understood without prior knowledge of 1113ff. and 174 without knowledge of 1109f. (5) There is not the slightest need to see a reference to Hellenistic astronomical language in the -ζων-part of λιπαροζώνου (175n.).

Of Dihle's linguistic objections, several are quite misconceived: there is nothing strange about the use of ὁμόγαμος (137n.) or suspicious about hapax λευκολόφας (119n.), transitive ἐπαντέλλων (105n.), intransitive περᾷ (145n.), the use of λιπαρόζωνος for a male (175n.), or the structure of the χρῆμα-idiom (198n.). To others one need not ascribe very much force: the use of πρόπαρ (rare in any case) in a spatial sense 'in front of' is not difficult, nor is ἀμφέπει virtually meaning 'follow' or intransitive ἰθύνει (120n., 149n., 177–8n.); the stilted expression of 162 has a point.

The meaning of σάκος *implied* by σακεσφόροι in 139 remains very unusual. If one studies the passage with awareness of the variety and mannerisms of tragic style rather than with the goal of detecting arguments for suspicion, it is not suspicious. Both the metrical form and some specific linguistic traits are characteristic of Euripides: in addition to the items cited above (p. 170), see the notes on ποδὸς ἴχνος 105, γαῦρος 127, αὐτοκασιγνήται 136, ἀτρεμαῖα 177, εἴσβα 193, ἀφορμᾶς ... λόγων 199. The teichoskopia should be regarded as genuine with as much confidence as the bulk of the prologue and of the agon-scene are so regarded.

88–201 Metre:[1] The Servant speaks in trimeters throughout, while Antigone speaks (or chants or sings?) a few trimeters (with antilabe 123, 132, 160, 171; cf. 133, 180) and sings 12 brief astrophic systems featuring dochmiacs with an admixture of syncopated iambic, anapaestic, dactylic, and 'prosodiac/enoplian' elements. Lyrics of dochmiac character interspersed with trimeters are found in strophic construction in Aesch., Soph., and Eur. *Alc., Hcld., Andr.* The earliest extant astrophic lyrics in an iambic/dochmiac amoibaion occur in *Hipp.* 565–600, where the rhythm is purely dochmiac with almost no word-overlap between metra. Comparable to the present passage are *Hec.* 681–725, *Tro.* 235–91, *Her.* 1178–213 (all scenes of strong grief), *IT* 827–99, *Hel.* 625–97, *Ion* 1439–509, *Hyps.* fr. 64, 74ff. (all joyful scenes of reunion or reconciliation). Counterpointing of a purely iambic voice (usually male) and a lyric voice (usually female) is a standard feature of such scenes. The present scene is unique in the use to which it puts this typically Euripidean form.

On Eur.'s development of complex mixed rhythms of the kind used here, see Dale, *LMGD*² 111, 157–76, 208. On dochmiacs in drama see Conomis; West, *Greek Metre*, 108–15; Diggle (1990b).

---

[1] The metrical analyses presented here were originally completed some years ago, before the appearance of T. Cole's book *Epiploke*. On the value and the problems of this book, see, e.g., Diggle, *LCM* 15.5 (1990) 74–9; Haslam, *CP* 86 (1991) 229–39; R. L. Fowler, *EMC* 10 (1991) 1–20. Without relying on Cole's terminology or theory, I hope that I have (in the footsteps of Dale and Stinton) made appropriate comments on the ambiguities and affinities of the cola to which I assign conventional names. I should also state that I regard much of these analyses as tentative, as possible interpretations of the metre of the text I have printed in the Teubner edition. James Diggle has shared with me in correspondence (and now published in 1989, 1990a, 1990b) his objections or alternative proposals. On several points he prefers to eliminate rare phenomena by transposition or other emendation, while I have tended to offer a more conservative interpretation and note the difficulties.

103	⏑⏖–⏑⏖⏑⏑––⏑–‖	2 dochm
104	–⏖–⏑–‖	dochm
105	⏑⏑–⏑⏑–––‖	an, sp
109	×–⏖⏑–‖	dochm
110	––⏑⏑–⏑⏑–⏑⏑–‖	2 an
111	⏑⏖–––‖ʰ	dochm
114	–⏖––––⏖⏑–⏑∩‖ᵇ	dochm, dochm hex
		(or 2 cr?)
115	–⏖–⏑––⏖–⏑–‖	2 dochm
116	–⏖–––‖	dochm
119	⏑–⏑⏑–⏑⏑–‖	⏑ D
120	⏖⏑–––⏑–‖	cr, ia
121–2	––⏑–⏑–⏑⏑–⏑⏑–––‖	ia penth, D – –
127	××––⏑–⏑⏖–⏑–‖	exclam, ia, dochm
128	⏑–⏑–⏑⏑–⏑⏑–⏑‖	ia, an ⏑ (or ◡e ⏑ D ⏑)
129	–⏑–⏑⟨–⟩–⏑–⏑–⏑–	hypod, lec
130	⏑⏑–⏑⏑–––‖	an, sp
135	–⏑⏑–⏑⏑–⏑⏑–⏑⏑‖	4 da
136	–⏑⏑––––‖ᶜ	4 da∧∧
137	⏑⏖–⏑–‖ʰ	dochm
146	⏑⏑–⏑⏑–⏑⏑–⏑‖	enopl paroem
147	–⏑–⏑–⏑–‖?	lec
148	⏑–⏑–◡–⏑–⏑–⏑∩‖ᵇ	ia trim
149	⏑⏖–⏑–‖ʰ	dochm
151	–⏑⏑–⏑⏑–⏑⏑–⏑⏑‖	4 da
152	–⏑⏑–⏑⏑–––⏑⏑–⏑⏑–∩‖ᵇ	6 da∧
153	⏖⏑–⏑⏖–––‖	cr, dochm
156	–⏖–⏑–⏑⏖–––‖	2 dochm
157	⏑⏖–––‖ʰ	dochm
163	⏑⏑–⏑⏑–⏑⏑–⏑⏑–‖	2 an
164	⏑⏑–⏑⏑–⏑⏑–⏑–‖ᶜ?	enopl
165	⏑⏖⏖⏑⏖⏑⏖–⏑–‖	2 dochm
166	⏑––⏑–⏑––⏑–‖	2 dochm
167	⏑⏖⏖⏑–‖	dochm
168	⏑–⏑–⏑–⏑–⏑∩‖ᵇ	ia trim
169	⏑––⏑–⏑⏖–⏑–––⏑–‖ʰ	2 dochm, cr
		(or ba, 2 dochm?)
175	–⏖–––⏑⏖–⏑–‖	2 dochm
176	⏑––––⏑⏖––∩‖ᵇ	2 dochm
177	–⏖–⏑–⏑––⏑∩‖ᵇ	2 dochm
178	––⏖⏑––––‖	dochm, mol
182	◡–‖	exclam

174

182bis	υ‿‿–υ–υ‿‿–––		2 dochm
183	υ–υ–υ––‿‿–υ–		dochm hex, dochm
184	υυ–υυ–υυ–υυ–––‖	2 an, sp
185	υ–υ–υ–υ∩‖ᵇ	2 ia
186	–‿‿–––υ––υ–		2 dochm
187	–––υ––υ––		mol, 2 ba
188	υ––υ–υ––υ–		2 dochm
189	υ‿‿–––‿‿υ–‖?	dochm, cr
190	–υυ–υυ–––υυ		4 da
191	–υυ–υυ–υυ–∩‖ᵇ	4 da∧
192	–υυ–υυ–––‖ᶜ	4 da∧∧

NOTES TO METRICAL SCHEME

105 I regard this as a type of enoplian colon (cf. Cole, 109–10, on 'prosodiac' with dochmiac) and tentatively suggest the same for 130. Cf. 184 below and *Ion* 716 (2 an, sp) for a longer dragged enoplian also associated with dochmiacs. The tendency to dragged close (in 8 of 11 systems) is noteworthy; in many cases the 'enoplian-prosodiac' elements thus show their affinity to the nearby dochmiacs. Bothe's deletion of ποδός will produce a purely dochmiac system, but pleonastic ποδὸς ἴχνος is well attested in Eur. Diggle (1989) suggests ἐπανατέλλων (ia, ba) or transposition of ποδός or ἴχνος to the end of the line.

109 Π³ may attest ὤ, yielding ––υυ– (anapaest); cf. *ZPE* 49 (1982) 10.

110 Anapaests among dochmiacs: *Hec.* 1104, *IT* 880, *Hyps.* fr. 64, 77.

114 On dochmiac hexasyllable cf. Conomis, 28ff.; Dale, *LMGD*² 115f.; Dodds on *Ba.* 982–4; Barrett on *Hipp.*, p. 268. It is controversial whether period-end without strong rhetorical pause can be assumed as readily among dochmiacs as among other kinds of lyric metres: Conomis argued against such period-end, but Stinton, 'Pause' 46–7, seems to me to have made a good case for regarding Conomis' claim as extreme. (Cf. on 177 below.) There may be a very minor rhetorical break here between the subject-term χαλκόδετά τ' ἔμβολα and the predicate (the dative in 115 goes with the following verb, not with ἔμβολα as some have assumed). Still assuming period-end, we may alternatively scan χαλκ. τ' ἔμβ. as 2 cr; cf. *Ag.* 1136, 1143 and the Sophoclean cola cited by Stinton, 'Notes II' 130 and n. 16, which are treated by some as dochmiacs and by others as syncopated ia. But note the quadruple 'internal rhyme' of –‿‿ in the dochmiac interpretation. If period-end is rejected, then Seidler's χαλκόδετ' ἔμβολά τε (–‿‿–υ‿‿ dochm) is the best alternative, though it introduces a postponement of τε (cf. *Tro.* 1064, *Cycl.* 190; Fraenkel on *Ag.*, II.131;

below 331–3n., 1249n.). Diggle rejects the possibility of brevis here (see note below on 177) and of cretic interpretation; for his emendation see comm. on 114–16.

119 The colon × −∪∪−∪∪− occurs, likewise in association with iambo-trochaic rhythm, in *Ant.* 354f.; Dale, *LMGD*² 162.

121–2 This dicolon is an extended form of the iambelegus; it also occurs in dochmiac contexts in *Ion* 718 and *Her.* 1185–7 (divided between two voices); Dale, *LMGD*² 174.

127 I have left this line as in Teubner, but it is probably better divided as exclamation / ia, dochm. Dochmiac with initial anceps resolved is doubted by many, firmly denied by Diggle, *CR* 34 (1984) 68; see Kannicht, ii.180, on *Hel.* 670, with further references; West, *Greek Metre* 111. It can rarely be verified whether ĕ ĕ is intended to be ∪∪, ∪−, or −−: *Ag.* 1114 (=1125) attests −−, *Septem* 327 (=339) attests ∪∪ (ionic ∪∪−∪−∪−−), but other responding passages feature period-end (cf. also *OC* 150 (=117), best analysed by Wilam., *GV* 257), or are ambiguous (*Hel.* 661–2, *Tro.* 1216). If ĕ ĕ is not *extra metrum* here (followed by ia, dochm), it is perhaps best taken as ∪∪.

128–30 Analysis of these lines is quite uncertain, and doubts about the sense compound the difficulty. Maintaining the transmitted text in 128, we have what Dale, *LMGD*² 171, calls a 'pendant inverted enoplian' (others have called it ia + reizianum). The same colon occurs (with probable period-end) at *Med.* 207 and (without period-end?) at *Ba.* 1190, where Hermann's slight change θήραι / τοῦδε gives long link-anceps and a hypodóchmiac following (there are insufficient grounds for Wilam.'s emendation, favoured by Dodds, which alters the rare rhythm). With the latter passage in mind, we can assume synapheia between 128 and 129 and retain ἀστερωπός with true initial longum (with ἀστρωπός we would have to assume period-end at προσόμοιος before the anceps of the following iamb). Without further emendation, we can treat the first part of 129 as hypodóchmius or lecythion or cretic. If ἀμερίωι γένναι is left on its own as a final dochmiac, there are a number of ways to treat 129, all with brevis in longo at πρόσφορος. But πρόσφορος is a rare usage (see comm.), perhaps preferred to the commoner προσφερής because the final short syllable was desired for the rhythm. Thus I have tried to treat -φορος ἀμερίωι γένναι as the final colon (enoplian with affinity to dochmiac, identical to 105; cf. 184). 129 is then, without emendation, lec + ia (or hypod + dochm hex); but on grounds of sense I favour the addition of ὡς, yielding hypod + lec. But the rhythm of 129 can be adjusted in many different ways by combining different choices between ἀστερ-/ ἀστρ-, γραφαῖσιν/ -αῖς, οὐχὶ/ οὐ (Tricl.), ἐν/{ἐν}. Diggle (1990a) notes that ⟨ὥσπερ⟩ would be preferable for metre: e.g., 129–30 ἀστερωπός ⟨ὥσπερ⟩ ἐν / γραφαῖσιν οὐχὶ πρόσφορος ἀμ. γ. = lec followed by same colon as 121–2.

136 The colon is ambiguous (the pattern is compatible with dochm + sp and da + dochm), as often in transition from one rhythm to another.

146–7 See Dale, *LMGD*² 175, and Diggle, *ICS* 6.1 (1981) 90–2, for other dicola beginning with the enoplian paroemiac with short link syllable, and cf. 128–9 and 191–2. This analysis requires true longum εἰσ- and rules out dochmiac ἐσιδεῖν νεανίας. It is unnecessary to seek dochmiacs here (Schroeder: 2 anap, 2 dochm, with ὄμμασι⟨ν⟩).

153 Objecting to the sense and the rhythm, Nauck wanted to delete πέρσων. But the word is pointed and emphatic; cretics are commonly intermixed with dochmiacs (Conomis, 48), and cr + dochm as clausula occurs also *Septem* 107 (*Her.* 920–1 is corrupt, but may have presented 2 cr + dochm). (See now Diggle (1990b) for a thorough review of cretics in association with dochmiacs: this pattern is possible, but he suggests we may create 2 dochmiacs by doubling ἐμάν.)

166 See comm.

169 ἀελίου as choriamb does not yield a probable clausula (to my knowledge, the only single choriamb associated with dochmiacs is *Hipp.* 1275 dochm + chor, often emended to 2 dochm, and in any case occurring in a passage that combines dochmiacs and enoplian or aeolic cola). Thus it is best scanned as cretic, with synizesis of αε, as often in choral lyric and as again in 175 below. Hermann and subsequent editors (including Diggle) regularize by writing ἁλίου for ἀελίου in *Med.* 1252, *Her.* 661 (already Tricl.), *Ion* 122, *Hel.* 342, *Or.* 1002, and these passages of *Phoen.* (so too at *Hipp.* 850, where θ᾽ ἁλίοιο is read for corrupt ἀελίου τε); forms of ἅλιος are transmitted in six passages, ἀελ- without synizesis in twelve. Cf. Barrett on *Hipp.* 848–51. Pure dochmiacs can be easily restored by deleting ἀελίου as a gloss (Wecklein). For dochm + cr cf. perhaps 189 below (but text may be lacunose or corrupt) and dochm + mol 178 below (also doubted by many). See Diggle (1990) 108–9.

175 see on 169.

176 Overlap of four syllables between the two dochmiacs of a dimeter is very rare (also *Septem* 693; *Rhes.* 131); JD notes that word-division after second long anceps is objectionable (cf. Parker, *CQ* 16 (1966) 12) and commends Paley's ⟨πότνα⟩ Σελ. χρυσο- for eliminating both anomalies.

177 Semantic or grammatical grounds seem not to require emendation (comm.). There remains the brevis in longo σώφρονα without change of rhythm or strong rhetorical break, a phenomenon doubted by many in dochmiacs, though it surely exists in other lyric metres of tragedy (see esp. Conomis, 43–4; for Eur. only Diggle *ICS* 6.1 (1981) 96). Stinton, 'Pause'

46–7, has tried to show that such doubts are not justified on statistical or theoretical grounds, and I tentatively accept the phenomenon here (as well as 114 above). The closest parallels for brevis (or hiatus) in dochmiacs without rhetorical pause are *Eum.* 783 (emended by West), *Choe.* 958 (see Garvie *ad loc.*), *Andr.* 833 (emended by Diggle); at *Her.* 1061 (emended by Diggle, but see Bond) and Aesch. *Su.* 649 (emended by Weil) there may be a slight pause; cf. also for hypodochmii *Aj.* 401ff., 422. If it is accepted that change of metre after the dochmiac makes no theoretical or practical difference to this question, cf. also *Ag.* 1090, *OT* 1350. Since the acc. ἀτρεμαῖα ... σώφρονα cohere as a phrase, there may be here (as in 114) a very mild rhetorical break. Cole, 106 n. 118, 113 n. 125, offers an analysis with division after πώλοις, allowing σώφρονα to be – ∪∪.

178 For molossus in the clausula cf. on 169 (dochm + cr) and the colon mol + dochm in responsion to cr + dochm at *Or.* 168 = 189.

183 Replacement of the dochm hex by a plain dochm is unnecessary (cf. on 114), and the paraphrast's gen. in ὦ κεραυνοῦ φῶς is not a reliable indication that anything other than κεραύνιον was in the text.

187 Since the context is apparently lacunose (see comm.), this colon is quite uncertain; Conomis, 48, describes it as dochm + tro, but the only other example he cites, *Ag.* 1123 = 1134, is often analysed otherwise (e.g., Fraenkel or West). For paired bacchiacs in close association with dochm see on 1289–90 = 1301–2.[1]

191–2 Dale, *LMGD*² 175, treats this as a dicolon of pendant prosodiac with short anceps + dragged prosodiac, comparing 146–7 (cf. Cole, 109). Link-anceps should perhaps be recognized in some passages (e.g. 128, 146 above), but here I prefer the dactylic treatment with dual clausulae. On the problem of the existence of link-anceps, see Parker, 'Catalexis' 26–7, and Stinton, 'Pause' 64–6.

88–201: COMMENTARY

88ff. staging The actors appear on the flat roof of the skene-building, either by a ladder leading up from the rear or by one from within the building, through a trap-door. For full discussion of the use of the roof, see 'Actors on High', esp. 255–7 on this scene. The Servant ascends the ladder by 99 (and probably before beginning his speech at 88) and speaks to Ant. while she is yet unseen or while only her head is visible (to that part of the audience seated higher in the *theatron*). Ant. climbs into view during 100–8.

---

[1] For another treatment of 182–9 cf. Cole, 109, 115 n. 128 (but there are misprints in the scansion, or he tacitly emends).

At the end of the scene the Servant tells Ant. 'Enter the house' (193), which she does by going back down the ladder. Cf. 90n.

88–102 in delaying Ant.'s appearance, the Servant's speech (1) characterizes Ant. as a sheltered maiden and as a girl with a special tie to her father (88) and an eager interest in Pol. and his allies (91); (2) ironically asserts (as in Jocasta's prologue) conventional social proprieties in a family in which relations are anything but normal; (3) identifies the Servant as the messenger referred to in 83. These functions suffice to justify the lines without recourse to Σ's explanation (on 93) that Eur. is padding to allow the actor who played Jocasta to reappear as Ant. Joc. and Ant. are played by separate actors in 1264–83, and it is perfectly possible to assign their roles in their entirety to separate actors. But if only the protagonist had an excellent singing voice, it would be reasonable (though taxing) for him to play all of Joc.'s scenes and to play Ant. in the scenes in which she sings (88–201, 1485–end). If Ant. is not at all visible during this speech, the dramatic technique is highly unusual (if, on the other hand, Ant.'s head is visible before the Servant speaks, nothing unusual occurs). It is common enough for visible actors (or chorus) to shout a summons or a command indoors (cf. 296ff., 1067ff., 1264ff., 1530ff.), but the closest parallel for a newly emerged character conversing behind his back, as it were, to someone indoors is the comic technique seen in Men. *Dysk.* 206 and 427 (and frequently in Latin comedy: P. Legrande, *Daos: Tableau de la comédie grecque pendant la période dite nouvelle* [Ann. Univ. Lyon, nouv. série, Droit II: Lettres, fasc. 22 (1910)], 449f.; E. Fraenkel, *Elementi Plautini* 137, 155–6). In the comic instances the addressee remains indoors, here Ant. soon appears. The unusual technique perhaps creates an impression of conspiratorial caution, reinforcing the theme of Ant. as sheltered maiden.

88 pers. nota in the mss and *index personarum* the Servant is called παιδαγωγός, and Σ88 views him as a τροφεύς (κατ' ἐπιτροπὴν μὲν μητρός, παιδαγωγίαν δὲ τροφέως) or guardian (ἀλλ' ὁ διὰ τὸ γῆρας σώφρων καὶ φρόνιμος [φυλάττει]). But a pedagogue is the slave who accompanies and oversees a boy from the age of first schooling, when the boy leaves the care of the female τροφός; Greek girls remained in the care of the nurse throughout childhood and are often attended by the nurse even after marriage (as Deianeira, Phaedra, Medea, Hermione in tragedy). From the text we can see that Ant.'s companion is an old, trusted retainer, solicitous of the family; he is to be termed θεράπων or perhaps πρέσβυς/πρεσβύτης, as in *El.* or *Ion.*

88 ὦ κλεινὸν κτλ. extended vocative with grandiloquent interlaced or enclosing order. Probably originating in elaborate lyric invocations (Pindar *O.* 14.3–4; fr. 76 ὦ ταὶ λιπαραὶ καὶ ἰοστέφανοι καὶ ἀοίδιμοι, Ἑλλάδος ἔρεισμα, κλειναὶ Ἀθᾶναι, δαιμόνιον πτολίεθρον), such complex order is typical of formal invocations of the gods and of especially ceremonial address: *OT* 14, *Hipp.* 63–4, *Ion* 1606, *Or.* 1673, esp. Eur. *El.* 880–1 ὦ καλλίνικε, πατρὸς ἐκ νικηφόρου / γεγώς, 'Ορέστα, τῆς ὑπ' 'Ιλίωι μάχης; with purpose, *Hel.* 386–7, *Or.* 72. Here the style lends special dignity to Ant.'s role.

οἴκοις ... πατρί some comm. make a neat distinction: οἴκοις with κλεινόν, πατρί with θάλος. This is overprecise; both datives accompany κλεινὸν θάλος, and the sense is 'Antigone, scion in the house who brings glory to your father' or 'Ant., scion who brings glory to the house for your father'. Cf. Schwyzer II.153; K–G 1.428 Anm. 1(a).

θάλος originally a metaphor of special emotional force (*Il.* 22.87 Hecuba of Hector; *Od.* 6.157 Odysseus describing Nausicaa's parents' pride in her), later an honorific synonym for 'child' in Pindar; but in Eur. it varies from colourless in *El.* 15 ἄρσενά τ' 'Ορέστην θῆλύ τ' 'Ηλέκτρας θάλος to emotional in *IT* 232 ἔτι βρέφος, ἔτι νέον, ἔτι θάλος; probably honorific if not positively emotional here.

89 παρθενῶνας ἐκλιπεῖν Ant.'s maidenhood and the seclusion it requires according to conventional etiquette become a leitmotif which articulates her action in the play, illustrating her emergence from a protected innocence into the harsh realities of adult life: cf. Introd. I p. 6, n. 1 and 194, 1265, 1275, 1485–90, [1637], 1691–2, [1739]. For the conventional sentiment, cf. *Hcld.* 43–4 νέας γὰρ παρθένους αἰδούμεθα / ὄχλωι πελάζειν κἀπιβωμιοστατεῖν; *Or.* 108 ἐς ὄχλον ἕρπειν παρθένοισιν οὐ καλόν.

90 μεθῆκε μεθίημι 'let go' + acc. + epexegetic inf. can denote physical release (*Hec.* 1128: presumably Polymestor gyrates menacingly at 1125–6 and Agamemnon puts a hand on his shoulder at 1127) or figurative release (*Ant.* 653–4, Soph. *El.* 628 with Lloyd-Jones and Wilson's με for μοι) and can connote the granting of verbal permission to go (here, *Ion* 232, and Hdt. 1.37.3 and 1.40, where the inf. is ἰέναι).

ἐς διῆρες ἔσχατον since ἔσχατος used of physical position never means 'highest' (in Pindar *O.* 1.113 τὸ δ' ἔσχατον κορυφοῦται βασιλεῦσι the spatial metaphor is carried by the verb), it must mean 'outermost' here, implying an unobstructed view (rather than 'furthest ⟨from the maiden-chambers⟩', suggested by Roux, *REG* 74 (1961) 34f.). The meaning of διῆρες is harder to ascertain: (1) 'two-storied building' or (2a) 'upper storey' or (2b) 'upper-storey room' or (3) 'rooftop terrace'? Etymology favours (1): on the analogy of μονήρης ≈ μόνος, a δῶμα διῆρες, for instance, could be the whole of a two-storey structure (cf. οἰκίδιον διπλοῦν Lys. 1.9, where the further description indicates that a house could be of two storeys in some parts and not in others). But meaning (2) is implied by other attestations: the only other classical use extant is in Plato Com. fr. 120 K–A ὁρᾶτε τὸ διῆρες ὑπερῶιον, cited in ΣFrogs 159 as an example of μετάληψις (interchange, substitution) of synonymous words; this citation and glosses in Pollux 1.81, Hesych., Moeris, Et. magnum prove that διῆρες was later taken to be synonymous with ὑπερῶιον, the upper storey only of a two-storied structure (cf. Plut. *Mor.* 77E καταβαλεῖν ἑαυτὸν ἔκ τινος διήρους). And (3) is possible if διῆρες came to refer to anything above the main storey. If (1) or (2a) is correct, 'to the outermost two-storied part of the palace' implies height and unobstructed view, and the audience imagines that the skene-roof is the roof of an (unrepresented) upper storey. (2b) should not be accepted, since no upper-storey room was represented on the roof: 'Actors on High', 256 n. 23.

91 ἰδεῖν inf. of purpose (Moorhouse, *Syntax Soph.* 236-7): either ἐκλιπεῖν implies a verb of motion like ἐξελθεῖν (cf. *Phaethon* 97; *Eum.* 938; Neophron *TrGF* 15 F 1.1; the inf. in Soph. *OC* 12 is not of the same kind – see Jebb),[1] or ἐκλιπεῖν μεθῆκε implies ἔπεμψε (e.g., Soph. *El.* 406 πέμπει ... τυμβεῦσαι; *Rhes.* 26); neither construction is common in tragedy.

92 προὐξερευνήσω hapax (but cf. *Rhes.* 296 προὐξερευνητάς); the double compound is more precise here than ἐξερευνάω, which occurs four times in Soph. and Eur. and is then found in post-classical prose.

92-3 στίβον ... τρίβωι similar variatio in *Or.* 1269, 1274; cf. *IT* 67 ὅρα, φυλάσσου μή τις ἐν στίβωι βροτῶν.

93-4 μή ... φαντάζεται ... ἔλθηι although semantically very close to indirect question εἰ φαντάζεται, the use of an indicative μή-clause for the object to be examined/ascertained carries an undertone of anxiety (cf. *IT* 67) and here allows for a neat progression from the fact immediately to be ascertained to the more remote bad consequences that result if someone is present. This progression from ind. to subj. is also attested in *Eccl.* 495 (μή-clause expressing apprehension: cf. Ussher *ad loc.*); cf. *Or.* 1533-4 (εἰ-clause, restoration uncertain: see Willink).

94-8 since 97 is identical to 143, it is a natural assumption that one of the two lines is spurious (143n.). Wecklein (1901) contemplated eliminating 97 rather than 143; but to do so one must eliminate all of 94-8, surely the wrong solution. The audience needs to know from the beginning of the scene that this Servant is the man Jocasta referred to in 83 and why he can identify the attackers for Antigone. Nor is the caution evident in 92-3 effectively exploited without 94-5.

94-5 κἀμοὶ μὲν ... σοὶ δ' ὡς ἀνάσσηι two interpretations have been given: (a) 'and to me there may come a reproach that can be deemed of small account, since I am a slave, but to you, as mistress, a reproach ⟨that cannot be ignored⟩' (Σ, Hartung, Paley); (b) 'and to me, as a slave, and

---

[1] Perhaps also *IT* 938, though δρᾶσαι might be felt to depend on κελευσθείς rather than ἀφικόμην.

to you, as mistress, there may come some evil [or mean-spirited] reproach' (recent comm., but so already Arsenius and Barnes). (a) involves a more common sense of φαῦλος, 'trivial, unimportant', which the juxtaposition with ὡς δούλωι might initially suggest; but the brachylogy or ellipsis assumed is too great. For the meaning of φαῦλος in (b) – κακός (Arsenius), 'schimpflich' (Wecklein), 'humiliant' (Méridier), or 'mean-spirited' (JD) – most parallels are later, but earlier cf. Democritus 68 в 177 D–K φαύλην πρῆξιν, *IT* 390 τὸ φαῦλον, fr. 259 ὀργῆι φαύληι (not *Andr.* 870: see Stevens).

96 the imbalance of ἅ τ' εἶδον εἰσήκουσά τ' is due to the omission of a second ἅ; for comparable instances cf. Denniston, *GP*² 518f.

98 δεῦρό τ' αὖ κείνων πάρα the truce is reciprocal since the Argives must agree not to attack while the Theban commander is busy negotiating (note πρὶν ψαῦσαι δορός 82) and Pol. must agree not to attack his brother in the city (600f.: καὶ σέ). Paulson falsely assumed that the truce was on Et.'s side only and so deleted 98. If the less obvious κείνων (V, supported by ᴾΣ) is correct against κείνου (assimilation to sing. κασιγνήτωι in 97), the point may be that Pol. is not commander-in-chief of the Argives.

99 ἀλλ' here, in its breaking-off function, introduces an observation of a new (or newly ascertained) situation. As after ἀλλὰ γάρ (1308n.; cf. Denniston, *GP*² 99, 103f.) or ἀλλὰ μήν (*Or.* 1549), the remark prompted by the observation (usually a command, expression of intention, or the like) follows in asyndeton: Aesch. *Pers.* 150, *Alc.* 136, *IT* 64, *Phoen.* 274.

100 κέδρου παλαιὰν κλίμαχ' the ladder is old because cedar, a sturdy material (τὸ τοῦ δένδρου ἄσηπτον καὶ εὐῶδες Eust. 1344, 60; *materiae … ipsi aeternitas* Plin. *Nat.Hist.* 13.53), was favoured for expensive structures, fixtures, and coffins: (rooms, beams) *Il.* 24.192, *Or.* 1371; (clothes-chest) *Alc.* 160; (coffins) *Alc.* 365, *Tro.* 1141, *Or.* 1053; (doors and ceilings) A. Trevor Hodge, *Woodwork of Greek Roofs* (Cambridge 1960), 124; R. Martin, *Manuel d'archéologie grecque* I (Paris 1965) 22ff.; R. Meiggs, *Trees and Timber in the Ancient Mediterranean World* (Oxford 1982), *passim* (pp. 410–26 on the confusion of juniper and cedar). It is a mark of Eur.'s 'realism' that almost all the literary citations for the use of cedar are from his plays.

κλίμαχ' ἐκπέρα an unusual phrase: 'traverse the full extent of' so 'climb to the top of' (cf. 299n.).

101 πεδία the object of σκόπει, not of παρ'. Looking north, Antigone will first see the expanse of the Teneric and Aonian plains and then focus on the details of the two famous streams and the enemy army adjacent to them.

Ἰσμηνοῦ the rough breathing is treated as secondary by Schwyzer 1.306, but there is no doubt that it was present in Boeotian at least until the epichoric alphabet died out (*c.* 350) as well as in old Attic and

Corinthian; cf. Teubner *praef.* ¶20(1); Hutchinson on *Septem* 273. M has rough breathing here and in 57 (but not 347, 794, 827). The scribe makes so many errors with breathing signs that these cases may be accidental; but JD reports that codd. at Plut. *Dem.* 45.5 attest (*fere*) νάμαθ' Ἰσμηνοῦ at *Ba.* 5 and refers to W. Schulze, *Kleine Schriften* (Göttingen ²1966) 393.

102 στράτευμ' ὅσον for the elliptic indirect question following the proleptic noun cf. 1370 δάκρυα τῆς τύχης ὅση, Soph. *Aj.* 118 ὁρᾷς ... τὴν θεῶν ἰσχὺν ὅση; (instances with ὅπου in E. Bruhn, *Anhang zu Sophokles* (= *Sophokles* erklärt von F. W. Schneidewin und A. Nauck, vol. VIII, Berlin 1899) 19).

103 ὄρεγέ for the dramatic significance of this gesture, 1710–66n. For the typical repetition of the imperative in dochmiacs, cf. Diggle (1990b) 109.

νῦν the long vowel is guaranteed in the enclitic also in *Alc.* 1077, *IT* 1203, *Hel.* 1419, *Ion* 970, *Or.* 795, 1291, 1678, *IA* 654, *Cycl.* 630 (there are about thirty-five instances of νῦν in Eur., about fifty-five others where the vowel-length is indeterminate).[1]

νέαι sc. χειρί, as position and context (ξύναψον) suggest (Σ paraphrases ἐμοὶ τῆι νέαι, but νέα = νεᾶνις is apparently not found).

104 until about 1850 ἀπὸ κλιμάκων was usually taken wrongly with ὄρεγε rather than ἐπαντέλλων.

105 ποδὸς ἴχνος a Euripidean mannerism (see *Concordance*); there are insufficient grounds to prefer pure dochmiacs here (see under Metre), so the deletion of ποδός is unwarranted.

ἐπαντέλλων ἀντ- for ἀνατ- is the preferred tragic form for this verb and for ἀντολή and is here supported by either my own or Bothe's treatment of the metre; but ἐπανα-, as proposed by Diggle (see Metre 105n.), cannot be excluded. For transitive use of the verb cf. transitive ἀνατέλλω in Homer, Pindar, Aesch. fr. 300.7.

106 ἰδού 1714n.

109–10 παῖ Λατοῦς Ἑκάτα syncretism of Artemis and Hecate is either recorded or alluded to in Aesch. *Su.* 676 (see Friis Johansen and Whittle *ad loc.*) and Artemis Hecate is listed in *IG* I³ 383, 125–7 of 429/8 B.C. (cf.

---

[1] I do not agree with C. J. Ruijgh, *L'élément achéen dans la langue épique* (Assen 1957) 66, that we should follow ancient grammarians in writing νῦν whenever the vowel is long, even in enclitic position. Granted that we, like the ancient grammarians, are trapped in inconsistencies in our accentuation of postpositives and enclitics, it does not help to follow a tradition which obscures the real difference between emphatic temporal adverb and enclitic logical particle.

even earlier *IG* XII:8.359, *c.* 450 B.C., Thasus). Invocation of Hecate elsewhere has apotropaic force (*Hel.* 569; Arist. *Plut.* 1070), and wonder and fear are combined here. Antigone invokes virgin goddesses throughout the scene; apotropaic force is evident in 152, 182, 190–2, but not in 175–7.

110–11 an imitation of *Il.* 20.156 τῶν δ' ἅπαν ἐπλήσθη πεδίον καὶ λάμπετο χαλκῶι. Cf. also *Hyps.* fr. 1 ii.32f. Bond ἀστράπτει χαλκέοισιν ὅπλοις Ἀργεῖον πεδίον πᾶν. Π³ has ὅπλοις after ἅπαν, and ὅπλοις may have been in the text of Heliodorus (unless his imitation 9.14.1 καὶ ἀργυροῖς τε καὶ ἐπιχρύσοις τοῖς ὅπλοις τὸ πεδίον καταστράπτων was based on *Hyps.* rather than *Phoen.*). The word is probably a gloss; if it is retained, the metre is less simple (ὅπλοις πεδίον ἀστράπτει could be sp + dochm or ia + mol) and (if there is synapheia) we have ἅπαν (the vowel is indeterminate in almost all tragic instances: exceptions are Eur. fr. 898.3–4 τὸ δ' ἄκαιρον ἅπαν ὑπερβάλ- / λον τε μὴ προσείμαν¹ and (by emendation) ἅπαν in *Choe.* 788, 967; cf. 1504 below πρόπαν, also ἅπαν *Plut.* 493, anap.; ἅπαν Men. fr. 117.5 K–T, trimeter).

114–16 'Have the portals been tightly closed with doors and have the bronze-bound bars been fixed to the walls, product of Amphion's stoneworking?' In simple terms, 'Are the gates closed and are they locked/barred?' ἥρμοσται is used in zeugma; κλήιθροις is better taken as 'closed doors' than as 'bars' or 'bolts'; ἔμβολα are simply 'things which are inserted', hence 'bars' (elsewhere μοχλός: cf. Xen. *Anab.* 7.1.12 and 15 ἐμβάλλειν τὸν μοχλόν, an action which in each case follows συγκλείειν τὰς πύλας; also Aen. *Tact.* 18); ὀργάνοις here means 'thing produced' rather than 'tool' (so too Soph. fr. 398.5 ξουθῆς μελίσσης κηρόπλαστον ὄργανον = honey); τείχεος is defining gen. with ὄργανον, Ἀμφίονος subjective gen. with the phrase (cf. defining and possessive gen. *Trach.* 1191 τὸν Οἴτης Ζηνὸς ... πάγον). Greek double-leaved gates could be routinely fastened to sill and lintel with vertical pins (sometimes in one leaf only, the other leaf being held in place by the offset of the sill and overlap of the pinned leaf), but for greater security a strong horizontal bar (μοχλός) was affixed across the leaves to the jambs. (Wherever μοχλοί are referred to in tragedy, a special effort at security is implied.) This bar could be metal-plated for added strength: so χαλκόδετα here, iron plating in Aen. *Tact.* 20.2.² Cf. D. Barends, *Lexicon Aeneium* (Assen 1955), 162–4 with Diagram 1; F. E. Winter, *Greek Fortifications* (Toronto 1971), 257–64 with figures 295–309. A possible alternative is to take κλήιθροις as equivalent to μοχλοῖς

---

¹ This instance disappears with the emendation of Page given in Diggle, *ICS* 6.1 (1981) 91.

² We cannot exclude the possibility that χαλκόδετος is here an ornate variation on χάλκεος (Diggle (1989) 197–8).

and ἔμβολα as the βάλανοι, the metal pins which fix the μοχλός to the door-leaves or to a housing in the jamb. Aen. Tact. attests the phrase ἐμβάλλειν τὸν βάλανον, and in various passages scholars have attempted to take κλῆιθρον as 'bar' or in some other more precise technical sense distinct from that of μοχλός (e.g., Di Benedetto on *Or.* 1551). But Barrett on *Hipp.* 577–81 shows that κλῆιθρα in tragedy is generally 'barred doors'; and the notion 'fixed to the walls' is more obviously true of a bar than of a locking-pin. The simpler rendering given above should therefore be favoured. The suggestions of Σ that a bronze portcullis is described or that ἔμβολα are the pivots of the doors do not stand up to examination. The interpretation given here works with the transmitted reading or with Seidler's small correction (see Metre, note on 114). I argued against further emendation in *ZPE* 49 (1982) 10–12; I still find the zeugma suitable in this style. Diggle (1989) 197–9 prefers to remove the zeugma with πυλᾶν and is sympathetic to Fritzsche's χαλκόδετ' ἔμβολ' ἐν.

118 †τὸν πρῶτον ... μαθεῖν† the sequence of dialogue in 118–24 is defective, and this seems to be the weakest point of the text. It is perhaps not an insuperable difficulty that τὸν πρῶτον (sc. λοχαγόν, vaguely inferred from χωρίζουσι ... λόχους 108) abruptly introduces interest in the seven leaders, but it is unacceptable (1) for Ant. to frame her question as if she is picking out an object of inquiry after the Servant has pointed to a single λοχαγός and (2) for the Servant to reply λοχαγός in 123 if his line 118 implies λοχαγόν. The problem was noted independently by Burges and Hermann and has recently been discussed by Jouanna, 'Remarques' 40–6. Hermann changed λοχαγός 123 to acc. and transposed (ἀλλ' εἰσόρα τὸν πρῶτον εἰ βούληι μαθεῖν / λοχαγόν, ὦ δέσποινα, τίς πόθεν γεγώς). The resulting structure is convoluted, the lively τίς πόθεν is proper only in a *direct* question, and the naturalness of 125–6 as an answer to 123b–24 is lost. Dindorf's deletion of 123–4 reduces the liveliness of the scene and leaves objection (1) untouched.[1] Grotius and a few others punctuate after εἰσόρα, not πρῶτον; but this leaves objection (2) unanswered and involves a pause after the fourth position, which is extremely rare in Eur. (cf. Denniston (1936)). Jouanna (as already A. Schoene, *Hermes* 9 (1875) 499) favours emending to adverb τὸ πρῶτον, and translates (too loosely) 'allons, commence par regarder'; but the adverb must imply 'first, *before* something else', which makes no sense here. Polle's τοι πρῶτον suffers from the same fault, and against τοι with such an imperative cf. N. V. Dunbar, *CR* 20 (1970) 272. If the passage as a whole is by Eur., then corruption

---

[1] Somewhat more attractive would be deletion of 123 alone: a gloss λοχαγός could have been filled out to a trimeter. This would give some justification to the Doric alpha of αὔδασον.

must be assumed (unless 118 alone is deleted: Diggle 1990a). Either μαθεῖν is intrusive and we may read e.g. τὸν πρῶτον, εἰ βούληι, λόχον, with polite εἰ βούληι (*Su.* 569 (ironic), cf. Arist. *Lys.* 194; εἰ βούληι conceding free choice or freedom of action is more common: *Alc.* 1112, *Med.* 1358, Soph. *Ant.* 1168). Or τὸν πρῶτον is intrusive and we need something on the lines of ἀλλ᾽ εἰσόρα τὸ πεδίον (anon.) or ἀλλ᾽ εἰσόρα δή, ⟨ – ∪⟩ εἰ βούληι μαθεῖν (e.g. πάντας or πάντα γ᾽).

119 λευκολόφας hapax; the Doric-style formation is more elevated than normal λευκόλοφος (cf. φοινικόλοφος 820) and not at all suspicious in tragic lyric (cf. parodic Γοργολόφας in *Acharn.* 567). For variation between -ος and -ᾱς in compounds for metrical and stylistic reasons, cf. ἁβροκόμας *Ion* 920, κατάκομος *Ba.* 1187, χρυσοκόμας *Su.* 975, χλωρόκομος *IA* 759, εὔλυρος fr. 477, εὐλύρας *Alc.* 570.

120 πρόπαρ perhaps from προπάροιθε rather than πρό + παρά (cf. Wackernagel, *Syntax* II.232–4), so probably not to be written πρόπαρ᾽ (West on Hes. *Th.* 518), though the word is attested before a vowel six times (probably all prepositional) vs. πρόπαρ θανούσας (adv.) Aesch. *Su.* 791. The gen. στρατοῦ must be governed by πρόπαρ, since ἡγέομαι + gen. is 'be leader of a group' (*Ba.* 1334) and the sense here is 'lead the way' (absolutely; or with dat. 'lead someone along the way'). πρόπαρ as prep. usually means 'alongside' (cf. 827; whether 'before, beyond' or 'alongside' is intended in Hes. *Th.* 518 is unclear); but 'in front of a man' seems the likelier interpretation of *Ag.* 1019 πρόπαρ ἀνδρός; and even if πρόπαρ is taken as temporal adverb there, the local sense 'in front of' is paralleled for πάροιθε and προπάροιθε.

121–2 πάγχαλκον ἀσπίδ᾽ cf. *Se.* 590–1 (Amphiaraus), but the juncture of the adj. with weapon or armour is not quite rare enough to ensure that there is a deliberate allusion (as Saïd, 508, suggests).

ἀμφὶ βραχίονι the dative is the more poetic case and also more precise here, expressing actual position, not mere proximity (contrast *Tro.* 1137 [ἀσπίδα] ἣν πατὴρ τοῦδ᾽ ἀμφὶ|πλευρ᾽ ἐβάλλετο).

κουφίζων a common verb, but the special meanings 'lift lightly', 'bear lightly' , 'make (or leap) lightly' are affected by Soph. and Eur. (LSJ s.v. II.1). Antigone consistently notes details of reflected light and graceful movement (110–11, 119, 129, 138, 146, 168–9, 172, 177–8), even as she expresses fear and utters hostile prayers.

123 the banality of the Servant's answer may simply be intended to counterpoint Ant.'s excitement and impatience. Here for the first time in the scene she uses trimeter speech, but with antilabe; τίς πόθεν in asyndeton also marks excitement; repetition of questions may convey excitement (*Contact and Discontinuity* 39ff.; Kannicht on *Hel.* 84–6 for repetition in requests for identification). Depending on what is read in 118, it may be preferable or necessary to recognize Ant.'s question as an interruption (so first Geel); if it is one, it forces the Servant to abandon the sentence he had begun (*Contact and Discontinuity* 58–9). I prefer to punctuate with a period. Deletion of 123–4 (Dindorf; supported by Diggle 1990a) seems to me too drastic a reaction to the dialogue-sequence (118n.).

124 αὔδησον the form with η is due to Matthiae. There are two possible explanations for αὔδασον with Doric ᾱ. (1) The Doric tint of Ant.'s lyrics spills over into her trimeter (Hermann; deletion of 123 alone would make this slightly more probable). But this does not occur elsewhere in the scene (cf. 145, 172, 179; μορφᾶς 162 (L𝄐) has little chance of being an ancient variant), nor to my knowledge in the trimeters of comparable scenes in other plays. (2) αὐδᾶν is a poetic word not native to Attic and so retains its non-Attic vocalism even in trimeters: so λοχᾱγός, ὀπᾱδός, etc.; verbs πόρπᾱσον *Prom.* 61 (like πόρπᾱμα), ποινᾱσόμεσθα *IT* 1433 (like ποινᾱτωρ). But Eur. himself may have ἀναύδητος (*Ion* 782, *sed locus corruptus*) and αὐδήσειεν fr. 1064.7 (*sed lectio dubia*); Soph. has αὐδήσει *OT* 846, προσαυδήσω *Aj.* 855, αὐδῆσαι *Trach.* 171, αὐδηθείς *Trach.* 1106; αὔδασον is not to be read in Aesch. fr. 20. Björck, 139–42, does not defend αὔδασον convincingly. It is better viewed as a scribal error than as an idiosyncratic Euripidean decision.

126 Λερναῖα δ' οἰκεῖ νάμαθ' for the close identification of a local river or spring with the citizens of the locality cf. Fraenkel on *Ag.* 1157, Kannicht on *Hel.* 1–3. See also 222n., 347–8n., 368n., 574, 613. The supposed ruin of Hippomedon's house at Lerna was displayed in Pausanias' day (2.36.8).

127 γαῦρος almost a *Lieblingswort* for Eur., who also has γαυρόομαι and γαύρωμα, whereas Aesch. and Soph. have none of these.

128–9 a very difficult passage. There are two basic approaches to the transmitted text, already present in Σ. (a) 'How haughty, how terrible to look upon, like an earthborn giant in painting,[1] dazzling-faced, not like the mortal race!' References in tragedy to something seen only in art may imply the speaker's lack of first-hand experience or the monstrosity or foreignness of the thing referred to: Aesch. *Su.* 282–3, *Eum.* 49–51; *Hipp.* 1005, *Tro.* 687, *Ion* 271. Here both connotations would be involved. The principal difficulty with this view is the need to take ἐν γραφαῖσιν as attributive with γίγαντι, despite its position. Hyperbaton of various kinds is found in tragedy (lists in Pearson on *Hel.* 719, Wilam. on *Her.* 222, Kaibel, *El.* p. 279 n. 1; cf. Stinton, *PCPS* 201 (1975) 82ff., 'Notes II' 131f.), but I know of no case closely comparable to this one. The difficulty here seems to lie in the facts that (1) the attribute is not an adjective which by

---

[1] I see no justification for Craik's 'in outline' for ἐν γραφαῖσιν.

its termination clearly shows where it belongs in sense and (2) the intervening term is not προσόμοιος, but includes the adjective ἀστερωπός in apposition, a sequence which makes γίγαντι ... πρόσφορος seem to be a closed phrase (in most hyperbata there is an obvious sense of suspension after the first element which is only resolved when the accompanying element is reached: cf. 88 κλεινὸν ... θάλος). Despite the difficulty, most scholars from Hartung on have adopted (a). (b) 'How haughty, how terrible to look upon, like an earthborn giant, star-bedecked in the painting ⟨of his shield⟩, not like the mortal race.' This view takes seriously the rhetorical phrasing which may be implied if there is period-end after προσόμοιος. The -ωπ- element of ἀστερωπός will here carry no etymological meaning: Eur. affects compounds in -ωπός/-ώψ (cf., e.g., F. Sommer, *SBAW* 27 (1948) 6), and in a few the -ωπ- element is merely an adjectival suffix with no semantic contribution (*IT* 1279 νυκτωπός = νύκτερος), though usually there is some imagistic or personifying force (cf. Jebb on *Aj*. 954f. κελανώπαν θυμόν; I would argue that -ωπ- is not meaningless in *IT* 263 κοιλωπὸς ἀγμός, *Ba.* 553-4 χρυσῶπα ... θύρσον). This reading has seemed to many to receive support from the picture on Hippomedon's shield described in 1115-17, but even if those lines are by Eur. they cannot induce an audience which has not yet heard them to interpret line 129 accordingly. (On Dihle's view, see 88-201n. Authenticity.) The most serious objection to (b), however, is that ἐν γραφαῖσιν cannot refer either to 'painted garment' (Σ and translators before Valck.) or to a shield-painting (Valck.) in the absence of τῆς ἀσπίδος (esp. after 121 πάγχαλκον ἀσπίδ᾽), and even if ἀσπίδος could be supplied mentally, the sense assumed for ἐν is dubious. (One who favours (b) might do well to delete ἐν.)

I conclude that (b) cannot be right and that (a) should be right, but one cannot be confident in the transmitted text. There are many emendations, none attractive: some eliminate γίγαντι as a gloss; some alter ἀστερωπός to a proper name (Aster, Steropes, Asteropos or -opes), usually introducing ὅπως, οἷος, or ὡς; Fecht softens the hyperbaton by transposing ἐν γραφαῖσιν and ἀστερωπός. The deletion of ἐν γραφαῖσιν would eliminate all problems, but the phrase is earlier than Π³ and not a likely gloss, and the motif fits well with Ant.'s character and with reference to a giant. The simplest change is ἀστερωπὸς ⟨ὡς⟩ ἐν γρ. (cf. *Ag.* 242 and Nauck's (1859) στερρωπὸς ὡς γραφαῖσιν or στερρωπὸς ὥσπερ ἐν γραφαῖσιν). Since dochmiacs are often corrupted into iambic or near-iambic form, further adjustments in rhythm can be made by reading γραφαῖς and/or οὐ (Tricl.), but note that Π³ already reflects the text found in mss.

128 γίγαντι γηγενέται the jingling sound is not inexpressive, the rhythm rare but paralleled; this reading should be retained. Π³'s garbled version does not seem to me to reflect a better text: *ZPE* 49 (1982) 12 against Levitt, *AJP* 83 (1962) 422-3, approved by Ferrari, *ASNP* ser. 3,

11:2 (1981) 284–6. Comparison of one of the Seven with a giant may recall *Se.* 424 (Capaneus).

129 ἀστερωπός 'starry-faced', i.e. 'with dazzling visage'. Ant. can see the crest and note Hippomedon's arrogance, so it is reasonable to assume that she can observe his face (cf. 146–7). The epithet is in part explanatory of 'like a giant'. Giants in Greek art were depicted as hoplite-warriors until about 500 B.C., and thereafter as nude savages or savages clothed in animal skins (F. Vian, *EAA* s.v. Giganti). There is nothing particularly star-like about them (Σ129 ἀστεροειδεῖς τὸ σῶμα καὶ τὴν ἐσθῆτα γράφουσι τοὺς Γίγαντας πρὸς τὸ φοβερὸν αὐτῶν is scholiastic invention). But in a painting the facial expression is an obvious tool for conveying savagery, and brightness of glance is associated with ability to inspire terror in γοργός, γοργωπός, μαρμαρωπός, etc. (cf. Wilam. on *Her.* 130 and 883). In other interpretations ἀστερωπός = ἀστερόεις (128–9n.).

129–30 ἐν γραφαῖσιν if the meaning 'star-bedecked in his shield-painting' is preferred, ἐν should probably be deleted (128–9n.).

πρόσφορος here only = 'similar to' (+dat); the slight shift from its common sense 'suitable to' is made clear by the typical polar opposition γίγαντι προσόμοιος ... οὐχὶ πρόσφορος ἀμ. γέν. Compare προφερής, which is commonly 'similar to', but at least once 'suitable to' (Hdt. 5.111.3). The unusual choice is presumably metrically conditioned (see above under Metre).

130 ἀμερίωι the variant ἀμερίων (cf. *IA* 1330–1 γένος ... ἀμερίων; *Aj.* 398–400, probably to be construed γένος ... ἀμερίων ... ἀνθρώπων) is more obvious and therefore rejected. Cf. 1512 αἵματος ἀμερίου, taken by many to mean 'of the mortal race' (but see *ad loc.*).

131–2 Two problems intersect in these lines: whether to leave 131 in the mouth of the Servant and whether to read 132 as a full trimeter or not. Hamaker (apud Geel) assigned all of 127–33a to Ant. on the ground that Ant. should do all the asking, the Servant answer only (for the resulting mix of lyric and iambic cf. 145–9, 161–9). This is an insufficient reason: whatever we read at 118, the Servant takes some initiative there, and it is arbitrary to assume that Eur. did not vary the pattern at all. The transmitted division gives superior dramatic sense: Ant. is absorbed in the dazzling terror of Hippomedon's appearance, but the servant urges her on to the next leader (cf. 114–18). As for λοχαγόν, its presence has respectable authority, including Π³ and B,[1] and it could easily have been omitted

---

[1] It is best to regard Π³'s nominative as one of the scribe's many errors of case-ending. K. Matthiessen, *Studien zur Textüberlieferung der Hekabe des Eur.* [Bibl. d. kl. Altertumswiss. n. F., 2. Reihe, 52 (Heidelberg 1974)] 57, recommends, however, that Ant. be assigned the reply λοχαγὸς ἄλλος· ἄλλος ὅδε τευχέων τρόπος.

when, in ancient and medieval fashion, it occupied a line by itself. Without the word, Ant. would have an isolated short lyric intervention (in similar scenes such short lyric lines occur only when there is an interlacing of short utterances by both voices). If these words are Ant.'s, three features mark her excitement even in iambic trimeter: the repetition ἄλλος ἄλλος (cf. *Hec.* 689 (leading into dochmiacs) ἄπιστ' ἄπιστα, καινὰ καινὰ δέρκομαι; *Ion* 1472, where I believe a full trimeter should be restored: ἄλλοθεν ⟨σὺ⟩ γέγονας, ἄλλοθεν); the fact that she comments on the strangeness of the armour before asking 'who?'; and the antilabe in successive lines which gives 132a and 133b to the servant, 132b–33a to Ant. (cf. *ZPE* 49 (1982) 13 n. 11; W. Köhler, *Die Versbrechung bei den griechischen Tragikern* (Darmstadt 1913) 51–2). Diggle (1990a) 9 commended Buchholtz's λοχαγὸν ἄλλον;, suggesting that 131–2 in their entirety belong to the Servant (whereas Buchholtz followed Hamaker in giving 127–33a to Ant. without break); he now prefers to follow Nauck and Leutsch in deleting 132, noting that the latter half anticipates 138. If λοχ. is not printed, Ant's line gives 2 hypodochmiacs or 3 cretics (or 2 cr, ia with trisyllabic τευχέων): cf. Parker, *CQ* 18 (1968) 261.

131   Tydeus is presumably imagined to be crossing from the area north of the Cadmeia (between Dirce and Hismenus) to the west bank of Dirce in order to reach the west side of Thebes without approaching too close to the walls and exposing his troops to missiles. See Appendix on Topography.

133   Π³ has τίς οὗτός ἐστι; For word-order there is little to choose between this and the mss text, but the asyndeton seems doubtful: *ZPE* 49 (1982) 13–14 (add *Hipp.* 1050).

134 Ἄρη   'warlike spirit' as in *Ag.* 78, Aesch. *Su.* 749, Soph. *El.* 1242, perhaps *Ant.* 952; Gorgias 82 в 6 D–K (p. 286, 10–11). The warlike nature of the Aetolians has literary tradition behind it (*Il.* 9.529 Αἰτωλοὶ μενεχάρμαι) and contemporary historical support (Thuc. 3.94.4 τὸ γὰρ ἔθνος μέγα . . . καὶ μάχιμον). Thuc. also attests contemporary judgment of the Aetolians as culturally backward (still living off plunder and bearing arms in daily life, 1.5–6; dwelling in scattered villages only, without fortification, 3.94.4) and militarily unorthodox (σκευῆι ψιλῆι χρώμενον, 3.94.4; ψιλοί and the repeated verb ἐσακοντίζειν, 3.97–8). Ἄρην is often a variant for Ἄρη in tragic texts (Teubner app. here, 939, 1006, 1124), but it is nowhere required by metre and unlikely to be original (at *Se.* 45 read Ἄρη τ', not Ἄρην with Page); cf. 72n.

ἐν στέρνοις   for στέρνον as seat of manly spirit cf. Soph. fr. 201e ἀνδρῶν γὰρ ἐσθλῶν στέρνον οὐ μαλάσσεται; for other feelings, cf. LSJ s.v. 1.2.

135–8   the rhetorical question probably has a tone of surprise verging on disbelief ('apistetic': *Contact and Discontinuity* 12f.), and the tone is explained by the exclamation which returns to the strange (non-hoplite) appearance of Tydeus' arms.

136 αὐτοκασιγνήται the style is deliberately convoluted, but the gen. of the mss (kept by Craik) renders the whole too obscure. Reiske saw the solution and Π³ confirms it. αὐτοκασιγνήτη (used outside of epic only here), like the hapax συγκασιγνήτη (*IT* 800), seems to be an intensifying compound, 'very own sister'. See *LfgrE* s.v. αὐτοκασίγνητος; cf. αὐτάδελφος, αὐτανέψιος and αὐτεπώνυμον (769n.)

137 ὁμόγαμος as with many compound adjs. involving kinship-words (*EMC* n.s. 2 (1983) 102), the meaning varies with the context: *Her.* 339 'who shares the same wife/husband', like σύλλεκτρος *Her.* 1, σύγγαμος *Her.* 149, *Andr.* 182, ὁμόλεκτρος *Or.* 476; but here 'who shares marriage with' = 'spouse' (LSJ errs), like σύλλεκτρος *Her.* 1268, σύγγαμος *El.* 212, *Andr.* 836, ὁμόλεκτρος *Or.* 508 (cf. 428n.). All these compounds are extant in Eur. alone among classical authors.

138 ἀλλόχρως attested only in Eur. (*Andr.* 879; *Hipp.* 175 heteroclite form -χροος) before the late fourth century (Theophrastus, [Arist.] *Probl.*). A few compounds in -χρως are found in earlier Greek (Homeric ταμεσίχρως, μελάγχρως Hdt., κελαινόχρως Aesch. *Su.* 785 [restored]), but Eur. is the first to coin or employ several ornate compounds (αἰολο-, ἁπαλο-, κυανο-, λευκο-, πολιο-, χιονο-), a mannerism revived by late Greek poets. Eur. varies freely among -χρως, -χρωτος (308bis below, *Hec.* 1106, *Or.* 321); -χρως, -χροος (acc. -χροα 323 below, *Hel.* 373; -χρων? *Ba.* 1365); -χροος, -χρόου (*Hipp.* 175, *Hel.* 1502; contracted -χρουν *Rhes.* 716).

μειξο- cf. Meisterhans³, p. 51 n. 400 (also p. 36 n. 193, p. 181 n. 1496). For this judgment of the Aetolians, 134n.

139 σακεσφόροι apparently 'bearing (light) shields of leather (or hide)'. From the context one assumes that the Aetolian σάκος differs in weight and material from the bronze (or bronze-and-wood) shield of the standard hoplite, although σάκος in poetry is often used loosely to refer to a shield of any material and may be synonymous with ἀσπίς (*Il.* 13.130–1; *Se.* 387, 389, *et passim*, Eur. *El.* 455, 464, *Tro.* 1136, 1222, *Phoen.* 1105, 1107). σάκος seems, however, to have retained its etymological connection with leather or hide when used of Ajax: cf. his famous σάκος χάλκεον ἑπταβόειον (*Il.* 7.219–20, whence *Aj.* 576) and esp. *Aj.* 19 Αἴαντι τῶι σακεσφόρωι (the only other occurrence of the adj.). Note that in the shield-descriptions of 1104–40, suspected by many, Tydeus has a lion's hide on his shield, not a painted or sculpted design (1120–2n.). Craik sees the contrast rather as between a larger Mycenean-style body-shield and a smaller hoplite's shield.

πάντες Tydeus leads a contingent of Aetolians (1165–7).

140 ἀκοντιστῆρες the use of javelins rather than the heavier thrusting-spear of the hoplite is another feature of light-armed warfare (134n.). The word is hapax in classical Greek (revived in Oppian and Nonnus), coined for metrical convenience as an alternative to ἀκοντιστής.

141–4 this exchange first came under suspicion because of the verbatim repetition of line 97 in 143 (143n.), but there are other serious problems. (1) What does 141 mean? (a) If Ant. is digressing from the survey of leaders to ask 'How do you recognize (know?) these facts (the identifications of all the leaders) reliably?', the Servant's answer is suitable. But αἰσθάνηι = 'recognize ⟨a fact⟩' is poorly supported by the use of the aorist ἠισθόμην = 'recognize ⟨a voice⟩', as in *Hec.* 1114, *Ba.* 178, *Rhes.* 608 (and the sense 'know' seems to be unparalleled: *Her.* 1312 εὖ τόδ' αἰσθάνηι is 'perceive, realize'; cf. *Or.* 752); τάδε is ambiguous after 139–40, and (given that Ant. has heard 95–8) there is no good reason for the poet to have Ant. ask this here. (b) If Ant. is not digressing but means 'How do you know these facts ⟨about Aetolian soldiers⟩?', the Servant's answer fits poorly and αἰσθάνηι is still abnormal. (c) If Ant. means 'How do you perceive (see) these facts (Aetolian weaponry) clearly?' (as if she cannot see clearly herself: cf. 161; Barlow, 58, believes that the whole scene implies the half-mist of early dawn), this is not congruent with her own pinpointing of details before and after this passage, and the Servant's reply is convoluted (virtually 'I can tell by the shield-symbols who they are and don't need a clear view of the details'). (2) (a) If ἐγνώρισα in 142 is an instantaneous aorist ('I've recognized them now'), as the Homeric precedent *Il.* 5.182 ἀσπίδι γιγνώσκων implies, then προσδεδορκώς and οἶδα are woefully redundant. (b) If ἐγνώρισα refers to the past ('I got to know them then'), then 144 'seeing which now, I know the men ⟨so⟩ armed' is less redundant, but still 'a lame and paltry addition' (Pearson). It seems best to delete the whole passage.[1] Less drastic solutions are to delete 143 alone (Burges, Geel) or to delete 143–4 (Busche). In either case τότ' in 142 is left rather bare,[2] but the usage is perhaps possible. τότε sometimes gets its definite reference from the immediate context: *Hel.* 1081 ἐς καιρὸν ἦλθε, τότε δ' ἄκαιρ' ἀπώλλυτο; Soph. *El.* 278–9 ἱεροῦσ' ἐκείνην ἡμέραν, ἐν ἧι τότε πατέρα . . . κατέκτανεν; *Aj.* 650 ὃς τὰ δείν' ἐκαρτέρουν τότε; see Bond on *Hyps.* fr. 60, 30; Pearson on *Hcld.* 970 (but Pearson believes that τότε is sometimes indefinite 'formerly'; I would say rather that the context always implies definition). So here ἰδών, with 95–8 in the background, could imply the definite time 'when I went there and saw them'. Bergk, *Phil* 16 (1860) 616–18, believing that Eur. must have devoted some space to

---

[1] Here for once the theory of interpolation to compensate for a cut (Friedrich) seems plausible (428n.): if 88–102 were cut, the addition of 141–4 (or perhaps only 141–3, 144 deriving from a reader's erroneous elaboration) would supply an identification of the Servant and a rapid nod to verisimilitude.

[2] Hartung's τάδ' for τότ' is unattractive.

Adrastus, proposed a lacuna after 140 (with 141–4 perhaps a spurious filler); this is unnecessary (160n.).

143 Verbatim repetition of a line within the same play is generally accepted to be a strong index of suspicion of deliberate or accidental interpolation (1282 (=976) is an obvious case of the latter), but few editors are willing to judge such repetition absolutely impossible. The repetition at *Hcld.* 221–2a = 97–8a is retained by Diggle; that at *Or.* 536 = 625 is retained by many edd.: the emphasis created by such repetitions has a dramatic value (as does the all but verbatim repetition *Hipp.* 898 = 1049, defended by Barrett). Here the repetition has no such value: it does not even 'characterize' the Servant, as some allege, it merely identifies him again, superfluously. Nor is there room to argue that Ant. did not hear 97 because there is imperfect dialogue-contact at 97 (cf. the cases discussed in *Contact and Discontinuity* 28–32), since she is addressed at 88 and obeys the orders of 92 and 100. 143 should be deleted even by an editor who retains 141–2. On Wecklein's alternative proposal (1901), to delete 94–8 and retain 141–4, cf. 94–8n. and Friedrich, 269. See also 756n., 1376n., 1282n.; for verbatim repetition of a line from another play, 972n.; for near-verbatim repetition within a play, 912n., 1243n., 1360n.; between two plays, 372n., 778n., 1634n., 1758–9n.[1]

145 μνῆμα τὸ Ζήθου just north of the citadel of Thebes is a mound, called Ἀμφεῖον, considered in later antiquity and probably in Eur.'s time to be the common tomb of Amphion and Zethos (see Appendix on Topography; cf. Schachter 1.28–9).[2] This monument is also cited in *Se.* 528 (Amphion's tomb) when Parthenopaeus is described. Moving alongside this mound, Parthenopaeus and his troops are imagined to be not far from Tydeus' Aetolians (131n.).

---

[1] Major discussions of *versus iterati*: C. G. Firnhaber, *Die Verdächtigungen Euripideischer Versen beleuchtet und in den Phoinissen und der Medea zurückgewiesen* (Leipzig 1840); P. Wesener, *de repetitione versuum in fabulis Euripideis* (Bonn 1866); F. Schroeder, *de iteratis apud tragicos graecos* [Diss. phil. Argent. selectae 6:1 (Strasbourg 1882)] (little more than a compilation of lists); Page, *Actors' Interp.* 103–5; P. W. Harsh, 'Repetition of lines in Eur.', *Hermes* 72 (1937) 435–49; P. D. Arnott, 'Line-repetitions and diptychal structure in Eur.', *Philological Quarterly* 40 (1961) 307–13; J. Baumert, *ENIOI ΑΘΕΤΟΥΣΙΝ. Untersuchungen zu Athetesen bei Eur. am Beispiel der Alkestis und Medea* (Tübingen 1968); Mueller-Goldingen 280–330.

[2] Part of the difficulty Dihle has with the topographical references of this scene and 1104–40 is due to his rejection of this identification.

πέρᾱι   used absolutely, either 'passes, moves along (by the Ampheion)' or 'crosses over (the Dirce, at a spot near the Ampheion)'; for the former cf. 844 below, for the latter *Pers.* 721.

146 καταβόστρυχος   probably 'with abundant curls' (Σ τὸ γὰρ κατά πλήθους ἐμφαντικόν) rather than 'with down-flowing locks'; cf. *Ba.* 1186–7 γένυν ... κατάκομον (simply 'hairy') and see Schwyzer 11.495 on κατα-compounds of this kind. κατάσκιος is found from Homer on, κατάπτερος is shared by *Prom.* 798 and *Or.* 176, Soph. has κάθυδρος (*OC* 158), but it is Eur. in his later plays who first extends the use of these adjs. (καταβόστρυχος, κατάκομος, κάτοινος are all hapax in classical Greek, κάθαιμος occurs only in Eur.), and the tendency is carried on in post-classical prose and poetry. For Parthenopaeus' beauty, cf. *Su.* 889, 899–900, Aesch. *Se.* 532ff., and below 1159–62.

ὄμμασι γοργός   'with bright and terrifying eyes' (129n.); an imitation of *Se.* 537 γοργὸν δ᾽ ὄμμ᾽ ἔχων. On the variant γοργός τ᾽, see *Text. Trad.* 108.

147 νεανίας   Parthenopaeus' youth is emphasized for pathetic effect in 1160–2.

148–9   Markland and Hermann independently restored sense by re-moving change of speaker before and after λοχαγός. The assignment in the mss (only L reliably reflects a correct treatment, either as a unique survival or under Triclinian influence) results from reminiscence of 123 and misconstrues causal ὡς as exclamatory.

ὑστέρωι ποδί   'coming behind', as in *Her.* 1040 and (in a more preg-nant sense) *Hipp.* 1243; cf. 301–3n.

ἀμφέπει   the phrase is somewhat artificial (but typical of the style) in that the ἀμφ- element in 'throng *around*, attend upon' is nullified by the modifier ὑστέρωι ποδί, so that the sense is almost simply 'follow'.

150   enough has been said about Parthenopaeus; Wesener's suggestion that a second verse spoken by the Servant has been lost is quite improbable.

151–3   after repeated expressions of fear and wonder (and a note of familial curiosity in 135–7), Ant. finally curses an enemy; but the mixture of emotions continues as the Servant remarks on justice and Ant. expresses love, longing, and wonder before reaching a new climax in the implied curse of 181a–92.

154 σὺν δίκηι   Polynices' claim to δίκη (along with Eteocles' ἀδικία) becomes a leitmotif of the first third of the play: 258, 319, 369, 452, 467, 470, 471, 490, 492, 496, 524–5, 532, 548, 549, 608.

155 ὃ καὶ δέδοικα μή   the same half-line occurs at 263 (and at Arist. *Eccl.* 338), but there is no reason to suspect either occurrence on that account; in writing 263 Eur. had the phrase fresh in his mind, but the repetition carries no special meaning. The two parallels (cf. also *Od.* 4.206

COMMENTARY 155-60

ὃ καὶ πεπνύμενα βάζεις, Dem. 19.86 ὃ καὶ θαυμάζω, and perhaps *Hec.* 13–14 ὃ καί με γῆς ὑπεξέπεμψεν [sc. Πρίαμος]), and the idiomatic responsive καί preceding δέδοικα (Denniston, *GP*² 294–5) indicate that ὅ is 'wherefore' rather than 'which fact' (as object of σκοπῶσ'). Absolute σκοπεῖν is normally confined to the sense of physically looking or watching out (*IT* 68, 76, *Hel.* 578, *Or.* 1291, *Ba.* 1279), but in *Rhes.* 339 καιρίως σκοπεῖς = 'you look ⟨to what is advantageous⟩ in a fitting manner' the object is implicit in the context, and so here the meaning will be 'and that is the very reason why I fear that the gods may look rightly ⟨to the justice of his case⟩'.

156 Ant.'s concern to see her brother alludes to Helen's final comment in her teichoskopia (*Il.* 3.236–42), where she wonders why she cannot see Castor and Polydeuces. The allusion marks Ant.'s position, deceptively, as more fortunate, since she sees her brother and is told she will see him up close when he enters the city (170n.).

ἐμοὶ μιᾶς . . . ἐκ ματρός both the sense 'from one and the same mother' and the dative construction (either of advantage/possession or on the analogy of dat. with τῆς αὐτῆς) are borrowed from *Il.* 3.238 τώ μοι μία γείνατο μήτηρ (cf. 19.293). For 'same mother' as a mark of the closest kinship ('same father' being understood), cf. 11n. and *IT* 497 πότερον ἀδελφὼ μητρός ἐστον ἐκ μιᾶς;

157 πολυπόνωι probably with a deliberate reinforcing echo in Πολυνείκης in the next line, as also in 1492–4 πολύστονον . . . Πολύνεικες; cf. 1022n.

159–60 ἑπτὰ παρθένων τάφου . . . Νιόβης Paus. 9.16.4 (with no allusion to conflicting traditions) mentions the tomb of the daughters of Niobe among the sights located outside the Proetid Gate and north of the road to Chalcis, in the vicinity of the theatre and the agora of the lower town. If Eur. has the same location in mind, Pol. and Adrastus are to be imagined to have crossed the Hismenus, but to be farther east than Parthenopaeus. See Appendix on Topography. Aristodemus of Thebes or Alexandria (*FGrHist* 383), active *c.* 150–130 B.C., at a time when the portion of Thebes outside the acropolis lay waste and abandoned, denied the existence of a tomb of the Niobids at Thebes (perhaps because he found no epigraphic evidence, perhaps partly because he favoured a different location on mythographic grounds): fr. 3 Jacoby = Σ on this line. It is of course possible that Eur. indulges in autoschediasm (as Σ concludes) and freely invents the monument, but more likely he conveys a contemporary tradition which, for whatever reason, Aristodemus could not verify in his day (cf. Jacoby). The number of Niobids varied in different sources: see Barrett apud R. Carden, *The Papyrus Fragments of Sophocles* (Berlin 1974), 227. For παρθένων = 'daughters' cf. Diggle, *Phaethon*, p. 76 n. 1.

160 Ἀδράστωι πλησίον παραστατεῖ a token of the relationship of Pol.

195

and Adrastus; A. receives no separate description here, but this is not objectionable in such an informal survey (141–4n. *ad fin.*), and the omission may be due to Adrastus' lack of marked traits of personality in the tradition (Adrastus is not counted as one of the Seven in *Se.* and Eur. *Su.*).

161 ὁρᾶις; ὁρῶ . . . ὁρῶ . . . the notion of the difficulty of viewing from a distance is deployed emphatically at just this point not as a matter of realism, but in order to heighten the poignancy of Ant.'s separation from her brother. There is no comparable reason for the reference to difficulty in viewing some critics detect in [141–4] above.

162 μορφῆς τύπωμα στέρνα τ' ἐξηικασμένα 'the moulded outline of his form and the semblance of his chest'; the language emphasizes that there is something unreal, unoriginal, or unconcrete about what Ant. can experience of her brother. τύπωμα occurs in classical Greek only here and in Soph. *El.* 54 ('urn of moulded metal') and was probably coined as a high-style variation on τύπος. ἐξηικασμένα (here only in Eur.; twice Aesch., once Arist.) in the sense 'made in the form of a (mere) likeness' is similar to *Ag.* 1244 οὐδὲν ἐξήικ. 'things not (spoken) in images' (see Fraenkel *ad loc.*; but the sense in *Se.* 445 is different and simpler (446 is not to be deleted: cf. Hutchinson)).[1]

163–7 the wish to fly is typically found either in escape-wishes prompted by desperation or (as here) in impossible wishes to be where one cannot be and witness what one cannot witness; add this passage to those cited by Barrett on *Hipp.* 732–4 and 1290–3.

163 ἀνεμώκεος (only occurrence in Eur.) 'wind-swift', i.e. 'borne swiftly on the wind'; cf. *Birds* 697 ἀνεμώκεσι δίναις 'swift whirls of the wind' (*PMG* adesp. 958 ἀνεμώκεα κόραν).

163–4 δρόμον . . . ἐξανύσαιμι a periphrasis for δράμοιμι; δρόμον = 'racing' rather than 'path' (cf. *Alc.* 245 νεφέλας δρομαίου, *Hel.* 1488 σύννομοι νεφέων δρόμου); cf. *Tro.* 232 στείχει ταχύπουν ἴχνος ἐξανύτων 'comes accomplishing a swift-footed pace'.

165 ὁμογενέτορα hapax in extant Greek, a variant *metri gratia* for ὁμογενῆ (the fully resolved dochmiac marks a climax of Ant.'s emotion at the mention of her dear brother). The compound is unusual in two ways: (1) formation from adverb element + verbal element is unique (Breitenbach, 58); (2) the suffix -τωρ is in origin suited only to verbal compounds with transitive meanings. But (1) ὁμο- is very much like συν-,

---

[1] West (*Aeschylus*, xlii) has accepted the speculation of Wackernagel, *Kl. Schr.* 1.584, that (like ἐργάζομαι: 1062n.) εἰκάζω had augment in ἠι- but reduplication in εἰ-; this is possibly correct, but Wackernagel made a rather partial use of the evidence of the mss, which is of uncertain value in any case (cf. K–B II.410).

and Eur. has two other hapax compounds formed from preposition + verbal element (*Hipp.* 1380 προγεννήτωρ, *El.* 746 συγγενέτειρα); (2) as Ernst Fraenkel, *Nom. agentis* 1.48, indicates, the tragedians artificially extended the use of these suffixes to form lyric compounds of unusual shape, and passive -γενέτωρ is precisely paralleled in συγγενέτειρα = 'sister' (so rightly Fraenkel and Denniston *ad loc.*; not 'mother', as Breitenbach and LSJ). Cf. 128 γηγενέτης for γηγενής.

165–6 περὶ δ' ... βάλοιμι tmesis of περί is rare in tragedy, but four of the six instances involve περιβάλλω (here, *Andr.* 115, *Ag.* 1559, all modelled on *Od.* 11.211 φίλας περὶ χεῖρε βαλόντε; *Ba.* 619; other verbs *Hel.* 628, *Pers.* 872). From Homer on περιβάλλω χεῖρας vel sim. (usually absolute, but with dat. here and 1459 below) is idiomatic, but Eur. varies the construction in *Or.* 372 (Ὀρέστην) φίλαισι χερσὶ περιβαλεῖν and *IT* 796 σ' ἀπίστωι περιβαλὼν βραχίονι. V²'s variant ὠλέναις δέρην φιλτάταις is thus grammatically possible, but it departs from the Homeric precedent and is probably a conjecture or gloss designed to ease or clarify the construction of φυγάδα (167n.).

166 βάλοιμι χρόνωι many follow Hermann in reading -μ' ⟨ἐν⟩ χρόνωι to avoid metrically heavy treatment of final short vowel before initial mute and liquid, in the belief that this is to be doubted either in tragic lyrics in general or in dochmiacs in particular (e.g., Conomis, 39–40). But it is not justifiable to eliminate all instances of this phenomenon in tragic lyric in general (Fraenkel, *Ag.* comm. III.826f.; Barrett on *Hipp.* 760 with addenda, pp. 434, 439). And if the phenomenon is admitted in tragic lyric in general, then there seems to me to be no statistical or theoretical justification for eliminating it from dochmiacs: what is already very rarely attested in non-dochmiac lyric will naturally be extremely rarely attested in dochmiacs, since the sample studied is less extensive. At Soph. *El.* 853 Lloyd-Jones and Wilson print εἴδομεν ἃ θροεῖς (= 864 ἄσκοπος ἃ λώβα), noting in *Sophoclea*, 59, Diggle's elimination of the example; Barrett accepts ὁ τλάμων *Hipp.* 837 (Diggle prints Elmsley's ὦ τλάμων); Murray printed γελῶντι προσώπωι at *Ba.* 1021, but himself suggested transposition (accepted by Dodds and Kopff). *IA* 1285 is too uncertain to be considered. On the other hand, it might be argued against βάλοιμι χρόνωι that the words do not cohere closely like ὁ τλάμων and perhaps ἃ θροεῖς. There has been disagreement whether ἐν χρόνωι improves the diction, ruins idiom, or is idiomatically identical to plain χρόνωι. Certainly in the sense 'after a while, with the passage of time' (in contrast to αὐτίκα expressed or implied) χρόνωι and ἐν χρόνωι are used synonymously (cf. *Alc.* 1036, *Ba.* 294 with *Andr.* 782, *OT* 613; Jebb on *OC* 88); and with an adj. we find ἐν χρόνωι μακρῶι *Phil.* 235 = 'now at last after a long time'; but otherwise the sense 'now at last after a time' (as commonly found in scenes of reunion and recognition) is conveyed by χρόνωι alone (Eur. *El.* 578–9 ὦ χρόνωι φανείς, / ἔχω σ' ἀέλπτως. κἀξ ἐμοῦ γ' ἔχηι χρόνωι; *Her.* 607 χρόνωι δ' ἀνελθών; *Phoen.* 295 ἔβας ὦ χρόνωι; cf. *IA* 640 ἐσεῖδόν σ' ἀσμένη πολλῶι χρόνωι, Soph. *El.* 1273 χρόνωι μακρῶι, *Trach.* 227–8 χρόνωι / πολλῶι φανέντα). In 304–5 χρόνωι ... μυρίαις τ' ἐν ἁμέραις it is ambiguous whether ἐν applies back to χρόνωι. Possibly there is a slight idiomatic preference for χρόνωι over ἐν χρόνωι in phrases of this kind. One may retain χρόνωι and eliminate the metrical anomaly with Diggle's βάλοιμεν (1989); West 1990 commends Pluygers' χρονία.

167 φυγάδα μέλεον this acc. has troubled scholars since antiquity. (a) I print περὶ δ' ... χρόνωι as parenthetic or διὰ μέσου, so that φυγάδα is in apposition to ὁμογενέτορα (so Σ, Pearson; earlier King and Musgrave, but with comma wrongly placed before χρόνωι). For parenthetic sentence or phrase of similar length, cf. *Hipp.* 304b–305a, *Andr.* 573b–74, *El.* 608–9a, 788–9a, *Ba.* 1316b–17, *IA* 66b–67, 392b–93 (*Rhes.* 220b–21, unless 222f. are interpolated; 939–40a). Especially striking is the lyric instance *Hel.* 1471–5. Formally, the present instance is comparable to *Il.* 11.738–9 and *Hec.* 919–21, cited by Diggle, *ICS* 6.1 (1981) 92 (cf. K–G 1.80 and see Diggle p. 100 n. 28 for further references). In most cases of parenthesis the audience can feel the incompleteness of the suspended element and can expect the construction to be resumed after interruption (for a list of shorter parentheses in which this is always the case, cf. Diggle, *Studies* 115–16); but in a few cases, as here with the appositive, the continuation cannot have been anticipated: *El.* 787–9 ἀλλ' ἴωμεν ἐς δόμους ... οὐδ' ἀπαρνεῖσθαι χρεών; *Hel.* 1465–76 κόρας ... ἂν λάβοις ... μόσχον θ'; *IA* 392–4 φιλόγαμοι μνηστῆρες ... οὓς λαβὼν στράτευε (*Rhes.* 222). Most parentheses feature γάρ, καί, or asyndeton, but for δέ as here cf. *Or.* 1516, *IA* 66, 392 (*Rhes.* 220, 939). (b) φυγάδα has been taken as object of the whole phrase περὶ δ' ... βάλοιμι (≈ ἀσπάσαιμι) by most edd. since Porson (earlier Grotius and Barnes, with comma before χρόνωι). Accusatives governed by phrases are esp. common with phrases denoting singing (Diggle, *Studies* 58, 62; R. Renehan, *Stud. Gk. Texts* 51ff.), but are also found in phrases denoting fear, anxiety, and grief (*Ba.* 1288 τὸ μέλλον καρδία πήδημ' ἔχει; *El.* 208–9 ψυχὰν τακομένα ... φυγὰς; τεθνάναι τῶι δέει / φόβωι in Dem.) or when some other verbal noun or adj. is present (see Page on *Med.* 206, Dodds on *Ba.* 1288, and below 1549n.; also 293n.). Here no verbal noun is present, and it is especially troubling that Pol. is already referred to as an object of the action of embrace in the locative dat. δέραι. For these reasons (a) is to be preferred to (b). Other expedients: (1) in antiquity some texts carried interpolated ἴδω after ὡς, with comma before χρόνωι; (2) V² implies double acc. of the part and the whole (ὠλέναις δέραν ... περιβάλοιμι ... φυγάδα; similarly

Wecklein 1921, with φιλτάταν for V²'s φιλτάταις); (3) Brodaeus put a stop after χρόνωι and left φυγάδα μέλεον as exclamatory acc.

168 ὅπλοισι χρυσέοισιν Saïd, 509, suggests this detail is a transposition of the golden warrior shown on Pol.'s shield in *Se*. 644.

169 ἀελίου I hesitantly leave this in the text, since it is not impossible that Eur. preferred the fuller expression and we cannot assume that he preferred pure dochmiac close (cf. 153, 178, perhaps 189). On scansion of this word see under Metre.

170 ὥστε σ' ἐμπλῆσαι χαρᾶς effectively anticipating a meeting that will not be allowed to occur (cf. 377–8, 616).

171 τίς κυρεῖ an ancient variant τίς πόθεν (Π⁴ and χ) has produced conflated τίς πόθεν κυρεῖ in the medieval tradition; the answer suits τίς κυρεῖ better, and τίς πόθεν may derive from reminiscence of 123 or of Homeric passages (cf. Bremer (1983) 304f.).

172 ἅρμα . . . ἡνιοστροφεῖ βεβώς the verb occurs here in Eur. and in Aesch. *Choe*. 1022 (a certain emendation), then in Lycophr. *Alex*. 166; noun ἡνιοστρόφος in Soph. *El*. 731, then in *Anth. gr*. 9.777 (Philippus): both are typical tragic coinages. ἅρμα may be governed by both verb and participle: cf. Diggle on *Phaethon* 175 νῶτα . . . βεβώς.

174 Γῆς φιλαίματοι ῥοαί '(sources of) streams of abundant blood for (sacrifice to) Earth'. For the gen., cf. *Hel*. 1333 θεῶν θυσίαι, *Ion* 1235 θύματα νερτέρων.¹ For φιλαίματος cf. φιλόθυτος = *sacrificiis abundans*, *Se*. 179, φιλόσπονδος = *abunde libatus*, *Choe*. 292; the usual meaning of the word is 'bloodthirsty' (Anacr. epigr. 1.3 (*Epigr. Gr*. 37 Page); *Se*. 45; *Rhes*. 932), whence the trivialization φιλαιμάτου in some mss. ῥοαί is often used in connection with αἷμα (cf. *Concordance*), but its sense is stretched here (χοαί Musgrave). σφάγια are propitiatory/prophetic sacrifices made by μάντεις just as a battle begins, different from standard sacrifice in that no altar is required and the victims are not to be eaten. Cf. *Hcld*. 819–22 and see Pritchett, *Greek State at War* I.109–15; III.83–90; Jameson, 'Sacrifice before battle'. Pearson argues that the victims are newly slaughtered and are being carried around to purify the whole area; this makes ῥοαί a little easier. Jameson suggests that σφάγια προύφερον τὰ νομιζόμενα in Thuc. 6.69.2 refers likewise to carrying forward dead victims, not bringing victims forward to slaughter in front of the troops. But elsewhere the victims are kept in readiness for the moment when battle begins and (e.g., in *Hcld*.)

---

¹ In apposition to σφάγια, ῥοαί assumes a wider meaning that seems to me to justify the gen. as with θυσίαι; if the gen. is deemed too hard, Paley's γῆι φιλαιμάτωι produces the same meaning.

are not killed until hope of averting battle is lost. Since there is a truce, it would be premature for Amphiaraus to be carrying dead victims here. Here Earth (I now prefer to capitalize the word) is specified as recipient, not simply because the blood of such sacrifices is poured on the earth, but because the Argives are trying to take possession of Theban soil (the Thebans too will need Earth's favour: 931–40). Amphiaraus' routine behaviour is in deliberate contrast with the tradition of his opposition to the attack (*Se.* 568ff., esp. 584–6; cf. Eur. *Su.* 158, 230).

175 λιπαροζώνου θύγατερ Ἀελίου Hesiod, *Th.* 371 makes Selene the sister of Helios, other later sources make her his wife (*RE* 2A (1921) 1137), but Σ on this line credits Aesch. (fr. 375a = 457 Nauck²) as the earliest to use the genealogy based on the dependence of the moon on the sun for its light (cf. ΣAratus 455 παρὰ τοῖς τραγικοῖς). It is quite arbitrary of Nauck and others to accuse Σ of writing Aeschylus in error when they meant Euripides and to assume that the plural in ΣAratus is a vague reference to Eur. alone. Of course, when Selene is identified with Artemis (via Hecate), she has Zeus and Leto for her parents: so first in Aesch. fr. 170; cf. Soph. fr. 535 and Pearson' s comm.; *IT* 21 (*IA* 1570–1). Helios, the charioteer, naturally wears a belt: cf. the bronze charioteer at Delphi (R. Lullies–M. Hirmer, *Greek Sculpture²* (New York 1960), plates 102–4) and a golden-belted Helios on a late fifth-century red-figured vase (Vienna 1771: W. Hahland, *Vasen um Meidias* (Berlin 1930), Tafel 19a; cited by Barlow, 147 n. 73). The noun ζώνη itself is occasionally used of a man's belt (LSJ s.v. I.I.c, II.I.a), and cf. εὔζωνος and 'masculine' uses of ζώννυμι. λιπαρο-compounds (epic, Pindar, Bacchylides; in tragedy only here and *Eum.* 806 λιπαροθρόνοισιν ... ἐπ' ἐσχάραις) are usually epithets of females (e.g., λιπαροζώνων θυγατρῶν Bacch. 9.49–50), but all gods, and esp. Helios, are associated in poetry with the brightness of shining light and gold. Burges' -ζωνος (-ζωνε Barnes) or Badham's Λατοῦς for Ἀελίου (metrically poor, whence ἁ Λατοῦς Nauck, with odd article) are quite unnecessary (cf. M. Haupt, *Hermes* 1 (1866) 26–8). For Ἀελίου see under Metre (169).

176 χρυσεόκυκλον hapax in extant Greek; so too at least three other χρυσεο-compounds in late Euripidean lyric (-νωτος fr. 159 (*Antig.*), -στολος *Her.* 414, -φάλαρος *Tro.* 520), and χρυσεοβόστρυχος 191 is nearly so (190–2n.). For possible emendation of this line, see Metre 176n.

177–8 'How calm and controlled the goad he applies in turn to the horses as he drives straight on.' ἀτρέμα(ς) and ἀτρεμαῖος are favourite words of Eur. (eight occurrences vs. none in Soph. or Aesch. (unless Butler is right at *Su.* 686)). σωφροσύνη is a traditional characteristic of Amphiaraus (*Se.* 568, 610; below 1112 σωφρόνως ἄσημ' ὅπλα). The sense of μεταφέρων ('shifting from one place to another in turns/alternately') is exactly paralleled in Plato, *Tim.* 73e4 μεταφέρων δ' [τὸ ὀστοῦν] οὕτω πολλάκις εἰς ἑκάτερον [sc. πῦρ ἢ ὕδωρ] ὑπ' ἀμφοῖν ἄτηκτον ἀπηργάσατο; cf. Longus 1.5.2 τὸ παιδίον ... εἰς ἀμφοτέρας τὰς θηλὰς μεταφέρον τὸ στόμα, *Hipp.* 1194f. ἐπῆγε κέντρον ... πώλοις, and for the μετα-compound ΣPindar *I.*2.31 ῥαιδίως καὶ ἀμεταγώγως (= 'without shifting') τὰς ἡνίας εὐθύνοντα. A similar sense of alternating movement is found in some δια-compounds (1371n.). ἰθύνει is probably here intransitive/absolute, like ἐλαύνω; cf. *Od.* 5.255, 270 (of Odysseus steering his raft) and intransitive ἰθύω. In some emendations the verb has its normal transitive use, governing κέντρα. Wilam.'s ἰθύνει ⟨δρόμον⟩ (after Paley) completes a dochmiac dimeter and provides an object. Many emendations have been offered (1) in the false belief that Eustathius read μετάφρενον, an epic word, found nowhere else in extant tragedy, and always used of human anatomy (in fact Eust. wrote μεταφέρων and his use of the line to exemplify periphrasis for μάστιξε does not imply anything other than μεταφέρων), (2) out of concern about the use of μεταφέρων and absolute ἰθύνει, (3) in the belief that brevis in longo at σώφρονα cannot stand and that pure dochmiacs are required (see under Metre). A typical example is Wecklein's ... σώφρον' ἐν / πώλοιν μεταφρένοις φέρων ἰθύνει; JD, building on the deletion and supplement proposed by Paley, suggests, e.g., ὡς ἀτρεμαῖα {καὶ σώφρονα} κέντρα πώλοις νέμων / ἰθύνει ⟨δρόμον⟩.

179 τὰ δεινὰ ... ἐφυβρίζει 'makes those arrogant threats of violence (of which we have all heard)': cf. Jebb on *Trach.* 476 (appendix).

πόλει see L. Threatte, *The Grammar of Attic Inscriptions* I (Berlin 1980) 381–3, for the strong evidence that in fifth-century Attic the dative of πόλις (unlike other i- or u-stems with gen. in -εως) was πόληι, not πόλει. For convenience I retain the conventional spelling. West (*Aeschylus*, p. xxxvii) advocates printing πόληι in tragic texts.

180 Geel's reason for assigning Καπανεύς; to the Servant is nugatory (*convenientius duco ut nomen Capanei aut non recordetur [Antigona] aut nunc certe non dicat, quippe in terrore nil nisi alienas minas cogitans*), and the change should never have been accepted by Murray. The change of speaker after Καπανεύς left that word on a line by itself in some ancient and medieval texts (cf. Π⁴), causing the insertion of ἑπτά (from 159) to make the Servant's reply a full trimeter.

180–1 προσβάσεις τεκμαίρεται πύργων κτλ. 'calculates/estimates approaches to/assaults upon the ramparts, (visually) measuring the walls upwards and downwards'; for προσβάσεις πύργων cf. 744 τειχέων προσαμβάσεις 'assaults upon the walls' and *El.* 489 πρόσβασιν ... οἴκων 'approach to this house'; πρόσβασις often implies movement uphill (LSJ) and is here used as a slightly less precise equivalent of προσανάβασις. ἄνω τε καὶ κάτω implies reciprocal movement, up and down or back and forth, either once or repeatedly. For the action of estimating height, cf. the Plataeans in Thuc. 3.20.3.

182bis Νέμεσι personified as a goddess in Hes. *Th.* 223 (daughter of Night, sister of Moirai and Keres) and *Op.* 200 (paired with Aidos), Pindar *P.* 10.44 (ὑπέρδικον N.); invoked, as here, against a blasphemous remark in Soph. *El.* 792. In the later fifth century Cratinus' *Nemesis* gave popularity to Nemesis' role in the birth and adventures of Helen; as a mythological subject she appears as early as *c.* 420 on a painted amphoriskos by the Heimarmene Painter, Berlin inv. 30036 (Beazley, *ARV*² 1173). In archaic and classical times Nemesis had important cults at Rhamnous and Smyrna, but it is difficult to see (at this period) any connection between these cults and the poetic/mythological personality.

183 φῶς for πῦρ as intrusive gloss cf. *Phil.* 297; the phrase πυρὸς κεραυνίου in *Alc.* 129, *Ba.* 288 may have aided the intrusion.

183–4 σύ τοι . . . κοιμίζεις both the presence of τοι (Denniston, *GP*² 545, cites only *Ag.* 974 μέλοι δέ τοί σοι τῶνπερ ἂν μέλλῃς τελεῖν for τοι with opt.) and the emphatic σύ ('it is *your* function, *remember*, to . . .': for 'remember' cf. *GP*² 542f.) show that the indicative is genuine, the opt. κοιμίζοις an error. For κοιμίζω of the taming power of the thunderbolt cf. *Hec.* 472–4.

184 μεγαληγορίαν ὑπεράνορα Σ present a confused mixture of glosses implying the two readings μεγαλανορίαν and μεγαληγορίαν, and Valck. was correct to restore the latter. It was Capaneus' overweening speech that drew the attention of Zeus (1175n.); and the two compound words in μεγαλανορίαν ὑπεράνορα would be redundant in a different way from such full tragic expressions as *Hipp.* 200 εὐπήχεις χεῖρας or 1549 below πόδα . . . τυφλόπουν.[1] The closest parallel, less objectionable because the noun is simple and disjoined from the epithet, is *Hcld.* 387–8 φρονημάτων . . . ὑπερφρόνων (ὑπερκόπων Schroeder). For -ηγορ- preferred to -αγορ- in tragic lyric, see Björck, 167. μεγαληγορία may be a Eur. coinage (*Hcld.* 356; Xenophon and later prose).

185–9 punctuated by many as a rhetorical question (marking surprise and indignation: 'apistetic'), comparable to 135–7 (where there is however an element of surmise); but Ant. has already mentioned Capaneus' threat, so there is less room for apistetic force. As a statement 185–8 are explicative of 182–4, hence the asyndeton.

186–9 ὅς δορὶ . . . περιβαλών text and interpretation are quite uncer-

---

[1] In addition to the instances in Eur. cited by Breitenbach (1549n.), JD refers to *Ant.* 502, *Phil.* 894, *Prom.* 585, A. *Su.* 817–19 (?), E. *Su.* 1197.

tain, but I think the general sense was 'who says that he will make the women of Thebes slaves to the women of Argos, fetching water at Argive springs'. I would tentatively translate the text printed as 'who ⟨says⟩ he will, by force of spear, give Theban women to women of Mycenae (= Argos) ⟨as slaves⟩ and to the Lernaean trident (= spring at Lerna, where they will fetch water), having cast about them (the Theban women) slavery to the Posidonian waters of Amymone (= the spring at Lerna)', with 188–9 explicating the allusive reference in 187. The main index of corruption is the lack of a verb to govern δώσειν, but critics have also been troubled by the indirection of expression, the impure rhythm of 187 and 189, by the double epithet of 188, and by the succession of datives in 187–9. The most conservative solutions may be rejected: (1) Canter's δώσει gives defective sense (what precedes and what follows prove that Ant. is speaking of a threat); (2) the assumption of *sermo fractus* (emotional ellipsis of a verb of saying was posited by Barnes, Battier, and Valck.) is no more convincing than most such suggestions (cf. in general *Contact and Discontinuity*, 66–73). The most likely place for a supplement is after 186, as Wecklein's Μυκήναις φησίν (a remnant of which he saw in M's μυκήνησι) or Hermann's[1] and Matthiae's Μυκήναις εὐ- / χεται. But the vulgate Μυκήναις is more likely to be secondary: readings of MO against the other mss generally deserve serious consideration, this reading is close to presenting a correct dochmiac, and MO are not otherwise prone to datives in -η(ι)σι. Despite the accent (misreported in the past), the form originally intended was probably Μυκηνῆισιν (for the unusual formation, 186n.). With this, ⟨εὔχεται⟩ gives cr, mol, 2 ba in 187 (acceptable), but involves brevis in longo without strong sense-pause (see under Metre, 177); ⟨κομπεῖ⟩ does not require brevis and also scans well (dochm, 2 ba). Or we may assume the loss of a whole line, e.g., λατρεύειν θήσειν αὐτίκα κομπάζει, or with very rare form of dochmiac (*IT* 894),[2] κομπάζει λατρεύματ' αὐτίκα θήσειν. A less likely location for supplement is after περιβαλών, where two extra syllables will give pure dochmiacs; but the verb is then strangely placed: ⟨ἔφη⟩ Spiro (ἔφα Murray); ⟨λέγει⟩ or ⟨βοᾶι⟩ (with other changes) Paley. Mention may also be made of versions which change ὅς to ὁ and insert a participle: δώσων for δώσειν Seidler, ὁ ⟨φάς⟩ (with other changes) Nauck 1854; περιβοῶν for περιβαλών (with other changes) F. G. Schoene.

186 Μυκηνῆισιν the feminine adj. otherwise attested in poetry (including Eur.) and by Steph. Byz. is Μυκηνίς. Although Μυκηνῆις has not

---

[1] In *de usu antistrophicorum* (Leipzig 1810), later abandoned.
[2] But JD reminds me how doubtful *IT* 894 is (split resolution before long anceps).

been acknowledged in dictionaries or the major grammars, the form is a possible one. -ῆῖς feminines arise as patronymics from α-stems (Χρυσῆῖς from Χρύση/Χρύσης: Μυκηνῆῖς from Μυκηνᾶ- ionicized?) or corresponding to -εύς masculines (βασιλεύς > βασιληῖς *Il.* 6.193: cf. Μυκηνεύς, the name of the eponymous hero of Mycenae mentioned by Acusilaus apud Paus. 2.16.4) or in a number of other ways (cf. epic Καδμῆῖς as alternative to Καδμεία): cf. Chantraine, *Formation des noms* 335ff., who notes how the -ῆῖς suffix is occasionally extended even to other stems (e.g., χλωρῆῖς *Od.* 19.518, ἀλσῆῖς and ποταμῆῖς Ap. Rhod.).

187 Λερναῖαι ... τριαίναι the major named spring at Lerna was called Amymone after the daughter of Danaus; the spring was also sometimes called Lerna, and Amymone was also the name of the stream flowing from the spring and of the λίμνη formed by it and other streams. It appears from this passage that the spring was also called 'Trident' because it originated when Amymone pulled Posidon's trident from the rock after he rescued her from a satyr (so Σ; cf. Hyginus 169, 169a). Elsewhere 'Trident' is attested only in Nonnus, *Dion.* 8.240–2, presumably reflecting the same mythographic scholarship as Σ; but the name may have appeared in Aesch.'s satyr-play *Amymone*. To give the maidens to the spring is to impose upon them the water-fetching function of slaves (coupled with weaving by Hector in *Il.* 6.456–7 καί κεν ἐν Ἄργει ἐοῦσα πρὸς ἄλλης ἱστὸν ὑφαίνοις, καί κεν ὕδωρ φορέοις; cf. *Tro.* 205f.).

188–9 Ποσειδανίοις Ἀμυμωνίοις ὕδασι patronymic adj. in -ιος in place of gen. noun is a familiar idiom (Schwyzer II.177), but this phrase is unusual in combining two such adjs. (for one adj. and one gen. cf. Pindar, *O.* 2.13 Κρόνιε παῖ 'Ρέας, more stately than, e.g., *Hcld.* 210 Ζηνὸς Ἀλκμήνης τε παῖς). Ἀμυμώνιος is not extant elsewhere except in Eustathius' allusion to this line (461, 4–5). Σ and most editors treat the phrase as an apposition which explains the allusive Λερναῖαι ... τριαίναι, and some print a comma after ὕδασι. But it is conceivable that ὕδασι is governed by the verbal force of δουλείαν (cf. 334n.) and that the participial phrase restates more explicitly the import of δώσειν τριαίναι: 'casting (upon them [Θηβαίαις understood from Θηβαίας 186]) servitude to the waters of Posidon and Amymone'.[1] The metaphor in περιβαλών is of entrapment in a snare or binding in a noose (*Ba.* 619, 1021; cf. *Ion* 1273).

---

[1] West (1990) suggests Ποσειδανίοις Ἀμυμωνίαν ὕδασι δουλείαν περιβαλών, 'casting Argive slavery upon the Posidonian waters (of Dirce)': the general connection of Posidon with springs (*Se.* 307–10) is insufficient to identify Dirce here, 'Amymonian' for Argive is too precious, and the motif of water-carrying is missed.

190–2 for the elaborate heaping of vocatives cf. *Hipp.* 61ff. πότνια πότνια σεμνοτάτα, Ζηνὸς γένεθλον, ... ὦ κόρα Λατοῦς Ἄρτεμι καὶ Διός, καλλίστα... For χρυσεοβόστρυχον (elsewhere only Philoxenus *PMG* 821), cf. 176n.

193 εἴσβα this imperative form, confined to compounds, is typically Euripidean: cf. *El.* 113 ~ 128, *Ion* 167, *Alc.* 872, all lyric, vs. ἔκβηθι *IT* 1086 (trimeter); it seems not to be inherently lyric or elevated: cf. Stevens, *Colloquial Expr.* 63. On the origin of the form, see O. Lautensach, *Die Aoriste bei den att. Tragikern und Komikern* [Forsch. z. gr. u. lat. Grammatik, 1 (Göttingen 1911)] 4–5.

194–5 πόθου εἰς τέρψιν ἦλθες 'have attained gratification of your longing'. Like διά + gen. + verb of motion (20n.), εἰς + acc. of verbal noun + verb of motion is a periphrasis well suited to tragic style: cf. 361 εἰς φόβον τ' ἀφικόμην, *IT* 797 εἰς τέρψιν εἶμι, *Tro.* 60 εἰς οἶκτον ἦλθες, *Ion* 389 ἔλθηι μητρὸς εἰς ὄψιν; with ἐπί *Phoen.* 1300 μονόμαχον ἐπὶ φρέν' ἠλθέτην; with πρός e.g., *Su.* 882f. πρὸς ἡδονὰς Μουσῶν τραπέσθαι.

ὧν ἔχρηιζες εἰσιδεῖν gen. also dependent on τέρψιν, amplifying the content of the πόθος.

196–201 ὄχλος γὰρ κτλ. the Servant 'sees' the chorus approaching (whether or not they are really on the entrance-ramp and visible to him or to any of the audience) and hustles Ant. in to avoid contact with them. The closest parallels to this in tragedy are the hiding/eavesdropping scenes *Choe.* 10–21 and *OC* 111–16; cf. also Eur. *El.* 107ff. (hiding at Electra's approach, remaining hidden when chorus arrives) and *Hipp.* 51ff. (Hipp. and secondary chorus approach), *Hec.* 52ff., *Ion* 76ff. Even more similar are the act-ending remarks in New Comedy which motivate the lack of contact between characters and the entering chorus (Men. *Asp.* 245–9, *Dysc.* 230–2 with Handley's note, *Epitr.* 169–71, *Peric.* 261–6: in two of these the chorus is termed ὄχλος). Cf. Fraenkel, *Beobacht. zu Arist.* 22–6 (but *Phaethon* 54ff. is not fully comparable: see Diggle). The sententious conclusion of this scene has two main effects. The Servant's exaggerated concern for proprieties reinforces the 'sheltered maiden' motif introduced in the beginning of the scene. Moreover, there is a strong ironic effect in the conventionally misogynistic generalization about women, for the problems of the day, much more serious than carping tongues, are the results of men's ambitions and actions. Such irony at the expense of conventional assessments of male superiority and female inferiority is typical of tragedy (esp. *Ag.*, *Ant.*, *Med.*, *Ba.*); and in this play Eur. seems to be fond of ironic scene-ending words: cf. 84–7 (futile prayer), 636–7 (traditional etymology used for woefully one-sided placement of blame), 780–3 (claim of justice and prayer to Eulabeia in the mouth of unjust Et. whose lack of εὐλάβεια has just been illustrated in 713–36). These effects are lost if 196–201 (Friedrich) or 198–201 (Hartung 1837, abandoned later) are deleted (neither scholar offered any adequate ground for deletion; Friedrich thought 196–201 were added when, in a later performance, 88–102 were omitted; but the ψόγος motif in 196–201 is less readily understandable if the audience has not heard 92–5).

196 ὡς ταραγμὸς εἰσῆλθεν πόλιν 'now that panic has entered the town' (Pearson). This line has been needlessly suspected, mainly because of excessive concern for realistic details that Eur. had no reason to elaborate (where were the women before? why do they come here?). He is merely providing a motive for the arrival of the chorus. Fear, panic, and uncertainty were likely to prompt Greeks to leave their houses and converge upon a public place, and such motivation is often put to use in the parodoi of tragedy: cf. *Ag.*, *Pers.*, *OC*, *Alc.*; for women, the parodos of *Se.* is of course the obvious precedent, but cf. the Trojan women who hover near the city gates awaiting news of the latest battle (*Il.* 6.238ff.) or assemble at a temple for prayer (*Il.* 6.379f.). It is not necessary to infer (with Craik) that the imagined panic in the city is reflected in 'a disorderly and noisy advance' of the chorus (a staging that is certainly not supported by the metre or content of lines 202ff.).[1]

198 φιλόψογον δὲ χρῆμα θηλειῶν 'females are a carping lot', a colloquial and contemptuous way of saying φιλόψογοι αἱ γυναῖκες. The idioms with χρῆμα are well analysed by L. Bergson, *Eranos* 65 (1967) 79–117; see also Stevens, *Colloquial Expr.* 20–1. This phrase may be viewed as a brachylogy for φιλόψογον χρῆμα τὸ χρῆμα (τῶν) θηλειῶν, but see Bergson, 98–9, showing that it makes no difference how exactly this mixed form is analysed.

δέ rather than γάρ because γάρ is often a gloss on this sort of δέ and sometimes intrudes: cf. Σ and Rf at 250; Denniston, *GP²* 169 n. 1. δέ in this quasi-causal sense also at 86, 200, 745, perhaps 250.

199 ἀφορμὰς ... τῶν λόγων ψόγων in Stob. is a gnomologist's trivialization and is lame after φιλόψογον; λόγων is the *mot juste* with ἀφορμαί, a favourite word of Eur. in this quasi-technical rhetorical/legal sense (Dodds on *Ba.* 266–9, Wilam. on *Her.* 236).

200 ἐπεισφέρουσιν ἐπ- connotes a heaping on of more than is justified or more than can be borne; cf. *Ag.* 864–5 τὸν δ᾽ ἐπεισφέρειν κακοῦ κάκιον ἄλλο πῆμα.

---

[1] Cf. Foley, 114, on Eur.'s playing with the precedent of *Septem*: 'The Pedagogue ... leads us to expect a chorus of women as troublesome and disorderly as they were in Aeschylus, whereas Euripides' chorus is in fact orderly and distant.' Cf. Hose, *Chor* 143.

202-60: PARODOS

FUNCTION AND STYLE

Self-introduction occupies more than half of the parodos, reasonably in view of Eur.'s need to explain the presence of this exotic group of young women. Only with ἄφοβος in 236 does the current situation of war clearly intrude (there may be a minor intimation in πύργους 219), and then its danger dominates the final two stanzas. As in the previous scene, fear and apotropaic prayer are combined with recognition of the justice of Pol.'s claim and the possibility that the gods may be on his side. Mention (without name) of Polynices at the end of the ode prepares the audience for his arrival (83n.). Themes of importance in subsequent odes and outside the odes are introduced or touched upon here: kinship (216–18, 234–9); peaceful worship and joyful dancing (Delphi and Dionysus), esp. as activities of maidens (203, 205–7, 215, 220–5, 226–38), viewed as the antithesis of war (Thebes and Ares) (216–19, 238, 239–41, 250–3); arrival from a distance (202, 216) and other movements from place to place (237–8, 240, 258–60); the curse of Oedipus upon his sons (254–5); the justice of Pol.'s cause (258–60).

The chorus enters upon an empty stage, probably the more archaic technique (in many plays of Eur. and Soph., esp. later ones, the parodos is not only directed to a tableau present on stage, but is shared by actor and chorus). The five stanzas are constructed of very simple and uniform cola, and the glyconic (and related) cola of the first three are perhaps reminiscent of popular song (cf. the 'refrain' in *Her.* 348–441, similar to the concluding quatrain of each stanza in Aesch. *Su.* 630–97 and *Ag.* 367–474). The simplicity is reinforced by repetitions of content and of words or word-shapes (see below), by syntax (numerous appositions and participial phrases in sequence, the polysyndetic series 226–34), and by the avoidance of word-overlap between cola (entirely in second pair of stanzas, almost entirely in the first; the epode seems to provide a deliberate contrast). An almost monotonous clarity is thus created for this chorus.

Verbal repetitions or near-echoes are a characteristic of many tragic odes and are a striking feature of the odes of *Phoen.* Such repetitions occur at beginning and end of ode or stanza or group of stanzas (λιποῦσ' 202 ~ προλιποῦσα 238) or at approximately the same position in adjacent stanzas (φλέγει 241 ~ 251),[1] or without similarity of location (νιφοβόλοις

---

[1] Hermann thought of placing 240 after 241 to make the placement precisely the same; but note that 240–1 and 251–2 are isometric as transmitted, but not with the transposition.

206 ~ νιφόβολον 234; ἐγενόμαν 221 ~ γενοίμαν 236; κάλλιστον 213 ~ καλλιστεύματα 215; Φοίβωι δούλα 205 ~ Φοίβωι λάτρις 221 ~ Φοιβείαισι λατρείαις 225). For repetitions of words and phrases between odes, see 638–89n. Similar in effect is anaphora in succeeding cola (κοινά 243–4) and within a colon (κοινὸν ... κοινά 247): for further effects of this kind, see on 1284–307. Finally, isometric echoes are present: ἀκροθίνια Λοξίαι 203 ~ καλλιστεύματα Λοξίαι 215 (reinforced by identical semantic and syntactic function within nearly tautologous sentences); ὧν μέτεστί μοι πόνων 249 ~ ὃς μετέρχεται δόμους 260.

THE IDENTITY OF THE CHORUS

The chorus consists of Phoenician maidens sent by the Agenoridae of Tyre to be *hierodouloi* at Delphi. They are ἀκροθίνια ('choicest offerings', from a harvest or esp. from war-booty: 203n.), chosen for their beauty from their entire city (214–15); they identify strongly with the Agenoridae (217) and the kinship of the Agenoridae with Thebes (cf. also 291–2), and this identification is thematically important to their odes. They are proud of their holy servitude. The audience is therefore probably to assume that they are daughters of citizens of Tyre, selected as *hierodouloi* to be a thank-offering to Apollo (for some favour: 281–2 later reveal that the favour was victory in war). Their free movement in the city (196–7) also suggests such status. They give no sign of being captive maidens, daughters of people defeated by the Agenoridae of Tyre, which the use of ἀκροθίνιον in 203 and esp. δορὸς ἀκροθίνιον in 281–2 has led some to believe.[1] The chorus' prayer for children at 1060–1 may suggest that the maidens' service to Apollo has a fixed term (but see *ad loc.*). On *hierodouloi* see Hepding, *RE* 8 (1913) 1459–68, esp. 1464–6: most *hierodouloi* are captives or slaves, and the custom is more eastern than Greek, but in some Greek foundation-legends citizens are dedicated to Apollo at Delphi and subsequently migrate to colonies from Delphi (e.g. Strabo 6.1.6; Plut. *Thes.* 16.2).

Why did Eur. invent this chorus for his Theban play? The best explanation is in terms of his literary/dramatic goals. Positively, he wanted to give his Theban play the resonance of parallels with and causation deriving from the Cadmus-story. The Phoenician chorus, arriving from Tyre as

---

[1] Mueller-Goldingen, 66, 72, is the most recent critic to view the chorus as slaves. For those who believe that the Phoenician maidens are war-captives, the slave-chorus of *Choe.* (75–83) is relevant, for it identifies fully with the house of Atreus. But there is no hint in that play that the women are captive *Trojans*: M. McCall, 'The Chorus of Aeschylus' *Choephori*', in *Cabinet of the Muses*, 17–21.

Cadmus had and connected with Delphi as Cadmus was, becomes an ideal
exponent of the common ancestry from Io and of the archetypal fratricide
of the foundation-legend. Negatively, Eur. likes to concentrate the action
and the strongest emotional stresses and reactions in the actors and accordingly favours in general powerless choruses, sympathetic but not too inti-
mately tied to the fate of the protagonists (hence, women, slaves, old men).
A chorus of Theban women might have seemed too personally involved to
be an appropriate vehicle for the distant perspective of the ode-cycle of
Phoen. The foreign chorus can sympathize adequately, but be pushed to
the side when (around line 1200) the theme of city-salvation reaches a
climax and salvation of the family becomes the dominant focus of attention.
In comparison with these literary/dramatic motivations for Eur.'s choice,
other suggestions must be assigned a minor importance, if any: desire to
be different from *Septem*; opportunity to display the exotic (several critics
assume that the chorus' costumes were especially striking: they must at
least have looked non-Greek: 278–9n.); need to justify the open criticism
of Eteocles in 526–7 (cf. 258–60); cryptic (and, I would say, pointless)
allusion to Phrynichus' *Phoenissae.*

THE VOYAGE OF THE MAIDENS

Unlike military vessels or slave-galleys, broad-bottomed vessels carrying
cargo and passengers relied mainly on wind-power, a crucial fact ignored
by most commentators (and flatly contradicted by Pearson).[1] It is also
important to remember that most vessels kept their course close to shore
whenever possible and that during much of the sailing season the Etesian
Winds blow from the north in the Aegean. In such circumstances, a voyage
from Tyre to Thebes was most easily made by passing along the coast of
Crete, rounding the Peloponnese, and entering the Gulf of Corinth from
the Ionian Sea, disembarking at Creusis, the port of Thespiae, whence one
could reach Thebes overland without difficulty. The Thebans, as kin and
proxenoi of the Tyrians, could then escort the maidens by land to Delphi
for dedication to Apollo (cf. 280–5). The literary precedent for the latter
part of this voyage is important: in *Hom.h.Ap.* 388–439 Apollo comman-
deers a vessel in the sea north of western Crete; to take the men to Delphi
he directs the vessel not east of the Peloponnese to Corinth, but around the

---

[1] Cf. John Morrison, *Long Ships and Round Ships. Warfare and Trade in the
Mediterranean 3000 BC–500 AD* (London 1980), 51–8; Lionel Casson, *Ships
and Seamanship in the Ancient World* (Princeton 1971), 65–8, 157, 169–82,
270–3.

Peloponnese to the mouth of the Gulf of Corinth, where a west wind (Ζέφυρος 433) carries the vessel to Crisa.[1] The audience is here informed that the route around the Peloponnese was taken by the references to the Ionian and Sicilian Seas (both names apply to the waters west of the Peloponnese: 208n. and 210–11n.) and to Zephyrus with its lovely sound (which must therefore have been a favourable wind, as it would be on the last stage of the voyage). The route should not have been surprising or obscure to an ancient audience.

From the scholia to Powell and the Budé edition, however, the passage has seemed obscure, and a great deal of nonsense has been proposed, including (among the ancients) misidentification of the Ionian Sea and invention of a different Sicily and (among moderns) the historicist fantasy that Eur. means to allude to Carthage rather than Tyre and to a contemporary military triumph of the Carthaginians over Greek enemies of Athens in Sicily. Not only is such allusion wholly uncharacteristic of tragedy[2] and a thoroughly gratuitous assumption in a passage capable of normal explication; here it would create confusion about what must be recognized as the main thematic function of the chorus – the kinship with the Agenoridae of Tyre, the homeland of Cadmus.

202–60 Metre The parodos consists of a triad of glyconic cola (including wilamowitzian and the usual clausular pherecratean) followed by a pair of stanzas in lecythia (with a few trochaic cola). For the former, compare the predominantly glyconic stanzas that are common in late Eur. (*Her.* 348–407, *IT* 1089–122, *Ion* 184–9 = 194–200, *Ba.* 403–32, 862–901), but also used earlier (*Alc.* 962–83, *Hipp.* 141–60 in Barrett's division; in actors' lyric duet *Andr.* 501–14 = 523–36); cf. too the predominantly wilamowitzian stanzas *Hel.* 1301–68, 1451–78, *IA* 543–72 and mixed stanzas such as *IT* 1123–52. On the wilamowitzian (also called choriambic dimeter B or aeolic dimeter B or gl ˙ ˙ or gl³ or gl^c), sometimes used on its own and sometimes (as here) as a variant of glyconic, see K. Itsumi, 'The

---

[1] Cf. the cargo-ship in Heliod. *Aethiop.* 4.16, which sails from Tyre for Carthage by way of Malea and the western Peloponnese and makes a detour to Delphi when it reaches Cephallenia and the winds are adverse. Another voyage to the Corinthian Gulf from Ionia with mention of the west wind may have been present in the *Rhadine* ascribed to Stesichorus (*PMGF* fr. spur. 278): Pausanias 7.5.13 places this Rhadine in Ionian Samos, but Strabo 8.3.20 insists that Samikon in Elis must once have been called Samos and that the poet meant the Elean town. It is not impossible that Strabo is misinterpreting the poem and wrongly forcing the name Samos on the Elean site.

[2] Cf. Zuntz, *Political Plays* 58–71, and 'Contemporary Politics'.

"Choriambic Dimeter" of Euripides', *CQ* 32 (1982) 59–74. For the internal epode 226–38, linked in rhythm to the preceding strophic pair, cf. (all parodoi) *Pers.* 93–100 (which, with O. Müller's transposition, close the ionic section of the parodos), *Ag.* 140–59 (closing the dactylic portion of the parodos), and perhaps *IA* 206–30 (final, not internal, if 231ff. are spurious). Final epodes are much more common, esp. in late Eur. (cf. first and third stasimons of this play). The internal epodes of the stasimon *Her.* 348–441 are in responsion with mesodes and are rhythmically equivalent to ephymnia (cf. Rode apud W. Jens, *Die Bauformen der gr. Tragödie* [Poetica. Beiheft 6 (1971)], 99 n. 44). The term 'mesode' has sometimes been applied to 226–38, but the ancient definition reserves that term for astrophic elements between corresponding stanzas (cf. K. Münscher, *Hermes* 62 (1927) 154–78). The unusual structure has prompted various unconvincing proposals of assignment and textual dislocation: R. Arnoldt, 124–7, assigns 202–38 to the whole chorus, 239–49 and 250–60 to semi-choruses; Wecklein (1894) suggests that the coryphaeus sang 202–38, the whole chorus 239–60 or that the epode be transposed to follow 260; Craik speculates that the stanzas may have been sung by five separate soloists; Hermann and Burges rewrote 226–38 as strophe and antistrophe; A. L. Brown even questions the authenticity of 239–60 (see *ad loc.*). It is much better to recognize that Eur. is experimenting with the form, probably as a deliberate archaism.

As for the second strophic pair, stanzas of trochaic cola containing many lecythia (catalectic dimeters) and often otherwise divisible into full or syncopated dimeters (although periods are in fact built of larger sequences, the phrasing and the rarity of word-overlap suggest dimeters) are characteristic of late Eur.: cf. the first stasimon, third stasimon, and *Hel.* 167–252, 348–74 (preceded by lecythia and many iambic dimeters in 330–47), and the suspected portion of the parodos of *IA*. Cf. in Aesch. *Su.* 1062–73, *Ag.* 160–91, 975–1000. The sequence we find here of seven lecythia without resolution is unusual (cf. *Ag.* 1008–13 = 1025–30: six lecythia).

202/214	⏑⏑⏑–⏑⏑–⏑–|	gl
203/215	–⏑͜–⏑⏑–⏑–|	gl
204/216	–––⏑⏑––‖ᶜ	pher
205/217	––ū–⏑⏑–|	∧wil
206/218	⏑⏑⏑–⏑⏑⏑͡⏑⏑–|	gl
207/219	–––⏑⏑––‖ʰ¹ᶜ	pher
208/220	ū⏑⏑–⏑⏑–⏑⏑͡⏑	gl
209/221	–––⏑⏑⏑͡⏑⏑–| (‖?)	gl
210	⏑⏑⏑–––⏑⏑–|	wil
=222	⏑⏑⏑–⏑⏑–⏑–|	=gl

211/223	⌣⌣⌣ – ⌣⌣ – ⌣ – |	gl
212/224	– – – ⌣⌣ – ⌣ – |	gl
213/225	– – – ⌣⌣ – – ‖||^{b1c}	pher
226	– – – ⌣⌣ – ⌣ – |	gl
227	⌣⌣⌣ – ⌣⌣⌣⌣⌣ – |	gl
228	– – – ⌣⌣ – – ‖^{hc}	pher
229	– – – ⌣ – ⌣⌣ – |	wil
230	– – – ⌣⌣ – ⌣ –	gl
231	– – × – ⌣⌣ – ‖^{c}	‸wil
232	⌣⌣⌣ – ⌣⌣ – ⌣ –	gl
233	– – – ⌣⌣ – ⌣ – |	gl
234	⌣⌣⌣ – ⌣⌣⌣⌣⌣ –	gl
235	– – – ⌣⌣ – ⌣ – |	gl
236	⌣ – ⌣ – – ⌣⌣ –	ia, chor (≈ wil)
237	⌣⌣⌣ – ⌣⌣⌣⌣⌣ –	gl
238	– – – ⌣⌣ – ⌒‖||^{bc}	pher
239/250	– ⌣ – ⌣ – ⌣ – ‖^{b2}	lec
240/251	– ⌣ – ⌣ – ⌣ – |	lec
241/252	– ⌣ – ⌣ – ⌣ – |	lec
242/253	– ⌣ – ⌣ – ⌣ – ‖$^{?}$	lec
243/254	– ⌣ – ⌣ – ⌣ – |	lec
244/255	– ⌣ – ⌣ – ⌣ – ‖^{h1}	lec
245/256	– ⌣ – ⌣ – ⌣ – |	lec
246/257	– – – – – – – – ‖$^{?}$	mol, 2 sp
247/258	– ⌣⌣⌣ – ⌣⌣⌣⌣|	2 tro
248/259	– ⌣ – ⌣ – ⌣ – ⌣ – – ‖^{h2}	2 tro, sp (lec, ba)
249/260	– ⌣ – ⌣ – ⌣ – |||	lec

NOTES TO METRICAL SCHEME

202/214 Itsumi, 70, argues against interpreting ⌣⌣⌣ base in tragic glyconics as a resolution of – ⌣; but the statistical predominance of – – and – ⌣ as base (Itsumi, 67) at least suggests that the hearer may have had an expectation of – × and so received ⌣⌣⌣ as ⌣⌣⌣.

205/217 ‸wil may also be termed aeolic heptasyllable B or telesillean c or (West) tl˙˙. The same colon probably begins a new period also at *Hipp.* 145 = 155, *IT* 1100 = 1117.

206/218 Resolution of the sixth or eighth element of gl is a Euripidean mannerism (sixth: twenty-three times in Eur., two in Soph.; eighth: twenty-one times in Eur., one in Soph, according to Itsumi, 77–8): in this ode the sixth element is resolved also in 221, 227, 234, 237, the eighth at 208 only.

208/220 Many assume a short initial iota in 'Ιόνιον, but the iota is long in Pindar, Apollonius, and all Latin instances[1], and since the Greeks (rightly or wrongly: 208n.) associated the Ionian Sea with 'Ιώ, it is natural to assume that the iota was universally treated as long. In *Prom.* 840 'Ιόνιος, $-\cup\cup-$ (anapaest in fourth foot of trimeter in proper name) is equally possible with $\widehat{\cup}\cup-$ (resolution of third longum). As for this passage, glyconics with base $-\cup\cup$ do exist (Itsumi, 71–2: cf. *IT* 1098 = 1115, *IA* 169 = 190, 759 = 770), and responsion of base $-\cup\cup$ with $\cup\cup\cup$ is rare but not unexampled, esp. when a proper name is involved. In glyconics cf. *IT* 1129 ($\cup\cup\cup$) = 1144 ($-\cup\cup$)[2], 1092 ($-\cup\cup-\cup\cup-\cup-$) = 1109 (wil $\cup\cup\cup---\cup\cup-$); in wilamowitzians *Ba.* 410 ($-\cup\cup$: Πιερία) = 424 ($\cup\cup\cup$), *IA* 553 ($-\cup\cup$: ὢ Κύπρι) = 568 ($\cup\cup\cup$), 753 ($\cup\cup\cup$) = 764 ($-\cup\cup$ Τρῶες), 754 ($\cup\cup\cup$) = 765 ($-\cup\cup$: πόντιος)[3]; Itsumi, 72 n. 17, would add *Hel.* 1347 ($-\cup\cup$ τύμπανα) = 1363 ($\cup\cup\cup$), but emendation to the attested form τύπανα is easy. This sort of responsion could indicate an inversion of the common sequence $-\times$ to $\times-$ appearing as $\overline{\times}\ \widehat{\cup}\cup$: cf. *EMC* n.s. 2 (1983) 114–15; Dale, *LMGD*[2] 134, 153; note, however, that Itsumi, 70, 72, finds 'resolution' an inappropriate description of the trisyllabic base. If, on the other hand, the iota of 'Ιόνιος is deemed to be short in tragedy, then we should probably assume that it was short etymologically (208n.) and that the long iota was a metrical licence of dactylic poetry, taken over by Pindar (cf. Elmsley, *Edinburgh Review* 19 (1811–12) 70).

Resolution of the eighth element with word-overlap into the next colon is unusual (Kannicht II.336–7 and Itsumi, 78, cite only *Hel.* 1348 = 1364 and this line); cf. on 234.

209/222 Period-end is perhaps to be assumed here, to avoid a period of too great length: cf. Stinton, 'Pause' 40, 50.

---

[1] Ovid *Her.* 14.103 and *Ibis* 622 formerly carried as *false* readings the same Io scanned $\cup-$. The iota is also long in *Tro.* 225 'Ιονίωι ναύται πόντωι, but ναύται at least is corrupt, and L. P. E. Parker, *CQ* 8 (1958) 86, believes that 'Ιονίωι may also be wrong because of the rarity of word-end after $-\cup\cup-$ in paroemiacs.

[2] *Locus corruptus*, but suggestions which remove παρθένος 1144 seem to me to remove an essential element of the nostalgia expressed by the lines; read perhaps παρθένος εὐδοκίμοις γάμοις (after Paley) or παρθ. εὐδοκίμους γάμους (as object of 'dance in celebration of', with Monk's θιάσοις in 1146). If $-\cup\cup$ is accepted in 1144, Markland's transposition ἑπτατόνου κέλαδον in 1129 regularizes responsion, but to do so is *petitio principii*.

[3] The theory of Page (*Actors' Interp.*) that these stanzas of *IA* are half Euripidean and half not seems to me unlikely.

210/222   wil in responsion to gl is a familiar phenomenon: Euripidean instances are listed by Itsumi, 72–74; cf. Denniston, *El.* comm., p. 215.

230–1   I owe this division to Stinton. The lines are usually divided at πολύκαρπον/, pher ‖ ᵇ wil; but rhetorical structure favours period-end at 231, and 229–31 thus echo the structure of 226–8.

231   The quantity of the iota of ἰεῖσα cannot be determined: long iota is more common overall in Attic poetry, but short is common in lyric instances (*Septem* 310, Soph. *El.* 131, *Hipp.* 124, 1125, Eur. *Su.* 281, *Hec.* 1104, *Hel.* 188, etc.) and even found in trimeters (*Septem* 493, *Hec.* 338, *IT* 298, *Hel.* 1236, *IA* 1101, Arist. *Birds* 946, Strato com. fr. 1.3 K–A).

234   Two-syllable overlap after resolution (of the sixth element) is unique; one-syllable overlap, as in 237, is not uncommon (Itsumi, 78).

246/257   This colon, apparently syncopated trochees, provides a striking transition from the regularity of the lecythia (with which it is isosyllabic) to the trochees of the concluding cola, with their syncopation. Cf. perhaps the colon of five longa *Hel.* 1307 = 1325 in transition from aeolic to syncopated iambics.

248–9/259–60   Textual solutions other than deletion of παῖς involve the desire to avoid hiatus and period-end between the penultimate and the ultimate cola of the stanza. Although the final lec is catalectic in comparision with the full trochees that dominate in the two previous cola and so provides a suitable stanza-end, 248 = 259 is also catalectic with respect to 247 = 258 by virtue of the contrast between unsyncopated and blunt syncopated form (on the concept of contrast cf. Parker, 'Catalexis'). Some parallels for period-end at the penultimate colon of a stanza: *Prom.* 134b = 151; 587 = 607; *Trach.* 139, *OC* 253a (hiatus), 1083 = 1094; *Hipp.* 129 = 139, *Andr.* 139 = 145 (hiatus, with ⟨ὤ⟩ in 140), 299 = 307 (brevis), Eur. *El.* 1225 = 1231 (brevis), *Hel.* 384, probably *Phaethon* 93 = 100 Diggle. Similarly, it must be recognized in general that period-end (proved by hiatus or brevis) sometimes occurs without catalexis in tragic stanzas: so in this ode 239 = 250,[1] 244 = 255;[2] cf. *OT* 1193 = 1201 with Dawe's note on 1201, which correctly defends the hiatus but wrongly adds that 'the phenomenon remains highly abnormal'.

202-60: COMMENTARY

202–13   this stanza, like the epode 226–38, consists of a single sentence, a characteristic of the so-called 'dithyrambic' style of late Eur. lyric (see

---

[1] Brevis in longo at 250 could be avoided by Heimsoeth's transposition πυκνὸν ἀσπίδων, but cf. 676–7 below (JD cites *IA* 279–80).

[2] For hiatus at 244 after lec when lec (or trochees) follows JD refers to 1721, *IA* 273, 1490, *Hel.* 353; cf. Stinton, 'Pause' 60–1.

on 638–89). It is built from two nominative participles and a genitive absolute, a relative clause of place, a predicate noun and its appositive, and an internal accusative phrase. The epode has a long series of vocatives (with a relative clause) and one nominative participial phrase.

202 Τύριον οἶδμα λιποῦσ' ἔβαν choral self-introduction often mentions point of departure (Aesch. *Su.* 4–5 Δίαν δὲ λιποῦσαι χθόνα, *Choe.* 22 ἰαλτὸς ... ἔβαν; *Hec.* 99 σκηνὰς προλιποῦσ', *Tro.* 176 σκηνὰς ἔλιπον, *Ba.* 64–5, *IA* 168 Χαλκίδα ... προλιποῦσα). The similarity of Phrynichus, *Phoen. TrGF* 3 F 9 Σιδώνιον ἄστυ λιποῦσα καὶ δροσεράν Ἄραδον resides in the formula and is no safe indication that literary reminiscence was intended.[1] In other contexts as well participial phrases with λιπών are formulaic: e.g., *Alc.* 580, *Hec.* 2, *Her.* 770, *Tro.* 1, *Ba.* 13, 172.

203 ἀκροθίνια 'choicest offering', the best chosen from a gathered heap. It is uncertain whether the notion originated with heaps of harvested crops or heaps of war-booty. War-booty is meant in the prose examples and most poetic examples, but Aesch. means other offerings in *Eum.* 834, Pindar fr. dub. 357 refers to offerings from the catch of hunting and fishing, in *IT* 459 the word may mean simply 'choicest offerings', and Eur. coins the verb ἀκροθινιάζομαι to mean 'select the choicest' (*Her.* 476). Later we find Plato referring to the three best citizens of his state as dedicated ἀκροθίνιον Ἀπόλλωνι κατὰ τὸν παλαιὸν νόμον ... κοινὸν καὶ Ἡλίωι (*Laws* 946b–c). The generalised sense seems to be intended here: 202–60n., 281–2n.

204 Φοινίσσας ἀπὸ νάσου after Jocasta's mention of Phoenician Cadmus (5–6) and Τύριον 202, it is impossible to take this phrase as anything but a reference to Tyre (Polle suggested the meaning was Sicily, Radermacher saw an allusion to the Carthaginian peninsula). Tyre was an island until joined to the mainland by a mole during the siege by Alexander in 332 B.C.

205 Φοίβωι δούλα μελάθρων the normal objective genitive (here of the sphere of servitude, cf. *Hipp.* 1249 δοῦλος ... σῶν δόμων) is combined with the personal dative dependent on the same noun (17n.). For this uncommon dat. cf. *Tro.* 250–1, *Ion* 132, *OT* 410, Thuc. 6.76.4 σφίσιν ... καταδουλώσεως.

206 νιφοβόλοις true (cf. E. Meyer, *Der kl. Pauly* s.v. Parnassos), but also a poetic commonplace for this and other tall mountains: Panyassis apud Paus. 10.8.9; *OT* 473; 234 below; (other peaks) 802 below; *Aj.* 696, Arist. *Clouds* 270.

207 Παρνασσοῦ under the influence of Boeckh and Cobet, editors of poetry tend to print Παρνασός, etc., but for -σσ- cf. Riemann, *BCH* 3

---

[1] For another passage wrongly identified as imitative of this line of Phrynichus, see R. Renehan, *Stud. Gk. Texts*, 66–7.

(1879) 494f., H. v. Herwerden, *Lexicon Graecum suppletorium et dialecticum*[2] (Leiden 1910) 1123, and Teubner *praefatio*, ¶20 (2). Eur. apparently used non-Attic Παρνᾶ- even in trimeters (*Tro.* 9, *Her.* 240 vs. *Andr.* 1100, *Ion* 1267), though in Aesch. (*Choe.* 563, *Eum.* 11) editors accept Παρνη-.

κατενάσθη a certain emendation by S. Thirlby, now found in Ad (but probably by accident: Diggle, *Textual Trad. Or.* 68 n. 5). Just as 205 expands upon ἀκροθίνια 203, so 206–7 make explicit ('at Delphi') what is implied in the name Loxias in 203; cf. the identifying topographic relative clause or participial phrase so common in invocations of gods (Richardson on *Hom.h.Dem.* 490–5). Defences of κατενάσθην (Σ and some comm.) all involve impossible assumptions: the chorus has not yet been to Delphi; the verb cannot mean 'I have been destined to dwell'.

208 Ἰόνιον on the quantity of the initial iota, see note above under Metre. In the fifth century the name Ionian Sea (or Gulf) referred to the Adriatic (Hdt.; *Prom.* 840) and to the sea separating Corcyra, Epirus, Acarnania, Leucas, and the mouth of the Corinthian Gulf from Southern Italy and Sicily (cf. Pindar, esp. *P.* 3.68, an imagined voyage from Thebes to Sicily; Thuc.; Eur. here and *Tro.* 225 (if sound)). At the south it overlaps (and later became interchangeable with) the Sicilian Sea (or Gulf), which in Thuc. and Eur. (*Cycl.* 703, *El.* 1347) applies to the sea between Sicily and western Peloponnese or Ithaca. In Latin poets *Ionius* comes to be used for *Ionicus*, and *Ionium mare* can refer to the Aegean (Ovid, *Fasti* 4.566, Sen. *Ag.* 506, *Phoen.* 610); even later Ἰόνιον πέλαγος was alleged by some to refer to the sea off Gaza as far as Egypt (Steph. Byz. s.v.; Eust. on Dion. Perieg. 92), but this is equally irrelevant to the Euripidean usage. The popular derivation of Ἰόνιος from Io (*Prom.* 840 and later) is perhaps false, but pays more attention to linguistic and historical facts than some modern theories. Against Frisk s.v. Ἴωνες, Schwyzer 1.80, and H. Treidler, *Klio* 22 (1929) 91–4, see R. L. Beaumont, *JHS* 56 (1936) 204; Chantraine s.vv. Ἰώ, Ἴωνες and cf. 238n.

208–9 ἐλάται 'ship' by metonymy, as *Alc.* 444, *IA* 174, 1322, not 'oar' (twice in Homer) as the scholiasts thought, believing the vessel was rowed against an adverse wind.

209–11 περιρρύτων . . . Σικελίας this phrase must be taken with Ζεφ. ἱππεύσαντος, not with πλεύσασα. Few commentators are explicit on this point, and after a period of overpunctuated texts most editors since Dindorf have eliminated all punctuation and left the issue open. Many translators, from Barnes to Méridier and Craik, have associated the phrase with πλεύσασα in the sense 'along, over the waters of the Sicilian Sea', but ὑπέρ + gen. is thus misused (and the phrase is redundant with Ἰόνιον κατὰ πόντον). With Ζεφ. ἱππ. the prepositional phrase probably means simply 'above the Sicilian Sea' (Eur. *El.* 459 ὑπὲρ ἁλὸς ποτανοῖσι = '(in flight) above the sea'; *Ag.* 576 ὑπὲρ θαλάσσης καὶ χθονὸς ποτωμένοις; prob. Soph. fr. 476.2 ὡς ἀμποταθείην ὑπὲρ ἀτρυγέτου). The sense 'along, over the waters . . .' would require the acc.: *Eum.* 77, Soph. fr. 956, epic ὑπεὶρ ἅλα. If taken with πλεύσασα, ὑπέρ + gen. would have to be 'across the Sicilian Sea (from one bordering land to another)': cf. e.g. Hes. fr. 204.60 M–W ὑπὲρ 'Ωγυγίου πόντου (from Crete to Tyndareus' home), Pindar *P.* 9.52 ὑπὲρ πόντου (from Thessaly to Cyrene), *Aj.* 702 'Ικαρίων δ' ὑπὲρ πελαγέων (from Delos to Troy; text corrupt? – cf. Lloyd-Jones and Wilson). Such a sense is possible with ἱππεύσαντος if Zephyrus is viewed as coming all the way from Sicily to western Greece.

209 περιρρύτων the adj. is elsewhere in classical Greek 'passive' and an epithet of islands or land-masses. If gen. pl. is correct, it is here 'active', of the waters encircling an island (cf. Eusebius *de vita Constantini* 2.31 περιρρύτωι περικεκλεισμένοι θαλάσσηι). This is a legitimate variation for compound adjs. in -τος: cf. Barrett on *Hipp.* 678 (δυσ-/-τος and ἀ-/-τος types, but for other kinds cf. *Hipp.* 1346 καταληπτόν and Fraenkel on *Ag.* 12 with further references, also p. 137 n. 1). For -ρυτος in particular JD reminds me of nominal compounds like αἱμόρρυτος or ἀργυρόρρυτος and 'active' ἐπίρρυτος (*Eum.* 907), ἀπόρρυτος (Hes. *Op.* 595). With περιρρύτων governing Σικελίας (cf. ὅ τε γῆς περίρρους 'Ωκεανός, Aristides *or.* 43(1).24 Keil), the whole phrase is a poetic periphrasis for the Sicilian Sea, i.e. the waters on the western coast of the Peloponnese (208n.; cf. Thuc. 4.53.3 πᾶσα [ἡ Λακωνική] . . . ἀνέχει πρὸς τὸ Σικελικὸν καὶ Κρητικὸν πέλαγος). There is no implication that the maidens sailed close to Sicily. περιρρύτωι has uncertain attestation (V¹ wrote -των (as at *Andr.* 802 κακῶν), M¹ -τω*, which seemed to be -τωι to Wecklein's collator, but -των to me: the erasure and rewriting may in any case imply knowledge of a variant). Hiatus and period-end would be acceptable here, and the adj. would be 'passive', but 'sea-girt ship' is not a very pointed expression (contrast *Ant.* 953f. ἁλίκτυποι . . . νᾶες), and ἀκαρπίστων πεδίων Σικελίας is harsh, if not impossible, for 'seas adjacent to Sicily' (the natural meaning would be 'unharvested plains of Sicily', where the epithet is false). The last objection also applies to Stinton's περιρρύτου.

210 ἀκαρπίστων hapax in extant Greek, a reminiscence of Homeric ἀτρύγετος.

πεδίων 'plains of the sea', as the epithets make clear; cf. *Hel.* 1117, Aesch. fr. 150, Ion *TrGF* 19 F 60, Tim. *Pers.* (*PMG* 791) 78, and poetic usage of νῶτα and Latin *aequor*.

211–13 Ζεφύρου . . . ἱππεύσαντος . . . κελάδημα 'while Zephyrus rode with his breezes, producing a lovely music in the sky' (κελάδημα internal acc.: Wilam. on *Her.* 59, Barrett on *Hipp.* 752–7). πνοαῖς is here modal dative with ἱππεύσαντος, though the phrase Ζεφ. πν. is reminiscent of Homeric πνοιῆι Ζεφύροιο, in which the noun depends on instrumental πνοιῆι (*Il.* 19.415; cf. *Od.* 4.402, 10.25, Bacch. 5.28f. σὺν ζεφ. πνοιαῖσιν). One might have expected ἱππεύοντος for this accompanying action (so tacitly Wilam. on *Her.* 59, then Wecklein), but perhaps the aorist participle can be viewed as coincident with πλεύσασα, although other instances are of nom. part. coincident with finite aorists or aor. inf. (1507n.; but for acc. part. see 964n.). JD suggests instead that the aor. indicates the earlier stage of the voyage, the Sicilian Sea being distinguished from the Ionian (208n.). For the sound of Zephyrus cf. κελαδεινόν *Il.* 23.208, κελάδοντ᾽ *Od.* 2.421, λιγὺ πνείοντος 4.567; for this wind as favourable or delightful cf. *Od.* 2.421, 4.567 (Elysium), 7.119 (garden of Alcinous), 10.25 (the only wind not trapped in the bag by Aeolus), 'sweet blast' Philoxenus *PMG* 835; Bacchyl. epigr. 1 (*Epigr. Gr.* 430 Page). Zephyrus would have been the favouring wind on the final leg of the voyage, from Cape Chelonatas in north-western Elis to Creusis. ἱππεύσαντος (imitated by Horace, *Odes* 4.4.43–4 *vel Eurus per Siculas equitavit undas*) may allude to an old belief that wind-gods may be equine in form (cf. Lloyd-Jones, *CQ* 7 (1957) 24 with references) and probably means 'riding like a horse' rather than 'riding on a horse' (see Bond on *Her.* 1001).

214 ἐκπροκριθεῖσ᾽   hapax in extant Greek (cf. hapax ἐκπροτιμάω *Ant.* 913, ἐκπροίημι *Ion* 219).

215 καλλιστεύματα   either 'offering of what is fairest' as a variation on the more usual καλλιστεῖον (*IT* 23 and inscr. cited by LSJ), or repersonified abstract (21n.), 'persons pre-eminent in beauty' (cf. true abstract in *Or.* 1639 'by means of the pre-eminent beauty of this woman ⟨Helen⟩'). Unless κ]αλλισ[in Aesch. fr. 154a.21 is to be restored as a form of καλλίστευμα, the word may be a Euripidean coinage (otherwise only in Lycophron).

216 Καδμείων ... γᾶν   Diggle, in a note on *Ba.* 1 (forthcoming in *Euripidea*), notes a preference for adj. Θηβαία/Καδμεία with χθών (and perhaps γῆ) and for gen. noun Θηβαίων/Καδμείων with πόλις or ἄστυ and proposes to accept Καδμείαν here (which happens to be recorded from the worthless codex Thessalonicensis). Most mss carry δ᾽ after Καδμείων, the result of punctuating at Λοξίαι 215 rather than κελάδημα 212, a mistake aided by *horror asyndeti* and the failure to perceive the epodic form of 202–38, first restored by Canter.

217 Ἀγηνοριδᾶν   the Phoenicians (or Tyrians) are simply 'descendants of Agenor' and Eur. is here no more specific about Agenor's relation to Cadmus; in *Ba.* 171 Cadmus is son of Agenor, in *Phrixos B* fr. 819 Cadmus may have been grandson of Agenor and son of Phoenix, unless Θάσος in line 9 is emended to Κάδμος; so too Europa is daughter of Phoenix in Homer, Hesiod, and Bacchyl., but of Agenor in later sources. Cf. A. W. Gomme, *JHS* 33 (1913) 53–72 (68 n. 114 favouring emendation in fr.

819.9); Jacoby's comm. on *FGrHist* 3 F 21; E. Wüst s.v. Phoinix (4), *RE* 20 (1941) 412–14. Already in Σ we find the alternative punctuation (adopted by some comm. and transl.) that makes κλεινῶν Ἀγηνοριδῶν appositive to Καδμείων rather than dependent on ὁμογενεῖς, where it has more point. This patronymic is otherwise extant only in the singular (of Phoenix or Cadmus) in Ap.Rhod. and a few later texts.

218–19 ὁμογενεῖς . . . πύργους like συγγενής, ὁμογενής is easily used in the extended sense 'belonging to kin' (1291 below; cf. *Med.* 1268).

220–1 χρυσοτεύκτοις 2n.

221 λάτρις ἐγενόμαν this describes the maidens' status from the time of selection in Tyre and does not imply (as Σ and others have believed) that the maidens have already been to Delphi. To forestall ambiguity Eur. immediately adds ἔτι δὲ κτλ.

222 Κασταλίας the spring is used as a symbol of the location (126n.) and was probably of real importance for ritual purification, a daily preliminary to service in the temple (cf. *Ion* 94–7). Cf. H. W. Parke, 'Castalia', *BCH* 102 (1978) 199–219.

223 περιμένει the minority reading of MO+ probably deserves preference over ἐπιμένει because of the quality of the source. ἐπιμένω and περιμένω are synonyms in Soph. (metrically distinct: *Ant.* 1296 τίς ἄρα, τίς με πότμος ἔτι περιμένει vs. *OC* 1715f. τίς ἄρα με πότμος / ἐπιμένει σέ τ'; cf. Eur. *Su.* 623f. τίς ἄρα πότμος ἐπιμένει, *Phoen.* 1734, *Her.* 432) and in prose (Plato, *Rep.* 361d οἷος ἑκάτερον βίος ἐπιμένει vs. 614a ἃ τελευτήσαντα ἑκάτερον περιμένει). In Aristophanes, Menander, and Attic prose, however, περιμένω is more frequent than ἐπι-, and in later Greek 'await' + acc. is normally περιμένω, whereas ἐπιμένω is usually 'persist in' + dat. Thus it is not impossible that περιμένει (not elsewhere extant in Eur.) originated as a gloss on ἐπιμένει. Either verb can govern acc. + inf. ('waits for me to moisten', with personification) or have the sense 'is in store for me, awaits me, so that I may moisten' (epexegetic inf.).

223–4 κόμας ἐμᾶς . . . παρθένιον χλιδάν 'the maidenly luxuriance of my hair', a typical lyric periphrasis for 'my luxuriant hair, in which a maiden takes pride' (χλιδή implies a subjective as well as an objective richness; cf. Orestes' dedication at his father's tomb, Soph. *El.* 52 καρατόμοις χλιδαῖς, Aesch. fr. 313.1 χλιδῶν τε πλόκαμος ὥστε παρθένοις ἁβραῖς). For maidens' pride in their hair, cf. Alcm. *PMGF* 1.51–3, 3.71–2, and perhaps *IT* 1149.

225 λατρείαις a vague sociative dat. of attendant circumstances (Schwyzer 11.162): 'in my service to Phoebus'. Parke's inference (*BCH* 102 (1978) 222) from the picturesque detail of 222–5 that washing the hair in Castalia was a part of contemporary initiation into service at Delphi seems to me a risky one.

226–38 a stanza consisting of a single sentence (202–13n.).

226 ὦ monosyllabic pronunciation of ἰώ is not impossible (*Phil.* 759 has been widely accepted; the emendation accepted in Lloyd-Jones and Wilson is not attractive), but given the frequency of ἰώ / ὦ (ὤ) confusion (see *Concordance* s.vv.) there is little reason to choose ἰώ (mss) over Π⁴'s ω. For the variation see also 109 (Π³), 1500 Π⁵, *Andr.* 1009, *Hec.* 716.

226–8 λάμπουσα . . . βακχείων 'crag shining with the twin-peaked gleam of fire above the lofty sites of revelry', an ornate periphrasis for the twin peaks of Parnassus looming over Delphi, the Phaedriades (on the other hand, 234 refers to the whole mountain). The more natural juncture of epithets in Kirchhoff's δικορύφων . . . βακχεῖον is not necessarily preferable if the style is 'dithyrambic', as it often is in the odes of this play. The Phaedriades, seen from the point of view of Delphi, are probably responsible for the poetic commonplace of a twin-peaked Parnassus, though the mountain as a whole has in fact many peaks of nearly equal height (J. Schmidt, *RE* 18:2 (1949) 1595–603). σέλας is internal acc., as in *TrGF* adesp. 33 πυρὸς δ' ἐξ ὀμμάτων ἔλαμπεν αἴγλην (see too LSJ s.v. ἐκλάμπω II); closely related is the acc. of the object effected in *Hel.* 1131 ἀστέρα λάμψας (*Ion* 82–3 would be even bolder, an acc. of the object affected, but Diggle's punctuation removes the anomaly).

227–8 ἄκρων βακχείων either 'bacchic (revel-filled) heights' or, less redundantly with Διονύσου, 'lofty sites of revelry'; for this sense of βακχεῖον see 21n. Σ wrongly ascribes this sense to βακχειῶν, which would in fact be *nomen actionis* and would have the inappropriate meaning '(lofty) bacchic dancing'. At Delphi Dionysus was second in importance to Apollo: Farnell, *Cults of the Greek States* v.153; Fontenrose, *Python* 373–94; Burkert, *Gr. Religion* 342f.(= Engl. transl. 224f.). Nocturnal mountain-top dancing is a feature of Bacchic cult in many places, Delphi/Parnassus the most famous among them: see Dodds, *The Greeks and the Irrational*, 270ff.; *IT* 1242–4, *Ion* 716–17, 1125–6, *Ant.* 1126–9 (three of these share with our passage the allusion to the torch-light on the peaks of Parnassus).

229–31 οἶνα . . . βότρυν 'vine, which daily drips (wine?) *or* grows ripe (?), putting forth (every day) the full-fruited grape-cluster from the grape-bloom'. This is obscure to us, but Eur. could assume in his audience some knowledge of this magical vine which put forth each day a new bloom that matured within a few hours. Soph. described a similar one in Euboea (*Thyestes* fr. 255, from Σ; Radt quotes other scholia discussing ἐφήμεροι ἄμπελοι). στάζεις is difficult: it cannot govern βότρυν = 'grape-cluster' (so LSJ) and so must be absolute, in one of two rare or unparalleled senses. (1) 'drip (liquid)', presumably wine: we are told by Σ (who may be doing no more than inferring from this passage) that each day's libation came from the ripe cluster; in Soph. and the other scholiastic sources it is said that pure wine is provided directly from the harvested clusters. Here we are to imagine the grapes so full of wine as to exude it even before crushing. The only parallel for στάζω so used is *Andr.* 532–4 λείβομαι δάκρυσιν κόρας, στάζω λισσάδος ὡς πέτρας λιβὰς ἀνάλιος. (2) 'grow ripe': the only potential parallel is one possible sense of the corrupt passage Aesch. *Su.* 1001 καρπώματα στάζοντα (see Friis Johansen and Whittle *ad loc.*). On the whole, (1) is preferable.

τόν the article is emphatic, 'that well-known': cf. 179 τὰ δεινά; K–G 1.598; perhaps also *Hyps.* fr. 765 οἰνάνθα τρέφει τὸν ἱερὸν βότρυν.

ἱεῖσα another unique usage: compare ἀνίημι of production from the earth or womb (LSJ s.v. 1.1; *Hom.h.Dem.* 332; *OT* 270), and in later prose the use of ἀφίημι of putting forth mature fruit, leaf, or flowers (Theophr. *HP* 3.4.5, 6.5.1, 7.7.3; LSJ wrongly see this sense in *Od.* 7.126, where ἀφιεῖσαι is rather 'shedding'; cf. also προΐενται τοὺς βλαστούς, Theophr. *CP* 1.12.9). The separative gen. (of source) without preposition is paralleled in ἀνιέναι γῆς (*Hom.h.Dem.* and *OT*, cited above) and προϊεῖσα κρημνῶν *Hipp.* 124 and makes better sense than adnominal gen. 'grapecluster of the grape-bloom'. So explained, the passage is probably sound. Nauck's περκάζεις for στάζεις τόν (cf. ὑποπερκάζουσιν *Od.* 7.126, in the passage from which Eur. probably borrowed πολύκαρπον; περκάζουσαν Chaeremon *TrGF* 71 F 12.2) removes only one of the oddities, and that at the expense of the idiomatic article.

232–3 ἄντρα δράκοντος . . . σκοπιαὶ θεῶν the chorus thus alludes to the Corycian Cave on Parnassus inhabited by Python, site of the conquest of the serpent-monster by Apollo, and to the Lookout Place or Archer's Hill from which Apollo shot his arrow; on the myth see Fontenrose, *Python*, esp. 78, 409–12 on cave and lookout. The chorus' allusion to this myth in a context of longing will have an ironic resonance when Cadmus' conquest of Ares' serpent (a myth of parallel form and function) later becomes a focus of attention and anxiety. θεῶν is allusive: gods in general possess and dwell on peaks (24n.) and reference to Apollo's battle is included; I do not find it suitable poetically to limit θεῶν to the Corycian nymphs (Σ; so now West (1990), reading θεᾶν), nor does the comment on Apollo necessarily imply that a scholiast once read θεοῦ (Wilam. *GV* 279 n. 1).

234–8 εἱλίσσων . . . προλιποῦσα the long series of invocations is finally revealed to be a prelude to an escape-wish, with ἄφοβος introducing the fear of the present situation and the rejection implied by Δίρκαν προλιποῦσα saved emphatically for the end. γενοίμαν is typical of such wishes, most of which involve the desire to fly away (163–7n.); for desired change of place without flight cf. *Hipp.* 230–1, *Aj.* 1217.

εἱλίσσων use of this verb for dancing is a Eur. mannerism; it is so used

221

both in active and middle/passive (*Ba.* 569–70, *IA* 1055), and when active may have an object such as πόδα (*Tro.* 333 (Diggle's text); perhaps *IT* 1145) or the god celebrated (*Her.* 690 (γόνον is ἀπὸ κοινοῦ object), *IA* 1480) or be intransitive/absolute as it must be here unless we emend (cf. *Tro.* 333 in other treatments of the text). Ever since Matthiae's misreporting of L's reading as ἀθανάτους many have given εἱλίσσων an object (ἀθανάτους θεούς Seyffert, εἱλίσσουσ' ἀθανάτους θεοῦ χοροῖς Paley, simply ἀθανάτους Wecklein), at the same time eliminating the obscurity of the unnamed goddess (see below). But unless we adopt Paley's multiple correction, εἱλίσσων is an attribute of χορός and the phrase produced by the smallest and easiest change ('a dancing-to-the-immortals chorus of the god ⟨Apollo⟩') does not seem to me felicitous. Seyffert's solution would be *lectio facilior*. I am still inclined to accept intransitive εἱλίσσων.

ἀθανάτας θεοῦ granted that ἀθανάτου θεοῦ (= Apollo) arose as an attempt to bypass the problem presented by this phrase, we are left with three choices for the goddess. (1) Artemis, proposed by Σ and accepted by most, is sister of Apollo and patroness of maidens. No separate cult of Artemis is attested at Delphi, and the non-literary evidence for her presence there as sister of Apollo is slight: she was with Apollo in the pediment of the sixth-century temple of Apollo, and an Amphictyonic oath inscribed in 379 B.C. is sworn by Apollo, Artemis, and Leto (*SIG* 145); cf. Farnell, *Cults of the Greek States* II.466–7; Burkert, *Gr. Religion* 335 (= Engl. trans. 219). On the other hand, in the literary tradition Pindar includes Artemis with Apollo in reference to the Pythian games at *P.* 4.3 Λατοΐδαισιν ὀφειλόμενον Πυθῶνί τ' αὔξῃς οὖρον ὕμνων and *N.* 9.4–5 ματέρι [Leto] καὶ διδύμοις παίδεσσιν αὐδὰν μανύει Πυθῶνος αἰπεινᾶς ὁμοκλάροις ἐπόπταις (only Apollo has been mentioned in the preceding lines); cf. too *P.* 8.66 ἑορταῖς ὑμαῖς (the Delphinia at Aegina) in an address to Apollo, where ὑμαῖς implicitly includes Artemis with Apollo. Further literary evidence for Artemis at Delphi comes from *Hom.h.* 27 (of uncertain date): Artemis goes to her brother's house at Delphi after the hunt and there leads a chorus of Muses and Graces (cf. Allen–Halliday–Sikes on lines 13–15). It is thus possible that Eur. expected θεοῦ to be unambiguously understood to be Artemis. (2) Athena, worshipped at Delphi as Pronaia, was proposed by Hermann, with unconvincing reasoning (*Attici tragici quum non addito nomine deam dicunt, Minervam, ut consentaneum est, cogitant, cuius honorandae ubicumque fieri potest occasionem captant*).[1] (3) Ge is proposed by Craik; but although

---

[1] Wecklein wrongly claimed that reading ἀδαμάτας would identify Artemis more unambiguously than ἀθανάτας: ἄδμης or ἄδμητος is used of her at Aesch. *Su.* 149 and Soph. *El.* 1239, but ἀδάματος of Athena at *Aj.* 450.

she is prominent in the remaining odes (where she is explicitly named), I see no clue or tradition of worship that would induce an audience to think of her here. Diggle (1990a) 10 notes that ἀθάνατος is redundant and is not used elsewhere in Eur. of a god (and (JD) that he would expect ἀθανάτου θεᾶς rather than ἀθανάτας θεοῦ), and so accepts Wecklein's version. For fem. form of ἀθάνατος in drama, cf. *Choe.* 619, *Clouds* 289, *Thesm.* 1052 (? = Eur. fr. 122).

237 παρά παρά gives glyconic opening ⏑⏑∪, very common in Eur., whereas preposition πάρ (MO) is otherwise unattested for him (but *Trach.* 636 is the only Sophoclean instance; Aesch. has three examples, *Su.* 553, *Eum.* 229 (trim.), fr. 204b.3). Cf. 1139-40n.

γύαλα Delphi is located in the hollow of Parnassus and so this word became a poetic commonplace for the shrine of Apollo. It provides no support for the later fantasy that there was a cavern or chasm in the temple itself (cf. Fontenrose, *The Delphic Oracle* 200-3).

239-60 the chorus now openly turns to the present situation, leading up to the important concession of the justice of Pol.'s cause. Movement in a choral ode from the more remote or general to the more immediate or specific is commonplace. The content of these stanzas is necessary, and the language and rhythm are thoroughly Euripidean. The unusual internal epode (see on Metre) is a wholly inadequate ground for suspecting the authenticity of these lines (so, in an *obiter dictum*, A. L. Brown, *Eranos* 74 (1976) 8 n. 8).

241 αἷμα δάϊον φλέγει 'kindles the bloodshed of destructive war'; for the metaphor cf. *Aj.* 195 ἄταν οὐρανίαν φλέγων and, with intransitive 'blaze', *Il.* 20.18 μάχη πόλεμός τε δέδηε, 12.35 μάχη ἐνοπή τε δεδήει. By juxtaposing δάϊον with φλέγει, Eur. may be playing on the etymological confusion of the word ('destructive, hostile' vs. 'blazing'); cf. Chantraine s.v. δήϊος.

242 ὃ μὴ τύχοι like ὃ μὴ γένοιτο an apotropaic interjection meant to cancel the effect of ill-omened words: cf. 571 below and Diggle, *Studies* 104. The idiom is probably colloquial, contributing to the straightforward tone of the passage.

243 κοινὰ γὰρ φίλων ἄχη κοινὰ τὰ (τῶν) φίλων was proverbial, ascribed to Pythagoras (see Biehl's testimonia on *Or.* 735; in Eur. also at *Andr.* 336-7). By specifying ἄχη as what is shared, the chorus alludes to the truest test of friendship, sharing in misery as well as in happiness (cf. 403 below, *Or.* 665-6, *Her.* 55-9 with Bond's notes). The fourfold anaphora of κοιν- is comparable only to ἐκεῖσ' ... ἐκεῖ ... ἐκεῖ ... ἐκεῖ ... in *Ba.* 412ff.; but threefold anaphora is more common (Breitenbach, 231).

248 κερασφόρου ... 'Ιοῦς for the epithet cf. *Hyps.* fr. 1.iii.29-31 'Ιώ ... ἀμεῖψαι [κερ]άσφορον ἄταν. Io's name is of uncertain derivation (Chantraine s.v.); the suggestion that it is a short form of Iole (cf. Iokaste,

Iolaos) founders on the quantity of the iota, always long in Io, short in the other names.

249 ὧν the antecedent τέκεα includes Thebans and Agenoridae, implying 'whose troubles (whether they be Thebans or Agenoridae) are a care to me'.

250–2 νέφος ἀσπίδων ... μάχας 'A dense storm-cloud of shields blazes (flashes lightning?), producing a vision of bloody battle.' This seems the most probable rendering, although πυκνόν could be adverbial with φλέγει, some have taken σχῆμα as in apposition to νέφος rather than as internal acc. with φλέγει, and one could even take σχῆμα as subject and νέφος as object (with little difference in overall effect). Metaphorical use of νέφος / νεφέλη is discussed at length by Wilam. on *Her.* 1140 (cf. Bond as well). νέφος here implies both darkness and the vehemence of storm, and φλέγει as verb is strongly oxymoronic unless the image is of lightning flashing in a dark cloud (at *Med.* 107 νέφος οἰμωγῆς ὡς τάχ' ἀνάψει the reference is rather to sound than light, according to Diggle, *CQ* 34 (1984) 53). The range of meaning of πυκνόν is especially suitable here: it is used (1) of vehement weather or thick-falling snow; (2) of dense darkness (especially with νέφος, but also with ὄρφνη *Rhes.* 774); (3) of massed weaponry or missiles.

σχῆμα basically 'form' or 'shape' but often connoting 'external appearance' or 'visual impression' (*Ion* 238, 240, fr. 688.2, *Med.* 1072), sometimes with a suggestion of familiarity (*Alc.* 912 ὦ σχῆμα δόμων, *Phil.* 952 ὦ σχῆμα πέτρας δίπυλον) or even pride (*Hec.* 619 ὦ σχῆμὰτ' οἴκων; *Ant.* 1169 τύραννον σχῆμ' ἔχων) or beauty (*Andr.* 1 Ἀσιάτιδος γῆς σχῆμα = 'ornament of Asia' (*contra* Stevens, who favours an empty periphrastic rendering here and elsewhere) and perhaps fr. 476 and fr. 360.27; cf. the connotation of seemliness which makes possible the idiom ἔχει σχῆμα *Tro.* 470, *IA* 983). Here, as Pearson noted, σχῆμα 'denotes the sensual presentation of an object by which we are aware of its identity' and seems to me superior to σῆμα (variant based on gloss) in sense and poetic vividness.

253 ἂν Ἄρης τάχ' εἴσεται 'which Ares will soon witness'; cf. *Andr.* 258 θεοὶ γὰρ εἴσονται τάδε [Hermione's murder of a suppliant], 998 τελουμένων δὲ Δελφὶς εἴσεται πέτρα, *Hel.* 1295 σὺ δ' αὐτὸς ἐγγὺς ὢν εἴσῃ τάδε. Ares' presence as a witness (and bringer of πημονὰν Ἐρινύων) may imply he will be βραβεύς of the contest (for the notion cf. *Trach.* 515–16, *Hel.* 703), but the usual rendering 'will decide, will put to the test' involves an unattested and unlikely sense of οἶδα. The parallels alleged do not stand up: εἴσεται in *Choe.* 305 is not 'it will be decided', but 'he will find out'; in *Hcld.* 269 πειρώμενος δὴ τοῦτό γ' αὐτίκ' εἴσομαι the notion of testing is in the participle (and the object again is 'this fact'); in *IA* 970–2 τάχ' εἴσεται σίδηρος ... εἰ ... 'determine whether' is possible but so is 'will find out whether' and the εἰ-clause is not comparable to μάχην as object.

257–60 the fear that the gods may support the justice of Pol.'s cause echoes 154–5 and further disposes the audience to give Pol. a sympathetic hearing.

259 ἔνοπλος ὁρμᾶι cf. *Or.* 1289 ἔνοπλος ὁρμήσας.

259–60 ὁρμᾶι {παῖς} / ὅς granted that there can be no objection to hiatus and period-end at ὁρμᾶι (see under Metre), the deletion of παῖς restores the smoothest and most effective text. εἰς ἀγῶνα τόνδ' goes well with verb ὁρμᾶι, but is clumsy with μετέρχεται δόμους in Battier's version (ὁρμᾶι as noun, ὅς deleted); Hartung's ὁρμῶν / παῖς μετ. and ὁρμᾶι [verb] καὶ μετ. assume multiple changes and (like Battier's text) destroy the isometric echo 249 = 260, which should be viewed as an intentional effect. παῖς was apparently added to supply an explicit antecedent for ὅς. As the connective γάρ and the chorus' question in 286–7 prove, this is a general comment ('not unjust is this contest ⟨of war⟩ toward which he presses with armed force, the one who comes to recover his patrimony'), not an announcement of Pol.'s entrance (cf. *Contact and Discontinuity* 100 n. 14; Hose, *Chor* 193 n. 6, well compares *Choe.* 648–51 for choral preparation for an entry).[1] For μετέρχομαι = 'go / come to recover', cf. μετῆλθε 1655 and μεθήκω 441 and the sense 'pursue to recover / avenge' in *IT* 14, *Andr.* 992, *Cycl.* 280.

261–442: FIRST EPISODE, PART 1

The longest and most quoted 'act' of *Phoen.* (261–637) consists of two large sections. In the second we have the famous ἀγὼν λόγων of Eteocles and Polynices with Jocasta as arbitrator (443–637n.). In this first section, however, Polynices alone shares the stage with his mother and his dilemma is given a full and sympathetic exposure through three self-descriptive rheseis (261–79, 357–78, 427–42), an emotional aria of reunion and grief (301–54), and a two-part stichomythia (388–426). The cautious entry of Pol., glancing from side to side, sword in hand, is similar to that of Orestes and Pylades in *IT* 67ff. or of Odysseus and Diomedes in *Rhesus* 565ff. and underlines the distrust between the brothers as well as the poignancy of Pol.'s situation. In his native city he feels as endangered as Orestes in the

---

[1] Without denying the general nature of these lines, Craik and Saïd, 519, believe an audience will detect a secondary meaning descriptive of Pol. ('armed he approaches the house for this contest ⟨of words⟩').

land of the Tauri and even subsumes his case under those in which one walks on enemy soil (270-1). As is typical in Eur., Pol. is both endowed with self-awareness and blindly trapped in his assumptions. On the one hand, he is aware of the irony of his position and frequently employs antitheses and paradoxes (272, 357, 431-2), and his statements of love for his family and fatherland may be taken at face value. On the other hand, his assumptions about wealth, self-respect, and justice are disastrously inflexible, and he seems not to perceive the divine plan which is leading him to his doom (413n.). Jocasta's aria gives lengthy expression to the emotions which drive her to attempt to reconcile her sons, but it is striking that the lyric is uninterrupted by contributions from Pol. himself (contrast traditional scenes of reunion/recognition, e.g. *IT* 827ff., *Ion* 1437ff.). Pol.'s response is rather the self-contained rhesis which follows the aria. This one-sidedness dramatizes a reserve and stiffness in Pol. which do not evince a lack of feeling (warmth is evident in such lines as 359-60, 366, 371ff., 387, 407, 431, 437, 615-18, 633) but which foreshadow the ineffectiveness of Jocasta's appeals and the irrevocable separation that follows. The stichomythia is prompted by Jocasta's curiosity and concern and, apart from the variety of form which it affords, is an effective expression of Jocasta's close interest in what her son has to tell her. The first part (388-407), with its generalizations about exile, lays the groundwork for both the content and the failure of Jocasta's later plea to Pol.: the preciousness of one's fatherland is the final deduction from the survey of the ills of exile, and if Jocasta wants to evoke the former to ask Pol. to give up the attack, it is ironic that the full force of the latter militates against such a concession. The second part of the stichomythia (408-26) narrates in detail a part of the background known only in general terms to Jocasta (and likewise to the audience which has depended on her prologue-speech) and leads to Pol.'s final statement of his position before the agon proper.

261-2 εἰσεδέξατο . . . τειχέων ἔσω μολεῖν 450n., 451n.

εὐπετείας the noun here alone in tragedy, probably a prosaic word (adj. εὐπετής is used by all three tragedians).

263 ὃ καί 155n.

δικτύων ἔσω cf. *Cycl.* 196 ἀρκύων μολεῖν ἔσω; metaphors from hunting are of course common and ominous in tragedy (*Pers.* 99, *Ag. passim*); for δίκτυον or ἄρκυς used of an ambush cf. *El.* 965, *Her.* 729, *Or.* 1315, Soph. *El.* 1476-7.

264 ἐκφρῶσ' for Attic *φρέω and compounds see Barrett on *Hipp.* 866-7; Schwyzer 1.689, Chantraine s.v. *πίφρημι. The verb is not used by Aesch. and Photius' ascription of it to Soph. (s.v. οὐκ ἐκφρῶσιν – not recorded as a fr. in Radt) may well be an error (Renehan, *Gk. Text. Crit.*, 51). The verb was not current in later Greek and its forms were often

226

corrupted. In this passage Philoxenus (first cent. B.C.), fr. 16 Theodoridis (from Σ), still read ἐκφρω- but the mss have μεθω-, simple substitution of a more familiar word. That actors made the change διὰ τὸ δυσέκφορον (or at all) is strongly to be doubted. For actors wrongly adduced by scholiasts to explain real (or supposed) errors in the text, cf. W. Malzan, *de scholiis Euripideis quae ad res scenicas et ad histriones pertinent* (Darmstadt 1908), 29; E. Bruhn, *Lucubr. Eur.* 247–51.

ἀναίμακτον predicative with με (not χρόα, as LSJ); a rare epithet, also in Aesch. *Su.* 196 and *Rhes.* 222.

265 ὄμμα πανταχῆι διοιστέον cf. *IT* 68 ὁρῶ, σκοποῦμαι δ᾽ ὄμμα πανταχῆι (Monk: -χοῦ L) στρέφων, *Ion* 205 πάνται (Musgrave: πάντα L)[1] τοι βλέφαρον διώκω, *Or.* 1267 κόρας διάδοτε (Canter: κόραισι δίδοτε codd.) ... πάνται (Weil: πάντα L, πάντη(ι) rell.), 1295 σκοπεύουσ᾽ ἁπάνται (Nauck: fere σκοποῦσα πάντα vel ἅπαντα vel πάντη codd. (πάνται Brunck)); Arist. *Thesm.* 660, 665, 958. These parallels show that πανταχοῦ is a trivialization (*IT* 68; variant here and *Or.* 760) and not a pointer to a genuine πανταχοῖ (van den Es).

268 τὰ πίστ᾽ ... τοῦ θράσους 'the guarantee of my confidence/ fearlessness'. The phrase is borrowed from legal terminology and perhaps has a prosaic ring. Cf. Xen. *Anab.* 4.8.7 ἠρώτων ... εἰ δοῖεν ἂν τούτων τὰ πιστά; Arist. *Clouds* 533 πιστὰ ... γνώμης ... ὅρκια ('pledges of your ⟨favourable⟩ judgment'); Andoc. *myst.* 41 πίστιν δὲ τούτων δοῦναί τε καὶ δέξασθαι; Xen. *Hell.* 3.4.5 ἔξεστιν ... σοι τούτων πίστιν λαβεῖν. The singular τὸ πιστόν is used with the gen. in periphrases of a different sort: e.g. Soph. *Trach.* 398 ('the reliability of the truth' = 'the whole truth'), Thuc. 6.72.4 ('the confidence derived from trained skill'). For the notion of self-defence as the ultimate pledge, cf. Xen. *Cyr.* 4.2.13 ἔχομεν τὰ πιστὰ ἐν ταῖς ἡμετέραις ψυχαῖς καὶ ταῖς ἡμετέραις χερσίν.

269 A similar nervous reaction to a real or imagined sound occurs in *Rhes.* 565–6 οὐκ ἤκουσας – ἢ κενὸς ψόφος / στάζει δι᾽ ὤτων; – τευχέων τινὰ κτύπον; and in Soph. *Acris.* fr. 61.1 βοᾶι τις, ὤ· ἀκούετ᾽; ἢ μάτην ὑλῶ; which is cited in the margin of gB (fol. 30ʳ) as a parallel to 269–71 (see next note). This detail again underlines the danger and distrust felt by Pol. The scholiasts (on 267, 274, 275) reflect a carping criticism of Pol.'s behaviour as unheroic (θρασύδειλος; ἀσθενοῦς ψυχῆς τεκμήριον), and Hermann agreed (*praef.* xiv: *paene ridiculum; stultum*). In reaction a few critics have claimed the scene has an intentionally comic effect – surely an inappropriate response to the lively melodrama of these lines. For correct refutation of Σ see Elsperger, 33, 45ff.

---

[1] For the corruption, cf. 312–16n.

270–1 cf. Soph. *Acris.* fr. 61.2 ἅπαντα (Gesner, τὰ πάντα gB, πάντα Stob.) γάρ τοι τῶι φοβουμένωι ψοφεῖ. Line 271 is suspected by Nauck and Wecklein, but without it 270 is much too sweeping and bald.

272 πέποιθα ... κοὐ πέποιθ' a rhetorical schema expressing ambivalence: cf. 357 φρονῶν εὖ κοὐ φρονῶν, *Hec.* 566 οὐ θέλων τε καὶ θέλων; similarly in other contexts of confusion *Hipp.* 1034 ἐσωφρόνησε δ' οὐκ ἔχουσα σωφρονεῖν, *Hel.* 697 ἔλιπον οὐ λιποῦσ' ἐπ' αἰσχροῖς γάμοις (with Kannicht's note), *Hel.* 138 τεθνᾶσι κοὐ τεθνᾶσι (cf. *Alc.* 521, *Ion* 1444).

273 cf. 81–2.

ἥτις = *quippe quae*.

274 ἀλλ' equivalent to ἀλλὰ γάρ (99n.), pointing forward to the self-addressed command of 276–7.

274–5 βώμιοι ... πάρεισι parenthetic to ἀλκή, while κοὐκ ἔρημα δώματα continues the ἀλλά-clause, the first part leading to 276, the second to 277: cf. Weil as quoted in Fraenkel, 17. The vulgate punctuation (κοὐκ κτλ. as part of the γάρ-clause) was assumed by the carping scholiast (269n.). ἐσχάρα and βωμός are distinct in Homer but synonymous in tragedy (cf. Soph. fr. 730); βώμιοι ... ἐσχάραι is just a periphrasis for βωμός. This reference perhaps implies that the stage-altar (presumably located in front of and to one side of the door) was a standard feature of the palace-set, even in plays in which it is not used for refuge or sacrifice. Cf. 631n. for refs.

275 κοὐκ ἔρημα δώματα now at last Pol. catches sight of the women of the chorus. They were not, of course, in any way concealed from him earlier, but by convention he is imagined to be moving and speaking in a space where he does not yet see them and they do not yet hear him (they hear him only after he addresses them): cf. *Contact and Discontinuity* 22–3. δώματα is of course the palace, not 'shrines' (Craik).

276 σκοτεινὰς περιβολάς a rather ornate periphrasis for κολεόν; Eur. is fond of periphrases of περιβολαί + gen. (see *Concordance* s.v.; cf. Chaeremon *TrGF* 71 F 17), whereas the noun (with its necessary resolution) is absent from Aesch. and Soph.

278–9 ξέναι ... Ἑλληνικοῖσι δώμασιν unlike Pelasgus in Aesch. *Su.* 234–7, Pol. gives no reason for his assumption that the women are non-Greek. From this we can infer that the chorus' costumes were of exotic appearance and that Pol.'s assumption thus seemed utterly natural to the audience.

281–2 δορὸς ... ἀκροθίνιον without context δορὸς ἀκροθίνιον would be taken as 'finest offering from the booty of war' and the maidens would be understood to be captives. But if the audience has (as I think) already understood that the maidens are themselves Tyrians, it will interpret the phrase rather as 'choicest offerings in thanks for victory in war'. So in

Pindar *O.* 2.3–4 Ὀλυμπιάδα δ' ἔστασεν Ἡρακλέης ἀκρόθινα πολέμου may be 'founded the Olympian festival as a thank-offering for his victory in war' rather than a compressed version of what we read in *O.* 10.56–8 ὁπᾶι τὰν πολέμοιο δόσιν ἀκρόθινα διελὼν ἔθυε καὶ πενταετηρίδ' ὅπως ἄρα ἔστασεν ἑορτάν. Cf. 203n. Robert, *Oidipus* II.151 n. 82, removes all ambiguity by emending to δόμοις/Φοίβου.

283–5 *Musterbeispiel* of nom. pendens participle (see Testimonia; cf. K–G II.108–9; Barrett on *Hipp.* 23; Diggle, *Studies* 107).

284 μαντεῖα σεμνὰ Λοξίου τ' ἐπ' ἐσχάρας the governing preposition is expressed with the second item of the pair, as often in high-style poetry (Wilam. on *Her.* 237; Kiefner, 27–9, 43).

285 ἐπεστράτευσεν ... πόλιν Eur. twice has dat. of person after ἐπιστρατεύω, but πόλιν is confirmed against πόλει (RVr, Eust.) by 605 below, *Su.* 646, *Tro.* 22, Soph. *Trach.* 75, 362.

287 ἐπτάστομον like ἑπτάπυργος (Eur. only) and ἑπτατειχής (Aesch. only), a variant on the traditional epithet ἑπτάπυλος (79n.).

288–90 a formal identification-triplet, including parentage (here both parents, often only the father), city/nation, and name: *Ion* 260–1, *Hel.* 87–8, fr. 591.1–2, Soph. *Phil.* 232–3 + 239–41; cf. *Od.* 9.19–21, *Birds* 184–5; *IA* 695–6, 827–8, *OC* 571–2; Simonides, *Epigr. Gr.* 191–2, 197–8 Page. The formality of Pol.'s reply is increased by the inclusion of both parents and the addition of his grandfathers, which may betoken a tone of pride (undimmed by the ominous descent from Laius). Renewed mention of Menoeceus is relevant to the kinship-theme: see Introd. I.

289 ἔτικτε a timeless imperfect (perhaps 'registering' like the present: see on 13 γαμεῖ and cf. K–G I.137), inherited from Homer (*Il.* 2.628; 5.547, preceded by τέκετ' and followed by γενέσθην; etc.) and used by other poets as well. ἔτικτε is normally used of the father in Homer, but of the mother in *Il.* 16.180, etc. and in Hesiod and later poets, and timeless use of the present stem is extended to ἡ τίκτουσα (= ἡ τεκοῦσα) in Soph. *El.* 342, *OT* 1247. It is debated whether ἔτικτε actually emphasizes an enduring effect of the action or expresses a mere stylistic variation: cf. F. Hartmann, *Zeitschr. f. vergl. Sprachforschung* 49 (1920) 39; H. Meltzen, *Indogerm. Forschungen* 17 (1904) 226; H. Koller, *MusHelv* 8 (1951) 92–3; Chantraine, *Grammaire hom.* ¶287; Rijksbaron (1991) 4.

291–300 Metre this choral prooemium provides a gliding transition from the iambic exchange with Pol. to Jocasta's extended aria. If 291–2 are genuine (see *ad loc.*), we have a transition from iambic address (by the coryphaeus alone) to the excited lyrics (by the whole chorus?) which actually accompany the welcoming gesture of kneeling, and then the lyric excitement is continued in the summons to Jocasta, who herself emerges singing. For modulation in the choral voice *without* intervening actor's

utterance, cf. *Cycl.* 654ff., *Hec.* 1024ff., *Su.* 263ff., *El.* 1168ff., *Her.* 815ff. (it
is rarely certain whether such lines should be given to the coryphaeus alone,
divided among separate choreutae, or divided between coryphaeus and
chorus). Eur. uses this technique in a variety of astrophic settings, Soph.
either not at all or only in *Trach.* 885 (see Easterling's text and comm.),
Aesch. in epirrhematic scenes (*Su.* 347ff., 734ff., cf. Eur. *Hcld.* 73ff., *Her.*
740ff.) or before a stasimon or exit-song (*Su.* 1014ff., *Ag.* 351ff., *Choe.* 931ff.,
1063ff.; in these cases the shift from coryphaeus to whole chorus seems
clear). For lyric proem to actor's song, cf. *Hipp.* 811–16 (chorus' lyrics
prepare for Theseus' shift to song), *IA* 1276–8 (Clytaemnestra introduces
Iphigenia's aria); *Hec.* 170–6 (Hecuba summons Polyxena at the start of
a lyric duet). This may be a variation on the use of choral anapaests to
introduce an actor's singing entrance (*Hipp.* 1342–6; *Andr.* 1166–72, *Su.*
980–9, *Phoen.* 1480–4).

291	− − ∪ − ∪ − ∪ − ∪ − ∪ − ‖	ia trim
292	∪ − ∪ − − − − ∪ − ∪ − ∪ ∩ ‖	ia trim
293	∪ ͜∪ ͜∪ − ∪ − − ∪ − ∪ − |	dochm, hypod (2 dochm?)
294	∪ − ∪ − ∪ − ∪ − ∩ ‖ᵇʰ	dochm hex, ba (ia, ia penth)
295	∪ − − ∪ − − ∪ − − ‖	3 ba
296	͜∪∪ ∪ − ∪ ͜∪ ͜∪ ∪ ͜∪ |	cr, dochm
297	− ͜∪ ∪ − ∪ − ‖?	dochm
298	∪ − − ∪ − ∪ − ∪ − − ‖	dochm, ia penth (ba, ia, ba)
299	∪ − − ∪ − ∪ ͜∪ ͜∪ ∪ − |	2 dochm
300	∪ − − ∪ − ∪ − − ‖	dochm, ba

NOTES TO METRICAL SCHEME

293 Π¹³'s προσπίπτω produces a regular dochmiac, but (προσ)πίπτω
tends to intrude upon the more poetic (προσ)πίτνω. At *Or.* 1507
προσπίπτω is ruled out by the metre; in metrically indifferent positions
πιπτ- is a variant rejected by editors at *Alc.* 183, *Med.* 1195, 1205, *Andr.*
358, 537, *Tro.* 762, *Phoen.* 924, 1278, *Septem* 834; moreover, in Euripidean
passages without variants προσπίτνω appears thirteen times, προσπίπτω
once (*Hec.* 339; but cf. *Tro.* 762). It is not impossible to scan προσπίτνω
to obtain a dochmiac: πῑτν- in a princeps position occurs at *Pers.* 152
(anap.), Soph. *El.* 1380 (ia. trim.), *Tro.* 762 (ia. trim.) (also in biceps
position of anap. at *Andr.* 537). But in lyric πῑπτ- is commoner at princeps
positions: Aesch. *Su.* 91, *Eum.* 377, Soph. *El.* 216, *Ant.* 595, 782, Eur. *Su.*
44, 63, *Alc.* 913, *Or.* 1489 (also in biceps of anap. at *IA* 137).

293–4 Π¹³V and some *recc.* divide at ἄναξ, as I have done. An alternative division at προσπίτνω is in MOB+ and used to be adopted: this

yields cr, dochm (or dochm, cr) | 2 ia, ba ‖ and cannot be decisively rejected.

294 for the ia penthemimer in the alternative description see on 298. Murray produced simple iambics by eliding σέβουσ'; but stage-action and rhetorical pause point to period-end at this point, and 'there is no parallel for elision of an iambic dimeter before an iambic line beginning with a bacchiac' (Diggle (1990b) 123 n. 122). Diggle doubts the colon produced here and would transpose to σέβουσα νόμον, 2 ia with final longum resolved.

295 for bacchiacs in association with dochm see metrical note on 1290.

296 with different scansion of the exclamation, this could be ia, dochm.

297 with ἀναπέτασον this is dochm hex; but ἀμπ- is preferable rhythmically and otherwise (see comm. *ad loc.*).

298 the preferred alternative is a dicolon found also at *Rhes.* 457 = 824 and Arist. *Thesm.* 1047, cited by Stinton, 'More rare verse-forms' 93. To Stinton's references add West, *Greek Metre*, 111; but many (or most) of the possible examples can be otherwise interpreted. For isolated ia penth in dochmiac context, cf. *Ion* 763.

300 the mss present ba, ia (or perhaps dochm, sp), both rare sequences, though the former seems to be a mannerism of later Eur. (Stinton, 'More rare verse-forms' 84–5, 94; Conomis, 48). With a small change we get a colon whose end echoes 294, 295, and 298.

291–300: COMMENTARY

291–2 omitted by Π¹³. Haslam (1976) 4–10 argues that any tragic verses absent from papyri should be subject to strong suspicion of interpolation and condemns this couplet, commenting that 'the chorus's relationship to Polyneices is not in point'. On the contrary, kinship is the major reason for the existence of this chorus (202–60n.), and the kinship-theme is a vital one in the play. In general, extant papyri of tragedy are less carefully controlled copies than those produced in the Middle Ages (this is not to say that they may not contain true readings lost to the later tradition), and if accidental omission of verses can occur in the medieval tradition it can occur just as well in ancient copies. In papyri of plays other than *Phoen.* we find incorrect omission of *Med.* 1300, *Hipp.* 43 (and of all of *Hec.* 756–9, where at least something must, I think, be retained) vs. correct omission of the interpolated lines *Andr.* 7, *Med.* 725–6, *Ba.* 1091–2 (cf. *Hec.* 756–7). In the present passage, the scribe knew he was recording a dialogue of chorus and Pol., and it would not be surprising for him to turn back from writing out 290 and focus on the indented lyrics of 293ff. as the next choral passage to be copied, ignoring 291–2. See also 387n., 436n., 778n., 780–1n.

Parallels for the formal technique presented by 291-2 (shift from iambic to lyric) are listed under 291-300 Metre. Presumably the coryphaeus speaks 291-2 and is then joined by the whole chorus in 293-300 (Jocasta addresses νεάνιδες on her appearance); Arnoldt assigned 291-5 to the coryphaeus, 296-8 and 299-300 to the leaders of semichoruses. JD suggests that one should assign some corroborating weight to Haslam's claim (*Arktouros* 91-100) that vocative addresses are especially prone to expansion by interpolators; he also remarks that the intrusion (in mid sentence, as it were) of the full chorus after the vocative I ascribe to the leader is strange and may be taken as a sign of interpolation.

291 συγγένεια abstract for concrete, a repersonification more common with neuter abstracts (21n.; λόχευμα 803n.). The noun is not found in Aesch. or Soph., and the sense 'kinsman' or 'kinsmen' is a Euripidean mannerism (*Tro.* 754, *Or.* 733, 1233 (singular, as here), fr. 497.3; earlier Pindar *Paean* 4.33), although the collective sense may have been ordinary Greek (LSJ s.v. II.1 cites fourth-century prose and inscr.). So too *Her.* 663 ἁ δυσγένεια = ὁ δυσγενής (see Bond *ad loc.*).

293 γονυπετεῖς ἕδρας internal acc. to προσπίτνω, which also has its usual external object in σ'. The epithet occurs here and Tim. *Pers.* 176 (of Xerxes in grief: γονυπετὴς αἴκιζε σῶμα) and reappears in late prose. ἕδρα here means 'suppliant posture', a common tragic usage (LSJ classifies wrongly).

προσπίτνω on variant -πίπτω see under Metre.

294 τὸν οἴκοθεν νόμον σέβουσα cf. (more servilely expressed) *Or.* 1507 (Phrygian to Orestes) προσκυνῶ σ', ἄναξ, νόμοισι βαρβάροισι προσπίτνων; *Tro.* 1021 (Hecuba to Helen) καὶ προσκυνεῖσθαι βαρβάρων ὕπ' ἤθελες. Kneeling acknowledges the honoured man as master and marks the kneeler as his subject or slave and so was incompatible with Greek custom except in prayers to gods or supplication to gods or men: cf. *Pers.* 152 (with 241-2), Hdt. 7.136 (Lacedaemonian envoys refuse to kneel to Xerxes).

295 ἔβας on the significance of the arrival-motif see Introd. I.

χρόνωι 'at last', as typically in reunion-scenes (166n.; cf. 305).

296-8 Π¹³ had a different text in these lines: 296 was somewhat longer than in the mss, and 297-8 were considerably shorter. JD, re-examining the alignment, feels that there is little doubt that 297 was omitted (as Haslam (1976) proposed) and establishes that the words transmitted in the mss would fit in 298,¹ and that, e.g., Haslam's ιωιωποτνιαποτνια could

---

¹ The size of the second gap was incorrectly reported in *Text. Trad.* 219, correctly in the Teubner as 18-20 letters lost before ματερ.

well fill the gap before μο]λε in 296 (though he rejects this reading as producing a lyric iambic trimeter without caesura: 673n.). Deletion of 297 ἀμπέτασον πύλας deserves consideration, especially in view of the nearby omission of 291–2. But omission may be accidental in both cases or in one or the other. The traditional text is quite satisfactory in sense and rhythm, and the phrase ἀμπ. πύλας simply serves to help fill the time between summons and emergence from the door. Mueller-Goldingen, 73 n. 4, believes 297 is an actor's interpolation supplying a stage-direction.

πρόδομος the adjective serves adverbially in place of the common δόμων (δωμάτων) πάρος, πρὸ δόμων (δωμάτων), ἔξω δόμων (δωμάτων). The adj. is rare (Bacchyl. 6.14, Aesch. fr. 388; Nicarchus, *Anth. gr.* 6.285) and here preferred to πρὸ δόμων in order to maintain synapheia. The variant πρόδρομος (also falsely transmitted in most witnesses of Aesch. fr. 388) would mean 'running headlong' (*Se.* 211, *Ant.* 108) and is unsuitable to a summons to an aged queen, even one who is to be joyfully reunited with her son.

ἀμπέτασον ἀμπ- is transmitted solely in V, but is probably not to be regarded as a learned conjecture (*Text. Trad.* 56). *Apokope* of ἀνα- in verbs is normal in tragic lyric, and corruption to ἀνα- is common (105n., 504, 1410).

299 ὑπώροφα the epithet means simply 'surmounted by a roof' and opposes the indoors to the outdoors (cf. *Or.* 147 with Di Benedetto's note; on *Her.* 107 see *EMC* 2 (1983) 105).

μέλαθρα περᾶν 'cross (the threshold of) the house (and come out)'; on the flexibility of meaning of περᾶν cf. 100n. and Barrett on *Hipp.* 782–3.

301–54 The monody of Jocasta, echoing the confused emotions of Antigone in the teichoskopia, presents a unique combination of joy and sorrow, unlike the uniformly sorrowful arias of an Electra (*Or.*) or a Creusa (*Ion*) but like the duets of reunion in which joy is tempered by remembrance of the sorrows of separation or by contemplation of death or kin-murder narrowly escaped. The sequence of topics is straightforward: emergence (301–3); sighting, embrace, and caressing dance (304–16); lamentation of separation, including general statement (317–21), effect on Jocasta herself (322–6), and effect on Oedipus (327–36); (turning back to Po. himself) lamentation of the foreign marriage and lost ceremonies (337–49); final curse on the cause, with climactic self-reference (350–4). On the use of an unbroken monody rather than amoibaion, cf. 261–442n.

301–54 Metre the monody of Jocasta presents a rather simple combination of dochmiac and iambic rhythm (with some syncopation and very little resolution) with a dactylic coda. Contrast the more complex mixture of rhythms in Antigone's aria (1485ff.) or in the contemporary arias of Electra and Phrygian in *Or.* The rhythm is well modulated to match

233

the shifting subjects and emotions of the aria. Jocasta's halting gait is accompanied by dochmiacs; when she sees her son at 304, the rhythm shifts to pure iambic, and in 312–17 her dance of joy is marked by syncopation. The lamentations which centre on Jocasta herself (318–26) are almost entirely dochmiac, while the following description of Oedipus' despair (327–36) is more varied. Almost pure iambic rhythm returns for the lament over the foreign marriage (337–43), but as Jocasta evokes her own absence from the ceremony and the lack of participation of the local river and the city, dochmiacs insistently return. The concluding curse is dactylic with dochmiac clausula.

301	– – – ∪ –|	dochm
302	∪ – – ∪ – ∪ – – × –|	2 dochm
303	∪◡∪ – – – ∪∩‖ᵇ	2 ia
304	∪ – ∪ – ∪ – ∪ –	2 ia
305	∪ – ∪ – ∪ – ∪ –|	2 ia
306	∪ – ∪ – ∪ – ∪ –	2 ia
307	∪ – ∪ – ∪ – ∪ –‖ˀ	2 ia
308	∪ – ∪ – ∪ – ∪ –	2 ia
308bis	∪ – ∪◡∪ – ∪ –	2 ia
309	– ◡∪ – ∪ – – ∪ – – – ‖	dochm, cr, sp
310	∪ – ∪ – ∪ – ∪ –|	2 ia
311	∪ – ∪ – ∪ – ∪ – ∪ – ∪ –‖ˀ	3 ia
312	∪ – ∪ – ∪ – –‖ᶜ	ia, ba
313	– – ∪ – ∪ – ∩‖ᵇᶜ	ia, ba
314	◡∪∪ – ∪ – ∪ –|	lec
315	∪ – ∪ – ∪ – ∩‖ᵇ	ia, ba
316	◡∪∪ – – ∪ – – ∪ – – ∪ – – ∪ –‖	5 cr
317	∪ – ∪∩‖ᵇ	ia
318	∪ – – ∪ – ∪◡∪ – ∪ –|	2 dochm
319	∪◡∪ – ∪ – ∪ – – – – –‖ʰ	2 dochm
320	– ∪ – – ∪ –|	2 cr
321	– ∪ – – – – ‖	cr, mol
322	∪◡∪ – ∪ – ∪◡∪ – ∪ –|	2 dochm
323	∪◡∪ – ∪ – ∪ – – ∪ –|	2 dochm
324	∪∪ – ∪∪ – – – – –|	2 anap
325	∪ – – ∪ – ∪ – – ∪ –|	2 dochm
326	∪◡∪ – ∪ –‖ʰ	dochm
327	∪ – ∪ – ∪ – ∪ – ∪ – ∪ –‖ˀ	3 ia
328	∪ – – ∪ – ∪ – – ∪ –	2 dochm
329	∪ – – ∪ –|	2 dochm
330	∪∪ – ∪∪ – ∪∪ – ∪∪ –‖ˀ	2 anap

331	∪–∪–∪–∪–	2 ia
332	∪–∪–∪–∪–	2 ia
333	∪–∪–∪–∪–	2 ia
334	–∪–––‖ᶜ	cr, sp
335	∪⏖–∪–∪––∪–|	2 dochm
336	∪⏖–∪–‖	dochm
337	∪–∪––∪–∪–∪–|	ia, cr, ia
338	∪–∪–∪–∪–∪–|	dochm hex, ia
339	∪–∪–∪–∪–|	2 ia
340	∪–∪–∪–∪–|	2 ia
341	∪–∪–∪–∪–	2 ia
342	∪–∪–∪–∪–|	2 ia
343	∪–∪–∪––‖ᶜ	ia, ba
344	∪––∪–∪⏖–∪–|	2 dochm
345	∪⏖–∪–|	dochm
346	–∪––⏖∪⏖∪–‖ʰ	cr, dochm
347	∪⏖–∪––⏖–––|	2 dochm
348	–⏖–∪–∪⏖–––|	2 dochm
349	∪⏖––––⏖–––‖	2 dochm
350	∪–∪∪–∪∪–∪|	∪D∪ (∪D◠‖ᵇ?)
351	–∪∪–∪∪–∪∪–∪∪|	4 da
352	–∪∪–∪∪–∪∪–∪∪|	4 da
353	–∪∪–∪∪–‖	D
354	∪⏖–∪–∪⏖–∪–‖‖‖	2 dochm

NOTES TO METRICAL SCHEME

301–3 the dochmiac version of 301–2 must be the original, but the reading in 303 is less certain: see comm.

304 Jocasta turns and sees Pol. for the first time here, so it is best to start a new period at ἰώ.

307 perhaps one should posit period-end here; without it 304–9 form a very long period.

309 dochm, hypod can be obtained by accepting ἐμάν, but this form is likely to be a trivialization. With ἁμάν and the transmitted word-order, we have –∪– – –, which might be regarded as a dragged form of hypod: so (without reference to this line) Dale, *LMGD*², 114 on *IT* 870 δείν' ἔτλαν ὤμοι, and Di Benedetto on *Or.* 1267–8 (which in his text is dochm hex + –∪– – – [= 1248 ∪∪∪– – –]). This interpretation is disputed by Diggle, *PCPS* 22 (1976) 43, who emends *IT* 870 to ἔτλαν δείν' ὤμοι and rejects dochmiac interpretation of clausular –∪– – – in mixed contexts such as *Tro.* 283, 286, *Her.* 899, 909, *Phaethon* 235, 244. At *Or.* 1267–8 =

1247–8 the text is too uncertain to be of help (see commentators). Here, whether we call the sequence cr + sp or hypod, it is possibly legitimate (word-overlap only here and Soph. *El.* 487 = 503 (*Or.* 1248?) and in 334 below, where other interpretations are possible (see below)). The regularizing transposition of Kirchhoff (σκ. ἀμὰν δέραν) or Fritzsche (δέραν σκ. ἀμάν) is, however, easy (see Diggle, *Studies* 49–50; (1990b) 119 n. 96).

312 on this colon cf. Stinton, 'More rare verse-forms' 94; it is the same whether we read ἅπαντα with brevis in longo or ἁπάνται. Note the staccato effect of the short periods in 312–15, reinforced by the rhetorical phrasing and threefold repetition of ia + ba. This I take to be a deliberate effect suited to the dance-movements and gestures of Jocasta, and so I reject the view of Wilam. (*GV* 571) that 312–16 are continuous iambics.

313 Brevis in longo can be eliminated by Fritzsche's λόγοισιν, but may as well be kept if 315,with its brevis, is retained (see comm. below).

316–17 I follow Wilam. in having a new period begin at ἰὼ τέκος; for 5 cr as a period, cf. 1524–5 below; the isolated iamb of 317 is suited to an exclamation. JD recommends instead 4 cr | lec ‖, pointing to the example of *Tro.* 1091–2 = 1110–11 (4 cr + lec, with word-overlap) and exx. of shorter lengths of cr with lec following (*Andr.* 275–6 = 285–6, *Her.* 386–7 = 399–400, *IA* 297–8, *Or.* 1377–8, *Eum.* 491–2 = 500–1, S. *El.* 854–5 = 865–6, *Phil.* 1170–1).

320–1 in this context, these cola have the effect of dochmiacs extended with an initial longum.

324 anapaests among dochmiacs as in 330 below and in 110 (cf. 105, 184). On the alpha of φαρέων, here short as in *Andr.* 831, *Or.* 840, etc., see LSJ s.v. Pure dochmiacs are unnecessary, but can be easily obtained by Dindorf's addition ⟨ὦ⟩ τέκνον with ἄπεπλος (rare: Conomis, 38–9) and disyllabic φαρέων.

330–4 to avoid dochm. hex. in 331 Murray divided κατ-/ ἔχων, which is impossible (anceps iuxta anceps in synapheia). I have followed Wilam. (*GV* 572; cf. Stinton, 'More rare verse-forms' 93) in treating ἀνῇιξε κτλ. as purely iambic down to a clausula of cr + sp (cf. on 309 above) or cr + ba with τέκνοισι (as Wilam.). Others divide at ξίφους/ ... σφαγὰν/... ἀγχόνας/, creating dochm hex in 331 and ba + ia in 334 (not objectionable in late Eur.: see on 300); the hexasyllable is perhaps legitimate as a transition from the predominant dochmiacs of the previous lines, and 334 could possibly be treated as dochm + sp (but see on 300). With this division, which harmonizes cola and sense, it would be attractive to write ἀνῇιξε⟨ν⟩ in 331 (Stinton in private communication), producing ba + ia, and then clausular dochm + ba in 334 (with τέκνοισιν Stinton).

337–8 Hermann's deletion of καί would make these lines straightforward iambics and may be right; see comm. There are other possibilities with syncopated iambics. The anaphora of ξεν- seems to define 339 and 340 as dimeters, so unless a syllable is added to 338 (⟨τὰν⟩ παιδ. Fritzsche), we must (keeping καί) either accept a hexasyllable in 338 or consider some other reading which also abandons pure iambics (see comm.). If we end the first colon at δή rather than (as in 2 papyri and most mss) after κλύω, the result is no simpler (ia + hypod, 3 ia).

301–54: COMMENTARY

301–3 the text of 303 can be no more than tentative; but in 301–2 the value of other minority readings of MO, the vacuity of the additional phrases in the iambic version of the majority, and the well-known tendency of dochmiacs to be corrupted to iambic or approximately iambic form (Barrett on *Hipp.* 565–600, 853–4) all favour the dochmiac version, which (despite the iambic-form lemma) is also reflected in the comment of Σ. Perhaps ποδός intruded as a gloss in 303 (or ποδί fell out and was incorrectly restored before and adjusted to βάσιν, after which conflation led to the majority text): the duplication of ποδ- prompted the emendations γήραι … ποδός and γηραιῶι … ποδί, further conflation led to γήραι τῶι παιδί. Although γήραι τρομεράν would be excellent idiom (*Her.* 231 γήραι … τρομερὰ γυῖα), it is not attractive metrically. On the other hand, the modal dative epithet + ποδί is a Euripidean cliché (twenty-one other instances, unfortunately mixed with other expressions in *Concordance* s.v. πούς), as is γηραιὸς / γεραιὸς / γέρων πούς (1536–7 below; *Alc.* 611, *Andr.* 546, *Tro.* 1275, *Ion* 1041, *Or.* 456, fr. 876). With ποδί and with period-end assumed at βάσιν (where there is a strong rhetorical break and a dramatic shift of focus), the deletion of ποδός gives possible metre,[1] and it is not necessary to restore a dochmiac (e.g., ποδὶ τρομὰν ἐξέλκω βάσιν, dochm + cr).

301 Φοίνισσαν βοάν reference to the foreign accent is purely conventional; the tragic choreuts use their normal Attic stage-voices, as does the actor playing Orestes in *Choe.* 653ff. despite 563–4. βοάν implies an indistinct sound, and Jocasta's ἰώ in 304 suggests that she is only then aware of Pol.'s presence: for hearing a summons but not taking in the content of the summoner's remark, cf. *Contact and Discontinuity* 27–30 and below 1070–1n., 1265–9n. Thus I would rule out O's παιδί and emendations based on it.

302 κλυοῦσ' for interpretation (and accentuation) as aorist, see West,

---

[1] But JD points out to me that the divided resolution is unwelcome and that, with long anceps, the second metron runs very awkwardly.

BICS 31 (1984) 172–80, esp. 178, comparing *Se.* 239–41 ποταινεὶ κλυοῦσα πάταγον ... ἱκόμαν, *IA* [1534] φθογγῆς κλυοῦσα δεῦρο σῆς ἀφικόμην.

304 χρόνωι see 166n., 295n. and compare χρόνιος in *El.* 585, *Hel.* 566, 645. Other standard motifs of recognition/reunion found in this passage include: face and sight (*Choe.* 238, Soph. *El.* 1263, 1277, 1286; *Hel.* 636, *Ion* 1437); embrace (*OC* 329, 1105, 1112; Eur. *El.* 579, *IT* 796, 828, *Hel.* 624, 627, *Ion* 560, 1438); μόλις (*OC* 325–6, *Hel.* 652); φανείς and similar forms (Soph. *El.* 1261, 1274, 1285, *OC* 328; Eur. *El.* 578); unexpectedness (ἀέλπτως and negated ἐλπίζω: Soph. *El.* 1263–4, *OC* 1105; Eur. *El.* 579, *IT* 802, *Hel.* 656, *Ion* 1444; ἀδόκητος and negated δοκέω: Eur. *El.* 580, *Hel.* 657, *Ion* 1447); pleasure (χάρις, χαρά, χαρμονή, τέρψις, ἡδονή: Soph. *El.* 1266, 1267; Eur. *El.* 596, *IT* 794, 797, 842, *Hel.* 626, 634f., 654, 655, *Ion* 1448, 1449). See also F. L. Shisler, 'The Technique of the Portrayal of Joy in Greek Tragedy', *TAPA* 73 (1942) 277–92.

305 μυρίαις τ' ἐν ἁμέραις cf. *Hel.* 652–3 ἡλίους δὲ μυρίους μόλις διελθών. ἐν = 'after' develops from the phrase ἐν χρόνωι, usually 'during the course of time', but becoming in some contexts 'at the end of a period of time' or 'after a time': cf. 166n., *OC* 88 ταύτην ἔλεξε παῦλαν ἐν χρόνωι μακρῶι. The extension of this sense to phrases without χρόνωι seems to be a Euripidean peculiarity (here and *Hel.* 629 ἐν μακρᾶι φλογὶ φαεσφόρωι, on which see Kannicht).

306–9 'Embrace your mother's breast with your arms and ⟨bring close (to my face)⟩ your outstretched cheek and the dark-coloured curly locks of your hair, shading my neck.' If the text is sound, ἀμφίβαλλε is used in zeugma (cf. 114–16n.), shifting from acc. of object encircled (μαστόν) with instrumental dat. (ὠλέναισι) to acc. of objects placed around (ὄρεγμα ... πλόκαμον) with implied locative dat. or dat. of direction παρηΐδι (for these alternatives, 26n.). The presence of the verbal abstract ὄρεγμα probably assists the construction, which also involves the mental substitution of a more suitable prefix for -βαλλε (cf. παρειὰν προσβαλεῖν παρηΐδι *Hec.* 410). The metre gives no hint of corruption, and the transmitted text is essentially the same in Π⁸ of the sixth century. To avoid the harsh zeugma, some have referred μαστόν to Polynices ('surround your own chest with your mother's arms'), but μαστός in tragedy is always used of women and the request is unnatural (contrast *Tro.* 761–3). Pearson makes ἀμφίβαλλε ... ματέρος parenthetic, taking παρηΐδων τ' ... as additional objects of προσεῖδον (and reading σκιάζοντ' in 309), but both ὄρεγμα and σκιάζειν imply embrace and not just vision. Emendations provide a different verb for the later objects: Hermann δέραν ⟨χρίμπτ'⟩ ἐμάν (partly prompted by a futile search for strophic structure); Camper ὄρεγμα δὸς τριχῶν (with other, improbable changes); better is JD's suggestion (after Camper and

Fritzsche) δὸς τριχῶν τε, κυανόχρωτι χαίτας πλοκάμωι δέραν σκιάζων ἀμάν.[1] See 308-9n.

306-7 μαστόν normally used specifically of the female breasts and not of the chest as a whole. Its use here probably implies 'put your arms around my chest, pressing close to my breasts': cf. *Andr.* 510-11 κείσηι δή, τέκνον ὦ φίλος, μαστοῖς ματέρος ἀμφὶ σᾶς; *Su.* 1159 ἀμφὶ μαστὸν ὑποβάλω σποδόν.

308 παρηίδων ὄρεγμα virtually παρῆίδας ὀρωρεγμένας; cf. 1529n.

308-9 βοστρύχων κυανόχρωτα χαίτας πλόκαμον similar two-word combinations are a Euripidean mannerism (*El.* 882 κόμης σῆς βοστρύχων, 515 χαίτης βοστρύχους, 527 χαίτης πλόκος, 1071 πλόκαμον κόμης, *Tro.* 1183 πολὺν βοστρύχων πλόκαμον, *IA* 1437 πλόκαμον ... τριχός; cf. Pindar *P.* 4.82 κομᾶν πλόκαμοι); but here the extreme fullness of expression has caused suspicion. Perhaps χαίτας is more general (χ. πλόκ. = 'hair-locks') and βοστρύχων more specific, a quasi-synonymous gen. ('hair-locks which are curls'),[2] and the intervening epithet may mitigate the redundancy. The closest parallels in Breitenbach, 194, are 645 below καλλιπόταμος ὕδατος ... νοτίς (with single gen. and more distinct denotative contributions from the repetitive elements) and the corrupt phrase *Her.* 413-14 πέπλων χρυσεόστολον φάρος (not *Hipp.* 149-50, where πελάγους goes with χέρσον). Reiske's βόστρυχον (now attested in R^s), with πλόκαμον in apposition, is easier but flatter. With κυανόχρωτι ... πλοκάμωι (Fritzsche after Geel and Hartung), βοστρύχων must be taken with ὄρεγμα (Hartung deleted τε and retained double gen.). Brodeau thought of χαίταις, which now appears in Π^8: this could have been intended as dat. of respect with the epithet or as dat. with implied πρόσβαλλε (Barnes: *comaeque caeruleam ad meos capillos caesariem applica*). The former is unnatural when the noun is πλόκαμον; the latter is scarcely understandable at such a distance from the verb without a preposition or possessive pronoun and gives an inappropriate sense (Jocasta, whose hair is shorn, wants the sensation of Pol.'s cheek and abundant hair against her own cheek and neck).

308bis κυανόχρωτα probably a Euripidean coinage (138n.; cf. κυανόχροος *Hel.* 1502; later Alcidamas apud Arist. *Rhet.* 1406a4, post-

---

[1] Ferrari, *ASNP* ser. 3, 11:2 (1981) 286ff., deletes τ' and treats ὄρεγμα as acc. in apposition; Mueller-Goldingen, 74 n. 8, thinks ὄρεγμα is an internal object sandwiched between external objects: both fail to note that πλόκαμον must be Pol.'s, not Joc.'s.

[2] Cf. phrases with double defining gen. (Wilam. on *Her.* 170, Jebb on *Aj.* 308-9), in which one of the two gens. is normally more general, the other more specific.

classical poetry), an elaboration of Homeric κυανοχαίτης. Other words in this aria first attested in Eur. and occurring only here in Eur. are πολυέλικτον 314, περιχορεύουσα 316, λευκόχροα 322 (but see *ad loc.*), δυσόρφναια 325 (hapax in extant lit.), ἀμφιδάκρυτον 330 (hapax), κατακωμάζω 352 (hapax); cf. λουτροφόρου 348n.

312 τί φῶ σε; The opposition καὶ χερσὶ καὶ λόγοισι in the next line implies that Jocasta is overwhelmed by the abundance of things she would like to say and of ways she would like to touch and caress her son. Accordingly we find for τί φῶ σε; translations such as *quid dicam tibi?* (Stiblinus), 'wie soll ich dich begrüssen?' (Wecklein, based on Barnes' *quomodo te compellam?*). But σε is not σοι, and φημί is not 'begrüssen'. The sense must rather be 'what am I to say about you?' or 'in what terms am I to mention you?' (cf. Craik, and perhaps Méridier's 'de quel nom te saluer?', but 'saluer' again implies address). For the latter cf. κακὰ λέγειν + acc. of person (a bold variation on this in *El.* 907 τίν' ἀρχὴν ... σ' ἐξείπω κακῶν;). The former probably involves an ellipsis of an indirect discourse infinitive which need not be specified: e.g., Xen. *Hell.* 3.5.12 Κορινθίους δὲ καὶ Ἀρκάδας καὶ Ἀχαιοὺς τί φῶμεν, οἳ κτλ., which is easier because the acc. nouns form a phrase at the head of the sentence (cf. K–G 1.330f, Schwyzer II.88 ¶2). Hartung's deletion of σε produces attractive style and metre (2 bacchiacs), but why would σε have intruded?

312–16 πῶς ... χαρμονᾶν 'How in every way, both with hands and with words, dancing about (you), to that side and this side, many turns that bring me pleasure, am I to get the delight of joys long missed?' The passage is well discussed by Renehan, *Gk. Text. Crit.* 107–10. 313 is a poetic variant on ἔργωι / λόγωι (cf. *OT* 883–4 εἰ δέ τις ὑπέροπτα χερσὶν ἢ λόγωι), although I assume that the words are in fact accompanied by gestures of caressing (see below). πολυέλικτον ἀδονάν is internal acc. to περιχορεύουσα, and ἐκεῖσε καὶ τὸ δεῦρο (wrongly deleted by Murray on the basis of similarity to 266)[1] is as much in place as τᾶιδ' ἐκεῖσε in *Tro.* 333. I have hesitantly preferred ἁπάνται to ἅπαντα (for the common corruption, a simple misinterpretation of ΑΠΑΝΤΑ, cf. πάνται *Eum.* 967 and *Concordance* s.v. πάντηι; 265n.). It is of little moment that ἅπαντα is not found as an adverb elsewhere in tragedy: adv. πάντα is found with adjs. in Aesch. and Soph. (also *OC* 337 with adjectival κατεικασθέντε, cf. ὁμοίαν *Ag.* 609); in Eur. the adverbial internal acc. is used closely

---

[1] Also by Mueller-Goldingen, 334, alleging that the adverbs do not suit περι- (but they simply mark repeated change of direction, a mark of excitement). Diggle (1990b) 114 n. 75, in the interest of removing brevis in longo, says the deletion may be right, but does not bracket it in his OCT.

with verbs (δυστυχῶ Hec 429; ἀνεσκευάσμεθ' El. 602, πειθόμεσθα Or. 593, εὐδαιμονεῖ Sthen. 1 Page). Internal acc. ἄπαντα λάβω ('get in every manner of getting') is possible, but ἄπαντα is rather distant from λάβω. Renehan argues that the Homeric idiom ἀμφότερον (adv. acc.) + two dative specifications (747n.) supports a simple adverbial sense for ἄπαντα, taken in conjunction with the following datives. Unlike πάνται (-ηι), ἀπάνται is not securely attested in tragedy, but may be right at Or. 1295 (Diggle, Textual Trad. Or. 122; the two instances might defend each other against Willink's 'not in Attic poetry'). πάνται in tragedy usually (and ἀπάντηι in Homer and Plato always) means 'in every direction, everywhere', and the translation 'on every side' (preparing for ἐκεῖσε καὶ τὸ δεῦρο) is possible here, but more likely the adverb prepares for 'both with hands and with words' and means 'in every way': cf. Ba. 844 πάντηι 'at all events'; Med. 853–4 (restored) πάνται πάντως, a very emphatic 'in every way'.

316 περιχορεύουσα I assume that after 311 Jocasta breaks from the embrace, steps back to look at her son, and then steps repeatedly from side to side, stroking him with her hands. This 'dance' need not have been so sprightly as to seem incongruous with γηραιῶι ποδὶ τρομερὰν ἕλκω βάσιν above; but in any event the point is that the presence of her son has suddenly animated Jocasta. (It is unnecessary to posit a ritual apotropaic function for the dance: C. Longo Rubbi, Dioniso 41 (1967) 398–409.)

παλαιᾶν 'of long ago', i.e. which have not recently been enjoyed, and so in this context 'long missed'.

319 ὁμαίμου λώβαι in this emotional scene we find Jocasta's strongest statement of Eteocles' injustice. In the calm of the prologue and of the stichomythia 388ff. she avoids passing judgment. In the agon she is neutral at first (see on ὡς σὺ φήις 467), and even in her long rhesis she neither dwells on the past in her argument to Eteocles that he is doing wrong nor explicitly seconds Pol.'s view that he is being intolerably wronged.

320–1 ἢ ποθεινὸς ... ἢ ποθεινὸς for this rare anaphora Denniston, GP² 281, cites IA 1330 ἢ πολύμοχθον ἄρ' ἦν γένος, ἢ πολύμοχθον ἀμερίων and (a simple anadiplosis) Prom. 887 ἢ σοφὸς ἢ σοφός; JD adds Pers. 647 ἢ φίλος ἀνήρ, ἢ φίλος ὄχθος.

322 τε syntactically, a smooth response would be ἐμάν τε ... κείρομαι ... ἄπεπλός τε ... ἀμείβομαι, pairing the two standard signs of grief; instead we have an irregular responsion with δ' and an irregular contrast, since ἄπεπλος φαρέων λευκῶν, a part of the first member, anticipates the sense of the second member. Perhaps it is better to recognize a stronger anacoluthon and view δ' not as responsive to τε but as contrasting 324 ('without white') with 325f. ('with black'). (Some have identified δ' in 327 as responsive to τε, but with so much intervening the effect will still be similar to anacoluthon.) On τε ... δέ ... see Denniston, GP² 513f. (not mentioning this passage) and cf. 344n., 1313n. Emendations: Valckenaer proposed γε in 322 (pointless); Wakefield proposed τ' for δ' in 325 (leaving the rhetorical imbalance untouched: Hartung accordingly added the deletion of 324); Fritzsche and F. G. Schoene moved δέ to 324 (ἄπεπλος δὲ φ. λ. τέκνον), but had to accept unconvincing changes in 325.

λευκόχροα   138n.; first extant in Eur. (308bis n.), but common of persons in fourth-century comedy (Eubulus fr. 34 K–A, Alexis fr. 103.18 K–A, Men. *Sic.* 200, 258), and the medical/scientific use of the word may have been contemporary with Eur.

323   The transmitted text does not scan, δακρυόεσσαν is not likely to be an epithet of κόμαν (when not used of persons, it means 'causing tears' or (speech, lament) 'accompanied by tears'), and the scholia had a somewhat different version before them (although they could make no good sense of it). The first step toward a solution is to redivide to obtain nom. δακρυόεσσ' (which perhaps survives in FP). -ιεῖσα must be an emendation of the impossible simplex *εῖσα which presented itself after the false division -όεσσαν. πενθήρη κόμαν is excellent idiom and Euripidean (cf. *Tro.* 141f. πενθήρη κρᾶτ' ἐκπορθηθεῖσ') and a metrical text can be had with Hartung's δακρυόεσσ' ἀεί preceding it; but Σ points to a two-syllable form and πενθήρη could be due to conflation with or reminiscence of the passage in *Tro.* Unfortunately, doubt must remain about the meaning and hence the truth of ἀνεῖσα πένθει κόμαν, which Hermann deduced from Σ's εἰς σ' ἀπενθῆ and εἰς σὰ πένθη. Theoretically, ἀνιέναι κόμαν could be *crinem solvere* ('undo' as in undoing a garment: 1491n.), but in practice the verb is found with κόμην (τρίχας, etc) in Plut. *Lys.* 1 and Hdt. 2.36.1, 4.175.1 (with inf. αὔξεσθαι) as 'let grow long', the antithesis of κείρομαι. Nor does Hermann's explication (*soluerat crines prae dolore; tum absciderat*) make any sense with the real present tense 'I keep my hair cut short.' Wecklein proposed ἀνιέναι = 'dedicate', but this verb means 'dedicate' only in the sense 'leave [land] untilled' or 'let roam free and uninhibited, saved for a sacral purpose', not in the more general sense of ἀνατίθημι. Intransitive meanings have been proposed: Pearson's 'yielding to grief' (but intrans. ἀνιέναι implies a relaxing from some tense state, and it is harsh to view Joc.'s previous state, the absence of grief. as something tense like madness or wrath); Mueller-Goldingen's *nachgeben.* If ἀνεῖσα is correct, perhaps the meaning is 'neglect' or 'leave unattended', a sense akin to LSJ s.v. II.6 or II.7.b; but there is no exact parallel. The neglect would consist in leaving the hair defiled with dirt as a sign of grief: cf. *El.* 184 σκέψαι μου πιναρὰν κόμαν (from grief, cf. 305), *Or.* 225 βοστρύχων πινῶδες ... κάρα (from sickness: cf. ἀλουσίας 226).

324   ἄπεπλος φαρέων λευκῶν   a typical locution, with defining gen. of a quasi-redundant noun of related stem (the gen. approaches a separative sense as well): cf. *Hipp.* 147 ἀνίερος ἀθύτων πελανῶν and Breitenbach, 192, with refs. Cf. in Hdt. and Attic oratory phrases like ἄπαις ἀρρένων τέκνων.

325 δυσόρφναια (hapax: 308bis n.) 'unhappily dark-as-night', δυσ- adding a negative emotional connotation to a stem which would otherwise be neutral (cf. *Ag.* 774 δύσκαπνος = 'unpleasantly smoky') or reinforcing a stem which is already negative (*Ant.* 359 δύσομβρα ... βέλη, 1276 πόνοι ... δύσπονοι; δύσκωφος in medical writers; cf. intensifying δυσ- in δυσάθλιος, δύσταλας, δυσάμμορος, δυσάνολβος). Use of -ορφναῖος as a colour-epithet with a noun like τρύχη is perhaps a poetic innovation (the simplex is either an epithet of night or means 'of the night'; ὄρφνινος as a colour-epithet is first attested in fourth-century prose).

ἀμφὶ τρύχη ἀμφί is adverbial (as *Trach.* 787, *Hipp.* 770, *Ion.* 224), 'around ⟨my body⟩' as in ἀμφιβάλλω or -έννυμι. The ghost-word ἀμφιτρυχῆ (or -τρυγῆ) in the lexicographers derives from misunderstanding of this passage: here we need an explicit substantive as object, and no compound in -τρυχης is known.

328–9 ἀπήνας ὁμοπτέρου τᾶς ἀποζυγείσας δόμων either 'the team of (two) kinsmen which has been unyoked from the house' or 'the wagon-yoke-mate, kin to his partner, who has been unyoked from the house'. The latter gives a more precise correspondence between the metaphorical periphrasis and Pol.'s exile and concentrates Oedipus' *pothos* on Pol. (just as the whole context concentrates on him). But there is no parallel for ἀπήνη = 'one member of a team that draws a wagon'. Nor is there, strictly, for the former sense; but ἅρματα can mean 'team of chariot-horses' and ζεῦγος can be 'team/pair of draught-animals' (ζεῦγος in general often implies pairing, but may mean a team of four in Plato *Apol.* 36d8 ἵππωι ἢ συνωρίδι ἢ ζεύγει νενίκηκεν), and it is likely enough that a mule-car was usually drawn by two mules.[1] In either case Oedipus imagines a team which should serve the household, but is unyoked from service to the house through the absence of one member. ὁμοπτέρου brings in a separate (but perhaps faded) metaphor: cf. *Choe.* 174 ὅδ' [βόστρυχος] ἐστὶ κάρτ' ἰδεῖν ὁμόπτερος, Eur. *El.* 530 βοστρύχους ὁμοπτέρους; Pollux 6.156 Στράττις [fr. 88 K–A] τοὺς ὁμήλικας εἴρηκεν.

330 κατέχων 'holding fast', an intensified ἔχω. Just as ἔχω can have states, conditions, and emotions as either subject or object (LSJ s.v. A.I.8: e.g. *Ion* 572 κἄμ' ἔχει πόθος vs. *Or.* 189 πόθον ἔχει βορᾶς), so too can κατέχω.

---

[1] The racing ἀπήνη, which is two-wheeled, unlike the normal four-wheeled car, was drawn by a pair: Paus. 5.9.2; coins of Rhegium and Messene, pl. 45 of C. Kraay, *Archaic and Classical Greek Coins* (Berkeley 1976).

Locutions with the emotion as subject are more common (LSJ s.v. II.6), but the inverted form (neglected by LSJ) is found here and in *Med.* 760f. ἐπίνοιαν ... κατέχων, *IA* 987 κενὴν κατέσχον ἐλπίδ', *Phil.* 689f. πῶς ἄρα πανδάκρυτον οὕτω βιοτὰν κατέσχεν; (Pearson thinks our passage may echo *Phil.*; I doubt it).

331 ἀνῆιξε   in this description of Oedipus' unchanging (ἀεί 330, αἰέν 335) reaction to Pol.'s absence, this is not a simple narrative aorist, but expresses a typical repeated act of the grief-stricken father. The aorist is most similar to those used in typical situations (with indefinite or generic subjects) illustrated by Schwyzer II.283, ¶6. After ἀεὶ κατέχων there may also be a nuance of suddenness or climactic action, as in many of the instances assembled by Schwyzer under ¶5-6. Pearson terms the aorist 'gnomic', but it would at most be a close kin of the gnomic aorist if the latter is understood as derived from the expression of a single past event considered exemplary of many like events: but see Schwyzer II.285-6, ¶10.

331-3   the sword and the noose are the standard means of suicide in tragedy, leaping to one's death or drinking poison are occasionally alternatives: see Kannicht II.113 on *Hel.* 353-6 and Fraenkel, *Phil* 87 (1932) 470-3. The position of ξίφους makes the placement of τε irregular (add this to Denniston's exx., *GP*² 517 (iv)); but the actual position of τε ensures that ἐπί will be carried over to govern ἀγχόνας. On τέραμνα = 'roof-beams' see Barrett on *Hipp.* 418.

333-4 στενάζων ἀρὰς τέκνοις   in isolation, ἀράς in στενάζων ἀράς could be internal or external object; here the context makes an audience decide that it is external[1] and that τέκνοις goes closely with the verbal noun ἀράς (as in 67 ἀρᾶται παισίν; cf. Plato *Symp.* 182d8 παρακέλευσις τῶι ἐρῶντι; K-G I.426f.). Grammar thus does not require an epithet for ἀράς which would govern τέκνοις (ἀραιάς Hermann, ἀτηράς Weil), although these supplements restore a double dochmiac.

335   The assonance of α and αι may be a deliberate onomatopoeic effect, reinforcing the description of grief; the same effect is sought more strongly in 1519-21 αἴλινον αἰαγμάτων ἃ τούσδε προκλαίω μονάδ' αἰῶνα διάξουσα τὸν αἰεὶ χρόνον. Cf. the traditional punning on the sound αι in connection with the name Aias (*Aj.* 430ff. with Jebb's note).

ἀλαλαῖσι   cf. Kannicht on *Hel.* 1341-5; Deubner (1941) 9. I suspect that the variant ἀλαλαγαῖσι which occurs here and at *Trach.* 206 is, for

---

[1] The external-object interpretation is perfectly justifiable, *pace* Craik, who adopts the internal-object interpretation, believing that the inconsistency of Oedipus' longing for his sons and continued cursing of them is a mark of his derangement.

classical texts, a ghost-word arising from scribal confusion, despite the use of ἀλαλαγή by a scholiast commenting on *O.* 7.37 ἀλάλαξεν. ἀλαλάζω derives from ἀλαλαί and produces ἀλαλαγμός or -γμα, just as αἰάζω derives from αἰαῖ and produces αἴαγμα or -γμός. But cf. ἰυγή and ἰυγμός, ὀλολυγή and -υγμα or -υγμός; for recent support of ἀλαλαγαῖς in *Trach.* see Davies and Lloyd-Jones and Wilson, *Sophoclea* 157; the instance restored at *Ion* 677 (Hermann on the basis of Triclinius' supplement for responsion) is too uncertain to count for the issue.

336 σκότια internal/adverbial acc., virtually 'in the darkness (of his closed rooms)'; cf. 1541 σκοτίων ἐκ θαλάμων, *Ba.* 549 σκοτίαις κρυπτὸν ἐν εἰρκταῖς. σκότιος, found earlier only in *Il.* 6.24 (?Democritus 68 в 11 D–K), is a favourite word of Eur., used both literally and metaphorically (of sexual liaisons outside of marriage, the sense in *Il.* and Eubulus fr. 67.1 K–A (imitation of Eur.: cf. Hunter *ad loc.*)). Adverbial σκότια occurs only here and [1746] below (imitation by the interpolator?); the adj. in later tragedy, *TrGF* adesp. 127.7.

337 καὶ γάμοισι δή the metrical simplicity of the result makes it very tempting to delete καί with Hermann. A plain δή would add emotional intensity to the word γάμοισι (cf. in lyric *Hec.* 909 δορὶ δὴ δορὶ πέρσαν; *Su.* 815 περιπτυχαῖσι δή): 'I hear you're *married.*' καὶ ... δή seems to me slightly more pointed in this context: 'and as for you, child, I hear that (in addition to your absence from us in exile) you are *even married*'. καὶ ... δή with adverbial rather than connective καί is not very common in Attic prose (Denniston, *GP²* 254f.) and is rare in tragedy (Denniston lists none, but I find *Prom.* 298, *Ant.* 726, *IT* 526), so it is hard to see why καί would intrude, esp. since without it the line runs smoothly as iambic. If dochmiac hexasyllable amidst iambics is rejected, then one may consider (as Griffith points out to me) the reading of Π¹³, καὶ γάμοις·ἤδη (but Π⁸ probably had καὶ γάμοι]..νδη): ἤδη would go with ζυγέντα and imply 'already now before I could play my proper role'; dividing after ζυγέντα we then have ia, cr | ia, ba ‖ lec |. Wilam. (1991) 19 had independently proposed καὶ γάμοισιν ἤδη; Diggle (1989) 199 proposes {καὶ} γάμοισιν ἤ- / δη κλύω ζυγέντα (2 ia, ithyph); West (1990) suggests a redivision as ia, lec, ba ‖ lec, retaining καὶ ... δή.

338 παιδοποιὸν ἀδονάν Breitenbach, 207, notes Eur.'s use of compound epithet to replace the gen. of an abstract noun; cf. 1300 μονόμαχον ἐπὶ φρέν', *Ba.* 139 ὠμοφάγον χάριν, *Her.* 385 χαρμοναῖσιν ἀνδροβρῶσι. This is a high-style locution, although παιδοποιός, through its association with παιδοποιέω (prose, Aristophanes, often in Eur., once Soph. *El.* 589), is probably not *per se* an elevated term (*Andr.* 4 with δάμαρ; Hdt. 6.68 with σπέρμα).

339–40 ξένοισιν ... ξένον τε though παιδοποιόν rather than ξένοισιν is the first word in the rhetorical unit, the effect of 339–40 is akin to anaphora, if Eur. intended the phrases to be recognized as dimeters, as many have assumed. In true anaphora we would expect δέ (as in Π¹³) rather than τε: Denniston, *GP²* 163 (2) and 502 (f); Diggle (1990a) supports δέ, pointing out that Σ paraphrases with δέ; see also *Studies* 55–6. In this unbalanced structure the single τε has a normal explicative or consequential function (K–G ii.242).

341 ἄλαστα internal acc. to ἀμφέπειν, a construction difficult enough to make Σ and medieval scribes understand ΤΑΔΕ as τάδε rather than τᾶιδε. On the sense of ἄλαστος see Barrett on *Hipp.* 877–80. For the resentment of foreign connection cf. the disapproval from the Argive side implied in *Su.* 134–7 and the Athenian attitude in *Ion* 293–8, 588–92, 1056–60, etc.

341–2 Λαΐου τε τοῦ πάλαι γένει so Hermann. Transmitted Λαΐωι τε τῶι παλαιγενεῖ involves two or three curious features. (1) παλαιγενής is used of a person who is dead. The only parallel seems to be *Med.* 421 παλαιγενέων ... ἀοιδῶν (sed v. l. ἀοιδᾶν). The Homeric sense is 'aged', of living men. Aesch. extends the word to gods 'of ancient birth' and to acts 'that happened long ago' and even to 'an enemy from of old' (ἐχθρὸς ... παλαιγενής *Ag.* 1637). (2) More important, it assumes that the dead can be saddened by the acts of the living without providing a mechanism for the dead to learn of those acts. There is ample poetic precedent for the dead taking delight in news of their offspring, but always through a messenger to the Underworld: *Hcld.* 320–2 ὅταν θάνω, / πολλῶι σ' ἐπαίνωι Θησέως, ὦ τᾶν, πέλας / ὑψηλὸν ἀρῶ καὶ λέγων τάδ' εὐφρανῶ; *Od.* 11.492–540 (Achilles–Neoptolemus), 24.106ff. (Agamemnon and the suitors); Pindar *O.* 8.81–4 (Ἀγγελία as messenger), 14.20–4 (Ἀχώ); for grief at the misfortunes of one's offspring, cf. Darius in *Persae*, who is his own messenger. Cf. also Aristotle's *aporia* in *EN* 1099b18ff., 1101a22ff., with the commentary of Gauthier and Jollif on 1101a34–b1, citing orators' cautious statements (e.g. Dem. 20.87 εἴ τινες τούτων τῶν τετελευτηκότων λάβοιεν τρόπωι τινὶ τοῦ νυνὶ γιγνομένου πράγματος αἴσθησιν) as opposed to Plato's pious claim at *Laws* 927b (τὰς τῶν κεκμηκότων ψυχάς, αἷς ἐστιν ἐν τῆι φύσει τῶν αὐτῶν ἐκγόνων κήδεσθαι διαφερόντως καὶ τιμῶσίν τε αὐτοὺς εὐμενεῖς εἶναι καὶ ἀτιμάζουσιν δυσμενεῖς). (3) Finally, it is hard to see why Laius personally should be presented as distraught at Pol.'s marriage in particular. On the other hand, the notion that the whole clan or household shares in the grief is commonplace, and τοῦ πάλαι of dead forebears is good tragic idiom: *Ion* 1429 Ἐριχθονίου ... τοῦ πάλαι, *OT* 1 Κάδμου τοῦ πάλαι, 268 τοῦ πάλαι τ' Ἀγήνορος. (Geel's less drastic change Λαΐου τε τῶι πάλαι γένει will not do, for πάλαι cannot, it seems, mean 'ancient', i.e. 'begun long ago', as if it were παλαιῶι.)

343 ἐπακτόν   used in its normal sense 'brought in from abroad, foreign', not 'brought upon oneself' (LSJ s.v. II).

344-7 οὔτε . . . δ'   for the combination, usually implying some contrast in the second member, see Denniston, *GP*² 511 and below 891-2n. With ἐγὼ δ' preceding οὔτε there is a slight anacoluthon here in any case.

345 νόμιμον ἐν γάμοις   The nocturnal procession from bride's house to groom's house was accompanied by many torches (cf. *Il.* 18.492, *Ion* 1474), but the torch-bearing of the mothers of the couple had a special emotional and probably ritual significance: cf. Σ here and on *Tro.* 315 and on Ap. Rh. 4.808; *Med.* 1026-7 πρὶν λουτρὰ [Burges, λέκτρα codd.] καὶ γυναῖκα καὶ γαμηλίους εὐνὰς ἀγῆλαι λαμπάδας τ' ἀνασχεθεῖν; *IA* 732-4 τίς δ' ἀνασχήσει φλόγα; κτλ. See W. Erdmann, *Die Ehe im alten Griechenland* [Münch. Beitr. z. Papyrusforschung u. Rechtsges. 20 (München 1934)], 256.

346 ὡς πρέπει   Nauck found an impression of overfullness in 345-6 and deleted this phrase to obtain pure dochmiacs. But fullness is no defect in a lyric of this kind, and ὡς πρέπει adds something valuable to the sentence, working together with μακαρίαι to evoke Jocasta's sense of loss more effectively than a bare dat. depending (with a little strain) on νόμιμον. Diggle (1990b) 108 calls all instances of cr sandwiched between dochmiac into question and suggests that here ἐν γάμοις (omitted in ΣAp. Rhod. 4.808-9) could be an intrusion; so already Wilam. (1991) 19.

347-8 ἀνυμέναια . . . χλιδᾶς   'and Hismenus was deprived of wedding-songs and deprived of the luxuriant joy of the ritual water-bearing when he received this marriage-tie'. Through supplying water for the rite, the personified river becomes not only a participant but virtually a kinsman. ἐκηδεύθη is bold. κήδευμα can mean 'relation by marriage' (*OT* 85, *Or.* 477), and κηδεύσων τινά in *Hec* 1202 must be 'intending to make some Greek your kinsman by marriage', a unique meaning of which ἐκηδεύθη here is the passive counterpart. Likewise, ἀνυμέναια . . . χλιδᾶς is bold because the bath and the song are not synonymous (ἄπεπλος φαρέων: see on 324) or genus and species (ἄχαλκος ἀσπίδων *OT* 191) but two species of the genus 'wedding-rituals'. But such boldness is not suspicious in this context. Water for rituals is drawn from a particular source, which thereby becomes strongly identified with the locality and its people: see 222n. (Castalia) and 126n., and Thuc. 2.15.5 (Callirrhoe). For the ritual, cf. *Med.* 1026, *IT* 818, and see W. Erdmann, *Die Ehe im alten Griechenland* [Münch. Beitr. z. Papyrusforschung u. Rechtsges. 20 (München 1934)], 252-3; Herkenbach, *RE* 8:2 (1913) 2129-31 s.v. Hochzeit. λουτροφόρος as an epithet of χλιδά seems to be a Euripidean innovation. The word must have been current both as an epithet or title of the ritual water-bearer and as the name of the vessel used, though the first extant citations for these uses happen to be later than *Phoen.*

348–9 Θηβαίαν πόλιν Diggle (216n.) prefers Θηβαίων (AaFSa); in this lyric passage I prefer the untypical expression.

349 ἐσιγάθη σᾶς ἔσοδοι νύμφας the argument *utrum in alterum* suggests that ἐσιγάθησαν ἔσοδοι and ἐσιγάθη σᾶς ἔσοδος are 'corrections' of the unusual but possibly genuine syntax, the so-called *schema Pindaricum*, adopted here as a lyric artificiality. Many apparent examples are textually uncertain, but in a few cases we find the schema seen here, a singular verb (other than ἔστι or ἦν) followed by a plural noun (often abstract and singular in sense): Pindar *P.* 10.71 κεῖται ... κυβερνάσιες, 4.236 τέλεσεν ... πλαγαί. Barrett, addendum on *Hipp.* 1255, notes the dithyrambic style of several instances in Pindar; perhaps such an effect is sought here, following on the artificiality of the previous clause. In addition to Barrett's note and K–G 1.68, Schwyzer II.608, see Gildersleeve on Pindar *O.* 11.6, Dodds on *Ba.* 1350, Richardson on *Hom.h.Dem.* 279; R.S. Haydon, *AJP* 11 (1890) 182–92 (who discounts or explains away many examples; he finds our passage intolerable unless it is explained by a shift of construction – the subject was to be ἡ σὴ νύμφη εἰσιοῦσα). Craik adopts Wölfflin's dative ἐσόδωι, requiring an unparalleled impersonal use of σιγάω that is more suspect than the *schema Pindaricum* (on the rarity and restricted use of impersonals in Greek, cf. Schwyzer II.239). JD reminds me that Bremer and Worp (255) thought they could read εσιγαθεν in Π¹³ (but the reading could not be confirmed on the original) and notes that Willink independently conjectured ἐσίγαθεν (short 3rd pl. ending: 1246n.), which would well account for the transmitted readings and perhaps for Π¹³.

350–1 τάδ' ... αἴτιος the acc. is governed by αἴτιος (ἐστι) as if it were ἔκρανε or ἔπραξε; *Hel.* 261 τὰ δὲ τὸ κάλλος αἴτιον is not necessarily the same, since τὰ μὲν ... τὰ δέ can be quasi-adverbial acc. of respect; but cf. χοὰς προπομπός *Choe.* 23 [χοᾶν Casaubon], σε ... φύξιμος *Ant.* 786, and Schwyzer II.73 (c), K–G 1.296 Anm.4. αἴτιος or τὸ αἴτιον followed by acc. articular inf. (Plato, *Lach.* 190e; Dem. 8.56, 9.63) is probably not comparable, as it may derive from a particular development of the articular inf. (Schwyzer II.371, ¶7).

350–3 εἴτε ... εἴτ' ... εἴτε ... εἴτε by canvassing so many possibilities (malevolent magic, the competitiveness of human nature, specific curse, or general demonic persecution), Jocasta expresses an indifference to knowing the precise cause which emphasizes the importance to her of the resulting grief. The openness of the question of causation is, however, a typical feature of tragedy and an important theme in this play: see Introd. I and cf. 49, 413. That Oedipus is here cursed by Jocasta (whereas elsewhere in the play she is seen as loyal and loving toward him) is another index of the confusion of emotions caused by the brothers' quarrel.

350 σίδαρος iron is endowed with magical properties in the superstitious thinking of several primitive tribes (Frazer, *Golden Bough*³ 1.159f., III.167, 176, 225–36; see also M. Cary and A. D. Nock, 'Magic Spears', *CQ* 21 (1927) 122–7), and a trace of such superstition is probably present in *Od.* 16.294 = 19.13 αὐτὸς γὰρ ἐφέλκεται ἄνδρα σίδηρος (cf., slightly rationalized, Hdt. 1.68.4 τὸν δὲ ἐξελαυνόμενον σίδηρον τὸ πῆμα ἐπὶ πήματι κείμενον, κατὰ τοιόνδε τι εἰκάζων, ὡς ἐπὶ κακῶι ἀνθρώπου σίδηρος ἀνεύρηται). There may also be a more specific literary allusion to the role of iron in *Septem* (and in earlier sources?). In *Se.*, as in *Phoen.* 68, 'by means of iron' is specified in the curse, and much is made in the crucial ode *Se.* 720–91 of iron as the foreign arbiter of the quarrel (727–33); σίδηρος or its compounds appear at *Se.* 52, 730, 788, 817, 884, 911, 912. *Phoen.* has more iron-words than any other play (26, 68, 517, 672 (an echo of *Se.* 52?), 1130, 1383, 1393, 1420, 1677): cf. five instances in *Or.*, four in *Prom.* (in many fewer lines).

352 τὸ δαιμόνιον Eur. shares this generalized abstraction (also *Ba.* 894, fr. 152) with Hdt. and Attic prose; it is perhaps a coinage of intellectuals who doubt the specifics of traditional polytheistic myths and cults but believe nevertheless in divinity.

κατεκώμασε for the idea cf. *Ag.* 1189–90 κῶμος ἐν δόμοις μένει, δύσπεμπτος ἔξω, συγγόνων Ἐρινύων. The hapax would remind hearers of ἐπικωμάζω, and the dat. δώμασιν probably combines the locative and the true dat.: 'has brought a revel of destruction upon the house / has held a revel of destruction in the house'. Cf. dat. with καταγελάω in Hdt. (analogy of ἐπιγελάω) and with καθυβρίζω in Hdt. and Soph. (analogy of ἐφυβρίζω): Jebb on *Aj.* 153, K–G 1.407.

355–6 if the chorus is present, the conclusion of any substantial lyric sung by an actor or actors is normally marked off by two or three lines expressing the chorus' sympathy or general reaction to the song (in an antistrophic aria the chorus may react after each stanza). The words κακά, κακῶς, συμφορά are frequent in such comments. Outside *Phoen.* there are at least twelve examples in Eur. (from *Hipp.* 680–1 to *IA* 1336–7) and two in Soph., plus eight instances (five iambic, three anapaestic) where the chorus instead announces an entering character. For the few exceptions, see 1582–3n.

δεινὸν γυναιξὶν κτλ. 'Bearing children through the pains of labour has a wondrously powerful effect upon women ...' For δεινόν compare *Prom.* 39 τὸ συγγενές τοι δεινόν, *Andr.* 985 τὸ συγγενὲς γὰρ δεινόν, *Tro.* 616 τὸ τῆς ἀνάγκης δεινόν, and esp. Soph. *El.* 770 δεινὸν τὸ τίκτειν

COMMENTARY 356–60

ἐστίν and *IA* 917–18 δεινὸν τὸ τίκτειν καὶ φέρει φίλτρον μέγα / πᾶσίν τε κοινὸν ὥσθ' ὑπερκάμνειν τέκνων. For the neuter adj. as predicate see Barrett on *Hipp*. 443–6. See also 30n.

φιλότεκνον in *Her*. 634–6 Heracles universalizes love of children, as does Creon in 965 below (q.v.) and later Aristotle, *Rhet*. 1371b24–5, but the superior love shown by the mother is also a commonplace, as in Eur. fr. 1015 αἰεὶ δὲ μήτηρ φιλότεκνος μᾶλλον πατρός· / ἡ μὲν γὰρ αὐτῆς οἶδεν ὄνθ', ὁ δ' οἴεται; Lycurgus, *Leocr*. 101 (following quotation of Praxithea's speech, *Erectheus* fr. 50 Austin) φύσει ... οὐσῶν φιλοτέκνων πασῶν τῶν γυναικῶν; Aristotle, *EN* 1168a25–6 αἱ μητέρες φιλοτεκνότεραι· ἐπιπονωτέρα γὰρ ἡ γέννησις, καὶ μᾶλλον ἴσασιν ὅτι αὐτῶν. That Eur. dwells explicitly in many of his plays on the love of children and the pathos of separation from them shows his greater interest in domestic emotions and women's emotions: there is nothing like this in extant Aesch., and in Soph. only Oedipus' outpourings to his daughters in *OT* and *OC* are comparable (note how differently Eurydice is treated in *Ant*.).

357–78 Pol. recapitulates the themes of his entrance-monologue 261–73 (being among enemies, fear of treachery, divided emotions, reliance on his mother's pledge of truce) and also responds to those of Joc.'s aria (arrival, emotion at return to familiar sites, Et.'s injustice, effect of separation on other loved ones). The speech progresses first through two stages of self-centred remarks: 357–66a, love of fatherland compels him to risk entering the city (note the framing elements ἀφικόμην ~ εἰσήγαγεν, πατρίδος ~ πατρῶια); 366b–70, tearful return and tearful exile (note πολύδακρυς ~ δακρυρροοῦν). Then Pol. shifts to observation of Joc.'s appearance and generalizes about the cost of the feud. Cf. 376–8n.

357 φρονῶν εὖ κοὐ φρονῶν 'with proper feelings and yet against proper prudence' (272n.).

358 ἀλλ' strongly opposing the damning admission in οὐ φρονῶν; in a less emotional, rhetorically neater style the cryptic pairing in 357 would probably have been followed by an antithesis with μὲν γάρ ... δέ.

359 πατρίδος ἐρᾶν cf. with similar connotations of homesickness Aesch. *Ag*. 540 ἔρως πατρώιας τῆσδε γῆς and probably adesp. comic. 431 Kock οὕτως ἔρως ἰσχυρὸς ἐντέτηκέ μοι τῆς πατρίδος; of a more general patriotism Eur. fr. 729.2 πατρίδος ἐρῶντας.

360 λόγοισι χαίρει 'delights in (insincere) disputation', that is, makes the argument not from conviction but for the eristic pleasure of denying a well-known truth. Here, as later (469–72n.), Pol.'s no-nonsense approach to values dissociates him from the methods and amorality of sophistic relativism (cf. τὸν ἥττω λόγον κρείττω ποιεῖν, δισσοὶ λόγοι).

τὸν δὲ νοῦν ... ἔχει 'his real belief lies in that direction'. Contrasted with λόγοισι, νοῦν ἔχειν is here more than 'direct attention' (as 1418 below,

250

Ion 251, *Or.* 1181, like prosaic προσέχειν τὸν νοῦν); νοῦς contains – and, since it is opaque to one's fellow-man, conceals – one's inmost convictions: e.g. Theognis 87 μή μ' ἔπεσιν μὲν στέργε, νόον δ' ἔχε καὶ φρένας ἄλληι and 119–28 (on the difficulty of knowing another's νοῦς).[1]

ἐκεῖσ' i.e., εἰς τὸ ἐρᾶν τῆς πατρίδος; cf. ἄλληι in Theognis; *Phaethon* 265 with Diggle's note.

361 οὕτω δ' ἐτάρβησ' a phrase like ὧδε τάρβους ἔχειν would be possible (K–G 1.382–3; Diggle, *Studies* 34–5), but transmitted οὕτω δε τάρβους is unidiomatic with ἀφικόμην and does not combine smoothly with εἰς φόβον. If a verb-form is to be restored, Hermann's aorist (anticipated in Rw) is better than Porson's ἐτάρβουν and no less likely to have been corrupted through faulty division. (1) εἰς φόβον ἀφικόμην is a periphrasis for an aorist: e.g. *Ba.* 610 εἰς ἀθυμίαν ἀφίκεσθ', 879 below εἰς ἔχθος ἦλθον (both ingressive, as here), *Med.* 872–3 ἐμαυτῆι διὰ λόγων ἀφικόμην κἀλοιδόρησα. (2) The line should present two synonymous phrases, a *variatio* that produces full-ness and emphasis: cf. *OT* 296 ὧι μή 'στι δρῶντι τάρβος, οὐδ' ἔπος φοβεῖ; *Or.* 312 τὸ ταρβοῦν κἀκφοβοῦν σ' ἐκ δεμνίων; *IA* 1535 ταρβοῦσα ... κἀκπεπληγμένη φόβωι; also Aesch. *Su.* 736 περίφοβον ... τάρβος, *Se.* 240 ταρβοσύνωι φόβωι; *Trach.* 176 φόβωι ταρβοῦσαν; *Her.* 971 ταρβοῦντες φόβωι. Triclinius' τάρβος features a similar coupling of synonyms (with postponed preposition: 284n.) and is championed by Kiefner, 101, but is stylistically flatter. Craik proposes οὕτω δὲ φόβον ἐς ταρβόσυνον ἀφικόμην, suggesting a deliberate echo of *Se.* 240; but there is virtually no caesura, and the overwrought phrase suits dochmiacs (so too *Su.* 736), but not trimeters.

ἀφικόμην three times at line-end within ten lines; the two literal uses at 357 and 366 help to mark two sections of the speech (357–78n.), but the periphrastic use here (194–5n.) has no such force. On insignificant repetition cf. 22n.

363 ξιφήρη a favourite word of Eur., the only classical author who uses it (later in prose from Strabo on); here only it modifies 'hand' rather than a person.

364 κυκλῶν πρόσωπον a unique combination, but cf. the phrases cited on 265 ὄμμα ... διοιστέον; κυκλεῖν is elsewhere used with πόδα/βάσιν (*Aj.* 19, Eur. *El.* 561, *Or.* 632); πρόσωπον is an alternative of ὄμμα: cf. 457 πρόσωπον ... στρέφε, *IT* 68 ὄμμα ... στρέφων, *Med.* 27–8 οὔτ' ὄμμ' ἐπαίρουσ' οὔτ' ἀπαλλάσσουσα γῆς πρόσωπον.

---

[1] The difference of meaning in 1418 does not militate against the contex-tually determined meaning in 360, as Craik believes; nor do I see how Craik's translation (or paraphrase) 'plays with words, but is devoid of sense' can be obtained from the Greek.

365 σὴ πίστις 'the pledge you have given' rather than 'my trust in you', since 'the truce and your pledge' are 'one thing'.

365-6 εἰσήγαγεν τείχη 'brought me inside the walls'; not a simple acc. of the goal, but more or less governed by εἰσ-, 'into', as εἰσάγειν δόμους *Alc.* 1112, etc. (Diggle, *Studies* 116). Cf. 451n.

366 πολύδακρυς it is a Eur. mannerism to use epic πολυδάκρυς / -υτος of a person in the active sense. πολυ-compounds are more frequently used in anapaests or lyrics; when used in dialogue, they seem to carry the dignity of epic colouring, and there may be some emotional force here (the only use of πολυδακρ- in dialogue).

367 χρόνιος 304n.

μέλαθρα καὶ βωμοὺς θεῶν it is a sign of piety and warm emotional attachment when a returning character thankfully addresses the holy places and images as well as the house itself: *Ag.* 518-19 (herald), *Her.* 523-4, 609 (Heracles); Agamemnon, whose relationship to the house is more ambivalent and dangerous, concentrates on the gods (*Ag.* 810-11, 851-3); in *Or.* 356-7 a cool and amoral Menelaus greets only the house. In this survey of favourite sites, μέλαθρα is more likely to be 'the palace' than 'the temples' (with θεῶν taken ἀπὸ κοινοῦ: so e.g. Buschor).

368 γυμνάσια a favourite haunt of (well-born) youths, for equestrian and personal exercise, both in the heroic world of Eur. tragedy (*Hipp.* 229, 1131-4, *Tro.* 834 (Ganymede), *Hel.* 209 (Tyndaridae), *Phaethon* fr. inc. sed. 4 Diggle) and in contemporary Athens (Aristoph. *Clouds* 417, 1002, etc.).

ἐνετράφην another sentimental touch; cf. *Hipp.* 1095-6 ὦ πέδον Τροζήνιον, ὡς ἐγκαθηβᾶν πόλλ' ἔχεις εὐδαίμονα.

Δίρκης θ' ὕδωρ one's native stream is emotionally important in general (126n.), but *Tro.* 833-4 τὰ δὲ σὰ δροσόεντα λουτρὰ γυμνασίων τε δρόμοι βεβᾶσι suggests that bathing and swimming connected with the gymnasium are also implied.

369-70 West (1981) deletes this couplet as an out-of-place digression and finds that Pol.'s weeping in exile clashes with his weeping on return (366). The claim of injustice, however, is usefully introduced at this point; ξένην πόλιν ναίω is a response to 339-40, and Pol.'s unhappiness in exile is the mirror-image of the grief of his loved ones at Thebes (357-78n.).

370 ναίω ναίων (cf. Π¹³) ... ἔχω (cf. Eust.), rhetorically much less effective, is preferred by Valck. and Heath only because their conjectures require the nu of ναίων.

†δι' ὅσσων ὄμμ'† ἔχων δακρυρροοῦν since ὄσσε is exactly synonymous with ὀφθαλμός/-οί, ὄμμα/ὄμματα, the transmitted phrase can be defended only by giving ὄμμ' the sense 'look, expression' (as in 454 σχάσον δὲ δεινὸν ὄμμα); but although 'having a ... expression in one's eyes' is idiomatic English, it seems intolerably redundant in the Greek, despite such pleonasms as ὄμμασιν ὁρᾶν. νᾶμ' ἔχων has been a popular remedy, but the verb seems to me much too colourless: in the parallel passages we find ῥήξασα, ἵει, ἐξανίετε (*Trach.* 919, *Med.* 1187, *Her.* 625: cf. Burges' στάζουσι νᾶμα in *Choe.* 1058), whence Hemsterhuys' original (unmetrical) νᾶμα χέων. L's αἶμ' is likely to be a bevue of the scribe, not a corruption of an alternative reading. On the other hand, ὄμμ' ἔχειν + epithet is common: *Se.* 537 γοργόν, *Prom.* 569 δόλιον, *Hcld.* 633 κατηφές, *El.* 503 διάβροχον, etc. The corruption thus seems more likely to lie in δι' ὄσσων. We need either an adverbial modifier of ἔχων (Schoene's δι' οἴκτων is the best available: Eur. affects plural οἶκτοι; but the plural in the sense 'pity' or 'feelings of pity' is doubtful (JD, referring to *Studies* 46) and δι' could be an intrusion from the line above) or a predicate adjective with πόλιν ναίω (e.g. μέτοικος, after Paley) rather than another epithet of ὄμμ' (e.g. κατηφές Valck.).

δακρυρροοῦν δακρυρροεῖν is used with a person as subject in Soph. and Eur., but Eur. also has ὄμμα as subject in *Alc.* 826 ὄμμ' ἰδὼν δακρυρροοῦν and *Ion* 246 ὄμμα σὸν δακρυρροεῖ. If νᾶμ' is read, the change to δακρύρροον is justified: cf. *Her.* 98–9 δακρυρρόους τέκνων πηγὰς ἀφαίρει.

371–2 Fraenkel, 18–20, well traces the misinterpretation and mispunctuation from which 371 has often suffered. For the parenthetic γάρ-clause Valck. compared *Tro.* 706–7 ἀλλ' ἐκ λόγου γὰρ ἄλλος ἐκβαίνει λόγος, / τίν' αὖ δέδορκα κτλ. αὖ must go with ἄλγος (1) because ἐκ ... ἄλγους implies 'another', so that αὖ is idiomatic as in ἄλλος αὖ (417) and the like and (2) because it cannot stand at the head of a colon, as Pearson's punctuation after ἄλγος has it. The pains referred to are Pol.'s (those of exile, now that of seeing Joc.'s condition), not Joc.'s; thus 372 is indispensable in providing an object of 373 ἔχουσαν. Kirchhoff wrongly deleted 372 as interpolated from *Alc.* 427 κουρᾶι ξυρήκει καὶ μελαμπέπλωι στολῆι (LP: μελαγχίμοις πέπλοις OV), but it is likely that OV there reflect contamination from *Phoen.*

372 ξυρηκές or perhaps ξύρηκες, probably not ξυρῆκες (*Text. Trad.* 228, Teubner app.).[1]

[375] the line was absent in some copies known to ancient or early Byzantine scholars (Σ), a strong cause for suspicion but not in itself irresistible grounds for deletion (see below); here the case is clinched by the

---

[1] The rule in Chandler, *Gk. Accentuation* §698 (compounds in -ηκης are paroxytone) is an uncertain inference from the ancient sources, which dispute whether such words are oxytone or not, but give no grounds for deciding whether, if not oxytone, neuter singular forms would be proparoxytone or properispomenon.

unidiomatic pairing of genders in the predicates δεινόν and ἔχουσα (normal idiom requires either expansion with an independent verb καὶ ... ἔχει or parallel predicates – as Pindar N. 9.32 φίλιπποί τ' ... καὶ κτεάνων ψυχὰς ἔχοντες κρέσσονας; exx. in Attic prose listed by W. J. Alexander, AJP 4 (1883) 295–6, 298) or by the loose connection with καί if ἔχουσι (subject φίλοι) is the original form. The objection cannot be overcome by claiming that ἔχουσα is attributive, coupled with οἰκείων φίλων: this would be a rhetorically feeble afterthought. Many have believed that δυσλύτους as epithet of διαλλαγάς can only mean 'hard to dissolve', which makes no sense; but the meaning 'reconciliations that entail difficult dissolution ⟨of hatred⟩' seems to me possible. The range of meanings of verbal adjs. in -τος is very wide. If one wishes to analyse the logic of the compound, one may say that δύσλυτος ἔχθρα implies a direct-object phrase such as χαλεπῶς (δια)λύειν τὴν ἔχθραν while δύσλυτος διαλλαγή implies an internal-accusative phrase such as χαλεπὴν (δια)λύειν διαλλαγήν and features synonymous roots in adj. and noun, διαλλάσσειν ≈ (δια)λύειν. Such analysis is not, however, necessary: Barrett on Hipp. 677–9 πέραν δυσεκπέρατον, Williger, 43ff. Cf. Aesch. Eum. 496–7 παιδότρωτα πάθεα, Soph. Aj. 254 λιθόλευστον Ἄρη, 631–4 χερόπληκτοι ... δοῦποι, Trach. 357 ῥιπτὸς ... μόρος, Ant. 36 φόνον ... δημόλευστον, 1115 below στικτοῖς ... ὄμμασιν. The line probably began as part of a gnomic marginal parallel. The abruptness of the one-line gnome 374 may have assisted the intrusion. Perhaps ἔχουσι (as in Π¹³) was the original form (e.g., 'when kinsmen have a falling out, they are bitterest enemies, and hard to fashion are the reconciliations they afford'), but the sense of ἔχω (LSJ A.I.11) is easier to parallel with an abstract subject (besides LSJ's passages note El. 1085 παράδειγμα ... εἴσοψίν τ' ἔχει, Hel. 506 ἔχει φυλάξεις (as explained by Kannicht), Thuc. 2.62.1 κομπωδεστέραν ἔχοντι τὴν προσποίησιν; Thuc. 2.41.3 has ἡ πόλις as subject); ἔχουσα could have followed a line containing fem. pred. adj.

For eleven passages in five of the select plays of Eur. we have scholiastic evidence about the absence (οὐ φέρεται/φέρονται; ΣOr. 1394 οὐ γράφεται, ΣAlc. 820 οὐκ ἔγκειται) of the verse(s) in some or many copies (ἔν τισιν ΣHipp. 871, Alc. 820, here; ἐν ἐνίοις ΣOr. 957; ἐν πολλοῖς (ἀντιγράφοις) ΣHipp. 1050, Phoen. 1282, Or. 1394;[1] ἐν τοῖς πολλοῖς (τῶν ἀντιγράφων / ἀντιγράφοις) ΣAndr. 1254, Phoen. 1075?, 1225; ἐν τῶι ἀντιγράφωι ΣOr. 1229). The collations on which such remarks are based may have occurred as late as the ninth or tenth century (the scholia are almost all in B or M; ΣAlc. 820 in V only), but it is more likely that they occurred in late antiquity

---

[1] Or. 1394 is absent from P.Oxy. 53.3717.

COMMENTARY [375]–378

(whenever the selection and the compilation of scholia took place) or much earlier in Alexandria (at the best the basis of the notes would be marginal signs in the edition of Aristophanes of Byzantium).[1] Reeve, 'Interp.' 253–5, reviews all the passages and concludes that all are in fact interpolated. I agree that deletion is justified in eight passages (if the vaguely placed scholion on *Phoen.* 1069–73 belongs to 1075: see *ad loc.*), but I think (with Jackson and Diggle) that *Andr.* 1254 is better transposed than deleted, and I am not convinced (*pace* Reeve and Willink) that *Or.* 957–9 and 1227–30 are spurious. Cf. 291–2n. (verses omitted in papyri); 1346n. (verses omitted in major mss).

376–8 discussed in detail in *Contact and Discontinuity* 121–4. Pol.'s speech can well end at 374, with ὡς δεινὸν κτλ. as a conclusive gnome, albeit more abrupt than most. The three lines have been suspected mainly because of the loose connection to what precedes (γάρ interpreted as progressive, at a change of topic) and because Joc. appears not to answer Pol.'s questions. On the usual reading, these are fatal objections because one must assume an unparalleled and illogical combination of casualness in Pol. and emotional distraction in Joc.[2] If the lines are interpolated, the author (in this case surely an actor/producer) has captured Eur.'s characterization of Pol. very well and seems to have chosen to anticipate 615–17; but it is hard to see how he wanted these and the surrounding lines to be performed – unless in the way I ascribe to Eur. himself. If the lines are genuine, the gnome in 374 may be viewed as pivotal in function (a common use in choral lyric; for Eur. cf. *Her.* 57, *Tro.* 400–2): that is, it generalizes upon the circumstances described in 371–3 but also leads to further explication in 376–8. Just as Pol.'s rhesis responds to other themes of Joc.'s song, so here mention of blind old Oedipus in the house echoes 327. On this view, γάρ has a normal inferential sense ('for my father and sisters are also suffering, aren't they?'), and the complex of questions suggests in itself a surmise which is tacitly acknowledged by Joc.'s confirming larger generalization about the family's plight. Joc. cuts off her detailed list of woes before reaching the present and turns to a new topic at 383. The demonstration

---

[1] At the worst, such notes would not be based on collation of copies of the plays, but on suggestions made in ancient commentaries: cf. W. J. Slater, 'Problems in Interpreting Scholia on Greek Texts', in *Editing Gk. and Lat. Texts* 37–61 (57, suggesting ἐν ἐνίοις refers to ὑπομνηματισταί, not ἀντίγραφα).

[2] Further objections adduced by Mueller-Goldingen, 81–2 n. 19, have little force: he thinks it does not fit Pol.'s ethos to seek pity and that Joc. has already told Pol. enough about Oed. in 327–36 (but this assumes that τί δρᾷ; = 'how is he?').

255

of Pol.'s familial solidarity, answering 163–70 and anticipating 615–17, is dramatically effective, and the similarity of 376–8 and 615–17 is typical of the repetitions by which Eur. emphasizes Pol's claim to justice, feeling of danger, and affection for kin and country.

376 τί ... δρᾶι 'What is he doing?', δρᾶν serving, like ποιεῖν, as a catch-all verb and leading, as often, to a more specific verb in the following question (ἤ που στένουσι;). The sequence is common with first- and second-person verbs, but occurs in other forms as well: *Ba.* 803 τί δρῶντα; δουλεύοντα δουλείαις ἐμαῖς; *Andr.* 66–7 τί δρῶσι; ποίας μηχανὰς πλέκουσιν αὖ ...; esp. Libanius, *Basilii et Libanii commercium*, ep. 2.3 (XI.574 Foerster) τί νῦν ἡμῖν (cf. μοι) ὁ Βασίλειος δρᾶι καὶ πρὸς τίνα βίον ὥρμηκεν; ἆρ' ἐν δικαστηρίοις στρέφεται τοὺς παλαιοὺς ῥήτορας ζηλῶν ἢ ῥήτορας εὐδαιμόνων πατέρων ἀπεργάζεται παῖδας; Fraenkel held that τί δρᾶι; is here used mistakenly in the sense πῶς πράσσει; and assumed that such a use of δρᾶν betrays post-classical authorship. In fact, there is no evidence that a Greek of any period would or could have made such an error of idiom (further examples adduced by Reeve and Dihle are not cogent: *Contact and Discontinuity* 122 n. 34).

ἐν δόμοισι 66n.

377 σκότον δεδορκώς either 'whose glance hits darkness', with direct object as in *Ba.* 510 σκότιον εἰσορᾶι κνέφας ('look upon the dark gloom ⟨of a prison-cell⟩') and βλέπειν φάος, or 'whose glance is darkness', as in *OT* 419 βλέποντα νῦν μὲν ὄρθ', ἔπειτα δὲ σκότον, if σκότον is grammatically parallel to ὄρθ'. Either will fit the Greek conception of vision, which assumes rays from the seer's eyes. This phrase, together with πρέσβυς, forms a not unsympathetic reference to an essential characteristic of Oed.'s present life (cf. 327 πρέσβυς ὀμματοστερής, 1088 γέροντα τυφλόν, 1530–5). Despite the similarity of *OT* 419, we probably have here a clichéd poetic periphrasis rather than a specific reminiscence: Soph. uses σκότος of blindness at *OT* 1273 and 1313 as well and Eur. himself again at 1534 (q.v.). σκότος traditionally comes over the eyes at the moment of death (cf. 1453), and 'those who do not see' are the dead: σκότον δεδορκώς is thus another detail which suggests that Oed. is little more than a living ghost (1540n.).

378 τλήμονες thrice elsewhere Eur. has τλήμονας φυγάς ∪ – at line-end (*Hipp.* 1177, *El.* 233, 505, the last even ending στένεις), whence Brunck's proposal to read τλήμονας here; but in those cases the speaker is lamenting the exile of a third person (but cf. *Ba.* 1350 τλήμονες φυγαί at line-end, Agave speaking of the exile of Cadmus and herself). Pol. is inclined to self-pity, but in the present context he is also showing concern for the sufferings of others: στένουσι τλήμονες yields a subtle and rhetorically effective mixture of compassion and self-pity. Triclinius' τλήμονος is needlessly precious (cf. *OC* 344 τἀμὰ δυστήνου κακά, metrically convenient) and even more self-centred in tone.

379 κακῶς θεῶν τις .. φθείρει it is typical to ascribe extraordinary misfortune to an unspecified divine malevolence (cf. 352–3 εἴτε τὸ δαιμόνιον κτλ.). As with Polydorus speaking of Hecuba in *Hec.* 57–8 σε φθείρει θεῶν τις, Joc. avoids going into the details of causation and the fateful contributions of specific individuals. Her reticence is dramatically convenient (the audience has heard the prologue) and psychologically apt (specific recriminations are painful and will not do any good now). κακῶς is 'wretchedly' (as usual with φθείρω and similar verbs), not 'incorrectly' (Burian and Swann: 'it was wrong for one of the gods to destroy').

380 ἦρξατ' 'the god' is subject, and the verb may be absolute ('began his work') rather than govern understood φθείρειν. The following infinitives are epexegetic/consecutive; cf. K–G II.17; Schwyzer II.362–3. The usage here is more striking than those in 91, 262, and 450, where the verbs imply permission and motion.

380–1 note the reticence (379n.) of ellipsis here: unlawfully ⟨because Laius had been forbidden by Apollo⟩ I gave birth ⟨to Oedipus⟩, Oedipus married ⟨me⟩ for ill and ⟨for ill⟩ you were born ⟨to us⟩. φῦναι fits this pattern better than the more obvious φῦσαι.

382 ἀτὰρ τί ταῦτα; for the cut-off formula cf. *Su.* 750 and (without ἀτάρ) *Hel.* 991; (with verb added) [1762] below, *Andr.* 397, *Hipp.* 971; also *Hel.* 860 φεῦγ'· ἀτὰρ τί φευκτέον;

383–4 cf. Fraenkel 24–5. The expression of hesitation is reinforced by the interlacing of clauses (ὅπως goes with δέδοικα; ἃ χρήιζω with ἔρωμαι; μή ... δάκω is a purpose clause); the effect is weakened, along with Joc.'s solicitude, with Weil's emendation μήτε [μηδὲ debuit: Diggle (1990a) 10] σὴν δάκηι. For the general sense Pearson well cites *Or.* 544–5 ἐγώ τοι πρὸς σὲ δειμαίνω λέγειν, ὅπου γε μέλλω σὴν τι λυπήσειν φρένα (as restored by Musgrave; note idiomatic τι).[1] For interrogative ὅπως with δέδοικα ('I am fearful and uncertain') cf. *IT* 995–6 τὴν θεὸν δ' ὅπως λάθω δέδοικα καὶ τύραννον. K–G II.397 and Schwyzer II.677 give examples of similar questions (fut. ind., vivid present ind., χρή + inf.) after verbs of fearing; note esp. Xen. *Cyr.* 4.5.19 ἀποροῦντες μὲν πῶς χρὴ καλοῦντος ἀπειθεῖν, φοβούμενοι δὲ πῶς χρὴ ἀπειλοῦντι ὑπακοῦσαι.[2]

δάκω φρένα cf. *Hcld.* 483 δάκνει φ., *Or.* 545 λυπήσειν φ., *Med.* 599

---

[1] Deletion of *Or.* 545 is proposed by Diggle (1990b) 102.

[2] Cf., with a different kind of question, *Hipp.* 1204–5 ἦν φόβος ... πόθεν ποτ' εἴη φθόγγος. Note that constructions of verbs of fearing with ὅπως μή are different: with subj., as in simple μή clause, *Hipp.* 518 and prose; with fut. ind., as after verbs of effort, *OT* 1074–5 and prose.

κνίζοι φ., all antonyms of the common τέρπειν φρένα; also *Ant.* 317 ἐν τοῖσιν ὠσὶν ἢ 'πὶ τῆι ψυχῆι δάκνηι;

διὰ πόθου . . . ἐλήλυθα tragic periphrasis for ποθῶ [sc. ἐρέσθαι], but with perfect aspect; see 20n., 479n.

386 ταῦτ' the simple correlatives ἅ . . . ταῦτ' are not impossible here, but the identity of interests is better expressed with emphasis (cf. *Or.* 1123 ταῦθ' ἅπερ – see Willink).

387 absent in Π¹³ and condemned by Haslam (1976: 'we would be well rid of 387'); yet the politeness of prefacing an introduction to the interrogation, acknowledging Pol.'s permission (καὶ δή σ' ἐρωτῶ answering ἐξερώτα; cf. *Se.* 473, *Alc.* 1118, Denniston, *GP*² 251–2), fits Joc.'s stance in this dialogue better than an abrupt entry into the stichomythia; and for a pair of couplets as introduction to Euripidean stichomythia cf. *Alc.* 803–6, *Med.* 663–6, *Hipp.* 311–14, *Hel.* 441–4, *Or.* 1177–80. The absence of the verse in a papyrus should not be an automatic cause of suspicion (291–2n.).

388–407 the first part of the two-part stichomythia makes heavy use of gnomic material on the theme of exile, as Joc. in her marked sensitivity (cf. also 418) inquires closely into her son's experiences, paradoxically evoking Pol.'s sense of loss and injustice even as she is laying the groundwork for her appeal to his love of fatherland later in the scene (261–442n.). The dialogue falls into three sections. The first stage of Joc.'s inquiries (388–95) reflects sympathetic curiosity, and Pol. concentrates on the lack of independence he has suffered. In the second section (396–9) Joc.'s topic has the ulterior motive of questioning Pol.'s hopes of a successful return (cf. 578–83, and the proof of her failure in 634–5), and in the third (400–7) she aims to evoke love of fatherland, preparing for 571–7.[1] Joc.'s use of gnomes serves in part to prepare the audience for her intellectual argumentation in the agon; Pol.'s gives a succinct view of the assumptions about independence, wealth, and nobility which are crucial to his insistence on pressing his claim. Moreover, the theme of exile has a wider relevance in the play (to Cadmus (see on 638ff.), to Menoeceus, to Oedipus). The ancient criticism (Σ388 οὐκ ἐν δέοντι δὲ γνωμολογεῖ τοιούτων κακῶν περιεστώτων τὴν πόλιν. τοιοῦτος δὲ πολλαχοῦ ὁ Εὐριπίδης) is typical of negative comments in the scholia (cf. 269n., 395n.) and is not justified. Nevertheless, as usual, the scholiasts' 'authority' strongly influenced early modern critics of the play (e.g. Hermann, *praefatio* xv), some of whom believed the passage could be partially excused because the audience was meant to recognize the exiled Alcibiades behind the mask of Pol. This

---

[1] For a similar division, but different analysis of the motivation of the dialogue, see Schwinge, *Stichomythie* 202–10.

view originated with H. Zirndorfer in *de chronologia fabularum Euripidearum* (Marburg 1839) and was naturally espoused by Goossens and Delebecque; for refutation see in general Zuntz, 'Contemporary Politics', and *Political Plays*, and, for this particular case, J. de Romilly, 'Les Phéniciennes', esp. 29–31.

389 ἔργωι . . . λόγωι this antithesis, found in *Prom.* 336 (cf. 1080), *Alc.* 339, and frequently elsewhere in Eur. and in Thuc., usually implies criticism of λόγος as insubstantial, insincere, or false (499–502n.), but here we have a rather colourless contrast ('worse in fact than people say it is').

390 δυσχερές for the concurrence of δυστυχ- with δυσχερ- in the mss cf. *Hipp.* 484, *Tro.* 357, *Or.* 606 with Diggle, *Textual Trad. Or.* 52, 86; note also the variant δυσμεν- in Soph. *El.* 929. For the question itself, cf. *Med.* 733 ἢ τί σοι τὸ δυσχερές;

391–5 the vexation cited as first and greatest by Pol. is a slavish sense of dependency on persons who are not really, in Pol.'s view, his superiors. The same attitude is prominent in the statement with which Pol. concludes this dialogue with Joc., 438–42, although here the emphasis is on free speech and independent judgment, there on wealth. For the connection between wealth and free speech, see 438–42n. παρρησία is one mark of freedom vs. slavery, of self-respect vs. crippling shame (Democritus B 226 οἰκήιον ἐλευθερίης παρρησίη; Alexis fr. 150 K–A, Plato *Rep.* 557b4–5). It was a trait on which the Athenian democracy prided itself (Demades fr. 115 de Falco τοῦ τῶν Ἀθηναίων ὀνόματος ἀξίαν παρρησίαν; Moschion *TrGF* 97 F 4 τὴν . . . ἐντεθραμμένην ἀστοῖς Ἀθάνας τῆι τε Θησέως πόλει . . . παρρησίαν), and in Eur. even 'aristocratic' characters view it as part of the good life (*Hipp.* 422, *Ion* 672–5, esp. τό γε στόμα δοῦλον πέπαται κοὐκ ἔχει παρρησίαν), although one can also see in *Or.* 905 (θορύβωι τε πίσυνος κἀμαθεῖ παρρησίαι) a sign of the backlash against it as affording prominence to base speakers (e.g. [Xen.] *AthPol.* 1.6, Arist. *Frogs* 948–55, Isocr. 8.14).

391 οὐκ ἔχει in asyndeton after μέγιστον, as in the figure illustrated in 999n. οὐκ ἔχειν (Arnaldus) had a brief vogue (Valck. to Porson), but οὐ for μή with this infinitive would be extraordinary. The subject of ἔχει could be 'the state of exile' (following from αὐτοῦ in 390) or 'an exile', varying from the generalizing plural φυγάσιν.

393–4 393 presents, as it were, the other side of the coin of not having the παρρησία to speak one's own mind; hence asyndeton is proper, and Markland's and Paley's proposals to introduce a conjunction are not needed. On the other hand, Joc., reacting sympathetically to each statement, treats the aspects separately (καὶ τοῦτο).[1]

---

[1] West (1990) favours Czwalina's deletion of 393–4, but gives no reason, and I have not been able to see Czwalina's discussion.

τῶν κρατούντων τῶν πολιτῶν probably derives from contamination with a version of the line current independently as a maxim, modified to make a point with an anti-democratic political bent.

ἀμαθίας ἀμαθία (with ἀμαθής), a favourite word of Eur., stems from the intellectual vocabulary of the mid and late fifth century (Heraclitus, Democritus, Gorgias (three times in his *Helen*), *Dissoi Logoi*, Thuc., Hippocratic corpus, Arist. *Frogs* 1109, Soph. fr. 924, etc.). The pejorative tinge of ἀμαθής/ἀμαθία derives from the implied (rationalistic and optimistic) belief that the ignorance is culpable and could have been cured by effort. Cf. Bond on *Her.* 347, Denniston on *El.* 294-6. The plural (not attested again until Diodorus and later prose) means, as often with an abstract noun, 'displays of, instances of' the quality. Cf. 584n., 763, 874.

συνασοφεῖν hapax in extant Greek, surely coined for this passage (to create a rhetorical figure with τοῖς μὴ σοφοῖς); it is a regular denominative formation[1] from ἄσοφος (Pindar *O.* 3.45, Theognis 370, *El.* 1302, Xen. *Mem.* 3.9.4; possibly ἀσοφία *Or.* 491 – cf. Willink), like ξυναδικέω (Thuc. 1.37.4, etc.) or συνασεβέω (Antiphon *Tetr.* 3.1.3) or συνατυχέω (Lycurgus *Leocrat.* 131), except that the simplex verb is not found and ἄσοφος is a less common adj. Cf. also Alcaeus' ἀσυννέτημμι. There is no reason to insist on a more precise analogy (namely, monosyllabic adjectival roots forming adjs. X-ος, ἀ-X-ος, and verb ἀ-X-έω), as Valckenaer did in doubting the word; but an analogous formation does exist if ἀδηλοῦμεν, 'we are uncertain, ignorant' in *OC* 35 is from ἀδηλέω.[2]

395 ἀλλ' εἰς τὸ κέρδος 'but with one's eye fixed on profit', 'in order to attain profit' (sc. the profit of sustenance in exile);[3] for this sense of εἰς, cf. *El.* 1073 ἐς κάλλος ἀσκεῖ, *Hipp.* 277 ἀσιτεῖ γ' εἰς ἀπόστασιν βίου, *Her.* 869 ταῦρος ὡς ἐς ἐμβολήν, *Su.* 1057, *Tro.* 485. This is far more to the point in

---

[1] Unfortunately, this verb escaped the notice of H. von der Pfordten, *Zur Geschichte der griechischen Denominativa* (Leipzig 1886) and of L. Sütterlin, *Zur Geschichte der Verba Denominativa im Griechischen. Erster Teil: Die Verba Denominativa auf -άω, -έω, -όω* (Strassburg 1891).

[2] Cf. Philo *de somniis* 2.17 ἀδηλοῦντος καὶ ἐνδοιάζοντος, Didymus Caecus *comm. in Eccl.* pt. 3, p. 173 Kramer τοῖς ⟨ἀ⟩δηλοῦσιν; the passive forms meaning 'be obscure, invisible' are generally indistinguishable between ἀδηλέω and ἀδηλόω (Philo and Sextus Emp. both use forms of ἀδηλούμενος frequently, but the former also has ἀδηλοῦσθαι at *de conf. ling.* 119, the later ἀδηλεῖσθαι at *adv. math.* 11.233, alibi); nor is Hipp. *mul. affect.* 1.2 ἀδηλεύμενα decisive (cf. K–B I.212, II.150).

[3] Craik correctly notes that 391–4 have a general force and are not meant to apply specifically to Pol.'s relationship with Adrastus; yet she wrongly glosses κέρδος as securing military help.

this context than ὅπου τὸ κέρδος (testimonia), which is a generalizing gnomologic corruption (*Text. Trad.* 71–2).

The criticism in Σ οὐκ ἀξιόχρεως ἥρωος ὁ λόγος is misconceived. Eur. is not concerned to portray a 'hero' but to show the strain between Pol.'s aristocratic beliefs and the situation in which he has found himself. 269n. and 388–407n. discuss similar carping, and note that Pol.'s statements are also attacked in Σ402 (πῶς δὲ ταῦτά φησιν, ὅπου γε ὑπὸ τῶν φίλων εἰς τὴν πατρίδα κατάγεται; correctly refuted in the following comments) and Σ405 (ἐψεύσατο· πρῶτον γὰρ διὰ τὸν χρησμὸν ὁμολογουμένως ὁ Ἄδραστος, ἔπειτα δὲ καὶ διὰ τὸ γένος συνώικισεν αὐτῶι τὴν θυγατέρα Ἀργείαν. οὐκ ἂν γὰρ οὐδὲ ὁ Ἀπόλλων τὸν τυχόντα ἔλεγεν ἑλέσθαι: but Pol. is speaking of the time before his marriage, and the relevance of his noble birth to the marriage and oracle is pure invention). Such criticisms may be an indirect reflection of the use of Pol. as a negative example by the philosophical schools which attacked conventional Greek beliefs about the importance of one's homeland and the misery of separation from it. From this genre of περὶ φυγῆς literature we have Stobaeus' excerpts from the Cynic Teles and the Stoic Musonius (30.40.8–9) as well as Dio Chrys. *or.* 12, Favorinus, and Plutarch (*Mor.* 599–607): all except Dio quote from *Phoen.*, and Dio perhaps alludes to the situation of Pol. at 12.6.

396 for the proverbial notion expressed here and for related locutions see Fraenkel on *Ag.* 1668 οἶδ' ἐγὼ φεύγοντας ἄνδρας ἐλπίδας σιτουμένους. For the shape of the line, cf. Men. *sent.* 51 αἱ δ' ἐλπίδες βόσκουσι τοὺς κενοὺς βροτῶν.

397 καλοῖς βλέπ. ὄμμασιν the language of erotic attraction (Ibycus 287 *PMGF*, Pindar *N.* 8.2, Barrett on *Hipp.* 525–6, 530–4).

βλέπουσαί γ' Hermann's restoration, perhaps still read by one of the scholiasts, is necessary: the elliptic participle with γε (cf. Denniston, *GP²* 133–4) conveys Pol.'s assent and prepares for the adversative clause μέλλουσι δέ. 398–9 indicate that Pol. does assent, though he recognizes one unsatisfactory aspect of hope. Indicative βλέπουσι (with γ' doing duty – improbably – for corrective μὲν οὖν or γοῦν?) would express a more negative attitude toward hope and render 398 superfluous.

398 διεσάφησ' a distinctly prosaic, even bookish, verb, found in Plato and subsequent philosophers, historians, and scholiasts, but absent in Attic oratory and from all poetry except here and Machon 9.81 (which scarcely counts as poetry). Despite this, no one has ever suspected the verse (cf. 52n.), and only Scaliger emended (to ghost-word διεσάφισ', based on an itacistic error in a ms of 2 Maccabees 1.21).

κενάς a conventional epithet of hopes from Hesiod to the orators and beyond, e.g., Hes. *Op.* 498, Simonides 542.22 *PMG*, Pindar *N.* 8.45, *Pers.* 804, Soph. *El.* 1460, *Aj.* 478, Isocr. 8.75, Dem. *proem.* 35.4. For κενός applied instead to the men who are deluded by hope, cf. Men. *sent.* 51 (quoted 396n.).

399 Ἀφροδίτην τιν' ἡδεῖαν κακῶν Pol. is explaining why the delays which prove hope to be delusive have not caused him to abandon his hopes. The language of 397 has already alluded to the erotic seduction exerted by hope, so the most probable interpretation of this unusual phrase is 'hopes have (contain, afford) a certain sweet compulsive desire for evils', 'hopes compel one to be pleasantly in love with evils'. In this case, Ἀφροδίτη is by metonymy 'a compulsive longing', just as in *IA* 1264–5 μέμηνε δ' Ἀφροδίτη τις Ἑλλήνων στρατῶι πλεῖν, and κακῶν, in an oxymoronic juxtaposition with ἡδεῖαν, is a normal objective gen., referring not to the evils of exile but to the evils which attend upon delusive hope: cf. the traditional association of man's delusive hopes with 'being in love with evils' (Semonides 1.23 West) or 'being in love with the impossible, or the absent' (ἀμηχάνων, ἀπράκτων, ἀτελέστων, ἀπόντων ἐρᾶν vel sim., collected in Young, 116–20). This sense is perhaps intended by LSJ's 'enjoyment' placed under the same heading as 'vehement longing' and by translations like 'eine süsser Reiz für das Unglück' (Klotz–Wecklein) or 'ein süsser Reiz des Unglücks' (Wecklein). But from the scholiasts on, most commentators have not been very clear about the exact sense of the line, either providing vague paraphrases or mixing separate possibilities. At least two other readings of the transmitted text can be contemplated. With Ἀφροδίτη in the sense 'charm, attractiveness' (cf. *venustas*; *Ag.* 419 ἔρρει πᾶσ' Ἀφροδίτα, later prose – LSJ II.3) and κακῶν as a genitive of connection or content, there is still a strong oxymoron and the sense is 'a certain sweet seductive charm of ⟨exerted by, consisting of, attached to?⟩ evils' (sc. the evils of delusive hope). Or if Ἀφροδίτη can be given a more pregnant sense, 'seductive charm *that soothes*', then κακῶν, 'the evils of exile', can be quasi-objective gen., on the analogy of *Hom.h.* 16.4 θελκτῆρ' ὀδυνάων, *Choe.* 670 πόνων θελκτηρία, *Hipp.* 509–10 φίλτρα ... θελκτήρια ἔρωτος, or like the gen. with πόρος or μηχανή (cf. Barrett on *Hipp.* 716 εὕρημα τῆσδε συμφορᾶς). This view is favoured by e.g. Hartung, Geel, and apparently Pearson (but his translation 'charm in misfortune' is like the vague and wishful ἐν κακοῖς of Σ). But there seems to be no justification for reading the connotation 'soothing, lightening, curing' into Ἀφροδίτη,[1] and this reading also renders ἡδεῖαν less pointed, even superfluous. The variant θεόν for κακῶν is possibly a sign that the end of the line was

---

[1] By contrast, the phrase μοῦσα ἀμηχανέων μελεδώνων in *Hom.h.Herm.* 447 alludes to the topos of the enchanting power of poetry to bring forgetfulness of pains and troubles.

damaged and κακῶν not original (so formerly Nauck; Musgrave's νόσον is not much help), but more probably it is an intrusive gloss prompted by the difficulty of the line and the odd use of Ἀφροδίτη. If one wants to obtain a sense like Geel's *mali lenimentum*, then the corruption is probably in ἡδεῖαν: Herwerden's ἴασιν (1875) seems too strong in sense (Soph. uses the word, Eur. does not elsewhere); Jackson's εὐδίαν is clever, but I am not convinced by the sense 'a certain charm, ⟨which is or which produces⟩ a tranquil freedom from one's trouble'.

401 note the double *variatio* ποτὲ μὲν … εἶτ' and εἶχον … εἶχον ἄν (there is no compelling reason to retroject ἄν to accompany the earlier verb). For the 'iterative' past potential indicative, cf. K–G I.211; Moorhouse, *Syntax Soph.* 189, 194; R. C. Seaton, *CR* 3 (1889) 343–5; the construction, not common in general (and perhaps 'colloquial': Stevens, *Colloquial Expr.* 60), is rare in tragedy, found only here in Eur. and in Soph. only in *Phil.* (289–97 (three times), 443, 701–2). Not recognizing this use of the ind. with ἄν, Reiske, Valck., and others changed to αὖ.

403 εὖ πρᾶσσε 'always have good fortune' (sc. if you want friends to pay attention to you); not 'good luck to you' (sc. who are so naive as to think my father's friends helped me), as suggested by Valckenaer and apparently still assumed by Pearson, who calls the imperative 'concessive' ('go ahead and …', like βλάπτεσθ' in *Hcld.* 264).

δ' is either adversative (with the understood condition 'if you want friends …') or equivalent to γάρ (86n.). Explanatory asyndeton (which probably arose by separate accidents in Ab and Πᵃ a.c.) is not impossible (for interpolation of δ' cf. 405 and 456).

οὐδέν (sc. ἐστι), 'amounts to nothing', so here 'is no help'; cf. *Andr.* 50 παιδί τ' οὐδέν ἐστ' [sc. the absent Neoptolemus], *Her.* 314 νῦν δ' οὐδέν ἐσμεν, fr. 393 γνώμης γὰρ οὐδὲν ἀρετὴ μονουμένη. Cf. 442n., 598n., and for the whole phrase *Hel.* 1421 τὰ τῶν θανόντων οὐδέν.

ἤν τις δυστυχῇ τις in this position, it is now generally conceded, does not violate Porson's bridge (885n.). There is no reason to prefer the indefinite second person τι δυστυχῆις, proposed by Elmsley (not for sense, but to satisfy Porson's bridge) and ill attested in the indirect tradition, where it may have arisen under the influence of εὖ πρᾶσσε (which is not, however, indefinite, but addressed to Joc.). Cf. 407n. For the sentiment, cf. Theognis 209 and *Her.* 55–9 with Bond's note on 57–9.

404 μέγαν restored by Wecklein; proleptic adj. after αἴρω, as *Hcld.* 321–2 σ' … ὑψηλὸν ἀρῶ, *Med.* 1297 πτηνὸν ἆραι σῶμ', *Hel.* 606 ἀρθεῖσ' ἄφαντος, Andoc. 3.7 ὑψηλὸν ἦρε. εἰς ὕψος needs no adj.: cf. fr. 1040.1 πρὸς ὕψος ἡρμένον τινά, *OT* 914 ὑψοῦ … αἴρει θυμόν.

405 ἔβοσκέ rounds off the treatment of physical sustenance begun in 400 (ἐβόσκου); the verb was also used to begin the preceding theme of psychological support (396). βόσκω, properly used of feeding animals, is a poetic synonym of τρέφω, often transferred to human objects with no pejorative tinge (*Od.* 11.365, *Choe.* 27, *Trach.* 144, *OT* 1425, etc.). In some uses βόσκω emphasizes more than τρέφω the weakness or dependency of the object in relation to the power or generosity of the subject; so here Pol. may be emphasizing pathetically the dependency of his position; but, esp. after 396 and 400, it is excessive to see 'a certain degree of contempt' (Pearson) in this use. Cf. Neil on *Knights* 256, who presses too far the 'irksomeness or contempt' of βόσκω applied to human objects and is cited too concisely by Pearson.

406 πατρίς closes the ring begun at 388, and signals the close of the ethical, gnomological half of the stichomythia.

407 ὀνομάσαι here simply 'express in words', a recherché synonym of εἰπεῖν, as in *OC* 293–4 λόγοισι γὰρ οὐκ ὠνόμασται [no different from εἴρηται] βραχέσι. Cf. 502n.

δύναι' ἄν the corruption to δύναιμ' ἄν perhaps results from failure to recognize the presence of elision: also *Prom.* 758 ἥδοι' ἄν (ἥδοιμ' ἄν in most mss), *Andr.* 351 (M); cf. fr. 362.2. The second person here is specifically Joc., but in context the second person is generalizing, verging on the indefinite (cf. 403 εὖ πρᾶσσε followed by τις with 3rd pers.). This may be compared to the 'indefinite' second person with verbs of perception, as in *Andr.* 1135 εἶδες ἄν (cf. Schwyzer II.244).

408–26 the second half of the stichomythia (cf. 388–407n.) has a basically narrative function; the story, though broken up, is told in chronological sequence (408–14n.), and the form is dramatically justified by the co-operative and sympathetic contributions made by Joc.

408–14 for a detailed defence of the transmitted order of the lines against Jacobs' transposition of 413–14 to precede 409, see *Contact and Discontinuity* 48–51. Pol. answers the question 'How did you go to Argos?' by starting *ab ovo*, with the earliest event, and moving forward in chronological order, with co-operative contributions from Joc. In Jacobs' order, Pol.'s introduction of ὁ δαίμων in 413 is abrupt, and Joc.'s acceptance of the explanation in 414 (σοφὸς γὰρ ὁ θεός) is unmotivated if she has not yet heard that an oracle is involved. The contrast in 413 between Pol.'s own lack of knowledge and the action of the god works better when the emphatic σοί of 412 immediately precedes. One may also wonder whether οὐκ οἶδα in 413 could be a proper response to 408 as a whole or to τίν' ἐπίνοιαν ἔσχεθες; in particular: it would be more natural to say 'I had no fixed intention'.

408 ἐπίνοιαν 'intention, purpose', as in *Med.* 760 (but 'second thoughts' in *Ant.* 389, the only other tragic instance). The word's intellectual tinge is at home in late fifth-century prose and Aristophanes (cf. ἐπινοέω, in tragedy only at *Rhes.* 195).

410 most of the line is 'filler', commonly used in reply to an interlocutor who has begun a gradual answer or statement *ab ovo* in stichomythia; cf. τί τοῦτ' ἔλεξας; *Hel.* 1037, *IA* 1010 (in lyric antilabe *Ion* 1478), οὐκ ἔχω μαθεῖν *Hec.* 761. Such fillers (and the frustration they convey) are typically used at the very start of the process of gradual answering – another point against Jacobs' transposition.

411 κάπρωι λέοντί θ' neither here nor in the similar stichomythic narrative of *Su.* 131–46 is there any hint of which hero corresponds to which animal, and in both places Adrastus recognizes the relevance of the oracle because of the quarrelling between Pol. and Tydeus, not because of any emblems they wear. The lacunose lyric description in *Hyps.* fr. 8/9 mentions fighting and refers to marriage to beasts without specification. No emblems or animal skins appear in the two illustrations of Tydeus and Pol. which are extant (*LIMC* I:2.172 no. 2, 350 B.C.: Adrastus intervenes upon fierce fighting; I:1.723, 530 B.C.: the youths seated on floor, wearing identical cloaks, before Adrastus on *kline*). Lions and boars are two notably fierce creatures exploited in legend and in epic similes (so too Et. and Pol. fight like boars at 1380–1 and like lions at 1573), and this may be the whole reason why the oracle, in the (epic?) version known to or preferred by Eur., used these metaphors. Σ and other mythographic sources (cf. Fontenrose, *The Delphic Oracle* 96 n. 9, 365–6; Bond on *Hyps.* fr. 8/9) provide various speculations that seem to be attempts to embellish the oracle by inference, suggesting that they knew no details from any early literary source: either the two have taken dedicated lion- and boar-hides from a shrine (for warmth or bedding), or they wear skins or bear shield-symbols that reflect their respective origins, the Calydonian boar for Tydeus (but see 1120n. for Tydeus' lion-skin) vs. the lion for Pol. in allusion either to the lion slain by Theban Heracles or to the lion-faced Sphinx. The later sources also disagree as to whether they fight or simply arrive and are recognized as the right bridegrooms. The hexameter oracle cited by Mnaseas fr. 48, FHG 3.157 (apud Σ) implies a shrine (ἐξ ἱεροῖο) out of which the pair is seen (peacefully) approaching Adrastus' house, but in Eur. they come directly to his porch and Adrastus becomes aware of them because of the fight.

412 'What part did *you* have in the beasts named?' or 'What did the beasts named in the oracle have to do with *you*?' Joc., following up her inquiry about Pol.'s intentions, wonders whether Pol. deliberately went to Argos because he recognized something in himself that would satisfy the oracle.

413 οὐκ οἶδ' this perhaps conveys not only Pol.'s lack of intention, but also a broader blindness to the quarrelsomeness of his own nature and the force of the pattern being worked out in accordance with Apollo's prediction to Laius and the curse of Oedipus. Cf. 23n., 49n.

ὁ δαίμων in the transmitted position of the lines, probably specifically Apollo (cf. *Ion* 1353 ὁ δαίμων = Λοξίας 1347) rather than 'the spirit who controls my fate'; with Jacobs' transposition the later meaning is necessary. Joc.'s ὁ θεός in the next line will be accordingly either Apollo himself (and σοφός will be especially apposite) or 'god' as divine providence, with σοφός implying simply that 'god works in mysterious and cunning ways' (but such a reaction is less well motivated: 408-14n.).

416 ματεύων 36n.

ἧι the only correct change made by Ioannes Gregoropulus in preparing the Aldine text of *Phoen.* (for his errors see Teubner *praef.* §15). Pol.'s answer in 417 (which would have to be less vague than ἦν ταῦτα if an alternative question preceded), the renewed reference to bedding in 421, and the fact that Pol.'s lack of intention has already been noted all show that ἤ cannot stand. ἧι here has its normal meaning 'in the way in which' (sc. a wandering exile is accustomed to do). But the ellipsis of a verb other than ἐστι seems unparalleled with ἧι, though it is common with ὡς. For the easier ellipsis of ἐστι cf. fr. 743.2 (if the sentence is complete) γνῶναι τὸν ἐχθρὸν ἧι [Gesner: εἰ codd. Stob.] μάλισθ' ἁλώσιμος, Xenophon's use of ἧι with superlatives, and Aristotle's use of it in the philosophical sense *qua*.

417 κᾆτά γ' the γε (Denniston, *GP*² 157) here stresses the whole addition made by καί, not just the intervening word; for its use after the assent of ἦν ταῦτα, compare its use in stichomythic answers where the answerer implicitly confirms the questioner's surmise and adds a further point (423 below, *Andr.* 1063, *Cycl.* 178, *Hec.* 993, *Hel.* 106, etc.). Nauck's κᾆτ' ἐπῆλθεν is quite unnecessary. The variant κᾆτα δ' (Π⁶ and *recc.*) is to be rejected: in drama καὶ ... δέ combines connective δέ and adverbial καί, with the latter providing special emphasis to the word that follows (often a personal pronoun); εἶτα here does not need or deserve such weight (contrast *Peace* 632, where κᾆτα δ' (often emended to κἀνθάδ') follows on κᾆτα in 619 and 625 after an intervening comment). For the corruption, cf. *Wealth* 838.

ἄλλος αὖ an intensifying pleonasm, not unlike αὖθις αὖ et sim. or ordinals with αὖ (e.g., *Su.* 881, fr. 382.8); cf. ἄλλος αὖ *Ag.* 1280, *Thesm.* 664, χἄτερ' αὖ *Hyps.* fr. 60.91 (sed v.l.), ἕτερος αὖ in Aristophanes.

418 ὡς ἄρ' ... ἦν best taken, with Wecklein, as a causal clause, explaining the tone of sympathy in the question τίς οὗτος; (Hermann: *satis mira est haec Iocastae miseratio hominis ignoti*). ἄρα conveys the lively realization 'I see this from what you have said about the ills of exile'; cf. the few tragic exx. given by Denniston, GP^2 35–6, under ἄρα ii. (1) and (2). The collocation of ὡς and ἄρα is thus coincidental, unrelated to the dissociating ὡς ἄρα of prose, found uniquely in *Her.* 758. Some have preferred to interpret as an exclamation, but in the cited parallels *Knights* 1170 ὡς μέγαν ἄρ' εἶχες ὦ πότνια τὸν δάκτυλον and *Acharn.* 990 ὡς καλὸν ἔχουσα τὸ πρόσωπον ἄρ' ἐλάνθανες we have idiomatic ἄρα with the imperfect expressing sudden realization of a fact that has always been true.

420 τί θηρσὶν ὑμᾶς δῆτ' normal inferential δῆτα in a question, post-poned (Denniston, GP^2 270–1), marking the return to explanation of the oracle. The majority reading τί θηρσὶ δ' ὑμᾶς δῆτ' involves an extremely rare combination of δέ and δῆτα and would mean 'and why did he liken *you* . . .', with δῆτα, like δή, emphasizing only the preceding word (the only tragic parallel seems to be *Se.* 813 αὐτὸς δ' ἀναλοῖ δῆτα).

423 κἄδωκέ γ' 417n. The necessary emendation was made by Schaefer (Diggle (1990a)) before Kirchhoff.

δύο δυοῖν on the tendency of numerals and other quantity-words to be juxtaposed, cf. 38n. For the verbal play with the two cases cf. *Hec.* 45, *Ant.* 13 (reinforced in 14 by μιᾶι . . . διπλῆι), *Phaedo* 71a13, c7, *Gorg.* 481d3, *Phileb.* 53d12.

424 τοῖς γάμοις instrumental dative of specification or respect, as fr. 143 χρήμασιν γὰρ εὐτυχῶ, ταῖς συμφοραῖσιν δ', ὡς ὁρᾶις, οὐκ εὐτυχῶ, *IT* 850, fr. 285.12 and 20, perhaps *Ion* 1426 (μόνωι τῶιδ' L: μόνον τόδ' Usener); synonymous with ἐν + dat. (fr. 1056 οὐ πάντες οὔτε δυστυχοῦσιν ἐν γάμοις οὔτ' εὐτυχοῦσι) or εἰς + acc. (*Ion* 567, *Or.* 542).

425 εἰς τόδ' ἡμέρας 'up to the present moment' (Barrett on *Hipp.* 1003); here as in 1085 below and *Alc.* 9 the phrase leaves an opening for a change in the foreseen or unforeseen future (no such implication in *Hipp.* 1003 or *OC* 1138).

426–32 Eur. reduces this part of the background-story to a bare minimum: Adrastus' oath and the χάρις of the Argive chiefs explain the expedition, and no allusion is made to the deceit used to force Amphiaraus' participation or the bad omens on the journey, elements exploited by Aesch. in *Septem* and Eur. himself in *Su.* and *Hyps.*, and further developed by Soph. in *OC*. Cf. 431–2n.

[428] the verse is to be deleted as not merely superfluous, but also intrusive (between τόδε and κατάξειν) and feeble (the filler γάρ-clause is less explicit than what it allegedly explains). The sense of σύγγαμος, however, should not be deemed objectionable: its meaning could be specified by the context (137n.) as 'is one who shares marriage' (sc. by the same oracle, to one of two sisters). The interpolation may be due to a reader who filled out a glossing proper name (cf. R. Merkelbach, 'Interpolierte Eigennamen', *ZPE* 1 (1967) 100–2). If actors were involved, the addition would make sense only if the preceding lines (e.g. 408–25) were cut in performance (so Fraenkel apud Page, *Actors' Interp.* 27). Friedrich argued that a number of interpolated passages in the play should be viewed as additions made to compensate for cuts, but this is one of only two passages in the play where I find such a hypothesis remotely attractive (141–4n.). In the Homeric scholia the charge of being περιττόν is connected to athetesis (e.g. Σ *Il.* 1.96, 8.528), but since the Homeric texts had a special problem of textual variation (different in kind and in degree from what was found in tragic texts), I do not think it safe to assume that wherever the Euripides scholia judge a verse περιττόν (here, Σ973 referring to 974, Σ *Med.* 87 and Σ *Tro.* 863) there was in fact uneven attestation of the verse in the copies known to ancient scholars (Reeve, 'Interp.' 249–50, argues from the Homeric case that one may perhaps make such an inference when athetesis is mentioned). Perhaps, however, in three of these cases a proposal to delete (and not just a carping criticism of Eur.'s style) was involved, but has been obscured in the truncation of the scholia (note the hanging γάρ in Σ428 and the other problems which *Tro.* 862–3 raise). I retain 974 (see n.).

429 πρόσθεν δ' ἐμέ   the promise to restore both sons-in-law is recorded also in Apollodorus, Diodorus Siculus, and Statius *Theb.* 2.199–200, but no one offers a reason for restoring Pol. first, except Σ, which with characteristic *horror vacui* says that Pol. was first because he married the elder daughter.

430 Δαναῶν καὶ Μυκηναίων   the terms are both synonyms for Ἀργείων; in *Phoen., Or., Hyps., Su.,* and fr. 305 (*Bellerophon*) Δαναοί and Δαναΐδαι are 'the inhabitants of Argos', whereas in the Trojan War plays *Hec., Tro., IT, IA* these terms refer to 'the (assembled) Greeks', as does Δαναοί in Soph. and Aesch. The force of using the two terms side by side is uncertain, unless with both high-style synonyms Pol. is magnifying their worth.

ἄκροι   equivalent to ἄριστοι or ἀριστῆς, as in 1245 below, *Su.* 118, fr. 703.1 (*Telephus*).

431–2 λυπρὰν χάριν ἀναγκαίαν δέ μοι διδόντες   the second adj. explains that Pol. must accept the oxymoronic 'favour which brings pain ⟨to me⟩', and the following clauses (432–4) explicate the two adjs. in parallel order. Pol.'s pain at attacking his fatherland (cf. 437, 629) is consonant with his expressions of love for his country (358–9, 366–70, 406–7), but his sense that he has been the passive victim of injustice and that his status has been intolerably reduced (cf. 395, 405, 442, 492–3, 607–13, 627–30) produces a situation of ἀνάγκη: he cannot see (or cannot admit to others that he can see) any alternative to pressing his claim. Wecklein was wrong

268

to interpret 'a favour painful to them, but forced on them ⟨by Adrastus⟩', assuming unwillingness in the Argives (426–32n.).

δέ μοι I prefer the enclitic because ἀναγκαίαν bears more emphasis than 'to me' and the pronoun is primarily the ind. obj. of διδόντες or ἀπὸ κοινοῦ the ind. obj. and dat. of reference with *both* adjs. Cf. *Hel.* 1006 (δέ μοι Matthiae: δ' ἐμοί L), *Alc.* 433, *Hec.* 982, and contrast 1314 below and passages like *Med.* 1037, *Cycl.* 148. If there is a pause before and after ἀναγκαίαν δ', however, ἐμοί will be necessary.

433 θεούς the traditional nature of Pol.'s values is suggested by the number of times he invokes and refers to the gods (cf. 367, 413, 481, 491, 604–8, 626, 631–2, 634); Et. refers to the gods only in mocking repartee (604–8) and in his prayer to the abstraction Eulabeia (782–3n.), though there is a reported prayer in 1372–5.

ἐπώμοσ' is instantaneous aorist (1561n.), like ἀπώμοσ' in *Cycl.* 266, *Phil.* 1289, κατώμοσα in *Birds* 630.

433–4 ἀκουσίως ... ἑκοῦσιν for the contrast cf. *OC* 985–7 ἀλλ' ἐν γὰρ οὖν ἔξοιδα, σὲ μὲν ἑκόντ' ἐμὲ κεινήν τε ταῦτα δυσστομεῖν· ἐγὼ δέ νιν ἄκων τ' ἔγημα, φθέγγομαί τ' ἄκων τάδε; *Trach.* 198–9 οὕτως ἐκεῖνος οὐχ ἑκών, ἑκοῦσι δὲ ξύνεστιν. More common are expressions underlining mutual unwillingness or willingness, such as *Cycl.* 257–8 κἀδίδου πιεῖν λαβὼν ἑκὼν ἑκοῦσι, *Hipp.* 319 φίλος μ' ἀπόλλυσ' οὐχ ἑκοῦσαν οὐχ ἑκών, fr. 68.2, *Ant.* 276 πάρειμι δ' ἄκων οὐχ ἑκοῦσιν, *Prom.* 218 ἑκόνθ' ἑκόντι Ζηνὶ συμπαραστατεῖν, *Prom.* 19 (cf. Aesch. *Su.* 227). See 630n. for another rhetorical play with ἑκών.

τοῖς φιλτάτοις 'my nearest kin', that is, Et. (generalizing plural); Pol.'s traditional values are marked by his frequent use of kinship-words, even of his brother (also 436, 1446). Because of the accompanying ἑκουσιν, I take φιλτάτοις as masc.; for neuter idiom τὰ φίλτατα see Page on *Med.* 16.

435 εἰς σὲ τείνει 'looks to you', almost 'depends on you'; cf. Hdt. 6.109.6 ταῦτα ... πάντα ἐς σὲ νῦν τείνει καὶ ἐκ σέο ἄρτηται; not a difficult use of the verb, but apparently unique in tragedy (*Hipp.* 797 is not quite the same: 'refers to, concerns'; cf. the curious phrase in *Rhes.* 875–6 ἐς σὲ τείνεται /γλῶσσ').

διάλυσις through the rest of this scene of attempted reconciliation Eur. echoes legal and diplomatic terminology: διάλυσις here (one of only two occurrences in tragedy: cf. fr. 502.6 of divorce), διαλλάξασαν 436, διαλλαγάς 443, 515 (also 701, [375]; elsewhere in this sense *Hcld.* 820, Aesch. fr. 132c.35, and often in Aristophanes and prose), διαλλάξεις 445, διαλλακτής 468 (hapax in classical poetry, cf. διαλλακτῆρι in *Septem* 908), σύμβασις 587 (cf. 85, ξυμβαῖμεν 590: Eur. is the only classical poet who uses the noun), βραβείας 450; cf. also 81 λύουσ', [375] δυσλύτους.

436 ὁμογενεῖς φίλους probably an intensifying redundancy ('kin of one blood': for the kinship theme, see Introd. I) rather than separate accusatives ('reconcile those of shared blood so that they become friends', as Pearson suggests). Nauck and F. W. Schmidt found the juncture strange and proposed the deletion of the line; now Π²² apparently lacks it, and the absence may be taken as supporting suspicion (291–2n.). I still find the urgency of the vocative attractive, and the complex διαλλάξασαν ... παῦσαι a more suitable explication of τῶνδε διάλυσις κακῶν than παῦσαι alone (or, in asyndeton, imperative παῦσον, suggested by Wecklein).

437 the appeal is made emphatic by the alliteration and assonance: π̲α̲ῦ̲σ̲α̲ι̲ π̲ό̲ν̲ω̲ν̲ σὲ κἀμὲ καὶ π̲ᾶ̲σ̲α̲ν̲ π̲ό̲λ̲ι̲ν̲.

σὲ κἀμέ Π²² now shows]εκἀμε[, that is, σὲ κἀμέ, as Elmsley proposed (on *OT* 376); and, as Haslam notes, with this reading there is no reason not to take σέ as emphatic (here used reflexively: K–G 1.559 Anm. 8). The mss reading με καὶ σέ couples unemphatic and emphatic pronouns in a way not exactly paralleled in K–G 1.557 (exx. with ἤ = 'than' or with unemphatic pronoun linked to noun; cf. also Diggle *CR* 32 (1982) 134 n. 4). Pearson's explanation ('the leading emphasis is on παῦσαι πόνων: σέ and πόλιν are not so much contrasted with με as added to it') is in principle possible, but no longer necessary.

438–42 an (implicitly) explanatory gnomic conclusion of the rhesis following the final appeal in 435–7; for the pattern of appeal and generalizing reflection cf. 84–7, 584–5, 951–9, *Or.* 448–55, *Hel.* 939–43, *Ion* 392–400, *Hec.* 369–78, 841–5; see also Friis Johansen, *General Reflection* 151–9 on 'conclusive reflections', esp. 155–6 on the tendency to close with a gnomic passage an episode or another important break in the action (such as we have here at the entrance of Eteocles). Pol. moves from longer gnome (elaborately introduced) to personal application and back to the gnome in a pithy alternative form. For a man of conventional aristocratic thinking, the status of high birth is inseparable from the wealth that maintains one's standing among peers and ability to act independently. Honour, power, and wealth were already Pol.'s main concerns in 391–405, and although Joc. made a distinction between the time before and after marriage in regard to simple physical sustenance (400–5), there was no such distinction for the complaints of 391–9. Pol.'s wider concerns for status are not relieved by his marriage to a princess, for it is a commonplace that a man dependent on his wife's wealth has a precarious status. On aristocratic notions of wealth see the excellent note of Denniston on *El.* 253; cf. Theognis 173–8, 619–20, 683–6 and *Erectheus* fr. 53.14–17 Austin ἔχειν δὲ [sc. χρήματα] πειρῶ· τοῦτο γὰρ τό τ' εὐγενὲς / καὶ τοὺς γάμους δίδωσι τοὺς πρώτους / ἔχειν. / ἐν τῶι πένεσθαι δ' ἐστὶν ἥ τ' ἀδοξία, / κἂν ἦι σοφός τις, ἥ τ' ἀτιμία / βίου, *El.* 37–8 χρημάτων δὲ δὴ / πένητες, ἔνθεν ηὑγένει' ἀπόλλυται. For freedom of speech guaranteed by *independent* wealth or reduced status consequent on lack of it, cf. *Andr.* 147–53, fr. 502.3–4 τὰ τῆς γυναικὸς γὰρ κρατοῦντ' ἐν δώμασιν / δουλοῖ τὸν ἄνδρα, κοὐκέτ' ἐστ' ἐλεύθερος, Anaxandrides fr. 53 K–A, Menander fr. 579 K–T, *sent.* 517. Racine *Thébaïde* Act 4, Scene 3 correctly explicates Pol.'s motivations in more detail. There is thus no inconsistency in Pol.'s insistence on his need for wealth despite his marriage; it is merely an index of the conventionality of his values and the fatal inflexibility of his self-image. Nor does this speech, for a Greek audience, 'unmask' Pol. as a hypocrite motivated by greed rather than a sense of justice, as some critics suggest. For Eur. the dramatic interest lies, as often, not in exposing a simple hypocrisy but in unfolding the complexity of human motivations and the tragic entrapment of a character in his or her own system of beliefs. (Naturally, Eur. himself and other Greeks could contemplate a separation of nobility of birth and behaviour from wealth. Eur. has made Pol.'s position conventional and understandable, but not unassailable. Pol. is a 'sympathetic' character, but not a saint or a sage.)

Misunderstanding of the traditional value-system, along with an over-simplified reading of Eur.'s characterization of Pol. as a sympathetic figure, has been the major impetus behind the proposal to delete 438–42 (esp. favoured by German scholars, from Hartung to Fraenkel, though Hartung recanted; most recently Mueller-Goldingen, who alleges that the final gnome in 442 goes significantly farther than 405 and that 'Die gegen den Wert der εὐγένεια gerichtete Spitze dürfte nicht im Sinne des Euripides sein.'). Prejudiced against the lines on these grounds, critics have sought other reasons for suspicion but found nothing that stands up to careful scrutiny. (1) The gnome of 442 is just as good an end to the speech (and scene) as 437. (2) The echo of 435–7 in 443–5 (435n.) is just as effective if the gnomic passage intervenes; indeed σὸν ἔργον, μῆτερ κτλ. in 444–5 seems unusually redundant if it follows closely on εἰς σὲ τείνει ... μῆτερ. (3) The different sentiment about wealth in 597 is a debating point in a frantic stichomythia and any 'contradiction' is just the sort tolerated by conventional wisdom. (4) The construction of μεθήκω is not difficult or suspicious (see below). (5) The threat or boast of μυρίαν is not much different from the grandiloquence of line 430. (6) Mueller-Goldingen adds the argument that after saying that he is entirely dependent on his mother, Pol. should not refer threateningly to his army. But Pol. has already alluded to his army in 430 and 434, and his dependence on his mother is limited to the prospect of getting what he wants without having to attack the city, without causing 'toils' to himself and the city. Throughout there is the assumption that if reconciliation fails, force will be used.

438 πάλαι μὲν οὖν ὑμνηθέν acknowledging the repetition of conventional wisdom: cf. *Aj.* 292–3 ὁ δ' εἶπε πρός με βαί', ἀεὶ δ' ὑμνούμενα· γύναι, γυναιξὶ κόσμον ἡ σιγὴ φέρει; fr. 25 φεῦ φεῦ, παλαιὸς αἶνος ὡς καλῶς ἔχει· γέροντες οὐδέν ἐσμεν ἄλλο πλὴν ψόφος κτλ.; fr. 285.1–2 ἐγὼ τὸ μὲν δὴ πανταχοῦ θρυλούμενον / κράτιστον εἶναι φημὶ μὴ φῦναι βροτῷ.

ὑμνηθέν may here (as in *Ajax* 292) carry a connotation of 'mentioned with approval, praise, or admiration', but is mainly 'uttered in (a ritual-like) repetition'; cf. *Sthen.* 12 Page [= prol. 18 von Arnim] ὑμνεῖ τὸν αὐτὸν μῦθον and Plato's frequent use of the verb (LSJ s.v. II).

439–40 τὰ χρήματ' κτλ. the form of the statement suggests that the maxim was intended as an answer to a question like 'What is the best thing, most valuable thing for man?' – a traditional way of elucidating values (and debating against other possible answers). Cf. in particular Soph. fr. 354, where the speaker says (4–5) κἄστι πρὸς τὰ χρήματα / θνητοῖσι τἄλλα δεύτερ', rejecting the view of those who praise health as most important. Eur.'s couplet is a rephrasing of Theognis 717–18 ἀλλὰ χρὴ πάντας γνώμην ταύτην καταθέσθαι, / ὡς πλοῦτος πλείστην πᾶσιν ἔχει δύναμιν, perhaps incorporating an echo of the famous slogan χρήματα χρήματ' ἀνήρ (Pindar *I.* 2.11), associated with the (?) Argive sage Aristodamus (on a visit to Sparta?: cf. Alcaeus fr. 360 L–P, who finishes the line with πένιχρος δ' οὐδ' εἷς πέλετ' ἔσλος οὐδὲ τίμιος). Cf. also Menander *sent.* 612 ὅπλον μέγιστον ἐν βροτοῖς τὰ χρήματα, *sent.* 181 δύναμις πέφυκε τοῖς βροτοῖς τὰ χρήματα, Soph. fr. 88 τὰ χρήματ' ἀνθρώποισιν εὑρίσκει φίλους κτλ., Eur. fr. 642 [= ?Polyidus *TrGF* 78 F 2] οὐ γὰρ παρὰ κρατῆρα καὶ θοινὴν μόνον / τὰ χρήματ' ἀνθρώποισιν ἡδονὰς ἔχει, / ἀλλ' ἐν κακοῖσι δύναμιν οὐ μικρὰν φέρει.

For the repetition of ἀνθρώποισ(ι) in successive lines, cf. *Hipp.* 615–16 (separate speakers), *Aj.* 760–1 (within three lines *Andr.* 1162–4, *Cycl.* 337–9), and see Jackson, *Marg. Scaen.* 220–2.

441 μεθήκω a very rare verb, occurring also at *Tro.* 1270, *Knights* 937 (and in post-classical Greek only μεθήξειν in Dio Cassius 64.7.1). In the other three passages the verb has a person for object (understood in *Knights*), but there is no reason to be suspicious because the object is here ἃ (χρήματα). A similar allowance of non-personal and personal objects is found with μεθέπω, μεταδιώκω, μετακιάθω, μεταπορεύομαι, μετατρέχω, μέτειμι, μετέρχομαι, μετοίχομαι (another very rare word, with non-personal object only in *IT* 1332, wrongly termed 'odd' by Platnauer).

442 πένης γὰρ οὐδὲν εὐγενὴς ἀνήρ the sense is 'for a well-born man is nothing if he is impoverished', restating the gist of 404–5; not 'a beggar is no nobleman' (Burian–Swann) or 'a man who is poor is in no way noble' (Craik), which distorts Pol.'s attitude toward his own worth. We have here a brachylogy for πένης γὰρ ὢν or ἐὰν γὰρ πένης ᾖ, οὐδὲν κτλ.; cf. *Hipp.* 94 τίς δ' οὐ σεμνὸς [sc. ὢν] ἀχθεινὸς βροτῶν; and esp. *Ant.* 1327 βράχιστα [sc. ὄντα] γὰρ κράτιστα τἀν ποσὶν κακά. The ellipsis of ὧν here is not difficult, but has (along with a few other Eur. examples) escaped the notice of authoritative grammarians (K–G II.102–3, Goodwin *MT* §875, Moorhouse, *Syntax Soph.* 341): cf. *Andr.* 594–5 ὡς δὴ γυναῖκα σώφρον' ἐν δόμοις ἔχων / πασῶν κακίστην [οὖσαν], 1113, *El.* 1294 θέμις, οὐ μυσαραῖς [οὔσαις] τοῖσδε σφαγίοις. For οὐδέν = 'worthless, powerless' cf. *Eum.* 38, Aesch. *Su.* 749, *Ajax* 1231, *Andr.* 134, etc. and cf. 403n. For the sentiment expressed cf. esp. fr. 95 ἀλλ' οὐδὲν ηὐγένεια πρὸς τὰ χρήματα· τὸν γὰρ κάκιστον πλοῦτος εἰς πρώτους ἄγει, Soph. fr. 354.6–7 ἐμοὶ δ' οὐδεὶς δοκεῖ / εἶναι πένης ὢν ἄνοσος, ἀλλ' ἀεὶ νοσεῖν.

443–637: FIRST EPISODE, PART TWO

The second part of this long episode is an agon-scene with typical elements: preliminaries (446–68), three-cornered debate of rheseis (469–587), and degeneration into argumentative stichomythia/antilabe (588–624, concluding in a brief farewell-speech with final taunt, 625–37). The versatility of the agon-form is demonstrated by the unusual features of this scene, which is modelled on the pattern of a debate between plaintiff and defendant before a judge: cf. *Eum.*, *Hec.*, *Tro.*, and the variations in *Hel.*, where both speeches press the same position, and *Or.*, where the position of judge is thrust unwillingly on Menelaus and instead of a verdict we find a secondary agon between Orestes and Menelaus. Joc. presides like a neutral judge but, unlike Agamemnon in *Hec.* or Menelaus in *Tro.*, she has no power of decision and becomes indeed also a participant in the debate. The agon fails to produce persuasion or reconciliation, and this is exactly Eur.'s intention (and in general the intention of most tragic agones). Instead, the formal speeches allow the incompatible world-views and values of the speakers to emerge clearly, and the articulation of positions leads to their hardening. Joc.'s hope that words and wisdom can solve problems is undercut, and the ensuing argument even introduces the idea of a fratricidal duel. For fuller discussion, see 'The Optimistic Rationalist', 204–6; Strohm, 37–46; on the agon-form see J. Duchemin, *L' Agón dans la tragédie grecque* (Paris 1945,²1968), C. Collard, 'Formal Debates in Euripides' Drama', *G&R* 22 (1975) 58–71; M. Lloyd, *The Agon in Euripides* (Oxford 1992), esp. 83–93 on *Phoen.*

443 καὶ μὴν . . . ὅδε introducing the arrival of Eteocles (cf. Denniston, *GP*² 356), who is probably accompanied by a pair of attendants. They are not alluded to in this scene, even when he is threatening Pol. at 593, 596, 603, 614, but are certainly present in the next episode (690n. and 779n.), and it would seem more natural for the king to have his attendants with him all the while than to fetch them from the palace only at 690, if, as is likely, Et. goes inside between episodes (690n.). On mute attendants in Eur. see Stanley-Porter.

διαλλαγάς (and 445 διαλλάξεις) cf. 435n.

444 σὸν ἔργον the phrase is often used with some urgency, and some of the comic examples seem paratragic in tone (so too Plato *Meno* 75d1-2 and *Symp.* 188e2 are formal if not solemn), so Sandbach on Men. *Dysc.* 630 doubts (rightly, I think) that the idiom is 'colloquial', as believed by Stevens (*Colloquial Expr.* 39-40).

446-51 Eteocles' brusqueness and haste are well conveyed by the crowding of four blunt and grudging sentences into the two lines 446-7, and Joc. responds to this haste in ἐπίσχες and τὸ ταχύ in 452. Nauck argued that someone who says ἀρχέτω δέ τις λόγου should stop speaking and wait for an answer, and because he found τί χρὴ δρᾶν; inconsistent with Et.'s knowledge that he has come for peace-negotiations (450) he concluded that 447 was spurious (and emended to τήνδε σοι χάριν διδούς in 446). But τί χρὴ δρᾶν; should not be taken so literally: it is another impolite, even sarcastic feature, as if Et. does not know what would be the appropriate course of action in a mediation he does not really want. And it can be argued that Et. need not be so logically consistent that he cannot add a reason for his haste (thereby also informing the audience where he has been up to this moment). Yet there are other problems in this passage, and a smooth and rapid transition from Et.'s haste to Joc.'s reply in 452 would also be produced by the deletion of 448-51, advocated by Diggle (1989) 200. Wecklein had earlier suspected 450-1 on the grounds that βραβείας would make Et. concede too much and that εἰσεδέξω τειχέων is suspicious (see below). Diggle (1) finds the construction of μολεῖν in 450 unsatisfactory (I explain it below as epexegetic); (2) rejects *Aj.* 1274 as support for εἰσεδέξω τειχέων (see note); (3) deems πείσασά με a feeble appendage; (4) finds the uniqueness of βραβεία in an otherwise suspect context also suspicious. The larger deletion also removes the serious difficulties of 448-9 (the sense and juncture of ξυνωρίδας, the use of πόλιν in τάσσων πόλιν) which have led others to view the lines as corrupt. Diggle's proposal has considerable attraction and is perhaps to be accepted, but I do not concede as much strength to some of his arguments as he would: βραβείας, though a hapax in tragedy, is typical of the technical language used in the scene and the root is typical of tragedy and of Eur.(435n.); I would interpret πείσασά με not as feeble and pointless, but as a grudging reference to the truce, worthy of Et., and as another detail suggesting the difficulty of Joc.'s task (82n.). Perhaps, moreover, the actor needs more time than just 446-7 to mime the gestures of anger and hatred to which Joc. immediately refers.

446 δέ σοι the pronoun is not in a prominent position, and if Eur. had wished to make the point 'in deference to *you*, not to satisfy Pol.', he could easily have written σοὶ δὲ τὴν χάριν; thus I prefer the enclitic, despite the claim of Σ (ὀρθοτονητέον τὴν σοί διὰ τὴν πρὸς τὸν ἀδελφὸν σχέσιν). The point is rather to give a grudging hint of Et.'s disinclination to negotiate with his brother ('*only* as a *favour*'). The article (almost 'the favour you requested') also indicates that Et. had to be asked for the favour.

447 ἀρχέτω δέ τις λόγου cf. *IT* 1060 τοῦ λόγου τάδ' ἀρχέτω.

448–9 ὡς ἀμφὶ τείχη . . . τάσσων ἐπέσχον †πόλιν† if the text is sound, the meaning will be 'for around the walls and the pairs of divisions I interrupted my arrangement of the citizens'. But 'pairs of divisions' is odd as object of ἀμφί paired with τείχη and much more natural as an object of τάσσων, and τάσσων πόλιν is also odd. πόλις can be equivalent to πολῖται or at least 'inhabitants', esp. when accompanied by πᾶσα or by a genitive like Ἀθηναίων or Ἀργείων, or when performing the action of a political entity. For a military context, however, cf. *Held.* 399 πόλις τ' ἐν ὅπλοις and 712 below ἐξοιστέον τἄρ' ὅπλα Καδμείων πόλει; but whereas these emphasize the united action or appearance of the citizen-body (and the latter has the defining gen. with it and possibly echoes 710: see *ad loc.*), the present context and phrase imply division of the citizen-body. The passage therefore requires emendation, unless it is the work of a particularly incompetent interpolator (446–51n.). I prefer to posit a lacuna (with Paley): e.g. ⟨καὶ πύλας ἑπταστόμους ἱππηλάτας τε⟩, bringing in both the gates as a natural locus of defence and the cavalry which is so often paired with infantry in tragic battle descriptions. Emendations which do without a lacuna either require an unconvincing filler to replace καί or assume a jumbling of the word order (e.g. Wecklein (after Herwerden) καὶ πύλας ξυνωρίδας τάσσων λόχων ἐπέσχον {πόλιν} ὡς).

ξυνωρίδας λόχων this will have to mean 'pairs of divisions', a rather cryptic anticipation of what is described more clearly (and, at that point, naturally) in 1095–6 (reserved units of cavalry and infantry at each gate to back up the primary force). συνωρίς in tragedy is normally a high-style word for 'pair' (seven times vs. twice of 'pairs of horses', fr. 675.2 and *Rhes.* 987, both times with other clues to the equine meaning in the passage). There is nothing in the context to support either part of Pearson's ξυν. λοχῶν, 'seeking to waylay the chariots'.

τάσσων ἐπέσχον supplementary participle as with παύομαι or λήγω, elsewhere (only?) *Knights* 915 and Menander fr. 516.1 K–T (cf. ἄπαγε, 1733n.).

πόλιν it is not impossible that the omission of the word in L is a distant reflection of the corruption that the passage has suffered; note that the old Σ give no gloss for πόλιν and take ξυνωρίδας as the object, dismissing καί as redundant (ὁ καί παρέλκει). On the assumption of a lacuna, the word will have been supplied as an object for τάσσων once ξυνωρίδας seemed to go with ἀμφί; if so, the missing word need not have been palaeographically similar (Hartung's πάλιν is unidiomatic, Badham's μόλις possible).

κλύοιμί probably aorist: West, *BICS* 31 (1984) 179.

450 βραβείας βραβεύς is used by all three tragedians, but Eur. also has βραβεύειν (*Hel.* 996, 1073 only) and is the only poet to use it before Men. *Aspis* 148 and ps.-Epicharmus 87.7 Austin; and the derived fem. abstract βραβεία appears only here and in Lycophron *Alex.* 1154 πάλου βραβείαις (cf. βράβευμα, only in Soph. fr. 314a26). A hapax of this sort is, in my view, not an index of interpolation (52n.); indeed, such a rare word seems much more likely to have been coined by Eur. than by an interpolator.

αἷς a loose dative of circumstances (= ἐφ' αἷς), perhaps with an admixture of purpose.

μολεῖν epexegetic inf. with εἰσεδέξω ('admitted' almost becomes 'permitted'): cf. 261–2 above (where the time-relation between the admitting of εἰσεδέξατο and the coming of μολεῖν is no more logical than here) and 90n.

451 εἰσεδέξω τειχέων εἰσδέχομαι is most commonly used absolutely or with εἰς + acc., but Eur. alone once has a plain acc. (*Su.* 876: cf. 365–6n., and see Diggle, *Studies* 116), and the dative is attested three times in classical authors (most clearly locative in Men. *Samia* 517 εἰσεδεξάμην μελάθροις τοῖς ἐμοῖς, modal in *IA* 1228–9 ἐσδέξομαι ἐμῶν φίλαισιν ὑποδοχαῖς δόμων, a mixture of the two in *Cycl.* 35 καθαροῖσιν ἄντροις ... ἐσδεχώμεθα). The gen. here is explained by grammarians as a partitive/locative use (K–G 1.384–5, Schwyzer II.112), commoner in epic and in certain fixed phrases. The closest tragic parallel is Soph. *Aj.* 1274 ἕρκέων ποθ' ὑμᾶς ... ἐγκεκλημένους, which differs in having a verb of rest (see the explanation of Moorhouse, *Syntax Soph.* 59: 'in the area of' becomes 'within' under the influence of the verb). Here, it is possible that the idea of rest/position is proleptically conveyed by the verb of motion[1] ('received into ⟨so that he is inside⟩'), so that a similar explanation applies. Or (an admittedly harsher construction) the notion of ἐντός or εἴσω, and not just the 'region of the action', consciously or unconsciously under the influence of 261–2 μ' εἰσεδέξατο τειχέων ἔσω μολεῖν may have been in the author's (and audience's) mind. Possibly the compressed expression is meant to reflect Et.'s haste. One who deletes 448–51 or 450–1 will suggest instead that the interpolator has solecistically imitated 261–2.

452–68 the solemnity of Joc.'s rhesis is marked by her use of gnomes in 452–3 and 461–4 (with 460 openly labelling the wisdom of the thought)

---

[1] Cf. the use of πίπτω ἐν in place of πίπτω εἰς.

and by elevated language in the opening lines (454 σχάσον, 455 λαιμότμητον).

452–3 ἐπίσχες this imperative occasionally interrupts a speech (*Knights* 847, *Wasps* 829, *Frogs* 851), more commonly halts a departure or incipient action (e.g. 896 below, *Andr.* 550, *Ion* 1320, *Or.* 1069, *Phil.* 539, *OC* 856), but here simply slows down the haste urged by Et. without interrupting his speech or changing what he was about to do (cf. *El.* 962, *Hipp.* 567, *Clouds* 1047). If 448–51 are genuine, then Joc.'s plea 'Wait, slow down!' responds especially to Et.'s first words and perhaps to a rapid delivery of and grudging tone in the intervening lines.

οὔτοι . . . σοφόν rejection of haste as inimical to good judgment and justice is traditional (cf. *Hipp.* 1051–2, 1055–6, 1321–4, *OT* 613–14, 617 φρονεῖν γὰρ οἱ ταχεῖς οὐκ ἀσφαλεῖς, *Andr.* 550 μὴ τάχυν' ἄνευ δίκης; Theognis 329 καὶ βραδὺς εὔβουλος εἶλεν ταχὺν ἄνδρα διώκων). In this maxim, as in the rest of the scene, Joc. is shown to value τὸ σοφόν very highly and to believe that it consorts well with justice and harmony: cf. 460 παραινέσαι δε σφῶϊν τι βούλομαι σοφόν, 529–30 ἀλλ' ἡμπειρία ἔχει τι λέξαι τῶν νέων σοφώτερον; and the opposed accusations of ignorance, 569–70 ἀμαθεῖς . . . ἀσύνετα, 584 ἀμαθία.[1] But Et. represents a different view (499–525n.), and Eur., as in other plays, is exploring the possible meanings and values of σοφία/τὸ σοφόν in the difficulties of human life.

ἀνύτουσιν Porson was probably correct to call for the restoration of ἀνυτ- for ἀνυ- in tragedy (in the Teubner I wrongly failed to mention the suggestion even in the app.). Aesch. has ξυνανύτει and ἠνυτόμαν, Soph. ἤνυτον (twice), ἀνύτουσαν, διανύτων (*Ichneut.* 314.70 Radt), and Eur. ἐξανύτ- thrice against ἐξανυ- once (*Tro.* 232, changed to ἐξανύτ- by Diggle), and ἤνυτον in *Ba.* 1100 as well as transmitted in H at *Hec.* 1167 against all other mss; cf. also *TrGF* adesp. 659.14, 660.3. Contemporary Attic prose uses ἀνυτ- (Thuc., Xen., Plato), though the few instances in orators are all ἀνυ-. Editors of Aristophanes generally print ἀνυ- (*Frogs* 606, *Wealth* 413, 607 (v.l.); διανύτομεν in fr. 950 Kock is a ghost-example); Menander fr. 148.35 *CGFPR* has ἀνύεται. It is possible that in colloquial Attic (and Aristophanes) the verb had a rough breathing, as grammarians allege for Attic, but mss of Eur. and Soph. uniformly present κατανυ- and it is best to keep the smooth breathing in tragedy.

---

[1] Thus σοφόν should not, I think, be changed to σοφοῖς (Markland, West; JD notes that he feels the lack of an article). I take πλεῖστον as predicative in force: 'accomplish a wise result to a very great extent' or 'with a very wide effect'; but the meaning will be similar if it is adverbial with the verb.

454 σχάσον δὲ δεινὸν ὄμμα in anger, as in madness, the eyes may be wide open or distorted, the brows raised or gathered in a frown, so relaxing the 'eye' denotes a restoration of calm, as elsewhere relaxing the brow (ὀφρὺν λύειν et sim.) marks an end of distress (cf. Seaford on *Cycl.* 167). σχάσον here in place of the usual λύειν was sufficiently unusual that this use is glossed in the lexicographers. Of course, the expression on Et.'s mask cannot change, but Joc.'s comment helps the audience imagine or exaggerate its fierceness, and the bearing and gestures of the actor playing Et. must also have assisted the impression first of hostility and agitation and then of the calming counselled by Joc.

θυμοῦ πνοάς cf. *Ba.* 620 θυμὸν ἐκπνέων, *Rhes.* 786 θυμὸν πνέουσαι, *Septem* 52–3 θυμὸς ... ἔπνει, and see R. B. Onians, *The Origins of European Thought about the Body, the Mind, the Soul, the World, Time, and Fate* (Cambridge 1951) chapter 3, esp. 49–50, 53–4; agitated breathing is another sign of madness or anger (*Her.* 869 ἄμπνοὰς δ' οὐ σωφρονίζει, 1059; cf. *Her.* 1092–3, *Or.* 277 for abnormal breathing noticed on recovering from a fit of madness). Presumably the actor has actually put on a display of deep and rapid breathing.

455 λαιμότμητον ... κάρα 'head severed at the throat' (cf. *IA* 776 λαιμοτόμους κεφαλάς (text and authorship doubtful)), a rather precious use of the adj., and even more striking here in that synonymous and related compounds are all coinages of Euripidean lyric – λαιμοτόμας, λαιμοτόμος, λαιμότομος (*Ion* 1055 Γοργοῦς λαιμοτόμων ἀπὸ σταλαγμῶν); λαιμότομος is taken over by Timotheus *Pers.* (*PMG* 791) 130, and λαιμότμητος is specifically mocked in *Thesm.* 1054 λαιμότμητ' ἄχη δαιμόνι' (the word must have appeared in *Andromeda*).

456 Γοργόνος Eur. uses either Γοργόνος or Γοργοῦς for metrical convenience in dialogue and lyric, and this is the only place where either form will fit; Valck. unconvincingly advocated Γοργοῦς here as more 'Attic'. Et. responds to the sight of his brother as if he were a loathsome monster (cf. *Eum.* 48ff.), but his response was probably not merely a ferocity of stance and gesture (as I suggested in the Teubner *actio*), but also a turning away from the sight, the standard action: *Alc.* 1118 (Admetus offers his hand but does not look in the woman's face until ordered to do so by Heracles); *Or.* 1520 (Phrygian turns away from the gleam of the sword); Antiphanes fr. 164 K–A. For the initial dactyl, cf. 3n.

456 ἀδελφὸν εἰσορᾷς the rhetorical opposition, marked by chiastic order (modifier, verb, noun :: noun, verb, modifier), exact repetition of the verb, and direct juxtaposition of Γοργόνος and ἀδελφόν, is heightened by asyndeton. This may be called the asyndeton of antithesis (K–G II.342): cf. *Ant.* 1334–5 μέλλοντα ταῦτα· τῶν προκειμένων τι χρὴ πράσσειν, *Hec.* 264–5 ἀλλ' οὐδὲν αὐτὸν ἥδε γ' εἴργασται κακόν· Ἑλένην νιν αἰτεῖν χρῆν

278

τάφωι προσφάγματα, *Ant.* 360 ... παντόπορος· ἄπορος ..., 370 ... ὑψίπολις· ἄπολις ... The majority reading with δ' is likely to be due to scribal elimination of asyndeton.

458 εἰς ... ταὐτὸν ... βλέπων literally 'looking at the same point', but in context (and reinforced by the position of the actors: the brothers would best be placed to either side of Joc. in the centre) equivalent to 462 ὄμματ' ὄμμασιν διδῶι, 'look face-to-face'. *Pace* Pearson, the similar phrase in Xen. *Eq.* 6.1 is not comparable: εἰς τὸ αὐτὸ βλέπων τῶι ἵππωι ('facing in the same direction as the horse') is there contrasted with ἀντία τῶι ἵππωι ὁρῶν ('looking in the opposite direction to the horse').[1] There is no need for εἰς ... τοῦτον (Geel), which consorts ill with τοῦδε in the next line.

459 ἐνδέξηι λόγους 'be receptive to' or 'give serious attention to', a frequent locution in prose (where the meaning sometimes verges on 'approve' – LSJ s.v. ἐνδέχομαι ΙΙ): cf. fr. 139 [= *Thesm.* 1128–9] αἰαῖ, τί δράσω; πρὸς τίνας στρεφθῶ λόγους; ἀλλ' οὐκ ἂν ⟨ἐν⟩δέξαιτο [suppl. Kuster] βάρβαρος φύσις, Moschion *TrGF* 97 F 5.1 μόνον σὺ θυμοῦ χωρὶς ἔνδεξαι λόγους. ἐκδέξηι λόγους (*recc.*) has the wrong sense ('take up in turn, speak in reply'), and ἐκδέχομαι is not extant in Eur.

462 ὄμματ' ὄμμασιν διδῶι Eur. affects a range of periphrases with ὄμμα(τα), κόρας, βλέφαρα as object of verbs like διαφέρω, ἑλίσσω, διώκω (*Ion* 205, *Or.* 1261, *Ba.* 1087, 1123, fr. 764); phrases with the less colourful διδόναι (cf. Wilam. on *Her.* 1403) occur here and *Or.* 893–4 τὸ δ' ὄμμ' ... φαιδρωπὸν ἐδίδου, *IA* 1238 ὄμμα δὸς φίλημά τε; cf. 1370–1n., 1371n.

464 κακῶν δὲ τῶν πρὶν μηδενὸς μνείαν ἔχειν a clear echo of the political principle or ideal μὴ μνησικακεῖν, found in Hdt., Thuc., and the orators as well as *Clouds* 999 and *Lys.* 590, and most famously exemplified a few years after *Phoen.* in the settlement following the expulsion of the Thirty (Andoc. *Myst.* 81 and *passim*, Xen. *Hell.* 2.4.43, *Wealth* 1146). Even in the years preceding *Phoen.* the concept will have become more important in the wake of the civil strife in many cities during the Peloponnesian War (e.g., Thuc. 4.74.2, 8.73.6).

465 λόγος ... σὸς πρόσθε in an allusion to legal procedure (that is also typical of the tragic agon in general), Pol. speaks first as the plaintiff (ἄδικα πεπονθώς 467), the one who is pressing the action (στράτευμα ... ἄγων 466).

467 ὡς σὺ φῄς whereas Joc. could speak vehemently of Et.'s wrongdoing in the reunion-scene (319n.), now, as mediator, she must adopt a neutral stance and so dissociate herself from Pol.'s claim: for this force of

---

[1] On this consult J. K. Anderson, *Ancient Greek Horsemanship* (Berkeley 1961) 164 and *JHS* 80 (1960) 2.

the phrase cf. *Ba.* 333, fr. 451 [*Cresph.* fr. 69 Austin], *Aj.* 1234, *OC* 940, and οὐχ ὡς σὺ φῆις in *Ba.* 686.

467–8 κριτὴς δέ τις κτλ. this prayer and that by the chorus in 586–7, both as futile as the one in 84–5 (see *ad loc.*), frame the formal rheseis of the agon. For διαλλακτής see 435n. There should be no objection to the objective gen. κακῶν (τέκνων Polle; Wecklein would connect κακῶν to κριτής): it represents the separative genitive complement of the verbal phrase (cf. *Med.* 896–7), and in any case there is the analogy of διαλύειν ἔχθραν vs. διαλύειν τινάς or ἰατρὸς κακῶν vs. ἄλλων ἰατρός (Eur. fr. 1086).

469–96 Pol.'s speech is remarkably clear in structure and straightforward in argument. The framing elements, 469–72 and 494–6, are elaborate and, in line with Pol.'s (almost unthinking) reflection of traditional values earlier, contain an attack on sophistic rhetoric, suggesting that there is in fact one obvious view to take of the situation. With ἄδικα πεπονθώς (recalling judgments of neutral observers, the Servant at 154 and the chorus at 258), Joc. had given an opening for Pol. to argue in terms of the injustice he has suffered, and Pol. presents his case strictly in terms of δίκη (492n.). A narration of the 'facts' fills the first half of the body of the speech, 473–83, showing Pol.'s own foresight and piety in contrast to Et.'s treachery. The second part of the speech, nearly equal in length (484–93), contains Pol.'s proposal for settlement (484–91a) followed by a climactic appeal to the gods as witnesses and an assertion of justice (491b–93). In the narrow terms he adopts, Pol.'s case is unimpeachable. But the clear narrative of his brother's past wrongdoing, true though it is, is a form of μνησικακεῖν and thus contrary to Joc.'s admonition; and Pol.'s narrow vision is blind to the moral complexity introduced into the situation by the threat he poses to the (largely or at least partially) innocent population of Thebes and by the mere fact that he is attacking his own country. Apart from these moral ironies, there is an irony of style, for the brother who rejects sophistic rhetoric delivers a speech which in structure and particular effects is strikingly skilful rhetoric. Again, this should not be viewed as evidence of hypocrisy (438–42n.), but as an exposure of the partiality, inconsistency, and blindness which Eur. presents as inherent in the human soul.

469–72 Pol.'s insistence on the accessibility and clarity of truth and on the deceptive enchantment of speech and (one kind of) σοφία constitutes an attack on sophistic conceptions of truth and on positive evaluations of rhetoric (Protagoras, Gorgias). Simplicity or singleness (ἁπλοῦς) is traditionally associated with straightforward honesty. Line 469 is very similar to Aesch. fr. 176 ἁπλᾶ γάρ ἐστι τῆς ἀληθείας ἔπη (from *Hoplon Crisis*: spoken by Ajax?), but the expression may well have been proverbial before Aeschylus. Cf. Pindar, *N.* 8.35–6 κελεύθοις ἁπλόαις ζωᾶς ἐφαπτοίμαν, *IA*

927 ἔμαθον τοὺς τρόπους ἁπλοῦς ἔχειν (Achilles), *Wealth* 1158 οὐ γὰρ δόλου νῦν ἔργον, ἀλλ' ἁπλῶν τρόπων; also ἁπλῶι λόγωι (*Prom.* 46, 610, etc.), ἁπλοῦς λόγος *Hel.* 979; and conversely the implications of doubleness: cunning or treachery, Archil. 196a.36 West σὺ] μὲν γὰρ οὔτ' ἄπιστος οὔτε διπλόη, *Rhes.* 394–5 φιλῶ λέγειν τἀληθὲς αἰεὶ κοὐ διπλοῦς πέφυκ' ἀνήρ, 422–3 ... εὐθεῖαν λόγων τέμνων κέλευθον, κοὐ διπλοῦς πέφυκ' ἀνήρ; ambiguity, *Alc.* 519, *Her.* 950, *Hipp.* 385; moral relativism, fr. 189 and *Dissoi Logoi.* ποικίλος and derived words frequently denote cleverness, sometimes neutrally (fr. 27.2 ποικιλία πραπίδων, *Knights* 196 ποικίλως πως καὶ σοφῶς), but usually with a connotation of suspicion or disapproval (cf. ποικιλομήτης, ποικιλόφρων, ποικιλόβουλος, and ποικίλος itself in Hes. *Th.* 511, *Prom.* 308, *IA* 526; also Pindar *O.* 1.29 ψεύδεσι ποικίλοις, *N.* 5.28 ποικίλοις βουλεύμασιν, Theognis 213 ποικίλον ἦθος, 221–6 ποικίλα δήνε', *Thesm.* 439 ποικίλους λόγους, *Knights* 686 δόλοισι ποικίλοις). Although ἑρμήνευμα (a Euripidean word – *Her.* 1137, *Andr.* 46 – not found again until Philo and St Basil) does not elsewhere have any connotation of falsehood, to be ἑρμηνεύς is normally to have some expert or privileged access to an interpretation not obvious to laymen, and in this context Pol. insists that laymen can see the truth for themselves (cf. 495–6 καὶ σοφοῖς καὶ τοῖσι φαύλοις). As for ὁ ἄδικος λόγος, it is possible that this was already widely known as a (hostile) synonym for ὁ ἥττων λόγος of sophistic terminology: cf. *Clouds* 116 ἦν οὖν μάθηις μοι τὸν ἄδικον τοῦτον λόγον, 657, 885 with Dover's remarks on pp. lvii-lviii of his edition. Finally, although the metaphor in φαρμάκων continues that in νοσῶν, the word also calls to mind Gorgias' view of the power of λόγος in *Hel.* 14, which is itself based on traditional ideas about the enchanting power of poetic speech (used for deceit, e.g., Pindar *O.* 1.28–9, *N.* 7.22–3): the clever drugs which the ἄδικος λόγος needs are specious λόγοι which compel assent to unjustified propositions.

470 δεῖ τἄνδιχ' acc. personal pronoun is common in Eur. with impersonal δεῖ + gen. (*Concordance*; K–G 1.297), but τἄνδικα here may well be nom. with personal δεῖ (so Pearson, cf. K–G 1.399, citing two Platonic instances, to which add Xen. *Mem.* 4.2.10).

471 ἔχει γὰρ αὐτὰ καιρόν 'Just claims have all by themselves the proper measure (sc. so as to persuade an audience).' For αὐτά cf. LSJ s.v. αὐτός 1.3; for καιρός see Barrett on *Hipp.* 386 and for its use of rhetorical propriety cf. Pindar *P.* 9.78, *N.* 1.18.

472 νοσῶν the metaphor of illness is very widely applied by the tragedians, esp. Eur., but this seems to be the only place where a λόγος is ill; cf. however the use of ὑγιές for 'truthful' (201n.).

473–80 this passage has been handled rather roughly by some critics, mainly because of the uncertain construction of 473–74a and the asyndeton between 475 and 476. Nauck cut out 473b-74a and 475; but it is hard to see a reason for the *Binneninterpolation* to have arisen, and it weakens Pol.'s presentation if he starts with willing departure rather than a claim of prudent forethought. Hartung and Paley removed 476, which contains no internal faults, and left δούς κτλ. a rather loose appendage of 473-5. Wecklein considered deleting 474-6, but 'concern for my father's house' – 473 by itself – is a too generous view of what happened. The doubts attached to 479-80 are not related to the difficulties of 473-6 and may be discussed separately *ad loc.* The asyndeton between 475 and 476 is adequately explained as explicative: Pol.'s forethought and avoidance of the curse consisted in his voluntary departure on the terms of an annual alternation of rule. The problems of 473-4 should be faced by exegesis or emendation rather than athetesis.

473 ἐγὼ δέ δέ 'marks the transition from the introduction to a speech to the opening of the speech proper' (Denniston, *GP*[2] 170-1); or in the terminology of Friis Johansen, *General Reflection* 138-9, 110 n. 28, the pronoun + δέ marks the beginning of the 'descriptive application' of the introductory gnome.

473-4 πατρὸς δωμάτων προὐσκεψάμην τοὐμόν τε καὶ τοῦδ' τὸ σὸν προσκοπεῖσθαι ('looking out for your interests') is a Euripidean locution (*Med.* 460, *Andr.* 257; cf. *El.* 1114 τοὐμὸν δ', οὐχὶ τοὐκείνου σκοπῶ, Soph. *El.* 251-2 τὸ σὸν σπεύδουσ' ἅμα καὶ τοὐμὸν αὐτῆς), so it is best to take τοὐμόν τε καὶ τοῦδ' with the main verb, 'looked out for both our interests'; the gen. δωμάτων may then be explained (with Hermann) as a partitive gen. depending on τοὐμόν κτλ., 'my share in, my interest in our father's house'. The father's house implies the inheritance of property and kingship (cf. 68 δῶμα διαλαχεῖν), and Pol. moves freely from house to kingship in describing what he has lost: 477 ἀνάσσειν, 478 ἄρχειν, 483 τυραννίδ' ... καὶ δόμων ἐμὸν μέρος, 484 τἀμαυτοῦ, 486 οἰκεῖν ... τὸν ἐμὸν οἶκον. An alternative construal, taking δωμάτων with προὐσκεψάμην, as *Ant.* 688 σοῦ δ' οὖν πέφυκα πάντα προσκοπεῖν,[1] Antiphon fr. 51 Blass–Thalheim (fr. 1.4 Gernet) τῆς ... ταλαιπορίας προὐσκέψαντο, Dio Cassius 44.33.3 τῆς κοινῆς σωτηρίας προσκοπεῖν, is unattractive since the idiomatic parallels will have to be discounted and τοὐμόν τε καὶ τοῦδ' will then have to be taken either as subject of ἐκφυγεῖν (which does not need one) and as baldly equivalent to ἐμὲ καὶ τόνδε (which such periphrases never really are: 775n.) or (uniquely) as equivalent to τοὐμόν μέρος as limiting adverbial acc. with προὐσκεψάμην. If one doubts Hermann's explanation, there are

---

[1] I prefer this reading to the variant σὺ δ' οὐ πέφυκας κτλ.

no very convincing emendations: Schenkl's δ' ὑπὲρ τῶν δωμάτων lacks a legitimate caesura; Weil's δ' ἰατρὸς δωμάτων is too abrupt, as there is no reinforcement of the metaphor in the rest of the sentence and δωμάτων must be taken as δωμάτων συμφορῶν or δωμάτων νοσούντων; Munro's πάτωρ is untrue, irrelevant, and an uncertainly attested word (cf. *TrGF* 43 F 17.4 with app.); Pearson's πρόσθεν δωμάτων extends the 'preferential' sense of πρόσθεν (LSJ s.v. A.I.3) suitably found with verbs of ranking, choosing, or placing (like ἄγειν, ἡγεῖσθαι, τιθέναι, ζητεῖν, ἀξιοῦν) to a less suitable verb and produces a false antithesis between the brothers' interests and the inheritance. Nauck's rearrangement ἐγὼ δὲ πατρὸς ἐκφυγεῖν χρῄζων ἀρὰς / τοὐμόν τε καὶ τὸ τοῦδ' ὁμῶς προὐσκεψάμην gives a good sense, at the cost of deleting 475. JD recommends something like δ' ἀπάρας δωμάτων.

474 τοὐμόν τε καὶ τοῦδ' for the omission of the article with the second possessive word, cf. *El.* 301 τύχας ... τὰς ἐμὰς κἀμοῦ πατρός, *OC* 606 τἀμὰ κἀκείνων (in general, Collard on *Su.* 486–8; Renehan *CP* 80 (1985) 150–1). Accepting explicative asyndeton, Matthiae placed the colon after τοῦδ' rather than at the end of 475 (and Craik so punctuates in her translation, though her text has a comma at both τοῦδ' and ποτε); he had earlier suggested ⟨δ'⟩ ἀράς, following Musgrave's ⟨τ'⟩. There is better balance with the colon at 475 (477–80 explicate 474b–75).

475 this verse must necessarily be deleted if one accepts either of Nauck's treatments of 473–4; otherwise, despite its detachability, it gives just the sort of specific detail which one would expect in a clear narration within a plaintiff's speech.

ἐφθέγξατ' here, as often, of a solemn, authoritative, or oracular utterance.

476 although ἑκὼν αὐτός is not precisely paralleled elsewhere (for other emphatic redundant phrases with ἑκών see 433–4n., 630n.), the emphatic coupling of quasi-redundant terms is a device typical of tragic style; αὐτός, 'on my own initiative', may carry a self-serving implication (cf. ἐγὼ ... προὐσκεψάμην) that Pol. originated the plan of alternation. Since this phrase is not suspect, the only possible source of complaint against this verse is the asyndeton (for a false numerological argument, see 479–80n.). Barnes proposed κἀξῆλθον (for καί in crasis lost in the tradition cf. 683n., 878n., 1215n., 1249n.; Davies on *Trach.* 1046–7), but explicative asyndeton is acceptable here (473–80n.).

478–80 deleted by Diggle (cf. Craik's apparatus); for discussion see on 479–80.

478 ὥστ' *ea condicione ut*, like prosaic ἐφ' ᾧ (K–G II.504–5).

ἀνὰ μέρος λαβών I believe that, in context, there is no difficulty in the lack of explicit object: λαβών answers δούς, just as ἀνὰ μέρος answers ἐνιαυτοῦ κύκλον and ἄρχειν answers ἀνάσσειν. Cf. the less integral use of λαβών with understood object in *OC* 475 οἵός νεαροῦς νεοπόκωι μαλλῶι λαβών. Wecklein's ἀρχήν ... λαβεῖν needlessly weakens the expression: Pol. wants to *rule*, not just to *take up* the rule. The whole phrase recurs in 486, but this I view as a purposeful rather than a careless repetition (cf. also 484 τἀμαυτοῦ λαβών, 486 μέρος, to which Pol. recurs again in 601, 603): Pol. wants to return to the original terms of the agreement, guaranteed sharing. ἀνὰ μέρος for the more common prosaic κατὰ μέρος, ἐν μέρει occurs only here and 486 in Eur., then thrice in Aristotle *Pol.* (in varying senses) and in Men. fr. 740.18 K–T ('proportionately').

479–80 nothing is more typical of Greek rhetoric than to express an idea both in its positive and in its negative formulation; so this couplet elaborates 478 in polar opposition. The elaboration is no longer pure *narratio*, but by innuendo Pol. puts Et. in the wrong even before he states the fact of Et.'s breach of faith. Such a tendentious use of *narratio* is typical of prose oratory as well, and Wecklein's suspicion (1901 app.) that the couplet as a whole is spurious seems to me unjustified. The larger deletion proposed by Diggle (removing 478 as well as 479–80) weakens Pol.'s rhetoric by making him move without comment from his departure to Et.'s failure to keep his promise. A larger number of critics have deleted 480 alone, finding the line flat and judging ἃ γίγνεται a mere filler. If φόνου is read in 479, then κακόν τι δρᾶσαι καὶ παθεῖν is intolerably anticlimactic and 480 deserves to be removed. But the γρ-variant φθόνου gives excellent sense in conjunction with ἔχθρας; φθόνος is just the right term in connection with Pol.'s anxiety over μέρος (478n., cf. 545); and the participial phrase in 479 then has its proper logical and rhetorical subordination to the infinitive phrase of 480. The resulting understatement strikes me as effective: there is an undertone of both menace and regret here, in contrast to the open threat in the climactic declaration of 490–1. The fact that the deletion of one line from Pol.'s speech would produce exact equality of length with Et.'s speech (twenty-seven lines if nothing is deleted from Et.'s speech) has been cited by some in favour of deletion of 480 (Paley made the same observation in favouring removal of 476). Such numerological considerations deserve no weight at all: in the theatre, no one is counting the verses of the two speeches (nor did Greek book-rolls make awareness of exact symmetries *on this scale* easy to detect in reading); the audience is expected to perceive the balanced length of the speeches, but this perception will tolerate approximation.

δι' ἔχθρας ... καὶ φθόνου μολών for the type of idiom, 20n. The two nouns may be in hendiadys: cf. *Med.* 297 φθόνον ... δυσμενῆ, Pindar *Pae.* 2.54–5 ὁ δ' ἐχθρὰ νοήσαις ... φθόνος. For confusion of φθόνος and φόνος in mss cf. *Andr.* 780, Soph. *El.* 1466, *OC* 1234–5.

ἃ γίγνεται 'which is now happening', with the relative picking up the whole infinitive phrase, like *Ion* 559 ὃ σοί γε γίγνεται (after Διὸς παιδὸς γενέσθαι παῖς), *Hec.* 408 ἃ πείσηι (after πεσεῖν ... ἑλκῶσαί τε ... ἀσχημονῆσαί τ'). So interpreted, the phrase is part of the implied indictment of Et., not the empty filler it seems to some critics who follow Σ in interpreting ὁποῖα εἴωθε γίνεσθαι καὶ συμβαίνειν τοῖς φίλοις εἰς ἔχθραν ἥκουσιν.

481 ὁρκίους ... δοὺς θεούς an informal periphrasis on the analogy of πίστιν or δεξιὰν διδόναι, cf. *IT* 735 ὅρκον δότω; this usage differs from the technical legal one, in which ὅρκον διδόναι is the action of one who demands or proposes the oath, not of the one who swears it (Dem. 39.3–4, 39.25, 49.65, Isaeus 9.24, Arist. *Rhet.* 1377a8ff.).

483 δόμων ἐμὸν μέρος Za's reading may well be accidental, and it is impossible to be certain that the scholiast who wrote γρ. καὶ δόμων ἐμῶν μέρος had ἐμόν before him, but ἐμόν must be correct. A possessive which might go with a gen. noun is sometimes attached instead to the noun on which the gen. depends (30n.), but here we have the reverse phenomenon, which is unparalleled. No audience could fail to understand δόμων ἐμῶν μέρος on first hearing as 'a part of my house' (which is factually false), and Eur. had no reason to require an audience to rethink the sense of the phrase. The error arose by assimilation of ending (and δόμων ἐμῶν is a common phrase: *Med.* 562, *Ion* 34, *Alc.* 304, *Phaethon* 251).

484–9 Pol. states his present position with the mild 'I am prepared ...' and offers a full diplomatic solution: (1) removal of invasion army; (2) assumption of his turn at rule; (3) after a year, release of the rule back to Et. for the agreed time-span. But Pol. backs up his offer with the threat of force, first implied in 488–9, which provide in polar opposition the alternative to 484–7 (the parallelism of structure with 476–80 is deliberate: Pol. wants the original deal restored), then more openly declared (though with modesty and vagueness: πειράσομαι δρᾶν) in 490–1. The clarity and power of Pol.'s proposal and its presentation are spoiled by the suggested deletion of 486–7, which originated in Valckenaer's improbable idea that 486 alone be deleted. Valck. objected to the repetition of ἀνὰ μέρος λαβών (478n.), though he also suggested that οἶκον ... οἰκεῖν betrayed interpolation because of its similarity to 1231 below and *IA* 331 (but explaining how an interpolator might have cobbled together a line is no part of a case indicting the line: 6on.). Instead of acknowledging that Valck. was simply wrong (his deletion destroys the μὲν–δέ structure and leaves ἀφεῖναι without its needed object), Hartung, Geel and others extended the suspicion to the equally necessary 487, which contains no fault except the loss of a syllable by corruption in transmission. Nauck confined his suspicion to 487, objecting to the reference to the future in between the present actions described in 485–6 and 488–9; but οἰκεῖν in 486 already refers to the future, and diplomacy requires the assurance offered by 487.

487 αὖθις ⟨εἰς⟩ so Jackson, positing an easier corruption than for Triclinius' ⟨αὖ⟩, though the latter is good Euripidean idiom. Eur. uses εἰς ... χρόνον with several modifiers that also occur with the plain acc. χρόνον (see *Concordance*).

488 προσφέρειν the proper word for applying siege-devices to a wall: Σ *Lys.* 309 κριὸς γὰρ χαλκοῦν μηχάνημα ὃ τοῖς τείχεσι προσφέρουσιν οἱ βάρβαροι; Pollux 4.90 τείχει προσέφερέ τινα μηχανήν; one should not be led by the error μηκέτι or μήτε τι (ΤΙ by dittography of Π?) to introduce μήτ' ἐπεισφέρειν (Paley). Note also the alliteration of π in 488–9, to which the 'rhyme' of προσφέρειν and προσαμβάσεις contributes.

489 πηκτῶν κλιμάκων προσαμβάσεις a tragic periphrasis for 'ladder' based on *Septem* 466 κλίμακος προσαμβάσεις (στείχει), with the -σις abstract converted to a concrete noun under the influence of the defining gen.; Eur. reuses the phrase in 1173 and a few years later in *Ba.* 1213 (including πηκτῶν), but had probably already used it in *IT* 97; cf. 744n.

491 δρᾶν the enjambed monosyllable with such strong punctuation following is very rare (Denniston (1936) 74, 76); here the feature probably adds emphasis. Monosyllables followed by weaker punctuation occur in 85, 939, 941, 1182, 1357, 1403.

μάρτυρας ... δαίμονας for Pol.'s invocations of the gods, 433–4n. For the gods as witnesses of the rights and wrongs of a dispute leading to war, cf. Thuc. 1.78.4 εἰ δὲ μή [sc. maintain the truce and submit differences to arbitration], θεοὺς τοὺς ὁρκίους μάρτυρας ποιούμενοι πειρασόμεθα [cf. 490 πειράσομαι] ἀμύνεσθαι πολέμου ἄρχοντας, 2.74.2 ἐς ἐπιμαρτυρίαν καὶ θεῶν καὶ ἡρώων τῶν ἐγχωρίων Ἀρχίδαμος ὁ βασιλεὺς κατέστη, λέγων ὧδε· θεοὶ ὅσοι γῆν τήνδε Πλαταιίδα ἔχετε καὶ ἥρωες, ξυνίστορές ἐστε ὅτι οὔτε τὴν ἀρχὴν ἀδίκως, ἐκλιπόντων δὲ τῶνδε προτέρων τὸ ξυνώμοτον, ἐπὶ γῆν τήνδε ἤλθομεν ... οὔτε νῦν, ἤν τι ποιῶμεν, ἀδικήσομεν.

492 σὺν δίκηι δίκης ἄτερ chiastic juxtaposition for emphasis. Again Pol. makes his point by simple repetition, which is intended, not careless: 490 δίκης, 492 δίκηι δίκης, 496 ἔνδιχ'.

493 ἀνοσιώτατα beyond the lack of fair play as man to man, Et. has, by conventional standards, offended the gods by violating his oath; hence the use of this strong religious term here and in 609 ἀνόσιος πέφυκας (capping an appeal to the gods in 604–8). In tragedy ἀνόσιος (more frequent in Eur. because of its metrical shape) almost always refers to polluting violations of fundamental moral laws (matricide and other kin-murder, incest, cannibalism, human sacrifice, theomachy, adultery, neglect of burial); when applied to other situations, it shows that the speaker regards the criminal act as tantamount to such violations (*Or.* 1213 and *Phil.* 257 of betrayal, *Her.* 567 of attempted mass murder of one's family). For a real contemporary concern for divine sanctions against violation of an agreement secured by oaths, cf. Thuc. 7.18 on the Spartans' belief that their reverses in the Archidamian War were due to their violating the truce with Athens.

494–6 the concluding frame deliberately recalls the opening gnomes: note ἔνδιχ' ≈ τἄνδιχ'; αὔθ' ἕκαστα ≈ ἁπλοῦς ... ἀληθείας; περιπλοκὰς ≈ ποικίλων ... ἑρμηνευμάτων; σοφῶν ≈ σοφοῖς.

αὔθ' ἕκαστα 'the precise facts, plain and simple'; cf. *Prom.* 950 (contrasted with μηδὲν αἰνικτηρίως), *Ichneut.* fr. 314.106 Radt (coupled with σαφῶς), *Or.* 1393 (coupled with σαφῶς), 1400, *Lys.* 1100; with no contrast with obscurity or dishonesty, Hdt. 1.107.1 ('the full details'); see Griffith on *Prom.* 950.

περιπλοκὰς λόγων although 'weaving' of words was traditionally a complimentary metaphor for the craftsmanship of the rhapsode/poet or orator (cf. e.g. *Il.* 3.212 μύθους καὶ μήδεα πᾶσιν ὕφαινον, Pindar *O.* 6.86–7 πλέκων ποικίλον ὕμνον), the metaphor also applied more sinisterly to cunning contrivance of plots and deceptions (for πλέκω see Diggle, *Studies* 115; for ὑφαίνω see *Il.* 6.187 πυκινὸν δόλον ἄλλον ὕφαινε, *Od.* 5.356, etc.; cf. μηχανορραφέω, -ραφος), so that in *Rhes.* 834 πλέκων λόγους connotes lying. περιπλοκή is used neutrally in scientific and philosophical writing, but Eur.'s pejorative use of the plural is imitated by Antiphanes fr. 75.1 K–A περιπλοκὰς λίαν ἐρωτᾷς (opposed to σαφῶς) and Straton fr. 1.35 K–A (= *CGFPR* 219.35) τί οὖν ... περιπλοκὰς λέγεις; (opposed to ἁπλῶς and σαφέστερον).

ἀθροίσας perhaps the military metaphor 'mustering' is to be felt here, but in any case the word implies gathering together what is not already present and thus further denigrates the ploys to which the clever but unjust speaker is forced.

καὶ σοφοῖς καὶ τοῖσι φαύλοις given Pol.'s opposition to sophistic argument and rhetoric, this means 'the clever people and the ordinary laymen' (cf. the contrast in *Ba.* 427–33, and Dodds' note on 430–3) rather than 'the wise and the undistinguished'. For the article supplied ἀπὸ κοινοῦ from the second term to the first see Fraenkel on *Ag.* 926; Kiefner, 41–2; 474n.; 1258n.

497–8 this is a remarkably forthright judgment for a neutral chorus to express after hearing only one speech (contrast the indirection of the sympathetic chorus in *Med.* 520–1 after Medea demonstrates the injustice of Jason); for the effect of such a partisan comment between the speeches of an agon see Hose, *Chor* 222. There are also two points of mild irony in the speech. First, the chorus concedes its non-Hellenic origin yet offers a judgment with which the audience is invited to agree: Eur. plays elsewhere

287

with the stereotype of the non-Greek who is supposed not to share the moral values or moral sense of a Greek, e.g. *Med.* 1330–1, 1339–40, *Hec.* 328–31, *IT* 1174. Second, although Pol. has tried to dissociate himself from 'modern' rhetoric, the chorus finds his speech ξυνετά, a 'modern' intellectualist word affected by Eur.

ἐμοὶ μὲν . . . μοι for repetition of the personal pronoun, mitigated by the intervening clause and the resumptive force of ἀλλ' οὖν, cf. K–G 1.660; Fraenkel, *Beobacht. zu Arist.* 89–91, 216; Diggle, *Papyrologica Florentina* 7 (1980) 58. In most other cases both pronouns are unemphatic, but for emphatic pronoun picked up by unemphatic cf. [Dem.] 47.74 ᾤοντο . . . ἐμέ, εἰ πολλά μου λάβοιεν ἐνέχυρα, ἄσμενον ἀφήσειν με κτλ., *Trach.* 287–9 αὐτὸν δ' ἐκεῖνον, εὖτ' ἂν . . . , φρόνει νιν ὡς ἥξοντα. For μέν *solitarium* with the personal pronoun ('whatever others may think, *my* view is . . .'), cf. Denniston, *GP*² 381. For the use of ἀλλ' οὖν ('still, however that may be' after a concessive condition), cf. Denniston, *GP*² 444 and *Cycl.* 651–2 χειρὶ δ' εἰ μηδὲν σθένεις, ἀλλ' οὖν ἐπεγκέλευέ γ'.

499–525 in contrast to Pol.'s speech, Et.'s lacks symmetrical framing and a clear internal structure. His opens with a four-line gnome and concludes with a two-line gnome, but these do not form a ring with echoes of content and vocabulary. There is no *narratio*, but only repeated declarations of his attachment to kingship (504–6, 507–8, 519–20, 523), enclosing two emotional arguments justifying this attachment (ἀνανδρία 509–10a, αἰσχύνομαι/ὄνειδος 510b–14), a recommendation of non-military means of redress which seems to be naive and cynical at the same time (515–17), and the briefest possible proposal of a 'compromise' (518–19a). Both the language and the content of Et.'s speech are meant to associate Et. with the clever young men who used the training of the sophists to discomfit their traditionally minded elders and to justify selfish and aggressive behaviour. The denial of a stable foundation for assigning crucial moral predicates (499–502) recalls Protagorean relativism, Gorgianic scepticism, and sophistic manipulations of the *nomos–physis* dichotomy (here realized in the common disjunction of name and reality: ὀνομάσαι vs. ἔργον). The acceptance of ἀμφίλεκτος ἔρις (500) as a fact of life recalls Protagoras' *Kataballontes* and the *Dissoi Logoi*. The use of τὸ πλέον (509, cf. τὸ ἔλασσον 510) instead of πλοῦτος and χρήματα, the terms used by Pol. and Joc., reflects the terminology of political theory (553n.). The celebration of the power of speech (516 πᾶν γὰρ ἐξαιρεῖ λόγος) also has a sophistic ring (cf. the claims for rhetoric made in *Gorgias*), as does the willingness to concede his own ἀδικία yet boldly term it κάλλιστον (cf. Odysseus in *Phil.* 81–5). All these features mark Et. as a young man who can use the glittering σοφία of the sophists for personal advantage.

499–502 instead of disputing Pol.'s version of the facts, Et. declares that he is not bound by the moral terms and perceptions adopted by Pol. Values are, he argues, a matter of *nomos*, not *physis*; agreement among men exists only at the verbal level, but diverse (and equally valid) values are revealed in men's actions. See in general Guthrie, *Hist. Greek Phil.* III.148ff., 164ff., G. B. Kerferd, *The Sophistic Movement* (Cambridge 1981) chap. 10, M. Ostwald, *From Popular Sovereignty to the Sovereignty of Law* (Berkeley 1986) 250–73, F. Heinimann, *Nomos und Physis* (Basel 1945), esp. 110–62. Tyndareus makes the opposite assumption in *Or.* 492ff. εἰ τὰ καλὰ πᾶσι φανερὰ καὶ τὰ μὴ καλά, κτλ.

499 ταὐτό for my preference of this over ταὐτόν cf. Teubner *praef.* §20.[1] The preliminary publication of Πᵏ shows it as reading τοαυτο.

καλὸν . . . σοφόν θ' ἅμα in this pairing σοφόν is taken by Et. to be a term of praise, 'prudent, wise', rather than 'clever, cunning', as Pol. used the word.

ἔφυ a common tragic synonym for ἐστι/ἦν which by itself need not evoke the *nomos–physis* controversy. Likewise, dispute over the question τί τὸ κάλλιστον; is a tradition much older than the sophists: cf. e.g. Sappho 16 L–P, M. Griffith, 'Contest and Contradiction in Early Greek Poetry', in *Cabinet of the Muses*, 185–207. But 501–2 firmly place Et.'s statement in a modern-sounding, sophistic context.

500 ἀμφίλεκτος 'in which there is speech on two sides', only here quasi-active ('⟨strife⟩ which disputes on both sides') rather than quasi-passive ('disputed, challenged' in *Ag.* 1585; '(spoken as) twofold' in *Ag.* 881; cf. adv. οὐδ' ἀμφιλέκτως *Se.* 809). Coined as a variation on ἀμφίλογος (*Pers.* 904 οὐκ ἀμφιλόγως, *Ant.* 111 νεικέων ἐξ ἀμφιλόγων, *Med.* 637 ἀμφιλόγους ὀργὰς ἀκόρεστά τε νείκη), the word is not again extant (except in quotations of this line) until late Christian authors.

501–2 νῦν δ' κτλ. 'but in actual fact there is nothing that is like or equal for men except in their use of ⟨like or equal⟩ words. The reality is not that (sc. like or equal).' Et. is not denying the existence of equality in particular, but arguing that no terms whatever have a firm foundation in reality. Words are merely groups of sounds shared by different speakers, but what each man really understands by each word is not the same as what another man understands, and so one man's καλὸν ἔργον is not καλόν to another.

---

[1] I do not accept the judgment of Barrett on *Hipp.* 1178–9 that the proportion of metrically guaranteed (and required) ταὐτόν to metrically guaranteed (and required) ταὐτό establishes a 'preference' for the former that can be applied to the metrically indifferent cases; on the other hand, the evidence I cited points to a *scribal* tendency to prefer ταὐτόν.

ὀνομάσαι   for the sense 'express in words', cf. 407n.; for the contrast with ἔργον, here very dismissive of λόγος/ὄνομα, cf. 389n. and *Hipp.* 501–2 κρεῖσσον τοὔργον ... ἢ τοὔνομ', *Hel.* 792 τοὔργον μὲν ἦν τοῦτ', ὄνομα δ' οὐκ εἶχεν τόδε, *Or.* 454–5 ὄνομα γάρ, ἔργον δ' οὐκ ἔχουσιν οἱ φίλοι οἱ μὴ 'πὶ ταῖσι συμφοραῖς ὄντες φίλοι. The epexegetic/result infinitive following πλήν = 'except so much as to' is distinct from various other constructions in which the inf. after πλήν serves as a nom. or acc. substantive or as complementary inf. with an appropriate verb. This construction has not been treated in the standard grammars, but is well established by this passage and *Su.* 534–5 οὔτι γὰρ κεκτήμεθα ἡμέτερον αὐτὸ [sc. τὸ σῶμα] πλὴν ἐνοικῆσαι βίον, *Hec.* 356 ἴση θεοῖσι πλὴν τὸ κατθανεῖν μόνον (for equivalence of articular inf. with plain inf. see K–G II.43–5), *Or.* 717–18 ὦ πλὴν γυναικὸς οὕνεκα στρατηλατεῖν τἄλλ' οὐδέν. I would also interpret this way Soph. *El.* 414 οὐ κάτοιδα πλὴν ἐπὶ σμικρὸν φράσαι, where Jebb and Kamerbeek take πλήν with ἐπὶ σμικρόν only and consider φράσαι as epexegetic by itself (K. also considers taking it as complementary with κάτοιδα = 'I know how to', but that will hardly do); and Men. *Dysc.* 679–80 πλὴν ἀεὶ ἕλκειν ἐκεῖνον.[1] Cf. also *Andr.* 322–3 ἔχειν οὐκ ἀξιώσω, πλὴν τύχηι φρονεῖν δοκεῖν (321–3 are deleted by Diggle; but whoever wrote the lines, the construction could still be as Stevens explains it). Porson sought a more typical antithesis by substituting ὀνόμασιν for the inf., but there is no syntactical or semantic reason to change ὀνομάσαι, which I would prefer as *difficilior* if ὀνόμασιν were a competing variant; Pearson favours ὀνόμασιν as 'more idiomatic and clearer'. Some of the shorter Σ use ὀνόματι or ὀνόμασι in paraphrase, but this is not a reliable indication that ὀνόμασιν was ever in the text (the fullest Σ clearly had ὀνομάσαι: note μέχρι ὀνόματος and ὀνομάζομεν).

τόδε   this is best taken as predicate, 'the reality is not this (sc. τὸ εἶναί τι ὅμοιον ἢ ἴσον)': cf. *Hel.* 792, where τοῦτο = τὸ προσαιτεῖν βίον, understood from 791 (also 550n.). Or can τόδε perhaps be simply equivalent to the adjs. ὅμοιον ἢ ἴσον?[2] Some take τόδε as attributive (Paley: 'this reality (the reality of this boasted fairness) exists not'; cf. Pearson); but the point

---

[1] I punctuate as Sandbach: 'For the stricken man below I didn't care a whit, except so as to be always pulling on Gorgias – *that* was a real nuisance!' Handley and Arnott put a stop before πλήν and treat it as equivalent to ἀλλά and then take ἕλκειν as subject of ἐνώχλει, resumed (rather superfluously) by τοῦτ'.

[2] Cf. Aristotle *EN* 1099a22–3 ἀλλὰ μὴν καὶ ἀγαθαί γε καὶ καλαί, καὶ μάλιστα τούτων ἕκαστον, where ἕκαστον refers to each of 'good' and 'noble'.

of an ἔργον is that its existence is indisputable, and the antithesis is weakened by this reading.

503 γάρ introducing an instance which exemplifies a proposition (Denniston, *GP*² 66); that is, Et.'s view that rule is a καλόν (504–8) is no less valid than Pol.'s view that it is right to abide by the oath-sanctioned agreement.

οὐδὲν . . . ἀποκρύψας perhaps a rhetorical formula, asserting a claim of utter frankness and complete disclosure in order to defuse anticipated resentment at an unwelcome or blunt statement: *Trach.* 474 πᾶν σοι φράσω τἀληθὲς οὐδὲ κρύψομαι (Lichas finally telling the truth); *Phil.* 915 οὐδέν σε κρύψω· δεῖ γὰρ ἐς Τροίαν σε πλεῖν; *Wealth* 343 οὐδὲν ἀποκρύψας ἐρῶ (wrongly alleged to be a reminiscence specifically of our line); Dem. 6.31 τἀληθῆ μετὰ παρρησίας ἐρῶ πρὸς ὑμᾶς καὶ οὐκ ἀποκρύψομαι (cf. 8.73, 13.10, 19.3), Isocr. 15.140 οὐκ ἀποκρύψομαι πρὸς ὑμᾶς, 12.100 οὐ γὰρ ἀποκρύψομαι τἀληθές; Plato *Ion* 535c5 οὐ γάρ σε ἀποκρυψάμενος ἐρῶ (replying to 535b1–2). The personal object need not be expressed (σ᾽ ἐρῶ Rw from Σ; ἐγὼ δέ σ᾽ Kirchhoff).

504–5 ἄστρων . . . καὶ γῆς ἔνερθε it is obvious that Et. is offering an *adunaton*[1] featuring polar opposition, so the sense ought to be 'I'd climb to heaven and I'd delve beneath the earth' (for this conventional pairing of the 'sky and underworld' see Barrett on *Hipp.* 1290–3 on escape-wishes to fly away or plunge beneath the earth). This sense can perhaps be obtained from ἄστρων . . . αἰθέρος πρὸς ἀντολάς, which survives only in Stobaeus. Plutarch, Σ, and mss all give ἡλίου πρὸς ἀν(α)τολάς, which may have arisen by accidental reminiscence (same phrase in same position in *Ag.* 1180, *Prom.* 707, cf. 791) or as a deliberate change by someone unsure how to take αἰθέρος. Suggested constructions of ἡλίου are unacceptable: (1) redundant gen. ἐκ παραλλήλου with ἄστρων, as proposed by Kannicht on *Hel.* 1–3 (in *Hel.* 1–3, if πέδον and γύας are both sound, there is at least a part-and-whole relationship between the two objects); (2) possessive with ἄστρων (the stars belong to οὐρανός, not to the sun (1n.); Powell offers no parallel to show that in Eur. ἄστρα ἡλίου could be understood as 'planets'); (3) subj. gen. with ἀντολάς (Hermann: *qua sol ad astra ascendit*; so Craik: 'the rising of the sun up to the stars'). Moreover, with ἡλίου there would inevitably be a confusion with the sense 'to the east', spoiling the antithesis, unless one posits a lacuna containing a longer list of impossible destinations ('to the sky, to the far west, to the far east, beneath the earth'

---

[1] The passage is not treated in E. Dutoit, *Le thème de l'adynaton dans la poésie antique* (Paris 1936).

seems more Senecan than Euripidean). If αἰθέρος is correct, two worries remain. (1) Is it possessive gen. with ἄστρων (cf. *Prom.* 1049 οὐρανίων ἄστρων; for αἰθήρ and ἄστρα associated, *Ion* 1147 Οὐρανὸς ἀθροίζων ἄστρ' ἐν αἰθέρος κύκλωι, *El.* 991–2 οἳ φλογερὰν αἰθέρ' ἐν ἄστροις ναίουσι) or gen. of description with ἀντολάς ('heavenly risings', 'risings in the aether')? It is not likely to be dependent on the preposition in ἀντολάς, as suggested by Wilam. on *Her.* 170, paraphrasing τὰ ἄστρα τοῦ αἰθέρος ἀνατέλλει: verbs in ἀνα- govern only a separative gen. (K–G 1.394, 396), and the gen. with ἀνά itself is limited to the Odyssean phrase ἂν ... νηὸς βαῖνεν and an inscr. cited by LSJ. (2) Why does Eur. refer to 'risings' at all in a contrast between underworld and sky? Why not 'paths of the stars' or 'expanse of the heavens'? In *Prom.* 457–8 and *Ag.* 7 'risings' are naturally paired with settings; fr. 482 lacks a full context but probably had the same point as *Prom.* 457–8. Among emendations, apart from wholesale recasting (e.g. Seyffert ἄστρ' ἂν διέλθοιμ' ἡλίου παρ' ἄντυγας), some attack ἄστρων (ἄισσων Schumacher, ἑκών Rauchenstein, σπάσων Harry, ἄνω τ' Wecklein), but I find the emphatic placement of ἄστρων effective and most of the substitutes rather otiose (but if ἄστρων is altered, then Zakas' αἰθέρος πρὸς ἀμπτυχάς is attractive). Others attack πρός in order to introduce a conjunction (τ' ἐπ' repud. Valck., τ' εἰς Schoene), leaving the superfluous and ambiguous reference to the sun. Hannemueller's ἡδέως displaces the sun, but does not ring true rhetorically or, I think, in word-order. Like Pol.'s complaints about exile (395n.), Et.'s frank praise of tyranny and willingness to acquire it at any cost became targets for the criticism of later philosophers: there is a trace of complaint in Σ504 and Σ507; Epictetus (*diss.* 4.5.29–30) pairs Et.'s false dogma about what is good with Pol.'s about what is bad; and 524–5 come in for criticism from Cicero *de off.* 3.21.82 and Plutarch *Mor.* 18D and 125D–E. Euripides was clearly criticized by some for writing the lines (Cicero: *capitalis Eteocles vel potius Euripides*), but in this case we find an intelligent defence offered in Σ and in Plutarch *Mor.* 18.

506 τὴν θεῶν μεγίστην ... Τυραννίδα on the identification of highly valued or powerful emotions, states, or events as 'gods' see Kannicht on *Hel.* 559–60 θεὸς γὰρ καὶ τὸ γιγνώσκειν φίλους. For Tyrannis as a goddess cf. fr. 250 Τυραννίδ' ἢ θεῶν δευτέρα νομίζεται and the milder personifications in *Ion* 621 (her πρόσωπον), Hdt. 3.53.4 (her ἐρασταί: cf. *Her.* 65–6, fr. 850); also the goddess Basileia in *Birds* and later the allegory in Dio Chrys. 1.78 (contrasted with Basileia, 1.73). Although τυραννίς can be a non-pejorative synonym for βασιλεία in tragedy, Eur. is surely counting on the negative associations of the word here and in 523–4: Et.'s valuation of the tyranny is in line with the tradition that views it as a god-like licence to do with impunity whatever one wishes: cf. Solon fr. 33 West, Plato *Gorg.*

469c, *Rep.* 343–4. See J. L. O'Neil, 'The Semantic Usage of *tyrannos* and Related Words', *Antichthon* 20 (1986) 26–40.

508 παρεῖναι from παρίημι, not πάρειμι; Et. emphasizes his unwillingness to let go by heavy repetition, cf. 509 ἀπολέσας, 514 παρείην, 519 μεθήσομαι, 523 παρήσω.

509–10 ἀνανδρία . . . ὅστις for ὅστις equivalent to εἴ τις, giving the conditions of a general statement, cf. K–G II.441–2; Diggle on *Phaethon* 160–2. For this argument, Pearson compares Callicles' claim (*Gorgias* 483) that it is unmanly or slavish to let oneself be treated unjustly, which by nature is to allow oneself to be left with the smaller share, and Thrasymachus' claim (*Rep.* 338ff., esp. 344c) that injustice, taking a bigger share, is characteristic of personal freedom.

τὸ πλέον . . . τοὔλασσον 539–40n., 553n.

510–14 having made the selfish argument justifying retention of what he values (τὸ χρηστόν) and the personal argument from 'manliness' (ἀνανδρία), Et. now exploits the issue of shame (αἰσχύνομαι, ὄνειδος) in a patriotic fashion in order to imply an identity of interest between himself and the city as a whole – a typical ploy of politicians for generating public support in defence of a policy actually dictated by individual imprudence or vice.

510 αἰσχύνομαι the acc. and inf. construction used here (different from that attested in LSJ s.v. B.II.3) is analogous to οὐ βούλομαι τόνδε τυχεῖν and is exceedingly rare (the only other classical instance I find is Xen. *Cyr.* 8.4.5 τὸν δὲ πρωτεύοντα ἐν ἕδραι ἡισχύνετο μὴ οὐ πλεῖστα καὶ ἀγαθὰ ἔχοντα παρ' αὐτοῦ φαίνεσθαι); more usual is αἰσχύνομαι εἰ, as *Ion* 1074ff. αἰσχύνομαι . . . εἰ . . . [sc. Ἴων] ὄψεται.

511 πορθοῦντα γῆν the present part. could be merely conative ('seeking to ravage') or Et. may be stretching the truth for the sake of argument; but the Athenian audience would be accustomed to the notion that an army marching through enemy territory would loot and destroy crops and property on the route before facing battle or beginning a siege. Eur.'s sympathetic portrayal of Pol., however, requires that he downplay any destruction wrought before the opening of the play.

512 ταῖς . . . Θήβαις city-names in tragedy, when used without an epithet, are most often anarthrous. Calling ταῖς *inutilis*, Hermann emended to καὶ γὰρ ἂν Θήβαις, perhaps because this would be the only passage in Eur. with the article (among over thirty-five instances). Paley also mentions the separation of the article from its noun by two (separate) postpositives, but himself cites *Hel.* 922 τὰ μέν σε θεῖα and the even bolder *Aj.* 311 (cf. also K–G I.610, Wackernagel *Kl. Schr.* I.38, 62; an exact parallel at Thuc. 6.64.1 τοὺς γὰρ ἂν ψιλούς, cf. 6.11.3 ὧι γὰρ ἂν τρόπωι). But Soph. has the article only twice (*OT* 1380, *OC* 616), and for other cities use of the article is also relatively infrequent (e.g. Ἄργος over 100 times in tragedy (over 80 in Eur.), with the article 8 times, all in Eur.; Ἀθῆναι about 70 times in tragedy, with the article 18 times); cf. Moorhouse, *Syntax Soph.* 147. The article may add some dignity to the name (cf. 717).

516 πᾶν γὰρ ἐξαιρεῖ λόγος 'Speech captures full well every goal.' Et. uses a paradoxically violent word, boastfully glorying, it seems, in the quasi-military power of rhetoric (cf. Gorgias *Helen* 8 λόγος δυνάστης μέγας ἐστίν, ὃς σμικροτάτωι σώματι καὶ ἀφανεστάτωι θειότατα ἔργα ἀποτελεῖ; Plato *Gorg.* 456). The verb can of course be paraphrased with 'accomplish' (LSJ s.v. IV.2, a very lonely heading, not related to IV.1), but that is not its actual meaning. Since there is no notion here of taking one thing from a larger group, ἐξ- should be taken as intensifying (as it probably is in the common meaning 'kill, destroy'), and the verb granted some of its physical force ('seize, get into one's power' rather than a more bland 'win, gain'). The metaphor is chosen because of the following comparison with war, and Plutarch had the military sense in mind when he quoted the lines in *Pyrrh.* 14 and explained ὁ γοῦν Πύρρος ἔλεγε πλείονας πόλεις ὑπὸ Κινέου τοῖς λόγοις ἢ τοῖς ὅπλοις ὑφ' ἑαυτοῦ προσῆχθαι (Plut.'s translator H. Cruser used *expugnare* to render ἐξαιρεῖν).[1] Pearson's interpretation of ἐξαιρεῖ as 'removes' cannot be accepted: (1) unlike Isocr. 12.165 πρεσβείαις καὶ λόγοις ἐξαιρεῖν ἐπειρῶντο τὰς διαφοράς and the other passages he cites, here there is no clue that suggests taking πᾶν as 'every obstacle or point of disagreement'; (2) if δράσειεν is substitute-verb 'do' (= 'remove') instead of 'accomplish', then ὅ will have to be 'which thing (sc. removal of obstacles)' (Pearson unjustifiably paraphrases ὅ with 'as well as'), i.e. πᾶν will not be its antecedent, and as a result the idiomatic responsive force of καί (517n.) will be spoiled. The other interpretation of the transmitted letters is ἐξαίρει, but 'raise up' makes no sense and the meaning 'carry off, earn' is confined to the middle ('make away with', LSJ I.5, is late Greek, perhaps by conflation with ἐξαιρεῖν). For the gnome itself, cf. *Su.* 748–9 πόλεις τ', ἔχουσαι διὰ λόγου κάμψαι κακά, φόνωι καθαιρεῖσθ' οὐ λόγωι τὰ πράγματα and other passages cited by Collard *ad loc.* Et.'s confidence in the power of speech, implicit in the showiness of his argument and explicit in this gnome, is ironic. The main point of this agon is that λόγος does not accomplish anything good. By mouthing this gnome in this inapposite context (cf. Creon at 900, 902, 1320–1), he reveals a naive blindness which is perhaps

---

[1] Cf. *Ion* 60–1 ... πολέμιος κλύδων· ὃν συμπονήσας καὶ συνεξελὼν δορί, where συνεξελών could perhaps be interpreted as 'having joined in capturing, controlling, defeating', a more military sense, rather than 'dispose of' (recommended by Owen, comparing our passage).

the one feature which allows an audience to have some tragic sympathy for his plight. Joc. will suggest that his wisdom is suspect, and the next episode will prove it. But his use of the gnome is also cynical, since he refuses to engage in discussion of Pol.'s grievance and has already depreciated the possibility of useful communication through ὀνόματα. Such intellectual and psychic inconsistency is a hallmark of Euripidean characterization.

517 ὃ καί καὶ marks the antithesis between λόγος and σίδηρος, with a sort of inverse responsion (Denniston, *GP*² 295–6) in place of the more logical 'speech too can do what war might do'.

518 ἄλλως i.e. without taking away my kingship.

519–20 among the problems of these lines are (1) to what does ἐκεῖνο refer? (2) can it stand as object of μεθήσομαι? (3) does the variant δουλεῦσαι throw more doubt on ἐκεῖνο or μεθήσομαι? (4) is 520 genuine? (1) ἐκεῖνο δ' is contrasted with εἰ μὲν ἄλλως, and this contrast and Et.'s obsession with retaining the rule are enough for an audience to understand ἐκεῖνο as 'my rule, which he wants to take away or share' without an explaining inf. in apposition to it. Such an inf. could have been added, but there is, on my view, instead an emotional shift of construction, making ἄρχειν instead a subordinate element of the rhetorical question in 520. (2) The most natural sense for middle μεθήσομαι in this context is 'give up, surrender'. When used of physically releasing an object one holds, the separative gen. is normal (cf. 1661 οὐ μεθήσομαι νεκροῦ). But the holding and releasing are not physical here, and it is possible that the acc. can stand (as it usually does with active μεθίημι): cf. MacDowell's defence of transmitted τόνδ' in *Wasps* 416, and perhaps *Med.* 736 ἄγουσιν οὐ μεθεῖ' ἂν ἐκ γαίας ἐμέ.[1] O's ἐκείνου may be a conflation of ἐκεῖνο and ἐκείνου (coni. Valck.), but I suspect that the gen. is more likely to be a grammatical regularization than a survival of the truth. (3) The inf. δουλεῦσαι could be the explication of ἐκεῖνο only if μεθήσομαι were given the unexampled meaning 'permit (to happen) to myself' (for active μεθίημι approaching the sense 'permit' see 90n.) or 'submit to' (a proper meaning for προσήσομαι, LSJ II.3), or if it were emended (e.g. Geel' s μαθήσομαι, clever but not quite right, since 'learn one's lesson to do X' is normally said hostilely of someone else –

---

[1] One could of course claim that ἐμέ is here solely the object of ἄγουσιν, but it seems very likely to me that it would be felt as ἀπὸ κοινοῦ object of μεθεῖ as well (cf. Stinton, *PCPS* 21 (1975) 87 n. 1); less useful for my purpose is Soph. *El.* 1277, where μεθέσθαι is an afterthought by position and redundant in sense, so there is less impetus to connect the preceding acc. with it. I do not regard *Trach.* 196–7 as an example (as Kamerbeek does); for later Greek cf. Herodas 3.87 μέθεσθε … αὐτόν.

second or third person, not first). δουλεῦσαι is, I believe, simply a graphic error (ω/αι confusion is easy in minuscule). There is no likelihood that δουλεῦσαι is exclamatory (Valckenaer) or epexegetic (Matthiae). (4) Kirchhoff regarded 520 as *interpretis additamentum*. Unless he meant that the line was filled out from a single-word gloss ἄρχειν, this is unlikely, since an interpreter would have made a more obvious expansion of ἐκεῖνο (such as an inf. phrase meaning 'to rule'), not the effective rhetorical question we find.

520 δουλεύσω a rhetorical exaggeration, but it is also true that the simplistic opposition of ruling or being enslaved, with no admission of a middle ground, is typical of Greek political thought in the fifth century (cf. Herodotus' depiction of the rise and fall of empires and the political rhetoric used by all parties in Thucydides' account of the Peloponnesian War).

521 πρὸς ταῦτ' 'with a view to the facts (as I have just stated them)'; this phrase and πρὸς τάδε are commonly used in drama to introduce an imperative with a tone of admonition or (esp. in tragedy) defiance. See Barrett on *Hipp*. 304-5, Jebb on *Ant*. 658, Diggle, *Studies* 38; and cf. *Prom*. 915, 992, 1043, *Aj*. 971, *OT* 343, 426, S. *El*. 820, *OC* 455, *Med*. 1358, *Cret*. fr. 82.35 Austin.

522 the asyndeton between ζεύγνυσθ' and πίμπλαθ' marks the rising intensity of the four-term series; similarly, the increasing length of the members within each pair of terms adds rhetorical weight to the final item, which is hyperbolic, as in Dem. 8.74 οὐκ ἐμπλήσετε τὴν θάλατταν ... τριήρων; (contrast Xen. *Hell*. 7.1.20, literally ἐμπλήσαντες τὸ πεδίον).

524-5 despite his opening denial of common values, Et. here shamelessly adopts the traditional moral terminology of Pol., conceding his own ἀδικία and ἀσέβεια (violation of oaths). With τἄλλα ... εὐσεβεῖν χρεών cf. Odysseus' δίκαιοι δ' αὖθις ἐκφανούμεθα in *Phil*. 82.

526-7 again the choral comment is remarkably partisan (497-8n.). *Med*. 576-8 is similar, but not quite so strong, and the Corinthian women are clearly Medea's partisans (likewise *Hec*. 1183-4, *Tro*. 966-8). More commonly the chorus is deferential to a king, whether or not they approve what he says (*Aj*. 1091-2, 1118-19, 1264-5, *Andr*. 181-2, 364-5). Presumably Eur. counted on a similarly disapproving reaction in the audience, one that makes them eager to hear a rebuttal, regardless of its practical effectiveness, just as in *Tro*. an audience is eager to hear, with sympathy, Hecuba's reply to Helen, regardless of the balance of truth between the opposing speeches. For disapproval of eloquence used in the service of moral wrong – a conventional complaint against sophistic rhetoric – see Dodds on *Ba*. 266-71, with refs. (add fr. 583 ὅστις λέγει μὲν εὖ, τὰ δ' ἔργ' ἐφ' οἷς λέγει / αἴσχρ' ἐστι, τούτου τὸ σοφὸν οὐκ αἰνῶ ποτε). εὖ λέγειν is of course 'speak skilfully, eloquently' here, not 'praise' (Burian–Swann, Buschor).

526 μὴ 'πὶ τοῖς ἔργοις καλοῖς   the positions of μή and καλοῖς (predicative) have bothered some critics, but are explained by recognizing that we have a compressed expression for μὴ λέγοντα (i.e. ἐὰν μὴ λέγηι τις) ἐπὶ τοῖς ἔργοις οὖσι καὶ αὐτοῖς καλοῖς. For the position of μή and the conditional ellipsis, cf. Jebb on *Aj.* 950 οὐκ ἂν τάδ' ἔστη τῆιδε, μὴ θεῶν μέτα and *OT* 1456–7 οὐ γὰρ ἄν ποτε θνήισκων ἐσώθην, μὴ 'πί τωι δεινῶι κακῶι.

527 πικρόν   βαρύ Stobaeus, cf. Mosch. gloss and lemma. Both πικρός ('bitter, hateful') and βαρύς ('annoying' or 'oppressive' or, of persons, 'severe') are good tragic words, and both readings are ancient. πικρός attracts a gloss here and in 956, but βαρεῖα does too in Σ *Med.* 38. βαρύ is perhaps less obvious (and so more likely to have attracted substitution of πικρόν than vice versa), but I retain πικρόν because (1) none of the uses of βαρύ seem quite like this construction (sc. τὸ εὖ λέγειν … βαρύ ἐστι τῆι δίκηι), and (2) the gnomological tradition is prone to error.

528–85   Joc.'s great speech, about equal in length to her sons' speeches combined and among the longest of extant agon-speeches, argues in turn against the positions of both brothers, reacting first and at greater length to Et. because he has just spoken, he is more glaringly in the wrong, and he has just put forward a view of the world to which Joc. is eager to oppose (and the audience is eager to hear) an alternative view. Like Theseus in *Su.* and Tiresias in *Ba.* (see 'Optimistic Rationalist'), she combines traditional wisdom with modern-sounding terms and arguments and with sophisticated theorizing about the order of the universe (for details, see notes on 528–9, 533, 536, 536–8, 538, 539–40, 541–2, 543–5, 546, 549, 553, 556). What she provides is a construct of an orderly and intelligible universe in which divine power not only provides man with examples but gives him the tools of order. Equality has given man measure and number, and equality is the binding element in nature as well as society. The balance structured into night and day is a service to man: that is, both as an example (which Et. refuses to follow) and as a guarantor of the seasons, the order of nature is provided by divine powers for man's good. Man in turn should feel that he is a temporary guardian and user of what is ultimately the gods'. This is an impressive and intellectually exciting performance, rhetorically varied (including gnomes and specific statements, rhetorical questions, varied sentence-lengths), with marks of earnestness and emotion (e.g. 532 μὴ σύ γ', 546–7 indignant εἶτα-question, 567 telegraphic final rebuke φιλότιμος δὲ σύ). But its dramatic impact is complex, for the tragic world of the play shows that Joc.'s faith is futile. She may 'win' the debate by a test of audience approval, but she loses by the test of results. Her rhesis receives no detailed response: Pol. says nothing, and Et., shifting gears into the quicker tempo of trochaic tetrameters, returns to the brusqueness and haste that characterized his entering speech as he dismisses Joc.'s effort. The structure of the speech is as follows. (1) 528–67, addressed to Et., consisting of (a) 528–30 introductory gnome; (b) 531–5a attack on Philotimia; (c) 535b–47 (or –48?) praise of Isotes (535b–40 gnomic, 541–5 illustrations in human life and nature, 546–8 application); (d) 549–67 renewed attack on Tyrannis/Philotimia (549–51 τυραννίς, 552–7 emptiness of πλεονεξία, 559–67 costs of τυραννίς/φιλοτιμία). (2) 568–83, addressed to Pol., consisting of (a) 568 formula of transition; (b) 569–83 attack on his decision to invade (569–70 general condemnation, 571–7 costs of victory over one's fatherland, 578–83 costs of defeat). (3) 584–5, final appeal to both brothers, with conclusive gnome. The first section in particular is marked by elements which specifically answer parts of Et.'s speech: 530 σοφώτερον (rejecting relativism of σοφόν, 499); 531 τῆς κακίστης δαιμόνων (506 τὴν θεῶν μεγίστην); 535 κάλλιον (525 κάλλιστον); 536 (with 538, 542, 544, 547) Ἰσότης/ἴσον (rejecting denial of ἴσον, 501, and desirability of τὸ πλέον, 509); 539–40 (with 553) τῶι πλέονι/τοὔλασσον (509–10); 546 δουλεύει βροτοῖς (reappropriating 520 τῶιδε δουλεύσω); 553 ὄνομ' ἔχει μόνον (502). In addition, 545 φθόνον picks up Pol.'s use of the word in 479, and 547 δωμάτων ἔχων ἴσον recalls his emphasis on μέρος and equal exchange. There are also framing repetitions which mark the beginnings and endings of subsections of (1): 532 Φιλοτιμίας / 567 φιλότιμος (cf. 549 τυραννίδ' / 560–1 τυραννεῖν); 532 ἄδικος / ?548 δίκη / 549 ἀδικίαν; 536 Ἰσότητα / 547 ἴσον. Finally, both main sections contain parallel presentations of the likely costs of the sons' decisions; and the theme of wisdom vs. folly frames the whole speech (the opening gnome accuses Et. of inexperience and lack of, or inferior, σοφία; the second section begins with ἀμαθεῖς and ἀσύνετα in anaphora; the concluding gnome refers to the ἀμαθία of both).

528–9 οὐχ ἅπαντα τῶι γήραι κακά . . . πρόσεστιν κακά is predicative, 'not all things attending old age are bad'. Joc. is adapting and correcting proverbial wisdom about old age: Soph. fr. 949 πάντ' ἐμπέφυκε τῶι μακρῶι γήραι κακά, νοῦς φροῦδος, ἔργ' ἀχρεῖα, φροντίδες κεναί, *OC* 1237–8 γῆρας . . . ἵνα πρόπαντα κακὰ κακῶν ξυνοικεῖ, *Wasps* 441 εἶτα δῆτ' οὐ πόλλ' ἔνεστι δεινὰ τῶι γήραι κακά;, Antiphanes fr. 251 K–A πρὸς γὰρ τὸ γῆρας ὥσπερ ἐργαστήριον / ἅπαντα τἀνθρώπεια προσφοιτᾶι κακά, cf. Mimnermus 1 West, Lysias 24.8, Men. *Sent.* 39. But her adaptation is also based on traditional wisdom, e.g., fr. 291 ὦ παῖ, νέων τοι δρᾶν μὲν ἔντονοι χέρες, / γνῶμαι δ' ἀμείνους εἰσὶ τῶν γεραιτέρων· / ὁ γὰρ χρόνος δίδαγμα ποικιλώτατον; Soph. fr. 260 . . . ἀλλὰ τῶι γήραι φιλεῖ / χὼ νοῦς ὁμαρτεῖν καὶ τὸ βουλεύειν ἃ δεῖ; cf. Diggle, *Studies* 23, Hutchinson on *Se.* 622, Friis

Johansen and Whittle on A. *Su.* 361. For the form of expression cf. the proverb of Chilon (or Sodamus) in Critias 7 West, μηδὲν ἄγαν· καιρῶι πάντα πρόσεστι καλά.

529 ἡμπειρία the noun, which first appears in late fifth-century authors and in Eur. alone among high-style poets, contributes to the scientific or intellectualist tenor of the speech. Eur.'s other use of the word is in a similar context: fr. 619 τὸ γῆρας, ὦ παῖ, τῶν νεωτέρων φρενῶν / σοφώτερον πέφυκε κἀσφαλέστερον, / ἡμπειρία [Porson, ἐμπ- Stob.] τε τῆς ἀπειρίας κρατεῖ. The γρ-variant dative ἐμπειρίαι arose after the omission of ἡ, which was probably due to what seemed to be an excess of syllables when the line was written in *scriptio plena* (for such omission cf. 21 and 476n.). There is no reason to believe that πρόσεστι, τῆι δ' ἐμπειρίαι was ever read (as Paley thought).

530 λέξαι attested already in the curious Delphic inscription, which J. Bousquet, *Fouilles de Delphes*, II: le Trésor de Cyrène (Paris 1952) 107, dates to the end of the fourth century B.C. (others to the third), this word in Joc.'s exordium matches Pol.'s μῦθος (470) and Et.'s ἐρῶ (503). δεῖξαι in Stobaeus (variant in Sextus) is due to the carelessness of gnomologic transmission: it is too boastful or demonstrative for this context (contrast *Su.* 340 ἔθος τόδ' ... ἐξεδειξάμην [Hermann, -ελεξά- L]). For δείκνυμι of a statement cf. *Phaethon* 106 περὶ γὰρ μεγάλων γνώμας δείξει (a proclamation); cf. *Rhes.* 39–40 πολλὰ γὰρ εἰπὼν οὐδὲν τρανῶς ἀπέδειξας; *Phil.* 426 is corrupt, but -λεξ- seems more likely than -δειξ- there.

531 κακίστης answering 506 μεγίστην (528–85n.).

532 Φιλοτιμίας Joc. means this to be a synonym for Τυραννίς, as is clear from the equivalence of 561 τυραννεῖν and 567 φιλότιμος (cf. the use of τὸ φιλότιμον in *IA* 342, 385 to mean virtually 'the supreme command'). Another implied synonym for τυραννίς is πλεονεξία (540–1n.), which Dio Chrys. actually has here in his extraordinarily unreliable quotation of 531–40 (see Teubner app., which fails to record βροτοῖς for τέκνον in 535): πλεονεξία is just as prosaic a word as φιλοτιμία, occurring in classical poetry only at *IA* 509 and a few times in Menander and Philemon, but is the more obvious word here and intruded for that reason. φιλοτιμία in the sense 'ambition for power/rule' corresponds to the pejorative sense of φιλότιμος that arose in the late fifth century. For the earlier, favourable sense of the adj. cf. Aesch. *Su.* 658, *Eum.* 1032. Pindar fr. 210 would give the earliest attestation of the noun and of this pejorative sense if Plutarch is quoting verbatim, which is far from certain. In Hdt. 3.53.4 the noun means 'stubborn pride'; but for 'ambitious rivalry' cf. Thuc. 2.65.7 (his disparaging comments on politicians after Pericles), 3.82.8 (the *stasis* passage: note the combination of terms in ἀρχὴ ἡ διὰ πλεονεξίαν καὶ φιλοτιμίαν), 8.89.3 (private ambitions leading to dissolution of oligarchy of 411); *Thesm.*

383 (an imitation of oratory in the assembly, cf. Lysias 19.56 for a similar excusing formula); *IA* 527 φιλοτιμίαι μὲν ἐνέχεται [sc. Odysseus], δεινῶι κακῶι. J. de Romilly, 'Les Phéniciennes' 36–41, suggests that condemnation of φιλοτιμία as harmful to the city arose in the period around 411 and that Eur.'s use of the term is especially topical.

μὴ σύ γ' for this earnest elliptical appeal, cf. *Hec.* 408 (also with explication following: μὴ σύ γ'· οὐ γὰρ ἄξιον), *Ion* 439, 1335, *IA* 1459, *OC* 1441, Men. *Georg.* 28; without ellipsis e.g. *Med.* 1056, *Lys.* 189.

533 οἴκους καὶ πόλεις Joc. is fervently trying to save her family, but she speaks also as protector of the wider concerns of the city, esp. in 559–67 and 571–7. After she has failed to reconcile her sons, the salvation of the city becomes more clearly separated from that of the royal house in the next three episodes (see Introd. I). The ruinous effects of political rivalry on the wider population are underscored by Thuc. (see previous note), but the idea is traditional (Solon fr. 4 West, Pindar fr. 210), based on the even older notion that the injustice of the 'kings' can bring destruction on all (Hes. *Op.* 238–69). For the rhetorical pairing cf. Isocr. 20.9 εὑρήσετε ... πολλοὺς μὲν οἴκους δι' αὐτὴν [sc. ὕβριν] διαφθαρέντας, πολλὰς δὲ πόλεις ἀναστάτους γεγενημένας; also *Ant.* 296–7, 673–4, *Tro.* 892–3, *Se.* 190. Nauck's deletion of 533–4 would leave ἄδικος woefully unsubstantiated and reduce the force of 535 ἐφ' ἧι ('this is the sort of goddess ...').

534 εἰσῆλθε κἀξῆλθ' ἐπ' ὀλέθρωι ἐπ' ὀλ. probably goes with the latter verb only: 'she has visited many prosperous households and cities and has departed only after the destruction [ἐπί = 'on the condition of', LSJ B.III.3] of those who associated with her'. It is also possible to consider εἰσῆλθε κἀξῆλθ' as an inseparable pair meaning 'visit' and take ἐπί as expressing purpose (LSJ B.III.2): commentators cite *Hel.* 1167 ἐξιών τε κἀσιὼν δόμους, where ἐκ δόμων can easily be supplied with ἐξιών (but hardly needs to be). Π^c offers και εισηλθε, which would be 'visited many ... and visited only in order to destroy those who ...', a weaker expression.

535 ἐφ' ἧι σὺ μαίνηι 'with whom you are madly in love'; cf. Anacr. 359.2 *PMG* Κλεοβούλωι δ' ἐπιμαίνομαι, and μαίνομαι ἐπί in Theocr. 10.31, 20.34 and *Eccl.* 966 μ' ἐκμαίνεις ἐπὶ ταύτηι; for the infatuation of love as madness cf. also Anacr. 428 *PMG*, *Ant.* 790, *Trach.* 1142, *Med.* 433, *Hipp.* 1274.

536 Ἰσότητα another prosaic/philosophical word, occurring in classical poetry only here and 542 and in the imitations at Men. *Sent.* 362 and 366. The conceptual connection of equality with justice and political harmony is, however, traditional as well as a topic of late fifth-century philosophical discussion: cf. Solon 36.18 West and the older terms ἰσονομία, ἰσηγορία (Attic scolia 893, 896 *PMG*; Hdt., Eupolis fr. 316.3 K–A); Plato *Gorg.* 507e6–508a7 φασὶ δ' οἱ σοφοί ... καὶ οὐρανὸν καὶ γῆν καὶ θεοὺς καὶ ἀνθρώπους τὴν κοινωνίαν συνέχειν καὶ φιλίαν καὶ κοσμιότητα καὶ σωφροσύνην καὶ δικαιότητα ... ἀλλὰ λέληθέν σε ὅτι ἡ ἰσότης ἡ γεωμετρικὴ καὶ ἐν θεοῖς καὶ ἐν ἀνθρώποις μέγα δύναται, σὺ δὲ πλεονεξίαν οἴει δεῖν ἀσκεῖν, *Laws* 757a5 παλαιὸς γὰρ λόγος ... ὡς ἰσότης φιλότητα ἀπεργάζεται (cf. Aristotle *EN* 8.6–8 on friendship and equality). See M. Ostwald, *Nomos and the Beginnings of Athenian Democracy* (Oxford 1969); G. Vlastos, 'Equality and Justice in Early Greek Cosmologies', *CP* 42 (1947) 156–78; Guthrie, *Hist. Greek Phil.* III.148–51. For speculation that Eur. drew (esp. here and in *Su.* 429–56) upon a specific contemporary 'sociological' treatise that celebrated the rule of law and justified it by reference to the order of nature, see F. Dümmler, *Prolegomena zu Platons Staat und der Platonischen und Aristotelischen Staatslehre* (Basel 1891) 10–20.[1]

536–8 ἢ φίλους ἀεὶ φίλοις ... συνδεῖ the gnomologic tradition spawned a feeble variant καὶ φίλους εἶναι φίλοις [or φίλους] πόλεις τε πόλεσι ... συνδεῖν; parts of this have intruded in various witnesses.[2] For the sequence of three polyptota, cf. A. fr. 38 and see B. Gygli-Wyss, *Das nominale Polyptoton im älteren Griechisch* [Erganzungshefte zur Z. f. vergl. Sprachforschung, 18 (Göttingen 1966)] 91; Fehling, 226. The close relation of equality with justice and law is suggested by the similar claim of the binding power of the latter in Anon. Iamblichi (89 D–K) 3.6 (how will one perform a lasting, non-monetary benefaction to one's fellow-men?) ὧδε οὖν ἔσται τοῦτο, εἰ τοῖς νόμοις τε καὶ τῶι δικαίωι ἐπικουροίη· τοῦτο γὰρ τάς τε πόλεις καὶ τοὺς ἀνθρώπους τὸ συνοικίζον καὶ τὸ συνέχον. The helpfulness of equality in interstate relations has little relevance to the Thebes–Argos conflict, but in this section Joc. is generalizing as much as possible to show the universal applicability of the principle she recommends.

538 νόμιμον 'characterized by, and characteristic of, accepted usage and law', and therefore 'just' as opposed to the injustice of φιλοτιμία/τυραννίς/πλεονεξία. Equality binds through its lawful precision and regularity and through its provision of a common, known standard. This produces the opposite of the 'state of nature' as envisioned by a Callicles or Thrasymachus, in which the stronger seizes as much as he can (Joc., however, like the chorus in *Ba.* 894–6 would prefer to acknowledge no opposition between *nomos* and *physis*). The allusion to *nomos* here prepares for the opposed theme of πλέον ἔχειν in the next lines (see next note), and

---

[1] Mueller-Goldingen, 104 (with refs. in n. 68), follows those who believe there is specifically Pythagorean background to Joc.'s world-view.

[2] Dio Chrys. has φίλοις; the ascription of φίλους in *Text. Trad.* and Teubner app. is my error.

then the regularity and conventional acceptance of weights and measures are used in illustration in 541–5. νόμιμον and δίκαιον are nearly synonymous: cf. Xen. *Mem.* 4.4.12–25, *Cyr.* 1.3.17, Plato, *Gorg.* 504d, *Rep.* 359a4, Isocr. 15.179, Anon. Iamblichi cited on 536–8; for τὸ ἴσον associated with these terms, cf. (in addition to the passages cited on 536) Aristotle *EN* 5.1, esp. 1129a34–b1 τὸ μὲν δίκαιον ἄρα τὸ νόμιμον καὶ τὸ ἴσον, τὸ δ' ἄδικον τὸ παράνομον καὶ ἄνισον, *Pol.* 6.3, esp. 1318b1–5 ἀλλὰ περὶ μὲν τοῦ ἴσου καὶ δικαίου, κἂν ἦι πάνυ χαλεπὸν εὑρεῖν τὴν ἀλήθειαν περὶ αὐτῶν, ὅμως ῥᾶιον τυχεῖν ἢ συμπεῖσαι τοὺς δυναμένους πλεονεκτεῖν· ἀεὶ γὰρ ζητοῦσι τὸ ἴσον καὶ τὸ δίκαιον οἱ ἥττους, οἱ δὲ κρατοῦντες οὐδὲν φροντίζουσιν. For lawfulness associated with συνέχειν cf. also *Su.* 312–13 τὸ γάρ τοι συνέχον ἀνθρώπων πόλεις / τοῦτ' ἔσθ', ὅταν τις τοὺς νόμους σώιζηι καλῶς.

Part of the indirect tradition offers μόνιμον for νόμιμον. When Plutarch quotes 536–8 at *Mor.* 481A, he makes no paraphrase of the final words and there is nothing in the immediate context to prove which reading he meant (the mss offer both); but at 484B–C he mixes paraphrases of Plato (jumbling words from both *Rep.* and *Soph.*) and *Phoen.* 536–8 and 539 (ὁ δ' ἐν οἰκίαι παραινῶν ἀδελφοῖς μάλιστα μὲν ὡς ὁ Πλάτων παρήινει τοῖς πολίταις 'τὸ ἐμόν' ἐξαιρεῖν 'καὶ τὸ οὐκ ἐμόν', εἰ δὲ μή, τὴν ἴσην ἀγαπᾶν [cf. Ἰσότητα τιμᾶν] καὶ τῆς ἴσης περιέχεσθαι, καλὴν κρηπῖδα καὶ μόνιμον ὁμονοίας καὶ εἰρήνης καταβαλλόμενος ἀεὶ ⟨φανεῖται⟩ [suppl. Pohlenz]). It is clear that at this point Plutarch believed that μόνιμον was in the Euripidean text, and the existence of ἀσφαλές as a gloss in Σ confirms that the word was actually in the tradition and not merely due to a trick of Plutarch's memory. The rest of the indirect tradition has νόμιμον, but none of the quotations paraphrase this exact word or rely on it for their appropriateness. μόνιμον is found elsewhere in tragedy only in *Or.* 340 of ὄλβος (cf. 558 below) and in *OT* 1322 of a faithful friend. As opposed to νόμιμον, it would here make the point that equality is 'long-lasting' or more accurately 'supportive of prolonged stability'; this seems to me a narrower and a weaker point than Joc. intends, and than she is entitled (on her construct of the universe), to make, for she views peace as not merely long-lived, but as the natural, permanent condition when equality is present.[1] In

---

[1] I do not think two places in Aristotle where ἴσον and μόνιμον are conjoined speak in favour of μόνιμον here: in *Pol.*5.7, discussing forms of state which are more or less μόνιμοι, he mentions that polities sometimes deviate into oligarchies because they lose the only thing making them stable, namely, equality according to worth and each class's possession of its own property (1307a26–7 μόνον γὰρ μόνιμον ['producing stability'] τὸ κατ' ἀξίαν ἴσον καὶ τὸ ἔχειν τὰ αὐτῶν); in *Pol.* 1302a2–8

discussing the choice of reading, Valck. (who in the end adopts νόμιμον) notes that μόνιμον would be more suitable than νόμιμον for persuading Et., who does not believe in νόμος, and Hartung presses this point even more strongly. But in a Euripidean agon we cannot insist that the debaters use the best argument to persuade their opponent and avoid what will alienate their opponent: indeed, the opposite is very often the case (cf. Jason and Medea, Theseus and Hippolytus), because Euripides considers it more important that his characters reveal the strong contrasts of their world-views.

539–40 for the notion that unjust men cannot live in harmony but inevitably quarrel among themselves, cf. Plato *Prot.* 322b–d, *Rep.* 352b–c, Anon. Iamblichi (89 D–K) 6.1.

τῶι πλέονι ... τοὔλασσον Joc. takes up the terms used by Et. in 510–11, and from the discussions in *Gorgias* and *Republic* 1 we can see that sophistic theorists like Callicles and Thrasymachus used these terms, esp. τὸ πλέον, to describe the competition of men for goods and power, and in such discussion the *tyrannos* is the supreme example of the πλεονέκτης, just as *tyrannis* is the strongest temptation to the unwise in choosing a life (*Rep.* 619b–c). Note esp. *Gorg.* 483c–d [οἱ πολλοὶ καὶ ἀσθενεῖς] ἐκφοβοῦντες τοὺς ἐρρωμενεστέρους τῶν ἀνθρώπων καὶ δυνατοὺς ὄντας πλέον ἔχειν, ἵνα μὴ αὐτῶν πλέον ἔχωσιν, λέγουσιν ὡς αἰσχρὸν καὶ ἄδικον τὸ πλεονεκτεῖν, καὶ τοῦτό ἐστιν τὸ ἀδικεῖν, τὸ πλέον τῶν ἄλλων ζητεῖν ἔχειν; *Rep.* 344a τοῦτον οὖν [τὸν μεγάλα δυνάμενον πλεονεκτεῖν] σκόπει· ... πάντων δὲ ῥᾶιστα μαθήσηι, ἐὰν ἐπὶ τὴν τελεωτάτην ἀδικίαν ἔλθηις ... ἔστιν δὲ τοῦτο τυραννίς, 349bff, 359b; cf. also Aristotle's discussion of ὁ ἄδικος in *EN* 5.2 (cf. *Magna Moralia* 1.34.4) and the conventional association of πλεονεκτεῖν with ἀδικία in, e.g., Thuc. 1.77.4, Xen. *Mem.* 2.6.23. Anon. Iamblichi (89 D–K) 6 argues for the proposition that οὐκ ἐπὶ πλεονεξίαν ὁρμᾶν δεῖ. Later in her speech Joc. shifts to the terms πόλλ' ἔχειν (552), χρήματα (555), and πλοῦτος (566), which she equally associates with πλεονεκτεῖν (note πλέον 553), τυραννίς, and φιλοτιμία, reflecting a traditional linking of wealth and tyranny (Solon 33.5–6 West πλοῦτον ἄφθονον λαβὼν καὶ τυραννεύσας; *O T* 380 ὦ πλοῦτε καὶ τυραννί, *Ant.* 1168–9 πλούτει τε γὰρ κατ' οἶκον ... καὶ ζῆ τύραννον σχῆμ' ἔχων).

ἐχθρᾶς ... ἡμέρας a periphrasis for 'day of enmity' (= 'condition of enmity') based on epic locutions of the type δούλιον ἦμαρ (LSJ s.v. ἦμαρ

---

he remarks that no state is μόνιμος in which either numerical equality or equality according to worth is applied alone, without admixture of the other type.

1.2); most of the other examples in LSJ s.v. ἡμέρα 1.2 refer to a time of life rather than a state or condition, so this phrase has a strong epic colouring which contributes to the solemnity of Joc.'s speech.

541–2 measures and numbers are cited in fuller accounts as important steps in the progress of man from a bestial state toward civilization, whether they are the gift of a god (*Prom.* 459–60, paired with writing; cf. perhaps *Su.* 202 διεσταθμήσατο; Theuth, Plato *Phdr.* 274c–d, paired with writing; Thoth, Stobaeus 1. proem. 6) or an invention of man (Palamedes: Aesch. fr. 181a , Soph. fr. 432, Gorgias *Palam.* 30 [82 B 11a D–K]; paired with writing in Gorgias); see Collard on *Su.* 201–13, 203–4.

543–5 for the alternation of day and night as an example of justice or order and balance, cf. Heraclitus B94 D–K Ἥλιος οὐχ ὑπερβήσεται μέτρα· εἰ δὲ μή, Ἐρινύες μιν Δίκης ἐπίκουροι ἐξευρήσουσιν, Parmenides B1.11–14 (gates of the paths of Night and Day controlled by Dike), B9.3–4 D–K πᾶν πλέον ἐστὶν ὁμοῦ φάεος καὶ νυκτὸς ἀφάντου, / ἴσων ἀμφοτέρων, ἐπεὶ οὐδετέρωι μέτα μηδέν, Hippocr. περὶ διαίτης 1.5 χωρεῖ δὲ πάντα καὶ θεῖα καὶ ἀνθρώπινα ἄνω καὶ κάτω ἀμειβόμενα· ἡμέρα καὶ εὐφρόνη ἐπὶ τὸ μήκιστον καὶ ἐλάχιστον; *Aj.* 672–3 ἐξίσταται δὲ νυκτὸς αἰανὴς κύκλος / τῆι λευκοπώλωι φέγγος ἡμέραι φλέγειν.

543 νυκτός τ' ἀφεγγὲς βλέφαρον 'the lightless eye of night', that is, night with its darkness that neither sees nor helps men see (whereas day has the sun, which sees all and lets men see); there is a similar oxymoron in fr. 386a Snell νυκτὸς ἀμβλωπὸν σέλας, presumably, in view of ἀμβλωπόν, a periphrasis for night, not for the moon; milder cases in *Pers.* 428 κελαινὸν νυκτὸς ὄμμα and *IT* 110 νυκτὸς ὄμμα λυγαίας. The 'eye of night' can also be the moon (*Septem* 390; 'eye of evening' Pindar *O.* 3.19–20), but that sense is ruled out here by the adj., by the rephrasing of 543 in 546, and by Joc.'s point (over the course of a year, there is the same amount of daylight and of darkness). For the metaphor cf. also *El.* 102 ('dawn's white eye') and *Ant.* 104 ('golden day's eye'). Pearson identifies the metaphor instead as 'eyelid of night' (the night as a shroud which closes over the light sky), but this seems unnecessary.

544 βαδίζει this verb, quite frequent in comedy and used by orators, Xen., and Plato, is rare in serious poetry: only here in Eur., once in Soph. (*El.* 1502: Orestes' brusque command to Aegisthus), plus *Hom.h.Herm.* 210, 320, Chaeremon *TrGF* 71 F 20, *TrGF* adesp. 177.1. If the verb is rather colloquial in tone (unlike βαδιστής *Med.* 1182, hapax in classical Greek), it is perhaps chosen to 'humanize' the celestial phenomena which are being offered as an example.

τὸν ἐνιαύσιον κύκλον though the division of the time-span is different in the two cases, this phrase echoes 477 ἐνιαυτοῦ κύκλον and so prepares for the application of the celestial example to the brothers.

545 κοὐδέτερον αὐτῶν possibly αὐτοῖν (VrPRwZZbTᶻ) is the truth; αὐτοῖν is not otherwise attested in Eur. (L's αὐτοῖν in *IT* 317 was corrected to αὐτοῖν by England), but cf. αὐτώ in *Or.* 1555, and with a word like οὐδέτερος the dual is likely to occur (cf. *Clouds* 953 ὁπότερος αὐτοῖν, *Thesm.* 11 αὐτοῖν ἑκατέρου). οὐδέτερος is used in tragedy only here and *Or.* 1577, but the form has epic precedents (could this passage be a reminiscence of Parmenides B9.4, quoted on 542–5?).

φθόνον ἔχει νικώμενον 'neither ... is defeated and (so) feels envy', not 'neither ... feels envy when ousted' (Craik); the single negative at the head of the sentence applies to both verbal forms, as usual in Greek (K–G II.199 Anm. 1), and it is essential to Joc.'s argument that there is no 'defeat' or worsting in a case of equality.

546–7 [or **8**?] for the form of the argument and use of natural phenomenon, cf. *Clouds* 1292–5 (after the creditor admits that it is not δίκαιον for the sea to become larger) κᾆτα πῶς / αὕτη μέν, ὦ κακόδαιμον, οὐδὲν γίγνεται / ἐπιρρεόντων τῶν ποταμῶν πλείων, σὺ δὲ / ζητεῖς ποῆσαι τἀργύριον πλέον τὸ σόν; Also similar is the argument from divine example, esp. as used in *Hipp.* 451–9, ending in σὺ δ' οὐκ ἀνέξηι; (see Barrett on 459–61).

546 δουλεύει βροτοῖς 'do service to mankind', that is, by marking off the year into predictable seasons, which make possible agriculture, seafaring, etc. For the notion that the world, or aspects of it, has been designed by the gods for man's benefit, cf. Theseus in *Su.* 195ff., Tiresias on the benefits of Dionysus in *Ba.* 272ff., and esp. Xen. *Mem.* 1.4.11–15 (advantages of body and mind given to man by the gods), 4.3.3–17 (esp. 3 on day and night, 4 on seasons, 8–9 on annual movements of the sun); cf. also West on Hes. *Op.* 398 θεοὶ διετεκμήραντο. Though the expression δουλεύει βροτοῖς verges on extravagance, it is merely a development of the thought of the previous lines: 541 ἀνθρώποισι shows that mankind is the beneficiary of the arrangements made by Isotes, and the connection of 543–5 with τ' already implies that the seasonal variations of day and night are also for man's benefit. It is the boldness of δουλεύει βροτοῖς, I think, that attracted Strattis' attention and that makes his parody so funny (*Phoen.* fr. 48 K–A εἶθ' ἥλιος μὲν πείθεται τοῖς παιδίοις / ὅταν λέγωσιν 'ἔξεχ' ὦ φίλ' ἥλιε'). The parody loses a great deal if we believe (with Weil and Fraenkel) that Eur. actually wrote δουλεύει μέτροις. It should not be regarded as significant that the paraphrase of Σ simplifies to δουλεύει τῶι ἴσωι; Origen's use of the line proves that he (or Celsus before him) had βροτοῖς in the text. Finally, in view of Strattis' attestation of the line so early in the history of the text, no serious thought should be given to deleting 546: it rephrases and sharpens 543–5 as a lead-in to 547; εἶθ' adds to the tone of indignation, and μέν in 546 makes the δ' in 547 more forceful (though it is of course possible to have both the indignation and the contrasting force of δ' without such an explicit lead-in, as in *Alc.* 634–5 and *Hipp.* 459 σὺ δ' οὐκ ἀνέξηι;).

547-8 548 comes under strong suspicion. A phrase conveying 'and allot to him ⟨an equal share⟩' or 'allot to him also ⟨an equal share⟩' would make sense here and make the comparison fully balanced (οὐ νικώμενον ≈ ἔχων ἴσον; οὐ φθόνον ἔχει ≈ τῶιδε [ἴσον] ἀπονέμειν), and the vehement question κᾆτα ποῦ 'στιν ἡ δίκη; would reintroduce the term used at the beginning of the section (532 ἄδικος) and smooth the transition to 549 ἀδικίαν. Yet the problems of 548 are serious. (1) The 'transmitted' text has an unmetrical anapaest in τῶιδ' ἀπονεῖμαι (cf. 1637n.). In calling this the 'transmitted' text, we are trusting the *veteres* and assuming that ἀπονέμειν (in a few *recc.* and χ) arose from it by a grammatical regularization (to match ἔχειν in 547). Cf. Σ547 ἐὰν γράφηται ἔχειν, καὶ ἀπονέμειν· ἐὰν δὲ ἔχων, καὶ ἀπονέμων, which seems to be counselling against a mixture of participle and infinitive after ἀνέχομαι. Such a counsel may have been prompted in the first instance by ἔχων/ἀπονεῖμαι, but as it stands, it seems to imply that the commentator already found ἀπονέμ- present in the text. But given our current understanding of the nature of the tradition, we must at least ask whether ἀπονέμ- is a genuine variant and not secondary to ἀπονεῖμαι. Three major scenarios of corruption may be reviewed. (a) If ἔχων/ἀπονέμειν was the original reading (whether by Eur. or an interpolator), it invited the substitution of ἔχειν (already in the text in antiquity), and the existence of the variant then invited the comment of Σ, and the comment in turn led to ἀπονέμων in the text (A only). But in this scenario, corruption to ἀπονεῖμαι is not explained. (b) If Eur. actually wrote ἔχων/(τῶιδε) νεῖμαι, this may have attracted the gloss ἀπονεῖμαι. ἀπονέμω is not attested in tragedy (in Soph. fr. 144.2 as transmitted in ΣPindar the word intrudes as gloss or misplaced lemma, ἀπόνειμον νέμει τις for (probably) νέμ' εἴ τις), though it is frequent in late prose (in classical poetry only Pindar *I.* 2.47, Antiphanes fr. 204 K–A, Simonides 118.3 Diehl [= *Anth. gr.* 7.253]). The gloss then ousted the truth, and then was adjusted to the present ἀπονέμειν and produced further variations as above. (c) An interpolator wrote unmetrical τῶιδ' ἀπονεῖμαι, and this was adjusted to ἀπονέμων, etc. None of these scenarios is impossible, but I do not find (a) more plausible than (b) or (c). (2) If an infinitive was originally present along with a participle, it is highly unusual. The supplementary part. with ἀνέχομαι is well attested in Eur. and occurs a few times in Soph. and Aesch. The complementary inf. (occurring more often with negated verb than with unnegated) is much less common in any age. In classical authors one can cite *Eum.* 914–15 οὐκ ἀνέξομαι τὸ μὴ οὐ τήνδε ... τιμᾶν πόλιν; *Her.* 1254 οὐκ ἂν ⟨σ'⟩ ἀνάσχοιθ' Ἑλλὰς ἀμαθίαι θανεῖν (acc. and inf. analogous to constr. with κωλύω, οὐκ ἐάω; or, perhaps better, expressing a thought which would be intolerable); Cratinus fr. 344 K–A κοκκύζειν τὸν ἀλεκτρύον' οὐκ ἀνέχονται; Hdt. 7.139.6 καταμείναντες ἀνέσχοντο τὸν ἐπιόντα ἐπὶ τὴν χώρην δέξασθαι; some post-classical uses in LSJ c.ii.5 (also K–G ii.74), and cf. Plut. *Marius* 20.5 οἱ Τεύτονες οὐκ ἠνέσχοντο καταβαίνοντας αὐτοῖς ἐξ ἴσου διαγωνίζεσθαι τοὺς Ῥωμαίους. If the combination of part. and inf. is authentic, then we should not view it as a mixture of the two constructions (with conjunction καί), but (with Hermann, Klotz, and Geel) consider the inf. the complement of ἀνέξῃ, καί adverbial, and ἔχων as a circumstantial participle subordinate to the inf. (or the main verb): 'will you not bring yourself to give him too an equal share, having an equal share yourself?' Cf. καταμείναντες and καταβαίνοντας in Hdt. and Plut. quoted above. (3) 548 is not quoted by Oenomaus, who cites 546–7;[1] Paley claims it would have been cited if present in the text. But (a) the line was not suitable to the point Oenomaus was making (he wanted the rhetorical question to suggest a positive response, but 548 implies a negative one); (b) if the passage was anthologized as a gnome, 548 was apt to be omitted because of the specificity of τῶιδε; (c) the variant ἔχειν (present in these testimonia) is likely to have arisen by assimilation to an inf. in the following line (καί being taken as a conj.), and so the quotations probably derive ultimately from a text including 548. To conclude: if 548 is kept, I would endorse an explanation such as offered by Hermann and Klotz and give slight preference to Salmasius' τῶιδε νεῖμαι over τῶιδ' ἀπονέμειν (*utrum in alterum*; also, aorist aspect perhaps preferable in 'bring yourself to do X'). If 548 is deleted (as histrionic, in view of the declamatory style of κᾆτα ποῦ κτλ.), then ἔχων should be read in 547 (as the far more common constr., from which Eur. had no reason to depart). For κᾆτα in indignant questions, cf. 598, *Ion* 1408, *Andr.* 339, etc., and Denniston, *GP*[2] 311, Stevens *Colloquial Expr.* 47. The force of ποῦ is similarly expressive of indignant incredulity ('Justice is nowhere to be found if things will be like that!'); cf. *Aj.* 1100, *OT* 390, *Andr.* 591 with Stevens' note.

549–67 the entire final section of the portion of the speech directed to Eteocles (527–85n.) is deemed spurious by Kovacs, 42–5. Kovacs' arguments are of three kinds. (1) He finds the disquisition in these lines irrelevant to the concrete dramatic situation, alleging that desire for great wealth is distinct from Eteocles' desire for τυραννίς. But the point is that Joc. is here identifying these desires, and that this identification is in line with contemporary views of πλεονεξία and τυραννίς (532n., 539–40n.,

---

[1] Apud Euseb.; Theodoretus similarly cites 546–7, but he derived this and many other quotations from Euseb.: P. Canivet, *Théodoret de Cyène. Thérapeutique des maladies helléniques* i (Paris 1958) 57–8.

550n.). The speech thus moves freely from τυραννίς to πολλὰ ἔχειν and back to τυραννεῖν and again to πλοῦτος. The different terms of the discourse of Pol. and Joc. on the one hand and of Et. on the other are a crucial index of the intellectual drama of this scene, which goes well beyond the immediate needs of the concrete dramatic situation in a way that is thoroughly typical of Eur. Any argument that challenges the value of the χρηστόν on which Et. is staking everything is suitable to Joc.'s attempt at reconciliation. Furthermore, the consideration of the probable costs of Et.'s insistence on his rule (559–67) is precisely paralleled in the section of the speech addressed to Pol., and Joc.'s appeal to Et. would be deficient without it. (2) Kovacs believes that the ethical import of most of what Joc. says here 'runs counter to the basic presuppositions of Greek thought in the classical period'. Here I believe he is guilty of a fatal oversimplification of the Greek ethical tradition, misrepresenting heroic and aristocratic ethics as the whole of a rich and ambiguous (even at times contradictory) system of values. For instance, Kovacs claims that 'no one doubts that it [eminence, περιβλέπεσθαι] is in itself desirable', ignoring, e.g., the tradition of appeals for moderation (from Hesiod and Solon on), the challenge to the κλέος-ideal embodied in Achilles' speech in *Od.* 11.487ff., and the challenge to the ideal of wealth and power (τυραννίς) in Solon's confrontation with Croesus, Hdt. 1.29–33. Likewise, the notion of wealth as a cause of toils, though more prominent in the later tradition because of the influence of the philosophical schools, is not foreign to classical thought, as *Ion* 629–32 (cited along with other passages on 552) shows. (3) Kovacs cites four internal features of the lines to show 'that the author is not completely at home in the diction of fifth-century tragedy' and faults the rhetoric at various points. The points of diction are addressed below on 550 (perfect ἥγησαι, resumptive τόδε), 554 (double γε), and 559 (δύο λόγω προθεῖσ' ἅμα), and I do not consider them difficult enough or suspicious enough to add any weight to Kovacs' case. The rhetoric of 559–65 and 566–7 are explained *ad loc.* Finally, it is in my view no improvement (as Kovacs believes) to have Joc. address to the two brothers speeches of more closely similar lengths (527–85n.; Et. himself refers grudgingly to the length of Joc.'s speech, 592n.).

549 ἀδικίαν εὐδαίμονα   a striking oxymoron, combining two opposing strains in the Greek tradition, admiration of tyranny as the opportunity to satisfy all one's desires and condemnation of it as the ultimate injustice. In context, of course, Joc. speaks εὐδαίμονα with irony, and the next lines are devoted to arguing that the supposed advantages of tyranny are really empty. (For the traditional theme of rejection of tyranny, see Archilochus 19 West, Solon 32, 33, 34 West, Hdt. 5.92; Young, 1–26 on Pindar *P.* 11.) Again the similarity to themes in Plato is remarkable: cf. *Gorg.* 470d–71d, on the theme ὡς πολλοὶ ἀδικοῦντες ἄνθρωποι εὐδαίμονές εἰσιν (Archelaus of Macedon as example); *Rep.* 360e–62c, on whether the ἄδικος or the δίκαιος is εὐδαιμονέστερος; see also Anon. Iamblichi (89 D–K) 6.

550 ὑπέρφευ in all three other tragic uses (*Pers.* 820, *Ag.* 377, *Her.* 1321) the adverb is associated with excess that is dangerous for a mortal, so there may here be a suggestion of overstepping folly in the degree of Et.'s attachment to Tyrannis. Cratinus fr. 393 K–A μηδὲν ὑπέρφευ is the only other extant use of the word outside Herodian and lexicographers. It is hard to decide whether the word is an artificial coinage (by Aesch.: Wilam. on *Her.* 1321) or a borrowing from lively popular language, like ὑπέρευ(γε) (Plato, Menander, but not Arist.), or an 'old-fashioned' word (Denniston–Page on *Ag.* 377; cf. Fraenkel).

καὶ μέγ' ἥγησαι τόδε a rhetorical filler, adding weight, but no new content, to the question τί ... ὑπέρφευ; τόδε refers backwards and is equivalent to τὸ τυραννεῖν, understood from τὴν τυραννίδ', a perfectly normal construction, *pace* Kovacs (549–67n.): cf. *Su.* 432 τόδ' = τὸ ἕνα κρατεῖν, 444 τόδε = τὸ ὑπεῖναι νεανίας, *Hec.* 427 τόδε = τὸ χαίρειν. Some critics have wanted to give this question a more independent content and make τόδε refer forward rather than backward. But if the question is continued to περιβλέπεσθαι τίμ., then τίμιος will, I believe, have to be read (a pred. adj. after an inf. is regularly attracted to the case of the implied subject of the inf., here nom., 'you, Et.'), and a false division will be created between wealth (πόλλ' ἔχων) and tyranny, which are equivalent concepts (532n., 539–40n.). As ἤ in 552 indicates, two aspects of tyranny's 'blessedness/prosperity' are considered and devalued in turn: first, being the object of attention of all eyes; second, having more than others; the first is κενόν, the second ὄνομ' ἔχει μόνον. Nor does it help to punctuate after ἥγησαι and read either τί δέ (Valck., with question-mark after both περιβλέπεσθαι and τίμιον) or τὸ δέ (Porson): Eur. rarely begins a new sentence after the tenth element of the trimeter, and Porson's reading would give a Sophoclean, not a Euripidean, verse-structure.

For μέγ', 'a thing of great value', cf. *Tro.* 259 οὐ γὰρ μέγ' αὐτῆι βασιλικῶν λέκτρων τυχεῖν;, *Ant.* 836 καίτοι φθιμένηι μέγα κἀκοῦσαι κτλ., *Rhes.* 198; but in this context spoken with some irony (cf. English 'a big deal').

ἥγησαι the use of the perfect for a settled opinion is found several times in Hdt., in Attic only here in Eur. and a few times in Plato (*Laws* 837c6, *Tim.* 19e3, *Hipp.Min.* 374d6); cf. νενόμικα used with a similar force in Hdt., comedy, Plato. I see no serious cause for suspicion in the isolation of this usage in extant drama (*pace* Kovacs: 549–67n.); there are many unique usages of a similar sort in unsuspected passages of the play.

551 περιβλέπεσθαι hapax in Eur., and the sense 'to be admired by all observers' is first found in Eur. and not common (cf. Xen. *Hieron* 7.2; *OC* 996 is surely 'look around carefully to discover/ascertain'); cf. adj. περίβλεπτος, used thrice by Eur., otherwise prosaic except Antiphanes 173.5 K–A.

μὲν οὖν   rejecting τίμιον (Denniston, *GP²* 478–9).

552 ἤ   not ἦ, since περιβλέπεσθαι is only one part of tyranny's supposed advantages, and a surmise-question with ἦ would begin a new topic, spoiling the cogency of the condemnation of tyranny.

552–3 πολλὰ μοχθεῖν . . . βούληι;   'Do you want to toil?' is an argumentative way of saying 'Do you want to cause yourself ⟨unnecessary⟩ toil and worry?' The objection that amassing and protecting abundant property entail abundant worry is traditionally made by those who recommend moderation: e.g., (cited but discounted by Kovacs) *Ion* 629–32 εἴποις ἂν ὡς ὁ χρυσὸς ἐκνικᾶι τάδε, / πλουτεῖν τε τερπνόν· οὐ φιλῶ ψόγους [Brodaeus; ψόφους L] κλύειν / ἐν χερσὶ σώιζων ὄλβον οὐδ' ἔχειν πόνους· / εἴη γ' ἐμοὶ ⟨μὲν⟩ μέτρια μὴ λυπουμένωι; (not cited by Kovacs) Soph. fr. 592 ἀλλὰ τῶν πολλῶν καλῶν / τίς χάρις, εἰ κακόβουλος / φροντὶς ἐκτρίψει [Herwerden: cf. Radt's app.] τὸν εὐαίωνα πλοῦτον;, Menander fr. 619 K–T, 'Philetas' apud Stobaeus 4.33.19 [= *Men. et Philist. Comp.* II.59–67 Jaekel], Horace *Odes* 3.1, etc.; cf. the association of μέριμναι with wealth in Theognis 1153–4 εἴη μοι πλουτοῦντι κακῶν ἀπάτερθε μεριμνέων / ζώειν ἀβλαβέως μηδὲν ἔχοντι κακόν. For the rhetorical play on πολλὰ cf. *Su.* 577 τοίγαρ πονοῦσα πολλὰ πόλλ' εὐδαιμονεῖ and for both rhetoric and sense cf. Men. fr. 12 K–T τί πολλὰ τηρεῖν πολλὰ δεῖ δεδοικότα;

553 τί δ' ἐστὶ τὸ πλέον   perhaps reminiscent of the Socratic form of question τί ἐστι . . . ; but here the point of the question is to cast doubt ('τὸ πλέον is really nothing substantial'), not to elicit an investigation.

ὄνομ' ἔχει μόνον   389n., 502n.; again Joc. uses Et.'s own terminology against him.

554 ἐπεὶ τά γ' ἀρχοῦνθ' . . . τοῖς γε σώφροσιν   the appearance of γε twice within the same clause is very rare (as Kovacs notes: 549–67n.), but each γε can be given a proper force, as explained by Denniston, *GP*² 142, 144. The first γ', despite its position, goes in sense with ἐπεί (cf. *Med.* 495) and marks the whole clause as a defiant assertion ('no matter what you may think or what else you may say'); the second, by emphasizing the class of moderate men, makes an implied comparison with the class of immoderate men, to which Et. has shown his allegiance. The sound parallels (all unique instances within their authors' works) rightly accepted by Denniston are *OC* 387 ἔγωγε τοῖς νῦν γ', ὦ πάτερ, μαντεύμασιν (eliminated by Lloyd-Jones and Wilson), Hdt. 1.187.2 μὴ μέντοι γε μὴ σπανίσας γε ἄλλως ἀνοίξηι, Xen. *Cyr.* 2.2.3 εἴ γε ἀφ' ἡμῶν γε τῶν ἐν μέσωι οὐδεὶς οὐδέποτε ἄρξεται, Lysias 31.29 εἰ μή γε ἄλλωι τινὶ μείζονι, τῆι γε παρούσηι ἀτιμίαι, to which I can add *Birds* 816 οὐδ' ἂν χαμεύνηι πάνυ γε κειρίαν γ' ἔχων (there are also several cases in Homer: *Il.* 5.258, 5.827, 16.30, *Od.* 8.138-9, 11.444, 22.116-17). Anyone who is still troubled by the double γε may prefer to read τοῖσι σώφροσιν with χZZbTᶻ (positing that this is a survival of truth and γε a metrical restoration repairing τοῖς σώφροσιν, rather than vice versa as suggested in *Text. Trad.* 102). For the sense, in addition to the passages cited on 552 cf. Solon fr. 24 West.

555-[8] Valckenaer believed that 558 was a Euripidean gnome cited in the margin and then incorporated into the text (for this type of interpolation, see Fraenkel, *Eranos* 44 (1946) 82ff., Kannicht on *Hel.* 905, Reeve, *GRBS* 11 (1970) 288-9). Most critics have followed him, rightly: if 555-7 are genuine, 558 is repetitious, enfeebling rather than strengthening or clinching Joc.'s argument. Such an interpolation is due to readers or copyists, not to actors. Lines 555-7 deserve to be judged separately (*pace* Page, *Actors' Interp.* 29: 'all four lines are spurious, if any'). Valckenaer considered 555-7 dispensable to the debate, but conceded that Eur. may have written them here. Nauck deleted, and Fraenkel supports this deletion by insisting on a rigid distinction between consideration of πλεονεξία and reflection on the perishable nature of material wealth. The issue here depends almost entirely on a critic's judgment of Eur.'s sense of relevance; for a single possible linguistic point, cf. 556n.[1] Fraenkel's distinction of topics is here misconceived. It is relevant to Joc.'s case to demonstrate the futility of Et.'s πολλὰ μοχθεῖν and the emptiness of τὸ πλέον; indeed 555-7 may almost be said to be necessary fully to substantiate 553 ὄνομ' ἔχει μόνον. Furthermore, the espousal of a proper relationship between men and gods is consonant with Joc.'s optimistic rationalist's world-view: the gods are provident, allowing mankind to oversee and enjoy what is theirs.[2] (For this reason it is certainly preferable to keep 555-7 without

---

[1] The confusion in the indirect tradition does not add any weight to the suspicion of 555-7. Soph. fr. 88.1 τὰ χρήματ' ἀνθρώποισιν εὑρίσκει φίλους is clearly not part of the same quotation as 555-7, which follow in Stob. 4.31d.104 without an intervening lemma. The rest of Soph. fr. 88 is actually given in Stob. 4.31a.27, and omission of lemma is a frequent error in the mss of Stobaeus; moreover, the missing lemma may be the one present at 4.31d.98.

[2] Mueller-Goldingen, 106, supports deletion of 555-7 by making a distinction between Joc.'s belief that by rational behaviour based on measure and equality humans can avoid disaster and the implication here that man's fortune is subject to the whims of the gods; he concludes that 555-7 contradict Joc.'s express beliefs. This distinction seems unduly strict. He also argues that if 555-7 are spurious, they are due

558 than to keep 558 without 555–7, as Wecklein once proposed.)   For the thought of these lines, cf. the traditional notion of the gods as 'givers of goods (and evils)' (e.g., Solon fr. 13 West, Theognis 133–4, 165–6). The idea that man has his life and his material goods on loan from higher powers (such as φύσις or τύχη) was later popular among the Stoics and Cynics,[1] but it should not be doubted that a kindred notion was current in classical times. Cf. *Alc.* 788–9 τὸν καθ' ἡμέραν / βίον λογίζου σόν, τὰ δ' ἄλλα τῆς τύχης; *Su.* 534–6 οὔτι γὰρ κεκτήμεθα / ἡμέτερον αὐτὸ [τὸ σῶμα] πλὴν ἐνοικῆσαι βίον, / κἄπειτα τὴν θρέψασαν αὐτὸ δεῖ λαβεῖν. It fits Joc.'s stance that she here refers to the gods as owners rather than τύχη and describes men as 'overseers', introducing a pious twist to the relationship between men and gods.

556 τὰ τῶν θεῶν δ'   for such postponement of δ' cf. Denniston, *GP*[2] 186 (4).

ἐπιμελούμεθα   the compound verb is prosaic and colloquial (attested in comedy) and occurs only here in tragedy (Luzac's conjecture in fr. 185.1 is too uncertain to count). The related noun ἐπιμέλεια is found only in prose and comedy, while the adj. ἐπιμελής occurs once in tragedy (Soph. fr. 472). The rarity of this usage is related to the prosaic, 'scientific' tenor of Joc.'s speech (532n., 536n.) and should not be deemed suspicious. Dindorf claimed that ἐπιμελούμεθα in place of ἐπιμελόμεθα betrays an interpolator, but ἐπιμέλομαι is not found in serious poetry either!

557 αὖτ'   it is highly unusual for unemphatic oblique cases of αὐτός to appear first in a clause or first in a phrase after a comma (at *Hel.* 421 αὐτά is emphatic, 'the facts themselves'; at *Phaethon* 114, if αὐτῶι δέ is correct, it must be 'for the king himself'; at *Med.* 1055 αὐτῶι is emphatic). Here one cannot argue for an emphatic use (such as 'the things themselves' as opposed to man's enjoyment of them), since when the gods take back possession they also terminate enjoyment. Rather, the subordinate clause is treated as a word-unit that occupies first position in the sentence, and αὖτ' is thus felt to be in the unemphatic second position. For a comparable case with μοι cf. *Hipp.* 1154–5 with Barrett's note and Add. (citing *Cycl.* 676). Perhaps the comma after χρήιζωσ' should be omitted (cf. Barrett on *Hipp.* 327). (One might take αὖτ' as object of χρήιζωσ' to avoid the rare phenomenon, but this is rhetorically less apposite and weaker.)

[558] ὁ δ' ὄλβος οὐ βέβαιος   a commonplace, cf. *Her.* 512 (ὄλβος), *El.*

---

to actors (the same ones who added 438–42), not to marginal annotation by a reader (107 n. 81).

[1] A list of relevant passages is given by R. Heinze, *De Horatio Bionis Imitatore* (diss. Bonn 1889) 28 n. 1.

941 (χρήματα); also Soph. fr. 201d and the moralized version of the maxim, Eur. fr. 303 (κακοῦ ἀνδρὸς … ὄλβον), 354 (πλοῦτος … ἄδικος).

ἐφήμερος 'short-lived' of things is not common in poetry (Pindar *I.* 7.40 is not an example, *pace* LSJ), but it is Euripidean (*Hcld.* 866 ἐφήμεροι τύχαι).

559 ἄγ' a transitional exclamation, usually accompanying an imperative or self-exhortation, but for this lively use introducing a challenging question within a rhesis and without a change of addressee, cf. *Med.* 499, *IA* 1171.

δύο λόγω προθεῖσ' ἅμα 'setting before you two statements ⟨of choice⟩ side by side'; this may be a variation on the prosaic locution προτιθέναι γνώμας = 'set forth resolutions for public debate and decision' (Thuc. 3.36.5, 6.14, LSJ s.v. προτίθημι II.4, mixed with examples of προτιθέναι λόγον = 'give an opportunity for debate'). I do not understand why Kovacs (549–67n.) considers this phrase unclear.

560 πόλιν σῶσαι the choice put to Et. here will later be put to Creon and Menoeceus (952; cf. 834–1018n.). Joc. had prayed for the family's salvation in the prologue (85), and Et. had used σώιζειν in a selfish sense in 508. 'Saving the city', introduced explicitly here (and implicitly in 437; cf. 533n.), becomes a major leitmotif in the third episode (864n.). Aorist σῶισαι ('rescue, act to save from a specific imminent danger') fits better here than Kirchhoff's present ('keep safe ⟨over time⟩, keep what one already holds').

561–5 I treat ἣν δὲ … πορθουμένας as a conditional statement (period at 565; many mss have full stop at both 563 and 565), but two other punctuations have been proposed. (a) Following Σ561 (562n.) one may treat the protasis as a separate question, with ellipsis of the apodosis (1684n.), and have 563–5 as a statement. (b) Grotius puts a question mark not only at 562, but also at 565. (b) is better than (a), and would be rhetorically lively. But Joc. is here drawing a stark contrast between ruling (and destroying the city) and yielding (and saving the city). It is to her purpose to present as a fact rather than a question the destruction that will result from the wrong choice.

562 Murray deduced from Σ^M 561 ἐὰν δὲ νικήσηι σε οὗτος, τί; λείπει δὲ τὸ τί that the commentator may have had a text without 562, and so he deleted 562. This seems to me an unsafe inference: the scholiast was interpreting the protasis as an elliptical question, and he had no need to extend his paraphrase to the end of 562 to make this point. The case is not comparable to that of 1225 below or *Or.* 1024, where the interpolation fills in that which the commentator says is omitted. Line 562 itself is in my judgment blameless: it is an expansion with *variatio* of νικήσηι σ' ὅδε, and the expansion forms an excellent and needed transition to the evocation of the public costs of Et.'s selfishness. (Mueller-Goldingen 108 n. 82 agrees that Murray's reasoning was invalid, but deletes 562 as an unnecessary repetition of 561, since 561 already refers to Argive victory, not to Pol.'s defeat of Et. in a duel; but the repetition may be normal tragic fullness of expression. JD tells me that Willink would delete 563–5 as a supplement supplying the ellipsis.)

563–5 ὄψηι ... ὄψηι δέ for anaphora with δέ see Denniston, *GP*² 163, supplemented by Diggle, *Studies* 55–6.

δαμασθὲν ... πορθουμένας δαμάζω/δάμνημι is sometimes used of the conquest of cities (*Se.* 338, *Trach.* 432, *Phil.* 200; cf. *Her.* 374), but more commonly has persons as its object and can be used of women subdued, theoretically or actually against their will, to marriage or concubinage. πέρθειν/πορθεῖν πόλιν (ἄστυ, etc.), on the other hand, is an almost formulaic juncture, and persons are not often the object (with the sense 'kill': *Aj.* 1198, *OT* 1456, Eur. fr. 605.3). Here Eur. applies the two verbs in the less obvious (or even unobvious) junctures for a stylistic effect of surprise and elevation (cf. Wilam. on *Her.* 883, who somewhat exaggerates the inversion). The unusual pregnant sense of πορθουμένας = 'taken as captives ⟨through the capture of their city⟩' is exactly paralleled in *El.* 316 δμωαὶ ... ἃς ἔπερσ' ἐμὸς πατήρ. The γρ-variant λεληισμένας is clearly a banalization.

566–7 Dindorf proposed the deletion of this couplet, wrongly leaving the major section of Joc.'s speech without a conclusion or climax; Paley added the worthless numerological argument that without the couplet Joc.'s speech is exactly twice as long as her sons' speeches. On Valck.'s suspicion of 567 alone, see note.

566 δαπανηρὸς ... ὁ πλοῦτος δαπανηρός (Π¹⁵, supralinear or γρ-variant in a few mss) is a prosaic word (once in Men. *Sent.* 153 γυνὴ τὸ σύνολόν ἐστι δαπανηρὸν φύσει), never very common (about a dozen times in classical authors, a couple of dozen in post-classical), while ὀδυνηρός (all mss in linea) is used by classical poets (in tragedy only *Hipp.* 189), but is also very common in late prose. Both are possible here, but δαπανηρός was slightly more likely to evoke a variant than ὀδυνηρός, since it is a more strained and precious usage ('costly ... wealth'; the adj. usually applies to spendthrift persons or expensive projects), and the cleverness of δαπανηρός gives a better climax, whereas ὀδυνηρός is perhaps too understated after 563–5.

567 Valck., who deleted this line, showed that he did not understand it by asking '*cur* [ὀδυνηρός] *Thebis potius quam Eteocli?*'; he also attacked φιλότιμος δὲ σύ as *frigidum*. The cost to Thebes of Et.'s selfishness is just the point of the whole section 559–67, and φιλότιμος δὲ σύ closes a framing ring with 532 Φιλοτιμίας and ends the speech on a note of sharp rebuke.

Commentators disagree about the ellipsis or fail to see its rhetorical point (so most recently, Mueller-Goldingen 108 n. 83 claims that if εἶ is understood the sentence lacks continuity). Pearson suggests that one should understand φιλότιμος δὲ [ὢν] σὺ [ὀδυνηρὸς γενήσηι Θήβαις], but that would be expressed idiomatically by ὁ φιλότιμος σύ. Old Σ understand ἔσηι, Moschopulus supplies γενήσηι from γενήσεται. The ellipsis is best treated, however, as one of εἶ, which is quite normal in tragic dialogue (and lyric), e.g. *Prom.* 42, 178, 373, *Ant.* 549, 1059, *OC* 806, *Hipp.* 949 σὺ σώφρων καὶ κακῶν ἀκήρατος;, *Hcld.* 360 σὺ δ' ἄφρων, *Andr.* 245 σοφὴ σοφὴ σύ, *Ba.* 655, *Hec.* 417 οἰκτρὰ σύ, *Hel.* 446 σὺ δ' αἴτιος. As in many of these examples, the tone of Joc.'s elliptical remark is sharp and impatient or exasperated: '(Thebes will suffer greatly . . .), but you are ambitious ⟨and don't care⟩!'; cf. Craik: 'yet you remain ambitious'; Buschor: 'nur dein Ehrgeiz bleibt dir treu'.

568 For this formal transition from one addressee to another cf. (with nearly identical first half-lines) *Su.* 1213, *Hel.* 1662, and [774] below; also *El.* 1276, where the δέ-clause carries third-person futures instead of second-person address; Diggle, *Studies* 39, refers also to *Antiope* 84 Page (fr. 48.90 Kambitsis) and *El.* 692 + 694. The formality is desirable here to mark clearly the turning to Pol. after the long harangue to Et.

569 ἀμαθεῖς cf. 393–4n. Adrastus' folly is of course his sponsoring Pol.'s impious and risky expedition, not his 'superstitious folly' (Pearson) in taking Pol. as his son-in-law.

χάριτας . . . ἀνήψατο ἀνάπτω is a favourite word of Eur., and he uses the expression κῆδος ἀνάπτεσθαι in *Tro.* 845 and *Her.* 35 (for the still living metaphor involved, see Bond and Σ here). The locution here is similar, but χάριτας is not the marriage itself, but (as the parallelism of 569 and 570 shows) the promise of help which accompanied the marriage (427–9). (Plutarch uses active τὴν χάριν ἀνάπτειν in a different sense, *Brut.* 6.12, *Ant.* 46.5.)

570 ἀσύνετα like ἀμαθής/ἀμαθία, an intellectualist word of which Eur. is fond (1506n., 1727n.).

571 φέρ', ἢν κτλ. with no long moral disquisition such as she had directed to Et., Joc. proceeds straight to the consideration of the probable outcome for Pol.; this line recalls 559 ἄγ', ἢν σ' ἔρωμαι κτλ., and the two sections of 571–83 correspond to the section 559–67. Hoping to play on Pol.'s conventional religious feelings (367n., 433–4n.), Joc. refers to religious activities connected with victory and rule of Thebes and suggests the impiety he will involve himself in.

ὃ μὴ τύχοι ποτέ 242n.

572 πρὸς θεῶν in Soph., Eur., and comedy this exclamation (elliptical for πρὸς θεῶν λίσσομαι, φράσον or εἰπέ) can accompany a question asked

315

with some special urgency or surprise: cf. Barrett on *Hipp.* 219, *IT* 509, *Hel.* 660, *Or.* 747, etc.

τροπαῖα on 'older' Attic τροπαῖον and 'younger' Attic τρόπαιον, cf. K–B 1.326, Ellendt, *Lex. Soph.* s.vv. τροπαῖον, ὁμοῖος, ἑτοῖμος, ἐρῆμος. The grammarians who inform us of this distinction had no way to date the shift, nor do we; in a conservative genre and in an author whose speech-habits were formed in the first half of the fifth century perhaps the older prosody still applied (but see West, *Aeschylus, praef.* xxxii).

ἀναστήσεις the technical phrase in Attic prose was τροπαῖον στῆσαι, and tragedy naturally tends to deviate from the commonplace in various ways: (a) by varying the verb (ἀναστήσεις here, θήσειν τροπαῖα in *Se.* 277, *Hel.* 1380, τροπ. ἱδρύεται in *Hcld.* 786); (b) by adding an unusual subj. gen. (*Se.* 957 ἔστακε δ' Ἄτας τροπαῖον) or obj. gen. (*Trach.* 1102 τροπαῖ' ἔστησε τῶν ἐμῶν χερῶν, *Or.* 713 τῶν κακῶν); (c) by using τροπαῖον βρέτας in place of plain τροπαῖον (below 1250–1, 1473, cf. *Hcld.* 936–7). Wrongly believing that ἀνίστημι must mean *deiectum erigere*, Porson needlessly restored the commonplace locution by writing ἆρα στήσεις. ἀνίστημι is later used with τρόπαιον in Plutarch *Alcib.* 29.2 (cf. *Mor.* 873B), Paus. 9.40.9, Athen. 350B.

Διί Zeus (τροπαῖος) is the proper god to name in connection with the trophy (below 1251, 1473, *Su.* 647, *Hcld.* 937). On the conjecture δορός in the mss, made to repair a defective line-ending, see *Text. Trad.* 51. On the custom of victory-trophies, see Pritchett, *Greek State at War* II.246–75.

573 πῶς δ' αὖ for the corruption of δ' αὖ to δαί in Π[15], cf. probably *El.* 244, 1116 (so Diggle against Denniston, *GP²* 260–2). δαί is too colloquial in this context (Page on *Med.* 339), and in all the probable Euripidean uses, and about 90 per cent of the Aristophanean, the particle occurs in stichomythia or antilabe, not in continuous speech (but cf. *Thesm.* 139–40 for τίς δαί continuing a series of τί-questions within a speech).

κατάρξηι θυμάτων since Joc. is emphasizing the impiety of Pol.'s possible actions, these sacrifices are probably to be understood as ones made either in dedicating the trophies on Theban soil or in other religious observances subsequently, when Pol. is ruler of Thebes. A person in authority, king or priest, 'begins' by taking the first ritual steps (such as sprinkling of water and barley or cutting a lock of hair), while the physical management of the victim before, during, and after the slaughter is often left to subordinates: cf. *Od.* 3.430–63, *IT* 40, 56, 1154.

574 for dedication of captured armour, see Pritchett, *Greek State at War* III.240–95.

σκῦλα γράψεις although the object of γράφω is most commonly the message or text produced (with prep. phrase giving the medium: *Il.* 6.169 γράψας ἐν πίνακι; fr. 506.2–3 ἐν Διὸς δέλτου πτυχαῖς γράφειν τιν' αὐτά;

316

with εἰς in Soph. fr. 811 and in prose and inscriptions), there is no theoretical or practical obstacle to γράφω being construed with an external object of the thing affected. This is the case in the sense 'graze' found in *Il.* 17.599, and Eur. himself uses the construction in *IT* 584–5 δέλτον ... ἣν ... ἔγραψεν, *IA* 35 (cf. in a more pregnant sense Pindar *O.* 3.29–30 ἔλαφον ... ἄν ποτε ... ἔγραψεν ἱεράν; *Thesm.* 770–1 and 773–4 are not relevant since γράφων is probably absolute). Cf. also passives like *Trach.* 157–8 δέλτον ἐγγεγραμμένην ξυνθήματ' and Philostratus *VA* 2.20 πίνακες γεγραμμένοι τὰ Ἀλεξάνδρου ἔργα, where there is also a retained object of the thing produced. Valckenaer's κὰς σκῦλα is unnecessary.

ἐπ' Ἰνάχου ῥοαῖς that is, in Argos (126n.), when thank-offerings are made at the temples of local gods, who are assumed to assist the citizen-army even when it is fighting abroad. Herwerden (1878) and Wecklein wanted to delete 574, wrongly believing that it separated actions in 573 and 575 that belonged together; but 573 takes place on the battlefield at Thebes, 575 at Argos.

575 τάσδε with ἀσπίδας, not with Θήβας (as Craik). The demonstrative is normal in verse dedications and funeral epigrams, though non-verse inscriptions may simply name the dedicator, the divine recipient, and the source of the booty. See e.g. Meiggs–Lewis, nos. 4, 11, 15 and Thuc. 1.132.2 vs. Meiggs–Lewis nos. 19, 29, 57. In the next line ἔθηκε for ἀνέθηκε is also traditional: Meiggs–Lewis nos. 11 and 15 provide better parallels than the doubtful Homeric examples in LSJ s.v. τίθημι A.III.2; cf. also *El.* 7.

577 ὑφ' Ἑλλήνων as if κλέος λαβεῖν were ἐπαινεθῆναι.

578 ὑπερδράμηι the majority reading ὑπεκδράμηι would imply escape from danger (cf. 873; this is the sense even in *Trach.* 167, where LSJ wrongly creates a separate heading); but that is too weak here, where τὰ τοῦδ' κτλ. is in polar opposition to κρατηθῆις and should mean 'prevail, emerge triumphant', the normal sense of ὑπερτρέχω in tragedy. The direction of corruption is more commonly from ὑπεκ- to ὑπερ- (873 below, *Su.* 1049, *Med.* 988), but cf. *Pers.* 100.

579 μυρίους λιπὼν νεκρούς perhaps a deliberate reminiscence and rebuttal of Pol.'s μυρίαν ἄγων λόγχην in 441–2.

580–2 ἐρεῖ δὲ δή τις κτλ. Joc. plays upon the fact that Pol. is conventionally sensitive to what others think of him, evoking the kind of shame shown by Hector in *Il.* 22.105–7 αἰδέομαι ... μή ποτέ τις εἴπηισι κακώτερος ἄλλος ἐμεῖο· / Ἕκτωρ ἧφι βίηφι πιθήσας ὤλεσε λαόν; cf. Aethra's similar evocation of Theseus' sense of shame in *Su.* 314 ἐρεῖ δὲ δή τις ὡς ..., and Admetus in *Alc.* 954 ἐρεῖ δέ μ' ὅστις ἐχθρὸς ὢν κυρεῖ τάδε. Apart from the specific reminiscence of *Il.* 22.107 here, διὰ μιᾶς νύμφης γάμον additionally alludes to the traditional 'because of a/one woman' used in complaints about the Trojan War.

317

δὲ δή δή stresses the addition as being of special weight: cf. Denniston, *GP²* 259, 460.

μνηστεύματα extant only here and *Hel.* 1514, probably a Eur. coinage (but it is unknown what noun was current for 'wooing' in contemporary Attic: Homer has μνηστύς, and μνηστεία is not attested until post-classical times).

προσθείς probably 'impose, inflict (on us a baneful betrothal)' (LSJ s.v. A.II.1); less vigorous and pointed would be 'attached, gave (to Pol. a baneful betrothal)', though this sense is attested in *Med.* 1356 ὅ σοι προσθεὶς γάμους. A third possibility is to give μνηστεύματα a transferred meaning: 'adding ill-fated betrothal gifts (sc. the promise of military aid) ⟨to the gift of the bride herself⟩' (cf. *Hipp.* 628–9 προσθεὶς ... φερνάς); but διὰ ... γάμον is against this.

583 κείνων στέρεσθαι τῶνδέ τ' ἐν μέσωι πεσεῖν '(sc. if you are defeated) to lose what you have there in Argos and to fall without attaining your goal here'. The expression of only a single limit (the future or more distant one) with ἐν μέσωι, implying 'in between your starting-point and these things you seek here', is best paralleled in the use of μεταξύ: *Hec.* 436–7 πλὴν ὅσον χρόνον ξίφους / βαίνω μεταξὺ καὶ πυρᾶς Ἀχιλλέως (the two gen. here are in hendiadys: 'the sword which awaits me at the funeral-mound of Achilles'); *OC* 291 μεταξὺ τούτου ('until that point in time' = 'between now and that time'), *Acharn.* 434 μεταξὺ τῶν Ἰνοῦς ('⟨above Thyestes' rags⟩ before you get to Ino's'). With ἐν μέσωι itself the nearest parallels are in an idiom with ἐστί + single gen. meaning 'be in the way of, block access to': *Birds* 187 ἐν μέσωι ... ἀήρ ἐστι γῆς; Xen. *Cyr.* 5.2.26 ἐν μέσωι ἐστὶ τοῦ συμμεῖξαι.[1] I prefer the explanation supported by these approximate parallels to Lloyd-Jones' emendation τῶνδέ τ', ἐν μέσωι πεσών (*CR* 7 (1957) 98–9): this introduces a proverb ('fall between the two') not actually attested in Greek and reduces the impact of the dual δύο κακώ, which instead of two infinitives in apposition would have only one inf. with two complements whose pairing is not emphatically enough marked. Powell's much different rendering ('if you conquer, in the hour of success you will fail ⟨for a victory over one's country is a loss⟩') puts too much strain on τῶνδε and πεσεῖν.

584 μέθετον ... μέθετον an expressive doubling, comparable to the scheme ἤλγουν μὲν ἤλγουν (Stevens on *Andr.* 980); cf. Soph. *El.* 459, *Phil.* 1241; in general Schwyzer II.699–700. Asyndeton and omission of

---

[1] Pearson also cites *Hcld.* 803 μεταιχμίοις δορός, which is somewhat different, since there are military forces (δόρυ) on both sides of the 'space between the armies'.

the copula in the gnome also give force to the concluding couplet, while this line has the remarkable accumulation of three resolutions.

τὸ λίαν 'excessive behaviour', closest to *Andr.* 866 τὸ λίαν οὔτ' ἐκεῖν' ἐπῄνεσα, but the noun τὸ λίαν occurs a number of times in Eur. (see *Concordance*) and not in other classical authors (Plato's use at *Phileb.* 24e8 is a 'quotation' of the adverb).

ἀμαθία 393n. There is no reason to understand this form as dual nom. (the subject of μόλητον is the same as that of μέθετον, the same pair as δυοῖν), or to accept the plural. For the thought cf. Soph. fr. 924 ὡς δυσπάλαιστόν ἐστιν ἀμαθία κακόν.

585 ἔχθιστον confusion with αἴσχιστον is easy (cf. *Alc.* 1037, *Hec.* 200, *Tro.* 1059, *Aj.* 1059, *OT* 1519, *Phil.* 1284); αἴσχιστον makes sense here, but ἔχθιστον is much more to the point (cf. fr. 230.2-3 ἔτι γὰρ θάλλει πενία / κακὸν ἔχθιστον).

586-7 for the prayer, 467-8n.; for ξύμβασίν 435n.

ἀπότ|ροποι syllabic lengthening in a prepositional prefix before initial mute and liquid of a verb-stem is extremely rare. JD reminds me of Porson's note on *Or.* 64[1] and notes that for ἀπο|τρ- we find 9-11 instances, in lyric except as noted (*Pers.* 203 (ia. trim.), *Cho.* 44, 155, A. *Su.* 891 = 901, *Aj.* 606, *OT* 1314, *Trach.* 1013 (corrupt), *Her.* 821, *Hel.* 360, *Or.* 410 (ia. trim.; emended by Diggle 1990b), *IA* 336 (tro. tetr.)), but for ἀποτ|ρ- only *Pers.* 217 (tro. tetr.), A. *Su.* 880 (lyric), [A.] *Se.* 1060 (anap.). For other prepositions or other verbs, JD cites *Prom.* 24, S. *El.* 1193, *OT* 640, *IT* 51, *Tro.* 995, *Hel.* 404, and 60 above ἀνατ|λὰς (cf. 166n.).

588-637 a fifty-line passage of trochaic tetrameters concludes the episode. This metre was revived in the last decade of Eur.'s activity as one of his many experiments with varying and renewing the formal elements of tragedy. See in general W. Krieg, 'Der trochäische Tetrameter bei Euripides', *Philologus* 91 (1936) 42-51; M. Imhof, 'Tetrameterszenen in der Tragödie', *MusHelv* 13 (1956) 125-43; T. Drew-Bear, 'The Trochaic Tetrameter in Greek Tragedy', *AJP* 89 (1968) 385-404. The tetrameter had a more pronounced 'beat' than the trimeter: Aristotle considered it less like normal speech and more suitable to dance. In scenes in which it is used not only are the emotions more agitated or the tone somehow altered by frenzy or demonic authority (*Tro.* 444-61, *Her.* 855-73, *Ba.* 604-41), but physical movement is either being initiated or becoming more rapid. This passage is one of the longest extant continuous passages, surpassed

---

[1] See also Tucker, *CR* 11 (1897) 341-4, for a classified list of words with syllabic lengthening before mute and liquid in trimeters, tetrameters, and marching anapaests in tragedy.

only by (in the early days) *Pers.* 697-758 and (from Eur. himself) *Ion* 510-65, *Or.* 729-806, and three passages in *IA* (counting 317-401 as single despite the iambic couplet of the chorus between the rheseis). Here the change of metre marks more forcefully the quickening of tempo after the formal speeches of the agon (note the internal reference to haste at the outset, 588-9, 592, and cf. *Or.* 729 and 447 above) and underlines the exacerbation of tone (which is typical in any case of dialogue following agon-rheseis, but the metre may here provide an undertone of increasing irrationality). The longer line also accommodates more easily than the trimeter an extended and effective use of antilabe. Short passages of tetrameter antilabe occur in Soph. *OT* and *Phil.*, but the extended use is characteristic of Eur. Cf. *IT* 1203-21 (after a lengthy iambic stichomythia), *Ion* 530-62 (after tetr. stich. 517-26), *Or.* 774-98 (after tetr. stich. 734-73), *IA* 1341-68, and here 603-24 (after tetr. stich. 596-602; the alternation of three speakers in 618-24 is paralleled in *Ion* 1616-18).

588 οὐ λόγων ἔθ' ἀγών cf. Willink on *Or.* 1292 οὐχ ἕδρας ἀγών; the converse expression ('hurry, time for action') is here left implied.

ἔθ' ἀγών the article (Musgrave) is welcome here and ἔθ' (Canter) is pointed, so this correction is better than Grotius' transposition ἀγών ἐστ'. For confusion of ἔτι and ἐστι cf. *Pers.* 348, *Ag.* 1322, *IT* 1040 (P), perhaps *Ion* 514 (JD).

588-9 ἀναλοῦται χρόνος οὐν μέσωι ὁ ἐν μέσωι χρόνος takes its sense from its context. In *Her.* 94 it is 'between now and our inevitable death', while in *Ion* 1393-4 it is 'between the time it was abandoned and now'. Here, after Et. says it is 'no longer' time for words, the prospective sense 'from now to the time of decisive action' is better (cf. *Med.* 819 οὐν μέσωι λόγοι 'between now and the accomplishment of my plan'; A. *Su.* 735, *OC* 583), whereas the retrospective sense 'between the beginning of our peace-conference and now' would involve a remote limit that is not so easily supplied. So Valck.'s restoration of the present ἀναλοῦται is to be accepted. If the perfect were kept, Elmsley's ἀνήλωται would be required (Meisterhans³ 173); the Eur. mss always carry the Koine form ἀναλω- (*Hipp.* 1336, *Andr.* 455, 1154, *El.* 681), but at *Aj.* 1049 ἀνηλω- is in most mss. For the sense of the verb here, cf. *Med.* 325 λόγους ἀναλοῖς ('you're wasting your breath'), *Aj.* 1049 τοσόνδ' ἀνήλωσας λόγον.

ἡ προθυμία clearly Joc.'s 'eager (but futile) good intention' (for this connotation, cf. 1683 below, *Her.* 309-10, *Hcld.* 410), not Et.'s (Klotz: *promptus et paratus ad componendam litem animus*). For emphasis on Joc.'s responsibility for the effort at reconciliation, cf. 81-2, 273, 435-7, 444-5, 446, 449-51.

590 ξυμβαῖμεν picking up (and dashing the hopes expressed in) the chorus' ξύμβασιν in 587.

591 σκήπτρων κρατοῦντα the same juncture also at 1253 below, but nowhere else except *orac.Sibyl.* 8.68 and 12.24 σκήπτρων ἐπὶ πουλὺ κρατήσει.

592 μακρῶν this acknowledges not only the overall length of Joc.'s speech, but in particular the relative length of the portion directed at Et. himself. The word would make less sense if the length of Joc.'s admonition to Et. were cut in half by a large deletion (see on 549–67).

νουθετημάτων the -μα abstract (in place of normal prose νουθέτησις) is typical of tragic style (four times in tragedy, then with poetic colouring in Pl. *Gorg.* 525c8, and in post-classical Greek).

593 ἤ 'or else': LSJ A.i.3, K–G ii.297, citing prose authors; but cf. *Phil.* 983, *Alc.* 628, *El.* 308, etc.

594 τίς ὧδ' ἄτρωτος see Kannicht on *Hel.* 810 for Homeric precedent (add *Il.* 4.510–11) and Euripidean parallels for such a declaration of vulnerability. τίς δ' ὧδ' is to be rejected. When two questions are essentially different formulations of the same query, asking for a single response, asyndeton is normal: cf. 408, 1706, *Cycl.* 229 ὑπὸ τοῦ; τίς ἐς σὸν κρᾶτ' ἐπύκτευσεν, γέρον; , *Andr.* 1104–5, 1125–6, etc. δέ is used when a true double question is asked (e.g., *Su.* 758–9), when the first question is quasi-exclamatory (*Su.* 756 πῶς φήις; ὁ δ' ἄλλος ποῦ κεκμηκότων ὄχλος; , *Or.* 1072: cf. Denniston, *GP*² 174–5), or in anaphora (*Tro.* 153 τί θροεῖς; τί δὲ θωΰσσεις;). But one cannot draw too fine a distinction, since metrical convenience may play a role (cf. *Hel.* 578).

595 ἀποίσεται μόρον 'will win for himself, will earn for his troubles'; the middle is used somewhat differently in 1161 οὐδ' ἀποίσεται βίον (τῆι ... μητρί), 'won't bring back (his own) life to his mother'. Cf. 1546n.

596 ἐγγύς, οὐ πρόσω βέβηκεν Pol.'s mocking use of the third person in his question is parried by Et.'s use of the third person to refer to himself. The same rhetorical gesture, with a different tone, appears in *Il.* 14.107–10: Agamemnon's wish εἴη ὅς κτλ. is equivalent to a question τίς κε κτλ., and Diomedes replies ἐγγὺς ἀνήρ, οὐ δηθὰ ματεύσομεν, referring to himself. Cf. also Theocr. 22.68–9 ΠΟ. τίς γὰρ ὅτωι χεῖρας καὶ ἐμοὺς συνερείσω ἱμάντας; / ΑΜ. ἐγγὺς ὁρᾶις· οὐ γύννις ἐὼν κεκλήσεθ' ὁ πύκτης.[1] In the majority reading βέβηκας, the ending has been assimilated to λεύσσεις,

---

[1] The passage is misrepresented by Gow. At line 65 ἑνὶ ... ἀνδρί is a designedly vague third person and should not be turned into an explicit first person 'me'; after settling the ground rules of the fight in 66–7, Polydeuces asks, 'Who is it, then, that I am to fight?', and Amycus answers, 'You see him near before you.'

spoiling the subtlety and reducing the point of οὐ πρόσω (cf. οὐ δηθά in *Il.* 14.110). For ἐγγύς reinforced by the negative οὐ πρόσω see Bond on *Hyps.* fr. 10.3.

εἰς χέρας λεύσσεις ἐμάς; cf. *Phil.* 1254–5 χεῖρα δεξιὰν ὁρᾶις / κώπης ἐπιψαύουσαν; In both places the actor puts his hand on the hilt of his sword, but does not draw it from its scabbard.

597 δειλὸν δ᾿ ὁ πλοῦτος the association of wealth and its luxuries (ἁβροσύνη, τρυφή) with lack of military prowess was a traditional stereotype, applied e.g. to the Ionians, the Lydians, the Persians, etc. (Xenophanes fr. 3 W; Hdt. and Thuc. *passim*; for wealth, luxury, and δειλία cf. Plato *Rep.* 422a, 556b, 590b, *Laws* 919b). Cf. fr. 54 κακόν τι παίδευμ᾿ ἦν ἄρ᾿ εἰς εὐανδρίαν / ὁ πλοῦτος ἀνθρώποισιν αἵ τ᾿ ἄγαν τρυφαί· / πενία δὲ δύστηνον μέν, ἀλλ᾿ ὅμως τρέφει / μοχθεῖν τ᾿ ἀμείνω τέκνα καὶ δραστήρια, fr. 235 πλουτεῖς, ὁ πλοῦτος δ᾿ ἀμαθία δειλόν θ᾿ ἅμα; *Wealth* 203. It is more likely that Pol. alludes to this stereotype than to the sort of considerations adduced here by Σ: οἱ πλούσιοι δειλοί εἰσι πρὸς θάνατον ὡς μεγάλων ἀγαθῶν στερούμενοι· οἱ δὲ πένητες ῥιψοκίνδυνοι κτλ.

598 κᾆτα mockingly granting Pol.'s claim in order to point out an inconsistency: cf. *Or.* 419 and see also 547–8n. *ad fin.*

οὐδὲν ἐς μάχην sc. ὄντα, 'a man who is worthless for fighting'; for οὐδέν cf. 442n., and for the limiting phrase cf. *Aj.* 1094 μηδὲν ὢν γοναῖσιν and phrases of the type ἐσθλοὶ ... εἰς ἀλκὴν δορός (fr. 298.3), θρασὺς εἰς ἀλκάν (*Or.* 1405). Pearson wrongly connects εἰς μάχην with ἦλθες (whence *Concordance* and some recent translators, but not older ones): ἐλθεῖν εἰς μάχην is of course a known idiom, but Et. means 'You came here with many helpers planning to fight me' and the idiom would mean 'You entered battle with me' (as *Ba.* 636, *Her.* 579).

599 θρασὺς στρατηλάτης the theme so lightly touched on here becomes a major issue in relation to Et. himself in the next episode: 690–783n., 713n., 714n., 746n.

600 κομπός the adj. is rare: Epicurus *Gnom. Vat.* 45, Callimachus fr. 96.1, Herodian, Et. magn. (κομπὸς λόγος, presumably from a lost literary text).

σώιζουσιν θανεῖν the inf. construction with this verb seems to be confined to Eur., here and *Hcld.* 577 πειρῶ δὲ σῶσαι [τοὺς παῖδας] μὴ θανεῖν; in both cases θανεῖν is quasi-redundant. For the variation between inf. with and without μή, cf. κωλύω and K–G II.209 Anm. 7 (μή) vs. II.215 Anm. 9(a) (without μή). Similar is *Alc.* 11 ὃν θανεῖν ἐρρυσάμην vs. *Her.* 197 ῥύεται μὴ κατθανεῖν, *Or.* 599.

601 καὶ σέ· δεύτερον δ᾿ Wilam.'s punctuation and emendation of γ᾿ to δ᾿ produce excellent repartee. In transmitted καί σε δεύτερόν γ᾿ ἀπαιτῶ, the rhetorical connection is faulty and the emphasis on δεύτερον misplaced (for the position of σε and γ' cf. *Cycl.* 684 καί σε διαφεύγουσί γε and examples in Denniston, *GP*² 158): Pol. would be agreeing, 'Yes, I do talk big', and adding 'what is more, I demand *again* ...'.

δεύτερον the first demand was made in 484–7.

602 οὐκ ἀπαιτούμεσθ' a dynamic use of the present tense, with the force almost of a future: 'I don't/won't admit any such demand!' Cf. Goodwin, *MT* §32 and below 1718n. Some have instead explained οὐκ ἀπαιτούμεσθ' as a rejection of Pol.'s use of ἀπαιτεῖν: 'I am not subject to any demanding back ⟨since the house is mine alone⟩.' But this is weaker rhetoric and ignores the defiance of the future οἰκήσω. ἐγὼ γὰρ ... δόμον as a whole deliberately repeats the idiom used by Pol. in 486.

603–24: on tetrameter antilabe see 588–637n. The repartee is structured as follows: 603 transitional; 604–13 a calling to witness of city-gods, parents, and city itself; 614–20 farewell to kin; 621–4 suggestion of duel. The complex effect of this dialogue is created by the skill with which the 'bad' brother interrupts and undercuts the statements of the 'good' brother, exploiting and reappropriating the very details that suggest Pol.'s traditional piety and real care for his kin and city. Et.'s taunting is cruel, but (spoken by anyone else) justified. The combativeness of the repartee is sometimes reinforced by the structure of the antilabe. The most usual division (11 out of 22 lines) is at the main diaeresis, dividing the 15 elements in the ratio 8:7. In the sequences at 611–13 (8:7, 4:11, 3:12) and 615–17 (11:4, 8:7, 5:10) I would take the progressive shortening of Pol.'s part and lengthening of Et.'s part as a deliberate technique to underscore the frustration of Pol.'s appeals: cf. perhaps 606–8 (10:5, 8:7, 5:10); in trimeters cf. *Or.* 1609–11, 1615–17, and (with different effect) *OT* 1173–6.

603 τὰ πλείω so probably Π¹² (unless it had τὰ πλ[εῖστα, cf. τὸ πλεῖστον in some *recc.*; for the interchange, cf. *Tro.* 644); more easily corrupted into τὸ πλεῖον than vice versa. πλεῖον is rarely secure in tragedy (Teubner *praef.* §10).

604 βωμοί like the temple of Amphion and Zethus invoked in 606, these altars are presumably addressed from afar and imagined to be elsewhere in the city, not represented on stage. See 631–2n. for the on-stage altar(s).

605 κλύετέ ... κλύοι the latter is almost certainly to be taken as aorist, the former probably so: West, *BICS* 31 (1984) 175.

πατρίδ' ἐπεστρατευμένου for the acc. cf. 285n.

606 θεῶν τῶν λευκοπώλων in a Theban context these are the Dioscuri Amphion and Zethus (cf. *Her.* 29, *Antiope* fr. 48.98 Kambitsis), although in a Laconian or panhellenic context the same phrase would refer to the Dioscuri Castor and Polydeuces: cf. Kannicht on *Hel.* 204–9 with refs., to which add Burkert, *Gr. Religion* 324–5 (= Engl. transl. 212–13); Schachter 1.28–9.

607 ἐξελαυνόμεσθα πατρίδος Blomfield transposed these words to eliminate the resolution next to long anceps in πατρίδος, but JD compares *Herc.* 866 (conj.), *Ion* 512, *Or.* 786, and several exx. in *IA* (cf. Cropp and Fick, 67, types 4.1cP, 4.1cL, 4.2cP).

ἐξελῶν understand με: 'yes, and you for your part came to drive me out'; both Craik ('to destroy it' (sc. the city)) and Burian–Swann ('which you have come to destroy') resurrect the error of Σ who glosses ἐξελάσων πορθήσων.

608 γ' Denniston, *GP*² 138 (cf. *l*) notes how γ' here marks a continuation of Pol.'s own sentence across Et.'s interruption; but he is not quite right to say that Pol. 'ignores' the interruption. He 'ignores' it in the sense that he does not yet turn to Et. with an explicit second-person address and does not abandon his own sentence. But γ' actually acknowledges the interruption by insisting that his own ἐξελαυνόμεσθα is crucially different (ἀδικίαι) from the ἐξελῶν thrown in his face by Et.

γ' ὦ θεοί σῆι is an intrusive gloss; γ' ὦ may be a metrical correction or a survival (consciously recognized as preferable?) channelled through the 'Moschopulean' tradition. Some critics have suggested accepting γε σῆι in place of γ' ὦ θεοί, but in this close repartee Et.'s θεούς answers Pol.'s θεοί, not the more remote θεῶν in 604a and 606a. On synizesis of θεός, θεά, and cases in Eur.'s trimeters see Diggle, *PCPS* 20 (1974) 31–6, with 36 n. 1 on cases in tetrameters.[1]

609 ἀνόσιος 493n.

610 καὶ . . . γε πρός these particles with adverb πρός also in *Prom.* 73 and *Peace* 19; both this combination and καὶ πρός γε (*Med.* 704, *Hcld.* 641, *Hipp.* 893, *Hel.* 110, *Acharn.* 1229) make emphatic additions, but the former gives even more weight to the intervening word.

611 ἃ πάσχω . . . οἷα δρᾶις perhaps this plays upon the traditional δράσαντι παθεῖν, as comm. suggest, but there is no exact correspondence of doing and suffering here; οἷα is not mere *variatio* for ἅ, but deliberately taunting: 'Yes, and he also hears what sort of things you do ⟨attacking your own fatherland, assaulting shrines of your ancestral gods, etc.⟩.' For καὶ γάρ see Denniston, *GP*² 109–10.

---

[1] Of the other eight instances in Eur.'s tetr., four occur in the 8th element, three in the 9th (i.e. on either side of the diaeresis, corresponding to the most frequent positions in the trimeter, before and after caesura), one in the 4th (*IA* 1339). The position here in the 5th element is analogous to the position in the 2nd element of the trimeter.

612 ἀθέμιτόν Bothe's correction of transmitted οὐ θεμιτόν creates a hapax in Eur., but is superior to Grotius' οὐ θέμις, a common phrase in Eur., but less likely to have produced the corruption οὐ θεμιτόν. θεμιτός itself is hapax in Eur. (*Or.* 97), though it is also used a few times in earlier poets (always negated), while ἀθέμιτος is attested a few times in Antiphon and Xen. and then in post-classical authors.

613 ὦ πόλις this and similar exclamations call the citizens in general as witnesses to one's sufferings or mistreatment. Cf. *Hipp.* 884 (with Barrett's refs. to discussions of the quasi-legal force of a βοή),[1] *Andr.* 1176, 1211, *Su.* 808, fr. 713 (= *Knights* 813 and *Wealth* 601), *Knights* 273, *Wasps* 418, *OT* 629, *Ant.* 842, *OC* 833, and perhaps Aesch. *Su.* 23.[2] Cf. 1494n.

Λέρνης ὕδωρ see on 126.

614 μὴ πόνει 'don't trouble yourself needlessly ⟨to give me advice⟩', almost 'don't worry'. In two other passages this is like English 'no, thank you' (*Prom.* 340-2 τὰ μέν σ' ἐπαινῶ ... ἀτὰρ μηδὲν πόνει, *El.* 1007 μὴ σύ μοι πόνει); since there is no evidence that the phrase is colloquial, it appears to be an artificial idiom of tragic style. Cf. *Prom.* 44 τὰ μηδὲν ὠφελοῦντα μὴ πόνει μάτην, Men. fr. 1101.2 μὴ κενῶς πόνει.

αἰνῶ for the use of this verb in an expression of thanks, cf. *Prom.* 340 (just quoted) and 1683n.

χθονός here and in 636 below ἔξιθ' ἐκ χώρας the words for 'territory controlled by a state' are used where one might expect the more accurate term πόλεως or ἄστεως; but the broader terms may be more appropriate legally in a situation where the end of a truce is being proclaimed (cf. Thuc. 2.12.2), and in any case the city itself is at this moment all the territory that the state of Thebes actually controls.

615-16 Pol.'s request to see his father and sisters is an important token of the value of kinship-ties to him and reinforces the impression made by 376-8, if those lines are genuine. These lines also recall the false suggestion in 170-1 that Ant. will see Pol. during his visit to the city and continue the preparation for Pol.'s request for burial in 1447-50 and Ant.'s effort to comply.

οὐκ ἂν τύχοις deliberately recalled in 1666 (Creon's refusal to Ant.); for the emphatic pot. opt., 926n.

---

[1] Also Richardson on *Hom.h.Dem.* 20; Taplin, *Stagecraft* 218-21; D. Bain, *ZPE* 44 (1981) 169-71, 45 (1982) 270, 49 (1982) 42; R. Kassel, *ZPE* 44 (1981) 172; C. Willink, *CQ* 40 (1990) 77 [JD].

[2] Add perhaps *Hipp.* 817: the distinction which Barrett makes between this and the other passages in order to support τάλας over πόλις seems to me rather forced.

ἀλλά 'but if not that, then instead (at least)', introducing an alternative request after one has been refused; likewise in 618, cf. Denniston, *GP²* 9 and below 1665n. Valckenaer suggested ἀλλὰ παρθένους γ' (cf. 1671 ἀλλὰ στόμα γε), but in tragedy ἀλλά is more common than ἀλλά . . . γε in this idiom (Denniston, *GP²* 12).

617 In 611–13 Pol. calls to witness his father (as a figure of authority), his mother (as one present and also as a figure of authority) and the citizens (as public witnesses and potential helpers). His invocation of his sisters is different: it represents a protesting farewell from afar in reaction to his inability to see them in person. F. G. Schoene's placement of 617 before 613 would wrongly place the sisters in the context of witnessing, for which they have insufficient authority. It would also bring the triple repetition of forms of ἀνακαλεῖν (608, 613, 617) into even closer proximity.

618 ἀλλά μοι σύ the word-order σύ μοι is much more common (over twenty-five times in tragedy and Aristophanes, including *Pers.* 640 ἀλλὰ σύ μοι), but an enclitic pronoun often attaches itself to ἀλλά, and μοι σύ is found in passages where it is, as here, metrically convenient (*Med.* 964, *Aj.* 574, 823–4, *OT* 957, *Acharn.* 299).

χαῖρε . . . χαρτά comm. since Valckenaer have collected passages that play on the ambiguity of χαῖρε: cf. in particular *Hec.* 426–7 ΠΟ. χαῖρ', ὦ τεκοῦσα . . . ΕΚ. χαίρουσιν ἄλλοι, μητρὶ δ' οὐκ ἔστιν τόδε, *Ba.* 1379–80 χαῖρ' ὦ μελέα θύγατερ. χαλεπῶς ⟨δ'⟩ ἐς τόδ' ἂν ἥκοις.

γοῦν the sarcastic or ironical use of γοῦν appears to be colloquial (Denniston, *GP²* 455, Stevens, *Colloquial Expr.* 45; cf. esp. *Eccl.* 794 χαρίεντα γοῦν πάθοιμ' ἄν). Emendation of γοῦν to γ' οὐ (G) or δ' οὐ (Kirchhoff) is misconceived.

619 οὐκέτ' εἰμὶ παῖς σός 'you have lost your son' (Burian–Swann), not 'I your son exist no longer' (Craik). This is probably not a renunciation of his family-ties, such as is made by Admetus in *Alc.* 636–41, for Pol. continues to show solidarity with his mother by using ἡμᾶς in 620 and maintains his attachment to Thebes in 631–3. Rather, Pol. acknowledges the cessation of a normal and valued tie caused by the now-inevitable state of war.

621 the idea of meeting in a duel during battle arises naturally out of the anger of the scene, in which the brothers have already threatened each other and almost drawn swords (593–7, 600–1). But the curse of Oedipus is already established in the background and is immediately recognized as applicable by Joc., so there can be no question of giving precedence to the 'realistic' psychological motivation over the the supernatural one. The two work in harmony.

ὡς τί probably an ellipsis for ὡς τί θέλων (so *IT* 557, cf. *Med.* 682 ὡς τί χρήιζων, *Rhes.* 99 ὡς τί δράσων), since ὡς τί almost always implies 'What have you got in mind?' or 'What are you thinking of?' (*Her.* 1407, *Or.* 796, *IA* 1342; but in *Ion* 525 the phrase is not much different from plain τί). Others explain the ellipsis as subjunctive of purpose, as in the more colloquial ἵνα τί: cf. Stevens, *Colloquial Expr.* 29.

623–4 ascribed by Helmbold, 131, to 'the actor's natural desire to keep a good three-cornered scene rolling a little longer'; on the contrary, it is the needed conclusion to Jocasta's tragic frustration, and 624 is deliberately recalled by Eur. in 919.

623b–624b the *pers. notae* have become confused in the tradition. Joc. speaks to both sons, so one should assign 623b and 624b to different speakers, not both to one son or the other. The vehement tone of 624b, the order Pol.–Et. that has been established in the preceding dialogue, and the inconcinnity of ἐρρέτω πρόπας δόμος with Pol.'s previous concern for his family and with the regretful tone of 625ff. all indicate that 623b belongs to Pol. and 624b to Et. The confusion arose because of failure to recognize the idiomatic use of ὡς = ἴσθι ὡς at the change of speaker in 625.

623 αὐτὸ σημανεῖ cf. *Ba.* 976; the fuller idiom occurs in *Andr.* 265 τὸ δ' ἔργον αὐτὸ σημανεῖ τάχα (cf. *Hel.* 151 πλοῦς ... αὐτὸς σημανεῖ). This seems to be Eur.'s reformulation of colloquial (αὐτὸ) δείξει (τάχα), Soph. fr. 388, *Lys.* 375, (?) *Eccl.* 933, and other passages cited in LSJ s.v. δείκνυμι 2.

625 ὡς equivalent to ἴσθι ὡς, introducing a defiant asseveration, as also in 720 and 1664 below and often elsewhere (*Concordance* s.v. II [b]; Diggle, *Studies* 88).

οὐκέθ' goes closely with ἀργήσει, equivalent to 'will soon be busy', a sense which can more naturally support the proleptic adjective αἱματηρόν ('and be stained with blood').

626–8 μαρτύρομαι 433–4n. The fullness and repetitions within Pol.'s expostulations are in part self-pitying, but they also reflect his frustration and helplessness in the debate with his brother. With ἄτιμος cf. 610 ἄμοιρον; with οἰκτρὰ πάσχων cf. 611 κλύεις ἃ πάσχω; with ἐξελαύνομαι cf. 607, 610; δοῦλος ὡς recalls his keen sense of noble birth in 395, 442.

630 ἐξελαύνομαι χθονός this phrase is certainly wrong here: it is rhetorically feeble with ἄκων and inapposite in explanation of 629. The words have clearly intruded from 627, where they formed the climax of the repeated theme of 'being driven out'. Valckenaer deleted 630 as a whole, but 629 is more cogent with the justifying γάρ-clause: any harm Pol. does is ἀκούσιον, so blameless, for the ἀρχή of the harm lies in Et.'s power. The sense must originally have been 'and unwillingly do I attack my own country'. For the emphatic repetition with *variatio* οὐχ ἑκὼν ... ἄκων cf. *Hcld.* 531 ἑκοῦσα κοὐκ ἄκουσα, *Andr.* 357 ἑκόντες οὐκ ἄκοντες, *OT* 1230; also *Tro.* 373 ἑκούσης κοὐ βίαι (*IA* 360–1, *Hcld.* 885, *Hel.* 395–6), *Hcld.* 551 ἑκοῦσα ... ἀναγκασθεῖσα δ' οὔ; see 433–4n.

631 Φοῖβ' . . . **Ἀγυιεῦ** as Agyieus or προστατήριος Apollo protects the entrance of a house, just like Hermes. In the lexicographic tradition the image of Apollo Agyieus is reported to have been a simple pillar with a pointed top, but there is also reference to an apparently flat ἀγυιεὺς βωμός, and it is unclear whether in classical Athens (and in the theatrical representation) the pillar and altar regularly coexisted or were alternative representations of Apollo's presence: cf. Fraenkel on *Ag.* 1081; MacDowell on *Wasps* 875; Gomme–Sandbach on *Dysc.* 659 for further refs.; Diggle, *Studies* 33–4; and see now the discussion of J. P. Poe, 'The Altar in the Fifth-Century Theater', *Classical Antiquity* 8 (1989) 116–39, esp. 130–7. The archaeological evidence, assembled and discussed by E. de Filippo Balestrazzi, 'Apollon Agyieus', *LIMC* II:1.327–32, II:2.279–83, confirms the aniconic nature of the image (pointed column or alabastron-shaped column), but is all non-Attic and post-classical (the earliest images are South Italian vase-paintings no earlier than 375). Yet it at least provides some ground to speculate that the Agyieus pillar may sometimes have stood on a wider base which could have served as an altar (cf. Poe, 136). As for the stage-prop implied here, it is possible that Pol. merely turns to the low altar by the central door. But the address here and in some passages of comedy will be more effective, I think, if there is at least a pillar (cf. the herm interrogated by Strepsiades in *Clouds* 1478–85). And wherever a palace is portrayed in tragedy I wonder whether there may not have been a prop of a real image rather than the more mundane pillar: the relevant scenes are *Ag.* 1081 (Cassandra); *OT* 919 (Joc. addresses Apollo with epithet Λύκει', but ἄγχιστος alludes to his position as Agyieus; she lays offerings before him); Soph. *El.* 634–59 (addressed as Φοῖβε προστατήριε and as Λύκει' ἄναξ, and later in 1379 as Λύκει' Ἄπολλον); in the humbler setting of Eur. *El.* 221 Φοῖβ' Ἄπολλον is perhaps addressed to a plain pillar or altar. On statue props in general, see P. Arnott, *Greek Scenic Conventions in the 5th Century B.C.* (Oxford 1961) 66–9.

632 ἡλικές θ' οὑμοί the young men with whom he spent time in shared training and leisure, as implied earlier in 368 γυμνάσιά θ' οἶσιν ἐνετράφην. Cf. the farewell of Hippolytus, *Hipp.* 1098 ἴτ' ὦ νέοι μοι τῆσδε γῆς ὁμήλικες, 1179–80 μυρία δ' ὀπισθόπους / φίλων ἅμ' ἔστειχ' ἡλίκων ⟨θ'⟩ ὁμήγυρις.

θεῶν τε δεξίμηλ' ἀγάλματα ἀγάλματα here are perhaps simply 'altars', from the general sense '(sacred) objects in which the gods delight' (cf. *Andr.* 1138 βωμοῦ ... δεξίμηλον ἐσχάραν, and the ref. to altars in 274 above). But it cannot be ruled out that the meaning is 'statues' and that several prop-statues were present on stage, each with a small altar before it. For multiple statues in front of a stage-palace, cf. *Hipp.*, Soph. *El.* 1374–5, *Ag.* 519.

δεξίμηλ' extant in Eur. alone (three times), apart from the phrase in *Etymologicum genuinum* which may attest another literary passage or be a corrupt ref. to this one.

633 προσειπεῖν αὖθις ἔσθ' ... **ποτε** one might strictly expect ἔσται, but the adverbs and the timeless force of the infinitive make the reference to the future quite plain, and it may be that the present ἔσθ' adds an undertone of resignation, as if Pol. were to say 'whether it is granted by fate (which is already fixed)'.

634 ἐλπίδες cf. 396.

635 action after his speech, Pol. heads off alone by the eisodos by which he entered. Probably at the same time Joc. turns and re-enters the palace in silence, a dramatic token of her defeat and despair, even though her movement is not commented on explicitly as in the well-known cases in Soph. (*Ant.* 1244ff., *Trach.* 813ff., cf. *OT* 1073–5).

636–7 ἐκ χώρας 614n.

ἀληθῶς ... **θείαι προνοίαι** cf. *Ag.* 681–4 τίς ποτ' ὠνόμαζεν ὧδ' ἐς τὸ πᾶν ἐτητύμως ... προνοίαισι τοῦ πεπρωμένου, and on ἀληθῶς and similar words in etymologies see Griffith, *HSCP* 82 (1978) 83–6. Quintilian 5.10.31 criticizes this etymology as *frigidum*, and he may well be echoing what he read in (or was taught from) ancient commentaries, the authors of which delighted in finding fault with Eur. Here the criticism is unjustified. The use of the etymology for accusation (echoing the words of Amphiaraus in *Septem* 576–8) provide a deliberate scene-concluding irony (196–201n.): the brother who has been clearly displayed as an equal or greater instigator of the strife and obstacle to peace selfishly (and perhaps blindly) appropriates the traditional etymology in a woefully inadequate summary of the preceding action. See in general Van Looy, ' παρετυμολογεῖ ὁ Εὐριπίδης'.

637 action Et. and his attendants apparently go into the palace at this point and re-emerge after the choral ode: 690n.

638–89: FIRST STASIMON

FUNCTION AND SYTLE

To the collapse of the effort at reconciliation and to the open threat of fratricide, Eur. (who is shaping the action so as to retard and complicate the duel of the brothers) makes the Phoenician chorus respond with notable detachment. Instead of anticipating the outbreak of battle or commenting openly on the brothers' rush toward doom (like the citizen-women of Aeschylus' *Septem*), they begin, in a relatively unemotional metre, a remote narrative replete with pictorial description. In the epode the language (and to a lesser extent the metre) becomes more agitated, but the divinity addressed is again exotic, and the prayer itself is for general aid to Thebes, without any specific reference to the royal family, thereby contributing to the shift of interest at this point in the play toward the question of the city's salvation.

The most obvious relevance of the Cadmus story is in providing, in the mutual slaughter of the Spartoi with which it ends, a mythical prototype for the coming fratricide. But Cadmus' arrival (in exile) at Thebes is relevant in other ways too: (a) as the first origin of Theban misfortunes (as already suggested by Joc. in 4–6, and confirmed by Tiresias in 931–40); (b) as the earliest arrival guided by Apollo of Delphi, parallel to Oedipus' arrival at Thebes (1043–5) and Pol.'s arrival at Argos (409–14) and then at Thebes (fulfilling the oracle to Laius, 20), and comparable also to the arrival (806, 1019) of the dread Sphinx (sent by a god, 810, 1031–2); (c) as the first example of the ambivalent relationship with the gods enjoyed by Thebes. Cadmus is blessed by Apollo and aided by Athena, but his founding actions anger Ares and Earth. Thebes is correspondingly blessed with well-watered, fertile fields, the joyful worship of Dionysus, and the protection of Demeter and Kore; but the fertility is jealously guarded by a monster serpent, the Theban earth gives birth to the fratricidal Spartoi, and the forbidden fertility of Joc. leads to the visitation of the monster Sphinx and the return of Oedipus and the birth of incestuous offspring. The slaying of the chthonic serpent at the spring lays claim to the natural riches of the land for civilized human settlement, but the founding acts are also crimes which represent an 'original sin' of civilization from which it cannot be totally freed – a theme which reinforces the play's meditation on the fallibility of λόγος and σοφία and the power of the irrational/ supernatural elements in human life. On the 'civilization' theme, see Arthur; on Cadmus and the serpent in general, see Vian, *Origines de Thèbes*, and Fontenrose, *Python*, esp. 306–20.

The ode has been severely criticized by some: although there survives no scholiastic condemnation such as that directed at the third stasimon, Hermann supplied the deficiency (*hanc neminem defensurum, nedum laudaturum arbitror*), and even Kranz, who was more sensitive to Eur.'s lyric style, lamented the lack of 'inner necessity' justifying this ode in this position in the play. But the allusive narration of myth as paradigm and aetiology is a traditional feature of Greek choral lyric, an 'archaic' technique revived by Eur. in his late plays (cf. esp. *IT* 1234–83 and perhaps *Helen* 1301–68).

There are several links between the parodos and the first stasimon, and with this and subsequent odes it becomes apparent that the choral odes of *Phoen.* form a 'song cycle', as recognized by Kranz (*Stasimon* 260) and demonstrated in detail by Riemschneider, Parry (diss. and *Lyric Poems* 166–73), Panagl, and Arthur. The trochaic/lecythion metre of this stasimon is similar to that of the second pair of stanzas in the parodos and is echoed later in the third stasimon. Verbal echoes include: Τύριον/-ος 202, 639; ἔμολον γᾶν/ἔμολε τάνδε γᾶν 216, 638 (cf. also μολών 240, 662, and βᾶθι βᾶθι τάνδε γᾶν 681); (?) ὑπὲρ ἄκρων 227, 671; (?) φοινίου 252, φόνιος 657, 664; ἔνοπλος/πάνοπλος 259, 671; πνοαῖς ... ἐν οὐρανῶι 211–12, αἰθέρος πνοαῖς 675. Repeated personalities and motifs in parodos and first stasimon include: Ares (240, 253, 658), Io (248, 677), Dionysus and Dionysiac revelry (227–8, 649–56), chthonic serpent (232, 657), sacred local spring (222–3, 645–8, 659–60), magic fertility (blessed 229–31, 651–4, 677–8; monstrous 670–2). For further parallels of this type, cf. 784–833n., 1019–66n.

Internally, the ode displays the so-called 'dithyrambic' style affected by Eur. in his later plays (see esp. Panagl). The main characteristics of this are short cola, an abundance of compound epithets (several unique in extant Greek or used in a uniquely eccentric sense), run-on appositions, accumulation of relative clauses and imbalance between main clauses and subordinate clauses, verbal repetition, and the paradoxical wedding of beautiful language and sensuous description to violent content. The clause-structure of the strophe and antistrophe is remarkable: there is a single five-word main clause at the opening, followed within the strophe by four relative clauses of greater length ('to whom' ... 'where' ... 'and where' ... 'where'); then the antistrophe opens with a further relative connection ('where'), which is followed in turn by three more relative clauses ('which' ... 'whence' ... 'who'), two of which run on into quasi-independent δέ-limbs. There is also a plethora of verbal repetition within the ode: δικε(ν)/δικών 641, 665, 667 (see notes for defence of second and third occurrences); βαθυσπόρους γύας 648, 669; χλοηφόρους, -οισιν 647, 653 (cf. χλοερά 660); φόνιος, -ον 657, 664; ὠμόφρων/σιδαρόφρων 658, 672; ὄλεσε/ὀλεσίθηρος 663–4; γᾶ/γαῖα/γαπετεῖς eight times; ritual anadiplosis three times in 679–81, and a similar anaphora in 686 (πάντων, cf. πάντα beginning the colon at 689). The inexact echo of πυρόφορα 644 in πυρφόρους 687, the accumulation of water-words in 645–6 and 659, and the variations on μάτηρ in this context of wondrous and horrible births (649–50, cf. ἀμάτορος 666, προμάτορος 676, perhaps τροφός 686) are also to be noted. The text of the ode is in many places uncertain, and at least one repetition is due to corruption (γύας 646); but because repetition appears to be integral to the style affected in this song, I have generally rejected solutions which rely on or aim for the elimination of repetitions (e.g., Wilam.'s deletion of both 648 and 669, or reduction of anadiplosis in the prayer to Epaphus).

638–89 Metre The pair of narrative stanzas is in simple iambo-trochaic rhythm, with a preponderance of lecythia. For the use of this rhythm in late Eur. see the note on 202–60 metre (at end). The final seven cola clearly form two periods (hiatus and brevis in antistrophe), but there is no firm proof of period-division in the first 13 cola, and it is possible that the lines (or a section of them) form a *pnigos*, reinforcing the run-on 'dithyrambic' style (cf. *Hel.* 169–78, a much more emotional lyric). I have preferred, however, to assume period-end after 638 = 657 (in 639 Τύριος is quasi-appositional, and the phrase in 658 may be felt as such) and after 642 = 661 and 646 = 665 (clausular effect of lec after 2 tro, also sense-break in antistrophe at both places). The text can be no more than provisional at several places, and thus the metrical analysis is equally tentative. The epode is similar in rhythm, but more agitated (note resolutions in 679, short cola and exclamation in 679bis–68obis) and varied (note esp. the sequence of cola introduced by sp). Again the text and analysis can be no more than provisional, esp. since responsion is lacking; by emendation and deletion of repetitions some have produced more regular rhythm (Burges and Hermann, followed by Wecklein, even produced strophe and antistrophe out of this epode).

638/657	– ∪ ⏑⏑ – ∪ – ‖?	lec
639/658	⏑⏑ – ∪ – ∪ –		lec
640/659	– ∪ ⏑⏑ – ∪ – ∪|	2 tro
641/660	⏑⏑ – ∪ – ∪ – ∪|	2 tro
642/661	‾‾∪ – ∪ – ∪ – ‖c	lec
643/662	⏑⏑ – ∪ – ∪ –		lec
644/663	– ∪ ⏑⏑ – ∪ –		lec
645/664	– ∪ ⏑⏑∪⏑⏑∪⏑⏑∪|	2 tro
646/665	⏑⏑∪ – ∪ – ∪ – ‖c	lec
647/666	– – ∪ – ∪ –		sync tro, cr
648/667	– ∪ – ∪ – ∪ –		lec
649/669	⏑⏑∪ – ∪⏑⏑∪ –	lec
650/668	– ∪ – ∪ – – ‖b2c	ithyph
651/670	– ∪ – ∪ – ∪ –		lec
652/671	∪ – ∪ – ∪⏑⏑∪ –		2 ia
653/672	∪ – ∪ – ∪ – ∪ –		2 ia
654/673	∪ – ∪ – ∪ – ∪ – ∪ – ‖h2	3 ia
655/674	– ∪ – ∪ – ∪ – ∪	2 tro
655bis/674bis	– ∪ – – ∪ – ∪|	cr, tro
656/675	– ∪ – ∪ – ∪ – ‖‖‖	lec
676	– ∪ – ∪ – ∪∩‖b	lec
677	– – ∪ – ∪∩‖b	sync tro, cr
678–9	⏑⏑∪ – ∪ – ∪⏑⏑∪⏑⏑∪⏑⏑∪|	3 tro
679bis	– ∪ – ∪ – ‖h	Kurzvers

680	∪–‖	exclam
680bis	–∪–∪–‖	Kurzvers
681	–∪–∪–∪–‖	lec
682	–∪–∪–∪–|	lec
683	–∪–∪–∪–|	lec
684	–∪–∪–∪–|	lec
685	–––∪–|	sp, cr
686	––∪–⌒‖ᵇ	sp, ba
686bis	––∪–∪–|	sp, ia
687	––∪–∪–∪–∪–|	sp, 2 ia
688	∪–∪–∪––‖ᶜ	ia, ba
689	–∪–∪–∪–‖‖	lec

NOTES TO METRICAL SCHEME

649–50 I do not think the corrupt antistrophe should be accepted as the pattern for the strophe: the sense here does not require any supplement (see *ad loc.*). As for metre, many critics end 649 at μάτηρ (2 tro) and expand 650 to a full lecythion. But a dimeter ending in μάτηρ would produce a long anceps (highly exceptional in Eur. lyric trochees)[1] or period-end without sense-pause (if -ας in corresponding ὀδόντας is treated as brevis in longo). Dale, *Metr.Anal.* 3.246, also presents this as a lec-ithyph dicolon.

651–4 could easily be redivided as trochaic with repeated word-over-lap, but the avoidance of word-overlap may be a deliberate effect of the style (cf. parodos and third stasimon).

652 if ἕλικος is read (see *ad loc.*), then this is another lec, and in 671 we have the somewhat more usual πάνο|πλον instead of πάνοπ|λον, but for the latter in lyric cf. ἔνοπ| λον in 259 above, ὁπ|λοφόροις in 789 below and

---

[1] Cf. Dale, *LMGD*² 92; instances known to me are doubtful or involve a proper name: *Hel.* 171 (Kannicht accepts two long ancipitia, Dale has one, internal; but see now C. Willink, *CQ* 40 (1990) 83, arguing against long anceps), *Or.* 1396, 1467–9 (-τα μέλεον ... 'Ορέστας: trochaic in Di Benedetto, not in Murray or Willink), 1492–3 (see Willink against Murray or Di Benedetto); and various places in *IA*, for all of which Euripidean authorship is disputed: 281 (long anceps in proper name, but the line may be either cr, 2 ia or 2 tro, cr), 1300–1 (as divided in Günther's Teubner, but a different division is better), 1307 (apparently unavoidable), 1314 (at period-end); cf. also *IA* 241, sp, lec with long central anceps in lec in proper name. I distinguish between lyric trochees and 'trochaic' passages in dactylo-epitrite context (e.g. *Hipp.* 759–65 = 770–5, where long anceps predominates).

IA 190, ὅπ|λοις in *IA* 211, καθοπ|λίσασα in Soph. *El.* 1087 (in anap. *Tro.* 574, *Ant.* 130).

656 Θηβαῖαισι   in the only other attestation of diaeresis of the diph-thong in this word, the second syllable is treated as short (*Ant.* 1135 Θηβαῖας, a choriamb in aeolics).[1] Eur. may have formed Θηβαῖα on the analogy of Θηβαῖς, Θηβαϊκός (explained by Schwyzer 1.266; for diaeresis in general see K–B 1.243–52).

673   on the lack of caesura in this lyric iambic trimeter, see comm. below.

676–7   the double appearance of brevis in longo coincides with possible semantic pause before appositive proper names.

677   this could also be called sp, ia; but whatever it is called, by its opening the colon anticipates 685–7.

678–9   Bothe deletes ἐκάλεσ', which produces an iambo-trochaic line that can be variously scanned, depending on the treatment of the second syllable of γένεθλον and the presence or absence of brevis in longo. JD notes that the repetition of the verb that I accept produces an anadiplosis that does not conform to Euripidean usage as described in *Text. Trad. Or.* 135 n. 13 (anadiplosis fills the iambic or trochaic metron or overruns it by one short syllable).

679bis   for this iambo-trochaic Kurzvers, see metrical note on 1023–4. I prefer this treatment because it reinforces the repetition βαρβάρωι βοᾶι / βαρβάροις λιταῖς; others remove ἐκάλεσ' to produce 3 tro, cr (or cr, 3 ia) in Ἔπαφον ... βοᾶι.

685–7   for spondee opening iambo-trochaic cola, cf. 1039–40 = 1063–4 and sp, lec or sp, ithyph *passim* in *IA* 231ff. With this division, the metrical phrasing again echoes the verbal repetition. It is possible that a new period starts at κτήσαντο, after the appositive phrase.

688   if ἀμῦναι is read (see *ad loc.*), then read γᾶι as well and scan as ba, cr. With γᾶι instead of γαίαι, Willink, 196 n. 14, proposes ἄμυν' ⟨ἄμυνε⟩ τᾶιδε γᾶι.

638–89: COMMENTARY

638 ἔμολε τάνδε γᾶν   like the parodos (202) and like both stanzas of the third stasimon (1019, 1043), this ode begins with the arrival-motif (see Introd. I); here Τύριος in 639 contributes to the echo of the parodos (202 Τύριον οἶδμα λιποῦσ').

---

[1] Diaeresis of αι in the adj. termination -αιος seems not to be attested any-where else: K–B 1.250 list none, and C. A. Lobeck, *Pathologiae graeci sermonis elementa* II (Königsberg 1862) 11 cites only Hermann's two emendations.

639–41 τετρασκελὴς μόσχος ἀδάματον πέσημα δίκε τετρασκελής, a tragic coinage, is elsewhere used more picturesquely and pointedly than here, where it is almost an ornamental epithet: *Her.* 181 τετρασκελές θ' ὕβρισμα, Κενταύρων γένος, 1272-3 τετρασκελῆ κενταυροπληθῆ πόλεμον, *Prom.* 395, Soph. fr. 941.10. Thus, Bergk's τετρασκελὲς ... ἀδάματος has some attraction; but the epithet in ἀδάματον πέσημα is characteristically clever and pregnant: 'spontaneous, unforced, of her own free will', with a play on 'unmated/unyoked' in enallage. Ritual often requires a pure and free animal, but in this context non-intervention by human agents in the path chosen by the animal and in its decision to rest is the more significant ritual requirement, and this is best conveyed by ἀδάματον πέσημα.[1] One might consider τετρασκελὲς ... ἀδάματον, but that would leave μόσχος without an epithet, unlikely (though not impossible) in this style.

ἀδάματον in Eur. only here; Elmsley (on *OT* 196 ed. suae (= 205)) showed that this is the proper tragic form, though the word appears in codd. as -αστος or -αντος.

πέσημα δίκε πέσημα is a specifically tragic word (cf. com. adesp. 621 Kock καταπεσεῖν τι βούλομαι / τραγικὸν πέσημα; later only in quotations of tragedy, in pseudo-Lucian's paratragic *Ocypus* 44, and grammarians); normally a *nomen actionis*, it serves in Eur. (like other abstracts in -μα) also as concrete 'thing fallen', either 'corpse' as in 1701 below or 'statue (fallen from heaven)' in *IT* 1384. Some regard it as concrete here, 'living body', and direct object of δίκε (cf. *Ba.* 600 δίκετε πεδόσε δίκετε τρομερὰ σώματα). I prefer to view it as *nomen actionis* and internal object, 'threw a spontaneous falling down', i.e., 'threw herself down spontaneously': cf. Lycophron, *Alex.* 531 πήδημα λαιψηρὸν δικῶν, 'swooping a swift leap' (the only post-classical use of δικεῖν before *Christ. Pat.*, possibly an imitation of πέσημα δίκε); and perhaps *Or.* 990–1 Μυρτίλου φόνον δικῶν, 'murdering Myrtilus by throwing (him into the sea)' (cf. West against Willink). For δίκε, 664–5n.

641 τελεσφόρον διδοῦσα χρησμόν διδοῦσα is here a vague equivalent of τιθεῖσα or ποιοῦσα, but the construction with pred. adj. τελεσφόρον is similar to that of Soph. *El.* 646 εἰ μὲν πέφηνεν ἐσθλά [sc. τὰ φάσματα], δὸς τελεσφόρα ('grant', addressed to a god), and perhaps *OC* 1489-90 τελεσφόρον χάριν / δοῦναί σφιν [θέλω] (spoken by hero-to-be Oedipus).

642-4 οὐ κατοικίσαι ... ἔχρη the corruption of κατοικίσαι to a finite form and that of νιν to μέν (via μιν) are interrelated and older than our Σ;

---

[1] Cf. *Hom.h.Herm.* 103 ἀδμῆτες δ' ἵκανον [sc. βόες] ἐς αὔλιον ὑψιμέλαθρον, where ἀδμῆτες is equivalent to αὐτόμαται (Allen–Halliday–Sikes *ad loc.*).

335

Valck. first restored the sentence structure by accepting the infinitive and by deleting punctuation after 642 (but he retained μέν, soon repaired by Morus and Musgrave). With the additional change of ἔχρησε(ν) to ἔχρη, the clause is restored to responsion with the antistrophe (which is free of corruption once the temporal augment is removed in 663) and to good sense, except for the troubling δόμων. Those who accept δόμων treat it as gen. with κατοικίσαι on the analogy of verbs of filling ('settle the fertile plains, filling them with homes'). It might instead be interpreted as a loose gen. of description (or possession?) with πεδία ('the fertile plains, site of ⟨future Theban⟩ homes'; cf. Craik: 'to settle lands, wheat producing, for his home'). None of the emendations is attractive. δόμοις would be easier, but why would it have been corrupted to δόμων? Valck.'s Ἀόνων has often been praised and adapted, but although another synonym for Theban and Cadmean would have been handy to Pindar and the tragedians, the word is not attested in poetry before Hellenistic times (cf. Pfeiffer on Call. fr. 572), when it became a learned synonym for 'Theban'. Moreover, Ἀον- elsewhere has long alpha, so either transposition or assumption of prosodic licence is needed to make it fit in this trochaic passage. Geel's δόμους involves as much grammatical peculiarity as δόμων, if he meant 'establish houses throughout/upon the fertile plains' (taking κατ- as governing πεδία). δόμον τ' (Nauck) and μολόντ' (Wilam.) seem to me superfluous and anticlimactic.

οὗ '⟨at the place⟩ where' rather than gen. relative with θέσφατον (antecedent χρησμόν), as Panagl (see on 645 ἵνα τε).

644-5 πεδία . . . πυρόφορα a Homeric juncture, *Il.* 21.602; cf. similar phrases at *Il.* 12.314, 14.123, Solon 13.20, 24.2 West, Theognis 988.

νιν the proper tragic form; mss frequently present the Homeric/Ionic μιν, which probably intruded here before corruption to μέν.

ἔχρη the imperfect of this verb (Bergk, Hermann for transmitted aorist) is not found elsewhere in Eur. and is otherwise rare (the aorist is common; Hdt. also uses historical present often): cf. alternate version of Tyrtaeus 4.1-2 West (ὧδε . . . Ἀπόλλων / χρυσοκόμης ἔχρη), Pindar *O.* 7.92 (ἔχρεον), *OC* 87 (ἐξέχρη), Ap. Rh. 1.302 (ἔχρη), 2.454 (ἔχραεν). The form has no true imperfective force in [Tyrtaeus], Pindar, and Ap. Rh. 1.302, so the simple past meaning required here is not a problem (cf. 27n., 289n.).

645 καλλιπόταμος hapax in extant literature. For the abundance of the epithet (and gen. ὕδατος) with νοτίς, cf. Breitenbach, 189, 194.

ἵνα τε I take τε as the conjunction, joining this clause to οὗ κατοικίσαι κτλ. So too perhaps *IA* 1495, 'and where' being correlative with the indication of place conveyed in Χαλκίδος ἀντίπορον = 'in Aulis'. So-called epic τε cannot be established securely in Eur. (1751n.). ἵνα γε (Valck.) is not found in tragedy, and its γε would not have any useful force (ἵνα γε introduces purpose clauses three times in Aristophanes).

646–8 ἐπέρχεται ... βαθυσπόρους γύας   γύας cannot stand in both 646 and 648, since outside of invocations apposition of a modified noun to the same noun unmodified is contrary to Greek poetic style, though found in other languages.[1] If one assumes that the strophe is sounder than the antistrophe at this point and that the echo of 648 in 669 is a deliberate effect of style rather than an accident arising from corruption, then γύας in 646 must be considered corrupt. The variants and omissions in the mss at 646 and 648 seem to reflect awareness of the corruption, but do not, I think, provide any lead toward a solution. With other treatments of the antistrophe, more radical solutions may be proposed (e.g., Geel's removal of 648 as a whole). But for minimal intervention here, at least two approaches may be considered. (1) Suppose that καί in 648 joins χλοηφόρους and βαθυσπόρους: this is stylistically unusual in high-lyric and dithyrambic style, where multiple epithets are most often in asyndeton (e.g., 653–4 χλοηφόροισιν ἔρνεσιν κατασκίοισιν); but there are a few exx. in Pindar (Slater, *Lex. Pind.* s.v. καί A.2.b, esp. *P.* 9.6–7 πολυμήλου καί πολυκαρποτάτας ... χθονὸς) and Bacchylides (D. E. Gerber, *Lexicon in Bacchylidem* (Hildesheim 1984) s.v. καί (a)(iii)), and cf. *Ba.* 399–402 μαινομένων ... καί κακοβούλων ... φωτῶν, *Hel.* 1485 ἄβροχα πεδία καρποφόρα τε γᾶς. Then γύας in 646 might be emended to an epithet of Δίρκας, which may modify νοτίς, or perhaps better (since νοτίς already has two modifiers) γύας in 648: this was Hermann's approach with ῥυτᾶς, but ῥυτός is elsewhere in tragedy an epithet of general 'water' words, not of a proper noun. Or a noun might be supplied that with Δίρκας would form an appositive to νοτίς (e.g. γάνος Δίρκας, 'the shimmering water of Dirce': cf. *Su.* 1149, *Hel.* 462). (2) Suppose that καί joins βαθυσπόρους γύας with a previous noun-object. Then one might consider τόπους Δίρκας χλοηφόρου (cf. 1026–7 Διρκαίων ... ἐκ τόπων) or perhaps γάνος Δ. χλοηφόρου, if this could mean 'land by the gleaming Dirce' (cf. the metonymy in *Hel.* 462, where Kannicht renders τὸ Νείλου γάνος as 'das Land am glitzernden [schimmernden] Nil').

χλοηφόρους 'rich in young green shoots' ; many epithets in -ηφόρος are Aeschylean coinages; Eur. uses several of these (νικ-, ζυγ-, δαφν-,

[1] Fehling, 175, lists only *Choe.* 627–8 ἐπ' ἀνδρί, τευχεσφόρωι ἐπ' ἀνδρί, but punctuation before rather than after τευχεσφόρωι is uncertain and the second ἐπ' ἀνδρί begins an incurably corrupt colon and may itself be an error. The figure is well established in invocations, esp. with proper names, but for a common noun cf. e.g. *Hec.* 444 αὔρα, ποντιὰς αὔρα.

COMMENTARY 648–52

ἀσπιδ-, ξιφ-; Soph has only νικ- and coins παρδαλήφορος in fr. 11.2), and apparently originates others: στεφαν- *Ba.* 531 (lyric), ἀστραπ- *Ba.* 3 (cf. ἀστραπηφορεῖ, fr. 312), and χλο-, used twice in this ode and not found again until post-classical prose (but χλοηφορέω as botanical term as early as Theophrastus).

βαθυσπόρους 'deeply sown', i.e., 'with deeply fertile soil', as opposed to farmland with very shallow top soil (λεπτόγεως). This meaning is confirmed by passages like Ap. Rhod. 1.685–7, [Moschus] *Megara* 37 Ἀονίου πεδίοιο βαθεῖαν βῶλον ἀροῦντες, Philo Jud. *De Somniis* 2.170 περιαθρεῖν τὴν ἄπασαν ἀρετῆς χώραν, εἴτε εὔγειος καὶ βαθεῖα καὶ χλοηφόρος καὶ καρποτόκος ἐστὶ ..., *De Spec. Legibus* 4.29 βαθύγειον πεδιάδα χλοηφοροῦσαν.[1] The adj. is attested only in Eur. (also fr. 7.1 βαθυσπόρου χθονὸς); Hsch. glosses the nom. sing.

649–56 the birth of Dionysus is a source of pride and fame for Thebes, and this description emphasizes the god's relation to Zeus, the magic fertility that accompanied his birth, and the joyful worship he inspires. No doubt the idea of the destruction of Semele that occasioned his birth provides a negative undertone suitable to the ambiguity of interactions with the divine in this ode (and others in the play). But the chorus should not, I think, evoke the dark aspect here with an open reference such as Wecklein's ⟨ἀστραπᾷ⟩ would supply. The other suggested supplements are metrical fillers unnecessary to the sense, and it seems to me better to obtain responsion by emending only the antistrophe.

649 τέκετο the middle is rare in tragedy relative to the active, and is as likely to be used of the mother (*Choe.* 419, *Tro.* 265, *Or.* 196) as of the father (*Hel.* 214, *Her.* 1023, 1184).

651 περιστεφής only here in the 'active' sense 'encircling as a wreath'; the 'passive' is found in Soph. *El.* 895 (with gen. ἀνθέων) and later in Apollonides, *Anth. gr.* 9.791.1, Plut. *Fab.* 6.3 (both with dative).

652 ἑλικτός after one appearance in *Hom.h.Herm.* 192, this poetic adj. is used in various senses in tragedy (*Trach.* 12 δράκων ἑλικτός, *Andr.* 448, *El.* 180, *Ion* 40, Chaeremon 71 F 7, Theodectas 72 F 6.4, trag. adesp. 626.57; cf. Lycophron *Alex.* 1466) and a few times in Hellenistic poets (it is also a scientific descriptive word in Aristotle and Theophrastus). Here it means 'coiling about', reinforcing περιστεφής. Given the style of the ode, such quasi-redundant fullness cannot be ruled out (cf. the *figura etymologica* in *Her.* 398–9 ἄπλατον ἀμφελικτὸς ἕλικ'). A different, less redundant abun-

---

[1] W. J. Verdenius, in J. Bremer *et al.*, eds., *Miscellanea Tragica in hon. J. C. Kamerbeek* (Amsterdam 1976) 465, wrongly argues that the meaning is 'bearing tall vegetation', comparing *Prom.* 652 and Hdt. 5.92ζ.2.

dance is offered by Hermann's ἕλικος, going with ἔρνεσιν. This is a good Euripidean usage (*Hel.* 1331 βοσκὰς εὐφύλλων ἑλίκων; cf. *Thesm.* 999–1000 κύκλωι δὲ περί σε κισσὸς / εὐπέταλος ἕλικι θάλλει, *Frogs* 1321 βότρυος ἕλικα παυσίπονον); but ἕλικος ... ἔρνεσιν strikes me as somewhat odd ('shoots of tendrils', i.e., 'tendril-shoots'?). Elsewhere the gen. with ἔρνος is usually of the variety of tree (cf. *Concordance*).

654 ὀλβίσας ἐνώτισεν juxtaposition of the semantically free use of two verbs in -ιζω produces a recherché effect. ὀλβίζω is a specifically tragic word, but Eur. typically extends the meaning: *Tro.* 229 (Κρᾶθις) εὐανδρόν τ' ὀλβίζων γᾶν ('making the land well-peopled and prosperous'), *Hel.* 227–8 πάτρια μέλαθρα καὶ τὰν Χαλκίοικον ὀλβιεῖς ('bring joy to' with μέλαθρα and perhaps by zeugma 'hail as ὀλβία' with the divine object: cf. Kannicht). Here it probably means 'mark the blessed status of' or 'acknowledge as blessed' by a bold transfer to the ivy of the 'cultic' use (Kannicht cites *Thesm.* 117 (and 107?)). An alternative is to take it as simply 'making wealthy ⟨with ivy⟩', so (as Craik) 'in abundance'. νωτίζω as well is a tragic word and is given *ad hoc* meanings for various contexts: *Ag.* 286; *OT* 193 and *Andr.* 1141 (cf. Soph. fr. 713); here 'covering the back of', similar to ἐπινωτίσας in *Her.* 362, either 'putting on one's back' (with understood object) or perhaps absolute 'covering one's back'. Cf. Eur.'s use of νώτισμα in fr. 83.8 Austin ('what the Sphinx had on its back'). In later Greek only κατανωτίζομαι is found (add to LSJ's refs. Longus 3.14.4).

655 χόρευμα by a variation typical of Eur., the abstract is used for a person, here the object rather than subject of the verbal action (21n., 215n.): 'who is worshipped in dancing', 'inspiration of dancing worship', based on the trans. use of χορεύω, LSJ II.2.

655bis Θηβαῖαισι for the scansion see note under Metre above. If the apparent scansion is doubted, εὐαλίοισι may be changed (674bis–75n.); keeping 674bis as is, West (1990) suggests παρθένοισιν ἐγχωρίαισι (the adj. is common in Aesch., rare in Eur. and Soph., and always in trimeters except A. *Su.* 705; JD notes that in Eur. it would be ἐγχωρίοισι).

656 εὐίοις the cult-epithet Εὔιος may apply in tragedy to implements, acts, and places of Bacchic revelry (*Ant.* 964, Eur. often), but here only applies to the revellers themselves.

658 Ἄρεος probably to be taken in common with δράκων and φύλαξ. Eur. is not as explicit as other sources (cf. Fontenrose, *Python* 308 n. 61) in making Ares father of the Theban dragon, but the warlike nature of the dragon's offspring fits this genealogy. That Ge is the mother (as one would expect for a monster, esp. a serpent) is confirmed by Tiresias (γηγενής 931, 935); but Σ *Ant.* 126 records an alternative (Erinys Tilphossa: cf. Fontenrose, *Python* 308 n. 61). In myth dragons and serpents often guard what is particularly valued or reserved for divinities and/or forbidden to mortals. The guarding of the spring is a mark of jealous retention by primordial forces of the Theban land, made valuable by the precious water of its abundant source. Thebes can be colonized and civilized by a human community only if this dragon is slain (cf. Apollo's acquisition of Delphi by the slaying of Python). For an overview of Ares' role in the play as opposite of Athena and Dionysus, see Masaracchia.

660 δεργμάτων the word is used as normal *nomen actionis* once in Aesch. (*Pers.* 82), but Eur. typically treats the plural as a synonym of ὄμματα (also 870 below, *Hipp.* 1217, *Hec.* 1265; as 'glance' only in *Med.* 187). In later Greek the word survives only in [Orph.] *Lithica* 339, δέργμα δράκοντος, borrowed from Aesch.; and the late medical writer Meletius says δέργματα is a term for 'whites of the eyes' (*De Nat. Hominis* 69).

662 ἐπὶ χέρνιβας it is emblematic of the tragic entrapment in which the family of Laius is involved that Cadmus' offence against Ares and Earth results from obedience to an oracle and performance of a ritual: Cadmus is about to offer sacrifice in acknowledgment of the fulfilment of the oracle; in some sources the animal that led him is specified as the victim.

663 μαρμάρωι the phrasing suggests to me that this goes with ὄλεσε, though it may be taken ἀπὸ κοινοῦ with the following phrase; Wilam. (*GV* 279) punctuates before μαρμάρωι, producing a combination of datives of instrument and manner (βολαῖς). The word and the action have an epic colouring (*Il.* 12.380, 16.735 of warriors, *Od.* 9.499 of Polyphemus; cf. Alcman 1.31 *PMGF*, and a mock-epic use in *Acharn.* 1172). Cadmus uses a stone at the suggestion of Athena (1062; 666–8n.), who is the protecting goddess aiding the hero in his dangerous feat. The dragon may have had invulnerable skin, rendering the usual weaponry useless (cf. Caeneus), or the ploy may have been designed to keep Cadmus at a safe distance. This stone is perhaps a chthonic symbol (cf. the story of Deucalion), suggesting that the earth-born dragon can be killed only by a kindred element (just as the Spartoi kill each other, in some versions only after Cadmus throws a stone among them).[1]

664 ὄλεσε for the omission of temporal augment in Eur. see Diggle, *Studies* 65–6, 120.

ὀλεσίθηρος hapax in extant Greek, gen. with ὠλένας. Σ, perhaps reacting to a corrupt text with ὠλέναις, considers the epithet either gen. with understood δράκοντος (implying a meaning contrary to all analogy for compounds in ὀλεσι-/ὠλεσι-) or nom. with Κάδμος (with legitimate mean-

---

[1] Fontenrose, *Python* 312–13, sees instead a survival of a detail of a story in which a weather-god overcomes a monster with a thunder-weapon.

ing, but no other compound in -θηρος has a verbal prefix, except late μιξόθηρος, used by Church Fathers for classical μιξόθηρ).

665 δικὼν βολαῖς δικεῖν (with its compounds: ἐπι- Pindar, ἀπο-Aesch., Eur., ἐκ- glossed by Hesych.) is a rare high-style substitute for ῥῖψαι or βαλεῖν, used only in Pindar, Bacch., Aesch., and esp. late Eur. (five of his nine instances in *Phoen.*, three in this ode), then once each in Lycophron (quoted 639–41n.) and *Christ. Pat.* 466 (apart from lexica and grammarians). Its object is usually the thing thrown, and Pindar uses it absolutely, *O.* 10.72 μᾶκος ... ἔδικε πέτρωι ... ὑπὲρ ἁπάντων ('for a length [acc. of extent] beyond all others he made a cast with a rock'). Some have doubted whether it can here govern an object of the thing struck (κρᾶτα), but the analogy of βάλλω is available, and it may be that κρᾶτα is the object of the phrase δικὼν βολαῖς rather than of δικών itself. Note, moreover, that pseudo-Herodian twice (*Epim.* 20.9–10, 247.5 Boissonade) glosses δίκω· τὸ τιτρώσκω, perhaps reflecting interpretation of this passage; and, for what little it is worth, *Christ. Pat.* 466 has καρδία μου δίκεται in the sense 'my heart is struck (with grief and fear)'. Another way to treat the repetitions of δικ- (and the doubt about its syntax in 665) and the faulty structure of 664–9 is to consider the first δικών intrusive and replace it with another participle of striking, such as Geel's θενών or Kock's κιχών (the latter does not normally mean 'reach ⟨with a weapon⟩' in tragedy and would here be a reminiscence of the unusual use in *Il.* 10.370 σε δουρὶ κιχήσομαι, cf. 5.187 βέλος ... κιχήμενον).

666–7–9–8 in the mss δίας ἀμάτορος Παλλάδος φραδαῖσιν runs on as part of the previous sentence, linking Athena's advice to the slaying (as in the brief recapitulation of the story in 1062–4), but the additional run-on of 668–9 with another participial phrase is impossible semantically (we cannot have a coincident participle like that in 1507) and clumsy stylistically.[1] The lines are also metrically defective, given the text adopted in the strophe (but the strophe could be rewritten if one prefers to stick closer to the transmitted text here). Athena's advice is more suitable to the otherwise unexplained action of sowing the dragon's teeth, and with a conjunction restored in 666 a finite verb is also needed. I think it best to restore a lecythion in 667 and think it likely enough that Eur. used another form of δικεῖν. Another possibility is Παλλάδος φραδαῖς ⟨ἐνῆκ'⟩, after Wecklein; Wilam. placed ⟨δίκεν⟩ after φραδαῖς, but this requires the

---

[1] It is no help to punctuate after μαρμάρωι and make Cadmus throw the whole head in order to sow the teeth: so, e.g., Buschor, following a hint in Σ; but apart from the impracticality of the technique, this requires the illegitimate meaning of ὀλεσίθηρος.

unjustifiably violent remedy of eliminating both 669 and 648. By the near echo between strophe and antistrophe Eur. plays on the ambivalence of the fertility of Theban soil.

668 γαπετεῖς another hapax. Like Aesch. (βαρυ-, δακρυο-), Eur. coins new -πετής compounds (γονυ- [293n.], διο-, δορι-) as well as using the more obvious and traditional ones shared by Soph. (εὐ-, περι-, ὑψι-, etc.).

671 πάνοπλον ὄψιν 'a vision of fully-armed men', a recherché equivalent of 'fully armed men, a wondrous sight'. The precious style continues in ἄκρων ὅρων χθονός, 'the earth's limiting shell'; the odd use of ὅρος perhaps reinforces the note of transgression of norms in this miraculous birth.

672 σιδαρόφρων an Aeschylean echo (Se. 52; cf. Prom. 242; the adj. is not found again before Athanasius); on 'steel' as an ominous word, 350n.

673 Diggle, Textual Trad. Or. 138 n. 18, notes that lyric iambic trimeters in Eur. usually have a caesura; he there notes about half a dozen exceptions but now believes all can be eliminated by redivision. This line, as restored by Triclinius, has no caesura, but can be given one by adopting Porson's ξυνῆψε γᾶι φίλαι πάλιν (his additional transposition φόνος δέ νιν σιδαρόφρων is unnecessary and deprives the impressive epithet of its emphatic position); JD proposes σιδαρόφρων / δέ νιν φίλαι ξυνῆψε γᾶι φόνος πάλιν (or πάλιν φόνος). I would not insist on restoring a caesura in all the lines that lack it. The textual confusion probably arose from omission of φίλαι (under the influence of 670?), which was then inserted above γᾶι and restored incorrectly. The omission of πάλιν in PRw may be due to the faulty reinsertion of φίλα rather than to a separate problem.

νιν probably 'them', the Spartoi, understood from πάνοπλον ὄψιν.

ξυνῆψε although Eur. is in general fond of this verb, I regard its repetition in this play as thematically significant, associating the fatal linkage of marriage with fatal and violent meetings of other kinds: 37 the meeting of Laius and Oedipus; 702 meeting of Et. and Pol. for debate (cf. 1241 of oath-taking before the fatal duel); 1230, 1381 meeting of Et. and Pol. for battle (cf. 1192 of general battle); 49, 1049 incestuous marriage of Joc. and Oed. Here I would detect a sexual, almost incestuous undertone in the use of the verb: the Spartoi die in their mother's embrace (cf. the imagery of 1458-9, Joc. and her sons), wetting her with blood.

674 αἵματος δ' ἔδευσε Eur. avoids too-obvious reminiscence of the Homeric αἵματι δὲ χθὼν / δεύετο, Il. 17.360-1, by exceptionally using gen. instead of dat. with δεύω, as if it were a verb of filling.

674bis-75 εὐαλίοισι δεῖξεν αἰθέρος πνοαῖς the paradoxically gentle, sensual image adds pathos to the picture of violence. δεῖξεν has the force of an English pluperfect, and δεῖξεν ... πνοαῖς is an artificial variation on 'brought forth to the light, gave birth to'. The image may also recall the contrast between sun/bright sky and human misfortune in the prologue (3–5, 84) and that between the beauty of Pol.'s armour and the violence of his mission in 168–9. If the diaeresis of αι in 655bis is not accepted (see n.), Musgrave's εὐείλοισι will produce responsion: εὔειλος is ascribed to Aristophanes by Photius (fr. 823 K–A) and is found in botanical works of Aristotle and Theophrastus; cf. Aesch. fr. 334 ἄειλα. But Eur. has εὐάλιος in lyric at *Hipp.* 129 and *IT* 1139 (cf. *Frogs* 242; εὐηλίως in trimeters *Eum.* 906; δυσάλιος in *Rhes.* 247).

676 καὶ σέ such a transition is common in a sequence of prayers to various gods (as in *Se.* 128–65, *OT* 158–67, 203–15); here we have rather a shift from narrative involving many gods (some well-disposed, some hostile) to invocation of a specific god to ward off the evil implied by the narration.

προμάτορος possibly another echo of *Se.*, where the Theban chorus appeals to Aphrodite (mother of Harmonia) as γένους προμάτωρ (140), but by contrast Eur. plays upon the foreignness of his chorus. The noun is found in tragedy only in *Se.* 140 and *Phoen.* (again of Io at 828) and does not reappear until late prose.

677 ἔκγονον for the form (vs. ἔγγονον) see Barrett on *Hipp.* 447–50.

679bis βαρβάρωι βοᾶι repeated (in reverse order) in 1301 (cf. Φοίνισσαν βοάν 301); same phrase in *Or.* 1385. βοά is a favourite term in tragic lyric, and I prefer to ascribe the repetitious phrase here to Eur., not to a gloss on βαρβάροις λιταῖς (though the latter has suffered contamination from βοᾶι in the tradition).

682–3 σοί νιν ἔκγονοι κτίσαν κτλ. this passage occasioned considerable confusion of interpretation early in the tradition. The most straightforward sequence of thought is procured by σοί ... ἔκγονοι κτίσαν: 'come to this land, because it was your offspring (Cadmus and his people) who founded it'. The main alternative, σῶι ... ἐκγόνωι κτίσαν αἱ ... θεαί, is probably the result of corruption and short-sighted reading (ignoring the verb in 687: see *ad loc.* for the question of this word's presence).[1] It was

---

[1] Σ perhaps implies the secondary nature of the reading as dative when it cites the theory that the text was originally written in the old Attic alphabet (ΣΟΙ ... ΕΚΓΟΝΟΙ) and was wrongly converted to Ionic lettering. This theory is presumably wrong. Athenians were using Ionic letters in graffiti and dipinti from the middle of the fifth century, and Eur. had a herdsman in *Theseus* (before 422) describe Ionic letters forming the hero's name (fr. 382). It seems probable to me that well before the time of *Phoen.* scribes writing books (and poets composing

defended by Wilam. with an irrelevant and illegitimate historicist argument about the actual prehistory of Boeotia; moreover, to suggest that Demeter/Ge founded Thebes *for* Cadmus consorts ill with the narrative just completed, in which Cadmus wins the land from its chthonic guardian through Apollo and Athena, angering (as is clear later) Ge. Finally, κτίζειν is normally a function for humans, not for deities, with the exception of Apollo, who through his oracle is sometimes regarded as a founder (e.g., Apollo κτίστης for Cyrene). The letters after κτίσαν were clearly ΑΙ in the time of the ancient commentators, but αἱ leaves an implausible asyndeton and ἅι prevents τάνδε γᾶν from being understood as object of the verb in 687, as it should be. ΑΙ, then, seems to be a corruption of ΚΑΙ or ΚΑΙΑΙ or ΑΝ. Since it is unidiomatic for a relative to follow upon νιν, I prefer καί (Major) or χαί (mine) to ἄν (Scholefield); these also dispense with brevis and pause in 682. If χαί is right, the corruption may be due to *scriptio plena* representation of vowels in crasis (476n.). But crasis of καί and article does not occur elsewhere in Euripidean lyric or anapaests, though it is found in *OC* 706 (pherecratean) and four times in anapaests (*Pers.* 45, Soph. *El.* 97, *Phil.* 1467, *OC* 1767). So καί is probably the better choice.

683 διώνυμοι 'who are addressed as a pair' (e.g. as τὼ θεώ, the Eleusinian goddesses), not 'having two names each' or simply pleonastic for 'two'. This is a unique use, and the word is not attested again until Hellenistic times, when it is a grammatical term, esp. as substantive τὸ διώνυμον = 'alternative name'.

686bis πάντων δέ δέ is not to be emended to τε; for δέ in anaphora see Denniston, *GP*² 163, 502; Diggle, *Studies* 55-6; cf. 340n.

Γᾶ τροφός it is likely that the view that the Δη- of Demeter is a variant of Ge was already current in Eur.'s time, and so this phrase is a poetic etymologizing of the preceding Δαμάτηρ: cf. *Ba.* 274-6 and A. Henrichs, *ZPE* 3 (1968) 111-12.

687 κτήσαντο Wilam.'s treatment of 682-3 entails the deletion of this verb. The ancient scholars who took αἱ ... θεαί as subject of κτίσαν need

---

plays) would have used the Ionic alphabet, while the conservatism of official record-keeping maintained the old alphabet in many inscriptions until the official abandonment of it in 403. For denial of a general μεταχαρακτηρισμός cf. Pfeiffer, *Hist. Cl. Schol.* 30; on the use of Ionic letters in literature, including Attic literature of the second half of the fifth century, see Wilam., *Homerische Untersuchungen* [Phil. Unters. 7 (Berlin 1884)], 301-5, esp. 302 n. 12. For use of the notion of change in alphabet by Hellenistic scholars, cf. ΣPindar *N.* 1.34b Drachmann; see also R. Janko, *The Iliad: a commentary. Volume IV: books 13-16* (Cambridge 1992) 34-7.

not have had a text without this verb, for ancient commentators are notoriously apt to take too short-sighted a view of a text that they are worrying. On the other hand, the commentators who understood AI as ἅι in 683 must have had a verb here. In any case, as argued above, the goddesses should not be the sole subject of κτίσαν, and it would be no improvement to have them as conjoint subject of κτίσαν, with καὶ in 683.[1] The *veteres* and Σ read ἐκτίσαντο, which Σ interpret as ᾤκησαν, relying on the false analogy of the epithet ὀρείκτιτον. The middle of κτίζω is confined to Pindar, and though Eur. might in lyrics have taken over this use, the sense 'founded for themselves' is still implausible. Most have therefore accepted ἐκτήσαντο or Porson's κτήσαντο. This would mean that upon the foundation of Thebes, Demeter and Kore chose and acquired it as a major cult-site, implying a relationship of favour. In reality, it appears that Demeter Thesmophoros, whose shrine was on the Theban citadel (even, according to Pausanias' sources, on the site of Cadmus' house), was the protective city-goddess at Thebes as well as an agricultural deity: cf. Schachter, *Cults of Boeotia* I.165–8, and for Persephone II.200–1. So it is natural for Demeter to be called upon for protection in time of war, although it remains a problem how we are to understand the identification of Demeter and Ge in relation to Ge's role in the story of Cadmus and the dragon. Perhaps the chorus is wishfully reappropriating Ge's favour for Thebes by renaming her and by describing a propitious selection of Thebes as a favoured site.

πέμπε probably 'escort', since Epaphus has himself been called upon to come.

πυρφόρους Demeter is associated with torches in her search for her kidnapped daughter, and torches played an important role in Eleusinian processions and rituals: cf. Richardson on *Hom.h.Dem.* 47ff. Persephone is connected to torches by her pairing with Demeter, but also by her identification with Hecate: cf. Diggle on *Phaethon* 268 ὦ πυρὸς δέσποινα Δήμητρος κόρη.

688 ἄμυνε if πέμπε is taken as 'send', then ἀμῦναι as inf. of purpose is possible, but this leaves Epaphus too indirectly involved in aiding his descendants. The γρ-variant of Σ, ἀμύνεται δὲ γᾶ, is a misdivision of the text adopted here (with variant γᾶι written without silent iota).

689 πάντα δ' εὐπετῆ θεοῖς acknowledgment of the god's power to give aid is a tactful element in a prayer for help: cf. *Alc.* 219–20 θεοῖσιν

---

[1] This juncture is apparently intended by Willink, 196 n. 14, who deletes Δαμάτηρ in 685 as well as ἐκτίσαντο.

εὐξόμεσθα· / θεῶν γὰρ δύναμις μεγίστα. The motif of the 'ease' of divine action (see e.g. West on Hes. *Op.* 5ff.) also contributes to the *captatio benevolentiae*.

690–783: SECOND EPISODE

STRUCTURE AND FUNCTION

This unusually short episode consists of two roughly equal sections: a deliberation-stichomythia between Eteocles and Creon, and a sort of 'fare-well'-rhesis in which Eteocles makes his final dispositions before disappearing as a speaking actor in the play. Two major functions are served by the scene. First, mainly in the stichomythia but partly also in the preliminaries and in the long rhesis, Eteocles is ironically exposed: the flashy sophistry that in the previous scene he opposed to the traditional wisdom of Joc. and deployed against Pol.'s just claim and conventional values is now seen to be insubstantial, as his failed strategic suggestions reveal youth, rashness, and inexperience; and his blindness to his own failings and to the moral complications of the situation is highlighted, particularly in the ironic scene-ending prayer (781–3n.). Second, mainly in the rhesis but partly also in the stichomythia, dramatic preparation is supplied for significant developments: the interview with Tiresias and the essential presence of Menoeceus, the major battle at the Seven Gates and the fratricide, and the conflicts of the exodos over burial and marriage. The separation of the fate of the family from the fate of the city begins in this scene, and Euripides marks the novelty of his construction of events by inviting comparison with *Septem* (including a very explicit allusion in 751–2: see note). In *Septem* Eteocles was, however we may judge his other qualities, without doubt a competent military leader: the plan for defence of the city and the selection of the seven defenders belong firmly to him, his actions as general are central to the action of the play, and these actions are inextricably tied to the suddenly revealed inevitability of the fratricidal duel (so that although Et. does not in fact view his decision to fight his brother as a straightforward *Opfertod* for the city, there is in essence no disjunction between his personal motivations and his civic duties). Here, instead, the plan of defence is not Eteocles', but Creon's, presented to Et. only after the rejection of several rash ideas leads Et. to *aporia*; and later the sacrifice of Menoeceus (in conscious *Opfertod*, unknown to Et.) and the separation of the main battle from the fratricide (in separate messenger-speeches in separate episodes) undermine Et.'s connection to the ultimate success of the city. The sharp difference from *Septem* is also marked by Et.'s refusal to name the defenders of the seven gates (751–2).[1] Whereas Eur. gives an unusually lengthy and sympathetic build-up to Pol. before and within the first episode, he treats Et. more harshly by devoting the episode he dominates to undercutting his pretensions.[2]

The major controversies over the possibility of interpolation in this scene arise in the final rhesis of Et. (751–6n., 751–2n., 753n., 754–[6]n., 753–5n., 757–65n., 763–5n., 774–7n.), although for a few critics the opening speech raises doubts because of its possible reference forward to what they suspect later in the scene (690–6n.).

690 action there is no clear indication of Et.'s movements in the words either at the end of the previous episode or here, and the view that he stays on stage during the first stasimon has been espoused (against Σ: δεῖ νοεῖν ὅτι τοῦ χοροῦ ᾄδοντος ἔσω ἦν ὁ Ἐτεοκλῆς) by a few commentators (most recently Craik) and vigorously supported by Riemschneider in particular, in whose Nazi-influenced reading of the play Et. is said to hold the stage in triumph after disposing of the threat to the fatherland posed by Pol. and Joc. But if Et. initiates (even if abortively) an action at the opening of the scene, this is a strong indication that he went inside at the end of the previous episode and is re-emerging from the palace at this moment. If we set aside cases in which an actor is immobilized on stage by the need to supplicate or some other factor, there remain a certain number of instances in which an actor remains on stage during a stasimon: e.g., Medea during the four stasimons of *Med.*; Creon during the second stasimon of this play; Pentheus during the first stasimon of *Ba.*; in Sophocles, Creon during the second and fourth stasimons of *Ant.*; Oedipus during the third stasimon of *OT*; Electra during the first three stasimons of *El.*; also Hector during the first two stasimons of *Rhesus*. But in every such case, the next episode begins with the arrival of a new character, and if (as rarely happens) the lingering actor speaks first in the new episode, it is always in order to announce or comment on the entrance (as in *OT*

---

[1] Cf. Foley, 124, for the idea that Et. is not only refusing to behave like the Aeschylean model, but usurping functions of other characters in the literary tradition in his instructions about marriage, care of Jocasta, and the body of Pol.

[2] I mention as a historical curiosity that does not merit discussion the suspicion expressed by G. Norwood, *Essays on Euripidean Drama* (Berkeley 1954) 36, that this whole episode is inauthentic. In my Teubner (p. 140) I wrongly ascribed this suspicion also to Leidloff (who doubted instead the next episode).

1110).[1] So it would be extraordinary for Et. (with his attendants) to stand inactive during the stasimon and then to give a command (which could have been given before the stasimon) only after the song is finished.[2] The technique used here is closely paralleled in *Su.* 381ff., where Theseus re-enters from one side with a herald, opening the episode by giving instructions, but the herald's departure is checked by the entrance of the Theban herald. (If, on the other hand, 690–6 are deleted with Willink (1990) 193–4 (see note below), the above argument does not apply, and parallels support Et.'s presence on stage during the stasimon.)

If Et. speaks while he and the attendants are still moving forward from the door, there may be created an impression that the actor has been making other dispositions just before he emerged, and the technique points the way toward the representation of an ongoing conversation that becomes audible to the audience in mid-stream. The closest that extant tragedy comes to such a technique is *Phil.* 1222, *IA* 303, and *Alexandros* fr. 23 Snell (in all of which two characters enter hastily in disagreement or uncertainty about what is to be done); for comedy see Gomme–Sandbach on *Dysc.* 233 and their Introd. p. 13; also Fraenkel, *Beobacht. zu Arist.* 103–4. A few other abrupt scene-opening speeches that may create an impression similar to that of this scene are *Su.* 381, *Andr.* 147 (see Stevens, and *Contact and Discontinuity* 116–17), and *Eum.* 64.

690–6 this passage is deleted by Willink (1990) 193–4 in conformity with his reconstruction of the second part of the scene without any testamentary dispositions (757–65n.); cf. Dos Santos Alves' proposed deletion of 692 alone (with 753–65). Willink argues (1) that Creon is adequately identified without 690–6 and that Et.'s desire to see Creon (700) is adequately explained by 701–2 (to me, 701–2 appear insufficient, since to be explanatory they need the unstated premise 'I have something to say to you before I go to battle, now imminent', which the audience has heard in 692–4); (2) Et. had no reason to go in at 637 (637n., 690 action n.; on the other hand, Et. had no reason to stay on stage at 637: his staying when he was in such a hurry (446–7, 450–1, 588–9, 592) is just as 'unrealistic' as his going in and coming out); (3) the initiative in the following sticho-

---

[1] So too if Clytaenmestra speaks *Ag.* 489ff. after staying on during the first stasimon (but I now believe that she exits at 354 and returns at 587). The same episode-opening technique applies in cases where 'immobilized' actors remain during a stasimon (cf. *OC* 710, 1251).

[2] Cf. Mueller-Goldingen, 120 n. 1. Contrast the episode-ending order of Medea in *Med.* 820, preparing for the entrance of Jason at the start of the next episode; likewise, *Phoen.* 768–70, *Ba.* 352–7.

mythia comes from Creon, not Et., as these lines suggest (but the course of the dialogue can effect a change, and it may have dramatic point that the initiative is taken away from Et. in the strategic planning: 692n. 706–7n.); (4) the passage functions as preparation for the later passages (agreed, but this has force only after one agrees that 757–65 are a later addition).

691 ἀδελφὸν μητρὸς 'Ιοκάστης ἐμῆς the appositive phrase is not necessary for identification of Creon (either for the audience or for the attendant), but serves to reinforce the kinship theme (see Introd. I) and provides the ground of ἀγχιστεία for the choice of Creon as the confidant of Et.'s οἰκεῖα ... βουλεύματα. On the other hand, Κρέοντ' and hence the whole line are necessary, since the bare τὸν Μενοικέως left by Zipperer's deletion of 691 is too abrupt: without apposition to or of the name itself, the periphrasis of article plus genitive of the father's name is proper to lyric style rather than dialogue (cf. however *Phil.* 628).

692 οἰκεῖα καὶ κοινὰ χθονός in οἰκεῖα Et. already has in mind the 'testamentary' dispositions to be made in his rhesis (757ff.), in the event that he dies and the Thebans win, leaving Creon as eldest male relative κύριος of the household and its female or incapacitated members. Dos Santos Alves[1] and Mueller-Goldingen object to this understanding of the line because in the event Et. does not in fact deliberate with Creon about the family's affairs, but simply gives instructions to which Creon makes no reply. But (1) at the conclusion of the stichomythia on strategy there is a dramatic advantage in varying the form by shifting to a long rhesis; (2) the lack of true discussion between Et. and Creon concerning the testamentary dispositions may be read as suggestive of Et.'s egocentric confidence and Creon's subservience (cf. 766–73n., 774–7n., 782–3n.). κοινὰ χθονός refers, at the minimum, to the instruction to receive Tiresias' advice, but may perhaps also be taken by defenders of 774–7 as preparation for the burial-edict (which likewise assumes the case in which Et. is dead but the Thebans triumphant). It is unclear from the available evidence whether Et. had intended from the beginning to discuss strategy with Creon. That topic arises from Creon's insistence (706) and the course of the dialogue either postpones Et.'s own βουλεύματα or covers that part of his intended topics.

κοινὰ χθονός the genitive depends on the noun βουλεύματα and not on κοινά, though it reinforces and clarifies the sense of the adj.; just as

---

[1] He in fact deletes line 692 as a side-effect of his deletion of 757–65, which contain all the familial dispositions. He exaggerates the rarity of the gen. with κοινός, which is explained here.

οἰκεῖα represents 'of the household' in a 'pertinentive' rather than a 'possessive' sense ('about, concerning the household'), so χθονός is 'about, concerning the land' (for this type of gen. see Barrett on *Hipp.* 129–30 with refs.). The phrase is nevertheless closely comparable to the use of κοινός in conjunction with a possessive gen. found in all three tragedians: e.g., *Eum.* 109 ὥραν οὐδενὸς κοινὴν θεῶν, *Trach.* 207–8 κοινὸς ἀρσένων / ἴτω κλαγγά, *Ion* 366 τρίποδα κοινὸν Ἑλλάδος.

συμβαλεῖν βουλεύματα a precious expression for 'join counsel with, share counsel with, deliberate with'; cf. *Pers.* 528 πιστοῖσι πιστὰ ξυμφέρειν βουλεύματα. For συμβαλεῖν cf. *IA* 830 αἰσχρὸν δέ μοι γυναιξὶ συμβάλλειν λόγους. Eur. is perhaps creating a variation on συμβάλλεσθαι ('contribute') λόγους, γνώμας, etc. (cf. LSJ s.v. 1.10; *OC* 1151 συμβαλοῦ γνώμην).

695 cf. *Su.* 397–8 (at sight of the Theban herald) ἐπίσχες, ἤν σ' ἀπαλλάξῃ πόνου / μολὼν ὕπαντα τοῖς ἐμοῖς βουλεύμασιν.

ἐκλύει 'undoes (by relaxing the tension/intensity of)', so 'puts an end to', a meaning that is common enough in the simplex (cf. 81 ἔριν λύουσ'), but rare in this compound: in *OT* 35–6 ἐξέλυσας ... δασμόν is probably a financial metaphor ('paid off in full'), in *Trach.* 654 ἐπιπόνων ἀμερᾶν is to be preferred to ἐπίπονον ἀμέραν; but LSJ 11.2 cites Dem. 9.14 and 18.26 (add Hippocrates *De Locis in homine* 27).

696 it would be uncharacteristically abrupt for the approach of Creon to be acknowledged by 695 alone, as Geel and Herwerden (1903) assume in suggesting that 696 be deleted as inorganic. The line is, to be sure, helpful to a reader, but the verbal marking of movement and action is nevertheless typical of the dramatic scripts themselves.

697 ἦ πόλλ' affirmative ἦ often strengthens an emphatic adjective of quantity or magnitude (cf. Denniston, *GP*[2] 280); there are over a dozen instances of ἦ πολ-/πολλ- in tragedy.

†ἐπῆλθον† some have defended the appearance of this verb in both 697 and 699 as an instance of careless and insignificant repetition; but the offence here is not the mere repetition of the word, but (1) the identity within repetitious clauses that otherwise aim for variation (πόλλ' vs. πέριξ ... πύλας φυλακάς τε; εἰσιδεῖν χρήιζων σ' vs. σὸν δέμας θηρώμενος) and (2) the weakness of the expression πόλλ' ἐπῆλθον, 'I visited many spots'. This weakness makes it preferable to deem 697 corrupt by contamination from 699 rather than vice versa (as Burges, Paley, Nauck). Of possible corrections, verbs of motion are too strong (Polak's ἐπῆισσον) or consort ill with πόλλ' (with Stadtmüller's ἐφοίτων I would expect εἰς πόλλ', but ἦ πόλλ' should not be altered). A verb of filling (Schoene's ἐπλήρουν, based on Burges' proposal for 699, ἔπληθον) assumes a doubtful idiom, since *Ion* 1108, the passage the conjecture is based on, is defective. A verb of toil seems more likely: Geel's aorist ἐμόχθησ'[1] is better than Valck.'s imperfect, but both introduce a jingle with μόχθον in 695, which is odd since an entering character normally does not 'hear' his own announcement; ἀπήντλουν, without the support of πόνον or the like, is unsatisfactory; Willink (1990) 200 n. 48 suggests πολλά γ' ἤθλουν or ἤθλησ'.

699 φυλακάς τ'   although φύλακας ἐπελθεῖν by itself could be good idiom ('approach' or 'consult the guards'), the pairing with πύλας favours φυλακάς here ('visited the guardposts at the gates').

700 καὶ μήν   the particles mark agreement and reciprocation of intention (also conveyed by the echo of 697 in σ' ἔχρηιζον εἰσιδεῖν); cf. in general Denniston, GP² 353–6 and compare perhaps the use of καὶ δή to mark compliance with a request.

701 πολλῶι ... ἐνδεεῖς   'very far from meeting the need'; for the dative as if with a comparative word, cf. *Held.* 170 πολλῶι τοῦ παρόντος ἐνδεές. πολλῶν ('lacking many needed features') gives a weaker, less apposite sense. Willink (1990) 200 n. 50 doubts πολλῶι in a context in which ἐνδεής has no gen. of comparison expressed and finds ὡς 'a little odd'; he proposes ἐνδεῆ διαλλαγῆς / ὅσ' εἰς κτλ., which seems to me unnecessarily elaborate.

702   the phrasing could be analysed as εἰς λόγους μολών and συνῆψα [ἐμαυτὸν] Πολυνείκει, but the prep. phrase and the dative could both be felt with either verb-form (for εἰς λόγους συνῆψα cf. Soph. *El.* 21 ξυνάπτετον λόγοισιν and esp. *Lys.* 468 τοῖσδε σαυτὸν εἰς λόγον ... συνάπτεις), and the word-order suggests that μολών may be a quasi-redundant filler. Cf. 673n.

703 εἰς Θήβας   transmitted μεῖζον ... ἢ Θήβας φρονεῖν is difficult. Most, following Σ, believe that Pol. is said to have grand ambitions beyond the conquest of Thebes (cf. Hartung's 'dass er über Theben stolz hinweg schaut'; Méridier's 'il va plus loin que Thèbes'). But the implied construction of Θήβας as internal acc. of φρονεῖν is harsh (contrast *Knights* 1216 τὰ τοῦ δήμου φρονεῖ). And why should Creon think this, or what point could Eur. be making by putting such a misconception in Creon's mouth? More appositely, others translate 'spurns, shows contempt for Thebes' (e.g., Grotius' *nempe ille spernit Thebas*),[2] for which one can compare the idiom 'think oneself better/grander than' seen in *Andr.* 700 φρονοῦσι δήμου μεῖζον

---

[1] Cf. line-initial καὶ πόλλ' ἐμόχθησ', *Telephus* fr. 102.8 Austin, unknown to Geel; but Valck. had already quoted Greg. Naz. *Carm. de se ipso* 14.59 = *PG* 37.1249, 10 ἢ πόλλ' ἐμόχθησ'.

[2] Di Benedetto on *Or.* 1568 is too fanciful in detecting a resonance of the idiomatic use of πυργοῦμαι, as if we had here 'towers in his pride higher than Thebes' walls'.

351

[= ἢ δῆμος φρονεῖ], Alexis fr. 16.4 K–A μεῖζόν τι τῶν ἄλλων φρονεῖν [= ἢ οἱ ἄλλοι φρονοῦσι], or Dem. 23.205 Θεμιστοκλέα λαβόντες μεῖζον ἑαυτῶν ἀξιοῦντα φρονεῖν [= ἢ αὐτοὶ φρονοῦσι]: but this requires us to take ἢ Θήβας as ἢ Θῆβαι [φρονοῦσι] attracted into acc. because of the indirect discourse. The same construction is assumed in Craik's 'has more confidence than Thebes', which misrepresents the pejorative force of μέγα φρονεῖν (though her note correctly speaks of pride) and is an odd concession for Creon to make so baldly. A more natural expression of the desired sense is Wecklein's εἰς Θήβας (suggested in his revision of Klotz), 'has overproud thoughts in regard to Thebes', that is, 'thinks of Thebes and her strength with proud contempt'; he compared *Hcld.* 386–7 οὐ σμικρὸν φρονῶν / ἐς τὰς Ἀθήνας (where the phrase contributes more when taken with φρονῶν than with εἶσι in 386); cf. also *Hipp.* 6 φρονοῦσιν εἰς ἡμᾶς μέγα. Nauck's ἢ θέμις or Wecklein's later ἢ θνητόν bring in unwanted connotations.

703–5 ἤκουσα the dramatist need not tell his audience how Creon heard what he heard, but the intervening choral ode provides a gap in which an audience can assume, if it wishes, the spread of the report; cf. Creon's entrance (from the side) at *OT* 512 (πεπυσμένος, but source not specified), and the failure to inform the audience of the source of Menelaus' knowledge of the attack on Helen in *Or.* 1554–5.[1] As for the content of his knowledge, Creon echoes the patriotic line that Pol. is the leader of a foreign force (cf. 512–14) and makes no reference to the issue of justice debated in the previous scene. Likewise, although his cut-off formula refers to the gods, he shows no sign of the anxiety about divine favour expressed by the Old Servant (154–5) and the chorus (257–8).

705 for this cut-off formula, cf. *Il.*17.514 ἀλλ' ἤτοι μὲν ταῦτα θεῶν ἐν γούνασι κεῖται. Metaphorical ἀναρτάω, 'leave fully in the power of', is first extant in Eur.: *Su.* 735 σοῦ [Zeus] γὰρ ἐξηρτήμεθα, fr. 626.1 δήμωι δὲ μήτε πᾶν ἀναρτήσηις κράτος (where the dative functions like εἰς θεούς here). Whether some particular image (such as suspending of offerings in a temple or from an image, or the gesture of supplication) lies behind the usage is unclear; Homeric commentators have a similar uncertainty about ἐν γούνασι κεῖται. For the periphrasis ἀναρτήσαντ' ἔχειν serving as 'resultative' perfect, see Moorhouse, *Syntax Soph.* 206.

706–7 after dismissing the topic broached by Et., Creon introduces his

---

[1] I do not believe that the Phrygian is Menelaus' informant; the chorus' deliberation in *Or.* 1539 shows that the Phrygian has gone back indoors, not been dismissed by Orestes to report to Menelaus, as Verrall, West, and Willink believe.

own in a vague anticipatory manner typical of tragic dialogue, thus taking the initiative in the incipient stichomythia and evoking from Et. a first line that is in a sense 'filler', but also confirms the relationship between the speakers that will hold throughout. 707 differs only in two syllables (μῆτερ for ταῦτα) from *Trach*. 78. τὰ ποῖα ταῦτα; is found also in *OT* 291, 935, *OC* 893, which all have more vigorous post-caesura halves. Cf. 1704n.

709 δὲ δὴ τί the particles and the postponement of τί throw emphasis on λέγει (cf. Denniston, *GP*² 259), probably marking impatience (cf. λέγεις δὲ δὴ τί; in Pl. *Phdr.* 242d3); cf. 1277 below.

710–11 three objections have made reduction of the couplet to a single verse an almost universal choice: (a) the stichomythia is disturbed; (b) πέριξ is nowhere else construed with the dative; (c) Καδμείων πόλιν in 710 is suspiciously similar to Καδμείων πόλει in the same position in 712. But the case for excision is inconclusive. (a) Some nineteenth-century critics believed it justified to regularize every stichomythia by deletion or assumption of lacunae; more recent studies usually concede that there are some genuine cases of irregularity, esp. at the beginning or end of a sequence: A. Gross, *Die Stichomythie in der gr. Trag. u. Kom.* (Berlin 1905) 25–40; Denniston on *El.* 651–2, Dodds on *Ba.* 927–9, Kannicht on *Hel.* 780–1; Diggle, *Studies* 110–11. For expressive irregularity cf. *Alc.* 1133–40, *Hipp.* 1057–63, *El.* 558–9, 573–4, *Or.* 255–7, *Ba.* 927–9, 1269–70, perhaps *Antiope* fr. 48.32–3 Kambitsis. Less expressive cases are *Hec.* 239–41 (beginning of story) and perhaps 759–60 (in transmitted order: *CP* 83 (1988) 157), *IT* 69–70 (identification of shrine), 735–6 (content of oath), 811–12 (beginning of proofs), *Ion* 936–7 (beginning of story), *Ba.* 842–6 (end of sequence). If the couplet here is genuine, it would fall into the latter class, since it conveys the essential news, the first mention of the full encirclement, which is a prerequisite of a simultaneous attack on the seven gates. (b) Not only is the dative with πέριξ otherwise unattested, but the sense required here is 'all around the towers', which would correctly be expressed by περὶ/πέριξ + acc. (of extension), as in *IA* 774–5 Πέργαμον δὲ Φρυγῶν πόλιν λαΐνους περὶ πύργους κυκλώσας; *Pers.* 368 [τάξαι νεῶν] ἄλλας ... κύκλωι νῆσον Αἴαντος πέριξ; *Her.* 243 βωμὸν [Brodaeus for -ῶν] πέριξ νήσαντες ἀμφήρη ξύλα (prose authors from Hdt. on have the acc. with πέριξ and less often the gen.). The dative should be like that with περί, expressing static, clinging encirclement or attachment (such as of armour on a body, or in an embrace or supplication). So something is amiss in 710, but it is not clear that the fault is due to an interpolator. (c) Careless repetition is possible, but here the repetition could be viewed as deliberate and emphatic: Et. parries the threat to the city by picking up Creon's words (also 711 ὅπλοις, 712 ὅπλ').

The corrected couplet or single line should contain at least a subject, an object, the verb ἑλίξειν (a favourite of Eur.) and the dative ὅπλοις (without which ἑλίξειν can scarcely be understood: for the phrase cf. *Or.* 444 κύκλωι ... εἱλισσόμεθα ... ὅπλοις). The redundancy of adverbial πέριξ with ἑλίξειν is also idiomatic, and the adv. is the *mot juste* in such a context (cf. Hdt. 3.155.6, 3.158.1, 5.115.2, Thuc. 6.90.3); nor is the precision of μέλλειν unwelcome in context. Moreover, in view of the course of the following discussion of strategy Creon's speech should refer to the encirclement of the city but not to the attack upon the gates (see next note). The most straightforward excisions fail to produce a convincing line because they omit one or more of these elements, and several emendations introduce the notion of attack. Kirchhoff's μέλλειν πέριξ πύργοισι προσβαλεῖν λόχους eliminates ἑλίξειν and lacks an explicit subject. With 710 deleted (Burges, Dindorf) 711 lacks an object, which can be supplied by Dindorf's Ἀργείους πόλιν; Rauchenstein and Herwerden (1875) wrongly eliminate ὅπλοις to make room for an object. Both object and ὅπλοις are missing from the *Binneninterpolation* suggested by Verrall and Wilam. and approved by Murray. It seems best to retain the couplet and recognize, with Reiske, a corruption in πύργοισι; he proposed πυκνοῖσι.[1] Assuming a wider corruption one could also try e.g. πύργωμα Καδμείων πυλῶν.

712–47 Despite the earlier indications that an assault on the walls (180, 488–9) or a pitched battle before the walls (522, 621–2, 694) is now imminent, this dialogue is somewhat artificially structured to consider first (through 735) possible responses to a static siege, and only after 737 does the notion of repulsing a seven-pronged assault on the gates arise. By making room for a full range of strategic options, Eur. allows Et. to display thoroughly his lack of εὐβουλία in contrast to the caution of Creon: note the terms of perception, counsel, and caution in 713, 721, 731, 735–6, 745–7. The technique of exploring false trails before lighting on the appropriate scheme is typical of stichomythiae of plotting and planning (cf. Schwinge, *Stichomythie* 117ff.), and the dramatic and ethical point seems to me a sufficient justification for the dialogue's content and style. Critics who do not recognize this technique and function attribute extra-dramatic significance to the bulk of this passage: Eur. is taken to be displaying his own strategic knowledge and preferences, adopting a 'Periclean' position in the contemporary dispute (actually two decades old by the time of *Phoen.*) about the proper reaction to Peloponnesian invasions of Attica (cf. Y. Garlan, 'La poliorcétique dans les "Phéniciennes" d'Euripide', *REA* 68

---

[1] West (1990) proposes μάργοισι or μαργῶσι, too highflown for the sober Creon of this scene. D. I. Jacob proposes ὅπλοις ⟨θ'⟩, so that πύργοις is understood as a siege-device of the Argives (implausible in tragedy, esp. in this context).

(1966) 264–77). One critic (Jessen) eliminates the review of possible strategies by deleting 710–36 (reading φησιν for φασιν in 737); he believed that 710–11 must have conveyed as new the information that an attack on all the gates was imminent and that the topics covered through line 735 were thus pre-empted.

713 νεάζων implying rashness and lack of circumspection, as νέος often does: cf. esp. *Pers.* 782 νέος ἔτ' ὢν νέα φρονεῖ, Aristotle *EN* 1095a3–8. Pearson proposed a concessive reading, 'for all thy youth', with allusion to the notion that the young have keener vision; but the vision meant by Creon is intellectual, not physical.

χρή the variant χρῆν is more sharply critical ('what you should be seeing ⟨and are not⟩') and less suitable to Creon's tactful style of admonition (note the reluctant force of μῶν: Barrett on *Hipp.* 794).

714 ἐκτὸς τάφρων τῶνδ' a trench at a distance from a wall is a standard defensive feature: see 1100–3n. and cf. 1100, 1188, *Rhes.* 111, 213, 989. Aeneas' admonition to Hector in *Rhes.* 105–30 suggests the rashness of crossing one's own defensive trench before one is certain of victory.

μαχουμένους the plural follows on the collective πόλει in 712 *ad sensum* (K–G 1.53–4), and the acc., common by itself when a participle accompanies a verbal adjective in -τέος, occurs here in conjunction with the previous dative (K–G 1.448 Anm. 2, citing Pl. *Rep.* 453d ἡμῖν νευστέον καὶ πειρατέον ... ἐλπίζοντας). The reading -μένοις (O, *recc.*, Porson) is a regularization.

716 τοῖς λόγοις implying καὶ/ἀλλ' οὐ τοῖς ἔργοις; cf. *IT* 794 τὴν ἡδονὴν πρῶτ' οὐ λόγοις αἱρήσομαι, *El.* 47 τὸν λόγοισι κηδεύοντ' ἐμοί, *Held.* 5 οἶδα δ' οὐ λόγωι μαθών. For the article, which has quasi-possessive force, cf. *Or.* 287 τοῖς μέν λόγοις ηὔφρανε, τοῖς δ' ἔργοισιν οὔ. Nauck's ἐν λόγοις is not needed.

717 ὄγκον 'reputation for proud standing ⟨in warfare⟩', cf. *Tro.* 1158 ὦ μεῖζον' ὄγκον δορὸς ἔχοντες ἢ φρενῶν, 'you who are held in greater repute for warfare than for wise judgment'.

τἄργος The article, if genuine, may add some dignity to the name (512n.).

719 for omission of ὄν after ὁρῶ, 1100n. The predicative gen. has the sense 'requiring much toil', 'no easy task', rather than 'causing much hardship' (Craik).

721 πᾶν nom. agreeing with τὸ νικᾶν, 'in its entirety', 'taken as a whole', but with adverbial meaning: 'victory is entirely a matter of, depends solely on, good counsel'. For πᾶν cf. fr. 545.1 πᾶσα γὰρ δούλη πέφυκεν ἀνδρὸς ἡ σώφρων γυνή, *Phil.* 386 πόλις γάρ ἐστι πᾶσα τῶν ἡγουμένων; and for the concise and pregnant nominal predicate cf. Hdt. 1.32.4 πᾶν ἐστι ἄνθρωπος συμφορή. Failure to understand the idiom perhaps led to variant dative εὐβουλίαι, which cannot properly be instrumental or possessive. Gen. εὐβουλίας (F. G. Schoene) is good idiom, and may be right; as Diggle (1990a) 8 points out, Σ probably implies the gen. (two different explanations of πᾶν are given, and the genitive in the first one may be taken from the text and not be a further element of paraphrase).

723 κίνδυνον ... μολεῖν Wecklein's note suggests that he took κίνδυνον to be subject of μολεῖν, but translators have followed Arsenius' paraphrase πρὶν ἐλθεῖν εἰς κίνδυνον, rightly (cf. 1080n.).

724–31 whereas a sally from the gates (now rejected) could apply both to a long-term siege of the city and to an impending attack, the suggestions of attack by night or during a meal presuppose a long-term siege (712– 47n.). Both types of attack have some parallel in the recent events of the Athenian campaign in Sicily, presumably well known to the audience: cf. Thuc. 7.44 for νυκτομαχία and the trouble caused by confusion and difficult terrain, Thuc. 7.40 for a naval attack that caught the Athenians by surprise as they were tending to their meal.

724 for the elliptical question, 561–5n., 1684n.

725–7 Burges and Wecklein interchange 725 and 727, but this sequence alters for the worse Creon's tactful mode of response. In the transmitted order Creon merely intimates the danger of an attack by night, and only after Et. tries to minimize the risk does he make a more sweeping condemnation. In Burges' order Creon is first blunter than usual and then too mild in response to Et.'s espousal of τολμή, so that it is hard to see why Et. moves on to a new tactic in 728. Wecklein addresses only the last objection by placing 730–1 after 727–6–5 (see below).

725 εἴπερ σφαλείς γε εἴπερ by itself implies consent to the question, but γε here goes closely with σφαλείς rather than simply strengthening εἴπερ: cf. *Hipp.* 501 εἴπερ ἐκσώσει γέ σε.

727 ἐνδυστυχῆσαι δεινόν for this type of epexegetic inf. see Barrett on *Hipp.* 1096 ἐγκαθηβᾶν.

728 -βάλω the aor. is correct (against Π¹²B, *recc.*), as in 724 (guaranteed by metre) and 732.

730–1 whether placed after 729 or after 725 (Wecklein: 725–7n.), this line contains a concession by Et.: 'if we don't actually defeat them, it would be difficult to make a smooth flight back across the deep channel of Dirce' (for the strategic risk cf. *Rhes.* 110–18). For γέ τοι of partial agreement or partial explanation see Denniston, *GP*² 550–1; *Cycl.* 224 is the only other Eur. example. With Wecklein's transposition the topic of nocturnal assault is abandoned only at 731 and then 728–9 alone deal with the next proposal. But 729 almost needs the further concession and conclusive rejection in 730–1, and this transposition depends on the earlier one, rejected above.

Helmbold suggested deletion of 728–9, leaving the equally unrealistic proposal of nocturnal attack (724–31n.). Dihle, 75, 77, uses this reference to Dirce to claim that Eur. thought only of an attack from the west side of the citadel and thus to allege that the teichoskopia (in which the army seems to be on both sides of the city) and 1100–3 (with the approach of the Argives from the east) cannot be Euripidean. But 710–11 (however they are restored) refer to encirclement of the city; the artificial presuppositions of this dialogue on strategy do not sanction wider inferences about topography; and the channel of Dirce may be cited simply as a prime example of a danger.

733 πέφαρκται for restoration of -φαρκτ- for -φρακτ- see Barrett on *Hipp.* 657.

734 -οισι δῶ not -οις δώσω: τί δράσω; is normally to be taken as deliberative subj, not fut. ind., and if a suggested action is expressed in a following question, this is normally aor. subj. as well: in drama eight certain aorists, four ambiguous forms, one pres. subj. vs. one future (*Or.* 309). See also Rijksbaron (1991) 175–90.

736 'Then what thought-out plan proves to be more wise ⟨than what I have so far considered⟩?', not 'What prudence is more sensible than forethought?' (Craik). For πρόνοια in the sense 'a plan' cf. *Choe.* 605–6 μήσατο πυρδαῆ ... πρόνοιαν, Thuc. 8.95.4 ἀπὸ προνοίας τῶν Ἐρετριῶν, and perhaps *Or.* 1179; γίγνεται is a dynamic present (='will be').

737 αὐτοῖς within its own line can be heard as a vague dat. of interest/advantage, and with προστετάχθαι in 738 can be felt as dat. of agent.

738 τὸ γὰρ σθένος βραχύ a sly allusion to the improbability of the traditional myth (or specifically of *Septem*), with its emphasis on the champions and their individual efforts to storm the gates. The critique is playful and does not prevent Eur. himself from later making the defeat of a champion tantamount to victory at a gate (1153–63, 1170–86).

739 †λόχων ἀνάσσειν† προσκεῖσθαι ('press', 'attack', as in *IT* 316, 319, 325, Hdt., Thuc.) is not convincing as epexegetic inf. with ἀνάσσειν, and Σ's λείπει ὁ καί is a response to obscurity and corruption, not attestation of another reading. As an answer to 738 this line should contain some allusion to whole companies of attackers, and the intrusion from 742 could have been caused by homoeoarcton: hence Matthiae's λόχων ἄνακτας, Wecklein's λοχαγετοῦντας (an unattested word). But the similarity of 737 and 741 may have created enough confusion without homoeoarcton in 739 and 742, in which case restorations without λοχ- may be considered (e.g. πολλῶν μετ' ἄλλων).

741 αὐτοῖς 'to face them', a dat. of disadvantage, creating a deliberate extended echo of 737, with change of reference in ἔπτ' ἄνδρας and αὐτοῖς. Grotius' αὐτὸς καὶ σύ appears to be unidiomatic: if emphatic αὐτὸς σύ or σὺ δ᾽ αὐτός is to be further intensified, it should be σὺ . . . καὐτός, like ἐγὼ δὲ καὐτός *Med.* 1142, *Phil.* 319, σοι καὐτῶι *Phil.* 620–1 (also ἐγώ τι καὐτός *IA* 1349 [Musgrave: τιν᾽ αὐτός Blomfield]).

742–3 deleted by Czwalina and Jessen on the grounds that 742 is inept (but Eur. is here still alluding to and rejecting for his own version the tradition of duels between Theban and Argive champions) and that 746 is too repetitive of 743 (but Et. takes the cue of 746 προκρίνας from 743, and audacity vs. good judgment is a distinction that may supervene upon might in defensive battle).

742 μονοστόλου δορός 'an armament of a single spear'; the adj. is used as a lyric variant of μόνος in *Alc.* 407 μονόστολος τε ματρός and then reappears in the sense 'travelling alone' only in Lycophr. *Alex.* 690 (Odysseus) and Dion. Hal. *Ant.Rom.* 1.41.2 (Heracles).

744 ἀμύνειν τειχέων προσαμβάσεις 'to ward off scalings of the wall', with the noun used here only in its etymologically proper sense as *nomen actionis* (489n.); not 'to defend the places where the wall may be approached' (cf. LSJ, assuming an illicit construction of ἀμύνειν).

745 ξυστρατήγους hapax in tragedy, a technical military term for members of a board of generals. The acc. looks back for its syntax to 741 ἄνδρας . . . ἑλοῦ via the implied subject of 744 ἀμύνειν. Σ's view that Creon was advising appointment of seven colleagues for the seven Theban gate-commanders seduced translators and commentators until Pearson explained correctly; the sense is of course 'generals along with yourself', and εἷς ἀνήρ refers tactfully to Eteocles. The conclusion of the discussion is marked by repetition of key concepts: οὐ πάνθ᾽ ὁρᾶι ~ οὐχ ὁρᾶις 713, εὐβουλία 746 ~ εὐβουλίαι 721.

⟨γ᾽⟩ (Lenting) is welcome to emphasize the crucial added point.

δ᾽ equivalent to γάρ (198n.).

746 θάρσει . . . ἢ φρενῶν εὐβουλίαι a traditional dichotomy in the assessment of what is needed for military leadership, often exemplified in pairs of leaders in poetry and history, e.g., Hector and Polydamas in *Il.* 18, Xerxes and Darius in *Pers.*, Adrastus and Theseus in *Su.*, Hector and Aeneas in *Rhes.*, Alcibiades and Nicias in Thuc. 6, Minucius Rufus and Fabius Cunctator in Livy 22, etc. The person of rash boldness is often, but not always, also portrayed as physically strong, so that the topos of rashness/boldness vs. good sense/caution sometimes intersects with that of brawn vs. brains. The latter is more prominent in the topos of Sall. *Cat.* 1.5–7 cited by Wecklein: diu magnum inter mortales certamen fuit, vine corporis an virtute animi res militaris magis procederet. nam et prius quam incipias consulto, et ubi consulueris mature facto opus est. ita utrumque per se indigens alterum alterius auxilio eget.

358

747 'By both tests; for either one, if separated ⟨from the other⟩, is worthless.' The transmitted text seems to me defensible. Singular acc. adv. ἀμφότερον is used as in Homer and Pindar (but not elsewhere in tragedy; acc. pl. adv. only in *Pers.* 720), though the alternatives precede instead of following as in the common schema. ἀπολειφθέν is used absolutely (sc. 'from the other of the two') as in *Or.* 80 (sc. τῆς ἀδελφῆς, from 78) and Pl. *Phdr.* 240c7 (sc. τοῦ νεωτέρου, from c6). The indefinite sense of θάτερον, 'whichever of the two you like', is legitimate (as *Prom.* 778, τὸν ἕτερον in 952 below, etc.); or the sense may be 'only one', 'just one of the two' as in *Wasps* 497 παραβλέψασα ... θατέρωι, *Dysc.* 796 ἱκανὸν δ' ἐστὶν ἡμῖν θάτερον. Both the sense of οὐδέν and the concise syntax are exactly paralleled in 442 πένης γὰρ οὐδὲν εὐγενὴς ἀνήρ. Nonetheless, the reading of Wecklein is neat: ἀμφότερ'· ἓν [Burges] ἀπολειφθὲν γὰρ οὐδὲν θατέρου [Reiske], and the postponement of γάρ (Denniston, *GP*² 96) could easily have caused the corruption. Diggle, *CR* 40 (1990) 10, regards Sallust *Cat.* 1.5-7 (cited above) as a reminiscence and views *alterum alterius auxilio eget* as supporting ἓν ... θατέρου, but both the variation in the topos and the rhetorical amplification make uncertain the inference that Sall. read θατέρου here. For disyllabic forms of οὐδείς preceding a final cretic, see West, *Greek Metre* 85.

748 ἔσται τάδ' a phrase expressing agreement to a request, common in Euripides (also *Phil.* 893; plain ἔσται in *Choe.* 514); cf. Fraenkel, *Beobacht. zu Arist.* 79-80.

ἐλθών for asyndeton (wrongly removed in OV, *recc.*) with a fuller statement of intention after ἔσται τάδε, cf. *Tro.* 87-8 (ταράξω), *Or.* 1041 (οὐ λελείψομαι), *IA* 1033 (με ... χρεών); also *Her.* 332 (Lycus issues requested command). The synonymous version with μολών is likely to be secondary (it has to be if στόμα is correctly restored): if ἐλθών were omitted, accidentally or deliberately (to remove the oddity of 'going' to the city when in it, commented on in Σ), a restoration or correction at the end of the line was likely to follow; no similar motivation for inserting ἐλθών in mid-line is available.

στόμα transmitted πόλιν cannot stand, since bare πόλις cannot mean 'lower city' in contrast to acropolis (and the mythical topography in any case assumes identity of city-walls and acropolis-walls); Craik's interpretation of ἑπτάπυργον ἐς πόλιν as 'to the seven towers of the city' lacks parallels. Jackson's στόμα (*Marg. Scaen.* 117-18) is palaeographically easy and seems to me stylistically apt: cf. *Ant.* 119 ἑπτάπυλον στόμα, 287 above ἑπτάστομον πύργωμα (στόμα in 1166 is different). Willink (1990) 198 n. 32 finds στόμα too 'fancy' and argues for Musgrave's κύκλον (cf. perhaps *Ba.* 653 κλήιειν ... πάντα πύργον ἐν κύκλωι; *Ant.* 118, which he cites, is hardly relevant).¹ Geel's πόλον, 'circuit', assumes a sense unattested in the fifth century and scarcely found thereafter ([Pl.] *Epin.* 986c4).²

751-6 all of the lines between Et.'s consent to Creon's advice and his provisions for the kin over whom he is κύριος (757ff.) have been doubted in various proposals of deletion. Apart from individual points of style or usage, critics have objected to (1) the inconsistency of objecting to διατριβή and then continuing on other topics for 20-30 lines; (2) the long delay between the formula ἀλλ' εἶμι and Et.'s actual exit; (3) the verbatim iteration of 756 in 1376. These issues are considered in the following notes.

751-2 there is certainly an intertextual allusion to *Septem* here, but the spirit of the allusion has long been disputed. One school sees the couplet as a polite, even complimentary, acknowledgment of Aeschylus within Eur.'s deliberately different treatment: so Didymus (cited in Σ: πεφύλακται τὰς ὀνομασίας αὐτῶν εἰπεῖν ... διὰ τὸ ὑπὸ Αἰσχύλου εἰρῆσθαι ἐν τοῖς Ἑπτὰ ἐπὶ Θήβας), Grotius, Geel, *et al.* Another sees here a sarcastic rejection of Aeschylus' technique as unrealistic: so Brumoy, Valckenaer, Hermann, *et al.* These alternatives are overdrawn. Eur. likes to let slip every now and then self-conscious references to the actualities and conventions of tragic writing and performance, but such playful acknowledgment does not mean that he himself rejects or does without those artificialities and instead endorses a wholly naturalistic style.³ Thus, in *El.* there is mockery of the recognition-scene of *Choe.*, but simultaneously the mocker, Electra, is shown to be guilty of self-delusion, and later Eur. employs an equally hoary device, the scar, for recognition. Here the criticism of A. is captious, at best, since A. himself marks the suspension of action necessary for the pairs of speeches at the outset of the sequence (*Se.* 378-9 πόρον δ' Ἰσμηνὸν οὐκ ἐᾶι περᾶν / ὁ μάντις· οὐ γὰρ σφάγια γίγνεται καλά), and the symbolic import of the scene obviously outweighs any interest in chronological realism (as Eur. himself would surely have conceded if pressed); nor is Eur. a naturalist who refrains from exploiting the suspension of time and action that tragic speech may entail (e.g., Medea takes time to hear a long messenger-speech when an attack on her is felt to be imminent; cf. the second messenger-speech in *IT* and that in *Ion*). Apart from its intertextual import, the couplet has local meaning: it shows Et.'s impatience with further details of military planning, continuing the impression created

---

¹ Taplin, 143 n. 2, for a similar reason, suggested ὁδόν (not listed in Teubner edn).

² For a careful survey see E. Maass, *Aratea* [Phil. Untersuchungen, 12 (Berlin 1892)] 123-38.

³ Cf. R. Scodel, 'Euripides and *Apatē*', in *Cabinet of the Muses*, 75-87.

earlier (446–8n., 588–637n., 709n.), and it prepares the way for Et.'s own topics (692–3 οἰκεῖα καὶ κοινὰ χθονός . . . βουλεύματα).

No adequate argument has been offered for viewing 751–2 as interpolated; rather, they have been attacked only because of 753. A. Trendelenburg (*Grammaticorum graecorum de arte tragica iudiciorum reliquiae* (Bonn 1867) 54 n. 56) had specific objections to 753 and thought the speech would be more forceful without 751–3; he went so far as to suggest that the couplet was based on Didymus' explanation of the absence of the names of the Theban champions, while Zipperer speculated about an earlier, histrionic addition. Friedrich again argued specifically against 753 and the join between 753 and 754. The intertextual allusion is characteristically Euripidean (I do not believe that the allusions to *Choe.* in *El.* can be ascribed to an interpolator).

751 διατριβὴ πολλὴ λέγειν seems excellent idiom: cf. *Ant.* 780 πόνος περισσός . . . σέβειν, *Ba.* 1279 βραχὺς ὁ μόχθος εἰσιδεῖν. M here conveys a confusion, not the truth, in διατριβὴν πολλὴν ἔχει (cf. Xen. *Oec.* 4.8.13 ὥστε διατριβὴν παρέχειν): as Fraenkel (*Ag.* comm. III.824 n. 2) points out, it would be very harsh for subject ὄνομα to be treated virtually as *nomen actionis* (cf. *Prom.* 637–9 τἀποκλαῦσαι . . . ἀξίαν τριβὴν ἔχει). διατριβή is hapax in Eur. (and appears but once, meaning 'pastime', in Soph. fr. 479.2); the pejorative sense has contemporary parallels in Thuc.

753 ἀλλ' εἶμ' in tragedy this phrase has two functions, as an announcement of the intention to exit and as a cut-off formula that dismisses words in favour of action (sometimes expressing assent to a suggestion) or one topic in favour of another. In most examples departure follows within 1–6 lines, which may contain some final gnome or explanation or instruction: *Pers.* 849 (two lines follow), *Choe.* 781 (one line: prayer γένοιτο κτλ.), *Aj.* 810 (two lines: exhortation to chorus), *Trach.* 86 (five lines: explanation and reply with gnome), *OC* 503 (six lines: question to chorus and their answer, instruction to Antigone), *Alc.* 209 (three lines: explanation), *Andr.* 89 (one line: gnome), *El.* 1132 (six lines: intended subsequent action, instruction to attendants), *Tro.* 1153 (two lines: purpose clause), *IT* 636 (six lines: instruction to attendants, self-directed conclusive comment), *Ba.* 857 (four lines: prediction), *Phaethon* 266 (three lines: explanation and prayer); cf. also 1009 below, where the genuineness of some of the following lines is in question. Thus Fraenkel is able to lay emphasis on the 'grammatical' oddity of Eteocles' departing so long after ἀλλ' εἶμι here. But there are some cases where the departure is not so rapid. *Trach.* 389 and *Hcld.* 678 are not relevant because the intended departure is forestalled by a sudden development (Lichas emerges before Deianira can go in; Iolaus announces his intention to accompany the herald, provoking further discussion). At *Ag.* 1313 the formula renews the intention to depart (cf. 1289), dismissing

the loathsome terrors of the house which turned back Cassandra's initial approach (1306); the playwright then (despite conclusive-sounding
ἀρκείτω βίος in 1314) dwells on the pathos of a conscious exit to cruel
slaughter in fifteen further lines. Perhaps most nearly relevant is *Aj.* 654,
where ἀλλ' εἶμι follows on the scene-opening proem about softening and
pity, dismissing that topic. There an audience clearly expects more to be
said before departure, and the addition of a purpose clause and further
elaboration of Ajax's intention (μολών τε ... κρύψω) provide a gliding
transition to 'gifts of enemies', change, friendship, etc. After this exposition
instructions to Tecmessa and the chorus follow (684–9) and then a renewed
announcement (690 ἐγὼ γὰρ εἶμ' ἐκεῖσ' ὅποι πορευτέον) two lines before
exit. Our passage can be read as in part similar. ἀλλ' εἶμι strongly dismisses
ὄνομα λέγειν in favour of action, previously described fully in 748–50. The
prayer that follows in 754–5 is not unlike short appendages in other
examples (cf. esp. *Choe.* 782), and by introducing the notion of face-to-face
confrontation with Pol. (recalling 621–2) provides a gliding transition to
Et.'s 'testament' (758 ἐάν τι τῆς τύχης ἐγὼ σφαλῶ). After the intervening
topics, the announcement of departure is resumed in 781–2. If 753 is
genuine, then Eur. has manipulated the 'rule' on the use of ἀλλ' εἶμι in
order to present more strikingly Et.'s eagerness to get on with the military
action off-stage and to highlight a dissonance between such vehemence
and the run-on, matter-of-fact style of the 'testament', which thus gives the
impression of an afterthought (766–73n., 774–7n.). Yet there remains a
residual doubt, since ἀλλ' εἶμι in this passage is absolute (unlike *Aj.* 654–5
ἀλλ' εἶμι πρός τε λουτρὰ καὶ παρακτίους λειμῶνας), leaving the supplement 'to choose them there' to be understood from the preceding, and since
it would also have been easy enough for Eur. to write an explicit transition
to the 'testament', such as 'but before I go, I must say what I intended
before'.

Objections to 753 apart from the above are not, to my mind, cogent.
Paley thought καταργεῖν χέρα 'a strange phrase', translating tendentiously
'to be idle in action'. The verb is hapax in classical Greek, but quite
common as a transitive verb ('put a stop to', 'bring to nought', 'defeat',
etc.) in Septuagint, NT, and Church Fathers; but here it may well be not
transitive 'leave idle', but intransitive (with χέρα as acc. of specification),
an intensified form of intrans. ἀργέω (only twice in Eur., once in Soph. fr.
842; cf. 625).[1] In either case, the phrase conveys Et.'s eagerness to have

---

[1] καταργεῖν is also intransitive in the only other use by a pagan author:
Suda κ 1055 κατηργηκέναι· ἀνενέργητον εἶναι· τὸν δὲ καθήμενον περὶ
τὰ Τύανα κατηργηκέναι καὶ καταπροΐεσθαι τοὺς καιρούς (the quota-

a personal role in the fighting, not merely name the defenders (there may be a reminiscence of 625 and its immediate context).

754-[6] If Et. is assumed to be a prudent and thoroughly logical general, it would be out of place for him to look forward at this point to a face-to-face fight with Pol., since he has just agreed to defend the attack on the seven gates from inside and to appoint seven others to supervise. But Et. has been shown to be callow and reckless, is known to be under a curse, and has previously expressed this desire (622), so it is not implausible that the desire press forth here too (esp. after 753 ὅπως ἂν μὴ καταργῶμεν χέρα). Paley, in suspecting 753-6, thought the wish 'out of place' and suggested that both the idea and the word ξυσταθέντα were borrowed from *Se.* 672-3 εἶμι καὶ ξυστήσομαι / αὐτός. But in intrans./passive forms συνίστημι is a common term for military confrontation (LSJ в.ιι.1-2); the redundancy noted by Fraenkel is not suspicious, but typical of tragic fullness; and Mueller-Goldingen, 125, notes that a deliberate reminiscence of *Se.* serves to mark the difference of Eur.'s treatment. Fraenkel also objects to the predicative use of ἀντήρη (attributive in four or five exx. in Soph. and Eur.), but this is a perfectly normal construction with λαμβάνειν: *Andr.* 628 χειρίαν λαβών, *IT* 350 δύσνουν ... λήψεσθ', *Hel.* 1411 πλήρη λάβω, *Her.* 223 κακίστην λαμβάνων.

ἑλεῖν δορί 'kill', not simply 'capture' (cf. *Med.* 385 φαρμάκοις ἑλεῖν, *Tro.* 376, *Her.* 994, 1380, *Rhes.* 257); to be preferred to variants both in idiom and by *utrum in alterum*. Both ἐλθεῖν δορί (M^{γρ}BO*recc.*) and ἔχειν δόρυ (B^{γρ}) seem to be designed to remove the redundancy with following κτανεῖν θ'. The latter is obviously wrong, and δορί would be super-fluous with διὰ μάχης ἐλθεῖν (Pearson implausibly assumes a quasi-lyric hyperbaton ξυσταθέντα ... δορί).

756 = 1376. It is improbable that both are genuine (96n.), and if one is genuine, 1376 is more organic in its context than 756; but 1376 is itself suspect (see *ad loc.*). Here κτανεῖν is intolerably redundant and acceptable only with inferior ἐλθεῖν in 755. The interpolation may have arisen from supplementation of a simple gloss κτανεῖν (cf. gloss/variant at *Med.* 385) to create a full trimeter (the ὅς-clause is reminiscent of 153). No force should be granted to Valck.'s additional argument against this line, that Et. should have given an 'objective' reason, such as 'who is attacking his own city'.

753-5 To sum up: these lines cannot be acquitted of all suspicion, yet

---

tion was ascribed by Valesius to Polybius, fr. 176 Büttner-Wobst). LSJ ignores the gloss and unjustifiably treats καιρούς as object of transitive καταργεῖν.

the case against them is not conclusive. I tentatively retain them, principally because the text without them still leaves an odd transition from 752 to 757, whereas the 'testament' follows better after an allusion to Et.'s own dangerous activity; furthermore, the characterizing force of 754–5, in contradistinction to the Et. of *Septem*, seems to me just as important as the intertextual allusion to plot-mechanics in 751–2. Critics who doubt the unusual dramatic 'grammar' of ἀλλ' εἶμι may consider removing 753 alone; but the wish follows more smoothly on 753 than on ἐλθὼν ... τάξω (with 751–2 treated as parenthetic). If deletion is preferred, 753–5 should go as a unit, and they might be viewed as an alternative scene-ending for a performance omitting 757–83 (or 757–77). Walter also would keep the triplet 753–5 together by transposing it to precede 779 (with 774–7 deleted), so that ἀλλ' εἶμι is close to Et.'s exit (but in this arrangement 780–1 is redundant with 753 ὅπως ἂν κτλ.).

A different solution is proposed by Willink (1990) 186–9: he takes very seriously Et.'s prayer to Εὐλάβεια (782–3n.) and postulates that from the end of the previous episode until his death Et. concentrates his attention solely on defending the city, while the notion of a duel with his brother is both suppressed by Eur. and disregarded by Et. until the challenge to the duel in 1219ff. Thus he regards the prayer of 754–5 as out of place here and the testamentary dispositions as likewise unmotivated by Et.'s present attitude (if he is not going to fight a duel, there is no need to make such plans). His solution is to have 766–73 follow directly on 753 and then to close the scene with 779–80 + 782–3, removing the testament entirely as well as the burial-decree (774–7). I doubt this solution: (1) I am convinced that Eur. is playing with the expectation of the duel throughout these scenes, retarding its fulfilment but teasing his audience all the while; (2) Et.'s attitude should not be interpreted in such a simple and favourable light (see esp. 780–1n., 782–3n.; also 1217–63n.(penultimate paragraph)); (3) the join of 766 to 753 is clumsy (so is the transmitted text, but at least there the prayer to face his brother provides a transition of sorts to the change of topic); (4) it is unconvincing to doubt 754–5 for the shocking nature of the prayer, since such unconventional thinking is quite in tune with Et.'s previous words and behaviour and the undercutting purpose of the whole scene (as for Creon's failure to comment, cf. 782–3n.). See also next note.

757–65 Oed. has not been κύριος of the household since the discovery of incest and the incapacitation caused by self-blinding. The sons became κύριοι on coming of age (63), and Et. is solely κύριος since the departure of Pol. Et. here provisionally passes responsibility for his household to Creon, who, as twice in the past, would take over as the senior male next-of-kin. Mention of the betrothal provides an allusion to Soph. *Ant.*

(where the betrothal is understood to predate the Argive attack) and within *Phoen.* prepares for the exclusion of Haemon in 944-6 and the issue of the marriage in the exodos. It seems unlikely to me that Eur. would have laid emphasis on the betrothal here solely for the sake of 944-6.[1] Dos Santos Alves, objecting to the delay caused by the 'testament' after the expression of haste in 751-2 and to the pessimistic attitude of Et. in making such provisions at all, proposes the deletion of 757-65 as a whole (as well as of 692, which anticipates them). He cites no convincing internal faults apart from those alleged against 763-5, discussed below. Willink (see previous note) has made a similar proposal, arguing principally in terms of character and limitation of theme.

757-9 γάμους ... σοὶ χρὴ μέλεσθαι middle μέλομαι is a stylistic variation on the active 'be a concern' (LSJ s.v. μέλω A.III.1; cf. 1303 below ἰαχὰν ... μελομέναν νεκροῖς); Valck.'s γάμου (Paley γάμων) is unnecessary.

758 ἐάν τι τῆς τύχης ἐγὼ σφαλῶ mildly euphemistic, 'if I at all fail of attaining the success I hope for'; for the 'sinister euphemistic' use of τι see Diggle on *Phaethon* 93.

759 ἐχέγγυον the adjective has a legal flavour but is in fact probably poetic (five times in tragedy, in classical prose only Thuc. 3.46.1). ἐχέγγυον ποιῶ virtually = 'reconfirm'.

761 τί δεῖ μακρηγορεῖν; another sign of Et.'s brusqueness, underlining his reluctance to express conventional affection or duty (though 762 is in fact dutiful). Cf. Thuc. 1.68.3 νῦν δὲ τί δεῖ μακρηγορεῖν; (Corinthian dismissing need to elaborate on Athenian wrongdoing), 4.59.2 τί ἄν τις ... μακρηγοροίη; (Hermocrates to assembled Greeks of Sicily).

763-5 Paley found the lines on Oed. superfluous, and Fraenkel argued for excision;[2] Friedrich had attacked 764 alone as a false expansion of 763. The specific objections to οὐκ ἄγαν, ἐς αὐτόν, and the anticipation of mutual fratricide are answered below. In general, reference to the father fits in perfectly in the sequence (757-65n.), and the harsh light thrown on Et. by the bitterness of 763-4 is consonant with Eur.'s characterization: after 762 the implication is 'Let Oed. shift for himself; he is to blame for his troubles and mine.' It is to be noted how Fraenkel's deletions in this speech (here, 753-5, 774-7) all tend to improve the image of Et. He would assign the crassness and cynicism to a post-classical *Bearbeiter* and thus tame the

---

[1] 944-6 have now been deleted by Willink, unjustifiably, I believe (see *ad loc.*).

[2] The three lines were already ascribed to actors, without further argument, by Helmbold, 131.

tone of the text with a classicizing decorum. The complexity, as I would prefer to call it, is likely to be Euripidean.

763 ἐς αὐτὸν ἀμαθίαν ὀφλισκάνει 'incurs the charge of senseless behaviour toward himself', ἐς αὐτόν being attached to the noun, like *Andr.* 905 [τίς] συμφορὰ πλὴν ἐς λέχος, *Ba.* 9 μητέρ' εἰς ἐμὴν ὕβριν (cf. 375), 779 ψόγος ἐς Ἕλληνας, *Tro.* 666 τὸ δυσμενὲς γυναικὸς εἰς ἀνδρὸς λέχος. This expresses Et.'s assessment of Oed.'s action, but the omission of the specification of the judge implies tendentiously that this view is widely shared. This sense of the verb is common in tragedy (LSJ II.2); cf. esp. with obj. ἀμαθίαν *Hec.* 327, μωρίαν *Alc.* 1093, *IT* 488, fr. 150.7 Austin, *Ant.* 470, σκαιότητα *Ant.* 1028. Fraenkel insisted on taking ἐς αὐτόν with ὀφλισκάνει ('in his own eyes', 'by his own judgment': a clearly inferior sense) and then damns the line as the unidiomatic Greek of a *Bearbeiter*: the person judging, if expressed, is plain dative or παρά + dat. or πρός (ἀπό) + gen., except for πρὸς ὑμᾶς found in *Hippias Maior* 282a1 only.

764 ὄψιν τυφλώσας Friedrich thought Oed.'s ἀμαθία consisted in the curse and regarded 764 as the improper insertion of mythological detail.[1] But Oed.'s blindness was a permanent reminder of his shameful deeds, one that mortified his sons (63–5, cf. 870–4); so this expression of resentment is not out of place.

οὐκ ἄγαν a bitter meiosis, implying 'not at all', just as in *Med.* 583 ἔστι δ' οὐκ ἄγαν σοφός, *Eum.* 339–40 θανὼν δ' οὐκ ἄγαν ἐλεύθερος, and perhaps A. *Su.* 409 δεδορκὸς ὄμμα μηδ' ἄγαν ὠινωμένον (but not, e.g., *Med.* 305, *Knights* 598). The more colloquial οὐ πάνυ (τι) is used similarly (*OC* 144 and comedy). Friedrich's objection to the phrase as too weak cannot be sustained.

ἐπήινεσα instantaneous aorist (433n., 1561n.), as in *Alc.* 1095, *Med.* 707, *Tro.* 53, 718, *Or.* 1672.

765 some critics have ascribed any lines anticipating the mutual fratricide to interpolation (774–7n., 880n., 1263n., 1269n.) on the ground that they destroy suspense. But suspense in a Greek tragedy on a familiar theme involves how and when the usual result will come about, not whether it will happen at all. The theme of curse and fratricide is well established by 67–70, 333–4, 351, 623–4, 670–5. The allusion here adds nothing to Fraenkel's case against 763–5.

766–73 with this passage Et. moves from οἰκεῖα to κοινὰ χθονός βουλεύματα (692n.), and Eur. prepares for the next episode, creating a further retardation of the battle and the duel of the brothers and putting

---

[1] The omission of 764 by the careless scribe of Ad is unlikely to be other than accidental.

a key element of the city's salvation out of Et.'s knowledge and responsibility (again a marked deviation from *Septem*).

766 based on the transposition in MR+ and the Aldine, Scaliger suggested ἐν δ' ἀργὸν ἡμῖν ἐστιν, but the majority reading is superior, with emphatic ἀργόν at the end of its colon.

769 αὐτεπώνυμον hapax in extant literature; αὐτ- is intensifying, as in tragic αὐτάδελφος etc. (136n.) and comic αὐτοδάξ, αὐτέκμαγμα. For naming after the grandfather, see 57–8n. The clarity and emphasis of this naming line have two functions: to introduce a new figure into the family of Creon (see Introd. IV for argument that Menoeceus is an innovation; for the technique cf. *Her.* 31–2 on invented Lycus); to underscore the kinship-theme, which will be exploited later (965n., 1317–21n., 1665n.). The line is wrongly deleted by Zipperer for being over-precise.

770 λαβόντα πέμψω δεῦρο the command to Menoeceus could be λαβὼν Τειρεσίαν ἄπελθε πρὸς τὸν πατέρα, and the same aorist participle can be used with πέμψω, 'after he has fetched Tiresias', 'with Tir.'. There is no need for a future part. (Markland, Valck. ἄξοντα, Burton καλοῦντα), despite the superficially similar *Hcld.* 136–7 πέμπει ... δεῦρό μ' ... ἄξοντα τούσδε. The interlaced word-order (πέμψω δεῦρο between λαβόντα and Τειρεσίαν) is unusual, but not obscure, since πέμψω finally provides a construction for the preceding acc. phrase and λαβόντα creates an expectation of an object that Τειρεσίαν fulfills.[1] Because of the word-order, Willink proposes ἄγειν for Κρέον so that Τειρεσίαν will be object of λαβόντα and ἄγειν.

771 ἡδύς 'in an agreeable mood' (*libens* Wecklein), like *Hipp.* 289 ἡδίων γενοῦ; thus without objection or refusal, such as Tir. might offer if called to advise Et. himself (cf. 865–7). σοί is thus to be taken with εἰς λόγους ἀφίξεται, not with ἡδύς. See Stinton, 'Notes 1' 131–2, on possible meanings of ἡδύς in general and on the superiority of 'sweet-tempered', 'agreeable' here vs. 'well-disposed', espoused by Lloyd-Jones, *YCS* 22 (1972) 263–4. Pearson, who rightly notes 'adverbial ("gladly")', suggests that the sense 'welcome to you' is ambiguously latent here and that there is dramatic irony; but if Menoeceus' sacrifice is an innovation, the audience could not detect such an irony at this moment.

772 Prophets could be attacked (1) as bearers of bad news (*Il.* 1.105ff.); (2) on the ground that particular prophets lacked a genuine access to the supernatural and to truth (*OT* 390ff., 489ff., *Ant.* 1033ff.); (3) on the

---

[1] Cf. perhaps Stinton, *PCPS* 21 (1975) 84–5, noting that nom. part. λαβών = 'with' is more easily used in interlaced order than other participles.

367

ground that the gods (if there are gods) do not give signs to men (*Hel.* 744ff.; cf. the Epicurean position in later disputes with the Stoics over divination).[1] After Et.'s sophistically amoral arguments in the agon and given the abstractness of τέχνη μαντική, an audience might here think that Et. had used argument (3), despite the inconsistency of his now authorizing a consultation on behalf of the city. It later is made clear (878–9) that the brothers quarrelled with Tir. because they disliked his unwelcome advice and warnings (1).

773 πρὸς αὐτόν the prep. expresses 'not the person against whom the charge is laid, but the audience (who may be more or less interested) before whom it is brought' (Gow on Theocr. 30.24).

ὥστε μοι Willink (1990) 199 n. 37 prefers ὥστ' ἐμοί, to emphasize mutual reproach; this may be right, but the contrast is primarily between Creon and Et. (σοὶ μὲν ... ἐγὼ δέ), and the weaker pronoun may be correct (cf. perhaps *Hipp.* 49–50 παρασχεῖν τοὺς ἐμοὺς ἐχθροὺς ἐμοὶ / δίκην τοσαύτην ὥστε μοι καλῶς ἔχειν).

μομφὰς ἔχειν phrases like μομφήν/μέμψιν/αἰτίαν ἔχειν may be either 'active' or 'passive' in sense depending on the context: 'have cause to reproach/blame' here and in *Prom.* 445, *Aj.* 180, *Or.* 1069, *Peace* 664 (μέμψιν *Phil.* 1309, αἰτίαν *IT* 1036, *Hel.* 469); but 'to be reproached/blamed' in *Hcld.* 974 (μέμψιν) and (αἰτίαν) *Eum.* 99, *Ant.* 1312, E. *El.* 213, *Wasps* 506, *Samia* 51, etc. In Pindar *I.* 4.37 commentators are split between active and passive interpretations. In tragedy the subject of a natural result clause is often understood from the context, even when it is not the same as the subject of the main clause (e.g., *Hipp.* 50, *Andr.* 153, *Hec.* 248, *Her.* 234–5); there is no need for ἔχει (West, *BICS* 28 (1981) 67).

774-7 Critics who remove the burial-motif from the exodos also remove these four lines as an insertion preparing for the later addition.[2] Since the burial-motif is firmly entrenched in 1447–50,[3] I believe the motif was also present in Eur.'s exodos (see 1582–709n.), and I do not ascribe weight to the external argument regarding 774–7. On the other hand, defenders of 774–7 cite 1646 Ἐτεοκλέους βουλεύματ', οὐχ ἡμῶν, τάδε

---

[1] See in general L. Radermacher, 'Euripides und die Mantik', *RhM* 53 (1898) 497–510.

[2] For this methodologically dubious procedure, cf. Verrall's suspicion of the teichoskopia, a consequence of his decision to remove Antigone from the exodos and thus from all earlier parts as well; or G. A. Seeck, *Hermes* 97 (1969) 9–22, who deletes *Or.* 1618–20 and then proceeds to remove all earlier mentions of fire.

[3] See *ad loc.* for Hose's recent proposal to delete 1447–50 for consistency with the hypothesis that the burial-motif had no place in Eur.'s play.

as external support, though Mueller-Goldingen (e.g.) accepts 1646 and its surrounding as authentic while denying a reference back to 774-7 (1646n.). In view of the controversy, this external index must likewise be left to one side. The internal objections (as made principally by Friedrich and Fraenkel) are: (1) 766 ἓν δ᾽ ἐστὶν ἡμῖν ἀργόν sounds to some like the introduction to the last thing Et. means to say before departure; Fraenkel even translates 'Eins ist noch unerledigt (ungesagt)' and compares *Hipp.* 1021 ἓν οὐ λέλεκται (introducing the oath of 1025–31, to which a conclusive comment is attached in 1032–5); (2) τἀμά in 775 should be simply equivalent to ἐγώ, but this produces nonsense; (3) Et. is assuming that both brothers will be dead; (4) the passage reflects badly on the character of Et.; (5) Creon makes no response. I believe these can be diminished by careful scrutiny. (1) ἀργόν is 'undone', not 'unsaid'. Both 766-73 and 774-7 are, in my view, 'public counsels', but the former is something that must still be done before the battle, the latter is a provision contingent on a certain outcome of the battle. The order of treatment is logical, and the emphasis in 766 is appropriate and no obstacle to Et.'s continuing in the run-on style that characterizes his whole speech.[1] For a different view, see Mueller-Goldingen 127–9, who believes that 774-7 would more properly conclude the 'private' topics and that ἀργόν must signal a final instruction; also West (1990), who considers the passage clearly an addition to the speech, but ascribes it to Eur. himself in the process of writing his play. (2) It is true that τἀμά is often a stylistically more weighty variation on pronoun ἐγώ: Fraenkel cites, e.g., *Andr.* 235 ὡς δὴ σὺ σώφρων, τἀμὰ δ᾽ οὐχὶ σώφρονα, *Hel.* 1194 ὄλωλα· φροῦδα τἀμὰ κοὐδέν εἰμ᾽ ἔτι. But this does not mean that it is a pure synonym for ἐγώ (it is often 'I and my interests, situation, behaviour',[2] as *Ant.* 501, *Ion* 1397, *IT* 1195) or that context has no effect on meaning. ἐπισκήπτω in 774 reaffirms that this is another testamentary (but public) instruction to be followed in the event of Et.'s death in battle, and τἀμά is thus easily (and inevitably: a competent user of a language rejects nonsensical interpretations in the very process of listening) taken in context as 'my side (in the Theban–Argive battle)'. (3) The assumption that both brothers will be dead is not strictly logical (as Musgrave already noted, judging the verses *paullo negligentius scripti*), but if Et. is alive he will see to the matter himself and if Pol. is alive he may well be ruler of Thebes and Creon have no authority any longer. The crucial case arises if both die, but Creon takes over power; and this case

---

[1] For the retarding of Et.'s exit by the continuation of his speech see also Saïd, 519–21.

[2] Cf. Diggle, *Studies* 106: 'When used as the subject of a verb, it [τὸ ἐμόν] always expresses something of the speaker's condition or behaviour.'

has already been implied by the curse and referred to in 765.[1] (4) It is a *petitio principii* to whitewash the character of Et. (763–5n.). (5) On the silence of Creon, see 782–3n.

776 ταφῆναι ... χθονί the dative perhaps blends 'in this land of Thebes' and 'with this Theban soil' (cf. plain χθονί in *Su.* 17 θάψαι ... χθονί or phrases like κρύψαι χθονί); in 1447–8 below we have θάψον ... ἐν γῆι πατρώιαι, and Wecklein tentatively suggested ταφῆναι 'ν here.

777 κἂν φίλων τις ἦι this specification plays primarily on the audience's knowledge of the story of Antigone (just as 156–71, 377(?), and 616–17 did), so that Mueller-Goldingen's objection that it makes Et. 'allzu vorausschauend' is somewhat beside the point. One can, moreover, say that the remark is not implausible from the point of view of Et., since he has heard 615–17, and since an audience is entitled to assume that he is aware of the longing for the absent Pol. that they have heard repeatedly expressed, and since funeral rites in general are the responsibility of the kin, esp. of the female kin. This specification, like the posthumous spitefulness of the whole injunction, is unflattering to Et. (774–7n., objection 4).

[778] rightly deleted by Kirchhoff, whose suspicion receives confirmation from the absence of the line in Π10 (on the principle involved, 291–2n.). As Fraenkel well argues, such an elaborate transition is appropriate to the carefully balanced persuasion of Jocasta (568) or to *dei ex machina* who dispense instructions and predictions to separate persons or groups (*Su.* 1213, *El.* 1276, *Hel.* 1662). I think the line is likely to be a reader's addition for clarification, as Kirchhoff proposed; but Fraenkel ascribes it to the *Bearbeiter* to whom he assigns 774–7. The first half of this line occurs also in *Su.* 1213, *El.* 1276, and with αὐδῶ in *Hel.* 1662 and 568 above (whence variant here); the second half is similar to *Su.* 1213 παισὶ δ' Ἀργείων λέγω, *Hel.* 1662 συγγόνωι δ' ἐμῆι λέγω.

779 the call for armour is another point of contact with the contrasted central scene of *Septem* (675–6 φέρ' ὡς τάχος κνημῖδας κτλ., without explicit vocative to attendant). Here I believe the attendants quickly fetch a panoply (stowed just inside the skene-door) and carry it off behind Et. as he exits; Et. does not pause to put the armour on. I believe the staging of *Se.* was similar, but for other views see Taplin, *Stagecraft* 158–61 (who deletes *Se.* 675–6, which are thus an imitation of our line) and Hutchinson *ad loc.* (who thinks the armour never appears, the call for armour being forgotten by the audience as the scene develops).

τεύχη πάνοπλά τ' ἀμφιβλήματα a hendiadys equivalent to πάνοπλα

---

[1] Note that Pol. in *Se.* 636–8 is quoted as mentioning, illogically, only two alternatives: both brothers will be dead or both alive.

τεύχη ἃ ἀμφιβάλλομαι, cf. *Hel.* 423 πέπλους τε τοὺς πρὶν λαμπρά τ᾽ ἀμφιβλήματα. Eur. affects a grandiose style for Et.'s military exit. πάνοπλος is a high-style epithet, used elsewhere in Eur. only in lyric and before him only in *Se.* 22 and Tyrt. 11.38 West. ἀμφιβλήματα is a late Eur. coinage (also *Hel.* 70, 423); later only in Aretaeus *SD* 2.6 and Nonnus *Paraphr. Joan.* 21.40 (both singular).

780–1 781 is omitted in Π¹⁰ (not an automatic condemnation: 291– 2n.) and Haslam (1976) deletes, objecting that Et. would not claim δίκη for himself. He classes the interpolation as a supplement to fill out apparently incomplete grammar (1225n.), since the ὡς in 780 could idiomatically be used to reinforce the notion of intention already hinted at in εἰς (as in 1361 + 1363 below and *Held.* 672). But 780 without 781 is poor idiom: when ὡς emphasizes purpose or intention it properly marks the intention of the subject of the clause, but here the subject is the attendants and the intention is Et.'s.[1] Objection to Et.'s reference to justice is valid only on the questionable premise that Eur. is presenting a wholly consistent character. In this scene Et. is blind to his own shortcomings and fully capable of the inconsistency. He has by implication already claimed justice for his defence of the city in his mocking accusations of Pol. for attacking it (604–6, 608, 611, 613, 636–7). The irony of this Et.'s being swept up in the spirit of the Aeschylean role is typical of Eur. and of the intertextual allusions of this play.

ὁρμώμεθ᾽ ὁρμῶμεν (R+) is possible, but the middle/passive is commoner in tragedy than the intrans. active.

782–3 there is scene-ending irony (198–201n., 636–7n.) in Et.'s appropriation of the position Creon had to teach him. The silence of Creon at the end of the scene has bothered some critics, and together with the irony of 782–3 in Et.'s mouth led Pohlenz to assign the final couplet to Creon instead. But the personification of the abstraction εὐλάβεια[2] and the enthusiasm of the superlative (cf. 506 τὴν θεῶν μεγίστην ... Τυραννίδα) as well as the criterion of usefulness (χρήσιμος of a god apparently paralleled only in the cynical or whimsical Men. fr. 614.3–4 K–T ἐγὼ δ᾽ ὑπέλαβον χρησίμους εἶναι θεοὺς / τἀργύριον ἡμῖν καὶ τὸ χρυσίον) give an unconventional air to the piety that better suits Et. It would also be odd dramatic technique for such a scene-closing prayer to be uttered by the

---

[1] Willink (1990) 199 n. 38 accepts Haslam's deletion and cites instances of ὡς ἐπί as well, but my objection still applies.

[2] On the associations of this word see Willink (1990) 183–5 (but I disagree when he takes the term as an unironic index of Et.'s attitude during the scene: 754–5n. at end).

subsidiary character rather than by the warrior departing to battle. As for the silence, some consider the lack of verbal reaction to 754-5 and 774-7 to be indicative of the spuriousness of these passages. There are hardly any comparable scenes in extant tragedy to give us guidance in evaluating the dramatic technique here. Choruses, who are inherently weaker and more remote from the decisive action, sometimes fail to comment on what might be thought shocking.[1] A character's failure to react may be underlined by a comment and so carry undeniable dramatic effect, as in *Ant.* 1243 and *Trach.* 812 (Eurydice and Deianira) or *Phil.* 1062. More relevant to our instance, perhaps, is the way Soph. does not allow Tecmessa to react with words of joy or approval to Ajax's apparent decision to live on (*Aj.* 692; but the choral ode reflects her feelings); and the way Hermione is given no chance to comment after Orestes' revelation of the plot to murder her husband (see Stevens on *Andr.* 1005-6). In the latter case, we must be uncertain whether Eur. expected an audience to make an inference about Hermione's character; the chief point of the technique is rather the dominance of Orestes at the scene-ending and the offhand manner in which he reveals the plot after his disingenuous self-presentation. So here one might argue that the casual spitefulness of Et. and his blind appropriation of the Aeschylean role are being foregrounded and that Creon is simply shown to be a subordinate figure. For despite the prudence of his strategic advice to the rash Et., he is a subordinate character, a political loyalist, with no fondness for Pol., no openness to the issue of Et.'s injustice, no emotional impulse, like Joc.'s, to forestall familial disaster. Creon's own weakness will be laid bare in the next episode, and his subordination seems to continue even when he is regent (1308-53n., 1582-709n.). Furthermore, an audience familiar with the tragic tradition would not find Creon's acquiescence in such a decree unbelievable.

782 θεῶν   θεῶι (Π[10]) may yield a milder sense, 'a very useful goddess', but the true superlative sense with θεῶν is more suitable if Et. is the speaker of this couplet.

---

[1] *Med.* 374-5 (first threat by Medea to kill Corinth's king and princess) arouse no protest, nor do 788-9 (Medea immediately thereafter mentions child-killing, and the chorus concentrates on this issue); at *Andr.* 425ff. Andromache herself protests at Menelaus' treachery, but the chorus fails to comment; the chorus of *Or.* is a collaborator in the plot against Helen and Hermione, showing compunction only at 1539-40; textual doubt makes it unclear what the chorus says or does about Alcmene's violence at the end of *Hcld.* There is one case in which a chorus modifies a harsh command by expressing disapproval (*Ant.* 770, saving Ismene).

783 προσευχόμεσθα the present (Π¹⁰MAa; first adopted by Kirchhoff) is very common in performative utterance of a prayer (as *Trach.* 1190, *Alc.* 334, *Hel.* 646, etc.); a future sometimes has a performative sense in lyric poetry, but εὔξομαι and compounds are normally true futures (as *Ag.* 317, *Choe.* 112), and in the performative use in *Hipp.* 116 προσευξόμεσθα further lines of address to the goddess actually follow.

διασῶισαι the choice between aor. 'bring safely through to the end' and present 'keep safe through to the end' (MO +) is far from certain, but the aor. is used in connection with the critical issue of the battle in 560, 864, 900, 948, 952, so I prefer it here. The final words of this episode anticipate the major theme of the next.

784–833: SECOND STASIMON

FUNCTION AND STYLE

After the discussion of strategy and the departure of Eteocles with his armour, the chorus suitably begins its ode with an invocation of Ares and an impressionistic evocation of the crazed violence that infects both sides in a war. The focus narrows at the end of the strophe to the cause of the violence, the *eris* afflicting the royal family, but the generalizing plural γᾶς βασιλεῦσιν and the epithet πολυμόχθοις in 800 (repeated from the opening line) also suggest a wider range of misfortunes. The antistrophe takes its cue from this suggestion and highlights some disastrous moments in the history of the royal family (and Thebes), leading up again to the present *eris*. The antistrophe ends with a reference to the incest of Oedipus and Jocasta (obscured by corruption), and the epode opens with a contrasting reference to the birth of the Spartoi, interpreted here in a positive light. The rest of the epode then promotes, albeit not without sinister undertones, a positive view of Theban history as a ground for confidence in the face of the present peril. By this contrast between the antistrophe and epode, the song intimates the separability of the fortunes of the family and city and prepares for the elaboration of this theme in the following episode and for the emergence of Menoeceus as a saviour to be contrasted with the doomed and baneful Labdacids (the theme of the next stasimon).

In style, this passage affects a dithyrambic heaping of polysyllabic epithets (see esp. 801–5, 820–1), perhaps imitating with a late Euripidean twist some of the weight and passion of warlike Aeschylean dactyls. There are Aeschylean reminiscences in the diction (791–2n., 792n., 797n., 808–10n.) as well as several words coined by Eur. or employed in novel ways. The style seems to me to suit the occasion, the subject-matter, and the exotic chorus, but Hermann's peevish judgment has often been quoted with approval: *tumidissimum inani verborum strepitu carmen*. In form, the stasimon appears to fall apart into three separate songs (so Kranz, *Stasimon* 250: 'drei völlig in sich abgeschlossene Lieder'), each with its opening apostrophe and emphatic close. But as in other odes in this play and elsewhere in Greek choral lyric, implicit connections may sometimes be more important than appearances. The above summary indicates the relevance of the stanzas to each other and to the preceding and following scenes. In addition, connections of diction and repeated motifs tie the stanzas into a unit and relate the song to other parts of the song-cycle. Within the strophe, for instance, we find πολύμοχθος 784 ~ -οις 800, καλλιχόροις 786 ~ χοροποιοί 788 ~ προχορεύεις 790bis, αἵματι 784 ~ 790, Ἀργείων ἐπιπνεύσας 789 ~ Ἀργείοις ἐπιπν. 794, ὁπλοφόροις 789 ~ ἀσπιδοφέρμονα 796. From stanza to stanza we may cite θανάτωι 785 ~ 803, τετραβάμοσι 792 ~ 808, ἔρις 798 ~ 811, and γένναν 795 ~ 810 ~ 821, along with many other terms of nurture, kinship, and birth (πολυθηρότατον 801, -τρόφον 802, λόχευμ' 803, θρέψαι and βρέφος 804, -γενῆ 808, θάλλει 812, λόχευμα 816, ἔτεκες 818, -τρόφου 820, -φυῆ 821, -τρόφον 826, προμάτωρ 828, ἐγείνατο 829). Links backwards to parodos and first stasimon include the opening contrast between Dionysus and Ares (a redeployment of that motif of the parodos), the motif of music and worship (parodos and 649–56), the dragon and Sown Men (first stasimon), foundation of city and fertile location (first stasimon), Io as προμάτωρ (cf. 218, 248, 676 προμάτορος, also κερόεσσα 828 ~ κερασφόρου 248), magical fertility (e.g., χλοερoτρόφον 826 ~ χλοηφορ- 647, 653, χλοερά 660, ζαθέων 801 ~ ζάθεά 232) and divine interventions. For further links back to this ode see on the third stasimon.

784–833 Metre This triad is almost entirely dactylic and may be compared with the stasimon *Hcld.* 608–17 = 618–29 and the actors' stanzas at *Andr.* 1173–83 = 1186–96, *Hel.* 375–85. The strophic pair is wholly dactylic, but there is variation between stichic-style construction in the first ten lines (actual hexameters, or tetrameters or pentameters in which a caesura can be felt after the hemiepes-portion) and a style in which word-end tends to coincide more often with metron-end (so in most of the remaining nine lines). The latter style is more akin to anapaests and, to judge from the use in Peleus' song in *Andr.* and in Antigone's aria later in this play, perhaps conveys a more emotional or threnodic effect. As in the other examples, it seems appropriate to assume period-end in the first half of the stanza whenever word-end coincides with spondee at the close of a dactylic run. On this assumption we obtain several hexameters, and hiatus confirms period-end at 788 = 805; in the tentative reconstruction offered here there is also hiatus at 791 = 808 and brevis at 792 = 809. In the second half of the stanza, spondee coinciding with word-end may not be a reliable criterion, but we are aided by brevis in 795 (see 810n.) and catalexis at 797bis.

The epode is again predominantly dactylic, but there is admixture of single-short rhythm in the opening cretic and in the clausula, and I take 825–7 as an anapaestic period rather than headless dactyls, with the anap. dimeters giving a smooth transition from the preceding hexameters to the following shorter dactylic cola.

STROPHE/ANTISTROPHE

784/801	–∪∪–∪∪–⋮∪∪–∪∪	4 da
785/802	–∪∪–∪∪–⋮∪∪–∪∪–∪∪– –‖	6 da∧
786/803	–∪∪–∪∪–⋮∪∪–∪∪–∪∪– –‖	6 da∧
787/804	–∪∪–∪∪–⋮– –∪∪–∪∪– –‖	6 da∧
788/805	–∪∪–∪∪–⋮∪∪– –‖ʰ¹	4 da∧
789/806	–∪∪–∪∪–⋮∪∪– – –∪∪– –‖	6 da∧
790/807	–∪∪– –‖	2 da∧
790bis/807bis	–∪∪–∪∪–∪∪– –‖	4 da∧
791/808	–∪∪–∪∪–⋮∪∪–∪∪– –‖ʰ¹	5 da∧
792/809	–∪∪–∪∪–⋮∪∪–∪∪–∪∪– –‖ᵇ¹	6 da∧
793/810	– – –∪∪–∪∪– –‖	4 da
794/811	– – –∪∪– – – – –∪∪– –|	6 da
795/812	– – – –‖ᵇ¹	2 da∧
796†/813	–∪∪–∪∪–∪∪–∪∪|	4 da
797/814	–∪∪–∪∪–∪∪–∪∪|	4 da
797bis/815	– – –‾∪∪‾–‖	hemiepes
		(3 da∧∧)
798/816†	– – –∪∪–∪∪–∪∪|	4 da
799/817†	–∪∪–∪∪–∪∪– –‖ʔ	4 da∧
800/⟨817bis⟩	–∪∪–∪∪– –‖‖	3 da∧

EPODE

818	‾∪∪– –∪∪–∪∪|	cr, 2 da
819	–∪∪–∪∪–⋮∪∪–∪∪–∪∪– –‖	6 da∧
820	–∪∪–∪∪–⋮– –∪∪–∪∪– –‖	6 da∧
821	–∪∪–∪∪–⋮– – – –∪∪–⌒‖ᵇ	6 da∧
822	–∪∪–∪∪–∪∪– –‖ʔ	4 da∧
823	–∪∪–∪∪–⋮– –∪∪–∪∪– –‖	6 da∧
824	– – –∪∪–∪∪–∪∪–∪∪– –‖	6 da
825	∪∪–∪∪–∪∪–∪∪–|	2 an
826	– –∪∪–∪∪–∪∪–|	2 an
827	∪∪– – –∪∪– –‖ʰᶜ	paroem
828	– – –∪∪–∪∪– –‖ʔ	4 da∧
829	– – –∪∪–∪∪–∪∪|	4 da

830	$-\cup\cup-\cup\cup-\vdots\cup\cup-\cup\cup$	4 da
831	$-\cup\cup-\cup\cup-\parallel^{c}$	hemiepes (= D)
832	$\cup\cup-\cup\cup----\cup-$	an, ia
		$(= {}_{\wedge}D - e)$
833	$\cup-\cup\cup--\parallel\parallel\parallel$	reiz ($= \cup d -$)

NOTES TO METRICAL SCHEME

789–90: the sequence 6 da ‖ 2 da ‖ is also found in 794–5, 1549–50, 1558–9, and in *Hcld* 608–9 = 619–20; cf. 1495–7 (10 da ‖ 2 da‖).

791: see comm. for possible alternatives.

796: if extensive recasting of the context is ruled out (as I argue in comm. below), then we find in ἀσπιδοφέρμονα θίασον ἔνοπλον a stylistically unexceptionable phrase which does not correspond to 813 Οἰδιπόδα κατὰ δώματα καὶ πόλιν. The short iota of θιασ- is established beyond doubt by numerous passages in Eur. and Arist., and late lexicographers' θείασος is a product of itacistic error (and perhaps false association with θειάζω, θειασμός). Those who accept long iota assume an *ad hoc* epic lengthening. Without the long iota, there is no point in conjecturing εὔοπλον, Triclinius' mechanical change (not found in tragedy, and the prettifying prefix is here unsuitable). Two unpalatable courses are open to us. (a) F. G. Schoene proposed ἐνόπλιον (with θίασον transposed before ἀσπιδοφ.), whence Murray suggested θίασον ἐνόπλιον with resolved dactyl. Whereas ἔνοπλος occurs six times in Eur. (in Soph. only *OT* 469), ἐνόπλιος is not extant in tragedy, although Pindar has ἐνόπλια χαλκωθεὶς ἔπαιζεν ('practised playful armed manoeuvres') in *O.* 13.86 and Gorgias fr. 6 D–K has οὐκ ἄπειροι ... ἐνοπλίου ἔριδος. Resolved dactyls are very rare in tragedy (cf. Dale, *LMGD*² 25 n. 2 and Diggle *PCPS* 20 (1974) 26): Diggle prints one at *Andr.* 490 (=482, 4 da$_{\wedge}$‖ or D²‖ in an iambic context), but has emended the possible instance in *Alc.* 120 = 130 (D² + ba as clausula to dactylo-epitrite stanza). But this stanza is (it seems) otherwise wholly dactylic, not dactylo-epitrite; moreover, ἐνόπλιον removes the coincidence of word-end and metron-end that is frequent in the context (and found in the corresponding position). (b) Wilam. *GV* 360–1, Dale, *LMGD*² 66, and West, *Greek Metre* 131 are inclined to accept 'light' dactyls with word-end matching metron-end and accents where the longa would normally be.[1] But there is no

---

[1] Cole, 246 (cf. 215), speaks of the possibility of 'a brief modulation into a contrasting rhythm' without saying what that rhythm would be here, with responsion to $-\cup\cup-\cup\cup$.

necessity to interpret other lines in this play as 'light' dactyls (1498, 1557: see metr. anal. *ad loc.*). Here the hypothesis remains seductive, but a unique instance in tragedy fails to inspire confidence.

797bis/815: the only responsion of biceps to longum in the ode. The double contraction of 797bis seems unparalleled, but contracted hemiepes is in any case uncommon: first biceps is contracted in *Alc.* 114 = 124 (preceding regular hemiepes), *Med.* 980 = 987 ((D−e−); second in *Med.* 840 (dactylo-epitrite, corresponding to uncontracted D).

800: for the trimeter as clausula after a tetrameter ending in spondee cf. *Ag.* 117 = 135 (ia, 4 da|, 3 da‖). If there is period-end at 799, then there is a double clausular effect (see metr. anal. on 248/249).

818: for initial cretic, cf. ia introducing dactylic runs in *Ag.* 109, 116. Editors before Murray accepted hiatus within the line with γᾶ, which cannot be justified by any special licence (contrast 1515–16 below).

830–3: many other treatments are possible (e.g., Diggle (1990b) 120 n. 104; JD (and Willink) ἄκροις / στεφάνοις ἔστακεν Ἀρείοις; Cole, 73, 202 n. 276), especially if one chooses to read ἔστακεν or ἀρήιοις or alter the dative endings. With division /πόλις ... ἔστακ' / Ἀρηΐοις στεφάνοισιν / we would have blunt 'enoplian' followed by pendant (cf., in different terminology, West, *Greek Metre* 130). With the colon in 832 cf. *Andr.* 1012–14: ᴧ D∪−∪ between D‖ and D.... Reizianum as clausula in dactylo-epitrite is found also in *Aj.* 911–14: ∪e∪D | ia, ba ‖ D | reiz ‖‖.

784–833: COMMENTARY

784–5 The conceit developed in most of this stanza is that Ares, in his personal revelling and in the revelry he inspires in others, is immune to and the opposite of Dionysus: rather than joining in the delights of Dionysiac music, he himself moves to an unmusical tune of bloodshed and death, and the bands of 'worshippers' he leads on both sides are similarly inspired by war-frenzy instead of joyful choral music. The conceit is properly introduced by 'Why are you possessed by bloodshed and death, ⟨ever⟩ out of tune with (at?) Bromius' celebrations?' For the underlying notion that Ares might be charmed into inactivity by music, cf. Pindar *P.* 1.10–12 καὶ γὰρ βιατὰς Ἄρης, τραχεῖαν ἄνευθε λιπὼν ἐγχέων αἰχμάν, ἰαίνει καρδίαν κώματι. For the opposition between Ares and music, cf. Aesch. *Su.* 681 ἄχορον ἀκίθαριν δακρυόγονον Ἄρη (also 635, but the text is doubtful), *Il.* 15.508 οὐ μὰν ἔς γε χορὸν κέλετ' ἐλθέμεν, ἀλλὰ μάχεσθαι. Jackson proposed κατέχεις ... ἑορτάς, 'Why do you possess the celebrations of Bromius with bloodshed ...?'; but this mistakes the conceit and

377

wrongly introduces the ἑορταί as a present reality within the world of the play.[1]

πολύμοχθος commonly quasi-passive, 'experiencing many toils' (as in 800 below), but quasi-active 'occasioning many toils' here and in fr. 916.1; cf. adesp. 127.10 Kannicht–Snell and later, e.g., Aristotle *PMG* 842.1 Ἀρετὰ πολύμοχθε γένει βροτείωι.

παράμουσος extant only here and in *Choe.* 467 παράμουσος Ἄτας / αἱματόεσσα πλαγά before Eust. *in Il.* 821,15. The notion that grief and violence are out of tune with or negations of joyful music is conventional in Eur.: cf. 790bis ἀναυλότατον, 807bis ἀμουσοτάταισι, *Her.* 889–93 χορεύματ' ἄτερ τυπάνων κτλ., *Cycl.* 425–6 ᾄδει ... παρὰ κλαίουσι ... ἄμουσα, 489–90 ἄχαριν κέλαδον μουσιζόμενος ... ἀπωιδός, *Tro.* 120–1 μοῦσα δὲ χαύτη τοῖς δυστήνοις ἄτας κελαδεῖν ἀχορεύτους.

ἑορταῖς the dat. is hard to classify: a true dative (as with ἐναντίος), locative, or sociative (as with ἀσύμφωνος)?

786 οὐκ some critics want to continue the question through 788 or 790bis or even 797bis and so emend to οὐδ' (Heath) or κοὐκ (Battier); but this is much too tangled. The 'epiplectic' question (*Contact and Discontinuity* 13) ends at 785 and 786–97bis divide into two elaborating comments, 786–90bis (clearly divided internally οὐκ ... ἀλλὰ ...) and 791–97bis (internal construction in doubt because of corruption).

ἐπὶ καλλιχόροις στεφάνοισι νεάνιδος ὥρας 'amidst garlands worn by beautiful youth in their fair dances', a precious equivalent of 'joining the lovely dances of beautiful youths in their garlands' (so essentially Geel, *non cantas ad pulcros choros formosae iuventutis coronis redimitae*, following the lead of Musgrave, who had, after Mosch., understood στεφάνοισι as 'circles of dancers'). ἐπί + dat. here expresses accompanying circumstance, 'at the time of', 'in the midst of'; cf. (probably) *El.* 163 οὐ μίτραισι γυνά σε δέξατ' οὐδ' ἐπὶ στεφάνοις. For similar datives see on 534, 1555–6. For the association of crowns with joyful music and choral dancing cf. *Alc.* 343–4 παύσω δὲ κώμους συμποτῶν θ' ὁμιλίας / στεφάνους τε μοῦσάν θ' ἣ κατεῖχ' ἐμοὺς δόμους, *Cresphontes* fr. 71.6–8 Austin (to Eirene) πρὶν σὰν προσιδεῖν χαρίεσσαν ὥραν καὶ καλλιχόρους ἀοιδὰς φιλοστεφάνους τε κώμους, *Her.* 677. καλλίχορος is used only of places in earlier poetry, but applied more widely in Eur.'s lyrics (*Her.* 690 of Delian maidens, *Hel.* 1454 of dolphins, *Cresphontes* fr. 71.7 just quoted), and Arist. imitates the wider usage in *Frogs* 451. Adjectival νεᾶνις is another Eur. lyric innovation (cf. *Ion* 477 νεάνιδες ἥβαι, but probably not *Ba.* 745 χειρῶν ... νεανίδων, iambic), and the

---

[1] Pearson suggested a meta-theatrical reference: Ares is out of tune with the Dionysiac festival at which the play is performed. This is to be rejected. On Ares in the play, see Masaracchia.

metonymy ὥρα = 'lovely young people' is also contrived (cf. ἥβη in *Hcld*. 282–3 μάτην γὰρ ἥβην ὧδέ γ' ἂν κεκτήιμεθα / πολλὴν ἐν Ἄργει and several times in Aesch.).

787 βόστρυχον ἀμπετάσας freeing one's long curls from a headband or other restraint is a sign of freedom from normal decorum (cf. 1490 and *Hipp*. 202 ἀμπέτασον βόστρυχον ὤμοις); and wild tossing of the loosened hair is characteristic of bacchic frenzy (*Ba*. 150 τρυφερόν ⟨τε⟩ πλόκαμον εἰς αἰθέρα ῥίπτων and Dodds' note on *Ba*. 862–5).

λωτοῦ = αὐλοῦ by metonymy (cf. Pindar fr. 94b.14 αὐλίσκων ὑπὸ λωτίνων), a Eur. mannerism, later imitated by minor Hellenistic poets.

788 χάριτες χοροποιοί after ἐν ᾆ, χάριτες is better taken as an ordinary noun rather than as personified goddesses. For the sense 'musical splendours', cf. Pindar *O*. 13.19, *I*. 3.8, *Hcld*. 379–80 τὰν εὖ χαρίτων ἔχουσαν πόλιν,[1] Dionys. Chalc. 1.3 West, Ion Chius *eleg*. 1.4 (*Epigr. Gr*. 471 Page). The weakened sense of the epithet, 'that is accompanied by dancing', 'that is the occasion for dancing', is paralleled in *Hec*. 916–17 χοροποιὸν θυσίαν, as against the etymological sense 'director of the dance' (*Aj*. 698 of Pan, and prose; also *Frogs* 353 χοροποιὸν ... ἥβαν, 'performing the dance'). The late Greek word χαροποιός intrudes in mss in all three of the tragic passages.

789 σὺν ὁπλοφόροις balances οὐκ ἐπὶ καλλιχόροις ... ὥρας in the first limb of the antithesis, goes with κῶμον ... προχορεύεις, and is explicated by the following participial phrase στρατὸν ... ἐπιπνεύσας αἵματι Θήβας (the 'arms-bearing men' are the Argives). The antithetic balance and the simplicity of metrical phrasing are spoiled by emendations that aim to supply a plural noun for ὁπλοφόροις (e.g. σάγμασι for αἵματι Wecklein) or to adjust ὁπλοφόροις to a singular noun (e.g. ὁπλοφόρωι ... ἅλματι Schenkl after Stahl, ἄισματι Badham). All of these also require Θήβαις, which I regard as secondary, based on confusion about the meaning of αἵματι Θήβας (see below): the paraphrasing Σ assumes contorted word-order, Θήβαις with ὁπλοφόροις and αἵματι with προχορεύεις.

ἐπιπνεύσας here and in 794 appears to combine two senses: as in *Se*. 343–4 μαινόμενος δ' ἐπιπνεῖ λαοδάμας μιαίνων εὐσέβειαν Ἄρης, Ares is a storm-wind, 'driving X hard against Y', a traditional image (see Hutchinson *ad loc*.); but in this context his action is also one of anti-musical inspiration (opposite to 787 above λωτοῦ ... πνεύματα), 'inspiring X against Y' (cf. ἐπίπνοια). So too in *Hipp*. 563 δεινὰ γὰρ τὰ πάντ' ἐπιπνεῖ (sc. Κύπρις), the violence of a storm-wind is primary, but there is a secondary implication of enchantment and inspiration (cf. *Hipp*. 525, Ἔρως Ἔρως, ὁ κατ' ὀμμάτων στάζεις πόθον). The use of the acc. is bold

---

[1] Cf. perhaps in a corrupt passage *IT* 1147 ἐς ἁμίλλας χαρίτων.

whether it is felt to be external or internal, both attested later in Ap. Rhod. 3.937 οὐδέ σε Κύπρις οὔτ' ... ἐπιπνείουσιν Ἔρωτες vs. 3.1327 λάβρον ἐπιπνείοντε πυρὸς σέλας. On (ἐπι)πνέω see M. Van der Valk in *ΚΩΜΩΙΔΟΤΡΑΓΗΜΑΤΑ. Studia ... Koster* (Amsterdam 1967) 131–43, esp. 137–8.

790 αἵματι Θήβας I view 794–5 Ἀργείοις ἐπιπνεύσας Σπαρτῶν γένναν as a deliberate reversal of the participial phrase of 789–90, and I understand these words (with Σ) as 'the race/offspring of Thebes' (cf. LSJ s.v. αἷμα iii and 247 above κοινὸν αἷμα, κοινὰ τέκεα). Because of the rare use of αἷμα and the bold construction of ἐπιπνεύσας many other interpretations have been proposed. Mosch. and Valck. punctuate after αἵματι (violating the metrical phrasing) and take Θήβας as gen. with προ- in προχορεύεις. LSJ and Van der Valk take αἵματι Θήβας as a directional dative or dat. of purpose, 'inspiring to slaughter of Thebes' (as in one of King's three renderings, *ut sanguine Thebano satientur*). Pearson adopts Θήβαις (which I consider an intrusion from a wishful paraphrase: Σ wanted a noun with ὁπλοφόροις; Pearson treats it as governed by ἐπιπνεύσας) and treats αἷμα as modal, 'with thirst for blood'; this has recently been endorsed by Craik and Mueller-Goldingen.

790bis κῶμον ἀναυλότατον a typically tragic use of a pejorative epithet ironically to negate the positive connotations of the noun. On 'fluteless' (= 'grim', 'joyless') music, cf. Diggle *PCPS* 200 (1974) 11–12.

προχορεύεις probably 'lead in the dance' rather than just 'send forth dancing', though the latter is closer to the causative meaning of χορεύω affected by Eur. (Bond on *Her.* 686), and an intrans. sense with κῶμον as internal acc. (as *Ag.* 31 φροίμιον χορεύσομαι) cannot be ruled out; the verb is not extant again until Greg. Naz. *PG* 35.1117.5 (intrans.).

791–2 a corrupt passage whose constitution can only be tentative. The principal issues to consider are the following. (1) Should 791 = 808 be emended to form a normal hexameter, or should we accept the truncated hexameter (6da$_{\wedge\wedge}$) presented by δινεύεις = χαλαῖσι(ν)? Against the hexameter it may be said that 808 seems sound as is, that Triclinius' expedient in 808 τετραβάμοσι⟨ν ἐν⟩ χηλαῖσιν is unattractive both because of ἐν and because of the final double spondee, and that a supplement like δινεύεις ⟨ἀλλ'⟩ or ⟨ἐν δ'⟩ in 791 has the same double spondee and an implausible elision at a position where period-end should probably be recognized. 6da$_{\wedge\wedge}$ has no parallel in the ode (3da$_{\wedge\wedge}$ in 797bis is the familiar hemiepes). 5da$_{\wedge}$ is also unparalleled in the ode, but if 800 is accepted there is a case of 3da$_{\wedge}$, and *Hel.* 163 could be 5da$_{\wedge}$ as clausula after two hexameters (see Kannicht ii.60). 5da$_{\wedge}$ may also be deemed another Aeschylean echo (cf. *Ag.* parodos, *Pers.* 880 = 889). (2) Can θυρσομανεῖ by itself be understood to identify Dionysus, or does the epithet need a noun, such as Hermann's δίναι or Musgrave's οὐ πόδα θυρσομανῆ? One would expect the article (except in vocatives with ὤ), since anarthrous epithets are normally felt to be appositive or predicative in sense (e.g., *IT* 1236 χρυσοκόμαν, *Hipp.* 1275 χρυσοφαής; *Thesm.* 315 χρυσολύρα, cited by Geel, is vocative and is immediately followed by Δῆλον ὃς ἔχεις ἱεράν). Moreover, ὑπό + dat. of person in tragedy connotes '⟨enslaved or defeated⟩ under the mastery of', not 'under the influence, leadership of' (for the latter cf. LSJ s.v. ὑπό B.II.4, e.g., *Scutum* 282 ὑπ' αὐλητῆρι πρόσθ' ἔκιον; the uses under B.II.1 are not close enough). A few have assumed that κώμωι can be understood from 790bis, but the intervening strong adversative makes this unlikely. The use of the dat. in ὑπὸ θυρσομανεῖ δίναι would be idiomatic, as in *Hcld.* 782-3 ὀλολύγματα παννυχίοις ὑπὸ παρθένων ἰαχεῖ ποδῶν κρότοισιν, *Eum.* 1034 (LSJ B.II.4). (3) How is the antithesis between Dionysus and Ares expressed in these lines? Some (Geel, Parmentier) see an allusion to a Dionysiac procession in which the god enters on a four-wheeled carriage and so refer the chariot and horse of 792 to the Dionysiac image of 791; but the connection with τε in 793 is then impossible. Most rightly follow Σ in detecting an antithesis between 791 (Dionysiac revelry) and 792 (tumult of war). (4) What of the tangle of cases and variants in 792? To start at the end of the line, metre guides us to accept μώνυχα πῶλον rather than μωνύχων πώλων or μώνυχα πώλων (with indeclinable μώνυχα, as proposed by Barnes and by Parmentier *REG* 36 (1923) 54-5: completely implausible in tragedy; see Chantraine *Grammaire hom.* 1.200 for the Homeric peculiarity εὐρύοπα, Schwyzer 1.560(α) for late epic indeclinable -α). For rejection of Weidgen's μωνυχοπώλων see below. Early editors did not question ἅρμασι καὶ ψαλίοις, but fuller knowledge of the tradition has suggested that ἅρμασι καὶ ψαλίων should be regarded as the transmitted reading. Yet there is no convincing explication of this (without recasting of the following lines as well): καὶ ψαλίων cannot go with νεβρίδων μέτα. So even though dat. ψαλίοις in Σ may be the result of wishful paraphrase and in the mss may be a secondary adjustment, the dat. is what is needed, and ψαλίοις τετραβάμοσι is a preciosity worthy of this ode and less frigid than Hartung's τετραβάμονα μώνυχα πῶλον. I suggest, then, that ἅρμασι καί is the result of an intrusive gloss, and that the missing phrase made explicit the antithesis, made 792 co-ordinate with τ' ... βαίνων in 793, and provided a verb to govern πῶλον and perhaps referred to noise or otherwise provided a construction for ψαλίοις. For instance, ⟨ἀλλὰ κροτῶν⟩, based on *Il.* 15.452-3 ὑπερώησαν δέ οἱ ἵπποι κείν' ὄχεα κροτέοντες, *Peace* 155 χρυσοχάλινον πάταγον ψαλίων, Aelian *NA* 6.10 ψαλίων κρότον (but there is some strain in 'make a horse sound with rattling curb-chain' for 'make a horse's curb-chain rattle'). Of the other treatments, Murray's is cleverest. It retains ψαλίων by adopting Weidgen's μωνυχοπώλων (cf. *Tro.*

536 ἀμβροτοπώλου) and provides a function for καί and a noun for
τετραβάμοσι by transposing ἱππείαις to 793 and eliminating the connective (as in MnSVr): ἅρμασι καὶ ψαλίων τετραβάμοσι μωνυχοπώλων
ἱππείαις ... θοάζεις, 'with chariots and with the four-footed coursing of
single-hoofed-horse bridles' (i.e. 'of single-footed horses in their bridles').
The expression is stylistically possible in late Eur. lyric, but this text leaves
the adversative in 792 implicit and intervenes in 793–4, which are not
otherwise in doubt and are idiomatically superior in the transmitted form
(see below); nor do I believe (with Powell) that the same meaning can be
obtained without the transposition.

791 θυρσομανεῖ hapax in classical Greek, recurring much later in
Orphic hymn 50.8 Quandt and eight times as epithet of Dionysus in Nonnus.
νεβρίδων μέτα perhaps 'together with ⟨other worshippers dressed in⟩
fawn-skins' (so T. Mommsen, *Beiträge zu der Lehre von den gr. Präpositionen*²
(Berlin 1895) 109 n. 44), but possibly just 'dressed in fawn-skins' (for plural
νεβρίδες see Dodds on *Ba*. 251, for μέτα cf. *Ba*. 363 ἕπου μοι κισσίνου
βάκτρου μέτα).

δίναι elsewhere in Eur. used only of eddying water or motions of air
and clouds, but for δινέω of dancing cf. *Il*. 18.494, 606, Xen. *Anab*. 6.1.9,
and for the later association of root διν- with ecstatic revelry cf. E. Rohde,
*Psyche*⁹ (Tübingen 1925) II.9 n. 4. If one can satisfy oneself about other
problems in the lines, δινεύεις or δινεῖς (Geel) πῶλον can be paralleled in
Se. 461–2 ἵππους ... δινεῖ and *IT* 192 δινευούσαις ἵπποις.

792 τετραβάμοσι a coinage of Eur. lyric (five instances from *El*. on),
recurring later only in *Orphic hymn* 8.5 Quandt; the juncture with ψαλίοις
is slightly bold (other junctures are with ἵπποι, ἀπήνας, γυίοις, χαλαῖς). A
small index in favour of the dat. is the same form in similar position in 808,
not quite an isometric echo. Adjs. in -μων have an Aeschylean flavor, so
this and ἀσπιδοφέρμονα in 796 contribute to the Aeschylean tenor of the
stasimon.

μώνυχα πῶλον if this is correct, it is a deliberate variation on the
traditional juncture μώνυχες(-ας) ἵπποι(-ους) used exclusively in other
poets, and this is the only poetic use of the singular.

793 Ἰσμηνοῦ τ' ἐπὶ χεύμασι in the vast majority of cases in Eur. (and
more often than not in other high-style poets from Homer on), the genitive
of the proper name precedes the word for 'stream' or 'waters' (ὕδωρ, ῥοαί,
ῥέεθρα, νάματα, etc.); cf. in this play alone 101, 102, 131, 222, 368, 574,
613, 932. This idiomatic preference should count for something against
Murray's transposition ἐπὶ χεύμασι βαίνων Ἰσμηνοῖο. If 792 is so restored
so that τ' must be eliminated from this line, then Pearson's Ἰσμηνοῖ' ἐπί
should be accepted (for -οιο in Eur. see Page on *Med*. 135).

794 θοάζεις a favourite word of Eur., used by no other author until

382

Christ. Pat. 1144 ἀεὶ θεραπεύειν θοάζει τὸν θεόν; used both transitively (thus it governs πῶλον in some reconstructions) and intransitively; here it continues the imagery of bacchic frenzy (cf. *Ba.* 65, 219, *Tro.* 307, 349).

794–5 Ἀργείοις . . . γένναν cf. 789n., 790n. Because of the discrepancy between strophe and antistrophe, several critics have deleted words in the strophe, and Ἀργείοις ἐπιπνεύσας has frequently been a target because of the repetition.

796 ἀσπιδοφέρμονα hapax in extant Greek, coined as a dactylic variation on ἀσπιδηφόρος, 'bearing a shield'; on the suffix -μων see Schwyzer 1.522, and compare the ε-grade verbal stems in νεκροδέγμων *Prom.* 153 (vs. νεκροδόχος in Eust.), πολυθρέμμων *Pers.* 33 (vs. πολυτρόφος in Call.). Σ offers, beside the correct interpretation, a derivation from φέρβω,[1] wrongly endorsed by LSJ; Σ sees an allusion to the Spartoi 'born in full armour', LSJ give the even less plausible 'living by the shield, by war'.

†θίασον ἔνοπλον† the noun is surely appropriate to this context, its joyful connotations ironically perverted by the epithets; but see metrical analysis for doubts. Eichler proposed ἀσπιδοφέρμον' ἄθυρσον ἐνόπλιον, which obscures the construction of dactyls κατὰ συζυγίαν that prevails in 795–7bis and 799; West (1990) suggests κῶμον Ἀρήϊον; JD suggests (e.g.) ἀσπιδοφέρμονα χαλκῶι ἐνόπλιον . . . κοσμήσας θίασον. The acc. in 796 is felt initially as an appositive to γένναν and then as object of κοσμήσας in 797bis.

797 ἀντίπαλον possibly a reminiscence of *Se.* 417 or (and?) *Ant.* 125–6 (esp. if ἀντιπάλου . . . δράκοντος is read).

κατά not 'against' (Craik), but 'all along'.

797bis Triclinius' deletion of this colon has no authority; despite the metrical oddity the phrase is not to be doubted.

800 Λαβδακίδαις πολυμόχθοις given the discrepancy between strophe and antistrophe and the absence of this colon in Π[10], Nauck's deletion has a prima-facie attraction. But the antistrophe is so corrupt that it cannot be restored with any confidence and is an unreliable guide to judging the strophe. And although a proper name as gloss often intrudes into lyrics, here we also have a poetic epithet that makes a point within the ode (for the technique of meaningfully echoing at the end of a song or stanza the diction of its opening, cf. the ἄτη-ode in *Ant.* and πτεροῦσσα in 1019bis,

---

[1] There is an apparent parallel for φερβ- + -μων yielding -φερμων in Hsch. α 3188 ἀλλοφέρμονες· ἀλλαχοῦ τραφέντες (cf. Et. magn. 69,1), but that may be a post-classical coinage based on the false interpretation of ἀσπιδοφέρμων.

1042 below) and underlines a motif of the song-cycle picked up in 1022 πολύφθορος πολύστονος. In my Teubner app. I overstated the case in alleging a need for 800 as a clausula: 799 is already clausular with respect to 798; but at any rate successive clausulae are possible, so the shape of 799 does not count against 800.

801–2 ζαθέων πετάλων πολυθηρότατον νάπος the descriptive genitive[1] functions in parallel with the epithet, instead of the more obvious εὔδενδρον καὶ πολύθηρον; the mention of both fauna and flora underlines the theme of fertility (cf. 210, 230, 644–54, 659–61, 669), here with an emphasis on wild nature and a hint of the divine power underlying extraordinary fertility and reproduction. Cf. Pindar *P*. 9.58 (χθονὸς αἶσαν) οὔτε παγκάρπων φυτῶν νάποινον οὔτ' ἀγνῶτα θηρῶν (emphasizing the wild fertility as opposed to 9.6a–7 πολυμήλου καὶ πολυκαρποτάτας ... χθονὸς). ζάθεος, a traditional epithet of places, is here transferred to the foliage that characterizes the place.

πολυθηρότατον the adj. is exclusive to Eur. (also *Hipp.* 145 of Dictynna) apart from a few instances in later prose.

χιονοτρόφον ὄμμα the epithet is hapax in extant Greek (as is χιονοθρέμμονας in *Hel.* 1323); for snowy peaks cf. 206, 234. ὄμμα meaning 'precious delight' is a high-style conceit more commonly seen with ὀφθαλμός (Pindar and tragedy: cf. Stevens on *Andr.* 406, Jebb on *OT* 987), but this use is bolder than most because the attached genitive is virtually subjective (as if with ἄγαλμα or the like) rather than partitive, as in other examples.

803 λόχευμ' though used once as *nomen actionis* in *Ag.* 1392, the noun is a favourite of Eur., esp. as repersonified abstract (21n.), 'child (born of)', and is then unattested until late authors (in the sense 'child' only in Synesius *hymn* 5.29).

804 the division Οἰδίποδ' ἀνθρέψαι is inferior because the acc. Οἰδίποδα is late (ἀνατρέφω is doubtful in tragedy: *Eum.* 523).

ἔκβολον is another Eur. coinage, used with virtuosity in four or five contextually determined senses; cf. esp. *Ion* 555 ἔκβολον κόρης. The word recurs in the obvious sense 'cast out' in Call. *hymn* 6.115, Lucian *Podagra* 215, etc.

805 χρυσοδέτοις περόναις ἐπίσαμον for the 'contradiction' (already debated by the ancients, cf. Σ) between Joc.'s grim σιδηρᾶ κέντρα διαπείρας and this prettified lyric description (a royal baby should have golden adornments), cf. 26n. To avoid the contradiction, some ancients

---

[1] See 1491n. and Diggle, 'Euripides, *Orestes* 225', in H. D. Jocelyn, ed., *Tria Lustra: Essays and Notes presented to John Pinsent* (Liverpool 1993) 135–7.

and a few moderns have interpreted the phrase as an allusion to the self-blinding (cf. 62 χρυσηλάτοις πόρπαισιν), but such a reference would be thematically and chronologically out of place here. χρυσόδετος properly means 'bound with gold', that is, 'with golden adornments attached', but here it may be merely a high-style variation on χρύσεος (cf. 1091n. μελάνδετον).

806–7bis τὸ παρθένιον πτερόν ... Σφιγγὸς a lyric periphrase for 'the winged maiden Sphinx'; but the postponement of the gen. (and the possibility of taking it in its own colon with ὠιδαῖς) almost creates a *griphos* in 806 which is clearly resolved in 807bis. Nauck's Σφίγγ' ἀπομουσ- wrongly simplifies the style.

οὔρειον τέρας Eur. is probably associating the Sphinx with Cithaeron and not alluding to the separate hill Φίκιον/ Φίκειον known from Hes. fr. 195 = *Scutum* 33 (without reference to the Sphinx), Lycophr. *Alex.* 1465 Φίκιον τέρας (a reminiscence of this passage?), and later sources. Herbig *RE* 3A.1714 suggests that the version locating the Sphinx on Cithaeron was one in which the Cithaeronian Hera Gamostolos sent the monster.

ἀμουσοτάταισι cf. 784–5n. παράμουσος, 50n.

808–10 Καδμογενῆ ... γένναν the striking separation of epithet and noun reinforces the effective interlacing of impressionistic details (gripping claws, approach to walls, disappearance aloft). The adj. may be another reminiscence of *Se.* (302–3 πόλιν καὶ στρατὸν Καδμογενῆ ῥύεσθε); its only other extant use is *Trach.* 116 (Heracles). Cf. 1549n.

ἄβατον φῶς concisely implies the frustrating inability of the onlookers to pursue the monster or even to follow it for long with their eyes.

810 γένναν, τάν so, justifiably, Triclinius; the mss have γένναν ἄν, which would provide the only clear case of long alpha acc. (or nom.) for this word. The short alpha is established in Aesch., *Prom.*, Empedocles, Ezechiel, and in Eur. at 821 below and *Tro.* 531; all other passages are indeterminate because of following consonants or because of certain or probable brevis in longo at period-end, as at 795 above, *Andr.* 119, *Her.* 365, *IT* 155 (so too probably *Hec.* 159, or this may be emended to Porson's γενεά – cf. Diggle, *Studies* 97).

810–11 Ἅιδας ... ἐπιπέμπει probably Hades is implicated not as personally involved in some version of the story, but only in the general sense that the Sphinx's attack is deadly: cf. *Carmina Epigraphica Graeca* 120.1 (1.66 Hansen; Thessaly, *c.* 450) Σφίξ, Ἀΐδ[α]ο κύον. Eur., like several other authors, leaves the motivation of the Sphinx's attack obscure (1032n.).

811 ἔρις ἄλλα if the meaning is 'another strife', the adj. retrojects the description 'strife' upon the two incidents already alluded to: strife within the household is evident in the patricide made possible by the salvation of the exposed Oed., and the attack of the Sphinx could be viewed as 'strife' between the city and the divinely sent beast. The latest strife affects both the family and the city (813), but their fortunes will soon be separated. But possibly ἔρις ἄλλα is to be taken as ἄλλο κακόν, ἔρις (so Wecklein; cf. K–G 1.275, LSJ s.v. ἄλλος II.8). The alternative punctuation in OA (δυσδαίμων δ' ἔρις, ἀλλὰ / θάλλει) produces a harsh brevis in longo and a choppy sentence structure unsuited to this position in the period.

813 Οἰδιπόδα the gen. may be felt in common with παίδων and δώματα καὶ πόλιν.

814–17 The chorus ends the strophe with an assertion of faith in fundamental values. οὐ γὰρ ὃ μὴ καλὸν οὔποτ' ἔφυ καλόν implicitly opposes Et.'s amoral relativism (499–502), asserting that one can judge between good and bad and that faced with the history of the Labdacids a right-thinking person will gloomily accept the fact that an evil result was inevitable once incest had taken place. Mueller-Goldingen well cites the converse axiom in *Ag.* 761–2 οἴκων γὰρ εὐθυδίκων καλλίπαις πότμος αἰεί, *Her.* 1261–2 ὅταν δὲ κρηπὶς μὴ καταβληθῆι γένους / ὀρθῶς, ἀνάγκη δυστυχεῖν τοὺς ἐκγόνους. One may compare the moral attitude of the chorus at *Or.* 819–24 τὸ καλὸν οὐ καλόν κτλ. (where I follow West's explication, not Willink's): what Orestes has subtly argued to be a καλόν crime (cf. 823 τὸ δ' εὖ κακουργεῖν) cannot be accepted as such by right-thinking people. A similar strategy is employed more tendentiously in *Ba.* 395 τὸ σοφὸν δ' οὐ σοφία. Dodds on *Ba.* 877–81 sees here an allusion to the proverb sung by the Muses at the wedding of Cadmus and Harmonia (Theogn. 17 ὅττι καλόν, φίλον ἐστί· τὸ δ' οὐ καλὸν οὐ φίλον ἐστίν), and Valck. had already noted this and proposed emending to ἔφυ φίλον; but I fail to see the relevance of such a reminiscence to the themes of this ode and play.

The words which follow οὐδ' οἱ μὴ νόμιμοι seem irreparably corrupt, though it is clear that we have a kind of paratactic comparison, 'just as the foul can never be fair, so incest-begotten children can never be other than a polluting source of evil'. Some have attempted to restore 816–17 to respond to 798–9 (with 800 deleted), but this seems to me to leave too little room for manoeuvre, and I argued above that 800 ought to be retained. Two main lines of approach have been attempted. (1) A predicate 'good' may be supplied from the previous clause for the subject-copula phrase 'nor are unlawful children', and then the following nouns are taken in apposition: so e.g. Weidgen οὐδ' οἱ μὴ νόμιμοι / παῖδες, ματρὶ λόχευμα μιάσματος, / οὐδὲ σύναιμον ὃς εἰς λέχος ἦλθεν / ⟨e.g. πατροφόνος πολυπενθής⟩ = 'nor ⟨can⟩ unlawful sons ⟨ever be fair⟩, a polluting product of birth for their mother, nor ⟨can⟩ he who entered a kindred marriage-bed ...'; in this solution the gen. of description μιάσματος is harsh and the understood predicate is rather weak; cf. West (1990) παῖδες, ματρὶ

386

λόχευμα μιᾶι πατρός, 'nor ⟨are⟩ irregular children who are the brood of the same mother as their father' (but gen. and dat. here are both doubtful Greek). In Craik's adaptation of this, {παῖδες} ματρὶ λόχευμα, μίασμά τι πατρός = 'brood of their mother and pollution of their father', the dative is harsh and τι pointless. (2) λόχευμα is treated as the predicate, in which case it needs a favourable epithet, since the noun by itself cannot carry the burden of 'a genuine, wholesome, or glorious product of birth': so e.g. Pearson οὐδ' οἱ μὴ νόμιμοι ⟨νόμιμόν ποτε⟩ / ματρὶ λόχευμα μιάσματι πατρός· / ἣ δὲ συναίμων ἐς λέχος ἦλθεν, 'unholy ever are the children of an incestuous bed with taint of parricide; for she came to the marriage as kin ⟨of her husband⟩'; but this solution depends on the unjustified deletion of 797bis and Pearson's interpretation of μιάσματι πατρός as '⟨children born to⟩ Oed. tainted with the pollution of killing his father' is too strained both in the sense of μίασμα (not adequately supported by the sense 'source of pollution' seen in *Choe.* 1028 and *OT* 241) and in the use of the gen. I think the latter approach to 815–16 more likely to be right, but if μίασμα is to appear in the solution, it should, I think, refer to incest (cf. μιαίνει 1050), and 817, which seems weak and pointless if Joc. is subject, might better refer to Oed.; a rhetorically stronger conclusion of the stanza would also be welcome.

818–19 ἔτεκες … ἔτεκές … ἐδάην ἐδάην as in the epode of the previous stasimon, such iterations mark a heightening of emotional involvement as the chorus turns from narrative and commentary to prayer there and here to a more hopeful survey of the Theban past suggestive of salvation. βάρβαρον … ἀκοάν recalls 679bis–80bis βαρβάρωι βοᾶι … βαρβάροις λιταῖς.

Γαῖ' after consultation with Stephen Daitz, I now agree with him that H has γαῖ· and not γᾶι as in M.

820–1 the three compound adjs. are Eur. coinages, ὀδοντοφυῆ being hapax in extant Greek (ὀδοντοφυέω is a medical or zoological technical term), φοινικολόφοιο found later (of fighting cocks) only in Theocr. 22.72 and the *Geoponica*, and θηροτρόφος (also in *Ba.* 102, 556) in Hellenistic poets and late prose, always in its obvious sense 'nourishing wildlife' (of a place or divinity). Σ attest the false reading θηρότροφον, with a unique 'passive' sense 'born from the beast'; similarly, LSJ interpret 'feeding on beasts' (hardly relevant: the serpent was noted for feeding on Cadmus' men).[1] More likely, as in *Ba.* 102 ἄγραν θηροτρόφον ('their beast-brood

---

[1] LSJ is also in error (after Kühn) about θηριότροφος, 'fed on reptiles', and ἀσπιδότροφος, 'feeding on adders': both compounds should be paroxytone and are 'active' in sense in Galen 11.143 Kühn τοὺς

spoil', Dodds), the adj. is a 'sentence-compound' (=θήρ ὅς τρέφεται), a recherché variation on θηριώδης (as one Σ glosses it).[1] -τροφος thus has a weakened sense, but nevertheless has its effect within the diction of fertility and nurture in the stasimon.

821 ὀδοντοφυᾶ   see Addendum, p. 645.

Θήβαις κάλλιστον ὄνειδος   a deliberate paradox (suppressed by the Σ who wrongly claim that ὄνειδος can be a neutral word; for the doctrine cf. Eust. *in Il.* 88, 15 and 647, 36; for ironic uses of 'lovely reproach' cf. *Med.* 514, *Ba.* 652, *IA* 305); the Spartoi can be alluded to in reproach for their bestial origins and fratricide (cf. *Su.* 578–9, *Ba.* 537–44), but as a national emblem of Theban autochthony and as symbolic of martial spirit are a source of local pride (1006–8 below, *Her.* 797 Θήβαις ἱερὸν φῶς; *Se.* 412–14, *Ant.* 126; Pindar fr. 29.2 Σπαρτῶν ἱερὸν γένος ἀνδρῶν). The phrase crystallizes the ambiguous relationship of Thebes to its local divinities, so important in the next episode.

822–3   the attendance of the gods at the wedding of Cadmus and Harmonia was a mark of special privilege and glory: cf. esp. Pindar *P.* 3.88–93 (Cadmus and Peleus).

823–4   Thebes had a dual foundation-myth, with Cadmus responsible for the selection of the site and the origin of the chief families (with an emphasis on their military function), and the divine twins (like Romulus and Remus) responsible for the layout and construction of the walls that denote the consolidated polis (cf. Pindar *Pae.* 9.44 Κάδμου στρατὸν ἂν Ζεάθου πόλιν). The magical movement of the stones by Amphion's music is another source of pride.

ἀνέσταν   preferable to ἀνέστα as the more difficult juncture after τείχεα ... τε ... πύργος and as the less familiar form: for listing of rare short-vowel 3rd pl. personal endings in intrans. aor. or aor. pass. in tragedy see Barrett on *Hipp.* 1247–8, and cf. 1246 below ἔσταν.

825 διδύμων ποταμῶν πόρον ἀμφὶ μέσον   'on the narrow land between the two rivers' (sc. Dirce and Hismenus), topographically apt but involving unusual senses of ἀμφί and πόρον ignored in the loose paraphrases of most commentators. I take ἀμφί in the sense 'along through' (cf. the temporal 'during' as in Pindar *O.* 2.30 τὸν ὅλον ἀμφὶ χρόνον); this is

---

θηριοτρόφους καὶ ἀσπιδοτρόφους Μάρσους, 'the Marsi, who raise reptiles and adders' (for magical purposes: for Marsi as snake-charmers cf. Plin. *NH* 25.11, 28.19, 30; Sil. Ital. 8.495–7). In Joan. Chrys. *PG* 59.615 θηριοτρόφος should be written, since the meaning is 'devoured by wild beasts'.

[1] Rijksbaron (1991) 17–18 considers only the 'active' and 'passive' senses of the compound epithet and argues for θηρότροφον in *Ba.* 102.

somewhat different from the common 'near', 'alongside' found with places and bodies of water as object; cf. perhaps *Ba.* 1229 ἀμφὶ δρυμούς, 'scattered through' (if Bruhn's correction of the dat. is right), Pindar *P.* 5.24 γλυκὺν ἀμφὶ κᾶπον Ἀφροδίτας, *Mel.Desm.* 11 Page ἀμφὶ δ' ἀγνὰ Δωδώνης βάθρα ('at') and the sense 'somewhere in' as in *Andr.* 215, *Rhes.* 408, 932 (see Jebb on *Aj.* 1064). πόρος is basically 'a way from point A to point B' ; it is commonly applied to a strait of water (LSJ 1.2), but here must be the narrow land one must cross to get from one stream to the other (so probably Σ, περάσιμον τόπον, and explicitly Wilam. 'auf dem Werder' and Powell 'on the holm'). Blaydes' βαθύν for μέσον allows the easier sense 'along the deep channel', but is less natural with two rivers than it would be with one.

826 Δίρκα . . . ἅι the mss' Δίρκας would require ἃ πεδίον or, with ἀμπεδίον = ἃμ πεδίον, a lacuna for a conjunction to introduce καταδεύει. But the gen. makes no sense with 825: Dirce did not have two streams, and it is desperate to take διδύμων ποταμῶν as descriptive with πύργος (as Barnes and Valck.). As Burges (and later Schenkl) recognized, 826–7 should be a restatement of 825, with the two rivers mentioned explicitly and Dirce as subject of the clause. Original ΑΙΠ may also have given rise to ΑΜΠ.

χλοεροτρόφον another hapax in extant Greek (also the only compound of χλοερ-).

827 πρόπαρ 120n. After a roughly parallel course, the two rivers converge in the plain to the north of Thebes: see Appendix on Topography.

828 'Ἰώ θ' as pointed out by Bremer (1980) 282, the connection with τε here and in 824 means that marriage-banquet, wall-building, and descent from Io are treated as co-ordinate claims of fame and good fortune: there should be a comma at the end of 827 and a period or high stop at the end of 829; this is preferable to Wecklein's change to δ' in 828 and τ' in 830.

830–1 μυριάδας . . . μεταμειβομένα 'getting countless blessings in succession to other blessings', 'passing through a succession of countless blessings one after another'; this claim of a long sequence of goods is strong praise, since human fortune usually entails an alternation of bad and good, as in two of Pindar's three uses of μετ/πεδαμείβω, *P.* 3.96 ἐκ προτέρων μεταμειψάμενοι καμάτων, *O.* 12.12 ἐσλὸν βαθὺ πήματος . . . πεδάμειψαν. For the sake of the lyric style Eur. affects the unobvious shift of genders ἑτέροις ἑτέρας, regularized in GχT¹.

832–3 ἐπ' ἄκροις ἔστᾱχ' Ἀρηΐοις στεφάνοισιν the possible meanings of this are discussed in detail by H. Parry, *Phoenix* 21 (1967) 20–6, and Bremer (1980). I take the general tone of the stanza to be encomiastic and optimistic, and 830–1 are a 'summary priamel' that resumes the previous points and implies the existence of others unmentioned: see Parry, who provides the excellent parallel of *Ba.* 902–11, and Mueller-Goldingen 138–9, who notes the climactic adjectives and metaphors in two Pindaric parallels, *P.* 1.100 στέφανον ὕψιστον δέδεκται, *O.* 1.113–14 τὸ δ' ἔσχατον κορυφοῦται βασιλεῦσι; cf. also the structure of the praise in *I.* 5.44–50 τετείχισται δὲ πάλαι πύργος ὑψηλαῖς ἀρεταῖς ἀναβαίνειν. πολλὰ μὲν ... καὶ νῦν ... Given this structure, δέ in 831 should (in the absence of any clue that the participial phrase is concessive) be continuative, not adversative, so I believe that 832–3 is, in its surface meaning intended by the chorus, optimistic (as Parry argues). The sense is then 'has taken its stand (now) on its excellent crowns of war', implying in essence 'stakes its success in the coming battle on its military valour as proven by previous victories, won because of divine favour such as we see exemplified in other events'. Cf. one Σ: τὴν οὕτως μακαρίαν οὐκ ἀπεικὸς τοὺς ἐπελθόντας πολεμίους ἀπώσασθαι. The contrast with the terrible Ares of 784ff. and his separation from the crowns of joyful dancers (καλλιχόροις στεφάνοισι) is sharp and strained, and is meant to be felt as such. Pessimistic readings are also transmitted in Σ, νῦν ἐπὶ ξυροῦ ἔστηκεν and νῦν ἐν κινδύνοις ἄκροις ἔστηκεν, and such readings have been supported. I see no reason for an audience to think of the notion of the razor's edge and regard this as an arbitrary importation of meaning by the Σ. Pearson cites *Il.* 13.736 πάντηι γάρ σε περὶ στέφανος πολέμοιο δέδηε and suggests that the στέφανοι ἄρηιοι are 'the iron circles of the besiegers' force';[1] but 'on the verge of' for ἐπ' ἄκροις στεφ. does not produce a clear and sensible image. Bremer cites precedents from epic and Pindar (e.g., *Il.* 19.99 ἐϋστεφάνωι ἐνὶ Θήβηι, *O.* 8.32 Ἰλίωι μέλλοντες ἐπὶ στέφανον τεῦξαι) and notes Eur.'s use of στεφάνη for city-walls in *Hec.* 910 and *Tro.* 784, and so suggests that δέ in 830 is adversative and interprets 'but after all this good fortune, the city stands now on topmost crown of the walls', with the pessimistic implication that it is faced by a dire attack. But in this interpretation Ἀρηίοις seems to lack point (Bremer does not translate it); the metaphorical use of στέφανοι is not aided, as it is in both cited tragic passages by the crucial addition of πύργων (as also in *Ant.* 122 στεφάνωμα πύργων); and I doubt adversative δέ here (see also Mueller-Goldingen 137–9). So the optimistic interpretation is best, but it is a forced optimism, and there may be a secondary suggestion of danger (in the notion of standing upon a summit as well as

---

[1] By which he means, I suppose, the encirclement of the city by armed men; Bremer thinks Pearson imagines an Argive camp with walls, for which there is no place in this play. Cf. Mosch.'s paraphrase νῦν ἐπὶ μεγίστηι καὶ ἐσχάτηι πολιορκίαι τοῦ Ἄρεος ἔστηκεν and Thomas' κεκύκλωται νῦν ὑπὸ πολεμίων.

in the fate-tempting emphasis on continuous good fortune), just as the serpent-story also has its dark side, Cadmus' life its tragedies, and the Καδμείων βασιλῆας their toils.

834-1018: THIRD EPISODE

STRUCTURE AND FUNCTION

In Introd. IV, I argued that the self-sacrifice of Menoeceus should be regarded as an innovation. If that is correct, Eur. has not merely combined in one Theban play as many traditional elements as possible, but has chosen to make his play more complex by going beyond the tradition in the so-called Menoeceus-episode. The ensemble for the scene is created quickly, as the blind Tiresias is guided by his daughter and young Menoeceus to meet with Creon, who has waited on stage since the end of the second episode. After the entrance-speech (834-44, in function very like an entrance-monologue, since neither the daughter nor Menoeceus replies to Tir.'s addresses), there is a brief irregular dialogue of welcome (849-64, emphasizing politeness and a good omen). Then Tir. in two substantial rheseis (865-95, 930-59) provides an authoritative version of the intricate network of divine resentment: the first speech concentrates on the family of Laius and ends with a refusal to go on and reveal the requested prophecy; the second looks at the deeper past and the need to atone for Cadmus' founding act. In between (896-929) is a largely stichomythic passage in which Creon and Tir. argue first about revealing the prophecy and then about concealing it, with a further retarding ploy in 904-11. After Tir.'s departure, Creon elaborates his grounds for refusing to sacrifice his son (960-76), and in a hurried dialogue, mostly in antilabe (977-90), Men. appears to accept Creon's decision and prepares to flee. But as soon as Creon goes off, there is a surprising turn-around as Men. declares that he has deceived his father and will freely give his life as Tir. instructed (991-1012 or 1018).

The third episode is designed to disentangle the fate of the city from the fate of the family of Oedipus while further exploring the relative valuation of kinship, private interests, and the public good.[1] The danger to the city

---

[1] For a good discussion with a slightly different emphasis, see Foley's chapter on *Phoenissae*. She argues that the actions of the major male characters threaten to derail the mythical tradition of the salvation of Thebes, but that Menoeceus' action, like that of a *deus ex machina* placed in the middle of the drama, redirects the action to its traditional end.

becomes ever more prominent in teichoskopia, Joc.'s speech in the agon, and the sequence of choral odes. In this scene, σωτηρία for the city is the dominant theme (cf. 864, 890, 893, 898, 900, 910, 918, 952, 997). Citing the danger from the inherited communal guilt caused by Cadmus' slaying of the dragon (cf. first stasimon), Tir. provides a hope of salvation that is not dependent on the brothers (who have already rejected appeals to the good of the city), but on Creon and Menoeceus. The royal family is inescapably doomed, but the anger of Ares and Earth against the city, which threatens to be fatal only because of its present conjunction with the Labdacid guilt, can in fact be separately assuaged, allowing the city's fate to be separated from that of the brothers. Creon, used as a sensible foil to the rash Eteocles in the previous episode, is now tested in a parallel fashion and is shown to be almost equally lacking in self-knowledge and, in his own way, willing to sacrifice the city's interests for his own. The cordiality and patriotism of Creon is heavily marked in the opening of the scene to provide a stark contrast with his angry rejection of Tir. and of the city's need later in the scene (note esp. the echo of 560 in 952 and of 624b in 919). But Creon's preference for the salvation of his son is overturned by Men. himself (note 975 and esp. 989 vs. 997), as the apparent silent character and then pliant laconic interlocutor delivers himself of a brief but spirited rhesis infused with the idealism of innocent youth (note the contrast with the rancour and irony of the testament and 'farewell'-speech of Et. at the end of the previous episode). For him the interests of city and family come together (note 1003–4), and for him, unlike Et. and Pol., the rejection of exile can be combined with the safety of the city. He thus provides the key counter-example to faults of the three major male characters of the play, and his heroism, for the moment and for the duration of next ode and episode, should be regarded as effective, even decisive. Nevertheless, the isolation of this heroism in a naive youth, its location in a symbolic action which has no correspondence in contemporary political life, and the sordid final conclusion of the war with the Argives (see 1308–479n., 1427–79n.) retrospectively cast a bitter light on this self-sacrifice, just as the context of Iphigenia's free choice to die in *IA* creates an unbridgeable gap between her heroic gesture and the sordid political and military efforts it serves. The thematic connections and functions of the Menoeceus-scene described here are sufficient to rebut the orthodox criticism (made from Hermann onward) that it is an index of episodic composition without necessary relation to the remainder of the play. This criticism, like others made of the play, is based on an arbitrary notion of the 'proper' subject-matter of the play and a failure to recognize the writer's freedom to shape his audience's response by juxtaposition and counterpoint as much as by narrowly Aristotelian causal linkage in plotting.

The decision of Men. and, to a certain extent, the resistance of Creon are reminiscent of elements of the plot-pattern of human sacrifice, known esp. from *Hcld.*, *Hec.*, and *Erectheus* and later manipulated in *IA*. For study of this plot-type see the relevant chapters in the works of J. Schmitt, H. Strohm, and E. A. M. E. O'Connor-Visser, as well as Henrichs 'Human Sacrifice in Greek Religion'.[1] The cases of *Hcld.* and *Erectheus* are most relevant because they involve an invaded or besieged city state. What is remarkable in *Phoen.* is the strength and apparent decisiveness of Creon's opposition (if Erectheus opposed the sacrifice of his daughter, he was surely won over by Praxithea's speech, fr. 360; Clytaemnestra's opposition in *IA* is less successful because she is the mother) and the reduction of Men.'s role in the discussion of the demand as well as the brevity and isolation (only the chorus is present) of his acceptance of the sacrifice.[2] The earlier part of the scene plays on the general type-scene of the prophet scorned by the king and probably alludes in particular to earlier Theban plays such as *OT* (865–95n., 954–9n.) and *Ant.* (953n.). Such allusions reinforce the tragic theme that evils repeat themselves in similar forms from generation to generation.

834 action   as 836 δεῦρ' implies, the actor playing Tiresias has in one hand a staff (cf. 1539n.), perhaps recognizable as a seer's by some adornment (cf. the vase-painting in Roscher V.202, fig. 1, where Tir.'s staff has a small temple on top); he may have his other hand upon the shoulder of the extra playing his daughter, who precedes him (854 πάροιθε, 857 πρόβαινε) and carries in her hands the prophetic κλῆροι. Menoeceus is beside or behind Tir., but not yet assisting him. Cf. 845–9n. The daughter carries 'lots' of some kind (838n.). The tableau of daughter leading blind father is replayed on Tir.'s exit and then mirrored in the departure of Antigone and Oedipus at the end of the play.

834 πάροιθε   only here in tragedy is the plain adverb, unaccompanied by a gen., local rather than temporal in sense; cf. Homeric usage (*Il.* 6.319,

---

[1] See in general D. D. Hughes, *Human Sacrifice in Ancient Greece* (London and New York 1991), which does not add anything new so far as the literary representations are concerned.

[2] Given her interest in the social significance of ritual, Foley, 133–5, notes this deviation from the pattern and perhaps overemphasizes it. ('The Thebes of this play is a world that fails to perform its own sacrificial cure and hardly recognizes Menoeceus' gesture.' 'Menoeceus' secret gesture emphasizes his estrangement from his fellow men.') Dramaturgically, the isolation is necessary to the intrigue against Creon and the diminution of Et.'s responsibility for the city's safety; and there is acknowledgment from the Theban viewpoint in 1090–2.

etc.) and the unique local use of πάρος in Soph. *El.* 1502 σοὶ βαδιστέον πάρος.

θύγατερ not identified in the text as Manto, the name given by Σ. Manto is the name of a daughter of Melampous or Polyidus in Hes. fr. 136.5 M–W, and for the daughter of Tir. the name appears on an illustration of this episode on a 'Homeric' or 'Megarian' bowl of the late third century B.C. (Robert, *Oidipus* 1.452: London G104; the only certain illustration of Manto) and in Strabo and later sources; but Eur. presumably used the name in his lost *Alcmaeon B*, for she is the mother of the two children with whom Alcmaeon is reunited in that play.

835 ναυβάταισιν a high-style synonym for ναύτης affected by the tragedians (also Bacch. 17.48 and Lycophron) and rare in prose (Hdt. 1.143.2, Thuc. 1.121.3, 7.75.7, Plut. *Dio* 35.2, *Them.* 4.4). ναυτίλοισιν (L² or L¹ and Triclinius), though poetic in classical times, is commoner later and is a correction of corrupt ναύταισιν.

836 εἰς τὸ λευρὸν πέδον Tir. delivers this speech while slowly advancing from a visible position on the eisodos toward the centre-stage position where Creon has been waiting. There is a slight temptation to identify his detection of a 'smooth surface' with the transition from eisodos to orchestra, but the imagined physical conditions are created by the words and no inference should be made about the actual steepness or texture of the eisodos (845–9n.). Eur. is fond of forcefully marking the representation of old age by staging slow movement with comment on it: cf. *El.* 487–92, *Ion* 725–40, *Her.* 119–30.

838 κλήρους we have no other information about 'lots' of this kind, but the inference made by Barrett (on *Hipp.* 1057–8) is reasonable: 'evidently a note of some kind which the μάντις makes after observing the flight of birds; from the name κλῆρος I should suppose that he keeps a stock of them, recorded as occasion offers, and then when consulted takes one or more at random to use as the basis of his soothsaying.'[1] Cf. Pindar *P.* 4.190 μάντις ὀρνίχεσσι καὶ κλάροισι θεοπροπέων ἱεροῖς and the Latin use of *sortes*. On prophecy by lots in general see Ehrenberg, *RE* 13:2 (1927) 1451–504 (Losung). The props carried by the silent extra in this scene

---

[1] I suggest below (846n. at end) that Tir. might brandish the lots later in the scene, but he apparently does not actually pick one to interpret on the spot; it emerges during the speech 865–95 that he knows what is required by the gods. Helmbold would delete 838–40, asking how this action is possible for a blind man; the answer is partly supplied by *Ant.* 1001–4 and partly by the assumption that his daughter helps him (cf. *Ant.* 1012–14 and Sen. *Oed.* 301–83).

may have been small tablets of wood (with or without wax) or pieces of papyrus.[1]

840 θάκοισιν ἐν ἱεροῖσιν οὗ μαντεύομαι cf. *Ant.* 999–1000 παλαιὸν θᾶκον ὀρνιθοσκόπον ... ἵν' ἦν μοι παντὸς οἰωνοῦ λιμήν, *Ba.* 347 θάκους τοῦδ' ἵν' οἰωνοσκοπεῖ; Pausanias saw the οἰωνοσκοπεῖον Τειρεσίου καλούμενον on the citadel of Thebes, perhaps west of the palace of Cadmus and shrine of Semele, near the shrines of Ammon and of Tyche (9.16.1), whereas Manto's prophetic rock-seat (Μαντοῦς δίφρος) was at the Ismenion (9.10.3).

842 ἄστεως ὁδός 'path/journey through the city'; see on [1] οὐρανοῦ ... ὁδόν and cf. the metaphorical use in *Ion* 930 ἄλλων πημάτων κακὰς ὁδούς, *Or.* 633 διπλῆς μερίμνης διπτύχους ἰὼν ὁδούς.

844 πυκνὴν δὲ βαίνων ἥλυσιν 'proceeding with ⟨short and⟩ frequent steps', because of age, blindness, and weakness; Σ and Mosch. wrongly see an illusion to the length of the journey, treating πυκνήν as συνεχῆ (so too King: *continuum iter faciens*).

ἥλυσιν ἥλυσις is a Eur. coinage (also *Hec.* 67, *Her.* 1041), a back-formation from the root seen in ἔπηλυς, ἐνηλύσιος (Aesch. fr. 17.2), and in Hdt.'s περιήλυσις and ἐξήλυσις; in these words the eta is due to lengthening in composition.

845 Creon answers the question addressed to Menoeceus (841); this technique gives the impression that Menoeceus is to be a silent character, creating surprise when he finally does speak (*Contact and Discontinuity* 93).

846 εἰσώρμισαι transmitted ἐξ- cannot be correct, since it is Tir.'s arrival at a safe harbour that is described.[2] I do not find convincing

---

[1] See Robert, *JDAI* 23 (1908) 197, for speculation that on Homeric bowl *N* from London κλῆροι may be illustrated in Tir.'s left hand (perhaps with sacred fillets attached to them and hanging beneath Tir.'s hand; but the impression on the bowl is so unclear that interpretation is very uncertain). Cf. Séchan, 483 n. 1, who reports the suggestion of Svoronos that on this bowl the rectangular item seen a little way below Tir.'s hand is a box used for carrying the lots (but this rectangle receives quite a different interpretation from Robert 198–200). Three narrow, stiff lots (representing thin wooden ones?) are shown in the hand of Lachesis in two relief sculptures (in Madrid and Tegea) that go back to an original of the classical period: cf. *JÖAI* 6 (1903) 99 fig. 48 and Taf. 5–6; for the Madrid example see M. Robertson, *A History of Greek Art* (Cambridge 1975) 301–2.

[2] Out of context ἐξώρμισαι σὸν πόδα could mean 'you have launched your tread', but this could apply only to the outset of his journey and yields nonsense when combined with 'near to your friends' as in Craik's translation.

attempts to justify ἐξ- as merely intensifying: Wilam., *Herakles* III.25 n. 1, 'nur verstärkend' (cf. LSJ's 'hast come forth'); J. Jouanna, 'Remarques' 46–56, argues for the sense 'lance ton pied en avant', citing *Hel.* 1247 ἐς πόντον ὅσα χρή νέκυσιν ἐξορμίζομεν for an alleged conflation of ἐξορμίζω and ἐξορμάω. West and I have corrected to εἰσ-; the confusion of εἰς/ἐξ is easy in many medieval hands, but in this case the corruption goes back to antiquity, as Σ show (cf. *Text. Trad.* 59–60). Σ also had ΟΡΜΙΣΑΙ before them. The imperative interpretation does not fit the context. The aorist infinitive cannot well stand by itself, whether we translate with Wilam. 'Nahe ist es für deine Freunde, deinen Fuss ganz in den Hafen zu bringen' (an unidiomatic use of πέλας; more normal would be πέλας ... φίλοι γε σοί or φίλη στάσις (Stadtmüller)) or assume a harsh ellipsis of εἶ, 'you are close to your friends, so as to moor your foot'. Jouanna argues for ellipsis of εἶ followed by the imperative ἐξόρμισαι in asyndeton, but, apart from the dubious sense of ἐξόρμισαι, all his parallels (54 n. 28) show that with πέλας as predicate to an omitted copula Eur. would have used φίλοι as subject. The perfect indicative, restored in some *recc.* under the influence of Σ (τὸ ο ἀντὶ τοῦ ω), makes good sense if (with εἰσ- for ἐξ-) it is understood as 'have come into harbour' (i.e., have no more danger or long journey to face), which is consistent with Tir. continuing to move and then standing comfortably in one spot by 849. The verb εἰσορμίζω seems to occur elsewhere only in Xen. *Vect.* 8.3.2 and Plut. *Cimon* 12.6. Diggle (1990a) objects to this solution as involving an unwelcome middle form; he prefers Kvíčala's ἔσθ' ὁρμίσαι (*Listy filologické* 5 (1878) 171–2; *NJPP* 119 (1879) 533), 'you may now bring your foot to mooring close to your friends'.

λαβοῦ δ' αὐτοῦ, τέκνον Men. probably takes Tir. by the arm, guides him to his final position next to Creon, and releases his hold once Tir. has comfortably fixed the position of his staff and feet (at 904–5 Tir. has to ask where Men. is). It is tempting to see in this final assistance the point at which Tir. mounts the step(s) to the stage, as suggested by Paley and Jouanna; the existence of a low raised stage is by no means certain, but I regard it as more probable than not (cf. MacDowell on *Wasps* 1341), and climbing would give more point to the call for Men.'s help. But it is conceivable that Men.'s help is needed only *ad gradum stabiliendum post iter* (as I suggested in Teubner app.). Once Tir. is in position, perhaps he receives the κλῆροι from his daughter and is thus able to brandish them to reinforce lines like 865–7, 890, 903, 916, 922, 954–9.

847–8 ὡς πᾶσ' ἀπήνη πούς τε πρεσβύτου if sound, this phrase suggests a paratactic comparison: just as a woman descending from a cart (which was a normal form of transport for women and invalids) needs a helping hand from outside to step down (*El.* 998–9, 1004–6; *IA* 613–18), so an old man in walking needs help for any difficult or awkward movement (again the comment has more point if Tir. is in the process of climbing a step or two). The suggestion that ἀπήνη implies the woman about to dismount from a carriage was first made by E. Maltby (note on T. Morell, *Lexicon Graeco-prosodiacum*² (London 1824) s.v. πρεσβύτης) and accepted by Paley and Wilam.; Schaefer thought the sense was rather *senex, sive curru vehatur, sive pedibus incedat*. Roux (on *Ba.* 197–8) suggests that the compendious comparison implies rather 'just as a cart ⟨requires an outside force to move it⟩', χειρὸς θυραίας applying only to the old man; but this (partly antici- pated in Σ) is an even harsher compression than is assumed by Maltby. Many have found the comparison too compressed and allusive and have wished to emend (or in Dindorf's case, delete the difficulty entirely), but with no convincing result: Munro's στᾶσ' ἀπήνη leaves us with the allu- siveness of ἀπήνη but loses the appropriate universalizing force of πᾶσ' (which will be carried over to πούς) and the alliteration that characterizes the two phrases in 846; Hermann's παῖς ἔτ' ἀπτήν suggests rather an infant quite unable to walk than a toddler needing the help of an adult's hand. Jouanna ('Remarques'; also 'Texte et espace' 81–97) would interpret ἀπήνη as implying that Tir. is pushed uphill by Men., just as a cart sometimes needs to be pushed from behind on a hill; I do not believe that this inherently ridiculous gesture could have been used in tragedy (the illustration Jouanna offers is of drunken Silenus being pushed along by helpers).

κουφίσματα extant only here in classical Greek, later only in Menander fr. 782.2 K–T and in Crantor apud Plut. *Mor.* 114C, both in the quasi-medical sense of psychological alleviation (which is also the usual sense of later κουφισμός); Eur.'s concrete use of the verbal notion corresponds to the senses of κουφίζω affected in tragedy (121–2n.).

849 εἶἑν the internal aspiration is established by Apoll. Dysc. *Synt.* 318, 26 and Plut. *Mor.* 393B.

τί με καλεῖς the present is vivid, marking the continuing need, 'What is the need for which you summon(ed) me?' It is perhaps more gracious and complaisant than the imperfect (Valck.) τί μ' ἐκάλεις, which in the context of the parallel passage *El.* 1123 παῦσαι λόγων τῶνδ'. ἀλλὰ τί μ' ἐκάλεις, τέκνον; has an appropriately grudging and sceptical tone. But word-division has no ultimate authority in the tradition, and the imperfect is not certainly wrong.

850 οὔπω λελήσμεθ' 'not yet' here has, in my view, a colloquial tone of friendly irony.[1] Some deny the 'ironic' use of πω in tragedy and take

---

[1] Mueller-Goldingen, 142, regards the tone instead as condescending and believes the contrast between Creon's initial reception and his later abuse of Tir. is not as great as I suggest.

οὔπω here as simply 'not at all'. For the controversy see Jebb, Kamerbeek, and Dawe on *OT* 105 and Dawe, *Collation and Investigation of Manuscripts of Aeschylus* (Cambridge 1964) 122–3. The most likely cases of 'ironic' πω are *Hec.* 1278 μήπω μανείη Τυνδαρὶς τοσόνδε παῖς, *OT* 594 οὔπω τοσοῦτον ἠπατημένος κυρῶ.

σύλλεξαι σθένος cf. [Pl.] *Ax.* 370e4 ἔκ τε τῆς ἀσθενείας ἐμαυτὸν συνείλεγμαι; see Bond on *Her.* 626 σύλλογον ψυχῆς λαβέ.

851 πνεῦμ' ἄθροισον the common term for 'catch one's breath' is ἀναπνέω (ἀναπνοή); Eur.'s phrase perhaps has a medical colouring, as both ἀθροίζω and συλλέγω are used in medical writers of gatherings of bodily humours or fluids.

αἶπος ἐκβαλὼν ὁδοῦ 'casting off the ⟨effects of⟩ the steepness of the path'. αἶπος is used by Aesch. and later poets in the sense 'mountain peak', but Eur.'s two uses (here and *Alc.* 500 σκληρὸς γὰρ [sc. ὁ ἐμὸς δαίμων] αἰεὶ καὶ πρὸς αἶπος ἔρχεται) owe something to medical language: cf. Hipp. *Epid.* 7.107 ἦν ... καὶ ἀσθματώδης πρὸς αἶπος εἴ ποτε ἴοι, *Morb.* 2.51 καὶ ὅταν ὁδοιπορήσηι ἢ δράμηι, ἄλλως τε καὶ πρὸς αἶπος, ἄσθμά νιν καὶ ἀσθένεια ἐπιλαμβάνει, 2.52, 2.70, *Int.* 44. In the context there is no difficulty in perceiving the extended meaning 'effects of steepness' (namely, weakness and shortness of breath: so already Hsch. α 2054 κάματος and Σ). It is quite unnecessary to claim, with Pearson, that ἐκβαλών has a weakened sense 'forget' either here or in the prose passages he cites. As for the tradition, αἶπος is certainly what Eur. wrote; ἄπος/ἆπος in MBO+ and Eust. may be an early minuscule error; it is unclear whether there is a connection between the dialectically or metrically impossible κᾶπος/κάπος of *recc.* and κάπος (a ghost-word?) = πνεῦμα cited by ancient etymologists in relation to Homeric ἐκάπυσσεν (see Schwartz's app. to Σ851 and Frisk and Chantraine s.v. καπνός).

852 κόπωι παρεῖμαι loss of control of the joints is commonly pinpointed as an effect of sleep, death, exhaustion, or illness; cf. *Hipp.* 199 λέλυμαι μελέων σύνδεσμα φίλων, *Ba.* 634–5 κόπου δ' ὕπο / διαμεθεὶς ξίφος παρεῖται.

γοῦν 'selects a single instance in confirmation of what precedes' (Pearson; cf. Denniston's second explication, *GP²* 454). A blunder in some *recc.*, and later Hermann's false report of a γρ-variant in M, spurred unjustified doubts of γοῦν. τὰ γόνατα in Σ is probably the paraphraser's clarification, not evidence of a different reading. Another cause for doubt of γοῦν derived from the placement of the postpositive monosyllable in position 6, but such placement is now accepted even in Eur., who otherwise avoids a medial caesura without elision (P. Maas, *Greek Metre* (Oxford 1962) ¶137; Descroix, 284–7).

853 δεῦρ' ἐκκομισθείς in other instances of this juncture (*Tro.* 294, *IT*

1206), ἐκ- means 'out of the palace (tent, etc.)', but ἐκ- may also be applied to the movement from Attica (cf. *Hel.* 1182-3 γῆς τῆσδ' ἐκκομισθεῖσ'). Herwerden's εἰσκομ- (proposed in his note on *OT* 1007) is easy but not clearly superior.

τῆς πάροιθεν ἡμέρας i.e., before the Argives had encircled the city; Eur. tends to the minor detail of plausibility rather than, for instance, leaving it to be assumed that as a priest Tir. was given safe conduct.

854-5 cf. Σ854 ἐπίτηδες πρὸς ἔπαινον τῶν Ἀθηναίων ἀνακεχρόνισται, τέσσαρσι γενεαῖς προὔχοντα τοῦ Θηβαϊκοῦ πολέμου. The judgment that flattery of the Athenian audience is involved has been echoed in modern times, but the more important effect (and presumably purpose) of the anachronism is to allude to the story-pattern of patriotic self-sacrifice, evoking Eur.'s own *Erectheus* in order to provide a specific intertextual standard to be applied to Creon and Menoeceus. Understood as the citation of a model, this passage fits very well the view that the sacrifice of Men. is an innovation; but if the story were already known, the effect of citing a parallel would not be greatly different. Tir.'s contrived role in the success of the Athenians also gives extra authority to his prophecy for Thebes. There is no justification for detecting an allusion to a contemporary Athenian victory (Spiro, 6 n. 3, suggested that at Cyzicus, Xen. *Hell.* 1.1.14-19).

855 οὗ the antecedent is either δορός or πόλεμος (cf. 1048-9 καλλίνικος ὢν αἰνιγμάτων, *IT* 12 τὸν καλλίνικον στέφανον Ἰλίου); not adverbial 'where', as Σ (followed by Craik).

858 ἐθέμην instantaneous aorist, as elsewhere in welcoming a good omen (S. *El.* 668 ἐδεξάμην τὸ ῥηθέν, *Ion* 561).

καλλίνικα σὰ στέφη cf. *IT* 12 (just cited) and *Alexandros* fr. 43.41 Snell καλλίνικ' ἔχων στέφη. On the repetition of καλλίνικος in the play, 1048n.

859-60 ἐν . . . κλύδωνι . . . δορὸς Δαναϊδῶν the metaphor is perhaps not very lively by the date of *Phoen.* Imagery of ship of state and storm forms a major system in *Septem*, culminating in 795-6 πόλις ἐν εὐδίαι τε καὶ κλυδωνίου / πολλαῖσι πληγαῖς ἄντλον οὐκ ἐδέξατο (see Hutchinson on *Se.* 62-4, and in general Collard on *Su.* 267-9a). Eur.'s other uses are *Su.* 473-5 (κλύδων δορός), *IT* 316 κλύδωνα πολεμίων, *Ion* 60 πολέμιος κλύδων.

860 μέγας Θήβαις ἀγών μέγας (μείζων, μέγιστος) (ὁ) ἀγών (ἐστι) is an idiom of formal prose and colloquial speech (Arist., Plato com.), used in four other places by Eur. (as well as twice in *IA* and once in *Rhes.*), but absent from Aesch. and Soph. The sense of ἀγών in this idiom varies from 'struggle' or 'contest' to 'stakes of the struggle' and 'risk, danger of the struggle'.

861 μὲν οὖν marks the transition to and resumption of the topic postponed at 850.

κοσμηθεὶς ὅπλοις elsewhere this combination implies either 'dressing up' (as in a costume: maidens in Hdt. 4.180.3–4) or conspicuous adornment (*Phil.* 1063–4 σὺ τοῖς ἐμοῖς / ὅπλοισι κοσμηθεὶς ἐν Ἀργείοις φανῆι;; Xen. *Hipparch.* 1.25), but here and in 1359 (and *Rhes.* 993) the phrase is an artificial periphrasis for ὁπλισθείς; cf. also 797bis χαλκῶι κοσμήσας.

862 πρὸς ἀλκὴν . . . Μυκηνίδα The range of possible meanings of ἀλκή ('defence', 'strength', synonym for μάχη) and the ambiguity of the adj. serving as equivalent of a genitive (subjective or objective?) leave the precise sense indeterminate: perhaps 'to do battle against the Argives', though 'to the battle with the Argives' or 'to face the warlike strength of the Argives' (Craik: 'against Mykenaian might') cannot be ruled out.

863 ἐπέσταλκ' the resultative perfect emphasizes that the obligation lies firmly on Creon; similarly in prose this perfect marks a written message as a permanent trace of a communication.

865–95 Having prepared the audience for Tir.'s hostility to Et. (865–7 answer precisely to the prediction of Et. in 771–3) and displayed the cordiality that holds between Creon and the seer, Eur. now artfully manipulates Tir.'s revelation for maximum effects of retardation and reversal. The retarding moment is provided by Tir.'s insight into the past (867–79) and future (880–5). The review of past troubles, and of the errors made by those involved, makes the present crisis seem more desperate and underscores the need for an extraordinary measure to avoid the destruction of the city. Repeated reminders of the unwelcomeness of Tir.'s advice (878–9, 885, 886–8) lead finally to a reversal in which Tir. abandons the effort to convey his authoritative recommendation. This sequence may be viewed as a deliberate elaboration and variation of the depiction of the unwilling prophet in *OT* (see Mueller-Goldingen, 147). These functions of the speech (which follow naturally on the deliberately protracted opening of the scene) are seriously damaged by Fraenkel's proposal to remove 869–80 and 886–90 as the work of an interpolator. The reduced speech would feature a very clumsy transition from 868 to 881 (one would expect at least 'and on this day' or 'and now' to balance πάλαι) and a no less disturbing shift from the hopeful reticence of 885 εἰ μή ... τις to the sense of defeat in 891. Such a change of mind within a space of only seven lines is poorly motivated. Fraenkel's objections to 869–80 are all concentrated in 869–71 and 878–80: (1) the detail of 869 has, he claims, no proper place here; (2) 870 is judged to be an imitation of *OC* 552 and therefore post-Euripidean; (3) θ' in 870 is taken to be a meaningless filler; (4) the import of 871 is questioned; (5) transmitted ἅ in 878 seems to him syntactically indefensible; (6) 880 anticipates the mutual fratricide. These points (and two additional ones adduced by Reeve: see on 868) are answered in the notes below. Even the cumulative force of the separate weak or doubtful objections that may remain do not seem to me to outweigh the positive contribution of the passage and the evidence of Euripidean mannerisms within it. See also on 886–90.

867 γάρ introduces the following sentences as substantiation of the stated intention to inform: Denniston, *GP²* 59 (2).

868 'τεκνώθη 'was furnished with a child', an unusual sense that reflects Euripidean mannerism, as in *Her.* 6–7 οἳ Κάδμου πόλιν τεκνοῦσι παίδων παισίν (see Bond).

βίαι θεῶν a reminiscence of 18 δαιμόνων βίαι; other reminiscences of the prologue follow (869 ≈ 53–4, 59; 870 ≈ 61–2; 871–3 ≈ 64–5; 875–7 ≈ 66–7). Such repetition should be viewed as a device that collaborates with the perspective of the choral odes in emphasizing the weighty continuity of evil from distant past to present day. Reeve, 459, argues that Fraenkel's deletions may be perfected by assigning 868 as well to the interpolator. He sees an inconsistency between Tir.'s two explanations of Thebes' troubles (Laius' disobedience in this line and speech, Cadmus' slaying of the dragon in 930ff.). But the latter explanation answers a different question (Creon's 'why me and my son?'), and the combination of motifs is in fact intended (834–1018n., 886–90n.). Reeve also suggests that the use of μέλεον in an iambic trimeter here is a stylistic mistake of an ignorant interpolator. The word is, to be sure, predominantly used in lyric, but the emotional ὦ μέλεος first appears in trimeters in *Or.* (no less than four times; the only precedent is in troch. tetr. at *Pers.* 733) and fr. 517 (*Meleager*, probably a late play) has Μελέαγρε, μελέαν γάρ ποτ' ἀγρεύεις ἄγραν, discounted by Reeve because the use is forced by the etymology.[1] It is not unreasonable to allow that at the date of *Phoen.* Eur. himself could have used μέλεον in a trimeter, intending it to express sympathetic emotion.

869 μητρί 'for his (Oed.'s) mother' in context is perfectly understandable; the kinship word relies for its interpretation upon the knowledge of the audience (137n.). It presents no problem that taken out of context the phrase could mean 'for his (Laius') mother'. On the propriety of mentioning this event here, see next note. Paley deleted 869 alone, mainly for false reasons of numerical equality of passages.

870 θ' I understand this as co-ordinating νοσεῖ ... ἥδε γῆ with αἱ ... διαφθοραί (sc. εἰσιν); that is, Tir. highlights two areas of trouble, the begetting and birth of Oed. and the (patricide and) incest that followed

---

[1] Cf. Antiphanes' use in playful paronomasia in a line that also contains a lyric compound with Doric alpha: fr. 207.8–9 K–A ἀνθεσιπότατα μέλεα μελέοις ὀνόμασιν / ποιοῦσιν.

from it, and the self-blinding and the consequent imprisonment of Oed. and cursing of his sons. Mention of incest in 869 is appropriate because it was the crime that actually induced the self-blinding as opposed to another punishment solely for the killing of Laius. A theological import is ascribed to the blinding, so that the sons' response to it acquires an element of religious defiance or disobedience, parallel to Laius', in contrast to the purely psychological and secular terms in which Joc. described her sons' error. With proper enunciation it would be clear that θ' is not co-ordinate with τ' in 869; for such a sequence of non-related τε's cf., e.g., *Cycl.* 292–5, *Hipp.* 405–6, 927–8. There is no compelling need to change to δ' (so, before P's reading was known, Valck., inverting 870 and 871, and Paley, deleting 869). Nor, if the above interpretation is accepted, need we consider the text lacunose (Kirchhoff thought several verses missing after 869). The whole verse is very similar to *OC* 552 τὰς αἱματηρὰς ὀμμάτων διαφθοράς. Fraenkel judged the concept of blinding to be more organic to the passage of Soph. than to this one and concluded that this line is an imitation of *OC* 552 and hence post-Euripidean.[1] This argument ignores the possibility that both authors may have imitated a single earlier source, and it under-values the significance of the blinding in this play as a marker of Oed.'s disaster (61–2, 327, 377 [?], 763–4, 1088, 1531–5, 1539–40, 1549, 1562–4, 1613, 1686, 1708). The line features two Eur. mannerisms that should not facilely be ascribed to an interpolator (who would have been more likely merely to imitate his source in Soph.). Eur. in general affects adjs. in -ωπ- (F. Sommer, *ABAW* n.F. 27 (1948) 6), and αἱματώψ/αἱματωπός in particular are exclusively Euripidean words (with reinforcing etymological play, as here, in *Her.* 933 (ὄσσοις) and in fr. 870 (ὄμμα); also *Andr.* 978, *Or.* 256) until late Greek (Plut. *Mor.* 565c; an ostrakon, *TrGF* adesp. 737.8). δέργματα for ὄμματα is likewise peculiar to Eur. (66n.). Accepting this line as Euripidean, I do not see any difficulty in supposing that Soph. imitated it, characteristically substituting less mannered diction.

871 θεῶν σόφισμα κἀπίδειξις Ἑλλάδι almost a hendiadys, 'a subtle contrivance of the gods to give a lesson to Greece'. The blinding is a reminder to all of Oed.'s discovery of his unintentional crimes, and thus of the 'blindness' to the true meaning and τέλος of their actions that afflicts all human beings and marks their inferiority to gods. The coincidences of Oed.'s life, as shown for instance in *OT*, can be well understood as a subtle

---

[1] Some earlier critics had debated the priority of the two lines, but the issue was confused by the nineteenth-century theory that *OC* was written and circulated long before Soph.'s death and thus available to Eur. when he wrote *Phoen.*

contrivance of the gods, in which his success and prosperity and apparent understanding of the nature of man set him up for an exemplary fall that underscores not the particular failings of one man but the ignorance and fragility of all that is human (cf. *OT* 1186ff. ἰὼ γενεαὶ βροτῶν κτλ.). Moreover, when Oed.'s fall is viewed in this way, his sons' attempt to conceal him becomes an act of transgression against the gods. I thus disagree with Fraenkel, who (like Valck.) objects that the blinding is no σόφισμα ('bedürfte es doch keiner besonderen Erfindungskraft, keines besonders gescheiten oder listigen Einfalls') and conceives ἐπίδειξις so narrowly that it is held to be inapposite since Oed. is not physically displayed to Greece (see below).

θεῶν σόφισμα fr. 972 πολλαῖσι μορφαῖς οἱ θεοὶ σοφισμάτων / σφάλλουσιν ἡμᾶς κρείσσονες πεφυκότες is relevant; cf., in a different sense, *IT* 380 τὰ τῆς θεοῦ ... σοφίσματα. Cf. 65n.

κἀπίδειξις 'a visible demonstration', so conspicuous that it affects not only actual witnesses (as Fraenkel wrongly insisted) but also those who only hear of the event; cf. Ixion in Pindar *P.* 2.21–4, whom the gods compel to utter, in his exemplary punishment, a maxim for all mankind, though mankind will know of the advice only through indirect report. For ἐπίδειξις cf. Thuc. 6.31.4 εἰς τοὺς ἄλλους Ἕλληνας ἐπίδειξιν ... τῆς δυνάμεως καὶ ἐξουσίας; Lys. 18.13 αὐτῶι καλὴν εἶναι τὴν ἐπίδειξιν καὶ πρὸς τοὺς πολίτας καὶ τοὺς ξένους; Lycurg. *Leocr.* 102 ἐπίδειξιν ποιούμενοι πρὸς τοὺς Ἕλληνας ὅτι τὰ κάλλιστα τῶν ἔργων προηιροῦντο. ἐπίδειξις occurs here alone in extant tragedy (in comedy, *Clouds* 269), but a -σις noun of straightforward meaning is hardly unexpected in Eur.; similarly, ἀπόδειξις occurs only in *Hipp.* 196 and twice in comedy. The latter is a variant here in MB+, but 'revelation' or 'proof' is inferior in sense.

872 ἃ συγκαλύψαι the relative vaguely resumes all the shocking events just referred to and the verb alludes here not only to physical concealment of the blinded Oed., but to the obscuring of memory of the past by silence (cf. ἔκρυψαν and ἀμνήμων in 64; *Prom.* 522–3 τόνδε [λόγον] δ' οὐδαμῶς καιρὸς γεγωνεῖν, ἀλλὰ συγκαλυπτέος).

χρόνωι 'by the passage of time'; as suggested above, the ἐπίδειξις did not depend solely on display of Oed., but on the prevalent talk about him, which the sons hoped would gradually die away if no further reminder were given. χρόνωι is confirmed against Wakefield's σκότωι by 64–5, by the sense of this context, and by the following lines: the prolonged imprisonment (οὐ διδόντες, not δόντες in 875) finally exasperated the old man so much that he cursed them.

873 ὡς δή ironical, expressing Tir.'s disapproval of their plan and branding it as futile (Denniston, *GP²* 230).

ὑπεκ- is used of escaping the doom sanctioned by the gods, which includes both the death of the Labdacids (predicted even before the curse: cf. 20) and the exemplary display of Oedipus' fate; not ὑπερ- (RAa, Zakas, Mueller-Goldingen 144 n. 7), of prevailing over or against the gods (578n.).

874 ἀμαθῶς Tir.'s judgment echoes Joc.'s criticisms of her sons' folly (452–3, 460, 529–30, 569–70, 584–5).

γέρα the plural is less common than the singular in tragedy and occurs only here in Eur., so displacement by γέρας (MBHO+) was very easy (same corruption at *Prom.* 82, 107); the generalizing plural is also apt in sense (cf. *Prom.* 82, 107, 229, 439, *OC* 1396). The dishonour is vaguely alluded to here and in 877 ἠτιμασμένος; the specificity of *Thebaid* fr. 3 (the wrong cut of meat) is avoided.

877 νοσῶν τε καὶ ... ἠτιμασμένος Tir. expresses as a co-ordinate pair what Joc. seemed to express as cause and effect: see on 66 πρὸς δὲ τῆς τύχης νοσῶν.

878 Long a vexed passage for the critics, this line now seems securely established except for the first letters.[1] The omission of οὐ at some point in the tradition led to metrical adjustment (τί δρῶν ὁποῖα), to false replacement of οὐ (in Harleianus 6300), and to unidiomatic supplement τί μὴ δρῶν. But οὐ is rhetorically necessary in both participial cola,[2] the *variatio* τί ... ποῖα is well paralleled (*Andr.* 299 τίν' οὐκ ἐπῆλθε, ποῖον οὐκ ἐλίσσετο; Fraenkel cites Headlam–Knox on Herodas 6.74–8 for a collection of exx.), and the hiatus after τί seems adequately justified, even though this is the only tragic instance of τί οὐ that is extant. τί οὖν is extant nine times in tragedy (in Eur. only twice, *Hec.* 820 and *Telephus* 147.37 Austin) and τί εἶπας twice (only in Soph., *Trach.* 1203, *Phil.* 917).[3] Thus within the line there is no need for desperate measures like Porson's unstylish τίν' οὐ δρῶν. As for the beginning of the line, the ἃ of ἀγώ would have to be a vague relative comprising the actions just referred to and would serve as

---

[1] Helmbold unjustifiably deletes 878–9 from the context because of the unmetrical corrupt form of the verse and the similarity of 879b to 1331b.

[2] Cf. (possibly in imitation of our line) Ach. Tat. 5.22.4 τί γὰρ οὐ λέγουσα, τί δὲ οὐ ποιοῦσα τῶν ἀρέσαι δυναμένων; Eust./Eumathius 10.10.2 τί μὲν οὐ λέγουσαι, τί δὲ οὐ πράττουσαι.

[3] Compare the distribution of these phrases in comedy: over sixty instances of τί οὖν, about a dozen of τί οὐ (*Knights* 1207, *Wasps* 213, etc.), and only one of τί εἶπας (*Thesm.* 902, with Eur. speaking). For instances of τί in hiatus in Aesch. and Soph. cf. Friis Johansen–Whittle on A. *Su.* 306.

a loose adverbial acc. ('in regard to which') or acc. object of an action implied by the participial phrases ('do and say ⟨to ameliorate⟩ which'). Similarly, the mss at *Andr.* 660 present ἁγὼ προνοίαι τῆι τε σῆι κάμηι, with ἁ apparently 'in regard to which' or object of the action implied by προνοίαι (Stevens *ad loc.* defends both passages as instances of adv. 'wherefore', like the singular ὅ (cf. 155n.)). The two passages should be treated in the same way. I hesitantly print ἁγώ, but concede that κἀγώ (King here, Kirchhoff there) may be right: it is much easier to understand, and not a big change (for the disappearance from the tradition of a word written in full but requiring crasis, 476n.). In any case, ἁ should either be accepted as Euripidean or emended, not dismissed, with Fraenkel, as the impossible Greek of an interpolator.

879 εἰς ἔχθος ἦλθον 'became an enemy of', implying a mutual feeling of enmity. The γρ-variant εἰς ὄχλον looks superficially idiomatic but is inferior. Elsewhere we find δι' ὄχλου εἶναι/γενέσθαι (Thuc. 1.73.2, *Eccl.* 888, [Pl.] *Alc.* I 103a3); and for some words idioms with διά and εἰς coexist (*Or.* 757 διὰ φόβου γὰρ ἔρχομαι vs. 361 above, εἰς φόβον τ' ἀφικόμην). But the noun with εἰς normally implies an emotion of the subject or at least a mutual emotion, whereas with ὄχλον the emotion would be solely that of the 'object'. For Tir. advising or warning the sons of Oed., cf. Stesichorus 222 *PMGF* (Introd. IV p. 26 n. 1).

880: on anticipation of the mutual fratricide (cited by Fraenkel as an objection to Eur. authorship), cf. 765n.

αὐτόχειρ 'wrought by kindred hands', cf. *Med.* 1281 αὐτόχειρι μοίραι κτενεῖς;, *Ant.* 172 αὐτόχειρι σὺν μιάσματι (cf. *Ant.* 1175–6). For αὐτο- in compounds implying slaying of kin cf. also αὐτοφόνος, αὐτοκτόνος, αὐθέντης, with Fraenkel on *Ag.* 1091ff, 1573, Hutchinson on *Se.* 734–41.

881 νεκροὶ περὶ νεκροῖς cf. 1195 below and A. fr. 38 ἐφ' ἅρματος γὰρ ἅρμα καὶ νεκρῶι νεκρός, / ἵπποι δ' ἐφ' ἵπποις ἦσαν ἐμπεφυρμένοι, with refs. for polyptoton given on 536–8 above; also *Ant.* 1240 κεῖται δὲ νεκρὸς περὶ νεκρῶι. This line is imitated in a late anonymous poem, *Anth. gr.* 15.19.7 νεκροὶ δ' ἔκειντο περὶ νεκροῖς πεπτωκότες; cf. Philostr. maj. *Imag.* 2.29.2 τὰ μὲν δὴ ἐν τῶι πεδίωι νεκροὶ ἐπὶ νεκροῖς. The variation in prosody in νεκροί/νεκροῖς is an artistic device: *Ant.* 1240, *IT* 3 Ἀτρεύς/Ἀτρέως, *OC* 442 πατρός/πατρί, 883 ὕβρις/ὕβρις, *Phil.* 296 πέτροισι πέτρον (with Jebb's note); for lyric instances, Davies on *Trach.* 1005 (with Addendum).

882 μείξαντες βέλη probably 'having joined weapons in battle against each other', cf. LSJ s.v. μείγνυμι II.1, a poetic usage, but rare in tragedy (*OC* 1046–7 Ἄρη μείξουσιν). The more picturesque sense 'having produced a confused heap of weapons' cannot be ruled out. Markland and Earle proposed μέλη (accepted by Craik; for the error cf. *Ba.* 25), but the parallel passages cited on 881 do not support such a narrowing of focus upon the jumbled limbs of the corpses. (Nauck said of this verse *abesse mallem* but did not say why.)

883 γόους δώσουσι for δίδωμι in the sense 'produce, occasion' Pearson compares *IA* 585 (Paris) ἔρωτά τ' ἔδωκας and 641 above (but there the construction with pred. adj. makes some difference).

884 συγκατασκάπτηι a rare verb (add Strabo 12.4.3 to LSJ's four citations); elsewhere συγ- implies 'together with' (so too Lycophr. *Alex.* 222 συγκατασκάπτην) and Craik translates 'will be destroyed with them' (sc. the dead soldiers of 881–3), but here the prefix is probably intensifying, 'demolish utterly' (likewise, much later, in *Christ. Pat.* 2099). The prophetic present vividly pictures the terrible outcome: see Fraenkel on *Ag.* 126.

πόλις vocative πόλι (a variant here and at *Andr.* 1) seems to be confined to lyric passages (*Andr.* 1176, *Acharn.* 971, Arist. fr. 112.1 K–A, Eupolis fr. 316.1 K–A) except for com. adesp. 340 Kock; nominative used for vocative is common in ὦ πόλις and ἰὼ πόλις and is normally transmitted without variant in indifferent locations, as at verse-end *Tro.* 45, *OC* 108, *Acharn.* 75, *Thesm.* 839. So it seems more probable that πόλι is a clarifying correction of a scribe than a rare survival of truth here and in *Andr.* 1.

885 τις πείσεται Porson left τις δυστυχῆι at verse-end in 403 above, but suggested a transposition here (λόγοις τις τοῖς ἐμοῖσι πείσεται) to remove the long 9th element (JD notes that the transposition also produces a more natural position for τις). More likely, this is an acceptable licence when the 9th element is a monosyllabic enclitic: cf. *Andr.* 230 κακῶν γὰρ μητέρων, *El.* 275 οὐ γὰρ νῦν ἀκμή, *Tro.* 1182 πολύν σοι βοστρύχων; Descroix, 330–1, West, *Greek Metre* 85.

886–90 To accompany his deletion of 869–80 (argued against above), Fraenkel also ascribes these five lines to a *Bearbeiter*.[1] His grounds are weak: only the unusual use of πρῶτον in 886 should cause any pause, whereas his complaints about the alleged emptiness of expression in 887, about the unimpressive usage of δαιμονῶντας in 888 (when compared to *Se.* 1001), and the alleged lack of function of the lines are too subjective to have significant force. The passage serves to introduce, in a manner designed to postpone the revelation, the different natures of the conditions governing Thebes' possible disaster: the brothers' behaviour is a necessary condition of doom, but not a sufficient condition, since it must be conjoined to the city's failure to appease Earth and Ares.

886 πρῶτον the sense must be 'first choice', 'best possible course' (Σ πρωτεῦον, αἱρετώτατον), which is not clearly paralleled in tragedy,

[1] 886–8 were already deleted as 'very strange' by Helmbold, who would emend 890 to οὐκ ἔστιν κτλ.

though πρῶτον in fr. 572.1–2 ἕν ἐστι πάντων πρῶτον εἰδέναι †τουτί†, / φέρειν τὰ συμπίπτοντα μὴ παλιγκότως could well be 'best' or 'most desirable' rather than 'most important' (note Nauck's doubt: 'πρῶτον vide an in κρεῖσσον mutandum sit'; but the two passages may defend each other).[1] The related sense 'first in importance' is found (*Andr.* 241 οὐ γυναιξὶ ταῦτα πρῶτα πανταχοῦ; *Med.* 475, *Hec.* 350, *Ba.* 275, *Melan. Desm.* 8 Page = fr. 6.12 von Arnim), and both 'second-best' and 'second in importance' are well-established meanings of δεύτερος (*OT* 282, *Hipp.* 508, *Andr.* 373, *Tro.* 218, fr. 250). The notion of 'first choice' is implicit in the idiom δεύτερος πλοῦς, and the closest parallel to πρῶτον here comes from a Platonic passage in which that idea is present: *Politicus* 297e3–5 καὶ τοῦτ' ἔστιν ὀρθότατα καὶ κάλλιστ' ἔχον ὡς δεύτερον, ἐπειδὰν τὸ πρῶτόν τις μεταθῆι τὸ νυνδὴ ῥηθέν; cf. 300c2 δεύτερος πλοῦς, 303b3 πολὺ πρῶτόν τε καὶ ἄριστον ('by far the first choice and best'). To doubt the authenticity of the five lines because of this rare but understandable usage seems extreme. The best conjecture is Herwerden's λῷστον (1894), which West (1990) would improve to λῷον; but it is hard to see why this would be corrupted to πρῶτον.

ἦν 'it would be', 'it would have been', an imperfect of unfulfilled obligation in the impersonal expression: cf. ἦν ... καλόν in *Laws* 744b1, quoted on 889; also *fuit* in Ovid (in footnote).

886–7 τῶν Οἰδίπου μηδένα πολίτην μηδ' ἄνακτ' εἶναι χθονός in context this sounds as if it is limited to the two sons of Oed., though τῶν Οἰδίπου could be taken to refer to all his offspring; if 1590–1 (see note) are supposed to refer back to these lines, then Creon has treated τῶν Οἰδίπου as if it were τῶν περὶ (ἀμφὶ) τὸν Οἰδίπουν. Tir. is also making a stronger claim than anyone has made before: that in order to preserve Thebes the brothers should both be in exile (no longer a πολίτης). Such advice makes even more understandable the hostile reaction alluded to in 879.

μηδ' though οὐδέ/μηδέ after a preceding negative often has climactic force, 'nor even', it sometimes co-ordinates items in which the second is *a fortiori* ruled out by the negation of the first, 'nor (much less)': cf. *Alc.* 549–50 οὐ πρέπει θοινωμένους / κλύειν στεναγμῶν οὐδὲ λυπεῖσθαι ξένους,

---

[1] In Latin cf. Ovid *Met.* 9.618–19 nam primum, si facta mihi revocare liceret, / non coepisse fuit, coepta expugnare secundum est; Sen. *Phaedra* 140–1 honesta primum est velle nec labi via, / pudor est secundus nosse peccandi modum. This use of *primum* is just as rare as that of πρῶτον just described: it is not recognized by OLD and commentators cite no other instances. In both, however, 'second' is also expressed, as JD reminds me.

Hec. 277–8 μή μου τὸ τέκνον ἐκ χερῶν ἀποσπάσῃς / μηδὲ κτάνητε, Dem. 18.85 φαίνομαι τοίνυν ἐγὼ χάριτος τετυχηκὼς τότε, καὶ οὐ μέμψεως οὐδὲ τιμωρίας.

888 δαιμονῶντας 'driven by a possessing demon', in Tir.'s mouth a solemn term, reminiscent of the Aeschylean usages, *Choe.* 566 δαιμονᾷ δόμος κακοῖς, and esp. *Se.* 1001 (of the brothers) ἰὼ δαιμονῶντες ἄται; at a different level of style, (κακο)δαιμονάω may be more colloquial, 'be crazy', like μελαγχολάω (*Wealth* 372, Xen. *Mem.* 1.1.9, 2.1.5, Men. fr. 127 K–T). The plural participle follows by sense from τῶν Οἰδίπου μηδένα, reasserting the collaborative destructiveness of the two together.

889 ἐπεὶ δὲ κρεῖσσον τὸ κακόν ἐστι τἀγαθοῦ The vagueness of the explanation is a mark of resignation before an unmanageable problem. In this context, the reference of 'evil' and 'good' should be specific: 'but since the force of evil ⟨in this affair⟩ is stronger than that of good'. Σ cites *Il.* 1.576 (= *Od.* 18.404) ἐπεὶ τὰ χερείονα νικᾷ, 'since the worse ⟨of two possibilities⟩ is getting the upper hand'. For the pattern of thought in 886–890 cf. Plato *Laws* 744b1–4 ἦν μὲν δὴ καλὸν καὶ τἆλλα ἴσα πάντ' ἔχοντα ἕνα ἕκαστον ἐλθεῖν εἰς τὴν ἀποικίαν· ἐπειδὴ δὲ οὐ δυνατόν, ... δεῖ κτλ.

890 μηχανὴ σωτηρίας this half-line is shared by *Se.* 209, *Hel.* 1034, *Thesm.* 765, but it may have more force than a late Euripidean cliché, if an allusion to *Se.* is actually felt: in that play Et. is preoccupied with safeguarding the salvation of the city, here he is divorced from the issue and it is dominated by Tir. and Menoeceus.

891 ἀλλ' ... γάρ the particles function independently, and the intention expressed in ἄπειμι is comparable to the many cases where an imperative follows (Denniston, *GP*² 99).

891–2 οὔτ' ... τε Denniston, *GP*² 511, appears to favour οὔτε ... δέ (LZcZmZu) here, but I see no grounds for this preference, either in the quality of L as a witness or in the sense. With τε we have 'it is both unsafe for me to say this and bitter for them to comply', whereas δέ would probably suggest that the contrast between 'me' and 'them' is the chief point (for such a contrast of persons cf. *Or.* 292–3 εἰ μήτ' ἐκεῖνος ἀναλαβεῖν ἔμελλε φῶς, / ἐγὼ δ' ὁ τλήμων τοιάδ' ἐκπλήσειν κακά, with Willink's note approving δ'; and note editorial disagreements at *Trach.* 1153, *OC* 422, E. *Su.* 225). In 344–7 above there is a mild anacoluthon, a much longer first limb, and probably a general contrast between Joc.'s missed role as mother and Hismenus' missed role as ritual source. For emphatic οὐ preceding οὔτε Denniston 508 cites *Ant.* 763 and Pl. *Prot.* 360d6.

892 τοῖσι τὴν τύχην κεκτημένοις 'those who have acquired this gift of fortune' (with τύχη as in 897 and in 914 τὴν τύχην αὐτὸς καλεῖς) rather than 'diejenigen, welche das Schicksal (der Stadt) in der Hand haben' (Wecklein) or, even less likely, τῶι ἔχοντι τὴν τυραννίδα (Paley; cf. Σ).

893 φάρμακον σωτηρίας the objective gen. expresses the cure produced rather than, as more commonly, the disease cured (LSJ II.2 vs. I.2.b); likewise *Hel.* 1055 σωτηρίας ... ἄκος; Soph. fr. 302.1 σωτηρίας ... φάρμακα. Despite printing φάρμακον, Craik in her transl. and note wrongly treats the word as φαρμακόν, acc. of φαρμακός, a word which, despite modern preoccupations, is unattested in tragedy. Nauck judged this verse spurious, presumably as a false expansion and perhaps because of the repetition of σωτηρίας (but for salvation-theme see 834–1018n.).

894–5 εἷς γὰρ ὢν ... πείσομαι a variation of the consolation motif 'not you alone' (Stevens on *Andr.* 1041); cf. Pindar *Pae.* 9.21 (fr. 52k Maehler) ὀλοφύ⟨ρομαι οὐ⟩δέν, ὅ τι πάντων μέτα πείσομαι.

τί γὰρ πάθω; a colloquial idiom meaning 'What else am I to do?', 'What other choice do I have?', used as a mark of resignation also in *Hec.* 614 (parenthetic) and *Su.* 257 (conclusive, as here). γάρ is used because the question explains the tone or attitude of helplessness and resignation. For the origin of the idiom and a list of uses cf. Gomme–Sandbach on *Samia* 604 and *Phasma* 8, Stevens, *Colloquial Expr.* 57–8. The closest tragic parallels outside Eur. are *OC* 216 and [A.] *Se.* 1057. Mueller-Goldingen 146 thinks γάρ here should give a reason for refusing to reveal the prophecy and so takes τί γὰρ πάθω; to imply that Tir. is in fact certain that he will not have to suffer, any more than the others.

896–7 this brief use of antilabe accompanies physical action: Creon momentarily restrains Tir. with his hand.

897 μεῖνον· τί φεύγεις appears also in *Hel.* 548, *IA* 831 (cf. *Knights* 240, *Thesm.* 689).

ἡ τύχη σ' 'it is the ⟨terrible gift of⟩ fortune that is avoiding you...' (892n.). Σ wrongly paraphrases ἡ εὐτυχία φεύγει σε; the point is rather that Tir.'s silence would save Men. and that by detaining Tir. and forcing disclosure Creon is bringing the evil upon himself.

898 πολίταις καὶ πόλει the phrase is solemnly emphatic and perhaps reflects a cliché of ritual prayer: cf. *Eccl.* 414 ὡς τὴν πόλιν καὶ τοὺς πολίτας σώσετε, *Knights* 458 καὶ τῆι πόλει σωτὴρ φανεὶς ἡμῖν τε τοῖς πολίταις, *Lys.* 343 ῥυσαμένας Ἑλλάδα καὶ πολίτας, *OC* 1094–5 ἀρωγὰς μολεῖν γᾶι τᾶιδε καὶ πολίταις.

899 σὺ μέντοι for the emphatic particle after the pronoun, cf. Denniston, *GP*[2] 399; there is no need for an explicit contrast with τάχα (Blaydes σὺ νῦν ἀλλ' οὐχὶ).

900 deliberately recalls 560 ἢ πόλιν σῶισαι θέλεις.

901 δῆτα though postponed, emphasizes the interrogative tone of the whole line, as also in 909 (Denniston, *GP*[2] 271).

902 μᾶλλον the error μ' ἄλλο held sway in editions before Hartung, except for Porson. Patriotism, for Creon, is the supreme value, but not the only object of zeal; and the statement is more powerful without the specificity of μ' (⟨μ'⟩ ἔχειν Lenting).

903-4 the break in stichomythia is effective, reinforcing the pattern of twice delaying the revelation by self-interruption. The similarity of 903 to 911 is deliberate, and the digression in 905-10 needs 904 as an introduction: I would retain both lines (903-4 del. Zipperer; 904 susp. Nauck; 903 del. Diggle).

903 κλύοις ἄν an urbane potential opt. expressing consent or permission ('now you may hear'), a subclass of the use of pot. opt. for a softened command: cf. *Ion* 335, 1336 λέγοις ἄν, *IA* 863, etc.; K–G 1.233–4. κλύοις is probably aorist here: West, *BICS* 31 (1984) 174.

910 κλύων ... τῆς σωτηρίας 'hearing of the ⟨way to obtain⟩ salvation', the abstract noun, as often, having a pregnant sense; Wecklein's τῆι σωτηρίαι is unnecessary and rhetorically weaker. κλύων is here present, emphasizing Men.'s physical presence during the telling (cf. West, *BICS* 31 (1984) 176, 191 n. 25).

911-14 the stichomythia is again interrupted, reinforcing the long-awaited moment of revelation. Only 912 should be deleted; other interventions designed to restore stichomythia (911-12, 914 del. Nauck; 914 del. Paley, rewriting 912 for Creon) are misconceived.

911 θεσφάτων ἐμῶν ὁδόν the metaphor of the path may be rather trite by this date, but *Knights* 1014-15 ἄκουε δή νυν καὶ πρόσεχε τὸν νοῦν ἐμοί· / φράζευ 'Ερεχθείδη λογίων ὁδὸν κτλ. suggests that our whole line may be an echo of the solemn but clichéd language of oracle-mongers. Cf. also *Ag.* 1154 ὅρους ... θεσπεσίας ὁδοῦ, and the more general uses in *Hec.* 744 σῶν ὁδὸν βουλευμάτων, *Hipp.* 391 τῆς ἐμῆς γνώμης ὁδόν.

[912] The strongest argument against this line is the number and person of its verb: σώσαιμεν is clearly inappropriate, and σώσαιτε is hardly better, given ἄκουε, σ', σὸν, αἰτεῖς in the adjacent lines. Moreover, the line is superfluous in sense and an awkward appositive to ὁδόν, and the parallelism of two 3-line interruptions in the stichomythia is more likely than imbalanced interruptions (there are few suitable comparanda, but cf. *Med.* 59–66, divided 1:1:2:1:1:2). At least two theories of origin and corruption of 912 are available. (1) 864 may have been quoted in the margin and then more or less mechanically incorporated, with ἅ for τί; subsequently, a second-person version may have been produced, leading to the elimination of μάλιστα and the incorporation of Καδμείων (cf. 710); the reading of M and R resulted from conflation. (2) 912 may have been a deliberate (histrionic?) interpolation,[1] in the form found in most mss.

---

[1] So Fraenkel, *Beobacht. zu Arist.* 33 n. 2; West (1990) also argues that σώσαιτε was the primary reading.

(ἂν σώισαιτε Καδ. π.), and then in the written tradition conflation from 864 led to the version in M and R, and M's unmetrical reading was repaired in AaPRf. I prefer (1) because a deliberate interpolator had no need of Καδμείων and could easily have adjusted 864 to ἂν μάλιστα σώισειας πόλιν.

914 σὸν παῖδ', ἐπειδή the appositive is an emphatic acknowledgment of the horror, and ἐπειδή κτλ., spoken half as apology and half as accusation, here gives the reason why Tir. has revealed the truth (for ἐπειδή introducing the reason for making a statement cf. *Med.* 526–7 ἐγὼ δ', ἐπειδὴ καὶ λίαν πυργοῖς χάριν, Κύπριν νομίζω κτλ., *Hipp.* 946–7 δεῖξον δ', ἐπειδή γ' ἐς μίασμ' ἐλήλυθα, κτλ.).

915 τί φῄς; τίν' εἶπας τόνδε μῦθον for the disbelieving question expressing shock at information that the speaker has in fact understood, cf. *Contact and Discontinuity* 12–13 (where the examples from *Phil.* 1237 and *Ba.* 1032 show the same intensifying redundancy as here). Σ record an alternate version τί φῄς; ἐμὸν παῖδ' ἕνεκα γῆς σφάξαι θέλεις; Page and Snell (*Hermes* 87 (1959) 7–12) ascribe this to actors, Snell theorizing that 915 was so modified when the scene was performed without 916–27.[1] It could also be explained as a literal-minded reader/teacher's version, by someone who saw that Creon did understand what Tir. had said and thought 915 inconsistent with such understanding.

916 ἅπερ πέφηνε, ταῦτα· reading and punctuation are doubtful. If the whole line is one clause, then καί in κἀνάγκη is responsive, emphasizing the following phrase (not σε in particular). But the position of the ἅπερ-clause seems to me to fit better Hermann's punctuation after ταῦτα, and this also provides a sharper retort to Creon's objection. With this punctuation, I understand ἐστι, not εἶπον, as Hermann himself did, comparing *Prom.* 929 ἅπερ τελεῖται, πρὸς δ' ἃ βούλομαι λέγω.[2] On this view, ταῦτα must be supplied with δρᾶν, as occasionally elsewhere: fr. 572.4–5 ἀλλὰ ταῦτα γὰρ λέγειν / ἐπιστάμεσθα, δρᾶν δ' ἀμηχάνως ἔχει; cf. Soph.'s use of τὸ δρᾶν = 'the doing ⟨it⟩' in *OC* 442, *El.* 467, *Phil.* 118, 1421. As for the

---

[1] Before coming to the conclusion that the alternative version is spurious, Snell considers whether 915–27 might be the spurious version, highlighting some 'inconsistencies' of character and behaviour in Creon and Tir.; so too even more seriously Dos Santos Alves, pp. 93ff. In the end both concede that such arguments are in fact inappropriate and that the chorus-leader's comment on Creon's silence after 959 and Creon's use of δῆλον in 962 imply the presence of 915–27.

[2] To understand εἶπον, we must have Tir. take too literally Creon's questions in 915, which actually express shock and rejection rather than ask for clarification.

verb that follows ἅπερ, I no longer believe that πέφυκε can be retained, even doubtfully: it cannot be an emphatic way of saying 'be true' without a connotation of the naturalness and permanence (pre-existence) of the truth, which hardly applies here. Contrast *Ba.* 895–6 τό τ' ἐν χρόνωι μακρῶι νόμιμον / ἀεὶ φύσει τε πεφυκός; Alexis fr. 160.6–7 K–A ταῦτα γὰρ κατὰ φύσιν πέφυκεν οὕτως; *TrGF* adesp. 665.16 κοινῆι πέφυκεν ('it is naturally and commonly so').[1] Camper's πέφηνε is the most attractive emendation available. The closest parallel for φαίνεσθαι used of an oracle is in the more imagistic lyric context of *OT* 473–5 ἔλαμψε ... φανεῖσα φήμα; cf. its use for prophetic dream or portent, S. *El.* 646 (where πέφυκεν is a variant), Hdt. 9.120.1, and for other speech (τοὔπος in *OT* 525, 848, λόγος *Trach.* 1). The notion of revelation suits this context of delayed disclosure.

σε δρᾶν there is no reason to consider σε emphatic; such emphasis would more likely be expressed by σοί γε δραστέα or the like. With the punctuation after ταῦτα one may consider γε for σε, stressing the addition of ἀνάγκη δρᾶν. Wecklein's σ' ὁρᾶν gives too weak a response to Creon's resistance.

917 ἐν βραχεῖ χρόνωι rhetorical antithesis of βραχύς with a word of greater quantity (πολύς, πᾶς) is very common. For χρόνωι cf. *Pers.* 713 πάντα γάρ, Δαρεῖ', ἀκούσηι μῦθον ἐν βραχεῖ χρόνωι, but there variant λόγωι is accepted by Broadhead *et al.*, but not by Page or West. χρόν- is also a variant in *Prom.* 875 (ταῦτα δεῖ μακροῦ λόγου), an error at *Trach.* 731. Hence Nauck's λόγωι for χρόνωι here may be right. ἐν βραχεῖ without noun is common with expressions of speaking, esp. together with συλλαβών, συλλήβδην or the like; but ἐν βραχεῖ μύθωι or λόγωι is found a few times when a brief statement actually follows (fr. 362.5, *Phil.* 435, *Prom.* 505; add *Pers.* 713 if λόγωι is adopted). With χρόνωι there is reinforcing alliteration of χ and κ in the second half of the line and perhaps emphasis on the suddenness of the reversal of fortune (cf. Soph. fr. 646.4–5 ἐν γὰρ βραχεῖ καθεῖλε κὠλίγωι χρόνωι / πάμπλουτον ὄλβον δαίμονος κακοῦ δόσις; Neophron *TrGF* 15 F 2.14–15 ἢ πολὺν πόνον βραχεῖ / διαφθεροῦσα τὸν ἐμὸν ἔρχομαι χρόνωι).

918 πατρίδι ... σωτήρια cf. 893, 898, and in a similar context of human sacrifice, *Hcld.* 402, [405].

919 οὐκ ἔκλυον, οὐκ ἤκουσα the variation is probably simply a rhetorical intensification, like *Hipp.* 362 ἄιες ὤ, ἔκλυες ὤ, *Tro.* 1303 κλύετε, μάθετε,

---

[1] There is an odd use of the aorist of this verb in *OC* 1443–4 ταῦτα δ' ἐν τῶι δαίμονι / καὶ τῆιδε φῦναι χἀτέραι, where, if correct, φῦναι seems to be used for γενέσθαι or τυχεῖν or ἐκβῆναι.

and need not involve any subtle distinction in sense, such as merely hearing vs. comprehending or attending to, as suggested by Pearson, citing *Prom.* 448 κλύοντες οὐκ ἤκουον (but see Griffith *ad loc.*; also Garvie on *Choe.* 5, Page on *Med.* 67, where again I would see simple variation, not a distinction in sense). This is a passage where ἔκλυον is clearly aorist: West, *BICS* 31 (1984) 173.

920 ἀνήρ ἀνήρ codd., and K–G 1.629–30 lists this passage as one in which the article is omitted in a contemptuous use of ἀνὴρ οὗτος or ἀνὴρ ὅδε. In eighteen places in Eur. where edd. read ἀνήρ the mss (including Stobaeus for fr. 736.1, 1063.16) have ἁνήρ, except for P^ac here and a late corrector in P at *El.* 349. But metre proves that ἁνήρ is intended in fifteen of these, and thus it should surely be restored in the rest.[1]

οὐκέθ' αὐτός for the sense 'same as before', 'unchanged ⟨by an intervening event⟩', cf. *Her.* 931 ὁ δ' οὐκέθ' αὐτὸς ἦν, *IT* 729, Thuc. 2.61.2; also, with slight variation, *Hipp.* 1001, fr. 963.4, *OT* 557, *Phil.* 521, Thuc. 3.38.1. Craik's 'Kreon is no longer himself' is inexact.

ἐκνεύει the sense may be 'pulls back', a metaphor from a horse shying back its head (cf. LSJ s.v. I.1; also *IT* 1330 of nodding to motion people away), or simply 'changes course', 'veers aside/back', a less vivid extension of the literal sense of turning one's head out of position; the latter is presumably the sense in 1268 below, and *IT* 1186 σὺ δ' ἐς τὸ τῆς θεοῦ γ' ἐξένευσας εἰκότως is best so taken as well (rather than from ἐκνέω). ἐκνεύω = 'turn aside, change course' is paralleled in prose from Septuagint onward, even with acc. object ('turn aside to avoid'), but the only early parallel is noun ἔκνευσις in Plato *Laws* 815a3.

921 χαίρων ἴθ' ironic and dismissive as in *Alc.* 813, *Su.* 248, cf. *Trach.* 819 ἑρπέτω χαίρουσα; but the phrase can also be used sincerely, as in *El.* 1340, cf. *Med.* 756.

με δεῖ for the acc. pronoun, 470n.

μαντευμάτων θεσπισμάτων (many *recc.*) is perhaps due to reminiscence of 903; the two nouns are synonymous, but Creon would suitably avoid the word that etymologically implies divine origin (cf., however, 971).

922 if Creon's choice of word in 921 has implied that Tir. cannot be trusted to convey truly the gods' will, ἡ ἀλήθεια rebuts the implication.

923 the verb of supplication is often omitted in appeals prefaced by πρός σε + gen. noun (*Med.* 324, *Hipp.* 605, 607, etc.), so there is no strong interruption here; as in *Hel.* 1237–9, the stichomythia-partner

---

[1] ἀνήρ was not ousted from editions until Porson and his successors because epic/lyric trisyllabic forms in ἄνερ- suggested to critics that Attic poets could use ἀνήρ with short or long initial as need required.

acknowledges the supplication verbally (προσπίτνεις here, ἱκέτις in *Hel.*), and the speaker then continues with the request (σίγα here, θέλω in *Hel.*). Cf. *Contact and Discontinuity* 60–1.

γερασμίου τριχός   the rare epithet (to the four citations in LSJ add Aesch. *Dictyulci* 770 (fr. 47a, 1.6), Oppian *Hal.* 2. 655, *Orph. Arg.* 626) is properly 'honorific' or 'honoured', 'venerable'. Eur. alone, however, associates it with γέρων and assumes the sense 'aged' in *Su.* 95–6 γερασμίων ὄσσων and perhaps here; Σ gives gloss ἐντίμου, and it is possible that Eur. wanted both senses to be felt, since the *captatio benevolentiae* in 'venerable beard' would better reinforce Creon's supplication. See Fraenkel, 45 (arguing for 'aged' only). Supplication by both the knees and the beard/chin is found also in *Med.* 709–10 (cf. *IA* 909, right hand and chin). θρίξ by itself for the beard is unusual, but made clear by the actor's gesture and the conventions of supplication; cf. also *Pers.* 1056 γενείου πέρθε λευκήρη τρίχα; *Cycl.* 562 τὸ χεῖλος αἱ τρίχες τε (where χεῖλος limits the sense to 'moustache and chin-hairs'). The Homeric bowl illustrated in Robert, *Oidipus* 1.452, shows Creon clasping Tir.'s knees with both hands; on the stage the kneeling actor would probably have at least reached briefly for Tir.'s chin with one hand,[1] and then risen to his feet again at 929 or 930.

924 δυσφύλακτ' †αἰτῆι† κακά   Matthiae interprets the transmitted text as 'you are asking me for evils (sc. the escape of your son and the harm to the city that will follow) that are δυσφύλακτα'; cf. already Barnes' *inevitabilia postulas mala*. But if αἰτῆι is to be so taken, the epithet needs to be changed (so already Musgrave δυσμάλακτ'). More commonly, critics have taken δυσφύλακτα κακά as the demanded death of Menoeceus and tried to reinterpret or emend αἰτῆι. King translated as *deprecaris*, but this is the sense of παραιτῆι (cf. *Her.* 302–3 εἰ παραιτησαίμεθα φυγὰς τέκνων, Aeschines 2.19, 3.198, Dem. 21.5); or, in regard to a past charge or error for which pardon is sought, ἐξαιτεῖσθαι (*Andr.* 54, Aeschines 3.196). The prefixes are essential to these deflections of the sense of the simplex verb, so it is improbable that αἰτῆι can here be simplex used for compound. Craik's 'you ask about evils hard to avert' involves an impossible sense for αἰτέω. Emendation is thus necessary, but the popular αἰνεῖ ('accept') seems to preclude Creon's continuing with his request, unless he is taken to ignore it. Heath's ἐστίν and Porson's ἀρκεῖς are more suited to the course of dialogue; -ακτά τοι (Halm) or πηι (Harry) are palaeographically clever, but the particles are not convincing.

δυσφύλακτ'   first extant in Eur. (*Andr.* 728; fr. 320, virtually identical

---

[1] Because of the brevity of the references to supplication, Kaimio, 57, suspects that it was not acted out in a physical gesture.

to Alexis fr. dub. 340 K–A, the only other classical instance, if it is one). Both senses, 'hard to guard' (fr. 320) and 'hard to guard against, avoid' (*Andr.*, here), are found in later prose from Polybius on.

926 οὐ σιωπήσαιμεν ἄν an emphatic use of οὐ and the potential opt. for denial (K–G 1.233; Goodwin, *MT* ¶236 *ad fin.*); so even with the 2nd person in 615, 1666 οὐκ ἂν τύχοις.

929 After his initial rejection of the prophecy, Creon now seeks to understand why his family in particular has been chosen to supply the victim (868n.); this is a normal stage of reaction for a person trying to cope with a sudden disaster. Tir. recognizes it as a new tack by his approval of it, ὀρθῶς ἐρωτᾶις.

930 κἀς ἀγῶν' ἔρχηι λόγων same half-line at *Andr.* 234 (τί σεμνομυθεῖς κἀς ἀγῶν' ἔρχηι λόγων;), where there has in fact been a pairing of speeches in what we call the agon-form. Here the ἀγὼν λόγων consists only in the fact that Creon's question challenges Tir. to supply an explanation in defence of his prophecy. Cf. also 588 above, *Med.* 546, *Su.* 428 ἅμιλλαν γὰρ σὺ προύθηκας λόγων. The explanation would begin too baldly without 930 (del. Herwerden 1894).

931 θαλάμαις after two Homeric instances, Eur. is the only classical poet to use this word, in a variety of senses (see Collard on *Su.* 980). **δράκων ὁ γηγενής** 658n.

932 ναμάτων ἐπίσκοπος Tir.'s words closely recall the chorus' in 659–61 νάματ'... ἐπισκοπῶν and thus his explanation here retrospectively strengthens the chorus' suggestion of a significant link between Cadmus' founding and the current strife.

933–4 γῆι δοῦναι χοάς, Κάδμου παλαιῶν Ἄρεος ἐκ μηνιμάτων for the combination of two genitives with the verbal noun μηνιμάτων, Ἄρεος as subjective and Κάδμου as objective, cf. e.g. Thuc. 7.34.6 διά τε τὴν τοῦ ἀνέμου ἄπωσιν αὐτῶν, Pl. *Rep.* 329b1 τὰς τῶν οἰκείων προσπηλακίσεις τοῦ γήρως, K–G 1.337 Anm. 4, Schwyzer II.135–6. For obj. gen. Κάδμου with μήνιμα even though μηνίω takes the dat., cf. K–G 1.335–6 and *Or.* 123 νερτέρων δωρήματα (with Willink's note). In context there is no ambiguity ('because of the ancient wrath of Ares against Cadmus'), so Valck.'s adnominal dat. Κάδμωι is not necessary, even though objective gen. with μῆνις/μήνιμα is not found elsewhere: in *OT* 699 πράγματος is gen. of cause, as in E. *El.* 1261; in *IT* 1273 Πυθίων δόμων ἀφελεῖν μῆνιν θεᾶς, δόμων will be taken primarily as separative with ἀφελεῖν; in Plut. *Mor.* 558F τὰ δημόσια τῶν πόλεων μηνίματα the adj. makes possessive interpretation likely. Others have attempted to avoid the double genitive construction by punctuating differently. Reiske treated χοάς Κάδμου as appositive to αἷμα, but the sense *libationes nomine Cadmi* is hardly obvious. Geel put the comma after Κάδμου instead of after χοάς, improbably taking Κάδμου with γῆι (so now Craik); for this sense one would need Nauck's transposition of Κάδμου and δοῦναι, but the sense itself is inferior (it is the earth *per se* that needs the expiatory blood, and 935 explicates wrath against Cadmus: see also 1010n., 1315n.). Π¹² seems to have intended one of these interpretations, but extant Σ reflects only the view adopted here.

παλαιῶν . . . ἐκ μηνιμάτων the use of the same words in Pl. *Phdr.* 244d6 is either a reminiscence of Tir.'s speech or evidence that the phrase was traditional in religious or oracular language connected with expiation.

936 κτήσεσθ' the fut. ind. is more apt than the imperative (κτήσασθ' V, *recc.*) in an explanation and is confirmed by the parallelism of ἕξετ' in 938.

937 ἀντὶ καρποῦ καρπόν apart from biblical καρπὸς κοιλίας, καρπός appears not to be used elsewhere of human or animal offspring (though words like ἔρνος and θάλος are commonly so used). By using this term Tir. assimilates the human sacrifice to the first-fruits of a harvest: Earth produced the dragon, but she also produced the Spartoi and their descendants, and now she can be thought to demand a return of some portion of her bounty. A sacral tenor is given to this line by the parallel phrasing and double paregmenon.

939 Γῆν the personification is clear enough here so that (in modern convention) a capital letter is apt. I considered writing Γῆι in 933 and Χθών in 937, but the reference to chthonic ritual suggests a general sense rather than outright personification. Both the personification and the parallelism between 936 σύμμαχον κτήσεσθ' and 938 ἕξετ' εὐμενῆ suggest that Earth as well as Ares is to be placated: the ambivalent power of the Theban earth is emphasized in the choral odes, she is central to the depiction of mutual slaughter in 670–5, and the Sphinx's chthonic origin is highlighted in the next ode. I see no reason to insist that the sacrifice is directed at Ares alone (Mueller-Goldingen 149).

ἡμῖν although Tir. leaves it to the other Thebans to take the necessary action (928) and so uses 2nd pl. verbs in 936 and 938, his solidarity with the Thebans is clear earlier (894–5) and later (942), so ἡμῖν is preferable to ὑμῖν here.

χρυσοπήληκα this rare epithet alludes both to the wondrous appearance of the Spartoi (cf. 671 πάνοπλον ὄψιν) and to their warlike nature and relationship to Ares through the dragon. The only certainly earlier use is *Se.* 106 ὦ χρυσοπήληξ δαῖμον (Ares); cf. *Hom.h.* 8.1 (Ares); (χρυσεο-) Callimachus, *Hymn* 5.43 (Athena), Proclus, *Hymn to Athena* 4.

στάχυν 'crop ⟨of grain⟩', reinforcing the metaphor of Σπαρτῶν (Craik); cf. *Her.* 4–5 ἔνθ' ὁ γηγενὴς Σπαρτῶν στάχυς ἔβλαστεν, *Ba.* 264 Κάδμον τε τὸν σπείραντα γηγενῆ στάχυν.

940–1 ἐκ γένους . . . παῖς the sentence seems odd for two reasons. (1)

416

Not only is the indefinite subject of θανεῖν incorporated into the following relative clause, but it is reformulated under the influence of the verb in that clause (τινα or ἄνδρα has become παῖς): cf. Pearson's transl., 'one of this race must die, a child sprung from the dragon's jaw.' (2) There seems to be verbal play on ἐκ γένους / γένυος ἐκ-, but it is hard to see any of the aetiological significance that one expects to be attached to such play. Craik suggests that the punning may be an element of oracular style, along with other tautologies and emphatic juxtapositions in these lines. This seems more likely than that we are to see in this Tir. a precursor of the sophistic Tir. of *Ba*. Replacements for γένους are unconvincing (Busche λόγου, Wecklein ἐκ δὲ τοῦδε with ἄνδρ' ὅς in 941).

943 ἀκέραιος ἔκ τε μητρὸς ἀρσένων τ' ἄπο descent on both sides, rather than simply on the father's side, provides an intensification of kinship that ensures both the validity of the causal connection and the power of the suggested sacrifice. We have no further information about the maternal lineage of Creon himself or of his sons (for Eurydice in *Ant.* we have just the name); it is possible that Eur. is making an *ad hoc* claim to suit the innovation of the sacrifice. (Geel suspected the line because of lack of corroboration of this detail and failure to see its point.)

ἀκέραιος is a prosaic word used three times by Eur. as a variant on poetic ἀκήρατος (also *Hel.* 48, *Or.* 922), later in poetry only Men. *Epitr.* 910 (reminiscence of *Or.* 922) and three times in *Anth. gr.*

944-6 whether 946 is accepted as genuine or not, Eur. has indulged in a rather forced contrivance to narrow the choice of victim to Menoeceus alone. Haemon is disqualified by reference to his betrothal to Antigone, as if the act of betrothal is already an impairment of Haemon's pure status and begins a transitional phase between the status of ἤιθεος and that of married man. Normally, a youth or maiden is deemed to retain the immature status right up to the moment of marriage: a betrothed who dies on or just before the wedding day has not reached his or her τέλος.[1] The

---

[1] H. Foley, *Arethusa* 15 (1982) 162, cites *IA* 940 and a story in Paus. 4.9 as parallels for impairment of purity by betrothal as an objection to sacrifice, but neither passage is strictly relevant. In *IA* Achilles means that he will be impure with the blood-guilt of Iphigenia's death because he has been used as the means to entrap her. In the Messenian story in Paus. the man in love with the proposed virgin-victim first claims that the father is no longer κύριος because of her betrothal to him and so cannot satisfy the condition of willingly granting his daughter for sacrifice. Only after this ploy fails does the lover claim (falsely) that he has already had intercourse with the girl and that she is pregnant, and thus not an eligible victim.

forced interpretation of Haemon's status was necessitated, it seems, by Eur.'s desire to patch Menoeceus and the self-sacrifice motif onto the family of Creon and the battle against the Seven while retaining Haemon's relationship with Antigone, both out of respect for the tradition and in order to manipulate it in the exodos. The audience was prepared for this reference to the betrothal by 757–60, and the earlier arrangement there alluded to explains Tir.'s knowledge of it (if any explanation is needed).[1] The ritual requirement of the purity of virginity is widespread in ancient religion, for animal victims, for mythological human victims, and for certain functions in ceremony, such as virgin priestesses and prophetesses, choruses of unmarried boys and girls, arrephoroi, loutrophoroi, and the like. See R. Parker, *Miasma: pollution and purification in early Greek religion* (Oxford 1983) 79–81.

946 'For even though he has not ⟨yet⟩ touched the bed of sexual union, still (Denniston, *GP²* 11–12) he has a ⟨designated⟩ marriage/wife.' Valck. considered εὐνῆς ἥψατ' and ἔχει λέχος to be synonymous expressions (and the former to be foreign to Attic poetry, but cf. *Hipp.* 14 κοὐ ψαύει γάμων) and condemned the line as *inficetus*. Taken in isolation, the two phrases could indeed mean the same, but the meaning in context depends on the context, so that an audience will have no trouble understanding the distinction to be between physically experiencing sexuality in marriage (ἅψασθαι emphasizing physical touch, as probably in a somewhat different phrase at *Hipp.* 1026, τῶν σῶν μήποθ' ἅψασθαι γάμων, almost 'I never laid a hand on your wife/marriage') and possessing a partner who has been promised for an imminent union. The choice here is thus between (a) believing that after the pregnant use of γάμοι (944) = 'planned marriage' (cf. 757, 1678, *Hel.* 783, *IA* 941, 959) the catachrestic use of ἤιθεος (945) = 'unmarried *and unbetrothed* youth' can stand on its own and that 946 is an explanatory addition by a reader or actor, or (b) believing that only with

---

[1] Willink, 192–3, who believes that the testamentary mention of the betrothal is post-Euripidean and that in Eur.'s play Ant. had no other role than that given to her in the teichoskopia, 1265–83, and the aria and duet of lament for her brothers and mother, suggests that no mention was made of Haemon or of betrothal in Eur.'s play. Accordingly he proposes the deletion of 944–6. In this case, it is Creon only who is a pure descendant of the Spartoi (not Eurydice as well); the burden of atonement thus falls on him in the sense that he must sacrifice his son; Menoeceus is his only son (Willink: 'The episode proceeds as though Menoikeus is Kreon's only child'; but he has forgotten 1003 πατέρα καὶ κασίγνητον προδούς). I continue to believe that the contrivance in these lines is due to Eur. himself.

946 can Tir.'s unusual claim that Haemon is not ἤιθεος be made plausible to an audience and that the explanation is Eur.'s own. ἤιθεος elsewhere always means simply 'unmarried youth' and is frequently paired with παρθένος. I prefer (b).[1]

947 πῶλος ... ἀνειμένος πῶλος is more commonly used of an unmarried girl, marking not only immaturity but a 'wildness' that is to be tamed by marriage and its incorporation of the girl into the order of the city; cf. the use in erotic and ritual contexts, such as Alcman 1 or Anacr. 417 *PMG*. These connotations are relevant to the present use, though they seem to be absent when πῶλος is used of a male child with a gen. of the parent (*Choe.* 794, *Rhes.* 386–7). For the ritual senses of ἀνειμένος ('left untilled' or 'allowed to roam free' of land or animals dedicated to a god), cf. LSJ s.v. ἀνίημι II.6.

949–50 πικρὸν ... νόστον ... θήσει a combination of two familiar locutions: (a) giving or causing a bad return (λυγρόν *Od.* 1.326–7, 3.152; ἔχθιστον Pindar *O.* 8.68–9; κακόν *Hcld.* 1042–3, *Su.* 1209; πικρόν *Tro.* 66; δύσνοστον *Tro.* 75); (b) emphatic use of predicative πικρός for a result that has turned out to be or is threatened to be bitter (*Med.* 399–400 πικροὺς δ' ἐγώ σφιν καὶ λυγροὺς θήσω γάμους, / πικρὸν δὲ κῆδος καὶ φυγὰς ἐμᾶς χθονός; *Pers.* 473 πικρὰν ... ηὖρε; S. *El.* 470–1; more colloquial πικρὰν ... ὄψει *Birds* 1468, *Thesm.* 853, Eubulus 118.6 K–A, cf. *Ba.* 357 πικρὰν ... ἰδών, *Ba.* 634, *Med.* 1388.

950 μέλαιναν κῆρ' ἐπ' ὄμμασιν βαλών 'casting dark doom upon their eyes', primarily of the cloud of grief and misfortune (1311n.; Pearson aptly cites *OC* 1683–4 νῶιν δ' ὀλεθρία / νὺξ ἐπ' ὄμμασιν βέβακε, *Aj.* 706 ἔλυσεν αἰνὸν ἄχος ἀπ' ὀμμάτων Ἄρης), but also with a suggestion of the darkness that closes over the eyes of those who die in the battle (1453n.). For κῆρ' ἐπ' ὄμμασιν cf. Theognis 207–8 θάνατος γὰρ ἀναιδὴς / πρόσθεν ἐπὶ βλεφάροις ἕζετο κῆρα φέρουσα.

951 κλεινάς τε Θήβας sc. θήσει; since πικρόν is predicative (see above) as well as κλεινάς, there is only a very slight shift in sense, from 'bring about',

---

[1] Hartung and Wecklein (1872) argued that the author of the second explanation in the scholion ἢ καθὸ ἐμνηστεύσατο, ἢ ἐπεί, ὡς λέγουσι, λάθρα αὐτῆι συνῆλθε. τοῦτον (leg. τοῦτο?) δὲ ὡς μάντιν εἰδότα εὐφήμως εἰπεῖν did not have line 946 in his text. This is Σ946 in Schwartz, with the lemma as in MVC; B has no lemma, and the note follows Σ944 with only a divider symbol. But scholiastic commentators are frequently short-sighted, and this fantastic explanation could have been written to explain either 945 'not unmarried' or 946 'yet still has a marriage'; moreover, εὐφήμως is better taken as a reference to the convoluted language of 946.

'create' to 'cause X to be Y', hardly comparable to the Pindaric case (*P.* 1.40) cited by Pearson.

952 ἢ γὰρ παῖδα σῶισον ἢ πόλιν appositional γάρ, 'that is to say'; see Denniston, *GP²* 67, (9)(ii), citing *Ion* 844 (I would retain 844–58) and prose exx. with disjunctive ἤ (note Pl. *Apol.* 40c5–7 δυοῖν γὰρ θάτερόν ἐστιν τὸ τεθνάναι· ἢ γὰρ ... ἢ ...). With γάρ so understood, the imperative has its normal force: Pearson's interpretation as 'thou must save' is unnecessary.

953 τὰ μὲν παρ' ἡμῶν πάντ' ἔχεις a formula of closing (cf. Fraenkel on *Ag.* 1045f., also *Zu den Phoen.* 45 n. 3), indicating that Tir. has no more to say specifically to Creon.

ἡγοῦ, τέκνον cf. *Ant.* 1087ff. ὦ παῖ, σὺ δ' ἡμᾶς ἄπαγε πρὸς δόμους, ἵνα κτλ.: there too a scene which began cordially ends in hostility (865–95n., 954–9n.; cf. *OT* 444). Tir. probably hands his κλῆροι (838n., 846n.) back to his daughter and then places his hand on her shoulder. They may not actually begin moving toward the exit-ramp until 959. Note that in this context Eur. sees no advantage in referring, as earlier, to Tir.'s fear of slipping or the need to negotiate steps.

954–9 the concluding generalization is addressed to the environment at large, as often. Tir.'s complaint could apply to all his appearances in tragedy, so that by including it Eur. seems to be commenting on his exploitation of a familiar type of scene.

954 δ' perhaps answers μέν in 953, despite the intervening imperative ('There you have my prophecy; but prophecy is a wretched calling'); or μέν could be *solitarium*, with asyndeton at Tir.'s turning away, and δ' might be connective after ἡγοῦ (as if to say 'and/but I'll say this about prophecy'). Fraenkel, 46, asks: 'Wäre nicht 954 ohne δ' viel besser?'[1] Many conclusive reflections do feature asyndeton (esp. with an apostrophe), but for such reflections with 'a vague δὲ by which a close attachment to the preceding lines is avoided' see Friis Johansen, *General Reflection* 154. Note also that without δ' there would be four consecutive asyndeta in 953–9.

954 ἐμπύρωι ... τέχνηι strictly, 'art of divination by inspection of burnt offerings', but here clearly generalized to 'art of divination'.

955 μάταιος here probably 'is mistaken', 'labours in vain', or the like (cf. *Trach.* 863), rather than the stronger 'is a fool, is reckless'.

ἢν μὲν κτλ. explanatory asyndeton with antithetic limbs; γάρ intrudes

---

[1] Omission of δ' in Eustathius' quotation (*in Il.* 48, 42) is conditioned by the self-imposed limits of his inexact citation (ὃς ἐμπύρωι κτλ.) and is irrelevant to an editor's decision.

in MnSVr from Σ and should not be substituted for μέν (Markland, Blaydes).

σημήνας primarily 'has declared, proclaimed', but there is probably an interplay of the meaning 'give signs' (with god or omen as subject, rather than interpreter), so that the connotation is 'has proclaimed an interpretation of the signs'.

956 πικρός glossed with ἐχθρός, which has intruded in some mss (cf. *Phil.* 254 πικρός mss, ἐχθρός S^(γρ)). πικρός of a person is the more choice application, and one should not prefer Valck.'s pedestrian πικρά σημήνας ... ἐχθρὸς καθέστηχ'.

καθέστηχ' the perfect may be simply gnomic (Goodwin, *MT* §155; Moorhouse, *Syntax Soph.* 200) or may imply the rapidity and completeness of the arrival of the result (esp. in a conditional sentence: *MT* §51), as in what Wackernagel calls the 'anticipatory' use of the perfect (*Syntax* I.170-1, Schwyzer II.287; cf. the colloquial 'frequentative' use of the perfect noted by MacDowell on *Wasps* 494).

οἰωνοσκόπηι in classical authors extant only here and *Ba.* 347 (likewise οἰωνοσκόπον, *Su.* 500).

958 τὰ τῶν θεῶν 'what belongs to the gods', that is, their signs and their intention to reveal the future or influence human decisions.

Φοῖβον whereas the asyndeton at ἦν μέν in 955 is explanatory, this instance is contrastive (456n.).

959 χρῆν imperfect of unfulfilled obligation, typical of Eur. characters' suggestions for the smoother running of the world.

θεσπιωιδεῖν this verb (cf. *Ag.* 1161) and θεσπιωιδός are tragic words (*Wealth* 9 is deemed a quotation or paratragic); there are a few instances in later prose.

960 τί σιγᾶις γῆρυν ἄφθογγον σχάσας; the question calls attention to a brief period of silence following 959; this is the normal way to make a silence dramatically significant: *Contact and Discontinuity* 114-17; Taplin, *HSCP* 76 (1972) 57-97. The participial phrase is typically mannered in style, with three rather lofty words strikingly combined: ἄφθογγον is proleptic; σχάσας, 'relax', is a variation on παρεῖσα, cf. *Tro.* 695 ἄφθογγός εἰμι καὶ παρεῖσ' ἔχω στόμα.

961 γάρ a slightly illogical connection: Denniston, *GP²* 61, 'Yet I am not surprised at your silence: for I too am dumbfounded.' O's μέν could be a normal accidental substitution (Diggle, *Text. Trad. Or.* 83) or a deliberate simplification (based on 427 ἐμοὶ μέν, but μέν *solitarium* will not work with κἀμοί).

963 γάρ 867n.

εἰς τόδ' εἶμι συμφορᾶς 'bring myself to such a⟨n extreme⟩ degree of misery', the point being throughout the speech that he will never willingly allow the sacrifice to take place; cf. Demophon in *Hcld.* 413–14 ἑκὼν δὲ τίς κακῶς οὕτω φρονεῖ, / ὅστις τὰ φίλτατ' ἐκ χερῶν δώσει τέκνα; . συμφορά has its most common sense, 'misfortune', not the special sense 'guilt', as Pearson claims, citing Jebb on *OT* 99, who notes some places where συμφορά is a euphemism for 'blood-guilt', 'sacrilege', or the like. εἰς τόδε/τοῦτο + gen. + verb of going + ὥστε is an idiom of oratorical prose, not found in A. or S. Eur. has *Hipp.* 1332 ἐς τόδ' αἰσχύνης; *Med.* 56 ἐς τοῦτ' . . . ἀλγηδόνος; *El.* 918 ἐς τοῦτο . . . ἀμαθίας; also *Andr.* 170 ἐς τοῦτο . . . ἀμαθίας with relative clause of result instead of ὥστε; *Her.* 1294 ἐς τοῦτο . . . συμφορᾶς with γάρ-expansion; *Her.* 1281 ἀνάγκης ἐς τόδ' with asyndeton, cf. *Or.* 566 ἐς τόδ' . . . θράσους with appositional or epexegetic inf. From the orators one may cite εἰς τοῦτο in Antiphon *tetr.* 1.2.2, Isocr. 8.31, Isaeus 6.39, Dem. 22.74, *al.*; or the yet more common εἰς τοσοῦτον + gen., Lysias 12.22, Dem. 12.12, Isocr. 16.9, *al.*

964 σφαγέντα . . . προσθεῖναι the participle is coincident aorist (1507n.): sacrifice and gift to the city are essentially the same act. προσθεῖναι connotes surrender or delivery to a new possessor or authority: *Hec.* 368 Ἅιδηι προσθεῖσ' ἐμὸν δέμας, *Ion* 1545 ὁ δ' ὠφελῶν σε προστίθησ' ἄλλωι πατρί, *Antiope* 48.110–11 τὴν γὰρ ἀξίαν / σφῶιν προστίθησιν Ζεύς, ἐγώ τε σὺν Διί; LSJ s.v. 1.2. Cf. the use of δοῦναι in *Hcld.* 414 (quoted 963n.) and *Erecth.* fr. 50.4 Austin ἐγὼ δὲ δώσω παῖδα τὴν ἐμὴν κτανεῖν, 50.38-9 δώσω κόρην θῦσαι πρὸ γαίας.

965–9 contain a loose series of reasons for Creon's decision, including an offer of his own life as palliation of a possible charge of cowardice. There is no sufficient reason to doubt any of these lines (965–7 Harberton, 965 Conradt, 967–9 Herwerden (1894), 968–9 Hermann).

965 φιλότεκνος βίος 'a way of life that involves love of their children'; the reminiscence of 356, along with Men.'s reference to Joc. as his foster mother in 986–9, sets up a telling comparison between Creon and Joc. in their attitudes toward each other's children. Cf. 1317–21n., 1665n. For the motif in the context of sacrifice, cf. *Erecth.* fr. 51 Austin, *IA* 1256.

967 The connection of thought here is 'Nor can this natural affection be overcome by the knowledge that I'll be saving my city. I don't want to be praised for patriotism by someone who is killing (*or* trying to kill) my child.' κτείνων is either a vivid present or conative in force. The notion of praise for the sacrifice was implicit in 918 and 951, and is followed up (with limitation to Men.) in 1054–61, 1206–7, 1314. Since προσθεῖναι in 964 implies turning over his son to the city to do what it will with him and δοίη κτανεῖν in 966 reflects the same hands-off attitude toward the sacrifice, Markland and Nauck's κτείνειν does not fit the passage and involves an unparalleled construction ('say in praise that' with acc. + inf.).

τέκνα the generalizing poetic plural here adds vehemence to the protest.

968-9 the desperate offer of oneself as a substitute for the designated youthful victim is paralleled in *Hec.* 383-8; cf. also Iolaus' offer in *Hcld.* 453-7. In an overly logical argument Hermann branded this couplet spurious.

ἐν ὡραίωι . . . βίου 'in a stage of life ripe ⟨for such a fate⟩', the implied qualification being supplied by the immediately following words θνήισκειν ἕτοιμος; cf. *Alc.* 516 πατήρ γε μὴν ὡραῖος, εἴπερ οἴχεται, LSJ s.v. ὡραῖος III.1. βίου is Reiske's certain correction of βίωι, which does not yield any suitable sense (Hes. *Op.* 31-2 is different); for the partitive gen. cf. *Hipp.* 785 ἐν ἀσφαλεῖ βίου. Wecklein wrongly thought that the context could not supply the qualification of ὡραίωι and conjectured μόρου (cf. Σ's use of καιρῶι τῆς τελευτῆς, καιρὸν τοῦ θανάτου), but whereas Creon could be himself ὡραῖος μόρου (like ὡραῖος γάμου), ἐν ὡραίωι μόρου seems harshly obscure.

ἕτοιμος εἰμί is understood, as in *Med.* 612, *Hcld.* 502, *Rhes.* 959; *Aj.* 813, *OT* 92, *Thesm.* 59, *Dysc.* 370; cf. (ἐστί understood) *Ag.* 791, *Choe.* 1025. See J. E. Harry, *TAPA* 34 (1903) viii-x.

ἐκλυτήριον extant only here and *OT* 392 ηὔδας τι . . . ἐκλυτήριον; it is impossible to be sure whether it was felt as a true noun or as a substantivalized adjective (on the suffix see Schwyzer 1.467, 470). Here it is probably internal acc. after θνήισκειν, like σωτήριον after ξίφος λαιμῶν διῆκε in 1091-2 below, rather than nom. in apposition.

970 ἀλλ' εἶα the particles mark, as often, transition from a comment to an exhortation or imperative (cf. 1708 below, *Her.* 704, 833, *Or.* 1060, *IA* 111, 435, *Wealth* 292), and in this case also a shift from address to the chorus to address to Men. (cf. shift to command of silent extras in *Med.* 820, *Her.* 622, *Tro.* 880, *Hel.* 1429, *Or.* 1618). As Radt has pointed out, the rough breathing appears to be established by papyri of Soph. (fr. 221.4, 222b7.4, 314.93 and 174) and Σ^A *Il.* 9.262a.

971 ἀκόλαστ' 'unbridled', cf. *Or.* 10 ἀκόλαστον ἔσχε γλῶσσαν; this abusive word perhaps has a somewhat. colloquial air, since it and its derivatives are found mainly in comedy and prose, apart from six times in Eur. and once in Soph. fr. 744 (context unknown, not iambic trimeter). There is no reason to take the adj. as predicative (Craik: 'dismiss the prophecies of seers as wanton').

μάντεων generalizing plural as in 967 τέκνα.

972 = *Hel.* 780. The latter was branded an interpolation from *Phoen.* by Valck. Verbatim repetition of a line between two plays is in general less suspicious, a priori, than such repetition within a single play (143n.). In a formulaic line such as this, an accidental repetition is quite conceivable, and I am inclined to follow Kannicht in retaining *Hel.* 780.

ἀπαλλαχθείς by a large majority aorist passive forms in -λλαχθ-

423

outnumber those in -λλαγ- in tragedy, and there are rarely variant readings (here -αγείς B, *recc.*; cf. *Ag.* 336, *Med.* 896, *Hipp.* 1181, where edd. print -λλαχθ-). In optional locations only *Ant.* 422 and *Andr.* 592 have -λλαγ- without variant. Metrically necessary -λλαγ- is found in 592 above, 1409 below, *Antiope* 48.76 Kambitsis, *Prom.* 471, 750.

973-4 although Tir. originally refused to keep silent about the oracle (926) and said ἐμοὶ δ᾽ εἰρήσεται (928), at the end of his explanation he seems to leave the choice to Creon (952) and instructs his daughter to lead him πρὸς οἶκον (954). Creon, however, assumes the worst, ignoring the apparent implication of 952-4. Compare how Phaedra, convinced that Hipp. will spread the word of her shame, ignores or disbelieves the evidence to the contrary that she herself has heard (I believe) in *Hipp.* 601-68.

974 this line was judged to be περιττός by a critic whose judgment survives in Σ973 (ἤρκει οὗτος). For the reason given in 428n., I do not think it is a safe inference that 974 was unevenly attested in the copies known to that critic or even that he intended to athetize 974 rather than simply find fault with it. There is nothing wrong with the language of the line, and the argument that the feeble old seer could not go to all seven gates (Conradt) rests on an inappropriate rationalism. There is not sufficient reason for deletion, and the line perhaps makes a positive contribution (Powell: 'it brings out the fact that the "captains" are sentinels *at the gates*, who, if they were forewarned by Tiresias, would prevent egress'; cf. Mueller-Goldingen, 152 n. 20).

976 cf. 1282n.

977 the treatment of Men. at the beginning of the scene, during the dialogue of Creon and Tir., and immediately after Tir.'s departure all suggested that Men. was a silent extra, so there is an effect of surprise when he now turns out to be a speaking character.

τίνα ξένων; acc. of the person expressing direction or destination without a preposition is exceptional outside Homer: cf. K–G I.311–12, Schwyzer II.67–8 (who doubts the construction, excluding examples with compound verbs and with ἱκ- = 'reach' as only apparent cases). But both grammars have missed a number of tragic instances as well as this passage, where the oddity is made less striking by the anaphora with preceding normal τίνα πόλιν; Cf. *Ba.* 847 ἥξει δὲ Βάκχας, with Dodds' note; *OT* 713 αὐτὸν ἥξοι μοῖρα, with Kamerbeek's; and note Pindar *I.* 2.47–8 ὅταν ξεῖνον ἐμὸν ἠθαῖον ἔλθῃς (JD). Geel's τίν᾽ ἐς ξένον (ξένων Blaydes) is unnecessary.

979 for the interrogative interpretation of this verse (Wecklein; cf. Denniston, *GP*² 436), cf. *IT* 810 οὔκουν λέγειν μὲν χρή σέ, μανθάνειν δ᾽ ἐμέ; and (JD) *Rhes.* 161–2 οὔκουν πονεῖν μὲν χρή, πονοῦντα δ᾽ ἄξιον / μισθὸν φέρεσθαι; Here, as elsewhere, ἐκπονεῖν is 'carry out ⟨the task⟩', not 'endure it' (Craik).

424

980–6 the short passage of trimeter antilabe reinforces the sense of haste; a similar effect is to be seen in 1273–8.

980 Δελφοὺς περάσας Creon's finite verb (μόλε, ἐλθέ, or the like) is never uttered, but supplied from Men.'s intervention (*Contact and Discontinuity* 57–8; fully 'co-operative' syntax, implying a nominative for περάσας, would have been ποῖ μόλω;). φεῦγε in B²OV + is clearly the intruder, not πάτερ, as a Palaeologan scholar conjectured.

983 ἔγνως 'you've got it', 'you have it' (cf. *Trach.* 1221, *Andr.* 883, 920, *El.* 617, *Ion* 1115, *Or.* 1131, *Rhes.* 281); an instantaneous or 'dramatic' aorist in the second person, as commonly with ἔλεξας in stichomythia or any close exchange (e.g., *Aj.* 270, *Hel.* 141, *Choe.* 434).

τί δὴ τόδ' ἔρυμα transmitted δῆτ' ἔρυμα will not scan, since ῠ is well established in epic, tragedy, and later poets. Wilam., like Triclinius, suggests ἔρῦμα, which he also accepts in his emendation of *Eum.* 701, *Arist. und Athens* ii.336 n. 13; but if Eur. wanted ῡ he would probably have used the rarer alternate form ῥῦμα (five times in tragedy, once in Eur., *Hcld.* 260 (also sometimes restored in *IA* 791)) and written δῆτα ῥῦμα, as Valck. believed. But the demonstrative τόδ' is idiomatic and desirable to the sense ('What protection, then, will this (sc. going to Dodona) be for me?'), and δή and δῆτα are equivalent in questions like this, so Musgrave's emendation is best.

985 ἐγὼ πορεύσω χρυσόν 'I will have money conveyed ⟨to you there⟩.' ἐγώ emphasizes Creon's act as opposed to the god's, sc. giving counsel where to go and what to do (as Delphi did for the exiled Cadmus). The reference is to a future provision of funds for a long-term exile (cf. 400–1), not to supplying money to Men. before he departs (as held by Musgrave, Hartung, and others).

986–91 despite some confusion in a few mss, it is clear that the changes of speaker in 986 and 990–1 are part of the tradition from antiquity. The paragraphoi or dicolons marking change of speaker, though not infallible, are in general more reliable or 'authentic' than the identifications of the speakers, which were consistently applied rather late in the textual tradition of drama: cf. J. C. B. Lowe, *BICS* 9 (1962) 27ff.; Gomme–Sandbach, Menander comm., 40–1. In this passage the changes make good sense. After answering all Men.'s questions and obtaining his apparent full acquiescence (εὖ λέγεις, πάτερ), Creon resumes (from 972) the command that Men. depart (χώρει νυν, 'be on your way then'). Men. then turns toward the door rather than toward the eisodos, alleging that he must say farewell to Joc. Creon accepts this, and urges him on (ἀλλ' εἶα, χώρει, 'all right then, move along'). As Creon himself turns to depart (to the side), he says μὴ τὸ σὸν κωλυέτω, 'let not your own ⟨delaying action⟩ prevent ⟨your escape⟩', recalling the need for haste and the fear that Men. will be prevented by others from escaping (973–6). Musgrave removed the changes of speaker and subsequent edd. followed him; but Fraenkel well rebutted the received version. In Musgrave's arrangement, (1) Creon strangely surrenders the dialogue after 985 and has no final word; (2) Men. tells Creon 'be on the way, then', a command which both seems contrary to etiquette for a youth respectfully addressing his father and implies that Creon needs to get the money before Men. can depart (not true, and the reverse is implied by 985); (3) the reinforced χώρει in 990 is a further breach of etiquette (see Fraenkel, 48–50, for a full survey of the etiquette involved in use of εἶα with imperative), and τὸ σόν must again refer to the provision of money, as if the lack of money would stop Men. from escaping. Musgrave's assignment of the lines has been defended by Mueller-Goldingen 153 n. 22. He suggests that the etiquette identified by Fraenkel is deliberately broken to underline the fact that Men. is taking charge of the situation and the dialogue at 986; his argument that 986 could not be spoken by Creon depends on the assumption, rejected here, that Men. can't leave until supplied with money; his claim that ἀλλ' εἶα in 990 must be within a speech, not at the start of a speech, is refuted *ad loc.*

986 ὡς introducing a speech, 'know that', as in 625 above; Fraenkel, 51, cites *Cycl.* 472–3, *Hel.* 830–1, and *IA* 1367 for such a ὡς-clause beginning an answer to an imperative or equivalent.

987–8 this detail is not known from elsewhere, and although it is presumably designed for the needs of this scene, it has wider significance in connection with the kinship-theme (965n.).

μολών is antecedent to the action of προσηγορήσας in 989 (cf. 77–8n. for accumulation of participles in asyndeton); in this sequence there is nothing grammatically wrong in the combination of μολών with εἶμι in the same sentence (989n.).

'Ιοκάστην λέγω for the use of this idiom to identify more specifically someone not present, see *CP* 83 (1988) 156 n. 11 (add Soph. fr. 210.26, Philemon fr. 69.3 K–A).

988 ὀρφανός τ' ἀποζυγείς the verb is a Eur. *Lieblingswort* (once in Aesch., in a different sense; rare elsewhere until late prose) for bereavement (from wife and children, *Her.* 1375) or pathetic separation of kin (from children, *Med.* 1017; from brother, *El.* 284); cf. 328n.

989 Hartung's restored προσηγορήσας for -ήσων, based on a wishful paraphrase in the Thoman Σ (after clearly glossing fut. part., Thomas adds τουτέστι μετὰ τὸ προσειπεῖν ἐκείνην φευξοῦμαι καὶ σωθήσομαι), and he rightly accepted σώισω from a 'Moschopulean' source (by conjecture or a lucky survival: see *Text. Trad.* 102–3). This seems obvious once one accepts that 997 εἶμι καὶ σώισω πόλιν is a deliberate rephrasing of εἶμι καὶ σώισω βίον here and that εἶμι refers to departure from Thebes (answering Creon's χώρει). But it was easy for the future participle to arise next to εἶμι with the apparent sense 'I'll go inside' and then for σώισων to follow. The resistance of Nauck, Wecklein, and Murray to seeing the truth here was probably in part due to excessive distrust of *recc*. Craik retains the future participles, noting that the tenses are confused but improbably suggesting that Men.'s 'emotions may account for this'. Mueller-Goldingen 153 n. 22 follows Verrall in deleting 989, but there is nothing wrong with εἶμι after μολών (987–8n.) and the aposiopesis seems to me (like most of Verrall's suggestions of this sort) implausible.

εἶμι καὶ σώισω for εἶμι καί + fut. ind., cf. *Alc.* 209, *Su.* 346, 560, *Her.* 566, *IT* 636; *Pers.* 849, *Se.* 672, *Choe.* 781, comic. adesp. 133.2 Kock.

990 ἀλλ' εἶα, χώρει the particles mark, as often, the transition from discussion to action (Creon now turns to depart) and reinforce his previous command (986) after Men.'s comment. For ἀλλ' εἶα marking such a transition at the beginning of a speech, cf. *Hel.* 1429, *Wealth* 316, perhaps ἄγ' εἶα Soph. *Ichneut.* fr. 314.436.

μὴ τὸ σὸν κωλυέτω explained above, 986–91n. Some who follow Musgrave's attribution to Men. detect a double meaning here: to Creon, 'don't let your delay in getting the money prevent my escape' and to himself, 'don't let your action prevent my sacrificing myself'. But an audience could have no idea of this, unless they were absolutely certain that Men. was tricking his father (even if the sacrifice of Men. is not an innovation, they could hardly be certain of that).

991–1012 (or 1018?) Once Creon is far enough along the exit-ramp, Men. turns back from the door and addresses the chorus. His speech is a highly concentrated version of arguments and themes typical of characters accepting self-sacrifice or facing death without regret. After allusively overturning the apparent course of action, contrasting his position with that of Creon (991–6), Men. explicitly announces his resolve to die (997–8), revising the false words of 989. Then he contemplates in detail the shameful alternative to self-sacrifice (999–1005) and after vehement rejection (1006–8) recapitulates his intention, dismissing further deliberation or speech of any kind (1009–12). For those who accept 1013–18, he pauses in his movement off to redescribe his act and to append a concluding generalization with both internal and extra-dramatic relevance.

992 ὥσθ' ἃ βούλομαι τυχεῖν cf. 512 τυχεῖν ἃ χρήιζει, *Med.* 758 τυχοῦσ' ἃ βούλομαι.

993 τύχης 'the gift of fortune (or the gods)', that is, 'its chance for salvation'; the content of τύχη is the same as in 892, 897, and 914 above, but is here evaluated positively by Men.

994 δειλίαι δίδωσι 'delivers me up to a reputation for cowardice', not difficult in context, but there are no close parallels (cf. LSJ s.v. δίδωμι II.1, esp. *Il.* 5.397 ὀδύνηισιν ἔδωκεν, Pindar *P.* 5.60–1 ἔδωκ' Ἀπόλλων θῆρας αἰνῶι φόβωι); with this kind of object one would normally see a reflexive action, 'give oneself up to' (LSJ II.5, e.g. Diod. Sic. 17.108.4 δοὺς δ' ἑαυτὸν εἰς τρυφήν).

συγγνωστά for the neuter plural predicate in place of συγγνωστόν (the subject is implied inf. ταῦτα ποιεῖν, understood from 993–4a), cf. K–G I.66–7, Schwyzer II.606 (an archaic and poetic construction). Iolaus finds συγγνωστά the reluctance of Demophon to sacrifice his own child or force any of his citizens to do so (*Hcld.* 435).

995 γέροντι virtually causal in force, 'because he is an old man'. The implication is perhaps that Creon, being close to the end of his own life, attaches very great value to the children who represent the survival of his name and clan, or that, having served his city in the past, he cannot be too much blamed for refusing costly service now. Note also that Aristotle *Rhet.* 1389b13–90a23 lists among the stereotypical ἤθη of old men μικροψυχία, δειλία, and φιλαυτία, all in opposition to the stereotypical behaviour of young men, who are likely to be φιλότιμοι, ἀνδρειότεροι, and motivated primarily by τὸ καλόν (1389a3–b12).

συγγνώμην ἔχει here 'admits of forgiveness or pardon' with the questionable action as subject (so too *Trach.* 328, Antiphon *Herod.* 92, Antiphanes fr. 122.12 K–A, Dem. 19.133, 21.66); far more commonly (tragedy, comedy, prose) the sense is 'feels sympathetic understanding, grants pardon' with personal subject. For the reversibility of such idioms, see 773n.

996 προδότην a strong word (especially with πατρίδος as object), redefining an act of omission as one of commission. Cf. the use of προδοῦναι by Alcestis (*Alc.* 180, 290).

997–8 this is the first of three expressions of intention in the transmitted speech (cf. 1009–12, 1013–14), and there is too much overlap for all three to be genuine. Herwerden, *Exercitationes criticae etc.* (The Hague 1862) 132, deleted this couplet, and it would be possible for 999 to follow directly on 996. But emphatic opening statement followed by elaboration of reasons (999–1005) followed by emphatic reiteration of intention is rhetorically apt, 997 provides a meaningful echo of 989 (see above), and 1013–18 present serious problems (see *ad loc.*).

997 ὡς οὖν ἂν εἰδῆτ' giving the reason for uttering the statement, as often with ὡς ἂν (ἵνα) εἰδῆις/εἰδῆτε or μάθηις/μάθητε (cf. 1656, 1681); the formula prepares for the explicitness of εἶμι καὶ σώισω after the hints in 992 and 995.

998 ψυχήν τε δώσω a rare locution, also in *Hcld.* 550–1 (self-sacrifice of Her.'s daughter) τὴν ἐμὴν ψυχὴν ἐγὼ / δίδωμ' ἑκοῦσα τοῖσδ' (*Or.* 622

is different); cf. *Ant.* 322 ἐπ' ἀργυρῶι γε τὴν ψυχὴν προδούς; *IA* 1397 δίδωμι σῶμα τοὐμὸν Ἑλλάδι.

ὑπερθανεῖν final-consecutive inf. after διδόναι, K–G ii.16–17. Barnes cited in the margin '*al.* ὑπερθανών' (not found in any ms known to Matthiae or to me), and this apparent emendation is commended by Diggle (1990a). The participle (coincident aorist: 1507n.) would eliminate the slight oddity of ψυχήν as the implied subject of θανεῖν; but the inf. has more point since it more explicitly marks the patriotic purpose of the gesture. For the idea, cf. *Alc.* 284 θνήισκω ... ὑπὲρ σέθεν, *Hcld.* 532 θνήισκειν ἀδελφῶν τῶνδε κἀμαυτῆς ὕπερ, 545, 590; cf. *Erecth.* fr. 50.18 Austin ἐξὸν προπάντων μίαν ὑπερδοῦναι θανεῖν, 50.35.

999–1005 αἰσχρὸν γάρ· οἱ μὲν κτλ. γάρ here links all of 999–1005 to the declaration of intent. The asyndeton is a forceful brachylogy for τοῦτο γὰρ αἰσχρὸν ἔσται, εἰ οἱ μέν ... ἐγὼ δέ ..., made yet more vehement if it is correct to interpret οἱ μὲν κτλ. as a question with indignant, disbelieving force. In two other passages Eur. has αἰσχρόν ... εἰ (*Hec.* 311, *El.* 336), but the position of μέν ensures that asyndeton is correct here. So too the common orator's idiom δεινόν (ἐστι), εἰ has a rarer, more forceful cousin with asyndeton (Dem. 19.209, 59.107); cf. (Pearson) Antiph. *Choreut.* 9, Lys. 6.15, Dem. 20.79–80, Isaeus 3.63–5. In four of these exx. the second member has indignant interrogative force, and here too Matthiae's question mark at 1005 yields stronger rhetoric and a better lead-in to 1006 μά τόν.... Interrogative interpretation does not imply that Men. has any doubt about the proposition κακὸς φανήσομαι (*pace* Mueller-Goldingen 156–7). A similar argument contrasting others with oneself is used in *Hcld.* 503–6 τί φήσομεν γάρ, εἰ πόλις μέν ..., αὐτοὶ δέ ...;, *IA* 1387–90 ἀλλὰ μυρίοι μὲν ἄνδρες ..., ἡ δ' ἐμὴ ψυχή ...;

1000 εἰς ἀνάγκην δαιμόνων ἀφιγμένοι 'confronted with a fate ordained by the gods' or perhaps 'with a strong compulsion from the gods', since ἀνάγκη is applied here to a strong constraint or demand that Men. actually believes he has the chance to refuse (cf. Agamemnon at Aulis in Aesch.). It often depends on the rhetorical context whether ἀνάγκη is to be understood as something strictly inevitable. For the expression, cf. *IT* 620 εἰς ἀνάγκην κείμεθ', ἣν φυλακτέον, *Su.* 310 (ἄνδρας) ἐς τήνδ' ἀνάγκην σῆι καταστῆσαι χερί.

1005 κακὸς φανήσομαι cf. *Hcld.* 510 κακοὺς ὁρᾶσθαι, *Hec.* 348 κακὴ φανοῦμαι καὶ φιλόψυχος γυνή.

1006 μά plain μά in classical Attic drama always implies a negative (denying what has just been mentioned) or is followed by one. Here οὐκ ἄπειμι is understood, and ἀλλά follows the implied negation: cf. S. *El.* 881, *Knights* 85, 338, 1382, *Clouds* 330, *Dysc.* 358, etc. For later usage, which led to the intrusive gloss οὐ here, cf. Gomme–Sandbach on *Dysc.* 151.

τὸν μετ' ἄστρων Ζῆν' for Zeus '⟨dwelling⟩ in the company of the stars' Pearson well compares *Cycl.* 353–4 ὦ φαεννὰς ἀστέρων οἰκῶν ἕδρας Ζεῦ, *El.* 991 (Dioscuri), *Her.* 406–7 ἀστρωπούς ... οἴκους ... θεῶν.

1007 τοὺς ὑπερτείλαντας ἐκ γαίας ποτέ as in 671–2 and 939, the pictorial image inevitably associated with the Spartoi is of their rising full-grown and armed from the earth. There are no known illustrations of this moment, but comparable images are found for *anodoi*. Apart from one occurrence in Hdt., ὑπερτέλλω is a Euripidean verb (five instances), reappearing rarely in late Greek, often in imitation of Eur.

1009 ἀλλ' εἶμι for this formula occurring before departure, 753n.; with 1013–18 deleted (see below), there are three more lines before departure, containing an elaboration of the intended action and a reinforcing formula of closure in 1012.

εἶμι καί 989n.

στὰς ἐξ ἐπάλξεων ἄκρων as in 1223–4 below ἀπ' ὀρθίου σταθεὶς πύργου, the preposition of motion away from is used in an anticipatory sense, reflecting a subsequent action named or implied in the context: so here 'standing upon the edge of the battlements, letting my sacrificial blood flow *from there* into the dragon's lair'; or below, 'standing upon the steep tower, speaking *from there* to the troops'. Cf. *Tro.* 522–3, *Ant.* 411 with Jebb's note *ad loc.* (he calls this a 'surveying' use of the prepositions).

1010 σηκὸν εἰς μελαμβαθῆ σηκός only here in drama in the quasi-Homeric sense, 'lair, den' (cf. 931 θαλάμαις); elsewhere 'precinct'. μελαμβαθής may have chthonic and funereal connotations: it is associated with the underworld in *Prom.* 219, Soph. fr. 523.1, and is extant elsewhere only in Ap. Rhod. 4.516 (of a river). In sacrifice care had to be taken that the blood drained from the neck fell, or was collected, in the appropriate place: cf. *Od.* 11.35–6 ἀπεδειροτόμησα ἐς βόθρον, *Se.* 43 ταυροσφαγοῦντες ἐς ... σάκος. Human sacrifices in Eur. are normally assimilated to the ritual of σφάγια, in which the blood was shed directly upon the earth, not upon an altar: see Henrichs, 'Human Sacrifice in Greek Religion', esp. 208–24; O'Connor-Visser, 190–5. In the conditions of siege and haste, the easiest way for Men. to direct his blood to the proper ground was from above: see also 933–4n., 1315n.

1011 ἔνθ' ὁ μάντις ἐξηγήσατο cf. 931–3.

1012 ἐλευθερώσω γαῖαν climactically rounding out the sentence after the two participles (77–8n.) and relative clause, this forceful phrase combines the ideas of freeing the land from the wrath of Ares and Earth (934–9) and of keeping Thebes free of enslavement to the Argives.

εἴρηται λόγος a strong formula of conclusion (especially when following on ἀλλ' εἶμι in 1009). Although it is conceivable that it might be followed by some concluding comment of a general nature, it is not appropriately followed by lines which merely rephrase what has just been said (as 1013–14 do). Of similar formulae, only *Med.* 354 λέλεκται μῦθος ἀψευδὴς ὅδε is followed either immediately or very quickly by the departure of the speaker (Creon);[1] cf. *Hec.* 1284, where εἴρηται γάρ is followed by the forcible gagging and removal of Polymestor. The exact words εἴρηται λόγος appear at the end of speeches at *Eum.* 710 and *Or.* 1203 (Athena concludes her rhesis proclaiming the founding of the court, and the voting follows; Electra finishes her explanation of the plan to kidnap Hermione, and Orestes welcomes it). In *Phil.* 389 λόγος λέλεκται πᾶς closes Neoptolemus' tale of his quarrel with the Atreidae, but is followed by a line and a half of wish before a short choral stanza and Philoctetes' reply; and in *IA* 400 ταῦτά σοι βραχέα λέλεκται καὶ σαφῆ καὶ ῥάιδια closes Agamemnon's rhesis but is followed by a one-line warning to Menelaus, choral comment, and stichomythia. At this point Men. goes off, probably by the side opposite to that taken by Creon.[2]

[1013–18] the strongest charges against these lines are based on their poor relationship to what precedes. (1) The repetitious comment in 1013–14 is clumsy and inappropriate after εἴρηται λόγος (previous note). (2) The repetitions *per se* are clumsy (στείχω after 997 εἶμι and 1009 ἀλλ' εἶμι; θανάτου δῶρον ... δώσων after 998 ψυχήν τε δώσω; νόσου ... ἀπαλλάξω χθόνα after 1012 ἐλευθερώσω γαῖαν). Additional complaints have less certain force: (3) διέρχομαι in 1016 is used in a surprising or unexampled way; (4) λαβών in 1015 is clumsy. The serious charges are against 1013–14, which were separately deleted by Markland and Polle. But the connection with γάρ in 1015 coheres poorly with the strong sense of closure created in 1009–12, and it is better to delete the whole passage, with Scheurleer, Paley, and others.[3]

The only way that the passage might be made palatable on stage would be for Men. to begin to move off, then pause after several steps to draw a wider lesson from his action: for such a start-and-stop departure, cf.

---

[1] I am not persuaded by Nauck's deletion of 355–6 (deleted by Diggle, defended by Page). It is a *petitio principii* to delete 355–6 on the grounds that a *Schlussformel* must always be the end of a speech; and, in any case, 354 is not a straightforward *Schlussformel*, but a threatening assurance of truth and resolve meant to strengthen προυννέπω ... θανῆι.

[2] Men. naturally never says good-bye to Joc., a gesture that was mentioned as part of his ruse and that would needlessly delay or jeopardize his heroic act. The Budé editors contemplate, then reject, such a visit indoors.

[3] Mueller-Goldingen, 156–7, considers and rejects the hypothesis that 1009–12 are spurious and 1013–18 genuine. See also 997–8n.

Cassandra in *Ag.* 1285–330.[1] A defender of the lines may also compare
the repetitiousness of rheseis in which a character is saying farewell to life
(*Aj.* 815–65 (only some of the repetitions are removed by the deletion of
854–8, accepted by Lloyd-Jones and Wilson), *Hcld.* 574–96; *Hec.* 342–78,
402–37) or of Praxithea's lengthy explanation of her willingness to sacrifice
her daughter (fr. 360, with decision announced in line 4 and rephrased in
38–9, [42 del. Busche], 50–2). Yet in Men.'s compact and hurried speech
there is less place for such lingering, and in such a case one would expect
asyndeton after 1012 and a generalizing beginning to the afterthought (cf.
the conclusion of Praxithea's speech, fr. 360.53–5 ὦ πατρίς, εἴθε πάντες οἳ
ναίουσί σε / οὕτω φιλοῖεν ὡς ἐγώ· καὶ ῥᾳδίως / οἰκοῖμεν ἄν σε κοὐδὲν ἄν
πάσχοις κακόν; also *Dysc.* 743–5 with Gomme–Sandbach's note).

[1013] θανάτου   defining gen., wrongly glossed by Σ with λείπει ἡ
διά, leading to the simplification θανάτωι (Gχ), which imposed on some
edd.

δῶρον οὐκ αἰσχρόν   cf. *Tro.* 401 στέφανος οὐκ αἰσχρός, *IT* 593 μισθὸν
οὐκ αἰσχρόν.

[1014] νόσου δέ   transition to a finite clause is more idiomatic and gives
a more forceful lead-in to 1015–18 than a co-ordinated future participle
νόσου τε [γε Lenting] ... ἀπαλλάξων (Rf, Scaliger).

**[1015–16] λαβὼν ἔκαστος ὅ τι δύναιτό τις / χρηστὸν διέλθοι τοῦτο κἀς
κοινὸν φέροι**   the sense is probably 'if each man were to take whatever
useful thing he might ⟨do or contribute⟩ and examine it thoroughly and
apply it to the common good'. There is minor ambiguity or clumsiness in
1015 not so much because of λαβών (which can often be used quasi-
redundantly [K–G II.87 Anm. 10], but does, I think, contribute something
to the sense here) as because one is uncertain what, if anything, to understand with δύναιτο. The verb might be absolute ('whatever useful capacity
one has') or one might understand a general ποιεῖν or, from the following line, a more specific διελθεῖν καὶ φέρειν. Any initial temptation to
understand λαβεῖν with δύναιτο would presumably be suppressed by the
context: the point is to use properly whatever one has, not to acquire
something from another source. For διέλθοι no fewer than four meanings
have been proposed: (1) 'conduct, put into operation' (so apparently Σ
μεταχειρίζοιτο, cf. LSJ s.v. 3–4); (2) 'expend' (Paley, suggesting the phrase
is based on διελθεῖν χρήματα, an antonym of χρημάτων φείδεσθαι, but the

---

[1] Saïd, 519–21, views delayed exits (like delayed entrances) as characteristic of this play, and interprets both the final rhesis of Et. and these
lines of Menoeceus in that light.

former is never attested, 'go through one's money' being an anglicism);[1] (3) 'bring to an issue' (Pearson; Budé 'et le réalisant'); (4) 'go through, review, consider in detail' (cf. LSJ 1.6; Wecklein 'durchginge, um nichts auszulassen'). There is no warrant at all in Greek usage for (1) or (2). Pearson's proposal is based on the meaning he ascribes to the verb in Solon 36.15–17 West ταῦτα ... ἔρεξα, καὶ διῆλθον ὡς ὑπεσχόμην, and Her. 426 δρόμων τ' ἄλλων ἀγάλματ' εὐτυχῆ διῆλθε. But these are rather instances of the meaning 'go through, work through (a task or series of tasks) to the end', 'come through successfully' (cf. LSJ 1.2), which is also seen in Her. 1276, Xen. Oec. 9.6, 6.3 (absolutely), and (by implication) TrGF adesp. 514 K–S τῶι δ' ἔργωι κακῶς [sc. πάντα διέρχηι]; cf. διεξελθών Phil. 1419. This sense is not suitable here, since the good citizen is to bring the χρηστόν out for public use. (Cf. Craik's illogical transl.: 'seizing what he could of good, were to accomplish this and bring it to the common pool for his country'.) So I prefer (4), which is a development of διέρχομαι in the sense 'discuss ⟨a subject⟩ thoroughly', 'go through ⟨an argument⟩ in detail', 'enumerate'. This is very common in fourth-century prose, but is as old as Hom.h. Aphr. 276, Pindar N. 4.72, Prom. 874, Med. 530 (cf. LSJ 1.6); and already in Thuc. 1.21.1 'discuss, review' is applied to written rather than oral enumeration, and in IT 672 διῆλθον χἄτερον λόγον τινά is applied to mental review (cf. Hipp. Decent. 8 οὐ γὰρ οἷόν τε διέρχεσθαι πάντα τὸν ἰητρόν). Most nearly comparable is the close association of διέρχομαι with words of mental examination, as Isoc. 5.149 ταῦτ' οὖν ἐξετάσας ἅπαντα καὶ διελθὼν πρὸς αὑτόν, 11.47 σκέψαι δὲ κἀκεῖνο καὶ δίελθε πρὸς αὑτόν, 15.306 καὶ διέλθετε πρὸς ὑμᾶς αὐτοὺς καὶ σκέψασθε; cf. Alc. 15 πάντας δ' ἐλέγξας καὶ διεξελθὼν φίλους. The usage is unusual, but in view of Eur.'s innovative use of the verb in IT 672 it is difficult to argue that διέλθοι is a clear index of post-Euripidean authorship.

[1016] κἀς κοινὸν φέροι εἰς (τὸ) κοινόν is common with verbs of saying (LSJ s.v. κοινός B.III.1), in much the same sense as εἰς μέσον, but the phrase is also used for any contribution for general use, such as at a shared banquet (Xen. Mem. 3.14.1 εἰς τὸ κοινὸν τιθέναι) or in contexts of public service (Xen. Cyneg. 13.11 παρέχουσι, Isoc. 10. 36 ἀπεδίδου, Dem. 59.96 κατέθηκαν, Hyperid. epitaph. col. 6, 40–1 κατέθεσαν; cf. Pl. Crat. 384b7, Laws 796e1, Xen. Oec. 7.13, and with εἰς μέσον Cycl. 547, Eccl. 602, and esp.

---

[1] In Pindar I. 3.17 πλούτου διέστειχον, if πλούτου does go with διέστειχον and not with σύννομοι in the previous line (see Slater, Lex. Pind. s.v. διαστείχω, and Thummer ad loc.), the sense seems to be 'went their way amidst wealth', thus 'made use of their wealth', but not 'expend (fully) their wealth'.

Su. 438–9 τίς θέλει πόλει / χρηστόν τι βούλευμ' ἐς μέσον φέρειν ἔχων;). For χρηστόν as object cf. *Hel.* 1038 ὡς δή τι δράσων χρηστὸν ἐς κοινόν γε νῶιν.

[1017–18]   for the sentiment, cf. Praxithea's concluding gnome (quoted 1013–18n.).

κακῶν ... ἐλασσόνων πειρώμεναι   by an extension of meaning πειράομαι, 'make trial of and so get experience of' is simply 'experience' (LSJ B.II.2); cf. fr. 402.7 τῶν τρόπων πειρώμενοι, *Hec.* 1294–5 πειρασόμεναι μόχθων, fr. 198.2, 285.18; Dem. 18.253 πολλῶν κακῶν πεπείραται.

1019–66: THIRD STASIMON

STRUCTURE AND FUNCTION

The single pair of moderately long stanzas is in iambo-trochaic rhythm, recalling the rhythm of the second pair of stanzas in the parodos and of the first stasimon. Like the first stasimon, this ode begins with the arrival-motif and gives an impressionistic narrative of an important episode from the earlier history of Thebes. Both the earlier iambo-trochaic sections also feature crises in which the gods are ambivalently involved, as here; the final lines of this ode in fact recapitulate the founding event narrated in the first stasimon, now with the fuller awareness of its dangerous legacy thanks to the explanation provided by Tir. in the previous scene. More-over, without a rhythmical resemblance, the strophe recalls and expands on the description of the Sphinx's attack in the second stasimon (806–11). Other connections of diction and theme that make this ode a vital part of the 'song-cycle' are presented below.

As elsewhere in this play (and as often in the choral odes of tragedy), the movement is from past to present. The strophe presents the visitation of the Sphinx, the first half being an apostrophe to the monster in which the real content is all carried in appositives and a relative clause, as is typical of the 'dithyrambic' style. The rest of the strophe expresses the effects on the citizens in short phrases with frequent paralleling of structure. The antistrophe begins with another arrival, that of Oedipus, and in short sentences built of short phrases implicitly contrasts his flawed victory over the Sphinx and tainted rescue of the city with the apparently purer victory of Menoeceus in the present crisis, ending with a glance back to the founding act that began the recurrent troubles. Apart from the interest of its language and style, then, what this stasimon contributes is an important exposure of the disaster that lurks beneath victory, success, and rescue in the life of Oedipus and in the history of Thebes, and it exploits this darker theme as foil to a simple praise of Menoeceus. A number of critics have appreciated these functions of the ode (see esp. Panagl and Parry (diss. and

Lyric Poems 63–4)), but detractors of the play have often echoed incau-
tiously the captious complaint in Σ: πρὸς οὐδὲν ταῦτα· ἔδει γὰρ τὸν χορὸν
οἰκτίσασθαι διὰ τὸν θάνατον Μενοικέως ἢ ἀποδέχεσθαι τὴν εὐψυχίαν τοῦ
νεανίου. ἀλλὰ τὰ περὶ Οἰδίπουν καὶ τὴν Σφίγγα διηγεῖται τὰ πολλάκις
εἰρημένα (cf. ΣArist. *Acharn.* 442). In fact the chorus does express pity
(1057) and welcome the bravery of the youth (1054–5, 1060–1), and the
familiar story is 'narrated' mainly to set up an interpretation of past and
present in the antistrophe.

The structure of the ode is again marked by rings and parallelisms. Both
stanzas begin with arrival, using the same verb (ἔβας, ἔβα), the first has
the uncommon πτεροῦσσα at both beginning and end (reinforced by
μειξοπάρθενος and παρθένος), a larger ring is marked by ἁρπαγά in 1021
and ἁρπαγαῖσι in 1066, and the structure of 1042 ἁ πτεροῦσσα παρθένος
τιν' ἀνδρῶν and 1066 ἁρπαγαῖσι δαιμόνων τις ἄτα is isometric. There is
heavy use of anaphora and anadiplosis and other sound-figures, a feature
that will also be prominent in the next stasimon: 1019, 1022, 1030, 1031,
1033–4, 1036–7, 1038, 1047–47bis, 1054, 1061–2. Words for city, land,
and fatherland abound; the double use of πτεροῦσσα in the strophe is
reinforced by πτεροῖς in 1024; καλλίνικος/-α is significantly repeated (1048,
1059), and the sequence 1044 τλάμων, 1047bis τάλας, 1054 μέλεος emphasizes pity for Oedipus.

Motifs showing connections backward to the earlier odes include:
arrival-motif, earth-born monster (Sphinx), another serpent (Echidna),
birth and motherhood (note λόχευμα 1019–20 as in 803, but also 1060–1),
blood and slaughter, divine agency or sponsorship (Apollo, Athena,
and anonymous divinities in 1031–2, 1066). Specific items of diction
include τέρας (1023bis ~ 806), χαλαῖσι (1025 ~ 808), πτερ- (1019bis,
1024, 1042 ~ 806; more specifically, 1042 πτεροῦσσα παρθένος ~ 806
παρθένιον πτερόν), ἑπτάπυργα (1058, cf. 245), τάνδε γᾶν/γαῖαν (1045,
1065, cf. 245, 638, 681, 688), εἰς ἀγῶνα (1052 ~ 259). Other details of the
Sphinx's attack also echo 806–11 (lifting of victim, divine sponsorship,
unpleasant 'song' = riddle), just as 1062ff. (αἷμα λιθόβολον) recall 662ff.

1019–66 Metre cf. note on 202–60 metre (at end).

1019/1043	∪–∪–|	ia
1019bis/1043bis	–∪–∪–∪–	lec
1020/1044	∪–∪–∪––‖ᶜ	ia, ba
1021/1045	––––∪–|	mol, cr
1022/1046	∪–∪–∪–∪–‖ˀ	2 ia
1023/1047	–∪–∪–|	Kurzvers
1023bis/1047bis	–∪–∪–|	Kurzvers
1024/1048	–∪–∪–|	Kurzvers

435

1025/1049	‒ ‒ ⏑ ‒ ⏑ ‒ ‒ ‖ᶜ	ia, ba
1026/1050	⏞ ‒ ‒ ‒ ⏑ ‒ │	mol, cr = ba, cr
1027/1051	⏑ ‒ ⏑ ‒ ⏑ ‒ ‒	ia, ba
1028/1052	⏖ ⏑ ‒ ⏑ ‒ ⌒ ‖ᵇ	ithyph
1029/1053	⏖ ⏑ ‒ ⏑ ‒ ‒ ‖ᵇ²	ithyph
1030/1054	⏖ ⏑ ⏖ ⏑ ⏖ ⏑ ⏖ ⏑	2 tro
1031/1055	⏖ ⏑ ⏖ ⏑ ‒ ⏑ ‒ │	lec
1032/1056	‒ ⏑ ‒ ⏑ ‒ ‒ ‖ᶜ	ithyph
1033/1057	⏑ ‒ ⏑ ‒ ⏑ ‒ ⏑ ‒ │	2 ia
1034/1058	⏑ ‒ ⏑ ‒ ⏑ ‒ ⏑ ‒ │	2 ia
1035/1059	‒ ⏑ ‒ ⏑ ‒ ‒ ‖ᶜ	ithyph
1036/1060	⏑ ‒ ⏑ ‒ ⏑ ‒ ⏑ ‒ │	2 ia
1037/1061	⏑ ‒ ⏑ ‒ ⏑ ‒ ⏑ ‒ ‖ᵇ¹	2 ia
1038/1062	‒ ⏑ ‒ ⏑ ⏖ ⏑ ‒ ⏑ │	2 tro
1038bis/1062bis	⏖ ⏑ ‒ ⏑ ‒ ⏑ ‒ ‖ᶜ	lec
1039/1063	‒ ‒ ‒ ⏑ ‒ ⏑ │	sp, tro
1040/1064	‒ ‒ ‒ ⏑ ‒ ⏑ │	sp, tro
1041/1065	⏖ ⏑ ⏖ ⏑ ⏖ ⏑ ‒ ⏑ │	2 tro
1042/1066	‒ ⏑ ‒ ⏑ ‒ ⏑ ‒ ⏑ ‒ ‒ ‖‖‖	tro, cr, ba

NOTES TO METRICAL SCHEME

1019bis/1043bis the transmitted colon-division (Π²Π⁷ and almost all mss.) presents λόχευμα / and ἀποστολαῖσιν /, and a mixed scansion as ia, 2 tro, ithyph has been favoured by some (most recently Dale, *Metr. Anal.* 3.248); but see Stinton, 'More rare verse-forms' 96, for the pure iambic interpretation. The ancients regularly avoided (or eliminated) splitting a word between lyric cola, so there is no reason to ascribe special weight to the evidence of the papyri here.

1021/1045 for the molossus in the first metron of syncopated ia dim, see Dale, *LMGD²* 73; note that both instances are in proper names, as is the responsion of molossus Διρκαίων with bacchiac in 1026/1050.

1022/1046 period-division here is uncertain. There may be a single run of iambic metra from 1021–5, or period-end could be posited at 1021/1045 instead of 1022/1046. My preference is influenced by the antistrophe and by possibility that 1022/1046 is catalectic by the principle of contrast.

1023–4/1047–8 the same sequence of three cola occurs in *Or.* 992–5; in dochmiac contexts it is rightly called hypodochmius, but here it may be felt to be a short iambo-trochaic unit with no dochmiac connotations: Wilam. *GV* 406, Dale, *LMGD²* 114–15. Cf. 679bis above.

1026/1050 cf. (also opening a period) *Ion* 190 ἰδού, τᾶιδ' = 201 καὶ μὰν τόνδ'; (within a period) S. *El.* 485 -κτος ἀμφή- = 500 -ροις οὐδ' ἐν; further exx. in Diggle, *ICS* 6 (1988) 86–7.

1026–32/1050–6   to maintain pure iambic analysis, Wilam. *GV* 177–8 (reiterating *GGA* 1900, 47–9), followed in essentials by Dale, *Metr. Anal.* 3.248, treats this as one period: ba (mol), cr, ia | ba, cr, ia 5 ia ithyph. This does away with brevis in longo at 1028/1053 and absence of period-end at the ba πεδαιροῦσ' in 1027, both of which can be defended. On the other hand, it requires a ῠ in 'Ερινύν (or with ῡ an unlikely long anceps in heavily resolved context) and spoils the typical resolved trochaic dimeter ἔφερες ἔφερες ἄχεα πατρίδι with resolution over the first two syllables of each trisyllabic word (three out of four times with accent on the first syllable of the resolution) and coincidence of metron (and 'foot') with word-breaks (continued in φόνιος φόνια; cf. τέκεα μέλεος in antistrophe). As for the quantity of υ in 'Ερινύν, in tragedy nom. -υς and acc. -υν are in many words treated variously for metrical convenience (K–B 1.439 Anm. 2); but in thirty-two other instances of 'Ερινύς/ύν in drama there is not a single proved case of short vowel: LSJ allege *Med.* 1260 (dochmiacs), but apart from the problems of establishing the text of the line, ῡ is permissible there (first anceps of dochmiac, with inexact responsion as in 1252 = 1262 and 1258 = 1268). ῡ is certain in two places (in anap. *Med.* 1389, *Se.* 887; highly probable in dochmiacs *Se.* 700). In trimeters the nom. and acc. appear fourteen times, always in positions 3-4-5 (cf. in tro. tetr. *Tro.* 457), never in 1-2-3 or 7-8-9, which would require ῠ.

1027/1051   Dale, *LMGD*² 72, overstates the case for the need to recognize period-end after cr + ba or ia + ba; for qualifications, see Parker, 'Catalexis' 20 n. 17, and Stinton, 'Pause' 40. Here the fact that ba is followed not by anceps or short, but by resolved longum, makes a difference.

1039–40/1063–4   for the opening spondee, see metrical note on 685–7.

1019–66: COMMENTARY

1019 ἔβας   the parallel with other arrivals (see above) makes it clear that the sense here too is 'you came, you came', not 'you went, you went' (Craik, apparently in support of an alleged ambiguity, as if the line at first seems addressed to Menoeceus).

1019bis πτεροῦσσα   cf. *OT* 508 πτερόεσσ' ... κόρα; for the contraction of -όεσσα see Diggle on *Phaethon* 214–15.

1019bis–20 γᾶς λόχευμα νερτέρου τ' 'Εχίδνας   for λόχευμα cf. 803n. The Sphinx is an offspring of the earth (Γᾶς?) because Echidna's mother is Keto, daughter of Gaea and Pontus, and because she was born in the bowels of the earth, where Echidna lived. On Echidna's offspring cf. Hesiod *Th.* 295–332: ἡ δέ in 319 and ἡ δ' ἄρα in 326 are ambiguous enough to allow different interpretations of the descent of Sphinx, either directly from Echidna or from Chimaera (daughter or granddaughter of Echidna); see West *ad locc.*

1021 ἁρπαγά Σ and most mss read dative ἁρπαγᾶι, which could be construed as modal (and echoed in case by 1066 ἁρπαγᾶισι, as Craik notes); but the long sequence of nominatives (or vocatives) in apposition is characteristic of the dithyrambic and other high-lyric styles and seems better than an alternation of nominatives and datives. Π² gives some support to the nom.: the scribe uses adscript iota elsewhere and has none here. Since the style is allusive, one cannot insist that ἁρπαγά is required for ὦ πτεροῦσσα to be understood.

1022 πολύφθορος πολύστονος for this *Klangfigur* (Breitenbach, 227), cf. *Her.* 1197 πολυμοχθότερον πολυπλαγκτότερόν τε, *Hel.* 198–9 δι᾽ ἐμὲ τὰν πολυκτόνον, δι᾽ ἐμὸν ὄνομα πολύπονον; *Pers.* 83 πολύχειρ καὶ πολυναύτας, S. *El.* 489 καὶ πολύπους καὶ πολύχειρ, Pindar *P.* 9.6–7 πολυμήλου καὶ πολυκαρποτάτας; cf. S. *El.* 9–10, *Pers.* 71, and above 157n. πολύφθορος is found only here in Eur. (eight times A., S., Pindar).

1023 μειξοπάρθενος the rare compound (cf. hapax μειξόμβροτον in A. *Su.* 568 and the more common μειξοβάρβαρος, 138 above, etc.) is attested only in Hdt. 4.9.1 μειξοπάρθενόν τινα ἔχιδναν διφυέα, τῆς τὰ μὲν ἄνω ἀπὸ τῶν γλουτῶν εἶναι γυναικός, τὰ δὲ ἔνερθε ὄφιος and Lycophron *Alex.* 669 (Scylla) Ἐρινὺς μιξοπάρθενος κύων.

1023bis δάιον τέρας same phrase in *Prom.* 352 of Typhos.

1024–5 the instrumental datives by strict grammar go with ἔβας in 1019, but add to the accumulation of details in the intervening nominatives and thus may also be felt to go with the verbal force implicit in ἁρπαγά and πολύφθορος.

φοιτάσι for use of the substantive/adj. with generally fem. suffix to modify a neuter, cf. *Cycl.* 505 σκάφος ὁλκάς, *Hel.* 1301 δρομάδι κώλωι, *Or.* 837 δρομάσι βλεφάροις (Schwyzer 1.507 n. 5; cf. 1569n.).

χαλαῖσί τ᾽ ὠμοσίτοις a compressed expression, 'claws that grip prey to be eaten raw'; the deliberate echo of 807–10 in 1024–8 confirms that χηλή here is 'claw', not 'jaw'. For the latter sense, cf. Hesych. χηλή· ὁπλή, ὄνυξ βοός. γνάθος (where M. Schmidt refers to our passage), Σ's gloss σιαγόσιν, and Gow on Theocr. *Epigr.* 6.4. If Theocr. intended the sense 'jaw', his use may derive from a misinterpretation, or overly rational interpretation,[1] of our passage and of *Hec.* 90–1 ἔλαφον λύκου αἵμονι χαλᾶι σφαζομέναν. ὠμόσιτος is a rarer variation on ὠμοφάγος; this use

---

[1] The same desire to flatten the bold language prompted Herwerden's ὠμόσιτος (1878).

echoes *Se.* 541 Σφίγγ' ὠμόσιτον; elsewhere only *Ba.* 338, fr. 82.38 Austin, Lycophr. *Alex.* 654.

1026–7 Διρκαίων ... ἐκ τόπων probably a periphrasis for 'Thebes' rather than an allusion to a specific location of the Sphinx's assault; φοιτᾶσι πτεροῖς implies that the assaults were unpredictable. Paley suggested a reference to her snatching young men near the fountain of Dirce while they were fetching water, but young men do not fetch water when women are available to do it.

1027 νέους for the possible sexual element in the Sphinx's abduction of Theban youths, cf. *Oedipodeia* fr. 1 ἀλλ' ἔτι κάλλιστόν τε καὶ ἱμεροέστατον ἄλλων / παῖδα φίλον Κρείοντος ἀμύμονος, Αἵμονα δῖον and see Delcourt, chap. 3 (but Moret, 11, 147–8, objects that the iconography does not support such a view).

πεδαίρουσ' apart from πεδαίχμιοι in *Choe.* 589 and πεδοίκου in A. fr. 246d, tragic use of Aeolic-Doric πεδ- (never in Soph.) is confined to words from the root of ἀείρω: πεδαιρέω here, *Her.* 819, 872, *Rhes.* 372; πεδάρσιος *Choe.* 846, thrice in *Prom.*, *TrGF* adesp. 47.1, πεδάορος *Choe.* 590. In view of the apparent puns in *Her.* 819 πέδαιρε κῶλον, 872 πεδαίρουσ' ... πόδα, here too with χαλαῖσι preceding there may be a punning suggestion of 'lifting up in one's feet'.

1028 ἄλυρον ἀμφὶ μοῦσαν since ἀμφιφέρω (tmesis, assumed by Σ and Mosch.) is unattested before Quintus Smyrn. and would not yield any good sense here, ἀμφί must be the preposition and govern at least μοῦσαν (see next note). By extension of the local sense 'in the vicinity of', 'associated with', ἀμφί can mean 'in relation to', 'about, concerning' (with expressions of speaking or feeling: Schwyzer II. 439, Slater *Lex. Pind.* s.v. A.I.4; *Tro.* 511 ἀμφί ... Ἴλιον) or 'involved with', 'busy with' (as in ἔχειν ἀμφί τι). So here the sense must be 'in relation to your unhappy song' or '⟨busying yourself⟩ with your unhappy song', and so virtually 'because of' or 'with'. Cf. the equally unique use in Pindar *O.* 10.77 ἀείδετο ... τὸν ἐγκώμιον ἀμφὶ τρόπον, 'in close relation to the manner of encomium'.[1] For this interpretation cf. Σ's διά + acc., Thomas Mag.'s περί, *cum* in the transl. of Barnes and Musgrave, Hartung's 'unter Gesang', Paley's 'with a song'. Pearson suggests instead a temporal use, 'during', citing only *Cycl.* 5 ἀμφὶ γηγενῆ μάχην δορὸς (which could be local: see Seaford).

---

[1] The Pindaric parallel was already adduced by Musgrave, who also cited *O.* 9.96, wrongly, and more aptly Nonnus *Dionys.* 36.439 μετάρσιον ἀμφὶ χορείην (add 15.67 ἐνόπλιον ἀμφὶ χορείην). The latter are explained by Peek, *Lex. Dion. Nonnos* s.v., as instances of acc. instead of dat. (apparently instrumental) for metrical convenience.

ἄλυρον . . . μοῦσαν 'your singing that lacked the (joyful) accompaniment of the lyre', that is, the Sphinx's verse-riddle, already called μούσας in 50 above. This use of ἄλυρος is a tragic cliché (*IT* 146, *Hel.* 185, *OC* 1222, cf. ἀκίθαριν A. *Su.* 681, ἀφόρμιγκτος *Eum.* 332). Some interpreters (Σ) thought μοῦσαν referred to the θρῆνος of the mourners, anticipating 1033–5.

1029 ὀλομέναν τ' 'Ερινύν with the transmitted τ', this is a further object of ἀμφί, 'with (because of) an accursed force of demonic destruction', or with a slight shift in the sense of ἀμφί (cf. 1292n.) and a fully personified Erinys, 'in company with an accursed Erinys'. 1028–9 together could also be taken as lyric hendiadys for 'unjoyful demonically destructive riddle'. Given the dithyrambic style and the possibility that we do not have an identification of μοῦσαν and 'Ερινύν, I believe τ' may be retained. Σ1030 is confused and corrupt and may or may not reflect a text lacking τ'; Hartung was sure that it did and so removed the conjunction, taking 'Ερινύν as appositive to μοῦσαν, which does not produce a significantly different meaning from that proposed. Diggle (1989) also thinks 'Ερινύν is epexegetic of μοῦσαν and suggests that τ' be deleted or changed to γ' (citing Fraenkel on *Ag.* 1585, Denniston, *GP²* 502). Possibly in accepting the deletion and giving ἀμφί a temporal meaning Pearson intended to make 'Ερινύν object of ἔφερες (Mueller-Goldingen does so explicitly), with ἄχη as appositive, 'you brought an accursed demon of destruction, a bloody source of grief for their country'.

ὀλομέναν for the 'modal' use of the participle (reflecting ὅλοιο) see 1529n. But there may here be an admixture of an 'active' meaning, that is, 'damnably destructive' (cf. Willink on *Or.* 1364–5, Bond on *Her.* 1061).

1030 πατρίδι Wecklein remarks 'der Chor vergisst, dass er nicht aus thebanischen Jungfrauen besteht'; but in context the sense is 'their (sc. the young men's) fatherland' or 'the ⟨Theban⟩ fatherland'.

1031 φόνια· φόνιος this rhetorical figure is related to παλιλλογία (use of the same word at end of one verse and beginning of the next) and is cited from Eur. lyric elsewhere only at *Ba.* 373–4 . . . ἀίεις; ἀίεις . . . (Breitenbach, 234); but here we also have a variation in syntactic form (as in paregmenon).[1] There is a similar rhetorical effect in the inexact echoes of *Ant.* 360 παντόπορος· ἄπορος, 370 ὑψίπολις· ἄπολις.

---

[1] Breitenbach refers to P. Herrmanowski, *de homoeoteleutis quibusdam tragicorum et consonantiis repetitione eiusdem vocabuli ab Aeschylo effectis* (diss. Berlin 1881) 51–2, for comparable figures in Aesch. and Soph., but most are simply cases of anadiplosis split over two lines (at *Ag.* 1101–2 some older edd. and Lloyd-Jones' translation have . . . μέγα; μέγ' . . . ,

1032 ὃς τάδ' ἦν ὁ πράξας a mythographer would want to give a precise identification; Hera and Dionysus are mentioned in various sources (see Introd. IV), and some believe that φόνιος here points to Ares (cf. 1006 φοίνιος; see Masaracchia). But the tragic poet often prefers the ominous uncertainty of anonymity. Cf. 810–11n.

1034–5 the precise echoing of sound and structure in the two lines is probably evocative of the traditional style of ritual lamentation: see Stevens on *Andr.* 497 for exx. and further refs.; also Diggle on *Phaethon* 99. Lenting's τε in 1034 would needlessly mar the echo (Denniston, *GP*² 163).

παρθένων although lamentation is the function of the female relatives (so that παρθένων could be the victims' sisters), it is more likely that Eur. is alluding to the grief of the maidens betrothed to, or hopeful of being betrothed to, the young men of the city. Compare the similar mention of unmarried girls in the happier context of admiring an athletic victor: Pindar *P.* 9.98–100, 10.59.

1035 ἐστέναζον either the verb has a unique sense, 'sounded mournfully' (elsewhere the subject is a person or personified thing emitting the noise) or ἰάλεμοι ματέρων implies ματέρες ἰαλεμοῦσαι as subject: in either case, an artificiality of lyric style.

1036–7 Given the style of the passage, it is not certain where to punctuate. The mss show every possible variation. The stop after οἴκοις in · 1035 seen in most edd. since Porson is implied by a gloss in Σ^{MV}1036, by Grotius' translation (perhaps already by Arsenius' paraphrase). Σ^{V}1035 (marked as 'recent' by Schwartz) makes βοάν and μέλος the objects of ἐστέναζον, and punctuation after μέλος is shared by Mosch., Thomas, Tricl., and most edd. up to Porson. Wilam. wanted βοάν to go with ἐστέναζον, μέλος with the ἐπωτότυζε (a few mss have punctuation only after βοάν). The parallel rhetorical structure and the echoing pairing of γενοίμεθ' in responsion suggest to me that the two acc. should stay together. The preciosity of ἰάλεμοι ... ἐστέναζον becomes even more extreme if we add βοάν/μέλος to it, so like most edd. I attach βοάν/μέλος, as internal acc., to what follows.

1036 ἰηΐϊον the cry ἰὴ Παιάν may be used both to call for (a continuation of) blessings and to appeal for relief from sickness or distress. The exclamation also takes the form ἰὴ ἰὴ Παιάν and ἰὴ ἰὲ Παιάν and can be

---

but modern edd. tend to put the question mark before μέγα and accept a simple anadiplosis). The most relevant example cited is S. *El.* 1163–4 ... ὥς μ' ἀπώλεσας· / ἀπώλεσας δῆτ'. ...

shortened to plain ἰή ἰή (Bacch. fr. dub. 60.37, A. *Su.* 114 (followed by
ἰηλέμοισι), *Pers.* 1004, *Acharn.* 1206, Call. *hymn* 2.25, etc. (ἰὴ ἰή, aspiration
by learned etymology, cf. Ap. Rhod. 2.712); perhaps Simonides 519 fr.
78.i.10 *PMG*). ἰηϊήιος (not in LSJ or Suppl.) is extant only here, as a
metrically convenient variant on the ritual epithet ἰήιος, used in tragedy
also to mean 'mournful, grievous', *OT* 173 ἰηΐων καμάτων, E. *El.* 1211
ἰήιον γόον, *Hyps.* fr. 1.iii.9 ἔλεγον ἰήιον (cf. 657n. on εὔιος). Wilam. avoided
the hapax by writing ἰὴ ἰήιον; Pearson wrongly views it as a musical
innovation akin to εἰειειλίσσουσα in *Frogs* 1348. Before the unique form was
found in Π²Π⁷ editors were content with Tricl.'s βοὰν βοάν, . . . μέλος μέλος.

1038 ἄλλος ἄλλον ἐποτότυζε 'another person keened forth a mournful
cry for another victim'. I am now persuaded by JD that the more exquisite
unaugmented form of the verb (Brunck, now Π⁷; for lack of augment see
Diggle, *Studies* 65-6) should be preferred to the augmented form with
Battier's ἄλλ' ('another person keened forth another mournful cry, mournful song, in succession', with the asymmetry of having ἄλλ' agree with
only one noun of the rhetorical pair). With transmitted ἄλλον the verb
has both internal and external objects (cf. passive ὀτοτύζεται in *Choe.* 327,
with Garvie's note), or ἄλλον is object of the verbal notion βοάν/μέλος
ἐποτότυζε. Diggle's ἄλλος ἄλλοτ' ἐποτότυζε (*Mnem* 39 (1986) 244; Diggle
(1989) 201), with the adverb reinforcing διαδοχαῖς in a typical way, is
attractive.

ἐποτότυζε hapax in extant Greek; ὀτοτύζω only in *Choe.* 327 and four
times in comedy. Cf. ἐποιμώζω, ἐπολολύζω.

1039 βροντᾶι dat. noun, not 3rd sing. pres. of βροντάω (Kinkel;
accepted by Wecklein (with 1040 ὅμαυλος) and Pearson). The long descriptive passage is otherwise in the imperfect, and there is no place for a
present tense verb: Pearson compares ἐπιστέλλουσ' in *Hcld.* 938, but this
is the visibly fulfilled last action after a sequence of imperfects and aorists,
not a present sandwiched between imperfects. If one wants a verb, βρόντα
(3rd sing. imperf.) could be suggested instead, but ὅμοιος loses point
without the dative noun.

1040 ἀχά τ' ἦν ὅμοιος the nom. must be accepted, since ἀχά forms a
hendiadys with στεναγμός, 'loud groan of mourning', but would be anticlimactic if paired with βροντᾶι. Either ὅμοιος is fem. and here used as an
adj. with two endings (not recognized by LSJ or included in the lists of
K–B 1.535-8, but such treatment is always open to the tragedians and
fairly common with adjs. in -ιος; 1431n., 1575n.); or στεναγμός is felt to be
the more important word in the pair and ὅμοιος is masc. (for this schema
see K–G 1.80, esp. *Her.* 774-6 ὁ χρυσὸς ἅ τ' εὐτυχία . . . ἐξάγεται . . .
ἐφέλκων). Nom. pl. ἀχαί, apparently intended in Π², would create an even
harsher schema, but is not impossible: cf. *Thesm.* 977-81 Ἑρμῆν τε . . .

ἄντομαι καὶ Πᾶνα καὶ Νύμφας ... ἐπιγελάσαι ... χαρέντα. The error ἰαχ-
reflects a common scribal confusion (Elmsley on *Hcld.* 752): cf. *Med.* 149,
205, *Her.* 1027, *IT* 180 (1295n.).

1041 ἀφανίσειεν a sinister understatement, perhaps evocative of political and forensic uses of ἀφανίζω, such as the 'disappearing' of Helots
(Thuc. 4.80.4) or of witnesses (Antiphon *Herod.* 26, 38, etc.).

1043bis Πυθίαις ἀποστολαῖσιν this may mean no more than 'sent by
Delphic Apollo' in the general sense that the movements of Oed. were
controlled and orchestrated by Apollo, whose oracles were fulfilled by the
mysterious coincidences which led to Oed.'s preservation on exposure,
encounter with Laius, marriage to Joc., and discovery of his crimes. The
audience may also think of the version in *OT*, where Oed.'s reaction to the
oracle about his parents makes him decide not to return to Corinth and so
makes him seek his fortune elsewhere. If a more precise meaning is intended, 'sent ⟨with instruction to face the Sphinx⟩ by Delphic Apollo',
then Oed.'s experience more closely matches that of Cadmus in the first
stasimon, sent to found Thebes but thus also sent to battle the serpent and
to incur the consequence of fratricide and Ares' wrath. But such instruction
is not implied in the prologue (49–50 are vague) or in other sources, and
the general parallel with Cadmus is implied in any case. If a listener comes
to an interpretation that is inconsistent with the prologue, the inconsistency
in a detail of this sort is of no importance to the drama.

1046 τότ' ἀσμένοις, πάλιν δ' ἄχη an unbalanced antithesis, more
interesting than (e.g.) τότε μὲν χάρμα, ὕστερον δ' ἄχη (cf. Breitenbach,
212; note the interpolation of μεν in Π⁶).

1047–47bis γάμους δυσγάμους for this figure, see Breitenbach, 237,
Fehling, 287–9 and *Hermes* 96 (1968) 142–55 (list of exx., p. 150),
Kannicht on *Hel.* 363. This may intentionally recall *OT* 1214 τὸν ἄγαμον
γάμον.

1048 καλλίνικος the context undermines the value of the 'beautiful
victory', and a similar irony attaches to other references to 'victory' as a
fine achievement: at 1729 μοῦσαν καλλίνικον ... οὐράνιον the ruinous
victory over the Sphinx is again alluded to, and in 1253 and 1374 victory
polluted by fratricide is paradoxically called καλλίνικος; the chorus-leader's
καλὸν τὸ νικᾶν in 1200 is part of a guarded response that immediately
precedes the uncovering of the bad news concealed up to that moment;
νίκη is tainted with fratricide in 1258, 1368, is unreliably assumed in 1416
and 1461, is exposed as unreal in 1464 (θανόντων οὐδαμοῦ νίκη πέλοι),
and is finally secured in an ignominious rout of an unprepared and un-
armed foe (1464). Cf. also Et.'s use of δίκηι νικηφόρωι in 781. Such
devaluation of a conventionally positive term is typical of tragedy and of
Eur. in particular.

443

1049 αἰνιγμάτων for the gen., 855n.

συνάπτει for significant repetition of this verb, 673n.

1051–4 δι' αἱμάτων δ' ἀμείβει κτλ. 'he brings his sons through bloody deeds into a polluted contest, casting them down into it with his curse'; both μυσαρὸν εἰς ἀγῶνα and τέκεα are governed in common by main verb and participle. So Grotius, King, and Paley; note the reminiscence of 20 πᾶς σὸς οἶκος βήσεται δι' αἵματος, and Oed.'s curse as potential cause of bloodshed for his sons (69–70, 254–5, 474–80, 624,765, 876–80). Musgrave and Wecklein follow Σ in understanding πτόλιν as object of ἀμείβει; if this is preferred, one may consider τ' for δ'. Thomas Mag.'s intrans. gloss has been adopted by some (Pearson: 'passes from crime to crime'; Budé edn: 'au sang versé il fait succéder le sang'). But the two parallels cited have not the person, but an event or act as subject, and both feature paired terms: *Or.* 816–17 φόνωι φόνος ἐξαμείβων δι' αἵματος, 1503 ἀμείβει καινὸν ἐκ καινῶν τόδε.

αἱμάτων probably 'acts of bloodshed'; cf. 1062 below, 'bloody slaughter', and the sense 'bloodshed, murder' illustrated in 1502n.

μυσαρόν commonly applied in tragedy, like μύσος, to the special uncleanliness of kin-murder: *Choe.* 967, *Eum.* 445, *Med.* 1393, 1407, *El.* 1179, 1294, etc.

καταβαλών prob. a metaphor from wrestling (cf. Dodds on *Ba.* 201–3), cf. *IT* 605–6 τὰ τῶν φίλων ... καταβαλὼν ἐς ξυμφοράς; but if there is also a suggestion of the sense 'strike down a sacrificial victim' (*Or.* 1603, *Ba.* 1246), the perversion of ritual language would be characteristic of tragedy. The word is too strong to be simply a variation on καθιέναι εἰς ἀγῶνα (Pearson).

1059 καλλίνικα deliberately echoes 1048 καλλίνικος, but without the irony of the application to Oed. (cf. 855, 858).

1060–1 γενοίμεθ' ... γενοίμεθ' for this 'species of anadiplosis or epanalepsis, in which a word, standing at the beginning of a colon, is repeated for rhetorical emphasis at the beginning of a new colon', see Diggle (1990b) 105.

μάτερες ... εὔτεκνοι critics have noted that the prayer for children conflicts with the chorus' status as temple-servants of Apollo. It is possible to argue that as chosen representatives of their people (rather than war-captives) they are not necessarily consigned to permanent hierodoulia, and there are cases in legend of temporary temple-service in Delphi prior to a normal life elsewhere: 202–60n. (Identity of the Chorus). But this is probably to take too literal a view of the prayer. The first-person wish of a chorus is often intended to provide a model of proper behaviour, attitudes, or values in order to foster the listeners' adoption or endorsement

444

of the same values (cf. the 'ethical' first person in Pindar). This traditional choral function for the moment takes priority over concern about the specific status of the Tyrian maidens. Compare the wishes in *Alc.* 473 (for a wife like Alcestis, spoken by old men), *Andr.* 766–9 (for rich parents, spoken by slave-women). The wish to have a son like Men. is a high form of praise, one that assimilates him to an athletic victor (cf. 1052 ἀγῶνα, 1059 καλλίνικα, and Pindar *P.* 9.97–100 πλεῖστα νικάσαντά σε ... υἱὸν εὔχοντ' ... ἔμμεν).

1062 Παλλάς Athena is invoked as patroness of warfare and of heroic achievement in general, and so relevant to having a son like Men., and specifically as Cadmus' adviser and protector, who may be expected to take an interest in the final laying to rest of the threat of the dragon.

1062–62bis δράκοντος αἷμα λιθόβολον κατηργάσω 'accomplished the bloody slaughter of the dragon effected by a casting of stones'; for αἷμα, not to be taken as metonymy for σῶμα, cf. 1051n., 1502n. λιθόβολον with this accent and meaning is hapax in extant Greek (λιθοβόλος has military applications, of troops or machines that throw stones). Valck.'s λιθοβόλου is an unnecessary regularization. The meaning is of course that Cadmus threw the stones with the inspiration and support of Athena. Craik's transl. misleads ('who by hurling a stone caused to flow the blood of the dragon, thereby prompting the thought of Kadmos to his task').

κατηργάσω for the form, see Teubner *praef.* §20; West's *Aeschylus*, xlii.

1063 Καδμείαν μέριμναν 'Cadmus' zealous effort'; another quasi-athletic connotation: cf. 1052 ἀγῶνα, 1048, 1059 καλλίνικ-, 1061–2, and Pindar's use of μέριμνα to mean 'athletic ambition, endeavour' (Slater *Lex. Pind.* s.v.).

1064 ὁρμάσασ' for the Doric vocalism see Willink on *Or.* 1288–91.

1066 ἁρπαγαῖσι δαιμόνων τις ἄτα the Greek is ambiguous between construing the genitive with ἁρπαγαῖσι or ἄτα. Most have followed the paraphrases of Mosch. and Thomas in taking δαιμόνων with ἄτα; Arsenius and Craik are exceptions, and Wecklein (1881) cited the ambiguity in support of his unnecessary conjecture συναλλαγαῖσι (with γᾶν retained in 1065). For δαιμόνων ἄτα cf. *Hipp.* 241 ἐμάνην, ἔπεσον δαίμονος ἄτηι. The position of τις is not decisive, cf. 1042 (indeed, the isometric structure may support ἁρπαγαῖσι δαιμόνων). The echo of 1021 implies that the visitation of the Sphinx was one manifestation of divine persecution of Thebes, and those who opt for δαιμόνων ἄτα refer ἁρπαγαῖσι solely to the Sphinx's assaults. But the plural ἁρπαγαῖσι and the vagueness of τις at least suggest that the other misfortunes of Theban history, including the troubles of Laius' family, reflect the same disturbed relationship between the gods and Thebes, and that those horrors might be viewed as ἁρπαγαὶ δαιμόνων.

445

FOURTH EPISODE 1067–283

STRUCTURE AND FUNCTION

This episode opens with a stereotypical messenger-scene sequence: after Joc. is summoned out of the palace, the messenger engages her in a short irregular dialogue (1072–89) revealing the gist of the news and then embarks on a lengthy rhesis (1090–199) in response to her request for the full story. After a routine reaction to the narrative by the chorus-leader and then Joc. (1200–7a), Joc. presses for additional information about her sons. In a brief stichomythia (1209–16) she overcomes his resistance, and a second, substantial rhesis is delivered (1217–63). Finally, Joc. summons Antigone out of the palace (1263–9) and in a short dialogue with antilabe (1270–83) insists that the shy maiden join her in going to the battlefield to supplicate Et. and Pol. to call off their duel. The messenger then guides the two women off the stage (1263n.).

The entrance of a messenger-figure (in this case the παρασπιστής of Eteocles) at this point in a play would normally lead an audience to expect a definitive account of the completion off-stage of the actions awaited since the end of the first episode (and in fact anticipated from the very beginning of the play by anyone familiar with the main lines of Thebaid myth): the defeat of the attacking Seven and the mutual slaughter of the sons of Oedipus. Very early in the scene (cf. 1071, 1077, 1079, 1085), however, the audience receives the surprising news that the brothers are still alive. Despite the vague hint in 1085 εἰς τόδ' ἡμέρας and the pious caution of 1197 εἰς τὴν παροῦσαν ἡμέραν and 1198 τὸ λοιπόν, the standard structure of the scene up to 1206a, along with the conventional suspension of time and pressure to act during a messenger's rhesis, creates the impression that the messenger's function is fulfilled with this speech. The sense of reversal is thus all the greater when he is forced to append a continuation of his story and to urge haste upon Joc. The first rhesis has thus been used to retard still further the decisive moment in the brothers' fates and to reinforce the separation of the salvation of the city from that of the brothers. Whether or not 1104–40 are genuine (but more emphatically so if they are), Eur.'s rehearsal of some portion of the traditional account of the assault and defence of the city serves to underscore the one point on which his version differs most strikingly, the failure of the brothers to meet at the Neistid Gate (and this despite the apparent preparation in 621–2). Menoeceus' sacrifice, though mentioned only briefly (1090–2n.), appears to have been effective, as is confirmed by the acknowledgments of divine intervention or favour (1187, 1198, 1199, 1200, 1202), the framing references to salvation (1092, 1199), and echoes of the previous episode and

446

stasimon (esp. 1206–7 recalling 1057–9; also 1200 καλὸν τὸ νικᾶν, cf. καλλίνικ-).

The reversal contrived in the middle of the episode plays in part on the audience's feelings, but more strikingly on the feelings of Joc. as observed and sympathized with by the audience. The turn-around exploits the conventional notion of a messenger's reluctance to give bad news, which in this case also echoes the behaviour of Tir. in the previous scene. Many tragic messengers have no more to say after their rhesis and leave after delivering it. A few are held on stage for additional dialogue (usually very briefly: *Aj.* 792–802, *Ant.* 1246–56, *OT* 1287–96, *Hcld.* 883–91, *Hipp.* 1261–4, *Su.* 752–70; cf. named characters functioning as messengers, *Trach.* 815–20, *Alc.* 201–12). Very rarely the news is broken up into separate rheseis: 1356–479 below, *Pers.* 299–514, Soph. *Eurypylus* fr. 210. The only close parallel both for the emotional reversal and for the length of the appended rhesis is *Ag.* 617–80, to which Eur. may be consciously alluding. The psychological dynamic is by this point a familiar pattern in the play: previously we saw Joc.'s joyful greeting and hope to reconcile her sons reversed by a sorrowful farewell and an exacerbation of her sons' animosity; then Et.'s military overconfidence reduced to *aporia*, and Creon's confident patriotism shattered by Tir.'s harsh demand. For Joc., the reversal prompts a renewal of previous action. The messenger suggests that she might have σοφοὺς λόγους (1259) to apply in the crisis, recalling the claim of σοφία in her futile attempt to persuade her sons in the agon; and she tells Antigone (1277) that λύειν ἔριν is again her purpose (cf. 81, 445), although this time supplication will be the means. The parallelism between Joc.'s earlier and present role is marked also by the two summonses, 296–300 and 1067–71, which both allude to the old woman's slowness to appear.

At the beginning of the scene we are reminded of Oedipus' presence in the house (1088–9). In the rapid concluding sequence, it is Antigone who is called forth, with a deliberate evocation of the 'secluded-maiden' theme emphasized in the teichoskopia. We find already here suggestions that dire events no longer leave room for an etiquette of modest seclusion, a notion to be developed further in Ant.'s aria and in the exodos.

For the conventions and artistry of the Euripidean messenger's speech, see now DeJong, who provides full bibliography of earlier studies.

1069–71   for the stage-convention of shouting indoors and knocking cf. *Choe.* 653–8, *IT* 1304–6, *Hel.* 435–6, *Ba.* 170–5, perhaps *IA* 801–3. The visitor assumes a slave is stationed near the door or will come to the door either to open it or to hear and convey the visitor's request. In *Choe.* the summons is made thrice, to create suspense, play on the thematic number three, and allow for the ironic comment about φιλοξενία; in *Ba.* the summons is made twice, partly to allow for the emergence of a character slowed by age, as also here (cf. 299 τί μέλλεις).

ὠή this cry, 'halloo', is designed to make contact with someone unseen (cf. Kannicht on *Hel.* 435–6).

μάλ' αὖθις a strengthened form of αὖθις, commonly used with reiterated exclamations of grief and pain; the use here is most similar to that in *Choe.* 654. I assume a brief pause after 1068 before the renewed (knocking and) shouting. Jackson, *Marg. Scaen.* 173–4, suggests a second pause after αὖθις, then a noise at the door, and also punctuates with a period after ὅμως. The second pause is possible, but unnecessary. It is true that ἀλλ' ὅμως is often used elliptically, but what is to be understood here? (ἐκπορεύετε?) For ἀλλ' ὅμως with following verb cf. S. *El.* 450–1 σμικρὰ μὲν τάδ', ἀλλ' ὅμως / ἄχω, δός, *OT* 998, *Alc.* 218, cf. *Hipp.* 358. So here the sense is 'Even though ⟨it is⟩ after a long interval, nevertheless come forth, hear.'

διὰ μακροῦ sc. χρόνου ('after a long time'), as in Thuc. 6.15.4, 6.91.3, [Pl.] *Alc.* II 151b3; cf. *Cycl.* 439, *Hec.* 320, *IA* 1399 ('for a long time') and the two temporal senses of δι' ὀλίγου (LSJ s.v. ὀλίγος IV.2); not spatial, as in *IT* 480 (so Craik here 'even if from a long way off').

ἔξελθ', ἄκουσον same phrase in *Hcld.* 643; cf. *Clouds* 1165–6.

1070-1 a scholion reporting the absence of a verse in many copies (375n.) is unfortunately not accurately attached in our mss to any particular line (cf. *Text. Trad.* 310, correcting Schwartz); it lies between a note on 1069–70 and one on 1073. It probably referred originally to 1075 (see below), but critics have suggested other suspects. Zipperer saw no point in 1069, branded the sense of διὰ μακροῦ as late, and attached the scholion to it (Mueller-Goldingen, 171 n. 2, tentatively ascribes 1069 to actors, but places too much weight on the scholion). Bruhn (*Lucubr. Eur.* 271), aware of the pattern of interpolation after elliptical ἀλλ' ὅμως in our texts (*Or.* 1024, *Ba.* 1028, possibly *Her.* 1366, *Hcld.* 319), wished to leave an ellipsis here and thus deleted 1070 (writing λήξεις in 1071; but the shift to the second person without the vocative is unlikely). Reeve removed 1070–1, citing Joc.'s failure to hear the good news conveyed in 1071. But this failure to hear is conventional: see *Contact and Discontinuity* 28–30 (add *IT* 1306 as an ex. of a detail not heard by an emerging character who has heard a general noise).

1072 οὔ που on the tendency of this combination (a shortened form of οὔ τι που) to be displaced by ἦ που, as here, cf. Kannicht on *Hel.* 135, Denniston, *GP*² 492 vs. 286. ἦ που can have various tones, including sarcasm, but it is not particularly lively. In contexts of lively concern, whether fearful or indignant, οὔ που is appropriate. A number of passages remain open to dispute (see e.g. Willink on *Or.* 844), but here the earnest ὦ φίλτατ' and the high anxiety marked by the repetition in 1076 and confirmed by 1077 show that οὔ που is right.

1073–4 οὐ παρ' ἀσπίδα βέβηκας periphrasis for ὧι παρασπίζεις (1165n., 1435n.). The locution evokes both the heroic companion who fights beside a comrade acknowledged to be superior (as Iolaus with Heracles) and the ethos of the hoplite warrior, sworn to remain beside his comrades in the line. Cf. στάντες παρ' ἀσπίδ' in 1001 above (also *Med.* 250, *Hel.* 734, *Or.* 653) and the ephebic oath οὐδὲ λείψω τὸν παραστάτην (see Conomis' edition at Lyc. *Leocr.* 77). As 1074 shows, the messenger is not merely a 'squire' or 'shield-bearer' (DeJong 67 n. 17).

[1075] the question is repetitious, its calmer tone clumsily separates two more urgent appeals (*pace* Mueller-Goldingen, 173 n. 6), and its generality is inept after the specific surmise of 1073–4 (elsewhere καινός is used of news about which the recipient is in the dark: *Tro.* 238 ἥκω καινὸν ἀγγελῶν λόγον, *IT* 239 ἄκουε καινῶν ἐξ ἐμοῦ κηρυγμάτων, *Hel.* 1513 καίν' ἀκούσηι πήματ' ἐξ ἐμοῦ τάχα, *Her.* 530, *IT* 1160, *Tro.* 55, *Choe.* 659, *Prom.* 943, *OC* 722). The unattached οὐ φέρεται scholion (1070–1n.) probably once referred to this line (Valck.). It looks more like an intrusion of a parallel from the margin than an actor's addition. The objections to the line can be alleviated by moving it before 1073 (Geel), but it is better to have Joc. begin with the earnest ὦ φίλτατ', οὔ που....

1077 μὴ τρέσηις τόδ', ὡς punctuating after μὴ τρέσηις with τοῦδ' for τόδ' is tempting and may be right. Eur. uses μὴ τρέσηις alone in asyndeton (in mid-sentence) at *Hcld.* 715 and fr. 979.1 as well as (at end of sentence) *Alc.* 328 and *Hcld.* 654; but interjected μὴ τρέσηις ἡμᾶς in *Med.* 307 shows the longer phrase is possible here. Moreover, the ὡς-clause, giving the reason for making the statement ζῆι, is of a type in which the conjunction is normally not postponed. As for the sense of τόδ', it is probably external object 'this' = 'that he may be dead' (easily understood from the context), but could also be taken as internal object, 'don't have fear on this score' (i.e., whether he is alive or dead).

1078 τί δ'; for the various possible forces of τί δέ; see Barrett on *Hipp.* 608 and Denniston, *GP*² 175–6; here, if this punctuation is correct, we have Denniston's use (c), 'and what of the next point?' in transition to a new topic. Diggle (in a note on *Hel.* 873 forthcoming in his *Euripidea* advocates an excited self-interruption instead: τί δ' ἑπτάπυργοι – πῶς ἔχουσι; – περιβολαί; (based on *Hel.* 873 Ἑλένη, τί τἀμὰ – πῶς ἔχει; – θεσπίσματα;).[1]

---

[1] In the Teubner I ascribed this to Apitz, on the basis of a false inference.

περιβολαί   276n.

1080 ἦλθον δὲ πρὸς κίνδυνον   prob. a prosaic locution (Hdt. 6.109.3 ἐς κίνδυνον ἥκουσι μέγιστον, 7.10δ.1, Thuc. 2.11.3, 2.39.1, 8.27.3), also in *Hec.* 244 ἐς κίνδυνον ἐλθόντες μέγαν and 723 above. The subject of ἦλθον is still περιβολαί, the second half of 1079 being treated as parenthetic; ἦλθεν (FᶜP) is a simplification.

δορός   for the gen., either defining or of source, cf. Pindar *N.* 9.35 ἂν κίνδυνον ὀξείας ἀυτᾶς, Thuc. 2.71.2 τὸν κίνδυνον τῆς μάχης, *al.*

1081 ἀκμήν γ' ἐπ' αὐτήν   'yes, ⟨they reached⟩ the very moment of supreme crisis'; cf. Dem. 4.41 νῦν δ' ἐπ' αὐτὴν ἥκει τὴν ἀκμήν (the only other classical use of this idiom). *Her.* 532 εἰς ἀκμὴν ἐλθὼν φίλοις is similar.

1084 καὶ τόδ'   'this too', sc. in addition to her concerns about Et. and the city as a whole, not in addition to some other fact about Pol. (Hermann, inducing improbable conjectures and Paley's claim that εἰ λεύσσει follows ἕν and not τόδ').

1085 ξυνωρὶς   448–9n.

εἰς τόδ' ἡμέρας   ominously leaves an opening for a change in the future (425n.).

1086 εὐδαιμονοίης   a vehement, perhaps lofty 'thank you', as in *Alc.* 1137, *El.* 231 (note apposition μισθὸν ἡδίστων λόγων), *Hyps.* 64.69–70 (with Bond's note: a Eur. mannerism?).

πῶς γάρ   for γάρ here (wrongly emended by Brunck) see Denniston, *GP²* 82 and esp. πῶς γάρ in two other requests for full messenger-rheseis, *Su.* 647, *Ag.* 634 (also τίς γάρ in *Aj.* 282, *Phil.* 327). As with the exclamation εὖ γε in *Phil.* 327, εὐδαιμονοίης is parenthetic and unrelated to the force of γάρ.

Ἀργείων δόρυ   Π⁹ has αργειον, which Fix (on *Ba.* 1) had conjectured, and this may well be right (see now Diggle's note on *Ba.* 1 forthcoming in his *Euripidea*). With δόρυ used collectively or in metonymy for 'battle' or 'military force', Eur. uses a proper adj. twice as frequently as a gen. noun, and (nearly?) always elsewhere with Ἀργεῖον (1080, 1094, *Hcld.* 500 (but Ἀργείων Elsmley, prob. Diggle), 674, 834, 842, *Tro.* 8, 346; cf. Μυκηναίου δορός in 513, 1082; δορὶ ... Ἑλληνικῶι in *Hec.* 5, *Tro.* 868). For the gen. noun cf. 562 δόρυ τὸ Καδμείων and Καδμείων δορί/ός in *Su.* 1036, *Her.* 61; Ἑλλήνων δορί in *Hec.* 1112; and 860 above δορὸς Δαναϊδῶν. *Utrum in alterum* may very slightly favour Ἀργείων here, and in context there is no danger of misconstruing the gen. with πυλῶν, and variation may have been desired to avoid four repetitions of adj. + δόρυ within fifteen lines.

1088–9   the dramatist need not give a reason for the desire to hear the full details, but does so when a special point is to be made. Here we have another reminder of Oed.'s presence indoors and confirmation of his good will toward his city (and thus of his regret for his curse: contrast the wrathful Oed. of *OC*).

1090–2 S. A. Naber, *Mnem* 10 (1882) 148, objected to the fact that the messenger speaks of Men.'s death so briefly and in terms that seem to assume Joc. already knows its circumstances. We may also note that in 1204–7a Joc. herself speaks almost as if she were aware of what was said in the previous episode and stasimon. But these features should not be viewed as evidence that the rhesis has been altered by actors. Greek tragedy is not naturalistic, and characters often display knowledge they would not have in a real-life situation (cf. Barrett on *Hipp.* 1241, Stevens on *Andr.* 1047–288; on convention of messenger knowing where to start his story, see Rijksbaron (1976) 302–7). It is an artistic choice of the poet not to have Joc. react with surprise to the news, presumably because he wants to direct the emotions of Joc. and the audience in another direction (contrast the technique in *Phil.* 329ff., where Neoptolemus is embarking on what should be a lengthy narrative but is interrupted by Philoctetes so that the latter's sense of desolation may be highlighted). Similarly, Eur. has made the points he wants by the presentation of Men.'s decision and by the chorus' praise of it, and it is not dramatically necessary to the complex action of the play that more time be spent on the sacrifice, since other themes now take precedence. The brevity here is matched by the even more extreme case of the silence[1] about the daughter of Heracles after she leaves to be sacrificed at *Hcld.* 602: there too the real interest is in the dilemma posed by the demand for human sacrifice and in the representation of the decision, and there are other important events that take precedence for fuller treatment once the decision is made. In contrast, in *Hec.*, apart from the interest in Hecuba's resistance and Polyxena's reasoning, room is made to display more fully the defiance of the victim, the cruelty of the demand, and the contradictory emotions of the Greek spectators.

1091 μελάνδετον this epithet occurs six times in poetic texts (to LSJ's citations add [Hes.] *Scutum* 221 and E. fr. 373.2), always describing a sword (on the model of *Il.* 15.713 φάσγανα καλὰ μελάνδετα κωπήεντα) except in *Se.* 43 (σάκος). The element -δετος may have no semantic function, merely a stylistic function of high-style variation on μέλας (cf. Hutchinson on *Se.*

---

[1] In *Hcld.* 822 I follow Diggle in reading Helbig's βοείων for βροτείων (which could not in any case refer to the daughter of Heracles, since she was to be sacrificed to Kore without the attendance of males). I disagree with the view that an episode is missing containing a detailed narrative of the human sacrifice (cf. A. Lesky, *Die tragische Dichtung der Hellenen*[3] (Göttingen 1972) 356–7).

43 and cf. 805 above). The dark colour of iron weapons is a poetic commonplace; in tragedy epithets like μέλας and κελαινός often convey sinister overtones ('murderous'), and in *Or.* 821–2 μελάνδετον δὲ φόνωι ξίφος there is a clear reference to the dark stain of blood upon the sword. But I see no certainty that we are proleptically to understand 'dark with blood' here (Pearson) or in *Or.* 1472–3 παίειν λαιμῶν ἔμελλεν εἴσω μέλαν ξίφος (where Σ glosses μελανθησόμενον). See Willink on *Or.* 821, Kannicht on *Hel.* 1656.

1092 λαιμῶν διῆκε cf. *Or.* 1472–3 (just quoted) and *Ba.* 993 φονεύουσα λαιμῶν διαμπάξ. The acc. λαιμόν (O, *recc.*) is barely possible grammatically, but I do not believe that ξίφος λαιμὸν διῆκε and 1397–8 στέρνα ... διῆκε λόγχην defend each other, since the latter seems to me corrupt. A double acc. is found with e.g. διαβιβάζω, διαφέρω, διειρύω (for the type see K–G 1.329; cf. acc. retained with passive διαπεραιωθείς), but the second acc. in such cases is a river or isthmus, something travelled 'across', not 'through'.[1] Some intransitive compounds of δια- take an acc. (διαίσσω, διασεύομαι, διήκω; for διαπεράω, where the acc. is governed as much by the verb as by δια-, see 1394n.), in the sense 'across' or 'into' (*Prom.* 133–4 ἀχὼ ... διῆιξεν ἄντρων μυχόν) or 'through' (*Il.* 2.450–1 διέσσυτο λαὸν Ἀχαιῶν / ὀτρύνουσ' ἰέναι; *Ag.* 476–7 πόλιν διήκει ... βάξις), but not in connection with a piercing wound. δια-compounds denoting such wounding normally have the gen. (διελαύνω, διέρχομαι, διοϊστεύω), and the gen. is very common with prep. διά in this sense, though Homer has three instances of the acc. as well (*Il.* 7.247, 20.269, 23.806). On the whole, idiom and parallels favour λαιμῶν.

τῆιδε γῆι σωτήριον the dat. is supported by 918 above, *Hcld.* 1032, *Choe.* 505, *Se.* 183, etc., but the gen. τῆσδε γῆς (O, *recc.*) has parallels only in *Aj.* 779 and later prose (in *Eum.* 701 πόλεως goes primarily with ἔρυμα unless σωτήριον is taken as substantive). σωτήριον is either predicative with ξίφος or internal acc. (appositive: 'a thing which ...') after διῆκε (see Collard on *Su.* 1070): the meaning is the same in either case. Diggle attractively proposes σωτηρίαν (cf. his emendation of *Hcld.* 402; for corruption of internal acc. in apposition to the sentence cf. also 1131n.).

1093 ἔνειμεν the temporal relations of this narrative do not match the order of events implied by the rest of the play. I believe this is due to the internal needs of this narrative (and indifference to the inconsistency of such details) and not to revision of the passage by later actors. In this

---

[1] Note, however, Josephus *AJ* 10.7 τὴν χεῖρα διαπαρείς, not a valid parallel because here the acc. of the part is retained in the passive (from διαπείρειν αὐτὸν τὴν χεῖρα καλάμωι).

speech, Men.'s death is made to precede Et.'s military preparations (aorist ἔνειμεν as apodosis to ἐπεί + aor.). But Et. was represented as busy with them before the agon (448-9) and as returning to them urgently upon his exit at 783 (cf. 751-3), before Tir. had even arrived to give his prophecy. Similarly, the teichoskopia represented the Argive army close to Thebes and beginning to divide into separate divisions to encircle the city, and at 710-11 they were still about to encircle the city. But in this speech, their approach from the NE is described in 1100 after the Theban preparations are finished.

1095 this line may have suffered damage in a crucial stage of the medieval tradition, since V and O separately omit part of it and AMt lack the whole. But a subject like σὸς παῖς cannot be further postponed, and the rest of the line exactly suits what follows, so we may accept what the mss offer, only adding the conjunction θ' (perhaps already absent in Π⁹, which is hard to read and apparently corrupt at this point: Bremer and Worp, 249-50).

ἐφέδρους 'fresh reserves', to come into action if the Argives defeat the front line of defence; for the metaphor from wrestling contests see Garvie on *Choe.* 866.

1097 τῶι νοσοῦντι τειχέων 'any part of the walls that shows distress'; similarly 1171 τοῦτο παύσαντες νοσοῦν, 'having ended the distress of this section ⟨of the wall⟩'; *Hel.* 1606-7 Μενέλεως ... ὅποι νοσοῖεν ξύμμαχοι κατασκοπῶν.

1098 δι' ὀλίγου 'close at hand'; Musgrave already cited parallels from Thuc. for the spatial sense (2.89.9, 3.21.4, 3.43.4, etc.) against Σ's gloss διὰ βραχέος χρόνου. A temporal sense (also well attested in Thuc.) is possible with punctuation after ὀλίγου, but is necessary with the false punctuation after ἀλκή seen in the older mss and most *recc.* (cf. Σ^V 1095). Of edd. Grotius first had the correct division.

περγάμων extant as a common noun not applied to Troy only in *Prom.* 956, here, and 1176 below (context uncertain in *TrGF* adesp. 627.40).

1099 λεύκασπιν white shields are so firmly fixed as an attribute of the Argives that Aesch.'s chorus can refer to them simply as ὁ λεύκασπις .... λαός (*Se.* 91; cf. *Ant.* 106). The epithet occurs in tragedy only in these places, and one may conjecture that the plural was used in the epic *Thebaid(s)* (cf. *Il.* 22.294). It is uncertain what λεύκασπις actually means: perhaps the shields are painted white (Jebb on *Ant.* 106). Pritchett, *Greek State at War* III.262 n. 90, mentions ἀσπίδες λευκαί included in a treasure-list inscription and χρυσίον λευκόν, which may be an alloy containing silver. Craik, *Eranos* 84 (1986) 104-5, speculates that the shields may have been covered with white linen. For whitening of wooden weapons and of helmets cf. Xen. *Hell.* 2.4.25, 7.5.20.

453

1100-3 in 1104-40, if genuine, we have a description of the approach to the walls in progress; in 1141-3 we have the two sides engaged in *eminus* battle, implying that the Argive forces have come into range of missiles from the walls. At some point we need to be told that the Argives have arrived within such range and the battle is joined, and these functions are served by 1100-3, with reference to trench, trumpeting, and singing of paean. There is corruption in 1101, but excision of the difficulty does not seem helpful, whether one removes the whole passage (Dihle),[1] two lines (1100-1 Wecklein), or only one (1101 Kirchhoff). Without 1101, we must understand ὄντα with τάφρου πέλας: such an ellipse is paralleled (e.g., *OC* 29, 83, *Alc.* 24, esp. *Hcld.* 332 τόνδ' ἀγῶν' ὁρῶ πέλας; K–G II.66–7), but not, I think, when the omitted participle is paired, as here, with a different, expressed participle. Moreover, on reaching the trench an army comes into range of missiles from the walls (it makes best strategic sense to place such an obstacle where the enemy cannot overcome it at leisure and without harassment), and this is precisely the point at which a more rapid advance should begin in order to minimize exposure to enemy missiles. (This significance of the trench is confirmed by 1188.) Without 1101 there will be no indication of rapidity. Similarly, in Wecklein's version, the singing and trumpeting will be left bare and unmotivated if there is no preceding indication that the range for serious battle has just been reached.

1100 Τευμησσόν in mss. of many authors this name is frequently found with τελμ- for τευμ- and with either one or two sigmas; τελμ- is an error from confusion with Carian and Lycian Telmissus; the variation of ending is similar to that for Parnas(s)us and similar words (cf. Teubner *praef.* §20.2). Historically, the double sigma is correct, but we cannot be sure whether Eur. knew or used the historically correct form.[2]

ἐκλιπόντα Teumessus is said by Σ to be more than 100 stades from Thebes (about 12.5 miles or 20 km), but is actually about 5 miles or 8 km distant; of course, it is uncertain whether Eur. knew the distance or expected his audience to know it. Nevertheless it seems more likely that Et. and the messenger saw that the army had left Teumessus (and approached Thebes from the NE) than that they saw it 'leaving Teumessus' (ἐκλείποντα

---

1 Dihle, 72, 75, 81–2, 84, exaggerates the need for topographical and narrative simplicity and concludes that 1100–3, which he thinks imply an undivided Argive force attacking from one direction, are spurious because they contradict both the lines that precede them and 1104–40; he believes that 1100–3 were separately interpolated by a reader into a text that did not yet have 1104–40. But see 1100n.; also 730n.

2 *REG* 12 (1899) 74, line 73, presents a compound name Τευμασιγεν[in an inscription of 250 B.C. from Tanagra.

VC+ against Π¹MOB+; Craik prints aorist but translates present). The implication is that the Argives encamped near Teumessus and moved toward Thebes for this day of battle. Since it is clear from 107–8 and 710–11 that during the course of the play the Argive force has been dividing itself and placing itself all around the city to attack the seven gates, the messenger here is reaching back to the earliest point of the day's activities and telescoping his narrative, omitting the intervening events that the audience already knows and that are implied by 1093–4, 1163, and 1170. This procedure is no more objectionable than referring to Tydeus and Pol. as speaking in unison at 1144, though they are understood to be at separate gates.

τάφρου 714n.

1101 †δρόμωι ξυνῆψαν† the sense required by the context, with mention of ditch and of trumpets and paeans, is either 'they rushed toward the city' or 'they encircled the city'. Σ's gloss περιέλαβον περιεκύκλωσαν supports the latter, and Méridier translated 'vint à la course enserrer la ville'. The metaphor in συνάπτω would then be of 'binding, tying around', as seen in *Ba.* 545–6 ἔμ' ἐν βρόχοισι... ξυνάψει, 615 συνῆψε χεῖρας [Diggle: χεῖρα LP] δεσμίοισιν ἐν βρόχοις; but without some hint such as κύκλωι or βρόχωι I doubt that this metaphor can be operative, and encirclement of the city would in reality be accomplished before the attackers cross or even approach the ditch. For the former sense (assumed in Barnes' *cursu attigit* and by most others), Musgrave made the first attempt at explication, alleging that this is a Greek way to indicate speed: *cursu coniunxerunt urbem Thebanam ut vallo contigua esset* (but for this one needs τάφρωι rather than τάφρου πέλας). Paley hesitantly suggested 'joined the Theban citadel (to their own ranks)', as later Wecklein (1881) *urbem sibi contiguam fecit, i.e., muris ipsis successit.* But it would be normal idiom for ἑαυτούς, not ἑαυτοῖς, to be understood with the verb in an intrans. or absolute sense, with the thing in the dat. (ἄστει, metrically impossible). Some have taken the verb as absolute (as already a gloss, ὀξέως ἐπέβησαν, ἐπλησίασαν) and deemed ἄστυ an acc. of direction (Powell), but such an acc. is very harsh and ambiguous in juxtaposition to a verb that is usually transitive. Thus, no interpretation of δρόμωι ξυνῆψαν ἄστυ satisfies, and corruption is probable. Emendations usually change the verb or add a preposition or both: e.g., Blaydes' ξυνῆλθ' εἰς (but this keeps sing. verb), Carstens' δρόμοισιν ἦλθεν, my own δρόμοις ἐπῆιξαν. Emendations involving plural δρόμοις appear to go against the idiomatic use of modal sing. δρόμωι (about a dozen times in drama), but cf. perhaps *IT* 971, *Prom.* 838, and (lyric) A. *Su.* 819. That the verb in this line should be plural (subject Ἀργεῖοι) is confirmed by Π¹ and the plural glosses in Σ; but if there is corruption, it is old, and sing. verb (or participle) can't be ruled out.

ἄστυ Καδμείας χθονός   cf. *Ba.* 1202 ἄστυ Θηβαίας χθ., *Ag.* 503 οὖδας Ἀργείας χθ., 287 above, *Su.* 9, *Antiope* fr. 48.114, *Samia* 325. The expression seems genuine, but not so common that it might intrude on something else, such as ἄστυ Καδμείων ἔπι.

1102 παιὰν δὲ καὶ σάλπιγγες ἐκελάδουν   paeans or other war-cries and trumpeting are traditionally associated with attack in battle or with the beginning of a race: for both together see *Pers.* 388–95 (κέλαδος, παιᾶν', σάλπιγξ at start of naval battle), Achaeus *TrGF* 20 F 37 (trumpet and cry of ἐλελελεῦ); paean only, Thuc. 4.43.3, 4.96.1 (παιανίσαντες ἐπῇσαν); for trumpeting (also used at start of a race), *Held.* 830–1 (ἐσήμην' .. σάλπιγγι καὶ συνῆψαν ἀλλήλοις μάχην), 1378–9 below (σάλπιγγος ἠχὴ σῆμα φοινίου μάχης, ᾖξαν δράμημα of the duel), *Rhes.* 989, *Frogs* 1042, Thuc. 6.69.2 (σαλπιγκταὶ ξύνοδον ἐπώτρυνον τοῖς ὁπλίταις), *Se.* 393–4 (βοὴν σάλπιγγος, horse-race); S. *El.* 711 (ὑπαὶ σάλπιγγος ᾖξαν, chariot-race). On the paean see Pritchett, *Greek State at War* I.105–8.

1103 ἡμῶν πάρα   cf. *Pers.* 388 κέλαδος Ἑλλήνων πάρα.

1104–40   outside of the exodos this is the extended passage most subject to suspicion of interpolation. For a more detailed review of arguments against the passage made before 1977 see my article in *Phoenix* 32 (1978) 105–28. Since then Dihle, 73–84, and Mueller-Goldingen, 176–8, have added a few more observations in support of the hypothesis of interpolation. The most important arguments have been (1) the impression that the style of the whole is weak or demonstrably unlike Euripides and that particular lines are incurably obscure or corrupt; (2) the judgment that the passage is artistically irrelevant or even artistically in conflict with genuine features of the play. As for (1), I am (after reading it innumerable times in the process of collation) more willing than before to concede that the style is less interesting and impressive than Eur.'s best work: note ἔχων five times in 1107–20, ἐν μέσωι σάκει 1107 and 1114, πεφρικότα/-κός in 1105 and 1121, προσῆγε in 1124 and 1129 (as well as 1104); on the other hand, there is also skilful variation, esp. in the second half of the passage, in referring to the shield-symbols and the positions of the leaders. Moreover, the question remains whether Eur. (or any other poet) may always be assumed to produce the best possible work. Judgments of style are notoriously personal, and for this passage we find the full range from Morus' *Euripideae orationi dissimilis* to Pearson's 'This admirable speech is a model of concise and lucid narration' (speaking, to be sure, of all of 1090–199) and Page's 'an original composition, carefully imitating the style of Euripides'. It is also noteworthy how much the passage differs from Aeschylus' famous descriptions in *Se.*, despite allusions to them: one might have expected an interpolator of the fourth century or later to look solely to Aeschylus for inspiration and so to produce something much more imitative than the present passage. Of the individual obscurities used as arguments for interpolation by critics, the most serious are in 1116–17 and 1135–7, although 1120–2 have also been controversial: see separate notes for discussion. Diction alleged to be evidence of post-Euripidean origin includes 1112 ὑβρισμένα, 1131 ὅλην, 1133 ὑπόνοιαν, but I believe that only ὅλην is somewhat worrisome to defenders of the passage. The detail in 1110 could be regarded as a blunder of careless imitation (see note). Other minor internal points to which objections have been made are answered in the notes on 1104, 1115, 1118, 1119, 1140.

As for (2) the artistry of the passage in the scheme of the play as a whole, the main problem has been the relation of this catalogue of the Seven to the survey of the Seven in the teichoskopia and to the captious 'criticism' of Aeschylus seen in 751–2 (see note). If one views the teichoskopia mainly as an innovative alternative to a report in trimeters by a spy or messenger, the catalogue here seems not merely superfluous, but perverse and anti-climactic. And if one takes too seriously the 'criticism' of Aeschylus, it seems perverse, again, to include the catalogue. But the two namings of the Seven have different characteristics and functions. The one is lyric, informal, uneven, not related to a clear topographical scheme, and keyed to Antigone's shifting subjective reactions. The other evokes the tradition-ally famous names and threatening symbols just before narrating the climactic battle that brings the city salvation; it gives the Seven roughly even treatment, and makes clear the disposition of the attackers all around the city, thus clearing the way for the exciting narrative of actions (which does not, in fact, deal with all seven attackers). The criticism in 751–2, moreover, cannot strictly be used against 1104–40: 751–2 speak of naming the defenders in the midst of the pressures of preparation before the battle; but 1104–40 name the attackers after the battle, in the timeless setting of a messenger's narrative (751–2n.), within a deliberately contrived pause before the revelation of the new danger posed by the duel of the brothers.

Mueller-Goldingen applies too strictly the notion that Eur. is reacting against the version of *Septem* when he insists that Eur. wants to avoid the idea of seven attackers at seven gates and that the catalogue stands in contradiction to the design of the play. Eur. is in fact engaged in sophisti-cated play with the idea of a seven-pronged attack, and even with the idea that Et. and Pol. will meet at a gate in the first battle (note esp. 621–2; also 737–41, 749–50, 754–5, 765, 775, 880, 1093–4). And to place Pol. at one of the gates may simply go along with this manipulation and does not conflict with the notion that he is to be kept alive to fight in the duel with his brother. Dihle's new arguments depend on an expectation of topo-graphical clarity that is not appropriate in an audience of poetry and on the unprovable claim that Eur. avoided the names of the gates entirely in order to underline his difference from the tradition and to avoid the contradictions present in the tradition.

Other objections to 1104–40 may be discounted. The brevity of treatment of Men.'s death is discussed above, 1090–2n. Fraenkel wrongly supposed that 1146 implied that the first stage of battle was carried out by the Seven as *Einzelkämpfer* and that 1104–40, in which the Seven lead λόχοι, could not be genuine. But Eur. has abandoned the notion of *Einzelkämpfer* much earlier in 737–44 (738n.), and 1146 (see note) is about *comminus* vs. *eminus* battle, not about fighting with λόχοι as opposed to alone. Wecklein suggested that Adrastus could not both lead a division against a gate and call for a retreat after the death of Capaneus (1187–8). But he is the senior general and sponsor of the expedition, and the audience can easily assume that some, probably most, of the Seven have been killed by this time, so it is logical for Adrastus to issue this vital order to his whole army.

If the passage is genuine, then the speech ranks with the longest messenger-rheseis in Eur. (cf. *Ba.* 1043–152, *Ion* 1122–228), and its very length contributes to the contrived impression that this speech fulfills the main function of the messenger (1067–283n.). In my opinion,[1] the passage also gives a helpful clarity to what follows: 1100–3 view the Argive army as a whole and mark the initial charge; 1104–40 shift to a detailed view, making clear the disposition around the seven gates; 1141–52 return to an overall view of the *eminus* and then *comminus* fighting, then 1153–86 treat a selection of three gates in fuller detail. The lengthy preliminary description is paralleled in *Ion* 1132–66 (tent), and there was a catalogue of heroes with brief descriptions of their weapons and dress in *Meleager* (fr. 530 preserves nine lines of the messenger's speech).[2] Without 1104–40, the speech is unusually short (comparable only to those in much earlier plays, *Hcld.* 799–866 and *Hec.* 518–82), and the sevenfold division of the attackers is implied only by 1093–6 until, after the composite description of 1100–3 and 1141–52 (including 1144, which gives the impression that Tydeus and Pol. are together), we suddenly find separate gates described in 1153ff., but only three and none of them named, an odd limitation after the previous emphasis on the number seven.

---

[1] Note, on the other hand, Dihle's conviction that the speech with 1100–3 and 1104–40 is confused and contradictory in its topographical implications.

[2] There was perhaps a 'catalogue' of Argonauts in Aesch. *Kabeiroi* and Soph. *Lemnians* (A. fr. 97a = Soph. fr. 385).

Some critics have recently argued that 1104–40 make a positive contribution to *Phoen.* as part of the intertextual play with *Septem*: the catalogue is viewed as a deconstruction of the weight and symbolism of the central scene of that play[1] or as a series of symbols whose meaning must be interpreted by the audience rather than by Et. or the speaker of the lines and which often work against their bearers.[2] While such analyses are of interest if one is certain the passage is Euripidean, the strategies of reading adopted in them might produce very similar results on a spurious passage. Thus it is hard to adduce these readings in the argument over authenticity.

1104 καὶ πρῶτα μέν here not in a temporal sense (before the other leaders led their divisions toward their gates), but enumerative (see *Phoenix* 32 (1978) 112–13), the remaining items in the series being joined with δέ and the end of the series being signalled by 1134 ταῖς δ' ἑβδόμαις. Morus long ago pointed to the occurrence of this phrase in both 1104 and 1141 as a possible index of interpolation, and Fraenkel made the stronger claim that it was meaningless in 1104, a careless borrowing from the genuine 1141.

Νηΐσταις I print the spelling found in Π¹ and C (and advocated as genuine by Unger), but there is no decisive evidence extant to ensure that Νηΐταις is not correct instead. With the σ the sense may be 'Lowest Gates', opposed to the Ὕψισται named in Paus. 9.8.5. Cf. Schober, *RE* 5A (1934) 1431, 28ff., Bremer (1983) 298.[3] On the gates of Thebes, see F. Schober, *RE* 5A (1934) 1428–34; and Wilam. 'Sieben Thoren'. For their imagined locations, see Appendix on Topography. Wilam. argued that the seven gates were an invention of 'the' Thebaid poet:[4] they were not the sites of individual battles, only separate sally-points all on the east side of the citadel through which seven Thebans went to face the Seven in a battle on the plain east of Thebes. On this view, Aeschylus was the originator of the gate-by-gate assault all around the city. The order of treatment and the matching of heroes and gates are quite different in *Se.* and this catalogue (and the order also differs from that in the teichoskopia):

---

[1] Cf. Vidal-Naquet, 'The Shields of the Heroes' (p. 142) in J.-P. Vernant and P. Vidal-Naquet, *Tragedy and Myth in Ancient Greece* transl. J. Lloyd (Atlantic Highlands, N.J. 1981) 120–49; Foley, 128; Saïd, 506–9.

[2] B. Goff, 'The Shields of the Phoenissae', *GRBS* 29 (1988) 135–52.

[3] The reading I report from Hesychius differs from Latte's report and is based on J. M. Bremer's report of his examination of a microfilm of the manuscript H.

[4] Burkert, 'Seven' 39–46, argues that the tale of the seven attackers is an eighth-century epic transposition of an Assyrian ritual.

TEICHOSKOPIA	PHOEN. 1104–40		AESCH. *SE*	
Hippomedon	Neistae	Parthenopaeus	Proetides	Tydeus
Tydeus	Proetides	Amphiaraus	Electrae	Capaneus
Parthenopaeus	Ogygiae	Hippomedon	Neistae	Eteoclus
Polynices	Homoloides	Tydeus	of Onca	Hippomedon
Adrastus	Crenaeae	Polynices	Boreae	Parthenopaeus
Amphiaraus	Electrae	Capaneus	Homoloides	Amphiaraus
Capaneus	seventh	Adrastus	seventh	Polynices

Note that in *Su.* 860–908 the order Capaneus, Eteoclus, Hippomedon, Parthenopaeus, Tydeus more nearly matches the Aeschylean order. There is yet another order in the brief catalogue in *OC* 1313–25. Cf. 1107n. for variation in the shield-symbols.

1105 ἀσπίσιν πεφρικότα a Homeric reminiscence, suitable to the context: *Il.* 4.281–2 φάλαγγες ... σάκεσίν τε καὶ ἔγχεσι πεφρικυῖαι, 7.62.

1106 ὁ τῆς κυναγοῦ ... ἔκγονος cf. *Su.* 888 ὁ τῆς κυναγοῦ ... Ἀταλάντης γόνος.

Παρθενοπαῖος on the metrical awkwardness of the name, see Collard on *Su.* 888–91a.

1107 ἐπίσημ' the consonant-declension noun is a rare, metrically convenient alternative to normal τὸ ἐπίσημον, τὰ ἐπίσημα; cf. 1125, *Se.* 659, [Simonides] 63.2 (*Epigr. Gr.* 327 Page); LSJ also cites E. Schwyzer, *Dialectorum graecarum exempla epigraphica potiora* (Leipzig 1923) 607 for τόπισαμα (Thessaly, fifth cent.), and add ἐπισήμασι in Diod. Sic. 13.3.2.

The shield-symbols are not close imitations of Aeschylus:

HERO	PHOEN. 1104–40	SEPTEM
Parthenopaeus	positive image: mother's *aristeia* (Atalante subduing the boar)	negative image: threat to Thebes (Sphinx in metal relief attached to shield)
Amphiaraus	blank	blank
Hippomedon	Argos Panoptes (positive image of watchfulness?)	negative image: fire-breathing Typhos with many snakes growing from his waist
Tydeus	lion-skin covering (symbol of heroic ferocity and valour)[1]	full moon in centre of star-spangled sky (symbol of pre-eminence?)

---

[1] It is uncertain whether the lion is supposed to have any personal relevance to Tydeus: 411n.

Polynices	threatening image: crazed horses of Potniae	Justice leading armed man home
Capaneus	threatening image: giant carrying whole city torn from foundations	naked torch-bearer, proclaiming he will burn the city
Adrastus	threatening image: serpents (Hydra) snatching Thebans from within the walls	[Eteoclus instead: warrior climbing ladder to sack a tower]

1108 ἐκηβόλοις τόξοισιν a stereotyped juncture in tragedy, which removes the epithet from its original constant attachment to Apollo: *Eum.* 628, *Prom.* 711, *Her.* 472, *Or.* 273; cf. also 1142 below and Timotheus 800.3 *PMG*.

1110 σφάγι' ἔχων ἐφ' ἅρματι cf. 174n. Since the battle commences with the trumpeting in 1102, the σφάγια for this battle should (as Dihle notes) already have been sacrificed (cf. Thuc. 6.69.2: σφάγια and trumpeting are preparations for the pitched battle). Σ tries to obviate the difficulty by suggesting that Amphiaraus has further victims ready in case a need arises for further divination; a slightly more plausible escape would be to note that prophets needed a number of victims available in case the first offering did not give a good result (but once a good result was obtained, Amph. could have left the other victims behind). Pearson believes that the slaughtered animals are carried on the chariot to purify the ground they drip blood on; but Stengel, *Opferbräuche* 99, notes that we do not know what was done with the victims' bodies and cites a case where they were left where slain. More likely, we have here either carelessness by Eur. or the carelessness of an interpolator writing with an eye to the genuine 174 (or in Dihle's view, of an interpolator thinking of *Septem*). (The inconsistency also disappears if 1100–3 are spurious and 1104–40 genuine.)

ἅρματι plural ἅρμασιν (V²Rχ) is not impossible, since the plural is often used of a single chariot (LSJ; e.g., *Hipp.* 111).

1112 ὑβρισμέν' 'arrogant', a bold use, based on putative ὑβρίζειν σημεῖα, 'produce arrogant symbols' (object of thing effected), analogous to the passive τὰ ὑβρισμένα, 'wanton acts' (based on ταῦτα ὑβρίζειν): for the latter, cf. Lysias 3.7, Libanius *declam.* 5.1.3; for the former Xen. *Cyr.* 2.4.5 στολῆι οὐδέν τι ὑβρισμένηι, Aelian *VH* 1.31 οὐδέν τι τῶν ὑβρισμένων οὐδὲ τῶν ἄγαν πολυτελῶν; Diodorus of Tarsus apud Photius *Bibl.* 223.214a οὐδὲν ὑβρισμένον φέρει. Such a rare usage is no more likely to be an interpolator's than to be Euripides' own.

ἄσημ' cf. *Se.* 591 σῆμα δ' οὐκ ἐπῆν κύκλωι. This is the only shield that is precisely the same in *Se.* and *Phoen.*, unavoidably so. The moral distinction between Amphiaraus and the other Argive leaders was a traditional element of the story, but we cannot say whether the contrast in shield-symbol was an invention of Aesch. or had epic precedent.[1]

1115 στικτοῖς ... ὄμμασιν The dappled effect of eyes on the limbs is clear in some Attic vase-paintings (1116–17n., end). Valck. noted the unusual relationship of noun to quasi-passive :-τός verbal adj. (implying object of thing produced, στίζειν ὄμματα, rather than direct object, στίζειν Πανόπτην) and wrongly emended to πυκνοῖς. For such usage, typical of tragedy, cf. 375n.; cf. esp. *Trach.* 357 ῥιπτὸς μόρος, where as here we have a simplex and not compound adj.

Πανόπτην πανόπτης is an epithet of Argus in A. *Su.* 304, Plut. *Mor.* 93c, [Apollodor.] *Bibl.* 2.4, 2.6, Aristides 26.6 Keil, pseudo-Plut. *De Fluviis* 18.6 (*Geogr. Gr. min.* II.657 Müller), and is found alone as the name of Io's guard in *Eccl.* 80, Steph. Byz. s.v. Ἄργουρα, as well as inscribed by a picture of Argus on Louvre G229 (*CVA* France 9. Louvre 6, pl. 45, 7). There is no need to assume a lacuna in which the name Ἄργον appeared, as Hermann did.

1116–17 the most suspect individual passage within the suspect catalogue. Possible approaches are reviewed in detail in *Phoenix* 32 (1978) 118–21. If we reject emendations that make the participles unambiguously modify Πανόπτην in 1115 or that supply a finite verb for this couplet, then the likeliest interpretation is as follows: (1) the participles are neuter plural acc., (2) ὄμματα is in loose apposition to Πανόπτην, (3) κρύπτοντα is here used in an absolute, intransitive sense. The sense is then 'some eyes watching [i.e., opening] together with rising stars, others closing in unison with setting stars', describing a process of continuous relays of active eyes matching the continuous rising and setting of various stars in the course of the night; cf. perhaps Quintus Smyrn. 10.191 Ἄργον, ὃς ὀφθαλμοῖσιν ἀμοιβαδὸν ὑπνώεσκεν.[2] Bergk and others interpreted 'half of the eyes opening at sunset, the other half closing at sunrise', which produces non-

---

[1] I do not agree with the view that the allusion to tradition in σωφρόνως is too brief to have derived from Eur. (Mueller-Goldingen, 180 n. 20).

[2] Cf. the explication of Eustathius 182, 23–31 (on *Il.* 2.103) τὸν φονέα τοῦ Ἄργου καλεῖ, ὃν φύσεως τέρας ἡ ἱστορία παραδίδωσιν ὀφθαλμοὺς αὐτῶι ἀνοίξασα διὰ παντὸς τοῦ σώματος, οὓς ἄλλοτε ἄλλους ἀνοίγων καὶ τοῖς μὲν μύων, τοῖς δὲ βλέπων, ἄϋπνος ἦν διὰ βίου **ἄστροις μέν τισιν** ἀνατέλλουσιν ἐπανοίγων τοὺς μύοντας ὀφθαλμοὺς συνανατέλλοντας ὥσπερ καὶ αὐτούς, **ἑτέροις δὲ αὖ πάλιν** τῶν ἀστέρων δυομένοις ἐγκαταμύων τοὺς βλέποντας ὀφθαλμοὺς καὶ ὥσπερ συγκαταδύων τὸν ἐν αὐτοῖς ὀπτικὸν ἥλιον.

sense and features unparalleled use of σύν and μετά as equivalent of ἅμα + dat. In defence of (1), this agreement is the most natural given the word-order τὰ μὲν ... ὄμματα / βλέποντα. For the loose apposition of a part to the whole (2), the closest parallels come from prose: K–G 1.288 §8: cf. e.g. Hdt. 1.52 ἀνέθηκε σάκος τε χρύσεον ... καὶ αἰχμὴν ... χρυσέην, τὸ ξυστὸν τῆισι λόγχηισι ἐὸν ὁμοίως χρύσεον; for this construction with a person, cf. Plut. *Solon* 27.3 μέχρι πρὸς αὐτὸν [sc. Κροῖσον] ἤχθη, πᾶν ὅσον ... περὶ κόσμον ἐκπρεπὲς ἔχειν ἢ περιττὸν ἢ ζηλωτὸν ἐδόκει περικείμενον, where πᾶν περικείμενον is a description loosely appended to αὐτόν. This case seems harsher because 'eyes' has just been expressed in the dat., but what we have is a kind of *ad sensum* partitive apposition such as is well attested for nominative expressions (see Collard on *Su.* 406–8, cf. 1462–4 below, K–G II.107). For (3), cf. intransitive use of κεύθω in *Aj.* 635, *OT* 968, and of ἀποκρύπτουσι, apparently, in Hes. fr. 290 M–W; but S. *El.* 825 κρύπτουσιν and *Hom.h.Herm.* 416 ἐγκρύψαι, cited by others, are probably not intransitive. A further oddity detected by Munro is the incorporation of ὄμματα into the antithesis τὰ μὲν ... τὰ δέ (normal idiom would have ὀμμάτων or ὄμματα preceding the τὰ μέν), but this seems a possible variation, at least in poetry. If this combination of oddities is too much to stomach, then it is possible to delete 1116–17 (along with 1118) from the catalogue, but it is not clear why anyone other than the original author of the catalogue would have added them. One possibility is that they are designed to bring about conformity with 129 ἀστερωπὸς ἐν γραφαῖσι interpreted as 'star-bedecked in the painting ⟨of his shield⟩' (see *ad loc.*).[1]

The author of these lines seems to envision Argus depicted with eyes on many parts of his body (some open, some closed, and some half-open) against a background of the night sky with stars and some indication of the circular motion of the heavens (cf. *Ion* 1146–58 and the use of rising and falling chariots in the east pediment of the Parthenon). This is possible to imagine for a literary art-object, and it does not matter that archaic and classical vase-paintings of Argus do not depict the figure in this way.[2]

---

[1] 1116–17 have been said to imitate *Se.* 387–90 (Tydeus' shield-emblem, with full moon in starry sky), but apart from the use of 'stars' in both the passages are not similar.

[2] For catalogues of illustrations, see R. Engelmann, *JDAI* 18 (1903) 52–5 (esp. items 10, 11, 13, 14, 22, 24, 25), supplemented by F. Vian, *La Guerre des Géants. Le mythe avant l'époque Hellénistique* (Paris 1952) 44 (esp. items A*bis*, B, C, D, F, H); add Beazley, *Paralipomena*² 347 no. 8 *ter*, and K. Schauenberg, *Antike und Abendland* 10 (1961) 90 n. 147 with pl. 14, 28. See now also N. Yalouris, 'Io 1', *LIMC* v:1.661–76.

Argus is sometimes depicted as a two-eyed figure, but there are at least fifteen Attic vase-paintings earlier than or contemporary with Eur. that present a many-eyed figure, ranging from a Janus-like figure with two faces and only four eyes to a figure with about ninety eyes distributed over arms, legs, shoulders, and chest. The latter (Vienna 3729, Argos Painter, *c.* 500–480 = *CVA* Austria 2, Vienna Kunsthist. Mus. 2, pl. 66) is the best illustration of the dappled effect which is alluded to in 1115 στικτοῖς … ὄμμασιν. There are almost as many eyes on Louvre G229, Siren Painter, *c.* 500–480 = *CVA* France 9, Louvre 6, pl. 45, 7, but it is much restored and many of the eyes redone. These pictures mostly show Argus being slain by Hermes (in one Argus is simply guarding Io in her bovine form), and the artists show all of the eyes open, even when Argus has been mortally wounded and is collapsing in death, but this artistic convention should not be taken as proof that the notion of eyes that slept in alternation was unknown or inconceivable in Eur.'s time.

1118 Valck. first deleted this line (suspecting 1116–17 as well); Hartung and a few others delete 1118 by itself. The line is alleged to be 'inconsistent' with 1139–40, but it is possible to give a particular justification of knowledge here in addition to the general justification of knowledge of all seven attackers that 1139–40 provide.[1] The argument that we are nowhere else told that Hippomedon died is futile (the death of the attackers other than Adrastus was well known to the audience, and Eur. relies on that knowledge in the undisputed part of the messenger's report and the rest of the play, where most of the Seven are simply assumed to have perished).

θανόντος gen. abs. (70n.).

1119 The Homoloid Gate (Tydeus) is conjecturally placed on the east side of the citadel, half way around the city from the Neistan Gate (Parthenopaeus): see Appendix on Topography. Dihle detects an inconsistency between the catalogue and the battle-narrative because in 1163–4 Et. rushes from Parthenopaeus' gate to Tydeus', which Dihle assumes to be immediately adjacent. But a poet would not have expected his audience to keep track of such a detail (even if they actually knew the putative positions of the traditional gates), and the transitions at 1163–4 and 1170–1 do not necessarily imply that the gates visited are adjacent (rather, Et. is going wherever he sees the need of support or rallying).

1120–2 see *Phoenix* 32 (1978) 122–4 for detailed discussion. The passage is clearly inspired by the shield emblem of Capaneus, *Se.* 432–4 ἔχει

---

[1] For emphasis on autopsy in messenger-speeches, esp. those describing battle, see DeJong 10–11.

δὲ σῆμα γυμνὸν ἄνδρα πυρφόρον, / φλέγει δὲ λαμπὰς διὰ χερῶν ὡπλισμένη, / χρυσοῖς δὲ φωνεῖ γράμμασιν "πρήσω πόλιν". But there is deliberate variation: the torch-bearing warrior reminds our author of Prometheus, the torch-bearing is transferred from the artwork to the real warrior, and the painted quotation converted to a descriptive phrase, ὡς πρήσων πόλιν.

λέοντος δέρος . . . ἐπ' ἀσπίδος under the influence of *Se.* 432–4, some have believed that there are two images on Tydeus' shield, a lion-skin and Prometheus carrying a torch. But allusion may involve variation rather than exact imitation, and a lion-skin is not a suitable painted σημεῖον (hence δέμας Lenting, τέρας E. O. Schmidt), and two unrelated images on one shield are unlikely (unless part of a more complex adornment, such as on Achilles' shield in *Il.* 18 or that of Athena Parthenos). The run of the sentences suggests that the appearance of Tydeus' shield, naturally carried on his left arm, is first described, then the equipment of his right hand. The lion-skin will thus be an actual hide covering the shield, not a painting: the mane (and perhaps dangling paws) will have a threatening effect similar to impressive crests on a helmet. If a covering of the shield is intended, then ἐπ' ἀσπίδος (O +) has a good chance of being true against ἐπ' ἀσπίδι (assimilated to 1124), with a real distinction of meaning ('upon' as covering rather than 'on' as painting). Other authors, however, use ἐπ' ἀσπίδος but not ἐπ' ἀσπίδι in describing shield-emblems: Pindar *P.* 8.45–6, *Se.* 387, 400, 478, 512, 520, [519], 661, Hdt. 9.74.2; cf., however, πρὸς ἀσπίδι *Se.* 492.

δεξιᾶι given the run of the sentence, this is Tydeus' right hand, and thus he is the subject of ἔφερεν. Tydeus anticipates Parthenopaeus (1155) in his readiness to fire the gates and city (this answers the inappropriately naturalistic objection that Tydeus must have carried a more effective weapon than a torch). Pearson removes the unusual adornment of Tydeus' shield and obtains a closer imitation of *Se.* 432–4 by emending to ἐπ' αὐχένι . . . πεφρικός· ἐν σάκει δὲ . . . ; but the corruption is complex (gloss on σάκει ousts αὐχένι, then ἐν σάκει altered).

Τιτὰν Προμηθεύς same phrase in same position in *OC* 56, cf. *Ion.* 455 (lyric) Προμηθεῖ Τιτᾶνι. Unless we change to ὡς, we have here the figure 'identification' (or comparison without ὡς), 'a veritable Prometheus, another Prometheus' (cf. Σ αὐτόχρημα). For this figure see Fraenkel, *Plautinisches in Plautus* [Phil. Untersuch. 28 (Berlin 1922)] 51–2 (cf. *Elementi Plautini* 35–54, esp. 47–8), and *Ag.* comm. ii.206 (with further refs.); P. Shorey, *CP* 4 (1909) 433–6; R. Kassel, *RhMus* 116 (1973) 109–12. Identification is more frequent with animals (e.g. ταῦρος in *OT* 478) than with mythological figures, and in comedy or later authors (e.g. Lucian *Apol.* 3, Bellerophon) than in serious classical poetry (but cf. Pindar *P.* 4.289 κεῖνος Ἄτλας, 'that man [Damophilos], a second Atlas', with K. Braswell's note *ad loc.*).[1] Cf. also *Ag.* 870 Γηρυὼν ὁ δεύτερος, *Tro.* 618 Αἴας δεύτερος. The point of the comparison is the carrying of the torch: Prom. is often called πυρφόρος, and torch-bearing is a key element of his cult (W. Kraus, *RE* 23 (1957) 654–6); see E. Parabeni, *EAA* s.v. Prometeo, for a vase-painting showing a figure in theatre-costume bearing a torch who may be Prometheus; on Prom. in art see in general L. Eckhart, *RE* 23 (1957) 702–30. Tydeus' small stature (*Il.* 5.801) has not been evoked by Eur. and is not relevant here (Hermann thought the comparison less than apt, though genuine). The problem of identification and the uncertainty about ὡς/ὥς are eliminated if Προμηθεύς is an intrusive gloss: so West (1990) 316, suggesting Τιτάν τις οἷος.

ὡς πρήσων Musgrave's ὡς creates an actual simile, but ὡς is virtually obligatory with fut. part. in this kind of interpretation of someone's purpose or intention, unless the main verb expresses motion.

1123 ὁ σός West (1990) 316 suggests that this phrase requires a noun like ἔκγονος and that Πολυνείκης is an intrusion; ὁ σός by itself is very unusual, but cf. *Ion* 386 ὅς γ' οὔτ' ἔσωσας τὸν σὸν ὃν σῶσαί σ' ἐχρῆν; *Hel.* 226 ὁ δὲ σός [sc. πόσις]. (JD).

1124–5 Ποτνιάδες ... πῶλοι δρομάδες 'colts of Potniae, running wildly', that is, the mad flesh-eating horses of Glaucus of Potniae (10 stades from Thebes). The epithet should not be taken in a general sense, 'Boeotian' (LSJ); along with δρομάδες it evokes the specific mythological horses, out of control (this is almost always the connotation of δρομάς in Eur., for whom it is almost a *Lieblingswort*: *Hipp.* 550, *Su.* 1000, *Tro.* 42, *Hel.* 1301, *Ba.* 731). Ποτνιάδες is used in *Or.* 318 of the Erinyes (cf. Willink *ad loc.*, Dodds on *Ba.* 664), and here there may be a suggestion of 'maddened by the Erinyes', ironically relevant to Pol., who acts under the influence of his father's Erinyes.

φόβωι dat. of manner, 'in panic'; a mark of their possession by madness; for the converse, fear driving horses mad, cf. *Hipp.* 1229 φόβωι ... ἐκμαίνων. Thomas Mag., following up hints in Σ, interpreted φόβωι as active in sense, 'with fear' = 'so as to inspire fear'; active φόβος is possible (Diggle, *Studies* 54), but the plain dative (for ἐπὶ φόβωι) is harsh. If the author had wanted this sense, he could have written φόβον (cf. *Prom.*

---

[1] This interpretation of *P.* 4.289 is widely shared, but rejected by G. Kirkwood, *Selections from Pindar* (Chico, Calif. 1982) 199, who prefers 'the famous Atlas'. The use of καὶ μάν (moving from a gnomic statement to a directly relevant application, as in *N.* 2.13) and the obscurity of returning to Damophilus as subject with ἀλλ' εὔχεται in 293 are against Kirkwood's view.

355 συρίζων φόβον, *Se.* 498 φόβον βλέπων; cf. φόβον δρομάσι δινεύων βλεφάροις conj. Diggle in *Or.* 836, *Text. Trad. Or.* 119).

1126-7 as Heath saw, the sense of 1126 is *callide verticulis ab interiori clipei parte circumactae*, 'skilfully rotated by means of pivots from within'. For rejection of other views, see *Phoenix* 32 (1978) 124; I do not understand Craik's 'enclosed inside'. στρόφιγξ is a synonym of στροφεύς, 'pivot', and is never found in the sense 'circle, whirling motion' (the meaning of the poetic word στροφάλιγξ). The only other extant poetic uses of στρόφιγξ are *Frogs* 892 (Eur.'s invocation of the pivot of his tongue: is this an Aristophanic swipe at a mannerism of Eur.'s diction?) and Pherecrates fr. 270 K–A (quoted by Pollux for the meaning 'vertebrae'). ἔνδοθεν, 'from inside', 'from the back of the shield', is clarified by πόρπαχ' ὑπ' αὐτὸν, 'near/under the very handle', that is, the controls are within easy reach of the left hand that grasps the πόρπαξ behind the shield. For ὑπό + acc. in this sense, cf. *Se.* 561 ὑπὸ πτόλιν, S. *El.* 720 ὑπ' αὐτὴν ἐσχάτην στήλην ἔχων, E. *El.* 485 ὑπὸ δέραν, LSJ s.v. c.I.2. Moving parts on the literary shields of heroes are meant to inspire fear by sight or sound, but are deemed unseemly by some (Hartung once deleted 1126-7, Powell cites the device in impugning 1104-40); cf. *Se.* 385-6 ὑπ' ἀσπίδος δέ τῶι / χαλκήλατοι κλάζουσι κώδωνες φόβον (with Hutchinson's note), *Scutum* 164-5 τῶν [serpents] καὶ ὀδόντων μὲν κανаχὴ πέλεν, εὖτε μάχοιτο / Ἀμφιτρυωνιάδης. Several comm. regard 1126-7 as an imitation of *Se.* 541-2 Σφίγγ' ... γόμφοις ἐνώμα, but see art. cit. 121 n. 81 and Hutchinson *ad loc.*

ὥστε μαίνεσθαι δοκεῖν cf. perhaps Statius *Theb.* 10.658-9 *ipsa insanire videtur / Sphinx galeae custos.*

1128 οὐκ ἔλασσον Ἄρεος Ἄρεος goes with the comparative, not with μάχην (as Craik).

1130 σιδηρονώτοις δ' ἀσπίδος τύποις ἐπῆν 'upon the iron-backed hammered mouldings of the shield there was': this may mean either that the image was in hammered relief or that the image is painted on the shield, which is itself hammered into its convex shape and perhaps has hammered ribbing (cf. *Rhes.* 305-6 πέλτη δ' ἐπ' ὤμων χρυσοκολλήτοις τύποις / ἔλαμπε, which, if πέλτη is being used precisely of a light leather shield, implies hammered and moulded golden ribbing or rim). ἐπῆν is somewhat easier with the latter, and in either case we have a periphrasis for ἀσπίδι τετυπωμένηι. This is a far more interesting and precise expression than ἀσπίδος κύκλοις offered by Π¹; κύκλος for a shield is a stereotyped usage (*Se.* 489, 496, 591; below 1382, *El.* 455, 1257). Likewise, σιδηρονώτοις, with a half-transference of epithet (-νωτ- goes more naturally with ἀσπίδος), is more recherché than σιδηρονώτου (Π¹, but already conjectured characteristically by the prosaic-minded Valckenaer) and so likely to be original. For support of κύκλοις, see Bremer (1983) 299.

467

1131 γίγας . . . γηγενής a common etymological play; cf. 128 γίγαντι γηγενέται, *Her.* 178–9 τοῖσι γῆς βλαστήμασιν Γίγασι, *Trach.* 1058–9 ὁ γηγενὴς στρατὸς Γιγάντων. The giant on the shield may have been suggested by *Se.* 424 (of Capaneus) Γίγας ὅδ' ἄλλος.

ὅλην πόλιν Reeve has pointed out that if fr. 1041 is not Euripidean (the ascription rests on a τοῦ αὐτοῦ in the mss of Stobaeus), this would be the only place in extant Eur. tragedy that ὅλος is used; he would see this as an index of interpolation of 1104–40. But the word is not foreign to tragedy, as Soph.'s use proves (four times; also several instances in minor tragedians and adespota), and Eur. has the word once in *Cycl.* 217. So the force of this unique feature, if it is unique (fr. 1041 might be Eur. after all), is unclear. Note that ὅλην has a suitable note of hyperbole, and that πᾶσα πόλις has political connotations unsuited to this reference to the physical entity of the city. Cf. Call. *Hymn Dem.* 34 πάντας δ' ἀνδρογίγαντας ὅλαν πόλιν ἀρκίος ἆραι; N. Hopkinson comments *ad loc.* that our passage is 'either the source or a further representative of a τόπος of giants' strength'; if that line is genuine Callimachus (Hopkinson argues effectively, I believe, against the view that it is spurious), it may imply that Call. considered our passage genuine Euripides.[1]

1132 ἐξανασπάσας βάθρων the verb is extant only here and *Ba.* 1110 κἀξανέσπασαν [sc. ἐλάτην] χθονός and Hdt. 5.85.1 τὰ ἀγάλματα . . . ἐκ τῶν βάθρων ἐξανασπᾶν. Relatively rare compounds in ἐξανα- are somewhat more common in Eur. than in the other tragedians: cf. ἐξαναβρύω A., ἐξανευρίσκω A. and S., ἐξαναστρέφω S. vs. ἐξαναιρέω, ἐξανάπτω, ἐξαναρπάζω, ἐξανέρχομαι, ἐξαναστέφω in E. βάθρων is supported by the parallels (and possible imitations: Bremer (1983) 300) and is more vivid; βίαι looks like a careless scribal substitution or a stopgap filler for an illegible line-ending.

1133 Valck. wanted to delete this line from the context (*sapit interpolatoris ingenium*); if it is deleted, it adds nothing to the case against 1104–40 as a whole. If it is integral to the passage, as I believe, the internal acc.[2] (in apposition to the participial phrase πόλιν φέρων) is a usage characteristic of fifth-century tragedy and of Eur. in particular. A critic suspicious of

---

[1] F. Bornmann, *ZPE* 91 (1992) 15–17, now declares more decisively that the Callimachean line is an imitation of *Phoen.* 1131 and argues that this imitation gives a *terminus ante quem* for the interpolation of 1104–40. See also footnote 2 on 1184n, p. 478 below.

[2] υπονοια in Π¹ is a trivialization (corrupted because of unfamiliarity with internal acc. in apposition to the sentence: above 1092n.; *Phoenix* 32 (1978) 125 n. 82).

1104–40 could cite ὑπόνοιαν: it occurs nowhere else in serious poetry, and becomes moderately common in prose only from the fourth century on. But again, this is a doubtful argument. Like ἐπίνοια (408n.), the word appears to be a coinage of the late fifth century, and its meaning is still flexible: Thuc. uses in three different senses (2.41.4, 5.87.1, 7.49.4); Arist. has it once, *Peace* 993, in the sense 'suspicion' later seen several times in Menander. The sense here will be 'indirect [ὑπο-] suggestion' and is comparable to that in Thuc. 5.87.1 ('the truth of what actually happened will impair the notion induced in the audience by suggestion'). Cf. other uses in which ὑπόνοια is not the (uncertain) notion formed by the observer, but the suggestion implanted indirectly by someone else: 'indirect suggestion', 'allegory', Xen. *Symp.* 4.3.6, Pl. *Rep.* 378d6–7; rhetorical term καθ' ὑπόνοιαν or δι' ὑπονοίας, 'by suggestion or innuendo'.

πόλις in context surely 'our city', not 'a city' (Craik).

1135 The serpent-filled image may be a reminiscence of *Se.* 495 (serpents of Typhos), but our author has produced a highly original variation.

ἑκατὸν ἐχίδναις if 1136 is correctly deleted, this number of itself, reinforced by the Argive identification in 1137, probably suggests the Hydra rather than simply a large number of serpents. Argos was famous for its large population of serpents (A. *Su.* 262–7), but Hydra alone has the prestige-value to be an emblem and a threat. Artists generally show 5–12 heads in depicting Hydra (A. Rumpf, *EAA* s.v. Idra), but poets were free to imagine larger numbers (50 in Simonides acc. to ΣHes. *Th.* 313 and in Virg. *Aen.* 6.576; 100 in *Her.* 1188, Diod. Sic. 4.11.5, and *Aen.* 7.658 and other Latin poets; note μυριόκρανον *Her.* 419).

ἀσπίδ' ἐκπληρῶν γραφῆι the verb is used in a pregnant sense; Pearson notes that 'the verb transfers the function of the immediate agent to another person – here from the artist to the owner'; cf. κείραντες in *Hel.* 1124, which modifies the men whose death ultimately occasioned the shorn hair of mourning, not the direct agents of the shearing (see also Fraenkel, *Beobacht. zu Arist.* 157). The dative γραφῆι is modal, beside the more concrete, instrumental ἐχίδναις. The use of the verb, the double dative, and the repetitiousness of 1136 ἔχων after ἐκπληρῶν here have inspired various emendations (Reiske's γραφήν (with comma before) and Geel's ἐκπληροῦν are the least violent), but proper exegesis eliminates the first two motivations, leaving only the problem of repetition (see next note).

[1136] apart from the repetitiousness of this line (and its anticlimactically blander language), the plural βραχίοσιν in reference to a single arm is odd, not quite similar to plurals like στέρνα, νῶτα, etc. (see *Phoenix* 32 (1978) 126 n. 91). I accept Murray's deletion of this line, which may have begun as a gloss identifying the Hydra or may have been added to simplify the construction of the acc. αὔχημα in 1137 (cf. interpolated τε in *Ba.* 8; also interpolated ἴδω in 167 above, and Dodds' account of the interpolation of *Ba.* 1091–2). Valck. and others regard Virg. *Aen.* 7.657–8 *clipeoque insigne paternum | centum anguis cinctamque gerit serpentibus Hydram* as a reminiscence of 1135–6; if this is true, it provides a *terminus ante quem* for the intrusion of 1136.

1137 Ἀργεῖον αὔχημ' internal acc. (in apposition to ἀσπίδ' ἐκπληρῶν). Hydra is a famous emblem by which the Argives can proudly advertise their identity (hence Nauck's ἀχρεῖον is misconceived); cf. Minotaur on coins of Cnossus, Scylla on coins of Acragas and Cumae. The boast is, however, not only of civic identity but also of destructive power threatening Thebes, as the further description shows.

ἐκ δέ τειχέων μέσων by this phrase the threat is made to recall the depredations of the Sphinx (808–10, 1026–7). The internal allusion is strengthened by an external allusion to *Se.* 539–43 (Sphinx carrying off a Theban), but again there is effective variation (contrast τὸ πόλεως ὄνειδος in *Se.* 539 with Ἀργεῖον αὔχημα).

1139–40 for the justification of knowledge, cf. 95–8, [141–4], 1118n.; *Hcld.* 847–8.

θεάματα the flexible use of -μα nouns is a mannerism of tragedy; see A. A. Long, *Language and Thought in Sophocles* (London 1968) 18–19. For the unusual 'active' sense ('viewing', 'opportunity to see') here, cf. Chaeremon *TrGF* 71 F 14.4–5 γυμνὴ δ' αἰθέρος θεάμασιν / ζῶσαν γραφὴν ἔφαινε; also *El.* 1124 λοχευμάτων, 'my giving birth'; *IT* 410 ὄχημα, 'voyaging', which I take as int. acc. to ἔπλευσαν; 640 above πέσημα; *Ba.* 739 σπαράγμασιν. In all other instances θέαμα means 'sight', 'spectacle'; but the bold poetic usage is not more likely to be an interpolator's than Eur.'s own. For θέαμα in messenger-speeches in particular, see DeJong, 10 n. 21.

παρφέροντι this is one of two uncertain instances of παρ-*apokope* extant in the Eur. corpus; the other is *Hyps.* fr. apud Lydum (p. 48 of Bond's edn), where παραφρονήματ' is attested in Lydus, but παρφρονήματ' is now attested in a gnomology (Bartoletti, 12). The shorter forms could be due to scribal error (MO+ here have παραφ-), but παρφ- is here somewhat more likely to be a deliberate epicism, whoever wrote the line. Cf. *Eum.* 768 παρβαίνουσι (trim.; cf. in lyric *Eum.* 553, *Se.* 743, A. *Su.* 1048); Soph. *Ichn.* fr. 314.175 παρμένων (trim.); later Ezechiel (*TrGF* 128) *Exag.* 74 πάρδωκε. For παρφέρω cf. Sophron fr. 15 Kaibel, Philoxenus Leuc. *PMG* 836b.6; and for prepositional πάρ see 237n.. On *apokope* in general cf. K–B 1.180, Denniston on *El.* 868, Collard on *Su.* 984–6, Jebb on *Ant.* 1275 (JD).

ποιμέσιν λόχων for this tragic extension of epic ποιμένα λαῶν, cf. A. *Su.* 767 ναῶν ποιμένες, E. *Su.* 674 ποιμένες ὄχων.

1141 μεσαγκύλοις also in *Andr.* 1133, otherwise extant only in Men. fr. 745.2 K–T and a few instances in Polybius and later prose. Σ speaks of a javelin with a groove for the second finger, but other evidence shows that a javelin with a looped thong (ἀγκύλη, *amentum*; attached in the middle or toward the end) is intended. Cf. *Ba.* 1205 ἀγκυλωτοῖς [-ητοῖς Nauck] Θεσσαλῶν στοχάσμασιν with Dodds' note; for illustration see Daremberg–Saglio I.226–7 s.v. *amentum*.

1142 ἐμαρνάμεσθα Eur. is the only tragedian who uses this archaic poetic verb (five times).

ἐκηβόλοις 1108n.

1143 πέτρων τ' ἀραγμοῖς Lobeck on *Aj.* 727–8 demonstrated the usual distinction between πέτρα (massive, fixed, like a crag or cliff) and πέτρος (a piece of stone suitable in size and weight for use in combat, from Homer on); hence mss' πετρῶν is corrected here. Cf. esp. *Pers.* 460 πέτροισιν ἡράσσοντο, *IT* 327 ἤρασσεν πέτροις. ἀραγμός is an uncommon tragic word (once each in A. and S., four times in Eur. and *Rhes.*, then Lycophron and a very few times in later prose) and is here probably inspired by *Se.* 249 ἀραγμὸς δ' ἐν πύλαις ὀφέλλεται.

1145 πρὶν κατεξάνθαι βολαῖς cf. A. fr. 132c.2 πέτροις καταξανθέντα, *Aj.* 728, E. *Su.* 503, *Acharn.* 319–20; for βολαῖς cf. 665 above and *Or.* 59 ἐς πέτρων ἔλθηι βολάς.

1146 The subject of 1145 κατεξάνθαι is 'you children of the Danaans', that is, the whole Argive army, and this fact confirms that the initial attack is by the whole λόχοι (as implied by 1104–40), not by the Seven as μονόμαχοι, as Fraenkel supposed. πάντες here does not contrast with a single fighter, but reinforces ἐμπίπτειν (cf. *Pers.* 462 ἐφορμηθέντες ἐξ ἑνὸς ῥόθου). The exhortation here is thus very different from that of Sarpedon in *Il.* 12.409–12, where he urges his men to join him in the breach in the wall because he can hardly advance by himself. It is a topos of battle narratives that a period of *eminus* fighting is followed by *comminus* fighting: *Pers.* 459–64 (first assault with rocks and arrows, then a charge *en masse*); Hdt. 1.214.2 (first a battle with bows and arrows, then, arrows exhausted, the forces close to use spears and swords); *Andr.* 1132ff. (Neoptolemus, assaulted by βέλη of all kinds, leaps closer to his assailants to engage them with his sword); cf. Caesar *Gall.* 1.52.4 (forces close so fast that *pila* can't be used), Tac. *Ann.* 6.35 (need to charge and fight *comminus* to forestall battle with arrows). For the actual practice of preliminary skirmishes by light-armed missile-throwers before a pitched hoplite battle see Pritchett, *Greek State at War* IV.51–4.

τί μέλλετ' this question (like τί οὐ + pres. ind.) is equivalent to an urgent imperative: 299 above, *Hel.* 1593–4 τί μέλλετ' ... σφάζειν φονεύειν βαρβάρους, *Rhes.* 673, *OT* 678, *Hec.* 726; cf. absolute use adjacent to an imperative (*Or.* 275, etc.).

ἄρδην πάντες for this intensifying combination cf. *Thesm.* 274 (Eur. speaking) πάντας ἄρδην τοὺς θεούς, and prose exx. (Xen. *Anab.* 7.1.12, Pl. *Rep.* 421a6, Dem. 19.61, Polyb. 3.53.1, *al.*).

1147 γυμνῆτες κτλ. this line names only the auxiliaries of the full-armed infantry troops, in a partial apposition to πάντες, probably because these forces are the ones most likely to be damaged by prolonged bombardment, while the hoplites have the protection of their shields (cf. 1178). The γυμνῆτες would be the most active units in the *eminus* skirmish. The triplet 'hoplites, cavalry, and chariots' is more common (1190–1n.). Asyndeton between the first two nouns followed by connection with τε is paralleled in *Ba.* 694 νέαι παλαιαὶ παρθένοι τ' ἔτ' ἄζυγες (where again the third member is weightier than the first two) and exx. cited in Denniston, *GP*² 501. It is thus unnecessary to add τ' after ἱππῆς (Hartung) or remove τ' (Valck., om. V).

1149 πολλοὶ δ' ἔπιπτον same phrase in battle-narratives in *Hcld.* 838, *Andr.* 1142, also at the initial moment of close combat (cf. *Or.* 1489).

αἱματούμενοι the present is more vivid than the perfect, which could have been used (*Ba.* 1135–6 πᾶσα δ' ἡιματωμένη χεῖρας).

1151 κυβιστητῆρας ἐκπεπνευκότας the rare κυβιστητήρ (hapax in tragedy; Lycophron 296 πυκνοὶ κυβιστητῆρες imitates this line) and the conceit are taken from *Il.* 16.742–50: Cebriones falls from his chariot ἀρνευτῆρι ἐοικώς, and Patroclus exults ἦ ῥα καὶ ἐν Τρώεσσι κυβιστητῆρες ἔασιν. Eur. earlier used the image in *Su.* 692 ἐς κρᾶτα πρὸς γῆν ἐκκυβιστώντων, and cf. 1193 below. The juxtaposition of ἐκπεπνευκότας is striking, since it abruptly shifts from the image of flight 'toward the ground' (ἐς οὖδας going with the verbal force of κυβ.) to the final result of the expired corpses. For absolute ἐκπνέω = ἐκπνέω βίον, cf. *Hyps.* fr. 60.38 (perfect); *Aj.* 1026, *Hel.* 1123 (aor.), *Her.* 885 (fut.), *El.* 1220 (pres.). Madvig's ἐκπεπτωκότας gives a simpler picture and simpler grammar (ἐς οὖδας goes with it) and also creates a rhetorical balance with ἔπιπτον in 1149; but the more difficult juncture may be original. Diggle (1990a) 8–9 commends Markland's ἐκνενευκότας as completing the image, but I do not see how 'swim out' fits with the image of diving (or, if from ἐκνεύω, 'fall headlong' is not a meaning I accept for that verb: 1268n.).

1152 ἔδευον γαῖαν αἵματος ῥοαῖς another epic reminiscence (674n.), but also recalling 674 (death of Spartoi) and underlining the re-enactment of the original violence in this day's battle.

1153 Ἀρκάς, οὐκ Ἀργεῖος cf. *Su.* 890–1 Ἀρκὰς μὲν ἦν, ἐλθὼν δ' ἐπ'

Ἰνάχου ῥοάς / παιδεύεται κατ' Ἄργος, 896 λόχοις δ' ἐνεστὼς ὥσπερ Ἀργεῖος γεγώς; and *Se.* 547–8 Ἀρκάς ... μέτοικος, Ἄργει δ' ἐκτίνων καλὰς τροφάς. Here the phrase takes sides against another tradition that made Parthenopaeus an Argive by birth (Hutchinson on *Se.* 526–67), but probably also evokes the comments in *Se.* and *Su.* that declare the unusual devotion of the metic who fights enthusiastically for his adopted homeland.

1154–5 βοᾶι πῦρ καὶ δικέλλας lexicographers produce an entry 'call for, shout out for' as if βοάω is used like αἰτέω. But when this sense is intended, the acc. is actually internal, expressing the content of the shout, a kind of indirect quotation; cf. *Trach.* 772–3 'βόησε τὸν δυσδαίμονα Λίχαν, reflecting the shout ὦ Λίχα; see Fraenkel on *Ag.* 48ff.; Diggle's note on *Hel.* 1592 forthcoming in his *Euripidea.* For thing rather than person as invoked object Pearson cites *Frogs* 1073 μᾶζαν καλέσαι, *Wasps* 103 κέκραγεν ἐμβάδας. Singular δίκελλαν (O +) is a trivialization.

1156 μαργῶντ' perhaps a reminiscence of *Se.* 380 (of Tydeus),[1] but Eur. has the word in three other places as well as in 1247 below; it is a tragic word, twice in A., once in S. (later only in Call.).

1157 Περικλύμενος the only Theban champion named by Eur.; the name does not occur in *Se.* (where Actor faces Parthenopaeus), but is traditional, since Pindar in *N.* 9.26 says that Periclymenus (father not named) almost killed Amphiaraus. In Homer and Hesiod, Periclymenus is from Pylos, son of Neleus by a Theban woman, and thus grandson of Posidon. But Pindar *P.* 4.175 appears to make the Pylian a son of Posidon (see K. Braswell's note on 169–87 and 175). Craik's 'sea-goddess's son' is mistaken.

1158 ἀμαξοπληθῆ extant in three places. Lucian's use in *VH* 1.41 is a burlesque imitation of our passage: ἔβαλλον ... καὶ ἐτίτρωσκον ὀστρείοις τε ἀμαξοπληθέσι καὶ σπόγγοις πλεθριαίοις. Aeneas Tact. 32.5 advises besieged defenders of a city to drop a λίθος ἀμαξοπληθής from a projecting beam on the battlements down on the battering-ram's shaft to shatter it: perhaps the word was current in the construction trade to describe the largest stone capable of being carried in a wagon. Here the hyperbolic epithet recalls Homeric stones that not even two men οἷοι νῦν βροτοί εἰσ' could lift, esp. *Il.* 12.380–5 (Ajax), 12.445–50 (Hector). For coping-stones as a weapon, cf. *Or.* 1569–70.

γεῖσ' ἐπάλξεων ἄπο for prepositional phrase attributive to an anarthrous noun cf. Diggle, *Studies* 28–9.

1159–62 Homeric reminiscences continue in these lines: anatomical description of wound (cf. again *Il.* 12.384–5 σὺν δ' ὀστέ' ἄραξε / πάντ'

---

[1] Saïd, 506, suggests that βοᾶι in 1154 also looks to *Se.* 381.

ἄμυδις κεφαλῆς and 16.740–1 ἀμφοτέρας δ' ὀφρῦς σύνελεν λίθος, οὐδέ οἱ ἔσχεν / ὀστέον); pathetic reference to bereaved kin (e.g., *Il.* 13.645, 15.706, 17.300–3, 4.477–8, 5.24, 149–51, 688). The pathos is enhanced by allusion to Parthenopaeus' virginal beauty in ξανθόν (cf. 146 καταβόστρυχος) and ἄρτι δ' οἰνωπὸν γένυν.[1]

διεπάλυνε hapax in extant Greek; the meaning is probably 'shatter into small fragments'; 'stain, splatter ⟨with blood⟩' (Σ) is closer to senses of simplex παλύνω, but would make καθημάτωσεν anticlimactic.

ῥαφὰς . . . ὀστέων a quasi-technical anatomical term, also in *Su.* 503.

ἄρτι δ' οἰνωπὸν γένυν a mark of erotic attraction, applied to Dionysus, implying both the flush induced by imbibing and the effeminate beauty of his unbearded cheeks (cf. *Ba.* 236 with Dodds' note, *Ba.* 438, *OT* 211), and noted as a seductive feature by Pasiphae in *Cretans* fr. 82.15 Austin. The 'virginal' Parthenopaeus does not yet have a heavy, dark beard, but only a soft down: cf. *Se.* 534–5 ἄρτι διὰ παρηίδων ὥρας φυούσης; ἄρτι has the same sense here, 'freshly', 'just barely now', not 'at the same time' (as alleged by K–G 1.119–20). See 32n. and cf. Gow on Theocr. 15.85; *Anth. gr.* 11.36, 12.36; Dover, *Greek Homosexuality* (London 1978) 86–7.

ἀποίσεται here 'bring back' (595n., 1546n.), the middle expressing merely that it is his own life.

καλλιτόξωι almost hapax in extant literature.[2] Craik revives King's and Valck.'s idea of a word-play on βίος/βιός in juxtaposition with -τοξ-, comparing *Phil.* 931 ἀπεστέρηκας τὸν βίον τὰ τόξ' ἑλών; but whereas Philoctetes' bow *is* his livelihood and life, there seems no point in any play here, and Wecklein rightly doubts whether any play is intended.

Μαινάλου κόρηι perhaps, as Σ take it, 'the (well-known) maiden of Mt Maenalum', where Atalante was exposed and lived as a hunter, rather than 'daughter of Maenalus', an otherwise unattested eponym of the mountain, as understood by [Apollodorus] *Bibl.* 3.9.2 (the father of Atal. is usually Iasus or Schoeneus; there is also a Mainalus son of Lycaon, *Bibl.* 3.8.1). Μαιναλίαι[3] would have been more regular (cf. *Andr.* 128 Ἰλιὰς . . . κόρα, Antipater, *Anth. gr.* 7.413.7 Μαιναλίας . . . Ἀταλάντας, Ovid *Her.* 4.99 *Maenalia Atalanta*), but does not fit the metre.

1165 παρασπιστάς παρασπιστής and παρασπίζω are tragic alterna-

---

[1] DeJong, 78 and 82 n. 57, notes the use of the epic motifs 'beauty brought low' and 'bereaved parents': cf. J. Griffin, *Homer on Life and Death* (Oxford 1980) 134–8, 123–7.

[2] Pseudo-Aristides, *Ars Rhet.* 14.1 [= *Rhet. Gr.* 11.511 Spengel], has it in a list of epithets of Apollo.

[3] Or Μαιναλίδι: *Maenalis* appears in Latin poetry; in Nonnus Μαιναλίς = Μαινάς.

tives (esp. Eur., six of nine classical uses) to the somewhat more common παραστάτης and παραστατέω (Pindar *N*. 3.37, tragedy, and a few times in prose). See also 1073–4n.

1166–7 Αἰτωλίσιν λόγχαισιν ... ἀκοντίζοντας for the Aetolians' unusual weaponry, 134n., 139–40n.

ἄκρον στόμα 'topmost edge', perhaps with the same figure as in English 'lip of a wall', but in military contexts στόμα can be the front edge of an array of forces (LSJ II.1.b–c).

1168 ἐρίπνας elsewhere always 'lofty crags' (Pindar *Pae*. 5.21 (restored from scholion), *El*. 210; later in Ap. Rhod., Nicander, etc. and often in Nonnus); the metaphor is intended here, and prepares for the following simile (see next note).

φυγάδας 'those on the walls' is understood from εἰς ἄκρον στόμα πύργων as subject of λιπεῖν, and φυγάδας serves almost as a participle-equivalent, 'in flight'. The ellipsis of subject here is slightly harder than in the exx. cited in 773n., but not difficult enough, I think, to justify changing the vivid φυγάδας to φύλακας (commended by Diggle (1990a) 9, citing the corruption at *El*. 32). There is a similar case in *Hel*. 1609, ὥστ' ἐκκολυμβᾶν ναός, where the subject 'Egyptian sailors' is understood from the implied indirect object of ταύτηι προσῆγε ... ξίφος in 1608, with some help from the following clause (cf. Dale's note).

1169 κυναγὸς ὡσεὶ ... ἐξαθροίζεται the simile evokes a hunter who reassembles his panicked dogs after they are scattered by the attack of a cornered prey. The simile thus pivots on ἐξαθροίζεται, and there is no need for βοῶν (Wecklein for πάλιν) to make it work. The verb is hapax in extant Greek; ἐξ- probably suggests 'from the various directions in which they had fled', though it could simply be intensifying.

1171 νοσοῦν 1097n.

1172–86 the death of Capaneus is presented in much greater detail at the close of Statius *Theb*. 10, but there are no certainly identifiable close imitations of this passage (but see 1183n.). Quintus Smyrn. 11.450–73, describing the ladder-assault and death of Alcimedon at Troy, seems to echo Eur. in 452–3 σφετέρου ⟨δὲ⟩ καρήατος ἔμμεναι ἄλκαρ / ἀσπίδα θεὶς καθύπερθεν ἀνήιε λυγρὰ κέλευθα (cf. 1178), 458 ἤδη ὑπερκύπτοντι καὶ εἰσορόωντι πόληα (cf. 1180), and perhaps 463–4 ὁ δ' ὑψόθεν ἠΰτ' ὀιστός / ἔσσυτ' ἀπὸ νευρῆς (cf. 1182–3).

1172 πῶς εἴποιμ' ἂν ὡς the intrusion of such a rhetorical flourish in the middle of a messenger's rhesis (as opposed to beginning, as *Ag*. 636–48, or end, as *Pers*. 429–32) is unusual, but here marks the narrative of Capaneus' assault as climactic. Cf. the intensification provided at *Hcld*. 832–3 (beginning of battle after long preliminaries) by πόσον τιν' αὐχεῖς πάταγον κτλ.

1173 μακραύχενος extant only here in Greek poetry;[1] the word appears a few times in a prosaic anatomical sense in Hippocrates and Aristotle. Cf. however μακραυχενόπλους (meaning uncertain) in Timoth. *Persae* 89.

κλίμακος προσαμβάσεις 489n., 744n.

1174 ἔχων ἐχώρει for the repeated sound in adjacent words, see Diggle, *Studies* 75–6, and add Hopkinson on Call. *h. Dem.* 128, McKeown on Ovid *Am.* 1.2.52.

1175 τὸ σεμνὸν πῦρ ... Διός σεμνόν probably quotes Capaneus' blasphemous sarcasm. His challenge to Zeus in particular was traditional, and is elaborated in *Se.* 427–31 and 441–6.

εἰργαθεῖν Elmsley (on *Med.* 186) wanted to treat all verbs with suffix -αθ- as aorist; the aorist interpretation fits well here and in S. *El.* 1271. The other tragic instances of this verb are *OC* 862 ἀπειργάθηι, *Eum.* 566 κατειργαθοῦ or -άθου. It is possible that verbs in -αθ- were also used as present-stem forms. For the dispute, cf. Ellendt, *Lex. Soph.* s.v. εἰκαθεῖν, K–B 1.178–9, Schwyzer 1.703 n. 6, West, *Aeschylus praef.* LI.

1176 κατ' ἄκρων περγάμων a grandiloquent variation of traditional κατ' ἄκρας (for περγάμων, 1098n.).

1177 καὶ ταῦθ' ἅμ' ἠγόρευε καὶ same line-opening in *El.* 788, *Ba.* 1082; Pearson cites prose parallels for this idiom (Hdt. 8.5.2, 9.92.1 with ἠγόρευε, 1.112.1, 4.150.3 and Xen. *Hell.* 7.1.28 with ἔλεγε).

πετρούμενος πετρόομαι, 'to be stoned', is a late Eur. mannerism (*Ion* 1112, *Or.* 564, 946; cf. *Or.* 50 πέτρωμα, a hapax except as a proper name in Paus. 8.15.1–2); later authors (Lycophr. *Alex.* 401, 901, Antipater *Anth. gr.* 16.131.10, etc.) use it as 'to be turned to stone', 'to be frozen solid'.

1178 εἰλίξας δέμας for the protective stance ('coiling and contracting his body') under the shield Σ compares *Il.* 16.360 ἀσπίδι ταυρείηι κεκαλυμμένος (cf. 1382 below). The same phrase is used by Ion *TrGF* 19 F38.4 of a hedgehog.

1179 ἐνηλάτων βάθρα 'the footholds of the rungs', a periphrasis with defining gen.; so some Σ, but others wrongly take ἐνήλατα as the uprights in which the rungs are fixed.

1180 ἤδη δ' ὑπερβαίνοντα γεῖσα τειχέων the image of Capaneus cast down from the wall at the last moment was an exemplum of the punishment of the ὑβριστής: cf. *Su.* 729–30 ἐς ἄκρα βῆναι κλιμάκων ἐνήλατα / ζητῶν, in a description that evokes Capaneus; *Ant.* 127–37, *OT* 873–9 (esp. 876 ἀκρότατα γεῖσ' ἀναβᾶσ', if γεῖσ' is the correct emendation).

1182–6 ἐκ δὲ κλιμάκων ... εἰλίσσετ' Hermann complained that

---

[1] See DeJong, 83–4, for the idea that the epithet is chosen to suggest Capaneus' pride.

these lines present an unreal image of the effects of lightning, and Nauck found them so tasteless that he deleted 1183–5 (along with the parenthetic ἐκτύπησε ... πάντας). But this is the climax of the first battle-narrative, and Eur. (like the other tragedians) was not averse to describing horrific wounding and mutilation. Both the interesting verb ἐσφενδονᾶτο and the simile ὡς κύκλωμ' 'Ιξίονος[1] are worthy of Eur., and the text left by Nauck is simply too bare and brief.[2] The real source of difficulty is 1184. (1) "Ολυμπον for οὐρανόν is perhaps too high-flown: this epic use is affected in tragedy mainly in solemn references to the sky as sacred home of the gods, and even in more 'secular' uses is a feature of high style (Eur. fr. 114.5 = *Thesm.* 1068 (lyric anap.), *Birds* 1372 (lyric), perhaps adesp. 290a (lyric or anap.)). (2) Hair and blood are odd as partitive appositives of μέλη. (3) 1184 gives the impression of a body shattered into many pieces, but 1185–6 imply that the arms and legs are still attached to the trunk. (4) It is clumsy to have two items fall to earth (1186 εἰς γῆν after εἰς χθόνα). Deletion of 1184 seems the least intrusive solution to these problems. It may have arisen as an expansion of χωρὶς ἀλλήλων understood as 'separate from each other', equivalent to the common idiom χωρὶς ἕκαστον, a sense found in *Ba.* 1210 χωρίς τε θηρὸς ἄρθρα διεφορήσαμεν, where the verb affects the sense (cf. *Ba.* 1137 κεῖται δὲ χωρὶς σῶμα, τὸ μὲν ... τὸ δ' ...; with ἕκαστον, e.g., Eratosthenes (as quoted for the possible plot of Aesch.'s *Bassarae*, p. 138 Radt) αἳ διέσπασαν αὐτὸν καὶ τὰ μέλη ἔρριψαν χωρὶς ἕκαστον). The juncture χωρὶς ἀλλήλων occurs in fr. 346.4 τὰ δ' ἄλλα χωρὶς χρώμεθ' ἀλλήλων νόμοις (= χωρὶς ἕκαστοι).

1183 ἐσφενδονᾶτο the verb is attested mainly in prose, in its technical military sense, reflected even in Pindar fr. 183 Maehler and Men. *Dysc.* 120 (the only compound is διασφενδονάω, Xen. and later prose). In *Su.* 715 ἐσφενδόνα is used of Theseus swinging a club around like a sling, and here the verb could convey, with μέλη as subject and 1184 omitted, 'were swung around in a circle'. But the sense may rather be 'was/were flung violently off the ladder (as if shot from a sling)', as ἐκ κλιμάκων suggests; this interpretation has the advantage that ἐσφενδονᾶτο does not anticipate the striking Ixion-image. Cf. Josephus *BJ* 3.246 τὸ κρανίον ἀπὸ τριῶν ἐσφενδονήθη σταδίων, Photius *Bibl.* 243, 355b (Himerius) Παρνασσὸς ... ἐσφενδόνα τὰς κορυφάς.

χωρὶς †ἀλλήλων† μέλη if this phrase is sound and 1184 omitted, then

---

[1] DeJong, 92, notes that the comparison with Ixion serves to reinforce the messenger's view of Capaneus as ὑβριστής.

[2] Better in this regard is West's proposal (1990) to reduce 1183–5 to ἐσφενδονᾶτο χὼς κύκλωμ' 'Ιξίονος; but his objection to sing. εἱλίσσετ' after χεῖρες δὲ καὶ κῶλ' is not cogent (1186n.).

μέλη is subject and 'separate from each other' means in essence 'outstretched in different directions'; but then ἐσφενδονᾶτο must mean 'whirled around' and the image anticipates 1185–6. But a more interesting sequence of striking images results if we take the verb as 'shot' or 'flung' with Capaneus as subject and regard ἀλλήλων as a corruption of, or gloss intruding on, a nom. part. governing μέλη, describing the convulsive stiffening of Capaneus' limbs (ἐκβάλλων, ἀντείνων, and ἐκτείνων come to mind). Geel (as an alternative to deleting 1184) turned the passage into a source of Stat. *Theb.* 927–30 talia dicentem toto Iove fulmen adactum / corripuit: primae fugere in nubila cristae, / et clipei niger umbo cadit, iamque omnia lucent / membra viri by writing ἀλλήλων βέλη (or βέλει), / κόρυς μέν … αἰχμή δ’…. Hartung made Capaneus subj. by writing μεθεὶς / πνεῦμ’ εἰς … σῶμα δ’ εἰς χθονὸς πέδον, in imitation of *Su.* 532–4 ὅθεν δ’ ἕκαστον ἐς τὸ φῶς ἀφίκετο / ἐνταῦθ’ ἀπελθεῖν, πνεῦμα μὲν πρὸς αἰθέρα, / τὸ σῶμα δ’ ἐς γῆν. Both these leave the repetition of 'to earth', which is removed by Harry's αἱματοσταγεῖς. It is better to delete 1184 than to rewrite like this.

[**1184**] κόμαι probably meant literally, but if one wished to save the line from excess one might interpret it as synecdoche for 'head' (Capaneus having been decapitated by the force of the blast).[1]

εἰς Ὄλυμπον … εἰς χθόνα for the antithesis[2] cf. *Su.* 533–4 (just quoted) and *OC* 1654–5 γῆν τε προσκυνοῦνθ’ … καὶ τὸν θεῶν Ὄλυμπον.

αἷμα there is a superficial similarity in *Or.* 1086–7 μήθ’ αἷμά μου δέξαιτο κάρπιμον πέδον, μὴ λαμπρὸς αἰθήρ (see Di Benedetto), but here we have the different, gaudy notion of expelled blood raining down from

---

[1] Sir Basil Schonland, *The Flight of Thunderbolts* (Oxford 1964) 131, reports that in some cases of lightning-strikes upon a person the flesh is torn and that the generation of steam may cause clothes and boots to be stripped off and thrown some distance from the body. In the corrupt Aesch. fr. 17 the second line is probably to be restored as ἃ κεραυνὸς ἄρθρων ἐνηλυσίων ἀπέλειπεν, 'what the lightning-bolt left of the lightning-struck limbs ⟨of Capaneus⟩', implying partial consumption of the corpse; but not enough survives to tell whether the corpse was also shattered into pieces.

[2] F. Bornmann, *ZPE* 91 (1992) 15–17, suggests that the antithesis in Call. *Hymn Dem.* 58 ἵθματα μὲν χέρσῳ, κεφαλὰ δέ οἱ ἅψατ’ Ὀλύμπῳ is an imitation of *Phoen.* 1184 and that Callimachus' imitation would militate against the notion that 1184 alone is interpolated (apparently on the assumption that such a single-line expansion would be less likely than more extensive interpolations to arise before Callimachus). But I do not believe that *Hymn Dem.* 58 owes anything to *Phoen.* 1184: see Hopkinson's commentary *ad loc.* for the sources of Callimachus' conceit.

the corpse, while there αἷμά μου is more or less 'life-blood' and implies the whole body (cf. Willink).

1185 χεῖρες δὲ καὶ κῶλ' for this expansion of μέλη, cf. the epic formula (*Il.* 5.122, etc.) γυῖα δὲ θῆκεν ἐλαφρά, πόδας καὶ χεῖρας ὕπερθεν.

κύκλωμ' Ἰξίονος κύκλωμ' seems to be a Eur. coinage (also *Ba.* 124 βυρσότονον κύκλωμα; then Septuagint and a dozen times in later prose). Here, as in *Ba.*, it may be a recherché variant on κύκλος, 'wheel' (Ixion's τροχός, e.g. *TrGF* adesp. 680a.9, Diod. Sic. 4.69.5), or a verbal noun, 'wheeling', 'rotation'. For Ixion on his wheel, the human prototype of the magic iunx-wheel, see Gildersleeve on Pindar *P.* 2.40, Gow on Theocr. 2.17, and cf. *Her.* 1297–8 τὸν ἁρματήλατον Ἰξίον' ἐν δεσμοῖσιν. In illustrations the wheel is often winged or burning (partial list in *EAA* s.v. Issione), and Ixion flies through the air and is not (as later) confined to hell with other famous sinners.

1186 εἱλίσσετ' the verb (a favourite of Eur.: 3n.) is singular by attraction to the number of κύκλωμ' (or less likely, by agreement with the nearer of the two subjects, κῶλ'): cf. K–G 1.76 (end of §3).

ἔμπυρος here only in classical poetry in the simple sense 'aflame', elsewhere always of burnt offerings, altars for such offerings, or divination from them (as 954 above).

1187 Ἄδραστος regarded now as the commander-in-chief; the other leaders, apart from Pol., may be presumed by the audience to have died already or to die in the subsequent general engagement.

1188 ἔξω τάφρου by this withdrawal Adrastus attempts to end the battle (with an admission of the failure of this assault), since missiles from the wall will no longer strike the Argives (cf. 1100–3).

καθεῖσεν Barrett on *Hipp.* 29–32 defends the transmitted form against L. Dindorf's καθῖσεν (the later form).

στρατόν following στρατῶι in 1187 could be the result of corruption in one line or the other (e.g., 1187 στόλωι Bothe, 1188 ὅπλα Brunck); but unemphatic repetition like this is not always due to corruption (22n.).

1189 οἱ . . . παρ' ἡμῶν periphrasis for 'our people', the gen. with παρά being proleptically influenced by the idea of ἰδόντες (looking from the walls) or ἐξήλαυνον (driving out of the city) or both.

1190–3 the compressed phrasing suits the rapid action and the need to complete the narrative without lingering further over many details. Note (1) the asyndetic listing of the three divisions of Theban forces (cf. in a similarly rapid narrative Men. *Aspis* 60–1 οἱ δ' ἐπέρρεον / ἱππεῖς ὑπασπισταὶ στρατιῶται); (2) the brachylogy in κὰς . . . ὅπλα / συνῆψαν, for κὰς μέσ' Ἀργείων ὅπλα ὁρμηθέντες συνῆψαν Ἀργείοις ἔγχη (for the variety of constructions with συνάπτω see 37n.); (3) the asyndetic pair of verbs in 1193 (see note), with unexpressed subject ('men', i.e. on both

479

sides). Wecklein's proposal of a lacuna before and after 1191 is unnecessary. The only emendation needed is Musgrave's ὄχοι for mss' ὄχους. Earlier solutions, such as Scaliger's ὁπλῖταί τ' εἰς, illegitimately had ἱππῆς driving chariots. The three divisions mentioned are standard (cf. 1147 of the Argives; *Su.* 653–67), and it is not significant that in 1095–6 only Theban infantry and cavalry are named (cf. *Hcld.* 823–4, only charioteers and infantry). This general engagement outside the city after the attack on the gates has been repulsed is believed to have been present in the epic *Thebaid* (Vian, 203); but just as Eur. divides the duel of the brothers from the assault on the gates, he also allows this battle to end with the Argive army still in place near Thebes and reproduces the general engagement after the duel, when the Argives are finally put to flight.

1192 πάντα δ' ἦν ὁμοῦ κακά πάντα here connotes 'all manner of', cf. *Ba.* 1131 ἦν δὲ πᾶσ' ὁμοῦ βοή; elsewhere πάντα ... ὁμοῦ is an intensification of the numerical sense (1696 below, cf. *Trach.* 761, S. *El.* 715).

1193 ἔθνῃσκον ἐξέπιπτον verbal asyndeton at the start of a trimeter is an intensifying stylistic device used by all three tragedians, frequently in narratives of violence.[1] There are exx. with participles (listed by Bond on *Her.* 602 ἕλξων φονεύσων; add *Hec.* 840), with imperatival words (*Aj.* 811, 844, *Ant.* 1037, *Andr.* 260, *Hec.* 507; in anap. *Ag.* 1414), and with indicative verbs (mostly present or imperfect, aorist only at *Hcld.* 1014), as here. Cf. *Pers.* 426 ἔπαιον ἐρράχιζον, 463 παίουσι κρεοκοποῦσι, *Se.* 60 χωρεῖ κονίει, *Choe.* 289 κινεῖ ταράσσει, *Hec.* 1170 κεντοῦσιν αἱμάσσουσιν, *Her.* 999 σκάπτει μοχλεύει, below 1434 ἔκλαι' ἐθρήνει, *Aj.* 60 ὤτρυνον εἰσέβαλλον, S. *El.* 719 ἤφριζον εἰσέβαλλον, perhaps *Hcld.* 821 ἔσφαζον οὐκ ἔμελλον; also *Hec.* 86 (anap.) and *Phil.* 787–8 προσέρπει / προσέρχεται (exclaimed bacchiac followed by trimeter); cf. also in tricolon structure *Hipp.* 356–7 ῥίψω μεθήσω σῶμ', ἀπαλλαχθήσομαι / βίου, *Her.* 837, *Aj.* 896, S. *El.* 1380, *Her.* 494, 1226–7, 1390–1, *Hyps.* fr. 60.16, *Prom.* 937. In trimeters such asyndeton obeys a law of increasing members (the second verb has more syllables than the first), except in *Her.* 837 ἔλαυνε κίνει.[2] The two verbs are often synonymous, or the second is more specific and colourful than the first. A pattern with near synonyms can be obtained

---

[1] For prose K–G II.341 cites Xen. *Hell.* 2.4.33 οἱ ψιλοὶ ... ἐκδραμόντες ἠκόντιζον, ἔβαλλον, ἐτόξευον, ἐσφενδόνων, 4.3.19 συμβαλόντες τὰς ἀσπίδας ἐωθοῦντο, ἐμάχοντο, ἀπέκτεινον, ἀπέθνῃσκον. For comedy, cf. (with tricolon) *Acharn.* 531 ἤστραπτ', ἐβρόντα, ξυνεκύκα τὴν Ἑλλάδα.

[2] For adherence to this law in Eur.'s lyrics as well, see Diggle, *PCPS* 200 (1974) 10.

here by Earle's ἔθρωισκον for ἔθνησκον (recalling the leaper of *Il.* 16.742–50: 1151n.); then the subjects are by implication different (Diggle (1990a) 9, 'some leapt, some fell'); for less colourful ἐξέπιπτον in second position cf. *Hipp.* 356 ῥίψω μεθήσω. But in some cases a temporal sequence is implied in the pairing (*Her.* 602, *Hec.* 1170, *Pers.* 463), and that would be the case with ἔθνησκον, the subj. of the two verbs being the same – it is charioteers who are dying and then fall out of their chariots.

1194–5 τροχοὶ τ' ἐπήδων . . . ἐξεσωρεύονθ' ὁμοῦ after 'wheels leapt through the air' (implying the break-up of the chariots), one would like to translate 'and axles leapt ⟨and crashed down⟩ upon axles'. This is close in sense to Aesch. fr. 38 ἐφ' ἅρματος γὰρ ἅρμα κτλ. (881n.) and similar to the pairing in *Hipp.* 1234–5 σύριγγές τ' ἄνω / τροχῶν ἐπήδων ἀξόνων τ' ἐνήλατα; and though πηδάω normally takes a prep. + acc. to denote the landing-point of the leap, cf. for a dat. complement *OT* 1300–2 τίς ὁ πηδήσας . . . πρὸς σῆι δυσδαίμονι μοίραι; If such an interpretation of ἐπήδων seems too forced, then we must either understand ἀξόνες τ' ἐπ' ἄξοσιν as 'one axle after another' (so Pearson, but this has little point, unlike the cited parallel *Od.* 7.120–1 ὄγχνη ἐπ' ὄγχνηι γηράσκει κτλ.) or preferably write ἀξόνες δ' (*recc.*) . . . νεκροί τε (Fritzsche). With Fritzsche's reading, ἐπί is easily supplied with νεκροῖς. In the transmitted text the dat. may be adnominal (1495–6n.) or go with ὁμοῦ: cf. E. fr. 384.1, *Pers.* 426, *Trach.* 1225, etc.; the dat. with σωρεύω, 'heap something with something' (LSJ II) is late and different.

ἐξεσωρεύονθ' hapax in extant Greek; ἐκ- is intensifying.

1196–8 (–9?) the messenger concludes the rhesis with a note of caution (εἰς τὴν παροῦσαν ἡμέραν (cf. εἰς τόδ' ἡμέρας, 1085n.), τὸ λοιπόν) and an acknowledgment of divine power. κατασκαφάς in 1196 perhaps recalls Tir.'s prediction (884 συγκατασκάπτηι) and reminds the audience of Menoeceus' contribution; but if 1199 is genuine, the final emphasis is on the gods, whose favour Men. earned.

1199 survives only in M (its addition in the margin by L² reflects collation of an old ms in Triclinius' circle). Early nineteenth-century editors, ignorant of the importance of M as a witness, tended to regard it as spurious (so still Wilam. *Analecta Euripidea* (Berlin 1875) 206). Hermann argued that the verse is inappropriate because no hope has been expressed in the previous line, and he felt that the hopefulness of 1199 spoils the caution of 1196–8. But recognizing that the gods have helped in this victory (Zeus against Capaneus, Earth and Ares through the favour won by Men.) is not an assurance that the gods will help in the future; it merely asserts their power to help, if they so choose (a standard feature of Greek prayer). Klotz argued somewhat inconsistently that 1196–8 require no such addition and that 1199 is the work of someone who thought 1196–8 not sufficiently complete. An editor is left to personal judgment of rhetorical and dramatic appropriateness. I think that Joc.'s τὰ τῶν θεῶν in 1202 follows slightly better on the positive 1199 than on the neutral 1198 (she responds, of course, to the messenger, more or less ignoring the conventional choral couplet). 1199 could have been omitted by homoeoarcton (ΚΑΙ/ΚΑΛ).[1] On general suspicion of verses absent from major mss see 1346n.

1200–1 an unsolved problem. At least four interpretations have been suggested. (1) 'Victory is glorious. But if the gods have a better judgment (i.e., that justice is more on Pol.'s side than on Et.'s), then may I be fortunate ⟨if Thebes yet falls⟩.' (Σ, Wecklein) (2) 'Victory is glorious. But if the gods have a better purpose ⟨namely, that the brothers be peacefully reconciled⟩, then I would be fortunate.' (Σ alter; similarly Grotius, Barnes, Musgrave, but all with ἔχοιεν in 1201) (3) 'Good is victory, and if the purpose of the gods has better in store, may *I* be happy.' (Pearson) (4) 'Victory is good. And if the gods have still better purpose, I should be happy.' (Craik)[2] None of these is fully satisfactory. (1) has the apparent advantage that δ' is adversative: in light of the irony applied elsewhere to καλλίνικος (1048n.), one would expect a cautionary adversative here. Moreover, the sense of foreboding well explains the ellipsis or anacoluthon in the condition (Wecklein in fact prints a dash before εὐτυχής).[3] On the other hand, after Tir.'s assurances and Men.'s sacrifice and after the choral odes that have intervened since the parodos, it is strange, even unnatural, for the chorus to revert to the issue of justice. That issue was suitably expressed in 257–60 in preparation for Pol.'s entrance and the agon with Et., but Pol.'s justice was thereafter undercut by his refusal to bend for the good of the city. More troublesome still, ἄμεινον' ... γνώμην is an unlikely way to refer to a 'juster' purpose when that purpose would bring suffering to people about whom the chorus has expressed loyal concern. The phrase should rather mean either 'better γνώμη than someone else has' (as in fr.

---

[1] For precarious survival of a genuine line one used to cite *Ant.* 1167, but see N. G. Wilson, *Scholars of Byzantium* (London 1983) 201, for the argument that Eust. owes his knowledge to mss of Athenaeus, not to lost mss of Soph.

[2] Mueller-Goldingen, 185–6, apparently believes in yet another interpretation: if I interpret him correctly, the lines would mean 'But if the gods have a better judgment (i.e., that justice is more on Pol.'s side than on Et.'s), then I would be fortunate ⟨if they bring about a just resolution without military victory⟩.'

[3] K–G II.468 Anm. 2 lists a few cases of indicative protasis with opt. of wish in apodosis; none are closely comparable to our passage.

291.2) or, more suitable here, 'better γνώμη, kinder disposition, than they had before' (cf. *Or.* 119–20 πρευμενῆ ... γνώμην ἔχειν). (2) seems almost to require acceptance of ἔχοιεν, but this is surely a grammatical regularization of ἔχουσιν, upon which nothing should be built. Furthermore, it assumes that εἴην can be potential opt. without ἄν, which is extremely implausible, though recently advocated by Craik. Pindaric usage allows this (e.g., *O.* 11.20 and, in my view, *O.* 3.45 κεινὸς εἴην),[1] but that is not enough to justify the oddity in tragic trimeters. In five tragic passages cited by Paley (*Ag.* 552, 1375, *Choe.* 591, *Hel.* 992, *Her.* 1417), no modern editor accepts the bare opt. (3) assumes non-adversative δ', removing any overt doubt in καλὸν τὸ νικᾶν. But if an addition were the intended point, one would expect ἔτι or καί, 'also', in the εἰ-clause (in the sense illustrated by Denniston, *GP²* 303–4). With the positive sense, it is also difficult to see why the chorus prays so emphatically: why would it occur to anyone that the foreign maidens might be neglected if Thebes won a final victory and a firm peace were restored? (4), like (2), illegitimately assumes pot. opt. without ἄν, and we may note that Craik adds a 'still' to her translation that is not in the text. An uncured corruption may lurk here (the suggestions recorded by Wecklein are not encouraging).[2] The smallest change that brings some sense is Conradt's (ἔχουσ',) εἴην ἄν εὐτυχὴς ἐγώ, in the sense 'and if the gods ⟨now⟩ have a better disposition ⟨toward Thebes and the family of Oedipus⟩, I would be fortunate'.

1202 τὰ τῶν θεῶν καὶ τὰ τῆς τύχης it is more likely that Joc. is embracing all possibilities by this combined expression than that she has in mind any specific division of responsibility between the gods and τύχη (cf. the listing of alternative causes in 350–3). τύχη is not 'random luck', but whatever is not readily identified with a knowable purpose.

1204 νυμφευμάτων a favourite word: nine times in Eur., otherwise extant only in *OT* 980, Lycophron and Nonnus.

1205 ἀπολαῦσαι a prosaic word used by Eur. as a synonym for more poetic ἐπαυρέω, -ίσκω. For the ironic sense, 'reap an unpleasant harvest', cf. *Andr.* 543, *IT* 526, ἀπόλαυσιν in *Hel.* 77 (only use by a classical poet), and the similar use of ἐπαυρίσκω (Griffith on *Prom.* 28).

1207 ἄνελθέ μοι πάλιν 'go back over the details', as in *Ion* 933; cf. *Contact and Discontinuity* 67 n. 46; Diggle, *CQ* 34 (1984) 59.

---

[1] I interpret 'I would be a fool.' Gildersleeve alleges it is a wish-optative in the sense 'set me down a fool', and Powell would like to interpret 1202 in the same way.

[2] It is no solution to delete the difficulty (Paley and Harberton): a rhesis of this length by rule receives a conventional choral couplet if the dialogue is to continue.

1208 τἀπὶ τούτοις 'next', temporal adv. acc., as in τὰ νῦν or *Ion* 256 τἀπὶ τῶιδ', *El.* 1247 τἀντεῦθεν.

δρασείετον except for ἀκουσείων in Soph. fr. 991, δρασείω (also *Aj.* 326, 585, *Phil.* 1245, *Med.* 93) and ἐργασείω (*Trach.* 1232, *Phil.* 1001) are the only desideratives in -σείω extant in tragedy. Cf. in general K–B II.264, Schwyzer I.789.

1209 δεῦρ' ἀεί probably a specifically tragic locution (six more times in Eur., also *TrGF* adesp. 183 and *Eum.* 596 δεῦρό γ' ἀεί; in Pl. *Laws* 811c δεῦρο δή is the correct reading). The uncommon temporal use of δεῦρο is aided by the adjacent ἀεί, which here and in *Hel.* 761 serves to intensify, '*right* up to this point in time', rather than indicate true continuity over time.

εὐτυχεῖς 2nd. pers. verb, not nom. pl. adj. (as Craik).

1210 τοῦτ' εἰς ὕποπτον εἶπας 'this you have said in such a way as to rouse suspicion' or 'in a manner leading to suspicion'. For εἰς expressing manner, Pearson compares *Hel.* 904 ἐς ἁρπαγάς, 'by violent seizure'; Dale *ad loc.* cites *Hel.* 1297 ἐς ἀμβολάς, 'with delay'; cf. also *OT* 1312, *Birds* 805, K–G I.471 (εἰς καλόν, εἰς τάχος) and Pearson on Soph. fr. 612. Somewhat different is *El.* 345 εἰς ὕποπτα μὴ μόληις ἐμοί, 'don't become suspicious of me'; cf. 1400n.

1211 μεῖζον τί with Murray and the Budé edd. I find μεῖζον τί more forceful than μεῖζόν τι as a protest against Joc.'s probing. It also allows a more natural interpretation of καὶ ... γε in 1212. But the choice is hardly certain.

παῖδας ἤ the word-order prob. conveys 'what greater wish do you have for your sons than that they have come through safely?' But hyperbaton for ἤ παῖδας is perhaps possible (cf. hyperbaton with initial ἤ in 'either ... or', *Med.* 847, *Birds* 420).

1212 καὶ τἀπίλοιπά γ' 'I want to hear whether for my *future* fortune *too* I am faring well.' For the general sense, cf. *Ion.* 1456–7 ἀλλὰ τἀπίλοιπα τῆς τύχης / εὐδαιμονοῖμεν, ὡς τὰ πρόσθ' ἐδυστύχει. After μεῖζον τί, καί is to be taken as adverbial and both it and γε emphasize τἀπίλοιπα, which is the important word here, picking up τὰ λοιπά in 1209, which Joc. refuses to dismiss. For such use of καὶ ... γε, see Denniston, *GP²* 158, §(2)(i). For different views (with reading μεῖζόν τι), see Pearson and Denniston, *GP²* 159 (undervaluing the position of τἀπίλοιπα).

πράσσω a vivid present, reflecting the fact that Joc.'s future fortune is being shaped by what is developing at this very moment.

κλυεῖν equivalent to μαθεῖν, West, *BICS* 31 (1984) 179.

1213 μέθες μ' Joc. may be physically restraining the messenger, perhaps having begun to do so at 1210. Alternatively, she could step in front of and toward him and more or less block his exit. Either way, the gesture. or positioning should back up the threat in 1216 ('unless you fly away').

ὑπασπιστοῦ in this context the word seems to point to the subordinate function of a squire, but like παρασπιστής (1073–4n., 1165n.) it can also imply the relationship of a subordinate but fighting comrade (so ὑπασπίζων in Pindar N. 9.34, Hcld. 216; cf. Gomme–Sandbach on Aspis 61 addenda). For the interlaced word-order in this line, cf. Su. 133 τῶι δ' ἐξέδωκας παῖδας Ἀργείων σέθεν;

1215 κοὐκ ἄν γε καὶ ... γε here marks an emphatic addition, the commonest use (Denniston, GP² 157–8). The messenger is indeed admitting that he is concealing something, as he has implicitly admitted by trying to end the conversation in 1213 without satisfying Joc. Here he is defending his concealment: 'yes, *and* I refuse to speak of bad things after your good news.' Hermann, followed by Pearson, insisted *inepte, qui tacere de malis cupit, affirmaret se malum tegere*, applying too naturalistic a criterion to this artificially constructed belated revelation of trouble. A majority of edd. have followed Hermann in preferring οὐκ ἄν γε, but Elmsley (on *Med.* 867 = 836–7 ed. suae) already made the fatal objection that οὐκ ἄν γε cannot be paralleled. In drama (and elsewhere, to my knowledge), γε follows ἄν only when γε actually goes with a preceding word: Hcld. 966 ὅντιν' ἄν γε (ὅστις γε with ἄν; so too fr. 1132.48), Knights 961 πρίν ἄν γε (πρίν γε with ἄν; also Acharn. 296, Wasps 920, Eccl. 770); Or. 784 καί τις ἄν γε (καί ... γε emphasizing τις or the whole sentence, with τις ἄν interposed); Xen. Oec. 4.7 οὐδὲ ἄν γε νῦν ... ἑώρας (οὐδέ γε (Denniston, GP² 156) with ἄν). There is no case in drama or Xen. or Pl. of οὐκ ἄν γε. For corruption of κοὐκ to οὐκ cf. 476n. If κοὐκ ἄν γε is doubted, it is better to emend (e.g. Porson οὐκ ἄν τι ... κακόν) rather than accept οὐκ ἄν γε.

σοῖς Reiske conjectured σοι, which is possible; but position in the sentence probably favours σοῖς.

1216 ἢν μή γε here γε may both strengthen the condition as a whole and serve to mark an affirmation ('yes, you will tell me') in response to the preceding denial (Denniston, GP² 132); cf. Hcld. 272 ('yes, I'll strike him') εἰ μή γ' ὁ κῆρυξ σωφρονεῖν μαθήσεται, Alc. 493. The variant με (B+) is a typical intrusion of the understood object.

φεύγων ἐκφύγηις the coupling of simplex present part. φεύγων with an aorist form of a compound is not merely a matter of paronomasia (K–G II.99–100, Schwyzer II.388), but for this verb plays upon the conative aspect of the present and the complexive aspect of the aorist reinforced by the addition of the preposition ('get away', 'succeed in escaping'). Other classical instances of this schema: Il. 14.81 φεύγων προφύγηι, Hdt. 4.23 φεύγων καταφύγηι, Acharn. 177 φεύγοντ' ἐκφυγεῖν, Clouds

167 φεύγων ἂν ἀποφύγοι, Xen. *Anab.* 2.5.7 φεύγων ἀποφύγοι, [Pl.] *Hipp.Mai.* 292a6 ἐκφύγω φεύγων; cf. also *IT* 1326 (οὐ) φεύγουσιν, ὥστε διαφυγεῖν.

1217–63 After the build-up of the short stichomythia, the messenger surprisingly has another extended rhesis (see 1067–1283n. above). It is possible that this speech has attracted some accretions: 1225 is certainly spurious, and 1233–5 and 1262–3 are, in my view, the most suspect other lines in the passage; but others have wished to remove the arming and exhortation as a whole (1242–58) or parts of it. Powell followed up a suggestion of Paley in drawing up an indictment of 1221–58 as a whole, but he failed to recognize that many of Paley's objections were feeble and his own arguments were in part flawed (e.g., listing the interpolation of 1225 as weighing against 1221–58 as a whole, considering variation in the readings of manuscripts to be suggestive of interpolation). If Eur. were hastening to finish his scene, then he would have had Joc. express distress immediately after 1220 and not have her wait for the exhortation in 1259ff. But Eur. is not interested here in a realistic presentation of time, and since the messenger has been kept on for his surprise announcement, he may effectively be exploited for a detailed narrative explaining the essential point, how the duel that Eur. had eliminated from the main battle nevertheless came about.

In the Greek historical and literary tradition, a duel of single champions could be (1) a featured contest within or preceding a large-scale engagement of the opposing forces (so often in the *Iliad*; also, e.g., Hdt. 6.92.3 of Eurybates, leader of the Argive volunteers fighting the Athenians on Aegina); (2) less often, a contest solemnized by oaths and intended to settle the dispute without committing the full forces to battle; (3) an athletic contest (e.g., at funeral games, *Il.* 23.798–825 of Ajax and Diomedes, Hdt. 5.8 of Thracian customs; later as a challenge and entertainment, Diodorus 17.100 of Coragus and Dioxippus among the companions of Alexander). See Pritchett, *Greek State at War* IV.15–20, with refs. for parallels in Egypt and the Near East and a review of examples in Greek literature; also S. P. Oakley, 'Single Combat in the Roman Republic', *CQ* 35 (1985) 392–410. The contracted duel that forestalls wider bloodshed has as its major literary prototype the contest of Paris and Menelaus in *Iliad* 3, which has many parallels in the duel of Hector and Ajax in *Iliad* 7. Hdt. 9.26.3–5 records the contest of Hyllus and Echemus, which resulted in a delay of 100 years in the return of the Heraclidae. Athenian legend told of Melanthus and Xanthus, and there are similar stories involving more than one champion (e.g. Horatii and Curiatii in Roman legend, Livy 1.24–6, or a Greek version with triplets, Plut. *Mor.* 309D; contests of man, horse, and dog between Perinthians and Paeonians in Hdt. 6.92.3;[1] Spartan and Argive contingents of 300 deciding the fate of the Thyreatis, Hdt. 1.82). Eur. uses the motif in *Hcld.* 800–20 to highlight the bravery of Hyllus and the cowardice of Eurystheus, whose refusal to accept a duel necessitates a large-scale battle.

There are two striking features of the adaptation of the motif to *Phoen.* (1) The positioning of the challenge *after* a major battle in which many have already died on both sides undercuts the nobility of the gesture; the challenges of Hyllus in Hdt. 9.26 and *Hcld.* 800–20 indicate the normal timing of such a challenge, *before* others have lost their lives. It is another sign of the moral blindness of Et. that he utters the conventional noble reasons for the challenge with no awareness of the irony: a duel now should forestall the bloodshed of a further battle, but if offered earlier might have saved the lives already lost. One does not feel quite the same irony in the *Iliad*, because in narrative terms the duel of Paris and Menelaus (like the catalogue) seems to come at the start of the war. (2) The sworn compact breaks down, and a further battle of the two forces ensues anyway: cf. the outcome in *Iliad* 3, the contest over Thyreatis (despite the precaution of sending the two armies away so that they cannot watch and intervene, a dispute later arises as to the result, leading to a full battle), and the Paeonians' attack upon the Perinthians when the Perinthians seemed on the point of winning.

Many of the features of the duel-narrative here are matched in earlier examples of the type, and it must be emphasized (against Powell) that the similarities to the messenger-speech in *Hcld.* cannot be counted as evidence in favour of the hypothesis of interpolation. (1) 1224, silence before the πρόκλησις: *Il.* 3.84. (2) 1226–7, address to both sides: *Il.* 3.86, 7.66–7, cf. Hdt. 9.26.3 ἀγορεύσασθαι, *Hcld.* 803 (Hyllus stands μέσοισιν ἐν μεταιχμίοις, though addressing Eurystheus alone). (3) 1227–8 (and 1233–5?), provision for saving others: *Il.* 3.74–5 (Trojans dwell in their city, Argives νεέσθων), 3.98–100 (be reconciled, end of κακὰ πολλά), Hdt. 9.26.3 ὡς χρεὸν εἴη τὸν μὲν στρατὸν τῶι στρατῶι μὴ ἀνακινδυνεύειν συμβάλλοντα, *Hcld.* 805–7 (leave Attica alone, cause no loss of life to Argos), 811 ἀπαλλαγὰς πόνων. (4) 1229–32, terms of duel: *Il.* 3.71–2, 92–3, 7.76–86, Hdt. 9.26.4 ἢν μὲν Ὕλλος νικήσηι ..., ἢν δὲ νικηθῆι ..., *Hcld.* 805–7 ἢ κτανών ... ἢ θανών .... (5) 1236–7, response of challenged party: *Il.* 3.97–102, 7.92–102, Hdt. 9.26.4, cf. *Hcld.* 813–16 (silence or

---

[1] It is unclear whether this contest was meant to solve the dispute or whether the challenge was designed merely to establish bragging rights.

refusal, after others have been said to approve the idea). (6) 1238-9, response of the whole armies: *Il.* 3.111-15, joy and disarming; *Hcld.* 811-12 ἐπήινεσ'. (7) 1241-2, oaths in the μεταίχμια: *Il.* 3.105-7, 268-301, Hdt. 9.26.4. (8) 1242-5, arming: *Il.* 3.328-39 (note emphasis on fine appearance of equipment, use of borrowed breastplate), 7.206-13. (9) 1246, lack of fear: cf. the converse in *Il.* 3.35 ὦχρός τέ μιν εἷλε παρειάς, 7.93 (cf. 117, 129), *Hcld.* 813-16. Of features not in these parallel passages, the exhortation of the comrades (1248-54) is also an epic reminiscence (1249n.), but it may suggest athletic competition as much as battle (cf. *Il.* 23.681-4 and perhaps 306-48, Nestor's advice to his son). This speech and the next messenger's speech pay much more attention to audience-reaction than is usual in Homer: cf. *Il.* 3.297-301 (audience comments at oath), 7.178-80, 200-5 (at drawing of lots), 3.318-23 (before duel) and 7.214-15 (fear of onlookers, cf. *Phoen.* 1388-9), 3.342-3, 23.815 (wonder as duel begins), 7.307-12 (after suspended duel). Again, athletic competition offers a model too: *Il.* 23.728, 766, 840, 881 (watching in amazement, yelling, laughing). For further parallels see 1356-1424n.

1217-18 οὐκ εἴασας ... ἀλλὰ μηνῦσαι for the inf. after ἀλλά or δέ depending on the understood opposite of οὐκ ἐᾶν, cf. *Or.* 513-15 οὐκ εἴων περᾶν ..., φυγαῖσι δ' ὁσιοῦν, ἀνταποκτείνειν δὲ μή with Willink's note; K–G II.566-7.

εὐαγγέλου the adj. is Aesch. (five times in *Ag.*), adopted by Eur. (also *Med.* 975, 1010), and found once each later in Meleager, Oppian, Nonnus (then in *Christ. Pat.*). Its use here reinforces the echo of the situation in *Ag.* 617-48 (cf. 1067-1283n.): note esp. *Ag.* 636-7 εὔφημον ἦμαρ ... κακαγγέλωι γλώσσηι μιαίνειν and 646-7 σωτηρίων δὲ πραγμάτων εὐάγγελον ἥκοντα.

1219-20 τολμήματα αἴσχιστα int. acc. in apposition to the sentence μέλλετον μονομαχεῖν. τολμήματα is a Eur. word (six other places; otherwise in classical Greek only Aristoph., Thuc., Dem.). αἴσχιστα provides an alternative perspective that calls into question both Et.'s assumption of a noble attitude in offering the duel and the values of the soldier-comrades who approve and encourage the fratricidal duel. This force of the word is magnified by the fact that the speaker is Et.'s own attendant; 1222 οἷον μήποτ' ὤφελον λόγον has a similar effect.

μονομαχεῖν this verb and the adj. μονομάχος are not common in classical Greek: in poetry *Se.* 798 μονομάχοισι προστάταις, *Hcld.* 819, below 1300, 1325, 1363 (whence Arist. *Phoen.* fr. 570 K–A), Men. *Samia* 570; in prose only Hdt. (seven times) and Plato *Crat.* 391e5. Later μονομάχος meant gladiator (so prob. Posidippus fr. 23.2 K–A τῶν μονομαχούντων ἐσμὲν ἀθλιώτεροι; on *Samia* 570 see Gomme–Sandbach; cf. Athenaeus

154d–f on athletic or gladiatorial duels, citing Ephorus), and it is possible that Eur. means to evoke athletic contests by his choice of details.

1223 ὑπῆρξ' 'acted first, took the initiative', with supplementary λέγων easily understood from the preceding λέξαντες ... λόγον.

δ' used almost as in 473 above, in transition to the report of the actual speech after the introductory 1219–22. Such a transition could also have been effected by γάρ or by asyndeton, and Fraenkel suggested deleting δ'.[1]

1223–4 ἀπ' ὀρθίου σταθεὶς πύργου see 1009n.

1224 σῖγα κηρῦξαι σῖγα is a partial quotation of the herald's cry σῖγα ἀκούσατε (*Su.* 669–70) or σῖγα πᾶς ἔστω λεώς (*Hec.* 532) as object of the verb of speaking (1154–5n.). *Hec.* 530 has the alternative formulation σιγὴν ... κηρῦξαι, also in Xen. *Anab.* 2.2.20 σιγὴν κηρύξαντα.

[1225] Σ reveal that this line was absent in some ancient copies (see 375n.), and it was clearly absent in the copy of the commentator who noted the shift to direct speech in 1226 without an explicit ταῦτα λέγων. The interpolation is more likely to be one made for the benefit of readers than the work of actors. γῆς Ἑλλάδος στρατηλάται is empty padding, inept in that Et.'s speech is actually addressed to the full complement of warriors on both sides, not to generals.

1228 ἀπεμπολᾶτε except in *Cycl.* 257, this compound usually implies the selling of what ought not to be sold or illicit conveyance of what one has no right to deal with: *IT* 1360 (smuggling Iphigenia out of the country), *Ion.* 1371 (disposing of a baby), Xen. *Symp.* 4.8.21 (a boy selling his ὥρα), *Tro.* 973 and *Acharn.* 374 (of betrayal, 'selling out'). So here 'don't put your ⟨precious⟩ lives out for sale', almost 'don't squander your lives'. Σ, however, identifies the metaphor ἀπὸ τῶν ἐν τῆι θαλάσσηι κινδινευόντων διὰ τὸ κέρδος.

1229–30 'for I myself alone, dismissing this danger ⟨of the full armies⟩, shall join battle with my brother.' There are two uncertainties here. (1) Valck., on the basis of *Hipp.* 356 ῥίψω μεθήσω σῶμα, suggested that μεθιέναι κίνδυνον could be used in the same sense as ῥίπτειν κίνδυνον, 'take a risk'. The latter is attested in *Hcld.* 148–9, fr. 402.6–7, *Rhes.* 154–5; the more prosaic form is ἀναρρίπτειν κίνδυνον (Hdt. 7.50.3, Thuc. 4.85.4, *al.*), cf. *Se.* 1028 κἀνὰ κίνδυνον βαλῶ. This idiom derives from the throwing of dice, often conveyed by βάλλω and ῥίπτω (esp. κύβον ἀναρρίπτω, as

---

[1] Note that the absence of δ' in V*recc.* is due to intrusion of a gloss; in Vr its absence probably resulted from imperfect correction of προϋπῆρξ' by collation.

Arist. fr. dub. 929 K–A, Critias *TrGF* 43 F 7.27, Men. fr. 59.4 K–T, and later prose), but not found with μεθίημι (the closest locution is ἔσχατον κύβον ἀφιέντι, Plut. *Cor.* 3.1). Geel was thus right to reject Valck.'s idea and return to the traditional interpretation. μεθείς is used as in LSJ s.v. 1.2.d (though our passage is there placed under 1.2.e, a heading rather artificially separated from d, where the other two exx. have an explicit dat. of interest). I do not understand why Nauck thought this phrase corrupt. τόνδε κίνδυνον is very easily understood (*pace* Pearson) as 'this danger to you' (i.e., τὸ ὑμᾶς τὰς ψυχὰς ἀπεμπολᾶν ὑπὲρ ἡμῶν), less easily of the duel, whether τόνδε is supposed to point backward (i.e., τὸ ἐμὲ τὴν ψυχὴν ἀπεμπολᾶν) or forward (to μόνος συνάψω). The parallels (1217–63n., item 3, esp. Hdt. 9.26.3, *Hcld.* 805–7) support Geel, not Valck. and Pearson. (2) αὐτὸς . . . μόνος may be an emphatic redundancy, as in *Peace* 508 αὐτοὶ δὴ μόνοι and *Aj.* 1283 αὐτὸς Ἕκτορος μόνος μόνου (where the redundancy also serves the expressive paregmenon); cf. *Od.* 14.450, *El.* 1129, Pl. *Lysis* 211c11, *Polit.* 307e3. But one may at least consider whether the text was originally μόνωι συνάψω (Valck., cf. Rwˢ) or whether μόνος should be paired with μόνωι (for τὠμῶι, Pierson), as in *Aj.* 1283 and in *Hcld.* 807–8 ἐμοὶ μόνος μόνωι μάχην συνάψας. But since the characteristic paregmenon would require further changes (Schroeder μάχην συν. συγ. μόνος μόνωι) and since the emphasis of nom. μόνος and of the possessive is not unwelcome, I retain the transmitted text.

1231 οἶκον οἰκήσω μόνος cf. 602. If μόνος is correct in 1230, we have here a deliberate and effective repetition.

1232 ἡσσωμένος one might expect ἡσσημένος, but just as νικάω may have a perfective sense (1472n.), so may its opposite ἡττάομαι sometimes express 'be defeated' rather than 'be in the process of being defeated'. The former is probably the sense in *Hec.* 1252–3 (after Polymestor has lost the decision in the trial) γυναικός . . . ἡσσώμενος / δούλης ὑφέξω τοῖς κακίσοιν δίκην, and a particularly clear case is Andoc. 3.26 ἵνα ἡμῖν τί γένηται; ἵνα ἡττώμενοι μὲν καὶ τὴν οἰκείαν χώραν ἀπολέσωμεν πρὸς τῆι Κορινθίων, νικήσαντες δὲ τὴν Κορινθίων Ἀργείων ποιήσωμεν; cf. Thuc. 6.69.3, Agathon *TrGF* 39 F 7, Xen. *Hell.* 3.4.8, 7.5.25, *Anab.* 2.4.6, Dem. 18.273, etc.

πόλιν I believe this is genuine, used in deliberate variation after οἶκον in 1231. If so, it was accidentally ousted by μόνος from just above (both words are preceded by σω) and V¹ shows a conflation of truth and error, while μόνωι is a conjecture improving on feeble μόνος, and δόμον another such conjecture. But others believe that πόλιν too is a conjectural supplement of a line-ending that had become damaged or corrupt. If so, μόνωι (accepted by Murray, Budé edn, Craik) is preferable to any of the emendations.

1233–5   1235 has been deleted by many from Valck. on; but Fraenkel argued for the removal of all three lines.[1] Against 1233–4 he argues (1) that they do not contain anything not already conveyed in 1226–8, and Paley and Powell had noted as oddities (2) χθόνα, (3) νίσεσθε, and (4) βίοτον λιπόντες ἐνθάδε. But (1) 1233–4 form the positive counterpart of the negative 'don't risk your lives' of 1238, and such complementarity is often idiomatic, the repetition being a form of framing (ἀγῶν' ἀφέντες recalling κίνδυνον μεθέντες with a change of perspective): cf. 484–9, which this passage prob. recalls deliberately. (2) χθών is occasionally used absolutely in tragedy to refer to a particular land or fatherland, the identification of which is clear from the context: cf. A. Su. 425, Se. 477, 1007, Eum. 406, Ant. 368, Tro. 1119, Med. 723 σοῦ μὲν ἐλθούσης χθόνα, 112 ἦλθε . . . χθόνα, etc. Two instances where the identification of the land relies on careful attention to the context are A. Su. 583 πᾶσα βοᾶι χθών (= Egypt) and Med. 880–1 χθόνα φεύγοντας ἡμᾶς (= Thessaly). Here the preceding Ἀργεῖοι and the following νίσεσθε (which by etymology suggests 'return home') make it unambiguous that χθόνα means 'your own country'. As for νίσεσθε (3), elsewhere in tragedy it is rare and confined to lyric or anap. (six places, including compounds: Cycl. 43, Alc. 449, Hel. 1483, Ant. 129, OC 689, Prom. 530). But it is quite possible that the rare verb here deliberately evokes epic style in a messenger-speech that has epic models (esp. Il. 3.74 νεέσθων; cf. also 1246 ἔσταν). νίσεσθε may be present imperative, which makes the use of μή with the non-conditional λιπόντες easy (K–G II.200 Anm. 2). But many translators have assumed it is future indicative:[2] no other tragic use is future (though one might make an uncertain claim for Alc. 449), but it could be an imitation of Il. 23.76, Od. 10.42; future seems to me more apt rhetorically and would give 'not having died here' more point, but μή with the participle would then be harder, though not impossible.[3] (4) βίοτον μὴ λιπόντες ἐνθάδε is an emphatic expansion of

---

[1] So too Mueller-Goldingen, 190–1, regarding the lines as a clarifying explication of μήτε . . . ψυχὰς ἀπεμπολᾶτε.

[2] Eust. 1288, 54–9 teaches that νισσ- should appear in present forms and νισ- in future, but earlier grammarians (e.g. Et. Magn. 606, 12–16) speculate only on the variation between ει and ι. Variation in the mss between one and two sigmas seems to reflect scribal confusion, not any principle.

[3] On μή with participles that seem non-conditional and non-generic, see K–G II.201 Anm. 3 and Moorhouse, Syntax Soph. 331, with additional refs. (experts do not agree on the explanation of this phenomenon). The grammarians have regarded νίσεσθε here as imperative (e.g., G. E. Howes, HSCP 12 (1901) 282).

ἀγών' ἀφέντες, with ἐνθάδε contrasted with χθόνα: it cannot be faulted as idiom, since tragedians use βίοτος as an exact equivalent of βίος in a variety of expressions: with σώιζω, e.g., *Pers.* 360 vs. *Alc.* 146; ἐκ-/ἐμπνέω, e.g., *Hel.* 142 vs. *Hipp.* 1246; λείπω, e.g., *Andr.* 383, below 1428 vs. this line and *Hel.* 226 λέλοιπε βίοτον. I do not believe that an adequate case has been made against 1233-4.

1235 could be deleted separately. It is unmetrical in most of the mss, and this could be due to a false scansion of ἅλις, which would be a sign of very late insertion. But corruption of original ὅσος to ὅς would be very easy, and even if ὅσος is a metrical correction by Mosch. or a source of his, it may well hit upon the original form of the line. The sense is 'the number of Theban dead is ⟨already⟩ sufficient ⟨and there will be no more if my proposal is adopted⟩'. For ἅλις as predicate (instead of ἅλις + gen.: 1748n.) cf. *Alc.* 673, *Med.* 558, *Hec.* 394, etc.; for the sense cf. *Rhes.* 870 μὴ θνῆισχ'· ἅλις γὰρ τῶν τεθνηκότων ὄχλος, *Cycl.* 304 ἅλις δὲ Πριάμου γαῖ' ἐχήρωσ' Ἑλλάδα; also Theocr. 22.177-8 (in a passage that imitates the duel of *Phoen.*) ἅλις νέκυς ἐξ ἑνὸς οἴκου / εἷς. The truly unusual feature of the line is the use of νεκρός as an adj., a usage found in later Greek but cited in classical times only from Pindar fr. 203.2 νεκρὸν ἵππον (compare, however, Soph. fr. 210.51, where ἔκειντο νεκροί is prob. 'they lay dead' rather than 'the corpses lay', and appositional uses such as 1529 below). But even this is not inconceivable for Eur. The decision to keep or to delete 1235 thus rests mainly on one's sense of rhetorical aptness: those who delete say it is unneeded, those who keep it feel that rhetorical balance is to be expected (so Heath and Hermann, with whom I tend to agree: this is a formal proposal that should offer something to and win the approval of both sides). If deletion is contemplated, it may be better to remove 1233-5 rather than just 1235.

1236 τοσαῦτ' ἔλεξε for this formula concluding a direct quotation, cf. *Hec.* 542 and other exx. collected by Fraenkel, *Beobacht. zu Arist.* 40 n. 3.

1238-9 Fraenkel deletes both these lines, insisting that Eur. was only interested in the two brothers in this speech and that references to the reactions and actions of others are out of place, and branding ἐπερρόθησαν τάδε grammatically incorrect. The first argument is a *petitio principii*: one can just as well say that the proposal requires the fuller ratification, because the Argive army must agree to withdraw and the Theban citizens must agree to accept Pol. as their king should he kill Et. For the second argument, see next note. Powell noted 'a want of skill in the repetition of the cadence Κάδμου τε λαός in 1227, 1235, 1239'; but 1235 may be spurious, and if it is genuine it shows variation, since it has Σπαρτῶν τε λαός, and the repetition in 1239 is in any case at no small interval and serves to make explicit the formal acceptance by the two groups to which Et. addressed himself.

1238 ἐπερρόθησαν . . . τάδε this construction has long troubled the commentators. Valck. improbably placed a comma before τάδε to make it go with ἡγούμενοι rather than ἐπερρόθησαν. Pearson implausibly explicates τάδε as adverbial, 'thereat'. Fraenkel roundly declares it incorrect for normal τοῖσδε. It is clearly meant by the writer to be the direct object of ἐπερρόθησαν meaning 'clamoured in approval of'. The shouted response of an assembly or army to a proposal is a typical narrative element, starting with epic exx. (*Il.* 1.22 ἄλλοι μὲν πάντες ἐπευφήμησαν Ἀχαιοί, 8.542 ἐπὶ δὲ Τρῶες κελάδησαν) and accounting for half the surviving uses of ἐπιρροθέω: *Hec.* 553, *Or.* 901; Dion. Hal. *Ant.Rom.* 6.83.2, *Orph. Argon.* 294 (note ἐπήινει in 293), Greg. Naz. *De Vita Sua* 1389; *Christ. Pat.* 403. The verb is by no means common (eleven other places, to my knowledge) and is found with various constructions: six absolute (*Choe.* 427, 458, Soph. fr. 762.1, *Hec.* 553; Dion. Hal., Philostr. maj. *Imag.* 1.19.1), two with ὡς (*Or., Christ. Pat.*), one with acc. + inf. (*Argon.*), one with int. acc. (*Trach.* 264 πολλά), one with dat. (Greg.). Here the direct-object acc. construction is eased or influenced by the preceding ἐπήινει; I see little reason to think that it is less likely to be by Eur. than by an interpolator. For the acc. obj. where one might have expected a dat., cf. *Or.* 284 ἐπένευσας τάδ' and Aesch. fr. 350.3-4 θεοφιλεῖς ἐμὰς τύχας παιῶν' ἐπηυφήμησαν (where one could argue that τύχας is obj. of the phrase παιῶν' ἐπ.), ἐπαινέω with acc. of thing.[1] See in general K-G 1.300-1, and cf. *Ba.* 503 καταφρονεῖ με with Dodds' note.

1239 ὡς the particle serves to distance the speaker somewhat from the evaluation of the armies: he himself found the proposal shocking (1219-22).

1240-1 if 1238-9 are retained, the subject of ἐσπείσαντο is probably 'the Argives and the Thebans'; less likely, the plural subject becomes clear only with στρατηλάται in the following clause. If 1238-9 are deleted, there is ambiguity: is the subject 'Et. and Pol.' or 'the generals'? 'The generals' in 1241 should be the major surviving leaders on both sides, not just the brothers, since (1) the compliance of the rest of the forces is crucial to the agreement, (2) the emphatic subject in 1243 suggests that the subject of ἔκρυπτον is not the same as that of the previous verb, and (3) in 1462 'the generals' quarrel about the outcome when both brothers are dead.

---

[1] Cf. Xen. *Anab.* 5.8.25 εἰ δέ τωι ἢ χειμῶνα ἐπεκούρησα (ἐπεκούφισε Reiske).

1241 ἐμμενεῖν στρατηλάται for the fut. inf. (Markland, Elmsley) with ὅρκος, cf. *Su.* 1191, *IT* 735, *Ag.* 1290 + 1284 (with ἄξειν). In *Hel.* 977–8 aor. infs. follow ὅρκοις κεκλήιμεθ', depending on the overall sense of the phrase, 'be firmly resolved and bound', rather than on ὅρκοις alone. The variant στρατηλάτας (acc. adjusted to the adjacent inf.) yields poor sense: leaders other than Et. and Pol. must swear to accept the outcome. Cf. the oath exchanged by Priam and Agamemnon in *Il.* 3. τοῖσδε is understood as complement of ἐμμενεῖν from ἐπὶ τοῖσδε in the previous line.

1242–58 Fraenkel deletes this whole passage, but has very little linguistic evidence to support the excision, which is based principally on his belief that the interest here should be solely on the brothers and is backed up by identification of various lines and half-lines which the interpolator is supposed to have exploited in mosaic-fashion to write the passage. Shifts of perspective are common in messenger-speeches, and attention to the audience of a duel is found in the Homeric models. Possible sources of inspiration for an interpolator are of interest only after deletion has been shown to be probable on other grounds. As to specific points, see on 1244 ἐκόσμουν, 1246 ἔσταν (the only item within 1242–54 to which Paley and Powell had objected), 1247, 1253 κρατεῖς. The difficulties of 1255–8 (which could be deleted without affecting 1242–54) may be taken as a separate issue.

1242 ἔκρυπτον σῶμα παγχάλκοις ὅπλοις κρύπτω is occasionally a synonym for καλύπτω, with no notion of stealth or contrived concealment (*Ag.* 455, *Hec.* 726, *Hel.* 1222 of burial; *Hcld.* 561, *Tro.* 627 of covering with πέπλοι), but the use here may be a deliberate epicism: cf. *Il* 14.372–3 κεφαλὰς δὲ παναίθησιν κορύθεσσι / κρύψαντες. In *Hcld.* 823–4 L presents ὑπ' ἀσπίδων / πλευραῖς (-οῖς Elmsley, κύκλοις Wilam.) ἔκρυπτον πλεύρ', but Diggle convincingly emends to πλευροῖς ἔχριμπτον. παγχάλκοις adds to the epic colouring, since παγχάλκεος/-κος is Homeric and rare in tragedies (121 above, cf. *Se.* 591, *Ant.* 143).

1243 in most mss almost the same as 1360, identical in ORW by conflation with the later line. The specification of subject is needed here, and no one has proposed to delete 1243 by itself. Cf. 1360n.

1244 ἐκόσμουν Fraenkel objects that the comrades of Et. and Pol. should not be helping them put on their armour. When accompanied by ὅπλοις (861n.) the middle and passive of κοσμέω can mean 'arm oneself, be armed'. But here the active, without ὅπλοις and following the arming denoted in 1243, must be simply 'adorned, beautified', that is, by helping to remove the dust of the earlier battle and perhaps adding decorative elements like crest-feathers or spangles (cf. 1246 λαμπρῷ). This adorning of the champion by each side, like the verbal encouragement, creates the impression that the duel is like an athletic contest (or, to be anachronistic, a gladiatorial duel), a notion exploited more fully in the second messenger's narrative. Cf. *Il.* 23.681-4 (Diomedes helping Euryalus put on his boxing gear and exhorting him to victory).

1246 ἔσταν another detail of epic colouring. Paley cited this epic 3rd pl. aorist form as unlikely to have been used in trimeters by Eur.(for lyric see 823-4n.), and Powell noted suspicion of the similar form in *Hipp.* 1247 ἔκρυφθεν (also a messenger-speech). But the two cases defend each other, and neither should be suspected: cf. Barrett on *Hipp.* 1247-8.

χρῶμά τ' οὐκ ἠλλαξάτην a mark of fearlessness in the face of danger: *Il.* 13.279, 284 τοῦ μὲν γάρ τε κακοῦ τρέπεται χρὼς ἄλλυδις ἄλληι ... τοῦ δ' ἀγαθοῦ οὔτ' ἄρ τρέπεται χρὼς κτλ., *Od.* 11.529 οὔτ' ὠχρήσαντα χρόα κάλλιμον. The converse expression, Men. *Epitr.* 887 ἤλλαττε χρώματ', connotes overwrought emotion. χρῶμα is rare in tragedy: also Soph. fr. 307.1 (by emendation for σῶμα), *El.* 521 (deleted by Fraenkel!); Chaeremon (thrice), *TrGF* adesp. 201a.

1247 μαργῶντ' see 1156n. After the brightness and suggestion of calm in 1246 this line sharply reminds the audience of the messenger's disapproval and prepares for the use of bestial terms and images in the second messenger's report. Fraenkel objects to this description of the brothers as a brutal exaggeration; this judgment follows his tendency to oversimplify or whitewash the characterization in this play.

1249 λόγοις ἐθάρσυνόν another epic reminiscence: cf. *Od.* 13.328 θαρσύνας τ' ἐπέεσσι (also 9.377, *Il.* 4.233, 23.682), *Il.* 10.190 θάρσυνέ τε μύθωι; *Pers.* 215-16 (λόγοις).

τε κ(αί) perhaps the coherence of λόγοις ἐθάρσυνον as a phrase accounts for the postponed position of τε; of the exx. in Denniston, *GP²* 517, Hdt. 6.136.2 similarly has τε καί adding an explanatory phrase (ἑλὼν Λῆμνόν τε καὶ τεισάμενος τοὺς Πελασγούς).

1250-3 the two exhortations effectively display a dissonance between the enthusiasm of the warrior-comrades and the shock and revulsion that an audience will imagine to be felt by Joc. Note that Ζηνὸς ὀρθῶσαι βρέτας τροπαῖον recalls her disapproving question at 572 τροπαῖα πῶς ἀναστήσεις Διί; and that καλλίνικος now carries a pronounced irony (1048n.).

1252-3 νῦν ... νῦν for the anaphora and the asyndeton cf. *Med.* 765-7, 1401 (JD).

1252 ὑπερμαχεῖς a rare verb, no more likely to be chosen by an interpolator than by Eur. himself.

1253 κρατεῖς this dynamic, confident, virtually 'prophetic' present has wrongly been deemed the solecism of an interpolator by Fraenkel. This sentence is equivalent to εἰ γενήσηι καλλίνικος, κρατεῖς, with a confident use of the present that is idiomatic in conditions, such as Antiphon *tetr.* 1.4.10 οὐκ ἐὰν ἀποφύγω οὐκ ἔστιν ἐξ ὧν ἐλεγχθήσονται οἱ κακουργοῦντες, ἀλλ' ἐὰν καταληφθῶ, οὐδεμία ἀπολογία τοῖς διωκομένοις ἀρκοῦσά ἐστιν (cf. 1.3.9 εἰ μήτε ἐκ τῶν εἰκότων μήτε ἐκ τῶν μαρτυρουμένων οὗτος νῦν ἐλέγχεται, οὐκ ἔστιν ἔτι τῶν διωκόντων ἔλεγχος οὐδείς), Thuc. 6.91.3 καὶ εἰ αὕτη ἡ πόλις ληφθήσεται, ἔχεται καὶ ἡ πᾶσα Σικελία, *Andr.* 381 ἦν θανῇς σύ, παῖς ὅδ' ἐκφεύγει μόρον; without the explicit condition Thuc. 1.121.4 μιᾶι τε νίκηι ναυμαχίας κατὰ τὸ εἰκὸς ἁλίσκονται. See Schwyzer II.273 (with further refs.); Fraenkel on *Ag.* 126, Barrett on *Hipp.* 47, Broadhead on *Pers.* 241. For such exhortation, cf. Chariton 6.2.2 (supporters shouting to Chaereas and Dionysius) ἐπευφημούντων "σὺ κρείττων, σὺ νικᾷς"; 7.3.4 (Chaereas' confident prediction to the Egyptian king) νικῶμεν γάρ, ἂν θεοὶ θέλωσι, καὶ οὐ μόνον Τύρον ἕξομεν ἀλλὰ καὶ Βαβυλῶνα. For κρατεῖς in such a prediction, cf. *OC* 1332 (of an oracle) οἷς ἂν σὺ προσθῆι, τοῖσδ' ἔφασκ' εἶναι κράτος.

1255–8 prophecy is not a standard element of other duels; in *Hcld.* 821–2 the sacrifices are the standard ones before battle (174n., 1110n.), not related to the aborted duel. But the time taken for prophecy provides a suggestion of delay or pause that seems to leave room for Joc.'s final attempt to reconcile her sons. Eur. may have had in mind the σφάγια in *Se.* 378–9 that hold back the Argive assault during the central scene of that play. The purpose of this prophecy is similar, however, to that of military ἱερά / σφάγια:[1] it is to provide an omen of the outcome, though a bad omen will not, as for a battle, prevent the duel from occurring. There may be an allusion to other fire-prophecies in the literary tradition of Thebaid myth, e.g., *Ant.* 1005–11; an audience might also think of the motif of the divided flame on the funeral pyre of Et. and Pol. (attested only later, Statius *Theb.* 12.430; cf. Paus. 9.18.3).

The interpretation of these lines is quite uncertain. With Geel's ἐμπύρου τ' ἀκμῆς for ἐμπύρους ἀκμὰς (and removal of τ' after ῥήξεις), adopted here, the meaning is probably (a): 'They observed the fissures of the tips of sacrificial flame, ⟨a sign of⟩ opposing/unfavourable moistness, and the peak of flame, which holds the defining portents of two things, the sign of victory and that of the defeated.' On this view the prophets are looking for two things, the vigour of the fire (a strong flame is favourable, a sputtering smoky fire, overcome by the moisture of the entrails, is inauspicious) and the behaviour of the topmost flame (which may indicate good or bad either by its direction or by its height relative to the fire as a whole or by clarity

---

[1] Jameson, 'Sacrifice before Battle', notes the overall distinction between ἱερά as burnt sacrifices and σφάγια as fireless, but also shows the occasional functional equivalence of these rites. His discussion of our passage (208–9) is marred by an inaccurate description of the context.

or smokiness). The advantage of this reading is that it provides a defining gen. for ῥήξεις and avoids the apparent redundancy of ἄκραν λαμπάδ' with ἐμπύρους ἀκμάς. Many edd. have kept the reading of the mss, which may be interpreted in two different ways: (b) (after Pearson) 'They observed the tips of the flames and the fissures, an unfavourable flickering, and the highest peak of flame, etc.' (c) (as Stengel) 'They observed the tips of the flames and the ruptures [sc. of the gall-bladder], a moisture opposed to the fire, etc.' Several words in the passage have been interpreted in two ways. (1) ῥήξεις is interpreted as in (a) and (b) by Valck., Hermann and others: this gives a consistent reference to features of the fire (as in Sen. *Oed.* 309-13, Statius *Theb.* 10. 599-603).[1] Σ refer it instead to the bursting of the gall-bladder, as in (c), and this view is accepted by P. Stengel in *Hermes* 31 (1896) 478-80, 34 (1899) 642-3, and most strongly argued in the revised version of these articles in *Opferbräuche* 97-9.[2] The scholia on these lines contain various explanations, some of which are certainly false (e.g., that the ἄκρα λαμπάς is the heart of the victim or the tail, that the bile is examined for signs only about one's enemy) and some of which are mutually exclusive (e.g., the 'bursting' is either that of the gall-bladder or of the urinary bladder).[3] So it is unclear whether we should believe the explanation about the gall-bladder: Σ claims that the full bladder is placed on the fire and the seer observes how the bile is squirted out when it bursts. But a possible illustration of a gall-bladder used for prophecy shows it being

---

[1] M. H. Jameson (private correspondence) is inclined to think that only the behaviour of the fire is described, but fears that later interpretations have affected the text, making Eur.'s exact words unrecoverable.

[2] Stengel refers to Σ Thom. *Se.* 230d Smith (which Smith compares to Σ Thom. *Ant.* 1009) and puts special weight on Σ^A *Prom.* 476 Herington (prob. twelfth-century) as a source giving independent information. The latter reads in most witnesses ... καὶ ἀπὸ τῶν θυμάτων· οἷον τῆς χολῆς ἐμβληθείσης **τῶι πυρὶ** καὶ ἀνατιναγείσης πρὸς τὸ τῶν πολεμίων μέρος, ἧτταν τούτων ἐσήμαινεν, while Stengel relied on a later recension that reads καὶ ἀπὸ τῆς χολῆς ἥτις **ἐκ**βληθεῖσα καὶ ἀνατιναγεῖσα πρὸς κτλ., which seems to point to spurting of bile from a burst bladder. Thomas in his Σ on our passage interprets the direction of the spurting in the opposite way. I believe both the *Prom.*-commentator and Thomas are merely expanding on τηροῦσι ... πῶς τὴν ὑγρότητα ἀκοντίζουσιν in the old Σ on our passage.

[3] For the latter they cite Soph. fr. 394 τὰς μαλλοδέτας κύστεις, but without context we cannot say whether bursting was involved there. Stengel derives from the inconsistency of the Σ his view that both gall-bladder and urinary-bladder were regularly used for prophecy from σφάγια.

held over the fire and squeezed to produce a stream of bile for inspection, not being left on the fire to burst by itself.[1] Literary testimonia are indecisive (and not simply because χολή can mean either 'gall-bladder' or 'bile'): *Prom.* 493–5 isolates the colour of the bile as significant; *Ant.* 1009–10 καὶ μετάρσιοι χολαὶ διεσπείροντο is interpreted by Jebb (influenced by our Σ) as a description of the effect of bursting on a full gall-bladder deposited on fire, but it could just as well describe an unpropitious spluttering discharge from above by the seer; *Dysc.* 451–3 and com. adesp. 1205.3 Kock ὀστῶν ἀσάρκων καὶ χολῆς πυρουμένης [ἀπαρχαῖς] confirm that the gall-bladder was consumed on the fire, but do not tell whether its bursting on the fire was an expected event;[2] *Samia* 401 χολὴν ἱκανήν could be 'an adequate gall-bladder' or 'enough bile ⟨to squirt on the fire⟩'. Nor does the usage of ῥῆξις help: in poetry it is extant only here and in Call. fr. 23 (not relevant); it *may* have been easily recognizable as a technical term of prophecy for bursting of a bladder, but there is no other instance extant to confirm this. The word is common in medical and scientific writing, of ruptures and violent discharges, or in discussions of lightning and thunder. (2) If ῥῆξεις refers to the gall-bladder, then ὑγρότητ' ἐναντίαν could still be 'adverse moisture' (the way the gall spreads might suppress the flame), but Stengel (in the second article) preferred 'liquid shot out in opposite directions', which seems to me very far-fetched (in *Opferbräuche* Stengel himself returned tacitly to the view found in his first article). A third possible meaning of ὑγρότητ' (after Valck. and Hermann; LSJ II.1.b) is 'flickering' (from ὑγρός = 'supple, languid'), but this would be the only attestation of such usage, ὑγρότης elsewhere being applied to the flexibility of solid bodies or limbs or to human character. (3) Σ's notion that ἐναντίαν can mean something like 'giving a sign about the enemy' is to be rejected, as is the variant ἐναντίων (χ) which prob. intruded because of this explanation. The adjective rather combines the connotations of the natural opposition of the wet to fire and the specific opposition of this moisture to a favourably vigorous flame. Thus it arrives at the meaning 'unfavourable' only indirectly. (4) The meaning is also affected by how we identify the appositive: I view ὑγρότητ' ἐναντίαν as in apposition to ῥῆξεις alone, but some have put no comma after ἐναντίαν, apparently taking ὑγρότητ' and λαμπάδ' as in chiastic apposition to ἀκμάς and ῥῆξεις.

---

[1] See M. Jameson in *Greek Tragedy and its Legacy* 51–7 with plate following p. 364.

[2] Cf. Plut. *Mor.* 141E τὴν χολὴν οὐ συγκαθαγίζουσι τοῖς ἄλλοις ἱεροῖς when sacrificing to Hera Gamelia (also Plut. fr. 157.2 Sandbach). Porphyrius *De Antro Nymph.* 18 also mentions the offering of the χολή, giving it an allegorical interpretation.

In sum, I find (a) superior to (b), though the same meaning could perhaps be obtained without emendation if ἐμπ. ἀκμὰς ῥήξεις τ' is taken as hendiadys; and I prefer (a) to (c) in the present state of our knowledge. But if ῥῆξις had an established use in fire-prophecy, then (c) may be right. Paley, who doubts Euripidean authorship, claims that this passage sounds more like a Roman poet than a Greek one. It is true that description of such rites is favoured by, e.g., Seneca and Statius, but they are far more verbose. Such rites did exist in classical Greece, and the passages in *Prom.* and *Ant.* (also E. *El.* 826–9) show that they could have a place in tragedy. Fraenkel objects to the obscurity of the passage, *quo vitio minime tenebatur* (sc. Euripides). But what obscurity there is seems due to textual uncertainty and our ignorance of a practice that was perfectly familiar to Eur.'s audience. The difficulties of these lines do not contribute significantly, in my view, to indictment of 1242–58 as a whole.

1255 ἀκμῆς ἔμπυρος ἀκμή could mean 'vigorous sacrificial flame' rather than 'tip, edge of sacrificial flame', and Stengel perhaps intends something like the former when he speaks of the intensity of the fire. But such an expression would be rather high-flown for this context (contrast Pindar *O.* 1.48 ὕδατος ... πυρὶ ζέοισαν εἰς ἀκμάν, 'into vigorously boiling water').

1256 ἐνώμων 'observed', prob. a technical term for the observations of seers (cf. *Se.* 25, *OT* 300), though there are non-prophetic uses too (LSJ s.v. II.4).

1257 λαμπάδ' for the metonymic sense 'flame' cf. the use of λαμπάς for the sun (*Ant.* 879, *Med.* 352, *Ion* 1467) and for lightning (*Su.* 1011, *Ba.* 594); in *Ag.* 93 (οὐρανομήκης ... ἀνίσχει) the word could be translated as 'flame' rather than 'torch'.

ὅρους it is a small step from 'boundary marks' to 'defining portents'; this seems to be a unique application of the term, but it may be influenced by the notion of the 'path of prophetic speech' (911n.), even though speech is not involved here.

1258 Pearson notes the unusual sequence of anarthrous νίκης σῆμα followed by τὸ τῶν ἡσσωμένων and compares *El.* 1351 ὅσιον καὶ τὸ δίκαιον (for τὸ ὅσιον κτλ.), doubted by Denniston, but rightly kept by Diggle; the article here is more a matter of variation, as in *Phil.* 1312–13 μετὰ ζώντων ... νῦν δὲ τῶν τεθνηκότων; see also 494–6n. Here the variant τά (= 'the fate of, what belongs to, the defeated') is not impossible.

1259–60 the three alternatives are parallel to the traditional grouping of force, persuasion, and guile (Craik), and this tradition accounts for the presence of ἀλκήν, unnecessarily doubted by Valck.: '(physical) means of prevention' (cf. 'means of defence/prevention' in *Tro.* 729, *Her.* 326).

σοφοὺς ... λόγους an ominous reminiscence of the agon-scene, when

Joc.'s wisdom proved incapable of ending her sons' quarrel (445, 453, 460, 529–30, 584). There is no reason to expect a different result now, and the alternative ἢ φίλτρ' ἐπωιδῶν suggests that only an extraordinary power could be effective.

1261 ὁ κίνδυνος μέγας a common type of locution, e.g., Gorgias *Palamedes* 35, Antiphon *Herod.* 46, *tetr.* 1.3.3 (μείζων), Andoc. *Myst.* 137 (μείζων), Thuc. 1.32.5, 3.20.2, Lys. 2.34, *Peace* 264, *Eccl.* 287 (οὐχὶ μικρός), Pl. *Crat.* 436b2 (οὐ σμικρός), *Prot.* 314b1, *Rep.* 467b2 (οὐ σμικρός).

1262–3 Valck. deleted this couplet, objecting mainly to the prediction that both sons will die (an outcome implied by Oed.'s curse and well known to the audience, who cannot be in any suspense about this point: 765n.). He also thought tears an insufficient response to such a disaster (i.e. the conclusion is anticlimactic or bathetic). He could also have noted the repetition of δεινός, and the passage is rather weak in style if στερήσηι is retained and there is double asyndeton. Fraenkel supports Valck.'s analysis by adducing numerous exx. of ὡς-clause appended to an imperative at the end of a rhesis: but in only one case (*Hcld.* 866) is the ὡς-clause only one half-line, as it would be here; and several instances feature grammatically complex clauses (e.g., *Hcld.* 605–7, *Phil.* 1043–4, 1442–4). So the rhetorical form does not make it inherently more probable that Valck. was correct. The couplet may be an expansion, but there is not a strong enough case for the use of brackets in the text. As the couplet is punctuated in the tradition (after δεινά) and with Reiske's easy change to participle στερείσηι, both the death of the brothers (cf. Σ) and Joc.'s resulting grief can be understood as the 'prizes' of the contest (for tears as prize, cf. *Ba.* 1147 δάκρυα νικηφορεῖ). Valck. removed the punctuation after δεινά to make δάκρυα a predicate noun to ἔπαθλον (see below), comparing *Hel.* 480 θάνατος ξένιά σοι γενήσεται, which he thought the interpolator imitated. This punctuation has often been adopted: e.g., keeping καὶ τἆθλα, Klotz interprets 'the prizes for you will be terrible tears', Craik gives 'this struggle will mean terrible tears for you' (apparently taking ἆθλα in its rarer sense, = ἆθλος). But the article, not needed for such a construction, points rather to pairing of τἆθλα δεινά with ὁ κίνδυνος μέγας. Valck. alleged that a tragic poet could not use the crasis τἆθλα and suggested ἔπαθλον; Porson cited Σ (whose use of the later prose synonym (51n.) proves nothing about what he read in the text) to support his κἄπαθλα. But as Hermann pointed out long ago, there is no legitimate reason to ban crasis of the article with initial long alpha (a rare phenomenon in itself), and this case perhaps has the further excuse that ἆθλον is from ἄεθλον. The rare crasis may as well be kept and not weighed in with the doubts about authenticity.

1263 action Wecklein notes 'Der Bote rechts ab.' But with 1279 correctly ascribed to Joc. (see below), σύ in that line is best understood of the messenger, who is the logical guide to the site of the duel (so Jackson and Kassel). Less likely, the addressee in 1279 is a silent attendant (Taplin, *Stagecraft* 90, arguing from the 'finality' of 1259–61; but, e.g., 1196–9 are equally 'final' and do not mark departure). There seems no reason, however, for an attendant to come out with Joc. at 1072 or with Ant. at 1270.

1264–83 the theory of Verrall that Antigone did not appear in the original *Phoen.* entails the removal of this passage. Paley had already noted on 1268 'There is much that is unusual in the composition of this dialogue.' But the only unusual or difficult features are in lines 1266 and 1271, and Antigone's presence in the play is well established by the teichoskopia, which I regard (*pace* Dihle) as surely genuine, and by 1427–79, where not even the most active deleters have denied her presence, even granted the removal of 1430 and 1465.

1265–9 these lines are condemned by Fraenkel. The point of dramatic technique, that (as 1270–1 show) Ant. does not hear the content of the lines even though she hears the summons, should not be counted against the passage: see *Contact and Discontinuity* 28–30. The internal points cited as objections are (1) the obscurity or oddity of 1266, (2) the sense of ἐκνεύοντε, (3) the anticipation of the double fratricide. But ἐκνεύοντε can be adequately explicated, and (as argued before: 765n., 1262–3n.) the anticipation is objectionable only if we inappropriately posit that the dramatist was aiming for suspense on this point (Wecklein deleted only 1269 to remove the anticipation; note that Fraenkel himself does not remove 1283, which exploits the same anticipation). The difficulty of 1266 is not sufficient to justify removal of the passage. The lines cover the time for Ant.'s emergence, and if they are felt to be leisurely, they provide a strong contrast to the quicker pace of the following antilabe.

1264 this line is identical to *Or.* 112 except for Ἑρμιόνη/Ἀντιγόνη.

1265 οὐκ ἐν χορείαις οὐδὲ παρθενεύμασιν reference to dancing serves two functions. First, it evokes the world of the secluded maiden, in which public appearance is normally limited to ritual occasions, in particular to festivals in which maidens participate in choral dances (e.g., *IT* 1143–52). Thus this line, together with 1275–6, recalls the framing passages of the teichoskopia and prepares for manipulation and reversal of the motif of the secluded maiden in the exodos (1485–91, 1582–709n., 1691n.). Second, it plays upon the contrast between dancing and joyful or peaceful music and the disharmony of war that was developed in the parodos and second stasimon.

παρθενεύμασιν the noun is exclusively Euripidean, characteristically used in different senses inferrable from the contexts (cf. *Ion* 1425, 1473).

1266 νῦν σοι προχωρεῖ δαιμόνων κατάστασις '(not in choral dances nor in maidenly pursuits) does the fortune established by the gods now proceed for you', that is, 'the gods and fate do not now demand of you your normal behaviour'. This is the traditional interpretation (from Σ), but it has seemed to some a strangely elaborate periphrasis. κατάστασις denotes a fixed condition, and so here would apply to an unavoidable fate established by the gods: cf. θεσμός in *Eum.* 391–2 θεσμὸν τὸν μυριόκραντον ἐκ θεῶν, and LSJ s.v. I.1. Hermann thought Σ's paraphrase with τύχη and εἱμαρμένη pointed to δαίμονος κατάστασιν, but for the plural cf. 1000 above ἀνάγκην δαιμόνων, *Hipp.* 1267 δαιμόνων τε συμφοραῖς, fr. 37 τὰς δὲ δαιμόνων τύχας. For προχωρεῖ of the forward movement of events or fortune, esp. toward a good outcome, cf. LSJ s.v. II.1 and *Hcld.* 486–7 ἡμῖν δὲ δόξας εὖ προχωρῆσαι δρόμος [Jacobs, δόμος L] / πάλιν μεθέστηκ' αὖθις ἐς τἀμήχανον, where δρόμος is a metaphor for fortune. Blaydes' πραγμάτων κατ. leaves us with an equally elaborate periphrasis and the error would be hard to explain. Zakas' δωμάτων is an easier change, but the sense consorts ill with 1265. Fraenkel contemplated a wholly different approach, recalling the use of κατάστασις for dancing (*Ag.* 23 χορῶν, *Thesm.* 958 χοροῦ), but the anagrammatic μαινάδων yields poor sense, even for an alleged interpolator. I formerly proposed νῦν σὸν προχωρεῖν δαιμόνων κατάστασιν, but 'ordering of dances belonging to (*or* in honour of) the gods' is difficult, and confining the reference of 1265–6 to dancing necessitates treating παρθενεύμασιν as in hendiadys for 'maidenly dances' rather than denoting other activities. It is better to acquiesce in the traditional view.

1268 εἰς θάνατον ἐκνεύοντε 'veering aside ⟨from a straight course⟩ toward death' (920n.); the implied metaphorical straightness may connote either safety (going off the path onto terrain where an upset is more likely) or propriety (the course Joc. would want her sons to travel).

1269 see 1265–9n.

1270–1 like Alcmene in *Hcld.* 646, Ant. responds to the undifferentiated noise of the summons (αὐτεῖς, cf. αὐτῆς in *Hcld.*) and infers that there is reason for such an abnormal call. The detail τῶνδε δωμάτων πάρος is designed to underline the breach of normal decorum. Ant. would normally expect Joc. to express her grief or communicate her worries within the house: cf. *Ant.* 1246–50 (the hope that Eurydice has gone inside to grieve in dignity, out of the public eye); S. *El.* 328–9, 516–18 (Chrysothemis and Clytaemnestra on Electra's appearing and speaking outside the door); *Andr.* 876–7 (on Hermione's display of distress in public).[1] Nauck failed

---

[1] See also L. E. Woodbury, 'The Gratitude of the Locrian Maiden: Pindar, *Pyth.* 2.18–20', *TAPA* 108 (1978) 285–99, esp. 293–9 on πρὸ δόμων.

to see the point and removed τῶνδε δωμάτων πάρος as part of a *Binneninter-polation*, making other changes. In view of the embarrassment implied by 'before this house' φίλοις could perhaps refer to the chorus, or chorus and messenger (Craik: 'our friends before the house'): the chorus has shown solidarity with Joc. since the first episode (we need not ask how Ant. knows that). More likely, however, is the common view (cf. Σ, Klotz) that φίλοις means 'your kin/dear ones', that is, Ant. and Oed., to whom the ἔκπληξις more directly pertains. A third view (Σ), that φίλοις refers to Et. and Pol. (dat. of disadvantage going closely with ἔκπληξιν), is implausible.

1272 ἔρρει this 3rd sing. indicative form usually has a perfect meaning, 'is gone', 'is ruined', but here it must have the progressive aspect of a true present, since Joc.'s hope is that she can still save her sons by rapid intervention. In *Ion.* 699–700 νῦν δ' ἡ μὲν ἔρρει συμφοραῖς, ὁ δ' εὐτυχεῖ, πόλιον ἐσπεσοῦσα γῆρας, the sense could be present or perfect, but the more drastic perfect sense is more likely (there is a similar choice in *OT* 910 ἔρρει δὲ τὰ θεῖα). For present meaning, cf. (apparently) Eupolis fr. 232 K–A ὥσπερ ἐπὶ τὴν Λύκωνος ἔρρει πᾶς ἀνήρ.

1273–8 for the hastening effect of the antilabe see 980–6n.

1273 αἰχμὴν ἐς μίαν 'into single (spear-)battle'; for the metonymy cf. *Pers.* 999, *Tro.* 840, *Her.* 158, 437, *Or.* 1485. μίαν conveys both fighting separate from the others (for εἷς equivalent to εἷς μόνος cf. *Her.* 825, *Alc.* 883, etc.) and, when juxtaposed with the dual verb, the meeting of the opponents in one place (cf. 462 εἰς ἓν συνελθών). There is no need for emendation (Nauck αἰχμῆς ἐς πάλην).

1274 τί λέξεις; a Eur. idiom, a horrified 'what do you mean to say?' See Barrett on *Hipp.* 353, and cf. *Phil.* 1233, where τί λέξεις; likewise conveys shock and looks forward to an elaboration, but actually interrupts Neoptolemus' statement in mid-stream, so the future can be interpreted literally.

1275 παρθενῶνας ἐκλιποῦσ' a deliberate reminiscence of 89.

1276 αἰδούμεθ' ὄχλον cf. *Hcld.* 43–4 νέας γὰρ παρθένους αἰδούμεθα / ὄχλωι πελάζειν κἀπιβωμιοστατεῖν, *Or.* 108 ἐς ὄχλον ἕρπειν παρθένοισιν οὐ καλόν, *IA* 1338–41.

οὐκ ἐν αἰσχύνηι τὰ σά 'Your present situation does not allow (call for) a sense of shame.' Cf. *Ion.* 1397 οὐκ ἐν σιωπῆι τἀμά, 'my situation does not allow silence'; *IA* 1343 οὐκ ἐν ἁβρότητι κεῖσαι πρὸς τὰ νῦν πεπτωκότα (in a passage that exploits the same exaggerated sense of maidenly modesty). Cf. the predicative use of ἐν-phrases: *IT* 762 ἐν ἀσφαλεῖ, *Hel.* 1277 ἐν εὐσεβεῖ.

1277 δὲ δὴ τί see 709n.

λύσεις ἔριν cf. 81 ἔριν λύουσ'; the words remind the audience that Joc. is here desperately repeating what she has already failed to accomplish.

1279 σύ implies a change of addressee, and someone in antiquity made

the inference that Ant. speaks this line and Joc. the next. But if Ant. says
οὐ μελλητέον, there is no motivation for Joc. to reply with ἔπειγ' ἔπειγε;
and ἡγοῦ σύ is remarkably brusque for a daughter addressing her mother,
but normal for orders to subordinates (*Andr.* 551, *Alc.* 546). So Jackson,
Marg. Scaen. 174–5, and Kassel, *RhMus* 97 (1954) 96, independently restored the line to Joc. The addressee is prob. the messenger (1263n.).

1281 οὑμὸς ἐν φάει βίος 'my life is in the light of day', that is, 'my life
continues'. The understood verb may be ἐστι (cf. 1253n.) rather than
ἔσται. ἐν φάει is more common with negative expressions (cf. 1339) or with
a person as subject, and (*pace* Pearson) there may be here a suggestion of
salvation or prosperity in the use of the figure: in *Hec.* 1214 ἡνίχ' ἡμεῖς
οὐκέτ' ἦμεν ἐν φάει, Priam and Hector and other Trojans are dead, but
Hecuba herself has merely lost her prosperity.

[1282] 1280 ἦν μὲν φθάσω reminded someone of 975 κἂν μὲν φθάσωμεν,
leading to the citation of 976 in the margin, whence it intruded into most
surviving mss., though in the tenth century or earlier one could say ἐν
πολλοῖς οὐ φέρεται (Σ). This is a scribal or reader's, not a histrionic,
interpolation. Strangely, Valck. blamed it on actors (so too now Mueller-
Goldingen), and his note on this line is the first specimen of modern
research into histrionic interpolation.

1283 συνθανοῦσα κείσομαι κείσομαι, 'I'll lie (dead)', strengthens
συνθανοῦσα (see on 1687 πεσὼν ... κείσομαι). One should not translate
'shall lie over their bodies' (Craik).

1284–307: FOURTH STASIMON

As commonly happens in tragedy, the final stasimon is the shortest, as the
action moves toward a climax. In contrast to the earlier odes, the chorus
makes only the barest explicit reference to the past, recognizing the power
of the Erinyes at the very end. Instead the maidens fearfully anticipate the
duel and the mourning that will result from it. If the first and third
stasimons share a narrative bias and mainly trochaic rhythm, the second
and fourth can also be viewed, in part, as a corresponding pair. The second
starts and ends with an anticipation of the coming battle of the two armies,
the fourth has the narrower focus of the duel of the brothers. But while the
second ends with some grounds for hope that Thebes will again come
through safely, the fourth projects no hope at all for the brothers: although
the strophe asks 'which of the two?', the antistrophe treats the pair as
essentially joined in their fate.

The theme of duality is reinforced by the metrical pattern (familiar units
are used in pairs), by the rhetorical structure, with its use of anaphora,
anadiplosis, and polyptoton, and by repetitions of words and isometric

echoes between stanzas. These features are also, of course, traditional elements of cultic and (as here) threnetic song: see 1034–5n. and Bond on *Her.* 763ff. Words expressing kinship (1287 ματέρος, 1288 δίδυμα τέκεα, 1291 ὁμογενῆ, 1296 δίδυμοι) and bloodshed (1288/1299 αἵμαξ-, 1292 αἱμάτων, 1297 φόνιαι, 1304/1307 φόνος) abound here, as in earlier odes. The bestial serpent and Sphinx that were prominent in the earlier odes as emblems of the woes of Thebes' history now have their disruptive power embodied, as it were, in Et. and Pol.: with 1296 δίδυμοι θῆρες compare the similes used of the brothers in 1380–1 (boars) and 1573 (lions), and cf. also the oracle, 411–12 and 420–1, and the threatening animals of the shield-blazons (1120, 1124–5, 1135). Diction which is specifically reminiscent of the previous choral songs includes 1292 δι' αἱμάτων (1051), 1301 βοᾶι βαρβάρωι (cf. 679bis), and 1307 Ἐρινύς (255, 1029); less strikingly, 1289 πόνων (249), 1291 ὁμογενῆ (218), perhaps 1299 πέσεα (πέσημα 640), 1302 στενακτάν (1035, 1040).

Nothing in the content of the song supports a division between separate voices, as proposed by Arnoldt, 288–90. Asyndeton is quite normal in an excited lyric context (cf. Bond on the staccato style of *Her.* 734–62). The change of speaker Arnoldt indicates between 1304 and 1305 seems particularly unlikely.

1284–1307 Metre After an anapaestic introduction, the stanza is iambo-dochmiac, recalling the emotional lyrics of Antigone and Jocasta earlier in the play. (Cf. Dale, *Metr. Anal.* 3.124.)

1284/1296	$----\cup\cup---\mid$	2 an
1285–6/1297–8	$\cup\cup-\underline{\cup\cup}-\cup\cup-\cup\cup-\mid$	2 an
1287/1299	$\widehat{\cup\cup}\cup\widehat{\cup\cup}\underline{\cup\cup}\cup-\cup--\eightnote-\parallel^{?}$	lec, dochm
1288/1300	$\widehat{\cup\cup}\cup\widehat{\cup\cup}\cup\widehat{\cup\cup}\cup\widehat{\cup\cup}-\bar{\cup}-\parallel^{h1}$	lec, dochm
1289/1301	$\cup--\cup-\parallel^{h2}$	dochm
1290/1302	$\cup--\cup--\parallel^{h1}$	2 ba
1291/1303	$\cup\widehat{\cup\cup}-\cup-\cup\widehat{\cup\cup}---\mid$	2 dochm
1292/1304	$\cup-\cup-\cup-\mid$	2 ia
1293/1305	$\cup-\cup-\cup-\cap\parallel^{bc}$	ia, ba
1294–5/1306–7	$\cup\widehat{\cup\cup}\cup\widehat{\cup\cup}\cup\widehat{\cup\cup}\cup\widehat{\cup\cup}-\bar{\cup}-\parallel\mid$	do. hex, dochm

NOTES TO METRICAL SCHEME

1284/1296 for anapaests with dochmiacs, see metrical notes on 110 and 334 above.

1287–8/1299–1300 the combination lec + dochm is very rare: apart from fourfold use here, cf. *Or.* 1361–2 = 1545–6; also lec (separate period) between dochmiacs in *Hec.* 706; cretics and iambs are of course frequently combined with dochm. In 1287 we may have responsion of penultimate long anceps to short anceps in antistrophe (as in 1288/1300) or internal correption in δειλαίας (as in *Su.* 279, *Ant.* 1310, and δείλαιος at trimeter-end in Arist.).

1289/1301 The hiatus after this colon in antistrophe can be avoided by accepting the word-order στενακτὰν ἰαχάν from some *recc.*; but these *recc.* are in general less reliable than O and the *recc.* that exhibit ἰαχὰν στενακτάν, and there is no need to avoid hiatus. The exclamations of the strophe and the general rhetorical features of the passage show that a staccato delivery of short phrases is perfectly in place here. στενακτάν was omitted in part of the tradition (because of the sequence of three words ending in AN) and incorrectly replaced.

1290/1302 The hiatus in Ζεῦ/ἰώ is licensed by the exclamation, just as in dochmiacs (Conomis, 42); or it may be eliminated by reading καὶ Γᾶ (Diggle, Willink; cf. passages cited 1290n. below). 2 ba as a colon may be viewed as a dochmiac equivalent: cf. above 187 (mol + 2 ba preceding dochm), 295 (3 ba), below 1536–36bis, and *Ion* 1465, *Hel.* 642–3 (5 ba), *Or.* 1437–40.

1294–5/1306–7 Murray redivided τάλαινα, πό- / τερον κτλ. and μέλλον. ἄ- / ποτμος κτλ. in order to preserve a pure dochmiac interpretation of the final colon; but such division is contrary to the match between metrical and rhetorical structure that is characteristic of this stasimon and creates impossible or unlikely features in the penultimate colon (resolved ba, split resolution at strong rhetorical break). For emendations of both lines to produce 2 dochm see comm. Without emendation, we have an ambiguous sequence because of the number of resolutions. It is possible to treat the line as cr + ia + ia, with the final iamb taking the 'impure' form ∪ – ū – under the influence of the dochmiac context (cf. *El.* 1149 = 1157, *Or.* 171 = 192 and Parker *CQ* 18 (1968) 246, 261). This anomaly can be avoided by analysis as a combination of a dochmiac hexasyllable with a dochm. This seems an acceptable variation in this context, certainly preferable to the view that we have two dochmiacs with a resolved anceps in one of them. But there are anomalies here too, and it remains uncertain whether to interpret as hex + dochm or dochm + hex. In the first treatment, we have a fully resolved form of the hex. (not, I think paralleled, but cf. almost fully resolved form in *Eum.* 158 = 165, *Tro.* 311 = 328 (printed, but doubted by Diggle)); two-syllable overlap from the hex. to the dochm, which (for pure dochmiacs) is not uncommon; inexact responsion in the anceps of the dochm (a normal phenomenon); and one split resolution in the second long of the hex. (strophe only), with a normal split resolution in the first long of the dochm in both places. In the second treatment (adopted by Dale and Schroeder), we have fully resolved dochm (paralleled); three-syllable overlap between metra (rarer than two-syllable, but not unknown); the fifth element of the hex. treated as anceps (other apparent cases of this at *Her.* 1079 and *IT* 649 are easily emended; but cf. perhaps *Ion* 896); and a split resolution in the third long of the dochm of 1294-5 (rare, but not unknown) and no split resolution in the hex. For the sequence hex. + dochm, Dale's analyses offer *Hipp.* 594 (treated by Diggle, *Studies* 19 as 2 ia + cr), *Hec.* 1083 (printed, but doubted by Diggle), *Ion* 1454 (emended to 2 dochm in Diggle), 1472 (could be ia, ia, cr; others emend to ia trim.), *Or.* 186 = 207 (corrupt passage, but Willink and Diggle divide to produce 2 dochm).

1284-307: COMMENTARY

1284 τρομερὰν φρίκαι the same juncture in *Tro.* 1026; φρίκη occurs only a half dozen times in Soph. and Eur. (lyric except *OT* 1306) and is a particularly strong word.

1286 διὰ σάρκα the acc. with διά is used in poetry in the same senses as the more common gen.: contrast 1412 δι' ὀμφαλοῦ, 1457 διὰ ... αὐχένος, *Hel.* 356 διὰ σαρκός; cf. 164 δι' αἰθέρος vs. *IT* 29 διὰ ... αἰθέρα.

1287 ἔλεος appears in tragedy only in late Eur. (*Or.*, *IA*); same anadiplosis in *Or.* 968. It is common for a chorus to express the same sorts of fear and sympathy that the audience of tragedy may be presumed to feel, that is, to be, in part, an analogue of the audience within the drama. None the less, the collocation of 'pity and fear' in this passage is striking and may reflect a more self-conscious incorporation of contemporary critical discourse into the performance: cf. Gorgias *Helen* 9 τοὺς ἀκούοντας [sc. τῆς ποιήσεως] εἰσῆλθε καὶ φρίκη περίφοβος καὶ ἔλεος πολύδακρυς καὶ πόθος φιλοπενθής.

1288 δίδυμα τέκεα πότερος the partial apposition of singular to plural and shift to a singular verb make the sentence more forceful and excited than the normal partitive gen. would (although such force is absent from the prose exx. given in K–G 1.286–8): cf. *Ant.* 21, 561. Here we also have masc. following neuter *ad sensum*.

1290 γᾶ perhaps better Γᾶ; but it is hard to determine how vividly personified earth is here, as compared with invocations and mentions of the goddess in earlier odes (670, 686bis, 818). Earth is present in such an invocation as the polar opposite of Zeus/sky, in order to make the appeal comprehensive: cf. *Med.* 148 ὦ Ζεῦ καὶ Γᾶ καὶ φῶς (= *Or.* 1496, though the Phrygian adds καὶ νύξ), *Hipp.* 672 ἰὼ γᾶ καὶ φῶς, *El.* 1177 ἰὼ Γᾶ καὶ Ζεῦ, *Med.* 1251, *Hcld.* 748; also ἰὼ γᾶ *Erecth.* fr. 65.45 Austin (at the start of the earthquake), A. *Su.* 776, *Ag.* 1537.

1291-2 Strong emotion is conveyed here in several ways. The syntax of 1288 (part-objects of αἱμάξει, added to whole-object πότερον: K–G II.289–90) is continued after the interjections. The rhyming pairs of clipped phrases are in asyndeton, echoing the staccato structure of the preceding exclamations. Finally, the phrases themselves juxtapose terms of different kinds in an effective blurring: δέραν and ψυχάν, and ἀσπίδων and αἱμάτων. With the latter there is also a play on the senses of διά + gen.: δι᾽ ἀσπίδων at first seems concrete, '(stabbing) through the shield' (cf. Hcld. 738 δι᾽ ἀσπίδος θείνοντα πολεμίων τινά, fr. 282.20–1), but then δι᾽ αἱμάτων seems modal instead, suggesting a hendiadys 'in bloody armed battle'. Many critics have disapproved of these effects: Herwerden (1903) thought ψυχάν impossible, and many efforts have been made to replace αἱμάτων, some of which fail because they destroy the rhyming structure of the phrase (some remove δι᾽; Geel's ἐγχέων is not close enough an echo of the shape of ἀσπίδων), others because they replace a word with an important repeated root with a Homeric gloss or unknown word (ἀμάτων/ἡμάτων, αἰχμάτων). Breitenbach, 173, claims that αἱμάτων is here concrete, used by synecdoche for σωμάτων, but his parallels do not support this: in IT 880 πρὶν ἐπὶ [tmesis] ξίφος αἵματι σῶι πελάσαι, αἵματι is a vivid and proleptic substitute ('your flesh shedding blood') or pregnant in sense ('bring the sword close to ⟨the shedding of⟩ your blood'); see also 1051–4n., 1502n.

1295 νέκυν ὀλόμενον for the pleonasm cf. Hel. 178 νέκυσιν ὀλομένοις.

ἰαχήσω if this word is retained, it is presumably be to be scanned as ∪ – – – rather than ∪∪ – –: ἰαχέω is a favourite word of Eur. and has long alpha much more often than short (for the facts, see Diggle (1990b) 116).[1] Short alpha would not produce a less anomalous rhythm (2 fully-resolved ia + ba, with one split resolution in each metron), and in 1306–7 we would have to treat ἄποτμος ἄποτμος as ∪ – ∪∪∪∪, with varied treatment of τμ (881n.) and Ἐρινύων as trisyllabic (otherwise only in trimeters, IT 931, 970, 1456; for tetra. Tro. 457 see Diggle, Studies 62–3). Elmsley on Hcld. 752 noted how ἰαχ- sometimes is a corruption of ἀχ- (for the reverse see Diggle on Phaethon 82), but concluded that emendation was unnecessary here. Dindorf emended, in order to simplify to plain dochmiacs, and emended the antistrophe as well, where the transmitted reading is blameless. ἠχέω is often used with an internal acc. (e.g. ὅσα Aesch. fr. 339a, κωκυτόν Trach. 867, χορόν Her. 1027), but is not found with an external object. ἰαχέω is most often used absolutely, but sometimes has an internal object (μέλος Tro. 515), introduces indirect speech (a kind of

---

[1] Eur. always has long alpha in ἰαχή and has short in ἰάχημα (which is almost hapax).

internal object: *El.* 707, *Hel.* 1486), or has an external object (*Or.* 965–7 ἰαχείτω δὲ γᾶ Κυκλωπία ... πήματ' οἴκων; cf. *Hel.* 1147, where passive ἰαχήθης (so Hermann, rightly, I think, despite Kannicht's doubts) implies the same construction, cf. *Or.* 103 ἀναβοᾶι with Willink's note). Since ἰαχήσω seems metrically possible and is echoed by 1302 ἰαχάν in a way typical of the style of the ode, I prefer to keep it. But in the Teubner app. I overstated the difficulty of νέκυν ἀχήσω: ἰαχέω and ἀχέω are virtual synonyms, and Eur. could have used the latter once with an external object (cf. Diggle (1990b) 114 n. 74).

1296 φεῦ δᾶ for δᾶ, an exclamation of horror that reinforces other cries in tragedy, see Fraenkel on *Ag.* 1072 with Addendum. φεῦ δᾶ appears in *Lys.* 198.

1297–8 φόνιαι ψυχαὶ δορὶ παλλόμεναι 'murderous spirits' would be only a rough translation of φόνιαι ψυχαί. The noun alludes both to the emotional disposition of the brothers who are set on fratricide and to their living essence, emphasized because it is about to be extinguished. For the latter use, cf. *Ag.* 1457–8 τὰς πολλάς, τὰς πάνυ πολλὰς / ψυχὰς ὀλέσασ' ὑπὸ Τροίαι, *Hel.* 52 ψυχαὶ δὲ πολλαὶ δι' ἔμ' ἐπὶ Σκαμανδρίοις / ῥοαῖσιν ἔθανον, 1553 below. Σ, followed by early trans. and by Craik, treats δορὶ παλλόμεναι as if it were δόρυ πάλλουσαι (and Wecklein suggested δόρυ); but there is no parallel for such a middle use of πάλλω. Musgrave, after Heath, gives *hasta sortientes casus*, Hartung 'durchstossen vom Speer' ('jarred' would be more accurate than 'pierced'), but the sense is prob. 'excited by the fray' (Paley, after Σ ἐπὶ πόλεμον κινηθεῖσαι), with a grim variation on the standard phrase δείματι παλλόμεναι (*Hom.h.Dem.* 293) and the like (cf. A. *Su.* 566–7 δείματι θυμὸν πάλλοντ'; *OT* 153 φρένα δείματι πάλλων; oracle apud Hdt. 7.140.3): the brothers do not feel normal fear, only lust for battle. If this explanation is not accepted, Diggle's παλλομένωι should be read ((1989) 201–2). Kirchhoff suggested φονίαι ψυχᾶι (to which Paley added the necessary παλλόμενοι), but unless παλλόμενοι is middle, 'wielding', the dative is not likely (one would expect ψυχὰν παλλόμενοι, as in A. *Su.* 566–7).

1299 πέσεα ... αἱμάξετον 'will make bloody fallings', 'will fall amidst bloodshed', a bold lyric phrase, surpassed by *Ion* 168–9 αἱμάξεις ... τὰς καλλιφθόγγους ὠιδάς (but Diggle accepts Nauck's ἰάξεις). πέσος is hapax in extant Greek, an *ad hoc* alternative to πτῶμα or πέσημα; cf. poetic hapax γέμος, κλέπος (Schwyzer 1.512).

1300 μονομάχον ἐπὶ φρέν' 'to the thought of single combat'; for this lyric locution see 338n.

1303 μελομέναν νεκροῖς μέλομαι is here almost 'belonging to', 'dedicated to': cf. *IT* 644–5 τὸν χερνίβων / ῥανίσι μελόμενον αἱμακταῖς (and uses of μέλω cited by Platnauer *ad loc.*). By conjecture Markland and

Lobeck produced precise parallels at *IT* 182 and *Hel.* 178, but such emendation is not necessary in either place.

1304 σχεδὸν τύχα, πέλας φόνος Tiresias' prediction at 880 (ἐγγὺς δὲ θάνατος αὐτόχειρ αὐτοῖς) is recalled and confirmed. Scaliger's φόνος gives excellent sense and a structure that appropriately echoes that of the corresponding line, δι' ἀσπίδων, δι' αἱμάτων. It requires that σχεδόν, used here alone in tragic lyric, have the local meaning familiar to the audience from epic and Pindar, whereas in its uses in trimeters (Soph. four times, Eur. four times) it seems always to have its prosaic sense 'just about', 'almost'.[1] Transmitted φόνου does not give satisfactory sense. Σ simply tolerates the redundancy with the excuse ἐκ παραλλήλου τὸ αὐτό; Barnes rendered *prope fortuna [sc. est]; prope caedem est* (an ugly asymmetry), Klotz *paene fortuna prope caedem est* (too feeble for the context). Pearson, objecting that the sense 'near' is not found in Attic poets, accepts the Thoman explication of σχεδόν as ἄντικρυς, 'the doom of death is quite close' (whence Craik); but this intensifying sense is not found in any author! σχεδὸν πέλας could only have a softened sense, 'almost near', that does not fit the context. The only comparable expression I find is Pl. *Tim.* 21a8 ἦν ... σχεδὸν ἐγγὺς ἤδη τῶν ἐνενήκοντα ἐτῶν (context is lacking in *CGFPR* 244.189 Austin πλησίον σχεδόν).

1305 κρινεῖ ξίφος τὸ μέλλον the mss have κρινεῖ φάος, which is faulty because φάος lacks the requisite demonstrative (cf. *Aj.* 753, 756, *OT* 438, *Phaethon* 95, *Hel.* 1420, *Or.* 48, *Hipp.* 22, 57, etc.) and the disaster is now too close for 'the present day will decide' to be an effective topos. Nor does it help to take τὸ μέλλον with φάος and κρινεῖ absolutely (Klotz), since τὸ μέλλον φάος would be 'tomorrow'. Musgrave had proposed an emendation with ἄορ before Hermann hit upon the elegant change to ξίφος. Note that κρινεῖ ξίφος implies the fulfilment of the curse σιδήρωι διαλαχεῖν (68).

1306-7 ἄποτμος ἄποτμος ὁ φόνος ἄποτμος has the well-established meaning 'ill-fated' (like δύσποτμος or βαρύποτμος) already in Homer (of persons, *Il.* 24.388, *Od.* 1.219, 20.140), independent of the kind of oxymoron in which other alpha-private adjs. take on meanings equivalent to δυσ-compounds (for which see Fehling, *Hermes* 96 (1968) 142-55 and *Wiederholungsfiguren* 287-9); *Pers.* 280 ἄποτμον βοάν provides a parallel for its application to things. There is thus no stylistic reason to prefer Dindorf's πότμος ἄποτμος, based on *Hipp.* 1143-4 διοίσω πότμον ἄποτμον (also the

---

[1] In Eur. fr. 381 σχεδὸν παρ' αὐτοῖς κρασπέδοις Εὐρωπίας a local sense is possible, but so is 'just about at the very edge'; in fr. 676 σχεδὸν χαμεύνηι σύμμετρος Κορινθίας / παιδός the adv. prob. goes with σύμμετρος.

source of Hartung's unnecessary emendation of *IT* 864); conversely, in an ode with seven previous doublings ἄποτμος ἄποτμος fits the style perfectly. Acceptance of Dindorf's reading would be based solely on the desire for metrical simplification and would entail change in the strophe as well. In this case the gain in simplicity does not seem worth the cost.

1308–479 FIFTH EPISODE[1]

In several late plays Eur. has two messenger-scenes (*IT*; *Ba.*; *Hel.* abortively; *IA*?; cf. *Rhesus*), but only here do the scenes follow one another, as the battle to save Thebes from the assault of the Seven is deliberately separated from the duel of the brothers.

If Creon's entrance is genuine (1308–53n.), his presence for the messenger's report has several possible functions. His entrance retards the arrival of the expected messenger,[2] and it adds to the impression of repeated comings and goings of numerous characters, an index of the complexity of events and the separateness and weakness of each character's impact on the overall action. His position here is parallel to that of Joc. in the previous episode: both are concerned for their children, Joc. to save hers, Creon to provide his son's corpse with proper preparation and lamentation; both receive news of additional woes (cf. 1215, 1338). By providing a reminder of Menoeceus' noble sacrifice just before the narrative of the duel and the final (less than noble) victory of the Thebans, Creon keeps present the contrast between the fate of the city and the fate of the house of Oedipus. Moreover, his visible grief answers the expectations aroused by repeated statements that Men.'s death saves the city but pains Creon (918, 1057–9, 1204–7, and here 1314). His pious maxim about the treatment of the dead (1320–1), following on his assumption that his sister will loyally help him to mourn for *his* son, is an ironic preparation for his enforcement of the burial-edict against *her* son and his refusal to be swayed even by supplication in her name. The irony is exactly parallel to that seen in the third episode between Creon's confidently patriotic assertions before Tir. speaks and rejection of the city's needs thereafter.

As a messenger-scene, this passage has the usual structure of revelation of news in brief before detailed rhesis. The preliminaries to the rhesis are unusual in the variety of metres, with a few trochaic tetrameters

---

[1] The aria and duet that follow this scene are equivalent to a stasimon, and it seems best to designate 1308–479 an episode rather than the first part of a very long exodos.

[2] Cf. Saïd, 519.

(1308–9n.) and some dochmiacs (1341, 1345; (with related rhythm? see n.) 1350–1) among the trimeters. The narrative itself, presumably because of its length and complexity, takes the exceptional form of paired rheseis of sixty-six and fifty-two lines (by my text; these numbers will be slightly lower if one or another short suspected passage is deleted) divided by a choral couplet (1425–6): the first presents the duel itself, the second the arrival of Joc., the greetings of her dying sons, her suicide, and the quarrel and final battle of the armies. The narrative is closely tied to the previous episode: the story resumes just after the arming of the brothers (1359, cf. 1242–7) and with the brothers themselves praying for success (1364–75, cf. exhortations of comrades in 1248–54); Joc., the addressee of the first messenger, who departed with Ant. at the end of the episode, appears with Ant. in this narrative (cf. *Ba.*, where Pentheus is addressee of the first messenger and featured agent and victim in the narrative of the second). There is also clear preparation for the following scenes in the further re-minders of Oedipus' role in these events (1342, 1353, 1355, 1360, 1425–6), in Pol.'s direct request for burial, and in the messenger's expectation of the arrival of Antigone with the bodies.

The issues raised by the gladiatorial realism of the duel and by the means of final Theban victory are discussed below in 1356–1424n. and 1466–72n.

1308–53 Leidloff objected to the behaviour of Creon in this passage and suggested that his appearance here was due to a revision of the play by actors. Fraenkel (71–6), following up observations of V. Di Benedetto, independently developed an argument against the authenticity of Creon's entrance. The objections are of two kinds. First, there are several points of general dramatic technique and staging: (1) the messenger-speeches them-selves make no reference to Creon as addressee; (2) normally, a character on stage to hear a messenger speech gives a response to the speech, but Creon has none; (3) the silence of Creon from 1356 to 1583 seems to Fraenkel intolerable; (4) the stopping-action of Creon's words at 1584 is typical of a character who has just entered. To these points can be added, for those who think Creon arrives with the body of his son, (5) it is not clear what happens to the body later. Specific points are alleged by Leidloff and Fraenkel against 1310–11, 1313, 1317, 1327–8, and overly subjective objection is taken to the style of 1325–6, 1332, 1333. The specific points are addressed *ad locc.* below, and only 1313 seems to me to create serious concern (see also 1334n.). Point (5) is answered in 1308–9n. and 1316–17n., and (4) in 1584n. As for (1), Euripidean messenger speeches may contain 2nd-person address to a listening actor (like 1095 σὸς παῖς, etc., above) in order to heighten the intimacy of communication and the pathos of the speech, but such address is not mandatory and may be absent for long stretches of narrative, if the dramatist is more interested in the autonomous impact of the rhesis. In *Su.* 650–730 (where, admittedly, the messenger addresses the chorus even before the rhesis) Adrastus is never acknowledged; in *Andr.* 1085–165 nine-tenths of the rhesis passes before there is any address to Peleus (Neoptolemus is always 'my master' or 'Achilles' son').[1] It would have detracted from the inherent pathos of the narrative of the brothers' deaths and Jocasta's suicide if the messenger had personalized the reference by saying 'your nephews' or 'your sister'. If Creon's presence is genuine, the implication of the choice made by Eur. is that Creon is not important enough or emotionally involved enough to be brought into the speech as a renewed addressee. As for (2), messenger-speeches in Eur. are (almost?)[2] always followed by a choral reaction and then, if an actor is present, by a reaction from that actor: cf. the tabulation by Reeve, 254 n. 24.[3] But again, when considering a 'rule' of dramatic technique, we must ask whether an exception has any artistic purpose rather than simply deny its existence. Compare the case of *Andr.* 1166ff., which is unique among extant messenger scenes: the rhesis addressed to Peleus is followed by anapaests of the chorus announcing the arrival of the body of Neoptolemus, and the actor then launches a lyric *threnos*, the normal response to a messenger's rhesis being deflected by the entrance and the more important task of lamentation. At the end of this scene of *Phoen.* we have a similar sequence: the rhesis is followed by an entrance, marked by choral anapaests, and the new arrival Antigone, much more directly affected than Creon, is given the emotional lament. There is even a similarity in the linking of rhesis and anapaests (*Andr.* 1159–60 ∼ 1166–7; here 1476–7 ∼ 1480), marking the quick transition to the next scene. The unusual dramatic technique tells us that a response from Creon is not important enough here to take precedence over the spectacle of

---

[1] Cf. *Ant.* 1192–243: after the proem addressed to Eurydice, the messenger speaks only of 'master Creon' and 'the boy', not of 'your husband' or 'your son'. See now DeJong, 94–103 on the emotive use of 'denomination' by messengers and 103–6 on other features that she calls 'signs of the you'.

[2] Willink on *Or.* 960–1012 believes that Electra's portion of a shared lament came directly after the close of the messenger's speech (he deletes 957–9); but I would keep 957–9 or at least 957–8.

[3] Reeve's data need to be slightly corrected and supplemented: *Andr.* 1166 is wrongly listed as having no other character present; at *Phoen.* 1264 (the end of an appendix rather than a true messenger rhesis) the chorus is given no chance to comment; at *Phoen.* 1425 the choral comment merely provides a breather for the messenger to break up the exceptionally long narrative.

Antigone and the bodies. A similar argument applies to (3): if Creon is silent for almost 230 lines (some of them short lyric lines), that is because more important things are going on in the lyric aria of Antigone and her duet with Oedipus. Fraenkel knows of a suitable parallel: Adrastus speaks only five syllables between *Su.* 262 and 734, enduring silences of 250 and 220 lines each. But Fraenkel arbitrarily declares that Adrastus is a *Nebenfigur* and Creon is not.[1] The dramatic technique of this scene implies precisely that Creon is at this point a *Nebenfigur* in relation to Ant. and Oed. The important question is whether Creon's silent presence is awkward, noticeable, or distracting: not, I would say, to an audience focusing its attention where the dramatist wanted it to be. These three objections are thus much weaker than Fraenkel supposed, and they do not gain weight by accumulation of minor suspicions, because they are all fundamentally tied to a single issue: how important is Creon at this point in the play? In my view, he is important enough to be brought on to reveal his grief, to mouth pieties about the treatment of the dead, and to greet the news as a further burden of woe,[2] but not important enough to be addressed within the rhesis or be allowed to react to it prior to the entrance of Ant. or to join in or interrupt Ant.'s lyric lament.[3]

1308 action Enter Creon, alone or with two silent attendants. Since Creon's errand is a personal one to his sister and he is totally absorbed in his personal grief, not functioning as a king or regent, I believe he enters alone (as he does at 695). The attendants to whom he later gives orders will then be the soldiers who carry in the bodies with Ant. Grotius (in the Prolegomena of his 1630 edition and in the trans. of 1327 with a deictic) first stated that the corpse of Menoeceus is brought on stage at this moment;

---

[1] Adrastus is one of eight characters in *Su.*, is on stage most of the play, and speaks about 180 lines out of 1234; in *Phoen.* we have eleven characters and Creon is on stage about half of the play and is given about 150 lines out of a total of about 1700.

[2] Note also the argument of Mueller-Goldingen, 210, that the foreign chorus, as a distanced commentator on events, is not suitable as a recipient of the messenger's speech; he believes that the chorus could not have spoken lines like 1336 or 1352-3, which, on Fraenkel's hypothesis, would originally have been theirs.

[3] Hose, *Chor* 211-15, defends Creon's appearance, exploiting his idea that the chorus is too remotely involved to explain why it cannot serve as the recipient of this news, and suggesting that Creon is used because he is a family-member, but is not given a role in the lamentation because he is not so directly stricken (as, e.g., Peleus in *Andr.*). West (1990) instead applies the theory that Eur. decided late in the process of composition to have Creon appear here.

thereafter Paley and, e.g., Powell, Schmid, and Craik explicitly place the corpse on stage, and Fraenkel uses the alleged presence of the corpse as an argument against authenticity of this passage (he believes the interpolator was imitating the close of *Ant.*). But (1) it is extremely unlikely that even an interpolator would write the entry-announcement 1308–9 referring only to Creon's approach and evident gloom if the corpse were being brought on too (even more, if Creon were carrying the body in his arms: 1316n.); (2) Creon uses no deictics of his son (in other scenes with corpses there are apostrophes, deictics, and commands to look at them); and (3) 1316–17, properly interpreted, tell us the corpse is elsewhere (see below). Since there is no reference to the corpse in the final scene, a critic who believes that Creon enters with the corpse and that this scene and the final scene are essentially authentic must also assume that Creon removes the body (by a parodos) during Ant.'s aria and returns to the stage at 1584 (so Schmid and Grube).

1308–9 on trochaic tetrameters in general see 588–637n. In this scene tetrameters· are used for this two-line entry-announcement and for the initial five-line exchange (1335–9) in which the overwrought messenger reveals to Creon the death of the brothers. In 1308–9 they give a foretaste of the excitement to follow: grieving exclamations, more tetrameters, and dochmiac and related lyrics. Likewise in longer tetrameter scenes the use of the metre sometimes begins before the excitement that they are primarily used to reinforce (so 588–92 above, *Her.* 855ff., *Ion.* 510ff.). For the announcement, cf. *Or.* 1549–53, a five-line passage in which the coryphaeus announces the approach of Menelaus, following on excited lyrics of the chorus (but also echoing the tetrameters that preceded the lyric); also *IA* 1338 ἀνδρῶν ὄχλον εἰσορῶ πέλας (there, however, a long sequence of tetrameters follows). For the enhancement of emotional intensity in 1335–9 cf. the coryphaeus' reaction to the death-cries of Agamemnon in *Ag.* 1344, 1346–8, and *Rhes.* 730–1.

1308 ἀλλὰ γάρ ἀλλὰ γάρ is here used in its 'complex' sense, equivalent to ἀλλὰ παύσω, Κρέοντα γὰρ λεύσσω, paralleled in drama at *Ant.* 148 and *Wasps* 318. See Denniston, *GP²* 99, 103–4. But the cut-off force often seen in 'simple' ἀλλὰ γάρ is present explicitly here. ἀλλὰ ... γάρ is found in entrance-announcements only a few times (*Ant.* 155, *Her.* 138, 442 – all by coryphaeus at the end of a choral song; *Or.* 725), and since ἀλλὰ ... γάρ in general is more common than ἀλλὰ γάρ in tragedy, the isolation of this usage in proportion to the four of ἀλλὰ ... γάρ is not necessarily a suspicious feature. *Or.* 1549 ἀλλὰ μήν (tetrameter) is the only extant instance of that combination used to announce an entrance. Note, however, 'simple' ἀλλὰ γάρ in the spurious anapaestic announcement at *Se.* 861.

συννεφῆ 'clouded with gloom': the metaphor is traditional (*Ant.* 528 νεφέλη δ' ὀφρύων ὕπερ; *Hipp.* 172 στυγνὸν δ' ὀφρύων νέφος αὐξάνεται, cf. *El.* 1078 συννέφουσαν ὄμματα), and not confined to serious poetry (cf. Arist. fr. 410 K–A, Anaxandr. fr. 59.3 K–A). The metaphorical use of συννεφής and συννέφω is attested only here and *El.* 1078 before Meleager *Anth. gr.* 12.159.5 and later prose; the words are also used in description of the μέτωπον in [Aristotle] *Physiognom.* 811b–12a.

1310–11 οἴμοι, τί δράσω; πότερ' ἐμαυτὸν ἢ πόλιν στένω δακρύσας Valck. alleged that the similarity to *OC* 1254–6 οἴμοι, τί δράσω; πότερα τἀμαυτοῦ κακὰ / πρόσθεν δακρύσω, παῖδες, ἢ τὰ τοῦδ' ὁρῶν / πατρὸς γέροντος; could not be an accident, and Fraenkel uses the similarity as an indication that these lines were written after Eur.'s death. But οἴμοι, τί δράσω; is a stereotyped phrase (*Aj.* 809, 920, 1024, *Alc.* 380, *Med.* 1271, etc.), often followed by deliberative or alternative questions (*Her.* 1157, *OC* 1254, cf. *Hec.* 737 Ἑκάβη, τί δράσω; πότερα κτλ.), and it is a rhetorical commonplace in tragedy to deliberate which object of grief to address first (*Trach.* 947–9, *IT* 655–6, 1524–9 below, *IA* 1124–6, *Erecth.* fr. 65.35–42; cf. *Ant.* 1343–4). Thus the similarity may be due to a common rhetorical tradition rather than specific reminiscence. But if one grants a relationship of reminiscence, that does not decide the issue of temporal priority (see 870n. for a similar case). Fraenkel believed he could decide it by claiming that Creon's alternatives here make no sense, the city having been saved. But the city has lost many men in the battle, not just Menoeceus, and this reason for grief is given in the relative clause ἣν πέριξ κτλ. Creon's alternative question allows him to avoid appearing totally selfish in his concentration on his son (cf. Σ). So too in *Erecth.* fr. 65 (published later than Fraenkel's monograph) Praxithea, at a moment when the city has been victorious (and is not yet threatened by the earthquake that prompts the arrival of Athena *ex machina*), asks herself τίν' ἐπὶ / πρῶτον ἢ σὲ τὰν πάτραν ἢ σὲ τὰν φίλαν / παρθένων ... [ἢ τὸ]ν / κάτω πόσιν ἐμὸν στένω;

1311 νέφος this cloud too (1308n.) is metaphorical, implying a looming cover of dark grief, as in *Il.* 17.591 ἄχεος νεφέλη, *Med.* 107 νέφος οἰμωγῆς, *Her.* 1140 στεναγμῶν ... νέφος. Some early comm. seem to take νέφος literally here, following Valck. in citing Sen. *Phoen.* 394–6 vide ut atra nubes pulvere abscondat diem / fumoque similes campus in caelum erigat / nebulas as an allusion to this line; but literal gloom hiding the day is a commonplace in Seneca, and reference to actual clouds of dust would be pointless in Creon's mouth.

1312 Kirchhoff and Wecklein found this line so odd that they contemplated excision, and Wilam., in his long note on metaphorical νέφος (on *Her.* 1140), says: 'Phoen. 1310 hat Eur., als sein Stil immer mehr zur Manier ward, sogar gesagt πότερ' ... νέφος, ohne dieses Bild zu erläutern,

so dass ein Interpolator einen törichten Vers eingeschoben hat.' But while
the metaphor in συννεφῆ in 1308 is comprehensible without further clue,
that in νέφος in 1311 is, *pace* Wilam., certainly not, and 1312 should be
accepted as an integral part of this speech. Many early editors preferred
τοσοῦτον, but its authority is poor (the 'Thomano-Triclinian' circle) and
it is likely to be a simplification related to the glossing of νέφος with πλῆθος.
The sense is bold and drastic: 'such a cloud as to send it headlong across
the Acheron', that is, 'make the city itself experience sudden death'.
Compare *Se.* 321–2 πόλιν ὧδ' ὠγυγίαν / Ἀΐδαι προϊάψαι. Some try to
avoid this by seeing Acheron as a metaphor for extreme darkness (so Klotz,
citing inapposite Latin parallels) or by distorting the force of the result
infinitive (Pearson: 'such darkness as that of a voyage across Acheron').
δι' Ἀχέροντος is probably 'across', with gen. as Pindar *N.* 6.48 πέταται δ'
ἐπί τε χθόνα καὶ διὰ θαλάσσας, *Hyps.* fr. 64, ii.103 δι' Αἰγαίου, *IA* 166
Εὐρίπου διὰ χευμάτων κέλσασα, in the same sense as διά + acc. (*Se.* 856
δι' Ἀχέροντ' ἀμείβεται, *Hipp.* 753–5, *Her.* 838, etc.). To cross the Acheron
is to die. Less likely, διά is 'through', producing a phrase similar to *Hipp.*
541–2 διὰ πάσας ἱέντα συμφορᾶς θνατούς [ἱέντα Dobree, ἱόντα codd.].

1313 ἐμός τε γάρ   for Fraenkel τε here is the meaningless metrical filler
of an incompetent actor/director. For those not inclined to condemn this
scene or reluctant to assign such meaninglessness to an interpolator (who
would presumably be of the fourth or third century B.C.), τε γάρ must be
either a case of anacoluthon or due to corruption. Anacoluthon was already
assumed by Σ: τε γάρ suggests that two reasons will be given, one for
private and one for public grief; the private reason is given, but πόλις τε
πολλοὺς ἄνδρας ἀπώλεσε or the like[1] is not added, partly because Creon's
statement about his son becomes complex, partly because Creon is so
affected by his son's death, and partly because the public reason has
already been alluded to in ἣν πέριξ κτλ. The simplest emendation would
be Heimsoeth's ἐμὸς δὲ παῖς γῆς τῆσδ' (γάρ, an incorrect gloss on δέ, could
have intruded, the metre been adjusted by omission, and δέ later changed
to τε) or Pearson's ἐμός τε παῖς γῆς τῆσδ' (it is harder to see why γάρ would
intrude): in either case, the clause would be a continuation of the preceding relative clause, with a shift to independent construction (cf. 1317n.).
But the resulting construction is just as harsh as, or harsher than, the

---

[1] Whatever is omitted should be retrospective, not prospective, because
Creon knows that the battle has been won thanks to his son; thus
Hermann's *in summo discrimine urbis fortuna* and Paley's καὶ νῦν κινδινεύει
πόλις are false notions of the omitted thought.

anacoluthon it is meant to avoid, so I prefer to accept anacoluthon.[1] It is not plausible to take δέ in 1317 as corresponding to τε (Dindorf after Valck., who changed δέ to τε): the wailing of the household is a consequence of what happens in 1315–16, not a reason for Creon's *aporia* about his objects of grief.

1314 for the antithesis, cf. 918, 1057–9, 1204–7.

τοὔνομα λαβών for ὄνομα = 'fame' cf. LSJ s.v. ΙΙ and in tragedy *OC* 265, 306, *Tro.* 1278, *Su.* [905]; Blaydes' κληδόνα is not needed, nor is Valck.'s λαχών (cf. 574–5 κλέος ... λαβεῖν, fr. 134).

ἀνιαρόν with ῐ (so too ἀνία), like comic authors, unlike Homer and Soph. (ῑ).

1315 κρημνῶν ἐκ δρακοντείων Blaydes would change to σηκῶν, and Pearson unnecessarily construes the prep. phrase with αὐτοσφαγῆ rather than with ἑλών; but κρημνοί is here used loosely for the whole escarpment, from the top to the base, where the dragon's cave was located and where Men.'s body presumably fell after he cut his throat (933–4n., 1010n.). Less likely, it is δρακοντείων that is used loosely ('the crags *above* the dragon's cave'), and Men.'s body is presumed to have remained hanging over the edge of the battlements.

1316 αὐτοσφαγῆ otherwise attested only in *Aj.* 841 (twice, but one instance is deleted by most edd., both by Lloyd-Jones and Wilson) and in Herodian (discussing accentuation). The rarity of the word cannot be counted against Eur. authorship: cf. αὐτόχειρ, αὐτοκτόνος, αἱματοσφαγής, νεοσφαγής.

ἐκόμισ' ἐν χεροῖν κομίζω is the proper word for conveyance of a corpse[2] from the site of death to the household in which preparations for the ἐκφορά are to take place: *Andr.* 1158–9 ἡμεῖς δ' ἀναρπάσαντες ὡς τάχος χεροῖν / κομίζομέν νίν σοι κατοιμῶξαι γόοις, *Choe.* 683, Isaeus 8.21 ἧκον γὰρ ἐγὼ κομιούμενος αὐτὸν ὡς θάψων ἐκ τῆς οἰκίας τῆς ἐμαυτοῦ κτλ. A scholiast (M^g) and, e.g., Hartung (*Euripides Restitutus* ΙΙ.462) correctly understood Creon to mean that he carried the corpse to his house prior to coming to fetch Joc. The detail 'in his own hands' pathetically reinforces δύστηνος and is not a stage-direction (1308 action n.). If the corpse is present at this point, the force of ἐν χεροῖν must be watered down, or Creon

---

[1] Denniston, *GP*² 536, cites for anacoluthon with τε γάρ Dem. 19.159 (the sentence gets so complicated that τε is never picked up); Adam on Pl. *Rep.* 522b4 (τε γάρ anacoluthon due to an interruption) cites *Rep.* 373b2, 463d1, 575a2 for anacoluthon with plain τε (in each case the train of thought is lost in a complicated sentence).

[2] Not for 'carrying out for burial' as incorrectly claimed by LSJ s.v. ΙΙ.1: see *EMC* 12 (n.s.2) (1983) 113.

must already have set the corpse down (otherwise, it is unclear when hereafter he does so).[1]

1317 βοᾶι δὲ δῶμα πᾶν 'my entire household rings with cries of lamentation', the result of Creon's depositing of the corpse there. The construction becomes independent, but continues the thought of the relative clause that precedes. It is the job of the household women (slaves) to begin the ritual lamentation, even though the preparation of the corpse awaits the arrival of a female relative. Fraenkel, believing Men.'s corpse to be present, found this phrase nonsensical;[2] but it makes perfect sense if ἐκόμισα in 1316 is given its proper sense, 'brought home'. Craik incorrectly supposes that cries of grief may actually have been heard at this point and that δῶμα is the on-stage palace. Creon's house is off-stage (cf. 690, 978–90): for an off-stage house as a dramatic reality in tragedy, cf. *OT* 669–79 (Creon and Oed. are clearly to be sent to different destinations: Creon's house is off-stage, not, as in *Ant.*, the same as the Labdacid palace); *Med.* (the royal palace is off-stage, and people come and go from it to the visible house of Medea and Jason).

ἥκω μετά it is disputed whether to accent μέτα (μεθήκω with very rare tmesis and anastrophe)[3] or to write μετὰ or μετά and treat the preposition as separated from its acc. object because of the rhetorical effect of placing γέρων near γραῖαν (Wecklein).[4] I hesitantly now prefer the preposition.

---

[1] Note that corpses on the tragic stage are carried on litters by attendants or shown on the eccyclema or carried on the crane (*Med.*, *Rhesus*), not carried in the arms of a single speaking actor (Creon does not personally carry Haemon's corpse in *Ant.*: cf. Jebb).

[2] So too now West (1990), who proposes δῆμος πᾶς, which is inapposite because the city as a whole would welcome Menoeceus' saving gesture, whereas the grief is limited to Creon (918, 949–51, 1057–9, 1090–2, 1206–7).

[3] As JD points out to me, it can be disputed whether there is a parallel for tmesis with anastrophe for μεθήκω. In other instances an acc. object intervenes, so that one may interpret as simplex ἥκω with prepositional phrase in anastrophe (*Alc.* 46, *Su.* 670; cf. with μετέρχομαι *Phil.* 343). Tmesis with anastrophe is very rare outside of archaic hexameter poetry (K–G I.533–5, Schwyzer II.426): Semonides 7.63 West (λοῦται ... ἄπο) is a secure example, but Pindar *O.* 1.49 is not (κατὰ μέλη, not τάμον κάτα), nor *O.* 3.6 (ζευχθέντες ἔπι, but ἔπι may go with the preceding χαίταισι). *Hec.* 504 πέμψαντος ... μέτα would be an undoubted case, but the line is deleted by Jenni and Diggle.

[4] Scribal practice counts for little or nothing, but earlier treatments give the false impression that μέτα is poorly attested. The accent on μετα written with epsilon-tau ligature sometimes appears to be over the

Preposition at the end of a trimeter governing a noun in the next line is very rare (in Eur. only *El.* 852-3; the rarity is here compounded by the interposing of an emphatic word between prep. and object), whereas μεθήκω is Euripidean (441 above, *Tro.* 1270; cf. ambiguous ἥκω (...) μέτα with preceding acc. object in *Alc.* 46, *Su.* 670), and here γέρων and γραῖαν are not actually adjacent (*Od.* 5.155 παρ' οὐκ ἐθέλων ἐθελούσηι, *Prom.* 276 πρὸς ἄλλοτ' ἄλλον: Schwyzer II.427, K–G I.552–3). See Fraenkel on *Ag.* 1271 and West, *Greek Metre* 83 n. 22.

1318 γέρων ... γραῖαν the rhetorical play prob. has pathetic effect, suggesting Creon's desolation and the sad reversal of the old burying the young. Cf. *Ba.* 193 γέρων γέροντα παιδαγωγήσω σ' ἐγώ;

1319 λούσηι προθῆταί τ' preparation of the corpse (laying out, bathing, dressing) for official mourning, visitation, and burial is a duty of the female relatives: *Ant.* 901 ἔλουσα κἀκόσμησα, *Alc.* 664 περιστελοῦσι καὶ προθήσονται, *Hec.* 611–13 λουτροῖς τοῖς πανυστάτοις ... λούσω προθῶμαί θ'; cf. Garland, 24.

1320–1 this couplet was deleted as inappropriate by Schenkl, and some critics of the later part of the exodos have argued conversely that a Creon who utters this pious maxim could not be so cruel as the Creon of that scene. But the inconsistency is both possible and meaningful: 1308–1479n., 1663n.

θανοῦσι the aorist fits Creon's meaning ('those who have ⟨just⟩ died'), whereas the perfect ('the dead') in Stobaeus 4.57.9 might suit a gnomology better. Trisyllabic τεθνεῶσι(ν) would scan (see Diggle, *Studies* 93 on the synizesis), but the tragedians clearly favoured τεθνηκώς (τεθνεώς only in *Choe.* 682, ia.trim, and E. *Su.* 273, dactylic: the use in *Choe.* and in comedy might suggest that the 'second' perfect was too colloquial).

εὐσεβεῖν Valck. argued that in transitive phrases one should write εὖ σέβειν and accept εὐσεβεῖν only with a prepositional complement. But transitive εὐσεβεῖν is certain in *Tro.* 85 and probable enough elsewhere (cf. Fraenkel on *Ag.* 338), and the sense 'behave piously toward' is here superior to 'revere well'.

1322 δόμων ἔξω, Κρέον the word-order of O has a good chance of being genuine: *Text. Trad.* 53.

1323 κόρη τε μητρός ... κοινῶι ποδί μητρός goes with κοινῶι ποδί, not with κόρη (as Wecklein proposed, with inapposite parallels); the dat. is modal/circumstantial, lit. 'in the shared movement of her mother' (pos-

---

alpha (*Text. Trad.* 338), but comparison of μέτα in 1278 and 1349 and of other words with final alpha accented (e.g. κακά in 1347) usually shows that the scribes intended μέτα in all three places.

sessive gen.: 692n.; ποδί-phrases: 301–3n.). The phrase is artificial both because such a gen. with noun + κοινός normally denotes the whole or a collective (e.g. Ἑλλάδος, πάντων) and because of the interlaced word-order, a rhetorical device for juxtaposing the two kinship-words despite their lack of syntactic connection. It is a matter of taste whether this is deemed preciosity or clumsiness (Paley). Kvíčala (*Zeitschr. f. d. Österreich. Gymn.* 9 (1858) 624) deleted this line for symmetry 1 : 1 : 2 : 2 : 3 : 3 (but there is no strong reason to expect symmetry in a short dialogue of this kind); Zipperer agreed, objecting to μητρός and suggesting that Creon would have responded immediately to 1322. On the notion that lines have been added to incorporate Ant. where she was originally not mentioned see 1430n., 1465n.

1326 εἰς ἀσπίδ' ἥξειν 'will engage in battle'; for the use of ἀσπίδ', deemed 'very peculiar' by Paley and variously emended (e.g. Nauck ἥξειν ἐς αἰχμήν), cf. *Hcld.* 819 μονομάχου δι' ἀσπίδος (= μάχης), *Su.* [902]. The transferred meaning is made even more obvious by preceding μονομάχωι ... δορί. Fraenkel's objection to the style of the couplet 1325–6 is unjustified.

1327 τοι Denniston, *GP*² 541: 'revealing the speaker's emotional ... state', and hence explaining his surprise at the news.

ἀγαπάζων extant here alone in tragedy, but a poetic by-form of ἀγαπάω found in epic and Pindar. The sense 'show affection and honour to the dead' is found also for ἀγαπάω in *Su.* 764, *Hel.* 937 (the only instances of the verb in tragedy). There is no evidence that this is a general idiom, and it may be a Eur. mannerism.

1328 εἰς τόδ' ἦλθον ὥστε Fraenkel considers this an interpolator's erroneous version of the idiom εἰς τοσοῦτο / τοῦτο / τόδε + gen. noun + ὥστε, but there are parallels for the lack of gen. in prose and poetry: Lys. 27.10 εἰς τοσοῦτον ἥκομεν ὥσθ' κτλ.; Dem. 6.2 εἰς τοῦτ' ἤδη προηγμένα τυγχάνει πάντα τὰ πράγματα τῆι πόλει ὥσθ' κτλ. (cf. 19.42 ἐνταῦθ' ἦν ἤδη τὰ πράγμαθ' ὥστε κτλ., 45.83); Lycurg. *Leocr.* 3 περιέστηκεν εἰς τοῦτο ὥστε κτλ.; *Aj.* 729 ὥστ' ἐς τοσοῦτον ἦλθον ὥστε καὶ κτλ.; S. fr. 210.49 οὐκ ἐς τοσοῦτον ἦλθον ὥστ' ἐπεγχανεῖν; perhaps *Antiope* fr. 48.7–8 Kambitsis [μένου]σι δ' ἡμῖν εἰς τόδ' ἔρχεται τύχη / [ὡς ἤ] θανεῖν δεῖ κτλ.; cf., without ὥστε, *Her.* 1356 ἐς τοῦθ' ἱκέσθαι, δάκρυ' ἀπ' ὀμμάτων βαλεῖν. On constructions with εἰς τόδ' ἐλθεῖν *vel sim.* see also Diggle, *GRBS* 14 (1973) 267–8.

1329 πάλαι functions as an emphatic alternative for ἤδη, marking the relatively recent action as irrevocably past: cf. *Tro.* 624, *Or.* 1425; also *Ag.* 587, *Prom.* 845, and places where πάλαι reflects a subjective exaggeration of an anxious wait, *Med.* 1116, *Hipp.* 855, etc.

1330 δοκῶ apparently the chorus is making an inference solely from the passage of time, and it is Creon who first notes the approach of the messenger. Compare other brief dialogues that highlight waiting or uncertainty just before a messenger is seen approaching: *Med.* 1116-20, *El.* 758-60, *Or.* 844-51 (same technique for arrival of Creon in *OT* 73-84).

ἀγῶνα τὸν περὶ ψυχῆς   an elevated version of proverbial περὶ ψυχῆς δρόμος (refs. in Fraenkel on *Ag.* 119, MacDowell on *Wasps* 375); cf. *Or.* 847 ψυχῆς ἀγῶνα τὸν προκείμενον πέρι (deleted by Willink).

1332 τὸ μὲν σημεῖον   Kirchhoff labelled the verse *vix sanus*, and Paley and others have objected to τὸ μέν, suggesting e.g. τὸ γάρ, κακόν, τορόν; Fraenkel counts it as evidence of interpolation. The observations of Wecklein and Pearson seem adequate to defend the text: 'bei τὸ μέν ... schwebt vor: τὸ δὲ δρώμενον αὐτίκ' ἀκούσομαι'; 'μέν is without an answering δέ, since the contrast is otherwise expressed by the clause ὃς ... δρώμενον'.

1333 σκυθρωπὸν ὄμμα καὶ πρόσωπον   the fullness of expression and the parechesis of -ωπον are noteworthy (condemned as bombast by Fraenkel). ὄμμα and πρόσωπον are used synonymously in *variatio* in 454-8 above and in *Med.* 27-8, 1197-8, and with some distinction of reference in *Alc.* 826-7 ὄμμ' ἰδὼν δακρυρροοῦν / κουράν τε καὶ πρόσωπον. So here we either have a hendiadys or a slight distinction between the cast of the eyes and the expression of the face as a whole. The juncture of an adj. in -ωπον with ὄμμα is a Eur. mannerism: *Her.* 990 ἀγριωπόν, *Or.* 894 φαιδρωπόν, fr. 870 αἱματωπόν; and note the fullness of *Or.* 1319 σκυθρωποὺς ὀμμάτων ... κόρας. σκυθρωπός is used of the approaching messenger in *Hipp.* 1152, and the word occurs in seven other places in Eur., in comedy and prose, but in other poets only *Choe.* 738 (text uncertain). Porson avoided the parechesis by reading πρόσοψιν (Xa), but there is little likelihood that this is other than the slip of a fourteenth-century scribe; the source of XXaXb had πρόσωπον and Mosch. retains the latter in a paraphrase that glosses σκυθρωπόν.

1334 στείχοντος   Eur. uses acc. part. στείχοντα(ς) about a dozen times in announcements of entering characters (of messengers *Med.* 1119, *Tro.* 708). The use here is less integral, and the stylistically weak sequence ἀγγέλου ... ὃς ... ἀγγελεῖ seems to be without parallel (for ἄγγελος and ἀγγέλλω in close proximity, but spoken by different persons, cf. *El.* 759-62, *Tro.* 708-10). One might consider the deletion of 1334 as a reader's expansion.

τὸ δρώμενον   in this context, with πᾶν and with ἤδη πεπρᾶχθαι preceding, the present participle must have the force of the imperfect, 'all that was being done'; so too in [1358] below; in *Trach.* 588 τοῖς δρωμένοις is either conative present ('what you are trying to accomplish') or imperfect

522

('what you were just now doing'). For δρώμενα in connection with messengers see DeJong, 10 n. 21.

1335-9 for the use of tetrameters see 1308-9n.

1335 the messenger is not the same as the one in the previous episode (cf. *Ba.*). If the first messenger left as Joc.'s guide at 1283, as I believe, he would have arrived at the battlefield with her and missed the duel. Even if he left at 1263 or 1261 (1263 action n.), the resumption of the narrative from the point of arming (1359 ∼ 1242-7) would suggest to an audience that the duel began while the first messenger was still with Joc. There is no indication in the words or perspective of the second messenger that suggests his identity with the first.[1]

γόους even if this word were only attested in a few *recc.* (as edd. have believed, thanks to careless collation of B), it should have been accepted in preference to λόγους, which produces a pointless tautology. γόος is liable to be corrupted to λόγος in any case (1309 above; Diggle, *Studies* 102, *Text. Trad. Or.* 63), and here the process was favoured by λόγου in the next line and by the presence of μῦθον (glossed λόγον in some mss, and λόγον expels μῦθον in RfRv, which have γόους).

1336 οἰχόμεσθ' for this inference from the initial words of the messenger cf. *Or.* 855 αἰαῖ, διοιχόμεσθα· δῆλος εἶ λόγωι. Valck. assigned this word to the messenger and spoiled the stichomythia.

εὐπροσώποις φροιμίοις the epithet is used of a person's mood in *Aj.* 1009 and metaphorically, as here, in *Choe.* 969 τύχαι δ' εὐπρόσωποι (LSJ misplaces our passage under the heading 'specious'). The proem is what first greets the listener, hence the metaphor of a face: cf. Pindar *O.* 6.3-4 ἀρχομένου δ' ἔργου πρόσωπον / χρὴ θέμεν τηλαυγές (with admixture of architectural metaphor). The sound-echo of πρόσωπον in 1333 has no discernible purpose (Craik thinks 'Eur. repeats . . . perhaps in deliberate self-mockery').

ἄρχηι λόγου cf. *Her.* 538 Ἄπολλον, οἵοις φροιμίοις ἄρχηι λόγου.

1337 δισσῶς αὐτῶ δισσῶς is simply 'a second time', like μάλ' αὖθις (1069n.); adv. δισσῶς only here in tragedy, but cf. *Aj.* 432 δὶς αἰάζειν, 940 δὶς οἰμῶξαι. Hermann wrongly imported a distinction between the brothers' death (ἄλλοις πήμασιν) and Joc.'s (μεγάλα κακά) and treated δισσῶς as marking the distinction; see next note.

1338 Σ already were uncertain whether to punctuate the first part of

---

[1] DeJong, 67 n. 16, reports without rejecting the idea of Rijksbaron (1976) 305-6 that the two messengers might be the same character. Mueller-Goldingen, 214 n. 22, also refers to them as the same speaker, noting the similar use of ἐπεί-clauses at 1090 and 1359.

this line as statement or question. Among attempts to make 1338 a single sentence one may note Musgrave's πρὸς πεπρ. ἄλλο [ἄλλα Porson] πήμασιν λέγεις ἔτι; And Hermann continued the messenger's speech through to πήμασιν, spoiling the stichomythia. It is rhetorically apt for the recipient to comment on the accumulation (cf. *Ant.* 1281 τί δ' ἔστιν αὖ κάκιον ἐκ κακῶν ἔτι;), and with the first part of the line as a statement, the word-order λέγεις δὲ τί; suitably shows impatience, as in *Hel.* 604 παλαιὰ θρηνεῖς πήματ'· ἀγγέλλεις δὲ τί;, *Hipp.* 519 δειμαίνεις δὲ τί;, *Hec.* 1009 (cf. 709n.). But if πρὸς κτλ. is a disbelieving question, the tone of the second question does not fit so well. JD finds πεπραγμένοισιν ... πήμασιν odd and suggests that we want something like πρὸς πεπραγμένοισιν ἄλλα πήματ' ἀγγελεῖς ἔτι; But cf. perhaps *Hcld.* 960 πολλὰ πήματ' ἐξειργασμένον, *Rhes.* 808, *Pers.* 786 πήματ' ἔρξαντες τόσα.

1339 οὐκέτ' ... ἐν φάει cf. *Hec.* 707, *Ion* 726, *Phil.* 415, 1212; see 1281n.

1340-3 the metre of 1340-1 is exclamation + 2 dochmiacs. The older mss all assign this lyric outburst to the chorus, but edd. have followed the *recentiores* who assign it to Creon, arguing that Creon is the one addressed by the messenger and that μοι καὶ πόλει suits him rather than the foreign chorus. In modern editions 1342-3 (or 1342 with 1343 deleted) are then continued in Creon's voice, whereas earlier editions usually assigned them to the messenger (but after self-absorption and interaction with Creon it is too late for the messenger to be apostrophizing the house: contrast *Ba.* 1024-7). Change of speaker is well attested at 1342 (and change of speaker is usually more reliably transmitted than identification of speaker: 986-91n.) and fits the content and change of metre better than continuation in one voice. Moreover, the chorus has a lyric outburst in 1350-1 following the second piece of news (after 1349 is addressed to Creon), and its previous expressions of solidarity with the city make μοι καὶ πόλει possible in its mouth. I therefore retain not only the distribution[1] but also the attributions of the older mss, creating a parallel, though not responding,[2] sequence for the two parts of the news. The lyric outbursts thus belong to the female chorus rather than the male character (though Creon is left

---

[1] Hermann and Paley recognized that 1342 should be separated from 1340-1 and eliminated the messenger, but Hermann could give 1344 to the chorus as a reply to another speaker (note γ') only by giving 1343 by itself to Creon, and Paley, deleting 1343, made 1342 and 1344 continuous (chorus speaking), violating the force of γ'.

[2] Hermann, always apt to restore strophic responsion, by various small changes made 1340-4 respond to 1345-9, designating 1350-1 as epode. Hartung (1837) had anticipated this treatment.

with dochmiacs in 1345). Cf. *Su.* 1072ff., where Evadne's leap evokes lyrics from the chorus before any reaction from Iphis (who was just in conversation with Evadne), and Iphis' comments are confined to trimeters. For outbursts by a person not addressed cf. Soph. *El.* 671-9: Electra interrupts the dialogue between Clytaemnestra and the false messenger. The assignment of 1340-3 to Creon alone is defended by Mueller-Goldingen, 211-12 n. 19, who argues that the chorus has a more distanced attitude toward the brothers than toward Joc. and so appropriately intervenes in 1350 but not earlier; cf. also Hose, *Chor* 213 n. 40, who emphasizes the chorus' status as mere visitors and believes it cannot pair itself with the city. For such a sequence, cf. *Tro.* 235ff.: Hecuba, a female, is sole lyric respondent to the bad news given in trimeters; chorus remains silent until 292-3.[1]

1343 Valck. rather tentatively expressed a preference that this verse be deleted, and many have followed him. The objections are (1) obscurity of παίδων (Valck., Geel); (2) anticipation of details not yet heard (Wecklein); (3) interruption of sequence of thought from 1342 εἰσηκούσατ' to 1344 ὥστ' κτλ. But (1) in context it is completely obvious that παῖδες in 1339 means Et. and Pol. and that παίδων here has the same reference; (2) Valck. already noted that given Creon's knowledge of the single-combat and of the death of the brothers he is entitled to say ὁμοίαις συμφοραῖς; (3) the sequence of thought is still possible. More useful objections would be that the line is semantically superfluous (so Wecklein; but it may not be emotionally so), that it produces the only two-line speech in trimeters or tetrameters within 1335-49, and that the genitive absolute (if such it is) explicating τάδε is odd. The line may be spurious, but these are not fully cogent reasons to believe so.

παίδων . . . ὀλωλότων with τάδε as object of εἰσηκούσατ', it is best to take this phrase as genitive absolute, rather than as gen. of the topic dependent on the verb of hearing (K-G 1.360 Anm. 9b), as Matthiae and others did.

1344 ὥστ' ἐκδακρῦσαί γ' the infinitive with ὥστε presents a result as natural and potential rather than as actual, so it seems possible that the inf. may stand here by itself and need not have ἄν attached to it for congruence with the contrary-to-fact condition: 'Yes (γ': Denniston, *GP²* 134), ⟨it has heard well enough⟩ so as to burst out in tears, if . . .' Compare perhaps the absence of ἄν in the idiomatic impersonal imperfect of unfulfilled obligation. For corruption of ὥστ' ἐκδ- to ὥστε δ- cf. *Or.* 1122. The verb is otherwise attested only in *Phil.* 278 before Demades fr. 89 de Falco

---

[1] Cf., with no other character present, the dochmiacs of the chorus reacting to the trimeters of the messenger in *Ba.* 1030-42.

and late prose. For those who doubt that ἄν can be dispensed with, there is Hartung's correction of ὥστε δ- to ὥστ' ἄν δ-, but this produces a position for ἄν that, though not unexpected for an enclitic (e.g., ὥστε με *El.* 240), is paralleled only in Soph. *El.* 333 (with fut. less vivid condition, not inf.): see *Text. Trad.* 54.[1]

εἰ φρονοῦντ' ἐτύγχανεν for the topos of the animate house cf. *Ag.* 36-7, *Hipp.* 418, 1074, *Andr.* 924.

1345 two dochmiacs. In the arrangement accepted here, these are Creon's only lyrics. One may consider assigning the line to the chorus instead (giving 1344 to the coryphaeus alone), with Creon following in a trimeter. But 1348 δυσποτμώτερα looks like an echo of the same speaker's βαρυποτμωτάτας here.

βαρυποτμωτάτας a tragic adj. (Eur., Soph.), also a few times in later poetry and prose. The link-vowel ω here and in 1348 is for metrical convenience, exploiting alternative syllable-treatment -πο⌐τμω-, as also Men. *Mis.* A5 Sandbach and *TrGF* adesp. 325.2. Soph. fr. 568.3 has more normal εὐποτ⌐μοτάτα, and Philo and Plut. have βαρυ-/δυσποτμότερος and -ότατος.

[1346] if supposed to be spoken by the same voice as 1345, the redundancy seems too great, and the omission in MBV before correction, though possibly due to homoeoarcton, may be an index of interpolation. In an abundant tradition like that of *Phoen.*, there are naturally many instances where one or another ms accidentally omits a line, with no implication for the question of authenticity. But when a detachable line is missing in a major ms or a large number of mss, the situation is analogous to that of verses whose uneven attestation is recorded in Σ (375n.) or revealed by papyri (291-2n.). Condemnation is not automatic, but must be seriously considered. See 1199n.

1347 γ' again expresses elliptical assent: (with 1346 deleted) 'yes, ⟨you would truly cry woe⟩ if ...'; (with 1346 retained) 'yes, ⟨you would truly be wretched⟩ if ...'.

1348 καὶ πῶς expresses surprise or disbelief: Denniston, *GP*² 310.

1350-1 Metre as emended here (ἀνάγετ' ἄγετε, and choosing κρᾶτα), the metre is.

---

[1] ὥστε + inf. + ἄν is mainly a prosaic construction (Goodwin, *MT* §211, 592; K–G II.507-8); in tragedy I find *Her.* 234-5 (attached to a contrary-to-fact conditional sentence); *Trach.* 669-70, *OT* 374-5, S. *El.* 1316-17 (all representing pot. opt.); S. *El.* 755-6 (representing a past potential). For ἄν as quasi-enclitic in general, see E. Fraenkel, *Kleine Beiträge zur klassischen Philologie* I [Storia e Letteratura, 95 (Rome 1964)] 93-122.

∪⌣∪⌣∪ − −∪⌣∪| dochm, cr

−⌣∪ − ∪ − −∪ − ∪ − ‖   dochm, hypodoch

But the text is quite uncertain, because of the variant κάρα / κρᾶτα, the possibility that χεροῖν is a gloss, and doubt whether to restore pure dochmiacs or not. With transmitted ἀνάγετ' ἀνάγετε, 1350 could be ia + dochm. Dale, *Metr. Anal.* 3.124, posits brevis in longo at κωκυτόν and analyses 1350 as ia + ∪ − − (taken as dochmiac equivalent), leaving 1351 as lec + hypodoch (the reverse of what I create by emendation at 129; cf. also 1287-8 lec + dochm). Pure dochmiacs can be obtained, e.g., by Hermann's treatment (ἀνάγετ' ἀνάγετ', ἒ ἔ, κωκυτόν, χεροῖν / ἐπὶ κάρα τε λευκοπήχεις κτύπους), but it involves a postponed τε introduced by emendation. In Powell's adaptation of this, κωκυτὸν ⟨μέγαν⟩ (with χεροῖν deleted), the adj. is otiose (contrast *Aj.* 851, of Ajax's mother, ἤσει μέγαν κωκυτὸν ἐν πάσηι πόλει). Diggle, (1990b) 117 n. 90, doubts cretic sandwiched between dochmiacs and thinks the passage is not Euripidean, but suggests that more regular metre could be obtained with ἀνάγετ' ἄγετε κωκυτὸν ἐπὶ κάρα ⟨τίθε⟩τε κτλ. (dochm with 2 hypodoch).

1350-1 ἀνάγετ' ἄγετε this emendation produces simplex as rhetorical reinforcement of compound, a lyric mannerism of Eur. (for refs. see Willink on *Or.* 181; Diggle (1990b) 117). ἀνάγειν is here used with an effective zeugma, linking the two manifestations of mourning: with κωκυτόν it is figurative (raising the voice to a high volume, perhaps also bringing the breath up from within in song), as in *Trach.* 211 παιᾶν' ἀνάγετ', *El.* 126 ἄναγε πολύδακρυν ἀδονάν (= γόον); with κτύπους it may be physical (raising the arms to beat the head) with an admixture of the figurative ('stir up', like *Or.* 1353 ἐγείρετε κτύπον).

λευκοπήχεις κτύπους χεροῖν the quasi-redundant periphrasis for κτύπους λευκοῖν χεροῖν is typical lyric style (cf. 645 above; Breitenbach, 185, 189) and χειρῶν κτύπον occurs in *Alc.* 87, so one should not be too quick to treat χεροῖν as a gloss. λευκοπήχεις (extant elsewhere only *Ba.* 1206-7 λευκοπήχεσι / χειρῶν ἀκμαῖσι) is a recherché variation on λευκώλενος.

1352-3 οἷον τέρμον' . . . αἰνιγμοὺς ἔτλης 'as what an end of your life and marriage did you endure the Sphinx's riddle'. That is, the Sphinx's riddle has turned out to be the determining factor in the unhappy subsequent course of Joc.'s life. τέρμον' here is not just the temporal 'end' of life, but retains its more basic meaning of boundary and defined goal (cf. τέρμα and ὅρος). This reminder of the crucial role of the Sphinx fits with other references throughout the play (cf. 45-50, 801-11, 1019-54, 1505-7, 1688, 1728-33) and is suitably spoken by Creon, who proclaimed the marriage as reward for the solution of the riddle (47-9). For the construction Porson long ago compared *Il.* 4.155 φίλε κασίγνητε, θάνατόν νύ τοι ὅρκι' ἔταμνον. The τ' added in some mss is a simplification of the unobvious apposition; the false accent in M (αἰνιγμοῦς) is most likely a slip not uncharacteristic of this scribe, not a pointer to the truth of dat. αἰνιγμοῖς (Geel, approved by Pearson).

1354 πῶς καί postponed καί stresses the addition in the request for further information: Denniston, *GP*² 312-13 and Porson's note here. For this use in the question that prompts a messenger's rhesis, cf. *Hipp.* 1171, *Hec.* 515 (in both cases, as here, turning back to the messenger after apostrophe).

διπτύχων a favourite word of Eur. (eighteen times), often meaning no more than δύο; otherwise in classical drama it appears only in Soph. fr. 152.2 (which many have denied is Soph.) and Arist. fr. 570 K-A (parody of Eur., quoted below, 1361n.).

1355 ἀρᾶς τ' ἀγώνισμ' Οἰδίπου 'the contest/struggle caused by Oed.'s curse'; for the gen. Pearson well compares *Hec.* 699 πέσημα φοινίου δορός. Not 'achievement, issue of Oed.'s curse' (LSJ s.v. 1.2); this meaning is found only of creditable achievements, successful struggles against a worthy opponent. The noun is mainly prosaic (also *El.* 987, *Frogs* 284). Here it prepares for the gladiatorial tenor of the narrated duel.

1356-424 The narrative of the duel continues from the point reached in the speech of the previous messenger and contains further typical elements drawn from the literary tradition (1217-63n.). (1) 1361, the armed combatants proceed into an open space in the middle of the two armies: cf. *Il.* 3.340-1, 23.814 (also of athletes, 23.685, 710). (2) 1364-69, 1372-5, prayers of the duellists: cf. *Il.* 3.350-4. (3) 1369-71, 1388-9, 1395, 1399-1400, reactions of the onlookers: cf. 1217-63n. *ad fin.* (4) 1382-7, 1390-402, initial fighting done with spear: cf. *Il.* 3.345-49, 355-60, 7.244-62, 20. 259-83. (5) 1404-15, fighting with swords after failure to kill with spear: cf. *Il.* 3.361-3, 7.273, 20.283-90. Further epic reminiscences are mentioned in 1380-1n., 1401n., 1423n., 1453n. Eur.'s narrative also departs from the epic models for special effects. Throughout there is much more detail about the particular movements of the fighters, including a reference to a particular feint (1407-8). This aspect, combined with the repeated attention to audience-reaction, makes the fight more akin to an athletic event[1] and perhaps creates an impression of realism that under-

---

[1] One may ask whether in detecting a quality of athletic realism one is not being anachronistic, since combat in arms for entertainment is a familiar phenomenon of later times, esp. associated with the Romans. But for the classical Greek context one may point to (1) the contest of Ajax and Diomedes in *Il.* 23; (2) Athenaeus 4.154d citing Hermippus and Ephorus on the invention of ὁπλομαχία; (3) Diod. Sic. 17.100 for

cuts the stylized grandeur evoked by the Homeric models. Moreover, in Homeric combat the spears are usually cast without much delay, but here we find rather the style of athletic battle (as in *Il.* 23.816–19), an initial skirmish of jabbing spears (1382–7; cf., however, *Il.* 7.258–62, where jabbing follows the failed throws). The reference to sweating in 1388 may also suggest athletic endeavour: in Homer the sweating of the wounded or of one who has left battle is mentioned more often than the sweating of warriors (only in generalized descriptions, *Il.* 13.711, 17.385), but the sweating of athletic competitors is found in 23.688, 715 (cf. *Ba.* 620). One Homeric detail omitted is the terrible glance or grim look of the combatants approaching for battle (*Il.* 3.342, 7.212, 23.815); instead the attack is here accompanied by a vivid animal-simile (1380–1: for boars cf. *Il.* 7.256–7).

This narrative seems to be transmitted basically intact. I delete three individual lines (at least two of which are not histrionic additions). The only passages that have come under strong suspicion by those more inclined to detect interpolations are 1369–71 and 1388–9, both involving allusion to audience-reaction. See notes *ad locc.*

1355–6 τὰ μὲν . . . οἶσθ' the following rhesis in fact assumes that the listeners have heard not only of the success of Thebes in the pitched battle before the wall but also of the proposal of the duel and its acceptance. The internal motivation for the messenger to begin where he does is rather perfunctory, and it would be improper to ask how the messenger can be sure of this (cf. 1090–2n.). The essential point is that the poet does not want to bore his theatre-audience with the same details they have already heard. Cf. *Ag.* 598–9 (Clyt. has, I believe, just entered, but professes not to want details from the herald); *Prom.* 613–21 (Prom. refuses to repeat for Io what he has already told the chorus and audience). There is thus no implication in 1355–6 that the chorus rather than Creon is the addressee of this speech.

περιπτυχαί a Eur. favourite (four times in various senses, parodied in *Birds* 1241; cf. *TrGF* adesp. 91; extant later only in quotations of Eur.).

[1358] the normal negative with ὥστε + inf. is μή, and the few instances with οὐ (outside of indirect discourse) involve either negation of a single word (Goodwin, *MT* §597.2 – e.g., Isocr. 8.107 ὥσθ' . . . οὐ πολλοῖς

---

a single-combat arising from a challenge, but for no wider purpose than self-display of the combatants and entertainment of the onlookers; (4) the scant evidence for practice-combat with tipped weapons as a form of military training (1409–13n.). Thus it is possible that the language of this passage evokes not only racing and wrestling, but an ancient equivalent of fencing or martial arts.

529

ἔτεσιν ὕστερον … ἐπιπολάσαι; unconvincingly applied to this passage by Geel: οὐχ ἅπαντα = 'only a part') or an emphatic negative (so *Hel.* 108 ὥστ' οὐδ' ἴχνος γε τειχέων εἶναι σαφές, Soph. *El.* 780–1: cf. Jebb *ad loc.* with Appendix, K–G ii.188–9, Goodwin, *MT* §598–9). Dem. 53.2 is similar because of the negative main clause: οὐδ' αὖ οὕτως ἄπορος ἦν οὐδ' ἄφιλος ὥστε οὐκ ἂν ἐξευρεῖν τὸν ἀπογράψοντα. Jebb suggests that in our passage and Dem. 53.2 οὐ could be due to the influence of the preceding οὐ, but this is unconvincing, since a preceding οὐ regularly calls forth μὴ οὐ (as in τὸ μὴ οὐ in 1176, *Hipp.* 49, etc.). Dem. 53.2 is perhaps rather a case of emphatic negation. Goodwin tried to apply that rationale here ('a fact rather than a mere tendency is expressed'), but the context of inference is against that analysis. K–G ii.191, 220 are no more convincing in viewing οὐ as semantically redundant on the model of οὐ μᾶλλον … ἢ οὐ: that is, 'too far for you to know' becomes, with negation, 'not too far for you to know', with a superfluous addition of 'not' to the infinitive. Donaldson's ὡς μὴ οὐχ involves doubtful use of ὡς + inf. (Diggle, *Studies* 8–9); Shilleto's τὸ μὴ οὐχ is better. But it seems preferable to accept Wecklein's proposal that 1358 arose as an explanatory addition.

1359 σῶμ' ἐκοσμήσανθ' ὅπλοις see 861n., 1244n.

1360 with δισσοί for οἱ τοῦ, 1243 is almost the same, whence some have deleted this line as a false repetition; but as Valck. realized, despite his suspicions, an explicit subject is needed at this point, and the inexact repetition of a verse of this sort is not, in my view, suspicious. It is 1362 that is offensive.

1361 cf. *Hcld.* 803 ἔστη μέσοισιν ἐν μεταιχμίοις δορός (Hyllus about to issue his challenge).

[1362] the tautology is pointless. In defence Hermann cited passages which are in fact of a different stylistic level and tone. If 1360 is kept, there is no need for another nominative here, so it is better to delete than to emend the tautology away (e.g., Valck. δισσὼ ξυναίμω, Heath δισσὼ γ' ἀδελφώ). I suspect that a reader noted the similarity of 1243 to 1360 by writing δισσοί in the margin and that the word was later filled out into a trimeter placed in the text (cf. 428).[1]

1363 ὡς reinforces the notion of intention in εἰς (780–1n.).

εἰς ἀγῶνα μονομάχου τ' ἀλκὴν δορός hendiadys, 'to the battle-contest of the single-combat spear'; the true reading, barely surviving in γρ-variants and Σ, is confirmed by Arist. *Phoen.* fr. 570 K–A ἐς Οἰδίπου δὲ παῖδε, διπτύχω κόρω, / Ἄρης κατέσκηψ', ἔς τε μονομάχου πάλης / ἀγῶνα

---

[1] Helmbold's solution of deleting 1361b–62a μεταίχμιον … διπλῶ is inferior to the removal of 1362.

νῦν ἑστᾶσιν, which is based especially on this line, but prob. also owes something to 1354 for the Eur. διπτύχω.

1364 ἐπ' only in M, but perhaps more suitable for the sense 'toward ⟨a distant, unseen object⟩'; εἰς is the most common preposition with βλέπω and its compounds, either for looking at something within view or in a metaphorical sense, and so is prob. a trivialization. For ἐπ' cf. Thuc. 7.71.3 οἱ δ' ἐπὶ τὸ ἡσσώμενον βλέψαντες (viewing a object within sight), Dinarchus 1.72 ἐπιβλέψατε δ' ἐπὶ τὴν Θηβαίων πόλιν ('consider').

1365 ὦ πότνι' Ἥρα Pol.'s invocation of the foreign goddess evokes again the disenfranchisement of the exile and the new relationships on which he has been forced to depend (cf. 77–80, 337–40, 369–70, 427–33, 569, 580–1, 704, 1251).

1366 ναίω χθόνα many comm. understand σήν here, but Craik is correct, I think, to translate 'his land', supplying Ἀδράστου from earlier in the line: Pol.'s relation to Argive Hera is indirect, deriving from his marriage and his residency, both by Adrastus' good will.

1367 ἀντήρη cf. 755, which, if genuine, is clearly recalled by the prayers in this scene.

1368 καθαιματῶσαι δεξιὰν νικηφόρον perhaps recalls 625 οὐκέθ' αἱματηρὸν τοὐμὸν ἀργήσει ξίφος. Predicative νικηφόρον, parallel to καλλίνικον in 1374, continues the theme of a dubious victory positively valued by a speaker (1048n., 1250–3n.; cf. also the ironic σὺν δίκηι νικηφόρωι in 781).

1369 1369–71 have often been deleted as a unit, but the case of 1369 is mainly separate from that of 1370–1 (although the latter couplet is not well prepared for if 1369 is deleted, and 1369, if read as the comment of the messenger, would stand out as unbalanced without 1370–1). Valck.'s argument included untenable objections to the phrase αἴσχιστον ... στέφανον (a bitter oxymoron typical of tragic style) and to the use of κτανεῖν in apposition to στέφανον (cf. Her. 1334–5 καλὸς ... στέφανος.... εὐκλείας τυχεῖν, Tro. 401–2 στέφανος οὐκ αἰσχρὸς πόλει καλῶς ὀλέσθαι). The real question is whether, if αἰτῶ is read with the majority of mss, it makes any artistic or psychological sense for Pol. to undercut his own prayer by this admission. Many who observe Pol.'s reluctance and sensitivity to his dilemma in the first episode are prepared to see the same self-awareness in this line, but I agree with those who feel that such an admission does not cohere well with the tone of the preceding prayer. If Eur. had wanted to make Pol.'s prayer more reluctant or circumspect, he would, I think, have structured this into the whole utterance. Having rejected the propriety of the line with αἰτῶ, however, we must still consider whether the reading should be αἰτῶν (which could be true even if it is a conjecture in **z**) before acceding to deletion. The objection that the nominative on which αἰτῶν would depend (1364 Πολυνείκης) is too far away is refuted by *IT* 23 (ἀναφέρων goes back to 16 Κάλχας for its case; *El.* 808 λέγων, referring to 804). The judgmental comment by the messenger would be like that in 1219–20 τολμήματα / αἴσχιστα. One source of doubt remains: the comment is appended to the first prayer and no comment is made on the equally impious prayer of Et. But the judgment serves by implication for both, and I do not find this a big enough problem to justify deletion.

1370–1 In deleting, Valck. (1) saw a contradiction between 1238–40 and these lines and adduced a number of stylistic points: (2) πολλοῖς ἐπήιει δάκρυα struck him as *inaudita forma loquendi*: he felt one should have either ἐπήιει μοι + inf. meaning 'it came into my mind to do X' or εἰσῆλθέ με φόβος (vel sim.), 'an emotion came over me'; (3) δάκρυα τῆς τύχης ὅση was objectionable to him both for the obscurity of the gen. and for the elliptical ὅση; (4) διαδόντες κόρας seemed to him more suitable to the Graeae sharing their one eye. Critics who have conceded the weakness of some or all of Valck.'s points nevertheless suggest (5) that τύχης makes no sense (εὐχῆς Hermann) or (6) that the combination of ἔβλεψαν (absolute or with ἀλλήλοισι) with διαδόντες κόρας is unnatural. As for (1), it is possible either to accept that the poet sought different effects in the two scenes without concern for a contradiction of this kind or to infer that when confronted more immediately with the prayer for fratricide the soldiers lose the enthusiasm they felt when first offered the safety afforded by the duel. (Compare perhaps the shifting emotions of the Greek army in regard to the sacrifice of Polyxena in *Hec.*: a majority favoured it, but the sacrificer himself feels pity at the last moment and almost all show admiration.) For (2), a glance at LSJ s.v. ἔπειμι ‹B› 1.2, ἐπέρχομαι 1.2–3, εἴσειμι IV, εἰσέρχομαι VI, ὕπειμι 1.1, ὑπέρχομαι II, shows that Valck.'s restrictive view of this kind of idiom is unjustified: both dat. and acc. of the person are used with such verbs with little or no distinction in meaning, and if subjects like ἄλγος, δέος, οἶκτος are found there can be no objection to δάκρυα. From later Greek Musgrave cited Dion. Hal. *Ant.Rom.* 10.49.3 ἑαυτῶι μὲν ἐπελθεῖν δάκρυα τὴν συμφορὰν ... προανακλαιομένωι and Plut. *Mor.* 595D δάκρυα πολλοῖς ἐπῆλθεν ἡμῶν ... πρὸς τοὺς λόγους. (3) The gen. is unproblematic, objective as in Virgil's *lacrimae rerum*; and the whole phrase is equivalent to δακρύειν τὴν τύχην ὅση ἐστί (or εἴη) with exclamatory indirect question (cf. Pl. *Phaedo* 117c8–d1 ἀπέκλαον ... τὴν ἐμαυτοῦ τύχην, οἵου ἀνδρὸς ἑταίρου ἐστερημένος εἴην, but here τῆς τύχης is proleptic object[1] and the subordinate verb omitted, as in *Aj.* 118 ὁρᾶις ... τὴν θεῶν ἰσχὺν

---

[1] Cf. Thuc. 1.61.1 ἦλθε ... ἡ ἀγγελία τῶν πόλεων ὅτι ἀφεστᾶσι.

ὅση;). The use of δάκρυα as a virtual *nomen actionis* is not a problem: cf. 1303 above, *Hipp.* 1070, *Or.* 295, etc. (4) διαδόντες κόρας is very similar to Eur. expressions like *Or.* 1261 δόχμιά νυν κόρας διάφερ' ὀμμάτων (see further below), except that δια- in other passages conveys shifting movement of the eyes but here conveys (shifting?) interchange of glances. (5) τύχης may be adequately understood as 'the stroke of fortune' or 'the doom' that brought the brothers to this confrontation.[1] (6) Pearson wishes to take ἀλλήλοισι with ἔβλεψαν instead of διαδόντες, but the plain dative for direction of the gaze with simplex βλέπω is dubious (he cites an instance with ἀναβλέπω, *Ba.* 1308, otherwise explained by Dodds). Rather πρὸς ἀλλήλους is easily understood from (or preciously replaced by) the following ἀλλήλοισι διαδόντες κόρας. In sum, Valck. greatly exaggerated the oddities of these lines, but there is a residual accumulation of preciosity of style that is troubling. I do not regard the case for deletion as established, but suspicion remains.

1371 διαδόντες κόρας one might have expected a present part., but the aor. part. is to be explained as coincident in time with the main verb (1507n.). In addition to *Or.* 1261 (quoted above), the closest parallels would be *Ba.* 1087 διήνεγκαν κόρας (P, rightly, I think: κάρα P. Oxy. 22.2223, cf. *Christ. Pat.*, preferred by Dodds and Kopff), and *Or.* 1267 (with Canter's emendation κόρας διάδοτε; Willink prefers κόρας δίδοτε, which gives simpler metre but requires emendation of 1247 as well). Cf. also 265 ὄμμα πανταχῆι διοιστέον and the expressions illustrated above in 462n. The sense here is 'exchanging glances' (not 'cast one's eyes around', as LSJ), for which Musgrave cited Plut. *Philopoemen* 19.5 διαδιδόντες ἀλλήλοις λόγον and *Sulla* 35.5 ῥίψεις ὀμμάτων ἐπ' ἀλλήλους ἐγίνοντο . . . καὶ μειδιαμάτων διαδόσεις.

1372-5 are closely parallel to 1364-8: note βλέψας ἐπ' / πρὸς, ἧκε . . . ἀράς / ηὔξατ', ὦ πότνι' Ἥρα / ὦ Διὸς κόρη, δός, νικηφόρον / καλλίνικον, δεξιὰν / τῆσδ' ἀπ' ὠλένης.

1372 Παλλάδος χρυσάσπιδος Athena is invoked as war-goddess and patron of military skill. The epithet, not otherwise attested for her in the Theban context, is simply a poetic evocation of her warlike appearance. There is no useful point in detecting here an extradramatic nod to the image of the Parthenos on the nearby Acropolis. For worship of Athena at Thebes, see Schachter, *Cults of Boeotia* 1.129-33. χρύσασπις is used of Theba in Pindar *I.* 1.2, of Ares in Bacch. 20.11, and a few times in late Greek (Nonnus, *Dionys.* 34.47 of Athena).

---

[1] Mueller-Goldingen, 216 n. 23, who would keep 1369 and delete 1370-1, objects to the statement in 1370 because he takes τύχης specifically as 'das Unglück des Polyneikes'.

1374 †ἐκ χερός† the redundancy with τῆσδ᾽ ἀπ᾽ ὠλένης in the next line has been explained away by claiming this hand is Athena's ('give from your hand') or by glossing ἐκ χερός as 'in close combat', but neither explanation is convincing, nor is Σ's desperate ἐκ παραλλήλου τὸ αὐτό a solution. The words are prob. an intrusive gloss (εὐστόχως Wecklein).[1]

[1376] cf. 756; if the line is genuine in one of the two places, it seems more organic to this passage. But the conditions of the duel and the word καλλίνικον (and perhaps the word lost to ἐκ χερός) already imply the death of Pol., so the elaboration κτανεῖν θ᾽ is unnecessary here as well as after 755. If genuine, the line would present Et. still blindly cloaking his personal desire behind patriotic rhetoric (510-14n.). But Diodorus 10.9.8 cites the prayer-passage as beginning at 1364 and ending at 1375, so Valck.'s hypothesis that the verse is spurious here too should be accepted.

1377-8 ἀνήφθη πυρσὸς ὡς ... σάλπιγγος ἠχὴ the comparison of a sound to a flash of fire or light is traditional in Greek poetry: see Kamerbeek's note on *OT* 186 παιὼν δὲ λάμπει and the long list of comparanda given by Diggle, *PCPS* 195 (1969) 41. Only with his emendation ἀνήφθη does the synaesthesia have full force. With transmitted ἀφείθη the image depends weakly on ὡς and the verb is at best a different metaphor ('let go' rather than 'emit') and at worst colourless. The ancients incorrectly took πυρσός as subject and ὡς ... ἠχή as the simile, partly because of misplaced pedantry about the chronology of the use of trumpets in warfare (whatever Homeric practice, the tragedians assign it freely to the Trojan War and the heroic age in general: *Eum.* 568, *Aj.* 291, S. *El.* 711, etc.; see 1102n.). Σ allege that the casting down of a torch in the μεταίχμιον by sacred πυρφόροι was an ancient custom, but this may well be a fabrication inferred from this passage.[2] Pearson's citation of somewhat different

---

[1] Jacob, 435, offers the palaeographically easy εὐχερῶς, but this adverb seems to have little point.

[2] Σ also bring in an explanation of the proverb οὐδὲ πυρφόρος ἐσώθη / ἐλείφθη, which might lead one to believe that our passage was not the only source for this alleged custom. But the explanation is false, under the influence of the theory developed for our passage. Σ says the πυρφόρος was a priest of Ares on each side who began the battle and who was normally sacrosanct. But other evidence shows that the πυρφόρος was a priest charged with maintaining the sacred fire for ritual purposes: he had no connection with starting battles (except in so far as fire would be needed for any fire-prophecy or fire-sacrifice), and either because he was a non-combatant or because he was sacrosanct he survived all but the most ferocious battles. Cf. Xen. *Lac. pol.* 13.2 (Spartan army's πυρφόρος)

customs known from Frazer's *Golden Bough*[1] does not obviate the lack of Greek evidence for such a custom: Lycophr. *Alex.* 1295 is irrelevant, since it is an image of raising a signal-flare denoting enmity, not of dropping a torch to mark commencement of a particular battle; an Apulian vase (Naples 3253, last third of fourth cent.) with Apate holding two torches is relevant only by forced interpretation and circular reasoning.[2] The other explanation wrongly adduced for ἀφείθη has to do with the idiom ἀφιέναι τὴν λαμπάδα. Klotz, for instance, thought that the race described in *Frogs* 129-33 was started by the throwing down of a torch. But although the interpretation of *Frogs* 133 remains uncertain, it is clear that λαμπάδα in 131 is the race of torch-bearers, not the torch itself, and ἀφιεμένην means 'being started'.

1377 Τυρσηνικῆς Etruscan bronzework in general was famous (Critias B2.7-8 West) and the military trumpet was viewed as an Etrurian invention; so in tragedy the Etruscan trumpet is a cliché (*Eum.* 567, *Aj.* 17, *Hcld.* 830, *Rhes.* 988), and in Latin cf. Virg. *Aen.* 8.526 *Tyrrhenusque tubae ... clangor*, Sil. *Pun.* 2.19.

1379 ἤιξαν δράμημα the trumpet is a signal for a charge in battle, but also for the start of a race (1102n.), so the athletic metaphor in δράμημα fits nicely with the range of connotation of the trumpet-blast. The evidence that δράμημα was the older form, liable to be replaced by younger δρόμημα, comes from papyri (*Med.* 1108, Soph. *Ichneut.* fr. 318.80) and indirect tradition (Ion Chius *TrGF* 19 F 1.1) and from its precarious survival as a variant at *Pers.* 247, *OT* 193, *Or.* 1005. δράμημα is unattested in later authors, δρόμημα standard, though not common.

1380-1 for the use of bestial imagery of the brothers cf. 1284-307n. The clash of two warriors like wild boars is reminiscent of *Il.* 7.256-7 (duel

---

and for the proverb Hdt. 8.6, Philo *Mos.* 1.179, Dio Cass. 39.45.4, Gregory Naz. *PG* 35.681, 42, Eust. 893, 14-15 and Zenobius *Cent.* 5.34 (with further refs. cited in *Corpus Par. Gr.*).

1 Cf. Pritchett, *Greek State at War* III.88 n. 158.

2 F. M. Cornford, *Thucydides Mythistoricus* (London 1907) 194-6 (with plate), gives an interpretation of the painting and says the following of the goddess Apate, iconographically assimilated to a Fury: 'Her gesture shows that she is about to perform the ritual act proper to the declaration of war - the act of throwing a burning torch between the combatants [footnote citing ΣPhoen.].' It is not even clear that Apate is about to throw a torch: she may rather be swinging them, as is common in representations of torch-bearing maenads and other female figures. For more on the vase, cf. A. D. Trendall and A. Cambitoglou, *The Red-Figured Vases of Apulia* II (Oxford 1982) 495.

of Hector and Ajax) σύν ῥ' ἔπεσον λείουσιν ἐοικότες ὠμοφάγοισιν, / ἢ συσὶ κάπροισιν, τῶν τε σθένος οὐκ ἀλαπαδνόν; but θήγοντες ἀγρίαν γένυν more specifically recalls the similes at 11.414–18 (416 θήγων λευκὸν ὀδόντα μετὰ γναμπτῇσι γένυσσιν) and 13.471–5 (474–5 ὀφθαλμὼ δ' ἄρα οἱ πυρὶ λάμπετον· αὐτὰρ ὀδόντας / θήγει). The foam on the brothers' beards also has an epic precedent (Il. 20.168–9, lion-simile), but here, as elsewhere in Eur., is also a sign of madness or total loss of control (Her. 934, IT 308, Ba. 1122, cf. Med. 1174). In quoting 1380, Greg. Naz. De Vita Sua 1804–7 (PG 37.1155–6) has κάπροι ... γένυν / ὡς ἂν μιμήσομαί τι τῆς τραγωιδίας / λοξὸν βλέποντες ἐμπύροις τοῖς ὄμμασιν / συνῆπτον κτλ. It is completely ambiguous whether Greg. is signalling that 1806 is his own quasi-tragic line or a borrowing from tragedy. Some nineteenth-century editors put the line in the text (with Valck.'s ἐμπύροισιν ὄμμ.). If it was in late antique texts of *Phoen.*, which I doubt, it should be regarded as spurious, as it divides ἀφρῶι διάβροχοι γεν. from 1380. Statius' boar simile (*Theb.* 11.530–3 fulmineos veluti praeceps cum comminus egit / ira sues strictisque erexit tergora saetis: / igne tremunt oculi, lunataque dentibus uncis / ora sonant) contains characteristic expansion and variation and cannot be used as evidence that his text of *Phoen.* contained λοξὸν κτλ. (for the topos of flashing eyes, often combined with bristling hair, cf. Il. 13.474, Od. 19.446, Ovid *Met.* 8.284).

1381 ξυνῆψαν see 673n. For the absolute use 'join battle', cf. Ba. 52, Hdt. 4.80.2, *Acharn.* 686.

διάβροχοι a word of rather scientific flavour in prose, extant in classical poetry only in Eur. (also El. 503, Ba. 1051); later taken up by Callimachus, Nonnus, and poets in the Anthology.

1382 ἧσσον δὲ λόγχαις for this tentative jabbing with the spear see 1356–424n. Theocritus has this passage in mind (cf. 1233–5n.) as well as epic models when he describes the duel of Castor and Lynceus (22.183–204): note the opening of the duel, 187–8 ἔγχεσι μὲν πρώτιστα τιτυσκόμενοι πόνον εἶχον / ἀλλήλων, εἴ πού τι χροὸς γυμνωθὲν ἴδοιεν.

ὑφίζανον present-stem forms are extant only here and Rhes. 730 ὕφιζ' before Aristotle and later prose; Hdt. has aorist ὑπείσας.

κύκλοις 'shields' (1130n.).

1383 ἐξολισθάνοι μάτην 'slip off and achieve nothing': for this quasi-predicative use of μάτην cf. Barrett on *Hipp.* 916. The present form in -άνω is the older one, metrically guaranteed in Soph. fr. 960 and com. adesp. 222 Kock; there is variation in the mss also at *Knights* 491. ὀλισθάνω is found only here in Eur. (in Soph. also El. 746).

1385 στόματι early commentators followed one Σ in taking this as dative of direction or goal with ἐνώμα, but that construction is harsh in itself and requires that ὄμμα and στόματι be used loosely for 'face', although Eur. is clearly being quite precise in speaking of an eye peering over the rim of the shield (it is like the cliché of gunfights in Westerns: anyone who pokes his head slightly around a corner or above a barrier immediately draws fire). Geel saw that στόματι should be instrumental with προφθῆναι, and the same view is apparently intended by another Σ (ὥστε τοῦτον πλῆξαι τῶι στόματι). στόμα then means 'tip' of the spear, adequately supported by *Il.* 15.389 [ξυστὰ] ναύμαχα κολλήεντα, κατὰ στόμα εἱμένα χαλκῶι (I do not understand Pearson's objection to this parallel; cf. also LSJ s.v. III.1). Pearson and Major instead take στόματι as dat. of direction, 'at edge of the shield', a sense more dubious than the one Pearson objects to (for στόμα, 'edge', see 748n., 1166–7n.).

1386 κεγχρώμασιν probably 'embossed edges'; hapax in extant Greek. Σ are simply guessing when they offer definitions for this word; of the two offered, 'adornment at the rim of the shield' makes sense and 'eye-holes' does not (though accepted by LSJ, Frisk, and Chantraine). Having peered *over* the edge of the shield (there being no eye-holes to look through), the combatant draws his head back down when attacked, bringing his eye back under the protection of the rim (the top of his head is protected by the helmet). The decoration is probably embossing that makes the surface 'grainy' or rough, not golden nails as conjectured by Σ. Cf. A. Snodgrass, *Arms and Armour of the Greeks* (London 1967) 53: 'The whole shield sometimes had a bronze facing, and the rim was invariably faced with bronze, usually with a repoussé cable-decoration.' The root κεγχρ- is used of millet and of other things granular; κερχν-, on the other hand, probably conflates two origins, an alternate form of κεγχρ- with metathesis of nasal and ρ, and an onomatopoeic representation of coughing or hoarseness. Either form could well apply to an uneven embossed or studded surface, and I see no way to determine which Eur. used. For κεγχρ- cf. our mss and Σ, Hsch. κ 1972 κεγχρώμασι· ταῖς περιφερείαις, καὶ τοῖς καταστρώμασιν; for κερχν- cf. Hsch. κ 2371 κερχνώμασι· τραχύσμασι, κυκλώμασι, γαργαλισμοῖς.[1] καλοῦσι δὲ καὶ τὸν περὶ τὰς ἴτυς τῶν ἀσπίδων κόσμον καὶ ποτηρίων ἐπὶ χειλῶν; Soph. fr. 279 (ascription and text disputed: refs. in Radt), Erot. *voc. Hippocr.* κ 8 (p. 48, 9–13 Nachmanson), esp. ἀγγεῖα κερχνώδη, Hsch. κ 1162 s. v. κατακερχνοῦται and κ 2372 κερχνωτά· τετορνευμένα [sic; leg. τετορευμένα?] ἐπὶ τοῦ χείλους τῶν ποτηρίων ... τραχέα. πολύπαστα. Cf. the variants at *Prom.* 676 (Κερχνείας vs. Κεγχρείας).

1388–9 In a subjective and overrationalistic attack on this couplet,

---

[1] This word may not be corrupt, but rather a gloss of a medical use, for a 'tickling', hoarse throat.

Nauck argued that the effect of the report is weakened if the fight is presented as a spectacle (ὁρῶσιν and δρῶσι); he deleted 1389, with πᾶσιν for πλείων in 1388. Wecklein, with a better sense of method, deleted the couplet, alleging that the glimpse at the audience's reaction is a later embellishment (like that in 1370–1, if those lines are spurious). But there are no sufficient grounds for suspicion, not to mention deletion. For the narrative effect[1] of this comment (along with 1395, 1398–9) cf. Thuc. 7.71, a remarkable portrait of the anxiety of the onlookers of the great battle in the harbour of Syracuse. Cf. also the epic use of an imaginary spectator's reaction (Collard on *Su.* 684–7a, 719–20b). For the contrast between participants and onlookers (and greater response of the latter) cf. Aesch. T 149 Radt and Plutarch's comments on *Il.* 7.215–16 in *Mor.* 30A.

φίλων ὀρρωδίαν 'their fear on their friends' behalf'; the context makes unambiguous this poetic extension of the obj. gen. of the type seen in *Od.* 15.8 μελεδήματα πατρός, *Il.* 15.25 ὀδύνη Ἡρακλῆος (K–G 1.335). ὀρρωδία is a strong word, and not common: Hdt. has ἀρρωδίη six times, Thuc. uses ὀρρωδία twice in one passage (2.88.1, 89.1); Eur. is the only poet to use it (*Med.* 317, *Ion* 403, fr. 908.6); then Dem. and late prose.

1390–1 ποδὶ . . . ὑπόδρομον 'brushing aside with his foot a stone that was slipping under his step'; the stone caused unstable footing that could be fatal to Et. in a critical moment, but the sideways movement to push it aside leaves the leg momentarily out of the protection of the shield. μετα- conveys movement from one place to another, 'aside', so the verb is not 'brush against' (LSJ); ὑπόδρομον implies movement (τρέχοντα ὑπὸ τοῦ ἴχνους), the shifting of the loose stone under Et.'s foot, not 'in the way of his foot' (LSJ: so too apparently Pearson, wrongly comparing idiomatic use of ὑποτρέχω in *Knights* 676). μεταψαίρων is hapax, and adj. ὑπόδρομον is almost so (in a different sense *Orph. Arg.* 802).

1393 πληγὴν . . . εἰσιδών Paley compares *Il.* 4.467–9 νεκρὸν γὰρ ἐρύοντα ἰδὼν μεγάθυμος Ἀγήνωρ / πλευρά, τά οἱ κύψαντι παρ' ἀσπίδος ἐξεφαάνθη, / οὔτησε; *Scutum* 334–5; also Theocr. 22.187–8 (quoted 1382n.).

1394 κνήμην . . . δόρυ the conventional pattern of descriptions of wounding in Homer (26n.) makes it likely that δόρυ is the subject of διαπεράω in a normal sense, not the object of rare causative διαπεράω (LSJ s.v. III) with two acc. as in Eubulus 128.2 K–A (but δι- there is 'over, across', not 'through'). It also militates against Blaydes' Ἀργείωι δορί, which also offends by lack of variation with 1390. The acc. is the normal case with διαπεράω (as with περάω in similar senses), and the variant

---

[1] On interspersed comments of this kind, see DeJong, 77 n. 44.

κνήμης is prob. a simplification made by those who took δόρυ as object (for such a constr. cf. 1091-2 ξίφος λαιμῶν διῆκε; in *Aj.* 730 κολεῶν ἐρυστὰ διεπεραιώθη ξίφη the gen. is primarily separative).

1395 ἀνηλάλαξε for this cry of triumph, cf. *Su.* 719-20 (messenger, at the flight of the Thebans before Theseus' onslaught) ἐγὼ δ' ἀνηλάλαξα κἀνωρχησάμην / κἄκρουσα χεῖρας; Astydamas II *TrGF* 60 F 2a.16. The ἀλαλή in battle was the male counterpart of the female ὀλολυγμός (Xen. *Anab.* 4.3.19). Cf. Deubner (1941) 5-6.

1396 κἀν τῶιδε μόχθωι same phrase in messenger-speeches at *Ion* 1196, *Hel.* 1537, in the sense 'while this was going on', of busy activity that distracts from another event (landing of birds, arrival of Greek sailors), not of any particularly toilsome endeavour. We have the same here (Pol. is distracted by the celebration of his friends), rather than 'amid this toil (of the wound he just received)', which would anticipate the force of 1397 ὁ πρόσθε τρωθείς.

εἰσιδών the repetition from 1393 is deliberate, marking the evenness that characterizes the duel throughout (e.g., the two prayers, 1397 ὁ πρόσθε τρωθείς and 1422 ὁ πρόσθε ... πεσών – deliberate parallelism, neither to be deleted).

1397-8 †στέρνα Πολ. βίαι† διῆκε λόγχην the difficulty in this passage is confined, I believe, to this phrase. Many critics object that it is illogical to say that Et. sees a shoulder exposed but aims for the breast. This is not an insuperable problem, since Et. might be thought to raise his arm and direct his spear downward over Pol.'s shield to try to hit a more critical part of his chest. The serious objection, in my view, is that στέρνα διῆκε λόγχην would have to mean 'thrust his spear through Pol.'s chest', not just 'thrust it toward Pol.'s chest' (as Σ allege with λείπει ἡ εἰς, whence Klotz and K–G 1.312) or 'tried to thrust', as Valck. supposed, in defiance of verbal aspect.[1] In addition, such a double acc. with διῆκε is not well established (1092n., 1394n.; Porson proposed λόγχηι here – for such a construction, not found elsewhere with δίημι, cf. 26n.). Wecklein deleted 1397 as a whole, supplying the needed subject by reading τῶιδ' ὁ μοχθῶν in 1396; but even this implies that Et. thrust his spear *through* Pol.'s shoulder (the additional change of διῆκε to ἐφῆκε or εἰσῆκε might help). If the problem of shoulder vs. breast is considered explicable, then Paley's στέρνα Πολ. ἔπι is noteworthy (ἔπι occurs in anastrophe with acc. obj. in six

---

[1] Hartung followed Valck., citing *Aj.* 1126 κτείναντά με, which is not a conative use, but what I would call a 'drastic' use ('as good as killed me'; cf. *Ion* 1499, *Or.* 1512), and is recognized as such by Teucer in his mocking reply.

other places in Eur.), although δι- is then still odd (Paley proposed ἀφῆκε). Stadtmüller's σάρκα Πολ. βίαι seems rather vague, but cf. perhaps 1578. Pearson's στεγνά, supposed to mean 'harness', is palaeographically clever, but introduces a use of the word that is unparalleled and unexpected. If Πολ. is an intrusive gloss and στέρνα corrupt, one may consider phrases that mean 'through to the bone' or the like (e.g. ἐντὸς ὀστέων βίαι). JD suggests that there should be a reference to the thorax, as something that can both be pierced and break the spear-point, comparing *Il.* 17.605-7.

1398 κἀπέδωκεν ἀποδίδωμι is to give back what one has received in trust or to give that which is properly due. Et. may give back delight to his partisans either in the sense that his being wounded had just taken away their pleasure or in the sense that (again with a flavour of athletic competition) delight is what he naturally owes his 'fans'. Herwerden's κἀντέδωκεν is seductive (*Studia critica etc.* [Verh. d. k. Akad. v. Wet., Afd. Lett., 7. Deel (1872) no. 3] 21), but in fact ἀντιδιδόναι ἡδονάς would normally mean 'give pleasure in return to one who has given pleasure to you'.

1400 εἰς δ' ἄπορον ἥκων δορὸς similarly, without the gen., *Hel.* 813 ἐς ἄπορον ἥκεις, and for similar idioms cf. LSJ s.v. ἄπορος II.1. The gen. is separative, as with ἀπορία. The use of anarthrous neuter sing. adj. as abstract substantive with a preposition is a (mainly poetic) device not well treated in the standard grammars: cf. *Hipp.* 785 ἐν ἀσφαλεῖ βίου (with Barrett's note for similar phrases), below 1402 ἐξ ἴσου, S. *El.* 1429 ἐκ προδήλου, etc.

1400-1 ἐπὶ σκέλος πάλιν χωρεῖ cf. *Birds* 383 ἄναγ' ἐπὶ σκέλος and the military idiom in Xenophon, ἐπὶ πόδα ἀναχωρεῖν vel sim. (LSJ s.v. πούς 1.6b), of retreating gradually without turning one's back (cf. esp. *Cyr.* 7.5.6). Schwyzer II.472 lists ἐπὶ πόδα as directional, and the picture suggested is perhaps of the left (forward) foot being drawn back toward the right (rear) foot, as the hoplite backs up a half-step at a time, never putting the left foot behind the right (as this would be clumsy and risky for a line protected by shields carried on the left arm). F. W. Sturz, *Lexicon Xenophonteum* (Leipzig 1801-4) s.v. πούς, translates *pedetentim*, which catches only the gradualness, not the backward direction.

1401 the retreat and use of a stone after the loss of a spear imitate *Il.* 7.263-7, and the phrase μάρμαρον πέτρον is directly borrowed from *Il.* 16.734-5 and occurs nowhere else. In epic battle a stone usually hits a warrior or his armour; to break Pol.'s spear shows either great accuracy or luck. This line and 663 are the only uses of μάρμαρος extant in tragedy; apart from the epic reminiscence, the repetition may suggest that the battle of the brothers in this detail re-enacts the battle of Cadmus and the dragon.

1402 ἐξ ἴσου δ' Ἄρης comm. compare Latin *aequo Marte*; for ἐξ ἴσου (ἐκ τοῦ ἴσου), used in military and other contexts, see LSJ s.v. ἴσος IV.2. Cf. 1400n.

1403 χεῖρ' acc. of the part retained with the passive verb, implying the unattested construction ἀποστερεῖν τινα τὴν χεῖρα τῆς κάμακος; but cf. the retained external object in Thuc. 6.91.7 τὰς προσόδους ἀποστερήσονται (K–G 1.326–7).

1404 ἐνθένδε JD points out to me that there is no parallel for ἔνθεν δέ with backward-looking demonstrative sense: the tragedians use ἔνθεν as sentence-initial demonstrative in asyndeton (as is often the case for backward-looking demonstratives); ἔνθεν δ' in *Tro.* 951 either looks forward or is to be taken as relative.

1405 εἰς ταὐτὸν ἦκον cf. 38 above; εἰς ταὐτὸν ἥκειν is common in Eur. (cf. *Concordance*), more often in the transferred sense 'arrive at the same result'. ἦκον is used with aoristic aspect, as in *Ion.* 1177, *IT* 961; emendation is not needed (Blaydes' ἤιξαν or ἤισαν; West ἤισσον).

1406 ἀμφιβάντ' taken by some as acc. sing. (cf. LSJ), 'they had ⟨the sound of⟩ a great commotion of battle encompassing them'; but this lacks point, and nom. dual interpretation is likely after ἁρπάσαντε and συμβαλόντε. With the nom., some understand the verb of the circling movements, as each brother tries to get around the other's shield (Wecklein: 'indem sie einander umkreisen'), but this would require present, not aorist. The sense must be either 'with legs firmly straddled' (cf. Σ ἀμφοτέροις τοῖς ποσὶ βάντες καὶ στάντες and epic εὖ διαβάς) or 'standing firmly on either side' (cf. Pearson's 'close-locked', *Hcld.* 836 πούς ἐπαλλαχθεὶς ποδί): the face-to-face shoving requires good footing. Herwerden proposed ἀντιβάντ' (1874) or ἄγχι βάντ' (1894).

1407–8 for this couplet and the next five lines, see the discussion of E. K. Borthwick, *JHS* 90 (1970) 17–21, who argues well for recognizing a wrestling move in the language of this passage but comes to other conclusions that I do not share.

καί πως νοήσας ... ὁμιλίαι χθονός 'And somehow having thought of the Thessalian stratagem because he had visited that land, he applied (introduced) it.' σόφισμ' is common object of participle and main verb; the messenger knows how Et. would know of this trick, but cannot say how the idea came into Et.'s mind at this moment.[1] Other interpretations of νοήσας are (1) 'having observed', 'having learned through visiting that

---

[1] Valck. eliminated the messenger's act of guessing by reading κεῦ πως, but Porson pointed out that κεῦ is unattested in drama (I find it extant only in Theocr. 4.31; cf., however, with compounds *Alc.* 292 κεὐκλεῶς, etc.).

land' (Klotz, Wecklein); (2) 'contriving, as a present expedient' (Pearson); (3) 'being alert' (Borthwick). But in (1) πῶς is odd, since it either contradicts the confidence with which the messenger identifies the origin of Et.'s knowledge or must be taken to extend the conjecture to ὁμιλίαι χθονός as well (but πῶς is not που and is too distant from ὁμ. χθ.). For (2) one would expect the present, not the aorist. Note that simplex νοέω is rare in Eur.; the other attested uses are present stem (as for Soph.). (3) apparently requires that νοήσας be taken absolutely.

τὸ Θεσσαλὸν . . . σόφισμ' the article shows that this is a specific, familiar manoeuvre, not a generalizing use of the ethnic adj. for any species of trickery (as one Σ alleges). It must be a feint in wrestling or fencing or both (1409–13n.). Σ's collection of ethnic slurs against the Thessalians (Eur. fr. 426, *Wealth* 521, Dem. 1.22) is thus not relevant. σόφισμα and related verbs are used in later prose of military stratagems (E. L. Wheeler, *Stratagem and the Vocabulary of Military Trickery* [*Mnem* Supp. 108 (Leiden 1988)] 27).

εἰσήγαγεν not LSJ 1.5 'introduce a new custom', as if Et. were an innovative trainer, but rather LSJ ii 'bring forward' into the contest (perhaps with the connotation 'before an audience'), another detail presenting the duel as a spectator-sport.

ὁμιλίαι χθονός Et. is presumed to have spent some time in Thessaly, perhaps implying that the family had ξένοι there, as would be normal for an aristocratic house. This may be an improvisation of Eur., not a curt allusion to something in the epic *Thebais*, as Wecklein proposed. For ὁμιλ- of visiting a place, cf. LSJ s.v. ὁμιλέω vii and the personified collective use in *Eum.* 406 τήνδ' ὁμιλίαν χθονός, 'these visitors to my land'. Not recognizing that in context χθονός should be Thessaly, Σ made desperate attempts to explicate this phrase ('because of love of his fatherland', 'through desire for the kingship', 'bringing aid to his fatherland'). Mosch. glossed with κλίσει, πλησιασμῶι πρὸς τὴν γῆν, taking χθονός to be the ground under Et.'s feet, and Borthwick borrowed part of this in translating 'through familiarity with the terrain'. But, apart from the oddity of ὁμιλία in this juncture, there is no reason for Et. to be particularly familiar with the terrain on which the duel happens to be evolving at this moment, nor for him to be more familiar with it than his brother Pol., nor indeed does the terrain have anything to do with the manoeuvre he uses.

1409–13 Borthwick explains how the shifting of feet from the normal position (with left foot and left side forward) can confuse the opponent and draw him into an attack that might leave an opening for a lunge. In karate a sudden 180-degree shift of stance is supposed to upset an opponent. Yet Eur. does not give us quite enough detail to be certain how Et. gets around Pol.'s defences and lands the fatal blow. The 'trick' presumably consists in, first, giving the appearance of retreat: Et. backs away from the pressure of the clashing shields (τοῦ παρεστῶτος πόνου) and retreats with a movement similar to that in 1400–1. Then there follows a sudden lunge, right leg advancing (προβὰς δὲ κῶλον δεξιόν). When withdrawing his left foot, Et. must be careful that his shield does not turn to the left and leave an opening for a blow to his abdomen (just below his breastplate?). But Pol. is apparently not equally careful when he reacts to his brother's movement.

Borthwick cites evidence for the connection of Thessaly and wrestling-technique, and if wrestling is alluded to, then the terms σόφισμα, πόνος, ἀμφέρει, and προβάς also have parallels in the language of wrestling. In general see also M. Poliakoff, *Studies in the Terminology of Greek Combat Sports* [Beitr. z. kl. Philologie, 146 (Königstein 1982)], who regrettably does not treat this passage. But the terms are rather general, and it cannot be ruled out that Eur. is alluding instead to competitive sword-fighting, which was not an event of regular athletic games, but was practised (with tipped weapons) as part of military training: cf. 1356–424n.; Poliakoff, *Studies* 88–100, and *Combat Sports in the Ancient World* (New Haven 1987) 7, 164 n. 1.[1]

1410 ἀμφέρει for my preference for the form with *apokope* see 297n. μεταφέρει would scan (with change to τοὔπισθε), but is clearly a gloss: for ἀνα- cf. 1400–1 πάλιν χωρεῖ, and ἀναχωρεῖν, etc. in the idioms cited *ad loc*. Castor uses a similar manoeuvre in Theocr. 22.197–8 (ὑπεξαναβὰς ποδὶ ... σκαιῶι), but as a defensive move.

1411 τὰ κοῖλα γαστρὸς εὐλαβούμενος εὐλαβεῖσθαι usually takes as object a harmful thing one guards against, but Eur. affects a construction in which the object is that which is well guarded: so also *Or.* 699 καιρὸν εὐλαβούμενος (which LSJ glosses 'watch for', but this is an extension of 'preserve', 'guard'). The abdomen thus cannot be Pol.'s, as Powell thought. τὰ κοῖλα γαστρός is a poetic paraphrase for κοιλίαν, probably too colloquial for tragedy (anatomical term in medical writers; 'gut' or 'tripe' in comedy).

1412 προβάς ... κῶλον a somewhat precious variant on the βαίνειν πόδα idiom, surpassed by *Or.* 1470 ἀρβύλαν προβάς: see 1536–8n.

1413 καθῆκεν apparently implies a downward thrust over the top of Pol.'s shield when he is surprised by Et.'s sudden advance; cf. *Her.* 993 (of

---

[1] I am grateful to Prof. Roberta Park and Dr Ken Min of the Department of Physical Education at Berkeley for advice on this manoeuvre: they note that such a movement is likely to be found in all combative sports, but agree that it sounds more like fencing than anything else.

a blow with a club). But Borthwick attractively suggests that κατα- may refer instead to the depth of penetration of the sword in the body.[1]

σφονδύλοις τ' ἐνήρμοσεν cf. *Her.* 179 πλευροῖς πτήν' ἐναρμόσας βέλη, probably a Eur. juncture. Among poets only Eur. (*El.* 841) and comedy use σφόνδυλος/σπόνδυλος, but σφονδύλιον appears with the same meaning once each in Homer and Antimachus.

1416 ὡς κρατῶν δή the particles express irony (873n.).

1417 δικών see 665n. The use of the verb here may hint again at the present duel as a renewal of ancient events.

1418 τὸν νοῦν πρὸς αὐτὸν οὐκ ἔχων, ἐκεῖσε δέ 'not paying attention to himself, but to that task [πρὸς τὸ σκυλεύειν νιν]', that is, not being careful to protect himself. From ancient times interpreters have wavered between this view and, with αὐτόν, 'not paying attention to Pol., but to that task'. But the latter provides a poor antithesis, since Pol. is included implicitly in ἐκεῖσε; I would expect a stronger pronoun than αὐτόν if such a contrast were intended. The former, however, follows up the hint of Et.'s lack of awareness in 1416 ὡς ... δή. For the type of expression cf. *Trach.* 272–3 (a distracted Iphitus easily waylaid by Heracles) τότ' ἄλλοσ' αὐτὸν ὄμμα, θατέραι δὲ νοῦν / ἔχοντ'; for ἐκεῖσε,˜above 360n. and Diggle on *Phaethon* 265.

1419 ὃ καί 'and this is what tripped him up'; responsive καί as in 155 above, but here with ὅ = 'which'. ἔσφηλ' continues the athletic metaphors, as perhaps does πεσήματι (cf. πτῶμα in *Prom.* 919). Paus. 4.8.7 tells of a battle between Messenians and Lacedaemonians in which many of the victors were killed by the dying as they tried to strip their armour.

ἔτι ... ἐμπνέων βραχύ cf. *Alc.* 205 (σμικρὸν ... ἔτι), *Hipp.* 1246 (βραχὺν δὴ βίοτον ... ἔτι); *Ba.* 1132 (ὅσον ἐτύγχαν' ἐμπνέων (Reiske)). In this sense, ἐμπνέω is not treated as a compound of ἐν and πνέω, but as a quasi-denominative from ἔμπνοος = ἐν ὧι πνεῦμά ἐστι.

1421 μόλις μέν, ἐξέτεινε δ' for the ellipsis (or better ἀπὸ κοινοῦ construction (JD)) cf. *Ant.* 1105 μόλις μέν, καρδίας δ' ἐξίσταμαι, *Clouds* 1363.

1422 this line artfully rounds out the periodic sentence begun at 1419 ἔτι γάρ, containing the two names and marking the equality of doom as the apparent victor is brought low by ὁ πρόσθε ... πεσών (which also purposefully recalls 1397). Deletion (Paley, Paulson) would be folly.

---

[1] Prof. Park (previous note) tells me that plunging down with the sword would be mechanically difficult, although not impossible; an upward stroke is more usual with a lunge.

1423 γαῖαν δ' ὀδὰξ ἑλόντες a close imitation of *Il.* 22.17 γαῖαν ὀδὰξ εἷλον (similar phrases 2.418, 11.749). The other extant imitations (Lycophr. *Alex.* 1005–6, Ap. Rh. 3.1393) are not so close.

1424 κοὐ διώρισαν κράτος effectively underlines the futility of the duel and anticipates the argument that is to arise among the survivors (1460–4). I see no attraction in Denniston's καὶ διώρισαν (also in gE), 'and divided up the sovereignty' (*CR* 50 (1936) 116).

1425 pers. not. the ascription of the couplet to Creon in late antiquity derived from the false reading σὸς ὤν, where gender and sense pointed away from the coryphaeus as speaker. It was not the proposal of someone worried about Creon's long silence (1308–53n.), as Fraenkel suggested.

κακῶν σῶν goes with στένω, as in *Prom.* 397–8 στένω σε τᾶς οὐλομένας τύχας, *Hipp.* 1409 στένω σε . . . τῆς ἁμαρτίας, not with φεῦ φεῦ, as proposed when the end of the line was not yet corrected.

σ' presumably enclitic; for the position after the vocative, cf. Barrett on *Hipp.* 327 (vocative in second position), *Hcld.* 981 (vocative in later position, as here (JD)); also 557n. above.

1426 ἀρὰς . . . ἐκπλῆσαι the usual verb for 'bring ⟨a curse⟩ to fulfilment' is κραίνω, as in 70 above, *Prom.* 910–11; cf. also *Se.* 946 ἀρὰν πατρώιαν τιθεὶς ἀλαθῆ. Here the verb elsewhere used of the person who fulfills his duty or destiny (*El.* 1290, *IT* 90, etc.) is applied to the god instead. The prominence of the curse before and after the first rhesis prepares for the references to it in Antigone's lament (and in Oed.'s review of his life, 1610–14?).

1427–79 for the separation of the aftermath from the narrative of the fight itself, cf. the messenger-scene surviving in Soph. *Eurypylus* fr. 210: a rhesis describing the death of Eurypylus in battle is followed by a seventeen-line kommos (Astyoche and chorus), then a question about the fate of his corpse, then a second rhesis. The second rhesis begins with a general summary (49 οὐκ ἐς τοσοῦτον ἦλθον ὥστ' ἐπεγχανεῖν, which should be punctuated with a colon), then the narrative follows in asyndeton, beginning ἐπεὶ πάλαισμα κοινὸν ἠγωνισμένοι / ἔκειντο νεκροὶ τυτθὸν ἀλλήλων ἄπο. The present rhesis aims for a dignified pathos in the description of the deaths: 1428–59 are neither long-winded nor over-concise; direct speech is quoted three times; the gestures of hands and looks of eyes are carefully delineated; and the speaker's evaluative terms are few but telling (1429 τάλαινα, 1438 δύσθνητον, 1454 ἄθλιον, 1456 ὑπερπαθήσασ', 1457 δεινά). It is striking that Pol. is again allowed to speak, showing his split feelings (1445–6) and appealing for a forgiveness that Et. has spitefully forestalled (if 774–7 are accepted). Et., in contrast, though appearing here at his most sympathetic, is not allowed to speak, and his gesture of friendship seems directed exclusively at his mother. The heavy concentration of kinship-words in these lines is also noteworthy (twenty-four in thirty-one lines).

There is then an element of ironic juxtaposition in the return (1460-79) to the squabbling of the two armies over the outcome and the (not entirely noble) manner of the final defeat of the Argives. Through the brothers' lack of foresight in setting the conditions of the duel, the mutual fratricide leads to a renewal of ἔρις (1460, 1462) between the armies, who were supposed to have been spared further bloodshed. Some see this second Theban victory as entirely humanly motivated (see, however, 1466n.) and thus in sharp contrast to the victory assured by Menoeceus' sacrifice. Conacher goes so far as to detect a devaluing of Men.'s sacrifice and of the divine element in events.[1] The brothers seem to act in ignorance of the oracle and Men.'s heroic deed, but that reflects as much on their blind absorption in their own interests as on the importance of his deed. Nevertheless, the σωτηρία-theme had been played out in the previous episode and does not reappear here to create a competition for the role of saviour (though the city's safety is implicit in the final summation, 1478 εὐτυχέστατοι). If Creon's presence at the opening of this episode is genuine, then we have a final reminder of Men. before the focus shifts to the fate of the family. At the end, since the mutual fratricide is consonant with divine causation, an audience may interpret the Theban victory as the full pay-off of Men.'s sacrifice. Alternatively, Eur. may be playing with the notion that through their blindness and tendency toward dispute and violence the humans outrun the gods' ability to control events (as happens, but more obviously, in *Ion*). If the contrast between Men.'s sacrifice and the final victory is felt to be striking, one may compare the ironies of *IA*, where the audience seems to be guided to acknowledge the purity and nobility of Iphigenia's sentiments at the same time that they are shown the cynicism and unworthiness of the politician/warriors who benefit from it.

In this rhesis the text is again widely accepted as authentic: 1430 is almost universally condemned, and 1465 has been the object of a long controversy.

---

[1] Cf. the similar questions raised by Foley, 110; but I do not agree that the efficacy of Men.'s action is brought into doubt by Creon's continued selfishness ('the piety of Menoeceus has in fact set no abiding example for the rulers of Thebes') or by the failures of the other characters ('If Menoeceus' idealism has achieved precisely nothing in reconciling public and private interests, how can his ritual death have contributed to the city's actual salvation?'). Note that despite these doubts Foley later argues for 'the power of Menoeceus' sacrifice to redirect, however mysteriously, the action to its mythical tradition'.

1428 variant ὡς γάρ avoids asyndeton and so is probably secondary. The remaining confusion in the tradition was prob. occasioned by accidental substitution of παῖδε for τέκνω (16n.) and transposition to fix the metre; but it is not impossible that πεσόντε παῖδ' may be the original.

1429 προσπίτνει 'comes (suddenly?) upon the scene'; since προσπίτνουσα is used in 1433 in its common sense 'fall upon to embrace', emendations have been proposed here (the best is Harberton's ἐπεσπίτνει, but it is a little too violent a verb). But the repetition is not necessarily objectionable, and for the sense here cf. *Phil.* 46 μὴ καὶ λάθηι με προσπεσών (cf. 156).

[1430] the zeugma 'with maiden daughter and eagerness of foot' can only be comic, and the phrasing of 1435 suggests that that is the first mention of Ant. in this rhesis. It seems to me more likely that the line is a non-histrionic expansion of a marginal notation σὺν παρθένωι than a histrionic attempt to insert references to Ant. (cf. 1264–83n., 1323n., 1465n.). προθυμίαι ποδός is like σπουδῆι ποδός in *Hec.* 216, *Rhes.* 85, σπ. βημάτων in *Andr.* 880.

1431 καιρίους σφαγάς internal acc. retained with passive verb (K–G 1.326). καίριος is optionally of two or three terminations in tragedy: cf. *Choe.* 1064, *Phil.* 637 vs. *Ag.* 1292, *OT* 631.

1432 βοηδρόμος extant five times in Eur.; he also affects βοηδρομέω, which is also found in Aesch. fr. 46c.6, *Rhesus*, and later authors. Note the piquant use of the quasi-military term for Joc.'s mission of reconciliation, and cf. the use of παρασπίζουσ' of Ant. in 1435.

1433 προσπίτνουσα . . . τέκνα one might expect the dative, as in *Med.* 1205 προσπίτνει νεκρῶι, but both dat. and acc. are attested for the sense 'fall before/upon to supplicate' and *Ba.* 1115 προσπίτνει νιν is a relevant parallel, even though Agave's 'falling upon' her son is hostile. Stadtmüller proposed προσπτύσσουσα, removing repetition (1429) and the rare syntax.

1434 ἔκλαι', ἐθρήνει for the schema see 1193n.

μαστῶν πόνον cf. 30n. Joc. alludes to the particular functions that define the familial relation: her nurture of the helpless babies, and the expected return of nurture in old age (1436 γηροβοσκῶ). With nineteenth-century embarrassment, Nauck and Herwerden (*Mnem* 5 (1877) 34–5) preferred μάτην to μαστῶν, which would be both less pathetic and less clear (contrast the clarity of the topos in *Med.* 1029–30, 1261–2, *Her.* 901–3, *Tro.* 381, 760, cited by Diggle (1990a)).

1435 παρασπίζουσ' ὁμοῦ for the military term cf. 1432n. ὁμοῦ is not pleonastic with παρ-, but rather reinforces θ' in the ellipsis of 'cried, lamented'.

1436 edd. print this as Ant.'s words alone, allowing her to speak both of the betrayed filial duty to their mother and the betrayed brotherly duty to herself. But as Diggle (1989) noted (and earlier Geel, in his note, but not shown in his text), mother and daughter speak separately here, quoted directly with asyndeton (so too the two armies in *Su.* 702; cf. *Held.* 839–40).

γηροβοσκώ cf. 1434n.; the preferred classical prose words seem to have been γηροτροφέω and -ία (cf. τροφεῖα), while γηροβοσκ- and γηροκομ- and γηροτρόφος are variations better attested in poets, esp. Eur. (γηροβοσκός in classical prose, Xen. *Oec.* 4.1.13, 19, Hyperides fr. 233).

1436–7 γάμους ἐμοὺς προδόντ' just as the mother expects support in her old age from her son, so the sister has a right to expect that, with the death or incapacitation of the father, her brother(s) will provide for her placement in a legitimate marriage. In dying, the brothers leave her exposed to the whim of a more distant relative, and even if a marriage has been arranged (as here), they will be absent from a ceremony and a celebration that they should normally have attended. Hence the notion of betrayal (cf. Joc.'s lament at 337–49), an extreme of the reproach of abandonment, which is typical of traditional lamentation (Alexiou, 182–4 and index s.v. reproach).

1438 δύσθνητον hapax in extant Greek; cf. δυσθνήισκων (only Eur. *El.* 843, *Rhes.* 791); δυσθανατέω (somewhat more common); δυσθάνατος (*Ion* 1051, Hippocrates). The gloss δυσέκπνευστον and the corruption δύστλητον (a more obvious formation, but itself uncommon – add to LSJ Lycophr. *Alex.* 1281, Paulus Sil. *Anth. gr.* 7.560) indicate that M should be trusted here and that Hermann (who knew of M, but had an insufficient estimate of its value) need not have conjectured δυσθνήισκον. The verbal adj. in -τος means 'involving hard dying' and is perfectly apt as an epithet of φύσημα.

1439 ὑγρὰν χέρα best taken as 'flaccid', 'infirm', 'weak', reflecting Et.'s closeness to death (so first Heath and Musgrave); other interpretations include 'wet with blood', 'clammy with sweat (of the dying)', 'not yet stiff (with death)'. No suitable sense can be given to the variant λυγράν (contrast *Su.* 70 λυγρὰ μέλη, with Collard's note).

1442 ἔτ' ἔμπνους see 1419n., LSJ s.v. I.

1444 Ἀπωλόμεσθα like ἀπωλόμην, this is commonly used in Eur. (and once in Soph.) as a cry of despair with a meaning hardly different from the perfect, 'I am/we are undone'; the aorist is perhaps metrically more convenient, or perhaps it emphasizes the irrevocability of the action that has caused the ruin.

1446 a concise and paradoxical line (understand ὤν with first φίλος, ἐστι with the second), recalling Pol.'s earlier expressions of divided feelings (261–444n., 272n., 1652n.).

1447-50 even the critics most willing to posit interpolation in the exodos and related changes in the second episode had not, up to 1990, doubted this passage, with its clear allusion to the pre-existing story of the conflict over the burial of Pol. Those who delete the burial-theme take this as a passing allusion with no wider reference, just as they suggest that Ant.'s role in the teichoskopia, 1265-83, and in this narrative has the limited function of exposition and suitable mourning (so, most recently, Willink). Hose, 'Exodos' 69-70, has finally suggested deletion of these four lines for total elimination of the burial-motif (cf. Willink's desire to remove 944-6 and the instances cited in the footnote to 774-7n.). There is no fault in the lines; the reduced speech is remarkably less pathetic; and 1451 follows oddly on 1446.

1448-9 πόλιν . . . παρηγορεῖτον 'soothe by persuasion', 'use soothing persuasion on', a medical connotation of παρηγορ- seen in *Eum.* 507, *Pers.* 530 (with acc. object, as here most mss against dative in VRfRv), Aesch. fr. 348, *TrGF* adesp. 464a, and prob. *Hec.* 288.

γοῦν in its limitative sense, clearly the apt particle here; variant δή may be the simplification of someone who mistook the tone.

1450 Teles the Cynic (Stob. 3.40.8), in criticizing the conventional values that consider burial important, uses Pol. as his straw-man (cf. 395n. for Pol. as object of philosophical criticism). After quoting 1447-50 he asks εἰ δὲ μὴ τύχηις [-οις Gaisford] χθονὸς πατρώιας, ἀλλ' ἐπὶ ξένης ταφήσηι [-είης Halm], τί ἔσται τὸ διάφορον; ἢ ἐκ Θηβῶν μόνον [Gesner: μὲν codd.] εἰς Ἅιδου ὁ Χάρων πορθμεύει; Then he continues καὶ γῆς φίλης [-οις L] ὄχθοισι κρυφθῆι καὶ τάφωι· εἰ δὲ μὴ κρυφθείης, ἀλλὰ ἄταφος ⟨ῥιφθείης⟩, τί τὸ δυσχερές; ἢ τί διαφέρει ὑπὸ πυρὸς κατακαυθῆναι ἢ ὑπὸ κυνὸς καταβρωθῆναι ἢ ἐπάνω τῆς γῆς ὄντα ὑπὸ κοράκων, ἢ κατορυχθέντα ὑπὸ σκωλήκων; There follow 1451-52a and criticism of that request too. The underlined words are close to *TrGF* adesp. 281, quoted by Crantor (Diog. Laert. 4.25: ἐν γῆς . . . κρυφθῆναι καλόν). Many have inferred from this sequence that Teles read such a line interpolated into his text of *Phoen.*, but Hense remarks *diversa miscent Cynici haud raro*. The line would be poorly integrated with the text if καλόν is read, and even worse if τάφωι is kept (as by Hermann, who even thought the line possibly authentic). The inf. cannot be an explication of τοσόνδε, 'receive this much *from* my father-land', for the pronoun is object of τύχω and governs partitive χθονός (as Teles correctly understood).

1451 βλέφαρά μου the word-order μου βλέφαρα (Teles and the late gnomologies) is metrically permissible (monosyllabic enclitic following caesura, as in 852 above), but the enclitic pronoun may have been drawn to its common position after δέ.

1453 περιβάλλει σκότος another epic reminiscence, varying the formulae with σκότος covering (καλύπτειν) the eyes; elsewhere in tragedy only *Hipp.* 1444, fr. 806.3.

1456 ὑπερπαθήσασ' hapax in classical Greek (later in Josephus, 'Aesop', and Tzetzes).

ἥρπασ' ἐκ νεκρῶν the vigorous verb and the indefinite plural are clearly correct here; on the variants see *Text. Trad.* 52.

1457 κἄπραξε δεινά · ... γάρ for this rhetorical highlighting of the brutal detail, cf. *Med.* 1167-8 τοὐνθένδε μέντοι δεινὸν ἦν θέαμ' ἰδεῖν· χροιὰν γὰρ κτλ, *OT* 1267-8. In having Joc. use a weapon from her dead sons, Eur. may have had in mind Oed.'s snatching of the brooch for self-blinding from Joc.'s corpse in *OT*.

1458-9 mark the fulfilment of Joc.'s promise συνθανοῦσα κείσομαι in 1283 as well as recall the union of the dead Spartoi with their mother earth (673n.); cf. 1687n.

1460 ἀνῇξε δ' ὀρθός 'leapt to their feet', a common juncture (*Hel.* 1600, *Ba.* 693, *Rhes.* 792); it is implied that the onlookers were seated, like spectators.

1461-2 ἡμεῖς μὲν ... οἱ δ' the partitive apposition and the acc. absolutes with ὡς (serving in place of indirect discourse, whether this is the origin of the construction or not: K-G II.94 Anm. 5, 95-6; Schwyzer II.402-3) follow by sense from εἰς ἔριν λόγων, as if it were, e.g., ἀμφισβητῶν.

1462-4 ἔρις στρατηλάταις, οἱ μὲν ... οἱ δ' here the nom. follows as if after οἱ στρατηλάται ἤριζον: see Jebb on *Ant.* 259, K-G II.107. Note the artful variation in the indirect-discourse constructions. The soldiers simply argue, but the leaders try to make up for the incompleteness of the rules set before the duel, by referring to first blood or by conceding that one cannot determine a victor. θανόντων οὐδαμοῦ νίκη πέλοι is a final bitter assessment of the brothers' ambitions and lust for victory: taking θανόντων as gen. abs. without expressed noun and οὐδαμοῦ as local (so Paley), 'now that they are dead, victory is on neither side, nowhere to be found'. Pearson preferred 'victory is of no account', but in the cited parallels the transferred sense of valuation is supported by contextual clues that are absent here.

1465 This line should not be deleted from its context. Valck. deleted, but assumed that it had ousted a genuine line. He (1) thought Ant. would not have left the bodies and Eur. would not have referred to her at this point; (2) alleged that ἐν τῷδ' was borrowed from 1396; and (3) claimed that ὑπεξῆλθ' ... στρατοῦ δίχα was bad or inept Greek. Wecklein thought (4) that what is said of Ant. in 1476 showed that 1465 is spurious. Argument (2) is illegitimate in method (62n.). (3) is simply wrong: the meaning is 'withdrew (unnoticed and unmolested? cf. ὑπεκπέμπω, ὑπεκτίθημι), going apart from the ⟨quarrelling⟩ army', with a normal tragic pleonasm in combining δίχα with ὑπεξ- (cf. *Her.* 104 ἐξίσταται ... ἀπ' ἀλλήλων δίχα, *Ion* 775, fr. 484.3). (1) is entirely subjective. It would not be at all uncharacteristic for a Euripidean messenger to include such a minor detail in order to indicate briefly how the maiden was not hurt in the tumult. If 1465 precedes, 1476 simply informs us that after the dust of battle settles Ant. is reunited with the bodies for re-entry into Thebes. There is no contradiction (4). The grounds for suspicion are thus very weak, and as Valck. himself saw, removal of 1465 produces an impossible sequence of pronouns: οἱ δ' in 1466 should mean 'the men of the two armies', and it means that clearly and idiomatically only if the different subject Ἀντιγόνη precedes, but not if it follows directly on οἱ μὲν ... οἱ δ' (referring to Argive and Theban generals respectively). Nevertheless, deleting 1465 without a lacuna, Hartung took οἱ δ' of the Argives only (in his note; but his trans. is 'zu den waffen rennt man'), and Wecklein took it as 'milites utriusque exercitus'.[1]

ὑπεξῆλθ' this verb appears here only in classical poetry (false reading in Soph. fr. 757.2), but the same is true of other ὑπεκ- compounds (in Eur. -ακρίζω, -αντλέω, -βαίνω, -λαμβάνω), and the rarity of the word has, in my view, no relevance to the question of authorship.

1466 εὖ δέ πως προμηθίαι like τις/τι accompanying an adj., πως attached to an adverb may serve to soften or to strengthen it (K–G II.663-4): e.g., ὧδέ πως, 'in a manner somewhat like this', vs. κάλλιστα πως, 'extremely finely'. For εὖ πως, *Hec.* 902 and *IA* 66 may be emphatic, 'very well', but other Eur. instances (*Hipp.* 477, *Hel.* 712 (see Kannicht), 1126 above) are certainly softened expressions. If the indefinite, softening force is intended here, the messenger is suggesting that the origin of the προμηθία is unclear (which allows the audience to think either of divine guidance lurking in the background[2] or of the operation of inexplicable chance). Thus Barnes translates *bene quadam providentia*. I prefer this interpretation to 'and very well, with forethought', which would imply a confident ascription of forethought that does not consort well with the confusion described in 1460-4.

1467 καθῆστο ... ἀσπίδων ἔπι for the verb form cf. K–B II.228. The general sense is clear (the Thebans were able to get into their armour more quickly than the Argives), but ἀσπίδων ἔπι has been variously interpreted:

---

[1] So in the 1872 revision of Klotz's comm.; in his 1894 comm. his note on 1464 is apparently meant to go with 1466 ('οἱ δέ, die Argiver oder vielmehr die Mannen beiderseits' – the equivocation glosses over the difficulty). Helmbold suggested deleting 1463-7, but 1468 follows very poorly on 1462, and the accumulation of οἱ μὲν ... οἱ δ' to which he objects is strange only if 1465 is deleted. JD points out that οἱ δ' in 1466 can be understood if 1463-4 are deleted along with 1465 (Harberton).

[2] Contrast Foley, 109: 'This act of *promethia* (forethought, 1466) hardly suggests a further imprint of divinity on the battle.'

(a) literally, 'sitting upon their shields' (Valck., improbably suggesting that the Thebans were cunningly concealing their shields); (b) 'under arms', as opposed to setting arms aside (Pearson, comparing Xen. *Hell*. 2.4.12, where a force is said τὸ θέσθαι τὰς ἀσπίδας to open negotiations, but keep the rest of their armour on; cf. LSJ s.v. ἐπί A.I.2a); (c) 'in fighting lines' (Powell, citing Thuc. 7.79.1 παρατεταγμένην οὐκ ἐπ' ὀλίγων ἀσπίδων, 'lined up ⟨in rows⟩ several shields deep', a passage that was erroneously cited by earlier comm. for (b); same idiom *Lys*. 282, Xen. *Hell*. 2.4.11, 6.4.12, 6.5.19). (c) is disproved by καθῆστο and by the spirit of the truce. (b) may be right, but there seems to be no parallel. To remain with arms at the ready is elsewhere μένειν ἐπὶ τοῖς ὅπλοις (Xen. *Cyr*. 7.2.8; poetic version *Su*. 674, 357 ἐφ'/παρ' ὅπλοις ἧσθαι). Perhaps Valck. was close to the truth after all, if the gen. with ἔπι means 'by, near' (LSJ A.I.1 *ad fin*.) and implies that the Thebans removed their armour, but had it closer to hand than the Argives, who may have piled it to one side, creating confusion and delay when all rushed to get it at once. Cf. *Il*. 3.135, where the soldiers who are at ease during the truce, having taken off their armour (3.114), are described as ἀσπίσι κεκλιμένοι.[1]

1468 πεφαργμένον 733n.

1470–1 πεδία δ' ἐξεπίμπλασαν φεύγοντες cf. *Su*. 722–3 ἱερά τ' ἐξεπίμπλασαν / φόβωι, *IT* 324 φυγῆι λεπαίας ἐξεπίμπλαμεν νάπας.

αἷμα μυρίων νεκρῶν JD reminds me to consider the appeal of μυρίον (**rχ**): it produces a balance of nouns and modifiers, and the singular is a more exquisite, rarer use than the plural.

1472 ἐνικῶμεν the present stem of νικάω often has perfective force, as here, 'were victorious', 'were the victors' (cf. Pindaric usage and the Attic didascaliae, ἐνίκα Αἴσχυλος, etc.), not imperfective 'were winning' (Craik), though the latter is correct in 1143 above.

1473 Διὸς τροπαῖον . . . βρέτας cf. 572n., 1250–1.

1476–7 for the preparation for the next entrance cf. 1308–53n. and *Andr*. 1158–9 (quoted 1316n.: dative σοι there is like φίλοις here, the proper case accompanying the verb of carrying and the inf. of purpose).

1478–9 ἀγῶνες οἱ μὲν . . . οἱ δέ The scene ends with a striking rhyming couplet with artfully interlaced cola. The contest between Theban and Argive armies has twice been won by the Thebans, but the contest of the brothers (the second plural is due to rhetorical balance) had an unhappy

---

[1] Similarly, Themistius *Or*. 2, 37a, actually uses κεκλιμένοι ἐπὶ τῶν ἀσπίδων for soldiers at ease: ἐξαρκεῖ δὲ αὐτῶι [the philosopher-king] πολλάκις ὁ λόγος ἀντὶ τῶν ὅπλων καὶ τῶν στρατιωτῶν, καὶ οἱ μὲν ὁπλῖται ἑστήκασι κεκλιμένοι ἐπὶ τῶν ἀσπίδων, οἱ δὲ ἱππεῖς ἐγκεχαλινωμένοι τοὺς ἵππους, οἱ δὲ τοξόται τὰ τόξα ἀνέντες, οἱ δὲ σφενδονῖται χαλάσαντες τὰς σφενδόνας.

end. The paraphrase in the first Σ on this couplet is prob. simply a loose one, not evidence for the complex corruption supposed by Kock's τῆι μὲν ... τῆι δέ with οἷδ' for τῆιδ'. I see no justification for Helmbold's suggestion that this couplet be deleted.

1480–581: ARIA OF ANTIGONE, DUET OF ANTIGONE AND OEDIPUS

The messenger's rhesis is followed immediately by the entrance of Ant. accompanying the three corpses carried on litters by silent extras dressed as soldiers. If the opening of the previous scene is genuine, then Creon steps back or toward the side to allow the bodies and Ant. to become the centre of attention. The choral anapaests announcing the entrance replace the usual reaction to the speech itself. Cf. 1308–53n.

The emotional climax of the play is marked by a lyric effusion of grief, structurally balancing the lyric scenes of the first part of the play. The threnetic aria (1485–529) serves as a counterweight to and renewal of the partially joyous, partially grieving aria of Jocasta (301–54). The aporetic rhetoric of joy (312–17) is here matched by a similar rhetoric of grief; the physical symbols of mourning (322–6) are presented in a new context; and the concentration on Polynices is again evident. There are also parallelisms of thought and expression involving the δαίμων which afflicts the house (351–3 ~ 1495–6, 1503–4), the sounds of mourning (335–6 ~ 1519–21), and the surplus of evils (354 ~ 1511–13). The duet, on the other hand, recalls and reverses the situation of the teichoskopia: there Antigone is in need of the guidance and protection of an old man, is full of questions, and freely expresses almost childlike emotions; here she has matured to independence by the force of disaster, responds to the questions of the old man who is her partner in the duet, and articulates the griefs and serious reactions of an adult.

The first part of the scene shifts naturally among three topics: self-presentation as a mourner (1485–92, 1502, 1519–22); announcement and interpretation of the disaster (1493–7, 1504–7); the aporetic rhetoric of grief (1498–501, 1509–19, 1524–9). In the second part Oedipus, who has been mentioned repeatedly during the play as present in the house and affected by events (66, 88, 327ff., 376–8 (if genuine), 611, 614, 873–7, 1088–9), is finally summoned forth, his feeble ghostlike condition evoked in both the summons and his response (1530–45). He then receives the news in a lyric reworking (1546ff.) of the material already presented by the messenger. The climax is a beautiful passage of striking style and imagery presenting in even more pathetic terms the suicide of Jocasta as an act of solidarity with her unfortunate sons.

THE AUTHENTICITY OF THE SCENE

Verrall's fantastic theory that Antigone had no role in Eur.'s play entails the spuriousness of this lyric scene in which she plays such a large role. The important functions and effects of Antigone's role have already been explained in the discussion of 88–201 above (also 1264–83n.), so that we may safely reject Verrall's doubts (shared until recently only by Norwood). Nor has anything substantial been adduced against this scene in Dihle's recent study (pp. 92–7). Claiming to follow Fraenkel's strictures against the final scenes of the play, Dihle argues that in the transmitted form 1485–766 can hardly present the end of the play as composed by Eur. Fraenkel, however, regarded 1485–581 as an integral part of the Euripidean original.[1] Dihle (p. 36) also misdates the Strassburg papyrus (Π⁵) by two centuries, an error without which his theory that Hellenistic theatre-practice has contaminated our book-text tradition after the time of Aristophanes of Byzantium loses much of its already scant plausibility.

As for details, in a passage of almost 100 lines Dihle has real doubts about only two passages, 1533–5 and 1570–4 (for the unusual use of ἐπινωμάω in 1564 Dihle himself cites the appropriate parallel: see *ad loc.*). The latter passage is also suspected by Diggle, who proposes deletion of 1570–6 from the context, which he takes (I believe) to be genuine. Both passages are indeed difficult, but insufficient to support a wholesale rejection of 1485–581. In 1533–5 Dihle argues that ἐπὶ δώμασιν is to be understood as a dative of direction and that βαλών refers to the emission of vision-rays from Oedipus' eyes. He paraphrases 'auf der Haus hat er ein für alle Mal Dunkelheit statt erhellender, Erkenntnis bewirkender Sehstrahlen "geworfen"'; but σκότον by itself hardly suggests in such a context 'darkness *instead of bright rays*', and the sense which Dihle desires would more naturally be expressed with present participle βάλλων and with the complement 'from your eyes' rather than 'with your eyes'. The passage must

---

[1] Cf. Fraenkel, 76, where Creon's order to cease the lament (1485–581) is used to support the deletion of Creon's appearance at 1308ff.; also 86: 'Danach kommt mit Antigone, die den blinden Vater geleitet [sic!], der Zug der drei Leichen auf die Bühne. In dem Kommos, der aus dieser Situation herauswächst (1485–1581), bilden die Hauptmotiv die Klagen um den Tod der Brüder und ihrer Mutter; ein Nebenmotiv, das zum Schlussteil der Tragödie überleitet, ist die Klage um das Schicksal des Oedipus. Mithin gewahren wir in diesem ganzen ausgedehnten Szenenkomplex die streng durchgeführte Konzentration auf einen einzigen grossen Gegenstand. Dieses schöne Gefüge hat der Bearbeiter zerstört ...'

mean instead 'having cast the darkness of blindness upon your eyes' (see *ad loc.*). Even if Dihle's exegesis were acceptable, it would not follow that the line necessarily reflects Democritean vision-theory (and so is unlikely to have been written before the Hellenistic age), for (as Dihle himself notes) the notion of vision-rays is implicit in older beliefs (e.g., the evil eye and the glance of a beautiful person which inspires love (West on Hes. *Th.* 910)). Of 1570–5 Dihle can say only that the construction of the sentence is unusual (true, but this is late Euripidean monody; 1570–6n., 1572n.) and that he tends to prefer Porson's λέοντε συναύλω (wrongly, in my view: 1573n.). He also objects (by a circular argument) to the use of the proper name of the Electran Gate (1570n.). Until more careful and convincing arguments are adduced, we are justified in treating the bulk of 1485–581 as Euripidean beyond any serious doubt. The very form of monody is of course characteristic of late Euripides, and other typically Euripidean features of style are noted in 1485–6n., 1491n., 1497n., 1529n., 1536bis–38n., 1549n.

1485–581 Metre: The aria begins with a long passage of basically dactylic movement (1485–507), shifting from metra with affinities to hexameter structure to those constructed κατὰ συζυγίαν (showing affinities to anapaestic structure). As the content becomes even more passionate, a second, almost equally long passage displays mixed character (1508–29), starting off aeolic and shifting to choriambic/ionic. In the duet the summoning and emergence of Oedipus are accompanied by a further passage of mixed rhythm (1530–45), iambo-dochmiac with dactylic elements and ionics, expressive of a renewed or refocused agitation. The news is conveyed in a long passage (1546–81) which returns to the basically dactylic rhythm of the opening, now with an even more decided admixture of anapaestic elements.[1]

1485–6	$-\cup\cup-\cup\cup-\vdots\cup\cup-\cup\cup-\cup\cup-\cap\|^{b}$	6 da$_\wedge$
1487	$-\cup\cup-\cup\cup-\vdots\cup\cup-\cup\cup$	4 da
1488	$---\cup\cup-\cup\cup--\|^{h}$	4 da$_\wedge$
1489	$-\cup\cup-\cup\cup-\vdots--\cup\cup$	4 da
1490	$---\cup\cup-\cup\cup-\cup\cup$	4 da
1491	$-\cup\cup-\cup\cup-\cup\cup-\cup\cup-\|^{c}$	5 da$_{\wedge\wedge}$
1492–3	$-\cup\cup-\cup\cup-\cup\cup-\cup\cup-\cup\cup--\|^{h}$	4 da exclam
1494	$-\cup\cup-\cup\cup-\cup\cup-\cup\cup----\|$	4 da exclam
1495	$-\cup\cup-\cup\cup-\cup\cup-\cup\cup|$	4 da
1496	$-\cup\cup-\cup\cup-\cup\cup--$	4 da

---

[1] For another description of the metrical pattern cf. E. Cerbo, *QUCC* 32:2 (1989) 67–75.

1497	$-\cup\cup--\parallel^h$	2 da$_\wedge$
1497bis	$-\cup\cup--\parallel^c$	2 da$_\wedge$
1498	$\widehat{\cup\cup}\cup-\cup\mid$	tro
1499	$-\cup\cup-\cup\cup-\vdots\cup\cup-\cup\cup\mid$	4 da
1500	$-\cup\cup-\cup\cup-\cup\cup-\cup\cup\mid$	4 da
1501	$-\cup\cup--\parallel^c$	2 da$_\wedge$
1502	$-\cup\cup-\cup\cup-\cup\cup-\cup\cup\mid$	4 da
1503	$-\cup\cup-\cup\cup-\cup\cup-\cup\cup\mid$	4 da
1504	$-\cup\cup-\cup\cup-\vdots\cup\cup-\cup\cup\mid$	4 da
1505	$-\cup\cup-\cup\cup\mid$	2 da
1506	$-\cup\cup-\cup\cup-\vdots\cup\cup--\parallel^c$	4 da$_\wedge$
1507	$-\cup\cup---\cup\cup--\parallel^c$	4 da$_\wedge$
1508	$\times---\parallel^?$	exclam
1509	$\cup-\cup--\cup\cup-\mid$	ia chor
1510	$-\cup\cup--\cup\cup-\mid$	2 chor
1511	$\cup\widehat{\cup\cup}\cup-\cup-\cup-$	2 ia
1512	$-\cup\cup-\cup\cup-\mid$	hemiepes
1513	$-\cup\cup-\cup\cup\cap\parallel^b$	hemiepes
1514	$\cup--\cup\cup--\parallel^?$	2 io
1515	$\cup\cup--\cup\cup-\mid$	2 io
1516	$\cup\cup--\cup\cup--\cup\cup-\{-\cup\cup-\}\mid$	3 io
1517	$\dagger\cup\cup-\cup\cup\cup--\dagger\mid$	corrupt
1518	$\cup-\cup\widehat{\cup\cup}-\cap\parallel^b$	ia ba
1519	$-\cup\cup--\cup\cup-\mid$	2 chor
1520	$-\cup\cup--\cup\cup-$	2 chor
1521	$-\cup\cup--\cup\cup--\cup\cup-\mid$	3 chor
1522	$-\cup\cup--\cup\cup-\parallel$	2 chor
1523	$\{\cup\times--\}$	interpolated
1524	$\widehat{\cup\cup}\cup-\widehat{\cup\cup}\cup-$	2 cr
1525	$-\cup--\cup--\cup-\parallel$	3 cr
1526	$-\cup\cup--\cup\cup-\cup\cup-$	chor hemiepes
1527	$-\cup\cup--\mid$	chor $-$ (or adon)
1528	$-\cup\cup--\mid$	chor $-$ (or adon)
1529	$-\cup\cup--\cup\cup--\parallel$	2 chor $-$ (or chor adon)
1530	$\widehat{\cup\cup}\cup--\cup-\mid$	2 cr
1531	$\cup-\cup\widehat{\cup\cup}-\cup\cup-\mid$	ia chor
1532	$\cup-\cup-\cup-\cap\parallel^b$	ia ba
1533	$-\widehat{\cup\cup}-\cup--\widehat{\cup\cup}\widehat{\cup\cup}\cup\widehat{\cup\cup}\mid$	2 dochm
1534	$-\cup\cup-\cup\cup-\cup\cup-\cup\cup\mid$	4 da
1535	$-\widehat{\cup\cup}---\cup--\cup-\parallel^?$	2 dochm
1536	$\cup--\cup--$	2 ba

1536bis	∪−−∪−−	2 ba
1537	∪−−∪−	dochm
1538	−−∪∪−−‖ᶜ	reiz
1539	∪−−∪∪−−∪∪−−|	3 io
1540	∪∪−−∪∪−−‖?	2 io
1541	∪−−∪∪−−∪∪−−	3 io
1542	∪∪−−∪∪−−‖?	2 io
1543	⌣∪∪−⌣∪∪⌣∪∪−−∪−|	2 cr ia
1544	∪⌣∪−∪−|	dochm
1545	−∪∪−−‖ᶜ	adon (2 da∧)
1546	−∪∪−∪∪−⋮∪∪−−‖ᶜ	4 da∧
1547	∪∪−∪∪−∪∪−−‖ᶜ	paroem
1548	∪∪−∪∪−∪∪−−‖ᶜ	paroem
1549	−∪∪−∪∪−⋮∪∪−∪∪−∪∪−−‖ʰ	6 da∧
1550	−∪∪−−‖ʰ	2 da∧
1551–2	−∪∪−∪∪−⋮∪∪−∪∪−∪∪−−‖ᶜ	6 da∧
1553	−−−−−−−−|	4 sp
1554	−∪∪−∪∪−∪∪−−‖ʰ	4 da∧
1555	−∪∪−∪∪−∪∪−∪∪|	4 da
1556	−∪∪−∪∪−⋮∪∪−−‖ᶜ	4 da∧
1557	∪∪−−−|	an
1558	−∪∪−∪∪−∪⋮∪−∪∪−∪∪−−‖ᶜ	6 da∧
1559	−∪∪−−‖ʰ	2 da∧
1560	×−∪⌣∪∪−∪−|	2 ia
1561	−∪⌣∪∪−∪−‖ᶜ	lec
1562	−∪∪−∪∪−∪∪−−|	4 da
1563	−∪∪−∪∪−∪∪−−|	4 da
1564	−∪∪−−−∪∪−−‖	4 da∧
1565	−∪∪−∪∪−⋮∪∪−∪∪|	4 da
1566	−∪∪−∪∪−⋮∪∪−∪∪−∪∪−−‖ᶜ	6 da∧
1567	⌣∪∪⌣∪∪⌣∪∪−∪⌣∪∪−‖ᶜ	2 tro cr
1568	⌣∪∪−∪⌣∪∪⌣∪∪|	2 tro
1569	⌣∪∪⌣∪∪⌣∪∪−‖ʰᶜ	lec
1570	−∪∪−−−∪∪−∪∪|	4 da
1571	−∪∪−∪∪−∪∪−−‖ᶜ	4 da∧
1572	−∪∪−∪∪−‖ᶜ	hemiepes
1573	−−−∪∪−∪∪−−‖ᶜ?	4 da∧
1574	−∪∪−∪∪−∪∪−∪∪|	4 da
1575	−−−−−−∪∪⌒‖ᵇ	2 an
1576	−∪∪−−−∪∪−−‖ᶜ?	4 da∧
1577	−∪∪−∪∪−∪⋮∪−∪∪−∪∪−−‖ᶜ	6 da∧
1578	−∪∪−∪∪−∪⋮∪−∪∪−∪∪−⌒‖ᵇ	6 da∧

1579   −∪∪−∪∪−∪∪−∪∪| 4 da
1580   −∪∪−∪∪−∪:∪−∪∪−∪∪| 5 da
1581   −∪−∪−−‖ᶜ   ithyph

NOTES TO METRICAL SCHEME

1485–8 this can be read as a run of 14 dactyls if παρήϊδος is read; with either reading, the hexameter-style structure of the verse and the anaphora οὐ ... οὐδ᾽ suggest either colon-division or period-end after the first 6 dactyls.

1488–91 see Cole, 24 n. 23, on the 'dactylo-anapaestic' ambiguity of the demarcations in these lines.

1492–3 the intended form of the exclamations cannot be recovered; the first could be either 2 da or dochm (pentamakron), the second 2 sp (as printed) or dochm (pentamakron) with μοι doubled. In any case, the diaeresis after 4 da in each verse marks the affinity to nearby tetrameters.

1495–7bis construction κατὰ συζυγίαν comes to the fore here and diaeresis (or elision) after every second metron continues, with a few exceptions, in the dactylic cola down to 1507. For period of 2 da after a longer period see metrical note on 789–90. The longer period need not always be a hexameter, and the lack of caesura in ἀλλά φόνωι ... κρανθεῖσ᾽ is against such division here.

1498 isolated trochees among dactyls are very rare: *Hyps.* fr. 64, 86 (trochee between dactyls within a period); 1557 might be another example if ξίφεσι is read rather than ξίφεσιν; Wilam. created another in 1501 by reading ἀνακαλοῦμαι. Trochaic interpretation seems more likely, however, than the postulation of a 'light' adonean here (with brevis in longo) and in 1557 (see metrical note on 796 for refs.) or than Schroeder's scansion ∪−∪−− with rare lengthening of final short before initial mute and liquid (see metrical note on 166).

1501 dactylic clausula with syncopated form ἀγκαλέσωμαι is perfectly in place. Unsyncopated ἀνακαλέσωμαι (-έσομαι most mss) could be interpreted as ∪∪⏗∪−−, iambic penthemimer as clausula to dactyls; but other possible instances of this normally have initial long (so that the clausula deceptively begins with a dactylic shape) and are themselves subject to doubt. See below on 1581. Cf. *IA* 1332 (4 da +) ἀνδράσιν ἀνευρεῖν (εὑρεῖν Dindorf, producing 2daₐ); *El.* 456 (3 da +) Φρύγια τετύχθαι = 469 ὄμμασι τροπαῖοι (doubted on metrical and linguistic grounds by Diggle). Cf. West, *Greek Metre* 130, and *ZPE* 45 (1982) 3; Stinton, *CR* 15 (1965) 142–5; *contra* Diggle, *CR* 34 (1984) 68.

1512–13 the text is hardly certain, but if the mss are correct then for hemiepes among aeolic or choriambic cola cf. 1526 below and *El.* 723–5 (aristophanean + hemiepes + chor, aristophanean), Aesch. *Su.* 74–7 = 83–5, *Septem* 331 = 343, 350 = 361, *Ag.* 1505, *Trach.* 885. Without period-end at 1513, Wilam., e.g., treats 1512–14 (αἵματος … ἐλελίζει) as chor + 4 io, but there is no secure parallel for the fully resolved ionic metron he assumes; Dale (*Metr. Anal.* 3.296) treats 1513–14 as heavily-resolved chor dim A + adon.

1515 with the first ἤ omitted, 1514–16 are easily ionic: first metron shortened to ∪ − − as in 1539, 1541; shortened metron ∪∪ − occurs within the period as *Su.* 51–2 and *Pers.* 109–10 (Dale, *LMGD*² 121). If the first ἤ is retained, then with ὄρνῑς we may analyse as ionics with a single choriamb among them (possible parallels: 1528 below if an ionic scansion is preferred; chor leading into io in *Hipp.* 732; 1526 below in alternative scansion); Dale (*Metr. Anal.* 3.296) divides instead as 2 anapaests followed by 2 chor and pendant hemiepes. With ὄρνῑς the colon is ∪∪ − ∪ − ∪∪ −, which is found also in *Ag.* 689 (Denniston–Page comm., p. 231; Dale, *LMGD*² 130). For the hiatus ἤ ἐλάτας see comm.

1519–22 these could be printed as three cola of 3 chor each (JD; West (1990)).

1522 I assumed period-end both here and at 1525 after the run of cretics, without catalexis (cf. metrical note on 239 = 250). If δακρύοισιν is read in 1522, the period can be seen as ambiguous between choriambic (with added syllable at end) or ionic (with added syllable at start): cf. next note.

1525 σπαραγμοῖς yields an easy run of cretics (cf. Aesch. *Su.* 418ff., *Eum.* 491ff., *Hec.* 1080, 1100, *Tro.* 1091, esp. *Or.* 1419ff.); the majority reading -οῖσιν would give chor sandwiched between cretics, very unusual (cf. perhaps Timotheus *Pers.* 98–9, 106).

1526–9 the rhythm is ambiguous in a context which has featured both chor and io. The choriambic interpretation could also be expressed in dactylo-epitrite notation as dD−d−dd−. With different colon-division, one may have a mixture of chor and io: 2 chor, 2 io, chor, ∧∧io, 2 io (cf. West (1990) 314). Cf. *Pers.* 647 = 653, *Trach.* 849–50 = 860–1, and Stinton, 'More rare verse-forms' 102, Dale, *LMGD*² 120–2. Schroeder would omit ἐν in 1526 rather than emend it: the resulting colon −∪∪−∪∪−∪∪− (D²) occurs at period-end in Alcman 1 and in *El.* 141 = 158 and without word-overlap in *Ba.* 116 = 131 (period-end?), *IA* 1041 = 1063, *Rhes.* 244 = 255; a possible parallel for overlap is *Andr.* 1182–3 as redivided by Webster apud Stevens. See also on 1547–8. Cole, 47, analyses these lines as choriambic with syncopation, adding ⟨δίδυμ'⟩ before οὐλόμεν' in order to create two cola of the form −∪∪−−∪∪−. ∪∪−−∪∪−− (this is unnecessary and not attractive: Diggle, *LCM* 15.5 (1990) 79).

1530–2 the uncertainty of the shape and length of the exclamation and of colon-division makes any analysis tentative. Wilam.'s attempt to create more ionics is not convincing.

1533–5 the dactylic colon 1534 has been doubted in this context (e.g., by Wilam.). Dactyls are associated with dochmiacs elsewhere (cf. 135–7, 151–3, 188–92, 351–4). The difference here is that the dactyls form a single period with the preceding and following dochmiacs: cf. Conomis, 48, 'only "iambic-types" of metres are combined internally with dochmiacs'. Nevertheless, the dactyls assimilate well to the preceding and following dochmiac dimeters opening – ∪∪ (1581 may also present an exceptional combination with dactyls: see below). If dactylic scansion is rejected, then one may interpret as dochmiac + 2 cretics (brevis at the end of 1533, with ἔτι, not ἐπί), followed by 'prosodiac' (with ὄμμασιν, after Seidler): cf. the sequence in *Her.* 1055–7 and 1068–70 (Diggle's text). If 1534 is dactylic, 1535 could be scanned as 2 da + dochmiac, with μᾱκρόπνουν (Schroeder): syllabic lengthening before mute and liquid is rare in dochmiacs and can be avoided by Murray's μᾱκρόπνοον or Nauck's μακρόπονον; but there are undoubted cases in *Her.* and *Hel.* (Conomis, 38–9).

1536–8 for the striking series of bacchiacs (made more forceful by diaeresis) see Dale, *LMGD*² 101. The clausula here could be read as 2 more ba followed by an adonean.

1539–42 probably two pentameters, but for the ambiguity of the metron ∪ – – (λεχήρη) as possible period-end see Stinton, 'More rare verse-forms' 102.

1543 text (see *ad loc.*) and rhythm are disputed. Wilam. forced the passage into ionics (involving unparalleled features like iambic anaclasis and resolution in a shortened metron); Paley suggested dochm ‖ᵇ 2 cr |, but many doubt the possibility of brevis in longo in dochmiacs without strong sense-pause (see on 114 and 177, where I am inclined to accept brevis); Dale (*Metr. Anal.* 3.297) suggests '?doch equivalent' (⊻∪∪ – ∪∪).

1544–5 the adonean clausula may be taken as 'a sort of catalectic dochmiac' (Dale, *Metr. Anal.* 3.300); there is no reason to eliminate the dochmiac in 1544 (Cole, 73, emends to ἔνερθ' to produce ia or cr preceding what he calls 'heptadic aeolic' (here a reizianum)). For another analysis of 1543–5 cf. West (1990) 314.

1547–8 if these cola are recognized as quasi-anapaestic, they prepare for several of the following cola which present dactyls structured κατὰ συζυγίαν (1550, 1553, 1554, 1555, 1562, 1563, 1564, 1574, 1576) and for two cola which I take as openly anapaestic (1557, 1575). It does not seem helpful to insist on a purely dactylic division of 1546–8 such as 4 da∧∧ + 4 da∧∧ + 4 da, with word-overlap (see on 1526–9 [D² = 4 da∧∧]).

1550 with the supplement ⟨ὦ⟩ we have a familiar sequence in 6 da ‖ 2 da ‖ (see on 1496–7). Without it the clausula would be 5 da + reiz with word-overlap, unconvincing when -μόχθει can be perceived so naturally as the end of a hexameter.

1557 if anapaestic interpretation (see on 1547–8) is rejected and no lacuna is assumed, then I would prefer to recognize ξίφεσι βρίθων as an isolated trochee (cf. 1498) rather than as 'light' adonean (see metrical note on 796).

1560–1 if unambiguous dochmiacs were nearby, one might consider taking Oedipus' syllables as *extra metrum* and Antigone' s replies as dochm hex and dochm.

1562–4 since these dactyls are structured κατὰ συζυγίαν I have tentatively treated 1562–3 as acatalectic (contrast 1506–7).

1575 here (as in 1553) word-end fully matches metron-end, and the spondees may have a solemn, ritualistic effect. In such a context anapaestic interpretation seems to me suitable (see on 1547–8). Anapaests can be avoided by reading φοίνιον (West's φοινάν is not attractive).

1581 see above on 1501 for the problem whether iambic penthemimer (ὃς τάδε τελευτᾷ) as clausula to dactyls ought to be recognized. The very small change to τάδ' ἐ⟨κ⟩τελευτᾷ (Page) produces ithyph, a familiar clausula in other contexts; but it may be necessary to seek another solution. As Diggle (1990a) has noted, there is no parallel for ithyphallic as clausula after dactyls ending ∪∪. Ithyphallics are found after hemiepes (*Alc.* 440–1 = 450–1, *Tro.* 589–90 = 593–4, *Hyps.* fr. 1 ii.13–14 = iii.16–17), after hemiepes in longer dactylo-epitrite colon (e.g., *Andr.* 775–6 = 786–7), after dactylic tetrameter or longer length ending in a spondee (e.g, *Andr.* 117–18 = 126–7, *IA* 229–30), or dactylic tetrameter/pentameter catalectic (prob. *IT* 1136–7 = 1151–2; *Hel.* 384–5). Other syncopated iambic clausulae are found after dactyls ending ∪∪: *Cycl.* 610–11 and *Andr.* 293–4 (4 da + lec), *Cycl.* 615–16 (4 da + cr, ia, cr), *Ba.* 159–60 (4 da + 2 cr), *Hyps.* fr. 64.90–1 (4 da + lec (or 2 cr)), *Ant.* 339–41 (8 da + sp, ithyph). Apparent 4 da + ithyph at *Rhes.* 530 = 550 may be divided otherwise (W. Ritchie, *The Authenticity of the Rhesus of Euripides* (Cambridge 1964) 314–15). (I owe many of these instances to JD.) So ithyph here is uncertain; but if 2 cr follow dactyls in so few places, it is possible that this single instance of ithyph is to be accepted. If the ithyphallic is rejected, one possible approach is to transpose τάδ' ὅς, yielding dactylic pentameter catalectic (ending at μελάθροις) followed by ia + ba or by lec (with θεός di- or monosyllabic): Diggle (1990a) 10–11. Or 1580–1 could be divided as dactylic tetrameter catalectic (ending at ἄχη), followed by ∪∪–∪∪–∪–∪–– (JD, 9/92, referring to *Studies* 102, 121, for this colon).

1480–581: COMMENTARY

1480–1 οὐκ εἰς ἀκοὰς ἔτι . . . πάρα γὰρ λεύσσειν for such comment on the presentation of the reported outcome before the audience, cf. *Se.* 848 τάδ' αὐτόδηλα· προῦπτος [πρεπτὸς?] ἀγγέλου λόγος, *OT* 1294–6, *Ant.* 1293–5, *Hec.* 1049–53.

1482 πτώματα νεκρῶν τρισσῶν 'fallen bodies of the triple dead', with pathetic pleonasm. Eur. affects this use of πτῶμα even in trimeters (1697 below, *Or.* 1196; cf. fr. 728.2); there is lyric precedent in Aesch. *Su.* 662.

1484 σκοτίαν αἰῶνα λαχόντων 'having received as their lot the ⟨fated⟩ lifespan of darkness', that is, 'having met their death' (Σ, cf. Hartung's 'vom Dunkel des Todes umfangen'), rather than 'having met a dark fate' (Craik). αἰών is usually the shape and fortune of one's life before death, but here the epithet transfers the term to the after-life, viewed as separate allotment of existence. Cf. *IA* 1507–8 ἕτερον ἕτερον / αἰῶνα καὶ μοῖραν οἰκήσομεν; *Med.* 1039 ἐς ἄλλο σχῆμ' ἀποστάντες βίου; *TrGF* adesp. 279h.1–2 μακρὸν δὲ τὸν κατὰ γᾶς αἰῶνα τελευτῶμεν βροτοί; Pindar *I.* 7.41–2 ἔκαλος ἔπειμι γῆρας ἔς τε τὸν μόρσιμον αἰῶνα (virtually 'death'). For poetic fem. αἰών, only here and 1520 below in tragedy (unless Aesch. fr. 451l.10 conceals an instance), cf. *Il.* 22.58, *Scutum* 331, Pindar *P.* 4.186, 5.7, *N.* 9.44, [Simon.] *Epigr.* 70.3 (*Epigr. Gr.* 374 Page, *Anth. gr.* 7.515).

1485–6 προκαλυπτομένα here with object of the thing covered (as *Med.* 1147) rather than of the covering (as *IT* 312).

βοτρυχώδεος βοτρυχ- as alternative to βοστρυχ- occurs also in Pherecrates fr. 202 K–A ὦ ξανθοτάτοις βοτρύχοισι κομῶν, where metre appears to make Bergk's emendation likely (βοστρύχ- codd.). The two instances appear to defend each other.[1] For discussion of confusion or alternation of βοτρυ-/βοστρυ- see my article in *Scripta Classica Israelica* 12 (1993) 16–25. The adj. here means 'adorned with/shaded by spiralling or corkscrew curls', a reference to the curls which hang down in front of the ears in a hairdo characteristic of women, youthful gods and heroes (such as Achilles in E. Simon, *Die griechischen Vasen* (Munich 1976) plates 147 and XLIII), or effeminate men (*Ba.* 455–6 πλόκαμος . . . ταναός, . . . / γένυν παρ' αὐτὴν κεχυμένος, πόθου πλέως). The few mss which have the correct form perhaps owe it to metrical studies in the circle of Triclinius: see *Text. Trad.* 139–40 (tentatively identifying Tp with a young Triclinius); Diggle, *Textual Trad. Or.* 103–10 (against this identification). If one disbelieves in the form βοτρυχώδης for βοστρυχώδης, then Porson's βοτρυώδεος is an obvious

---

[1] Dindorf emended *Or.* 1267 to διὰ βοτρύχων (now found in Ad: Diggle, *Textual Trad. Or.* 68 n. 5), but recent edd. rightly reject this.

repair here. Eur. would still be referring to 'clustering curls', anticipating the use of βοτρυόεις in Ap. Rhod. 2.677 πλοχμοὶ βοτρυόεντες, unless βοτρυώδεος παρῆιδος could mean 'cheek like a ⟨ripe?⟩ grape-cluster (in colour and texture)', that is, with a delicate reddish bloom (cf. οἰνωπὸν γένυν, 1159–62n.).

ἀβρὰ παρῆιδος 'the delicate skin of my cheeks'. Both the cheek-curls (which are a part of the hairdo, not a result of the removal of the veil) and the soft texture (cf. ἀπαλάν Aesch. Su. 70, Prom. 400, Ant. 783) are tokens of delicate femininity, often veiled on a maiden like Antigone. The typical circumlocution (Breitenbach, 196ff.) gives more emphasis to the descriptive word (K–G 1.278).

1487 παρθενίας on the repeated motif of Ant.'s maidenhood, cf. 88–201n., 88–102n.

1488 φοίνικ', ἐρύθημα προσώπου a sort of γρῖφος; φοῖνιξ is not elsewhere used of the redness of a blushing face, and this is the first poetic use of ἐρύθημα, which is a medical term in Thuc. 2.49.2, Hippocr. et al., a simple colour-term in Xen. Cyneg. 5.18 (the sense 'blush' appears later in Chaeremon TrGF 71 F 1.4, late prose, and is a cliché in the novelists).

1489 αἰδομένα some take φοίνικ' as internal acc. (unparalleled for this verb) and understand 'not feeling shame and not displaying the cheek-blush', but the sense is rather 'not feeling shame at ⟨and so not concealing⟩ the blush on my cheek'. This involves a slight extension of the sense of the verb, but makes the proper point: Ant. blushes like a maiden (cf. IA 187–8), but in these circumstances does not bother to conceal herself (cf. 1275–6). There is no need for emendation (Wecklein adopted Huschke's ugly αἰθομένα).

1489–90 φέρομαι βάκχα νεκύων φέρομαι as a verb of motion with personal subject implies lack of rational or prudent control (Ant. 802, OT 1309, Soph. El. 922, Hec. 1076), and such frantic motion is typical of the distraught woman in literature (Il. 22.460 (Andromache) μεγάροιο διέσσυτο μαινάδι ἴση, cf. 6.388–9 ἐπειγομένη … μαινομένηι εἰκυῖα; Hom.h.Dem. 386 ἤϊξ' ἠΰτε μαινάς, with Richardson's note). βάκχα νεκύων 'frantic mourner of the dead' is superficially similar to Hec. 1076 βάκχαις Ἅιδα 'frantic agents of Death' (cf. Her. 1119, Aesch. Su. 564 θυιὰς Ἥρας), but actually closer to Septem 835–6 ἔτευξα τύμβωι μέλος θυιάς and ultimately descended from Homer's simile for Andromache.

1490–1 exposure of the hair for disordering, tearing, and defiling and release of the upper garment at the shoulder-brooch to expose the breast for beating are often paired in descriptions of mourning: cf. Andr. 829–35 and Gow on Theocr. 15.134. A woman's hair could be veiled either by pulling the large fold at the back of the peplos over the head or by donning a separate piece of clothing, the καλύπτρη (cf. Bieber, RE 11 (1922)

1690ff.), called λεπτόμιτον φάρος in *Andr.* 831 or κρήδεμνον in epic and here alone in tragedy (κρήδεμνον in tragedy elsewhere only *Tro.* 508 = 'battlement'). Here the unveiling of the maiden induced by grief probably plays upon the bridal ritual of unveiling (Seaford, 124). Comedy may have used an exaggeratedly padded and painted costume to represent the naked women who are the objects of obscene gestures and comments; tragedy clearly had to be more decorous, but there are three extant passages which imply baring of the breast by an actor (here, *Andr.* 832–3, *Choe.* 896–8 (see Garvie *ad loc.*)) and we cannot say how realistically or impressionistically or imaginatively this disrobing was portrayed on stage. If robes were really undone in these scenes, we may guess that they were refastened at the end of the lyric scene here (after 1581) and in *Andr.* (during 866–77 or 876–7) and almost immediately in *Choe.*

ἀνεῖσα   ἀνιέναι is the usual term for undoing or failing to secure a garment, esp. at the shoulder (*Il.* 22.80, Theocr. 15.134), but also at the closure of the peplos along the side of the legs (*Andr.* 598 πέπλοι ἀνειμένοι of Spartan girls, cf. Ibycus' φαινομηρίδες, *PMGF* 339). For another sense of this verb related to mourning see 323n.

1491 στολίδος . . . τρυφάν   this is Porson's conjecture, offered without argument. The periphrasis with genitive noun is an idiom typical of Euripidean lyric, and the locution is common with χλιδή, the synonym of τρυφή: above 224–5 κόμας . . . χλιδάν, *Andr.* 2 ἔδνων . . . χλιδῆι, *Rhes.* 960 πέπλων χλιδήν. στολίδα . . . τρυφᾶς (with rare but possible στολίδα κρο-: 166n.) would be a very unusual example of the gen. of description, but thanks to Moschopulus' paraphrase grammarians from Matthiae to K–G 1.264 and Schwyzer 11.129 cite τρυφᾶς = τρυφεράν as a standard example.[1] Of other examples the simplest type features a gen. noun with modifier, and the relationship to the governing noun may be paraphrased with 'full of', 'characterized by' (801–2 above ζαθέων πετάλων . . . νάπος; *Ant.* 114 λευκῆς χιόνος πτέρυγι; *Aj.* 888 μακρῶν ἀλάταν πόνων; *Andr.* 147 κόσμον . . . χρυσέας χλιδῆς) or 'consisting of' (*Prom.* 900 Ἥρας ἀλατείαις πόνων (I consider the line sound); Soph. *El.* 758 σῶμα δειλαίας σποδοῦ). More striking are cases in which the genitive is unaccompanied (although the governing noun may have an epithet which may seem to be transferred from the gen. or to which the gen. may be attached as a form of specification): again we may paraphrase 'full of', 'characterized by' (Aesch. fr.

---

[1] Σ treat the gen. as separative, as if 'casting my yellow dress from its luxuriance' were equivalent to 'causing my yellow dress to cease to be a luxuriant cover for my breast', but this ignores the idiomatic sense of ἀνιέναι explained above.

273a.6 δονάκων εἰς βένθος ἀμαυρόν; *Eum.* 954–5 δακρύων βίον ἀμβλωπόν; Soph. *El.* 19 ἄστρων ... εὐφρόνη; 1527 below γάλακτος ... μαστοῖς; *Or.* 225 βοστρύχων πινῶδες ... κάρα; *OT* 532–3 τοσόνδε ... τολμῆς πρόσωπον, 1463–4 ἡμὴ ... βορᾶς τράπεζα; *Ba.* 389 ὁ τᾶς ἡσυχίας βίος). From these examples[1] we may observe that the gen. usually precedes or is adjacent to the governing noun (and always precedes when the gen. is unaccompanied); that the gen. noun and governing noun are usually of the same type (concrete, abstract, activity- or agent-noun), but that when they are of mixed types, the governing noun wavers between concreteness and abstraction (κόσμον, ὄμμα, πρόσωπον) or the whole phrase is unified through hypallage (τοσόνδε in *OT* 532). In στολίδα ... τρυφᾶς both the position of the unaccompanied gen. and the combination of fully concrete στολίς with fully abstract τρυφᾶς seem to me exceptional.

κροκόεσσαν   the colour is associated with festivity, luxuriance, or femininity/effeminacy (cf. *Hec.* 468, *Ag.* 239 κρόκου βαφάς; *Pers.* 660 κροκόβαπτον; κροκωτός Arist. *Eccl.* 879, *Thesm.* 138, etc.).

τρυφάν   unlike Aesch. and Soph., Eur. uses τρυφή/τρυφάω as well as χλιδή (which is often glossed with τρυφή); and there is not sufficient cause to read χλιδ- here (Arsenius' χλιδᾶς· τρυφᾶς is probably a mistake for τρυφᾶς· χλιδᾶς, but the scholion is not present in either form in any ms I have seen).

1492 ἀγεμόνευμα ... πολύστονον   after the asyndetic series of nominatives, ἀγεμόνευμα is probably felt as nominative, a personal agent-noun (an extension of verbal root + -μα for a tool required for the action) like δούλευμα *Ion* 748, λάτρευμα *Tro.* 1106; but it could be a true abstract in appositional internal acc. With the latter, πολύστονον would be 'occasioning or full of groans of grief' (a common sense); in the former, 'groaning much' (rare; cf. *Od.* 19.118; *Sept.* 845 is different, *pace* LSJ). The *hapax* ἀγεμόνευμα governs the dat. because the epic verb ἡγεμονεύω does. The dat. would be very harsh if Seaford, 124 n. 185, were correct in taking ἀγεμόνευμα as passive in sense, implying that Ant. 'is led not in a bridal procession but by the dead'; moreover, in staging the entry, I would want Ant. in front of the procession to perform her song and dance most effectively (and φέρομαι βάκχα νεκύων suggests that she is not a passive follower: 1489–90n.).

---

[1] Others which are often cited are of dubious relevance: in 1574 below αἵματος should be taken with λοιβάν, not τραύμασιν; *Hel.* 1156 ἅμιλλα ... αἵματος is 'competition in bloodshed', like ἅμιλλα λόγων, 'competition in speech' (obj. gen.); *Aj.* 159 πύργου ῥῦμα is, as Jebb states, obj. gen. At *Ba.* 1218 transmitted μοχθῶν may be kept as imperfect participle (μόχθων μυρίοις ζητήμασιν Wecklein) – JD.

1494 ἔφυς ἄρ' ἐπώνυμος 'you were, it turns out, rightly named' or 'your name, after all, fit your destiny'. On ἄρα/ἆρα with past tense to express realization of a newly ascertained fact, cf. Denniston, *GP²* 36, 45, and for etymological play in such expressions cf. Griffith, *HSCP* 82 (1979) 83–6. In this context of new realization, ἔφυν does not have its strong sense, emphasizing 'be born with a natural disposition to be . . .', but a weaker sense equivalent to εἰμί or ἐγενόμην (as, e.g., *Pers.* 157, *Trach.* 36, *Hipp.* 272; see Ellendt, *Lex.Soph.* 777 col. i, although not all his examples are equally apposite). ἐπώνυμος = 'true to the name' also in 637 above, *al.*

Θῆβαι a dative of (dis)interest, either Hermann's Θήβαις or simply Θῆβαι, would (*pace* Wilam.) give perfectly good idiom with ἐπώνυμος (cf. *Sept.* 9, 404–5), but Peleus' exclamatory vocative ὦ πόλι Θεσσαλίας (*Andr.* 1176) within a very personal lament is probably sufficient to defend Antigone's invocation of the city in this similar context. Cf. ἰὼ γᾶ in 1290 above (where exclamatory ὦ Ζεῦ is a frozen expression, not fully comparable: cf. *Or.* 332, *al.*).

1495–6 σὰ δ' ἔρις . . . κρανθεῖσ' for interjection with οὐ used to reject a word in favour of a stronger alternative cf. *Hec.* 948–9 γάμος – οὐ γάμος ἀλλ' ἀλάστορός τις οἰζύς, 1121 ἀπώλεσ' – οὐκ ἀπώλεσ' ἀλλὰ μειζόνως, *Hel.* 1134 γέρας – οὐ γέρας ἀλλ' ἔριν –. These lines constitute an expansion of ἐπώνυμος, and ἔρις, though rhetorically rejected, remains the logical and grammatical subject of ὤλεσε; hence fem. κρανθεῖσ'. The sense of κρανθεῖσ' ('brought to fulfilment ⟨esp. by a superhuman power⟩': 7on.) recalls the motif of the curse and the self-perpetuating force of the family's woes (cf. 70, 350–3, 624, 765, 811–12, 1053, 1255).

φόνωι φόνος for this adnominal (locative) dat. see K–G 1.444 Anm. 4, Schwyzer II.156 and cf. 1194–5 above.

1497–7bis αἵματι δεινῶι αἵματι λυγρῶι the repetition is effective and characteristic, and hiatus and period-end are unobjectionable; neither deletion nor transposition is justified (the omission in a few mss is due to haplography).

1498–501 the most likely translation is perhaps 'what groaning lament of suitable tune or what artfully musical groan am I to summon up to use amidst my tears?', a proem-motif of *aporia* similar to *Hel.* 164–6 ὦ μεγάλων ἀχέων καταβαλλομένα μέγαν οἶκτον, / ποῖον ἁμιλλαθῶ γόον ἢ τίνα μοῦσαν ἐπέλθω / δάκρυσιν ἢ θρήνοις ἢ πένθεσιν; This assumes that προσωιδόν and μουσοπόλον are adjs. and that στοναχάν is direct object. But there are other possibilities. Some treat ἀνακαλέω here as equivalent to ἀναβοάω and regard στοναχάν as internal acc. (cf. *Her.* 910–11 ἀνακαλεῖ με τίνα βοάν;, where the presence of με makes a difference; also, ἀνα- retains its force there but here would have no point). Others believe that Antigone is here summoning to herself the musical accompaniment of others (just as she later in 1515–18 asks what bird will sing in tune with her grief). In this reading, προσωιδόν may be taken as a substantive (here only, but cf. substantival use of ἐπωιδός) or as an adj. implying *choral* accompaniment as opposed to a soloist's lament in μουσοπόλον στοναχάν. But this latter distinction is far-fetched.[1] A final possibility would be to take both προσωιδόν and μουσοπόλον as substantives and read στοναχάν ἔπι: 'what accompanist or poet shall I summon for my groaning lament *or* summon to lamentation [cf. *Ion* 361 ἐπ' οἶκτον ἐξάγειν] by my tears?' JD suggests that the difficulties of metre and sense point to corruption and offers, e.g., τίνα προσωιδὸν ⟨ὠιδάν⟩. Coupling of nearly synonymous alternatives with ἢ (προσωιδὸν ἢ ... μουσοπόλον) is typical of lyric lament: *Her.* 1025–7 τίνα στεναγμὸν ἢ γόον ἢ φθιτῶν ὠιδὰν ἢ τίν' Ἄιδα χορόν, *Hyps.* fr. 1 iv 6–7 τίς ἂν ἢ γόος ἢ μέλος ἢ κιθάρας ἐπὶ δάκρυσι μοῦσ' ἀνοδυρομένα; *Hel.* 165 (above).

ἐπὶ δάκρυσι as in the *Hyps.* passage just quoted, used of the circumstances of the action, modifying the verb (not attached to μουσοπόλον, as Pearson thinks): K–G i.502 (c), citing also *Tro.* 315 (corrupt?), *IA* 1175.

1500 for the successive anadiploses Breitenbach, 220, gives ten other examples in Eur.

1502 αἵματα σύγγονα a very bold expression, probably meaning 'slain bodies of kinsmen' (Brunck), whence the intrusive gloss σώματα (cf. the intrusions in 1482, 1697). The closest parallel is *Or.* 1357–8 τὸν Ἑλένας φόνον καθαιμακτὸν ἐν δόμοις κείμενον; some interpret *Hel.* 848 Αἴαντος ... σφαγάς similarly, but σφαγάς could be 'murderous wounds' or even simply abstract '(self-)murder' (Kannicht) rather than 'corpse' ; for *Or.* 990 Μυρτίλου φόνον δικὼν see 639–41 n.;[2] cf. also the difficult use of αἷμα in Soph. *El.* 1394 (with Jebb's note). Despite the boldness and its precarious survival, αἵματα deserves acceptance: the best available conjectures weaken the passage (Kirchhoff's φέρουσα πεσήματα loses the pathetic deictic; Wilam.'s φέρω τάδε σώματα loses the typical concatenation of clauses).[3]

---

[1] Pearson (misled by Neil on Arist. *Knights* 401) wrongly asserts that προσάιδω and προσωιδός inherently refer to choral singing. These compounds imply singing along with, in agreement with, or suitably (*Phil.* 405, *Ion* 359, Eur. fr. 631.2; Pl. *Phdr.* 86e). In *Knights* 401 (διδασκοίμην προσάιδειν Μορσίμου τραγωιδίαν) and Pl. *Laws* 670b (ὅσοι ... προσάιδειν ... καὶ βαίνειν ἐν ῥυθμῶι γεγόνασι διηναγκασμένοι) the point of the verb lies not in choral utterance but in learning a song by singing in agreement with a teacher.

[2] Breitenbach, 173, alleges that αἷμα = σῶμα also in *IT* 880, *Phoen.* 1062, 1293: but see 1051–4n., 1291–2n.

[3] JD notes that Rauchenstein's φέρουσ' ἅμα σώματα is worth considering.

By metonymy αἷμα can mean 'bloodshed' or virtually 'murder' (*Alc.* 733, *Or.* 285, *al.*; cf. αἵματος δίκη, often in Eur., and αἷμα = αἵματος δίκη, on which see Collard on *Su.* 148 αἷμα συγγενὲς φεύγων). But in many poetic passages translated thus the sense is really more concrete because of Greek notions of the pollution attached to unatoned bloodshed: 'blood that has been shed' or 'blood-guilt (pollution) incident upon murder' is more correct for αἷμα μητρῷον *Eum.* 230, ὅμαιμον αἷμα Aesch. *Su.* 449, αἷμα κοινόν *Choe.* 1038, *Her.* 831 (by emendation), πατρῷον αἷμα *OT* 996, αἷμα σύγγονον *Her.* 1077. Without context αἷμα σύγγονον would be expected to mean 'blood-guilt for kin-murder' or 'charge of kin-murder'; but in our passage context decides for the sense given above.[1]

1503 χάρματ' Ἐρινύος for the delight which the Erinyes take in slaughter cf. *Ag.* 1117-18, *Eum.* 190-2.

1504 πρόπαν tragedy affects πρόπας as emphatic alternative to πᾶς (cf. 624 πρόπας δόμος, with the same theme of utter destruction first signalled in 20). πρόπαν is not elsewhere used as adv. except in Nicander (*Ther.* 338), and Eur. could easily have written δῶμ'... πρόπαν (Jackson); but rhythmical considerations may have prompted the bolder δόμον ... πρόπαν (there is no spondee between 1499 ἢ τίνα and 1506 ἔγνω), and adverbial πρόπαν is not in itself suspicious. Simple πᾶν as adv. (as opposed to τὸ πᾶν and plural πάντα) is not attested with certainty: LSJ s.v. πᾶς D.III.a refers to idioms of the type seen in Hdt. 1.32.4 πᾶν ἐστι ἄνθρωπος συμφορή (cf. 721 above τὸ νικᾶν ἐστι πᾶν εὐβουλία), in which I take πᾶν as adj./pronoun accompanying the predicate term. But πάμπαν without article is unique in tragedy at *Med.* 1091, and πάνυ happens to be attested a few times in Aesch. and Soph. but only once in Eur. (*Cycl.* 646). JD reminds me that πρόπαρ (*recc.*), adverbial (120n.) anticipating ὅτε, is possible; but I prefer the drastic 'utterly' here.

1505 ὅτε κτλ. in families with a long history of woes the ἀρχὴ κακῶν can be variously identified depending on the perspective and intention of the speaker. Although Oedipus was doomed from birth, here and elsewhere (3rd stasimon, 1689, 1728ff.) the apparently positive achievement of defeating the Sphinx is viewed as the critical event of his life and of those of his mother/wife and children, since his victory brought incest, self-blinding, and curse.

1506 δυσξυνέτου ξυνετόν the verbal jingle is paralleled in *IT* 1092 εὐξύνετον ξυνετοῖς and *IA* 466 οὐ συνετὰ συνετῶς, and the phrase has a paradoxical quality suitable to what is being described. τᾶς ἀγρίας

---

[1] Musgrave, who divined αἵματα from the corrupt reading αἱμακτά, thought the sense was 'these kindred murders [*caedes*]'.

δυσξυνέτου functions as a kenning ('the fierce incomprehensible female') which is sufficient to indicate the Sphinx; position and the preceding period-end suggest that Σφιγγός 1507 does not complete the phrase τᾶς κτλ. but opens the new one ending in φονεύσαϛ. ξυνετόν (μέλος) is best taken as 'subtle, deep, clever' (with one Σ), a sense normally applied to persons, but Arist. has this sense in *Frogs* 876 ξυνετὰς φρένας, probably intended as a Euripidean locution (σύνεσις, συνετός, etc. are favourites of Eur.). Other Σ and LSJ understand 'intelligible ⟨to Oedipus, but not to others⟩' – unlikely without an explicit dative. Many have preferred to read δυσξύνετον ξυνετός, which I regard as a conflation of two separate simplifications of the genuine text. δυσξύνετον is used in a paraphrasing scholion which builds on previous exegesis of details and so is quite free in simplifying the grammar: the crucial phrase δυσξύνετον ἐκεῖνο καὶ ἀσαφὲς τοῖς πολλοῖς γνοὺς αὐτός (400, 5–6 Schwartz) in fact seems to presuppose the exegesis of another scholion which clearly explicates δυσξυνέτου ξυνετόν (399, 26–400, 2 Schwartz). δυσξύνετον in Rf may be due to contamination from Σ (*Text. Trad.* 63–4). ξυνετός has even weaker authority, since it is part of a wholesale simplification of the text of 1506–8, in which (with repunctuation) the interpolated πάτερ of 1508 is given a second-person verb (δυσξυνέτου ξυνετὸς μέλος ἔγνως ... πάτερ: 'Moschopulean').

μέλος ἔγνω 'solved the riddle' (48n.).

1507 φονεύσας in prose one would write μέλος γνοὺς τὴν Σφίγγα ἐφόνευσε, expressing in finite form the action that is logically or temporally last to be completed. Here we must recognize a 'coincident' use of the aorist participle, in which syntax lays emphasis on the underlying identity of the contents of the two verbal forms (here ἔγνω and φονεύσας). See Goodwin, *MT* ¶150–1; Barrett on *Hipp.* 289–92; Schwyzer II.300–1 (K–G I.198–9 jumbles together examples of different kinds). Just as *Od.* 24.199–200 κακὰ μήσατο ἔργα, κουρίδιον κτείνασα πόσιν is 'contrived evil deeds – an action which consisted in killing her husband', so here the meaning is 'solved the riddle – an action which involved/entailed the killing of the Sphinx'. This is perhaps harsher than other examples, but this is late Euripidean lyric of a deliberately complicated style. To avoid this exegesis, one may either consider φονεύσας corrupt (Π⁵ is defective at this point; but no useful conjecture has been made) or argue that Eur. did mean that Oedipus killed the Sphinx *before* solving the riddle (so Bethe, 20, believed that Eur. carelessly conflated two different mythic traditions; but this non-literary explanation flies in the face of Eur.'s clear emphasis on the intellectual triumph over the Sphinx as the starting-point of ruin).

1508–14 two almost universally transmitted details (vocative πάτερ in 1508 and second- or third-person verb in 1514) have created the impression that Antigone turns from self-directed laments to consideration of the grief and mourning of others. But outside of this passage Ant. concentrates, up to 1529, on self-presentation, on analysis of her own relation to the dead and to the ruin of the family, and on the *aporiai* facing her as she tries to find the appropriate response to the situation. The entire passage is more consistent and effective if 1508–14 are also self-directed. Hermann, for this good reason as well as two bad ones (responsion, misused Mosch. Σ), deleted πάτερ long ago, and Π⁵'s omission of the word should be accepted as evidence that the word is intrusive (cf. 1721). Without it, 1509 Ἑλλάς is much easier (see below) and 1509ff. describe Ant.'s own plight. Nor has any satisfactory explanation of ἐλελίζηι/-ει ever been offered. Ant. cannot be addressing Oedipus in the house (who does not yet know of the disaster), so Wilam.'s τάλας ὡς ἐλελίζηι is no help; the Palaeologan conjecture which has Ant. address her (dead!) mother in these lines is a token of desperation (*Text. Trad.* 123–4). Third-person ἐλελίζει prompted an impossible paraphrase in Σ, one which is instructive about Σ's approach to an obscure, corrupt text but which cannot serve as a basis for a transposition (Wecklein), since it is clearly a desperate attempt to force meaning on the words in their transmitted order. Murray's suggestion (ut tremule canit – lusciniam dico? immo quae tandem avium ...) misuses an obviously exclamatory ὡς as comparative and entails an impossibly obscure anacoluthon. Whether ἐλελίζω is a survival or a Palaeologan conjecture, it is the only reading which makes sense in 1514.[1]

1509 Ἑλλάς with πάτερ ejected from the text, this word can now have its ordinary meaning 'Greek woman' in antithesis to (fem.) βάρβαρος. It is unnecessary to assume the artificial usage whereby γῆ is understood and Ἑλλάς γῆ is taken as equivalent to Ἕλληνες (cf. *Trach.* 1060–1 οὔθ' Ἑλλάς οὔτ' ἄγλωσσος οὔθ' ὅσην ἐγώ / γαῖαν καθαίρων ἱκόμην) or to refer to the ancient doctrine conveyed by Photius and the Antiatticist (see Soph. fr. 17 in Radt).[2]

1510 προπάροιθ' an epicism, in tragedy only *Se.* 334 and here.

1511–13 Π⁵ had a longer version of these lines (see *ZPE* 38 (1980) 32),

---

[1] Craik translates with ἐλελίζει (3rd sing. active) as an impersonal verb (unexampled), but in her note also contemplates 2nd sing. mid. in self-address.

[2] Photius' entry has been shortened by corruption: read Ἕλλην· τὸ θηλυκόν· ⟨Φιλήμων Παιδαρίωι. Ἑλλάς· ὁ ἀνήρ· Σοφοκλῆς⟩ Αἴαντι Λοκρῶι (more or less what the Antiatticist gives).

but what we can discern of it is not superior to the traditional text, which has fairly convincing rhythm and phraseology.[1] For ἔτλα ... ἄχεα cf. *Ion* 764 ἔπαθον ἄχος, *Her.* 1411 ἔτλη κακά; for κακῶν ... ἄχη cf. 354 above. αἵματος ἀμερίου, however, presents problems. Many attach it to τίς or ἕτερος with the sense 'of the human race' (ἀμερίου used as in 130 above), but the phrase is then otiose after such detailed qualification of τίς in 1509–10 and the postponement of the gen. phrase is highly unusual (Breitenbach, 249–53, gives comparable cases from Euripidean lyric, but in no other case is the postponed gen. so otiose or open to such ambiguity as here; cf. Fraenkel on *Ag.* 1434 on avoidance of ambiguity in separation of a gen. from its noun, though he is considering usage in dialogue in Aesch. and Soph.). The latter objection can be overcome by transposition (Paley, Nauck), but Π⁵ already had the transmitted order. I prefer to take the phrase as defining gen. with the adjacent noun κακῶν: 'such pains of so many evils of human bloodshed' (cf. Σ κακῶν τοσοῦτον πλῆθος καὶ λύπης ἐπὶ ἀνθρωπίνωι σώματι: 'evils affecting a human being'?); or, as Mueller-Goldingen proposes, '... evils of bloodshed befalling on a single day' (but this sense of ἡμέριος is attested only very much later).

1514 τάλαιν', ὡς after the exclamatory, vocative (cf. *Hec.* 20, 913, *IT* 892), ὡς must be exclamatory 'how', not relative 'as' (correlative with τοιάδ' according to some critics). JD commends Brunck's οἷ' to reduce the abruptness of the exclamation.

ἐλελίζω on choice of reading see 1508–14n. The verb's two possible origins seem to have become confused. As a reduplicated form of ἐλίσσω, the verb means 'set astir' or the like and is applied in poetry to quivering strings (Pindar *O.* 9.13, *P.* 1.4). But it could also be felt to be derivative of ἐλελεῦ (as in Xen. *Anab.* 1.8.18 οἷον τῶι Ἐνυαλίωι ἐλελίζουσι; cf. ἀλαλάζω, ὀλολύζω); this is not just a war-cry but also a cry of grief or pain, as in *Prom.* 877. The contemporary uses in *Hel.* 1111 ὦ διὰ ξουθᾶν γενύων ἐλελιζομένα and Arist. *Birds* 213 are both middle and perhaps both absolute (text and punctuation in *Birds* are disputed): these could be regarded as middle of 'set astir' secondarily influenced by 'cry ἐλελεῦ'. But here we have the active used absolutely ('utter a shrill, mournful cry'), and the influence of ἐλελεῦ must be primary. Cf. E. Tichy, *Onomatopoetisch Verbalbildungen des Griechischen* [Oest. Ak. Wiss. Phil.-hist. Kl. Sitzungsber. 409 = Veröffentlichung der Kommission für Linguistik und Kommunikationsforschung 14

---

[1] JD notes that the anadiplosis of φανερά offered by Π⁵ is contrary to the general practice of having the doubled adjective begin the clause or syntactical unit.

(1983)], 239–41 (who wrongly, however, defends ἑλελίζηι, giving false parallels for the supposed use of ἄρα).[1]

1515–18 the verb in 1514 probably already evokes the mournful sound of the nightingale, and although there are severe textual uncertainties in these lines it is clear that when Ant. appeals here for suitable accompaniment from a bird, she has in mind the mourning nightingale concealed in foliage. The ἀηδών λοχμαία is described most fully in *Hel.* 1107ff., but the image is traditional: see Kannicht *ad loc.* and cf. *Od.* 19.518–22, *Hom.h.* 19.16–18, Arist. *Birds* 210–16 (also 737ff. μοῦσα λοχμαία), *OC* 671–3, *Phaethon* 67–70, Eur. fr. 88.

1515–16 δρυὸς ἢ ἐλάτας I prefer to follow Π⁵ and a few *recc.*, not the mss that have ἢ before δρυός as well: the rhythm is somewhat smoother without it (see note under Metre). Either form of text could have arisen through reminiscence of typical pairings in familiar passages (*Il.* 23.328 ἢ δρυὸς ἢ πεύκης, *Od.* 9.186 μακρῇσιν τε πίτυσσιν ἰδὲ δρυσὶν ὑψικόμοις; *Il.* 13.389 δρῦς ... ἢ ἀχερωΐς, *Ba.* 110 δρυὸς ἢ ἐλάτας). Wilam. on *Her.* 241 notes that δρυὸς ἢ ἐλάτας is a formulaic polar expression for all trees, those with leaves and those with needles (cf. Chantraine s.v. δρῦς); he also notes ((1903) 598 n. 1 = *Kl.Schr.* vi.356 n. 2) that the formulaic nature of the phrase (cf. *Hom.h.Aphr.* 264 ἢ ἐλάται ἠὲ δρύες) accounts for the hiatus without pause or epic correption both here and in *Ba.* 110, a licence not otherwise found in tragedy. The two passages appear to defend each other. Diggle (1989) 202 is sympathetic to Blomfield's ἢ ⟨'ν⟩ in *Ba.* 110 and proposes a similar avoidance of hiatus here: ἢ ⟨'ν⟩ ἐλάτας ἀκροκόμοισιν πετάλοις.

1516 ἐν πετάλοις {ἑζομένα} the metre does not decide whether we should prefer ἐν πετάλοις or ἀμφὶ κλάδοις or whether we should include or omit ἑζομένα, nor do other considerations allow a confident choice. On the whole I now incline to the version of Π⁵ (*contra* my previous opinion, *ZPE* 38 (1980) 28–9). ἐν πετάλοις is an epic locution (*Od.* 19.520, Hes. *Op.* 486, *Hom.h.* 19.17; compare Ibycus *PMGF* 317) and could here be a deliberate reminiscence (cf. 1510 προπάροιθ' and the nightingale-image itself); but it could also have intruded from reminiscence. The paraphrasing Σᴹᴮⱽ δρυὸς [ἐν add. V] πετάλοις ἐφεζομένη uses the less obvious word πετάλοις, either because the commentator had it in his text or because he remembered Hes. *Op.* 486 δρυὸς ἐν πετάλοισι. κλάδοις is a more obvious word: Eust. 1875, 43 glosses ἐν πετάλοις in *Od.* 19.520 with κλαδίον; cf. κλάδος as gloss (CMn) on ἔρνεσι in 653 above. Moreover, M, whose singular readings

---

[1] See also F. Skoda, "Ἑλελίζω I et II', *Revue de Philologie* 58 (1984) 223–32, who explains how onomatopoeic ἑλελίζω could have developed a variety of meanings referring to sound or to movement.

deserve attention, lacks ἀμφί, raising the possibility that κλάδοις intruded as a gloss and that ἀμφί was added subsequently (by someone who understood the metre). In addition, the use of ἀμφί here seems very odd for Eur. Grammarians speak of an 'inside' use of ἀμφί: Gildersleeve, Pindar comm., xcix, with reference to *O.* 13.37 ἁλίωι ἀμφ' ἑνὶ 'in a single day'; K–G I.490, Schwyzer II.438. But the ἀμφί of manner (ἀμφὶ φόβωι *Or.* 825) need not be explicated as 'surrounded by fear' and is hardly parallel to locative 'amidst, surrounded by the branches'. Other alleged Euripidean instances can be otherwise explained: 1578 below and *Andr.* 511 imply embracing and surrounding; *Ba.* 1229 ἀμφὶ δρυμοῖς may have a distributive sense 'here and there in the thickets' (but Bruhn's δρυμούς is attractive); *IA* 1291–2 τὸν ἀμφὶ βουσὶ βουκόλον is probably 'in the neighbourhood of' or 'in attendance upon'. Unless ἀμφὶ κλάδοις implies 'perched on', 'surrounding with its claws or body', the phrase is quite extraordinary. As for ἑζομένα, given its absence in both Π⁵ and B, the omission must be counted as a genuine variant that survived over centuries. It is more probable that it is an intrusion than that it was wrongly omitted. In the parallel passages (1515–18n.) a verb of sitting (καθέζομαι, ἵζομαι, ἐνίζω) is present in *Od.* 19.520, *Hel.* 1108, Arist. *Birds* 742 (cf. as well ἱζάνοισι in Ibycus 36), but not in the other five instances. Simplex ἕζομαι is poetic in classical Greek and could have been used by Eur., but it is a prosaic word in later Greek and could have been used as a gloss. Note that, as in the case of ἀμφὶ κλάδοις, even if ἑζομένα is not genuine it fits the metre.[1]

1517–18 †μονομάτερος ὀδυρμοῖς† ἐμοῖς ἄχεσι συνωιδός   no certain restoration is possible here in view of the difficulty of the mss text and the divergence of Π⁵ (μουνα[*c.* 14–15 letters]ρημαεμοισαχεϲιϲυνγωιδο[). μονομάτερος is corrupt (we can at the least be sure Eur. would have written μονομάτορος from -μάτωρ: cf. Chantraine s.v. μήτηρ) but must contain a reference to the nightingale as 'solitary, bereaved mother' (as Pearson recognized). The sense 'bereft of one's mother' (offered by Σ and earlier critics), though suitable to Ant. herself, will not fit the nightingale and defies analogy. μονο- + substantive stem X can mean 'having only one X' (μονόμματος), 'having nothing but X alone' (μονοχίτων), 'having X and being alone or apart from others' (μονοτράπεζος *IT* 949, μονόπωλος *Or.* 1004, μονόκωπος *Hel.* 1128 (see Kannicht)), or 'being X and being alone or single' (μόνιππος, μονογέρων, μονόβιβλος, μονόπαις *Alc.* 906), but not 'being alone, deprived of X'. Gen. μονομάτορος (agreeing with ἐμοῦ understood in ἐμοῖς) is thus impossible. Canter's μονομάτωρ is possible, but the fact that a paraphrasing Σ uses the nominative should not be assumed to

---

[1] JD notes 'Willink's ἀμ πετάλοις beautifully reconciles the variants.'

support it; if Π⁵ had μούνα ματέρος, the sense is wrong and the Ionic form μούνα (*Prom.* 804, Soph.) is dubious for Eur. (insecure attestation in fr. 646a Snell). If the evidence of Π⁵ is dismissed, the best emendation is Wilam.'s μονομάτορσιν ὀδυρμοῖς ('what bird ... with its mournful cries of a bereft mother sounds in unison with/suitably accompanies my pains?'): cf. Williger, 17, who well compares *Choe.* 334–5 δίπαις ... θρῆνος. But if, as Π⁵ suggests, ὀδυρμοῖς is corrupt (as some critics had already believed, because of the collocation of datives), then it is hard to find a convincing restoration (cf. *ZPE* 38 (1980) 33). Something on the lines of μονόματορ μέλπουσ' ὀδυρμ' (perhaps with συνῳδόν) might be attempted (cf. Nauck's μονομάτορ' ὀδυρμὸν ἵησιν); Mueller-Goldingen, 346, suggests / ἐξομένα μονομά-/ τωρ ἰαχοῦσ' ἔρημα / ἐμοῖς ..., comparing *Su.* 775 ἔρημα κλαίω. On the whole I favour Wilam.'s solution.

ἄχεσι συνῳδός the dat. with συνῳδός need not be a noun denoting sound (θρηνήμασι *Hel.* 174, *Or.* 133); cf. *Su.* 73 ξυνῳδοὶ κακοῖς (but for doubts about κακοῖς see Collard), *Med.* 1269–70 αὐτοφόνταις ξυνῳδὰ ... ἄχη (the dat. will be felt at least ἀπὸ κοινοῦ with ξυνῳδά, though it may also be governed by the verb lost to corruption in 1269); cf. προσῳδόν 1498 above.

1519–21 see 335n. for the onomatopoeic assonance of αι expressive of grief. Hence it is proper to read αἰεί rather than ἀεί in 1521: see *ZPE* 38 (1980) 23 (also p. 20 on 1549).

1520 τούσδε so Π⁵, as direct object of προκλαίω with αἴλινον internal acc. A similar sense can be obtained with mss τοῖσδε if it is taken as a loose dat. of interest (cf. Σ). Most translators have taken it with αἰάγμασιν, but then the demonstrative has less point.

προκλαίω προ- is to be taken not as temporal ('mourn in advance') but as spatial ('openly, in public') as in προτιθέναι νεκρόν. The word is rare, and in its few other uses προ- is temporal (*Alc.* 526, *Trach.* 963, Hdt. 5.8 (see Stein's comm.)). With temporal meaning, some interpret: 'who cry out *ailinon* in advance for my own ⟨future⟩ life of loneliness, since I am destined to spend all my time in the shedding of tears' (unsuitably self-centred). But αἰῶνα must go with διάξουσα and τὸν αἰεὶ χρόνον is acc. of duration: αἰῶνα διάγειν (*Hom.h.* 20.6–7; αἰῶνα διοιχνεῖ *Eum.* 315) is a poetic substitute for the common βίον/βίοτον διάγειν; for χρόνον cf. *Aj.* 342–3 τὸν εἰσαεὶ ... χρόνον, *Or.* 207 ἐς τὸν αἰὲν χρόνον.

1522 δάκρυσιν Π⁵'s δακρύοις could equally be right, or even δακρύοισιν (see note on Metre).

1523 {ἰαχήσω} the word intruded when μονάδ' was misinterpreted as μόνα δ' (already by some Σ); Π⁵ confirms the deletion by Burges (ed. of *Tro.*, p. 144).

1524–5 for illustration of the *dubitatio* of grief including the question 'which first?' see Tarrant on Sen. *Ag.* 649f. Π⁵'s version is inferior, probably the result of simplification (e.g., ἀπὸ χαίτας is placed before the verb, which seemed easier than connecting it as attribute with anarthrous σπαραγμοῖς (K–G 1.610)).

1526–7 ἐν and παρά cannot stand together. Alleged instances of pleonastic construction of prepositions ἐκ παραλλήλου are corrupt (*Phil.* 554, *IT* 1131, *Trach.* 1160, *Or.* 407: see Di Benedetto for an attempt to defend the last two, but cf. Diggle, *Text. Trad. Or.* 61–2); the conflated idiom ἀπὸ βοῆς ἕνεκα (Thuc. 8.92.9, Xen. *HG* 2.4.31) is a special case (cf. Pl. *Laws* 701d2 for τίνος δὴ χάριν ἕνεκα, a similar idiom if not the result of corruption). The metre seems to me more convincing with a syllable in place of ἐν, and King's ἤ is a likely solution; exclamation ἦν (Maas) is stylistically inapposite (in tragedy only in Lyssa's tro. tetr., *Her.* 867). On the omission/deletion of ἐν in RfRvW see *Text. Trad.* 107. For interrogative ἤ ... ἤ following on another question, Diggle (1989) 203 cites *Hec.* 447–61, *Ion* 429–32, K–G II.530–1 (Homeric usage); without a preceding question, the few instances of interrogative ἤ ... ἤ transmitted in the mss of tragedy have been plausibly replaced by εἰ or by non-interrogative interpretation (see Page on *Med.* 493).

There are two other problems in these lines. (1) The rhythm is ambiguous, but easiest to interpret if we read διδύμοισι rather than -οις or -οισιν and μαστοῖς rather than -οῖσιν. It would be possible to read διδύμοις if the alternative ionic interpretation of 1526–9 is adopted (1527 will then be ionic in the form ∪ – – ∪∪ – –, cf. 1539, 1541). (2) γάλακτος ... μαστοῖς is a very bold unaccompanied defining genitive (1491n.), not because of the words combined in the phrase, but because the context requires the meaning 'breasts that once nurtured me with milk' rather than the more straightforward 'breasts full of milk' or 'milky breasts'. Context, however, does often determine meaning, and we perhaps have here the inverse of the motif featured in 1434 τὸν πολὺν μαστῶν πόνον (cf. 30–1n.). As in 1434 some critics have found the reference to Jocasta's breasts tasteless and emended (e.g., Headlam's ἐν διδύμοισιν ἀγαλάκτοις ἄρα μαστοῖς (*CR* 15 (1901) 102): the particle seems to me pointless, though its late position can be defended by *Ion* 790); Diggle (1990a) would accept ἀγαλάκτοις, but not ἄρα.

1529 οὐλόμεν' this aorist participle often has a strong modal meaning (≈ ὅς ὄλοιτο); cf. Wilam. on *Her.* 1061, Schwyzer 1.524, II.17. This modal meaning is certainly present in 1029 above, *Med.* 1253, Soph. fr. 185. The alleged milder sense *infelix, miser* (LSJ s.v. II; G. Italie, *Index Aeschyleus*² (Leiden 1964) s.v. ὄλλυμι III) is not firmly established: a tone of deprecation or disapproval rather than of simple pity or self-pity may well be present in *Od.* 18.273, *Prom.* 397, *Hel.* 385, *Choe.*

575

152.[1] So here we have 'accursedly wounded bodies' rather than simply 'unhappy wounded bodies'.

αἰκίσματα νεκρῶν[2] probably equivalent to ἠικισμένους νεκρούς, a typical use of abstract noun with defining gen. in lyric circumlocution (cf. 308 παρηίδων ὄρεγμα and Breitenbach, 202), although αἴκισμα might be used as abstract for concrete, '(mutilated) wounds' (1502n. αἵματα). The characteristic and effective locution is diluted if one prefers the variant δισσῶν (already in Π⁵), which may be the result of assimilation to passages such as 55, 57, 1243, 1482, 1502.

1530 ὀτοτοτοῖ I now accept this spelling, supported by ὀτοτύζω (Aesch., Aristophanes) (JD).

λεῖπε in Attic drama the imperative of simplex λείπω is normally λεῖπε, not λίπε, regardless of the apparent aspect of the command. The sole exception would be 1682 below, but there is no reason to reject the variant λεῖπε there. The preference extends in part to compounds: -λειπε occurs five times, -λιπε twice (guaranteed by metre in Arist. *Lys.* 244 κατάλιφ', but not in Eur. *El.* 1250 ἔκλιπε: cf., with no discernible aspectual distinc- tion, Arist. *Birds* 660 κατάλειφ', *Her.* 1322 and *Ion* 1306 ἔκλειπε). For the occasional indifference of the imperative to distinctions of aspect, see 40n., Schwyzer ii.254f., Barrett on *Hipp.* 473–5, Gerber on Pindar *O.* 1.85.[3]

1532–3 δεῖξον . . . σὸν αἰῶνα μέλεον in asyndeton with λεῖπε, as often with imperatives in summons (cf. 296–7, 1068–70); a poetic periphrasis for 'wretched Oedipus, show yourself', just as ἀλαὸν ὄμμα φέρων is for 'being blind' (Breitenbach, 198–9). This is effectively followed by ὅς ('you who . . .') rather than ὄν or ὅσον as in Π⁵, which would throw further emphasis on αἰῶνα (cf. *ZPE* 38 (1980) 34 with n. 62).

1533 ἔτι so Π⁵, preferable to mss' ἐπί, for ἐπὶ δώμασι would be 'by the

---

[1] The use in *Choe.* 152 is conditioned by paregmenon ὀλόμενον ὀλομένωι, and the sense is perhaps 'tears which I would rather not have shed, but which are induced by the accursed murder': see Garvie *ad loc.* for another view, also rejecting the sense *infelix*.

[2] West, *Aeschylus* xlv, insists that Attic derivatives of ἀεικ- ought to be spelled ἀικ-, not αἰκ-; possibly so, but ἀϊκῶς (ᾰ) in *Il.* 22.336 could have led Attic poets to use αἰκ-.

[3] Cf. unexpected use of imperfect of λείπω: Tucker on *Septem* 55; Wackernagel, *Syntax* 1.182f.; Davies on *Trach.* 76–7. The distinc- tion 'imperfect of reluctance' vs. 'aorist of eagerness' proposed by Gildersleeve, *Problems in Greek Syntax* (Baltimore 1903) (=*AJP* 23 (1902)) 250 and on Pindar *O.* 6.45, is illuminating for some passages, but not for imperatives.

palace' (*Or.* 1255 μή τις ἐπὶ δώμασι σταθεὶς: the phrase is emended by Willink) or 'upon the palace'. It has earlier been emphasized that Oedipus is *inside*, so it is improbable that the poet would be vague about the distinction 'at/in' as Paley alleged (1570 below is different: see *ad loc.*). The closest potential parallel, *Wealth* 338 ἐπὶ τοῖσι κουρείοισι τῶν καθημένων, has often been emended to ἐν (cf. *Birds* 1441 ἐν τοῖσι κουρείοις; Eupolis fr. 194 K–A ἐν τοῖσι κουρείοις . . . καθίζων); and, if ἐπί is sound there, it need not mean 'inside', since the barbers' stalls may not have been enclosed and men may have congregated on benches outside the stall or under the same portico. Preposition ἐνί (Scholefield) is doubtful in tragedy (Fraenkel on *Ag.* 78). One may still doubt the appropriateness of ἔτι in Ant.'s mouth (*ZPE* 38 (1980) 18; cf. Mueller-Goldingen, 347), but it perhaps reinforces μακρόπνουν in an acceptable way ('you who still in the house, blind though you are, drag out a long-breathed life').

1534–5 δώμασιν ἀέριον σκότον ὄμμασι σοῖσι βαλών when ἐπί was read, several critics believed δώμασιν to be corrupt and suggested that it be replaced: δάκρυσιν Hermann, δέργμασιν Bothe (with ὄμμασι deleted), or ὄμμασι Wilam. (assuming that something was lost between it and the dochmiac ἀέριον σκότον). But if ἔτι is right, I see no strong objection to δώμασιν either on metrical grounds (see above under Metre) or because of repetition (blindness is referred to twice, 1531 and 1534, as well as by implication in 1536bis and explicitly in Oedipus' reply 1539; so too Oedipus' being indoors, 1530–1 and 1534, as well as 1541). δώμασιν may be pure locative (cf. *Pers.* 237, *Trach.* 950, *Hel.* 1043, etc.) or a combined locative/dat. of interest (cf. *Andr.* 620 δώμασιν λαβεῖν, combining locative, instrumental, and dat. of interest, or δόμοις/οἴκοις δέχεσθαι, combining locative, directional, and instrumental). As for the rest of the line, the sense must be 'having cast the darkness of blindness upon your eyes'. The verb may suggest the violence of the self-mutilation (cf. 61n.), but cf. also *Aj.* 51f. δυσφόρους ἐπ' ὄμμασι γνώμας βαλοῦσ', 950 above μέλαιναν κῆρ' ἐπ' ὄμμασιν βαλών; for simplex βάλλω as a more colourful substitute for ἐπιτίθημι or ἐφίημι cf. *Phil.* 67 λύπην πᾶσιν Ἀργείοις βαλεῖς.

ἀέριον outside Eur. the word is a scientific term in Democritus and the Hippocratic corpus and is used more widely in late authors; Eur. himself has the normal meaning 'of the ἀήρ' in fr. 27.4 (*Tro.* 546 has now been attractively emended by Diggle), but here the word is equivalent to epic ἠερόεις 'murky'. Thus both words in ἀέριον σκότον are suggestive of Oedipus' ghostly existence (1540n.).

1535 ἕλκεις μακρόπνουν ζοάν 'draw out a long-breathed life', i.e. 'a long life'. The metaphor in ἕλκω is of toilsome motion (as in *Or.* 206–7 βίοτον . . . ἕλκω), and μακρόπνουν is used with typical poetic redundancy of its second element (cf. *Pers.* 263 μακροβίοτος αἰών). As a medical term μακρόπνους refers to 'deep, slow breathing', a cure for continuous yawning in Hippocr. *Epid.* 2.3.7, 6.2.4, but here the sense 'draw a deep and laboured breath' (Powell) is less apposite. μακρόπουν (Π⁵, a survival in χ (*Text. Trad.* 66, 96)) would also give the sense 'long life' (from 'life that travels a long course'), but is stylistically inferior and might suggest an unwanted pun on Οἰδίπους. ζοάν¹ is to be preferred to ζωάν. The latter often intrudes: cf. *Se.* 939 (M vs. *recc.*), Theocr. *Ep.* 18.9 (Theocr. mss vs. *Anth. gr.* 9.600), Call. fr. 193.9, fr. 400.1 (*Anth. gr.* 13.10), Soph. frr. 592.4, 556, *Hipp.* 816, *Hec.* 1108 (also *El.* 121 unless responsion − ∪∪ − ῡ − is allowed). There are about ten instances in tragedy where the metre would allow either vowel, but omicron is required in the four (or five) just listed, omega only in *IT* 150, where the text is uncertain.

1536 bis–38 ἀλαίνων ... πόδ' ἤ ... δύστανος ἰαύων   Schoene's supplement is necessary, for πόδα must go with ἀλαίνων (not ἰαύων, as Σ) and Oedipus is *either* walking slowly and aimlessly in the courtyard *or* lying abed. ἀλαίνων πόδα is typically Euripidean: for this attachment of acc. πόδα or κῶλον to an intransitive verb of motion, cf. 1412 προβὰς ... κῶλον δεξιόν and idioms like βαίνειν πόδα illustrated by Porson on *Or.* 1427, Denniston on *El.* 94, Diggle, *Studies* 37. As Porson implies, the acc. is probably an external object of the part of the body affected by the action (cf. the retained acc. with passive: βεβολημένος ἦτορ), not an internal acc. (πόδα = βάσιν: so K–G 1.307).

δύστανος   the nominative is idiomatically correct (1205, 1316, *Su.* 1073, *Hec.* 683, etc.; likewise τάλας 53, 1414, *El.* 588, etc.). δύστανον would have to be adverbial, for which the only parallel is the superlative adv. restored in *Su.* 967. Corruption occurred by assimilation to πόδα after loss of ἤ.

ἰαύων   here and in *Her.* 1049 means 'sleep' or 'rest abed' rather than 'pass the night', the original Homeric sense still seen in *Aj.* 1204, *Rhes.* 740. Old people who are too weak to be fully active rest in bed by day: *Her.* 555.² The reading πόδα δύστανον δεμνίοις (metrically possible if ποδ' ἤ is read: dochm, cr + ba) is apparently due to deliberate transposition intended to simplify a passage made difficult by the loss of ἤ and the corruption to acc. δύστανον (*Text. Trad.* 112). The transposition in Π⁵

---

¹ The correct accentuation (ζόα/ζοά) cannot be recovered (*Text. Trad.* 56). Note that in *Se.* 938 M has ζοά. Mss of Hdt. also present great confusion over vowel-length and accent (cf. Hoffmann, *Gr. Dialekte* III.524). Paroxytone ζόη is found in Hdt. mss (along with ζοή, ζώη, ζωή) and in the marginal variant and scholion in Va at *Hec.* 1108.

² In *Tro.* 1181 V's λέχος would illustrate the same motif, but Diggle prefers P's πέπλους.

(πόδα δυστήνοις δεμνίοις) is on this view coincidentally the same. Though Paley conjectured ἐν δεμνίοις δυστάνοις, the dat. involves an improbable enallage (δύστηνος is normally used of persons or their sufferings).

1539 βακτρεύμασι either (a) 'by (my own) staff-supported movement of my blind feet', with ἐξάγαγες implying a verb of motion (cf. Mosch.'s gloss ἐξελθεῖν ἐποίησας) to which the dat. is in sense attached;[1] or (b) 'by (your) staff-like supporting of my blind steps', instrumental dat. more obviously attached to ἐξάγαγες. Etymology and usage do not decide the issue, but the probabilities of staging favour (a). The verb βακτρεύω could mean 'do anything in which a βάκτρον is involved', e.g. 'walk with a staff' or 'support like a staff' (as in the only attested use of the verb, *arg. metr. OC* 1–2 ἀλαὸν πόδα βακτρεύουσα / πατρὸς ... Ἀντιγόνη). Hence βάκτρευμα could also have various senses, each made clear by its context (as is true of other -μα nouns in tragedy). But though (b) receives some support from metaphorical uses of βάκτρον or σκῆπτρον of a human support as in *OC* 848, 1109, *Hec.* 281 (and the *arg. metr. OC*, which could be an imitation of our passage), it would imply that after finishing her monody in 1538 Antigone goes up to the door, latches onto Oedipus (who is supposed to have stumbled alone through the palace and courtyard without a staff), and guides him into position on stage (and if we take ἐξάγαγες fully literally, Ant. must go in to fetch Oed.!). The usual technique, however, is for the summoner simply to wait for the emerging character; indeed, the length of a summons may be designed to cover the time during which the character reaches the door from inside, opens it, and steps out. Moreover, the staff is a typical characterizing stage-prop for the old and feeble (*Ag.* 75, 80, *Andr.* 588, 1223, Arist. *Wealth* 272), and esp. in Eur. old men need both staff and guiding hand (*Her.* 107–8, 123–5, *Ion* 738–44, *Ba.* 193–8, 363–4).[2] Blind men ought to be guided by a companion or slave (*OT* 444, 1292, *Ant.* 988–90, 1087, *OC* 502, *Phoen.* 834, Arist. *Wealth* 13–16), but this does not exclude simultaneous use of a staff (see 1548n. and 1719n., where again the sense of the Greek and the staging are disputed).[3] When a blind man is unaccompanied, he ought to have a staff

---

[1] Cf. Σ and Hesych. s.v. βακτρεύμασιν, a corrupt entry which probably ought to be restored (with anon.) as τοῖς ἐρείσμασιν στηριζόμενον (-ος, -οις codd.).

[2] In *Ba.* Cadmus and Tiresias use *thyrsoi* as staffs (175–7, 251–4, 363). On support of old and blind characters, cf. Kaimio, 12–16. Old Priam supports himself on a staff at *Tro.* 150 (description, not staged).

[3] Characteristically, Soph. makes no reference to such a prop as a staff, and it is uncertain whether Tiresias has a staff as well as a guide in *OT*,

(*OT* 456, *Ba.* 170ff.)[1] except in circumstances like those of *OT* 1297ff., *Hec.* 1056ff. Another consideration in favour of the use of a staff here is that in the duet and the exodos Oedipus ought to be able to stand on his own, leaving Ant. free for her own movements and gestures.

1540 ἐξάγαγες εἰς φῶς Oedipus is presented as a ghostly being or demonic apparition by this phrase and other language in the passage: see above on 1534 ἀέριον σκότον; cf. 1541 σκοτίων ἐκ θαλάμων (θάλαμος is used metaphorically for the grave or the underworld), 1544 νέκυν ἔνερθεν, and Edmunds, *HSCP* 85 (1981) 230–1 on Oed. as revenant. It is as if a demonic power lurking in the background throughout the play (64 ἔκρυψαν, 336 σκότια κρύπτεται, 872 συγκαλύψαι, and refs. to the curse) is now brought before the audience's eyes; but there is an intended discrepancy between this intimation of demonic power and the realistic portrayal of Oed.'s feebleness with the evocation of his ordinary familial attachment to Jocasta, Antigone, and even his sons.

1542 δακρύοισιν 'by your pitiful tears': by convention Oed. has not heard the exact content of the summons, but has discerned its emotional tone (1265–9n.).

1543–5 all three items of comparison in this tricolon are traditional emblems of weakness and/or insubstantiality. For phantoms cf. *Ag.* 839 εἴδωλον σκιᾶς ('the superlative of the unreal': Fraenkel *ad loc.*), *Aj.* 126, and (most relevant) *Phil.* 947 and *OC* 109–10 ἀνδρὸς Οἰδίπου τόδ' ἄθλιον εἴδωλον. For the dead cf. *Phil.* 946, *Tro.* 193 νεκροῦ μορφά, νεκύων ἀμενηνὸν ἄγαλμα; likeness to the dead can also imply squalor, as *Or.* 385. For dreams (along with σκιά the most common such emblem), cf. *Ag.* 82, *Her.* 111–12 (see Bond), Eur. fr. 25.3, below 1722, etc.

1543 πολιὸν αἰθέρος ἀφανὲς εἴδωλον probably 'a grey and obscure image formed of ether', but the phrase is problematic in sense and metre (see under Metre). Some (from Σ to Méridier) have taken πολιόν with μ' in 1539; but whereas λεχήρη in 1541 gains force from its separation from μ', πολιόν is much less essential and would be bathetic if sandwiched

---

Ant., Phoen. (but I assume one: 834 action n.). Artistic representations are rare, but in Séchan, fig. 45, the figure which may be Tir. has a staff and is held by the arm by a little girl; in fig. 139 (Homeric bowl *N* in London: 838n.) there seems to be no staff; in fig. 142 Oed. extends his arms forwards, but the break prevents us from saying whether he has a staff or is feeling his way with his hands alone.

[1] That Tir. is unaccompanied is implied by *Ba.* 193–8, 363–5; cf. Stanley-Porter, 81. There is no mention of a staff in the prologue of *Wealth*, where the blind god is unguided.

between οἰκτρ. δακρύοισιν and the tricolon αἰθέρος … ὄνειρον.[1] πολιός is normally used of the whitish hair of the aged or, by transference, of any part or attribute of an aged person (*Her.* 1209 πολιὸν … δάκρυον); here it may suggest not just that the image is of a grey-haired old man, but that the image as a whole has the pallor of decrepitude. More serious are the doubts about ἀφανές. The αἰθήρ is usually bright (φαεννός, λαμπρός, etc.), and εἴδωλα in epic, in *Ba.* 291–3, and in *Hel.* (composed of οὐρανός ≈ αἰθήρ) are completely convincing images. Here, if πολιόν can suggest that the image is not a bright one, then ἀφανές perhaps can carry the unique sense 'obscure' or 'indistinct'.[2] If emendation is deemed necessary, two popular changes have been Hartung's deletion of ἀφανές as a gloss on πολιόν and Weil's αἰθεροφανές. Neither satisfies. πολιόν needs no gloss, and the glossator would himself be using ἀφανές in the untypical sense that prompts suspicion in our passage (Π⁵ should not be cited as support for this deletion, though it is possible that our text of 1543 would not fit in the gap in Π⁵). Compounds of noun-stem + -φανες are very rare in classical and even in Hellenistic Greek (and those in tragedy are all prepositional compounds, as Diggle notes), and αἰθεροφανές ought to mean 'appearing in the sky', which is inapposite for Oedipus. Diggle doubts both 'formed of ether' applied to Oed. and the unique sense of ἀφανές and proposes αἰθεροφαές, 'shining with the brightness of ether' ((1989) 203–4).

1545 πτανὸν ὄνειρον same phrase *IT* 571; cf. *Hec.* 704 φάσμα μελανόπτερον, Alcman *PMGF* 1.49 ὑποπετριδίων ὀνείρων.

1546 ἀγγελίας ἔπος poetic periphrasis for ἀγγελίαν; cf. ἔπος ἀγγέλλειν 1075 above, *OC* 302.

οἴσηι 'you will get' is effectively bitter, almost implying 'for the trouble of asking' (middle as in LSJ s.v. φέρω A.VI.3). The middle can have different implications in different contexts: contrast *Su.* 583 λόγοις …

---

[1] Note too that the combination πολιὸν αἰθέρ- appears in the contemporary aria at *Or.* 1376. On the basis of that passage Hermann proposed πολιὸν αἰθέρ' ὥς, but 'bright ether' (West on Hes. *Op.* 477) seems inappropriate here.

[2] The sense 'indistinct, hazy' is assumed by Meiggs and Lewis, no. 30B (=*SIG* 38), from Teos: (35–9) ὃς ἂν τὰ(ς) στήλας … ἢ κατάξει ἢ φοινικήϊα ἐκκόψει ἢ ἀφανέας ποιήσει. But the sense there is not 'make indistinct (by washing out the paint in the letters)', but 'conceal the stelae', the sense conveyed by the synonym ἀφανίζειν in Thuc. 6.54.7 προσοικοδομήσας … μεῖζον μῆκος τοῦ βωμοῦ ἠφάνισε τοὐπίγραμμα. Other senses of ἀφανής are 'unseen', 'unknown', 'indeterminate (because not yet apparent)' and even 'without fame or prominence' (*Tro.* 1244, Sappho fr. 55 L–P).

οὕσπερ ἤνεγκω ('which you brought with you as your own': cf. *Hel.* 664 λόγον, οἷον οἷον ἐσοίσομαι (Lenting's -ομεν is not needed; on metrical grounds Willink *CQ* 39 (1989) 62–3 argues for ἐσοισόμεθα or ἐσοίσω)); cf. 595 ἀποίσεται μόρον vs. 1161 ἀποίσεται βίον. Battier's flat εἴσηι seems to me unnecessary; for ἔπος εἴσηι JD compares *El.* 346 εἴσηι μῦθον, *Rhes.* 142 εἴσηι λόγον (both in trimeters); for εἴσηι/οἴσηι cf. 253 above.

1548 παραβάκτροις as in 1539 above, there is a dispute between a literal and a metaphorical use of βάκτρον in this hapax: either (a) '(with attendance) by your staff', the adj. being formed normally by hypostasis from παρὰ βάκτρωι (Schwyzer 1.436) and implying that Oed. always used a staff but also was assisted and guided by Jocasta; (b) '(with) staff-like (attendance)', the adj. being equivalent to *ἀντίβακτρος and implying that Oed. had only Jocasta for support. (a) is the more natural usage and is supported by the parallels (1539n.). Moreover, for an adj. compounded of παρα- and noun-stem X meaning 'like X' I know of no example other than Eratosthenes *FGrHist* 241 F 32 (Plut. *Dem.* 9.4) παράβακχος, but this could mean 'such as is found παρὰ Βάκχωι' rather than 'like a frenzied Bacchant'.

1549 πόδα σὸν τυφλόπουν direct object of the verbal complex θεραπεύμασιν ἐμόχθει (Schwyzer 11.74; Diggle, *Studies* 58). Both the fullness of πόδα . . . -πουν (cf. 808 Καδμογενῆ . . . γένναν) and the periphrastic reference to a person are typical: Breitenbach, 188, 199. There is further virtuosity in the expression if Eur. intends an ironic etymological play on Οἰδίπους vs. τυφλόπους (cf. *OT* 397).

1551–2 ὤμοι ἐμῶν παθέων the variant οἴμοι ἐγὼ παθέων is equally idiomatic (*Hipp.* 591, 817 (where παθέων is a variant for πόνων), *Rhes.* 902, *Or.* 671 (with variant: Diggle, *Text. Trad. Or.* 113); for ἐμῶν rather than ἐγὼ cf. *Hec.* 475, 1098, *Hel.* 676 (JD)).

πάρα γὰρ στενάχειν τάδ', αὐτεῖν for the first part, cf. *Tro.* 106 τί γὰρ οὐ πάρα μοι μελέαι στενάχειν; The unbalanced asyndeton and the use of αὐτεῖν (here apparently 'shout in grief': cf. perhaps *Pers.* 1058 αὔτει δ' ὀξύ) have prompted suspicion. Asyndeton between juxtaposed near-synonyms is a familiar device (1193n.), and in excited contexts cf. *Septem* 186 αὔειν λακάζειν, *Ion* 1446–7 τίν' αὐδὰν ἀύσω βοάσω; Sa's ἀυταῖς or ἀυτᾶι (after Wecklein) might satisfy, although ἀυτή will now be almost 'shouts of grief' rather than the normal 'yells, loud cries'. Jackson's τάδ' ἀύτει, anticipating 1554 αὔδα, seems too flat.

1553–4 ποίαι μοίραι πῶς if sound, the virtually redundant interrogatives are here emphatic (cf. *Hec.* 695–6 τίνι μόρωι θνήισκεις; τίνι πότμωι κεῖσαι;), but one may also compare the redundancy in how-questions preceding messenger speeches (Austin and Reeve, *Maia* 22 (1970) 17). Π[5] lacks the redundancy and presents a metrically and semantically equivalent text. The criteria between the two versions are generally inconclusive: cf. *ZPE* 38 (1980) 30. But Π[5]'s τάδε μοι, τέκνον, αὔδα is more pedestrian

(568, [778] [variant], *Hel.* 1662), absolute αὔδα more lyrical (124, *Hel.* 680, *Ion* 222 in Hermann's emendation). Diggle (1989) 204–5 proposes (after Wecklein, based on B^γρ μιᾶι μοίραι) τρισσαὶ ⟨δέ?⟩ μιᾶι ψυχαὶ μοίραι (or μοίραι ψυχαί).

1555–6 οὐκ ἐπ' ὀνείδεσιν . . . ἀλλ' ὀδύναισι ἐπί + dat. in this tricolon shifts from purpose (ὀνείδεσιν) to attendant circumstances, a closely related use. οὐδ' ἐπιχάρμασιν artfully gives an aural impression of anaphora without exact syntactic parallelism. ἐπὶ χάρμασιν cannot be read because χάρμα connotes malignant joy only when accompanied by a suitable dative (*Il.* 3.51 δυσμενέσιν, 6.82 δηΐοισι, Hes. *Op.* 701 γείτοσι) or gen. (1503 'Ερινύος). ἐπιχαίρω, ἐπίχαρτος, ἐπίχαρμα usually do carry that connotation (not always: Diggle on *Phaethon* 93).

1556 σὸς ἀλάστωρ an *alastor* is a destructive agent (Barrett on *Hipp.* 877–90), often a demon, usually one aroused by a crime (esp. murder) and capable of transmitting pollution (cf. *Her.* 1234, *Med.* 1333–5). The context, as well as repeated reference to Oedipus' curse earlier in the play, suggests that σός here is subjective, 'which your curse aroused': likewise *OC* 788 ἀλάστωρ οὑμὸς ἐννναίων ἀεί, of the destructive agent stirred by Oed.'s wrath and curse[1] (cf. *Septem* 723 πατρὸς εὐκταίαν 'Ερινύν, *OC* 1434 τῶν τοῦδ' 'Ερινύων, and probably *OC* 1299, *pace* Jebb). Less appropriate is 'which was sent against you for your sins' (Σ), for which cf. *Med.* 1333 τὸν σὸν δ' ἀλάστορ', 1593–4 below (and obj. gen. in *Ag.* 1501–2, *Trach.* 1092). Of course, in both *Phoen.* and *OC* the former type of *alastor* is, in a sense, just a new manifestation of the latter.

1557–8 ξίφεσιν . . . καὶ πυρὶ καὶ . . . μάχαις the typical destructive implements of war, fire (cf. 575, 1122, 1155) and sword, are coupled with a more general term: for such combination of concrete and abstract see 1292n. For the pairing cf. *Andr.* 105 δορὶ καὶ πυρί, *Hipp.* 551 σὺν αἵματι σὺν καπνῶι, Dion. Hal. *Ant.Rom.* 3.66.1 πυρὶ καὶ σιδήρωι καὶ πᾶσι λωβησάμενοι κακοῖς. The motif of fire-breathing Erinyes (*Eum.* 138, *IT* 288) or of torch-bearing Erinyes need not be evoked here: for the latter in literature cf. *Wealth* 423–5, perhaps earlier *Phaethon* 214 (Diggle's comm., p. 143); also fourth-century South Italian vase-painting.

βρίθων used (here only) in the way βαρύς (ὤν) or βάρος ἔχων are elsewhere: an Erinys or other malevolent demon or misfortune itself is often pictured as oppressing with its feet or swooping down from above upon the head of the victim (*Pers.* 515–16, *Ag.* 1175, *Ant.* 1272–4, 1345–6, *OT* 263, etc.).

σχετλίαισι μάχαις a bold use of the adj., since apart from *Od.* 10.68–9

---

[1] Cf. *Tro.* 941 ὁ τῆσδ' ἀλάστωρ, 'the destroyer to whom she [Hecuba] gave birth', not 'the bane or curse of this woman' (Lee).

ὕπνος σχέτλιος it normally qualifies a person or a neuter noun like κακόν (or *El.* 120 πόνων, a slight extension). The boldness probably prompted the gloss-variant φονίαισι.

1559 ὤμοι metre indicates that the change of speaker must follow, not precede, ὤμοι (Π⁵ vs. mss). 1550 suggests that ὤμοι is to be preferred to Π⁵'s οἴμοι (cf. variants at *Hec.* 158).

1560 τί τόδε καταστένεις; 'Why this groan?' (cf. *IT* 550 τί δ' ἐστέναξας τοῦτο;). Antigone's question is meant to elicit a more articulate response to the news, and Oedipus' reply τέκνα is marginally so. Compare the exchange of Electra and the chorus in Soph. *El.* 826ff. ἒ ἔ, αἰαῖ – ὦ παῖ, τί δακρύεις; – φεῦ – μηδὲν μέγ' ἀύσῃς. – ἀπολεῖς. τόδε (Π⁵) is slightly more idiomatic than the plural τάδε (mss): τί τόδ' *Alc.* 106, *Hec.* 187, *Tro.* 269, *OC* 209 (Diggle, *Studies* 42).

1561 δι' ὀδύνας ἔβας as in *Alc.* 874 and *El.* 1210 (where σάφ' οἶδα accompanies),[1] this phrase expresses an understanding response to grief-stricken cries or remarks. In *El.* the aorist is a true past tense, and the same is probably true in *Alc.* ('you *did* suffer pain, but your present lamentation does no good'); here, however, the aorist is an instantaneous one (Schwyzer II.281–2), a common usage in tragedy, usually in the first person (433 above ἐπώμοσα; ἀπέπτυσα, ἐπῄνεσα, etc.), sometimes in the second (983n. ἔγνως). Failure to recognize this idiom, along with the immediately following εἰ, led Σ to paraphrase with ἄν, which in turn has prompted many (from Triclinius to Pearson) wrongly to insert ἄν by emendation.

1562–3 εἰ δὲ ... γ' 'Granted, you have just now felt the pain of grief. But what if you were still sighted and saw the bodies with your own eyes?' Cf. *Trach.* 896–7 μᾶλλον δ' εἰ παροῦσα πλησία ἔλευσσες οἷ' ἔδρασε, κάρτ' ἄν ᾤκτισαο. Wilam.'s correction of εἰ τά to εἰ δέ finally made sense of this passage; for elliptical εἰ δέ see his note on *Her.* 1074, where he cites 1684 below (see n.), *Ion* 961, and compares τί δ' εἰ questions. He printed a period at 1564; the question-mark is due to Jackson. Without δέ, γε would not have a proper force unless we adopted ἔβας ἄν in 1561. With δέ the particle strengthens the adversative force, as in *Hipp.* 700 εἰ δ' εὖ γ' ἔπραξα (further exx. Denniston, *GP*² 155).[2]

τέθριππά ... ἔθ' ἅρματα λεύσσων ἀελίου ἔθ' must be read for transmitted ἐς because (1) τέθρ. ἅρμ. ἀελ. is a poetic substitute for φάος ἀελίου (whence φάος is interpolated in Π⁵) and with λεύσσων the whole is equivalent to λεύσσων φάος (cf. epic ὁρᾶν φάος ἠελίοιο); (2) when a preposition

---

[1] Whence Jackson's supplement of ⟨οἶδα⟩ at the beginning of Ant.'s speech, which makes 1561 a full iambic dimeter.

[2] Owen on *Ion* 961 wrongly groups our passage with instances of assentient γε in elliptical conditions (1347 above, *IT* 866, *Ion* 961); but these all follow change of speaker.

is used with βλέπω or λεύσσω special emphasis is thrown on the object, but such emphasis is inappropriate here. 'To see the light of the sun' is normally 'to be alive', but in this context Ant. literally means 'have sight', the inverse of 377 σκότον δεδορκώς; for the connection cf. the use of βλέπω to mean 'be alive'.

1563 σώματα νεκρῶν cf. *Su.* 358, *Tro.* 91, 599; above 1482 πτώματα νεκρῶν; *Andr.* 652–3 πεσήματα ... νεκρῶν.

1564 ὄμματος αὐγαῖς σαῖς for the agreement of the possessive cf. 30n.

ἐπενώμας σώμασι ὄμματα ἐπινωμᾶν would be a more obvious construction, but for alternative constructions with verbs like βάλλω cf. 26n. and note the use of simplex νωμάω in the sense 'observe' (LSJ s.v. II.4).

1564–6 I punctuate on the assumption that Ant. is not prevented from completing her syntax by a sharp interruption, but falls momentarily silent after rhetorical ellipsis (for similar examples see *Contact and Discontinuity* chap. 4). Oed. makes a concluding comment on the death of his sons and then resumes the question of Jocasta's death from 1553–4.

1567 δάκρυα γοερὰ φανερὰ πᾶσι τιθεμένα there are ample parallels to justify construing either (a) δάκρυα ... τιθεμένα = δακρύουσα or (b) φανερὰ τιθεμένα = φαίνουσα, δεικνῦσα. Word-order and sense seem to me to favour (b). In 1567–9 Eur. plays with sound for pathetic effect: γοερὰ φανερά, φανερὰ π̱ᾶσι, τιθεμένα, doubled ἔφερεν (cf. 1030 above, Breitenbach, 218), juxtaposed ἱκέτις ἱκέτιν.

1568 μαστὸν ἔφερεν for this form of supplication used by mothers to their children *in extremis* cf. *Il.* 22.80, *Choe.* 896–7, Eur. *El.* 1207, *Or.* 527, 841.

1569 ἱκέτις ἱκέτιν a bold use of the feminine-suffix agent noun ἱκέτιν as an adj. of common gender modifying masc. noun μαστόν, but ἱκέτιν is supported against ἱκέτην/-αν by considerations of style, metre, and recension. (1) Fully rhyming paregmenon is very apt here (1567n.). (2) In his lyric trochees, esp. when they are heavily resolved, Eur. almost entirely avoids long anceps (see metre note on 649–50). (3) The authority of M is strong when it disagrees with the majority; ἱκέτην is easily explained as a rationalization of or phonetic error for ἱκέτιν, and ἱκέταν may be a deliberate doricization of the former. Π⁵ is unhelpful (damaged context:]ϲιν̣ορ̣ο̣[extant), but the final ιν might point to original ἱκέτιν. For substantive used as adj.[1] cf. *Su.* 660 ἱππότην ὄχλον, *Cycl.* 505 σκάφος ὁλκάς, *Med.* 360 χθόνα

---

[1] This usage probably derived from appositional use of the substantive (e.g, Pindar *Paean* 6.13–15 στεφάνων καὶ θαλιᾶν τροφὸν ἄλσος Ἀπόλλωνος), but here ἱκέτιν is surely felt as an adj., not as a noun: Murray's suggested translation *tamquam feminam supplicem* is a subterfuge.

σωτῆρα κακῶν, *El.* 993 τιμὰς σωτῆρας (with Denniston's note), West on Hes. *Op.* 191 ὕβριν ἀνέρα, Pindar fr. 94b.13 σειρῆνα … κόμπον; for adj. with apparently gendered suffix used for common gender cf. *IT* 140–1 κώπαι χιλιοναύται (masc. -της suffix as common gender), 1024 above φοιτᾶσι πτεροῖς with 1024–5n.; *Titanomachia* fr. 4 Bernabé χρυσώπιδες ἑλλοί. See also Ernst Fraenkel, *Nom. agentis* II.49f. Here ἱκέτιν is unusual because it is a derived fem. form used instead of the coexisting masc., but the effects of sound and rhythm must have seemed worth the price of this boldness.

ὀρομένα ὄρνυμι is not common in Eur.; the thematic aorist ὀρόμενος (only here, *IA* 186, and four times in Aesch.) has usually been corrupted, often to ὁρώμενος, here also to αἰρ-(αἱρ-) – a change aided by the false assumption that the verb is transitive (Σ) and by reminiscence of *Il.* 22.80 μαζὸν ἀνέσχε.

1570–6 the remarkable style of these lines reinforces the pathos of the description of the mother who witnesses the fratricidal death throes of her sons. Separate details of the picture are presented in striking juxtapositions and hyperbata in an additive technique which postpones the final clues to the full meaning (cf. the effect of heaping of epithets *guttatim* in Aeschylus). The placement of λωτοτρόφον κατὰ λείμακα between τέκνα and λόγχαις … μαρναμένους again effects the ironic combination of beauty and fertility with violence which has been seen elsewhere in the play (e.g., 638–89n., 674bis–75n.). Similarly, μάτηρ, an appositive to the unexpressed subject,[1] evokes pathos by falling between ἐνυάλιον and ὥστε … μαρναμένους. The participle μαρναμένους, agreeing in gender κατὰ σύνεσιν with τέκνα, finally completes the construction which the listener has held in suspension after λόγχαις and κοινὸν ἐνυάλιον. Yet sense and syntax are uncertain in 1574–5, and the details are at variance with those in the messenger's report of the same events; accordingly, Diggle (1989) believes that 1570–6 are interpolated, suggesting that they interrupt the progress of the narrative. I concede the difficulty of 1574–5, but consider the variation in details to be allowable for pathetic effect and the passage a build-up to the climax rather than an interruption.

1570 ἐν … πύλαις the rare use of ἐν in place of the common ἐπί suits the style here; cf. *Se.* 451 λέγ' ἄλλον ἄλλαις ἐν πύλαις εἰληχότα. For ἐν = 'in the neighbourhood of' cf. K–G 1.464, who cite phrases in which the object is the city near which a battle takes place as well as *Od.* 5.466 ἐν ποταμῶι (but perhaps here and in *Il.* 18.521 ποταμός is 'bed of the river' referring to a portion that is seasonally dry) and *OT* 716 ἐν τριπλαῖς ἁμαξιτοῖς (cf. 730 πρὸς τρ. ἁμ.).

---

[1] In 'extraposition' : cf. Stinton, *CQ* 27 (1977) 33.

COMMENTARY 1570–3

Ἠλέκτραισι Eur. alone locates the duel outside the Electran Gate, on the east side of Thebes. In Pausanias' time one saw the alleged spot of the duel to the west of the city, outside the Neistan Gate, not far from the alleged tomb of Menoeceus (Paus. 9.25.2); in Aesch. the brothers meet at an unnamed seventh gate (Crenaean? – cf. 1123 above), while the Electran Gate is attacked by Capaneus (as in 1129 above). Dihle, 79, in line with his hypothesis that Eur. avoided reference to the proper names of the gates to maintain a strong distinction from the Aeschylean treatment (1104–40n.), finds suspect the use of the proper name here.

1571 λωτοτρόφον hapax in extant literature. The connotation is probably beautiful fertility (cf. *Il.* 14.348, *Od.* 4.603), not death (as Craik alleges).

1572 κοινὸν ἐνυάλιον after λόγχαις the listener expects a participle such as μαχόμενα and so holds ἐνυάλιον in suspense as internal acc. to the expected verb-form: 'waging mutual battle'. κοινόν perhaps carries also a suggestion of 'fraternal', as Eust. 612, 21 thought (see van der Valk's note *ad loc.*); and in this context, *pace* Pearson, the word may also evoke the horror of fratricide (cf. κοινὸν αἷμα). This is the only place in classical Greek in which ἐνυάλιος is used by metonymy for 'battle' (but cf. *Anth. gr.* 9.283.4 [Γερμανικὸς] ἀστράπτων Κελτοῖς πουλὺν ἐνυάλιον). The phrase may recall *Il.* 18.309 ξυνὸς ('impartial') Ἐνυάλιος, καί τε κτανέοντα κατέκτα, but Eur. has shifted the meaning of both words.[1]

1573 ὥστε λέοντας ἐναύλους 'like lions in a den', i.e., in this context 'like lions quarrelling over a lair (in a cave)'. For caves as lairs cf. *Eum.* 193 λέοντος ἄντρον αἱματορρόφου, Hes. *Op.* 529–33 (for κεραοὶ καὶ νήκεροι ὑληκοῖται); lions' lairs are elsewhere in thickets (*Il.* 18.318–20, *Od.* 4.335–9). Pairs of lions appear in epic similes as emblematic of co-operating warriors (*Il.* 5.554–8, 10.297, 13.198–200; cf. *Phil.* 1436),[2] but such a sense is inapposite here and would inevitably be conveyed by Porson's dual λέοντε συναύλω (σύναυλος is elsewhere used of peaceful cohabitation). For the hypostasized adj. (from ἐν αὐλῇ) cf. *Phil.* 157–8 στίβον ἔναυλον ἢ θυραῖον ('within his dwelling or outside'). αὐλή is used of a human dwelling or a cattle-fold, but in the verb αὐλίζομαι and the substantive ἔναυλος the

---

[1] The shift is slighter in the interpretation of Dihle, 97: he takes 'impartial battle' as apposition to the entire noun-participle complex, with 'impartial' in the sense 'having the same outcome for both'. But the syntax is already quite complicated and the phrase apparently has a noun in apposition in λοιβάν; it is better to regard ἐνυάλιον as internal acc. specific to μαρναμένους.

[2] Cf. C. Wolff, 'A Note on Lions and Soph. *Phil.* 1436', in *Arktouros* 144–50. In *Il.* 18.579 (shield-image, not simile) a pair of lions co-operates in killing a bull.

587

notion of shelter or sheltered resting-place is quite general. Σ glosses ἢ ἐν ἐπαύλει μαχομένους, but although epic lions are often portrayed attacking cattle-folds this notion again conflicts with the requirements of the context.

1574 μαρναμένους the switch to masc., as if παῖδας preceded, may have been influenced by the intervening λέοντας. Wilam. suggested that the participle is here timeless, conveying 'having fought', so that Ant.'s description agrees with that of the messenger. But it is more likely that the participle is used normally ('fighting') and that for pathetic effect Eur. tolerates a discrepancy between the two descriptions: here there is supplication before the catastrophe (1567–9; 1429–35 contain a different supplication *after* it), and Jocasta witnesses the ferocious strife; earlier maximum effect is obtained by separate concentration on the duel in 1377–1424 and on too-late arrival, lamentation, and suicide in 1427–59.

1574–5 ἐπὶ τραύμασιν, αἵματος ἤδη ψυχρὰν λοιβάν the meaning is probably '(fighting) to add wound upon wound, and their fighting was an act of libation, already cold, deadly, of blood ⟨not of wine⟩' (cf. Méridier's 'luttaient ensemble, couverts de blessures, ... et c'était, déjà froide, une sanglante libation de meutre'); but punctuation and interpretation are disputed. Some have followed Moschopulus and Thomas in connecting αἵματος with τραύμασιν as gen. of description (≈αἱματηροῖς), but the construction would be harsh (1491n.) and αἵματος is in any case needed with λοιβάν to provide the gruesome redefinition of the ritual term which is so typical of tragedy. With the punctuation adopted here, ἐπί is most easily taken as 'in addition to (previously inflicted wounds)': cf. the messenger's description of the duel; but with λόγχαις here one cannot have an exact correspondence. The ἐπί of purpose, however, cannot be ruled out (Thomas paraphrases ἐπὶ τῶι θανατῶσαι ἀλλήλους). λοιβάν, an internal acc. 'in apposition to the sentence' (Barrett on *Hipp.* 752–7, Wilam. on *Her.* 59, Schwyzer II.617), is then an abstract *nomen actionis*, although the epithet ψυχράν, transferred from the concrete αἵματος, creates some blurring of abstract and concrete. In the exegesis of Wilam. and Pearson (with punctuation before ἐπὶ τρ.) λοιβάν would be concrete (as *Ion* 1201, *IT* 164, 169, *IA* 1051) and the implication would be 'the libation of blood was already cold upon their wounds'; but a libation should fall upon the earth, and the concreteness of λοιβάν would be harsh if the noun is internal acc.[1] The scholiasts lacked the grammatical category of internal acc. and so

---

[1] Concreteness would not be a problem if μάρνασθαι λοιβάν could be treated on a par with τέμνειν ὁδόν = 'create a road by cutting' (external acc. of concrete thing effected). The sense would be 'and in their fighting they brought about a libation of blood'. But I know of no parallels for this bold construction.

fell back on the assumption that λοιβάν was a second object of ηῦρε in asyndeton. The source of O recognized the improbability of this and added τ' (i.e. ἐπὶ τραύμασι θ'), but this is a trivialization of what Eur. probably intended to be an impressionistic tangle.

1575 φόνιον if anapaestic rhythm is accepted (see on Metre), this (from Π⁵) may be preferred to the mss' φονίαν. The latter would perhaps add to the striking accumulation of α-sounds in 1575–6, but the more recherché common form was apt to be corrupted to the openly feminine form. Cf. *Choe.* 836 φόνιον edd. metri gratia, φοινίαν M; *Med.* 839 μετρίας codd., μετρι]ους P.Ant. 1.23. For dactylic rhythm one may read φοίνιον (odd rhythm after the three preceding spondees; if taken as anapaestic, – – –∪∪ is a rare metron – Diggle, *Studies* 45–6). For confusion of φόνιος/ φοίνιος see *Concordance* s.vv. and Teubner app. at 252, 595, 657, 933, 1006, 1378, 1558.

1576 Hades and Ares are paired here for the first time in the play, but have appeared separately in similar contexts in earlier lyrics : 240, 253, 658, 784, 810; cf. unnamed god(s) in 1030–2, 1066, 1580–1. ὀπάζω is constantly used of welcome divine gifts, but in a very few passages the gift is, as here, an evil: ὀῖζυν *Od.* 23.210; φόνια ... λάχεα *El.* 1192–3. For the bipartite structure of the line see Diggle on *Phaethon* 99, Davies on *Trach.* 834; G. Thomsen, *JHS* 73 (1953) 82–3.

1578 ἔβαψεν the ambiguous metaphor ξίφος (vel sim.) βάπτειν = 'dip and moisten / dye one's sword' is affected by tragedy (*Prom.* 863, *Aj.* 95); allusive association of the verb or of βαφή with shedding of blood is obvious in *Choe.* 1011, *Ag.* 239, and presumably latent in *Ag.* 612. Though already in Π⁵, ἔπεμψεν is banal: note that πέμπετε is interpolated after φάσγανα in *Or.* 1303; the verb is used of hurling rocks or shooting arrows, but of thrusting a sword only in this variant and in *Or.* 1303.

ἀμφὶ τέκνοισι implying embrace; cf. 1459 περιβαλοῦσ' ἀμφοῖν χέρας. The nominal paregmenon with intervening words in ἄχει ... τέκνων ... ἀμφὶ τέκνοισι might serve for intensification of pathos. Most of the examples cited by Breitenbach, 224 involve simple prepositional adjuncts (like *IT* 191 μόχθος δ' ἐκ μόχθων, *Tro.* 605 δάκρυά τ' ἐκ δακρύων), but cf. *Hipp.* 1348–9 πατρὸς ἐξ ἀδίκου χρησμοῖς ἀδίκοις, *Hel.* 164, *Cycl.* 511–12. τέκνοισι could easily have intruded by mistaken repetition, ousting (e.g.) Markland's νεκροῖσιν (commended by Diggle).

1579 ἐν ἄματι τῶιδε a gathering or culmination of evils 'on this present day' is a commonplace of tragedy: *Med.* 1231, *Andr.* 803, and see further 1582–3n.

συνάγαγεν doricized augment is in general exceptional in tragedy, but ἄγω and its compounds are treated differently from other verbs (Björck, 167). The doricized form here could be due to medieval correction, but the preponderance of α over η¹ suggests that it should be preferred here and restored in *Andr.* 104 (Dindorf), *Or.* 181 (Lautensach).

1580–1 with the combined reference to ἄχη and to divine participation in the fulfilment of the evil fate, Ant.'s lyric ends on a note that echoes the end of Jocasta's aria (352–4).

1580 ἀμετέροισιν ἄχη μελάθροις so Π⁵; ἀμετέροισι δόμοισιν ἄχη codd. Π⁵ also omits θεός, but the omission would be an easy accident (ΜΕΛΑΘΡΟΙCΘΕΟCΟC). The two versions are metrically and semantically equivalent: like δόμος, μέλαθρα can mean 'household, family', as in *Ag.* 771 (cf. Fraenkel), 1576, *Choe.* 1065, *Hipp.* 1345, *IT* 196, etc. I hesitantly follow Π⁵ because it has the less obvious noun in a less obvious order. But for μέλαθρον as an interpolator's word cf. *Hipp.* 749 and sch. *Tro.* 1113.

1581 τάδ' ἐκτελευτᾶι τάδε τελευτᾶι would have the same meaning (cf. *Alc.* 978–9 καὶ γὰρ Ζεὺς ὅτι νεύσηι / σὺν σοὶ τοῦτο τελευτᾶι), but the compound verb perhaps yields a clausula that is marginally more likely (but see under Metre for another possible solution). For ἐκτελευτάω of gods bringing fated events to their fulfilment, cf. Sem. 1.5 West, Pindar *P.* 4.19, 12.29; *Pers.* 741.

1582–1709: EXODOS (IAMBIC PART)

Through a careful combination (so at least I regard it: see below under Authenticity) of motifs, the exodos picks up, interweaves, and resolves the strands of the drama that are still left open after the death of the brothers, the suicide of Jocasta, and the final rout of the Argive invaders. (1) Oedipus, who has been kept before the audience's mind from the beginning and who finally emerged as a singing character in 1539ff., is given an opportunity for iambic speech as well. His life comes full circle to the condition of exile (the final application of this motif in the play). He voices a personal review of the disasters of his life, accepts his daughter's aid with just enough resistance to highlight her nobility, and makes his final farewells to his dead kin. Finally, with all issues settled, he reveals the ultimate goal of his wandering (1703–7n.), and then receives the support and guidance of his daughter (recalling the Tiresias-scene, and evoking the sort

---

¹ In Eur. I find eight doricized forms of augmented simplex (two in the *Hyps.* papyrus; in *Or.* 1365 Diggle reports that thirty-one mss have α, six have η) and five of compounds vs. two non-doricized simplex (*Andr.* 104, *Or.* 181; ἦγεν in *IA* 284 is probably corrupt) and the present passage with α/η variant (η in the majority and in Π⁵). For Aesch. and Soph. cf. *Pers.* 560, 863, *Choe.* 77, *Septem* 756 (η as variant), *Prom.* 559 (η in a few *recc.*), *Trach.* 858 vs. *Pers.* 550 (α in Tr).

of solidarity in misfortune that is prominent at the end of other Euripidean plays). (2) Antigone, whose relationship to Pol. has been hinted at from early in the play and who is now the only survivor on whom his appeal for burial can depend, continues to display the results of her rapid transition from a childlike sheltered status to adulthood as she vehemently disputes the propriety of Creon's orders. The burial-conflict is the logical conclusion of the poet's decision to use Ant. in this play and of the way in which he has portrayed her; the motif is firmly embedded in the play's fabric by Pol.'s appeal in 1447–50, even if 774–7 are deleted. Although alluding to the tradition of the heroic Antigone who defies Creon to bury her brother, this scene reinterprets her heroism so that it is turned in a somewhat more realistic direction, toward service to her helpless exiled father. (3) The betrothal of Antigone to Haemon, announced to the audience in Eteocles' 'testament', exploited in Tiresias' prophecy, and alluded to in Creon's assertion of authority at the beginning of the scene, now plays a crucial role in the see-saw contest between Creon and Antigone. Creon has the power to deny Ant. the right of burying her brother, and he refuses to allow any lesser token of attention to the corpse when Ant. abandons hope of burial and gradually reduces her requests (1667, 1669). He cannot, however, prevent her from kissing the corpse (1671), and his protestation reintroduces the notion of marriage to Haemon. This the exasperated Ant. now fiercely rejects, threatening first suicide and then, more tellingly for Creon, murder of her bridegroom. Creon's resolute refusal of supplication is now matched by Ant.'s resolve to avoid marriage with Creon's son by devoting her life instead to her father. For the second time in the play, Creon changes his mind when faced with a danger to a son's life: he allows Ant. to depart.

AUTHENTICITY OF THE SCENE[1]

Apart from stylistic and linguistic difficulties of particular lines (discussed in detail in the individual notes below), the general suspicion of the iambic part of the exodos is based on three general perceptions.

---

[1] Discussions of this problem are numerous, and for the purposes of this commentary I cannot summarize or respond to every argument ever adduced. There is no doubt that the controversy will continue. My purpose here is to lay out the main lines of the controversy and to offer the promised defence of the decisions I made in preparing the Teubner edition. I hope that my discussion will not appear dogmatic because of its necessary brevity, and that the commentary on detailed points will be of interest and use even to those who prefer a much different approach.

(1) To some critics (including an anonymous one in antiquity who complained ὅ τε ἐπὶ πᾶσι μετ' ᾠδῆς ἀδολέσχου φυγαδευόμενος Οἰδίπους προσέρραπται διὰ κενῆς), the play is already overfull of material and would be more satisfactory if it concluded with the deaths of the brothers and Joc. and some brief lament. But, as argued in the Introd. I, the conception of the action of this play as a complex one with ramifications back in time and across a large number of characters should be regarded as genuinely Euripidean (compare the nearly contemporary *Orestes*). The use of the Cadmus myth, the insertion of the sacrifice of Menoeceus, and other features all indicate that the a priori demand for a single or simple action made by Hermann and others is incommensurate with the actual artistry of the play. *Phoenissae* is 'overfull' not because it is intended as an 'historical pageant' and not because it is the third play of a trilogy and so eligible for episodic treatment, but because the dramatist wished to create an image of a world of a certain kind, fraught with explicable and inexplicable evil, with aspirations and frustrations, affecting an interlocking group of individuals and their community.

(2) Many have followed the example of careless scholiasts[1] and seen a contradiction between the theme of Pol.'s burial by Ant. and the theme of Ant.'s assistance to Oed. in his exile. Whereas the ancient critics ascribed the conflation to the arbitrary licence of the poet, modern critics prefer to believe that the mixture of motifs results from interpolation. But *within* this scene it is clear, as many others have recognized, that the two intentions of Ant. are not in contradiction because the second intention (accompanying Oed.) replaces the first (burying Pol.) after the latter has been forestalled by Creon's opposition. The sequence of diminishing requests in 1667ff. demonstrates that Ant. sees the impossibility of burying Pol. in defiance of Creon.[2] The confusion or conflation arises only in the lyric

---

[1] Σ^B 1692 οὐ τηρεῖ τὸ σύμφωνον, ἀλλὰ κατὰ τὸ δρᾶμα ὑποτίθεται. πῶς γὰρ θάψει Πολυνείκην Ἀντιγόνη συμφεύγουσα τῶι πατρί; πλεονάζει δὲ τῶι τοιούτωι εἴδει ὁ Εὐριπίδης; cf. Σ^B 1710 διὰ μὲν τοῦ ἐγώ σφε θάψω σπέρματα τῆι Σοφοκλέους Ἀντιγόνηι παρέσχε, διὰ δὲ τοῦ φεύγειν τῶι ἐπὶ Κολωνῶι Οἰδίποδι. ὡς βούλονται γὰρ οἰκονομοῦσι τὰ δράματα.

[2] I interpret Ant.'s abandonment of her intention as, for all intents and purposes of the drama, absolute. I do not see the point of making the distinction that Ant. has renounced only burial in Theban soil (Mueller-Goldingen, 249 n. 58), which seems useful only if one wants, inappropriately, to speculate about burial of Pol. outside of Theban territory after the end of the play (a point that Mueller-Goldingen agrees is not a concern of the play).

tailpiece, in lines 1744–6, and there the confusion is one among several reasons for denying the later passage to Eur. (1737–57n.).

(3) Some critics have an overly positive assessment of the importance and integrity of Creon as a figure in the play as a whole and find the actions and statements assigned to him in the exodos distasteful and inconsistent with such an image. I believe, however, that the subservience of Creon to Eteocles in the second episode, the blatant reversal of stance displayed in the third episode, the relative unimportance of Creon between the opening of the second messenger's rhesis and the end of Ant.'s lyric, and the unsympathetic attitude and ultimate retreat of Creon in this scene are all part of the same conception of this figure. We should not argue that a character who spoke 1320–1 (on duty to the dead) could never have been so harsh as the figure who issues the edicts in the exodos (for the inconsistency, the selfish partiality of Creon's ethics, is consistent and meaningful), nor should an audience now accept Creon as the champion of the interests of the state and agree with him that Oed. is still a threat. Some critics of the scene seem to mistake the emotional balance of an audience's sympathy, which surely tilts more toward Ant. and Oed., and to forget the force of the intertextual allusion to Soph.'s *Ant.* and the general disapproval of the refusal of burial to be seen in the moral universe of tragedy (*Aj.*, *Ant.*, E. *Su.*, A. *Eleusinioi*).

The particular passages doubted by critics may be divided into two classes. (1) Some individual lines, couplets and short passages could be deleted without major modification of our understanding of the scene: thus, 1596, 1634, 1637–8, which I delete; 1582–3, about which I am undecided; 1586b–90a, 1611, 1621, 1628b–29a, 1644, 1688–9, 1703–7, which I defend. (2) Other doubted passages make a real difference to how the scene develops and ends: see notes on 1595–624, 1625–38, 1639–82. I believe the most intractable problems are in the passage 1595–614, esp. 1596–607, where I conclude that the content is close to what we should expect but that the text has been affected by accidental corruption or deliberate alteration in such a way that one cannot neatly trim the spurious from the genuine. The other passages are not free of problems, but (with varying degrees of conviction) I believe that I have offered explications that may defend the text we have, except where diagnosis of corruption is preferable (as in 1653).

The main approaches to this scene offered by interpolation-critics are: (1) general rejection, with the assumption that Eur.'s play ended shortly after 1581: so first Leidloff, followed by Wecklein, then Powell and Page, and now Willink and Diggle; (2) rejection of the burial-theme (deleting most or all of 1627–82, along with 774–7, but leaving 1447–50 intact): so Balsamo, followed by Friedrich and Fraenkel; (3) rejection of the marriage-theme and departure of Ant. (deleting 1595–614, 1661–82 (or 1664–82), 1702–22): so H. D. F. Kitto, *CR* 53 (1939) 104–11. Defenders of the content, if not of the whole text, of the scene include Wilam., Robert, Pohlenz, Strohm, Conacher (book and, in more detail, *Phoenix* 21 (1967) 92–101), Valgiglio, Diller, Erbse, Mueller-Goldingen.

1582–3 it is normal for an actor's song to be followed by a sympathetic couplet spoken by the coryphaeus; reference to κακά is likewise conventional (355–6n.; note esp. *Ion* 923–4 μέγας θησαυρὸς ... κακῶν, *El.* 213 πολλῶν κακῶν. ... αἰτίαν ἔχει). Like other choral couplets, this kind helps the lyric stand forth as a distinct structural unit by defining its end and providing a pause before the next development. When a choral intervention is absent, there is a greater effect of continuity and urgency, or of an engagement between the actors that the poet does not want to loosen (cf. *Alc.* 273, *Hipp.* 1389, *Andr.* 866, *Prom.* 609, S. *El.* 1288; cf. Hose, *Chor* 233–4). At *Ant.* 833 Creon intervenes with an effective abruptness on Ant.'s kommos, but the situation here is different, and the punctuation of a choral couplet seems right. Thus, if it is granted that some of the following scene is Euripidean, it prob. began with a choral couplet, and if 1582–3 are intrusive in their context (Geel), they have ousted similar lines (so Zipperer). Choral couplets in Eur. are often vapid in content, but here two details are esp. troubling. (1) The day that is the beginning of many goods or evils is prob. a topos (a subtype of the topos of the ἀρχὴ κακῶν): Thuc. 2.12.3, *Peace* 435–6; for 'many evils/goods' and 'this day' conjoined see also *Med.* 1231–2, S. *El.* 918–19. But it is oddly applied to this day, which sees the culmination of evils that (as many earlier passages have made clear) began long ago (depending on one's perspective, with Cadmus' founding, with Laius' disobedience, with Oed.'s solution of the riddle, etc.). It is true that further troubles are to come (denial of burial and exile), but such a forward-looking comment by the chorus can hardly be intended here. (2) The reference of βίος is vague, but most likely Oed.'s remaining life is meant: he is the one with whom the chorus commiserates in 1425–6, and he has just received δυστυχὲς ἀγγελίας ἔπος from Ant.[1] Other uncertainties remain. (a) The word-order varies in the mss, apparently because of the omission and incorrect replacement of κακῶν. The order of the majority, πολλῶν κακῶν, is prob. correct (cf. *El.* 213), but not certainly so (S. *El.* 918–19, quoted below). (b) The end of 1582 was prob. damaged earlier in the tradition: variant δόμος could be a sign of damage to the ending of δόμοις, and τέκνοις and γένει may be conjectures to fill an empty

---

[1] Mueller-Goldingen, 226, suggests that the chorus may refer to its own future, as in 1200–1.

space. (c) The variant ὑπῆρξεν has been out of favour since the primacy of the older mss was acknowledged, but Valck. and Klotz correctly showed that κατάρχω is used as a gloss on ὑπάρχω (presumably to distinguish the sense 'begin' from the sense 'be available, exist'; cf. the clarifying corruption προϋπῆρξ' in 1223), and we now know that *recc.* sometimes carry the truth. *Andr.* 274 μεγάλων ἀχέων ... ὑπῆρξεν is a good parallel. With ὑπῆρξεν some have tried to give a different sense to the verb. Mosch. glossed as 'was in charge of, held power over'. More promisingly, Geel thought of the sense 'be', as in S. *El.* 918-19 ἡ δὲ νῦν ἴσως / πολλῶν ὑπάρξει κῦρος ἡμέρα καλῶν; but 'the day has turned out to be one of many evils' is doubtful: in the only classical instance of aorist ὑπάρξαι with predicate genitive, the sense is 'to be already', 'to be from the beginning' (Xen. *Oec.* 21.11 δεῖν ... φύσεως ἀγαθῆς ὑπάρξαι). Of emendations that rid the line of the idea of beginning, F. G. Schoene's ἔπλησεν Οἰδίπου δόμους may be mentioned; one might consider, e.g., πολλῶν τέλος συνῆψεν (κακῶν an intrusive gloss, leading to corruption of the verb).

1584 οἴκτων μὲν ἤδη λήγεθ' in arguing against Creon's appearance at 1308ff., Fraenkel noted that the stopping-action performed by him here is usually associated with an entering character. Of his five exx., I set aside *Or.* 1625 and *IT* 1425, which are instances of the stopping-action of a *deus ex machina* (on which see my discussion, 'Actors on High', 262-3 and *passim*), a separate convention. *Or.* 1022 is not parallel because Orestes' entrance is announced by the chorus at the end of Electra's song (1013-17) and his call for silence (1022) is in reference to Electra's incipient lament in 1018-21, not to her preceding lyric. The Soph. cases are to the point (*Ant.* 883, Creon enters; *OC* 1751, Theseus enters), but against them must be set cases in which a character already present intervenes to affect the action after being silent for some time. Diller cited *IT* 902 (most relevant structurally: after reunion-amoibaion and closing extended lyric by Iphigenia, a choral couplet, then Pylades intervenes – note 904 λήξαντα δ' οἴκτων) and *Hel.* 700. So dramatic technique provides no reliable indication that Creon enters here (or re-enters, for those who think he was present at 1310 but left during the lyric scene).

1585-6 τῶνδε ... λόγων ἄκουσον to be preferred to L's τόνδε ... λόγον: Fraenkel, 86 n. 2, shows that Eur. uses the singular λόγον with verbs of hearing only when it is accompanied by an adjective of some semantic weight.

1586-90 critics who deny the whole scene to Eur. criticize 1586-7 in particular, but Fraenkel argued that Eur.'s ἄκουσον· εἶπε Τειρεσίας οὐ μή ποτε (1586a + 1590b) was expanded by a *Binneninterpolation*. Apart from the traditional critique of 1586-7 (see next note), he can offer only the questionable claim that the shorter text better represents the milder, sympathetic Creon that Fraenkel attributes to Eur. (1582–709n.). But in the shorter text τῶνδε.... ἄκουσον is pompous, and more important, ἀλλ' + imperative in 1592 is too abrupt without 1589 preceding. With 1589, ἀλλ' restates the decision more forcefully, marking a transition from the statement of reason ('near the end of a speech, as a clinching and final appeal' – Denniston, *GP²* 14): 'I am in charge now. I won't let you stay. Tir. told me. Come then, leave.'

1586–7 ἀρχὰς τῆσδε γῆς ἔδωκέ μοι ... γάμων φερνὰς διδούς following the lead of Thomas' scholion, comm. have tried to be too specific about the constitutional arrangements. Thomas suggested that the kingship was to be part of Haemon's dowry (in the event, that is, of Et.'s death), and that Creon is to be regent only between the death of Et. and the consummation of the marriage of Haemon to Antigone. Accepting this view, Wecklein and others then brand the passage as not Euripidean because of lack of clarity and oddity of the arrangement. The emphasis of the sentence (ἀρχὰς ... ἔδωκέ μοι), the behaviour of Et. in the second episode,[1] and the mythic tradition agree, however, in making Creon the new ruler, not an interim officer. I do not agree with the view of Mueller-Goldingen, 129 and 229, that Eur. is making the point that Creon is misrepresenting the arrangement in his own selfish interests. The point of γάμων φερνὰς διδούς is that the arrangement for succession was ratified by Et. at the time when he was preparing for the war and for the possibility of his death, the time already referred to in reference to the dowry at 760 τὴν πρόσθε. The repetition ἔδωκε / διδούς has been deemed the clumsiness of an interpolator, but it may be a deliberate device to emphasize Creon's 'apologetic' tendency to shield his decisions behind the advice and actions of others (as in the references to Tiresias in 1590 and to Eteocles in 1646); for collocation of participle and finite form of same verb, cf. Diggle, *Studies* 66–7, 120, adding *Hec.* 655–6, *IA* 1221–2 (JD).

παῖς σός prob. right against σὸς παῖς in some *recc.*; word-order is metrically determined in the same phrase in 619, 1095, 1164, 1169, but at 1164 unmetrical σὸς παῖς has intruded in some mss.

φερνάς Eur. assigns the contemporary custom to heroic times and uses φερνή and even ἕδνα in the sense of the legal, non-poetic term προΐξ: cf. Stevens on *Andr.* 2, Diggle on *Phaethon* 158–9.

1588 Craik comments on the two resolutions in this line, but there are in fact three dozen such lines in *Phoen.* (for three resolutions in a line, 584n.).

---

[1] Even if 774–7 are spurious, Et. treats Creon as his main counsellor for both public and private matters (692–3) and as the legitimate spokesman for the city in consulting Tiresias.

1590 σαφῶς γὰρ εἶπε some comm. see an explicit reference to 886–7 τῶν Οἰδίπου / μηδένα πολίτην μηδ' ἄνακτ' εἶναι χθονός and claim that τῶν Οἰδίπου can be taken to include Oed. himself (comparing the idiom οἱ ἀμφί τινα). That is not a legitimate interpretation of 886–7 in its context, and an audience cannot be expected retrospectively to revise its understanding at this later point. Possible solutions: (a) the discrepancy is due to the carelessness of an interpolator; (b) the reference is not to the third episode, but to an earlier oracle delivered to Oed. or the Thebans (Valck.), which the audience may know of from the mythic tradition (if Eur. were introducing the motif here for the first time, one would expect a hint like πάλαι or ποτε); (c) the ref. is to the earlier scene, but Creon is guilty of misrepresentation, through unconscious wishful interpretation in the interest of self-exculpation; (d) same as (c), but Creon's misrepresentation is to be taken as cynical manipulation (Conacher; cf. Mueller-Goldingen). I do not detect enough clues in the scene to support (d); between (b) and (c), I incline slightly to the latter. It furthers the tragic pathos that Creon now applies a kind of reasoning that was useful before the terrible events (when Laius was warned, when Oed.'s crimes were revealed, when the brothers were warned) but is no longer so, now that the war has taken place and Oed. is clearly powerless by himself to stir further conflict, either within his family or for the city. Note that Creon's action could have been made to appear in quite a different light if explicit reference had been made to pollution; but for most of the play, as in this scene, Oed. has been viewed as a miserable sufferer and as a source of current woe through his curse, not through his crimes. Note the different tenor of Accius *Phoen.* fr. 12: *iussit proficisci exilium quovis gentium, / ne scelere tuo Thebani vastescant agri.*

οὐ μή ποτε the emphatic negative οὐ μή is most familiar in its construction with the aor. subj., but, as well explained by Wackernagel, *Syntax* II.305, this use was extended already in the fifth century to other contexts of strong asseveration about the future: thus, S. *El.* 1052 οὔ σοι μὴ μεθέψομαί ποτε (Goodwin, *MT* §295 *ad fin.*), *Phil.* 611–12 (another oracle quoted indirectly) ὡς οὐ μή ποτε / πέρσοιεν; Aeschines 3.177 τοὺς μὲν γὰρ πονηροὺς οὐ μήποτε βελτίους ποιήσετε. Thus Elmsley's advocacy of πρᾶξαι here and of πέρσαιεν in *Phil.* 612 is unjustified, nor need the unique usage (Goodwin, *MT* ¶ 296(a), 753.3) have any bearing on authorship.

1592 ἐκκομίζου the situation, and perhaps the word itself, recalls Et.'s treatment of Pol. (593 ἔξω κομίζου τειχέων, 614 ἔξιθι χθονός). Cf. 1666n., 1682n.

οὐχ ὕβρει Creon's interpretation of his own behaviour does not settle the issue for other characters or indeed for the audience. Since his previous and subsequent actions show him to be more sensitive to his own sufferings than to those of others, and since Ant. and Oed. have been shown in a

597

sympathetic light, it is possible to view Creon's brusque treatment of Oed. as harsh to the point of ὕβρις (cf. 1620–1, 1644), even the more so if the audience is unsure of the exact footing of the advice of Tir. (1590n.). If the writer had wanted to show someone inflicting suffering with great reluctance, the apology could have preceded the command and been more insistent (cf. *Tro.* 709–19); and if he had wanted Creon to seem sympathetic, one can imagine more kindly arrangements for exile (e.g., provision of house and servants just outside Theban territory).

1593–4 διὰ δὲ τοὺς ἀλάστορας τοὺς σούς 'the baneful spirits that attend you', σούς having the force of obj. gen. (1556n.).

1595–624 this speech contains perhaps the largest accumulation of odd features of any passage in the play. Paley suggested deleting all of it, together with 1625–6 (so now West (1990)), but it would be odd for Eur. to mention Oed.'s presence indoors throughout the play and then bring him on stage only for the few lines he sings in the duet and the few that follow 1682. It is normal for a sufferer in tragedy to provide a *Lebensrückblick* (Strohm, 156ff.; Bond on *Her.* 1258ff.), and that is exactly what an audience awaits here and what this speech provides. Fraenkel would delete only 1595–614, but this removes the review of Oed.'s life (spoiling the structure noted by Bond: review, then 'What can I do? Where can I go?': *Med.* 502ff., *Her.* 1281ff.) and deprives εἶέν of its point (1615n.).[1] Moreover, some lines of the speech are possibly alluded to in *Frogs* (1597n.). Although some of the oddity can be removed by separate deletion or recognition of corruption or a lacuna, the neat separation of genuine from spurious aimed at by Friedrich, Fraenkel, and others seems impossible here. We are left with a passage in which the general import seems appropriate and necessary, but the details unsatisfactory.

1595 ἀπ' ἀρχῆς . . . ἄθλιον for this motif, cf. *Her.* 1256–68, *Hel.* 255–6, *Hipp.* 1082. For the very common phrase ἀπ' ἀρχῆς see Diggle, *CQ* 34 (1984) 52.

[1596] the unidiomatic use of εἴ τις ἄλλος in a case different from τλῆμον' and with superfluous ἔφυ was already noted by Valck. (and perhaps by the author of the unmetrical τλήμων . . . ἔφυν in O), who emended but, acc. to Geel, later noted in the margin of his book that the line should be deleted. τλῆμον' adds nothing to ἄθλιον, and the line may

---

[1] See also R. L. Fowler, 'The Rhetoric of Desperation', *HSCP* 91 (1987) 5–38, who notes (31 n. 56) that the two-part structure is typical of what he calls desperation speeches. He suggests that the speech has been rewritten and would assume a lacuna before 1615 with something like τὸ δ' ἔσχατον so that δῆθ' in 1615 will be easier and a lacuna after 1621 so that the transition with οὐ μὴν . . . γ' in 1622 will be easier.

be an expansion of a marginal gloss. For normal idiom with εἴ τις ἄλλος, cf. *Andr.* 6, *OT* 1118, *Eccl.* 81, *Wealth* 655, Men. *Aspis* 18, *Samia* 300 and many prose exx., and the similar ellipsis in, e.g., *OC* 733–4 πόλιν ... σθένουσαν..., εἴ τιν᾽ Ἑλλάδος, μέγα. In a case like Pl. *Meno* 93c3–4 οὐκοῦν [φαίης ἄν] καὶ διδάσκαλον ἀγαθόν, εἴπερ τις ἄλλος τῆς αὑτοῦ ἀρετῆς διδάσκαλος ἦν, κἀκεῖνον εἶναι, the presence of the predicate noun explains the lack of attraction of case and the inclusion of ἦν.

1597–9 ὃν καὶ πρὶν ... ἄγονον ... μ᾽ ἐθέσπισεν φονέα γενέσθαι πατρός three odd features of this sentence have been attacked. (1) μ᾽ repeats the person referred to by ὅν; but this is paralleled in a few passages in which an intervening clause separates the relative from the verb that governs it (K–G ii.433–4, Anm. 2): so with unemphatic 3rd-person pronoun Pl. *Phaedo* 99b4–6, with demonstrative Xen. *Lac.Pol.* 10.4; see Stevens on *Andr.* 650 for discussion and a few other possible cases (though I accept emendation at *Andr.* 650 and 710). It is unnecessary to adopt the artificial explanation that ὅν is the subj. of μολεῖν and μ᾽ the object of ἐθέσπισεν (Wecklein 1872). (2) Fraenkel objects that if γονή is anatomical in sense, it is not so used elsewhere in tragedy, and that if it has the usual meaning 'birth' then instrumental ἐκ γονῆς consorts ill with local εἰς φῶς μολεῖν. I agree that poetic usage from Homer to tragedy makes it extremely unlikely that γονή means 'womb' here. But I see no problem, in poetic style, in combining the sense 'by my mother's bearing', 'in, by birth from my mother' (cf. *Ant.* 980 ματρὸς ἔχοντες ... γονάν) with 'come into the light', where εἰς φῶς is not local in a full literal sense (the phrase is a periphrasis for 'be born' : cf. *Su.* 532 ὅθεν δ᾽ ἕκαστον ἐς τὸ φῶς ἀφίκετο). For the phrase with ἐκ cf. fr. 839.10 τὰ δ᾽ ἀπ᾽ αἰθερίου βλαστόντα γονῆς. (3) The redundancy of ἄγονον after πρὶν ... μολεῖν is a device of rhetorical emphasis, reflecting indignation and pathos. For the sense 'not yet born' cf. *Il.* 3.40, Eubulus fr. 106.11 K–A. Arist. *Frogs* 1183–5, the response to the first line of Eur.'s *Antigone*, has several points of contact with our passage, as Valck. saw: ... ἀλλὰ κακοδαίμων φύσει· ὅντινά γε, πρὶν φῦναι μέν, Ἀπόλλων ἔφη / ἀποκτενεῖν τὸν πατέρα, πρὶν καὶ γεγονέναι. Note φύσει / φῦναι (1595 ἔφυσας), causal connection with relative, πρίν used twice (once πρὶν καί),[1] and the fact and content of the prophecy. Valck. and others have judged that Arist. alludes to our passage, cleverly using a parody of Eur.'s own

---

[1] This repetition is apparently for indignant emphasis, but may also be in mockery of Eur., either in general terms (cleverly reversing the criticism of Aesch.'s redundancies) or in specific reference to *Phoen.* Note, however, that there is no repetition if πρὶν καὶ γεγονέναι is assigned to Dionysus (as buffoon) and the rest to Aeschylus.

words from another play to undercut his opening line of *Ant*. (Most recently, Dover, *Aristophanes. Frogs* (Oxford 1993) 336, comments on *Frogs* 1184f. that 'there is a strong reminiscence here of E. *Pho*. 1595–1614' and quotes words from 1595 and 1597–8.) With so much of fifth-century drama lost to us, and with the possibility that we have a similarity of topos rather than direct allusion, Valck.'s hypothesis is far from certain, but I regard it as attractive, and certainly more probable than the hypothesis of Wecklein that *Frogs* 1184–5 parodies lost lines of Eur.'s *Ant*. and that the interpolator of our lines imitates *Frogs*. Chariton 2.8.7 ἄθλιον, πρὸ τοῦ γεννηθῆναι γέγονας ἐν τάφωι καὶ χερσὶ ληιστῶν παρεδόθης is prob. only a distant echo of the topos seen here.

1599   one γρ-variant, μητρί τ' ἀναβῆναι λέχος, is clearly a mythological supplement to produce conformity to the well-known oracle of *OT* 791–3. The origin of the other, πατρὸς ὅς μ' ἐγείνατο, is less clear, but the specification is superfluous here, and the interjection ὦ τάλας ἐγώ more effective.

γενέσθαι   for the aor. inf. referring to the future in a prophecy cf. *Wasps* 158–60 ὁ γὰρ θεός ... μοὔχρησεν ... ὅταν τις ἐκφύγηι μ', ἀποσκλῆναι τότε, K–G 1.195.

1600 αὖθις   possibly just 'in the next place', as in enumerating narratives (*IA* 350, *Aj*. 1283, *Trach*. 270, *Ant*. 1204, *Se*. 576), but there is prob. a suggestion of 'in (his) turn', implying that this is the second of a series of afflictions (the first being Apollo's dire prediction and attempt to forestall his birth). Cf. the compressed or elliptical use of πάλιν in Men. *Dysc*. 113 χάρακα λαμβάνει πάλιν τινά, 'for a second assault' (cf. Gomme–Sandbach). Erbse, 20–1, argues for the sense 'Laius, for his part ⟨in response to my threat to his life⟩', giving a reciprocal sense to αὖθις (cf. 479, 487 above, *Ion* 312), but this connection obscures the rhetorical division ὃν καὶ πρὶν / ἐπεὶ δ' ἐγενόμην and renders 1602a totally redundant. This use of αὖθις can be eliminated by emendation to αὐτίχ' (rejected by Geel) or αὐτός (Nauck); note that the same emendations have been proposed for αὖθις at *IA* 350.

1601 πολέμιον πεφυκέναι   MHBV all have intrusive δυσδάιμονα, and Kirchhoff thought that πεφυκέναι might be a conjecture rather than the original here. But it is hard to think of a more suitable word, unless one follows Nauck in ending this line with 1602b πέμπει δέ με, deleting the words in between. The similarity of the verse-ends 1599 and 1608 may have produced δυσδαίμων in the margin near 1601, whence the intrusion. In *Hipp*. 809 intrusive δυσδαίμονα perhaps began as a gloss on πικράν.

1602 χρῆν γὰρ θανεῖν νιν ἐξ ἐμοῦ   the repetition of this point may be pathetic; in 1597–9 the doom is viewed as an affliction of Oed., here as a motive for Laius' action.

600

1603 μαστὸν ποθοῦντα cf. 30–1 above.

θηρσὶν ἄθλιον βοράν ἄθλιον should be taken as fem. It seems to me too artificial to take ἄθλιον with με, as in the paraphrase apparently due to Arsenius (W. Dindorf, *Scholia Graeca in Euripidis Tragoedias* III (Oxford 1863) 387, 7; followed by Craik), although ἄθλιος is found interposed between related words in phrases that are unambiguous, as 1639 below and Lycophr. *Alex.* 903–4 ὦν οἱ μὲν Αἰγώνειαν ἄθλιοι πάτραν / ποθοῦντες.[1] ἀθλίαν in χ looks like a normalizing adjustment (cf. Σᵛ 1604). Treatment of ἄθλιος as of two terminations occurs elsewhere in Eur. only in the plural ἀθλίους (*Alc.* 1038, *Her.* 100, *Hel.* 797), but ἄθλιον ὄρνιν in *Trach.* 105 (in a simile for Deianira longing for Heracles) is apparently fem. These are the only instances of fem. ἄθλιος known to me. As for the sense, LSJ is wrong to put this passage under II.3 ('without any moral sense', that is, 'a sorry feast' from the point of view of the animals). 'Wretched, pitiable' in a moral sense is transferred from Oed. himself to what he was to become (cf. e.g. *Alc.* 204, *Ba.* 1216 ἄθλιον βάρος).

1604 οὗ σωιζόμεσθα 'where I am saved', the local adverb οὗ deriving its sense from 'to that place' (sc. Cithaeron) understood with πέμπει. Cf. *Held.* 19 πέμπων ὅπου γῆς πυνθάνοιθ' ἱδρυμένους, which is easier because ὅπου is indefinite and the relative clause more integral. The staccato transition reflects a shift of Oed.'s viewpoint, from pity at his treatment as a baby to regret that he had lived on. Craik wrongly follows Paley's suggestion that οὗ is gen. of separation, for οὗ κινδύνου.

1604–5 Ταρτάρου . . . χάσματα a hyperbolic expression, an extension (and adaptation to past time) of the usual 'may the earth swallow me up' (Barrett on *Hipp.* 1290–3) to include the whole mountain on which the baby was exposed. Cf. the lyric curse against old age in *Her.* 650–4 κατὰ κυμάτων δ' / ἔρροι μηδέ ποτ' ὤφελεν / θνατῶν δώματα καὶ πόλεις / ἐλθεῖν, ἀλλὰ κατ' αἰθέρ' αἰ- / εἰ πτεροῖσι φορείσθω (with Bond's note).

γάρ I believe that here, as in *Hel.* 1201 ἥκει· μόλοι γὰρ οἷ σφ' ἐγὼ χρῄζω μολεῖν, the wish is connected with γάρ because it explains the bitter tone with which the short preceding phrase was uttered: '⟨I say this with such bitterness⟩ because I wish . . .' Compare the use of γάρ to explain why a vocative is used (Barrett on *Hipp.* 88). Dale rejects such an interpretation of *Hel.* 1201 because she thinks the tone there must be ambiguous; but although the line has a secondary meaning for Helen, she is play-acting to deceive Theoclymenus and should, I think, utter ἥκει with bitterness.

---

[1] In view of ποθοῦντα here, one might take *Alex.* 903 as a learned allusion taking sides in a debate about the interpretation of ἄθλιον βοράν. But πόθος and ἄθλιος are also conjoined elsewhere, e.g. *Trach.* 103–7.

Badham proposed γ' ἄρ' here, which is not firmly established in tragedy[1] and has an inferential force that does not work here. Nor is Heimsoeth's δ' ἄρ' (favoured by Denniston, *GP*[2] 95) an improvement: in drama δ' ἄρα / δ' ἄρα is used to express sudden realizations (with imperfect) or sequence in a narrative or inference in questions ('what then . . .?').

ἄβυσσα χάσματα the adj. nowhere else in Eur., but attested three times in Aesch. and in *Frogs* 138 (also twice in Hdt.); χάσμα, on the other hand, appears several times in Eur., not in Aesch. or Soph. (but *Rhesus* 209 and Critias [?] *TrGF* 43 F 2.2). Cf. Hes. *Th.* 740 χάσμα μέγ' of Tartarus.

1606–7 unsympathetic ancient critics (269n., 395n.) had already criticized the εὐήθεια of Oed.'s curse on Cithaeron, saying that he should rather have cursed the herdsmen who picked him up or Polybus' wife (Σ1605), but the ancient reply ἀλλὰ μεμίμηται ὁ Εὐρ. τοὺς δι' ὑπερβολὴν συμφορᾶς καὶ τοῖς ἀναισθήτοις θυμουμένους is on the right lines. But the further complaint καὶ τοῦτο εὐήθως (Σ1606) applied to Oed.'s claim of 'serving as a slave to Polybus' is not so easily parried with a psychologizing reading. I find it unconvincing to argue that Eur. follows a different tradition, inconsistent with his prologue, in order to arouse pity: in some tales of exposed princes, the foundling has a humble or even servile status, but no such version is attested for Oed. It is true that δουλεύειν can be used in rhetorical exaggeration of a feeling of subjection or dependency that is not slavery in a legal sense (520n.; cf. *Ba.* 803, *Hel.* 1428), but again in the known versions Oed. leaves Corinth shortly after having doubts about his status and has no period of resentful dependency that could be subjectively viewed as δουλεία. Since the content of this couplet is thus so odd that it is not even the sort of thing that an interpolator of a whole speech would imagine, and since the details of expression are dubious (see below), I suspect that we have a badly cobbled repair of a defective text (cf. Murray's hypothesis of a lacuna). If Polybus was in the original, he should have been δεσπότης of his herdsmen, not of Oed. himself. The sense one might expect here is 'which didn't destroy me, but caused me to live out my terrible fate, rescued by Polybus' men'. Separate deletion of 1606–7 (Apitz) may be considered: the lines could have originated as an explanation for the curse on Cithaeron ('because it didn't destroy me'), badly filled out into trimeters. Hartung's larger deletion of 1604–7 seems to me to leave an unacceptable gap between 1603 and 1608 (one could assume a lacuna). There are three or four specific faults. (1) τε seems to be

---

[1] See in general J. C. B. Lowe, *Glotta* 51 (1973) 34–64, esp. 58–9; Lloyd-Jones and Wilson now read σοί γ' ἄρ' in *OC* 534 and Garvie considers γ' ἄρ' in *Choe.* 224.

unanswered: Denniston, *GP²* 513, lists the passage doubtfully under cases of τε ... δέ, but there is no perceivable contrast in the transition at 1608 κτανών δ', nor is the separation so great as to suggest anacoluthon. Elmsley (on *Med.* 560) proposed κτανών τ', now found in RfRv (perhaps as a correction of θ' (visual or phonetic error for δ'?) as seen in B), but in this step-by-step enumeration of his travails it is not suitable for Oed. to link in this way δουλεῦσαί τε ... κτανών τ'. (2) ἔδωκε + inf. is odd, since this construction is normally confined to prayers with δός, δότε, δοῖεν (LSJ III.1); the oddity remains even if we read τε με with O, which I suspect is a conjecture. (3) δουλεύειν ἀμφί τινα is a strange juncture, not adequately justified by idioms like οἱ ἀμφί τινα or ἔχειν ἀμφί τι ('be busy with some task'). (4) The change of subject from ὅς to δαίμων is not overly harsh, but it is interesting that δαίμων is absent in χ, though it is more probable that the omission arose *c.* 1300 than that it reflects an earlier stage of the tradition (*Text. Trad.* 98–9). Of the many emendations, Porson's δουλεύσοντά με eliminates two faults, but ἔδωκε would prob. have to be changed too (ἔθηκε Lenting, ἔσωιζε Wecklein), and the larger problem of what is here meant by 'slavery' is untouched. Caesar's δούλοισιν φέρειν starts out promisingly, but ἀμφί remains odd. Jackson's ὅς τ' οὐ διώλεσ' ἀλλὰ δουλεύσοντά με / δμώων ἔδωκε deserves mention for cleverness, but the position of δμώων is incredible and slavery to Polybus still present (*CQ* 35 (1941) 169–70, not repeated in *Marg. Scaen.*).

1611 ἀρὰς παραλαβὼν Λαΐου καὶ παισὶ δούς at least three interpretations have been offered. Σ believes that Laius cursed Oed. (Λαΐου subj. gen.), γνοὺς μὴ κατὰ βούλησιν θεῶν γεγονότα με. Mosch. referred the curse instead to Pelops (Λαΐου obj. gen.), which would provide the only allusion to the Chrysippus story within *Phoen.* Thomas also took the gen. as obj., but understood 'curse on Laius' in a generalized sense of Laius' misfortune. παραλαβών means 'take to oneself what had been another's', as in succession to office or inheritance of property but also in other contexts: *Ion* 814 (Xuthus) σὴν παραλαβὼν παγκληρίαν; *Or.* 552–3 πατὴρ μὲν ἐφύτευσέν με, σὴ δ' ἔτικτε παῖς, / τὸ σπέρμ' ἄρουρα παραλαβοῦσ' ἄλλου πάρα. So the view of Σ is unlikely, whether the curse is understood as uttered against the baby Oed. or as a result of the murder (on the assumption that any homicide arouses an *alastor*: cf. Barrett on *Hipp.* 1415). The play seems studiously to avoid Pelops and Chrysippus elsewhere, and it is by no means established that *Chrysippus* was part of the same tetralogy; so I doubt Mosch.'s view (see Introd. V). I prefer, therefore, the sense 'having in my turn suffered from an *alastor* (for patricide and incest) just as my father did (for disobedience to the gods' command to remain childless), I passed the curse on to my children'. In other words, Oedipus interprets his curse upon his sons as a continuation of the malevolent influence which pursued Laius and himself; he uses the word ἀράς in reference to Laius and himself in a loose and assimilating manner because his sentence is to climax in reference to the curse which has been so important in this play. For Oedipus as an intermediary in the transmission of troubles, see 1556n., 1593n. on ἀλάστωρ. I do not know why Wecklein, who considered the whole line unclear and faultily expressed, singled out παισὶ δούς as especially so. Dindorf deleted 1611 from the context, but 1612–14 are clearly an expansion of 1611 and do not follow well on 1610.

1612–14 Mosch. thought the indicative ὥστ' … ἐμηχανησάμην was irregular, and Paley, Pearson, and others deem the construction οὐ τοσοῦτον … ὥστε + ind. as improper in Attic and evidence of non-Euripidean origin. But the canon alleged by Paley (οὕτως ἀσύνετος ἦν ὥστε ταῦτα ἔδρασα, but οὐχ οὕτως ἀσύνετος ἦν ὥστε δρᾶσαι) is not clearly established; usage for this and similar expressions is quite flexible (cf. K–G II.506–7, esp. g and Anm. 5). It is relevant here that Oed. did in fact 'contrive these things', so that the unreality implied by an inf. is not mandatory.[1] In my view, then, the only suspicious feature in these lines is ἔμ' (see below). To delete the triplet from its context (Schenkl) would contribute little to solving the overall problems of Oed.'s speech.

1613 εἰς ἔμ' ὄμματα ἔμ' in context is immediately understandable as ἐμά and the anaphora with εἴς τ' ἐμῶν παίδων is vigorous and effective, but as Paley noted long ago, this is the only extant instance of elided ἐμά (as opposed to elided τἀμά, over 40 times in drama), not only in drama, but apparently in all poetry. ἔμ' is elsewhere ἐμέ (over 50 times in Eur., over 110 times in all drama).[2] To many this is a strong indication that Eur. did not write this line. Yet not every unique feature is inauthentic. Unelided anarthrous ἐμά is not very common: Aesch. once; Soph. four times (twice in lyric, once in a vocative, once elsewhere); Eur. five times (once as predicate, twice in lyric, twice in trimeters (1625 below, *Ba.* 59); Men. twice (once predicative). So one would not expect to find many cases of the anarthrous form elided. A critic who believes in Eur.'s authorship but refuses to ascribe this feature to Eur. could emend to τάδ', as Reeve noted.

---

[1] Cf. B. L. Gildersleeve, *AJP* 7 (1886) 172–3: 'The infinitive is preferred for failure to meet the conditions antecedent. [Isoc. 5.124] …, but the indicative can be used, as, after all, the failure is a fact … In negative statements, then, in questions that expect a negative answer, in conditions, we must look for a prevalence of the infinitive; but there is no mechanical rule.'

[2] In her translation (but not in her note) Craik implausibly treats ἔμ' as from ἐμέ: 'that on myself – my eyes –'.

1614 ἄνευ θεῶν του   this section of the speech ends, as it began, with reference to the powers controlling Oed.'s destiny. This point also brings us close to the present, since Creon had cited the afflicting demonic powers as a reason for the decree of exile; and Oed. now turns to his present situation.

1615-24   the remainder of Oed.'s speech is accepted as genuine by most critics of the scene, although Paley extended his suspicion all the way to 1626, without citing any linguistic faults in 1615-24 (he mentions Kirchhoff's suspicion that 1621 is intrusive, but not Geel's complaint about 1619: see below).

1615 εἶεν   makes excellent sense in a transition from comment about the past to contemplation of future action: cf. esp. *Su.* 1094 (after gnome about inability to correct mistaken choices by having a double life and description of suffering caused by death of a child) εἶεν· τί δὴ χρὴ τὸν ταλαίπορόν με δρᾶν; (followed by alternative questions). The particle normally marks the disposal of one topic and transition to another, or a move from delaying discussion to execution of action. Of about thirty-seven uses in tragedy (twenty-eight in Eur.), more than half occur in mid-speech or at a point of transition within a stichomythia. Fraenkel's deletion would have Oed. begin his speech with εἶεν, but Diller correctly objected to such an opening.[1] In the instances of speech-initial εἶεν (some are even scene-initial), we find (1) readiness to move the discussion and action forward after a lyric or messenger's narrative or other delaying element: *El.* 596, 907, 959, *Her.* 451, 1214, *IT* 342, 467, *Hel.* 761, above 849, *Phaethon* 313, *Prom.* 36; (2) miscellaneous Aeschylean uses (colloquial formula εἶεν ἀκούω in *Choe.* 657, marking the end of the wait for his arrival; transition to anapaests with act-dividing function at *Choe.* 719; re-entry of chorus and detection of the scent of the prey at *Eum.* 244).[2] Since Oed. has not yet spoken to Creon and no digressive element is present here without 1595-614, he cannot suitably open with εἶεν. Barrett apud Reeve suggests that Fraenkel's shortened speech can be saved by writing αἰαῖ for εἶεν. But rather than saving his hypothesis, I would rather conclude that Fraenkel's

---

[1] I do not accept the counter-argument of Reeve, 465 n. 18, who in rephrasing Diller's observation about εἶεν in terms of indicating 'acceptance, often resigned acceptance, of new information or a new situation' does not do justice to Diller's point or to the usage of the particle.

[2] Diggle reads αἰαῖ at *Ion* 756; transmitted εἶεν would apparently mark a transition from inarticulate responses to deliberation whether to answer Creusa's questions, but that ill suits the overall structure of the excited exchange.

confidence in the possibility of neatly separating Euripidean and non-Euripidean elements was unjustified.

τί δράσω δῆθ' Reeve questions the use of δῆτα if 1595–614 precede, since Oed.'s list of woes does not explicitly come back to the present situation. But the reference to blindness and loss of his sons provides some basis for the transition to 'what am I to do now? who will guide a wretched blind man?' Note also that in some passages the connective force of δῆτα seems subordinate to its emphatic force, and the circumstances that prompt the question are made clear in what immediately follows the question: *Ion* 253–4, *El.* 967, *Rhes.* 580–1.

1617 σάφ' οἶδ' ὅτι virtually an adverb, so best set off with a comma; for idioms of this kind see LSJ s.v. *εἴδω* B.8; cf. *Ant.* 276, 758; with σάφα *Wealth* 889, variant in *Med.* 963.

1618–19 ἀλλ' . . . / ἀλλ' introducing possible answers that are mentioned in order to be refuted (hypophora): Denniston, *GP²* 11.

οὐκ ἔστι μοι 'any longer' can be supplied from the context, and the more absolute '*that* I do not have' may be a rhetorical intensification. But οὐκ ἔστ(ι) ἔτι (Kirchhoff; cf. *Ant.* 567, *OC* 1270, οὐκ εἴμ' ἔτι *Hec.* 284) could easily have been corrupted by a kind of haplography, leaving a deficit of one syllable later filled with μοι.

1619 ἔτι νεάζων with bitter irony, 'am I still so young and vigorous that I could get my sustenance by myself?' Geel branded this line as bad rhetoric, noting that if Oed. were blind, being young would do him no good; and perhaps in response to this nitpicking analysis Nauck considered ἔτι νεάζων to be corrupt (and others offered unconvincing emendations).

εὕροιμ' ἂν βίον cf. 1626 ἐάσαιμ' ἂν χθόνα, both instances of a rare rhythm (long ninth element followed by monosyllabic enclitic, here with elision): Descroix, 329–30, gives five other instances with ἄν, to which JD adds *Held.* 456, *IA* 523 and notes the fact of double occurrence here within eight lines.

1620 πόθεν; 'impossible!'; a colloquial idiom (Stevens on *Andr.* 83).

1621 Kirchhoff remarked *interpretis manum prodere mihi videtur*; Wecklein brands the line as superfluous, Fraenkel judges it a bad climax to the series of questions. All of this is too subjective to justify the use of brackets in the text. The line may be viewed as a strong climax. Oed. uses the drastic term ἀκοκτείνεις in 1620, and then forestalls any objection ('I'm not putting you to death, I'm simply exiling you.') by justifying the term (Denniston, *GP²* 66): 'that's what you'll be doing, killing me, if you cast me from the land.'

1622–4 for the dramatic ploy of strong protestation followed by refusal to beg even in misfortune because of previous stature, cf. *Andr.* 459–63.

οὐ μὴν ἐλίξας γ' a strong adversative, 'but ⟨despite my protestations⟩ I am not going to clasp your knees and show myself a coward'. For οὐ μήν ... γε΄(twenty-four times in drama) see Denniston, *GP²* 335-6; but our passage belongs under his (1), not (2), cf. *Hipp.* 285 'but ⟨despite the failure of my previous attempts⟩ I am not going to let up'.

τὸ ... ἐμόν ποτ' εὐγενές 'the nobility I had of old'; the use of ποτε reflects the uncertainty whether one's noble stature is dependent solely on one's character or is subject to erosion by external circumstances. Here Oed. tries to live up to the standard, but is not sure whether he still possesses τὸ εὐγενές. Cf. 1688-9 with note. The Soph. Oed. characteristically has a surer sense of his lasting worth (*OC* 8 τὸ γενναῖον). For adjectival ποτε cf. LSJ s.v. III.1.a (citing Andoc. 3.22 τὴν ποτε φιλίαν), K-G I. 595.

κακὸς φανοῦμαι cf. κακὸς φανήσομαι in 1005 above, κακὴ φανοῦμαι *Hec.* 348, *Tro.* 663; also *Hel.* 1001, *Phil.* 906, *TrGF* adesp. 655.6.

οὐδέ περ only here in Eur., but the combination is rare in any case (Aesch. twice, Arist. once: Denniston, *GP²* 487).

1625-38 this speech has clearly been expanded by an interpolated parallel from the margin (1634), and I regard interpolation as the probable origin of the metrical and stylistic faults of 1637-8. Porson proposed a *Binneninterpolation* in 1628-9. But those who wish to remove the burial-decree and argument from the exodos either speak of rewriting that cannot be neatly separated from the genuine (Pearson) or try to identify a specific genuine core (e.g., 1625-6 + 1635-6, Fraenkel). The general arguments are addressed in 1582-709n. For particular points, see 1627n. (failure or delay in executing command), 1628-9n. (πόλιν πατρίδα and σὺν ἄλλοις), 1632n. (καταστέφων), 1634n., 1637-8n.

1625-6 σοί τ' ... ἐγὼ δέ δέ is appropriate since Creon is not only adding a point but emphasizing his own will ('and I *on my side* would not ...'): Denniston, *GP²* 513. The changes favoured by many edd. are graphically easy, but σοί γε puts too much weight on σοι, and ἐγώ τε is unnecessary (and not attested in V, as Kirchhoff led others to believe). JD notes the identity of *Hcld.* 333a and remarks that he would expect δέδοκται here.

χρώιζειν *Hel.* 831 ὡς οὐκ ἄχρωστα (leg. ἄχρωιστα?) γόνατ' ἐμῶν ἕξει χερῶν shows that γόνατα χρώιζειν (cf. *Med.* 497) is simply a precious alternative in Eur. for 'clasp the knees in supplication'. The verb does not imply defilement either here, as Thomas and Wecklein believed, or in *Med.* 497 (see Page, against LSJ s.v.3). Pearson notes the pregnant juncture λέλεκται ... μὴ χρώιζειν; but rather than say that λέλεκται is almost 'it is resolved' or that δεῖν is omitted, I would say that the present inf. is dynamic in force, 'that you are not going to be clasping my knees' (cf. L. Campbell's second explanation in his comm. on Pl. *Theat.* 197a τούτων τ' ἂν ἔφη ἀπέχεσθαι).

1627 action Creon announces the disposition of the bodies, but his commands are not immediately executed because of his attached comments and the appended order to Ant. The attendants would naturally wait for Creon to accompany them after finishing his comment and for Ant. to move away from the bodies, but Ant.'s resistance and the course of the dialogue prevents any action until at least 1682. The delay in execution of the order should not be counted as evidence of inauthenticity. See *Contact and Discontinuity* 106–7; D. Bain, *Masters, Servants and Orders in Greek Tragedy* (Manchester 1981) 39.

1627 νεκρῶν δὲ τῶνδε τὸν μέν it is self-evident that Joc.'s body is to be brought indoors for preparations for burial, and Creon acknowledges its presence in 1635 τριπτύχους. Et.'s body is directly referred to for the sake of contrast with Pol., whose case will receive fuller comment. To make clearer that Creon is speaking only of the brothers here, Elmsley (on *OT* 917) proposed νεκρὼ δὲ τώδε; West (1990) 316 suggests instead τὼ μέν (bodies of Joc. and Et.) so that 1627 may follow easily on 1594.

1628 ἤδη κομίζειν as in 1584 ἤδη means 'now' (as opposed to what has just been happening); it need not be translated 'sogleich', as by Fraenkel. Since no vocative is expressed, one should prob. understand ἡμᾶς as subj.; the attendants thus expect Creon to move indoors with them. The variant δμῶας may be the emendation of someone who wanted the subject of κομίζειν to be explicit. The mute characters present are the soldiers who accompanied the bodies, not household slaves (1308n.).

1628–9 τόνδε δ', ὃς . . . ἦλθε, Πολ. νέκυν many edd. have approved Porson's shortened text τὸν δὲ Πολ. νέκυν. He argued (1) that πόλιν πατρίδα is an unexampled combination; (2) that σὺν ἄλλοις is frigid; (3) that Creon is being brief and not taking time to give reasons, and that if Eur. wanted Creon to give a reason for his treatment of Pol., he would also have given a reason for treating Et. well. He considered the addition to be due to comparison with *Se.* 1013–24, esp. 1019 στράτευμ' ἐπακτὸν ἐμβαλὼν ᾔρει πόλιν and *Ant.* 198–206, esp. 199–201 ὃς γῆν πατρώιαν καὶ θεοὺς τοὺς ἐγγενεῖς / φυγὰς κατελθὼν ἠθέλησε μὲν πυρὶ / πρῆσαι. (1) has been answered by anon. Cantabr. (1810) with the claim that πόλιν is obj. of πέρσων, but πατρίδα is acc. with ἦλθε. Though accepted by Paley and not firmly rejected by Pearson, this reading is too artificial. Better to argue that πόλιν πατρίδα is used deliberately for special emphasis. The terms are conjoined in Pindar *O.* 10.36–8, but the presence of an epithet with πατρίδα and its separation from ἐὰν πόλιν give the impression of an emphatic apposition (cf. Gildersleeve): ἴδε πατρίδα πολυκτέανον ὑπὸ στερεῶι πυρὶ / πλαγαῖς τε σιδάρου βαθὺν εἰς ὀχετὸν ἄτας / ἵζοισαν ἐὰν πόλιν.¹ (2) σὺν ἄλλοις refers to the importation of a foreign army to further his treason (cf. 78, 431–2, 441–2, 466, 485, 598; *Se.* 1019). King already thought σὺν ἄλλοις jejune and σὺν ὅπλοις better here, and Valck. noted that σὺν ὅπλοις ἐλθεῖν is found in 511 and *Ion* 1292 (cf. *IA* 754). But σὺν ὅπλοις is somewhat otiose after πέρσων; ἄλλοις has more point. (3) The claim about Creon's brevity or the need for balance between Et. and Pol. is subjective and a priori. Pearson finds the ὅς-clause awkwardly placed before Πολυνείκους, but prob. τόνδε is the antecedent and there is a slight shift of thought as Πολυνείκους νέκυν follows instead of the expected Πολυνείκη νεκρόν (Dindorf suggested τοῦδε).

1630 ἐκβάλετ' . . . **ὅρων ἔξω χθονός** casting the corpse beyond the border was the contemporary legal treatment of traitors and some other malefactors (refs. in Hutchinson on *Se.* 1014); and this is all that Et. asked for at 776. But there is no necessary contradiction with the idea that Pol. will be food for the dogs (1650), since Creon expects that kin and Theban friends will be deterred by fear from attending to the body. The language in *Se.* 1014 is similar, ἔξω βαλεῖν ἄθαπτον, and there too it is assumed that this treatment will lead to mistreatment by birds and dogs (1014, 1020). This treatment of the corpse is thus not exactly the same as in *Ant.*, which interpolation-critics have regarded as the model of this passage (Mueller-Goldingen, 238–9). Hose, 'Exodos' 66–9, uses the apparent inconsistency between the *exorismos* motif and the non-burial motif to argue that the motifs are unintelligently combined: the author starts out with *exorismos*, in imitation of contemporary legal punishments (1630), but allows the situation of Soph.'s *Ant.* to intrude in 1631–3 and in 1645–70, seeking the strong effects of that argument; since the latter undercuts the former, this is inferior dramaturgy that is to be assigned to an interpolator rather than Eur.²

1631 κηρύξεται the future serves both as a performative utterance, proclaiming the decree to Oed. and Ant. and the Theban soldiers who are

---

¹ V's χθόνα at the end of 1629 is prob. an error from 1630, but it would be possible to regard it as a remnant of a lost reading πέρσων χθόνα in 1628. Another expedient is Blaydes' πολλοῖς σὺν ἄλλοις.

² Hose proposes that the genuine text after 1626 ran as follows: 1639–42, 1635–8, 1673–4, 1679–81, 1683–7, 1690–702, 1708–9. In this order, δ' in 1635 is odd, and the command in 1635–6 ('stop your lamentations for the dead') is unmotivated because Ant. has just spoken iambic trimeters on a different subject. Hose's explanation of ζῶσα in 1671 is also forced.

present, and as an acknowledgment that the rest of the citizens will need to be informed, since they are not represented by the chorus in this play. Et.'s instruction also calls for a proclamation (774 πόλει δὲ καὶ σοί). Fraenkel is wrong to brand the proclamation-motif unnecessary here and an uncritical imitation of *Ant.* (where it is stated with equal care that the proclamation has already been made to others and is to be repeated onstage τοῖσι μὴ εἰδόσιν, 27, 34). For the passive use of the so-called fut. middle, cf. K–G 1.114–16, but also Schwyzer 11.265–6, Wackernagel, *Syntax* 1.200–4, against seeing an aspectual distinction in the choice between κηρύξεται and κηρυχθήσεται.

1632 καταστέφων this refers to a ritual crowning of the corpse with σέλινον, along with bathing and dressing in fine clothes one of the standard forms of honouring the dead (Garland, 26; *Tro.* 1144). Here crowning is cited as representative of various acts of honour that might precede or follow burial. It is misplaced rationalism to say that someone illegally burying the corpse in the wilderness would not bother about this ritual (Fraenkel), nor need we seek another meaning for καταστέφων, understanding γῆι with it, or (as LSJ under the influence of *Ant.* 431, a transferred use of στέφω) 'with libations'.

1633 ἀνταλλάξεται twice elsewhere in Eur. (*Tro.* 351, *Hel.* 1088), also *Choe.* 133 and com. adesp. 1216.1 Kock, otherwise prosaic.

[1634] the change in construction from direct decree to indirect command ἐᾶν, the similarity to *Ant.* 29–30, and the repeated command (cf. 1630) after the striking climax of θάνατον ἀνταλλάξεται are strong grounds for recognizing this as a parallel passage once quoted in the margin (so Pohlenz; *contra*, Mueller-Goldingen, 239, ascribing it to actors). The theory that this interpolated line gives evidence of a *Binneninterpolation* (γλυκὺν ... χάριν) at *Ant.* 29–30 has not been accepted by the recent edd. (cf. Lloyd-Jones and Wilson, *Sophoclea* 116).

1635 Mueller-Goldingen, 242, rightly notes that Creon's order to Ant. to cease mourning follows well on the orders concerning burial (1627–33), but is poorly motivated if it follows 1626, as Fraenkel suggests.

τριπτύχους θρήνους νεκρῶν the variant τριπτύχων νεκρῶν γόους presumably began life as a paraphrase of the genuine text. Some edd. have preferred Valck.'s conflation of the main variants into τριπτύχων θρήνους νεκρῶν, on the ground that the hypallage is less acceptable than, e.g., 1351 λευκοπήχεις κτύπους χεροῖν. But the more precious reading is here to be accepted as *difficilior*. τρίπτυχος appears three times elsewhere in Eur., not in Soph. or Aesch. (unless Weil's restoration of fr. 74.6 is accepted); cf. 1355n. on δίπτυχος.

[1637–8] as transmitted, 1637 contains a serious metrical fault (impossible εἰσιοῦσαν, or ἐπιοῦσαν with illicit anapaest)[1] and one cannot be satisfied with the simplest correction (ἰοῦσαν); also, μένουσ᾽ . . . μένει is weak. A defender might argue that 1635–6 is too abrupt (note that Paley suspected that couplet only because he doubted 1637–8), that the preparation for 1672 is helpful, that ἰοῦσαν is after all the original (corrupted by a gloss in most witnesses), and that the punctuation should be 'and live as befits a virgin for the current day, awaiting the one on which the marriage bed of Haemon awaits you'. But this (or emendations that assume the same punctuation, like Marchant's ἔτ᾽ οὖσαν) does nothing about the weakness of 1638 (ameliorated somewhat by Heimsoeth's τηροῦσ᾽), and 1587–8 by themselves can prepare for emergence of the marriage-theme at 1672. Nor does it help to try to delete only one of the two lines, since either will be too cryptic without the other.

τὴν ἐπιοῦσαν ἡμέραν   with μένουσ᾽ in the next line, this should be its object and have its prosaic meaning 'the coming day', 'tomorrow'. Metrically correct ἰοῦσαν ought to mean not 'coming' (e.g., Craik), but 'passing', 'advancing', 'current', as in the use of νὺξ ἰοῦσα in Aratus 583 and Ap. Rh. 1.1015–16 ('as the night went along', not 'à la tombée de la nuit', as Vian), 4.979, 1634–5; this would require ἡμέραν to be acc. of duration, with translation as above. Porson, however, compared *Rhes.* 992 ἀκτῖνα τὴν στείχουσαν ἡλίου, spoken at night (cf. 988 πανούς (Reiske)), 'the approaching beam of the sun'.

1639–82   the dialogue between Ant. and Creon is denied to Eur. in its entirety by Fraenkel. Earlier, major portions were excised by Bakhuyzen (1639–60), and Balsamo and Friedrich (1639–72). The general objections to the presence of the burial-motif and to the characterization of the two figures are addressed above (1582–709n.). There is no contradiction between 1657 and 1679, as often claimed, because in 1667–71 Ant. retreats from her first resolve. Since I discount as based on inappropriately puristic taste Fraenkel's detection of grotesqueness and declamation, the specific complaints against the lines are in fact few in number. (1) 1653 is obscure. (2) The command in 1660 is not obeyed. (3) 1664 ὑγρὰν . . . κόνιν and 1673 ζῶσα are deemed inappropriate to their context and due to incautious

---

[1] The defence of even-foot anapaests not in proper names by C. Prato, *Maia* 9 (1957) 49–67, is misconceived. The statements of ancient metricians are to be explained by usage with proper names. Seventeen of Prato's nineteen examples involve split anapaests that arose when *scriptio plena* caused the insertion of nu to avoid apparent hiatus. Cf. Dale on *Hel.* 1660, Kannicht II.432.

imitation of Soph. *Ant.* These points are discussed *ad locc.* Only 1653 seems to me to be a serious problem.

1639 ἄθλιοι so Barnes for ἀθλίοις. ἄθλια κακά is a good juncture (*Tro.* 489, perhaps *Or.* 358), but Valck. correctly stated that οἴοις cannot be thus joined with ἀθλίοις.

1640 for the topos of the survivor being worse off than the dead cf. *Alc.* 864-9, 935-40, *Tro.* 630-40, *Se.* 336-7, esp. Aesch. fr. 138 Ἀντίλοχ', ἀποίμοξόν με τοῦ τεθνηκότος / τὸν ζῶντα μᾶλλον.

1641-2 parallels for this emphatic rhetorical periphrasis cited by comm. include *Pers.* 802, *Hel.* 646-7, *OC* 1671, Demodocus 2 West, Hdt. 1.139, 2.37.1, Pl. *Rep.* 475b5-7.

1643 ἀτάρ marks the transition from address to her father to address to Creon, not (as Valck. alleged) from one topic (Oed.'s exile) to another (the burial decree). So too *Ba.* 453; cf. (from comment to address) *Or.* 561, *Pers.* 333.

σ' ... τόν as Valck. already noted, this is not a polite form of address (e.g., *Prom.* 944, with Griffith's note), and Ant.'s lack of deference to Creon is also signalled by her addressing her father during 1639-42, even though Creon had just addressed her, and by her use of νεωστί.

1644 has often been deleted since Valck. because (1) Creon does not reply to it; (2) Ant. says no more in objection to the exile later in the scene; (3) her asking this question is pre-empted by Creon's explanation. But the question is 'epileptic', that is, indignant and disapproving (implying 'you ought not to be doing this'), not a request for information; Creon answers the double attack of 1644-5 by a chiastic response to the second element, and the course of dialogue (and the poet's choice of how to develop the scene) prevents a return to the first point. Like Oed. and the audience, Ant. is not required to accept Creon's reasoning as unquestionably valid (1592n.). For fuller discussion see *Contact and Discontinuity* 120-1.

1645 τί θεσμοποιεῖς τί is of course 'why' in vigorous anaphora; Méridier's 'que signifie la loi que tu forges' is wrong. θεσμοποιεῖς is hapax in extant Greek, possibly just a metrically convenient variation on θεσμοθετέω, but prob. here intended as mockingly grandiloquent.

1646 Ἐτεοκλέους βουλεύματ' cf. 774-7. The retreat behind the authority of another parallels that in 1590-1. If 774-7 are spurious and this passage is genuine, then this claim by Creon might seem particularly cryptic to an audience, unless (with Mueller-Goldingen, 129, 240, 244) they think Creon is stretching a point in claiming the regency and badly misrepresenting Tir.'s advice (1586-7n., 1590-1n.).

1647 ὃς ἐπίθου τάδε the aorist is pointed, 'who gave your consent', and the rebuke much sharper (matching ἄφρονά γε) than with a present, as in Hermann's ὃς πείθηι or Nauck's εἰ πείθηι. Aorist stem πιθ- is common in tragedy and often corrupted to πειθ-, as in the majority here, but this happens to be the only secure instance of an indicative form (*IA* 1017 is uncertain; but Arist. also has only one, ἐπιθόμην *Frogs* 1376). For τάδε cf. *IA* 1435, *Se.* 1065 (τά), *Birds* 661 (τοῦτο), *Or.* 92, *OT* 1434, *Clouds* 87, *Wasps* 761, *Birds* 164 (all τι or τί).[1]

1648 πῶς;   short for πῶς εἶπας; or πῶς φῄς; (above 1273, 1327), 'what do you mean?' For the following question cf. esp. *Su.* 943 πῶς; τὰς τεκούσας οὐ χρεὼν ψαῦσαι τέκνων;

τἀντεταλμέν'   Wecklein suggested that the word implies testamentary instructions in particular, but this is not borne out by the predominant usage of ἐντέλλω or ἐντολή. More likely, the word has an authoritarian flavour, of 'following orders': so in Hdt. and Xen. we often find λέγειν/ ἀγγέλλειν τὰ ἐντεταλμένα (also Soph. fr. 462.1) and in Hdt. ποιεῖν τὰ ἐντεταλμένα (4.9.5, 4.10.1, 4.112, 8.54), of which our phrase is a poetic variation.

ἐκπονεῖν   a favourite verb of Eur. (used in 979 above); the variant ἐκτελεῖν is possible (cf. *Trach.* 1187 τὸ λεχθὲν ἔργον ἐκτελεῖν; the verb also *Pers.* 228, *Hyps.* fr. 32.4 Bond), but in later Greek prose ἐκτελέω is commoner than ἐκπονέω by almost 2:1, and the former was familiar from Homer.

1650 κυσὶν δοθήσεται   for this assumed result of casting the body beyond the border cf. 1630n.

1651   '⟨No, not justly,⟩ because the penalty you exact from him is contrary to lawful custom.' For γάρ in dissenting answers cf. Denniston, *GP*² 74-5. The subj. of πράσσεσθε is prob. 'you and Et.' rather than 'you and the Thebans'.

1652 εἴπερ γε   γε reasserts ἔννομον, '⟨Yes, it is a just penalty,⟩ if he was an enemy of the state, being (by birth) no enemy.' The play on ἐχθρός / οὐκ ἐχθρός recalls 1446, and the contrast with the spirit of forgiveness shown there is deliberate.

1653 οὔκουν ἔδωκε †τῆι τύχηι τὸν δαίμονα†;   in this lively exchange a question with οὔκουν is better than a statement with οὐκοῦν (Σ; cf. 979n.). But no satisfactory explication has been given of 'gave his δαίμων to τύχη', and I believe that the problem is due to corruption rather than to the confusion of an interpolator. Σ interpreted δαίμων as 'fated death' and

---

[1] Paley complained of the unpleasing rhythm of the line. If unpleasant, the rhythm may be meant to match the tone and content. But lines containing two resolutions are not rare in *Phoen.* (1588n.), and the resolution in ὃς ἐπίθου is of a type attested in ten other places from *El.* on (incl. 471 above): cf. Cropp and Fick, 54, type 8.2c.

τύχηι as dat. of means, 'by the fortune he met in battle', but this gives no suitable force to ἔδωκε (one would expect 'meet' or 'fulfill' one's δαίμων). Thomas takes δαίμων instead of Pol.'s good fortune and life (τὴν κατ' αὐτὸν εὐτυχίαν καὶ ζωήν) and renders 'gave over to death (τύχηι dat. of ind. obj.) his life'. Barnes accepts Thomas' view of δαίμων, but not the rest, rendering *annon dedit fortunae suae animam?* (Compare Pearson's 'has yielded up his life to Woe', which he admits is doubtful.) King gives *annon dedit fortunae poenas?* (based on κόλασιν in the freer paraphrase in Σ). Musgrave renders *annon dedit bonam fortunam?*, omitting τύχηι, but in his note says the latter is equivalent to τῆι ἀτυχίαι. Matthiae is truer to the Greek than his predecessors when he suggests *sortem suam fortunae (s. incerti belli exitui) regendam commisit*; he concedes *insolens tamen locutio*, without specifying the oddity, which is that Pol. willingly puts his life on the line in a gamble, but the word used is not 'his prosperity' or 'his affairs' but the very word that suggests that a human does not have control over the outcome (cf. 1662).[1] The equivalence δαίμων = βίος is not normal to Greek, either in the classical period or later (in the time of a supposed interpolator).[2] In Pl. *Rep.* 617d–e (cited by Pearson) the two terms are not equivalent (there is one δαίμων, tutelary spirit, for each βίος, but the two are not the same thing); Xenocrates' identification of δαίμων with ψυχή (Aristotle *Top.* 112a38) is a special philosophical twist of the term (cf. Pl. *Tim.* 90a, god has given the highest part of the ψυχή to each man as a δαίμων).[3] Headlam, *Journal of Philology* 30 (1907) 305 n. 1, suggests that ἔδωκε δαίμονα is based on a (mis)interpretation of *Il.* 8.166 πάρος τοι δαίμονα δώσω, but this is unhelpful since in our passage the giver is the dead man, not the prospective killer. Wilam., *Glaube der Hellenen* I² (Leipzig 1955) 359 n. 1, after rejecting Matthiae's view and Headlam's, says 'Sein Dämon war, was Kreon eben angab, πόλεως ἐχθρὸς ἦν οὐκ ἐχθρὸς ὤν. Die Entscheidung über dieses Dilemma überliess er dem Zweikampf.' But such a definition of his δαίμων seems unjustifiably overspecific. Wilam. offers

---

[1] Contrast Lysias 2.79 οὐκ ἐπιτρέψαντες περὶ αὐτῶν τῆι τύχηι, οὐδ' ἀναμείναντες τὸν αὐτόματον θάνατον, ἀλλ' ἐκλεξάμενοι τὸν κάλλιστον.

[2] On δαίμων see G. François, *Le Polythéisme et l'emploi au singulier des mots ΘΕΟΣ ΔΑΙΜΩΝ dans la littérature grecque d'Homère à Platon* [Bibl. de la Fac. de Philos. et Lettres de l'Univ. de Liège, fasc. 147] (Paris 1957). In discussing the common sense 'an individual's lot in life' (pp. 340–2) François lists *Phoen.* 1653 as an instance without any discussion or explanation.

[3] Dihle, 100, argues that δαίμων here is used in a Hellenistic or Stoic sense of the immortal part of the soul in each man; I do not see how this makes the line any more comprehensible.

OC 76 as a parallel, 'wo der δαίμων des Ödipus seine Blindheit und auch sein Bettlertum ist', which seems to me much easier, if such specificity is in fact justified there.

If the line cannot be explicated, it is not much help to posit that an interpolator who writes lively stichomythia in a Euripidean style wrote the line as we have it. Nor is deletion of 1653–4 from the context (Harberton) attractive, since 1655 τί πλημμελήσας is better as an elliptic reply to the renewed edict παρασχέτω than to ἐχθρὸς ἦν. Emendations try to create a clearer sense of 'paying the penalty' in 1653 to which 1654 can aptly respond. Hartung's ἔτισε for ἔδωκε leaves a dubious sense of δαίμονα and removes the idiomatic variation ἔδωκε / παρασχέτω. Others put δίκην in 1653 to match 1654: note Purgold's ἔδωκε τὴν δίκην τῶι δαίμονι (τῆι τύχηι could have arisen as a gloss on δαίμονι, been incorporated, with subsequent change of case to δαίμονα),[1] Nauck's ἔδωκε τὴν δίκην θανὼν πόλει. For the notion that death ends the dispute and removes enmity, cf. *Su.* 528–30, *Aj.* 1344–5. F. W. Schmidt's ὅδ᾿ εἶκε τῆι τύχηι τῶν δαιμόνων cleverly retains τύχη and δαίμων in a convincing juncture, but is not so convincing as a lead-in to 1654.

1654 τῶι τάφωι 'by his burial', i.e., by the manner of his burial, thus in effect 'non-burial'. Pearson compares *Il.* 1.65 εὐχωλῆς ἐπιμέμφεται εἴθ᾿ ἑκατόμβης.

νυν καί is adverbial and coheres with τῶι τάφωι, postponing νυν to the third position; so too *Su.* 569 (κἀμοῦ νυν), *Cycl.* 568 (φέρ᾿ ἔγχεόν νυν), Soph. *El.* 1200, *Trach.* 1185.

1655 πλημμελήσας the verb only here in extant poetry (except for possible π[λημμελου]μένων in *CGFPR* 253.8 Austin), but note that πλημμελής is used three times by Eur. but is otherwise extant only in prose.

τὸ μέρος see 8on., 483, 601, 603.

μετῆλθε cf. 260, 441.

1656 Creon tries to end the argument by reasserting authority rather than replying to Ant.'s claim.

ὡς μάθηις is here argumentative (unlike *Cycl.* 143, *Andr.* 1073, etc. or 997 ὡς οὖν ἂν εἰδῆτ᾿), and is turned back on Creon by Ant. in 1681 ὡς μάθηις περαιτέρω; so too Men.'s ὡς μάθηις in *Hel.* 977 is slightly menacing.

1657 ἐγώ σφε θάψω same words in *Se.* 1028; cf. *Ant.* 71–2 κεῖνον δ᾿ ἐγὼ θάψω, *Se.* 1052 ἐγὼ δὲ θάψω τόνδε.

---

[1] I would understand Purgold's text as 'has he not paid the ⟨full⟩ penalty to the god ⟨that oversaw his life⟩?'; Wecklein, however, took τῶι δαίμονι as instrumental, 'durch sein Geschick', which leads well into instrumental τῶι τάφωι, but seems less probable after ἔδωκε.

κἂν ἀπεννέπηι πόλις these words magnify Ant.'s resolve, since they imply fuller authority for Creon and project a view of Ant. alone against all others. Soph.'s Ant. for most of the play treats Creon's decree as personal to him and without public support, although Creon aggrandizes his position by claiming to represent the state (on *Ant.* 44 see 1668n.). In *Se.* we have a clearer case of disobedience to the city (1030 ἄπιστον τήνδ' ἀναρχίαν πόλει), though the herald uses ἀπεννέπω in 1053, replying to θάψω.

1658 a similar threat in *Aj.* 1089–90 καί σοι προφωνῶ τόνδε μὴ θάπτειν, ὅπως / μὴ τόνδε θάπτων αὐτὸς ἐς ταφὰς πέσηις.

1659 cf. *Ant.* 72–3 καλόν μοι τοῦτο ποιούσηι θανεῖν· φίλη μετ' αὐτοῦ κείσομαι, φίλου μέτα.

1660 λάζυσθε this verb and its compounds are used about twenty times in Eur. (once *Rhes.*), otherwise in drama only *Lys.* 209. Here again Creon uses his authority to try to end the argument, but fails. Execution of the order by the silent extras is forestalled by Ant.'s protest and gesture (she at least clings to the corpse, perhaps also extends a hand toward the soldiers to signal 'stop'), and then Creon pursues the argument with Ant. rather than urging on the soldiers. See further *Contact and Discontinuity* 108 (against Fraenkel's insistence that the failure of the extras to obey is an interpolator's fault of dramatic technique).

1661 οὐ δῆτ' κομισθήσομαι or the like is understood from Creon's command κομίζετε; cf. *Cycl.* 198, where οὐ δῆτ' rejects the suggestion of flight in 197 (or perhaps rather Odysseus' own resolve to flee in 194).

1663 κέκριται a rejoinder to and variation on ἔκριν' in 1662, implying divine sanction against mistreatment of the dead, a theme well established in literature and mirrored in real life in the expectations about ἀναίρεσις of the dead after a battle. Cf. *Od.* 22.412; *Aj.* 1129–31, 1332–45, esp. 1343–4 οὐ γάρ τι τοῦτον, ἀλλὰ τοὺς θεῶν νόμους / φθείροις ἄν; *Ant.* 450–60, 1070–6; E. *Su.* 19, 558–63, *El.* 900–2, *Hel.* 1277, and Creon's own words in 1320–1 above. Just as Creon's confident patriotism was revealed to be shallow or empty by the reversal of the third episode, so his piety, expressed in the interests of his own son, is now shown to be selfish and shallow by his imperviousness to the same argument of piety.

ἐφυβρίζεσθαι as a putative divine injunction, this must be middle with active sense, not passive, but the use of the middle is hard to parallel. ὑβρίζω and its compounds are otherwise used in the active or in the passive, except in an inscription of Roman period that has παρυβριζόμενος in an active sense (G. Mihailov, *Inscriptiones Graecae in Bulgaria repertae* I² (Sofia 1970) no. 346, 6). ἐφυβρίζω itself occurs less than thirty times in extant Greek. Isolated middle for active is, however, a poetic licence found occasionally in tragedy (e.g. *Alc.* 1015 ἐλειψάμην). The verb takes a dat.

616

in *Aj*. 1385 θανόντι τῶιδε ... ἐφυβρίσαι and elsewhere, but acc. object (cited by LSJ from Plutarch) is in fact attested in *Hcld*. 947 as well as *Anth. gr.* 16.4.2 (νεκροῦ σῶμα λέοντος) and late prose. Characteristically, Blaydes removed the unusual features with μή 'ς νεκροὺς ἐφυβρίσαι (cf. *Andr*. 624).

1664 ὡς οὔτις again, Creon does not reply to Ant.'s argument, but uses strong asseveration (ὡς as in 625 above) to try to end the debate.

ὑγρὰν θήσει κόνιν since κόνις (like κονίη) connotes dryness, it is unlikely that ὑγράν is intended to be an attributive adj. It must be predicative, with the sense 'no one will make the dust moist around this man', a compendious way of saying 'no one will cover him with dust and pour ritual libations on his grave'. So already Wecklein in Klotz-Wecklein 1872, Bruhn on *Ant*. 431, and L. J. D. Richardson, *Hermathena* 92 (1958) 74-6. Σ offered two explanations of ὑγράν as attributive: (1) χυτὴν καὶ λεπτήν, 'broken up (pourable, granular) and fine', presumably based on ὑγρός = 'supple, flexible' (which sense is quite improbable with a noun like κόνις: 1255-8n.); (2) 'moist' because newly dug, but κόνις is against this. Fraenkel rejects the predicative interpretation, arguing that ἀμφὶ τῶιδ' requires that θήσει be 'place', not 'make'. I believe the brachylogy assumed above is possible, and I find incredible Fraenkel's theory that a *Bearbeiter*, however foolish, 'imitated' Soph.'s διψίαν κόνιν (*Ant*. 246-7, 429) by using an adj. with precisely the opposite meaning.

1665 ναί colloquial, 'imploring a person to relent from a refusal' (Barrett on *Hipp*. 605, with exx.; cf. ναί responding to other negatives, *Cycl*. 555 [L], *Knights* 338). Wecklein wrongly cited this usage as unusual.

πρός σε 923n. Creon supplicated Tir. in vain earlier, and now resists Ant.'s appeal. Supplication in the name of Joc. for the sake of Joc.'s son ironically recalls her relationship to Creon's son as nurse (987) and potential mourner and caregiver to the dead (1317-19). On the 'Homeric bowl' illustrated in Robert, *Oidipus* 1.452 Ant.'s supplication of Creon is immediately adjacent to Creon's supplication of Tir.

1666 οὐ γὰρ ἂν τύχοις τάδε recalls Et.'s harsh refusal to Pol. at 615. For τάδε cf. *Med*. 259 τοσοῦτον, 338 (τοῦθ'), *Alc*. 1023 (ὅ), etc.; also 992n.

1667 σὺ δ' ἀλλά the combination marks the beginning of Ant.'s retreat from the course she would most like to have followed (burial, 1657): '⟨if you won't allow the burial, then,⟩ at least permit me ...' (cf. Denniston, *GP²* 10). Many ancient and modern critics failed to note this surrender to *force majeure* and wrongly criticized the scene for combining resolve to bury her brother with decision to accompany her father.

λουτρὰ περιβαλεῖν a precious periphrasis for 'bathe' (for the practice, 1319n.). Either -βάλλω is reduced to the sense 'apply', or there is a transference from the (usually) closely related action of clothing the bathed corpse. περιβάλλω is a favourite verb of Eur., and there is no reason to believe that this expression is more likely to be by an interpolator than by Eur. himself.[1]

1668 τῶν ἀπορρήτων πόλει despite Ant.'s flourish κἂν ἀπεννέπηι πόλις in 1657, this is prob. 'the things forbidden to the city' (cf. 1631 κηρύξεται δὲ πᾶσι Καδμείοις), not 'forbidden by the city'. Creon does not elsewhere in the scene present himself as speaking on behalf of the city. In *Ant.* 44 ἦ γὰρ νοεῖς θάπτειν σφ', ἀπόρρητον πόλει; 'to the city' is also, I believe, the proper rendering.

1669 ἀλλ' the second stage of Ant.'s retreat: binding the ghastly wounds would not be of any ritual significance, but would at least be a comfort to herself. Cf. the modern notion that publication or broadcast of pictures of gruesomely killed bodies is a violation of the privacy of the dead person and his family.

τελαμῶνας an epic word, but not in the medical sense found here and *Tro.* 1232 (only uses in extant drama); cf. Hdt. 7.181.2.

τραύματ' ἄγρια cf. *Andr.* 1155 τραυμάτων ὑπ' ἀγρίων.

1671 ἀλλὰ . . . γε another retreat after a rebuff; γε seems both to stress the retreat and to add to the assertiveness of this final course of action. ἀλλά ... γε is rare in tragedy: *Andr.* 762, ten times in A. and S; cf. Denniston, *GP²* 12, 119. Ant. presumably kisses Pol. before Creon can protest against it.

στόμα . . . προσπτύξομαι the phrase is defended against Valck.'s desire to read σῶμα (invalidated in any case by the need for impossible ἀλλά γε) by *Med.* 1399-400 (also of a mourner bidding farewell to dead kin) φιλίου χρήιζω στόματος παίδων.... προσπτύξασθαι. The use of this verb perhaps reflects the customary gesture of the chief female mourner at a wake, clasping the dead person's head (*Il.* 24.724; Alexiou, 6; note that Creon classifies the act as γόοις).

1672 οὐ μὴ . . . κτήσηι the question with οὐ μή (Kirchhoff) + fut. is equivalent to an urgent prohibition, but this is not a prohibition that Creon can enforce, since Ant. is already kneeling by the body (since 1661). Fraenkel advocates keeping transmitted οὐκ and punctuating as a statement, citing Creon's use of statements in reply to other proposals or objections (1656, 1670). But in those cases, Ant. is seeking permission for a ritual act that she is unable to perform immediately and that Creon can prevent by the use of force; here she declares her intention to perform a personal act that can be done (and, I think, is done) immediately. It would

---

[1] West (1990) would regularize the expression with λουτρά γ' ἐπιβαλεῖν; but γ' here is a telltale *remedium Heathianum*, not attested with δ' ἀλλά.

be pointless for Creon to make a statement 'you will not' in this situation. Plain οὐκ + fut. in a question idiomatically has the opposite of the meaning needed here. If οὐ μή is correct, μή prob. dropped out of the text because of an apparent excess of syllables. If οὐκ is thought to be an intrusion from 1670, then Rauchenstein's ἀλλ' is possible (interrogative). Pearson accepted Heath's οὐδ', which seems too weak if there is a period at 1670 (as Pearson) and open to the objection made above if a comma is placed at 1670. To punctuate after οὐκ, with following statement (King) or question (Powell) in asyndeton, is possible (*Ion* 529, *Cycl.* 685, *Phil.* 631, Alexis fr. 223.13 K–A) but not, I think, lively enough in this context.

συμφοράν such close contact with the dead would be both polluting and ill-omened for one about to undergo marriage ritual and participate in a happy feast.

1673 Creon's renewed reference to the marriage provides the pivot for the course of the stichomythia; he has defeated Ant.'s desire to bury her brother, though defied in the end by her ability to kiss the corpse. Now Ant., frustrated by Creon's harshness, strikes back at him by refusing marriage with his son, first threatening suicide and then murder of Haemon, and finally insisting on departure with Oed. Friedrich's deletion of 1639–72 would have Ant.'s threats follow immediately on Creon's instruction to her to go in and await marriage (1635–8); but the violence of her reaction is not satisfactorily motivated without the intervening argument.

ἦ γάρ for the surprised and indignant tone cf. *Aj.* 1133, *Hipp.* 702, *Or.* 1600, etc.

ζῶσα the participle expresses compendiously the thought 'I'd rather die than marry your son'; cf. *Ant.* 525 ἐμοῦ δὲ ζῶντος οὐκ ἄρξει γυνή, almost 'I'd die before a woman could rule me'. Wecklein thought ζῶσα an inapposite reminiscence of *Ant.* 654 or 1240 (where ζῶσα does not appear), Fraenkel of *Ant.* 750 ταύτην ποτ' οὐκ ἔσθ' ὡς ἔτι ζῶσαν γαμεῖς. It may well be an allusion to the latter line, but in a clever and meaningful reversal of it that is not, in my view, a mark of carelessness or inauthenticity. Pearson wrongly suggests that Ant. expects to be put to death for burying her brother; but she has given up that intention. Creon's reply (ποῖ ... ἐκφεύξηι;) appears not to accept this threat as serious, since he still expects to be able to force the marriage. Noting this, Hose, 'Exodos' 70, suggests that 1681 explains Ant.'s meaning here (she will die with her father); but that meaning would be too obscure at this point, and ξυνθανοῦμαι should not be taken so literally (1681n.).

1674 πολλή σ' ἀνάγκη cf. πολλή μ' ἀνάγκη *Alc.* 378 (Monk; γ' codd.), *Med.* 1013 vs. πολλή γ' ἀνάγκη *Hec.* 396, πολλή 'στ' ἀνάγκη *Trach.* 295, S. *El.* 309, *OC* 293, Alexis fr. 46.3 K–A (variant γ' in Stobaeus). Many early edd. favoured γ' here, and Hartung proposed 'στ' (which could lie behind the reading of H).

ποῖ γὰρ ἐκφεύξηι λέχος; this question is a rhetorical transform (*Contact and Discontinuity* 7–8) of 'for there is no place for you to flee to' and need not be directly answered. Harberton proposed deleting 1675–8 from the context, which would let 1679 answer ποῖ and remove features some critics have found objectionable (see next notes); but the lines are needed to motivate 1682 (Harberton later removed 1680–4 as well).

1675 Δαναΐδων . . . μίαν such an allusive use of mythology is unique in extant tragic stichomythia (but much favoured by Seneca: B. Seidensticker, *Die Gespächsverdichtung in den Tragödien Senecas* (Heidelberg 1969) 159); cf., however, (in dialogue) Orpheus in *Ag.* 1629–32, *Alc.* 357–62, and (in lyric) Niobe, Itys, etc.

1676 εἶδες earlier comm. ignore the question, but Wecklein notes 'wie es scheint, an Ödipus gerichtet', and Pearson and others follow, explaining that εἶδες can be 'perceive' rather than 'see'. Fraenkel, 111 (with additional remarks in *MusHelv* 24 (1967) 190–3, 25 (1968) 179–80), well explains that such an indignant colloquial 'see', 'look' is not addressed to actor, chorus or audience, but to an imagined witness. Most exx. are from comedy (*Ach.* 366, 770, *Wasps* 799), but cf. *Or.* 128 εἶδετε (question, as here; Willink prefers ἴδετε); I would add *IT* 1298 ὁρᾶτ' ἄπιστον ὡς γυναικεῖον γένος (despite χὑμῖν in the next line, this is more sensibly addressed to an imagined witness than to the treacherous women themselves). Here εἶδετε in W^{ac} is not impossible, but prob. a mere slip.

τὸ τόλμημ' οἷον ἐξωνείδισεν one Σ takes τόλμημ' as descriptive of Ant. and as proleptic subject of ἐξωνείδισεν, but it is better taken as 'the bold gesture', 'the audacious claim'. Then either οἷον ἐξ. is in apposition, 'what an insulting utterance she let fly', or τόλμημα is also internal obj. of ἐξωνείδισεν, with the sense 'what a bold insult she let fly'. Ant.'s threat is an ὄνειδος because it treats Creon's authority with contumely and rejects Haemon, who would ordinarily have been deemed an excellent catch as bridegroom. The verb ἐξονειδίζω is found in four other tragic passages (S. *El.* 288, *Phil.* 382, *OC* 990, *IA* 305), then in late prose, and the int. acc. construction is characteristic of the tragic usage (later only Dio Cass. 47.8.3). Fraenkel judges the phrase 'recht Bedenklich', but it is striking and effective; nor do we need ἐξηκόντισεν (Walter after F. W. Schmidt).

1677 σίδηρος . . . ξίφος Ant. is presumably still kneeling by the body of Pol. and lays her hand on a sword there. With hendiadys, the meaning is 'Let the iron of this sword be witness to my oath.' Iron is thus not invoked in the abstract, but its malevolent magical qualities (350–3n.) are suggested. Critics who suspect the passage remark on the lack of a demonstrative or insist that there is no sword to hand for Ant. to refer to (Friedrich,

Fraenkel, Dihle). Mueller-Goldingen, 248 n. 53, takes the reference to be to the sword that Ant. imagines she will use on the fatal night.

1678 τί δ'   the fit between Creon's 'why are you so very eager to be free of this marriage?' and Ant.'s reply 'I'll go into exile with my father' is inexact, but this seems suitable in this altercation, as Ant. moves desperately from one idea to the next in rebelling against Creon's authority. The transition to 1681 καὶ ξυνθανοῦμαί γ' is similarly abrupt and passionate rather than logical. Reiske wanted to adjust the logic and remove ἐκπρο-. His τί δέ; προ- would have to be τί δ'; ἐκπρο-; cf. Hermann's τί δαί;, Hartung's τί δ' αὖ, Paley's ποῖ γάρ.

ἐκπροθυμῆι   hapax in extant Greek, an intensifying ἐκ-compound of προθυμέω (thus not strictly comparable to hapax compounds of ἐκπρο-, 214n.). There is nothing suspicious about such a formation.

1680 γενναιότης   the noun is not common in classical Greek (five times in Attic prose) and no other poet uses it, but Eur. has it *Hipp.* 1301, *Ion* 237, *Erecth.* fr. 65.69 Austin, fr. 527.2.

1681   Creon's backhanded compliment to her devotion to her father exasperates Ant. and prompts this hyperbolic claim, which she spits back at Creon; for ὡς μάθηις cf. 1656n. and for ξυνθανοῦμαι cf. 1283.

1682   Ant.'s vehemence causes Creon to back off, citing the important consideration of protecting his son (a re-enactment of his action in the third episode).[1] It is this threat that accounts for his retreat from πολλή σ' ἀνάγκη in 1674, and the retreat is problematic only if one has built up a false image of Creon's strength and importance as a character. It is possible that he departs (for his own house or into the palace?), as Paley and Wecklein indicate; but I think it would be slightly better for him to motion Ant. away, then break contact with her by stepping back, thus still maintaining his control over his soldiers and the bodies until Ant. and Oed. have departed as instructed.

λεῖπε   1530n.

1683–1709   the dialogue between Ant. and Oed. preceding their departure has been accepted by most critics who find fault with earlier parts of the scene. Critics have concentrated their suspicions on 1688–9 and 1703–7 as passages interpolated into the context. See *ad locc.*

1683 αἰνῶ μὲν   αἰνῶ is an expression of approval and thanks (614n., Bond on *Her.* 275), but in some contexts the approval is preface to a polite

---

[1] This view has been espoused by Robert and others; Mueller-Goldingen, 249 n. 57, rejects it, alleging that Creon desists from the argument because Ant.'s departure from Thebes ensures that she will not interfere with his goal of preventing burial of Pol.'s corpse in Theban soil.

refusal of an offer (*IA* 506, with ἀλλ' in 511; *Prom.* 340–1 ἐπαινῶ ... ἀτάρ; cf. West on Hes. *Op.* 643) or implies that the course approved is actually second-best (*El.* 396, *Hel.* 1232, fr. 603.1). Here the notion of refusal is suggested by μέν, preparing for an unstated but easily inferred 'but I don't want you to do this for me' (Denniston, *GP*² 381). Cf. J. H. H. Quincey, 'Greek Expressions of Thanks,' *JHS* 86 (1966) 133–59, esp. 146 (he would print no period here and view 1685 as the continuation, lacking δέ because of Ant.'s intervention; I disagree).

προθυμίας cf. in context of polite refusal *Prom.* 341 προθυμίας γὰρ οὐδὲν ἐλλείπεις, and in harsher rejection 589 above.

1684 ἀλλ' εἰ an elliptical question, as *Andr.* 845, and elsewhere with εἰ (724), τί δ' εἰ (732), εἰ δέ (1562–3n.). The bipartite fut. less vivid condition with φεύγοις is clearly superior to an unnatural mixed condition and alleged apodotic δέ, as with the majority reading φεύγεις, wrongly defended by some early edd.

1685 τἄμ' ἐγώ the asyndeton may be strongly contrastive (456n.) rather than simply explicative; for the intensifying juxtaposition of possessive and pronoun cf. *IA* 401 τἄμ' ἐγὼ θήσω καλῶς.

1686 θεραπεύσει cf. 1549 πόδα σὸν τυφλόπουν θεραπεύμασιν ... ἐμόχθει.

1687 πεσών ... κείσομαι the juncture suggests giving up a struggle: so of lovers in despair, *Eccl.* 963 and Theocr. 3.53 (cf. Gow's note), or of a hedgehog playing dead, Soph. *Ichneut.* fr. 314.127. Conversely, in *Clouds* 126 οὐδ' ... πεσών γε κείσομαι connotes spirited refusal to give up, like a tough wrestling competitor.

πέδωι I prefer this as more vivid and pathetic, but Hermann suggested that both θανών and πέδωι are supplements for a damaged verse-end and offered τέκνον. For intrusive clarifying gloss θανών (redundant after πεσών) cf. 1235, and contrast the correct use in 1459 θανοῦσα κεῖται.

1688–9 the couplet was first doubted by K. H. F. Müller, and Robert's statement of the indictment against it has been accepted by Friedrich, Fraenkel, and others. On this view, (1) the question in 1688 is said to have no point, since Ant. cannot be mocking Oed., nor can she be using the Sphinx-episode to encourage him, since that would contradict 1732–3; (2) the couplet disturbs the connection between 1687 and 1691 (Ant.'s hyperbolic ξυνθανοῦμαι is taken seriously); (3) the 'one day' of 1689 is an inapposite borrowing from *OT* 438. But (1), as Plutarch well understood,[1] Ant. is trying to rouse Oed. from the despair he has just shown in

---

[1] *Mor.* 72C–D: 'And such statements [*Phoen.* 1688, *Her.* 1250] too very

1687, and the appeal to former stature and achievement is suitable to that goal. 1732-3 should not be adduced against 1688-9: the audience has not yet heard 1732-3 (and some critics believe that the Eur. tailpiece ends before 1732), and 1732-3 occur in a different, lyric context, where Ant. is trying to terminate Oed.'s complaints as they depart. (2) μετασχεῖν τῶν σῶν κακῶν is not to be taken as 'die with you', but as 'share the sufferings of your exile', in line with 1685-6 and 1691-2. The force of 1690 οὔκουν after 1689 is 'then, if you *are* so ruined and wretched [ἀπώλεσεν], shouldn't I share your condition?'. If 1688-9 were deleted, οὔκουν would not have any proper force ('if you are going to give up and die, then shouldn't I share your condition?' is nonsense). (3) The 'one-day' motif is a legitimate variation of a flexible topos, not an imitation of *OT*: 1689n.

1688 the ποῦ-question implies 'is nowhere to be seen', that is, 'you are forgetting the fortitude that your fame and stature as Sphinx-slayer require'.

1689 ἐν ἡμάρ ... ἀπώλεσεν ἐν ... ἐν is here emphatic anaphora for 'one and the same', as, I believe,[1] in Pindar *N.* 6.1-2 ἐν ἀνδρῶν, ἐν θεῶν γένος· ἐκ μιᾶς δὲ πνέομεν ματρὸς ἀμφότεροι; cf. Soph. fr. 591 (ἐν φῦλον ἀνθρώπων restated, with anaphora and asyndeton, in μί' ἔδειξε κτλ.). The γρ-variant ὤλβισ' ἠδ' ἀπώλεσεν is not impossible (Denniston, *GP*[2] 277-8), but less vigorous. As implied by the context and confirmed by several other passages in the play (1043-50, 1204-5, 1352-3, 1504-7), the one day is, as Σ noted, that on which Oed. solved the riddle of the Sphinx (and consequently married Joc., had children by incest, etc.). The paradox of the misfortune that coincides with apparent success is typical of this play. For rhetorical play on paradoxically mixed experience on one day, as

---

plainly revive those who are giving way. For they not only soften the harshness and abasing quality of reproach, but they also instill in the hearer emulation toward himself as he feels shame at base acts because of the reminder of noble ones and as he makes himself an example of better behaviour.'

[1] I take this, with Farnell, Bury, and others, as 'single is the race of men and of gods, and from one and the same mother we both have life (*but* our powers are distinct, etc.)'. Others (e.g., Boeckh; E. L. Bundy, *Studia Pindarica* (Berkeley and Los Angeles 1962) 37-8; P. v. Kloch-Kornitz, *Hermes* 89 (1961) 370-1) have preferred the rendering 'there is one race of men, another of gods, *but* from the same mother we both have life (*but* our powers are distinct, etc.)'. Given the possibilities of Greek syntax, the dispute is probably unresolvable. But the latter view seems to me to ignore the fact that μιᾶς is in a kind of anaphoric relation with the preceding pair of ἐν, suggesting that it is not in opposition to that opening, but a restatement of what is, purposefully, a striking idea.

here, cf. Soph. *El.* 1362–3 μάλιστά σ' ἀνθρώπων ἐγὼ / ἤχθηρα κἀφίλησ' ἐν ἡμέραι μιᾷ, Apollonides *Anth. gr.* 9.243.1–2 γήθησαν περὶ παιδὸς Ἀριστίπποιο τοκῆες / καὶ κλαῦσαν· μοίρης δ' ἦμαρ ἓν ἀμφοτέρης; Philostratus *VA* 2.21 πάντα ἐν ἡμέραι μιᾷ καὶ ἀπώλεσα καὶ ἐκτησάμην; also *OT* 438 ἥδ' ἡμέρα φύσει σε καὶ διαφθερεῖ (if our line alludes to this, the discrepancy in meaning is not due to clumsiness but to a meaningful reinterpretation of the model). Most similar, structurally and rhetorically, to our passage is Sosiphanes *TrGF* 92 F 3.1–3 ὦ δυστυχεῖς μὲν πολλά, παῦρα δ' ὄλβιοι / βροτοί, τί σεμνύνεσθε ταῖς ἐξουσίαις, / ἃς ἕν τ' ἔδωκε φέγγος ἕν τ' ἀφείλετο; It too combines topoi a and b (below), but ἕν there is used of two different days, as is *una dies* in Ovid *Fasti* 2.235–6. Because of this parallel (or imitation) Geel doubted that ἕν ... ἕν could refer to the same day and proposed that the day of triumph over the Sphinx elevated Oed. and the present day has ruined him; but this ignores the established ambiguity of Oed.'s victory.

'One day' is a motif of various topoi, all connected to the notion that human fortune is so fragile that it may undergo a complete reversal in a single day. (a) one day may bring drastic change: Eur. fr. 549 ἀλλ' ἦμαρ ⟨ἓν⟩ τοι μεταβολὰς πολλὰς ἔχει, fr. 420.2–3 ὡς μικρὰ τὰ σφάλλοντα, καὶ μί' ἡμέρα / τὰ μὲν καθεῖλεν ὑψόθεν, τὰ δ' ἦρ' ἄνω; Soph. *El.* 1149 νῦν δ' ἐκλέλοιπε ταῦτ' ἐν ἡμέραι μιᾷ; *Aspis* 417–18 ὁ Καρκίνος φησ'· ἐν μιᾷ γὰρ ἡμέραι / τὸν εὐτυχῆ τίθησι δυστυχῆ θεός, *Dysc.* 187–8 πόλλ' ἐν ἡμέραι μιᾷ / γένοιτ' ἄν (cf. 864), Dion. Hal. *Ant.Rom.* 8.75.4 χρήσιμον δὲ πρᾶγμα ... ἀναβολή, καὶ πολλὰ ὁ χρόνος ἐν ἡμέραι μιᾷ μετατίθησι. For good fortune accomplished in a day, cf. Diggle's conjecture at *Hcld.* 788, ἥδε σ' ἡμέρα διώλβισεν, based on this line. (b) one day may deprive one of all prosperity: *Hec.* 285 τὸν πάντα δ' ὄλβον ἦμαρ ἕν μ' ἀφείλετο, *Her.* 509–10 καί μ' ἀφείλεθ' ἡ τύχη ... ἡμέραι μιᾷ; *TrGF* adesp. 638.13–14 ἀλλὰ τἀγάθ' ἡμέρα... σφάλλει μία; Isoc. 14.46, Dion. Hal. *Ant.Rom.* 5.3.2, 7.50.4. (c) one day brings many deaths (or other striking disaster) to a family or community: *Il.* 6.422; *Pers.* 431, Aeschines *Ctes.* 133, Polyb. 4.54.5, Diod. Sic. 4.13.3, 20.71.5; Dioscorides *Anth. gr.* 5.138.3. For Latin exx. see Tarrant on Sen. *Ag.* 626.

1690 οὔκουν   979n., 1653n.

1691 αἰσχρὰ φυγή   an unmarried girl should not be wandering in the open; cf. *OC* 337–45 and esp. 747–52, ending τηλικοῦτος, οὐ γάμων / ἔμπειρος, ἀλλὰ τοὐπιόντος ἁρπάσαι. Ant. rebuts this worry with σωφρονούσηι γ'. Oed.'s concern recalls the theme of Ant. as sheltered maiden, but she has gone beyond that condition; and her appeal to nobility matches Oed.'s in 1623 (cf. Mueller-Goldingen, 253).

1693 προσάγαγέ νυν   with this order Oed. acquiesces (νυν) in Ant.'s proposal to accompany him, and departure from the stage begins. At this point (and probably for the first time: 1539n.) Ant. goes to aid Oed. in his movements. He has been standing on his own, resting on his staff. The passage 1693–7 is illustrated on a 'Homeric bowl' (Robert, *Oidipus* 1.454) that even has a caption paraphrasing the lines: Οἰδί]πους κελεύει ἄγε[ιν πρὸς τὸ] πτῶμα τῆς αὐτοῦ μητ[ρός τε καὶ] γυναικὸς καὶ τῶν υἱῶν[.

1694 ἰδού marks compliance with a request (so too 1700, 1714).

παρειᾶς φιλτάτης F. W. Schmidt's excellent correction; the touch is suitably directed to the face, cf. 1671n. and 1699. Mss vary between φιλτάτης and φιλτάτηι, and it looks as if γεραιᾶι was also a variant on γεραιᾶς. Valck. proposed γεραιᾶι φιλτάτης, to give 'touch the dearest woman with your aged hand', but φιλτάτης without either article or partitive gen. is odd (closest parallel is in *Ag.* 329 φιλτάτων μόρον, where the same persons are referred to in the gen. pl. by the same speaker in 327–8), and 'aged' is rather otiose. Porson preferred γεραιᾶς φιλτάτηι, 'touch the old woman with a most loving hand', and Hermann defended γεραιᾶς φιλτάτης, but anarthrous γεραιᾶς as substantive (= γραίας) is not found except in the vocative, and γεραιᾶς has little point here.

1695 ξυνάορ' as with κυναγός and the like, this word is poetic and not current in an Attic form, so the long-alpha form is used in trimeters (Björck 221f.). Eur. has it twelve times, otherwise in tragedy only *TrGF* adesp. 634.3. Note Oed.'s pathetic pairing of his two relationships to Joc., reflecting the human loyalty that has abided in the family tainted by god-ordained incest (57–8n.).

1697 πτῶμα 1482n.

1698 ἐκτάδην a form suggested by Homeric ἐκτάδιος; *Tro.* 463 ἄναυδος ἐκτάδην πίτνει (ἐκτάδην restored convincingly by Verrall) is the only other classical usage extant (eight times in later prose; Luc. *DMort.* 12.5 and 17.2 both imitate the use with κεῖμαι for a dead body).

σοι a pathetic touch, almost 'awaiting your touch'.

1700 ἰδού again marking compliance (1694n.); for this use twice within a stichomythia cf. *Or.* 221, 229.

1701 πεσήματ' 639–41n.

1702 ὄμμα Purgold's correction of ὄνομα has more point in connection with the stage action here (1671n.) and picks up Oed.'s πρόσωπα (1699) just as φίλτατον δῆτ' echoes and intensifies φίλα (1701). The eye is the focus of affection in the face of the beloved (whence the idiom of 803n.), and ὄμμα can be used in affectionate periphrasis, as *Aj.* 977 ὦ φίλτατ' Αἴας, ὦ ξύναιμον ὄμμ' ἐμοί. For Ant.'s special fondness for Pol. within this play, cf. 156–71 as well as the protest over the edict of exposure. ὄνομα would inappropriately recall the ill-omened etymology of Pol.'s name, cited by Et. in 636–7 and by Ant. herself in 1494. ὄμμα and ὄνομα are variants in *Or.* 1082 (where ὄμμα is rightly preferred); P has ὄνομ' in error at *IA* 354;

ὄμμα replaces ὄνομα in a late apograph of L at *IT* 905, where the latter is perhaps correct (note κλεινόν), though Diggle reads ὄμμα.

1703–7 In Eur. the *deus ex machina* usually provides a glimpse of the future and reintegrates Eur.'s version of myth with some aspect of myth or ritual whose validity is secured outside of Eur.'s dramatic world. This may be viewed as an extension of an old poetic tradition whereby poets guarantee the validity of the creative and innovative aspects of their work (and thus advertise their own excellence) by relating their variations to more standard versions (e.g., Stesichorus' palinode, Pindar in *O.* 1). Even in plays without a *deus* Eur. usually manages to include such reference to the future: Medea's warning to Jason (*Med.* 1386–8), Eurystheus' prophecy (*Hcld.* 1028–36), Polymestor's prophecy (*Hec.* 1259–81), Theseus' promise of shrines for Heracles (*Her.* 1329–33). Of extant complete plays, this element is lacking only in *Alc.* and in *Tro.* (which has a glance at the future in the divine prologue). A connection to Attic legend and cult at Colonus is exactly what we should expect from Eur., and its belated introduction by Oed.'s suddenly remembering it is no more clumsy than the treatment of the prophecies in *Hcld.* and *Hec.* Nevertheless, Leidloff and later critics have branded these five lines an inapposite borrowing from *OC*, some alleging that the burial of Oed. on Attic soil was an invention of Soph. (1707n.), others detecting a contradiction between this oracle and 1687 on the one hand and 1736 on the other. But 1687 comes at an earlier point of despair and cannot be counted against this passage, whereas 1736 θανεῖν που is pathetically vague, reinforcing the regret at exile that is a theme of the duet (1710, 1723–4, 1735). Exile is throughout the play viewed as a great evil, and even this oracle implies wretched wandering before the final release in Attica (1705 ἀλώμενον). Compare the lamentations of Cadmus in *Ba.* 1353–62, unaffected by Dionysus' assurance in 1338–9 of his ultimate translation to the isles of the blessed. For 1708 ἀλλ' εἶα as evidence about 1703–7 see *ad loc.*

1703 Λοξίου it is fitting that Delphic Apollo, already involved at other stages of the story (15–20, 34–8, 409, 641–2, 1043bis), is mentioned one last time at the end of the play.

1704 ὁ ποῖος this lively form (apparently more pressing because the article makes the reference of the interrogative more specific) is more common in Soph. and comedy than in Eur., but cf. 707 above, *IT* 1319, *IA* 517. Cf. P. T. Stevens, *CQ* 31 (1937) 185–6.

ἀλλ' ἦ marks dismayed surprise or disbelief (Denniston, *GP*[2] 27); cf. esp. *Alc.* 58 πῶς εἶπας; ἀλλ' ἦ καὶ σοφὸς λέληθας ὤν; Early editors emended because misled by Mosch.'s mistaken ὁ ἀλλὰ περισσός.

1707 If 1703–7 are genuine, this is our earliest attestation of Oed. at Colonus, apparently based on a local legend (Daly, 782). There were of course various traditions about Oed.'s burial-place (e.g., Sparta, Eteonos, Attica: Robert, *Oidipus* I.1–47), and in Pausanias' time a tomb of Oed. was shown in the sanctuary of the Eumenides on the Areopagus (1.28.7) as well as a shrine of Oed. at Colonus (1.30.4). I see no reason to prefer the view that Soph. invented the connection of Oed. with Colonus (and that this reference is *ipso facto* post-Euripidean). E. Kearns, *The Heroes of Attica* [BICS Suppl. 57 (1989)] 50–2, 208–9, is sceptical of both traditions about Oed.'s burial in Attica, but concludes 'there is a little too much evidence connecting Oedipus with Kolonos to be explained simply by the influence of Sophocles' play' (she accepts Fraenkel's arguments against 1703–7).

δώμαθ' ἱππίου θεοῦ a periphrasis that distinguishes Κολωνὸς ἵππιος from Κολωνὸς ἀγοραῖος. ἵππιος, not ἵππειος, is the proper form of the epithet of Posidon (Archilochus 192 West; *IG* I³ 383, 59–60; *Se.* 131, ἵππιος favoured by metre) and hence of Colonus.

1708 ἀλλ' εἶα these particles predominantly occur within a speech, in transition from comment to action (970n.), and Diller cited this tendency in support of retaining 1703–7. But this point is not conclusive: there are a few cases of speech-initial ἀλλ' εἶα (990n.), and Oed. could be dismissing the apostrophes of farewell (1695–702) and reasserting his intention to accept Ant.'s accompaniment (1763n.).

ὑπηρέτει πατρί this is a more explicit acceptance of Ant.'s sacrifice, echoing 1686 σε τυφλὸν ὄντα θεραπεύσει. L's ποδί tempted Porson, but is not quite apt with ὑπηρέτει or with the following clause.

1710–66: LYRIC TAILPIECE AND SPURIA

Thematically, the play is complete at 1709. In a comparable situation in *Her.* Heracles and Theseus (whom one would not expect to sing at such a moment) make their way off together after a final gnome in trimeters. But in other plays there is a modulation from trimeters to actors' anapaests at the close: *Prom., Med., El., Or., Ba.*,[1] cf. *Aj., Trach., Phil.* Compare modulation to trochaic tetrameters in *Ion, Ag., OT.* In *Tro.* there is an exit-song in responsion shared by Hecuba and the chorus: cf. earlier A. *Su., Eum.*, and laments in *Pers., Se., Ant.*; *OC* has lyric lament followed by anapaests. Here the exit-song serves a similar function of accompanying the departure of characters from the stage. In this case the song and action also provide a significant echo of two earlier scenes. The joining of hands signalled by 1711 ὄρεγε recalls the teichoskopia (103): in that scene an old

---

[1] This is true of *Ba.* 1368–71 (plus whatever is lost) even if one has doubts about *Ba.* 1372–87, as Nauck did; see Dodds *ad loc.*

man gave help to the still child-like Antigone; now Antigone, changed and matured by the events of the day, gives help to Oed. At the same time, the daughter guiding her blind father is a scenic replaying of the arrival and departure of Tir., with the poignant difference that Tir., though scorned by Creon, departed for his home, having been true to his function, while Oed. leaves home behind and goes into exile. The theme of exile and wandering from home, so prominent throughout the play, comes to its pathetic conclusion here, as does the motif of the double-edged act of triumph over the Sphinx.

In such a tailpiece one expects only a restating of what has gone before, not a new twist in the action, such as appears in 1745–6 and 1747ff. The oddities of 1737ff., together with the external evidence of their absence from Π⁵, convince me that those lines are spurious (1737–57n.). Except for the few critics who try to defend the whole passage, most have placed the end of the Euripidean play near that point (1739, 1742, 1743); but Balsamo doubted the whole passage, Polle accepted only 1710–22, and Wecklein and Müller picked and chose widely separated pieces as the only genuine remnants. The problematic features in 1710–36 include 1714–15 (text and metre), 1722 (unusual construction), 1723–4 (defective or corrupt), 1730 (defective or interpolated), 1732–3 (odd usages, 1732 interpolated?). They are more concentrated from 1723 on, but I think still not enough to make a conclusive case against Euripidean authorship of these lines. The whole passage is spurious for those who view everything from 1582 on as not Euripidean (cf. 1582–709n.; so most recently Willink and Diggle).

1710–66 Metre the portion I accept as genuine is entirely iambo-trochaic of an unremarkable sort. The portion I consider spurious continues in the same vein, but introduces anapaestic elements in Ant.'s final piece before a trochaic coda.

1710–11	∪–∪–∪–∪⫶‿‿∪‿‿∪–‖	3 ia
1712	∪–∪–∪–∪–|	2 ia
1713	∪–∪–∪–∪–∪––‖ᶜ	2 ia, ba
1714	∪–‖	exclam
1714bis	∪–∪–∪–∪–|	2 ia
1715	∪–∪–∪–∪–‖	2 ia
1716	∪‿‿∪∪‿‿∪–∪–|	2 ia
1717	∪–∪–––∪–∪–∪–‖	3 ia
1718	‿‿∪∪‿‿∪–∪–∪|	2 tro
1719	–∪‿‿∪∪–∪–‖ᶜ	lec
1720	–∪–∪–∪–‖	lec
1721	–∪–∪‿‿∪∪–‖ʰ	lec
1722	–∪–∪––‖ᶜ	ithyph

1723	∪–∪– –∪–∪–∪–|	ia, cr, ia
1724	∪– – –∪–∪–∪–|	ba, cr, ia
1725	∪–∪– –∪–∪– –‖ᶜ	ia, cr, ba
1726	∪–∪– –∪–∪–∪–|	ia, cr, ia
1727	–∪–∪–∪–∪⏑⏑∪–‖	cr, 2 ia
1728	∪–∪–∪⏑⏑∪–	2 ia
1729	∪–∪–∪⏑⏑∪–|	2 ia
1730	–∪–∪–∪–|	lec
1731	– –∪⏑⏑∪– –‖ᶜ	ia, ba
1732	–∪⏑⏑∪–∪–∪	2 tro
1733	⏑⏑∪⏑⏑∪–∪–∪– –‖ᶜ	tro, ithyph
1734	⏑⏑∪⏑⏑∪⏑⏑∪⏑⏑∪|	2 tro
1735	⏑⏑∪⏑⏑∪⏑⏑∪⏑⏑∪	2 tro
1736	–∪–∪– –‖ᶜ	ithyph
1737	∪–∪⏑⏑∪⦙⏑⏑∪–∪–∪–|	3 ia
1738	∪–∪–∪⏑⏑∪⏑⏑∪– –‖ᶜ	2 ia, ba
1739	∪–∪–∪–∪–‖	2 ia
1740	–∪–∪–∪–‖	lec
1741	–∪–∪–∪–|	lec
1742	–∪–∪– –‖ᶜ	ithyph
1743	∪–∪– –⦙–∪–∪–∪–|	3 ia
1744	∪–∪–⏑⏑∪–∪–∪–|	ia, cr, ia
1745	∪⏑⏑∪–∪⦙–∪–∪–∪–|	3 ia
1746	⏑⏑∪–∪– –‖ᶜ	ithyph
1747	∪–∪–∪–∪–‖	2 ia
1750	⏑⏑∪–∪–∪–‖	lec
1749	∪–∪–∪–∪–‖	2 ia
1748	⏑⏑∪–∪–∪–‖	lec
1751	∪–∪⏑⏑∪⏑⏑∪–	2 ia
1752	∪⏑⏑∪⏑⏑∪–∪–‖	2 ia
1753	– – – –|	anap
1754	∪∪–∪∪–∪∪–∪∪–|	2 anap
1755	∪∪–∪∪∩‖ᵇ	anap
1756	⏑⏑∪⏑⏑∪⏑⏑∪–∪	2 tro
1757	⏑⏑∪⏑⏑∪–∪–∪–∩‖	tro, ithyph

NOTES TO METRICAL SCHEME

1714 for ἰδού *extra metrum* see comm. below.

1717 this lyric trimeter lacks a caesura, a feature that Diggle believes is not Euripidean (673n.).

1718   for γεραῖόν in tragic anap. and lyric cf. Denniston on *El.* 497 (add *Med.* 134 (with γεραιά) and this instance).

1721   for lec with hiatus and period-end before clausular ithyph cf. metrical note on 259–60. Murray's τιθείς is unnecessary.

1732–5   1733–5 are almost fully resolved and could be iambic (ia + ithyph, 4 ia), but if 1732 is genuine (see below) it gives a clear pointer to trochaic treatment, and the pattern of accentuation in 1734 in particular favours trochaic over iambic.

1744   this may be 3 ia, if the author intended νέκῦς: see note below.

1755   period-end within the phrase θίασον ἱερόν can be avoided by transposition (Porson θ. Σεμ. ἱερόν, Hermann Σεμ. ἱερὸν θ.).

1710–66: COMMENTARY

1710 action   after stroking his sons' faces (1701) Oed. has risen again on his own, and here he again lets Ant. hold his hand to guide him. Apart from the similar actions within *Phoen.* (1710–66n.), *Ion* 733–46 present a comparable action of helping the steps of an old man, and *OC* 173–83, 188–201 offer a parallel to (or imitation of?) this scene.

1712–13 πομπίμαν ... ναυσιπομπόν   the etymological play acoustically reinforces the simile. Wecklein branded the image inappropriate; but Greek poets are very fond of the imagery of the favouring wind, οὖρος (for πόμπιμος in this connection cf. *Hec.* 1290, *Hel.* 1073). Jouanna, 'Texte et espace' 81–97 (847–8n.), suggests that the image is proper because Ant. is pushing Oed.'s outstretched arm from slightly behind and compares the figures on a wall-painting (second–first cent. B.C.) in Delos (*Exploration archéologique de Délos*, fasc. 27: *L'îlot de la Maison des Comédiens* (Paris 1970) pl. 21,1).

ναυσιπομπόν   hapax in extant Greek; for the accent (against the mss) cf. Chandler, *Gk. Accentuation* §458. The element ναυσι- is properly dative or instrumental in force, but here by poetic freedom represents the object in ναῦς πέμπουσα, just as in Timotheus *Pers.* 144 ναυσιφθόροι αὖραι, *IA* 172 πλάτας ναυσιπόρους (same as ναυπόρωι in *Tro.* 877); this freedom is imitated by Hellenistic poets (cf. Schwyzer 1.446 with n. 6).

1714–15   the text of the mss had been suspected because it is two syllables too short or too long for straightforward iambo-trochaic scansion, and now Π⁵ seems to have too little room for the mss text (*ZPE* 38 (1980) 13). If the shorter text is not a mistake, then either ἰδού or τέκνον might be false additions to the text. But the cordiality of the vocative (answering Ant.'s πάτερ) is suitable here, whereas ἰδού might have intruded from 1694 and 1700. We find *extra metrum* ἰδού in trimeters at *Cycl.* 544 and *Ion* 742, however, so I believe it may be kept here. Hermann and Murray's ἰδού,

⟨ἰδού⟩ is stylistically suspect: double ἰδού is not used to indicate compliance (1694n.), but emphatically draws attention to something unexpected ('behold!', *Alc.* 233, *Tro.* 309, *Her.* 904, *Ag.* 1125).

τέκνον· σύ μοι the vocative goes better with the initial clause of compliance (as Musgrave and Porson saw; most edd. have only commas, but Murray put the colon after πορεύομαι, as Barnes had it). The asyndeton prob. expresses the interdependence of the actions ('I can move along only if you guide me'); JD suggests (e.g.) τέκνον· ⟨μόνον⟩ σύ μοι. Hermann eliminated the asyndeton with ⟨σύ δή,⟩ σύ μοι, Hartung with σύ δ᾽ ἀθλίου γενοῦ ποδαγός ἀθλία. μοι is preferable to μου because the dative better expresses service and interest.

ποδαγός cf. *Ant.* 1196, *TrGF* adesp. 692.17, then later ποδηγός adesp. 146a.3, Meleager *Anth. gr* 5.179.5, Heraclitus *Anth. gr.* 7.465.7, and rarely in late prose.

ἀθλία this is supported against ἀθλίου (which is secondary to μου) or ἀθλίωι by the verbal responsion of Ant.'s reply (a trait that lyric dialogue shares with stichomythia).

1716 γενόμεθ᾽ many transl. 'I am wretched indeed', with no punctuation after γενόμεθ᾽, but Murray correctly puts a comma there, as γε suggests. Understand ποδαγός as predicate, so that Ant. responds to the appeal in γενοῦ with an aorist that conveys instantaneous action, 'I have, I have taken that role'. Diggle notes that for anadiplosis of verbal forms this is the only instance in which an unelided form is followed by an elided one; he believes this is a mark of non-Euripidean origin ((1990b) 116–17); cf. 1725n.

ἄθλιοι Porson observed that mss' ἄθλιαι is contrary to idiom: a woman who refers to herself with the plural regularly used masc. pl. adj. (cf. K–G 1.83); for the corruption to fem. pl. cf. *Med.* 385.

1717 γε δῆτα the combination is rare (Denniston, *GP*² 278), in drama only *Su.* 1098 (ἥδιστα πρίν γε δῆθ᾽, restored by Canter) and *Peace* 630 ἐν δίκηι ⟨γε⟩ [add. Bentley] δῆτ᾽ (chorus picking up Trygaeus' ἐν δίκηι in 628), which is similar to this use (Denniston: 'there is little cohesion between the particles, γε marking the assent, δῆτα the repetition').

παρθένων most mss have δή added after this, perhaps a conflated remnant of a marginal restoration of δῆτα, which was omitted earlier in the tradition, as reflected in several of the mss that lack δή.

1718 πόθι rare in tragedy (lyric only), cf. *Trach.* 98, *Ba.* 556, *Rhes.* 252 (Hoffmann for ποτί).

γεραιὸν ἴχνος a variation on the favourite Eur. phrase γεραιὸς πούς (301–3n.).

τίθημι taken by Paley, Wecklein, and Méridier as a straightforward indicative, 'where am I (actually) placing my foot?'; to prompt Ant.'s answer, this should be spoken with a tone of doubt and fear (for worry about a false step, cf. 836–7, *Ion* 741 ἴχνος δ' ἐκφύλασσ' ὅπου τίθης). Because of the answer, others have taken the indic. as a dynamic one almost equivalent to τιθῶ or θήσω (Σ, Barnes' *ubi ponam*, Pearson). For various lively uses of the ind. cf. Schwyzer II.307, K–G I.203, *Il.* 4.26, *Andr.* 1036 πῶς πείθομαι;, *Hec.* 159 τίς ἀμύνει μοι;, *Her.* 942 τίς μοι δίδωσι τόξα;, Platonic τί (πῶς) λέγομεν (ποιοῦμεν);, as in *Euthyphron* 10d1, *Symp.* 214a7–b1, *Gorg.* 480b2, *Rep.* 530d9; cf. 602n. But some of these are colloquial, some have no specific addressee; Plato's τί λέγομεν; is 'what is our view?' rather than 'what are we to say?' Thus, although an equivalence to deliberative force cannot be ruled out entirely, I think it more likely that the indic. is a normal one.

1719 βάκτρα πόθι φέρω in *ZPE* 38 (1980) 35, I argued for Π⁵'s version in the sense 'where am I bearing my staff?' and against mss' βάκτρα πρόσφερ' ὦ (whether βάκτρα is taken literally or figuratively); for Oed.'s staff cf. 1529n. Mueller-Goldingen, 257 n. 69, once again supports Pearson's metaphorical interpretation of βάκτρα, making a distinction between Ant.'s joining hands with Oed. in 1710 and the firmer support Oed. here asks for, and objecting that φέρω cannot bear the same sense as ἐρείδω or τίθημι (but in this context the parallelism with ἴχνος τίθημι in 1718 makes it possible for φέρω to take on the requisite meaning). Irigoin's προσφέρων is better than πρόσφερ' ὦ, but still not the right verb (one expects προφέρων).

1720–1 τᾷδε Jouanna, 'Texte et espace' (1712–13n.), follows Roux on *Ba.* 364–5 in assigning these lines to the moment when the actors descend stairs from the stage to the orchestra. This is by no means certain, but if so, quadruple τᾷδε should not be taken (with Roux) as evidence that there were four steps (Oed. could not be moved quickly enough, or the anaphora sung slowly enough, to match words to steps). Cf. 846n.

τίθει· for the hiatus, see note to metre. Many mss. have interpolated πάτερ here (cf. 1508).

1722 ὥστ' ὄνειρον ἰσχύν ⟨being⟩ like a dream in strength', i.e., 'being as weak as a dream', a conventional image of the weakness of age (1543–5n.). ἰσχύν is acc. of respect with the adjective-equivalent ὥστ' ὄνειρον: C. J. Ruijgh, *Autour de TE épique* (Amsterdam 1971) §809. I take the phrase as modifying Oed. (ὄνειρον neut. nom.), not πόδα (ὄνειρον masc. or neut. acc.; so Geel, rejecting Hermann's view that ἰσχύν is in apposition to πόδα with ὥστ' ὄνειρον modifying ἰσχύν). The unusual regimen of the acc. of respect invited the gloss ἔχων. Some eliminate the oddity by emendation (Herwerden (1874) ἰσόνειρον, Wecklein ἀντόνειρον), but πόδα τίθει is complete in itself (a variation on βᾶθί μοι), and 'weak as a dream' better applies to Oed. than his foot. Sing. forms of masc. ὄνειρος are never clearly established in tragedy, whereas the neuter sing. is certain in four places (incl. *Her.* 517), although masc. sing appears in *Frogs* 1332 (parody of Eur. monody) and com. adesp. 157.2 Kock. For pl. Eur. has both masc. and neut. forms.

1723–4 φυγὰς ἀλαίνειν . . . ἐκ πάτρας the mss present ἐλαύνων, but the bare participle cannot be used to invoke Creon (whether present or not: 1682n.). The space available in Π⁵ does not suggest that it attested a longer text than that in the mss, but Hermann (who was creating strophes and antistrophes) added several words to preserve ἐλαύνων, and Nauck (after Grotius) tried ⟨Κρέων⟩ ἐλαύνει, Wilam. (after Dindorf) ⟨δαίμων⟩ ἐλαύνων. Valck.'s ἐλαύνειν (exclam. inf.) leaves the subject of the action unstated, so I prefer Musgrave's ἀλαίνειν. In view of *Eum.* 837, *Alc.* 410–11, one should not object to the use of exclam. inf. as too colloquial (Hermann). For ἀλαίνω of exile cf. *El.* 205, 589. Internal acc. φυγὰς ἀλαίνειν is a typical lyric variation on φεύγειν φυγάς (*Andr.* 976) and is preferable to accentuation as gen. of cause with ἰὼ ἰώ (for gen. with ἰώ cf. *El.* 1185, *Ag.* 1305).

1725 δεινὰ δείν' the iteration fits the metre and the style of the context; single δεινά is due to haplography, and the marginal notation of the omission led to incorrect reinsertion in AL and (in 1723) in OPW. Diggle (1990b) 116–17 notes the rarity of anadiplosis of noun or adjective in which the first form is unelided and the second elided (*Alc.* 270, *Ion* 1054); cf. 1716n.

1726 τί τλάς; 'Why say "suffered"?' The τί-question has dismissive force: for exx. see *Contact and Discontinuity* 14 (some with quoted word, some without) and add fr. 300 οἴμοι· τί δ' οἴμοι; θνητά τοι πεπόνθαμεν; Diggle, *Studies* 51. Such questions need not be as indignant as *Alc.* 807 τί ζῶσιν; Ant. is not being sarcastic in echoing Oed.'s word, nor is she unsympathetic to his plight. Rather, she considers lamentation at this point to be futile and advises her father to refrain from it, by implication in 1726–7 and explicitly in 1733.

1726–7 οὐχ ὁρᾶι. . . . ἀσυνεσίας The attitude of simple piety is that the gods are ever watchful and punish the bad (e.g., *Her.* 773 θεοὶ θεοὶ τῶν ἀδίκων μέλουσι, *Ba.* 882–90, *OT* 883–96, *Ag.* 369–72), but Ant., through bitter experience and her loyalty to her kin, has come to deny such a view: 'Justice does not watch the bad, nor does she punish men's acts of moral obliquity.' κακούς and ἀσυνεσίας must allude to Creon as the cause of Oed.'s immediate sufferings. Conacher, 244 n. 22, would make this a rhetorical question (implying 'Justice does watch and punish') and regard Ant. as being critical of Oed. But Ant.'s statement about Justice is not 'perverse' since it is equivalent to 'there is no goddess Justice who watches and punishes'. ἀσυνεσία is a coinage of late fifth-century intellectual language (Democritus 68 B 183 D–K; Thuc. 1.122.4, etc.), found also in fr.

257.2 and nowhere else in poetry, but it is typical of Eur. to import such a word into his lyrics (1506n. for his fondness for σύνεσις). Here, as often with σκαιός or ἀμαθής, a moral failing is assimilated to an intellectual failing. Wilam. (1903) 593 n. 1 (*Kl. Schr.* vi.350 n. 1) gives ἀσυνεσίας the artificial meaning ἀκούσια, 'was man παρὰ σύνεσιν συνείδησιν tut', but does not explain how that would make sense in the context.[1]

ἀμείβεται   for the sense 'requite (an injustice with punishment)' cf. (with personal obj.) Soph. fr. 12 τὸ χρύσεον δὲ τάς Δίκας δέδορκεν ὄμμα, τὸν δ' ἄδικον ἀμείβεται, *Prom.* 223 ἐξημείψατο.

1728–9 μοῦσαν ὃς ἐπὶ καλλίνικον οὐράνιον ἔβαν   'who attained to the song of fair-victory, ⟨a glory⟩ reaching high as heaven', an epinician metaphor, as καλλίνικος implies; for ἔβαν ἐπί Pearson compares *Il.* 8.285 τὸν … ἐϋκλείης ἐπίβησον (though the gen. complement has a different flavour: LSJ s.v. ἐπιβαίνω a.1.4, b.2). Recalling past glory as a contrast to present misfortune is a common tragic motif. On the irony attached to καλλίνικον cf. 1048n. There is no adequate parallel for the interpretation of μοῦσαν as σοφίαν favoured by Σ, Paley, and Wecklein, 'who attained to inspired wisdom that brought fair victory and fame as high as heaven'. Kinkel's view that μοῦσαν is the songstress Sphinx and ἔβαν 'attacked' is ruled out by the epithets. οὐράνιον recalls *Od.* 9.20 καί μευ κλέος οὐρανὸν ἵκει (cf. 8.74, 19.108, *Il.* 8.192, *Clouds* 460) and is better as an epithet of μοῦσαν than emended to nom. (Burges). The lyric collocation of epithets invited the prosaic interpolation of τ' in some mss.

1730 ⟨μειξο⟩παρθένου κόρας   transmitted παρθένου κόρας has been defended as an imitation of the epic mannerism of juxtaposing words for genus and species of *animals* (σύς κάπρος, ἴρηξ κίρκος, etc.: Hoekstra on *Od.* 13.86–7; for tragedy cf. Dodds on *Ba.* 1024–6; also Wilam. on *Her.* 465–6, Renehan *CP* 75 (1980) 348, 80 (1985) 148), but the mannerism seems pointless here as well as obscure. In poetry παρθένος and κόρη are usually synonymous, and defenders must appeal improbably to 'strict' definitions by which παρθένος is a sexually mature (unmarried) female whereas κόρη is an anatomically virgin female (Wilam. on *Her.* 834). Thus either παρθένου (which may have been absent in Π⁵) should be deleted as a gloss, with Haslam (*ZPE* 38 (1980) 35), or the epithet μειξοπαρθένου (as in 1023) should be restored with Wilam. I prefer the latter because παρθένου seems an odd gloss (unless it is a remnant of a longer note) and because the fuller

---

[1] Mueller-Goldingen, 258 with n. 70, follows Wilam., taking 1727 as consolation to Oed.; but οὐδ' should be additive, not adversative ('nor on the other hand'?).

form is more kenning-like (with κόρας alone, the identification depends wholly on the following words).

1731 αἴνιγμ' ἀσύνετον εὐρών for εὐρών cf. 48n. In this kenning-like phrase the characterizing epithet ἀσύνετον, used as equivalent to δυσξύνετον, is needed. Despite ξυνετὸν μέλος in 1506 (part of a paradoxical phrase), αἴνιγμα σύνετον, 'clever, subtle riddle' (RMnP, preferred by Wilam.) would be inferior here.

1732 Σφιγγὸς ἀναφέρεις ὄνειδος; Σ recommends that this be punctuated as a question, and early edd. did so, but from Kirchhoff on a period has been printed. A question seems to me livelier and more suited to the context; the tone is again disbelieving or disapproving, implying 'what good is it to speak of the Sphinx?', 'don't bother to mention that'. The ancient theory that ὄνειδος can be neutral or positive in sense (821n.) is mistaken. Ant. uses the word in a normal pejorative sense to correct emphatically the epinician language of 1728-31: the triumph over the Sphinx was no true victory, but a cause of shameful marriage and incestuous offspring (1689n.). ἀναφέρειν = 'call (back) to mind', 'mention' cannot be paralleled in poetry, but the similar usage found in prose is far from common ('remember' or 'consider mentally' rather than 'recall in speech': Pl. *Laws* 829e, Appian *Pun.* 112, Plut. *Pyrrh.* 32.8, *Mor.* 126F, 607E; cf. Lampe, *Patristic Greek Lexicon* s.v. B.1). Since Π⁵ has a shorter text in this area, Crönert and Lewis suggested that this phrase was absent there, and Haslam (*ZPE* 38 (1980) 35-6) has noted that in a text not yet written in colon-division there is no 'line' to be accidentally omitted and that absence is prima-facie evidence of spuriousness. The hypothesis of interpolation deserves strong consideration, but I find the bold usage of ὄνειδος, the uncommon sense of ἀναφέρεις, and the appropriateness of the trochaic rhythm hard to credit to an interpolator.

1733 ἄπαγε ... αὐδῶν the participle is supplementary, 'away with you and your talk of former success!' (cf. Hsch. α 5699 ἄπαγε· παῦσαι), and the unique construction is apparently an extension of colloquial ἄπαγε = 'away with you!' (in Attic with a prep. phrase attached, *Knights* 1151, *Peace* 1053, *Periceir.* 396, Theophr. *Char.* 25.5; in later Greek a frozen exclamation; for intransitive compound cf. *Cho.* 953 ἄναγε). For the part. cf. that with ἐπέχω (448n.).

1734 ἐπέμενε cf. 223n.

μέλεα πάθεα a stereotyped lyric juncture (*Hipp.* 363, 830, *Her.* 1180, *Tro.* 1117, A. *Su.* 111).

1736 που a pathetic vagueness, not, I think, a serious discrepancy with the oracle about Colonus (1703-7n.).

[1736-57] The evidence against this passage is of three kinds. (1) Π⁵ (third cent. B.C.), though terribly tattered, seems to have had, after clearly readable words of 1734 at the end of a line, 1735–6 on a new line, but has an extensive blank area on the right portion of this new line, where the papyrus has survived better. On the basis of the scribe's habits in copying lyrics of *Med.* and *Phoen.* in the rest of this roll, one can find no ready reason why he did not continue in the space available with 1737 if his exemplar contained 1737ff. (2) General arguments of coherence raise doubts, as Kampfhenkel first explained. (a) Ant. has renounced the burial in 1667–71 and replaced it with accompaniment of her father, but 1745–6 assert or reassert the intention to bury, with no indication of how this meshes with her helping her father in exile.[1] (b) Oed.'s suggestions to Ant. conflict with the hand-in-hand departure that is already well advanced. Indeed, it is very difficult to give a coherent explication of the stage-movements and emotions of the passage: the attempts of, e.g., H. O. Meredith in *CR* 51 (1937) 97–103 and Erbse, 30–4, do not convince, nor does Craik's view that Oed. 'makes her departure easier by naturalistic suggestion of acts of farewell'. (c) The tone changes between 1736 and 1737 without adequate explanation, esp. given the effect of closure afforded by the content and rhythm of 1734–6. (d) 1744 appears to imply that Pol.'s body has already been carried off, but this conflicts with normal dramatic technique. (3) Particular linguistic or stylistic faults have been alleged in 1743, 1744, and 1751, 1747–51, but some of the oddity may be due to the corruption that occurs normally (esp. at the end of a text) rather than to a mediocre writer, and only 'epic τε' in 1751 is truly problematic.

Various explanations have been given for the origin of these lines, which were presumably in the Alexandrian edition, since Didymus commented on 1747 (we cannot tell whether the passage was marked as suspect by the Alexandrians or whether, if so, Didymus was unaware of the marking or was aware but all trace of this knowledge has been lost in the truncation of the ancient *hypomnemata*). Friedrich sees them as a part of an expansion of Ant.'s role and ascribes them to the same *Bearbeiter* to whom he assigns 1646–89. He would have 1737–66 performed after 1646–89 (perhaps with 1708–9 in between). But I do not concede that Ant.'s importance in the play has been enhanced by interpolation, and the script Friedrich reconstructs still has Ant. give up the burial in the stichomythia and return to

---

[1] It is a desperate solution to reckon that Ant. can guide her father to Attica and leave him there for a few days (or profit from a quick fulfilment of the oracle of his death) in order to return to bury her brother (whose body has by then been cast over the border, and so could be buried *in situ* with impunity). In no other tragedy is an audience invited to exercise such ingenuity to deal with loose ends.

it in the lyric. Wilam. suggested that 1737–66 were simply a later replacement for 1710–36, with the later author failing to understand (or wanting to contradict) the import of Ant.'s backing down in the burial-argument. The oddity of 1747–57 led Hartung to suggest that a passage of Eur.'s *Antigone* had been conflated with the text of *Phoen.* in the ancient tradition (cf. Bakhuyzen and Balsamo for similar theories), but such confusion should have been easily detectable by Alexandrian scholars, including Didymus.

If 1710–36 are Euripidean, then there may have been some choral statement at the end, now lost: cf. Hose, *Chor* 233 n. 7. Cf. 1764–7n.

1737 ποθεινὰ δάκρυα 'weeping caused by their longing ⟨for me⟩' or 'weeping expressive of longing', not equivalent to 'a longing to weep' (Wecklein). ποθεινός is predominantly 'passive' in sense ('longed for', 'desired'), but the freer use seen here is paralleled in Xen. *Lac.* 1.5 ποθεινοτέρως ἔχειν + gen. ('be more desirous of each other'), Diod. Sic. 13.20.4 ποθεινοτέραν τὴν ὑπὲρ αὐτῶν μνήμην καταλελοίπασιν ('more productive of yearning', 'more imbued with yearning'). The usage is thus no secure index of post-Eur. authorship (cf., however, the odd use in *Med.* 1221 ποθεινὴ δακρύοισι συμφορά, deleted by Reeve and Diggle: 'a disaster arousing longing expressed by tears'?). Pearson compared *Od.* 8.531 ἐλεεινὸν δάκρυον, but Ameis–Hentze and Cunliffe treat this as 'caused by feelings worthy of pity' rather than 'expressing pity'. Note the isolated 'passive' use of ἀλγεινός, 'suffering pain', in *OC* 1664, against normal 'active' sense, 'causing pain'.

φίλαισι παρθένοις the reference to Ant.'s Theban age-mates (not the chorus) is rather abrupt, but the notion was implicit in 1265 χορείαις.... παρθενεύμασιν.

1738 ἀποπρό a good Eur. word (six times in lyric; also proposed in emendations by Diggle, *Dionysiaca* 165 (*Hel.* 694), and Willink on *Or.* 1500–2), adopted from *Il.* 7.334 (also perhaps 16.669, 679: cf. Schwyzer II.428), and recurring a few times in Hellenistic poetry.

1739 ἀπαρθένευτ' adv. (int.) acc. with ἀλωμένα, 'in a manner not proper for maidens' (for the notion cf. 1691n., but this self-pitying complaint is rather inconsistent with 1692). For this meaning, cf. *IA* 993 ἀπαρθένευτα μὲν τάδ'; for a different sense, cf. Soph. fr. 304, *Carm.Pop.* 5b.3 (*PMG* 851).

1740–1 φεῦ τὸ χρήσιμον φρενῶν under the influence of Hermann and Kirchhoff, many edd. have accepted the attribution suggested by the marginal note on 1740, τινὲς καὶ τοῦτο τῆς ἀντιγόνης. That attribution prob. arose from misunderstanding of the co-operative continuation of syntax (*Contact and Discontinuity* 55–6). It is not quite true to say with Neil (edn of *Knights*, p. 190) that γε is absurd if there is no change of speaker in

1740 and 1741, but parallels do support change of speaker (see below), and even for the self-pitying Ant. of this passage the exclamation of praise in 1740 strikes an odd note. If 1740 alone is Oed.'s, the nom. is unusual: with such an abstraction one would expect a gen. of cause after φεῦ (as *Hipp.* 936 τῆς βροτείας... φρενός), as compared with a voc. of address (*Med.* 1393), exclamatory nom. with self-reference (*Hipp.* 242 φεῦ τλήμων), or exclamatory articular inf. (fr. 439.1; K–G II.46), which may be nom. (but one wonders whether speakers actually sensed any case-usage in this idiom). Since Ant. takes the phrase as subject of her reply, it is possible that Oed.'s phrase is the beginning of an interrupted sentence. I see no advantage in emending to σε in 1742 so that 1740–2 can all be given to Oed. (Wilam., making a questionable inference from τινὲς καὶ τοῦτο τῆς ἀντιγόνης; supported by Mueller-Goldingen, 260 n. 77).

τὸ χρήσιμον   here 'the excellence' or 'the high worthiness'; for this rare sense of χρήσιμος cf. Theognis 406, *Aj.* 410 (Craik's strained 'my resources of spirit' is unnecessary). The phrase is also found in fr. 58 οἴμοι, θανοῦμαι διὰ τὸ χρήσιμον φρενῶν, / ἢ τοῖσιν ἄλλοις γίγνεται σωτηρία.

γε   if there is change of speaker, this can mark assent and continuation of the other speaker's thought (as Neil believed; Denniston, *GP²* 137), and the position after πατρός may be only a matter of postponement (Denniston, *GP²* 149: but in many of Denniston's examples the word before γε does carry emphasis). But there may also be limitative force, either (a) 'yes, in respect to my *father's* woes ⟨but not my brother's⟩', anticipating 1743, or (b) (as Σ and comm., with γε taken as postponed and limiting the whole phrase εἰς... συμφοράς) 'in respect to my father's *misfortune* ⟨though I would prefer to win fame in happier circumstances⟩'. Without change of speaker, (a) seems easier than (b), but neither is impossible.

1743 ⟨σῶν⟩   either this (Matthiae) or Musgrave's ⟨σοῦ⟩ seems justified by the paraphrase of Σ (ἀθλία εἰμὶ ἕνεκα τῶν σῶν κακῶν καὶ τῶν τοῦ ἀδελφοῦ Πολ. ὕβρεως), though it is barely possible that τῶν σῶν κακῶν was supplied by wishful thinking from πατρός γε συμφοράς. It is thus not safe to insist that the text of mss is due to an interpolator's misuse of θ' as a metrical stopgap (this would be a grosser blunder than the τε of 1751).

1744 νέκυς   like νέκυν, elsewhere in tragedy always has ὔ or indeterminate quantity; νέκῡς/-ῡν is found in half a dozen passages of Homer, in Ap. Rhod. 4.1534, Quintus Smyrn. 3.265, Greg. Naz. *Anth. gr.* 8.45.3, 8.198.2, and several times in *Christ. Pat.* It is a *petitio principii* to assume that the author of this line intended 3 ia, with νέκῡς, and then use the scansion as evidence of interpolation (Schmid). In any case, Eur. himself would have been capable of an isolated imitation of the Homeric scansion (note esp. *Il.* 22.386 νέκῡς ἄκλαυτος ἄθαπτος).

οἴχεται   there is no adequate parallel for giving this a present progressive meaning, 'is going',[1] or, in a dynamic sense, 'will be going', nor, in view of ἐκ δόμων, for understanding it figuratively, 'is ruined/wretched' (as, e.g., in fr. 187.5–6 ἡ φύσις γὰρ οἴχεται / ὅταν κτλ., Pl. *Laws* 945c7–d1, Dem. 21.60). Thus, the word seems to require that Pol.'s body has already been carried off stage, although it was still on stage at 1702. In normal classical dramatic technique, however, it is likely that such a distracting action would not occur simultaneously with the exit-duet or that, if it did occur, it would receive much fuller and more explicit reaction in the words of the text. This detail weighs strongly against authenticity.

1746 σκότια two interpretations have been given of this adv. acc. (as of σκοτίαι, the reading accepted before Hermann). Barnes rendered *clam*, followed by Hartung, Méridier, Craik (and now Mueller-Goldingen, 261, who argues that the interpolator's Ant. intends to bury Pol. in Theban soil, but that her action is tainted by the unheroic notion that she will escape notice). Others, after Valck. and Hermann himself, take the adverb as proleptic, reinforcing γᾶι καλύψω (= ἐν σκότωι γᾶς), 'so that it is hidden in darkness'. The inconsistency of 'secretly' with the defiance of 1745 and the similarity of 336 (see n.), of which this may be an imitation, favour the latter view. σκοτίαι γᾶι (all mss except F) would be good style, but an isolated ionic colon among iambics is unlikely.

1747–50 the omission and marginal replacement of 1750 in R and of 1748 in O may be accidental, or may reflect an older confusion about the ordering of these four lines. The difficulties of interpreting the motivation and exact sense of the lines make both emendation and reordering of them very uncertain. (1) Who are the ἥλικας of 1747? Presumably, the φίλαι παρθένοι of 1737, but then φάνηθι = 'go and show yourself to' is abnormal,[2] and why is Oed. suddenly surrendering his guide and companion? (2) Why should Ant. do this? Her rejection of the advice (whether 1748 or 1750 follows) shows that she interprets the purpose as getting sympathy by crying before them. Oed. can hardly mean 'after you (at some future date) bury your brother, show yourself to your age-mates to obtain their protection'. Didymus' desperate explanation ἵνα ἐρανίσωσιν αὐτήν, οὐδὲν γὰρ λαμβάνουσιν ἐξιόντες ἐφόδιον is laughable. (3) What does ἅλις ὀδυρμάτων mean? Valck. compared *TrGF* adesp. 76 ἅλις ἐγὼ δυστυχῶν,

---

[1] *IA* 1464 ὦ τέκνον, οἴχηι; at first glance seems to be 'are you going ⟨away from me⟩?', but it is continued by λιποῦσα in the next line, recalling idiomatic (ἀπο-/προ)λιπὼν οἴχεται and the like, so the sense is actually perfect, 'are you gone ⟨for me⟩?'

[2] Contrast Pl. *Epist.* 7, 348e3–4 (of a fugitive who is being summoned out of hiding) ἂν πρὸς τῆι σῆι ... φανῆι οἰκίαι.

which Aristotle *EN* 1171b18 cites to illustrate the reluctance to summon one's friends to share one's troubles; and edd. and comm. have interpreted 'Why should they weep too? My own laments are enough. Don't invite theirs.' But ἅλις + gen. is not the same as ἅλις as predicate to a nom. The gen. phrases imply 'No more of this', 'I'm through with this', 'Let's have no more of this', 'Stop this': *Cycl.* 248 λεόντων (to eat), *Alc.* 334 παίδων, *Hec.* 278 τῶν τεθνηκότων, *Her.* 1394 δακρύων, *Hel.* 143 μύθων, *OC* 1016 λόγων, etc. The nom. phrases mean 'the present bad (or good) is enough, I do not want to add to it': *Alc.* 673 ἅλις γὰρ ἡ παροῦσα συμφορά, *Med.* 558 ἅλις γὰρ οἱ γεγῶτες, *Hec.* 394 ἅλις κόρης σῆς θάνατος, *OT* 1061, *Trach.* 332, etc. (cf. Diggle (1990b) 106). The meaning assumed by Valck. would be given by ἅλις ὀδυρομένα ἐγώ or ἅλις ὀδύρματα ἐμά. Here Ant.'s words must mean 'no more wailing', 'let's have an end of wailing', dismissing Oed.'s advice and expressing the intention not to lament further herself. Pronoun μοι or ἐμοί is often found with ἅλις + gen., so χ's ἐμοί, perhaps implied by Σ αὐτάρκειά μοι τῶν θρήνων, is possible, but the other explanation (αὐτάρκως ὠδύραντο τὴν ἐμὴν ἀτυχίαν) implies ἐμῶν (taken improbably as equivalent to obj. gen. ἐμοῦ). (4) Is 1749 an interrupted sentence (Σ understands φάνηθι – unlikely; Oed. could have intended ἔχε, 'occupy yourself with prayers at the altars') that is never completed (*Contact and Discontinuity* 63–73), or does ἴθ' ἀλλά in 1751 complete it (Denniston, *GP*² 10, 170), or is it corrupt? With Ant.'s intervention, I find it hard to accept Denniston's proposal; more likely, σὺ δ' introduces one alternative after the rejection of 1747 and ἴθ' ἀλλά a third suggestion after rejection of 1749, with ἀλλά as in Denniston, *GP*² 13. In such a doubtful context, there is little gain in Elmsley's change to ἀμφιβωμίους (anticipated by Burges' δὸς ἀμφ. λιτάς; cf. Herwerden's ἴαλλε for ἴθ' ἀλλά in 1751), but Wecklein's ἀμφιβωμίοις λιταῖς is more promising, if 1751 continues 1749. Cf. *Tro.* 562 σφαγαὶ δ' ἀμφιβώμιοι, but *Her.* 984–5 ἀμφὶ βωμίαν ... κρηπῖδ', *Ion* 52 ἀμφὶ βωμίους τροφάς. (5) The subject of 1750 ἔχουσ', if it follows 1749, seems to be βωμοί understood from βωμίους (less likely, θεοί understood from βωμίους λιτάς, as Wecklein). The intrusive ἔχουσα in 1748 may suggest that someone once interpreted ἔχουσ' as fem. participle (and Craik has now done so in her translation, wrongly).

The passage may be marginally improved by transposition. Burges and Murray suggest 1749, 1748, 1747, 1750, so that 1749 is not incomplete (Burges emends, Murray would have 1747 complete it) and ἔχουσ' in 1750 gets its subj. more easily from ἥλικας. I suggest 1747, 1750, 1749, 1748, which helps 1750 in the same way, leaves σὺ δ' its force of introducing a *pis aller*, and puts the more drastic rejection (1748) after the second suggestion rather than the first. In this order 1749 is left incomplete because of a dismissive interruption. Diggle (1990a) 11 prefers to give 1749 a connection by accepting Wecklein's ἀμφιβωμίοις λιταῖς and putting the lines in the order 1749, 1747, 1748, 1750; 1748 + 1750 then mean 'They have enough of my laments, a surfeit of my woes.'; cf. *Or.* 240, with τοῦ.

1751 ἀλλά   see previous n. (4).

Βρόμιος ἵνα τε σηκός   early edd. had ἵνα γε from the χ-tradition (the combination is not found in tragedy: 645n.), and necessarily followed Mosch.'s treatment of Βρόμιος as adj. When ἵνα τε was accepted, adj. rendering remained (e.g. Craik, Buschor), although Wilam. branded the use of epic τε in ἵνα τε illicit for Eur. (for rejection of other possible instances see 645n.). But the author's intention cannot be fixed. Adj. use of Βρόμιος is plausibly rejected for Eur. by Diggle, as quoted by Bond on *Her.* 890 (βρομίωι ... θύρσωι L, Βρομίου Hartung); but it is found in *Clouds* 311 Βρομία χάρις and perhaps *Carm.Conv.* 4.2 (*PMG* 887) Βρομίαις (inspired by Dionysus)[1] ὀπαδὲ Νύμφαις. So the author may have meant 'precinct of Dionysus', with τε as a metrical filler. But it is also possible that the text is compendious for ἵνα Βρόμιος ἵνα τε σηκός (cf. perhaps *Hipp.* 550 δρομάδα ναΐδ' ὅπως τε βάκχαν, cf. 284n.); thus Méridier ('Va du moins trouver Bromios et l'enclos'), and Σ may have taken it thus, but inference from the paraphrase is not certain. The latter makes ὧι in 1753 easier. Musgrave's Βρομίου involves a corruption illicit in lyric iambics.

1751–2 σηκὸς ἄβατος ὄρεσι μαινάδων   prob. 'sacred precinct of (proper to, dear to) the maenads on the mountain' (Σ, Buschor, Craik), rather than 'sacred precinct on the mountain of the maenads' (Mosch., Barnes, Méridier). Σ correctly infers that the mountain (poetic pl.) is Cithaeron and that ἄβατος implies τοῖς βεβήλοις (such as Pentheus or the men of *Ba.* 677–768; for ἄβατος in this sense cf. *Ba.* 10, *OC* 167, 675). But there is no reason to accept the claim (inferred from 1755) that σηκός is the tomb of Semele (located on the Cadmeia in *Ba.* 6–12 and other sources: Dodds *ad loc.*): Keune, *RE* 2A (1923) 1342–3, incorrectly combines Σ with other data to invent regular worship by three thiasoi at the alleged tomb of Semele on Cithaeron.

1753 ὧι   the antecedent could be inferred from adj. Βρόμιος = τοῦ Βρομίου, if adj. was intended. Wecklein's οὗ (like Valck.'s ἧι) removes the obscurity, but the confusion in the mss points to ΩΙ as the transmitted reading, misunderstood and corrupted because of postponement of the relative.

---

[1] So Bergk and Diehl, rightly, I think, against Page, who prints βρομίαις (deep-sounding?).

1754 στολιδωσαμένα a metrically convenient variation on στολισαμένα, simply 'dressing myself in'. In the only other extant use, στολιδωθῆναι means 'become folded' (Soranus *Fasc.* 42), and στολιδωτός, στολίδωμα have the same connotation.

1755 Σεμέλας θίασον it is natural for a band honouring Dionysus to honour his mother: Pindar fr. 75.19 (dithyramb) οἰχνεῖ τε Σεμέλαν ἑλικάμπυκα χοροί; Gow on Theocr. 26.6.

1756 ἀνεχόρευσα the verb is a favourite of Eur. (five times; otherwise extant only *Thesm.* 994), with various constructions; here it may be 'set the band dancing' (sc. as leader), with external obj. as in *Or.* 582 ('set me madly dancing': cf. Willink), or 'performed the sacred dance', with internal obj. as in *Ba.* 482 (ὄργια).

1757 χάριν ἀχάριτον here, 'a favour that won no return', 'a gracious honour they did not accept'; for the paradox χάρις ἄχαρις or ἀχάριτος cf. *Ag.* 1545, *Choe.* 44, *IT* 566. Ant. believes that the sufferings of her family show that her worship of the gods was unrewarded. Pearson explains instead that 'her misery makes the joyful rite a mockery', but this is inconsistent with his own earlier paraphrase 'render an idle service to the gods'. ἀχάριτος, present by emendation here and *Choe.* 44, is perhaps a back-formation from the plural ἀχάριτα (Hdt. 1.207.1); cf. Hdt. 7.156.3 ἀχαριτώτατον, Xen. *Cyr.* 7.4.14, *Hieron* 1.24, Pl. *Laws* 761d5, com. adesp. 123.3 Kock.

διδοῦσα like Σ and most comm., I take this as dependent on ἀνεχόρευσα, 'offering, trying to give' (conative force). Pearson, perhaps prompted by the combination here of present participle with aor. main verb, makes διδοῦσα depend on ἴω understood from ἴθι and refers it to a prospective action (whence Craik: 'shall I render to the gods a service that is no service?').

[1758-63] The case against these lines rests on both general coherence and internal details. (1) If 1728-36, dismissing the Sphinx-theme, are accepted as the last genuine lines of the lyric, Oed.'s renewed use of it is odd. The lines follow rather abruptly even on 1757, but if 1737ff. were performed instead of 1710-36, then at least this passage could convey Oed.'s final resignation even as 1747-57 show Ant.'s despairing rejection of alternatives. (2) There are no representatives of the citizen-body on stage to be addressed: the chorus is foreign; the silent extras are a few citizen-soldiers under Creon's command and are not easily felt to be representative of the population at large (as the choruses of *OT* and *Ant.* are). It is possible to argue that Oed. is blind and does not know who is on stage, but this merely shifts the peculiarity to another aspect. The address is not general enough to be comparable to those in admonishments to mankind (e.g., *Hipp.* 916, *Su.* 744, fr. 816.6), and the content is not an urgent appeal, such as often justifies an address to someone absent (e.g., *Or.* 1621–2).[1] (3) 1758–9 are closely similar to *OT* 1524–5 (κλεινῆς πολῖται vs. Θήβης ἔνοικοι and ἔγνω καὶ μέγιστος vs. ᾔδει καὶ κράτιστος). This similarity is inconclusive for those who believe the final lines of *OT* are an interpolation, perhaps inspired by the present lines,[2] or for those who perceive some point in a deliberate allusion by Eur. to the Sophoclean *fabula docet*. (4) The change from 3rd person in 1758–9 to first person in 1760–2 is awkward. A. F. Braunlich, *AJP* 83 (1962) 395, defends this change by comparing *Her.* 4, *Tro.* 1212, *El.* 1239, but there is no change in *Tro.* and in *Her.* and *El.* there is an easy shift from 3rd-person introduction to 1st-person narrative, whereas here Oed. is not newly introduced, and we have ὅς-clauses in anaphora with different persons. On the other hand, perhaps ἔγνων should be accepted from **Vr**, and the clumsiness should be ascribed to corruption and not to an interpolator. (5) 1761 is more than half identical to 627, and 1762–3 is an expanded version of 382. Again, some might see a deliberate echo of 627 (Oed. now sharing Pol.'s fate of exile), and 1762–3 and 382 could be two versions of a commonplace. (6) αὐτός in 1761 is clumsy; but emendation is possible. In sum, the number of separate points, uncertain though some are, weighs in favour of deleting the whole passage (so first Boeckh (1808), together with 1764–6). Valck. originally deleted only 1758–9, a bad suggestion (1760 should not begin a speech); Kirchhoff assumed that 1758–9 had replaced something genuine. Many have deleted 1759 alone as incorporated from marginal citation of *OT* 1524–5, assuming either an interpolation into genuine tetrameters or an interpolation within an interpolation. For the use of tetrameters at the end of a play cf. *Ion, Ag., OT*.

1758 κλεινῆς has more point than κλεινοί and is understandable as a variation on Θήβης in *OT* 1524.

1759 τὰ κλείν' αἰνίγματ' Dawe, *Studies* 1.166–73, argues that 'the famous riddle' here (and in *OT* 1525) is an inappropriate borrowing from 1689 above, where he specifies the meaning as 'riddle that brought you

---

[1] Cf. *Contact and Discontinuity* 89–90 with n. 36. I still believe no Argive soldiers appear at the close of *Or.*, *pace* Willink and West.

[2] For the two sides of the debate see Dawe, *Studies* 1.267–73 and Lloyd-Jones and Wilson, *Sophoclea* 113–14. For my part, I believe that *OT* 1524–30, if genuine, are spoken by the coryphaeus and addressed to the members of the chorus representing the citizen-body; I do not believe that the priority of the *Phoen.* passage has been established by Dawe and think some details in *Phoen.* can be well understood as deliberate variations on the model in *OT* (cf. Mueller-Goldingen, 264–5).

fame'. In all the passages, however, the riddle is famous because the whole story is well known, and it is the context of 1689 that provides a refinement of meaning, if there is one.

ἔγνω (or ἔγνων? – 1758–63n.) cf. 48n.; this is a more obvious verb to use than ᾔδει, which may have been chosen in *OT* to allude to the pun οἶδα/Οἰδίπους that is exploited also in *OT* 397. If this is accepted, it seems to me to imply the priority of *OT* 1524–5. A similar argument can be made for μέγιστος, perhaps a deliberate variation on, but less pointed than, *OT*'s κράτιστος (which implies victory and the masterful power of kingship).

1760 κατέσχον . . . κράτη 'checked, overthrew her power', or perhaps 'victorious power', since κράτος in epinician contexts can mean 'victory': cf. *Ba.* 555 φονίου δ' ἀνδρὸς ὕβριν κατάσχες, and with ἔχω = κατέχω, Bacchyl. 18.39–41 ὃς τοσούτων ἀνδρῶν κρατερὸν σθένος ἔσχεν (and 18.26–7 τάν τε Κερκυόνος παλαίστραν ἔσχεν, 'put a stop to' rather than 'seized'?).

1761 νῦν νῦν δ' (**Orz**) could be correct, but is more likely to be due to scribal avoidance of asyndeton (possibly 1760 should end with colon rather than comma).

αὐτός 'for my part' (not 'alone', as e.g. Valck. and, by his punct., Porson); this implies a contrast either with the Sphinx or with the persons whom Oed.'s victory rescued, but in either case the use is clumsy. The Sphinx was killed, not deprived of honour, rendered pitiful, or driven out; and the saved Thebans are not clearly evoked (μόνος hints at 'all who tried' more than 'all who were threatened by her'). αὐτὸς οἰκτρῶς (Nauck) would improve the line, but if the speech is interpolated and based on 627, its obscurity may be original.

1762 ἀλλὰ γὰρ τί ταῦτα cf. 382n. In trimeters the usual particle is ἀτάρ, which has intruded in most mss here. ἀλλὰ γάρ marks a breaking off, as often in prose, but Denniston, *GP²* 103, cites from drama *Tro.* 444, *Andr.* 264, *Knights* 1086. Pearson incorrectly says that the usage is unique in drama and may support the hypothesis of interpolation.

ὀδύρομαι cf. *Andr.* [397] τί ταῦτα δύρομαι; [ταῦτ' ὀδύρομαι Porson], *IT* 482 τί ταῦτ' ὀδύρηι; The topos in these lines seems to me too commonplace for us to infer safely that the collocation of θρηνέω, ὀδύρομαι, and μάτην in Pl. *Tim.* 47b4–5 τἄλλα . . . ὧν ὁ μὴ φιλόσοφος τυφλωθεὶς ὀδυρόμενος ἂν θρηνοῖ μάτην attests to a specific allusion to our text; but for an argument to this effect see J. Whittaker in *Editing Gk. and Lat. Texts* 67, 74, and note the juxtaposition of τυφλωθείς. If the similarity is not fortuitous, one may imagine that there was a passage (spoken by Oed.?) in another play familiar to Plato and his readers that also attracted the interpolator's imitation.

1763 an expansion of the commonplace in 382 δεῖ φέρειν τὰ τῶν θεῶν, with the added detail θνητὸν ὄντα, for which compare *Med.* 1018 κούφως φέρειν χρὴ θνητὸν ὄντα συμφοράς, Soph. fr. 585.1–2 ... χρεὼν / τὰ θεῖα θνητοὺς ὄντας εὐπετῶς φέρειν, Men. *Sent.* 813 φέρειν ἀνάγκη θνητὸν ὄντα τὴν τύχην. The phrase may have been suggested by *OT* 1528, though there it is part of a different topos.

[1764–6] this choral prayer for victory, found also at the end of *IT* and *Or.* (and *Hipp.* in V²A), is spoken without dramatic impersonation and thus is not an artistic element of the tragedy it follows (thus, it is improper to say that the sentiment is unsuitable to *Phoen.*, but suitable to *IT*). Final prayer and self-referential break of illusion are familiar from comedy (*Clouds, Wasps, Thesm., Dysc., Mis., Sam.*), but the break of illusion is foreign to tragedy, so one may suspect that this tailpiece reflects a post-classical practice. In the ancient book-tradition, it may even have been imported by scribes, as a formula of completion, into texts of plays that had never been performed with such a close. Cf. Barrett on *Hipp.* 1462–6, Kannicht on *Hel.* 1688–92, Willink on *Or.* 1691–3.

1764 μέγα σεμνή perhaps a traditional ritual juncture; cf. A. *Su.* 141 σεμνᾶς μέγα ματρός, *Clouds* 291 ὦ μέγα σεμναὶ Νεφέλαι, com. adesp. = [Cratinus] fr. 75.8 *CGFPR*. For μέγα as adv. with adj. see Friis Johansen and Whittle on *Su.* 141 = 151.

Νίκη the goddess was apparently routinely invoked in later comedy: see Handley on *Dysc.* 968–9 and cf. the prayer to τὼ Θεσμοφόρω at the end of *Thesm.*

ADDENDUM

821 ὀδοντοφυᾶ JD has pointed out that L. Dindorf argued that in tragedy (and Attic authors in general) transmitted forms in -φυῆ should be emended to -φυᾶ: see his note in *Thesaurus Graecae Linguae* (Leipzig 1831–65) s.v. αὐτοφυής and his note on Xen. *Men.* 1.6.13. The evidence derives from inscriptions of the fourth century; see also Herodian, *Grammatici Graeci* III:2.676, 22–4; K–B 1.433–4, Schwyzer 1.189. The relevant passages in drama are (lyric) *Ion* 1480, *Ba.* 1196, *IA* 1516, E. fr. 186.1, *Thesm.* 968; (trimeters) *Phil.* 1014, *Trach.* 1095, *Knights* 141, *Clouds* 76, *Peace* 229, *Frogs* 611; (anapaests) E. fr. 593.1.

APPENDIX: THE POETIC
TOPOGRAPHY OF THEBES

Recent worthwhile discussions of the topography of ancient Thebes have appeared in P. Roesch, 'Thebes' in R. Stillwell, ed., *The Princeton Encyclopedia of Classical Sites* (Princeton 1976), 904–6; Ν. Δ. Παπαχάτζης, *Παυσανίου Ἑλλάδος Περιήγησις*, τομ. v, Βιβλία 9 καὶ 10: Βοιωτικὰ καὶ Φωκικά (Athens 1981) 64–5; N. H. Demand, *Thebes in the Fifth Century: Heracles Resurgent* (London 1982) 46–7; D. Müller, *Topographischer Bildkommentar zu den Historien Herodots: Griechenland* (Tübingen 1987) 584–6.[1]

A dramatist need do no more than project an imaginary setting in sufficient detail to serve the needs of his plot and of an audience which may not have firsthand knowledge of (and should not be primarily interested in) the actual topography of the play's locale. Sophocles does no more than this in his Theban plays, but it is not uncharacteristic that Euripides aims for a stronger impression of particularity and verisimilitude.[2] In *Su.* 650–65[3] and in *Phoen.*, Eur. refers readily to the gates of the Theban acropolis, the famous streams on either side of the acropolis, the adjacent plains, and mythologically significant sites nearby. The Thebes of heroic times is imagined as a small walled city covering the acropolis alone, and the more extensive lower city with its perimeter walls (the fifth-century reality) is usually ignored.[4] The tomb of Amphion and Zethus, the tomb of the Niobids, the dragon's cave, and the streams of Dirce and Hismenus are all imagined to be outside the defending walls of the acropolis.

Whatever the origin of the 'seven gates' (1104n.), it is clear that in the tragedians they are thought of as distributed all around the acropolis wall. Though rebuilt in the late fourth century after the destruction carried out by Alexander, by Roman times the city was again reduced to the inhabited acropolis, and the lower city abandoned. One can imagine that in this

---

[1] The treatment in S. Symeonoglou, *The Topography of Thebes from the Bronze Age to Modern Times* (Princeton 1985), is uncritical in its use of literary and mythographic evidence.

[2] Cf. Barrett on *Hipp.* 1198–200.

[3] On the topographical presuppositions of this passage, see Diggle, *GRBS* 14 (1973) 252–63.

[4] In *Antiope* 78–9 Page (fr. 48.84–5 Kambitsis), Hermes, in a *deus ex machina* speech looking to the future, invokes the real image of the Dirce flowing 'through the city'; the perimeter walls of the lower city did enclose both Dirce and Hismenus.

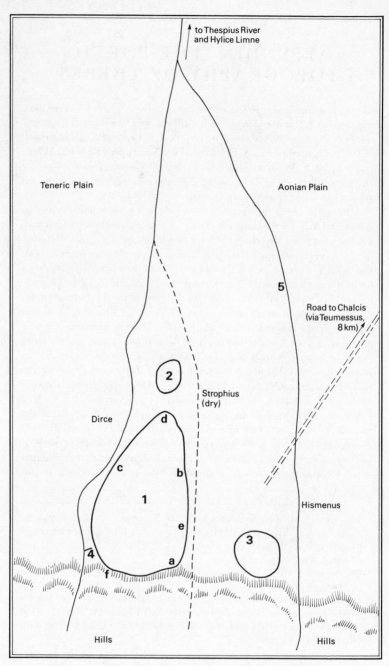

to Thespius River
and Hylice Limne

Teneric Plain

Aonian Plain

5

Road to Chalcis
(via Teumessus,
8 km)

2

Strophius
(dry)

Dirce

d

c

b

1

e

Hismenus

a

4

3

f

Hills

Hills

SCHEMATIC MAP OF THEBES AND
ENVIRONS

rebuilt city efforts were made to identify locations and features with the glorious names in classical poetry, and so it is no surprise that Pausanias (9.8.4–7) speaks in some detail of the names and etymologies of the famous gates. Yet Pausanias made use of only three of the gates for his sightseeing itineraries of the city's environs and of the major sites of Boeotia. The Electran Gate (Aesch., Eur., Paus.) is clearly on the south and is reasonably identified with the fortified gates excavated at the east corner of the south side of the acropolis. The Proetid Gate (Aesch., Eur., Paus.) leads to the road to Chalcis and various monuments identifiable on the NE side of the upper city, and so it is placed with reasonable certainty on the NE. Likewise, the Neistid Gate (Aesch., Eur., Paus.) is approximately fixed on the west by Pausanias' itinerary. As for the remaining gates, their position can be inferred only from their names or the possible location of sites assumed to be in their vicinity. Neither Pausanias nor the tragedians make any effort to suggest the relative positions of all the gates. The Paraporti spring (near the SW corner of the acropolis) is a significant one and the only one near the citadel walls, so it is rightly identified with the spring of Ares and Dirce,[1] and the Crenaean Gate (Eur., Paus.) is assumed to be nearby. The Boraean Gate (Aesch.) may be placed at the north end of the

---

[1] Paus. 9.10.5 places the spring of Ares in the hills above (south of) the Hismenion, on the east side of the Cadmeia; but it is clear that Eur. identified the spring of Ares with the major source of Dirce, on the west side of the Cadmeia: cf. 931–2; *Antiope* 76–8 Page (fr. 48.82–4 Kambitsis); Wilam., 'Sieben Thoren', 198–9.

KEY TO MAP
1 Cadmeia (acropolis, old city, site of the palace, protected by the walls and gates referred to in *Phoenissae*)
2 hill Ampheion, identified with the tomb of Amphion and Zethus
3 hill Hismenion
4 Spring of Ares or Spring of Dirce, assumed location of dragon's cave, also Crenaean gate
5 approximate location of Niobid tombs
a Electran gate (main south gate, confirmed by excavation)
b Proetid gate (main east gate, position inferred from Pausanias' description)
c Neistid gate (main west gate, position inferred from Pausanias' description)
d assumed location of Boraean gate ('seventh' in *Phoenissae*?)
e assumed location of Homoloid gate
f assumed location of Oncan gate (= Ogygian in *Phoenissae*?)

citadel. The name Ogygian (Eur., Paus.) gives no ground for inference (Keramopoullos thought it another name for the Boraean; others identify it with the Oncan Gate). The Homoloid Gate (Aesch., Eur., Paus.) was probably imagined to be near the shrine of Zeus Homoloios, but the site of the latter is unknown; *faute de mieux*, it has been placed by conjecture on the east, farther south than the Proetid Gate. The Oncan Gate (Aesch.) is assumed to have led to the shrine of Athena Onca, which appears to have been south of the citadel (somewhere west of the road to Plataea that entered the Electran Gate (Paus. 9.12.2)). Thus it is placed on the south. The Hypsistan Gate (Paus.) may be connected to the shrine of Zeus Hypsistos, but both shrine and gate are unlocated.

It is quite likely that the traditional topography known to Pausanias was a post-classical invention, a creative 'restoration' based on classic texts that did not in fact offer entirely real and consistent topographic information. Nevertheless, the tragedians were offering something similar in projecting an image of mythical Thebes. As far as modern topographical studies can show, the circumstantial details used for literary effect by Eur. do not introduce any proven gross improbabilities. See also 131n., 145n., 159–60n., 730–1n., 748n., 827n., 1104–40n., 1104n., 1119n., 1570n.

ABBREVIATIONS AND BIBLIOGRAPHY

In references to tragedies and to comedies of Aristophanes and Menander, the title is often used alone. The abbreviations used for tragedies are (Aesch.) *Pers.*, *Su.*, *Se.*, *Ag.*, *Choe.*, *Eum.*, *Prom.*; (Soph.) *Aj.*, *Ant.*, *Trach.*, *OT*, *El.*, *Phil.*, *OC*; (Eur.) *Alc.*, *Med.*, *Hcld.*, *Hipp.*, *Andr.*, *Hec.*, *Su.*, *El.*, *HF*, *Tro.*, *IT*, *Hel.*, *Phoen.*, *Or.*, *Ba.*, *IA*, *Hyps.* When *Su.* or *El.* is not otherwise identified, the reference is to Eur. rather than Aesch. *Su.* or Soph. *El.*

Fragments of Aesch., Soph., *tragici minores*, and tragic adespota are referred to from *TrGF* (ed. Snell, Kannicht, and Radt); fragments of Eur. are from Nauck² unless otherwise indicated. Fragments of comedy are from Kassel–Austin (K–A) whenever possible, otherwise reference is made to Kock or to Austin *CGFPR*.

Secondary literature included in the bibliography below is referred to in Introduction and commentary by author's name alone, or (when more than one work is listed) by name with short title or date. The bibliography does not include the major editions and commentators on *Phoen.* for which fuller information is available in my Teubner (xxvii–xxviii): Barnes, King, Valckenaer, Musgrave, Brunck, Porson, Burges, Matthiae, Hermann, Klotz, Geel, Hartung, Nauck, Kirchhoff, Paley, Kinkel, Klotz–Wecklein (1881), Wecklein (comm. 1894), Wecklein (ed. mai. 1901), Murray, Pearson, Powell, Méridier (trans.) and Chapouthier (text and notes) (Budé edn), Dos Santos Alves. The recent edition with translation of Craik, and the translations of Buschor and of Burian and Swann, are included below. These editors and commentators are referred to by name alone. If the origin of a conjecture mentioned in the apparatus or commentary is not explicitly mentioned, it may be obtained from the Conspectus Librorum of the Teubner edition.

KEY TO COMMON ABBREVIATIONS

Arktouros = Glen W. Bowersock *et al.*, eds., *Arktouros : Hellenic Studies presented to Bernard M. W. Knox.* Berlin, New York 1979

Beazley, *ARV*² = J. D. Beazley, *Attic Red-Figure Vase-Painters*, 2nd edn. Oxford 1963

Beazley, *Paralipomena*² = J. D. Beazley, *Paralipomena: Additions to Attic Black-Figure Vase-Painters and Attic Red-Figure Vase-Painters*, 2nd edn. Oxford 1971

Cabinet of the Muses = M. Griffith, D. J. Mastronarde, eds., *Cabinet of the*

BIBLIOGRAPHY

Muses: Essays on Classical and Comparative Literature in honor of Thomas G. Rosenmeyer. Atlanta 1990

CGFPR = C. Austin, *Comicorum Graecorum Fragmenta in Papyris Reperta.* Berlin 1973

Chandler, *Gk. Accentuation* = Henry W. Chandler, *A Practical Introduction to Greek Accentuation,* 2d edn. Oxford 1881

Chantraine = P. Chantraine, *Dictionnaire étymologique de la langue grecque: histoire des mots.* Paris 1968–80

Concordance = J. T. Allen and G. Italie, *A Concordance to Euripides.* Berkeley and Los Angeles 1954

Dale, *LMGD²* = A. M. Dale, *The Lyric Metres of Greek Drama².* Cambridge 1968

Daremberg–Saglio = C. Daremberg and E. Saglio, *Dictionnaire des antiquités grecques et romaines d'après les textes et les monuments.* Paris 1877–1919

Denniston, *GP²* = J. D. Denniston, *The Greek Particles².* Oxford 1954

Der kl. Pauly = K. Ziegler and W. Sontheimer, eds., *Der kleine Pauly. Lexicon der Antike auf der Grundlage von Pauly's Realencyclopädie.* Stuttgart and Munich 1964–75

D–K = H. Diels and W. Kranz, *Die Fragmente der Vorsokratiker⁶.* Zurich 1951–2

Dionysiaca = R. D. Dawe et al., eds., *Dionysiaca. Nine Studies in Greek Poetry ... presented to Sir Denys Page.* Cambridge 1978

EAA = *Enciclopedia dell'Arte Antica e Orientale.* Rome 1958–66

Editing Gk. and Lat. Texts = John N. Grant, ed., *Editing Greek and Latin Texts.* New York 1989

Ellendt, *Lex. Soph.* = F. Ellendt and H. Genthe, *Lexicon Sophocleum².* Berlin 1872

FGrHist = F. Jacoby, *Die Fragmente der griechischen Historiker.* Leiden 1923–58

Frisk = H. Frisk, *Griechisches etymologisches Wörterbuch.* Heidelberg 1954–72

Goodwin, *MT* = W. W. Goodwin, *Syntax of the Moods and Tenses of the Greek Verb.* Boston 1890

Greek Tragedy and its Legacy = M. Cropp, E. Fantham, S. E. Scully, eds., *Greek Tragedy and its Legacy: Essays presented to D. J. Conacher.* Calgary 1986

JD = James Diggle in comments privately communicated

K–B = R. Kühner and F. Blass, *Ausführliche Grammatik der griechischen Sprache, 1. Teil: Elementar- und Formenlehre³.* Hanover 1890–2

K–G = R. Kühner and Gerthe, *Ausführliche Grammatik der griechischen Sprache, 2. Teil: Satzlehre³.* Hanover 1898–1904

LfgrE = *Lexikon des frühgriechischen Epos.* Göttingen 1955–

LIMC = *Lexicon Iconographicum Mythologiae Classicae.* Zurich and Munich 1981–

BIBLIOGRAPHY

LSJ = H. G. Liddell, R. Scott, H. S. Jones, *A Greek–English Lexicon*[9]. Oxford 1925–40

Meisterhans[3] = K. Meisterhans and E. Schwyzer, *Grammatik der attischen Inschriften*[3]. Berlin 1900

Moorhouse, *Syntax Soph.* = A. C. Moorhouse, *The Syntax of Sophocles* [*Mnem* Suppl. 75]. Leiden 1982

Pfeiffer, *Hist. Cl. Schol.* = R. Pfeiffer, *History of Classical Scholarship from the Beginnings to the End of the Hellenistic Age.* Oxford 1968

PMG = D. L. Page, *Poetae Melici Graeci.* Oxford 1962

PMGF = M. Davies, *Poetarum Melicorum Graecorum Fragmenta* I. Oxford 1991

RE = A. Pauly and G. Wissowa, *Realencyclopädie der classischen Altertums- wissenschaft*, ed. W. Kranz *et al.* Munich and Stuttgart 1894–1978

Roscher = W. Roscher, *Ausführliches Lexikon der griechischen und römischen Mythologie.* Leipzig 1884–1937

Schwyzer = E. Schwyzer and A. Debrunner, *Griechische Grammatik.* Munich 1938–50

Slater, *Lex. Pind.* = W. J. Slater, *Lexicon to Pindar.* Berlin 1969

Stevens, *Colloquial Expr.* = P. T. Stevens, *Colloquial Expressions in Euripides* [Hermes Einzelschriften 38]. Wiesbaden 1976

TLG = Thesaurus Linguae Graecae (electronic texts: see Introd. p. 46)

TrGF = *Tragicorum Graecorum Fragmenta*, ed. B. Snell, R. Kannicht, S. Radt. Berlin 1971–85

Valck. = Valckenaer

Wilam. = Wilamowitz

My own works are referred to with the following short titles:

'Actors on High' = 'Actors on High: the Skene Roof, the Crane, and the Gods in Attic Drama', *CA* 9 (1990) 247–94

Contact and Discontinuity = *Contact and Discontinuity. Some Conventions of Speech and Action on the Greek Tragic Stage* [University of California Publications: Classical Studies, 21]. Berkeley and Los Angeles 1979

'Optimistic Rationalist' = 'The Optimistic Rationalist in Euripides: Theseus, Jocasta, Teiresias' in *Greek Tragedy and its Legacy*, 201–11.

Teubner = *Euripides. Phoenissae.* Leipzig 1988

Text. Trad. = D. J. Mastronarde and J. M. Bremer, *The Textual Tradition of Euripides' Phoinissai* [University of California Publications: Classical Studies, 27]. Berkeley and Los Angeles 1982

BIBLIOGRAPHY

Aélion, R., *Quelques grands mythes heroïques dans l'œuvre d'Euripide.* Paris 1986

Aélion, R., *Euripide Héritier d'Eschyle.* Paris 1983

653

BIBLIOGRAPHY

Alexiou, M., *The Ritual Lament in Greek Tradition*. Cambridge 1974

Arnim, H. v., *De prologorum Euripideorum arte et interpolatione*. Gryphiswald 1882

Arnoldt, R., *Die chorische Technik des Euripides*. Halle 1878

Arthur, M., 'The Curse of Civilization: the Choral Odes of *Phoenissae*', *HSCP* 81 (1977) 163–85

Bakhuyzen, W.H. van de Sande, *De parodia in comoediis Aristophanis*. Utrecht 1877

Balsamo, A., 'Sulla composizione delle Fenicie di Euripide', *SIFC* 9 (1901) 241–90

Barlow, S., *The Imagery of Euripides. A Study in the Dramatic Use of Pictorial Language*. London 1971

Bartoletti, V., 'Frammenti di un florilegio gnomologico in un papiro fiorentino', in *Atti dell'XI Congresso Internazionale di Papirologia* (Milan 1966) 1–14

Bergk, T., review of Dindorf, *Zeitschrift für die Altertumswissenschaft* 2 (1835) 945–68; 3 (1836) 44–83

Bethe, E., *Thebanische Heldenlieder. Untersuchungen über die Epen des Thebanisch-Argivischen Sagenkreises*. Leipzig 1891

Björck, G., *Das Alpha Impurum und die Tragische Kunstsprache: Attische Wort- und Stilstudien* [Reg. Upsal., 39:1]. Uppsala 1950

Boeckh, A., *Graecae tragoediae principum Aeschyli Sophoclis Euripidis num ea quae supersunt et genuina omnia sint et forma primitiva servata an eorum familiis aliquid debeat ex iis tribui*. Heidelberg 1808

Breitenbach, W., *Untersuchungen zur Sprache der Euripideischen Lyrik* [Tübinger Beiträge zur Altertumswissenschaft, Heft 20]. Stuttgart 1934

Bremer, J. M., 'Papyri containing Fragments of Eur. Phoenissae', *Mnem* 36 (1983) 293–305

'Euripides, Phoenissae 830–832', *Mnem* 33 (1980) 278–87

Bremer, J. M., and Worp, K. A., 'Papyri containing Fragments of Eur. Phoenissae (2)', *Mnem* 39 (1986) 240–60

Bruhn, E., *Lucubrationum Euripidearum capita selecta* [Jahrbuch für classische Philologie Suppl. 15, 225–326]. Leipzig 1887

Burian, P., and Swann, B., transl., *Euripides. The Phoenician Women*. Oxford 1981

Burkert, W., *Griechische Religion der archaischen und klassischen Epoche*. Stuttgart 1977 [= *Greek Religion* transl. by J. Raffan. Cambridge, Mass., 1985]

'Seven against Thebes: An Oral Tradition between Babylonian Magic and Greek Literature', in C. Brillante *et al.*, eds., *I poemi epici rapsodici non Omerici e la tradizione orale* (Padua 1981), 29–46

Buschor, E., transl., *Euripides. Sämtliche Tragödien und Fragmente* (herausgegeben von G. A. Seeck), Band IV. Munich 1972

BIBLIOGRAPHY

Chantraine, P., *La formation des noms en grec ancien*. Paris 1933

Grammaire homérique. Paris 1958–63

Cole, T., *Epiploke: Rhythmical Continuity and Poetic Structure in Greek Lyric*. Cambridge, Mass. 1988

Conacher, D. J., *Euripidean Drama. Myth, Theme and Structure*. Toronto 1967

Conomis, N. C., 'The Dochmiacs of Greek Drama', *Hermes* 92 (1964) 23–50

Craik, E., *Euripides. Phoenician Women*, ed. with comm. and transl. Warminster 1988

Cropp, M., and Fick, G., *Resolutions and Chronology in Euripides: the fragmentary tragedies* [*BICS* Suppl. 43]. London 1985

Dale, A. M., *Metrical Analyses of Tragic Choruses*, fasc. 2 Aeolo-Choriambic; fasc. 3 Dochmiac-Iambic-Dactylic-Ionic [BICS Suppl. 21.2–3]. London 1981–3

Daly, L. W., 'Oidipous', *RE* 17:2 (1937) 2103–17; Suppl. 7 (1940) 769–86

Dawe, R. D., *Studies on the Text of Sophocles* I: *The Manuscripts and the Text*. Leiden 1973

DeJong, I. J. F., *Narrative in Drama. The Art of the Euripidean Messenger-Speech* [*Mnem* Suppl. 116]. Leiden 1991

Delcourt, M., *Oedipe ou la légende du conquérant* [Bibl. de la Fac. de Phil. et Lettres, Univ. de Liège, fasc. 104]. Paris 1944 (reprint 1981)

Denniston, J. D., 'Pauses in the Tragic Senarius', *CQ* 30 (1936) 73–9

Descroix, J., *Le trimètre iambique des iambographes à la comédie nouvelle*. Macon 1931

Deubner, L., *Oedipusprobleme* [Abh. d. Pr. Akad. d. Wiss. Phil.-hist. Kl. 1942, no. 4]. Berlin 1942 [=*Kleine Schriften* (*Beiträge zur klassischen Philologie* 140, Königstein 1982) 635–77]

'Ololyge und Verwandtes', *Abh. Preuss. Akad. Wiss.* I (1941) 1–28 [=*Kleine Schriften* 607–34]

Diggle, J., 'Notes on the *Phoenissae* of Euripides', *SIFC* 7 (1989) 196–206

review of Teubner edn, *CR* 40 (1990) 6–11 (=Diggle 1990a)

'On the *Orestes* of Euripides', *CQ* 40 (1990) 100–23 (=Diggle 1990b)

Studies on the Text of Euripides. Oxford 1981

The Textual Tradition of Euripides' Orestes. Oxford 1991

Euripidea: Collected Essays. Oxford 1994

Dihle, A., *Der Prolog der 'Bacchen' und die antike Überlieferungsphase des Euripides-Textes* [Sitzungsber. Heidelberger Akad. Wiss. 1981, no. 2]

Diller, H., review of Fraenkel 1963, *Gnomon* 36 (1964) 641–50

Dodds, E. R., *The Greeks and the Irrational*. Berkeley and Los Angeles 1951

Edmunds, L., *The Sphinx in the Oedipus Legend* [Beitr. z. kl. Phil., Heft 127]. Königstein 1981

BIBLIOGRAPHY

'The Cults and the Legend of Oedipus', *HSCP* 85 (1981) 221–38

Oedipus. The Ancient Legend and its Later Analogues. Baltimore 1984

Elsperger, W., *Reste und Spuren antiker Kritik gegen Euripides gesammelt aus den Euripidesscholien* [*Philologus* Suppl. 11:1]. Leipzig 1908

Erbse, H., 'Beiträge zum Verständnis der Euripideischen Phoinissen,' *Phil* 110 (1966) 1–34

Farnell, L., *The Cults of the Greek States*. Oxford 1896–1909

Fehling, D., *Die Wiederholungsfiguren und ihr Gebrauch bei den Griechen vor Gorgias*. Berlin 1969

Foley, H. P., *Ritual Irony: Poetry and Sacrifice in Euripides*. Ithaca 1985

Fontenrose, J., *The Delphic Oracle*. Berkeley and Los Angeles 1978

Python. A Study of Delphic Myth and its Origins. Berkeley and Los Angeles 1959

Fraenkel, Ed., *Zu den Phoenissen des Euripides* [SBAW 1963, Heft 1] [referred to as Fraenkel]

Beobachtungen zu Aristophanes. Rome 1962

Elementi Plautini in Plauto. Florence 1960

Fraenkel, Ernst, *Geschichte der griechischen Nomina agentis auf -τήρ, -τωρ, -της (-τ-)*. Strassburg 1908–10

Frazer, J. G., *The Golden Bough*, 3rd edn. London 1911–15

Friedrich, W.H., 'Prolegomena zu den Phönissen', *Hermes* 74 (1939) 265–300

Friis Johansen, H., *General Reflection in Tragic Rhesis*. Copenhagen 1959

Garland, R., *The Greek Way of Death*. London 1985

Guthrie, W. C. K., *History of Greek Philosophy*, vol. III. Cambridge 1969

Hartung, J. A., *Euripides Restitutus*. Hamburg 1843–44

Iphigenia in Aulide. Praemittuntur de Euripidis fabularum interpolatione disputationes duae. Erlangen 1837

Haslam, M.W., 'The Authenticity of Euripides, Phoenissae 1–2 and Sophocles, Electra 1', *GRBS* 16 (1975) 149–74

'Interpolation in the Phoenissae: Papyrus Evidence', *CQ* 26 (1976) 4–11

Helmbold, W. C., review of Budé edition (vol. v), *CP* 48 (1953) 129–32

Henrichs, A., 'Human Sacrifice in Greek Religion: Three Case Studies', in J. Rudhardt and O. Reverdin, eds., *Le Sacrifice dans l'antiquité* [Fondation Hardt, Entretiens 27 (1980)] 195–235

Herwerden, H. v., *Adnotationes criticae et exegeticae ad Euripidem* [Verslagen en Med. Akad. Wet., Afd. Letterk., 2. r., 4 (1874) 81–112, 157–213]

Εὐριπίδου ˝Ιων. Utrecht 1875

'Novae lectiones Euripideae', *RPh* 2 (1878) 19–57

'Novae commentationes Euripideae', *RPh* 18 (1894) 60–98

'Novae curae Euripideae', *Mnem* 31 (1903) 261–94

BIBLIOGRAPHY

Hoffmann, O., *Die griechischen Dialekte in ihrem historischen Zusammenhange mit den wichtigsten ihrer Quellen dargestellt*. Göttingen 1891–8

Hose, M., *Studien zum Chor bei Euripides*, Teil 1. Stuttgart 1990
'Überlegungen zur Exodos der "Phoinissai" des Euripides', *WJA* 16 (1990) 63–74

Huxley, G. L., *Greek Epic Poetry from Eumelos to Panyassis*. London 1969

Itsumi, K., 'The Glyconic in Tragedy', *CQ* 34 (1984) 66–82

Jackson, J., *Marginalia Scaenica*. Oxford 1955

Jacob, D. I., review of Teubner edn, *ΕΛΛΗΝΙΚΑ* 40 (1989) 431–6

Jameson, M. H., 'Sacrifice Before Battle', in Victor D. Hanson, *Hoplites: The Classical Greek Battle Experience* (London 1991) 197–227

Jessen, J., *Quaestiunculae criticae et exegeticae*. Kiel 1901

Jouanna, J., 'Texte et espace théâtral dans les Phéniciennes d'Euripide', *Ktema* 1 (1976) 81–97
'Remarques sur le texte et la mise en scène de deux passages des Phéniciennes d'Euripide (v. 103–126 et 834–851)', *REG* 89 (1976) 40–56

Kaimio, M., *Physical Contact in Greek Tragedy. A Study of Stage Conventions* [Annales Academiae Scientiarum Fennicae, ser. B, tom. 244]. Helsinki 1988

Kiefner, G., *Die Versparung. Untersuchungen zu einer Stilfigur der dichterischen Rhetorik am Beispiel der griechischen Tragödie* [Klassisch-Philologische Studien, 25]. Wiesbaden 1964

Kirsten, E., 'Ur-Athen und die Heimat des Sophokles', *WS* 86 (1973) 5–26

de Kock, E. L., 'The Sophoklean Oidipus and its Antecedents', *Acta Classica (South Africa)* 4 (1961) 7–28
'The Peisandros Scholium – its sources, unity, and relationship to Euripides' Chrysippos', *Acta Classica (South Africa)* 5 (1962) 15–37

Kock, T., *Veri similia* [Jahrbuch für classische Philologie Suppl. 6.1, 161–272]. Leipzig 1872

Kovacs, D., 'Tyrants and Demagogues in Tragic Interpolation', *GRBS* 23 (1982) 42–5

Kranz, W., *Stasimon. Untersuchungen zu Form und Gehalt der griechischen Tragödie*. Berlin 1933

Lamer, H., 'Laios', *RE* 12:1 (1922) 467–512

Leidloff, H., *De Euripidis Phoenissarum argumento atque compositione*. Holzminden 1863

von Leutsch, E., *Phil* 29 (1870) 447

Lloyd-Jones, H., *The Justice of Zeus*. Berkeley and Los Angeles 1971

Lloyd-Jones, H., and Wilson, N. G., *Sophoclea. Studies on the Text of Sophocles*. Oxford 1990

van Looy, H., 'παρετυμολογεῖ ὁ Εὐριπίδης', *Zetesis. Album amicorum ... E. de Strycker* (Antwerp 1973) 345–66

BIBLIOGRAPHY

Ludwig, W., *Sapheneia. Ein Beitrag zur Formkunst im Spätwerk des Euripides.*
Tübingen 1954

March, J., *The Creative Poet: Studies on the Treatment of Myth in Greek Poetry*
[*BICS* Suppl. 49]. London 1987

Masaracchia, A., 'Ares nelle *Fenicie* di Euripide', *Filologia e forme letterarie:
studi offerti a Francesco della Corte* I (Urbino 1987) 169–81

Meiggs, R., and Lewis, D. M., *A Selection of Greek Historical Inscriptions to the
End of the Fifth Century* B.C. Oxford 1969

Moret, J.-M., *Oedipe, La Sphinx et les Thébains. Essai de mythologie iconogra-
phique* [Institut suisse de Rome. Bibliotheca Helvetica Romana, no. 23].
Rome 1984

Morus, S. F. N., *De Euripidis Phoenissis.* Leipzig 1771

Mueller-Goldingen, C., *Untersuchungen zu den Phönissen des Euripides* [Pal-
ingenesia 22]. Stuttgart 1985

Müller, K. H. F., *De Euripidis Phoenissarum parte extrema.* Jena 1881

Nauck, A., *Euripideische Studien* [Mémoires de l'Acad. imp. des sciences de
Saint-Pétersbourg, VIIe série, 1:12 (1859) 67–106]

O'Connor-Visser, E. A. M. E., *Aspects of Human Sacrifice in Euripides.*
Amsterdam 1987

Page, D. L., *Actors' Interpolations in Greek Tragedy.* Oxford 1934
Further Greek Epigrams. Cambridge 1981
Epigrammata Graeca. Oxford 1975

Panagl, O., *Die 'dithyrambischen Stasima' des Euripides.* Vienna 1971

Parker, L. P. E., 'Catalexis', *CQ* 26 (1976) 14–28

Parry, H., *The Choral Odes of Euripides: Problems in Structure and Dramatic
Relevance* (diss.). Berkeley 1963
The Lyric Poems of Greek Tragedy. Toronto 1978

Paulson, J., 'In Phoenissas Euripideam annotatiunculae', *Nordisk Tidskrift
for Filologi* 3. raekke, 5 (1896/97) 1–18

Peek, W., *Lexikon zu den Dionysiaka des Nonnos* [Alpha-Omega 3:1–4].
Hildesheim 1968–73

Podlecki, A., 'Some Themes in Euripides' Phoenissae', *TAPA* 93 (1962)
355–73

Pohlenz, M., *Die griechische Tragödie.* Göttingen 1930, ^{2}1954

Pritchett, W. K., *The Greek State at War* vols. I–IV. Berkeley and Los Angeles
1971–85

Purgold, L., *Observationes criticae in Sophoclem, Euripidem, Anthologiam Graecam
et Ciceronem.* Jena 1802

Rauchenstein, R., review of Kinkel's edn, *Neue Jahrbücher für Philologie und
Pädagogik* 103 (1871) 433–42

Reeve, M., 'Interpolation in Greek Tragedy, I–III', *GRBS* 13 (1972) 247–
65, 451–74; 14 (1973) 145–71

Renehan, R., *Greek Textual Criticism: A Reader*. Cambridge, Mass. 1969
Studies in Greek Texts: Critical Observations to Homer, Plato, Euripides, Aristophanes and Other Authors [Hypomnemata 43]. Göttingen 1976
Riemschneider, W., *Held und Staat in Euripides' Phönissen*. Würzburg 1940
Rijksbaron, A., *Grammatical Observations on Euripides' Bacchae*. Amsterdam 1991
'How does a Messenger begin his Speech?', in J. Bremer *et al.*, eds., *Miscellanea Tragica in hon. J. C. Kamerbeek* (Amsterdam 1976) 292–308
Robert, C., *Oidipus. Geschichte eines poetischen Stoffs im griechischen Altertum*. Berlin 1915
Romilly, J. de, 'Les Phéniciennes d'Euripide ou l'actualité dans la tragédie grecque', *RPh* 39 (1965) 28–47
Saïd, S., 'Euripide ou l'attente déçue: l'exemple des Phéniciennes', *ASNP* ser. 3, 15:2 (1985) 501–27
Schachter, A., *The Cults of Boeotia* [*BICS* Suppl. 38:1–2]. London 1981–6
Schenkl, K., review of Kinkel's edn, *Zeitschrift für die Österreichischen Gymnasien* 23 (1872) 267–81
Schmidt, F.W., *Kritische Studien zu den griechischen Dramatikern, 2. Band: Zu Euripides*. Berlin 1886
Schmitt, J., *Freiwilliger Opfertod bei Euripides. Ein Beitrag zu seiner dramatischen Technik* [Religionsgeschichtliche Versuche und Vorarbeiten 17:2]. Giessen 1921
Schoene, F.G., 'Kritische Bemerkungen zu Euripides', *Phil* 9 (1854) 213–22; 10 (1855) 82–96, 391–409
Schroeder, O., *Euripidis Cantica*. Leipzig 1910, ²1928
Schwinge, E.-R., *Die Verwendung des Stichomythie in den Dramen des Euripides*. Heidelberg 1968
Seaford, R., 'The Tragic Wedding', *JHS* 107 (1987) 106–30
Séchan, L., *Études sur la tragédie grecque dans ses rapports avec la céramique*. Paris 1926
Spiro, F., *De Euripidis Phoenissis*. Berlin 1884
Stadtmüller, H., 'Textkritische Bemerkungen zu Euripides im Anschluss an Studien zu Euripides von Holzner', *Blätter für das Bayerische Gymnasial-Schulwesen* 31 (1895) 416–18
Stanley-Porter, D. P., 'Mute Actors in the Tragedies of Euripides', *BICS* 20 (1973) 68–93
Stengel, P., *Opferbräuche der Griechen*. Leipzig 1910
Stephanopoulos, T. K., *Umgestaltung des Mythos durch Euripides*. Athens 1980
Stinton, T. C. W., 'More Rare Verse-forms', *BICS* 22 (1975) 84–108
[= *Collected Papers on Greek Tragedy* (Oxford 1989) 113–42]
'Notes on Greek Tragedy, I–II', *JHS* 76 (1976) 121–45, 77 (1977)

BIBLIOGRAPHY

129–54 [=*Collected Papers on Greek Tragedy* (Oxford 1989) 197–235, 271–309]

'Pause and Period in the Lyrics of Greek Tragedy', *CQ* 27 (1977) 27–66 [=*Collected Papers on Greek Tragedy* (Oxford 1989) 310–61]

Strohm, H., *Euripides. Interpretationen zur dramatischen Form* [Zetemata 15]. Munich 1957

Taplin, O. *The Stagecraft of Aeschylus. The Dramatic Use of Exits and Entrances in Greek Tragedy*. Oxford 1977

Thalmann, W. G., *Dramatic Art in Aeschylus' Seven Against Thebes*. New Haven 1978

Valgiglio, E., *L'esodo delle Fenicie di Euripide* [Univ. di Torino, Pubbl. della facoltà di lettere e filosofia 13:2, 1961]

Verrall, A.W., *Euripides the Rationalist. A Study in the History of Art and Religion*. Cambridge 1895

Vian, F., *Les origines de Thèbes. Cadmus et les Spartes* [Etudes et commentaires 48]. Paris 1963

Wackernagel, J., *Vorlesungen über Syntax*². Basel 1926–8

Kleine Schriften. Göttingen 1953

West, M. L., *Greek Metre*. Oxford 1982

review of Teubner edn, *CP* 85 (1990) 311–17

Wilamowitz-Moellendorff, U. v., *Griechische Verskunst*. Berlin 1921

*Herakles*². Berlin 1895

'Der Schluss der Phönissen des Euripides', *Sitzungsber. d. Preuss. Akad. Wiss.* 1903, 587–600 [= *Kleine Schriften* VI.344–59]

'Die Sieben Thoren Thebens', *Hermes* 26 (1891) 191–242 [=*Kl. Schriften* V:1, 26–77]

Wilamowitz-Moellendorff, U. v.: A. Bierl, W. M. Calder III, R. L. Fowler, eds., *The Prussian and the Poet. The Letters of Ulrich von Wilamowitz-Moellendorff to Gilbert Murray (1894–1930)*. Hildesheim 1991

Williger, E., *Sprachliche Untersuchungen zu den Komposita der gr. Dichter des 5. Jahrhunderts* [Forschungen z. gr. u. lat. Grammatik, 8]. Göttingen 1928

Willink, C., 'The Goddess ΕΥΛΑΒΕΙΑ and Pseudo-Euripides in Euripides' *Phoenissae*', *PCPS* 216 (1990) 182–201

Young, David C., *Three Odes of Pindar* [*Mnem* Supp. 9]. Leiden 1968

Zielinski, 'de Euripidis Thebaide posteriore', *Mnem* 52 (1924) 189–205

Zipperer, W., *De Euripidis Phoenissarum versibus suspectis et interpolatis*. Würzburg 1875

Zuntz, G., *The Political Plays of Euripides*. Manchester 1955

'Contemporary Politics in the Plays of Euripides', *Acta Congressus Madvigiani* I (Copenhagen 1958) 155–162 [= *Opuscula Selecta: Classica, Hellenistica, Christiana* (Manchester 1972) 54–61]

INDEX OF PASSAGES DISCUSSED

661

SUBJECT INDEX

INDEX

explanatory (explicative) 202,
263, 282, 283; pair of verbs in
582, at start of trimeter 480;
scribal elimination of 279, 359,
547, 589, 644

augment, temporal, omission of
340, 442

bacchiacs, associated with
dochmiacs 231
Bacchylides (poem 15) 26
blindness (moral or general) 9,
266, 280, 294, 487, 546
brachylogy 182, 206, 272, 429,
479, 617
breast, baring of (on stage) 564
brevis in longo 176, 177, 201, 203,
214, 236, 240, 333, 334, 385,
386, 437, 527, 558, 560
burial-motif 9, 10, 30, 42, 44, 325,
346, 349, 364, 368, 511–12, 549,
591–3, 607, 611

Cadmus 5, 143, 208, 209, 210,
218, 330, 340, 443, 445
caesura, absence of, in lyric iambic
trimeter 334, 342, 629
Callimachus, *pinakes* of 140;
possible imitation of *Phoen.* 468,
478
cedar, expensive structures and
fixtures made of, 182
change of speaker, mss authority
for 425, 524
Chrysippus 31–8, 603
choriambs, ambiguity with ionics
559; not associated with
dochmiacs 177
chorus, proem to actor's song 230;
response to messenger-speech
513; response to substantial
actor's song 249, 594
city vs. family 4–5, 29, 209, 300,
313, 330, 346, 373, 386, 390–2,
546
closing, formula of 420, 430
codex Bodmer (64) 49

colloquial words or expressions 47,
159, 205, 206, 223, 263, 274,
277, 304, 309, 312, 316, 325,
326, 327, 366, 397, 399, 408,
409, 419, 421, 423, 505, 520,
543, 606, 617, 620, 632, 633,
635
command, with execution delayed
or omitted 608, 616
comminus fighting 458, 471
compound adjs., 'active' and
'passive' meanings of 162, 217,
289, 338; formed by hypostasis
587; in -τος, flexible meaning of
254; involving kinship terms
191; replacing gen. of abstract
noun in lyric periphrasis 245;
sentence-compound 388
conative force of present stem 164,
293, 422, 485, 522, 642
contradiction *see* inconsistency
corpses (on stage), treatment of
and reference to 519
crasis, of article with initial long
alpha 500; words in, omitted
in transmission 283, 299, 344,
405
Creon as a subordinate figure 372,
593
criticism (often carping) found in
scholia, 164, 227, 228, 258, 261,
292, 329, 435, 602
curse of Oedipus 5, 7, 23–4, 26,
28, 163, 207, 248–9, 266, 282,
326, 363, 366, 370, 403–4, 444,
451, 500, 510, 528, 545, 566,
568, 580, 583, 597, 603–4
cut-off formula 257, 352, 361
Cypria (contained some version of
Oedipus' story) 17

dactyls, associated with dochmiacs
560; initial in proper name (in
trimeter) 143; 'light' 376, 558,
561; lyric, reminiscent of Aesch.
373; lyric (stichic-style
construction vs. κατὰ συζυγίαν)

664

and 43, 258, 370, 371; additions made to compensate for cuts in performance 267, 364, 411; caused by readers or copyists rather than actors 41, 311, 370, 411, 418, 504, 522; etymological interpolation, 151; filling out a gloss into a full trimeter 267, 363, 530; filling out an ellipsis 314, 448; *hapax legomena* and 45; incorporation of marginal parallels 41, 254, 311, 504, 610; notation of περισσότης and 43, 268, 424; repeated lines and 45, 193, 363; repeated words or phrases and 45

intransitive/absolute use of normally transitive verbs 146, 463

Ionian Sea 216

ionics, ambiguity with choriambs 559; shortened forms of metron 559

iron (steel), ominous superstitions connected with 249, 342, 620

ironic remarks at scene-ending 205

isometric echoes 207, 208, 225, 382, 435, 445, 504

iterative past potential indicative 263

ithyphallic (or other syncopated iambic colon) as clausula to dactyls 561

justice, Polynices' claim to 194, 207, 225, 280

kenning 569, 635

kinship 4, 7–8, 145, 195, 207, 208, 210, 229, 231, 269, 270, 325, 349, 367, 374, 391, 401, 417, 426, 505, 521, 546; compound adjs. involving terms of 191

Klangfigur 438

ladder (for access to roof of skene-building) 178, 182

Lebensrückblick 598

legal and diplomatic terminology 164, 206, 227, 269, 285, 356, 596

long anceps, rare in Eur.'s lyric trochees 333

Lycurgus degree 40

mannerisms of Euripides 143, 183, 191, 212, 221, 231, 232, 239, 252, 379, 394, 401, 402, 450, 467, 476, 521, 522, 527

medial caesura 398

Megareus, not to be identified with Menoeceus 29

meiosis 366

Menoeceus, creation of Eur. 28; not to be identified with Megareus 29

mesode 211

metaphor 142, 146, 149, 159, 164, 180, 204, 223, 224, 226, 243, 245, 265, 281, 283, 287, 294, 304, 315, 350, 352, 390, 395, 399, 410, 413, 416, 444, 453, 455, 475, 489, 502, 516–17, 523, 531, 534, 535, 544, 577, 579, 580, 582, 589, 632, 634

metonymy 152, 164, 216, 262, 337, 379, 445, 450, 499, 503, 568, 587

molossus, responding with bacchiac 436; among dochmiacs 178

Moschopulus 50–1, 153, 297, 315, 324, 378, 380, 390, 395, 426, 439, 441, 445, 492, 522, 542, 564, 569, 570, 579, 588, 595, 603, 604, 626, 641

mute and liquid, lengthening before, in lyric 197, 558; in prepositional prefix 319

mute characters: *see* silent characters

mythology, allusion to by a character 620

naming 139, 144, 152, 160, 367

GREEK INDEX

INDEX

INDEX